ANNUAL REVIEW OF ANTHROPOLOGY

EDITORIAL COMMITTEE (1985)

ALAN R. BEALS
EUGENE GILES
ALLEN W. JOHNSON
GREGORY A. JOHNSON
SUSAN PHILIPS
BERNARD J. SIEGEL
TERENCE S. TURNER
STEPHEN A. TYLER

Responsible for organization of Volume 14
(Editorial Committee, 1983)

ALAN R. BEALS
JOHN L. COMAROFF
EUGENE GILES
JANE H. HILL
FRANK A. HOLE
ALLEN W. JOHNSON
BERNARD J. SIEGEL
STEPHEN A. TYLER
RENATO ROSALDO (Guest)

Production Editor   JEAN HEAVENER
Indexing Coordinator   MARY A. GLASS
Subject Indexer   BARBARA LEE

ANNUAL REVIEW OF ANTHROPOLOGY

VOLUME 14, 1985

BERNARD J. SIEGEL, *Editor*
Stanford University

ALAN R. BEALS, *Associate Editor*
University of California, Riverside

STEPHEN A. TYLER, *Associate Editor*
Rice University

ANNUAL REVIEWS INC.   4139 EL CAMINO WAY   PALO ALTO, CALIFORNIA 94306 USA

ANNUAL REVIEWS INC.
Palo Alto, California, USA

COPYRIGHT © 1985 BY ANNUAL REVIEWS INC., PALO ALTO, CALIFORNIA, USA. ALL RIGHTS RESERVED. The appearance of the code at the bottom of the first page of an article in this serial indicates the copyright owner's consent that copies of the article may be made for personal or internal use, or for the personal or internal use of specific clients. This consent is given on the condition, however, that the copier pay the stated per-copy fee of $2.00 per article through the Copyright Clearance Center, Inc. (21 Congress Street, Salem, MA 01970) for copying beyond that permitted by Sections 107 or 108 of the US Copyright Law. The per-copy fee of $2.00 per article also applies to the copying, under the stated conditions, of articles published in any *Annual Review* serial before January 1, 1978. Individual readers, and nonprofit libraries acting for them, are permitted to make a single copy of an article without charge for use in research or teaching. This consent does not extend to other kinds of copying, such as copying for general distribution, for advertising or promotional purposes, for creating new collective works, or for resale. For such uses, written permission is required. Write to Permissions Dept., Annual Reviews Inc., 4139 El Camino Way, Palo Alto, CA 94306 USA.

International Standard Serial Number: 0084–6570
International Standard Book Number: 0–8243–1914-1
Library of Congress Catalog Card Number: 72–82136

Annual Review and publication titles are registered trademarks of Annual Reviews Inc.

Annual Reviews Inc. and the Editors of its publications assume no responsibility for the statements expressed by the contributors to this *Review*.

Typesetting by Kachina Typesetting Inc., Tempe, Arizona; John Olson, President
Typesetting coordinator, Dennis Phillips

PRINTED AND BOUND IN THE UNITED STATES OF AMERICA

PREFACE

In this, the fourteenth volume of the *Annual Review of Anthropology*, we continue to offer our readers a diverse and, we trust, interesting array of topics within the various subfields of the discipline. Some articles build upon prior research in different problem areas and others reach out in new directions. We would like to mention a few of the latter that are of general interest.

Carol Kramer's review of Ceramic Ethnoarchaeology provides a detailed analysis of the many questions archaeologists seek to answer in this domain of material culture, for which the study of living potters provides tests of alternative hypotheses. In a very welcome and firmly grounded article examining the diverse claims of "Scientific Creationism" to equal status with the biological theory of evolution, Jim Spuhler lays to rest the political controversy over this issue for any fair-minded, thinking individual. Among other things, it provides useful ammunition to counter these claims in public fora. We were also fortunate to have Aaron Cicourel review the new and burgeoning domain of Text and Discourse analysis, which now constitutes an important subfield of cultural anthropology and sociology.

This volume also includes three reviews of topics whose "time has come." A number of persons in the nursing profession, for example, have also acquired professional training in anthropology and have been instrumental in constructing new curricula for nurse training programs and for significant research bridging the two fields. Drs. Dougherty and Tripp-Reimer give us the history of this development as well as certain characteristics of nursing as a research area that distinguish it from other aspects of medical anthropology.

While agrarian systems have for some time commanded the attention of many anthropologists, Joel Kahn carries the reviewing of this work forward with his analysis of Peasant Ideologies. Anthropological studies of mining communities are much less well known, but Ricardo Godoy fills a gap in our coverage of this important domain with his critique of recent work; where it is coming from, and where it is going.

Finally, Renato Rosaldo has done a great service with his exhaustive review of Chicano Studies in anthropology over the past 15 years. From an earlier, rather acerbic, criticism of Anglo publications on Chicano societies, which seemed to imply that only Chicanos can properly interpret Chicano culture, research has moved to the mainstream—studies of youth, the aged, folklore, wage workers, and gender, to mention a few topics—drawing in a significant way upon a wide body of relevant literature. There is now a considerable amount of sophisticated work in print and soon to be published that has great promise for comparative treatment.

(continued)

PREFACE *(continued)*

The *Annual Review of Anthropology* seeks, as it has from the beginning, to address the needs and interests of diverse audiences in anthropology: students at all levels, academic and applied anthropologists of all persuasions, and scholars in related disciplines. The editors have been encouraged in their efforts by the positive response received over the years. They are also grateful for the dedicated contributions of the editorial committee members, who represent the major fields of anthropology as a whole. They have all been very broad gauged in their knowledge of current output in their respective subdisciplines, as well as in their perceptiveness about the qualifications of potential reviewers.

THE EDITORS

ARTICLES IN OTHER *ANNUAL REVIEWS* OF INTEREST TO ANTHROPOLOGISTS

From the *Annual Review of Psychology*, Volume 36 (1985):

Sex and Gender, Kay Deaux
Personality: Current Controversies, Issues, and Directions, Lawrence A. Pervin
The School as a Social Situation, Seymour B. Sarason and Michael Klaber
Social Cognition: A Look at Motivated Strategies, Carolin Showers and Nancy Cantor
Social Factors in Psychopathology: Stress, Social Support, and Coping Processes, Ronald C. Kessler, Richard H. Price, and Camille B. Wortman
Organizational Behavior, Benjamin Schneider

From the *Annual Review of Sociology*, Volume 11 (1985):

Social Theory and Talcott Parsons in the 1980s, David Sciulli and Dean Gerstein
Effects of Sibling Number on Child Outcome, David M. Heer
Organizational Culture, William G. Ouchi and Alan L. Wilkins
New Black-White Patterns: How Best to Conceptualize Them?, Thomas F. Pettigrew
Urban Poverty, William J. Wilson and Robert Aponte
Ethnicity, J. Milton Yinger
Macrosociolinguistics and the Sociology of Language in the Early Eighties, Joshua A. Fishman
The Organizational Structure of the School, William B. Tyler
Sociology of Mass Communication, Denis McQuail

From the *Annual Review of Ecology & Systematics*, Volume 26 (1985)

Approaches in Evolutionary Morphology: A Search for Patterns, L. B. Radinsky

From the *Annual Review of Public Health*, Volume 6 (1985)

The Community-based Strategy to Prevent Coronary Heart Disease: Conclusions from the Ten Years of the North Karelia Project, Pekka Puska, Aulikki Nissinen, Jaakko Tuomilehto, Jukka T. Salonen, Kaj Koskela, Alfred McAlister, Thomas E. Kottke, Nathan Maccoby, and John W. Farquhar

Annual Review of Anthropology
Volume 14, 1985

CONTENTS

OVERVIEW

An Individual's Participation in American Archaeology,
1928–1985, *James B. Griffin*   1

ARCHAEOLOGY

Ceramic Ethnoarchaeology, *Carol Kramer*   77
Context and Chronology of Early Man in the Americas,
William N. Irving   529

BIOLOGICAL ANTHROPOLOGY

Anthropology, Evolution, and "Scientific Creationism,"
James N. Spuhler   103
Dental Evidence for the Diet of Australopithecus, *Richard F.
Kay*   315
Human Genetic Distance Studies: Present Status and Future
Prospects, *L. B. Jorde*   343
Sexual Dimorphism, *David W. Frayer and Milford H. Wolpoff*   429
Bioanthropological Research in Developing Countries, *Rebecca
Huss-Ashmore and Francis E. Johnston*   475

LINGUISTICS

Modular Theories of Grammar, *Ann K. Farmer*   25
Text and Discourse, *Aaron V. Cicourel*   159
Mayan Linguistics: Where Are We Now?, *Lyle Campbell and
Terrence Kaufman*   187
Status and Style in Language, *Judith T. Irvine*   557

REGIONAL STUDIES

The Social Anthropology of West Africa, *Keith Hart*   243
Chicano Studies, 1970–1984, *Renato Rosaldo*   405

CULTURAL-SOCIAL ANTHROPOLOGY

Peasant Ideologies in the Third World, *Joel S. Kahn*   49
The Use of Statistics in Sociocultural Anthropology, *Michael
Chibnik*   135

(continued)   viii

Mining: Anthropological Perspectives, *Ricardo Godoy*	199
The Interface of Nursing and Anthropology, *Molly C. Dougherty and Toni Tripp-Reimer*	219
Issues in Divine Kingship, *Gillian Feeley-Harnik*	273
Sustenance and Symbol: Anthropological Studies of Domesticated Animals, *Eugenia Shanklin*	375

INDEXES

Author Index	583
Subject Index	601
Cumulative Index of Contributing Authors, Volumes 7–14	621
Cumulative Index of Chapter Titles, Volumes 7–14	623

ANNUAL REVIEWS INC. is a nonprofit scientific publisher established to promote the advancement of the sciences. Beginning in 1932 with the *Annual Review of Biochemistry*, the Company has pursued as its principal function the publication of high quality, reasonably priced *Annual Review* volumes. The volumes are organized by Editors and Editorial Committees who invite qualified authors to contribute critical articles reviewing significant developments within each major discipline. The Editor-in-Chief invites those interested in serving as future Editorial Committee members to communicate directly with him. Annual Reviews Inc. is administered by a Board of Directors, whose members serve without compensation.

1985 Board of Directors, Annual Reviews Inc.

Dr. J. Murray Luck, Founder and Director Emeritus of Annual Reviews Inc.
  Professor Emeritus of Chemistry, Stanford University
Dr. Joshua Lederberg, President of Annual Reviews Inc.
  President, The Rockefeller University
Dr. James E. Howell, Vice President of Annual Reviews Inc.
  Professor of Economics, Stanford University
Dr. William O. Baker, *Retired Chairman of the Board, Bell Laboratories*
Dr. Winslow R. Briggs, *Director, Carnegie Institution of Washington, Stanford*
Dr. Sidney D. Drell, *Deputy Director, Stanford Linear Accelerator Center*
Dr. Eugene Garfield, *President, Institute for Scientific Information*
Dr. Conyers Herring, *Professor of Applied Physics, Stanford University*
Mr. William Kaufmann, *President, William Kaufmann, Inc.*
Dr. D. E. Koshland, Jr., *Professor of Biochemistry, University of California, Berkeley*
Dr. Gardner Lindzey, *Director, Center for Advanced Study in the Behavioral Sciences, Stanford*
Dr. William D. McElroy, *Professor of Biology, University of California, San Diego*
Dr. William F. Miller, *President, SRI International*
Dr. Esmond E. Snell, *Professor of Microbiology and Chemistry, University of Texas, Austin*
Dr. Harriet A. Zuckerman, *Professor of Sociology, Columbia University*

Management of Annual Reviews Inc.

John S. McNeil, Publisher and Secretary-Treasurer
William Kaufmann, Editor-in-Chief
Mickey G. Hamilton, Promotion Manager
Donald S. Svedeman, Business Manager
Richard L. Burke, Production Manager

ANNUAL REVIEWS OF
Anthropology
Astronomy and Astrophysics
Biochemistry
Biophysics and Biophysical Chemistry
Cell Biology
Earth and Planetary Sciences
Ecology and Systematics
Energy
Entomology
Fluid Mechanics
Genetics
Immunology
Materials Science
Medicine
Microbiology
Neuroscience
Nuclear and Particle Science
Nutrition
Pharmacology and Toxicology
Physical Chemistry
Physiology
Phytopathology
Plant Physiology
Psychology
Public Health
Sociology

SPECIAL PUBLICATIONS
Annual Reviews Reprints:
  Cell Membranes, 1975–1977
  Cell Membranes, 1978–1980
  Immunology, 1977–1979

Excitement and Fascination
  of Science, Vols. 1 and 2

History of Entomology

Intelligence and Affectivity,
  by Jean Piaget

Telescopes for the 1980s

ERRATUM

Volume 13 (1984)

In the chapter, "The Problem of Informant Accuracy: The Validity of Retrospective Data," by H. Russell Bernard, Peter Killworth, David Kronenfeld, and Lee Sailer, several references were inadvertently omitted from the bibliography. The following should have been included:

51a. Kosa, J., Alpert, J. J., Haggerty, R. J. 1967. On the reliability of family health information: A comparative study of mothers' reports on illness and related behavior. *Soc. Sci. Med.* 1:165–81
53. La Pierre, R. T. 1934. Attitudes vs. actions. *Soc. Forces* 13:230–37
54. Linusson, E. E. I., Sanjur, D., Erickson, E. C. 1974. Validating the 24-hour recall method as a dietary survey tool. *Arch. Latinoam. Nutr.* 24:277–81
55. Lofland, J. 1976. *Doing Social Life: The Qualitative Study of Human Interaction in Natural Settings.* New York: Wiley
56. Loftus, E. F. 1979. *Eyewitness Testimony.* Cambridge, Mass: Harvard Univ. Press
57a. Loftus, E. F. 1980. The impact of expert psychological testimony on the unreliability of eyewitness identification. *J. Appl. Psychol.* 65:9–15

AN INDIVIDUAL'S PARTICIPATION IN AMERICAN ARCHAEOLOGY, 1928–1985

James B. Griffin

Museum of Anthropology and Department of Anthropology, University of Michigan, Ann Arbor, Michigan 48109

My participation in anthropology and archaeology did not come about as the result of a revelation or as a revolutionary departure from the ideas often acquired during one's early education in what was then called "grammar school," followed by four years of high school. I was attracted to history and geography at an early age in Atchison, Kansas, and in Denver, Colorado, but did poorly in arithmetic and continued to find any mathematics a difficult task. When we moved to Denver in 1912 our home was in easy walking distance of the Denver Museum of Natural History. Whether stimulated by the southwestern archaeological exhibits there or not, I remember writing an English theme in fifth grade on the "Cliff-dwellers."

My family moved to Oak Park, Illinois, in 1914, where I finished grammar school and high school. In those days the Field Museum was in one of the World's Columbian Exposition buildings in Jackson Park on the south side of Chicago. It is now the Rosenwald Museum. I made several trips on the elevated train (the "El") to see the museum. In high school I read a great deal, almost stumbling on books on evolution, *The Golden Bough,* European archaeology, and was also impressed by an admittedly fictionalized account of cultural evolution, *Wanderers* by Knut Hamsum (23). My selection of the University of Chicago was hardly the result of carefully weighing its advantages against those of other places. Compulsory military training was still in effect at the University of Illinois and Northwestern. It was available at Chicago but was not compulsory. Many colleges required modern language credits, but Chicago was content with the three years of Latin I managed to complete in four years. Furthermore, I could travel by "El" an hour and a half each way and live at home, which was a major factor as far as my parents were concerned.

In October 1923 I matriculated at the University of Chicago, embarking on a three-year program in business administration, then a three-year study of law. The first year was reasonably successful with courses in English, geography, history, and so on, but during the first quarter of my sophomore year my performance in accounting, the Manager's Administration of Finance, and economics caused me to shift to a social science major in the liberal arts college. The latter program was a potpourri of English history; Europe before, during, and after World War I; geography; ancient, medieval, and modern philosophy; political science; sociology and introductory anthropology; and a general course in ethnology from Fay-Cooper Cole. I was attracted both to Cole and to the breadth of view anthropology gave on human origins, cultural development, the many varieties of human culture within varied environments, and the many interpretations that had been developed on the relationship of people to the supernatural.

My father's illness was a factor in my embarking on a training program to become a junior executive in Standard Oil of Indiana, for I had no taste for selling securities as many of the 1927 graduates did. For a year and a half I manned service stations on the west side of Chicago, Cicero, and Oak Park. That experience plus some eight years of summer jobs produced dissatisfaction with business ethics. In the summer of 1928, Fred Eggan and I had a meeting with Fay-Cooper Cole about enrolling for graduate work in anthropology, and we were told that there were more positions open than PhDs to fill them. So in October 1928 I happily enrolled to become a member of a community of scholars in which there was little friction. It took me some years to learn how university competitiveness and the administrative bureaucracy worked.

Having taken only two courses in anthropology, I had a lot of catching up to do. The instructors were Cole, Edward Sapir, and Robert Redfield, who was taken into the department in the fall of 1928. I was startled when Sapir approached me to ask if I would be interested in studying linguistics with him, and I declined as gracefully as I could. I had had only a high school botany course, and to go into physical anthropology would mean spending considerable course time acquiring a biology background. While ethnography was interesting, it did not appeal to me as something I wanted to pursue. I was intrigued with archaeological fieldwork after the 1929 summer excavation of Parker Heights Mound north of Quincy, Illinois, and with the second summer of fieldwork in Fulton County, Illinois. I also found there was much more work to it than I had been led to believe in Cole's one-quarter course on field method with smatterings of Old and New World Archaeology.

In Redfield's course on Middle America, I had enjoyed preparing a class presentation on Maya burial practices, so when Redfield became my master's thesis advisor I set out to "test" Kroeber's proposal that burial practices were an affect-laden pattern and were slow to change. I picked the western half of the

Northeast Woodlands Culture area and collected information on the mortuary customs from historic accounts and prehistoric practices. The data I gathered did not confirm Kroeber's interpretation.

The course in which I did my best work was Cole's "The Peoples of Malaysia," and my class presentation topic was on the pygmy and negrito populations. Fortunately, there were not only the monographs but also the Field Museum collections to draw from, and Cole allowed me to talk in class for four days. He had mentioned that the Philippines were a promising area to do fieldwork in archaeology and I indicated my willingness to go, but H. Otley Beyer, of the University of the Philippines, did not, as far as I know, answer Cole's letter.

Some of the students with whom I associated were Fred Eggan, Richard Morgan, William Krogman, George Neumann, Frank Setzler, Paul Nesbitt, William Gilbert, J. Gilbert McAllister, Alfred Bowers, and later in the mid-1930s, John Bennett. Charlotte Gower and Paul Martin had been graduate student assistants to Cole and graded papers for my undergraduate courses. In the summer of 1930, Cole supervised the excavation in Fulton County conducted by Chicago students and a group supported by the Laboratory of Anthropology field training program. This latter group included Dorothy Cross from Pennsylvania, Rita Hahn from Columbia, J. O. Brew from Dartmouth and headed for Harvard, and Harold Driver from California. Thorne Deuel was the field boss.

The University of Chicago program in archaeology was fostered by Cole, beginning in 1925, as a visible demonstration of one of the benefits of anthropology and something which would appeal to some wealthy donors in the Chicago area. He also cultivated capable amateurs in the state such as George Langford and the Dixons in Fulton County. On the basis of the archaeological information that was obtained during the previous five years, Cole, in one of the Sunday morning discussion sessions in the 1930 season, proposed a chronological sequence for the area running from Black Sand and Red Ocher, the early Woodland complexes, through Hopewell to Late Woodland, and then Mississippian as represented at the Dixon mound and other sites. This sequence was applicable for the area from St. Louis north to Wisconsin and was a major development, paralleling a comparable potential sequence in Ohio interpreted in terms of the Northern Illinois findings. Short papers by a number of authors were published in the Transactions of the Illinois Academy of Science in the early 1930s (8, 26, 33) and one in the Illinois Blue Book by Kelly & Cole (25) entitled "Rediscovering Illinois."

In the summer of 1931 I was hired to direct excavations at Athens, Pennsylvania, for the Tioga Point Museum under a grant from the National Research Council. There was a strong local belief that the site of Carontouan, an Andaste Iroquoian village said to have been visited by one of Champlain's followers during A.D. 1615 from Canada, was located on Spanish Hill, an erosion remnant located between the Chemung and Susquehanna rivers near the New York-Pennsylvania state line. There were stories of bushel baskets of projectile points and other artifacts from the surface. I was not, however, told of the extensive testing there by a party under Warren Moorehead and Alanson Skinner in 1916, working for the Robert S. Peabody Foundation, that had failed to find evidence of Indian occupation. There was a low earthen "wall" around the brow of the hill, and when our surface collecting and a few exploratory pits failed to produce, we ran five or six trenches across the wall. These showed multiple stages of construction, leading to the interpretation that instead of having been constructed for an Indian fort, it was gradually built up by generations of farmers to prevent soil erosion. At other locations in the vicinity we excavated Second and Third Period Algonkian and Andaste Iroquoian material. On the Thatcher farm south of Athens we stripped rather large areas of top soil in order to reveal sub-plow zone features. In one of our excavation trenches we partly uncovered a large mammal, which was a bit puzzling until we found out that the farmer's recently deceased bull had been buried in one of Skinner's excavations. My report on the excavations was submitted in 1932 to the Director of the Museum but was never published, primarily, I think, because it ran counter to her cherished convictions. Recent attempts to have the report published were frustrated by failure of the museum personnel in 1931–32 to catalog the collections we obtained and documented, so that now the only published statement is a brief resume (7).

As a result of this excavation experience, I was selected to excavate and survey in the Susquehanna Valley near Wilkes-Barre in 1932. Richard Morgan was to do the same in Somerset County and William Ritchie in the west branch of the Susquehanna. We met in Harrisburg and were shown our equipment and cars by Donald Cadzow on the Tuesday morning after Decoration Day, but by noon we were informed that Governor Gifford Pinchot had vetoed the appropriation bill. By that time there was no possibility of joining other excavation programs. That summer I prepared a report on the Parker Heights excavation which, alas, was also never published. Some three years ago a copy of that report was turned over to Northwestern University to be included as an appendix to work they have recently done in the Mississippi Valley south of Quincy.

William T. Corlett, a Cleveland physician, had prepared a manuscript on "The Medicine Man of the American Indian and His Cultural Background" (5). He met rebuffs from publishers, and Paul Martin at the Field Museum was asked to revise it extensively. As a result, I was recruited to help and spent considerable time reading and writing, and produced necessary changes in the chapters on the Plains, the Northeast Woodland, and the Southern Woodland. For the latter area I made considerable use of the Field Museum Library and of the manuscript collections in the Ayer Library. J. Eric Thompson rewrote the Middle American section, Donald Collier did the Northwest Coast and perhaps the Arctic, while Martin did the Southwest chapter. We were paid for our work, but I was still startled when the book was finally published to find only Paul Martin's name mentioned as having aided its preparation. The rest of us turned out to be unmentioned ghostwriters.

There were a number of job opportunities which might have led to a PhD thesis topic. Sapir nominated me for a Bishop Museum Fellowship in Hawaii, but it went to Edwin G. Burrows. I tried to go with J. Alden Mason on his first trip to Piedras Negras, but instead he took Linton Satterthwaite. I also wrote to Ephraim Speiser, in order to go to the Near East, but his choice was Dorothy Cross, and I understood that. Then in late 1932 I was supported by Cole for a fellowship in Aboriginal North American Ceramics at the University of Michigan, administered by the Museum of Anthropology and supported by Eli Lilly through the Indiana Historical Society. I had met Carl Guthe and his secretary at a number of meetings. I was chosen and arrived in mid-February 1933. I learned the Fellowship was for three years, that I was to take graduate courses in geology, geography, history and a few in anthropology, write a thesis, and would receive a PhD in February 1936. The Fellowship stipend was one of the best in the country, $1000 on a 12-month basis, plus $200.00 for travel expenses.

My fellowship support was provided to aid in identifying ceramic complexes in the eastern United States, with special emphasis on those from the Ohio Valley and surrounding areas. This was to be done by studying the collections that Guthe had obtained since 1928 in the Ceramic Repository for the Eastern United States and by visiting and analyzing museum and private collections. I read extensively the pertinent publications and knew something of the then recognized achaeological cultures. On a late spring Sunday afternoon in 1933, I was escorting a young lady to a concert on the campus when, in front of the library, I suddenly realized that a study of the Oneota material in the Upper Mississippi Valley, Fort Ancient in the Ohio Valley, and Iroquoian in New York and Ontario might result in the recognition of an Upper Mississippi Phase of Mississippian in the terminology of the Midwestern taxonomic method. I excused myself, hurried back to the Museum, and worked until midnight. That was initially to be my thesis topic. I began with Fort Ancient, and Guthe arranged a loan from the American Museum of Natural History of the pottery from Fox Farm collected by Harlan I. Smith in north central Kentucky (32). In working with this material, functional forms such as salt pans, bowls, and jars were easily recognized, and these vessel shapes, along with other ceramic features such as tempering materials, surface treatment, handle forms, and animal effigy heads, made grouping them into ceramic types a relatively easy task. I remember showing my grouping or types to Guthe in the summer of

1933, and saying that we would be able to have pottery types in the East comparable to those in the Southwest. He thought I should write that idea down before I forgot it!

It was apparent early that my original thesis topic would take too long to complete, and I was often diverted to preparing reports on pottery submitted from many locations. A large consignment of pottery from the Norris Dam area in northeastern Tennessee, and one from the Wheeler Dam in northwestern Alabama were received in 1934. The Norris Dam material formed the basis for my PhD thesis in February 1936 (9), and the Wheeler Basin report was completed late in 1936 (10). Following completion of the thesis and a most beneficial marriage to Ruby Fletcher on February 14, 1936, in the University of Chicago Chapel, we pursued additional Fort Ancient collections at the University of Kentucky, the National Museum of Natural History, the American Museum of Natural History, and the Peabody Museum at Harvard. We were diverted for a week to Macon Plateau, where Arthur Kelley was struggling with a wide variety of ceramics from the extensive excavations in Bibb County, Georgia. A number of days were spent in Harrisburg, Pennsylvania, preparing a statement on the Susquehannock material from southern Pennsylvania, and we had a short visit at New Haven, where we saw Cornelius Osgood and his wife, Leslie Spier, Peter Murdock, and met Ben Rouse and Froelich Rainey for the first time. In New York and Cambridge, I saw large collections from New York Iroquoian sites which had never been studied and published.

My manuscript on Fort Ancient was completed in 1938–1939 and turned over to Carl Guthe for reading in early 1939. It reposed on his desk for a year, during which he had turned my writing style to his on only some 20 pages. He then agreed that editing should be left to the Museum editor, and the report was finally ready for distribution in early January, 1944 (11), five years after its essential completion. Another major study was begun in 1936 on the emerging recognition of local cultural sequences from the Plains to the east coast, and from the Gulf north into Canada so that a broad sequential cultural development could be identified over the whole area. This was discussed with students and colleagues in Ann Arbor, at archaeological meetings in a number of locations over a five-year time span, with a final formal presentation at the Andover meeting of the AAA in December, 1941, for a symposium on "Man in the Northeast." It was not published until 1946 (12), so I was able to update and annotate it during the intervening war years.

One of the highlights of the late 1930s was a meeting held in my office in Ann Arbor in the Museum of Anthropology at which a format for the typological identification and description of Southeastern and Eastern pottery was hammered together, using a binomial identification for the pottery type (18). In spite of Guthe's ten-year attempt to establish a major center for ceramic study in the Museum of Anthropology, he agreed only to welcome the 16 participants.

There was clear irritation visible on his part, as well as by some archaeologists in Washington and by W. S. Webb concerning this project. With the further refinement of the type variety system, it has become an effective guide to the eventual delineation of social groups within a small geographic region and within a relatively short time period. Probably the best formulations have been in Phillip's work on the Lower Yazoo Basin (28) and by Toth on the Marksville occupations of Mississippi and Louisiana (35).

In 1940–1941 I was involved with Jim Ford and Philip Phillips in a survey of part of eastern Arkansas and northwest Mississippi to identify the ceramic complexes in those areas before the appearance of the Mississippian complexes. This aim was successful in spite of a painfully low budget. By the time the publication appeared its scope had broadened to include presentations of the physiographic divisions of the area we surveyed, the importance of Mississippi River former courses as an aide to site chronology, a discussion of ethnohistory of the area, the settlement patterns through time and contemporary regional differences, a section on seriation of the pottery, and stratigraphic test results, as well as the presentation of the ceramic typology. The summary and conclusions were not based on our work alone but on integrated data from a broad area of the east. It was a fruitful collaboration even if some lemons appeared in the publication (30).

In early 1944 Carl Guthe resigned from his position as Director of the Museum of Anthropology and Director of the University Museum, and became Director of the New York State Museum. Guthe had been led to believe that the president of the university would support Guthe's recommendation that the head of the Museums Exhibit program should be removed from that office because of incompetence. The president did not do so, and in addition, refused to make a counteroffer to the one that Guthe had received from the New York State Museum. Guthe's recommendation to the president that I should succeed him as Director of the Museum of Anthropology was ignored. For a time requisitions and all other business of the Museum of Anthropology were handled by a budget clerk in the business office. I grew disenchanted with carrying requisitions to be signed across campus and was not provided with a messenger boy's uniform. The regents of the university had become dissatisfied with President Alexander G. Ruthven, and one of them was promoting the appointment of Froelich Rainey as Director of the Museum of Anthropology, while Ruthven was interested in appointing Leslie Spier as both Chairman of the Department of Anthropology and Director of the Museum of Anthropology. It was a stalemate, and I began to act as though I had the responsibility of some of the administrative chores of the Museum. The unfortunate state of affairs at the Museum was brought to the attention of the chairman of the department of botany, Harley H. Bartlett, who had been instrumental in the appointment of Hayward Kenniston as the new Dean of the Literary College. The Dean in his contacts with anthropologists learned that Leslie White had the best reputation of the department members, so he was appointed chairman of the department in 1945, and I was finally approved by the regents as Director of the Museum early in 1946. During one of the regents' meetings in 1945, Ray Baker, the University reporter for the Ann Arbor News, was in the Museum, and I expressed feeling puzzled by their failure to act. His reply was, "Look, Griffin, if Pendergast (the Kansas City Democratic boss) was on this campus, he would lose his pants in two weeks."

The reasons for the above discussion are to give a brief version of the activities involved in a quite minor affair in a university. It is an example that is certainly paralleled many times in universities and other complex bureaucracies. Mature and older professional anthropologists will recognize it as the normal functioning of such an institution. Younger, perhaps more naive, professionals should be aware of some of the problems they are likely to meet in the advancement or hindrance of their careers. Also, it is a recognition of the unforeseen circumstances which led to my appointment. My career would certainly have been much different from 1946 to 1976 if I had been rejected as Director, or if Guthe had not left the University of Michigan.

A major difficulty of being the Director in the late 1940s and early 1950s was that the Museum of Anthropology had very little support from the higher officials allocating university funds. There was no money in the Museum budget for fieldwork, and the current expense amount was at an absurdly low level. Salaries for the Museum staff, on a 12-month basis, were about half those for comparable people on the teaching staff of the college, who were on a 9-month basis. Volney Jones and I were allowed to teach courses in the department in the summer of 1944 and the academic year 1944–1945 without teaching titles, even though one member of the department staff opposed our continuing teaching and being given professorial titles. My spot in the staff budget was filled by the appointment of Albert C. Spaulding, and he was a fine asset until his departure in 1959–1962 to become the second Director of the Anthropology Program of the National Science Foundation.

My attendance at a lecture by Dr. Pablo Martinez del Rio in 1945 and our discussions the next day developed into support from the graduate school to spend six months in Mexico in 1946. I was to collaborate with Eduardo Noguera, the director of the Museum of Anthropology in Mexico City, on a study of the prehistoric connections between Mexican cultures and those of the eastern United States. I had attended the 1943 Mesa Redondo meetings in Mexico City on the connections between Mexico and the Southwest and southeastern United States. My immediate aim was to study the collections from the Valley of Mexico area in the museum in Mexico City, but I soon learned that substantial or even representative collections from the years of work by Mexican archaeologists were either not preserved or not available. As a result, I made collections from Archaic to Aztec sites in the Valley, in the western Cholula area, Tula, and in the state of Mexico. I also examined material from Monte Alban that Alfonso Caso and Ignacio Bernal were studying in a former monastery in southern Mexico City. This served to stir my interest in seeing that magnificent complex and the number of large ruins that were in the Valley of Oaxaca, many of which were occupied at the same times as Monte Alban. This opportunity to see a substantial number of the major highland Mexican population centers and to observe the considerable number of ancillary "contemporary" towns and hamlets gave me a comparative base for the cultural developments in the Southwest and eastern United States. In no way did the United States sites have the development or complexity of those in Mexico.

From my collections and observations I felt that the application of the binomial pottery typology in use in the United States might be an improvement on what had been done earlier in Mexico. Noguera declined to participate, but Martinez del Rio allowed me to work with the collections from Tlateloco in Mexico City. With the addition of material from Chalco, called Aztec I in the then current typology, given to me by Antonieta Espejo, and with her translation into Spanish, two papers were eventually published (21). I associated with many of the Mexican archaeologists, among whom was Miguel Covarrubias. He was interested in examining possible connections with the southeastern United States, but the only one that really stimulated him was on a photographic print I had with me of an engraved shell from Spiro in eastern Oklahoma (29) with individuals paddling a dugout; a portrayal similar to a mural painting on the Temple of the Warriors at Chichen Itza. Ignacio Marquina, Director of the National Institute of Anthropology and History, offered me the opportunity to direct excavations at one of the Tlaxcallan sites, and while I was honored by the offer, I did not feel that my temperament could adapt to a long exposure to Mexican archaeological culture. Among other handicaps, I was not able to even swear effectively in Spanish.

Noguera and I had many congenial hours together, and I went with him on quite a few excursions to Valley of Mexico sites for his course on Mexican ceramics and stratigraphy. We never did, however, get down to serious work together on the program that I had hoped would materialize. The six months' study in Mexico considerably improved my course in Mexican prehistory. I returned with a fairly impressive representative collection of pottery that I used in my teaching; it has also been an aid to Jeffrey Parsons, first in his thesis work and subsequently in his Meso-American course and training of graduate students. It also provided a base on which to build in my subsequent papers on Mexican-Eastern United States interaction. My confidence in such interaction or exchange has over the years been eroded to the point where in my last interpretation I could recognize only the spread of Mexican domesticated plants into the Southeast, some probably from northeast Mexico during the Late Archaic, 4000 to 1000 B.C., and corn arriving during the first millenium after Christ and probably from the Southwest (19). On subsequent trips to Mexico in the 1950s and 1960s, I was able to visit sites in eastern and northern Vera Cruz including Tajin, see some of the materials that Garcia Payon had excavated at the Formative Period site at El Trapiche, and see Chichen Itza and Mayapan in northern Yucatan and Uxmal and Kabah in the Puuc area. In 1955, I was also able to drive north from Mexico City along the highway on the east side of the Sierra Madre Occidental to Santa Fe. We stopped at the impressive site of La Quemada and obtained ^{14}C samples which supported the view that its T-shaped doorways, masonry construction, and some other features suggestive of the Southwest were probably indicative of interconnection between the two areas.

In the summer of 1946, Fred Eggan and I prepared an outline of a festschrift to honor Fay-Cooper Cole on his retirement in 1947 as chairman of the Department of Anthropology at the University of Chicago. Responsibility for editing the volume was turned over to me. If I had known the problems that would arise during the ensuing six years I would not have undertaken the task. The 28 chapters and an appendix on C^{14} dates for the eastern United States were a testimonial to Cole's leadership in establishing the University of Chicago as a preeminent trainer of archaeologists. The first chapter was received in April 1947 and the last one in April 1950. In the late spring of 1950 the complete manuscript was shipped to the University of Chicago Press. The Wenner-Gren Foundation and the Lichstern Fund of the department of anthropology provided substantial support. The contract with the Press provided that any royalties would be turned over to support archaeological research by the department of anthropology, and the editor at the Press for the volume agreed that archaeology would be spelled that way.

In the summer of 1950 I was asked by Robert Redfield and Sol Tax to come to Chicago and have lunch with them at the Quadrangle Club. I was told that the projected cost of the volume was $10,000 and that it was much too long. Redfield asked, "Jimmy, what would you do if you had $10,000? Would you expend it on this volume, or use it for research?" My reply indicated that I thought the volume was the result of years of archaeological research that was worth publishing by individuals who had the best knowledge of their subjects and that it was a valuable summation. I was astounded at their attitude. It was finally agreed that the volume size should be cut one-third and that several chapters should be returned to the authors. However, some individuals were out of the country or otherwise could not be contacted, so the task fell to me. I acquired the mailing lists of many of the state and regional archaeological societies for a prepublication reduced-price flyer. I read proof in July 1952 in Tucson and found to my consternation that the key word in the volume had been changed to archeology. The Press had also changed the contract and eliminated any royalties. By the time the volume appeared the cost was covered by an 11% return by subscribers, and by the subventions. The volume has had five impressions, and had sold 6513 copies as of 1978 and is now permanently out of stock (13). It is my interpretation that the sales represent a vote of 6513 in favor of publishing the Cole volume to two against it.

In the latter half of the mid-1940s W. F. Libby and his associates were developing radiocarbon dating (34). With the assured support of the Viking Foundation for Anthropological Research, the American Anthropological Association Executive Board appointed the Committee on Radioactive Carbon[14] with Frederick Johnson as Chairman, Froelich Rainey, and Donald Collier in February 1948, and in March 1948 enlarged by the addition of Richard F. Flint representing the Geological Society of America (24). I was asked by the Committee to obtain samples of Adena and Hopewell and related material. The results of these first assessments were surprising for they indicated that contrary to archaeological data, Adena was later than Hopewell, Tchefuncte was later than Marksville and that Marksville in the Lower Mississippi Valley, which should be essentially contemporary with Hopewell, was substantially later. Some archaeologists did not believe those results could be correct, including me, while others did (24). On the other hand, I was in error in my estimate of the chronological age of the time periods for Adena-Tchefuncte and Hopewell-Marksville. In the summer of 1949, with support from the Michigan Memorial Phoenix Fund, H. R. Crane of the department of physics began the construction of a radiocarbon counter, and an interdisciplinary committee was appointed by the graduate school to do the curatorial work on the specimens submitted and I was appointed chairman. Professor Crane constructed his counter and within a year it was in operation. I believe we were the second laboratory to produce dates. We functioned for 20 years until the pressure of other duties, inadequate financial support, and other factors caused the highly successful project to be abandoned. We issued reports on our results, first in *Science* and then in the journal *Radiocarbon,* with a total number of somewhat over 2000 dates. The curatorial responsibility of the Museum of Anthropology for the submitted samples provided financial support for quite a few graduate students in archaeology. The dates as they were obtained were of interest to staff and students and provided interesting discussion sessions.

The location of the University of Michigan made knowledge of the glaciation episodes of considerable importance so that with the formation of a Quaternary studies seminar of glacial geologists, botanists, paleontologists, and archaeologists, graduate students in archaeology were encouraged to enroll from the 1950s to the 1980s, and many of them did so. It was not only an advantage to them as an introduction to these supplementary sciences, but it also allowed them to understand something of the problems inherent in those fields.

One proposal that was prominent in the mid-years of the century was that the Eastern United States Woodland "pattern" had been introduced into North America from Northeast Asia (27). This concept, along with the more established derivation of the earliest human New World populations from that area, prompted me to obtain support from the Wenner-Gren Foundation for a study of northern Eurasian collections in Europe in 1953–1954. I particularly wanted to work with Russian and Siberian materials and applied to the Soviet Embassy in Washington for a visa in early 1953. My study of some of the Cape Denbigh ceramics for J. Louis Giddings had rekindled my interest (14), for it seemed possible to be somewhat more precise regarding the possible connections than was the case in the 1930s and 1940s. Needless to say, the Russian visa application was not approved. Nevertheless, some progress was made with the aid of Karl Jettmar in Vienna in 1954 in obtaining some comprehension of the southwestern Siberian prehistoric pottery. In addition, I had been intrigued with Grahame Clark's study of the mesolithic in the North Sea area (4). Visits to Norway, Sweden, Denmark, and England made me increasingly aware of the similarities of the environment in the North Sea-Baltic areas to that of the Great Lakes. Both areas had been glaciated, undergone subsidence and uplift with resultant changes in land-water relationships. Both had gone through a long period of reforestation, and of changes in fauna, with an important effect on the cultural adaptation of populations who moved to the north as the land became habitable. One of the results of this first European trip was the preparation of a manuscript of 50 or more pages on prehistoric connections between Siberia and North America for the International Congress of Prehistoric and Protohistoric Sciences in Hamburg in 1958. It was, of course, much too long, and I asked Grahame Clark if he would consider it for the Proceedings of the Prehistoric Society in England. The manuscript was returned about a year later with a rejection letter, and I submitted a shorter version to *Science* which was accepted (15).

I had been placed on the Permanent Council of the International Union of Prehistoric and Protohistoric Sciences as one of four United States representatives at the reorganization meeting of that body in Paris after World War II. This was probably done by Pedro Bosch Gimpera, whom I had met at the 1943 Mesa Redondo in Mexico City and again in 1946. The Permanent Council met every four years, and I was successful in obtaining support for frequent attendence. In Prague in 1962, where the Congress of the International Union was held, the other three United States representatives nominated me for the eight-man Executive Committee. To my, and their, surprise I was elected, and reelected for a second term, so that I attended most of the biennial meetings until I became an Honorary Member at the Congress in Nice in 1975. These European contacts were of considerable value in initiating the study in Poland of Saraunas Milisauskas and his later excavation program near Cracow, the introduction of Gregory Johnson to European prehistory, and the excavation program of Martin Wobst near Derventa in Yugoslavia.

In 1961, having noticed the approval of a cultural exchange between the United States and the Soviet Union, I applied to the American Council of Learned Societies to study the prehistoric collections in Yakutsk which had been gathered by A. P. Okladnikov from the Lena River, as well as other materials from northeast Siberia and the Lake Baikal-Angara river area in Irkutsk. I received word in April that others had been selected before me. However, within a month or so, another letter informed me that one of the five original selectees was unable to go. Later I learned that the ACLS had been asked by Soviet authorities if they really wanted to send one of the original group they had approved. Whoever it was did not go. I planned to attend the Sixth International Quaternary Congress in Warsaw, then Fred Matson's Ceramics and Man Conference at Burg Wartenstein in Austria, return to Warsaw, and take a train to Moscow on September 15, 1961. I immediately applied to the Soviet Embassy in Washington for a three-month visa, intending to return to Ann Arbor for Christmas. The visa had not been delivered when I sailed on the S. S. Flanders for France. I was told to visit the Soviet Embassy in Warsaw, which I did before and after my trip to Austria, but the visa did not appear. The American Embassy in Warsaw phoned our embassy in Moscow a number of times to determine what was holding up my visa. One of the Russian replies forwarded to Warsaw was "If Griffin is the man he says he is, he will get his visa." By mid-October the Cultural Affairs officer at the Warsaw office asked if there was anywhere else I wanted to go in Europe. So I retreated to West Germany, then north to Copenhagen, Stockholm, and finally to Helsinki, for somewhere along the way I was informed the visa would be at the Russian Embassy there. I spent about a week in Helsinki at the National Museum going over some of the early "Neolithic" pottery from Finland, which is very similar to that from the adjoining Russian area. Finally, a visa appeared in late October, and I was permitted to enter the Soviet Union and arrived in Moscow. I appeared at a formal gathering of the staff of the Institute of Ethnology, for they were my official host while I was in the Soviet Union. I was asked what I wanted to do even though my program had of course been approved by them. I was told that everything I wanted to see was in Moscow or Leningrad and that there was nothing in Yakutsk. Besides, I was told, it was very cold in Yakutsk. When it was suggested that an American ought to be able to stay there a few weeks if Russians lived there through the long winter, the inference was ignored. The real reasons were primarily "political," for major Soviet aboveground tests were taking place in northwest Siberia on Novaya Zemlya and no intruders were allowed to enter Siberia. Some of the reasons were also economic, because of the cost to the Institute of paying my way and that of an interpreter. However, during my three-month stay I did manage to see and work with a considerable amount of material from southcentral and northeastern Siberia. Some part of this work was later published (17).

A major conclusion was that while the earliest pottery in Alaska indeed derived from northeast Asia, about 1000 B.C. as the Norton Complex in Alaska, and then spread east to the mouth of the McKenzie River and south in Alaska, the tradition of pottery manufacture in the Eastern Woodlands or northern Plains did not come from Asia. A sidelight of this research trip is that if anyone reading this statement thinks an American is not presented with opportunities to stray from the paths of the righteous, I can testify that at least one was so opportuned. Both in Warsaw and Moscow, there were phone calls from young women which seemed to represent individual initiative but were so patently part of programmed professional patriots that it was diverting to engage in a bit of banter with the unseen callers. When it is understood that there were no telephone directories in Moscow in 1961, connivance was the only way the calls could have been made.

A program was put together in 1959 to correlate the gradual changes during the Holocene in the Great Lakes area, and particularly in Michigan, with prehistoric cultural changes. Initially the professional directorate was to be Griffin, George Quimby, and Albert Spaulding. However, Quimby was not able to participate because of his obligations to the Field Museum, and Spaulding took a leave of absence from the Museum in 1959 to become the head of the anthropology program of the National Science Foundation. With help from a great many people in the state, able graduate students, and adequate funding from a number of sources, we were able to support three field parties, in the Saginaw basin, on Bois Blanc at the Straits of Mackinaw, and at the Norton Mound Group in Grand Rapids. This was certainly the most extensive excavation program conducted by an institution in the state and perhaps still is. Major excavation reports were published, and the additional studies stimulated by the investigation made the period from 1960 to the early 1970s a rewarding one.

In the late 1950s I attended a lecture on campus by Erling Dorff, who had been captain of the University of Chicago swimming team (1924–1925) when I was a sophomore on the team. He was at the time professor of paleontology at Princeton and he talked on paleoclimates. The last segment of his presentation discussed briefly the Little Ice Age of about A.D. 1300–1500s in northwestern Europe. This set me off on my venture into identifying what North American prehistoric cultural changes might have been at least partly influenced by climatic change. As I associated with professionals in the various fields whose data were vital to identifying the effect of climatic variation on flora, soil changes, erosion, prehistoric agriculture, and other factors, I became aware of the complexity of each of these areas, and realized that our chronological controls in any of them were not adequate at the time to identify specific climatic or weather patterns that could have produced demonstrable cultural change. General trends of increasing warmth, or dryness lasting for millenia or even hundreds of years, inevitably contained fairly long and shorter periods when the trends were muted by variations. By 1963 I had decided that firm results from this approach were not likely to be reached in the near future, with the possible exception of the Southwest, where tree ring chronology provided a much tighter temporal framework than is now possible in most other areas. Since then considerable progress has been made with better excavation techniques in marginal vegetation areas and better identification and interpretational skills in the natural sciences, including the reconstruction of paleoclimates.

Another excavation program launched in the mid-1960s was in southeast Missouri on sites of the Powers phase. I became aware of this Mississippian complex in 1966 through James E. Price, a "native" of the area, when he was an undergraduate at the University of Missouri. A visit to the area in late July of 1967, with Price as a guide, convinced me that it was an unusual opportunity for investigation of a functioning prehistoric society. Powers Fort was the major site, with platform mounds, a palisade, plaza, and indications of houses. Within relatively short distances there were contemporary villages which from surface indications appeared to be members of the same polity. The locations of house structures were easily identified. Furthermore, there did not seem to be evidence of earlier or later occupations, and the surface debris and what was available from some clandestine excavations gave presumptive evidence of considerable interaction between near neighboring groups within a quite short period of time. In some 30 years of viewing sites in the east, I had never seen an area with such potential. Sitting in his vehicle parked at the Snodgrass site, Jim and I roughed out a proposal to the National Science Foundation to support an excavation program with Jim as the field director. A revised request was prepared and submitted to the National Science Foundation, and Price began his graduate studies at Ann Arbor. At that time random sampling was the golden key to unlocking the door to many archaeological questions, and some number of the graduate students, when we initiated the field program, were insistent that random sampling should be the procedure followed. However, we already knew where an adequate number of sites were located, their dimensions, the locations of house structures, and that the surface finds demonstrated rough contemporaneity. At that time there had not been a complete excavation of a Mississippian village or small town. Many sites had been sampled by stratigraphic pits, and a few houses in towns or villages, platform mounds, and cemeteries had been excavated. I thought it was more important to deviate from a then popular acceptable archaeological approach, and so the Snodgrass site of some 90 houses, with a barely discernible palisade wall, inner compound, and short-lived occupancy was almost completely excavated. Its "sister" village, the Turner site, was approximately three-fourths excavated, while the Powers

Fort and a few other villages had a few houses excavated to give additional guarantees of structural and artifactual similarities (31).

Again, a large number of students were able to participate in the pleasures and drudgery of field work, and some were able later to take charge of their own excavations and improve upon what was done in the Powers phase project. One of our strategies was to open large areas of the Snodgrass site, using power machinery to remove the plow-zone in order to reveal more accurately the house structures and also the areas between structures. We also were able to identify activity areas within houses, the essential homogeneity of projectile point forms, variation in vessel features and forms, and their normal location within houses. It was determined that the occupation of the site was short-lived on the basis of the physical evidence, and ^{14}C dates of some 29 samples from four sites on tree branches, while displaying a disturbing length of time, nevertheless clustered around A.D. 1300. A number of subsequent excavations in the Mississippi Valley adopted some of the procedures, modified by their own unique situations and funding. While this effort at complete exposure of subsurface features was not new, it was the first time that many archaeologists in the Mississippi Valley had witnessed it in operation.

The most stimulating excavation program in my recent experience has been, and still is, that of the Federal Highway I-270 project along the east side of the Mississippi flood plain opposite St. Louis (2). It began with an intensive survey of the then proposed right-of-way in 1975. In 1977 the University of Illinois at Urbana-Champaign signed an agreement as prime contractor, with Charles J. Bareis as the general director, and I use the adjective "general" advisedly. Several other institutions in the state were allotted subcontracts. Many of the professional archaeologists of the program had extensive experience in the American Bottom Mississippi flood plain and were also familiar with previous archaeological work within 500 miles, more or less, of the area of their investigations. The central Cahokia site, where most previous investigations has been conducted, has been recognized as the premier Mississippian period population concentration for almost 200 years. Excavations there, while contributing significantly to the attempt to understand the growth and development of the society, still suffered from the results of rebuilding and living activities so that separation of the sequent societies was difficult.

Very little was known about the populations outside the central area and how they might be related to the central area. The presence of Early and Middle Woodlands societies was known primarily from surface material, as well as the even earlier Archaic populations. Systematic studies of the subsistence base, the reasons for site locations, and many other pertinent delineations were not understood. In the published summary report (2), it is stated that almost 100 sites were excavated in the flood plain and the borrow pit locations on the adjoining bluffs. Many of these were not known to professional archaeologists before, especially those covered with alluvial and colluvial deposits. For the first time the geomorphology was studied, correlated with the periods of prehistoric occupation, and the temporal period was determined. Paleobotanical materials testified to the initial dependence upon local plant foods from the riverine environment in the Late Archaic populations and the gradual changes as domesticated plants were introduced, with native North American seed plants becoming domesticated. Tobacco was added in the first half of the first millenium after Christ and maize in the latter half. While there were clear indications of population growth from the third millenium B.C. to the introduction of maize, it is not until that domesticate arrives that the population expands and societal complexity, public works, and other Mississippian features make their appearance. Zooarchaeology studies were comparable in sophistication to those in paleobotany, and bioanthropology studies yielded interesting results on morbidity, diseases, trauma, and the influence of cultural practices on hard-tissue morphology.

Gradual changes in most artifact forms, house construction, village settlement pattern, and pit construction are seen to have evolved slowly, at varying speeds, in an almost unbroken sequence from A.D. 300 to A.D. 1450. It is certainly the most extensive continuing program in a concentrated area in eastern archaeology and has produced the most important results in regard to societal adaptation and structure. As this is written, nine final reports have been published by the University of Illinois Press with some eleven in progress on the excavations. There are other facets that will need to be studied and integrated into the available information from the central site and the interaction of American Bottom prehistoric populations over a large area of the Mississippi Valley. Much more can be learned by the expenditure of over six million dollars than by the comparatively paltry sums available in the earlier days. My participation in this program was miniscule as an advisor and commentator, and I am most grateful in my retired, but not retiring, years to have contributed in a small way to the major results it has produced.

For a volume of essays in honor of Emerson Greenman, Curator of the Great Lakes division of the Museum of Anthropology, I prepared a paper on "Hopewell and the Dark Black Glass" (16), which provided distributional data, assessment of the probably short time period in which obsidian appeared in the Midwest, differences in utilization between Ohio Hopewell sites and those of the Upper Mississippi Valley, the probable source, and if Yellowstone Park was the source, suggestions on how obsidian might have reached the Midwest. It was an antidote to the somewhat more casually constructed presentation of the diffusion or interaction sphere studies then in vogue. Shortly thereafter I became aware of the potential of neutron activation studies and enlisted Adon Gordus of the chemistry department to do the analyses. I gathered source material from 44 locations in the western United States, 4 in Meso-America, 2 from South America, 2 from Alaska, and others from Europe, the Near East, Iceland, Tenerife, and the Ascension Islands. I included some of the latter group to forestall suggestions that prehistoric immigrants or explorers from the Old World brought the obsidian with them. Sixty-three samples from 30 sites in five states and Ontario were analyzed, and all of them indicated Yellowstone Park as the source (22). What had been a topic of speculation for over a hundred years was thus placed in a much more secure framework. Unfortunately, how the obsidian arrived in the Midwest and its dispersal over the areas is still much less certain. This study apparently had an impact, for a number of papers have since appeared documenting the source areas for galena found in Late Archaic to Mississippian times (36, 37). The sources of Middle Woodland silver and copper have also been identified by their minute amounts of chemical elements (3, 6). It is much better to have such materials accurately pinned down to nonlocal sources because it is then possible to postulate how the raw material traveled. Unfortunately, the techniques of identification usually require expensive equipment and the time of specialists so that most such investigations are short lived.

In a recent manuscript I gave a brief resume of some of the concepts followed at the time of my introduction to archaeological research and for some time thereafter. The statement is quoted below:

> One of the major approaches to interpreting cultural activities was the recognition of culture areas which had a strong emphasis of the effect of environment on the development of material culture traits. This was based on museum studies in the last quarter of the nineteenth and the early twentieth centuries. Along with the identification of the area center went the identification of marginal tribes within and between areas. Trait associations were perceived as an important factor. Since many traits were assumed to have originated in or near the culture area center and spread outward from there, the age area hypothesis came into use. This may be regarded as at the base of the thinking which postulated that the Mississippian phenomenon originated in the central Mississippi Valley and spread outward from there. This is only one instance where anthropological theory led archaeologists astray. It was essentially a timeless framework applied to both ethnology and archaeology or when a temporal sequence was proposed it was not very accurate. The emphases on material culture traits in framing the culture area may be regarded as a forerunner of the University of California Trait Element lists and the Midwest Taxonomic Method.
>
> Diffusion was the means by which cultural elements spread. It was accomplished in some instances by borrowing from neighboring groups. A whole cycle of processes was required for the spread of the horse from the Southwest to the north and east and resulted in the several varieties of innovations developed by tribes or tribal groups. It accounted for the spread of maize and other agricultural crops. Trade and exchange were regarded as mechanisms for diffusion. Migration was a form of diffusion. Conquest and colonization resulted in the diffusion of new ideas and behavior.
>
> The psychic unity of man accounted for discovery and invention as similar needs produced similar results. There still lingered remnants of cultural evolutionary schemes of the nineteenth century, and the cultural evolution revival with energy as the engine which produced cultural change and development. Variations were convergent development and parallelism where historical connection could not be demonstrated. The direct historical

approach was utilized over much of the east as well as other parts of the country for many years where early historical records of tribal locations allowed it. Tribal traditions were extensively employed to explain separation of peoples who belonged to the same linguistic stock, and was partly responsible for the interpretation of the movement to the northeast of the Iroquois from a homeland in the central Mississippi Valley. Many archaeologists called for intensification of efforts to obtain a stratigraphic developmental sequence of culture in localized regions.

One of the major difficulties was a lack of adequate funds to explore and delineate village site remains. The long emphasis on mound exploration was giving way however to the excavation of village sites but these were not adequate to recover more than a small proportion of the settlement. Distributional and classificatory studies were pursued, ethnobotanical and faunal identifications were done wherever possible. It was an exciting period in the thirties as old interpretations were tested for their validity, particularly against the increasing evidence of prehistoric cultural depth and gradual change. The arrival of man in North America was pushed back to a period contemporary with extinct fauna at the Pleistocene-Holocene border (20).

Many facets of archaeology have changed a great deal in the last 30 to 40 years, as is true in many other areas of American culture. Much of this must be related to the growth and expansion of the economy and the accompanying population expansion. The research activities that accompanied the increase in students interested in higher education occurred in all fields of science. Existing universities and colleges expanded, and major new schools were established, in order to accommodate the need for instructors and research directors. Where one adequately trained individual was available in the 1930s, hundreds were pursuing careers by the 1970s. Many new developments took place in mammalogy, conchology, paleobotany, palynology, physiography, statistics, and dating techniques to name but a few of them. New theoretical models were proposed in the rapidly expanding fields of Anthropology, some of which were valuable for archaeological research, and some were applied which were either not applicable or could have been used with more caution.

The establishment of the Viking Fund, which later became the Wenner-Gren Foundation for Anthropological Research, provided a source for funds in many subdisciplines and to my own work in archaeology. It was followed about a decade later by the National Science Foundation, followed by the National Council for the Humanities. These federally funded sources enabled research activities to be conducted on a scale not normally possible earlier. Their proposal reviews and panel approval of projects raised the level of research activities in archaeology as well as in other fields. These funding sources enabled American archaeologists to operate in Latin America, Europe, Africa, and Asia in unprecedented numbers. This not only enabled American techniques and strategies to be introduced in many areas but also enabled Americans to incorporate new ideas into the American scene. It enabled American students to become familiar with a large number of areas, problems, and personnel while earlier they had relatively few sources written by little known individuals to broaden their knowledge of prehistory. Similar structural and economic growth was taking place in many countries. This cross-fertilization, dare I say diffusion, or interaction should produce more international similarities in the pursuit of archaeology than was the case in the past.

There has been a burgeoning of archaeological state and local societies in the United States, accompanied by a growth of regional organizations and conferences and national organizations such as the Society for Historical Archaeology, the Society of Archaeological Sciences, and so on. Each has its journals and a remarkable amount of information published, which means that an individual who tries to keep abreast of new programs and data over a large area is in a hopeless position. At one time I had read and knew much of what had been written on Eastern woodlands archaeology, somewhat less so on the Plains, and the Southwest. I had some knowledge of European prehistory and of Mexico.

The impact of federal legislation requiring surveys to determine if locations of highway construction, river and coastline changes, building construction, and pipeline routes would destroy sites has provided extraordinary funding and swollen the number of individuals identified as archaeologists to unprecedented levels. Some of those programs have produced admirable published reports, others are of lesser quality, and some have been disasters for a variety of reasons. Reports by the hundreds have been prepared and turned in to federal, state, and local agencies and private firms; many of these are languishing in files and are known to very few archaeologists. If the stated aims of archaeology are to be served adequately, it is vitally important that interpretation of prehistoric contemporaneous cultural systems be based on the most complete knowledge of the areal extent, density, and functional varieties that is possible. This is in contrast to the point of view recently expressed that "... it has seemed important to work towards filling in the gaps on maps or chronological charts. But except for remote corners and unusual circumstances, the need for descriptive inventories of the remains of human activity during successive epochs is long past" (1). The author then proceeds to identify other important goals and decry the purely descriptive approach. However, the eastern United States still is not adequately known and cannot provide definitive data to answer many legitimate questions of prehistoric research. I suspect that in most areas of the world a similar situation exists. This does not mean that interpretive studies of social organization, ideology, or adaptive strategies should not be pursued if they are regarded as studies which will inevitably have a relatively short life span.

One of my major objectives for most of my academically active career was to establish the Museum of Anthropology at the University of Michigan as a significant unit of the instructional and research activity of the university. In order to do this it was felt that the museum should be a separate administrative entity with its own budget and director. In addition, the staff should increase in size, in wider research interests, in additional space for offices for staff and students, and more space for research collections. The museum staff should be integrated on a half-time academic year basis with the department of anthropology so that its course offerings could provide a prehistoric background for the areal interests of social anthropologists in the department. In addition, the museum should provide a center for graduate students in archaeology to work on collections, their own research, and to be able to interact with each other and the professional staff in an agreeable cooperative social environment. At least some of these objectives have been accomplished. In spite of administrative personnel changes and shifts in attitudes toward the functions of research museums, persistent and reasonably polite presentation eventually established the museum as a significant program. The department's instructional interests were a great help in the staff additions from 1966 to 1974, particularly the efforts of William Schorger to add Near Eastern archaeologists.

An important part of a museum's responsibilities is to have a publication program as an outlet for staff research production, that of students, and of manuscripts of "friends" of the museum. The Museum of Anthropology had the *Occasional Contributions* series, which was established by Carl Guthe in 1932 and published by the University of Michigan Press. In the late 1940s a new director of the University Press was appointed, and publication of that series was abandoned. Shortly thereafter, a request came to me to publish a short manuscript by Frances Densmore that had been supported by a former governor of Michigan, Chase S. Osborn. As a result, the *Anthropological Paper* series was established in 1949, and by 1975 60 numbers had appeared. Later a *Memoir and Technical Report* series was begun, and seven Memoirs and three Technical Reports were issued by 1975. Almost all of the funds for these were obtained from outside sources and from income from sales.

There have been many areas of archaeological research in which I have not actively participated, not for lack of interest in them, but rather for lack of training, adequate skills, sufficient motivation, or because of more pressing duties. Various well- and ill-meaning criticisms have reached my eyes and ears over the years and will probably continue in the future. I am reminded of a presentation given by Alfred Kroeber to anthropologists at the University of Chicago in the mid-1930s which I happened to attend on one of my trips from Ann Arbor to my parents' home in Oak Park. After Kroeber's talk there were a number of questions, and then Radcliffe-Brown took Kroeber to task for his interests in cultural history when he could be doing much more meaningful studies such as those Radcliffe-Brown did. He asked Kroeber "Why do you continue to do hypothetical reconstructions of cultural history?" Kroeber's reply was, "Because I enjoy it. Do you mind?"

Along the path I have followed I have met and enjoyed association with a great many individuals and institutions. From most of these I have directly benefited and I trust such contacts have been of some benefit to them. It has been a long journey with many milestones and not too many millstones.

ACKNOWLEDGMENTS

I am grateful to the Department of Anthropology staff, National Museum of Natural History, Smithsonian Institution, for a Regents Fellowship for the 1984 calendar year and for office space in the department. This manuscript was prepared in December 1984 while I was away from my Ann Arbor office and the records there. It is as accurate as I can make it under that handicap.

Literature Cited

1. Adams, R. M. 1984. Smithsonian horizons. *Smithsonian* 15(8):14
2. Bareis, C. J., Porter, J. W., eds. 1984 *American Bottom Archaeology. A summary of the FAI-270 project contribution to the culture history of the Mississippi River Valley.* Urbana/Chicago: Univ. Ill. Press. 286 pp.
3. Brose, D. S., Greber, N. 1979. Hopewell archaeology: The Chillicothe Conference. *Midcont. J. Archaeol. Spec. Publ.* 3:253
4. Clark, J. G. D. 1936. *The Mesolithic Settlement of Northern Europe.* Cambridge, England: Univ. Press. 299 pp.
5. Corlett, W. T. 1935. *The Medicine Man of the American Indian and His Cultural Background.* Springfield/Baltimore: Thomas. 369 pp.
6. Goad, S. I., Noakes, J. 1978. Prehistoric copper artifacts in the Eastern United States. In *Archaeological Chemistry-II,* ed. G. F. Carter. *Adv. Chem. Ser.* 171:335–46. Washington, DC: Am. Chem. Soc. 389 pp.
7. Griffin, J. B. 1931. The Athens excavations. *Bull. Soc. Penn. Archeol.* 2(2):3
8. Griffin, J. B. 1934. Archaeological remains in Adams County, Illinois. *Ill. State Acad. Sci.* 2:97–99
9. Griffin, J. B. 1938. The ceramic remains from Norris Basin, Tennessee. In *An Archaeological Survey of the Norris Basin in Eastern Tennessee,* ed. W. S. Webb. *Bur. Am. Ethnol. Bull.* 118:253–358
10. Griffin, J. B. 1939. Report on the ceramics of Wheeler Basin. In *An archaeological survey of Wheeler Basin on the Tennessee River in northern Alabama,* ed. W. S. Webb. *Bur. Am. Ethnol. Bull.* 122:127–65
11. Griffin, J. B. 1943. *The Fort Ancient Aspect, its cultural and chronological position in Mississippi Valley archaeology.* Ann Arbor: Univ. Mich. Press. 392 pp.
12. Griffin, J. B. 1946. Cultural change and continuity in Eastern United States archaeology. In *Man in Northeastern North America,* ed. F. Johnson. Peabody Found. Archaeol. Pap. 3:37–95
13. Griffin, J. B., ed. 1952. *Archeology of Eastern United States.* Chicago/London: Univ. Chicago Press
14. Griffin, J. B. 1953. A preliminary statement on the pottery from Cape Denbigh, Alaska. In *Asia and North America, Transpacific Contacts,* assemb. M. W. Smith. *Soc. Am. Archaeol. Mem.* 9:40–42
15. Griffin, J. B. 1960. Some prehistoric connections between Siberia and America. *Science* 131(3403):801–12
16. Griffin, J. B. 1965. Hopewell and the dark black glass. *Mich. Archaeol.* 11:115–55
17. Griffin, J. B. 1970. Northeast Asian and northwestern American ceramics. *Proc. 8th Int. Congr. Anthropol. Ethnol. Sci.* 3:327–30. Tokyo/Kyoto: Sci. Counc. Japan
18. Griffin, J. B. 1976. A commentary on some archaeological activities in the Mid-Continent 1925–1975. *Midcont. J. Archaeol.* 1(1):5–38
19. Griffin, J. B. 1980. The Mesoamerican-Southeastern U.S. connection. *Early Man* 2(3):12–18
20. Griffin, J. B. 1985. The formation of the Society for American Archaeology. *Am. Antiq.* 49: In press
21. Griffin, J. B., Espejo, A. 1947. Tlatelolco a traves de los tiempos: La alfareria correspondiente al ultimo periodo de ocupacion nahua del Valle de Mexico. In *Academia mexicana de la historia correspondiente de la Realde Madrid. Memorias.* 6:131–47; t.9:118–67
22. Griffin, J. B., Gordus, A. A., Wright, G.

S. 1969. Identification of sources of Hopewellian obsidian in the Middle West. *Am. Antiq.* 4(1):1–14
23. Hamsum, K. 1922. *Wanderers.* New York: Knopf
24. Johnson, F., assemb. 1951. Radiocarbon dating. *Soc. Am. Archaeol. Mem.* 8 Suppl. *Am Antiq.* 17(1):1–3; 26–29
25. Kelly, A. R., Cole, F-C. 1931. Rediscovering Illinois: Springfield. *Blue Book of the State of Illinois 1931–1932,* pp. 318–41
26. Krogman, W. M. 1931. The archaeology of the Chicago area. III. *State Acad. Sci.* 23:413–20
27. McKern, W. C. 1937. An hypothesis for the Asiatic origin of the Woodland Pattern. *Am. Antiq.* 3(2):138–43
28. Phillips, P. 1970. Archaeological survey in the lower Yazoo Basin, Mississippi. *Pap. Peabody Mus. Am. Archaeol. Ethnol. Harvard Univ.,* Vol. 60. 999 pp.
29. Phillips, P., Brown, J. A. 1975–1984. *Pre-Columbian Shell Engravings from the Craig Mound at Spiro, Ohlahoma.* Cambridge, Mass: Peabody Museum Press. 6 vol. cloth, 2 vol. paper
30. Phillips, P., Ford, J. A., Griffin, J. B. 1951. Archaeological survey in the lower Mississippi Valley 1940–47. *Pap. Peabody Mus. Am. Archaeol. Ethnol. Harvard Univ.,* Vol. 25. 511 pp.
31. Price, J. E., Griffin, J. B. 1979. The Snodgrass site of the Powers Phase of Southeast Missouri. *Anthropol. Pap. Mus. Anthropol. Univ. Mich.* 66. 189 pp.
32. Smith, H. I. 1910. The prehistoric ethnology of a Kentucky site. *Anthropol. Pap. Am. Mus. Nat. Hist.* 6 (2):173–236
33. Snodgrass, R. M. 1933. Notes on the archaeology of Jo Daviess County. *Ill. State Acad. Sci.* 25:87–88
34. Taylor, R. E. 1978. Radiocarbon dating: An archaeological perspective. In *Archaeological Chemistry-II,* ed. G. F. Carter. *Adv. Chem. Ser.* 171:33–69. Washington DC: Am. Chem. Soc. 389 pp.
35. Toth, A. 1977. *Early Marksville phases in the lower Mississippi Valley: A study of culture contact dynamics.* PhD thesis. Harvard Univ., Cambridge, Mass. 520 pp.
36. Walthall, J. 1981. Galena and aboriginal trade in eastern North America. *Ill. State Mus. Sci. Pap.* 17
37. Walthall, J., Stow, S. H., Karson, M. J. 1980. Copena galena: Source identification and analysis. *Am. Antiq.* 45:21–42

MODULAR THEORIES OF GRAMMAR

Ann K. Farmer

Department of Linguistics, University of Arizona, Tucson, Arizona 85721

INTRODUCTION

The theories of grammar discussed in this paper are based on the hypothesis that language is modular. A language (a "linguistic system") is construed as a system of rules and representations factorable into independent but interacting subsystems. Such theories conform to what Pylyshyn (30, p. 121) characterizes as "an extremely general scientific maxim, namely, that a central goal of explanatory theories is to factor a set of phenomena, a problem, or a system into the most general and perspicuous components, principles, or subsystems." The modular theories of grammar presented here are Government and Binding (GB) theory (6, 7), Modular Grammar (MG) (9), and Lexical Functional Grammar (LFG) (2).

One interesting defense of various hypotheses about grammatical structure is based on anaphora phenomena, specifically intuitions about coreference and disjoint reference of referring expressions (e.g. *John, Mary, the man,* etc), pronouns, and anaphors (e.g. *himself, each other*).[1] Each of the three theories cited above offers partial answers to the question of how the linguistic system helps auditors to recognize the speaker's intents to refer. GB, MG, and LFG all offer a way of factoring the problem—i.e. of apportioning rules and principles to various components of the grammar. I here endeavor to acquaint the reader with these theories by showing how each treats reference. The discussion is not primarily critical, but it does confront several interesting questions.

I first present a concise overview and critique of GB theory, since many of the problems discussed in the literature today were first defined in GB theory and its two predecessors, Standard Theory (3) and Extended Standard Theory

---

[1]See references 10 and 32 for arguments of this type for Japanese, 18 for Hungarian, 19 for Chinese, 12 for Warlpiri, and 28 for Malayalam.

(5). Both MG and LFG draw on the successes of GB theory, and much of the crucial vocabulary used in numerous theories are introduced and defined in GB theory.

I then review MG and LFG, comparing them to GB on particular points of interest.

Finally, I compare and contrast the three theories.

GOVERNMENT AND BINDING THEORY

Recently Chomsky proposed decomposing the description of language into separate but interacting subsystems. For example, he distinguishes two classes of subsystems in the theory of grammar (6, pp. 5–6): (*a*) the "rule system" and its subcomponents, and (*b*) the "principle system" and its subcomponents. In current GB theory these are:

1. rule system:
    (*i*) lexicon;
    (*ii*) syntax:
        (*a*) categorial component;
        (*b*) transformational;
    (*iii*) Phonetic Form (PF)—component;
    (*iv*) Logical Form (LF)—component;
2. principle system:
    (*i*) bounding theory;
    (*ii*) θ-theory;
    (*iii*) binding theory;
    (*iv*) government theory;
    (*v*) case theory;
    (*vi*) control theory.

The "rule system" is depicted in *Figure* 1.

Chomsky summarizes the two systems as follows (6, pp. 5–6):

> The lexicon specifies the abstract morpho-phonological structure of each lexical item and its syntactic features, including its categorial features and its contextual features. The rules of the categorial component meet some variety of X-bar theory.[2] Systems 1.*i* and 1.*iia* constitute the base. Base rules generate D-structures (deep structures) through insertion of lexical items into structures generated by 1.*iia*, in accordance with their feature structure. These are mapped to S-structure by the rule Move-α, leaving traces coindexed with their antecedents; this rule constitutes the transformational component 1.*iib*, and may also appear in the PF- and LF-components. Thus the syntax generates S-structures which are assigned

---

[2]X-bar theory was first introduced by Chomsky (4) in "Remarks on Nominalization." One of the major innovations of X-bar theory is that it provides a simple definition of the notion "head." A central question of X-bar theory involves the nature of the S(sentence) node. See references 2, 9, 16, 20, and 27 for further discussion.

PF- and LF-representations by components *iii* and *iv* of 1. Bounding theory poses locality conditions on certain processes and related items. The central notion of government theory is the relation between the head of a construction and categories dependent on it. θ-Theory is concerned with the assignment of thematic roles such as agent-of-action, etc. . . . Binding theory is concerned with relations of anaphors, pronouns, names, and variables to possible antecedents. Case theory deals with assignment of abstract Case and its morphological realization. Control theory determines the potential for reference of the abstract pronominal element PRO.

In addition to the above subsystems there is an important wellformedness condition called the Projection Principle (PP), which requires that "representations at each syntactic level (i.e. LF, and D- and S-structure) are projected from the lexicon, in that they observe the subcategorization properties of lexical

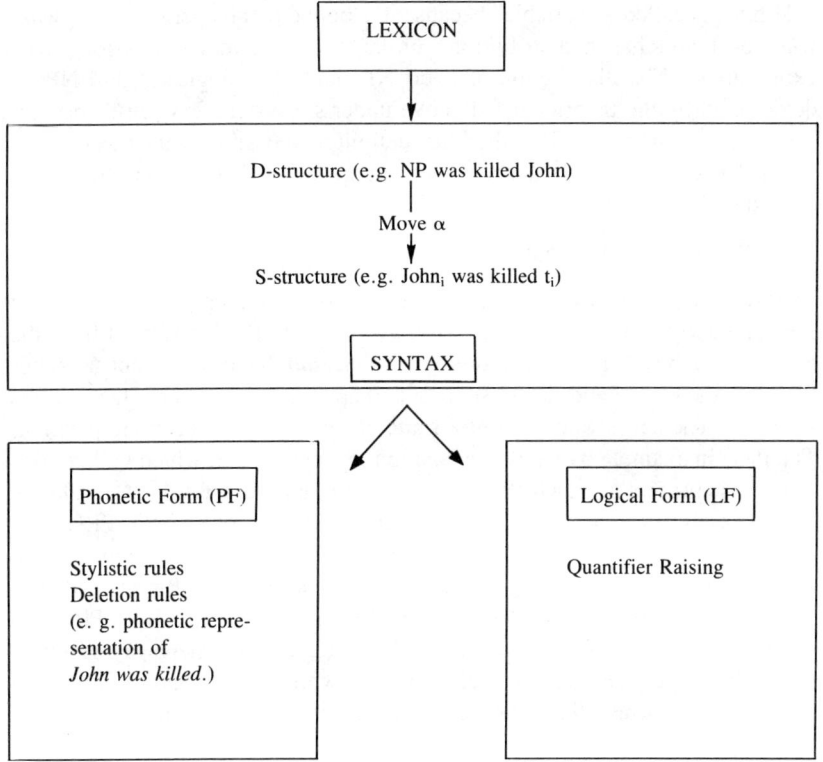

Figure 1 An account of the sentence *John was killed*. Quantified Raising (QR) is not applicable in this example. The sentence *Everyone loved her* does undergo QR in LF. QR yields the following representation: [Everyone$_i$ [t$_i$ loved her]], which is then mapped onto the representation: ∀x, x a person, x loved her. See May (27a) and Hornstein (17) for further discussion of QR and LF.

items" (6, p. 29).³ An immediate consequence of the PP is the presence of "empty categories" at all levels of syntactic representation. There are three types of empty categories (ec) for English: PRO, Noun Phrase-trace (NP-trace) and trace of WH words (WH-trace). The following examples exhibit each of the three types of ec:

3. John tried PRO to leave. (PRO; Control)
4. John$_i$ was killed t$_i$. (NP-trace; NP-Movement)
5. Who$_i$ did John kill t$_i$? (WH-trace; WH-Movement)

PRO has person, number, and gender features but lacks a phonological matrix. It is a pronominal-anaphor. NP-trace is called an "anaphor" because it shares certain distributional properties with overt anaphors (e.g. *himself, each other*)—i.e. the antecedent of the NP-trace and of overt anaphors is local. WH-trace is called a "variable" because it is bound by an operator, (e.g. *who, what* etc) and has a distribution similar to "referring expressions" (R-expressions). The distribution of overt NPs and phonologically null NPs is determined by the theories listed above under subsystem 2. Each theory has particular requirements. Together they delimit the possible syntactic positions in which each kind of NP can occur. For example, case theory and θ-theory rule out example 6:

6. *PRO was killed John.

The NP-*John* requires accusative case. *Killed* does not assign case to the object NP. The ability to assign case is taken away when *killed* is formed from the transitive verb *kill*. Thus, the requirement that *John* have case is not satisfied. PRO, on the other hand, is not supposed to appear in a position where case is assigned. The subject position of a finite clause is a case-receiving position. The PRO in example 6 then is in a position to receive case, which violates one of its basic properties. Each NP, *John* and PRO, requires a θ-role. A θ-role can only be assigned to an NP that is associated with case or is PRO. PRO does receive a θ-role, but *John* does not, thus violating the θ-criterion. The θ-criterion states that "each argument bears one and only one θ-role, and each θ-role is assigned to one and only one argument" (6, p. 36).⁴ Both PRO and *John* are arguments. Notice that it is possible for the requirements of one theory to be satisfied (e.g. PRO does receive a θ-role) while those of another are not. If any violations occur, the sentence is judged illformed, i.e. ungrammatical.

---

³The PP has been revised numerous times since it was first introduced in *Lectures on Government and Binding*. More technical versions are to be found in that work. The PP was augmented (7, p. 10) to require that all clauses have a subject. This version of the PP is referred to as the Extended Projection Principle.

⁴Chomsky (6, p. 35) uses the term "argument" to refer to NPs. He states that NPs like ". . . *the man, John,* [and] *he* are assigned θ roles, that is, are assigned the status of terms in a thematic relation. Let us call such expressions 'arguments'. . . ."

Binding Theory

Binding theory is devoted to accounting for the relation of pronouns, variables, anaphors, and names to their (potential) antecedents. It plays an important role in accounting for the distribution of NPs. In this theory, Chomsky claims that with freely assigned "referential" indexes in conjunction with Binding Conditions one can account for the distribution of anaphors and pronominals and their antecedents.

The Binding Conditions are defined over S-structure.[5] The principles of Binding Theory are as follows (6, p. 188):

7. (a) An anaphor is bound in its governing category.
   (b) A pronominal is free in its governing category.
   (c) An R-expression is free.

A governing category for an NP α is defined as the minimal S(entence) or NP containing α and a governor β.[6] The term *bound* is understood in the following way: an NP α is bound if and only if it is coindexed with an NP γ which c-commands α.[7] If it is not so coindexed with such a γ, α is free. The noun phrases in examples 8–10 are subject to free indexing and the Binding Conditions. After free indexing, each of the following sentences has two possible indexing arrays.

---

[5]Chomsky (6, pp. 196–98) discusses the possibility that Binding Theory applies at LF rather than S-structure. He concludes that Binding Theory applies at S-structure.

[6]According to Chomsky (7, p. 19), α governs β if $\alpha = X^0$ (in the sense of X-bar theory), α c-commands β, and β is not protected by a maximal projection. Examples: (V = α, NP = β, COMP = complementizer)

(i) V governs NP

(ii) V does *not* govern NP, since V does *not* c-command the NP.

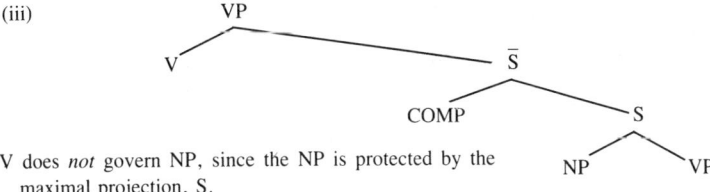

(iii) V does *not* govern NP, since the NP is protected by the maximal projection, S.

---

[7]The following is from Reinhart (31, p. 23): "A node A c(constituent) commands a node B if and only if the first branching node α that dominates A either dominates β, or is immediately dominated by a node α' which dominates β, where α and α' are of the same category type (e.g. S and S bar)." See also 6, 7, and 25 for other versions of "command".

8. (a) John$_i$ saw himself$_j$.
   (b) John$_i$ saw himself$_i$.
9. (a) John$_i$ saw him$_j$.
   (b) John$_i$ saw him$_i$.
10. (a) John$_i$ saw John$_i$.
    (b) John$_i$ saw John$_j$.

In sentences 8, the *John* is an R-expression, whereas *himself* is an anaphor. According to the Binding Conditions, only 8b is wellformed. This is because *himself* is an anaphor, so it must be bound in its governing category. In 8a, *himself* is free, thus violating condition 7a. NP-*John* is free in both cases, so Binding Condition 7c is not violated.

In sentences 9, *him* is a pronominal; therefore it must be free in its governing category. In 9b, *him* is bound—i.e. it is coindexed with *John*, and this *John* is in the minimal governing category of the *him* and also c-commands *him*. Therefore, in 9b, 7b of the Binding Conditions is violated; hence 9b is illformed. In 9a, however, since the indexes are not the same, *him* is free, thus not violating 7b, so the string is wellformed.

In examples 10, only 10b is wellformed because both *John*s are free. Example 10a is illformed because the second *John* is bound—i.e. coindexed—and this violates 7c of the Binding Conditions.

Now let us turn to examples involving empty categories.

11. To like John is difficult.
12. Who does John like?
13. John was bitten by the snake.

The S-structures for these sentences would be structures 14–16, respectively.[8]

14. PRO to like John is difficult.
15. Who$_i$ does John like t$_i$.
16. John$_i$ was bitten t$_i$ by the snake.

After free indexing, the structures would be as follows:

17. (a) PRO$_i$ to like John$_i$ is difficult.
    (b) PRO$_i$ to like John$_j$ is difficult.
18. (a) Who$_i$ does John$_i$ like t$_i$.
    (b) Who$_i$ does John$_j$ like t$_i$.
19. (a) John$_i$ was bitten t$_i$ by the snake$_i$.
    (b) John$_i$ was bitten t$_i$ by the snake$_j$.

In each case there are two possible indexing arrays, given free indexing. However, only one does not violate the Binding Conditions. Structure 17a involves a case where *John*, which is an R-expression and falls under 7c, is coindexed with PRO. This PRO c-commands *John*; hence, the PRO binds

---

[8]The indexes in structures 15 and 16 are the result of Move-α. An NP is automatically coindexed with the NP-trace that occupies the D-structure position of the "moved" NP.

John. But this situation violates 7c of the Binding Conditions, which states that an R-expression must be free—i.e. not bound. Notice that the PRO, though coindexed with *John,* is not bound by *John. John* does not c-command PRO. Structure 17*b* yields an indexing array that does not violate any of the Binding Conditions;[9] it is therefore wellformed.

In structures 18 the trace, t, is a variable. Variables fall under 7c. Structure 18*a* involves a case where the trace is coindexed with a c-commanding NP—i.e. *John.* The trace is not free, violating 7c. The trace in 18*b* is not bound since it is not coindexed with the c-commanding NP-*John.*[10] Structure 18*b* is wellformed while 18*a* is not.

The trace in 19 is an anaphor, which means it falls under 7*a* of the Binding Conditions. Condition 7*a* stipulates that an anaphor must be bound in its minimal governing category. In structures 19 the NP-*John* is automatically coindexed by the rule Move-α. Move-α, recall, maps D-structures onto S-structures. When the NP-*John* is moved from its D-structure position (i.e. is moved from the object position following *killed*) to the subject position, it is coindexed with the trace that has been left behind in the object position. The trace, then, is bound by *John. John* is also in the minimal S(entence) that contains the governor of the trace, t, (i.e. contains *killed*). The trace is therefore bound in its governing category. Turning to the NP-*the snake,* it should be noted that only structure 19*b* is wellformed. *The snake* is an R-expression, which means it falls under Condition 7c. It cannot be coindexed with *John* since *John* c-commands *the snake.*

The Binding Conditions are straightforward. It is always clear when any given Noun Phrase may or may not have the same index as another Noun Phrase in the sentence. But a fundamental question remains. What do these "referential" indexes mean? What intuition is being captured when two Noun Phrases have identical or different indexes? Are coindexed NPs representing "coreference" or "overlapping" reference? Are differently indexed NPs signaling "disjointness" or "non-overlapping" reference? Chomsky (6, pp. 285–89) raises this question and discovers a paradox, noting the following sentences as representative of the problem:

20. (*a*) I lost my way.
    (*b*) *We lost my way.
21. (*a*) We expected John to like me.
    (*b*) *We expected me to like John.

---

[9]PRO, which is a pronominal-anaphor in GB theory, does fall under the Binding Conditions, but the conditions apply vacuously. PRO must be *ungoverned,* and since it has no governor, it has no governing category. Recall that 7*a* and 7*b*, the relevant Conditions, refer to a pronoun or anaphor, respectively, as being bound 7*a* or free 7*b* in its *governing category*. The conditions, therefore, apply vacuously to PRO. See the section below on LFG for further discussion of PRO.

[10]The WH-word, *who,* is an operator that binds the trace. The trace is free, however, in the sense that it is not bound by another NP in an *argument* position (i.e. subject or object position). The WH-word occupies a non-argument position.

Chomsky notes that the idiom requires coindexing of *I* and *my* in 20*a* and of *we* and *my* in 20*b*. Example 20*b* is odd. Thus, Chomsky concludes, coindexing entails coreference. *We* and *my* are not coreferential but merely overlap in reference (i.e. they both have the speaker in their extension). In examples 21*a,b* the situation is slightly different. In 21*b*, *we* and *me* must have different indexes because *me* is a pronoun and falls under 7*b* of the Binding Conditions, which states that a pronoun must be free in its governing category. *We* is in the governing category for *me*, and therefore *we* cannot be coindexed with *me*. Example 21*b* is odd. This suggests that for *we* and *me* to be differently indexed is not wellformed, entailing that to be differently indexed is to be disjoint, which *we* and *me* are not. Example 21*a* is not odd. This means that *we* and *me* cannot be differently indexed but must be indexed the same way. Under this interpretation of coindexing, *overlapping* reference is sufficient. But this contradicts the account of the oddity of 20*b*, which concluded that overlapping reference was not sufficient when two Noun Phrases were coindexed.

Other examples have been noted in the literature (cf 6, 15, 26) that pose a problem for Binding Theory. Cases like those in examples 22–25, below, raise questions similar to the paradox just noted.

22. Tom informed Judy that they should leave.

Sentence 22 is an example of "split antecedents". *They* can be understood as having both *Tom* and *Judy* as antecedents. Other interpretations are possible. For example, *they* might include *Judy* and not *Tom;* it might exclude them both. Binding Theory stipulates that only two possibilities exist: NPs can be either coindexed or differently indexed. Each Noun Phrase is associated with only one index. *They* may be coindexed with *Tom* or *Judy* but not both. *They* may be indexed differently from both *Tom* and *Judy*. The question once again is, does being differently indexed entail "disjointness" or just "noncoreference"? If the answer is simply "noncoreference" then *they* could be associated with *Tom* and/or *Judy*, not via indexing but by context. At least two questions arise at this point. First, what work is the indexing doing? It is already clear that the words *Tom* and *they* cannot be coreferential—i.e. the indexing is redundant. The second question ties in with sentence 23.

23. They thought that Tom would win.

In this example, *they* cannot be coindexed with *Tom* because of Binding Condition 7*c*. If to be differently indexed only means "noncoreference," then *they* and *Tom* may be overlapping in reference. In this case the point discussed above applies. However, if to be differently indexed entails "disjoint reference," then *they* and *Tom* must be disjoint. Concluding that to be differently indexed entails "disjoint reference" suggests that to be coindexed necessarily involves coreference; recall that "overlapping reference" is insufficient to account for examples 20*a,b*. All this brings us back to the question of what it means when two Noun Phrases are coindexed. Are they strictly coreferential? But consider the following sentence:

24. They like John.

The Binding Conditions require that *they* and *John* have different indexes. If being differently indexed merely means "noncoreferential," then "overlapping" reference should be possible in example 24; yet, without contextual information to force that interpretation, *John* is not included in *they*.

Following now another avenue, what if coindexing only involves overlapping reference? (This possibility was noted above with respect to split antecedents.) There would then be a problem not only for examples like 20*a,b* but also for cases like 25:

25. *They like himself.

They and *himself* must be coindexed because *himself* is an anaphor and falls under 7*a* of the Binding Conditions. Example 25 is odd. It is clear that overlapping reference is not sufficient. The next example raises yet another question:

26. The woman who loved the man tolerated the boy.

The NPs of concern here are *the man* and *the boy*. Both NPs fall under 7*c* of the Binding Conditions. Since neither NP c-commands the other, the two may be either coindexed or differently indexed. Either way, both NPs are free. However, *the man* and *the boy* are not readily interpreted as coreferential or overlapping. They are interpreted as disjoint.

In short, the interpretation of coindexing is still uncertain. I have discussed three possible relations: coreferential, disjoint, and overlapping reference. These three cannot be captured simultaneously in the present theory. Such problems and questions are addressed in the recent GB literature (15, 26, and references cited therein).

Summary

GB theory is a rich and intricate theory. Each of its subtheories has its domain of application. The information encoded in the "old-style" transformations of Standard Theory are handled in the various components of the grammar. No rule alone accounts for, say, the passive construction, or "reference." The various rules and principles interact. A violation of any rule or principle yields an ungrammatical sentence.

MODULAR GRAMMAR

Modular Grammar (MG), as articulated in Farmer (9), is an outgrowth of GB theory. A number of basic assumptions, however, are different. For example, the Projection Principle and the θ-criterion are not wellformedness conditions that hold between the various syntactic levels of representation. An immediate consequence is that empty categories such as PRO, NP-trace, and WH-trace are not required at S-structure. A category, or terminal element appears at the Phrase Marker level of representation only if it is overt—i.e. associated with a phonological matrix. Such a position entails rethinking the question of anaphora in general, since it has been assumed and argued that empty categories fall under a general set of binding principles that also accounts for the construal and distribution of overt anaphors, pronouns, and referential expressions (R-expressions). I turn to the problem of reevaluating anaphora phenomena after a brief outline of MG.

The MG model differs from the GB model in a number of respects. First, in the syntactic component, lexical structure is kept distinct from the phrase structure (PS) level of representation. This means that the Valuation Component, which is the MG analog to GB's Syntactic Component (cf Figure 1), has the composition represented in Figure 2.

Rules of valuation associate overt NPs with argument slots of predicates. For Chomsky, these two levels are closely related in that the lexical structure is "projected" onto the PS level. In MG it is not assumed that the lexical structure is projected onto the PS level. Case theory is adopted in Modular Grammar. Case is what syntactically sanctions an NP. NPs associated with case are then associated with argument slots of predicates. Argument slots of predicates need not be associated with an overt NP. These "unevaluated" argument slots are the MG analog to empty categories. A second difference is that semantic and pragmatic principles, which are defined over both syntactic structure (the PS level) and lexical structure (the LS level), are posited. Principles of anaphora defined solely over the PS level of representation are inadequate, since they would fail to account for intuitions about such sentences as:

27. (*a*) Catch him!
    (*b*)

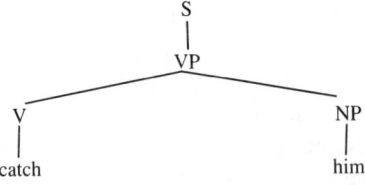

Without an overt subject NP it is still clear that the Hearer (intended addressee) is being ordered to catch a third person (male) and that the Hearer and this male are distinct. The general framework developed in Farmer (9) and Harnish & Farmer (14) is modular in the sense that distinct principles in distinct parts of the description of English interact to account for the facts. Oddity judgments are accounted for by using pragmatic and semantic principles that interact with

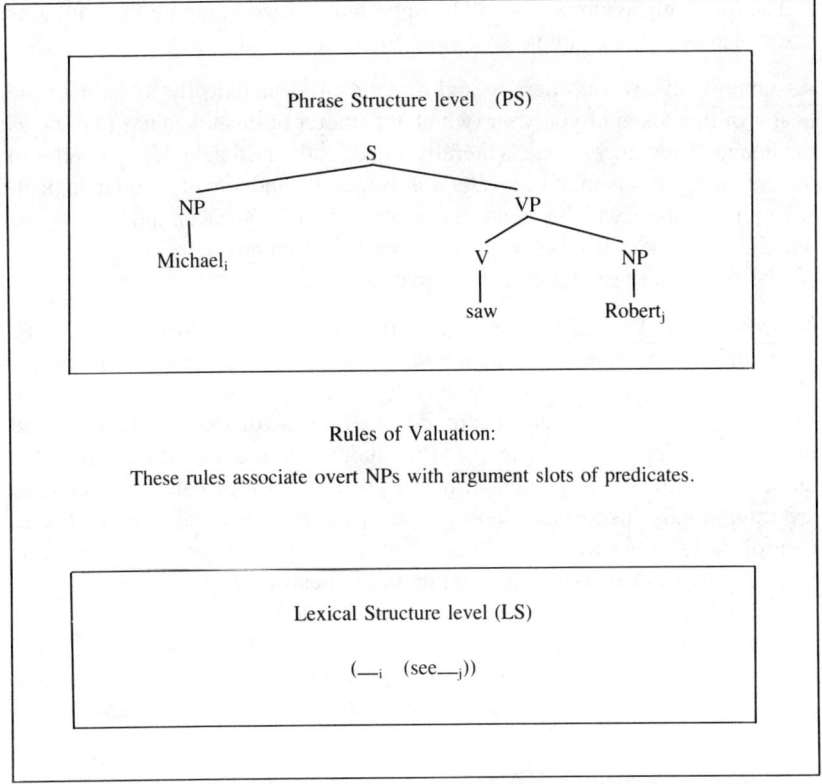

Figure 2 Valuation component: a sample. (See 9 for complete discussion of these rules.)

various levels of the grammar. The main concern, then, is to identify the contribution linguistic structure makes toward recognizing the referential intents of the speaker when the speaker is speaking literally and directly.

Anaphora Phenomena

One of the modules of MG is the Pragmatic Component. The output of the grammar is (*a*) a structural description of a string and (*b*) any information that is accessible via lexical items. It is not assumed that NPs are assigned a referential index freely. Much of the work of Binding Theory is accomplished in MG with Pragmatic Inferences, which are sensitive to structural properties of the string. The structure often imposes constraints on how a Noun Phrase or the argument[11] of a predicate is to be construed.

[11] In MG, *NP*, *argument slot*, and *argument* are distinct notions. NP is a syntactic category for constituents of sentences. An argument slot is not a syntactic category; it is not a sentence constituent. Argument slots mark terms of the relation expressed by the predicate. An argument is that entity which satisfies an argument slot of a predicate.

The following assumptions will be important in accounting for the intuitions associated with the example sentences to be discussed:

Assumptions:[12] *You* is literally and directly used indexically to refer to the hearer of this token of you/your (which the utterer of this token has in mind as the intended audience). *I/me* is literally and directly used indexically to refer to the utterer of this token of I/me. *He/him:* is literally and directly used indexically to refer to the x which is male and is other than the speaker and hearer, and which the speaker of this token of he/him has in mind.

The following principles will be invoked:

Noncoreference Principle (Pragmatic, defined over syntactic structure), P1: If a pronoun, P, c-commands a nonpronoun then noncoreference is intended. Disjoint Reference Principle (Pragmatic, defined over lexical structure), P3: The arguments of a predicate are intended to be disjoint, unless marked otherwise. Independence Principle (Pragmatic, defined over lexical and syntactic structure), P5: Argument structures of distinct predicates in a sentence are referentially independent unless one of the Ps is specially marked (e.g. control cases: *John tried to leave*). Predicate Argument Principle, P6: The lexicon provides the argument structure of predicates—e.g. verbs. Cosatisfaction Principle (Semantic, defined over lexical structure), P2: The semantics of some predicates is such that if xVy, then $x = y$; e.g. if "x gnashed y's teeth", then $x = y$. Cosatisfaction Principle (Semantic, defined over lexical and syntactic structure), P4: The semantics of "self" is such that if xV Pro:y+ "self", then $x = y$.

I now bring principles 1–6 to bear on the examples below.

28. He likes John.
29. To like John is difficult.
30. John likes John.
31. John likes himself.

Without any context to prejudice us, we judge sentence 28 to involve disjointness. If we ignore conversational situations, we assume that in uttering sentence 28 a speaker is referring to two individuals, *John* and *he*. The Disjoint Reference Principle, P3, codifies this intuition, asserting that the linguistic structure of sentence 28 signals pragmatic disjointness. On any given occasion a speaker may not intend disjointness, but this was not our question. P3 states that, out of context, the preferred interpretation is of disjointness.

In sentence 29 the question is whether the subject of *like* is disjoint from or "coreferential" with *John*. I enclose coreferential in quotation marks because there is no element in the subject position with which *John* can corefer. Is it therefore possible to take sentence 29 to mean *For John to like himself is*

---

[12]These words have other uses as well, and are characterized only to first approximations here. See Harnish (13) for the preliminary version of these assumptions.

difficult? Intuition tells us this is not the natural interpretation. Although the subject of *like* is left undetermined by the linguistic object, *John* is one entity the speaker of sentence 29 is unlikely to so intend. Once again, P3 accounts for this intuition.

Example 30 also involves disjointness. As was not the case with 28 and 29, however, speakers of English can fairly easily accept a coreferential interpretation of sentence 30, where the two *Johns* are taken as referring to the same individual. According to P3, the arguments of *like* are intended to be disjoint unless marked otherwise. It is the case that an individual who is named *John* is in the extension of the name *John*. *John* occurs twice in example 30. Thus a semantic property (i.e. what is in the extension of the name) here conflicts with P3. This conflict seems to account for the mixed intuitions associated with sentence 30. The hearer can force a literal coreferential interpretation on 30, but such an interpretation is not preferred.

Example 31 invokes P4, the Cosatisfaction Principle, which states that the semantics of *self* is such that if x V Pro:y + *self*, then is x identical to y. Sentence 31 meets the conditions specified in the principle; therefore, what satisfies the subject of *likes* is identical to what satisfies the object of *likes*. NP-*John* is associated with the subject of *likes* and the NP-*himself* is associated with the object of *likes*. No oddity is associated with this sentence. The name *John* usually refers to a male, who in this case can be taken to be someone other than the speaker or the intended addressee. The pronoun *him* is literally and directly used indexically to refer to the x which is male and is other than the speaker and hearer, and which the speaker of this token of *him* has in mind. Therefore, *John* and *him* can pick out the same individual, and P4 is satisfied. Note, however, than an NP can be changed, yielding an oddity. For example, the following sentences are odd:

32. John likes herself.
33. They like himself.
34. I like herself.
35. He likes yourself.

The case of sentence 32 is interesting because the oddity is purely pragmatic, traceable to the expectation that *John* refers to a male, while *her* is literally and directly used indexically to refer to an x which is female and is other than the speaker and hearer, and which the speaker of this token of *her* has in mind. One should not draw the conclusion that the sentence is "ungrammatical," since the speaker may not mean what the sentence means—may be said to be using utterance 32 nonliterally. Also, it is possible that the speaker intends to refer to a woman named *John*. In any case, one would not want to judge "grammaticality" on the basis of such aspects of the context of utterance.[13]

---

[13]See Lakoff (24), who does judge grammaticality according to certain aspects of the context of utterance.

The oddity in sentence 33 boils down to an incompatibility between the pronouns *they* and *him*. *Self* requires that whatever is the subject of *like* be coextensive with whatever is the object of *like*, but *they* and *him* cannot be taken as coextensive. Examples 34 and 35 are odd for the same reason.

P1 accounts for the intuition that NP-*John* and NP-*he* are disjoint in the following example:

36. He thinks that John will win.

The *he* c-commands *John*. Therefore, according to P1 the two NPs are taken as referring to two different individuals. This example contrasts with sentence 37 below, where the two Noun Phrases may be taken as coreferential, in accordance with the Independence Principle, P5.

37. John thinks that John will win.

The last principle to be discussed is the Cosatisfaction Principle, P2, which states that the semantics of some predicates is such that if xVy, then x is identical to y. The following sentence demonstrates this principle:[14]

38. John gnashed his teeth.

John is taken as coreferential with *his;* that is, one individual is being referred to. If the second NP is changed to *Mary,* an oddity results.

39. John gnashed Mary's teeth.

Unless *John* and *Mary* are the same individual, P2 is violated.

Notice that MG characterizes oddity judgments as conflicts between various principles and various facts. For example, the conflict may be between a pragmatic principle and a semantic fact (e.g. *We like me*) or between a semantic principle and a semantic fact (e.g. *They like himself*).

I now briefly compare MG theory with GB and GB-related theories.

A Comparison of GB and MG

For the purposes of this discussion I focus on examples 40–42:

40. John thinks that he will win.
41. John thinks that John will win.
42. He thinks that John will win.

Such examples have been discussed extensively in the literature, and the intuitions associated with them have been variously explained. No consensus concerning these intuitions has been reached. Most accounts use a version of

---

[14]Example 38 is similar to example 20, *I lost my way*. MG does not encounter the same paradox confronted by GB theory.

the structural notion, c-command (defined in Footnote 7). For example, Reinhart, who claims that her version of anaphora can be incorporated into GB theory, invokes the following indexing rule:

43. Coindex a pronoun P with a c-commanding NP α (α not immediately dominated by COMP or S). (Note: for "conditions," see reference 31, pp. 158–59.)

There are also many ways of stating a condition or rule with respect to the NPs involved. For example, Reinhart's coindexing rule is stated in terms of the nature of the c-commanded, rather than the c-commanding NP; this c-commanded NP must be a pronoun for rule 43 to apply. Chomsky (6, 7), on the other hand, assumes that indexing is free (not subject to a constraint as expressed in rule 43) and that the Binding Conditions (cf 7) in some sense "filter out" the overgenerated indexing relations. Binding Conditions 7c (R-expressions are free) and 7b (a pronoun must be free in its governing category) account for the above examples.

Like Reinhart, Chomsky accounts for examples 40–42 by referring to the properties of the c-commanded NP. Unlike Reinhart, however, Chomsky permits this NP to be an R-expression (in 41 and 42) and not a pronoun.

In yet another account, when Lasnik (25) states the properties of the two NPs he refers to the properties of the "commanded" NP. The commanded NP has to be a nonpronoun in order for his disjoint reference rule to apply.[15] Both Chomsky's principles and Lasnik's rule express the relation of noncoreference or disjoint reference between the two NPs, whereas Reinhart's coindexing rule expresses a relation of bound anaphora. Reinhart (31, p. 167) achieves the so-called disjoint interpretation via a Pragmatic Strategy:

44. Hearer's Strategy: If the speaker avoids the bound anaphora options provided by the structure he is using, then, unless he had reasons to avoid bound anaphora, he did not intend his expressions to corefer.

Unlike Chomsky's Binding Condition 7c and Lasnik's Disjoint Reference rule, statement 44 is not a rule of grammar.

MG proposes that the intuitions associated with examples 40–42 are explained, in part, by the Noncoreference Principle (P1), which is defined over the PS level of representation, and by the Independence Principle (P5), which is defined over both the lexical and PS levels. P1 and P5 should be viewed as principles which drive an inference. For example, in the sentence *John thinks that he will win,* what does the linguistic structure contribute to the hearer's recognition of the speaker's communicative reference? MG does not attribute

---

[15]The following is Lasnik's "Disjoint Reference" rule: If NP1 precedes and kommands NP2 and NP2 is not a pronoun, then NP1 and NP2 are disjoint in reference (25, p. 16).

indexes to the linguistic structure. Its principles are therefore stated in terms of hierarchical information (i.e. c-command) and the properties of the NPs themselves (e.g. "is a pronoun," "is not a pronoun," etc). In example 40, the NP-*John* c-commands the pronoun *he*. P1 is not applicable since the c-commanding NP is not a pronoun. Therefore, based on the structural relations in example 40 and the nature of the c-commanding NP, one cannot conclude whether or not the speaker intended for *John* and *he* to corefer. P5, the Independence Principle, has not been overridden by "Control." The arguments of the two predicates are therefore independent—i.e. free to be satisfied by the same argument or not. The structure and nature of the NPs are compatible with either interpretation; *John* and *he* may be coreferential or noncoreferential. In GB theory, sentence 40 would be structurally ambiguous. There would be two indexing arrays that would satisfy the Binding Conditions: *John* and *he* might be coindexed or they might be contra-indexed. MG characterizes the intuitions associated with sentence 40 not to structural ambiguity but to indeterminacy.

What about example 41, *John thinks that John will win?* Some hearers feel that two different *Johns* are referred to, others that there may be only one *John*. It is difficult to determine how such feelings arise. Do some hearers respond to intonation while others rely upon signals from the syntactic structure? MG claims that syntactic structure does not contribute to the determination of disjoint reference, which some speakers report as their preferred interpretation. Chomsky's Binding Conditions (7c specifically) would characterize example 41 as involving either noncoreference or disjoint reference (it's not clear which; see the discussion, above, on *Binding Theory*). But none of the Principles so far presented in MG necessitates either noncoreference or disjoint reference.

Many speakers agree without protest to the coreferential interpretation of sentence 41. Therefore we must ask whether, in order to allow such a coreferential interpretation, a principle of Modular Grammar has to be overridden. (Recall that in the case of the sentence *John likes John,* P3 was overridden to yield coreference.) If MG were to adopt a position like Chomsky's Binding Condition 7c, it would constrain contrasting judgments about disjoint reference in the following sentences:

45. Oscar thinks that Oscar will pass the exam.
46. Martha, who likes Oscar, knows that Oscar passed the exam.

In sentence 46, neither *Oscar* c-commands the other. In Chomsky's framework they can therefore be coindexed—i.e. interpreted as coreferential. In example 45, on the other hand, the first *Oscar* c-commands the second and the two cannot be coindexed. (If coindexed, the second *Oscar* would be bound, and this would violate Binding Condition 7c. Some hearers do not feel that sentences 45 and 46 differ strikingly, while others [e.g. Lasnik (25), Chomsky (6), and Reinhart (31)] note a contrast. Unmarked intonation contours associated with these two sentences no doubt influence the preferred interpretation of disjoint reference in example 45 as opposed to 46.

Now let us turn to sentence 42. While P5 states that arguments of separate predicates are independent, P1 states that if a pronoun c-commands a nonpronoun NP, then the speaker intends noncoreference. Syntactic and lexical considerations would produce this inference. On any given occasion, a speaker of this sentence may intend coreference, but the context must then provide the clue that will enable the hearer to recognize this intention.

If we change *John* to *he,* then P1 does not apply. The example is then much like *John thinks that he will win.* If *John* is changed to *she,* the nature of the pronouns compels one to infer disjoint reference. Note that nothing needs stating beyond the assumptions outlined earlier. If *John* is changed to, say, *administrators* then *he* and *administrators* are noncoreferential. This is certainly the case simply in virtue of the words themselves. In GB theory, Condition 7c would be invoked to yield contra-indexing between *he* and *administrators.* Should P1 of MG then be changed to yield an interpretation of disjointness? Are *he* and *administrators* to be interpreted as disjoint? This question is a familiar one in the GB perspective (see the section above on *Binding Theory*). It has also been confronted by Lasnik (25), who answered with the stronger, disjoint interpretation. In MG we have settled upon the "noncoreference" answer until independent criteria for choosing between the two are developed.

Summary

Both GB and MG are modular theories. Each postulates independent principles operating over particular domains, with each domain acting as a kind of filter on the others. GB theory posits Binding Conditions defined over a level of representation that enables them to govern empty categories as well as overt Noun Phrases. In MG, the Principles that account for judgments of coreference and disjoint reference are defined over different levels of representation, a necessary consequence of not projecting lexical structure onto the PS level of representation. In GB theory, sentences are characterized as ambiguous when coreference and disjoint reference are both possible interpretations. In MG, such sentences have indeterminate interpretations.

GB and MG both differ from Lexical Functional Grammar—for example in their claims about the nature of empty categories. I now turn to an overview of LFG.

LEXICAL FUNCTIONAL GRAMMAR

Lexical Functional Grammar (LFG) is a modular theory insofar as it posits levels of representation with various principles of wellformedness defined over them. Three important levels of representation are "configurational structure" (c-structure), "functional structure" (f-structure), and Lexical structure (LS) (see Figure 3). C-structure corresponds to GB theory's PS level of representation. Unlike GB theory, but similar to MG, LFG does not posit empty categories at the C-structure level of representation. The LFG analog to PRO is represented at the f-structure level of representation, which is the level where grammatical relations (e.g. "subject of," "object of") are encoded. As in GB theory, "PRO" is a consequence of conditions of wellformedness. In LFG, these conditions are conditions of wellformedness on f-structure:

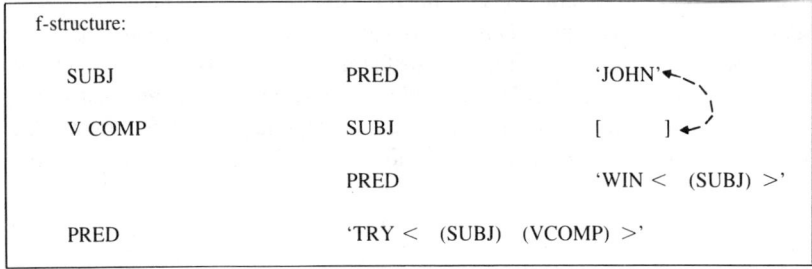

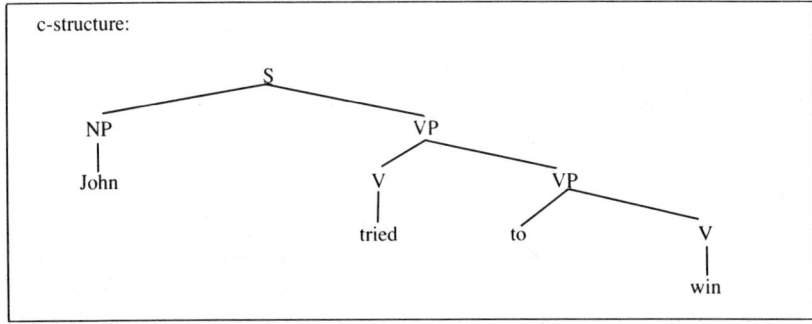

Figure 3 An analysis of *John tried to win* in LFG.

47. Definition of Completeness and Coherence (23, pp. 211–12):
    (a) An f-structure is *locally complete* if it contains all governable grammatical functions that its predicate governs. An f-structure is *complete* if it and all its subsidiary f-structures are locally complete.
    (b) An f-structure is locally coherent if all the governable grammatical functions that it contains are governed by a local predicate. An f-structure is *coherent* if it and all its subsidiary f-structures are locally coherent.

These conditions on f-structure fulfill much the same function as do the Projection Principle and θ-criterion in GB theory. While in LFG the "governed grammatical function" may not be realized at c-structure it must be realized at f-structure. F-structure is the level of representation that mediates between c-structure and lexical structure; it is the level of representation that forms the input to the semantic interpretation component.

Figure 3 illustrates the information encoded by each level of representation, using the sentence *John tried to win* as a basis. [This example is taken from Mohanan (29, p. 644).] The brackets in the f-structure of Figure 3 denote a "lexically unrealized grammatical function" (UR). The control equation, indicated by the double-headed arrow between "JOHN" and the brackets, indicates how the UR is to be interpreted. The control equation is defined over f-structure in LFG, which is necessitated by the absence of phonologically unrealized NPs of c-structure.[16] This example of control is called "functional control". Another type of control, "anaphoric control," is exemplified in the following sentence (29, p. 644):

48. John discussed scratching himself.

49(*a*) f-structure

```
[ SUBJ      PRED       "JOHN"                              ]
[                                                           ]
[ OBJ     [ SUBJ     PRED      PRO                   ]     ]
[         [                                           ]     ]
[         [ OBJ      PRED      'HIMSELF'              ]     ]
[         [                                           ]     ]
[         [ PRED     'SCRATCH' <(SUBJ) (OBJ)>'        ]     ]
[                                                           ]
[ PRED      'DISCUSS'  <(SUBJ) (OBJ)>'                      ]
```

(*b*) c-structure

    [[John] [discussed [[scratching himself]]]]
    S NP   VP   NP VP

The PRO is interpreted as "coreferential" with *John*. Example 50 involves a PRO that has no antecedent in the sentence:

50. Peeling apples bores John.

51(*a*) f-structure

```
[ SUBJ    [ SUBJ     PRED      PRO                   ]     ]
[         [                                           ]     ]
[         [ OBJ      PRED      "APPLES"               ]     ]
[         [                                           ]     ]
[         [ PRED     "PEEL"    <(SUBJ) (OBJ)>"        ]     ]
[                                                           ]
[ OBJ       PRED      "JOHN"                                ]
[                                                           ]
[ PRED      "BORES"   <(SUBJ) (OBJ)>"                       ]
```

[16]See Mohanan (29) for arguments for defining control over f-structure as opposed to c-structure.

(b) c-structure

```
   [   [  [peeling apples]]    [bores John]]
S   NP  VP                     VP
```

The subject of *peeling* is PRO.

Status of "PRO"

Bresnan (2, pp. 340–41) claims that in LFG 'PRO' has the following properties:

52. (*i*) 'PRO' is an unexpressed pronoun;
    (*ii*) 'PRO' may have either definite or indefinite reference, depending on context;
    (*iii*) 'PRO' is not assigned an antecedent within its minimal clause;
    (*iv*) 'PRO' may be obligatorily bound to certain thematically or grammatically specified antecedents;
    (*v*) an antecedent grammatically assigned 'PRO' must be superordinate to 'PRO' in the clause structure representing grammatical relations (in LFG, the antecedent must f-command 'PRO'); and
    (*vi*) 'PRO' has a restricted set of grammatical functions (either SUBJ alone as in the government and binding theory, or a subject of SUBJ, OBJ, OBJ2 as in the lexical-functional theory).

'PRO,' unlike GB's PRO, is a pronoun and *not* a pronominal anaphor. Bresnan (2, pp. 326–31) argues that 'PRO,' contrary to Chomsky's claim, *does* have the capacity for inherent reference.

LFG vs GB on the topic of PRO

Recall that Chomsky's Binding Theory accounts in part for the distribution of empty categories, which are present at the PS level of representation. PRO is an empty category. PRO appears in the subject position of infinitivals but not in the direct object position or as the subject of a finite clause. PRO may or may not have an antecedent within the sentence. The antecedent may be local or long distance. What emerges is a case of an entity that appears to be both a pronoun and an anaphor. The following examples illustrate each of the above cases.

53. John$_i$ tried PRO$_i$ to win. (antecedent local, PRO anaphor-like)
54. It's unclear what PRO to do. (no antecedent, PRO pronoun-like)
55. They$_i$ told Bill that it would be difficult PRO$_i$ to feed each other (long distance antecedent, PRO is pronoun-like)

If PRO is both an anaphor *and* a pronoun, however, a contradiction should result when the Binding Conditions are applied. Condition 7*a* would require that PRO be bound in its governing category, while 7b would require that PRO be free in its governing category. Chomsky's solution is to say that PRO cannot be governed and therefore has no governing category (see Footnote 10). GB's conclusions seem reasonable so long as PRO has the properties Chomsky has attributed to it—i.e. PRO is either definite in reference or is arbitrary (cf example 53, above).

Bresnan (2, p. 328) challenges this view: ". . . The assumption that 'PRO' is an anaphor in the sense of government and binding theory presents a serious problem: unlike anaphors, but like pronominals, 'PRO' does have the capacity to refer independently to specific extrasentential referents." In English, many examples arise in the context of indirect discourse, as the following sentences illustrate:

> 56. Mary was happy and excited. To have involved herself in the group was a risky action. But it was proving that she could change her life.

Bresnan (2, p. 329) notes that the 'PRO' subject of the infinitival is understood as referring to *Mary*. 'PRO' can also be used to refer to someone/thing that has not been mentioned—i.e. "presented in the nonverbal context of an utterance." For example, two people watch a third person's attempt to leap over a puddle. The leaper fails and ends up soaked. One observer says to the other:

> 57. *Trusting himself to make* that *jump was very foolish.*

The *leaper* is being picked out. Bresnan (2, p. 329) concludes that " 'PRO' does have the capacity to refer independently to specific extrasentential referents." If Bresnan is correct, then Chomsky can no longer assert legitimately that PRO is an anaphor. The status of PRO and the Binding Conditions must then be reevaluated.

Some interesting questions arise. First, what does it mean for phonologically null entity to refer? Although a speaker may have an individual in mind as the subject of *trusting* in example 57, the speaker may not be using a linguistic entity to signal the reference. That a particular person is understood as satisfying a particular role does not force one to conclude that a pronoun is present in the linguistic description of the utterance. Expressions greatly underdetermine the force and content (including reference) of a message. Use of the proper name *Paul*, for example, does not determine reference but instead picks out all individuals in the extension of the name *Paul*. Reference is underdetermined by the expression. The claim that sentences like 57 involve a phonologically null pronoun (cf sentence 36) has not yet been supported.

Chomsky's conception of PRO does not involve encoding reference via phonologically null entities. Chomsky asserts that PRO has no inherent reference and is not used to refer—i.e. that it is an anaphor. It is unlike an anaphor, however, in that it need not have an antecedent within its clause or sentence, and thus PRO sometimes has a "variable-like" interpretation (e.g. example 54 above). Neither variables nor anaphors can be used to refer.

Summary

Much of the LFG literature[17] has focused on motivating and defending the level of f-structure. One of the most important innovations of LFG is the position that c-structure encodes less structural information than the analogous level in GB theory.[18] LFG is therefore forced to capture coreference and disjoint reference phenomena via rules and principles defined over not only c-structure but f-structure as well. This situation is similar to that of MG.

OVERVIEW

What contribution does the linguistic system make to the recognition of a speaker's intents to refer?[19] In GB theory, indexes play a very important role in characterizing the intuitions of coreference and disjoint reference. These indexes are assigned at a level of representation that encodes both syntactic and lexical information—i.e. S-structure. Both MG and LFG have pulled this level apart. The analog to S-structure in MG is the pair, PS and LS. The analog in LFG is the pair, c-structure and f-structure. An interesting consequence of pulling S-structure apart is that rules and principles can be defined independently over PS or LS (in MG) or over c-structure or f-structure (in LFG). This means that principles defined over PS/c-structure will not affect "arguments" of LS/f-structure that are not represented at PS/c-structure.

LFG and GB both posit a phonologically null entity ('PRO'/PRO, respectively). In both theories, this entity is a pronoun at least. No such entity is defined in MG. In MG the analog to 'PRO'/PRO is simply an argument slot of a predicate that is not associated with an NP. MG attempts to derive all the properties attributed to empty categories from independent principles—i.e. the "properties" are derivative, not inherent.

Summary

Modular theories of grammar offer an interesting way of posing problems and questions. As can be seen from the above discussion, the solutions involve a

---

[17]See Bresnan (2), Mohanan (29), and references cited therein.

[18]This point should be qualified somewhat. The output of the PF-component in GB theory would be akin to c-structure in LFG. The crucial point is that c-structure never involves an isomorphism with lexical structure. In GB theory, D-structure is a projection of lexical structure.

[19]One could embed this question in a psychological theory such as Fodor's (11) theory of the modularity of mind. The question could then become, What is the structural description of an expression that hearers use in building hypotheses about the speaker's referential intents, i.e. what does the input to the Central Systems look like?

rich system of rules and principles. LFG, MG, and GB often posit analogous principles. At this time a definitive choice among these theories is not possible. The right theory will be the one that captures, elegantly, the properties and regularities of the language.

ACKNOWLEDGMENTS

I thank Peter Culicover, Mike Harnish, and Jeff Hershfield for discussing many of the points brought up in this paper. I also thank Mike for reading the many drafts and making several very helpful comments. All errors are, of course, my own.

Literature Cited

1. Abram, W., de Mey, S., eds. 1985. *Topic, Focus, and Configurationality*. Amsterdam: John Benjamins
2. Bresnan, J., ed. 1982. *The Mental Representation of Grammatical Representation*. Cambridge, Mass: MIT Press. 874 pp.
3. Chomsky, N. 1965. *Aspects of the Theory of Syntax*. Cambridge, Mass: MIT Press. 251 pp.
4. Chomsky, N. 1970. Remarks on nominalization. See Ref. 21, pp. 184–221
5. Chomsky, N. 1977. *Essays on Form and Interpretation*. New York: North Holland
6. Chomsky, N. 1981. *Lectures on Government and Binding*. Dordrecht, Holland: Foris Publ. 371 pp.
7. Chomsky, N. 1982. *Some Concepts and Consequences of the Theory of Government and Binding*. Cambridge, Mass: MIT Press
8. Davis, S., ed. 1984. *Studies in Native American Languages, Japanese and Spanish*. Coyote Papers, 5:236. Dept. Linguistics, Univ. Arizona, Tucson
9. Farmer, A. 1984. *Modularity in Syntax: A Study of Japanese and English*. Cambridge, Mass: MIT Press. 238 pp.
10. Farmer, A., Tsujimura, N. 1984. On the nature of syntactic structure: Implications for a theory of reference. See Ref. 8, pp. 32–52
11. Fodor, J. 1983. *Modularity of Mind*. Cambridge, Mass: MIT Press
12. Hale, K. 1983. Warlpiri and the grammar of non-configurational languages. *Nat. Lang. Linguist. Theory* 1(1):5–47
13. Harnish, R. 1984. Communicative reference: An inferential model. *Conceptus* 18(44):20–41
14. Harnish, R., Farmer, A. 1984. Pragmatics and the modularity of the linguistic system. *Lingua* 63:255–77
15. Higginbotham, J. 1983. Logical form, binding, and nominals. *Linguist. Inq.* 14(3):395–420
16. Hornstein, N. 1977. S and the X-bar convention. *Linguist. Anal.* 3:137–76
17. Hornstein, N. 1984. *Logic as Grammar*. Cambridge, Mass: MIT Press
18. Horvath, J. 1985. Remarks on the configurationality issue. See Ref. 1. In press
19. Huang, C.-T. 1984. On the distribution and reference of empty pronouns. *Linguist. Inq.* 15(4):531–74
20. Jackendoff, R. 1977. *X-bar Syntax: A Study of Phrase Structure*. Cambridge, Mass: MIT Press
21. Jacobs, R., Rosenbaum, P., eds. 1970. *Readings in English Transformational Grammar*. Waltham, Mass: Ginn
22. Jensen, J., ed. 1980. *Proc. 10th Ann. Meet. North East Linguist. Soc. Cah. Linguist. Ottawa* 9. Univ. Ottawa, Canada
23. Kaplan, R., Bresnan, J. 1982. See Ref. 2, pp. 211–12
24. Lakoff, G. 1971. Presupposition and relative well-formedness. See Ref. 33, pp. 329–40
25. Lasnik, H. 1976. Remarks on coreference. *Linguist. Anal.* 2:1–22
26. Lasnik, H. 1980. On two treatments of disjoint reference. *J. Linguist. Res.* 1:48–58
27. Marantz, A. 1980. English S is the maximal projection of V. See Ref. 22, pp. 303–14
27a. May, R. 1977. *The grammar of quantification*. PhD thesis, MIT
28. Mohanan, K. P. 1982. Grammatical rela-

29. Mohanan, K. P. 1983. Functional and anaphoric control. *Linguist. Inq.* 14(4):641–74
30. Pylyshyn, Z. 1980. Computation and cognition. *Behav. Brain Sci.* 53:741–88
31. Reinhart, T. 1983. *Anaphora and Semantic Interpretation*. London: Croom Helm. 223 pp.
32. Saito, M., Hoji, H. 1983. Weak crossover and Move α in Japanese. *Nat. Lang. Linguist. Theory* 1(2):245–59
33. Steinberg, D., Jakobovits, L., eds. 1971. *Semantics: An Interdisciplinary Reader*. Cambridge: Cambridge Univ. Press

PEASANT IDEOLOGIES IN THE THIRD WORLD

Joel S. Kahn

Department of Anthropology, University College London, London WC1E 6BT, England

In this review of recent work[1] by anthropologists, sociologists, and historians on peasant ideologies in the Third World, I argue that while a relatively wide range of foci and theories are manifest in the literature appearing in the last five or six years, it may be possible to discern a general tendency, which might be described as the "discovery" of peasant ideology. To make the point somewhat less dramatically, we might suggest that Western scholarship has increasingly tended to stress the positive features of peasantries in general and peasant ideologies, worldviews, and cultures in particular. In fact, this is not a discovery at all but a rediscovery, since these tendencies parallel in important ways intellectual trends manifest in earlier periods in the history of Western thinking on the agrarian question.

Having argued that a discovery of peasant ideology marks recent academic writing on the Third World, I must add that the term itself is a rather vague one. At one level it refers simply to the ideology held by or attributed to peasants—ideology being understood as "the system of meanings through which peoples interpret and understand the world," to quote one recent contributor (41, p. 215), and peasants being understood as a somewhat mixed bag of small-scale, primarily but not solely agricultural, producers who make a significant contribution to the national product of societies in which they are dominated by more powerful classes, bureaucracies, and the like. As discussed below, there is not necessarily anything specifically peasant-like about many of the ideological forms recently attributed to peasants. More specifically, much of the recent literature is concerned with documenting the presence and/or formation of ideologies in the rural Third World that are not exclusive to peasants, e.g.

---

[1]Because of the enormous volume of literature on this topic, I restricted myself almost completely to books and articles published from 1979 to the present.

class consciousness, (bourgeois) economic rationality, nationalism, and a consciousness of gender hierarchy.

At the same time the combined term peasant ideology conveys a more precise reference to systems of meaning that are in some sense nonmodern (or better, antimodernist). The discovery of peasant ideology, therefore, refers to a process of coming to grips with "what the peasants really think," but more specifically it refers to an increasing interest in these nonmodern or antimodernist forms of consciousness that are in one way or another seen as specific to the peasantry.

Since this process of discovery does not seem to be attributable to any single theoretical tendency in Western social science, I do not propose to organize the discussion solely along theoretical lines. Instead I divide the review by means of the following thematic categories:

1. The discussion of the development of "modernist" ideologies among Third World producers [what constitutes "modernist" depends, of course, on the stance of the analyst. For many Marxists it is class consciousness, for non-Marxists it is "rational" (Western) modes of economic calculation or political liberalism].
2. The analysis of what some take to be cultural or ideological obstacles to the development of modernist ideologies: here we look particularly at several neo-Marxist discussions of the obstacles to the development of class consciousness?
3. The study of other forms of peasant consciousness that are not seen to be specific to the peasantry, especially ideologies of gender and nationalism.
4. Studies that either implicitly or explicitly come to grips with antimodernism itself either by (*a*) focusing on the role played by religion, millenarianism, syncretism, or tradition in the formation of peasant political consciousness; or (*b*) querying the apparent rationality of modernism itself.

I conclude by offering some general remarks on the overall trends in this literature.

MODERNISM AND PEASANT CONSCIOUSNESS

As I have suggested, the meaning of modernism varies according to the theoretical stance of the observer. For liberal scholars, modernist worldviews are generally assumed to refer to rational, that is Western, economic outlooks and various forms of political liberalism. For Marxists, on the other hand, modernism refers to the emergence of class consciousness. We examine these writings separately in this section.

Marxist Approaches to Peasant Ideology: The Formation of Class Consciousness

Recent Marxist work on peasant ideology must be viewed in the context of changing analyses of the fate of small-scale producers in capitalist development within the Marxist tradition. Whatever the views of Marx himself on this issue, and at the risk of oversimplifying a complex set of often quite varied positions, it is possible to argue that a classical Marxist view crystallized out of the writings of Engels and Kautsky on Germany and Lenin on Russia, a view that posited the inevitable demise of the peasantry as a consequence of the capitalist penetration of agriculture.[2] Since these classical studies have an essentially political question behind them, namely what should be the attitude of the German and Russian social democratic movements to peasant demands, the argument about the inevitability of capitalist differentiation leads to the view that when rural producers adhere to specifically peasant, i.e. nonmodernist, forms of consciousness, then this must be treated as an anachronism in the modern world. In this sense peasant ideology per se was considered at best as irrelevant to the aims of the social democratic movement, and at worst as in conflict with its platform. Only when peasants manifest elements of proletarian consciousness should social democrats pay attention to their demands. Peasant ideology itself then was seen as a form of false consciousness.

To the extent that recent Marxist scholarship has questioned the implicit evolutionism of the classical model, it must similarly question traditional Marxist attitudes toward peasant ideology. It remains to be seen, of course, whether neo-Marxists have broken in any radical way with the classical attitude. But it is clear that recent Marxist writings on the subject cannot be considered in isolation from changing views on the agrarian question.

Since we are primarily concerned with Marxist analyses of peasant ideology, suffice it here to present only the weak and strong versions of the revisionist position on the agrarian question as they are found in recent writings on peasant consciousness. John Harris argues for a weak version in his study of agrarian structure and ideology in northern Tamil Nadu:

> ... the transformation of the agrarian economy under capitalism maintains in existence a large class of peasant producers who range from those who are wholly dependent upon merchant and financial capitalists, to those who may be independent of them. I have suggested that there is mobility along this range, and that the membership of the independent middle peasantry is thus somewhat unstable though as a category it may persist as a result of the conjunction of the economic structure and the organization of kinship (41, p. 264).

[2] For a recent analysis of the development of a classical Marxist position on the agrarian question, one differing in significant ways from Marx's own, see the two-volume work by Hussain & Tribe (46, 47).

A stronger form of this argument is presented by Roseberry in his work on Venezuela. According to Roseberry, it is inaccurate in this case to speak of the "persistence" of a peasantry through the period of capitalist transformation, because

> In broad terms, the process that has created peasants and proletarians in Venezuela has been world historical: the incorporation of Venezuela within the capitalist world system. But capitalist penetration of Venezuela did not encounter a peasantry on the ground to be destroyed or maintained . . . Rather, Andean peasants, like other Venezuelan toilers, were themselves precipitates of capitalist development (87, p. 110).

While there is already some room for disagreement here, it is clear that neo-Marxism at least provides the potential for a more positive evaluation of peasant ideology per se than does classical Marxism.

The reevaluation of peasant ideology suggested by revisions of the classical paradigm has taken a number of different forms in recent years. There has, for example, been a tendency to search for less orthodox intellectual precursors from within the Marxist tradition—precursors generally exhibiting Hegelian, humanist, and/or historicist tendencies. Roseberry, for example, attempts to develop Lukacian notions of totality and class consciousness in his discussion of Venezuelan peasants (87). Others have instead sought inspiration in the writings of Gramsci (6, 27, 38).

Related to this is the fact that a number of recent writers have sought to challenge in one way or another the interpretations of the French structural Marxists, and of Althusser in particular. More or less critical discussions of Althusser in the context of the analysis of peasant ideology are provided by Roseberry (87), Harriss (41), Chevalier (22), Kemp (55), and Turton (110). The challenge to Althusserianism usually revolves around a critique of the structuralist concept of social totality in which ideology is viewed as a superstructural instance of the social formation, albeit an instance with its own historicity. The critique is based less on a simple dissatisfaction with economic determinism than on the potential atomism of a concept of totality that separates economic, political, and cultural spheres of existence. Roseberry, for example, expresses unease with a view of society as composed of "factors or levels," a concept that "breaks up that totality and precludes historical understanding" (87, p. 106) Harriss, too, is unhappy with the base/superstructure dichotomy, a mode of thought that he argues "leads to the erroneous supposition that it is possible to deduce the rest of the structure of a reproductive totality from the process of material production alone" (41, p. 15).

At an empirical level, the negative evaluation of the political potential of the peasantry implicit in the work of at least some of the classical writings on the agrarian question has also been challenged. This is manifest in the recent literature on the formation of ideologies of class and class struggle among peasants in different parts of the Third World.

Quite a few recent studies have focused on the revolutionary potential of some peasants by examining the concrete roles played by different groups of peasants in revolutionary movements and the ways in which revolutionary ideologies take root among peasantries. The former focus is, of course, inherent in many earlier and now classic works on peasant revolutions, including the books and articles by Wolf, Barrington Moore, Paige, and Alavi. The latter concern, however, continues to be represented in recent literature.

Within the traditional framework, revolutionary ideology means, at least in the first instance, class ideology, and in such studies the focus tends to be on the formation of a "modernist" proletarian ideology among certain classes of rural producers. For example, Sumanta Banarjee examines the growth of a revolutionary peasant movement in West Bengal under the leadership of the Communist Party International (CPI; Marxist-Leninist) in his recent study of the Naxalite Uprising (8). Joshi (52) and Puri (82) discuss the recent development of rural class consciousness in India as a whole and in the Punjab respectively. An overview of Marxist approaches to the study of Indian peasant movements is provided by a collection of essays edited by Desai (30). Konings has written on the emergence of class conflict and consciousness among Ghanaian rice cultivators (61).

For Latin America we have numerous publications on the role played by peasants in revolutionary movements; these examine, among other things, class struggles and the development of class consciousness among rural producers. They include articles on the worker-peasant alliance in Nicaragua (29), on the way agrarian reforms in Chile actually served to heighten revolutionary consciousness among some peasant groups (14), and on class conflicts in Amazonia (92). The books provide, to varying degrees, material on the development of socialist peasant movements in El Salvador (76), Nicaragua (12), and Guatemala (13).

Liberals and Peasant Modernism

While Marxism takes the development of class consciousness, particularly proletarian consciousness, among peasants to be a manifestation of peasant modernism, such is obviously not the case for non-Marxist scholars. For them, peasants are modern/rational to the extent that they engage in Western forms of political and economic calculation.

Liberal discussion of peasant modernism has recently taken two forms. If we focus on the literature on calculation, which is the main expression of this tendency, there are those who posit a universal Western rationality. It is not so much, therefore, a question of establishing the conditions for the emergence of modern economic attitudes as a demonstration of their presence in concrete cases. On the other hand, there are also a large number of studies on the conditions under which peasants can be expected to engage in forms of behavior considered rational in the West.

An example of the first type of study is Popkin's book on the "rational" peasant (81). Taking issue with the position of what he terms the "moral economists," Popkin outlines an approach to peasant economic and political rationality that stems from "political economy." According to this approach, peasant norms and values are approached deductively by means of theories of individual decision making. This leads to the assumption that peasant attitudes toward investments and gambles, the village community, and political brokers and patrons are based on a kind of investment logic. While Popkin insists that this is merely a method of analysis, it is clear that it rests on attributing a particular form of rationality to concrete, individual peasants, as the following makes clear:

> By rationality I mean that individuals evaluate the possible outcomes associated with their choices in accordance with their preferences and values. In doing this, they discount the evaluation of each outcome in accordance with their subjective estimate of the likelihood of the outcome. Finally they make the choice which they believe will maximize their expected utility (81, p. 31).

Popkin's book is largely an attempt to demonstrate, therefore, that peasants in precolonial Vietnam did indeed manifest this "modern" form of economic and political rationality—that, for example, precolonial village-level cooperation was the product or outcome of the "individual interests of its members" (81, p. 132); that changes produced by colonial rule can be explained "by reference to local economic and political concerns" (81, p. 182); and, finally, that collective political action on the part of peasants also stems from a unifying investment logic. The participation of peasants in a variety of movements, from Cao Dai to Hoa Hao to Communism, must be understood not as "defensive reactions against threats to subsistence guarantees, loss of legitimacy for traditional elites, and moral outrage" but instead in terms of a rational, hence modernistic, "political competence" (81, p. 245).

Popkin's work has been widely discussed and subjected to greater or lesser degrees of critical scrutiny (see, for example, 72, 78, 85). But one criticism addressed to this kind of analysis even by those on the whole sympathetic to it is that, like the moral economy approach that it criticizes, it is overly generalized. This group of critics remain interested in the development of modernist forms of political and economic calculation among the peasantry, but are less inclined to see modernism as a universal feature of peasant ideologies. The contributors to a recently published symposium on peasant behavior, for example, are all relatively sympathetic to Popkin's approach, but in each case (Vietnam, China, Bengal, and Thailand) are concerned with documenting concrete instances of peasant economic or political behavior motivated by a rationality of calculated self-interest (56; see also 5, 57).[3]

A number of other studies have also appeared that bear on the problem of the conditions under which modernist economic and/or political norms take root among peasants, many of them concerned particularly with the conditions under which peasants develop innovative ideas and behavior. These studies include work on South Asia (20, 89), Costa Rica (9), Indonesia (10), northern Thailand (43), China (96), Kenya (70), Ethiopia (1), Tunisia (121), and even seventeenth and eighteenth century Holland (86).

IDEOLOGICAL OBSTACLES TO MODERNISM

This discussion leads quite neatly into a second set of concerns in the recent literature on peasant ideologies, concerns based on the recognition that peasants do not always manifest (often desired) adherence to modernist ideologies. The work cited immediately above can also be read in this way, to the extent that it examines both the causes for the emergence of norms of calculated self-interest as well as the reasons for its nonemergence. However, perhaps more interesting in this regard are a number of recent Marxist studies of the way the formation of class consciousness among peasants is blocked by means of ideological processes of "symbolic domination" or hegemony.

These studies represent somewhat of a break with Marxist orthodoxy since they challenge the use of simplistic notions such as false consciousness to explain the adherence of peasants to what these analysts in any case characterize as "non-class ideologies." An important and thought-provoking example of this kind of analysis is in Andrew Turton's recent paper on ideological domination in Thailand (110). Rather than treating manifestations of what he terms nonclass ideologies as theoretically unproblematic, Turton examines the degree to which "ruling power is maintained through a combination of ideologically and violently coercive forms of domination, rather than by morally persuasive, hegemonic leadership" (110, p. 19). In other words, he is interested primarily in the ways in which the non-class ideologies that serve to maintain ruling power by discouraging peasant opposition are formed. Now, for reasons discussed above, Turton's position on the "agrarian question" in Thailand is central to the whole project, since it determines the definition of particular forms of consciousness as class or non-class depending upon whether or not they reflect the posited class structure. To this end it is important to note that Turton is reluctant to use the term peasantry to describe small-scale

---

[3]A much more interesting approach to the problem is implied by analyses that examine the development of entrepreneurship as capitalist rationality [see for example Belasco's recent study of the commoditization of belief in Yoruba (11)].

agricultural producers in Thailand. He largely avoids the term because, in spite of the existence of relatively independent petty commodity producers in Thailand, there are in his view "greater numbers who might *appear* to be possessors or owners of the means of production . . . who should not be so regarded" (110, p. 34). If Thai rural producers are thus characterized as "wage-labor equivalents," then of course elements of peasant, as opposed to proletarian, ideology must be for Turton "non-class."

With this in mind, we turn to the central part of Turton's paper in which he looks "closely at the ideological aspect of the production and reproduction of this social formation, at the contexts, techniques and modalities of ideological domination, its inherent limitations and the limitations imposed by the resistance with which it is met" (110, p. 37). In a wide-ranging and thought-provoking discussion of these contexts, techniques, and modalities, Turton touches on a variety of state and non-state "ideological institutions of the dominant classes" showing how they serve to generate non-class forms of consciousness in "practical activity: in work, social and cultural reproduction, and in struggle." To this end he examines economic processes of commoditization and the "inculcation of new patterns and ideas, norms and values, of work and consumption, ideas which can be conceptualized as being simultaneously both forces of production and ideology" (110, p. 39). He also examines the ways, following Therborn, "in which the individual is formed, produced as a social subject" such that the dominant class "represents its interests as the universal interests of 'the people,' the whole society" (110, p. 44). Similarly, he examines the role of ritualized discourse in evoking a series of conjoined and mutually reinforcing non-class identities, existential, familial, and political. In addition to the formation of non-class identities through such positive means, Turton also discusses what he terms "restrictive ideological practices" that act to rule out the "free and creative response of dialogue, the ability to contradict (gainsay)" as well as actually to exclude while at the same time concealing the exclusion of rural producers in the discourse of the dominant classes (110, p. 46). It is ideological practices such as these, he argues, that produce the illusion of peasant apathy or silent indifference, since "in Thai society . . . participation in discourse of any kind is restricted according to age, gender, social rank and status" (110, p. 47).

Turton does not argue that the Thai social formation is reproduced by means of ideological domination alone. Indeed he is especially interested in the interaction between ideological and coercive domination by force. This analysis leads him to question the assumption that the greater the level of forceful domination, the less the degree of ideological hegemony. In Thailand, he asks

> Are we not bound to say that the level of forceful suppression is low relative to other comparable social formations? At the same time we have seen the ideological, and brittle, nature of claims to consensus, to a national culture etc. It is precisely this combination which

makes Thailand a particularly interesting case, requiring that we look more closely at, and conceptualize, the *combined* realities of coercion and consent, violent constraint and ideological domination, which has been the principal task of this paper (110, p. 60).

Turton's paper is one of a number of recent attempts within the Marxist tradition to examine closely the ways in which the (posited) class consciousness of peasants is overcome through concrete social and cultural practices, as well as how rural producers, in spite of this, may develop a "consciousness and discourse which is relatively resistant or oppositional to dominant ideological discourse, and to dominant relations of production and social power" (110, p. 65).

Another somewhat similar analysis is provided by Roseberry in an article as well as a very recently published book (87, 88). As we have seen, Roseberry uses Lukacs's procedures for imputing class consciousness in a discussion of the political role of Venezuelan peasants in the nineteenth century, the 1929 caudillo uprisings, and in the *guerillero* episode of the 1960s. The procedure, in Roseberry's view, involves imputing appropriate and rational reactions to particular positions in the production process and "outlining the possibilities for and limitations upon conscious activity by particular groups within a concrete whole" (87, p. 109). Imputing a "correct" form of peasant consciousness in this way leads him to characterize peasants in the nineteenth century as resembling the French peasants described by Marx in the *Eighteenth Brumaire*. In this period "peasant activity was conscious in that it was promoting particular economic interests" but "this consciousness was of particular rather than class interests" (87, p. 114). In 1929, the period in which Andean peasants came the closest to rebelling, "they did not initiate the movement but coalesced around a disaffected hacendado. . . . It centered around the leadership of a person; it was a factional rather than a class movement. It was not a peasant rebellion" (87, p. 123). Finally the 1960s movement failed because it did not address the class realities of Venezuela in this period characterized by "the increasing integration of the peasantry within the proletariat" (87, p. 125). Roseberry's work, like Turton's, demonstrates an interest in the ways in which these non-class ideologies are formed, in this case in political struggle.

Similarly John Harriss wishes to analyze the presence of non-class ideology among peasants, in this case the ideology of caste in northern Tamil Nadu. Unhappy with theories that treat caste as a mere "ideological screen for exploitation . . . ," Harriss argues for a form of structural analysis so that "it may be possible to explain forms of symbolic domination and so to understand the obstacles to the realization of class consciousness" (41, p. 217). Like Turton, then, Harriss discusses the processes of ideological domination. Like Roseberry, he shows how peasant political struggles may take place along non-class lines, furthering rather than challenging the hegemony of dominant classes. This latter focus is stressed in his concluding remarks on the effects of caste ideology. Its persistence, he argues,

> suggests that the expressions of protest that are heard amongst the exploited Paraiyans reflect a "subordinate meaning system" which has the effect of promoting an accomodative response to the facts of inequality, rather than a radical meaning system which explains and opposes them. (41, p. 257).

The expressions of solidarity that are manifest among the dominated castes "do not in the end offer a radical meaning system because they fails to identify the basis of exploitation" (41, p. 258).

Other recent work on the formation of non-class ideologies among peasantries includes analyses of the interaction of ethnicity and class consciousness in Malaysia (119a), Ecuador (115a), and Guadaloupe (21); the ways in which patron-clientage acts to prevent peasant rebellion in Malaysia (95); the interaction between class and vertical alliances on Lombok, Indonesia (18); and the ways in which state intervention in Brazil has historically separated Amazonian peasant producers from each other along non-class lines (76a).

PEASANTS AND IDEOLOGIES OF NATION AND GENDER

I have so far examined studies of the development of modernist forms of consciousness among Third World peasantries, as well as analyses of ideological or cultural obstacles to peasant modernism. One of the problems arising from studies of this kind stems from the radical dichotomy between modernism and nonmodernism on which they are based. The difficulties this can cause for an analysis of peasant ideology can be illustrated with the example of class consciousness. In spite of an attempt by neo-Marxists to overcome some of the theoretical problems of the classical paradigm, in particular problems with the concept of "false consciousness," many Marxist writers continue to view class consciousness among peasants as the main, if not the only, modern and hence correct form. They take this stance, I would argue, because they assume first that class struggle is the only effective mode of political action, and second, that liberation from relations of class exploitation is the only true form of liberation. It is for this reason that neo-Marxist analyses of peasant ideology revolve almost entirely around the issue of the emergence of class consciousness among peasants, or seek explanations for the absence of peasant liberation at the level of ideology. Finally, behind many of these analyses is a comparison with the assumed potential of the proletariat. In the classical paradigm such a comparison was almost inevitably unfavorable—the proletariat was the only class capable on the one hand of developing "true" forms of class consciousness and on the other of liberating all other classes through its own class struggle.

Analogous assumptions are implicit in much of the liberal writing, although in this case the issue is one of the conditions under which modern forms of economic and political rationality based on calculated self-interest do or do not emerge.

While these recent formulations of classical problematics have to some extent overcome the evolutionist and positivist pitfalls inherent in classical models of modernization, they must nonetheless be subjected to critical scrutiny at a number of levels. To illustrate again by means of the neo-Marxist approaches, I suggest there are three assumptions that need more careful thought.

First, it is necessary to examine the argument that class consciousness (and liberation from relations of exploitation) is the only liberating form of consciousness, and that all non-class ideologies are in some sense merely obstacles to the liberating struggle. Second, we must look more closely at the hidden yardstick against which peasant consciousness and peasant mobilization is continually being measured, namely the concept of a proletarian revolution. Third, we must look more critically at the concept of class itself as it is employed in these analyses.

In the final part of this paper I examine recent studies that contribute to this process of critical evaluation, either explicitly or implicitly. In this section I discuss ideologies that, like class consciousness and liberalism, may be manifest in the consciousness of (some) peasants but are not peasant ideologies per se; and in the next section, studies of ideologies more frequently associated specifically with peasant movements.

Nationalism

In a sense the career of the concept of nationalism in the history of academic discourse has been unique. For one thing, as Anderson points out, it is unique in being a force of undeniable political power in world history, but a concept characterized by extreme "philosophical poverty. . . . In other words, unlike most other isms, nationalism has never produced its own grand thinkers: no Hobbses, Tocquevilles, Marxes or Webers" (4, p. 14). As a concept it may be unique for another reason as well. Perhaps because of the very philosophical poverty of which Anderson has written, it has been appropriated by a wide variety of social theories, not to mention political movements, to be used in very different ways. A pertinent example here is the fate of the concept in liberal academia in the postwar years. In the 1950s and early 1960s at least American liberal academics seem to have looked very favorably on the development of national political consciousness. Indeed it might even be argued that the development of a national consciousness and the cultural modernization of Third World peasantries were seen as synonymous. More recently however, nationalism has been replaced in this equation by ideologies of political self-interest, as suggested above.[4]

In any case for a variety of reasons there appears to be a renewed interest in the phenomenon of nationalism in the West—both nationalism in the context of the nation state and nationalist movements within the boundaries of existing nation states [see for example (98)]. In spite of this growth in the literature on nationalisms in the West, however, the revival has yet to really manifest itself in writing on the Third World. This reviewer is aware of only a handful of recent works that deal explicitly with Third World nationalisms and that at the same time provide material of relevance to debates on peasant ideology. Foremost among these, if only because it raises important questions about the nature of liberation movements and nationalist revolutions in which peasants have played a significant role, is Anderson's book (4). Mention must also be made of a general study by Sathyamurthy (91), an edited collection on the Horn of Africa (65), and a recent article on Eritrea (35). In general, writers on the Third World continue to employ concepts such as ethnicity, communalism, primordialism, and the like, as though modern movements of this sort could be understood without reference to the hegemony of modern forms of nationalism.[5]

Although it makes little direct reference to the formation of national consciousness among peasants, Anderson's work is important for the subject at hand for two reasons. First, it suggests the need to look more closely at the nature of revolutionary consciousness, and the dangers of equating the ideology of revolution in movements with important peasant involvement with class consciousness on its own. He argues that recent history serves "to underline the fact that since World War II every successful revolution has defined itself in national *terms*—the People's Republic of China, the Socialist Republic of Vietnam and so forth—and in so doing has grounded itself firmly in a territorial and social space inherited from the prerevolutionary past" (4, p. 12). Any analysis of revolutionary ideology must, therefore, come to grips with the phenomenon of nationalism as a "cultural artefact" of a particular kind. Understanding nationalisms means careful consideration of "how they have come into historical being, in what ways their meanings have changed over time, and why, today, they command such profound emotional legitimacy" (4, p. 13f).

---

[4] Anderson offered a thought-provoking account of this shift among American Indonesianists (3). It is perhaps because of the shift that the profusion of postwar writings on ethnicity, communalism, tribalism, etc seems to have diminished in recent years, since their significance was a consequence of the way they were seen to be blocks to the development of modern national consciousness.

[5] For a review of this issue see (53). For a careful consideration of the problems in a treatment of ethnicity outside the framework of colonialism, see the work of William Henry Scott on the Philippines (94).

In addition to emphasizing the importance of the nationalist component of revolutionary ideology, Anderson makes a second point that has direct bearing on the topic at hand, and that is that nationalist aspirations must be treated with a degree of respect. National communities are "imagined communities," yes, but no more imagined than any other. This suggests that the desire for national liberation cannot be dismissed as in some sense false or pathological—but must be treated perhaps even on a par with the desire for economic liberation:

> In an age when it is so common for progressive, cosmopolitan intellectuals . . . to insist on the near-pathological character of nationalism, its roots in fear and hatred of the Other, and its affinities with racism, it is useful to remind ourselves that nations inspire love, and often profoundly self-sacrificing love. The cultural products of nationalism—poetry, prose fiction, music, plastic arts—show this love very clearly in thousands of different forms and styles. . . . Even in the case of colonized peoples, who have every reason to feel hatred for their imperialist rulers, it is astonishing how insignificant the element of hatred is in these expressions of national feeling (4, p. 129).

Anderson's work on nationalism, therefore, at least points to the pitfalls of assuming that only the development of particular forms of consciousness can be interpreted as liberating, and that all others are either forms of ideological domination or obstacles to the development of true liberationism.

Feminism

If such can be said of nationalism, then it can perhaps be argued even more clearly for the case of feminism. Unlike the literature on nationalism, however, there is an increasingly large feminist literature on the Third World. Unfortunately, not a great deal of this literature deals explicitly with the development of feminist consciousness among Third World peasant women, much of it dealing either with the economic and political relations of gender hierarchies or, when consciousness is discussed, on the relationship between gender and class consciousness among women wage workers. However, a number of recent publications do provide a discussion of the issues involved in examining the relationship between class consciousness and feminist consciousness in rural areas of the Third World. Among these are a recent collection of articles on sex and class in Latin America (75), works on the roles and perceptions of women, including peasant women, in liberation struggles in Nicaragua (83) and Angola (77), and an article on the experiences of Guatamalan women (42). Here one should also mention the recent publication in the West of a selection of articles from the Indian journal on women, *Manushi*, which has sought to collect "information about the life conditions of poor women, especially those living in villages" and their political and economic struggles (59), as well as a recently published overview of the Indian feminist movement including an analysis of *Manushi* by S. Renjen Bald (7). Other publications with at least some discussion of female consciousness and gender ideologies among peasants include works on patriarchy and social change in the Andes (15), the history of the Mexican feminist movement (66), and several edited collections that touch on issues of consciousness (17, 119). Finally there is a general collection of written materials from the Third World dealing with the relationship between women's struggles and national liberation (28).

The relevance of such studies to the theme under discussion here would seem to be the precise nature of female consciousness among concrete peasantries. The number of such empirical studies is remarkably small. Also relevant is the extent to which peasant participation in women's movements can be treated as liberating, if not from capitalist forms of economic exploitation, then liberating in other equally if not more valid ways. Mattelart's account of the way women's movements in Chile were coopted by the right to help bring about the downfall of government of Popular Unity is, of course, a counter case (68) and suggests the need to look closely at the relationship between feminist and class movements in the Third World. The progressive aspect of women's defense of tradition is discussed in a forthcoming article by Stivens (102).

NONMODERNISM AND ANTIMODERNISM IN PEASANT CONSCIOUSNESS

An examination of the relation between nationalism and feminism on the one hand, and class consciousness and liberal rationality on the other, leads us to consider more carefully the assumptions of both Marxists and liberals concerning the liberating implications of modernist ideologies. While under certain circumstances nationalist and feminine consciousness might be considered obstacles to the development of "true" consciousness of the peasants' situation, under others they are rational and liberating ideologies.

If, however, some Marxists and liberals have made inaccurate assumptions about the implications of nationalism and feminism, then how much truer is this for phenomena such as millenarianism, syncretism, and religious theology? The forms of consciousness encapsulated by these terms are obviously manifest in peasant ideology, even, one suspects, when it appears that peasants adhere to the rationalist ideologies of the leaders of revolutions and rebellions. The time has clearly come for a fresh look at the role played by these forms of peasant ideology, and the flood of literature in this area is a sign of what I termed the discovery of the peasantry in Western social science.

This literature, of course, is based on earlier works on peasants and political upheaval. But here again there seems to have been a movement toward a more positive evaluation of the ideologies and world views of peasant participants. There is thus a concern with "history from below," the experience of the peasant and the culture of the masses. As part of this, writers are directing their attention to the internal rationality of beliefs that have often been described but dismissed as anachronistic—millenarianism, nativism, syncretism, the Little Tradition, etc.

Speaking for this outlook, Michael Adas writes of five peasant rebellions (the Java War of 1825–1830; the Maori Pai Movement of 1864–1867; the Bisa Rising of East Central India in 1899–1900; the Tanzanian Maji Maji Rebellion; and the Burmese Saya San Movement in 1930–1932):

> In none of these movements was the response to change merely a blind retreat into an idealized pre-European past, although there was always some appeal to customary ways. Rather, they represented creative efforts to repair the fabric of societies rent by forces over which the indigenous peoples had little or no control. These prophet-inspired rebellions involved restoration and reformulation of customary ideas and institutions as well as the introduction of foreign elements and a millenarian vision of a new society. Their adherents were not faced with a choice between a traditional and modern order, but with the problems of coping with accelerated change and intense culture contact. In bits and pieces rather than by some grand design, they rejected or adapted, revived and reworked ideas, artifacts, and patterns of behavior in an effort to create a more viable social order (2, p.:xxvii).

This approach inevitably brings with it certain very thorny problems of method, problems that have to do with the difficulties of discovering or recovering the viewpoint of peasants in the modern period, or even more awkward, in the historical record. For anthropology, the problem is one of gaining genuine access to peasant systems of meaning. The most extended discussion of this is found in the work of the "interpretive" anthropologists. The advantages and disadvantages of an interpretive approach are nicely illustrated in a recent book on Minangkabau (32). This is a marvelously evocative study of the problems faced by the anthropologist in attempting to understand the culture of the other. The results are, however, somewhat disappointing in the sense that, as often seems to be the case in such studies, they bear on perhaps somewhat trivial aspects of peasant consciousness. At worst such studies confirm the impression that all an outside observer can really find out is the way his/her "object" of study chooses to present itself to outsiders.

The problems of discovering the view from below in the historical record is discussed by William Henry Scott, who argues that indigenous history can nonetheless be read through the "cracks in the parchment curtain" (94), and by Milner, who, arguing that it cannot, discusses the use of indigenous, written sources (71). Perhaps even more promising here is the use of techniques of oral history. For some discussion of one such project in the Third World, see the account by Nartsupha for Thailand (74).

Recent publications on peasant political mobilization, and peasant rebellions in particular, that consider in one way or another the role of nonmodernist ideology in peasant consciousness, are as follows: historical and contemporary work on peasant movements in South Asia (8, 26, 30, 38, 40, 41, 51, 52, 55, 58, 82, 103); writings on the Darul Islam movement in Indonesia (84, 100, 112); new analyses of the 1926–1927 Communist uprisings in Banten and West

Sumatra in colonial Indonesia (54, 116); studies of peasant political movements in southern Vietnam, including one of Cao Dai (115) and one on Hoa Hao (104); recent analyses of the role of religion and traditional forms of protest in peasant struggles in the Philippines (48, 93); and an edited collection with contributions from Southeast Asian, Japanese, and Anglo-Saxon scholars on Thailand, Indonesia, Vietnam, Malaysia, and Japan (111).

For Latin America, the classic remains Jean Meyer's 1976 study of the Cristeros in Mexico (69), although a recent re-study has been published (109). One should also mention analysis of: peasant resistance on the Colombian frontier (63), peasant movements in Paraguay (34, 39), campesino mobilization in Mexico (33), and peasants in Guatemala (99).

The work by Western scholars on Chinese peasant rebellions continues to proliferate. Recent contributions include studies of the long history of peasant movements in Haileng Country in the South (67); violence and political protest in the Ming and Qing periods (120); the ways in which the Chinese Communist Party adapted to the "Little Tradition" in the Shanxi-Hehei-Shandong border area in the 1930s and 1940s (106, 107); the Boxer Rebellion (31); peasant rebellions in northern China between 1845 and 1945 (79); and the cultural aspects of political action on Taiwan (49). We are also fortunate in having available a translation of some of the works by Chinese historians on the Nien rebellions (80). Here we should also mention the recent collection of writing on Minjung "liberation theology" in Korea (24).

For Africa we have a collection of articles on peasants and power (25), a discussion of peasnats and the state in the Cameroons that examines peasant egalitarian traditions (37), a look at the history of colonial protest movements in Kenya (117), a book on resistance to and collaboration with French colonial rulers among the Baule peoples (113), a study of peasant resistance in Ethiopia (105), and an edited collection of pieces by members of South Africa's History Workshop on capitalist penetration and popular response in the Transvaal (16). There is also a recent book on the role played by Iranian peasants in the overthrow of the Shah (44).

Although outside the scope of this review, it is interesting to note that there remains a considerable degree of cross-fertilization between Europeanists and students of peasant politics and ideology in the Third World. This is manifest in recent articles and books on agricultural disturbances in England (19), French peasants in revolution (45, 101), the late nineteenth century Crofters' Revolt in Scotland (118), the agrarian revolution in Russia (64), the role of traditional culture in fostering revolutionary attitudes among French peasants (73), and peasant violence in Ireland (23, 60).

Apart from these and other regionally specific studies of peasant rebellion and ideology, the last few years have also seen the publication of a number of general works on peasant ideology and the politics of rebellion. Perhaps most influential have been the two that appeared in 1979: Skocpol's important comparative study (97) of the role of peasants in the revolutions in France, Russia, and China; and Adas's comparison (2) of five prophet-inspired rebellions of non-Western peoples in European-dominated colonial areas. Mention should also be made of a collection of essays on rural unrest in Asia, Latin America, and Europe (114). Although not directly on our topic, there are the influential or potentially influential works on social movements by Louise and Charles Tilly (see, for example, 108) and the works of Sassoon (90) and Kreisberg (62). And finally, as part of a tendency to publish direct accounts of peasant experience of struggle, there is the collection compiled by Johnson & Bernstein (50).

Because of the incredible volume of these materials, this list is bound to be incomplete. Moreover, there is clearly no space in a review of this kind to even begin to summarize the literature in any detail. I therefore provide instead a brief summary of a few of these contributions.

"Traditional" Culture in Peasant Political Consciousness: Gramsci in India

Perhaps the most detailed examination of the interaction between traditional culture and political mobilization of the peasantry in the Marxist literature is found in the recent work of a group of Indianists calling themselves the "subalternists" (see 6, 38). In the words of one of their number, they seek to "examine Gramsci's ideas relating to the peasantry and then to consider how those ideas, particularly of subalternity, hegemony and passive revolution might be applied . . . to the specific case of the Indian peasantry in the nineteenth and twentieth centuries" (6, p. 156). Discussions of the pertinence of Gramsci's work in the analysis of peasants and ideology are also found in the works of Turton (110) and Davidson (27).

Two features of Gramsci's work are considered of particular significance for these writers. The first is that, after advocating a form of developmentalism that argued for the inevitable demise of the Italian peasantry in the transition to capitalism in Italy, Gramsci appears to have changed his views such that:

> No longer was it taken for granted that the peasantry were that section of the populace doomed to extinction and expropriation from their subsistence holdings, but it was recognised that international developments could result in their reproduction and growth in new forms to support new types of politics (27, p. 143).

The second important feature of Gramsci's writings was the way they suggested the presence of positive as well as negative elements in traditional peasant ways of seeing the world. In Davidson's words,

> To admit this was partly to reinstate popular culture not merely as something "folkloric" but as the starting point for the new socialist view of the world. In other words, in his *Prison*

Notebooks, coexisting uneasily with his earlier enlightened views and his developmentalism, there is present a reassertion of the value of some aspects of the peasant mode of production and the culture on which it rests in the face of the transformative pressures of centralising capitalism (27, p. 145).

Or, as Arnold argues,

> Gramsci validated the study of subaltern beliefs and consciousness not because he thought them objectively correct but because they were forms and expressions of the life of the masses which no exponent of the "philosophy of praxis" could afford to ignore (6, p. 159).

In the context of India, these ideas have been developed in the study of colonial peasant politics viewed as an autonomous domain and expressive of autonomous modes of peasant thought and action manifest in popular movements of all kinds. On the other hand, as Arnold points out, the subalternists are also concerned with understanding why, in spite of the autonomy of the popular modes of thought, the subordination of the subaltern classes has been perpetuated.

Prophet-Inspired Anticolonialism

Michael Adas's comparative study of five anticolonial millenarian or sectarian rebellions outlines similarities and differences in peasant anticolonial ideology and contributes to the study of the causes of peasant rebellion.

We have already looked briefly at his discussion of the general features of rebellious ideology. Overall, the movements he singles out for study are all centered on "prophetic figures and their divinely inspired revelations," although there are significant differences among them in terms of the form of their millenarian visions. Some, such as the Java War and the Maji Maji rebellion, are nativistic to the extent that the ideology of a new age, as well as the means adopted to achieve it derive largely from traditional cultural/religious heritage. Others, such as the Maori movement of 1864–1867, he describes as syncretistic in the sense that millenarian ideologies are supplied by outside religions. In the struggle with Europeans all the movements relied on what might appear to the observer, in any case, to be symbolic means to combat European superiority in military technology. Adas speaks of five main forms: preparatory rumors and omens (such as the earthquake in Burma in May 1930, taken as a sign of the coming of the struggle for a millennium); the use of legitimacy symbols (e.g. the traditional coronation rituals for Saya San); the organization of rituals to establish solidarity and invoke supernatural assistance; the use of talismans to overcome European technological superiority (e.g. Burmese tattoos); and the use of "sympathetic magic" or the imitation of the behavior of the adversary (such as the Burmese nin pole modelled on European creations like the telegraph pole and a ship's flagstaff (2, p. 140ff).

Adas's explanation for why rebellions took place when and where they did relies heavily on a somewhat modified concept of relative deprivation caused by the colonial displacement of elites; the challenge posed by colonialism to indigenous ritual and religious experts and the institutions and beliefs they represented; and the relative (but not absolute) economic deprivations caused by the imposition of new labor tributes and/or money taxes.

Millenarianism, Sectarianism, and Tradition in Peasant Rebellion: Three Case Studies

The above discussion suggests that it is necessary to take more care in our evaluations of concrete peasant ideologies rather than simply measuring them against the yardstick of (our own) ideological modernisms. A major obstacle to such careful evaluation is the relative absence of detailed case materials on the ideological content of struggles in which peasants have been politically engaged. All too often we are presented with an account of events, and the ideologies of the elites, or at least the almost invariably modernist ideologies of a rebellious or revolutionary leadership of such struggles on the one hand, or an account of certain relatively insignificant areas of peasant culture on the other. Three recent case studies have, with varying degrees of success, attempted to overcome this by focussing on the consciousness of the mass of peasant participants in historically significant, even formative, social movements.

The first, Elizabeth Perry's study of the roots of revolutionary ideology in the Huai-pei region of northern China (79), represents a further contribution to the debate over the role played by indigenous peasant traditions and ideologies in the actual formation of the revolutionary ideology of the CCP (see also 97, 106, 107). Perry's study is interesting for what it tells us of the nineteenth century Nien Rebellion, and the movement of the Red Spear society in the 1920s; for the suggestions it raises about the links between "traditional" predatory and protective strategies of peasant individuals and social groups and the nature of rebellious culture; for the way it raises questions about how peasants are and are not coopted by different social movements through the manipulation by elites of these traditional household and group strategies; and finally for its exploration of the links between CCP ideology and forms of mobilization and the earlier movements, particularly the Red Spear. It must be said that this last part of the study is, as Perry herself admits, its least successful part. Nonetheless the work is an important example of the kinds of research that might be pursued to produce a further positive appreciation of the insights offered by peasant consciousness and the historical importance of peasants, not just as passive followers of elites but as subjects of history in their own right.

A second and even more detailed account of a peasant-based political movement and the ideologies that motivated it is Hue-Tam Ho Tai's impressive account of the development and decline of the Hoa Hao sect in southern Vietnam. Hoa Hao, a religio-political organization, mobilized thousands of peasants first against the French and then in the late 1940s against the communists. Less has been written, however, about the tradition known as Buu Son Ky Huong out of which Hoa Hao emerged. Buu Son Ky Huong, which "represented a millenarian world-view and a communtarian way of life" (104, p. 3), had its origins in the southern part of what is now Vietnam in the middle of the last century. What is important about Tai's study, among other things, is the way it treats this form of peasant ideology not as some timeless form of peasant tradition but as a cultural and ideological formation that has particular social and historical roots. In examining the origins of Buu Son Ky Huong and its development and transformation through the period of the war against colonialism, Tai has given us significant insights into the ways in which peasant ideologies are formed without at the same time dismissing them out of hand as nonmodern or nonrational.

Finally, and perhaps the most interesting of all these studies, we have Ileto's excellent book on the history of popular movements in the Philippines between 1840 and 1910 (48). Ileto is explicitly interested in writing a history of the Philippines "from below," and does so by examining the revolutionary tradition associated with the Katipunan secret society of 1896. The tone of the book can be glimpsed in the following account of the Lapiang Maya affair given at the beginning of the book. Lapiang Maya (the Freedom Party) confronted the Manila police in May of 1967 armed "only with sacred bolos, *anting-anting* (amulets) and bullet-defying uniforms." This affair, writes Ileto was not

> ... an abberation in an otherwise comprehensible past. We should be able to find meaning in it, not reporting to convenient explanations like "fanaticism," "nativism," and "millenarianism," which only alienate us further from the kapatid (brotherhood) who lived through it. But what we modern Filipinos need first of all is a set of conceptual tools, a grammar, that would help us understand the world of the kapatid, which is part of our world . . . (48, pp. 2–3).

The search for these "conceptual tools" leads Ileto to a reexamination of the revolutionary period to escape the modernist readings of Filipino history that relegate movements such as this to the background, or argue that their suppression was essential to the rational development of Filipino politics.

Ileto's book makes fascinating reading because it succeeds in producing a history from below through the use of a range and diversity of source materials—poems, songs, scattered autobiographies, confessions, prayers, and folk sayings—often ignored in traditional histories (48, p. 13). In particular the study is based on a Tagalog version of an "Account of the Sacred Passion of Lord Jesus Christ" (known as the Pasyon Pilapil), which it is convincingly argued is significant not for its literary or theological merit but because it "stands out mainly as—to paraphrase Marc Bloch—a mirror of the collective consciousness" (48, p. 17).

While this reviewer is not qualified to judge the empirical accuracy of the results, he still finds Ileto's history of Tagalog popular culture and ideology of resistance in the Philippines to be one of the best works on peasant ideologies in the Third World to appear in recent years.

CONCLUDING REMARKS

In this review I have been largely concerned with summarizing a huge and growing body of literature on peasant ideologies in the Third World. The size of the literature together with limitations imposed by a review format prevent me from doing much more than briefly summarizing a few of these works that strike me as the most interesting. This may explain, for example the slight bias in favor of works on Asia in the review.

In any case it has not been possible to offer a comprehensive critique of any of the material discussed here, nor to suggest ways in which current interests and research might or should be extended. Indeed it would be presumptuous of a reviewer to set out to attack everything that does not simply reflect his or her own way of thinking. I would like to conclude, however, by making a few provisional and necessarily more personal remarks about the literature I reviewed for this article.

I noted what I take to be a general tendency in recent academic writings on the Third World, a tendency that I termed, perhaps somewhat overdramatically, the discovery of the peasantry. It may be somewhat early to explain why such a tendency should be manifest in the literature, but it is at least thought-provoking to recognize that while such a tendency can be observed for Western social science, it is not found everywhere. In her introduction to a recently translated collection of essays by Chinese historians on the Nien Rebellion, Elizabeth Perry writes:

> Following the demise of the "Gang of Four" and subsequent academic liberalization in China, a new outpouring of historical scholarship has commenced. As with historiography in the days before the Cultural Revolution, much attention continues to be focused on the subject of peasant rebellion. Now, however, along with the nationwide emphasis on productive forces rather than on class struggle as the primary motive force of history, there is room for a less positive appraisal of the role of peasant uprisings. As the perceived importance of class struggle recedes into the background, so too does the need to portray China's peasant rebellions as a glorious protorevolutionary tradition, leading inexorably toward communist victory in 1949. Quite the contrary in tune with the current dictum that China remains in large part "feudal" historians have set about the task of reevaluating the character of various peasant uprisings—stressing the many "backward" aspects of the movements (80, p. 3).

This apparent link between a stress on the development of the productive forces and a negative view of peasant ideology is found in a completely inverted form in the writings discussed above, and it suggests that the "discovery of the peasantry" is related in some way to a calling into question either the necessity or desirability of technological development as an end in itself. What is particularly interesting about this tendency is that in can be observed in the work of Marxists and non-Marxists alike.

Clifford Geertz, for example, in the published version of his 1983 Huxley Memorial Lecture, traces the development of his own discovery of culture in his experience of a particular kind of confrontation between Indonesia and the West in the 1950s:

> ... indigenous cultural traditions were thought [by many] to be a simple obstacle to social change, and especially to that particularly wished-for sort of social change called "development." The traditional family, traditional religion, traditional patterns of prestige and deference, traditional political arrangements were all regarded as standing in the way of the growth of properly rational attitudes towards work, efficient organisation, and the acceptance of technological change. Breaking the cake of custom was seen as the pre-requisite to the escape from poverty and to the so-called "takeoff" into sustained growth of *per capita* income, as well as to the blessings of modern life in general. For the economists, the thing to do with the past was abandon it; for the anthropologists, to study it before it was abandoned, and then perhaps to mourn it (36, p. 511).

Speaking for many liberal anthropologists working in Indonesia in this period, Geertz points out that such a negative evaluation of Indonesian culture was unacceptable to scholars who "were rather unsure, to put it mildly, how to go about trying to be of use in making Indonesia 'modern,' even if we so desired—which, distrusting the growth ethos as ethnocentric at best, imperialist at worst, we were very far from sure that we did" (36, p. 512).

What Geertz, perhaps, fails to appreciate here is that the shift to a more positive evaluation of the culture of Third World peasants is not restricted to liberal social science, but also, as we have seen, characterizes at least Western Marxism as well, and perhaps for similar reasons.

However, this kind of argument must be qualified. All the works cited above—however much they argue for a treatment of peasant ideology in its own terms, an appreciation of the internal rationality of peasant modes of thought, etc—inevitably draw back from any kind of absolute relativism. Adas, for example, is bound to say that however much we can appreciate the reasons for the particular "millenarian" practices of the political movements he studies, we must see them as, in the last instance, irrational, even if this judgment can only be taken with historical hindsight (see, for example, 2, p. 162). Ileto, perhaps the most sympathetic of all our observers, nonetheless talks of Lapiang Maya as an example of "cultural modes that reflect previous stages of development" (48, p. 3). Examples of similar language could be found in all the works cited above.

Does this not, therefore, testify to an unacceptable contradiction in the academic study of peasantries? I would argue that it does, and that what we are witnessing is not necessarily a discovery of the peasantry at all but a rediscovery of forms of discourse that are as much a part of the history of Western inquiry as are the sociological positivisms of which almost all the above writers disapprove. No one, not even Geertz, can escape from this.

If we ask ourselves why this should be, it seems to me that the answer has to do with the way even the most sensitive academic observers tend to treat the peasantry as an object of study. In other words, no matter to what extent the process of discovering peasant ideology and culture is a matter of self-consciousness dialogue between peasant and investigator, the longer-term evaluation of the academic text tends to have very little to do with peasants or, perhaps more accurately, the participants in the concrete struggles in which peasants are involved. This might be put in a less negative way, one that would serve at least partially to rescue much of the discovery that has been the topic of this paper. We as social scientists must self-consciously become aware of the fact that peasant ideology in the contemporary Third World is at least as much a critique of the modernism of which social scientific theory is an integral part as it is a survival from earlier "traditional" ways of thinking; only then shall we truly be able to claim to have discovered peasant ideology in academic discourse.

ACKNOWLEDGMENTS

I would like to thank Steve Nugent, Maila Stivens, John Gledhill, Josep Llobera, and particularly June Wyer for help in providing me with references for this review. I would also like to express thanks to Win Stivens and Fred and Mary Kahn for other assistance, without which this review could never have been completed.

Literature Cited

1. Abate, A. 1983. Peasant associations and collective agriculture in Ethiopia: promise and performance. *Erdkunde* 27:118–27
2. Adas, M. 1979. *Prophets of Rebellion: Millenarian Protest Movements against the European Colonial Order.* Chapel Hill: Univ. North Carolina Press
3. Anderson, B. O'G. 1982 (1973). Perspective and method in American research on Indonesia. In *Interpreting Indonesian Politics: Thirteen Contributions to the Debate,* ed. B. Anderson, A. Kahn. Ithaca, NY: Cornell Modern Indonesia Project, Interim Rep. Ser. No. 62
4. Anderson, B. O'G. 1983. *Imagined Communities: Reflections on the Origin and Spread of Nationalism.* London: Verso
5. Appadurai, A. 1984. How moral is South Asia's moral economy? A review article. *J. Asian Stud.* 43:481–97
6. Arnold, D. 1984. Gramsci and peasant subalternity in India. *J. Peasant Stud.* 11:155–77
7. Bald, S. R. 1983. *From Satyartha Prakesh to Manushi: An Overview of the "Women's Movement" in India.* East Lansing: Mich. State Univ. Pap. Women and Int. Dev. No. 23
8. Banerjee, S. 1984. *India's Simmering Revolution: The Naxalite Uprising.* London: Zed
9. Bartlett, P. 1982. *Agricultural Choice and Change: Decision Making in a Costa Rican Community.* New Brunswick: Rutgers Univ. Press
10. Batara-Goa, A. W. 1983. *A study of the impact of communication on the acceptance of technological innovations in a selected rural community in East Java, Indonesia.* PhD thesis. Cornell Univ.
11. Belasco, B. I. 1980. *The Entrepreneur as Culture Hero: Preadaptations in Nigerian Economic Development.* New York: Praeger

12. Black, G. 1981. *Triumph of the People: The Sandinista Revolution in Nicaragua.* London: Zed
13. Black, G. (with N. Jamal and N. S. Chinchilla). 1984. *Garrison Guatemala.* London: Zed
14. Bossert, T. J. 1980. The agricultural reform and peasant political consciousness in Chile. *Lat. Am. Perspect.* 7(4):6–28
15. Bourque, S. C., Warren, K. B. 1981. *Women in the Andes: Patriarchy and Social Change in Two Peruvian Towns.* Ann Arbor: Univ. Mich. Press
16. Bozzoli, B., ed. 1983. *Town and Countryside in the Transvaal. Capitalist Penetration and Popular Response.* Johannesburg: Raven
17. Caplan, P., Bujra, J., eds. 1978. *Women United, Women Divided: Cross-Cultural Perspectives in Female Solidarity.* London: Tavistock
18. Cederroth, S. 1981. *The Spell of the Ancestors and the Power of Mekkah: A Sasak Community on Lombok.* Gothenburg (Acta Univ. Gothoburgensis 3): Vasastaden Bokbinderi
19. Charlesworth, A. 1984. A comparative study of the spread of the agricultural disturbances of 1816, 1822 and 1830 in England. *Peasant Stud.* 11:91–110
20. Chaudry, M. A. 1984. Resistance to change: Fact or fiction? A study in selected areas of Punjab province in Pakistan. *Agric. Admin.* 16:131–43
21. Cherdieu, P. 1984. L'échec d'un socialisme colonial: la Guadeloupe (1891–1914). *Rev. Hist. Mod. Contemp.* 31:308–33
22. Chevalier, J. 1982. *Civilization and the Stolen Gift: Capital, Kin and Cult in Eastern Peru.* Toronto: Univ. Toronto Press
23. Clark, S., Donnelly, J. S., eds. 1983. *Irish Peasant Violence and Political Unrest: 1780–1914.* Madison: Univ. Wis. Press
24. Commission on the Theological Concerns of the Christian Conferences of Asia. 1983. *Minjung Theology: People as Subjects of History.* London: Zed
25. Copans, J., ed. 1984. Les paysans et le pouvoir en Afrique noire. *Polit. Afr., Vol. 13* (Spec. issue)
26. Copland, I. 1983. The Cambay "disturbances" of 1890: popular protest in princely India. *Indian Econ. Soc. Hist. Rev.* 20:415–38
27. Davidson, A. 1984. Gramsci, the peasantry and popular culture. *J. Peasant Stud.* 11:139–54
28. Davies, M. (compiler). 1983. *Third World-Second Sex: Women's Struggles and National Liberation.* London: Zed
29. Deere, C. D., Marchetti, P. 1981. The worker-peasant alliance in the first year of the Nicaraguan agrarian reform. *Lat. Am. Perspect.* 8(2):40–73
30. Desai, A. R., ed. 1979. *Peasant Struggles in India.* Bombay: Oxford Univ. Press
31. Doar, B. 1984. The Boxers and Chinese drama: Questions of interaction. *Pap. Far East. Econ. Hist.* 29:91–118
32. Errington, F. 1984. *Manners and Meaning in West Sumatra.* New Haven: Yale Univ. Press
33. Esteva, G. 1983. *The Struggle for Rural Mexico.* South Hadley, Mass: Bergin & Garvey
34. Fogel, R. B. 1982. *Avances teóricos en la explicacion de movimientos sociales rurales.* Cuadernos de Investigacion, Dept. Estud., Comité de Iglesias, Paraguay
35. Gebre-Medhin, J. 1984. Nationalism, peasant politics and the emergence of a vanguard front in Eritrea. *Rev. Afr. Polit. Econ.* 30:48–57
36. Geertz, C. 1984. Culture and social change: The Indonesian case. *Man* 19:511–32
37. Geschiere, P. 1982. *Village Communities and the Authority of the State.* London: Routledge & Kegan Paul
38. Ghua, R., ed. 1982. *Subaltern Studies I: Writings on South Asian History and Society.* New York: Oxford Univ. Press
39. Guiterrez, J. 1980. Paraguay: agribusiness is peasants. *NACLA Rep. Americas* 14(3):38–41
40. Gupta, A. 1984. Revolution in Telengara, 1946–1951. *South Asia Bull.* 4:1–26
41. Harriss, J. 1982. *Capitalism and Peasant Farming: Agrarian Structure and Ideology in Northern Tamil Nadu.* Bombay: Oxford Univ. Press
42. Herrera, L. A. 1980. Testimonies of Guatemalan women. *Lat. Am. Perspect.* 7:160–68
43. Hinton, P. 1983. Why the Karen do not grow opium: competition and contradiction in the highlands of North Thailand. *Ethnology* 22:1–16
44. Hoogland, E. J. 1982. *Land and Revolution in Iran, 1960–1980.* Austin: Univ. Texas Press
45. Hunt, D. 1984. Peasant politics in the French Revolution. *Soc. Hist.* 9:277–300
46. Hussain, A., Tribe, K. 1981. *Marxism and the Agrarian Question.* Volume 1: *German Social Democracy and the Peasantry, 1890–1907.* Atlantic Highlands, NJ: Humanities
47. Hussain, A., Tribe, K. 1981. *Marxism*

and the Agrarian Question. Volume 2: Russian Marxism and the Peasantry, 1861–1930. London: Macmillan
48. Ileto, R. C. 1979. Pasyon and Revolution: Popular Movements in the Philippines, 1840–1910. Quezon City: Ateneo de Manila Univ. Press
49. Jacobs, J. B. 1980. Local Politics in a Rural Chinese Setting: A Field Study of Mazu Township, Taiwan. Canberra: ANU Contemp. China Ctr.
50. Johnson, H., Bernstein, H., eds. 1982. Third World Lives of Struggle. London: Heineman Educational (with the Open Univ.)
51. Jose, A. V. 1984. Agrarian reforms in Kerala—the role of peasant organisations. J. Contemp. Asia 14:48–61
52. Joshi, P. C. 1982. Poverty, land hunger and emerging class conflicts in rural India. In Rural Poverty and Agrarian Reform, ed. S. Jones et al. New Delhi: Allied Publ.
53. Kahn, J. S. 1981. Explaining ethnicity: A review article. Crit. Anthropol. 4(16):43–52
54. Kahn, J. S. 1984. Peasant political consciousness in West Sumatra: A Reanalysis of the communist uprising of 1927. See Ref. 111, pp. 293–326
55. Kemp, C. 1984. Politics and class in Spring Valley, Sri Lanka: An "antistructuralist" interpretation. J. Peasant Stud. 12:41–64
56. Keyes, C., ed. 1983. Peasant strategies in Asian societies: Moral and rational economic approaches. J. Asian Stud. 42:753–868
57. Keyes, C., Moise, E. 1984. Comments on Keyes, 1983 (see Ref. 56). J. Asian Stud. 43:499–502
58. Kidd, R., Rashid, M. 1984. Theatre by the people, for the peoples and of the people: People's theatre and landless organising in Bangladesh. Bull. Concerned Asian Scholars 16:30–45
59. Kishwar, M., Vanita, R., eds. 1984. In Search of Answers: Indian Women's Voices from Manushi. London: Zed
60. Knott, J. W. 1984. Land, kinship and identity: the cultural roots of agrarian agitation in eighteenth- and nineteenth-century Ireland. J. Peasant Stud. 12:93–108
61. Konings, P. 1983. Riziculteurs capitalistes et petit paysans: la naissance d'un conflit de classe au Ghana. Polit. Afr. 11:77–94
62. Kriesberg, L., ed. 1982. Research in social movements. Conflict Change, Vol. 5 (Spec. issue)
63. LeGrand, C. 1984. Labor acquisition and social change on the Colombia frontier,

1850–1936. J. Lat. Am. Stud. 16:27–49
64. Lewin, M. 1984. Rural society in twentieth century Russia: an introduction. Soc. Hist. 9:171–80
65. Lewis, I. M., ed. 1983. Nationalism and Self-Determination in the Horn of Africa. London: Ithaca
66. Macias, A. 1982. Against All Odds: the Feminist Movement in Mexico to 1940. Connecticut/London: Greenwood
67. Marks, R. B. 1984. Rural Revolution in South China: Peasants and the Making of History in Haileng country, 1572–1930. Madison: Univ. Wis. Press
68. Mattelart, M. 1980. Chile: the feminine version of the coup d'etat. See Ref. 75, pp. 279–301
69. Meyer, J. 1976. The Cristero Rebellion: The Mexican People Between Church and State, 1926–1929. Cambridge: Cambridge Univ. Press
70. Meyers, L. R. 1982. Socioeconomic determinants of credit adoption in a semiarid district of Kenya. PhD thesis. Cornell Univ. Ithaca, NY
71. Milner, A. C. 1982. Kerajaan: Malay Political Culture on the Eve of Colonial Rule. Tucson: Univ. Ariz. Press
72. Moise, E. 1982. The moral economy dispute. Bull. Concerned Asian Scholars 14:72–76
73. Morgadant, T. 1979. French Peasants in Revolt: The Insurrection of 1851. Princeton: Princeton Univ. Press
74. Nartsupha, C. 1984. The ideology of "holy men" revolts in North East Thailand. See Ref. 111, pp. 111–34
75. Nash, J., Saffa, H. I., eds. 1980. Sex and Class in Latin America. New York: Berglin
76. North, L. 1981. Bitter Grounds: Roots of Revolution in El Salvador. Toronto: Between the Lines
76a. Nugent, S. L. 1979. Society, economy and national integration: An anthropological study of Santorem, a town on the Amazon River. PhD thesis. Univ. London
77. Organization of African Women. 1984. Angolan Women: Building the Future. London: Zed
78. Peletz, M. 1983. Moral and political economies in rural Southeast Asia: A review article. Comp. Stud. Soc. Hist. 25:731–39
79. Perry, E. 1980. Rebels and Revolutionaries in North China, 1845–1945. Stanford: Stanford Univ. Press
80. Perry, E., ed. 1981. Chinese Perspectives on the Nien Rebellion. Armonk, NY: Sharpe
81. Popkin, S. 1979. The Rational Peasant:

The Political Economy of Rural Society in Vietnam. Berkeley/Los Angeles: Univ. Calif. Press
82. Puri, H. K. 1983. "Green Revolution" and its impact on Punjab politics. *Indian Polit. Sci. Rev.* 17:98–111
83. Randall, M. 1981. *Sandino's Daughters—Testimonies of Nicaraguan Women in Struggle.* London: Zed
84. Robinson, K. 1983. Living in the Hutan: Jungle village life under the Darul Islam. *Rev. Indonesian Malay Stud.* 17:208–29
85. Roeder, P. G. 1984. Legitimacy and peasant revolution: An alternative to moral economy. *Peasant Stud.* 11:149–68
86. Roessingh, H. K. 1979. Tobacco growing in Holland in the 17th and 18th centuries: A case study of the innovative spirit of Dutch Peasants. *Acta Hist. Neerlandicae* 11:18–54
87. Roseberry, W. 1982. Peasants, proletarians, and politics in Venezuela, 1875–1975. See Ref. 114, pp. 106–31
88. Roseberry, W. 1983. *Coffee and Capitalism in the Venezuelan Andes.* Austin: Univ. Texas Press
89. Samanta, R. K., Reddy, M. N. 1982. Koya of Andhra and their sociopsychological and agro-economic characteristics. *J. Indian Anthropol. Soc.* 17:229–34
90. Sassoon, J. 1984. Ideology, symbolic action and rituality in social movements: the effects on organizational forms. *Soc. Sci. Inform.* 23:861–73
91. Sathyamurthy, T. V. 1983. *Nationalism in the Contemporary World: Political and sociological perspectives.* London: Frances Pinter
92. Schmink, M. 1982. Land conflicts in Amazonia. *Am. Ethnol.* 9:341–78
93. Schumacher, J. N. 1981. *Revolutionary Clergy: The Filipino Clergy and the Nationalist Movement, 1850–1903.* Quezon City: Ateneo de Manila Univ. Press
94. Scott, W. H. 1982. *Cracks in the Parchment Curtain and Other Essays in Philippine History.* Quezon City: New Day Publ.
95. Selat, N. 1981. Patron-client relationship and peasant rebellion. *Sarjana* 1:107–20
96. Sheridan, M. 1981. *Peasant innovation and diffusion of agricultural technology in China,* Spec. Ser. Agric. Res. Extension, No. 4. Ithaca, NY: Cornell Univ. Ctr. Int. Stud.
97. Skocpol, T. 1979. *State and Social Revolutions: A Comparative Analysis of France, Russia and China.* Cambridge Univ. Press
98. Smith, A. D. 1983. *State and Nation in the Third World.* Sussex: Harvester
99. Smith, C. A. 1984. Local history in global context: Social and economic transitions in Western Guatemala. *Comp. Stud. Soc. Hist.* 26:193–228
100. Soebardi, S. 1983. Kartosuwiryan and the Darul Islam rebellions in Indonesia. *J. Southeast Asian Stud.* 14:109–33
101. Sonenscher, M. 1984. The sans-culottes of the Year II: rethinking the language of labor in revolutionary France. *Soc. Hist.* 9:301–28
102. Stivens, M. 1985. *Sexual Politics in Rembau: Female Autonomy, Matriliny and Agrarian Change in Negeri Sembilan, Malaysia,* (Occasional Pap.). Canterbury: Ctr. Southeast Asian Stud. Univ. Kent. In press
103. Stokes, E. T. 1980. *Peasants and the Raj. Studies in Agrarian Society and Peasant Rebellions in Colonial India.* Cambridge: Cambridge Univ. Press
104. Tai, H. H. 1983. *Millenarianism and Peasant Politics in Vietnam.* Cambridge, Mass: Harvard Univ. Press
105. Tareke, G. 1984. Peasant resistance in Ethiopia: The case of Weyane. *J. Afr. Hist.* 25:77–92
106. Thaxton, R. 1982. Mao Zedong, Red Miserables, and the moral economy of peasant rebellion in modern China. See Ref. 114, pp. 132–56
107. Thaxton, R. 1983. *China Turned Rightside Up: Revolutionary Legitimacy in the Peasant World.* New Haven: Yale Univ. Press
108. Tilly, L. A., Tilly, C., eds. 1981. *Class Conflict and Collective Action.* Beverly Hills, Calif/London: Sage
109. Tuck, J. 1982. *The Holy War in Los Altos: A Regional Analysis of Mexico's Cristero Rebellion.* Tucson: Univ. Ariz. Press
110. Turton, A. 1984. Limits of ideological domination and the formation of social consciousness. See Ref. 111, pp. 19–74
111. Turton, A., Tanabe, S., eds. 1984. *History and Peasant Consciousness in South East Asia,* Senri Ethnol. Stud. No. 13. Osaka: Natl. Museum of Ethnology
112. van Dijk, C. 1981. *Rebellion under the Banner of Islam: The Darul Islam Movement in Indonesia,* (Verhandelingen van het Koninkklijk Inst. voor Taal-, Landen Volkenkunde, No. 94). The Hague: Nijhoff
113. Weiskel, T. C. 1980. *French Colonial Rule and the Baule Peoples: Resistance and Collaboration, 1889–1911.* Oxford: Oxford Univ. Press
114. Weller, R., Guggenheim, S., eds. 1982.

Power and Protest in the Countryside: Studies of Rural Unrest in Asia, Europe, and Latin America. Durham, NC: Duke Univ. Policy Stud.
115. Werner, J. S. 1981. *Peasant Politics and Religious Sectarianism: Peasant and Priest in the Cao Dai in Vietnam.* New Haven: Yale Univ. Press
115a. Whitten, N., ed. 1981. *Cultural Transformations and Ethnicity in Modern Ecuador.* Urbana: Univ. Ill. Press
116. Williams, M. C. 1982. *Sickle and Crescent: The Communist Revolt of 1926 in Banten,* Cornell Univ. Mod. Indonesia Proj. Monogr. Ser. 61. Ithaca, NY
117. Wipper, A. 1982. Protest movements in colonial Kenya. *Int. J. Sociol. Soc. Policy* 2:8–24
118. Wood, J. 1984. Transatlantic land reform: America and the Crofters' Revolt, 1878–1888. *Scottish Hist. Rev.* 63:79–104
119. Young, K., et al, eds. 1981. *Of Marriage and the Market: Women's Subordination in International Perspective.* London: CSE
119a. Zawawi, W. 1984. Investigating peasant consciousness in contemporary Malaysia. See Ref. 111, pp. 135–60
120. Zurndorfer, H. T. 1983. Violence and political protest in Ming and Qing China. *Int. Rev. Soc. Hist.* 28:304–19
121. Zussman, M. F. 1982. *The Fellahin of Tebourba: Rural development and farmer strategies in Northern Tunisia.* PhD thesis. Univ. Calif., Berkeley

CERAMIC ETHNOARCHAEOLOGY

Carol Kramer

Department of Anthropology, Lehman College, City University of New York, Bronx, New York 10468

INTRODUCTION

The enormous literature on potters and pottery reflects the diverse orientations and concerns of travelers, colonial administrators, ceramists, art historians, classical archaeologists, sociologists, anthropologists, and many others. There is a vast amount of information available, but much of it, reliable as it may be, fails to answer questions often posed by archaeologists. A number of ethnographic accounts of pottery-producing groups aim to aid archaeologists, often emphasizing continuities or "survivals" in the regions they describe. Many of these studies focus particularly on manufacturing techniques, and sometimes describe vessel functions as well. Some of them touch briefly on other matters of potential interest to archaeologists, such as learning routines, aspects of division of labor and social organization of production, scalar and spatial aspects of production and/or distribution (e.g. numbers of vessels manufactured, distances to resources and markets, workshop locations, sizes, and layouts), scheduling problems, secondary uses of pottery, potters' expenditures and income, vessel prices, and the like. Publications in this large corpus are not discussed at length here.[1] Rather, this survey focuses on studies which explicitly consider contemporary pots and potters in terms of particular problems with which archaeologists frequently struggle. Much of this work has been carried out by archaeologists and informed by questions raised in the study of ancient ceramics. Like other ethnoarchaeological research (that is, archaeologically oriented ethnographic research) its ultimate objective is an improved understanding of relationships between patterned human behavior and elements of material culture that may be preserved in the archaeological

---

[1]See 11, 14, 18, 22, 34, 38, 39, 41, 46, 49, 50, 54–56, 70, 74, 82, 84–86, 92–94, 98, 101, 103, 104, 110, 111, 116–121, 123–125, 136, 137, 142. The interested reader is also referred to a recent annotated bibliography (112).

record (33, 51, 75, 76, 133). The ceramic component of this record is inherently interesting to archaeologists because pottery is abundant, diverse, and nearly imperishable, it occurs in many geographic areas over long time spans, and it plays a critical role in many economic, social, and ritual contexts.

Archaeologists have traditionally used pottery to build chronologies, identify style zones and boundaries, and illuminate interaction on both regional and interregional levels. Some have also used ceramics to reconstruct household size (138), elucidate economic differentiation (97), and study the development of craft specialization (36), elements of social organization (31, 60, 87, 145), relationships between craft specialists and centralized administrations (37, 71), and other aspects of life in the past.

Ethnoarchaeological research with potters has sometimes been constrained by geopolitics (which can limit the movements of observers) and by the geographic distribution of contemporary traditional potters. Nonetheless, it too has covered a broad topical range, dealing with matters relating to technology, taxonomy, vessel function, longevity, recycling and disposal, division of labor, learning, style, ethnicity, distribution, and technological and stylistic change. Much of this work has been inspired by, or built directly on, a few seminal publications. These include Bunzel's (16) study of contemporary potters in the archaeologically well-known American Southwest, Shepard's (122) treatise on ceramic technology and analytic techniques useful to archaeologists, Thompson's (135) typological experiment with an ethnographic ceramic collection, and Matson's technological analyses of ancient and modern pottery (92, 93). The following pages review a sampling of recent ethnoarchaeological studies of potters and suggest additional avenues of investigation.

CERAMIC PRODUCTION

In the two decades following publication of the proceedings of a seminar organized by Matson (91), one of whose themes was the need for a "ceramic ecology," there has been a shift away from descriptive accounts of pottery production per se toward more focused studies of particular aspects of pottery manufacture and use in their larger social and economic contexts and their implications for archaeology. Although some of the findings of this body of research now seem banal, they have shattered some stereotypes and assumptions long cherished by archaeologists. For example, it is now clear that a single potter can use different clays and nonplastic additives ("temper"), with variation resulting from such factors as changes in availability of raw materials, seasonal shifts in potters' residences, and potters' standards concerning clay bodies for different kinds of vessels. Clay bodies can also vary within individual settlements even where potters' raw materials are accessible to all (2, 5,

24, 28, 29, 92, 105, 143). However, potters' "emic" classifications, based on the physical properties of their raw materials, have been shown in at least one instance (1) to be paralleled in distinctions revealed by "etic" X-ray diffraction analysis of clay minerals, and such patterning may be demonstrable in other settings. Raw materials are sometimes quarried by, or purchased from, middlemen, but they often come from a source within ten kilometers of the potter's place of work (7, 100). However, potters with access to mechanized transport or to boats may not only sell their wares but obtain their materials in locations at substantially greater distances (3, 12, 17, 28, 29, 35, 54, 81). In some systems, seasonally itinerant potters move to clay sources near anticipated buyers (32, 140). In some areas, clays are accessible only in dry seasons; threat of cave-ins at clay beds may be greater during the rainy season, or clays may only become available to potters when agricultural activities in clay-rich deposits have ceased, if only temporarily (5). Seasonality of access may impinge on production timetables or affect potters' strategies for securing or storing raw materials.

There are many ways to form a vessel, as well as to decorate and fire it; these need not be reviewed here (113). In some areas, such as highland Guatemala, variation in building technique appears to be associated with language group affiliation (6, 7). Here and elsewhere, size variation within form classes is often related to differential function, and such differences are often paralleled by potters' terminological distinctions (5, 13, 14, 29, 72, 79, 88, 141, 143). However, even where such distinctions exist, vessels of comparable form are sometimes differently named, and differences of vessel size or even form are sometimes not marked terminologically (13, 83).

Today, with the exception of potters in some industrialized nations, wheel-made wares are produced by men, whereas both male and female potters hand-build and use molds to form vessels. The reasons for the consistent association of the pivoted or "fast" wheel with male potters are not entirely clear, but the proposition that women are anatomically ill equipped to work with such devices seems implausible (44, 134). A more satisfactory if more complex explanation would probably involve such factors as increased demand for ceramics, artisans' household size, composition, and organization, their access to land, livestock, and alternate forms of employment, and the nature and seasonality of other demands on potters' time, energy, and capital. Where pots are consistently formed by members of one sex, children and adults of the opposite sex often participate in the productive process (obtaining raw materials, preparing clay, decorating vessels, assisting in firing) and in the distribution of finished products. There may be patterned relationships between division of labor in ceramic production and potters' commitments to other activities, such as child care and food production. There may also be religious or ideological reasons for gender specialization. In some Muslim areas, ceramic production is concentrated largely or exclusively in the male domain (18, 85,

114), perhaps partly because it is an activity involving considerable mobility and visibility, whereas women are meant to remain in the private sphere. This association is not invariable, however, and there are female potters in some Islamicized societies (10, 24, 83, 92, 103, 142).

Some comparatively specialized potters (generating high volumes for widespread trade, sometimes year-round) are reported in areas with limited or precarious food supplies, and some receive food in return for their vessels (22, 54, 81, 106, 115, 118, 126). Potters in many societies are described as working on a seasonal basis (often the dry season) producing vessels—sometimes in large quantities—when their agricultural work is at a standstill. This can occur even in cases where their wares are slated for a large and far-flung market (5, 12, 53, 54, 83). Some part-time potters are widows or women otherwise economically disadvantaged (24, 70, 78), and many full-time potters evidently do not have access to sufficient land or to other income-generating employment. Alienation from basic means of production may be one cause of potters' increasing specialization and, in some circumstances, of their urbanization (4, 21, 120, 135).

Comparatively little has been written on the subject of spatial and formal attributes of potters' workshops, but descriptions and maps in a number of publications indicate that most traditional potters work where they live, and suggest that sherd quantities and types in their household refuse are distinctive (18, 49, 85, 106, 110, 114, 132, 142). Ceramic workshops often contain settling vats and other structures used for clay storage and preparation, immovable containers for water and clay slops, firing areas or kilns, rotary devices or wheels, wheel pits, and platforms, benches, niches, and storage rooms for drying vessels. Stark (132) describes one contemporary workshop in Veracruz (Mexico) in some detail, specifying her expectations as to the ultimate archaeological visibility of various features and suggesting that a number of tools made of organic materials would perish, but also noting that while leather-hard vessels and stockpiled clay will probably melt, they might still be archaeologically recognizable. Deal (25), discussing residences of Tzeltal Maya potters and nonpotters, concludes that archaeological recognition of potter households would be feasible. For several reasons, it should be possible to distinguish craftsmen's industrial areas from those used primarily for other purposes and potters' workshops and houses from those of nonpotters.

Some differences among potters might relate to scale and context of production. Potters working on a large scale must either have sufficient space to store vessels or a mechanism for removing them to middlemen or buyers soon after they are fired. Urban potters must adapt to spatial constraints imposed by confined quarters and crowded neighborhoods, heavy street traffic, and neighbors' complaints about noxious smoke. As in parts of India, they may create and store vessels on their roofs, they sometimes work in streets and alleys (where passing vehicles or large animals occasionally break their wares), and they may have scheduling problems if such open but scarce areas as public squares are used for firing by many potters. The location of potters' workshops and quarters in settlements of varying size and function should be of interest to archaeologists working on craft specialization, and it would be useful to know whether—in situations where there is a prevailing wind—potters are often located downwind, and whether they are often near such other potentially esthetically displeasing areas as abattoirs, tanneries, cremation grounds, and middens (94, 106).

Many contemporary traditional potters use bonfires rather than kilns to fire their wares. Setting size and frequency are enormously varied, but, in general, temperatures are lower than those attainable in a kiln, and potters often have less control over the firing process. Where kilns coexist with simpler pits or bonfire areas, they may reflect some potters' more secure financial status (as reflected in building materials), their full-time commitment to the craft, their relatively greater technological expertise, or their willingness to experiment with a new technology. Kilns, as built structures, may be incorporated in archaeological deposits, and their firing chambers, which may vary in size, can be used to estimate a range of numbers of vessels fired at one time. Bonfire areas, in contrast, are often hardened and discolored earth, ash concentrations, or ash-filled pits of varying depth and area (5, 29, 132). They are frequently associated with scatters and piles of sherds, used in some productive systems as vessel props and to cover settings, and often reused over long periods. Such firing areas may be located at some distance from the potter's workshop (and, perhaps, the archaeologist's trench) to avoid competitors' observation of trade secrets, limit vessels' exposure to damage by witchcraft or sorcery, take advantage of prevailing winds to fan the flames or of shelter from unpredictable and potentially harmful winds, or minimize the annoyance caused by smoke (5, 70, 137, 141). Some potters do not fire their own wares. In Mexico, specialist firing crews are hired in Puebla (72), some Yucatecan Maya (135) and Mazahua potters (near Mexico City) sell unfired vessels to middlemen at a price lower than their fired wares would fetch (104), and Oaxacan potters habitually sell unfired pots when short of cash (134). Such division of labor may not occur often in nonurban, noncapitalist contexts, and hence might not be an important consideration in many archaeological reconstructions.

Bonfires and kilns alike can be fueled with a wide array of materials (animal dung, sawdust, wood, bamboo, coconut fronds, shrubs, leaves, grass, coal, cloth, kerosene, rubber tires, etc), and firing duration can range from a few minutes to more than a day. Overall coloration, and degree of color diversity on vessel surfaces, vary with firing techniques and fuels. The cores of vessel walls, in conjunction with mineralogical analysis and refiring experiments, can be used to reconstruct firing conditions such as temperature and duration (82,

92, 93, 102, 122). Intrasettlement variations in firing technology sometimes relate to potters' differing abilities to sustain fuel costs or their potential access to fuels (77, 78), and such variability might be detectable archaeologically.

Decoration is most often done prior to firing, but in some areas vessels are also treated after firing—sometimes to diminish their porosity, as by the addition of resins or other coatings (14, 29, 35, 53, 54, 121, 142). Glazed vessels, too, are not necessarily finished and distinguishable as to type immediately after firing. Glazed vessels are usually fired twice; the first (bisque) firing produces undecorated vessels, the second vitrifies the glaze coverant. "Wasters" broken in a bisque setting may not always be readily identifiable. My excavations in a Guatemalan potter's compound, used by his forebears for five or six generations, produced an array of fired but undecorated sherds which he was unable to name with certainty because he distinguished some types by their glazes and decorative motifs rather than by form or rim profile. He threw most of the vessels produced in his workshop, and, with various members of his household and a hired Guatemalan Indian assistant born and raised in another city, decorated them. Some vessels were thus the work of several individuals. Sharing of decorative work has also been described for the American Southwest (129, 130), Mexico (48), and Peru (29), and is seen in India and elsewhere (C. Kramer, unpublished information). Some potters use identification marks, but even in the absence of such marks, potters can usually identify their own products and often those made by other potters in their community as well (32, 49, 54, 57, 82, 83, 88, 92, 127, 131, 141). However, some potters use identifying marks only when firing jointly with another potter, and vessels are sometimes labeled with the name of the customer rather than the artisan.

Once decorated and fired, pottery is distributed. Ceramic distribution systems have rarely been the subject of systematic ethnoarchaeological research; while volume, spatial scale, and mechanisms of ceramic distribution vary widely (10, 70, 115, 118), a few salient and provocative points have already emerged. For example, several authors indicate that where production is carried out on a small scale and primarily for local use, vessels do not move far from their place of manufacture (24, 29). In contrast, particularly where boat or truck transport is available, some wares travel distances of several hundred kilometers, whether in the context of a complex marketing system or a ritually elaborated noncapitalist exchange network like the Melanesian *kula* or *hiri* (10, 17, 54; F. Hassan, personal communication; C. Kramer, unpublished information). While one might expect larger vessels to move comparatively shorter distances—as is reportedly the case in Nepal (13) and Tanzania (141), for example—under some conditions larger pots may have a wider spatial distribution than smaller vessels (104). Distance from manufacturer and transport cost can affect vessel prices in some areas (115) but are evidently insignificant factors in others (66). Some potters specialize in particular wares or forms to avoid competition and to monopolize a market (2, 4, 106); one aspect of such specialization can be the occurrence in both buyers' households and centers' markets of a relatively diverse ceramic assemblage whose component types—possibly regardless of vessel size—are derived from a number of sources at differing distances (C. Kramer, unpublished information). Several of the ceramic systems studied by ethnoarchaeologists are embedded in market economies, and some potters distribute their wares using trains, wheeled vehicles, and even planes; one may question the analogical value of such cases for a variety of archaeological contexts. Equally, one may question the long-held assumption that pottery was made in all prehistoric communities. Archaeological research has demonstrated that local, regional, and interregional exchange of ceramics has a long history, and that it can occur in the context of cottage industry (107), and ethnoarchaeological work has shown that complex nonmarket distribution strategies can coexist with formalized marketing systems (95).

PRODUCTION, SOCIAL ORGANIZATION, AND STYLE

Some of the recent interest in the organization of ceramic production was greatly stimulated by a small group of archaeological studies in the New World (31, 60, 87). These and other studies were predicated on a set of assumptions about interaction, learning, and stylistic variability (53, 108, 145). It was suggested that where residence is uxorilocal and women make pottery primarily for household use, processes of learning and production, in combination with limited mobility of women and their wares, will result in stylistic homogeneity within settlements and facilitate the identification of social units. The literature on ceramic production indicates that much contemporary pottery making in the Western hemisphere, Africa, Southeast Asia, and the Pacific falls in the female domain, that men control the craft in the Mediterranean and Aegean, the Middle East, South Asia, and Japan, and that in parts of Africa, Latin America, and the Middle East both men and women form vessels. This suggests that relationships among learning, residential patterns, content and spatial scales of different forms of interaction, and division of labor by sex are worthy of further investigation. Some ethnoarchaeological research has focused on aspects of this nexus of problems.

Predictably, this work reveals a diversity of adaptations. Residential patterns often deviate from normative preferences; in uxorilocal societies, not all female potters remain in their natal communities on marrying, and in virilocal societies, out-marrying female potters do not necessarily move very far from their families of orientation (24, 83, 88, 143). Potters learn their craft—very often by observation and imitation, without explicit verbal or manual instruction—from a variety of people and at diverse ages (24, 120, 125, 131, 141,

143). Potters sometimes work in groups whose composition is occasionally limited to household members but can also include residentially proximate non-kin (48, 53, 54, 131). As was noted above, even in the context of a single industrial household a given vessel may be formed or decorated by more than one person, and vessels are occasionally decorated by passersby, neighbors, visitors, specialists hired for the task, or purchasing vendors (19, 48, 72; C. Kramer, unpublished information). Where women make pottery, men may be knowledgeable about parts of the process, and in societies where men make vessels and women are prohibited from touching the wheel although they participate in other phases of the productive process, an absent potter is sometimes replaced by his wife, who issues a stream of verbal instructions and judgments to a young son experimenting with throwing vessels (142; C. Kramer, unpublished information).

Potters' skills and repertoires may vary with age. There is some evidence suggesting that skill in producing larger pots increases with age (22, 54, 125, 141–143), that particular vessel types are made by older potters whose work is not always as well executed as it was in their youth (135), and that decorative repertoires vary with potters' ages (53, 80, 83). The question of whether one potter's output over a lifetime of production retains distinctive and recognizable consistency—of whatever form—requires further investigation. Stanislawski (130) maintains that it does not, whereas Hill's (61) experimental work with handwriting suggests that it may. Among other things, this issue bears on the possibility of identifying the work of individual prehistoric potters, an endeavor that might be productive in a number of circumstances (62).

Female potters among Hopi-Tewa of Arizona reportedly often work in groups. Using data on learning obtained from 44 potters, Stanislawski argues that residential propinquity plays at least as important a role in the acquisition of artisans' knowledge as does kinship (129–131). In the learning relationships he outlines, a larger number of dyadic pairs of students and teachers involve matri-kin than non-kin. However, learning cross-cuts clan lines, and at least one style in the Hopi-Tewa assemblage is said to be made in seven settlements by women of two linguistic groups distributed over twelve clans. Hopi sharing of design elements (and, presumably, of motifs or configurations) is said to be common and, as elsewhere, designs evidently are not considered the property of individuals, families, clans, or work groups (48, 82, 125, 142, 143). Since Hopi clans today are not localized within settlements, Stanislawski argues that the spatial clustering of ceramic design units or types—such as might be identified archaeologically, were sherds deposited where they were made and used (which they often are not; see below)—would probably reflect such social units as neighborhood work groups involving learning across kin lines, rather than result from training and production within strictly localized kin groups.

Stanislawski has not illustrated the styles he discusses. He has not yet fully described the public for which Hopi-Tewa vessels are created; such information might clarify the role played by consumers in potters' selection of designs. He does not indicate which designs are used by individual potters in different locations and work groups, and with what frequency. His Hopi-Tewa studies argue against simplifying assumptions about the nature of learning and the role of kinship and residence in ceramic production, but do not constitute a conclusive refutation of the archaeological analyses which provided the catalyst for his research.

In his attempt to "test" Longacre's earlier conclusions about prehistoric ceramics from Arizona against an ethnographic case, Stanislawski returned to the same region and worked with modern potters. During the 1970s, Longacre himself went on to work in the Philippines, where the Kalinga potters he studied produce a less elaborately decorated assemblage than the Southwestern ceramics he had analyzed earlier. Despite a stated preference for uxorilocal residence, only approximately 60 percent of Kalinga postmarital residence conforms to the ideal. Nonetheless, grandmothers and mothers usually teach younger women (53, 88). As among Hopi, Kalinga potters' work groups comprise non-kin as well as kin, but most vessels are produced by a single potter, and potters are often able to identify their own work, even after some time. In addition to identifiable individual idiosyncrasies, there are reportedly distinctive Kalinga village styles (52, 53). Graves' work indicates that Kalinga designs vary with potters' birth cohort regardless of kin- or work group membership and that as women age, becoming more experienced potters, they employ a greater variety of designs. Where the number of designs used by individual potters increases with age, continuity between age cohorts appears to result in gradual rather than rapid design change. Rapid change might, in contrast, be expected in situations of large-scale population or birth cohort turnover (53), or following catastrophic events.

In Africa, as in the American Southwest and the Pacific, many potters are female. Among the patrilineal but not strictly virilocal Kisi of Tanzania, mothers and daughters are viewed as the primary pottery-producing units. However, learning continues into middle age and occurs in a variety of contexts, sometimes involving such tutors as elder sisters, co-wives, in-laws, and age-mates (141). As a potter ages, she learns to make more vessel types as well as larger vessels; it is not clear whether her decorative repertoire also expands. No one Kisi potter makes all vessel types; like Hopi (130), Tarascan (48), Huichol (143), Guatemalan (5), North African (10), and Indian potters, their houses contain ceramics made by a number of artisans. Because Kisi compounds have vessels made by more than one potter and because, depending on their functions and numbers in this polygynous society, vessels are located both within and outside of residential structures, Waane, like Stanislawski, concludes that social groups and basic elements of social organization could not be readily reconstructed from the spatial distribution of ceramics within houses.

Several of the studies cited above consider matters relating to ceramic style without describing in detail the style reviewed. The work of Hardin (48, 57–59) in Mexico and Arnold (8, 9) in Peru is unusual in attempting to specify the components of a single ceramic style. Using one of several wares produced in a Michoacan village, Hardin focuses on the spatial organization of vessel ornamentation and on the configurations (combinations of individual design elements) placed on vessels. She also describes some of the diagnostic features of individuals' painting of design elements. Hardin notes that potters borrow entire configurations fairly readily, and concludes that these could not be used to reconstruct the nature or frequency of interaction among potters. Rather, she suggests, it may be possible to monitor individuals by using, for example, distinctive features of brushwork, although she does not present an operational proposal for using such identifications to specify relationships among individuals. Arnold describes the decorative system used by Quinua potters and suggests that organization of surface treatment reflects potters' perceptions of the organization and use of their natural and social environment. Both Arnold and Hardin provide clear descriptions of selected wares in larger assemblages, although, in focusing on the distinctive components of these wares, neither specifies how they differ from similar wares and styles produced in neighboring communities.

As one part of a wide-ranging review of ceramic production and use in a Cameroon village, David & Hennig (24) discuss the products of female potters of three ethnic groups and illustrate differences in vessel form and surface treatment. They provide some information on ceramic distribution on a regional scale, but their primary focus is a single multiethnic community. Hodder, in contrast, has adopted an explicitly regional perspective in recent studies of pluralistic societies in Africa (63–69). Reviewing a Zambian sample, he notes that sharp ethnic distinctions are not evident in ceramic distributions among Lozi and most neighboring tribes. Until fairly recently these groups had been economically integrated under the traditional kingdom. Following the alteration of this administrative apparatus, first by colonial rulers and then by the postcolonial state, strains between some ethnic groups have developed. These strains, reflected in comparatively weak differential distributions of ceramic and other artifact types in Lozi and neighboring groups on the one hand, and recently settled Mbunda on the other, are construed as related to economic conflicts centering on resources increasing in the absence of the integrative kingdom, and to the recent use by some tribal groups of strategies designed to assert their distinctive identities for political ends (67). Hodder discerns clearer boundaries between three tribes in Kenya's Baringo district, which he attributes to various forms of long-standing competition among them and to internal tribal pressures for social and ethnic conformity (64). Interaction among tribal groups occurs in both the Zambian and Kenyan cases, but sharpness of boundaries in artifact distributions evidently differs. Hodder's attempts to define tribal and ethnic boundaries will interest many archaeologists, but some will be disappointed by his failure to specify criteria used in defining ceramic styles, the scanty documentation of ages, numbers, and locations of particular vessels and types in his samples, and the fact that the scale of the areas he discusses is considerable. While the issues he addresses are of fundamental importance, particular classes of material culture, including pottery, are—paradoxically, partly because of this laudable regional approach and thus the very scale of observation—used to paint a complex picture with very—sometimes overly—broad strokes.

To summarize: the ethnoarchaeological literature on production and style suggests that some archaeological assumptions are too simplistic. For example, in a range of ethnographic settings, a single vessel can be the work of more than one individual, who has not necessarily learned the craft from near kin. Both learning and production can occur in the context of potting "bees" whose participants are linked by residential bonds that for some purposes supersede those based on kinship. Where learning takes place along kin lines, it need not involve the mother-daughter (or, more rarely, father-son) dyad used in archaeological analogies. Members of some ethnolinguistic groups obtain, from considerable distances, pottery conforming to their own model of ethnic identity (69), while other consumers buy pots available locally, even if these are made by members of other ethnic groups and have alien diagnostic attributes. Some potters make a variety of wares for different ethnolinguistic markets (21, 35, 69, 127, 141). Potters also engage in other forms of style-switching; this can be related to scheduling constraints (57), market demand (24), or artisans' inclinations to experiment (79, 80). Finally, micromotor skills, range of forms, components and diversity of the decorative repertoire of individual artisans, and numbers of vessels produced, may change over time. If archaeological hypotheses involving kinship, ethnicity, interaction, and boundaries are to be better formulated and evaluated, it will be necessary to review our strategies for sampling within and among settlements and to develop appropriate measures for identifying the work of individuals and demonstrating the existence of localized groups. Strategies for identifying kin groups as opposed to other corporate groups and residentially proximate but unrelated potters require refinement, and it may be undesirable to base them on ceramics alone.

Style distributions have sometimes been viewed as reflecting interaction, such as occurs in individuals' learning, in the context of production units, and in exchange. Stylistic homogeneity—whose measurement remains a subject of ongoing discussion, and which has perhaps too often been associated with decorative attributes—is, in contrast to heterogeneity, sometimes taken to reflect interaction. Ceramic standardization, which can entail diminished heterogeneity, is often viewed by archaeologists as a corollary of increasing craft specialization; it is sometimes seen as reflecting greater control over production by centralized institutions, perhaps regardless of potters' social identities or interactions. Use of a recognized style may be one means of transmitting information regarding group affiliation and of marking boundaries (146), but some of Hodder's work suggests that stylistic boundaries can exist in the presence of social and economic interaction. If many ceramic vessels do not usually leave the household context and, when they do, do not travel far, one may ask to whom pots are signaling, what the information content of the message is, and why some household vessels are more elaborately decorated than others (10, 30). Wares and degree of diversity in ceramics produced primarily for a local market may differ substantially from those designed to appeal to a larger and possibly more diverse audience (13, 54). Degree of stylistic diversity within settlements may vary with their functional size, adding to the archaeologist's burden of selecting appropriate units for comparison. More detailed information concerning differences in diversity or standardization in differently organized production settings, and on relationships between decorative style and vessels' forms and functions, between potters' repertoires and styles desired by consumers, and between various forms of interaction and the character of boundaries, might further clarify these matters.

Some ceramic wares and assemblages are more complex than others, comprising more forms, a wider array of productive steps or techniques, or a greater variety of decorative motifs and configurations. For the archaeologist, this fact, and its attendant problems of devising appropriate measures of stylistic variability and complexity, underscore the difficulty of comparing styles with one another. It seems unlikely that less complex vessels convey less information to artisans and users than those that are more complicated technologically or elaborate decoratively; rather, the information load of ceramics and other classes of material culture probably varies across space and time. In some contexts, ceramic vessels may reinforce principles of social structure, including gender and power relationships, or reify other aspects of world view (15, 68, 73, 144). A few authors suggest that ceramics, in their symbolic capacity, can be manipulated to renegotiate and transform cultural behavior (69, 96). But the role of ceramics as "symbols in action" (69) must vary cross-culturally, and may not be demonstrable in many archaeological settings. More mundane uses of prehistoric pottery may be comparatively more accessible.

CERAMIC USE AND DISPOSAL

Many authors provide useful if scattered information about the use of ceramic vessels, but few have dealt systematically with vessel life expectancy, recycling, spatial distribution, and disposal. Such issues are not trivial, since archaeologists have often assumed that sherds found in a single context were used contemporaneously and in related activities. But vessels are often recycled, and sherds may be reused as scoops, drums, hearths, animal troughs or pens, construction and ornamental elements, and the like (25, 29, 128, 143). Potters' workshops often have more sherds and ceramic debris than residences of nonpotters, since they frequently retain ill-fired or damaged vessels for reuse in their work. Various authors suggest that ethnoarchaeological studies of vessel longevity, recycling, and discard might be useful to archaeologists in developing estimates of site population size and duration; analysis of disposal patterns should also be valuable in the development of archaeological sampling strategies aimed at locating and ultimately interpreting activity areas and discard contexts.

In an early account, Foster (45) described vessels in four Tzintzuntzan (Michoacan) households. He concluded that their life expectancy varied with ware, size, use frequency and location, and the presence of children or domestic animals likely to topple pots and cause breakage. Foster notes that life expectancy increases with vessel size and decreases with mobility and use frequency. He suggests that the life expectancy of about 1 year, and the population of 50 to 75 vessels per Tzintzuntzan household, are somewhat higher than might be expected in many archaeological situations, particularly in contexts where pottery was not readily accessible or was fired at lower temperatures and was thus more fragile.

Somewhat greater life expectancies and fewer household pots are reported for the Fulani. David (23, 24) notes that median vessel lifespans in one Cameroon village range from 2.5 to 12.5 years, that the average number of pots in a woman's quarters is 20.9, and that each woman in his sample replaced, on average, 3 pots in a year. Broken vessels are discarded both in pits and on village surfaces; contemporaneity of objects in rapidly filled pits is likely to be greater than it is on surfaces.

Like Foster, DeBoer (26–29) has found that use life is positively correlated with vessel size (partly because larger vessels are used less frequently and partly because their production cost is higher). The lifespan of Shipibo-Conibo vessels appears to be somewhat shorter than it is among Fulani, with a median use life of approximately 1 year (and a range of .25 to 2.25 years). DeBoer has also discussed the issue of vessel disposal. Since specific types are preferred for recycling as sherd temper, some vessels never enter the archaeological record, and some types are represented at lower frequencies than they are known to exist in their original contexts of manufacture and use. Larger discarded sherds tend to be found at the margins of heavily used areas, while frequently traveled paths are strewn with smaller sherds subject to ongoing comminution. Finally, sweeping of houses and plazas leaves many sherds in locations where cultural behavior relating to pottery is minimal.

Kalinga vessels can be recycled even before they break; when resined surfaces wear out, pots are consigned to some secondary use (88). Longacre's sample of Kalinga pots had use lives ranging from about 4 to 14 years; the average number of household vessels is fewer than 10 (90). Among the Kalinga, too, larger vessels seem to have comparatively greater life expectancies, and although children and dogs cause breakage as they do elsewhere, vessel replacement is evidently higher than among Fulani, at one vessel every month or two. Sherds are discarded in middens at the perimeters of habitation areas, and dense sherd deposits are also found on trails to water sources and at springs; as among the Shipibo, ceramic debris is likely to be found at some distance from original use contexts. Breakage rates vary with location and season, and breakage often occurs on slippery paths and during wet weather. Inventorying Kalinga households over a 4-year period, Longacre found a loss approaching 50 percent. During the interval between his censuses, the "missing" vessels had either been broken or given away as gifts, usually to relatives. However, missing vessels were not always replaced by containers of the same materials or in the same frequencies, so that even after a few years the profile of the censused ceramic population differed from that of the earlier one. Longacre found an increase in large rice cooking pots and a decline in water vessels. He attributes the former change to a greater availability of cash, used in part for feasting, which requires large rice pots; the latter shift evidently resulted from the introduction and greater availability of plastic water jars. This change was comparatively rapid, involved changing frequencies of forms rather than marked change in technology or decoration, and related to the increasing economic integration of one rural community in the larger Philippine world.

In the case just described, older vessels continued in use side by side with younger ones. Given the variation in use lives reported in the ethnoarchaeological literature, it is clear that in any ethnographic setting some pots will be older than others. Excavated assemblages will also include seemingly contemporaneous pots of differing age, and in surface collections, vessels and types presumed to have been contemporaneous need not have been so. David (23) has suggested that these factors might distort archaeological interpretations, particularly those based on seriation. Since smaller vessels in ethnographic contexts have higher turnover rates, archaeologists might focus on smaller vessels in seriating surface collections (90), but given the comparatively short use life of most vessels, archaeological analyses—based on comparatively longer phases—need not be seriously jeopardized by assumptions of vessel contemporaneity. Comparing two archaeological assemblages with an ethnographic one, DeBoer (26) points to specific discrepancies (for example, one of the archaeological sites was devoted primarily to mortuary activities), and observes that while the relative frequencies of types do not correspond exactly to relative frequencies of vessels in ethnographic use at any one time, a statistically generated archaeological assemblage suggests that after a period of approximately five years, types' relative frequencies would probably not differ markedly from the ethnographic assemblage from which they had derived.

Descriptions of ceramic longevity, recycling, and disposal raise questions not only about the practice and utility of seriation but about the value of conjoinability studies. Sherds of broken vessels are reused in a variety of ways and may also lie about unused, both within and outside household structures, for long periods. Sherds of a single vessel can have differing use lives and, when finally discarded forever, may come to rest in different locations and at different depths (130, 143). Vessel bases may have longer use lives than rim sherds, which may thus be discarded earlier and be found in deeper stratigraphic contexts. It would seem both desirable to attempt to join sherds even when they are not stratigraphically coeval and reasonable to assume that where pieces of the same vessel are found at different depths, those that are older more accurately reflect the vessel's age. Analysis of ceramics associated with joinable sherds from different stratigraphic contexts might then be designed to establish finer chronological distinctions among sherds and types of differing age. Although current thermoluminescence instrumentation for measuring ceramics' ages produces relatively wide standard deviations, it is conceivable that in the future such analytic techniques might be used in conjunction with attempts to join sherds to estimate site and phase duration through reconstructions of vessel age and reuse. The fact that vessels and types of differing age can enter a single archaeological sample need not be too vexing; if it can be demonstrated from stratified sequences that one type appeared at an earlier date than others, inappropriate groupings can be rectified. In the case of excavated sites it should probably be assumed that some vessels were older than others; however, it should not be forgotten that despite their differing ages they were all used together at some point in time. One of the excavator's problems is to distinguish between contexts of primary use and such secondary deposits as trash, roof collapse, "fill," and so forth, and to specify artifact distributions and type associations in different contexts.

Form and number of vessels may vary with function and use context, and perhaps also with household size, composition and wealth. Comparatively little work has been done on this subject, and it may be difficult to devise archaeologically relevant measures in ethnographic settings where vessels of other materials are being rapidly introduced and increasingly widely used (24, 90). DeBoer & Lathrap (29) found no correlation between number of vessels and

Shipibo household size or composition, and among Kalinga, the number of household pots reportedly has little to do with household size and is more closely related to status and wealth (89). Analyzing relationships between vessels' volumes and several attributes of households in a modern Mayan sample, Nelson (99) notes that total volume of cooking jars may vary with household size, but he also suggests that such variation among households relates to differences in status and wealth. A similar association is implied for at least one area in highland Peru (137), and socially prominent Tarahumara men in Chihuahua (Mexico) are said to have more cooking vessels for hosting fiestas (105).

In sum, several ethnoarchaeological studies have demonstrated that the number and kinds of vessels in a community's houses can vary substantially, that vessel breakage, replacement, and recycling occur at different rates and in a range of circumstances, and that replacement need not result in replication of the composition of immediately antecedent assemblages. They also reveal that much broken pottery is located in places that archaeologists do not necessarily investigate and that when it is found it is not always in original use contexts. Finally, this work suggests that additional empirical documentation of relationships among vessel numbers and types, and household size, composition, age, and wealth, is in order. Exotic imports such as Chinese porcelains or Wedgwood may be one reflection of differences in households' wealth, but archaeologists should also devise independent measures using locally made vessels to identify differences among households, if only because exotics are likely to be comparatively rare. Like local wares, their forms, frequencies, styles, and distribution change over time.

CERAMIC CHANGE

Because of the compressed nature of the archaeological record and the diachronic emphasis of much archaeological work, archaeologists' perceptions and descriptions of ceramic change are often comparatively coarse-grained. Nonetheless, such change is observable and is the meat of innumerable archaeological analyses and the very heart of most chronology building. Ethnographic studies tend to be carried out on a relatively small scale over short periods of time, and comparatively little ethnoarchaeological work systematically addresses the question or describes circumstances in which ceramic change occurs. Moreover, ceramic production is often characterized as a high-risk occupation involving little profit, much debt, and substantial loss in firing and transport. Given potters' desires to appeal to particular markets, one might endorse a stereotype of potters as psychologically and technologically conservative, unwilling to take risks and engage in innovative experiments, with conforming personalities and a low sense of self-esteem. This view, questioned by others (77, 104, 120, 121), is favored by Foster (47; see also 134). It would appear to be supported by Reina's account (109) of an inventive potter in the Guatemalan village of Chinautla. This young woman was virtually ostracized for her experiments. Her engagement to an agrarian innovator thwarted, she married only after her ceramic output once again conformed to the expected norm. Yet it is possible to imagine a variety of circumstances in which artisanal innovation would be rewarded rather than punished.

In a series of articles reviewing rotating devices utilized by potters, Foster (40, 43, 44, 47) suggests that the transition from slow-turning devices like the Guatemalan *kabal* to the pivoted wheel requires a fundamental shift in potters' motor activities, one unlikely to be deemed desirable unless substantial market demand is perceived or anticipated (see also 119, 135). Discussing potters in North Africa's Maghreb, Balfet (10) similarly observes that technological innovation is unlikely in the absence of consumer demand.

Potters' reluctance to change techniques and reorganize motor habits (such as are involved in a change from hand-building to wheel-throwing, for example) may be offset by their anticipation of an increased market or of greater economies in time and energy expenditures (2, 118, 121). Changes in technology and style, quantity of output, organization of production, and experimentation with new raw materials may occur in response to circumstances that impinge on potters but over which they have no direct control, as in the introduction of piped water or refrigerators that reduce the demand for water carrying or storage vessels, or the depletion of traditional fuels or exhaustion of familiar clay sources (12, 20, 93). In the Amphlett Islands, the use of new but sandier clays to replace clays no longer available resulted in vessels of poorer craftsmanship (82). In Rajasthan (India), the government has recently responded to increasing deforestation by limiting potters' access to traditionally foraged vegetable fuels; some potters now use rubber tires as fuel, and others who express concern about this policy claim that their output has diminished markedly as a result (C. Kramer, unpublished information).

If clays are associated with arable lands that cannot be quarried when potters most need them, those anxious to satisfy a highly seasonal buyer demand may experiment with new clays, and they may also reorganize their relationships with farmers owning clay deposits, middlemen who transport clays, and other potters from whom they can borrow clays. They may also modify their repertoire. For example, Indian potters who would normally expect to produce large, decorated, and comparatively costly water jars for Divali (a nationally important annual festival) can instead turn out many small, undecorated, inexpensive vessels, made with inferior clays but used on a large scale year-round, in the same unit of production time as fewer water jars. Where landowners limit access to clays, or lobby government agencies to limit potters' troublesome demands, traditional government grants and understandings with landowners allowing potters the freedom to quarry clays may be discontinued. Potters in some economic systems can form cooperatives, and these can affect technology (as when members of a Rajasthani cooperative recently used a low-interest government loan to acquire electric wheels). Division of labor, scale and standardization of production, and distribution of finished wares might also be affected by reorganization of relations among potters and between potters and their sources of materials and capital. Changed transport modes can affect the scale and distance of ceramic distribution, as well as frequencies of types marketed. Greater availability of trucks and tractors can alter frequency of shipments, sometimes destined for increasingly far-flung markets. It may result in shifts in types of vessels marketed, such as wider distribution of comparatively smaller, more easily stacked vessels. Certain forms of specialization may also develop, with one or two types in a potter's larger repertoire slated for particular distant markets where those same types are not locally manufactured.

Ceramic change can result from many other factors. Miller (96) describes a strategy by which low-ranking Hindus replicate vessel types associated with higher castes in an attempt to improve their status in the hierarchical Indian caste system; some higher-caste consumers respond by reorganizing their purchasing or using strategies to reestablish boundaries between groups of differing rank. With the introduction of Islam to West Africa, part of the ceramic assemblage related to production, storage, and consumption of beer dropped out of the household repertoire of a newly abstemious segment of the population; certain forms (and possibly also associated decorative techniques) disappeared and others, associated with Muslim activities, appeared (24, 83). In an ethnically mixed but predominantly Fulani village in Cameroon, the one Lame potter at first tried to conform to a perceived market of Fulani buyers. On realizing that Fulani would purchase non-"Fulani" vessels and that there was a Lame market among new immigrants to the region, the potter reverted to the production of "Lame"-style pots (24).

In Mexico in the 1970s when—for reasons having partly to do with the nature of personal relationships among particular potters, middlemen, and creditors— the organization of credit relationships changed, some Mazahua potters modified their productive strategies (building larger, roofed kilns and increasing production of the *piñata,* a disposable form used at *fiestas,* and much in demand in Mexico's urban centers) as well as the mechanisms by which their wares were distributed [increasing their reliance on trucks (104)]. Changes related to altered market demands are also reported for the Shipibo. Here, as elsewhere, potters have responded to growing tourist demand for ceramics by producing traditional vessel forms in different frequencies and sizes and by modifying and simplifying surface decoration (27, 79; see also 106, 111). In highland Peru, native potters created new forms for post-Conquest overlords and altered some aspects of their technology and decorative repertoires as well (137). In Japan, World War II government demand for particular ceramic vessels stimulated a production boom among potters and, as in parts of Mexico, a postwar demand for "folk" ceramics has been met by an increase in the number of active potters making different vessel types than they had previously (19, 46, 74, 98, 134). The conservatism of Chinautla potters referred to above was, in a few decades, overridden by a willingness to experiment with new forms for a cosmopolitan urban market [extending to New York City (110)].

Limited though the documentation is, ethnoarchaeological research suggests that ceramic change can result from a variety of causes, including change in forms and vessel frequencies as vessels of other materials become available, use of different body clays and cooking vessel forms as fuels or hearths are modified, alterations in quantities and seasonality of production as availability of raw materials changes, sometimes as a result of governmental meddling, and changes in productive and distribution strategies with tightened or eased access to loans and credit. Ceramic change is not simply a function of altered postmarital residence patterns or of the immigration of new peoples. It does not only affect design elements, and it occurs at different rates, with different effects. We must consider what kinds of change are most feasibly and usefully monitored in ethnographic settings, and at what scales, and decide which ethnoarchaeological observations are most relevant to the interpretation of the various kinds of change observable in archaeological ceramics.

CONCLUSION

Ceramic production, distribution, use, discard, and change are diverse and very complex processes. The foregoing review of recent ethnoarchaeological research outlines some of the directions already taken in studying them, but more work is needed, in the same and other geographic areas, and some of the issues addressed in earlier work should be explored further. Because archaeologists bring particular kinds of questions about behavior to the ceramics they unearth and study, they are singularly equipped to pursue some of the answers they seek by observing contemporary potters.

Much archaeological analysis involves classification. More work might be done on such aspects of indigenous systems of classification as the role of rims and decoration in potters' taxonomies and relationships between vessel name, form, and function. Much archaeological interpretation is concerned with vessel functions; further empirical documentation of vessels' locations, primary and secondary functions, use lives, and disposal would be illuminating. Relationships between vessel types and numbers, on the one hand, and household demographics, wealth, and cooking, serving, and storage practices, on the other, remain to be documented in many contemporary settings. Ceramic distribution, too, is a crucial but inadequately explored problem area; quantity, distance, differential directionality of distribution, and specialization in production for particular markets are matters of considerable interest to archaeologists. Assumptions concerning distance decay and scale of fall-off in artifact distributions are probably not uniformly applicable to all vessel types or sizes, nor to all economic systems; costs, scales, and modes of distribution under a variety of conditions remain to be specified and their implications for archaeological analysis more clearly delineated. Measures of other forms of interaction and of stylistic similarity or difference warrant further investigation, as do the nature of boundaries under various circumstances.

Some of the shortcomings of previous studies can be remedied in future work. For example, a number of ethnoarchaeological studies of potters do not reveal the sample size on which description and conclusions were based. Others describe the work of only one potter, often considered one of the most skilled in the community, and sometimes said to have made and fired vessels in demonstrations of "typical" events solicited by the visiting observer. The utility of descriptions that fail to specify sample sizes, the period of ethnographic observation, seasonal variation in potters' production schedules and output, content of potters' repertoires, and the possible role of consumers is limited. It has been suggested that observable variability grows with increased sample size; this may be the case not only with archaeological samples, but with ethnographic observations of potters and vessels as well. And when only one potter is studied for a brief period, it may be difficult to evaluate the extent to which she or he is representative of the community or how willing to experiment with novel materials, techniques, and designs. We require additional information on the content and scale of ceramic change, the variables involved, and their relationships and sequence.

The ethnographic and ethnoarchaeological literature reveals an enormous variety of productive strategies. Some "part-time" potters make only a few vessels in a year, while others produce hundreds albeit on a highly seasonal basis. The terms "part-time," "full-time," and "specialist" are used with some abandon by archaeologists, but ethnographic descriptions suggest that this craft involves diverse forms of specialization. The systematic development of such measures of specialization as potters' energy expenditures, seasonal differences in productivity, time devoted to other activities, number of vessels produced in a unit of time, composition, size, and distance of markets, repertoire content and diversity, as well as specification of the tangible and potentially archaeologically retrievable correlates of such variations, should enhance our ability to compare potters in a single community, potters in different areas, and productive systems across time. Further information on spatial and formal attributes of potters' workshops, on their locations within and among settlements, and on the differences between potters' household ceramics and those of nonpotters should also help us to locate prehistoric specialists and to refine evolutionary models concerning the content and development of craft specialization.

Ethnoarchaeological studies can shed light on division of labor and its relationship to modes of ceramic production in relation to other activities in which potters engage, but it seems unlikely that studies of contemporary technology and sex roles alone will resolve such evolutionary issues as the causes of transformations in productive systems, particularly where such changes occurred in the distant past and in the absence of written documentation. The coexistence of differing modes of production in some cultural contexts today would seem to militate against any universal or unilineal evolutionary model, but it is possible that at various times and in various places the organization of this craft has been affected by other aspects of economic and sociopolitical organization (6, 7, 10, 42, 121, 139). Factors that might figure significantly in organizational transformations include alterations in subsistence economy, changes in household size and organization, the development of suprafamilial kinship or other corporate groups, increased availability of wage labor, and changes in the structure of credit relationships, quantity and seasonality of demand, transport technology, and marketing mechanisms. An improved understanding of the development of ceramic specialization will entail the integration of ethnographic, historic, and archaeological data.

Ethnoarchaeological research in pottery-making societies has produced a number of cautionary tales. In clarifying many aspects of the productive process, as well as a range of circumstances in which vessels are acquired, used and abused, and discarded, it has also quashed some simplifying notions, illuminated a range of behavioral diversity, and begun to outline modal patterns of considerable potential value to archaeologists. Before the world's remaining traditional potters abandon their craft in favor of more lucrative work, and before their wares are replaced by vessels of metal, plastic, rubber, and glass, archaeologists must take to the field so that cross-cultural generalizations about this crucial specialization can be formulated, refined, and operationalized.

ACKNOWLEDGMENTS

I thank Warren DeBoer and Gregory Johnson, and am especially grateful to Bruce Byland, Matthew Stolper, and William Sumner, for their comments on an earlier draft of this paper.

Unpublished Indian data referred to here were collected by the author with support from the National Science Foundation (BNS-82–02992) and the Smithsonian Foreign Currency Program (TX003275; 20487600). Unpublished Guatemalan data were collected as part of a University of Pennsylvania project directed by Ruben Reina.

Literature Cited

1. Arnold, D. E. 1971. Ethnomineralogy of Ticul, Yucatan potters. *Am. Antiq.* 36:20–40
2. Arnold, D. E. 1972. Native pottery making in Quinua, Peru. *Anthropos* 67:858–72
3. Arnold, D. E. 1975. Ecological variables and ceramic production: Towards a general model. In *Primitive Art and Technology*, ed. J. S. Raymond, B. Loveseth, C. Arnold, G. Reardon, pp. 92–108. Calgary: Univ. Calgary Archaeol. Assoc.
4. Arnold, D. E. 1975. Ceramic ecology of the Ayacucho Basin, Peru: Implications for prehistory. *Curr. Anthropol.* 16:183–94
5. Arnold, D. E. 1978. Ethnography of pottery making in the Valley of Guatemala. In *The Ceramics of Kaminaljuyu, Guatemala*, ed. R. K. Wetherington, pp. 327–400. University Park: Penn. State Univ. Press
6. Arnold, D. E. 1978. Ceramic variability, environment, and culture history among the Pokom in the Valley of Guatemala. In *The Spatial Organisation of Culture*, ed. I. Hodder, pp. 39–60. Pittsburgh: Univ. Pittsburgh Press
7. Arnold, D. E. 1981. A model for the identification of non-local ceramic distribution: A view from the present. In *Production and Distribution: A Ceramic Viewpoint*, ed. H. Howard, E. L. Morris, pp. 31–44. Oxford: BAR Int. Ser. 120
8. Arnold, D. E. 1983. Design structure and community organization in Quinua, Peru. In *Structure and Cognition in Art*, ed. D. K. Washburn, pp. 56–73. Cambridge: Cambridge Univ. Press
9. Arnold, D. E. 1984. Social interaction and ceramic design: Community-wide correlates in Quinua, Peru. In *Pots and Potters: Current Approaches in Ceramic Archaeology*, ed. P. M. Rice, pp. 133–61. Los Angeles: UCLA Inst. Archaeol. Mongr. 24
10. Balfet, H. 1981. Production and distribution of pottery in the Maghreb. See Ref. 7, pp. 257–69
11. Bchura, N. K. 1978. *Peasant Potters of Orissa*. Delhi: Sterling Publ.
12. Birmingham, J. 1967. Pottery making in Andros. *Expedition* 10(1):33–39
13. Birmingham, J. 1975. Traditional potters of the Kathmandu Valley: An ethnoarchaeological study. *Man* 10:370–86
14. Bowen, T., Moser, E. 1968. Seri pottery. *The Kiva* 33(3):89–132
15. Braithwaite, M. 1982. Decoration as ritual symbol: A theoretical proposal and an ethnographic study in southern Sudan. In *Symbolic and Structural Archaeology*, ed. I. Hodder, pp. 80–88. Cambridge: Cambridge Univ. Press
16. Bunzel, R. C. 1929. *The Pueblo Potter*. New York: Columbia Univ. Press
17. Casson, S. 1938. The modern pottery trade in the Aegean. *Antiquity* 12:464–73
18. Centlivres-Demont, M. 1971. *Une Communauté de Potiers en Iran: le Centre de Meybod (Yazd)*. Beiträge zur Iranistik. Wiesbaden: Ludwig Reichert Verlag
19. Charlton, T. H. 1976. Modern ceramics in the Teotihuacán Valley. In *Ethnic and Tourist Arts*, ed. N. Graburn, pp. 137–48. Berkeley: Univ. Calif. Press
20. Charlton, T. H., Katz, R. R. 1979. Tonala Bruñida ware: Past and present. *Archaeology* 32(1):44–53
21. Crossland, L. B., Posnansky, M. 1978. Pottery, people and trade at Begho, Ghana. See Ref. 6, pp. 77–89
22. Curtis, F. 1962. The utility pottery industry of Bailén, southern Spain. *Am. Anthropol.* 64:486–503
23. David, N. 1972. On the life span of pottery, type frequencies, and archaeological inference. *Am. Antiq.* 37:141–42
24. David, N., Hennig, H. 1972. *The Ethnography of Pottery: A Fulani Case Seen in Archaeological Perspective*. McCaleb Modules Anthropol. No. 21. Reading, Mass: Addison-Wesley
25. Deal, M. 1983. *Pottery ethnoarchaeology among the Tzeltal Maya*. PhD thesis. Simon Fraser Univ., Burnaby, British Columbia
26. DeBoer, W. R. 1974. Ceramic longevity and archaeological interpretation: An example from the Upper Ucayali, Peru. *Am. Antiq.* 39:335–43
27. DeBoer, W. R. 1981. *Pots and pans do not speak nor do they lie: The case for occasional reductionism*. Presented at Ann. Meet. Soc. Am. Archaeol., 46th, San Diego
28. DeBoer, W. R. 1985. The last pottery show: System and sense in ceramic studies. In *The Many Dimensions of Pottery*, ed. S. Van der Leeuw, A. C. Pritchard, pp. 529–68. Amsterdam: Univ. Amsterdam Inst. for Pre- and Protohistory
29. DeBoer, W. R., Lathrap, D. 1979. The making and breaking of Shipibo-Conibo ceramics. See Ref. 76, pp. 102–38
30. DeBoer, W. R., Moore, J. A. 1982. The measurement and meaning of stylistic diversity. *Ñawpa Pacha* 20:147–62
31. Deetz, J. 1965. *The Dynamics of Stylistic Change in Arikara Ceramics*. Urbana: Univ. Ill. Stud. Anthropol., No. 4

32. Donnan, C. B. 1971. Ancient Peruvian potters' marks and their interpretation through ethnographic analogy. *Am. Antiq.* 36:460–66
33. Donnan, C. B., Clewlow, C. W. Jr., eds. 1974. *Ethnoarchaeology*. Los Angeles: UCLA Inst. Archaeol. Monogr. 4
34. Edson, G. 1979. *Mexican Market Pottery*. New York: Watson-Guptill
35. Ellen, R. F., Glover, I. C. 1974. Pottery manufacture and trade in the Central Moluccas, Indonesia: The modern situation and the historical implications. *Man* 9:353–79
36. Evans, R. K. 1978. Early craft specialization: An example from the Balkan Chalcolithic. In *Social Archeology: Beyond Subsistence and Dating*, ed. C. L. Redman, M. J. Berman, E. V. Curtin, W. T. Langhorne Jr., N. M. Versaggi, J. C. Wanser, pp. 113–29. New York: Academic
37. Feinman, G. 1980. *The relationship between administrative organization and ceramic production in the Valley of Oaxaca, Mexico*. PhD thesis. City Univ. New York, New York City
38. Fontana, B. L., Robinson, W. J., Cormack, C. W., Leavitt, E. E. Jr. 1962. *Papago Indian Pottery*. Am. Ethnol. Soc. Monogr. No. 37. Seattle: Univ. Wash. Press
39. Foster, G. M. 1948. *Empire's Children: The People of Tzintzuntzan*. Washington DC: Smithsonian Inst., Inst. Soc. Anthropol. Publ. No. 6
40. Foster, G. M. 1948. Some implications of modern Mexican mold-made pottery. *Southwest. J. Anthropol.* 4:356–70
41. Foster, G. M. 1955. Contemporary pottery techniques in southern and central Mexico. *Middle Am. Res. Inst. Publ.* 22:1–48
42. Foster, G. M. 1956. Pottery-making in Bengal. *Southwest J. Anthropol.* 12:395–405
43. Foster, G. M. 1959. The Coyotepec molde and some associated problems of the potter's wheel. *Southwest. J. Anthropol.* 15:53–63
44. Foster, G. M. 1959. The potter's wheel: An analysis of idea and artifact in invention. *Southwest J. Anthropol.* 15:99–119
45. Foster, G. M. 1960. Life-expectancy of utilitarian pottery in Tzintzuntzan, Michoacan, Mexico. *Am. Antiq.* 25:606–9
46. Foster, G. M. 1960. Archaeological implications of the modern pottery of Acatlan Pueblo, Mexico. *Am. Antiq.* 26:205–14
47. Foster, G. M. 1965. The sociology of pottery: Questions and hypotheses arising from contemporary Mexican work. See Ref. 91, pp. 43–61
48. Friedrich, M. H. 1970. Design structure and social interaction: Archaeological implications of an ethnographic analysis. *Am. Antiq.* 35:332–43
49. Gallay, A. 1970. La poterie en pays Sarakolé (Mali). *J. Soc. Africanistes* 40(1):7–84
50. Gasser, S. A. 1969. *Das Töpferhandwerk von Indonesien*. Basler Beiträge zur Ethnologie, Band 7. Basel: Pharos-Verlag Hansrudolf Schwabe AG
51. Gould, R. A., ed. 1978. *Explorations in Ethnoarchaeology*. Albuquerque: Univ. New Mexico Press
52. Graves, M. W. 1980. *Kalinga intercommunity ceramic design differentiation*. Presented at Ann. Meet. Soc. Am. Archaeol., 45th, Philadelphia
53. Graves, M. W. 1981. *Ethnoarchaeology of Kalinga ceramic design*. PhD thesis. Univ. Arizona, Tucson
54. Groves, M. 1960. Motuan pottery. *J. Polynesian Soc.* 69:2–22
55. Guthe, C. E. 1925. *Pueblo Pottery Making: A Study at the Village of San Ildefonso*. New Haven: Yale Univ. Press, Pap. Southwest. Exped. No. 2. (Published for Dep. Archaeol., Phillips Acad., Andover, Mass.)
56. Hankey, V. 1968. Pottery-making at Beit Shehab, Lebanon. *Palestine Explor. Q.*, pp. 27–32
57. Hardin, M. A. 1977. Individual style in San José pottery painting: The role of deliberate choice. See Ref. 62. pp. 109–36
58. Hardin, M. A. 1979. The cognitive basis of productivity in a decorative art style: Implications of an ethnographic study for archaeologists' taxonomies. See Ref. 76, pp. 75–101
59. Hardin, M. A. 1983. The structure of Tarascan pottery painting. See Ref. 8, pp. 8–24
60. Hill, J. N. 1970. *Broken K Pueblo: Prehistoric Social Organization in the American Southwest*. Anthropol. Pap. Univ. Arizona No. 18. Tucson: Univ. Arizona Press
61. Hill, J. N. 1977. Individual variability in ceramics and the study of prehistoric social organization. See Ref. 62, pp. 55–108
62. Hill, J. N., Gunn, J., eds. 1977. *The Individual in Prehistory*. New York: Academic
63. Hodder, I. 1977. A study in ethnoarchaeology in western Kenya. In *Archaeology and Anthropology*, ed. M. Spriggs, pp. 117–41. Oxford: BAR Suppl. Ser. 19

64. Hodder, I. 1977. The distribution of material culture items in the Baringo district, western Kenya. *Man* 12:239–69
65. Hodder, I. 1978. The maintenance of group identities in the Baringo district, W. Kenya. In *Social Organisation and Settlement*, ed. D. Green, C. Haselgrove, M. Spriggs, pp. 47–73. Oxford: BAR Int. Ser. (Suppl.) 47
66. Hodder, I. 1979. Pottery distributions: Service and tribal areas. In *Pottery and the Archaeologist*, ed. M. Millett, pp. 7–23. London: Univ. London Inst. Archaeol. Occas. Publ. No. 4
67. Hodder, I. 1981. Society, economy and culture: An ethnographic case study amongst the Lozi. In *Pattern of the Past*, ed. I. Hodder, G. Isaac, N. Hammond, pp. 67–96. Cambridge: Cambridge Univ. Press
68. Hodder, I. 1981. Pottery, production, and use: A theoretical discussion. See Ref. 7, pp. 215–20
69. Hodder, I. 1982. *Symbols in Action*. Cambridge: Cambridge Univ. Press
70. Howry, J. C. 1976. Fires on the mountain: Ceramic traditions and marketing in the highlands of Chiapas, Mexico. PhD thesis. Harvard Univ., Cambridge, Mass.
71. Johnson, G. A. 1973. *Local Exchange and Early State Development in Southwestern Iran*. Ann Arbor: Univ. Michigan Mus. Anthropol. Pap. No. 51
72. Kaplan, F. S. 1976. *Cognition and style, an analysis based on a Mexican pottery tradition*. PhD thesis. City Univ. New York, New York City
73. Kaplan, F. S. 1977. Symbolism in Mexican utilitarian pottery. *Centerpoint* 2(2):33–41
74. Kleinberg, M. J. 1979. *Kinship and economic growth: Pottery production in a Japanese village*. PhD thesis. Univ. Michigan, Ann Arbor
75. Kleindienst, M., Watson, P. J. 1956. Action archaeology: The archaeological inventory of a living community. *Anthropology Tomorrow* 5:75–78
76. Kramer, C., ed. 1979. *Ethnoarchaeology: Implications of Ethnography for Archaeology*. New York: Columbia Univ. Press
77. Krotser, P. H. 1974. Country potters of Veracruz, Mexico: Technological survivals and culture change. See Ref. 33, pp. 131–46
78. Krotser, P. H. 1980. Potters in the land of the Olmec. In *In the Land of the Olmec*. Vol. 2, *The People of the River*, ed. M. D. Coe, R. A. Diehl, pp. 125–38. Austin: Univ. Texas Press
79. Lathrap, D. W. 1976. Shipibo tourist pottery. See Ref. 19, pp. 197–207
80. Lathrap, D. W. 1983. Recent Shipibo-Conibo ceramics and their implications for archaeological interpretation. See Ref. 8, pp. 25–39
81. Lauer, P. K. 1970. Amphlett Islands' pottery trade and the *kula*. *Mankind* 7:165–76
82. Lauer, P. K. 1974. *Pottery Traditions in the d'Entrecasteaux Islands of Papua*. St. Lucia: Univ. Queensland Anthropol. Mus. Occas. Pap. Anthropol. No. 3
83. Linares de Sapir, O. 1969. Diola pottery of the Fogny and the Kasa. *Expedition* 11(3):2–11
84. Linné, S. 1965. The ethnologist and the American Indian potter. See Ref. 91, pp. 20–42
85. Lisse, O., Louis, A. 1956. *Les Potiers de Nabeul: Etude de Sociologie Tunisienne*. Tunis: Publ. Inst. Belles Lettres Arabes No. 23
86. Litto, G. 1976. *South American Folk Pottery*. New York: Watson-Guptill
87. Longacre, W. A. 1970. *Archaeology as Anthropology: A Case Study*. Anthropol. Pap. Univ. Arizona No. 17. Tucson: Univ. Arizona Press
88. Longacre, W. A. 1981. Kalinga pottery: an ethnoarchaeological study. See Ref. 67, pp. 49–66
89. Longacre, W. A. 1983. *Ethnoarchaeology of the Kalinga*. Weston: Pictures of Record
90. Longacre, W. A. 1985. Pottery use-life among the Kalinga, northern Luzon, the Philippines. In *Decoding Prehistoric Ceramics*, ed. B. A. Nelson. Carbondale: South. Ill. Univ. Press. In press
91. Matson, F. R., ed. 1965. *Ceramics and Man*. Viking Fund Publ. Anthropol. No. 41. New York: Wenner-Gren Found. Anthropol. Res.
92. Matson, F. R. 1972. Ceramic studies. In *The Minnesota Messenia Expedition*, ed. W. A. McDonald, G. R. Rapp, pp. 200–24. Minneapolis: Univ. Minnesota Press
93. Matson, F. R. 1973. The potters of Chalkis. In *Classics and the Classical Tradition*, ed. E. N. Borza, R. W. Carruba, pp. 117–42. University Park: Penn. State Univ. Press
94. Matson, F. R. 1974. The archaeological present: Near Eastern village potters at work. *Am. J. Archaeol.* 78:345–47
95. Miller, D. 1981. The relationship between ceramic production and distribution in a central Indian village. See Ref. 7, pp. 221–28
96. Miller, D. 1982. Structures and strategies: An aspect of the relationship be-

tween social hierarchy and cultural change. See Ref. 15, pp. 89–98
97. Miller, G. L. 1980. Classifications and economic scaling of Nineteenth Century ceramics. *Hist. Archaeol.* 14:1–40
98. Moeran, B. 1984. *Lost Innocence: Folk Craft Potters of Onta, Japan.* Berkeley: Univ. Calif. Press
99. Nelson, B. A. 1981. Ethnoarchaeology and paleodemography: A test of Turner and Lofgren's hypothesis. *J. Anthropol. Res.* 37:107–29
100. Nicklin, K. 1979. The location of pottery manufacture. *Man* 14:436–58
101. Nicklin, K. 1981. Pottery production and distribution in southeast Nigeria. See Ref. 7, pp. 169–86
102. Nicklin, K. 1981. Ceramic pyrometry: Two Ibibio examples. See Ref. 7, pp. 347–59
103. Ochsenschlager, E. L. 1974. Modern potters at al-Hiba, with some reflections on the excavated Early Dynastic pottery. See Ref. 33, pp. 149–57
104. Papousek, D. A. 1981. *The Peasant Potters of Los Pueblos: Stimulus Situation and Adaptive Processes in the Mazahua Region in Central Mexico.* Studies of Developing Countries No. 27. Assen: Van Gorcum
105. Pastron, A. G. 1974. Preliminary ethnoarchaeological investigations among the Tarahumara. See Ref. 33, pp. 93–114
106. Peacock, D. P. S. 1982. *Pottery in the Roman World: An Ethnoarchaeological Approach.* London: Longman
107. Plog, S. 1980. *Stylistic Variation in Prehistoric Ceramics.* Cambridge: Cambridge Univ. Press
108. Plog, S. 1983. Analysis of style in artifacts. *Ann. Rev. Anthropol.* 12:125–42
109. Reina, R. E. 1963. The potter and the farmer: The fate of two innovators in a Maya village. *Expedition* 5(4):18–30
110. Reina, R. E., Hill, R. M. II. 1978. *The Traditional Pottery of Guatemala.* Austin: Univ. Texas Press
111. Rice, P. M. 1978. Ceramic continuity and change in the Valley of Guatemala: A technological analysis. See Ref. 5, pp. 402–510
112. Rice, P. M., Saffer, M. E. 1982. *Ceramic Notes, No. 1: Annotated Bibliography of Ceramic Studies.* Part 1: Analysis. Technical and Ethnographic Approaches to Pottery Production and Use. Gainesville: Florida State Museum, Occas. Publ. Ceramic Technol. Lab.
113. Rye, O. S. 1981. *Pottery Technology: Principles and Reconstruction.* Manuals on Archaeology 4. Washington, DC: Taraxacum
114. Rye, O. S., Evans, C. 1976. *Traditional Pottery Techniques of Pakistan: Field and Laboratory Studies.* Smithsonian Contrib. Anthropol. 21. Washington, DC: Smithsonian Inst.
115. Saligan, D. P. 1982. The market system for earthenware potteries in southeastern Negros: A preliminary report. In *Houses Built on Scattered Poles: Prehistory and Ecology in Negros Oriental, Philippines,* ed. K. L. Hutterer, W. K. Macdonald, pp. 147–57. Cebu City: Univ. San Carlos
116. Saraswati, B. 1979. *Pottery-Making Cultures and Indian Civilization.* New Delhi: Abhinav Publ.
117. Saraswati, B., Behura, N. K. 1966. *Pottery Techniques in Peasant India.* Calcutta: Anthropol. Survey of India. Memoir No. 13
118. Scheans, D. J. 1960. The Pottery Industry of San Nicolas, Ilokos Norte. *J. East Asiatic Stud.* 9(1):1–38
119. Scheans, D. J. 1966. A new view of Philippines pottery manufacture. *Southwest J. Anthropol.* 22:106–19
120. Scheans, D. J. 1969. Sociocultural characteristics of Filipino potters. *Philipp. Sociol. Rev.* 17:83–96
121. Scheans, D. J. 1977. *Filipino Market Potteries.* Natl. Mus. Monogr. No. 3. Manila: National Museum
122. Shepard, A. O. 1956. *Ceramics for the Archaeologist.* Publ. 609. Washington, DC: Carnegie Inst. Washington
123. Solheim, W. G. II. 1952. Oceanian pottery manufacture. *J. East Asiatic Stud.* 1:1–39
124. Solheim, W. G. II. 1965. The functions of pottery in Southeast Asia: From the present to the past. See Ref. 91, pp. 254–73
125. Specht, J. 1972. The pottery industry of Buka Island, Territory of Papua, New Guinea. *Archaeol. Phys. Anthropol. Oceania* 7:125–44
126. Spriggs, M., Miller, D. 1979. Ambon-Lease: A study of contemporary pottery making and its archaeological relevance. See Ref. 66, pp. 25–34
127. Stanislawski, M. B. 1969. The ethnoarchaeology of Hopi pottery making. *Plateau* 42:27–33
128. Stanislawski, M. B. 1969. What good is a broken pot? An experiment in Hopi-Tewa ethnoarchaeology. *Southwest. Lore* 35(1):11–18
129. Stanislawski, M. B. 1977. Ethnoarchaeology of Hopi and Hopi-Tewa pottery making: Styles of learning. In *Experimental Archaeology,* ed. D. Ingersoll, J. Yellen, W. Macdonald, pp. 378–408. New York: Columbia Univ. Press

130. Stanislawski, M. B. 1978. If pots were mortal. See Ref. 51, pp. 201–27
131. Stanislawski, M. B., Stanislawski, B. 1978. Hopi and Hopi-Tewa ceramic tradition networks. See Ref. 6, pp. 61–76
132. Stark, B. 1984. An ethnoarchaeological study of a Mexican pottery industry. *J. New World Archaeol.* 6(2):4–14
133. Stiles, D. 1977. Ethnoarchaeology: A discussion of methods and applications. *Man* 12:87–103
134. Stolmaker, C. 1976. Examples of stability and change from Santa Maria Atzompa. In *Markets in Oaxaca*, ed. S. Cook, M. Diskin, pp. 189–207. Austin: Univ. Texas Press
135. Thompson, R. H. 1958. *Modern Yucatecan Maya Pottery Making*. Mem. Soc. Am. Archaeol. No. 15. *Am. Antiq.* 34, No. 4, Part 2
136. Tschopik, H. Jr. 1941. *Navaho Pottery Making*. Pap. Peabody Mus. Am. Archaeol. Ethnol. Vol. 17, No. 1. Cambridge: Harvard Univ. Press
137. Tschopik, H. Jr. 1950. An Andean ceramic tradition in historical perspective. *Am. Antiq.* 15:196–218
138. Turner, C. G. II, Lofgren, L. 1966. Household size of prehistoric Western Pueblo Indians. *Southwest. J. Anthropol.* 22:117–32
139. Van der Leeuw, S. E. 1983. Pottery distribution systems in Roman northwestern Europe and on contemporary Negros, Philippines. *Archaeol. Rev. Cambridge* 2(2):37–47
140. Voyatzoglou, M. 1974. The jar makers of Thrapsano in Crete. *Expedition* 16(2):18–24
141. Waane, S. 1977. Pottery-making traditions of the Ikombe Kisi, Mbeya region, Tanzania. *Baessler-Archiv N.F.* Band 25:251–306
142. Wahlman, M. 1972. Yoruba pottery making techniques. *Baessler-Archiv N. F.* Band 20:313–46
143. Weigand, P. C. 1969. *Modern Huichol Ceramics*. University Museum Mesoamerican Studies. Carbondale: South. Ill. Univ.
144. Welbourn, A. 1984. Endo ceramics and power strategies. In *Ideology, Power and Prehistory*, ed. D. Miller, C. Tilley, pp. 17–24. Cambridge: Cambridge Univ. Press
145. Whallon, R. Jr. 1968. Investigations of late prehistoric social organization in New York State. In *New Perspectives in Archeology*, ed. S. R. Binford, L. R. Binford, pp. 223–44. Chicago: Aldine
146. Wobst, H. M. 1977. Stylistic behavior and information exchange. In *For the Director: Research Essays in Honor of James B. Griffin*, ed. C. E. Cleland, pp. 317–42. Ann Arbor: Univ. Mich. Mus. Anthropol. Pap. No. 61

ANTHROPOLOGY, EVOLUTION, AND "SCIENTIFIC CREATIONISM"

James N. Spuhler

Department of Anthropology, University of Michigan, Ann Arbor, Michigan 48109

INTRODUCTION

According to a Gallup Poll reported 29 August 1982 (150, p. 21), 44% of the population in the United States does not accept an evolutionary origin for the human species, 9% are uncertain, and only 47% appear to be committed to a belief in human evolution, although most of those who believe in human evolution also expressed some theistic beliefs.

G. Evelyn Hutchinson warned in 1983: ". . . [T]he contemporary attacks on evolutionary theory . . . are terrifying, for they question the whole of the unity of knowledge and of the living world . . ." (85).

While a candidate, President Ronald Reagan stated at a meeting of Christian fundamentalists in Dallas on 22 August 1980 (83, p. 1214) that he supported the teaching of the biblical story of creation in the public schools and that he thought there were great flaws in the theory of evolution.

In 1976 President Jimmy Carter wrote (25, p. 2) in support of the separation of church and state and the importance of a well-rounded background in science, including the biological theory of evolution, for the development of young persons.

This review stresses publications during the years 1978–1984, but important works from earlier times are included. It does not present a full review of current facts and theories on evolution as such; rather it considers selected aspects of the ongoing controversy between the science of evolution and religious creationism, with special reference to those facts and theories that lead most scientists, many religious persons who are not fundamentalists insisting on a literal interpretation of the Bible, and the high courts to reject "scientific creationism" as a part of anthropological and other involved sciences.

For those who want a quick overview of the controversy, six works are recommended: Education Committee of the American Society of Zoologists,

Science as a Way of Knowing—Evolutionary Biology, 1984 (53a); Committee on Science and Creationism, *Science and Creationism,* 1984 (33); Godfrey, *Scientists Confront Creationism,* 1983 (67); Harris, *Evolution: Genesis and Revelations,* 1981 (76); Wood *"Scientific Creationism" and the Public Schools,* 1982 (210); and Zetterberg, *Evolution versus Creationism,* 1983 (218). J. R. Moore (133) supplies a bibliography of 200 titles concerning creationism, and McKim (122) provides a selected bibliography on the debate.

Definitions of Science and Religion

The legal definition of "religion" is of top importance in the controversy. Justice Black stated in Everson vs Board of Education (330 U.S. 1.15–16, 1947):

> The "establishment of religion" clause of the First Amendment means at least this: Neither a state nor the Federal Government can set up a church. Neither can pass laws which aid one religion, aid all religions, or prefer one religion over another. Neither can force nor influence a person to go to nor to remain away from church against his will or force him to profess a belief or disbelief in any religion. No person can be punished for entertaining or professing religious beliefs or disbeliefs, for church-attendance or non-attendance. No tax, large or small, can be levied to support religious activities or institutions, whatever they may be called, or whatever form they may adopt to teach or practice religion. Neither a state nor the Federal Government can, openly or secretly, participate in the affairs of any religious organizations or groups and vice versa. In the words of Jefferson, the clause . . . was intended to erect "a wall of separation between church and state."

Definitions of Facts and Theories

Many evolutionary scientists teach that "evolution is a theory." Because one dictionary definition of "theory" is "hypothesis, guess," some conclude that the theory of evolution is mere guesswork. The folk wisdom of America trusts "facts" and distrusts "theories."

Bertrand Russell (1929) made a useful classification of facts. A fact is not one of the simple things of the world; facts mean that a certain thing has a certain quality, or that certain things have certain relations. Facts are never simple; they have two or more constituents; they assign one or more qualities or relations to things. The fact itself is objective, and independent of our thought or opinion about it; but the assertion is something which involves thought, and may be either true or false (178, pp. 54–56).

Kluckhohn (1939), writing for anthropologists, gave a helpful dictionary-type definition of theory:

> "Theory" refers to a statement or statements of somewhat abstract nature covering the relationship between a number of descrete facts. The differentia of "theory" is primarily that the validity of operations of reasoning is at stake as well as the correctness of operations of perceptions. Theory is dependent on the logic of inference. Theories depend upon inferences from observations, but cannot themselves be observed directly (100, p. 344, footnote 32).

Cohen & Nagel (29) distinguish between two kinds of theories. Physical theories appeal to an easily imagined hidden mechanism which will explain the observable phenomena, for example, the atomic theory of chemistry and the theory of the gene in biological inheritance. Mathematical or abstractive theories avoid all reference to hidden mechanisms and make use of relations abstracted from the phenomena actually observable, for example, the theory of gravitation and the Darwinian theory of organic evolution. Neither kind of theory is more useful nor more fundamental than the other; some scientists use a fusion or synthesis of the two points of view as in most of neo-Darwinian evolutionary theory (see Mayr & Provine 120). Some anthropologists, especially archaeologists, prefer to avoid use of the term "facts" in the context of the present controversy and to speak instead of "data" in terms of some theoretical perspective, in reference to, for instance, a pot sherd or fossil bone.

Surveys on Belief in Evolution

Riddle found in 1942 that less than one half of high-school biology teachers in the United States taught evolution in their courses (173). Bliss (16) reported that a 1973 survey by a creationist group of a random sample comprising 2000 residents of Cupertino, California, gave these percentages: believe in creation 44.3, in evolution, 23.3, in both 3.5, in neither 10.6, and undecided 18.3.

FUNDAMENTALISM AND "SCIENTIFIC CREATIONISM"

Fundamentalist and Evangelical Churches

The Fundamentalist and Evangelical churches are a diverse group of theologically conservative Protestant churches with origins in the millenarianism of the 19th century. Some trace the movement back to the anabaptists of Zurich in 1523, who advocated a return to primitive Christianity. The word "Fundamentalist" was coined by Curtis Lee Laws of the *Baptist Watchman-Examiner* on page 834 of the issue of 1 July 1920 (J. R. Moore 134, p. 70). Sandeen (180) makes an excellent exposition, including an extensive bibliography, of the religious character of the fundamentalist movement back to its millenarian beginnings. Cole (32) gives an accurate description of beliefs, actions, and events in the 1920s, a period when several still existing fundamentalist churches were founded in the United States. Gasper (64) gives a descriptive account of the movement in America from the 1930s to the 1960s. H. L. Mencken (1880–1956), journalist, editor, and philologist, was perhaps the harshest critic of the movement, writing in his *Treatise on the Gods* (126, pp. 257–58): "In Fundamentalism it [Protestantism] reaches the nadir of theology. What is worst in Fundamentalism is common, perhaps, to all forms of Christianity, but it is only in the imprecations of the backwoods Wesleys that it is stated plainly. No more shocking nonsense has every been put into words by theoretically civilized men."

In the 1920s Mencken introduced the term "Bible Belt" for that region, chiefly in the southern states but now including parts of Oklahoma, west Texas, eastern New Mexico, and southern California, where churchgoing people held that the Bible is literally true. Among novels critical of the fundamentalist movement, probably the best known is Elmer Gantry (1927) by Sinclair Lewis (107), an account of certain ignorant, gross, and predatory preachers who operated midwestern fundamentalist churches in the 1920s.

J. R. Moore (134) shows that some of the early fundamentalists, including Augustus Hopkins Strong (1836–1921), author of *Systematic Theology* (193), and the leading Baptist theologian, Benjamin B. Warfield (1851–1921), and George Frederick Wright (1838–1921), glacial geologist, were strongly proevolutionists. " 'Evolution,' in short," said James Orr (1844–1914), Professor of Theology at Glasgow, "is coming to be recognized as but a new name for 'creation' " (156).

In America the religious antievolution crusade was delayed by the Civil War. Moore (134) argues convincingly that the campaign really got underway as an aftermath of World War I. Lewontin (110) outlines a social class explanation of the American fundamentalist movement.

In general, the fundamentalists of the 1920s claimed to defend the standards of orthodox Christianity against the church liberals and modernists who accepted 19th century and early 20th century biblical criticism and wished to make the activities of the church more relevant to contemporary social problems. The fundamentalists stress a complete, often verbal inspiration of the Bible and accept its full and final authority over religious faith and practice. Fundamentalists preach that a happy eternal life in Paradise after death is reached by accepting Jesus Christ as Savior; a view that moves a few rich and many not so rich fundamentalists to contribute money to support antievolutionary action and publications of the creed (134).

A coalition of fundamentalists called the "New Christian Right," and by some the "Moral Majority," took credit for having helped elect President Reagan and several members of the Senate and House. Most of the Christian Right were brought and held together by television evangelists, notably Rev. Jerry Falwell of Virginia, Rev. Jimmy Lee Swaggart of Louisiana, and Rev. James Robison of Texas.

The Christian militants claimed that liberals, humanists, and leftists had conspired to remove God from the public schools and to teach evolution as an alternative *religion*. Jorstad (90) showed that the fundamentalists had previously had some influence in electing rightest candidates in the United States, including Sen. Joseph R. McCarthy in the 1950s and Sen. Barry Goldwater and Gov. George Wallace in the 1960s, but these pioneers lacked the skillful use of television and computerized direct mailing shown by the New Christian Right during the 1980 and 1984 campaigns. Television fundamentalism is now a multimillion dollar business in Bible Belt America.

According to de Puy, in 1980 the conservatives defeated the liberals in the 13-million-member Southern Baptist Convention in electing as their president Bailey Smith, an avowed believer in an inerrant Bible (46, p. 597).

A reliable census of the number of fundamentalists who are antievolutionists, or special creationists, is not available. In 1984 fundamentalist organizations claimed nearly 40 million members. Probably about one half of these are antievolutionists of some degree. There were at least several hundred active "scientific creationists" in the United States in 1984; the Creation Research Society claims 3000 members (Encyclopedia of Associations, 18th edition, 1984).

TRANSLATIONS OF THE BIBLE A belief in the literal truth of the Bible presupposes designation of a particular version out of the many that have been written in the last 2000 years. By about 1450 A.D., when printing from movable type was introduced in Europe, there were 33 translations, and by about 1800 there were 71. For our purposes, *The Septuagint* (3rd–2nd century B.C.), *The Vulgate* (ca 383–405 B.C.), the *King James Version* (of 1611), and some modern translations are the most important. The three-volume *Cambridge History of the Bible,* 1963–1970, gives an excellent history of the translations.

Of several modern translations, the Anchor Bible is of special interest in the present context because William Foxwell Albright, a distinguished biblical scholar, archaeologist, and anthropologist, was the first general editor of the series: "Its object is to make the Bible accessible to the modern reader; its method is to arrive at the meaning of Biblical literature through exact translation and extended exposition, and to reconstruct the ancient setting of the biblical story, as well as the circumstances of its transcription and the characteristics of its transcribers (190, General Editor's Note, Vol. 1).

Creationist Literature

Boadt (1982), a theologian, pointed out that the literalist approach to biblical interpretation is not present in Judaism and Catholicism, but is present only in Protestantism, with its greater stress on the power of the word and lower stress on the power of the social community. He distinguished the descending, "transcendent," literal interpretation of the biblical text used today mostly by Protestant fundamentalists, from the ascending, "anthropological," critical interpretation employed by other biblical scholars. Boadt insists: "These are not simply different methods of arriving as the same insight. They are two distinct views. The conflict between creationism and evolutionary theory reflects these viewpoints, and it will not be resolved by a neutral discussion of how best to interpret evidence" (17, p. 17). The fundamentalist, transcendent interpretation of the Bible makes it the infallible, inerrant, and verbally inspired word of God (200, 201).

The nonfundamentalist, anthropological approach to interpretation of the Bible holds that the Old Testament is about but not by Jehovah, and that the New Testament is not written by Jesus Christ, but is about him. Inspiration does not mean dictation [see Benoit (11) for a full treatment of this question and also Megivern (124)].

The Catholic Church has long endorsed the historical, critical, anthropological method (36). Pope Leo XIII in his 1893 letter *Providentissimus Deus*, ordered Catholic scholars to attempt recovery of the ancient forms so as better to understand the intent of the text. Pope John Paul II stated in an address to the Pontifical Academy of Sciences on 3 October 1981:

> Cosmogony itself speaks to us of the origins of the universe and its makeup, not in order to provide us with a scientific treatise but in order to state the correct relationship of man with God and with the universe. Sacred Scripture wishes simply to declare that the world was created by God, and in order to teach this truth, it expresses itself in the terms of the cosmology in use at the time of the writer. The sacred book likewise wishes to tell men that the world was not created as the seat of the gods, as was taught by other cosmogonies and cosmologies, but was rather created for the service of man and the glory of God. Any other teaching about the origins and makeup of the universe is alien to the intentions of the Bible, which does not wish to teach how heaven was made but how one goes to heaven (167).

Gardner judges that of the thousands of "dreary and pathetic" books attempting to harmonize evolution and the Bible, published in the 19th century after Darwin's *Origin of Species*, only one stands out today—the book entitled *Omphalos*, by the English zoologist Philip Gosse (71). His delightful and fantastic theory is logical, in accord with geological theory, but untestable and not negatable. Gosse concluded that God created the earth, living species, and man about 4000 B.C., in six days, with the geological strata and their contained fossils all in the places and order that scientists discover; just as Adam and Eve were created with a navel that was never connected by an umbilical cord to a placenta, so the earth was created with stratified fossils that had no existence except in the mind of God (63).

The greatest of the 20th century Protestant creationists is George McCready Price, born in 1870, educated in Seventh Day Adventist schools, Professor of Geology at the Adventist Walla Walla College in Washington State, Bryan's chief authority in the Scopes Trial, quoted by nearly every fundamentalist antievolutionist. In 1923 he published *The New Geology* (168), a classic of pseudo-science. The heart of Price's argument is the literal six-day creation, the deluge, and the notion that the evidence for evolution is circular and thus invalid: the fossils are used to date the geological deposits and the sequence of fossils from "old" to "young" strata is used as evidence and proof of evolution. Price believed that the anthropoid apes are degenerate or hybridized men.

Probably the most influential of the Catholic antievolutionists is George Barry O'Toole, *The Case Against Evolution* (157), a work based mostly on Price. The Neo-Thomist philosopher Mortimer J. Adler has published (2, 3) several items against the evolutionary, gradualistic origin of species, claiming that species differ not in degree but, radically, in kind. The Catholic church now accepts the scientific theory of evolution with reservations about the original infusion of the soul (36, 167). Father Ernest C. Messenger, in *Evolution and Theology*, gives a full discussion on problems of the soul and evolution (127).

Is the Bible Literally True?

Apparently all "scientific creationists" are prior fundamentalists, who believe in the literal interpretation and absolute inerrancy of the Bible (56, 209), but many fundamentalists are not creationists and antievolutionists (25). Thus the claim that creationism is true and that evolution is false rests on a literal interpretation, free from error or mistake, of sentences in Genesis saying that God created man and all other species within six 24-hour days about 6000 to 10,000 years ago (217).

A classical statement of absolute inerrancy is by the 19th century English biblical scholar John William Burgon (21): "The Bible is none other than the voice of Him that sitteth upon the Throne! Every Book of it, every Chapter of it, every Verse of it, every word of it, every syllable of it (where are we to stop?), every letter of it, is the direct utterance of the Most High!" A modern statement is by Rev. Jerry Falwell, of the TV show "Gospel Hour," who holds that "the Bible is absolutely infallible, without error in all matters pertaining to faith and practice, as well as in the areas of geography, science, history . . ." (56). But the Bible literally interpreted makes contradictory statements, one or both of which must therefore be in error.

Of course, a wide variety of arguments may reconcile literally interpreted biblical contradictions. See, for example, Heidel's finding (79, pp. 245–48) that the numerical data in Genesis on the duration of the deluge are in perfect harmony. Many special creationists [see several mentioned in (147, 218)] perceive a unifying design in the final form of the creation and flood account in Genesis, notwithstanding dual origin and internal contradictions. Nevertheless, such rectifications are of no solace to those who believe in a strictly literal interpretation.

The contradictory statements are understandable if the Book of Genesis is a loosely edited compilation from more than one source, as modern biblical scholarship has conclusively demonstrated (61, 204). Often creationists argue on the basis of an English translation of the Hebrew or Greek texts, frequently accepting the King James Version despite its known lack of accuracy in identifying Hebrew roots (17, p. 19; 75). There is no reason to accept the creationist claims about the origin of man or Noah's flood if there are many factual errors elsewhere in the Bible. Here we will include errors in translation, but not obvious typographical errors [like that of a 17th century Bible which made the 7th commandment state (76): "Thou shalt commit adultery."] A partial list of biblical errors relevant to the evolution-creation controversy is given in references 17, 76, 190, and 218.

The view of a biologist regarding the virgin birth phenomenon in Matthew 1:18–25 becomes quite different upon learning that Hebrew *'almah,* "girl," is translated (uniquely in the New Testament) into Greek *parthenos,* "virgin" (6, p. 8). These authors explain further: "It is possible on some views that Isaiah was using mythological terms current in his own time to demonstrate an expected deliverer's birth. The LXX [Septiguent] translators would appear to have so understood the passage, and only later did Greek translations of the Hebrew appear with the word one would expect, *neanis,* 'young maiden,' instead of *parthenos.*" See also the comments by Fitzmyer (59) on the birth of Jesus narrative in Luke 1:26–38. If the birth was in fact virgin, that is, parthenogenetic without fertilization by a male gamete of the same species, then Jesus should have been a female with X chromosome(s) but no male sex-determining Y chromosome. Whether the conception of Jesus was "immaculate" is of course a religious and not a scientific matter.

A majority of Christians believe that the true Bible is religious, not scientific. As Alfred North Whitehead remarked (208, p. 17): "Collective enthusiasms, revivals, institutions, churches, ritual, bibles, codes of behaviour, are trappings of religion, its passing forms. They may be useful, or harmful; they may be authoritatively ordained, or merely temporary expedients. But the end of religion is beyond all this." And, to expand a phrase of Whitehead (208, p. 15): "You use arithmetic [or the facts and theories of evolution], but you are religious."

The "Creation Scientists"

Williams (209, p. 92) found that "An exegesis of the seminal works of Henry M. Morris, Director of the Institute for Creation Research, clearly reveals that scientific creationism is a religious doctrine. It is a necessary dogma of the conservative evangelical's particular form of Christianity, is premised upon a literal interpretation of the Bible, and has as its purpose the defense of Jesus Christ as Lord and Savior" (see also 137, 138, 142).

Three works by Morris are of special interest in the current controversy: 1. *Scientific Creationism,* issued in a General and a Public School Edition, 1974 (139), 2. *Many Infallible Proofs,* 1974 (140), and 3. *The Beginning of the World,* 1977 (141). The omission of material printed in the General Edition of *Scientific Creationism* from the Public School Edition is of particular importance in understanding the political strategy and the religious basis of scientific creationism. The final chapter of the General Edition (139), entitled "Creation According to Scripture," lays the theological foundation for a belief in creationism, gives documentation to the Bible, and defends against modern apostasy. This "religious" chapter is omitted entirely, and the references to God and the Bible in the opening chapter were removed from the Public School Edition.

After the Supreme Court invalidated a state antievolution law in Epperson v. Arkansas (1968), the creation scientists developed a "Creation Science Model" as a strategem to combat what they termed the "Evolution Model" (130–132). If creationism and evolution are really competing scientific models, then it is only fair, the creationists held, that the two theories should be given equal time in the public schools (130).

An advertisement by the Institute for Creation Research in 1981 (cited by Williams 209, p. 94) described Morris's *Many Infallible Proofs* (140) as: "A comprehensive and systematic handbook written as a survey of the unique truth and authority of Biblical Christianity. Contains evidence from science, prophesy, history, internal structure, and common sense. Used as a textbook in seminaries and colleges, and for church and home study classes, as well as for personal witnessing."

Benkov & Rothstein conclude that "Creation-science is a collection of statements that allege scientific support for the Biblical account of creation" (10, p. 1114). All acceptable individual applicants for membership in the Creation Research Society must sign a four-paragraph statement of belief (cited in Pipho 165, p. 224).

BIBLICAL CREATION AND FLOOD MYTHS

The Development of the Pentateuch

The Hebrew Old Testament consists of three parts: Torah, Nebhiim, and Kethubhim, the Law, Prophets, and Writings. The Torah is called the "Five Books of Moses," or, by the early Fathers beginning with Tertullian, the Pentateuch. The traditional view is that Moses was the sole author (with the possible exception of the closing verses) of the Pentateuch, including the Book of Genesis (205). Probably Moses was born in the late 14th century B.C. (5).

Jean Astruc (8), in his *Conjectures* (published 1753), accepted the Mosaic authorship but maintained that Moses incorporated in the Pentateuch several older written sources with little alteration (see Figure 1). During the later part of the 18th and the first part of the 19th centuries, biblical scholars continued and modified Astruc's views, first demonstrating, in the Supplement Theory, that the Elohistic portion of the Pentateuch was the older, and that it was later modified by Jehovist additions. The discovery in 1853 by Hupfeld (86) of a second Elohim source led to the Document Theory, the prevailing theory today as modified in the Graf-Wellhausen or Development Theory.

The four documents are identified by their initials as J, E, D, and P: the Jehovistic Document uses the divine name Jehova in the sections prior to the call of Moses. The Elohistic Document uses the divine name Elohim. The Deuteronomic Code provides most of the text of the Book of Deuteronomy. The Priestly Document, combining both history and law, is so named because it

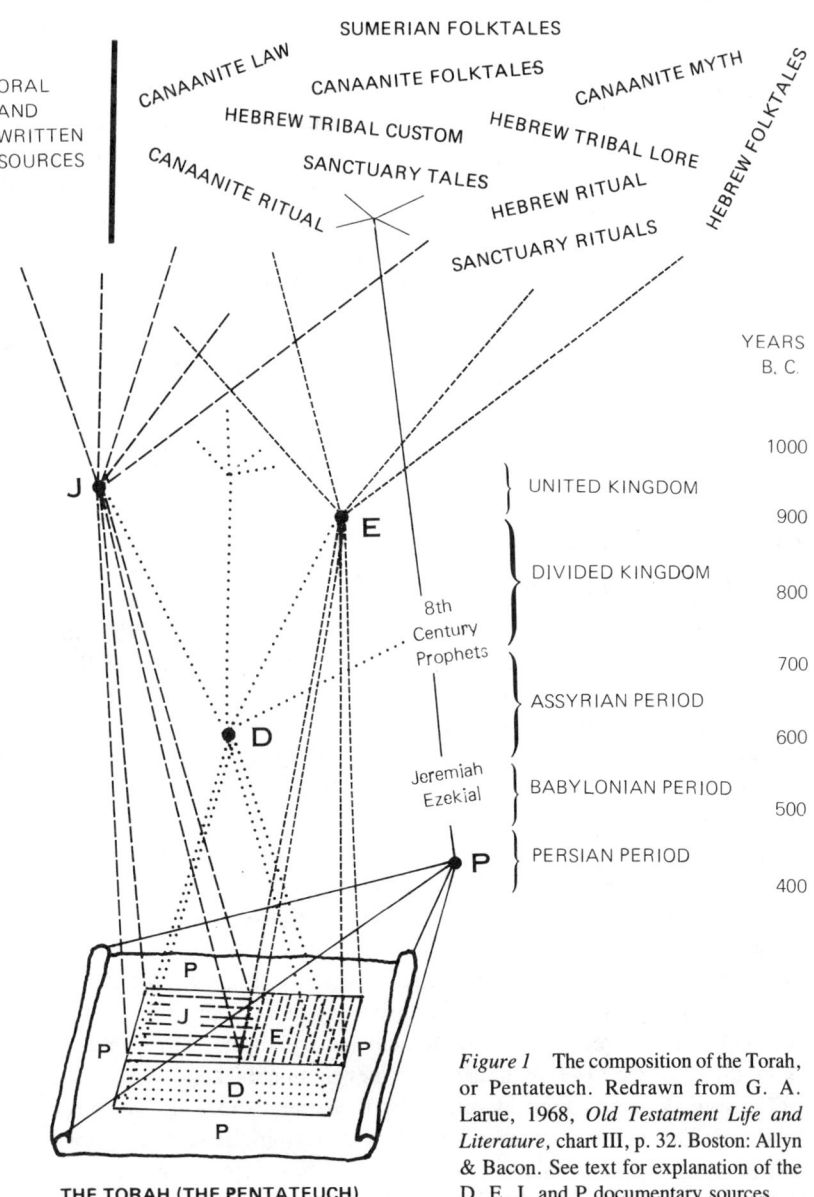

Figure 1 The composition of the Torah, or Pentateuch. Redrawn from G. A. Larue, 1968, *Old Testatment Life and Literature,* chart III, p. 32. Boston: Allyn & Bacon. See text for explanation of the D, E, J, and P documentary sources.

was written at a time when priests had a more dominant position in Judah than they had before the exile when prophets were dominant. According to Wellhausen (203, 204), the four documents are thought to have originated in the order J (about 850 B.C.), E (about 750 B.C.), D (about 650 B.C.), and P (about 500–350 B.C.) The language, style, and world view of the J and P documents are very different, and the linguistic pecularities of the P Document are numerous. The author of J is the best narrator of the Bible (see 58 and various chapters in 54). Noth (152, 153) holds skeptical views on the historical sources of the pentateuch and the traditional role of Moses in the history of Israel. Rowley (176) makes a serious attempt to relate the data of biblical tradition to archaeology, as is done in the works of Albright (5, 6). Some modern biblical scholars prefer to speak of traditions (southern vs northern, royal ideology vs priestly views) rather than, or in addition to, documentary sources (Beyerlin 12, DeVaux 47).

The Creation Stories

The most serious difficulty with a literal interpretation of the creation stories in the Bible is that two strikingly different and contradictory accounts of the creation of humans, male and female, are given in the first and second chapters of Genesis. Comparative mythology demonstrates that similar but somewhat variant creation myths are widespread in the earliest world literatures from the fourth to the first millenium B.C., and comparative linguistic and literary studies of the Bible and other documents in the ancient Near East show that the Genesis story can be traced to older Babylonian and Sumerian stories that are exactly parallel in numerous points but different in ways associated with known cultural differences in the area.

Among anthropologists, probably James George Frazer's *Folklore in the Old Testament* (61) is the best known source. Frazer shows, in the first chapter of Genesis, that on the fifth day God created the fishes and the birds, all the creatures that live in the water or in the air; on the sixth day God created all the terrestrial animals, and last of all man, whom he fashioned in his own image, both male and female. According to Genesis 1, man was the last to be created of all living species, and, incidentally, that bisexuality is shared also by the divinity. "So God created man in his own image, in the image of God created he him; male and female created he them" (Gen. 1:27). But the second chapter gives a totally different, and, indeed, contradictory account of the origin of man. There God created a male human being first, then other species of animals, and a female human being last of all, fashioning her out of a rib which he took from the male in his sleep. In the first story God starts with fishes and creates steadily up the chain of beings to man and women; in the second narrative God begins with man and works downward through the lower animals to woman. The second narrative says nothing about Adam and Eve being made in the image of God; rather "the Lord God formed man of the dust of the ground, and breathed into his nostrils the breath of life; and man became a living soul" (Gen. 2:7).

Speiser (1964) translated Genesis 2:7 as: "God Yahweh formed man from clods in the soil and blew into his nostrils the breath of life. Thus man became a living being." In the *Notes* Speiser explains (190, pp. 14–16) that here man is Mesoretic Text *'adam*, and "clods in the soil" *'dama*, in assonance with *'adam*, a play on words which the Bible shares with other ancient literatures, but not as mere punning: "Names were regarded not only as labels but also as symbols, magical keys as it were to the nature and essence of the given being or thing" (190, p. 16). Speiser finds the traditional "dust" hard to part with, yet inappropriate in Genesis 2:7, although preferable in Genesis 3:19: "For dust you are/And to dust you shall return." The theme that the gods created man from earth or clay is widespread in ancient creation myths (61). But as the great physical biologist Alfred Lotka remarked (113, p. 197): "We are indeed earth born, but yet not altogether common clay. Indeed, taken literally the expression 'common clay,' as applied to man, is an extreme case of poetic license; for aluminum and silicon—the chief constituents of clay, and taking second and third place in rank of abundance among the components of the earth's crust, are both present only in traces in the human body."

According to Graves & Patai, the writers of Genesis represented Eve as formed from Adam's rib, "an anecdote based apparently on the word *tsela*, meaning both 'rib' and 'a strumbling' (72a, p. 15)."

Modern biblical scholarship derives Genesis 1 from the P Document and Genesis 2 from the J Document (Speiser 190). As Frazer (61, p. 2) put it: "The flagrant contradiction between the two accounts is explained very simply by the circumstance that they are derived from two different and originally independent documents, which were afterwards combined into a single book by an editor, who pieced the two narratives together without always taking pains to soften or harmonize their discrepancies."

The striking correspondence in detail and order of events that preclude concidence and demonstrate derivation of the Genesis creation story from the earlier Enuma elish story is shown in the tabulation given by Heidel (79, p. 129):

Enuma elish	*Genesis*
Divine spirit and cosmic matter are coexistent and eternal	Divine spirit creates cosmic matter and exists independently of it
Primeval chasos; Ti'amat enveloped in darkness	The earth a desolate waste, with darkness covering the deep (tehom)
Light emanating from the gods	Light created
The creation of the firmament	The creation of the firmament
The creation of dry land	The creation of dry land
The creation of luminaries	The creation of luminaries
The creation of man	The creation of man
The gods rest and celebrate	God rests and sanctifies the seventh day

It is clear that the cuneiform Enuma elish story is older than the P Document Genesis story, and is most probably its cultural source. There is no basis in fact for assuming an unknown common source for both the Mesopotamian and the Hebrew stories (79, 190).

All well-qualified Old Testament scholars reject a literal interpretation of the Genesis creation poems, as well as the notion that Genesis 1 is a scientific account in the modern sense (57, 58, 79, 80, 172, 190). Paul Tillich (196, 1:252), a philosophical theologian, concluded regarding Genesis 1: "The doctrine of creation is not the story of an event which took place 'once upon a time.' It is the basic discription of the relation between God and the world." And in his extensive study of the biblical creation account, Langdon Gilkey (65, p. 260) wrote: "It is a true, although not literal, affirmation about the relation of the whole system of facts in the world to their Creator God."

The Genesis Flood Stories

The flood myth of Genesis 6:5 to 9:17, often called Noah's Flood or the Noachinan Deluge, repeats a theme found in many ancient Near Eastern traditions that describe a primordial destruction of the earth because of man's wickedness, with a faithful few being allowed to survive by intervention of God (or several gods), and the building of a huge boat or ark (61, 162). The biblical flood story clearly goes back to Mesopotamian sources originating with the Sumerians of the 4th millenium B.C. and is a part of the world's oldest known literature (166, 186). Reliable translations of the flood myth texts may be found in Pritchard (169); see also Jacobsen (87, 88), Kramer (97–99), and Speiser (190). Heidel provides a detailed discussion of Gilgamesh (79). Oppenheim (155) presents a good general account of the cultural background of Mesopotamia. Peake (163) reviews the world literature on flood myths.

Like the creation account, the Genesis flood story is a composite narrative; clearly one of the sources goes back to P, and probably J is the only other author involved (190). As in the Genesis account of the creation of man, there are obvious internal contradictions in the Genesis account of the flood, especially regarding the numbers of the various animals taken into the ark and the time schedule of the flood (190, p. 54).

Contenau (34, 35) speculates that the widespread flood myths of the ancient cultures record memories of the worldwide elevation in sea level at the end of the Pleistocene. Although the rise in sea level from the maxima of the Main Wurm and Wisconsin glaciations some 18,000 years B.P. was about 120 meters, and sufficient to drown the mouths of large streams in many parts of the world, the average rise in sea level was only 7–8 millimeters per year (60), so that is seems unlikely to be classified as a "flood."

In its full form, the Babylonian Flood Story contains nine points, and the same sequence of nine points occurs in the flood account from the Old Testament (58, pp. 42–43):

Babylonian Cuneiform	Genesis
1. The gods decide to make a flood	1. The Lord decides to destroy wicked mankind
2. The god Ea warns Artarhasis to build a ship	2. The Lord warns Noah to build an ark
3. He is to take his family and animals aboard	3. Noah is to take his family and animals aboard
4. The flood turns mankind into clay	4. The flood destroys all flesh
5. The ship grounds on Mount Nisir	5. The ark comes to rest on the Ararat mountains
6. Artarhasis learns when the waters have subsided by sending out a dove, a swallow, and a raven	6. Noah learns when the waters have subsided by sending out a dove, a swallow, and a raven
7. He offers sacrifice to the gods	7. He offers sacrifice to the Lord
8. The gods smell the sweet savor	8. The Lord smells the pleasing odor
9. The god Enlil blesses Artarhasis and his wife	9. God blesses Noah and his sons

The Historical and Archaeological Deluges

In 1929, excavating almost simultaneously, Langdon at Kish (101) and Woolley at Ur (211) announced archaeological evidence of the biblical flood. Mallowan (115) and Raikes (170) reexamine the historical and archaeological evidence on Noah's flood. Mallowan (116, p. 243–44) reached these conclusions: although the flood was not universal, it was exceptional among the long series of various cities in southern Babylonia; there are good reasons for claiming that alluvial mud deposits observed at Ur, Kish, and at Farah (Shuruppak) correspond with those described in the Gilgamesh epic and transmitted, perhaps through Canaanite myths, to the Old Testament; this flood was during the reign of the Sumerian king named Ziusudra at Shuruppak, precisely where a clean flood stratum has been found; and Ziusudra may be taken to mark the end of Early Dynastic I, for he was succeeded by a new dynasty at Kish which begins E.D. II.

In a review of Mesopotamian carbon-14 dates, Wright (212, p. 96) estimates that Early Dynastic I Period began after 3100 B.C. and ended 2800 B.C.

The Ur "flood" is now dated Late 'Ubeid at about 4500 B.C. The Abu Salabikh (Fara) flood is dated Early Dynastic I (about 2900 B.C.), and the Kish flood E. D. II (about 2700 B.C.), according to Moorey (135, p. 86). Thus the Fara and Kish floods, but not the Ur "flood," could be contemporary within their own range of carbon-14 dating errors. The floods at Fara and Kish, as Mallowan maintains, probably correspond to Noah's deluge.

Seemingly, in the absence of special field techniques not yet widely used in Mesopotamian excavations, "flood" layers are difficult to identify (103, 105). The Ur "flood" layers may be a dust dune (210a). The dune contains burials that are shallow and closely spaced throughout the period of deposition, precluding a long period under water (H. Wright 1984, personal communication). The "flood" clay at Ur may be from melted mud bricks (103). Kirkby (96) shows that the "flood" layer at Dar-Ul-Kazineh, investigated by Harmer & Thomas (cited in 105, pp. 32–33), is part of a piedmont colluvium.

A Post-Pleistocene Cataclysmic Flood

The Great Spokane Flood in Idaho and Washington at the end of the Pleistocene is probably the largest and most cataclysmic river flood known from geological evidence (7, 151). It occurred about 12,000 B.P. when a melting ice dam let out 3,300 cubic kilometers of water trapped in the Glen Fork tributary valley of the Columbia River in glacial Lake Missoula. According to Alden (7), the water reached a maximum flow of about 64 cubic kilometers per hour, equal to about ten times the normal flow of all rivers in the world. The flood covered nearly 8000 square kilometers of plateau land, extending far beyond the original river valley. Large current "ripples" of boulders and gravel were produced transverse to the direction of the flood torrent, forming a "channeled scabland." Newell (151) states, "While by no means a common event, the Spokane Flood is an example of a perfectly natural, if cataclysmic, process. If the flood geology of creationists were true, all the lands of the world would resemble the channeled scabland of Washington" (151, p. 40).

Biblical Chronology

The creationists accept 17th century estimates made by biblical scholars of the age of the world and of Noah's flood. Using several independent lines of evidence, most modern scientists estimate that the planet earth is older by six orders of magnitude (1), and that the origin of man (genus *Homo*) is greater by three orders of magnitude (19).

In order to have a critical understanding of "creation science" doctrine, it is necessary to examine the historical basis of such estimated biblical chronology.

James Ussher (1581–1656), sometimes written Usher, Archbishop of Armagh in Ireland and Vice Chancellor of Trinity College, Dublin, concluded from his extensive Old Testament studies, published 1650–1654 in *Annales Veteris et Novi Testamenti* (197), that earth and man had been created in 4004 B.C. His chronology was inserted in the margin of reference editions of English translations starting with a King James I Version issued in 1703 down to the Berkeley Version of 1959 (58). Carr (24) wrote a biography of Ussher.

Ussher inferred the date of the creation from the genealogies recorded in Genesis that tell the sequence of patriarchs and how old each patriarch was when his oldest son was born. Ussher followed the Hebrew text, adding the successive figures back from the Temple of Solomon (placed by modern scholars at either 968 B.C. or 959 B.C.), to date the Flood in 2349 B.C., 1656 years after the creation of Adam in 4004 B.C. Some difference of dating was possible because of textual ambiguities and differences between the Septuagint (with 2242 years from Adam to the Flood) and the Hebrew or Samaritan texts (with 2262 years). For example, Dr. John Lightfoot (1828–1889), Vice-Chancellor of Cambridge University and Bishop of Durham, placed the creation at 3928 B.C. Both scholars were more interested in establishing the birthdate of Jesus Christ, which most scholars today place either in the spring of 4 B.C. or in midwinter 5/4 B.C., say in December, 5 B.C. (59, p. 298), rather than the date of creation.

Daub (43) shows the widely quoted statement from A. D. White in *History of the Warfare of Science with Theology in Christendom* that ". . . man was created by the Trinity on October 23, 4004 B.C. at nine o'clock in the morning" (206, 1:9; Daub incorrectly cites 1895, p. 59). This quotation is not from Lightfoot's words (1822) but from the editor of his collected works, John Rogers Pitman, who accepted the year estimate of 4004 among several based on the Hebrew texts, and presented, in an editorial note to Ussher's text, the statement "Creation of the world (Sunday, Oct. 23) . . ." (111, 2:445.) Lightfoot himself supported the day as September 12 (then taken as the day of the autumnal equinox, as England had not yet adopted the Gregorian Calendar). Lightfoot supposed in commenting on Genesis 1:26 that man was created about the third hour of the Hebrew day, or about 9 o'clock in the morning. Opinion differs as to the day of the week, but some assume that the work of creation must have been completed on a Friday, since God rested the next day on the sabbath, Saturday.

Finegan (58) provides a detailed exposition on the principles of time reckoning in the ancient world and the problems of biblical chronology. It is interesting to note that Ussher's date for Noah's flood is 2349 B.C., the date from stratigraphic archaeology is about 3000 B.C., and that the modern estimate from carbon-14 is about 2800 B.C.!

"SCIENTIFIC" CREATIONISM AND THE COURTS

Of the three divisions of the American government, the courts have been more decisive in the evolution-creationism controversy than the executive or the legislative branches.

The courts have countered the creationist attempt to forbid the teaching of evolution in the public schools, to require that creationism be taught in the schools as science, to demand that it be given equal time with evolution; they have denied that "creation science" is a science. Three major trials require special mention: Scopes v. Tennessee in 1925, Epperson v. Arkansas in 1968, and McLean v. Board of Education in 1982.

The legal literature on the controversy is substantial. Le Clercq (104) considers at length the constitutional implications of the creationist efforts; his paper is an excellent starting place for the layman, with full citations of the cases. Wood (210) provides a nonlegal summary of issues on "scientific creationism" and the public schools. O'Neil (154) has a good introductory treatment of creationism, curriculum, and the constitution. Other valuable law review papers include Benkov & Rothstein (10), Lines (112), Greenberg (74), Gordon (69) with special attention to legal aspects of treating "creation science" as science, Dean (44) with regard to equal treatment problems, Taylor (195) concerning the McLean case, and Melnick (125), who argues that the influence of secular humanism has altered the very nature of the common law and the legal system away from the theistic concepts of law important in the foundation of western European civilization (125, 175). For philosophical and historical origins of constitutionalism see Friedrich (62) and Peaslee (164); for a general treatment of the United States Constitution see Corwin (38).

The complete text of the First Amendment to the Constitution is: "Congress shall make no law respecting an establishment of religion, or prohibiting the free exercise thereof; or abridging the freedom of speech or of the press; or the right of the people peaceably to assemble and to petition the Government for a redress of grievances." The 14th Amendment holds that citizenship rights are not to be abridged.

The Establishment and The Free Exercise Clauses have been of first importance in High Court decisions regarding the creation-evolution controversy (Le Clercq 104). A three-part test of the constitutionality of each law or act in question has emerged from establishment clause litigation: 1. a clearly secular legislative purpose, 2. a primary effect that neither advances nor prohibits religion, and 3. an avoidance of excessive governmental entanglement with religion. The Court repeatedly has recognized that tension inevitably exists between the Free Exercise and the Establishment Clauses. In order not to promote one without offending the other, states are required to maintain an attitude of "neutrality," neither "advancing" nor "inhibiting" religion [413 U.S. 788 (1973)].

Scopes v. State of Tennessee

Some legal scholars consider the Scopes or "Monkey" trial the most famous of all American court cases (106). Scopes was found guilty of teaching evolution as charged, but Tennessee's antievolutionary law was left intact. The trial received wide public attention because of the bizarre nature of the case, including the court's permitting Bryan to be a witness severely questioned by Darrow, but not permitting any of the defense scientific witnesses to take the stand. Scopes did much to defuse the political clout of the antievolutionary movement. The trial judge assessed a fine of $100.00 and Scopes appealed to the Tennessee Supreme Court. Although the court found that the statute itself was upheld, the assessment of the $100.00 fine against Scopes was found in violation of the Tennessee State Constitution which required any fine over $50.00 to be assessed only by jury. Since the statute in question provided for a minimum fine of $100.00, the court had no power to correct the error, and the lower court judgment was accordingly reversed. In order to put "the bizarre case" to rest, a *nolle prosequi* was suggested to the attorney general. Scopes went free, later to do graduate work in geology at the University of Chicago, and to work as a geologist for the Gulf Oil Company (30).

Kalven (92) concluded: "Along with the Sacco-Vanzetti case, it [Scopes] was one of the law cases of this century that drew the attention of the world to America. The case is at once regarded as a milestone in the history of American freedom and as a case that made America ridiculous in the eyes of the civilized world."

An exhaustive report of Scopes is in DeCamp (45). Fay-Cooper Cole, Professor of Anthropology at Chicago, was Darrow's expert on human evolution; Cole wrote an excellent account of the trial (30). Grabiner & Miller (72) hold that Scopes was not a victory for evolutionists, because the chilling effect of the antievolution laws from 1925 on resulted in a downgrading of evolution in nearly all high-school textbooks (see also 31).

When fundamentalist-sponsored legislation failed to eliminate the teaching of evolution in the public schools, the special creationists attempted to impose their minority view by way of school board regulation or state legislation requiring "balanced" teaching of a "theory of creation" alongside the theory of evolution (130, 199). The effort was nearly successful before the California Board in 1972 (129), but the attempt to secure their goals through litigation also failed (112).

McLean v. Arkansas Board of Education

The full text of the opinion by United States District Judge William R. Overton in McLean v. Arkansas has been reprinted (158–160); it is essential reading for anyone wishing to understand the current creationism-evolution controversy. Sullivan (194) presents an eyewitness account, and Parker (161) traces the history behind the McLean case.

The courts have avoided an inflexible definition of religion (10, p. 1140), using instead ideas and activities associated with traditional religions as a guide. For example, as in McLean, the courts have held that the concept of a supreme being is inherently religious and, therefore, because creation science presupposes the existence of supreme being and creator, will be considered religious.

The McLean court found that "a central premise [of fundamentalism] was always a literal interpretation of the Bible and a belief in the inerrancy of the Scriptures" (Judge Overton, 529 F Suppl. at 1259, 1981).

Creation science is a collection of statements that allege scientific support for the biblical account of creation of the earth, living organisms, and man. The creationists have attempted to secularize their religious beliefs in a "Scientific Creation Model" (13, 14).

In finding that the Arkansas Balanced Treatment Act had a primary effect of advancing religion, and thus was unconstitutional on the establishment clause, the court in the McLean case identified a legal definition of science based on the testimony of Ruse and other scientific witnesses. Judge Overton ruled that "... in a free society, knowledge does not require the imprimatur of legislation in order to become science. More precisely, the essential characteristics of science are: 1. It is guided by natural law; 2. It has to be explanatory by reference to natural law; 3. It is testable against the empirical world; 4. Its conclusions are tentative, i.e. are not necessarily the final word; and 5. It is falsifiable" (159, p. 175). Gordon (69, pp. 394–400) gives an excellent exposition of the scientific and legal aspects of the Overton definition. Background for the testimony of M. Ruse on the nature of science may be found in his *Philosophy of Biology* (177).

The court in the McLean case noted that settled case law rejected the contention that the theory of evolution is as unscientific as is creationism (see 69, notes 4 and 85, for legal details). Gordon (69, pp. 399–400) further shows that the theory of evolution exhibits the characteristics of science according to the legal definition.

"By utilizing the definition of science developed in McLean, courts facing future lawsuits in the creation-evolution controversy will be able to determine whether a state's activity is a legitimate exercise of its authority to determine the public school science curriculum" (Gordon 69, pp. 401–2).

"Since McLean is a trial court opinion, it can only follow the precedents of higher courts. However, this opinion demonstrates the difficulty ahead for other states which try to enact similar legislation. This case shows that under the present constitutional framework, no creation-science statutes which follow the approach of Act 590 will survive constitutional scrutiny" (Taylor 195, p. 329).

Bible study courses may be offered in public school without violating the constitution if they are "so planned and so taught as to constitute a secular and objective study of the Bible for its historic and literary worth" (Wiley v. Franklin 1979).

The federal courts have traditionally opposed state enactments prohibiting teaching evolution in public schools (10, 44, 74, 104). Also, state laws requiring equal time for teaching divine creation when evolution is taught have also been generally invalidated. Given the strength and organization of fundamentalist, Bible inerrant minority, and the nature of election and appointment to public office, antievolutionary regulations and state laws will continue to appear in the Bible Belt states. As Greenberg concluded (74, p. 486): "The persistence of the groups which back the bills has been unyielding, and the current reappearance of the laws in the form of balanced treatment acts indicate that the controversy is far from resolved."

The Creationist Textbook Watchers

Some fundamentalists claim that the teaching of evolution from public school textbooks is a root cause of the recent decline in the quality of grade and high school education in America, as documented by the Carnegie Report (23). Nelkin (148, 149) calls these critics the "Textbook Watchers." Her book is a defense of science against creationism with particular reference to the creationism-evolution controversy. She reports the dispute about a proposed curriculum in evolutionary anthropology called *Man: A Course of Study*.

In 1982, 17 states required that a public school textbook must be cleared by state authorities before a local district can buy it. The textbook watchers are particularly effective in Texas and California (129, 181, 188). The Texas textbook adoption system makes that state the largest mass purchaser of textbooks in the nation (53), with a textbook budget of $64 million in 1983 (81). Weinberg reports that, on Mrs. Gabler's initiative, "the [Texas] Board of Education adopted the requirement that texts which present evolution must treat it only as a theory, not as verifiable fact; must carry a statement to this effect in the front of the book; and must identify evolution as only one of several explanations of origins" (202, p. 543). Most of the watchers are intelligent, devoted, if misguided people. Sometimes their published statements exhibit more zeal than knowledge. Weinberg (202) relates that a lady from Mansfield, Texas, expressed skepticism that American cattle breeders use culling and artificial insemination as reported in a textbook, and asked: "On what facts are these assumptions based?" Hefley (78) gives a highly laudatory report on Norma Gabler of Texas, a leading textbook watcher.

The Textbook Watchers do have some effective, official opposition. The Board of Education of New York City decided in 1982 to reject the use of three biology texts because their treatment of evolution was not sufficiently thorough, and two texts were additionally unacceptable because of an uncritical endorsement of creationism. The texts were published by Prentice-Hall, Laidlaw Brothers, and Burgess Publishing Co. (*New York Times,* June 24, 1982, pp. A1, D23.) On June 25, 1982, a *New York Times* editorial entitled "A Fundamental Confusion" carried the following opening and closing paragraphs: "Censorship is shameful but bowdlerization is ridiculous. Textbook publishers commit both when, in surrender to certain fundamentalists, they put out texts on biology that soft-pedal its unifying explanatory system, the theory of evolution." . . . "The creationists' misplaced desire to protect their children's faith by attacking Darwin is a confusion that should not be extended into the classroom. Yet they have received misplaced encouragement from too many legislatures, school boards and compliant publishers. It was high time someone said no."

In 1984 two developments reversed the recent successes of the Textbook Watchers in Texas and Louisianna. Following a report critical of the quality of public education in Texas by a commission headed by industrialist Ross Perot, the sitting Board of Education was declared unconstitutional and replaced by a board more receptive to the teaching of evolution. Of the five biology texts approved by the new board, none mention biblical creationism (*Washington Post*, 2 Dec. 1984).

THE FACTS AND THEORIES OF EVOLUTION

The General Theory of Evolution

There are three great realms of general evolution: 1. cosmic evolution (22, 27, 37, 182), the development of the universe, the solar system, elements and substances, the continents, oceans, and atmosphere of earth; 2. organic evolution (50, 144, 183, 213–216), the development of living things; and 3. cultural evolution (123, 173, 192, 207), the development of human language and cultural behavior. The claims against evolution by "creation science" are contradicted by scientific facts and theories in all three realms of general evolution.

The general idea of "evolution," like that of "life," is difficult to define. Dobzhansky (48) suggests that "sustained change" comes as close as possible at present to a general definition. See Lewontin (108) for extensions of the general concept, and Bowler (18) for a convenient history of different meanings of the term "evolution."

Sorokin (189) held that evolution is "a dominant category of sensate mentality," and that "The standpoint of 'origin and development and evolution' is our main standpoint in studying anything, from religion to the stock market. It has rooted itself in our minds so deeply that many of us cannot even conceive of any other—nonhistorical, or nonevolutionary, or nondevelopmental—approach to the study of any phenomenon."

The central idea of evolution in its simplest form is that the current state of a system is the result of cumulative change from its original state, and that changes in structure and function of the system follow uniform laws. This may be called the narrow definition of general evolution. The narrow, minimal view becomes an increasingly broad set of views on evolution by adding one or more considerations: order, direction, progress, and perfectability (108). None of the broad evolutionary notions can be made a part of the minimal, narrow definition, because they do not hold for one or more of the important special realms of general evolution (37, 109).

The evolutionary view of things and events opposes a static view of the world, whether the stasis of a universe created only once, as in the Old Testament creation stories, or one created several times, as in the catastrophic view of Cuvier (42). Evolution involves the opposite ideas of persistence and change, but neither ceaseless change nor unchanging persistence is a part of evolution. Historically the conception of evolution is the development of a variety of entities, whether celestial bodies, chemical elements, geological formations, biological species, languages, items of material culture, economic or other cultural systems, by some dynamic process of cumulative change. New kinds of entities emerge as the outcome of change and then persist for a time after the new kind.

The theory of evolution is a fundamental part of a wide variety of modern sciences including astronomy, geology, botany, zoology, anthropology, linguistics, and economics (82). Today some consider evolution as mainly part of biology and as starting in 1859 with Charles Darwin. In fact, the theory is much older; Kant (93) and Laplace (102) published evolutionary accounts of the formation of suns and planets. The linguist William Jones (89) suggested that the similarities between Celtic, German, Greek, Latin, Persian, and Sanscrit languages could be explained by evolution from a common ancestral language (Greenberg 73). According to Singer (185), the first exact usage of organic evolution in the modern sense was in Lyell's *Principles of Geology* (114).

Organic Evolution

Life is not one of the fundamental categories of nature such as matter, energy, space, and time, which exist everywhere in the universe. Life was manifested only in certain biomolecules, especially nucleic acids and proteins. Life occurs in an environment where a system of macromolecules is capable of undergoing natural selection (41). This kind of environment and those kinds of large molecules could not exist when the earth was molten and will not exist when it becomes cold. Life on earth had a beginning and will have an end.

At an abstract genotypical level elegantly treatable with mathematics, the evolution of life is a history of cumulative change in gene frequencies (Dobzhansky et al 50, Wright 213–216). Evolution is the master concept of biology (49, 183). The ideas of evolution connect with and cut across all the large divisions of biology—genetic, structural, regulatory, developmental, and environmental.

The evolutionary path of life started when molecules capable of undergoing natural selection came into being, perhaps three to four billion years ago (22). Three processes define living organisms: 1. Organisms metabolize; they take raw materials from the outside and remake them inside into substances of the sort characteristic of the species and line. 2. Organisms replicate, then give rise to descendant organisms of the same variety. 3. Organisms mutate; some offspring are varied genetically but are capable of further replication in the mutant form.

Biological evolution proves that animals and plants living today are descended from different species living in the past, some leaving fossils that give historical evidence of phylogenetic relationships. The mechanism of evolution at the genotype-phenotype level is expressed in three principles: variation, heredity, and natural selection: 1. Members of a species are variable in structure, function, or behavior. 2. Some of the variation is inherited genetically. 3. Different variations have different rates of survival and reproduction in different environments, that is, the variation is subjected to natural selection. Four processes control the frequencies of genes in breeding populations: mutation, gene flow, selection, and genetic drift. Three systems of mating control the distribution of genes in genotypes: random, inbred, and assortative mating. The interaction of genotypes and environments control the expression of phenotypes. Varient phenotypes are subject to natural selection (77, 187, 213–216).

Evolutionary history displays both continuities and discontinuities, both unity and diversity. The unity of organisms is shown by the universality of the genetic code. Except for mitochondrial DNA, the genes of all organisms from virus to man are made of six molecules: two purines, two pyrimidines, a phosphate, and a sugar. All proteins of all organisms are synthesized from members of an identical set containing 20 amino acids, some of which are modified after being incorporated in the primary gene product.

Evidence for the facts of organic evolution, accumulated in the past 120 years, is from many different fields—biogeography, taxonomy, comparative anatomy, embryology, paleontology, biochemistry, genetics, cell physiology, and the study of cultivated plants and domestic animals (39, 183, 184, 215). Each field presents a body of data easily understandable on an evolutionary basis, but incomprehensible or even contradictory on any known theory in opposition. Everyone of open mind who has examined and understands the evidence—which takes some years of study to do—believes in the facts of evolution. There is a good deal of doubt as to some of the mechanisms of evolution, and as to the details of phyletic relations within some lines (55), but the general fact of organic evolution is as firmly established as the general fact of gravitation, or any other scientific theory (50, 109, 183, 187).

Molecular Evolution

There are two levels of organic evolution, the evolution of phenotypes and the evolution of molecules, especially the information molecules in the eukaryotic cell (95). Molecular biology has made spectacular progress in the three decades since Watson and Crick established the molecular structure of DNA, the genetic material (see 4). The concepts and methods of molecular biology furnish new insights into evolutionary processes and new methods in phylogenetics (9, 91). Molecular evolution makes possible identification of nodes in phylogenetic trees (points of origin of new species), and molecular clocks attach absolute dates to those branching points with acceptable accuracy (9).

CREATIONIST ARGUMENTS AGAINST EVOLUTION

The Second Law of Thermodynamics

Creationists repeatedly claim that evolution would violate the Second Law of Thermodynamics (Morris 141) because evolution implies the historical emergence of more highly ordered species that have lower entropy. Entropy is a quantity that measures the amount of energy in a system that is not available for doing work. One part of the Second Law, the Principle of the Increase of Entropy, states that the entropy of an adiabatically isolated system can never decrease (136). But the earth and the species that evolve on earth are not adiabatically isolated; for instance, they take in energy from the sun; thus the claim is false (15, 76, 143). Morris (141) accepts the fact that the earth is not an isolated system, but then repeals the Second Law by fiat: "the Second Law really applies only to open systems, since there is no such thing as a truly isolated system."

As Lotka (113) pointed out 60 years ago, if we consider that herbivores only appear to be hungry for grass, but that the grass is really hungry for oxygen with the animal performing a catalytic function, then energy is not diverted from its Second Law degradative trend in order to propagate and evolve species; rather the evolution of organisms is secondary to, in service of, and consonant with all natural processes that increase entropy (Black 15).

Failure to Observe Intermediate Steps in the Fossil Record

Creationists argue that gradual evolution is impossible because an eye or a middle ear must be complete and work perfectly in order to be favorably selected. Perhaps the most spectacular, gradual, morphological transition in the phylogeny of the vertebrates is the evolution of the mammalian masticatory apparatus and middle ear bones, a transition that is extremely well documented in comparative anatomy, embryology, and paleontology (40, 171, 174).

Failure to Directly Observe Evolution of Species

Creationists have claimed repeatedly that no living person has observed or will ever observe evolution from one "kind" of organism to another (66). The fact that plant and animal breeders have produced many new varieties of domesticated plants and animals led the creationists to redefine the biblical "kinds" as taxa above the species level or to make up undefined taxa (65, pp. 30–40; 139, p. 29).

Several new species have been created, or recreated, naturally or experimentally, and this trans-specific evolution has been observed directly (Stebbins 191). The grass *Spartina townsendii* is a wild species known to have originated in historic times under human observation. Huskins (84) showed that it is an allopolyploid derived from a natural cross between *S. alterniflora* × *S. stricta*. Several new artificial species were made by hybridizing two related species or even genera of plants; while many such hybrid plants are sterile, some that undergo chromosome doubling (polyploidy) are fertile, true breeding, and reproductively isolated from both parental species. Clausen & Goodspeed (26) synthesized a new species of tobacco, *Nicotiana digluta*, by hybridizing *N. tabacum* × *N. glutinosa*. One of the most spectacular of the experimentally created plant species is *Raphanobrassica* made by Karpenchenko (94), who crossed plants belonging to two different genera, a radish and a cabbage. Both the common radish *Raphanus sativus* and the cabbage *Brassica oleracea* have 9 pairs of chromosomes. The first-generation hybrid produced a few tetraploid seeds with 18 pairs of chromosomes, representing the entire genome of both parental species. *Raphanobrassica* is not important as a food plant because it has a cabbage-like root and a radish-like foliage. But the new species produces tall and vigorous plants which breed true and are reproductively isolated from both parental species. Muntzing (146) was the first to recreate experimentally a well-known Linnean species, the hempnettle *Galeopsis tetrahit*. A native of Eurasia, introduced into northeastern United States, this plant has $2N = 32$ chromosomes, while the related species of this mint family genus, *G. speciosa* and *G. pubescens*, has $2N = 16$. Muntzing crossed the latter two species to produce polyploid hybrid offspring with $2N = 32$. The newly created tetrahit plants are identical in morphology with the natural ones, cross freely with them, and produce fertile hybrids with normal mitotic and meiotic cell divisions. McFadden & Sears (121) experimentally resynthesized a species of bread wheat that is a naturally existing allopolyploid species. This is a case where a species that became completely extinct could be artificially recreated!

Species formation by allopolyploidy is widespread and important in some plant families; it is uncommon in vertebrates including mammals, mostly because the process upsets the specialized chromosomal, sex-determination mechanism (50). Among vertebrates, speciation often results from the gradual accumulation of genetic differences between geographically isolated (allopatric) populations followed by emergence of reproductive isolation between them (50, 118, 119). By means of laboratory selection through many generations, Dobzhansky & Pavlovsky (51) experimentally created the Llanos incipient species of *Drosophila* which exhibited behavioral (sexual) isolation from its ancestral Orinocan semispecies of *D. paulistorum*.

The H3 hemagglutinin genes of two strains of Hong Kong influenza virus illustrate very rapid evolution. Sequencing shows that each gene contains 1701 nucleotide sites. In the two strains, 63 sites have different nucleotides, 34 of these representing silent substitutions, so that the two strains differ by 28 amino acid substitutions. The degree of protein evolution by gene mutation and amino acid replacement corresponds to the evolutionary change in mammalian hemoglobin genes over 30 to 50 million years. Yet the time of divergence in the influenza virus strains is only 7 years (198).

Scientific refutations of other major arguments against evolution by "creation scientists" include: (a) the Young Earth claim, that the earth and universe are only about 10,000 years old (1, 20, 22, 28, 145); (b) improbability of the Random Origin of Life (22, 52); (c) the concept of natural selection is tautological and untestable (70, 76, 117, 128); (d) Noah's flood was universal and destroyed all living species not aboard the ark (68, 151).

CONCLUSION

"In all modern history, interference with science in the supposed interest of religion, no matter how conscientious such interference may have been, has resulted in the direst evils both to religion and to science, and invariably; and, on the other hand, all untrammeled scientific investigation, no matter how dangerous to religion some of its stages may have seemed for the time to be, has invariably resulted in the highest good both of religion and of science" (A. D. White, 206, p. viii).

Literature Cited

1. Abell, G. O. 1983. The ages of the earth and the universe. See Ref. 67, pp. 33–47
2. Adler, M. J. 1941. Solution of the species problem. *Thomist* 3:279–379
3. Adler, M. J. 1967. *The Difference of Man and the Difference it Makes.* New York: Holt, Rinehart & Winston
4. Alberts, B., Bray, D., Lewis, J., Raff, M., Roberts, K., Watson, J. D. 1983. *Molecular Biology of the Cell.* New York: Garland
5. Albright, W. F. 1957. *From the Stone Age to Christianity: Monotheism and the Historical Process.* Baltimore: Johns Hopkins Press
6. Albright, W. F., Mann, C. S. 1971. Matthew. *The Anchor Bible*, Vol. 26. Garden City, NY: Doubleday
7. Alden, W. C. 1953. Physiography and glacial geology of western Montana and adjacent areas. *U.S. Geol. Surv. Prof. Pap. 231*
8. Astruc, J. 1753. Conjectures sur les memoires originaux dont it paroit que Moyse s'est servi pour composer le livre de las Genese. A Bruxelles, chez Friex
9. Ayala, F. J., ed. 1976. *Molecular Evolution*. Sunderland, Mass: Sinauer
10. Benkov, J. L., Rothstein, M. 1982. The lessons of creation-science: Public school curriculum and the religious clauses. *Fordham Law Rev.* 50:1113–56
11. Benoit, P. 1961. *Prophecy and Inspiration.* New York: Cerf
12. Beyerlin, W. 1966. *Origins and History of Old Sinaitic Traditions,* transl. S. Rudman. Oxford: Blackwell
13. Bird, W. R. 1978. Freedom of religion and science instruction in public schools. *Yale Law J.* 87:515–70
14. Bird, W. 1979. Freedom from establishment and unneutrality in public school instruction and religious school regulation. *Harvard J. Law Public Policy* 28:125–205
15. Black, S. 1978. On the thermodynamics of evolution. *Perspect. Biol. Med.* 14:348–56
16. Bliss, R. B. 1978. *A comparison of two approaches to the teaching of origins of living things to high school biology students in Racine, Wisconsin.* PhD thesis. Univ. Sarasota, Fla.
17. Boadt, L. 1982. Countering the creationists: The theologian. *Academe* 68:17–20
18. Bowler, P. J. 1983. The changing meaning of "evolution." *J. Hist. Ideas* 36:95–114
19. Brace, C. L. 1983. Humans in time and space. See Ref. 67, pp. 245–82
20. Brush, S. C. 1983. Ghosts from the nineteenth century: Creationists arguments for a young earth. See Ref. 67, pp. 49–84

21. Burgon, J. W. 1861. *Inspirations and Interpretations*. Oxford: Parker
22. Calvin, M. 1969. *Chemical Evolution*. Oxford: Clarendon
23. Carnegie Foundation for the Advancement of Teaching. 1977. *Missions of the College Curriculum*. San Francisco: Jossey-Bass
24. Carr, J. A. 1895. *The Life of James Ussher, Archbishop of Armagh*. London: Gardner, Darton
25. Carter, J. 1976. Jimmy Carter on evolution. *Humanist* 36(6):2
26. Clausen, R. T., Goodspeed, T. H. 1925. Interspecific hybridization in *Nicotiana*, II. A tetrapoid glutinosa-*Tabacum* hybrid, an experimental verification of Winge's hypothesis. *Genetics* 10:279–84
27. Cloud, P. 1972. Scientific creationism—a new inquisition brewing. *Humanist* 37:6–15
28. Cloud, P. 1978. *Cosmos, Earth, and Man: A Short History of the Universe*. New Haven: Yale Univ. Press
29. Cohen, M. R., Nagel, E. 1934. *An Introduction to Logic and Scientific Method*. New York: Harcourt, Brace
30. Cole, F-C. 1959. A witness at the Scopes trial. *Sci. Am.* 200(1):120–30
31. Cole, J. R. 1983. Scopes and beyond: Antievolutionism and American culture. See Ref. 67, pp. 13–32
32. Cole, S. G. 1931. *The History of Fundamentalism*. New York: Smith
33. Committee on Science and Creationism. 1984. *Science and Creationism: A View of the National Academy of Sciences*. Washington DC: Natl. Acad. Press
34. Contenau, G. 1941. *Le deluge babylonien*. Paris: Payot
35. Contenau, G. 1954. *Everyday Life in Babylon and Assyria*, transl. K. R. & A. R. Maxwell-Hyslop. London: Arnold
36. Cooper, J. M. 1935. The scientific evidence bearing on human evolution. *Primitive Man* 8:1–56
37. Corson, D. W., ed. 1977. *Man's Place in the Universe: Changing Concepts*. Tucson: Coll. Liberal Arts, Univ. Arizona
38. Corwin, E. S. 1958. *The Constitution and What it Means Today*. Princeton: Princeton Univ. Press. 14th ed.
39. Cracraft, J. 1983. Systematics, comparative biology, and the case against creationism. See Ref. 67, pp. 163–91
40. Crompton, A. W., Parker, P. 1978. Evolution of the mammalian masticatory apparatus. *Am. Sci.* 66:192–201
41. Crow, J. F. 1958. Some possibilities for measuring selection intensities in man. In *Natural Selection in Man*, ed. J. N. Spuhler. *Mem. Am. Anthropol. Assoc.* 86:1–13
42. Cuvier, G. 1831. *A discourse on the revolutions of the surface of the globe, and the changes thereby produced in the animal kingdom*. Philadelphia: Carey & Lee
43. Daub, E. R. 1978. Demythologizing White's *Warfare of Science with Theology*. *Am. Biol. Teach.* 40:553–56
44. Dean, S. D. 1983. First amendment concerns regarding balanced science instruction in evolution and creation. *Ohio N. Univ. Law Rev.* 10:145–58
45. DeCamp, L. S. 1969. The end of the monkey war. *Sci. Am.* 220(2):15–21
46. De Puy, N. R. 1981. Baptist churches. *1981 Britannica Book of the Year*, p. 597. Chicago: Encyclopaedia Britannica
47. DeVaux, R. 1961. *Ancient Israel: Its Life and Institutions*, transl. J. McHugh. New York: McGraw Hill
48. Dobzhansky, T. 1967. *The Biology of Ultimate Concern*. New York: New Am. Library
49. Dobzhansky, T. 1973. Nothing in biology makes sense except in the light of evolution. *Am. Biol. Teach.* 35:125–29
50. Dobzhansky, T., Ayala, F. J., Stebbins, G. L., Valentine, J. W. 1977. *Evolution*. San Francisco: Freeman
51. Dobzhansky, T., Pavlovsky, D. 1971. Experimentally created incipient species of *Drosophila*. *Nature* 230:289–92
52. Doolittle, R. F. 1983. Probability and the origin of life. See Ref. 67, pp. 85–97
53. Edgar, J. W. 1976. *Proclamation/Textbook Adoption*. Austin: Texas Educ. Agency
53a. Education Committee of the American Society of Zoologists. 1984. Science as a way of knowing—evolutionary biology. *Am. Zool.* 24(2):421–534
54. Eiselen, F. C., Lewis, E., Downey, D. G., eds. 1929. *The Abingdon Bible Commentary*. New York: Abingdon Press
55. Eldridge, N., Gould, S. J. 1972. Punctuated equilibria: An alternative to phyletic gradualism. In *Models in Paleobiology*, ed. T. J. M. Schopf, pp. 82–115. San Francisco: Freeman, Cooper Publ.
56. Falwell, J. 1981. Quoted on absolute infallibility of the Bible. *Ecumenist* 19(1):26
57. Finegan, J. 1959. *Light from the Ancient Past; The Archaeological Background of Judaism and Christianity*. Princeton: Princeton Univ. Press. 2nd ed.
58. Finegan, J. 1964. *Handbook of Biblical Chronology: Principles of Time Reckoning in the Ancient World and Problems of Chronology in the Bible*. Princeton: Princeton Univ. Press
59. Fitzmyer, J. A. 1981. The Gospel

according to Luke, I–IX. *The Anchor Bible*, Vol. 28. Garden City, NY: Doubleday
60. Flint, R. F. 1957. *Glacial and Pleistocene Geology*. New York: Wiley
61. Frazer, J. G. 1923. *Folk-lore in the Old Testament: Studies in Comparative Religion, Legend and Law*, 3 vols. London: Macmillan
62. Friedrich, C. J. 1968. *Constitutional Government and Democracy: Theory and Practice in Europe and America*. Waltham, Mass: Blaisdell. 4th ed.
63. Gardner, M. 1957. *Fads and Fallacies in the Name of Science*. New York: Dover
64. Gasper, L. 1963. *The Fundamentalist Movement*. New York: Humanities Press
65. Gilkey, L. 1959. *Maker of Heaven and Earth: A Study of the Christian Doctrine of Creation*. Berkeley: Univ. Calif. Press
66. Gish, D. T. 1979. *Evolution? The Fossils say No!* San Diego: Creation-Life Publishers
67. Godfrey, L. R., ed. 1983. *Scientists Confront Creationism*. New York: Norton
68. Godfrey, L. R. 1983. Creationism and gaps in the fossil record. See Ref. 67, pp. 193–218
69. Gordon, R. M. 1982. Finding the science in "creation science." Case note, McLean vs. Arkansas Board of Education. *Northwestern Univ. Law Rev.* 77:374–402
70. Gould, S. J. 1983. Darwin's untimely burial—again! See Ref. 67, pp. 139–46
71. Gosse, P. 1857. *Omphalos*. London: Van Voorst
72. Grabiner, J. V., Miller, P. D. 1974. Effects of the Scopes trial. *Science* 185:832–37
72a. Graves, R., Patai, R. 1983. *Hebrew Myths: The Book of Genesis*. New York: Greenwich House
73. Greenberg, J. H. 1959. Language and evolution. In *Evolution and Anthropology: A Centennial Appraisal*, ed. B. Meggers, pp. 61–72. Washington DC: Anthropol. Soc. Washington
74. Greenberg, M. M. 1983. The constitutional issues surrounding the science-religion conflict in public schools: The anti-evolution controversy. *Pepperdine Law Rev.* 10:461–87
75. Hailman, J. P. 1982. Creation stories. *BioScience* 32:129–30
76. Harris, C. L. 1981. *Evolution: Genesis and Revelations*. Albany: State Univ. New York Press
77. Hartl, D. L. 1980. *Principles of Population Genetics*. Sunderland, Mass: Sinauer
78. Hefley, J. C. 1976. *Textbooks on Trial*. Wheaton, Ill: Victor Books
79. Heidel, A. 1949. *The Gilgamesh Epic and the Old Testament Parallels*. Chicago: Univ. Chicago Press. 2nd ed.
80. Heidel, A. 1951. *The Babylonian Genesis*. Chicago: Univ. Chicago Press. 2nd ed.
81. Hentoff, N. 1984. The dumbing of America. *Progressive* 48(2):29–31
82. Hirshleifer, J. 1982. Evolutionary models in economics and law. *Res. Law Econ.* 4:1–60
83. Holden, C. 1980. Republican candidate picks a fight with Darwin. *Science* 209:1214
84. Huskins, C. L. 1934. The origin of *Spartina townsendii*. *Genetics* 12:531–38
85. Hutchinson, G. E. 1983. What is science for? *Am. Sci.* 71:639–44
86. Hupfeld, H. 1853. *Qvaestionvm in Iobeidos locos vexatos specimen*. Italis Saxonvm: Prostat apud E. Anton
87. Jacobsen, T. 1970. *Toward the Image of Tamuz and Other Essays on Mesopotamian History and Culture*. Cambridge, Mass: Harvard Univ. Press
88. Jacobsen, T. 1976. *The Treasures of Darkness: A History of Mesopotamian Religion*. New Haven: Yale Univ. Press
89. Jones, W. 1788–1790. *Asiatick Researches*, Vols. 1–3. Calcutta: Asiatic Soc. of Bengal
90. Jorstad, E. T. 1970. *The Politics of Doomsday: Fundamentalist of the Far Right*. Nashville: Abingdon
91. Jukes, T. H. 1983. Molecular evidence for evolution. See Ref. 67, pp. 117–38
92. Kalven, H. Jr. 1960. A commemorative case note: *Scopes v. State*. *Univ. Chicago Law Rev.* 27:505–21
93. Kant, I. 1969. *Universal Natural History and Theory of the Heavens*, transl. W. Hastie. Ann Arbor: Univ. Mich. Press
94. Karpenchenko, G. D. 1928. Polyploid hybrids of *Raphanus sativis* L. × *Brassica oleracea* L. *Z. Indukt. Abstamm. Vererbungsl.* 39:1–7
95. Kimura, M. 1983. *The Neutral Theory of Molecular Evolution*. Cambridge: Cambridge Univ. Press
96. Kirkby, M. 1976. Land and water resources of the Deh Luran and Khuzistan Plain. *Mem. Univ. Mich. Mus. Anthropol.* 9:251–88
97. Kramer, S. N. 1961. *Sumerian Mythology*. New York: Harper & Row. Rev. ed.
98. Kramer, S. N. 1963. *The Sumerians: Their History, Culture, and Character*. Chicago: Univ. Chicago Press
99. Kramer, S. N. 1981. *History Begins at Sumer: Thirty-nine Firsts in Man's Recorded History*. Philadelphia: Univ. Penn. Press. 3rd ed.
100. Kluckhohn, C. 1939. The place of theory

in anthropological studies. *Philos. Sci.* 6:328–44
101. Langdon, S. 1929. *Excavations at Kish.* London: Luzak
102. Laplace, P. S. 1809. *The System of the World,* transl. J. Pond, 2 vols. London: Phillips
103. Larsen, C. E. 1975. The Mesopotamian delta region: A reconsideration of Lees and Falcon. *J. Am. Orient. Soc.* 95:43–57
104. Le Clercq, F. W. 1974. The monkey laws and the public schools: A second consumption. *Vanderbilt Law Rev.* 27:209–42
105. Lees, J. M., Falcon, N. L. 1952. The geological history of the Mesopotamian Plains. *Geogr. J.* 118:24–39
106. Levy, L. E., ed. 1971. The world's most famous court trial. *State of Tennessee v. John Thomas Scopes.* New York: Da Capa
107. Lewis, S. 1927. *Elmer Gantry.* New York: Knopf
108. Lewontin, R. C. 1968. The concept of evolution. *Int. Encycl. Soc. Sci.* 5:202–10
109. Lewontin, R. C. 1974. *The Genetic Basis of Evolutionary Change.* New York: Columbia Univ. Press
110. Lewontin, R. C. 1983. Introduction. See Ref. 67, pp. xxiii–vi
111. Lightfoot, J. 1823–25. *The Whole Works of the Rev. John Lightfoot, D.D.,* ed. Rev. John Rogers Pitman, 13 vols. London: Dove
112. Lines, P. M. 1982. Scientific creationism in the classroom: A constitutional dilemma. *Loyola Law Rev.* 28:35–59
113. Lotka, A. J. 1925. *Elements of Physical Biology.* Baltimore: Williams & Wilkins
114. Lyell, C. 1833. *Principles of Geology.* London: Mumford
115. Mallowan, M. E. L. 1964. Noah's flood reconsidered. *Iraq* 26:62–82
116. Mallowan, M. E. L. 1971. The Early Dynastic Period in Mesopotamia. In *Cambridge Ancient History,* ed. I. E. S. Edwards, C. J. Gadd, N G L. Hammond, 1(2):238–314. Cambridge: Cambridge Univ. Press. 3rd ed.
117. Mayer, W. V. 1982. Evolutionary theory vs. creationist doctrine. *J. Col. Sci. Teach.* 11:270–76
118. Mayr, E. 1970. *Populations, Species and Evolution.* Cambridge: Harvard Univ. Press
119. Mayr, E. 1976. *Evolution and the Diversity of Life.* Cambridge: Harvard Univ. Press
120. Mayr, E., Provine, W. B., eds. 1980. *Perspectives on the Unification of Biology.* Cambridge: Harvard Univ. Press
121. McFadden, E. S., Sears, E. R. 1946. The origin of *Triticum spelta* and its free-threshing hexaploid relatives. *J. Hered.* 37:81–89, 107–16
122. McKim, P. 1983. Evolution vs creation: A selected bibliography. *Anthropol. Newsl.* 24(7):5, 9
123. Mead, M. 1964. *Continuities in Cultural Evolution.* New Haven: Yale Univ. Press
124. Megivern, J., ed. 1978. *Bible Interpretation: Official Catholic Teachings.* Wilmington, NC: Consortium Books
125. Melnick, R. R. 1981. Secularism in the law: The religion of secular humanism. *Ohio N. Univ. Law Rev.* 8:329–57
126. Mencken, H. L. 1930. *Treatise on the Gods.* New York: Knopf
127. Messenger, E. C. 1932. *Evolution and Theology.* New York: Macmillan
128. Mills, S. K., Beatty, J. H. 1979. The propensity interpretation of fitness. *Philos. Sci.* 46:263–86
129. Moore, J. A. 1974. Creationism in California. *Daedalus* 103:173–89
130. Moore, J. A. 1975. On giving equal time to the teaching of evolution and creation. *Perspect. Biol. Med.* 18:405–17
131. Moore, J. A. 1982. Countering the creationists: The scientist. *Academe* 68(2):14–16
132. Moore, J. A. 1982. Evolution and public education. *BioScience* 32:606–12
133. Moore, J. R. 1975. Evolutionary theory and Christian faith: A bibliographic guide to the post-Darwinian controversies. *Christian Sci. Rev.* 4:211–30
134. Moore, J. R. 1979. *The post-Darwinian Controversies.* Cambridge: Cambridge Univ. Press
135. Moorey, P. R. S. 1979. *Kish Excavations, 1923–1933.* Oxford: Clarendon
136. Morowitz, H. J. 1970. *Entropy for Biologists: Fundamental Concepts of Thermodynamics.* New York: Academic
137. Morris, H. M. 1965. *Science, Scripture and Salvation.* Denver: Accent Books
138. Morris, H. M. 1973. Geology and the flood. *ICR Impact Ser. No. 6*
139. Morris, H. M. 1974. *Scientific Creationism,* General edition and Public School edition. San Diego: Creation-Life Publishers
140. Morris, H. M. 1974. *Many Infallible Proofs.* San Diego: Creation-Life Publishers
141. Morris, H. M. 1976. *Entropy and Open Systems.* San Diego: Inst. Creation Research
142. Morris, H. M. 1977. *In the Beginning of the World.* Denver: Accent Books
143. Morse, P. 1974. *Thermal Physics.* New York: Benjamin

144. Motulsky, A. G. 1974. "Brave New World?" *Science* 185:653–63
145. Moyer, W. A. 1983. Young earth creationism and biology textbooks. *BioScience* 33:113–14
146. Muntzing, A. 1930. Uber Chromosomenvermehrung in Galeopsis-Kreuzungen und ihre phylogenetische Bedeutung. *Hereditas* 17:131–54
147. Nebelsick, H. 1983. *Theology and Science in Mutual Modification.* New York: Oxford Univ. Press
148. Nelkin, D. 1977. *Science Textbook Controversies and the Politics of Equal Time.* Cambridge, Mass: MIT Press
149. Nelkin, D. 1981. *The Creation Controversy: Science and Scripture in the Schools.* New York: Norton
150. New York Times. 1982. Report of Gallup poll on belief in evolution in the United States. Aug. 29, p. 21
151. Newell, N. 1982. *Creation and Evolution: Myth or Reality?* Irvington, NY: Columbia Univ. Press
152. Noth, M. 1960. *The History of Israel,* transl. P. R. Ackroyd. London: Black. 2nd ed.
153. Noth, M. 1972. *A History of Pentateuchal Traditions,* transl. B. W. Anderson. Englewood Cliffs, NJ: Prentice-Hall
154. O'Neil, R. M. 1982. *Creationism, Curriculum and the Constitution. Academe* 68(2):17–200
155. Oppenheim, A. L. 1977. *Ancient Mesopotamia. Portrait of a Dead Civilization.* Chicago: Univ. Chicago Press. 2nd ed.
156. Orr, J. 1906. *The Problem of the Old Testament Considered with Respect to Current Criticism.* New York: Scribner
157. O'Toole, G. B. 1925. *The Case Against Evolution.* New York: Macmillan
158. Overton, W. R. 1982. Creationism in schools. The decision in McLean versus the Arkansas Board of Education. *Science* 215:934–43
159. Overton, W. R. 1982. Creationism in schools. The Arkansas decision. *Am. Biol. Teach.* 44:172–79
160. Overton, W. R. 1982. Rev. Bill McLean vs. Arkansas Board of Education. *Academe* 68:27–36
161. Parker, F. 1982. Behind the evolution-creation science controversy. *Coll. Board Rev.* 123:18–21, 37
162. Parrot, A. 1953. *The Flood and Noah's Ark.* New York: Philosophical Library
163. Peake, H. 1930. *The Flood. New Light on an Old Story.* London: K. Paul, Trench, Trubner
164. Peaslee, A. J. 1974. *Constitutions of Nations.* The Hague: Martinus Nijhoff. 4th ed.
165. Pipho, C. 1981. Scientific creationism: A case study. *Educ. Urban Soc.* 13:219–33
166. Poebel, A. 1947. *Miscellaneous Studies.* Chicago: Univ. Chicago Press
167. Pope John Paul II. 1981. Address to the members of the Pontifical Academy of Sciences. *Origins* 11:279
168. Price, G. M. 1923. *The New Geology.* Mountain View, Calif: Pacific Press
169. Pritchard, J. B., ed. 1969. *Ancient Near Eastern Texts Relating to the Old Testament.* Princeton: Princeton Univ. Press. 3rd ed.
170. Raikes, R. L. 1966. The physical evidence for Noah's flood. *Iraq* 28:52–63
171. Raup, D. M. 1983. The geological and paleontological arguments of creationism. See Ref. 67, pp. 147–62
172. Renckens, H. 1964. *Israel's Concept of the Beginning. The Theory of Genesis 1–3,* transl. C. Napier. New York: Herder & Herder
173. Riddle, O. 1942. *The Teaching of Biology in the Secondary Schools of the United States.* Washington DC: Union of Am. Biol. Sci.
174. Romer, A. S. 1966. *Vertebrate Paleontology.* Chicago: Univ. Chicago Press. 3rd ed.
175. Rosenfeld, M. 1982. Darwin and the Bible in federal court. *New York Law J.* 187(2):2
176. Rowley, H. H. 1950. *From Joseph to Joshua: Biblical Traditions in the Light of Archaeology.* London: Oxford Univ. Press
177. Ruse, M. 1973. *The Philosophy of Biology.* London: Hutchinson
178. Russell, B. 1929. *Our Knowledge of the External World.* New York: Norton. 2nd ed.
179. Sahlins, M. D., Service, E. R., eds. 1960. *Evolution and Culture.* Ann Arbor: Univ. Mich. Press
180. Sandeen, E. R. 1970. *The Roots of Fundamentalism.* Grand Rapids, Mich: Baker Books
181. Scheid, D. E. 1983. Evolution and creationism in the public schools. *J. Contemp. Law* 9:81–126
182. Shapley, H. 1960. *Of Stars and Men.* New York: Washington Square Press
183. Simpson, G. G. 1967. *The Meaning of Evolution: A Study in the History of Life and its Significance for Man.* New Haven: Yale Univ. Press. 2nd ed.
184. Simpson, G. G. 1977. A new heaven and a new earth and a new man. See Ref. 33, pp. 53–75
185. Singer, C. 1959. *A History of Biology.* London: Abelard-Schuman. 3rd ed.
186. Smith, G. 1880. *The Chaldean Account of Genesis.* London: Sampson Low

187. Smith, J. M. 1975. *The Theory of Evolution*. London: Penguin Books
188. Snow, T. 1976. *Bill of Particulars*. Austin: Texas Educ. Agency
189. Sorokin, P. A. 1937. *Social and Cultural Dynamics*, 4 vols. New York: Bedminster Press
190. Speiser, E. A. 1964. *Genesis. The Anchor Bible*, Vol. 1. Garden City, NY: Doubleday
191. Stebbins, G. L. 1950. *Variation and Evolution in Plants*. New York: Columbia Univ. Press
192. Steward, J. H. 1977. *Evolution and Ecology*. Urbana: Univ. Ill. Press
193. Strong, A. H. 1889. *Systematic Theology*. New York: Armstrong. 2nd ed.
194. Sullivan, L. L. 1982. The Arkansas landmark court challange of creation science. *Coll. Board Rev.* 123:12–17, 32–35
195. Taylor, M. F. 1983. Creation science's first confrontation with the Establishment Clause. Case note. McLean vs. Board of Education. *Arkansas Law Rev.* 36:326–37
196. Tillich, P. 1951. *Systematic Theology*, 3 vols. Chicago: Univ. Chicago Press
197. Ussher, J. 1847–64. *The Whole Works of the Most Rev. James Ussher*, 17 vols. Dublin: Hodges & Smith
198. Verhoeyen, M., Fang, R., Jou, W. M., Devos, R., Huylebroeck, D., et al. 1980. Antigenic drift between the haemoagglutinin of Hong Kong influenza strains A/Aichi/2/68 and A/Victoria/3/75. *Nature* 286:771–76
199. Wade, N. 1972. Creationists and evolutionists: Confrontation in California. *Science* 178:724–29
200. Watch Tower Bible & Tract Society. 1950. *Evolution Versus the New World*. Brooklyn: Int. Bible Students Assoc.
201. Watch Tower Bible & Tract Society. 1967. *Did Man Get Here by Evolution or by Creation?* Brooklyn: Int. Bible Students Assoc.
202. Weinberg, S. L. 1978. Two views on the Textbook Watchers. *Am. Biol. Teach.* 40:541–45, 56
203. Wellhausen, J. 1885. *Prolegomena to the History of Israel*, transl. J. S. Black. Edinburgh: Black
204. Wellhausen, J. 1963. Die Composition des Hexateuchs und der historischen Bucher des Alten Testaments, 4. Auf. Berlin: W. DeGruyter
205. West, J. K. 1981. *Introduction to the Old Testament*. New York: Macmillan. 2nd ed.
206. White, A. D. 1895. *A History of the Warfare of Science with Theology in Christendom*. London: Macmillan
207. White, L. A. 1959. *The Evolution of Culture*. New York: McGraw-Hill
208. Whitehead, A. N. 1926. *Religion in the Making*. New York: Macmillan
209. Williams, R. C. 1983. Scientific creationism: An exegesis for a religious doctrine. *Am. Anthropol.* 85:91–102
210. Wood, J. E. Jr. 1982. "Scientific creationism" and the public schools. *J. Church State* 24:231–43
210a. Woolley, C. L. 1956. *Ur: The Early Period (Ur Excavations IV)*. Philadelphia: British Museum and Univ. Penn. Museum
211. Woolley, C. L. 1929. *Ur of the Chaldees*. London: Benn
212. Wright, H. 1980. Problems of absolute chronology in protohistoric Mesopotamia. *Paléorient* 6:93–96
213. Wright, S. 1968. *Evolution and the Genetics of Populations*. Vol. 1, *Genetic and biometric foundations*. Chicago: Univ. Chicago Press
214. Wright, S. 1969. See Ref. 213, Vol. 2, *The theory of gene frequencies*
215. Wright, S. 1977. See Ref. 213, Vol. 3, *Experimental results and theoretical deductions*
216. Wright, S. 1978. See Ref. 213, Vol. 4, *Variability within and among populations*
217. Wysong, R. L. 1976. *The Creation-Evolution Controversy*. Midland, Mich: Inquiry Press
218. Zetterberg, P. 1983. *Evolution versus Creationism: The Public Education Controversy*. Phoenix: Oryx

THE USE OF STATISTICS IN SOCIOCULTURAL ANTHROPOLOGY

Michael Chibnik

Department of Anthropology, University of Iowa, Iowa City, Iowa 52242

INTRODUCTION

Sociocultural anthropologists have never used statistics as much as their colleagues in other social sciences. When sociologists (92), political scientists (33), and economists (98) were urging the increased use of statistics in their disciplines in the 1920s, Boas (7, p. 120) was asserting that the success of attempts to apply statistics to ethnographic phenomena was "more than doubtful." Kluckhohn (73, p. 350) wrote a decade later that the professional folklore included an a priori resistance to any use of statistics; and even as recently as the 1950s, Driver (28, p. 54) stated that anthropologists avoided mathematics and statistics "like the mother-in-law." Early statistical analyses, moreover, were largely restricted to cross-cultural comparisons (e.g. 29, 58, 90). Although quantitative data were sometimes collected in field work, analyses of such data rarely went beyond tabular presentations and calculations of means and medians.

In the 1950s and 1960s the use of mathematics in sociocultural anthropology increased dramatically (66; 123, pp. 2–5) and statistical analyses of field data became common. While new theoretical and methodological orientations in anthropology (see 62, 91, 96, 97) obviously influenced this increased emphasis on quantification, the changing nature of field work was also important. Whereas most ethnographers in the earlier part of the century tried to provide holistic descriptions of many aspects of culture, by the 1950s research tended to be problem-oriented, emphasizing intensive examinations of particular topics. Since problem-oriented studies often involved the systematic collection of quantitative data, the need for statistical methods of description and inference became apparent. The statistics used in the 1950s and 1960s, however, tended to be rather simple bivariate tests of significance and measures of association rather than the multivariate methods increasingly employed by psychologists and sociologists. Reviews of "mathematical anthropology" written at the end of this period (12, 59, 66, 132) emphasized model building and abstract algebra more than statistics. Kay (66, p. xvi) predicted that anthropologists in the future would use abstract algebra more than statistics and speculated that there would be a slight deemphasis on correlational methods and a great deemphasis on tests of significance.

Kay's predictions have not been fulfilled. While algebraic modeling is still occasionally attempted (e.g. 3, 126, 127), the most striking development in mathematical and quantitative anthropology in the past decade has been the increased use of multivariate statistical methods. Computer packages have allowed researchers with limited statistical expertise to use complex analytic methods such as multiple regression, path analysis, and multidimensional scaling. Furthermore, simpler bivariate statistics involving correlation measures and tests of significance are now routinely included in articles in North American journals and are not uncommon in publications elsewhere.

The types of data collected by sociocultural anthropologists conducting field work frequently pose problems for statistical analyses. Samples are usually small, and causal connections between numerous possibly important variables are often complex. The extent of quantification that is possible for many important variables is limited. An excellent book on research methods (97) and a sensible although unfortunately error-riddled text (123) discuss the use of bivariate statistics despite these problems. However, no comprehensive discussion of the use of multivariate statistics by anthropologists has yet been published.

This review of the recent use of statistics by sociocultural anthropologists emphasizes multivariate methods. I begin by discussing (a) how well the assumptions behind statistical tests and measures—especially those concerning sampling, level of measurement, and distribution—apply to data commonly analyzed by anthropologists, and (b) the extent to which such tests and measures can be used when these assumptions are violated. I then discuss problems associated with bivariate analyses. The next and longest section of the essay is a description of some of the multivariate methods most frequently used in sociocultural anthropology. I attempt to characterize these methods in simple, nontechnical language and provide examples of the use of each method. I conclude with remarks about the likely future role of statistics in sociocultural anthropology.

Space considerations preclude an exhaustive coverage of all the ways that sociocultural anthropologists have used statistics. For this reason I restrict my review for the most part to analyses of data collected within single field settings and do not examine problems associated with cross-cultural analyses. I also do not discuss the use of statistics in demography, nor do I treat other techniques either only occasionally used by sociocultural anthropologists (e.g. analysis of variance, time series analysis) or those superseded by newer methods (e.g. Guttman scaling).

This essay is not aimed at the few statistically sophisticated sociocultural anthropologists. Although such readers may find some of the citations useful, they will be familiar with much of the material and may regard the presentation as insufficiently critical of past statistical sins [for discussions of abuses of statistics in sociocultural anthropology and archaeology see (60, 75, 124)]. Instead, the essay is aimed at the majority of sociocultural anthropologists, who know something about statistics but would like to know more about how they have been and should be used in analyzing data collected in field work.

ASSUMPTIONS OF INFERENTIAL STATISTICS

Inferential statistics are methods and procedures used to make generalizations about a population (universe) from a subset (sample) of the population. The tests and measures that comprise inferential statistics make assumptions about the nature of the sample, the measurement of variables, and the distribution of the data. Introductory texts on statistics and research methods in the social sciences (e.g. 5, 62, 97, 123) characteristically contain statements about the perils of using tests and measures when these assumptions do not hold. Field work conditions and the nature of the variables being examined, however, often prevent sociocultural anthropologists from using data that completely meet such assumptions. Although anthropologists have sometimes been ingenious in devising techniques to overcome some of these difficulties, they have not sufficiently recognized the extent to which many assumptions underlying statistical tests can be relaxed.

Sampling

Inferential statistics require *probability samples*, where each member of the population has a known probability of being included in the sample. The best known probabilistic sampling method is random sampling, where each member has an equal probability of being selected; other frequently used methods are systematic, stratified, and cluster sampling. Several books (e.g. 62, pp. 54–59; 97, pp. 127–40; 123, pp. 439–40) discuss the special problems sociocultural anthropologists have in obtaining probability samples and the advantages and disadvantages of various sampling methods. Of the techniques devised to overcome sampling problems, Johnson's (61) method of random visits to examine productive activities is worthy of special note. While this method obviously could not be applied everywhere and can be difficult to use, researchers making random visits have generated useful information about the work activities of commercial Swiss farmers (85), Bolivian "peasants" (130), and remote Peruvian tribal groups (87).

Sociocultural anthropologists usually are inexplicit about what constitutes the population (universe) from which their sample is drawn. In many cases this population is hypothetical. For example, researchers often use inferential statistics to examine interrelationships of variables in villages where every household has been censused. The implicit universe in such cases is sometimes a limited geographical area that includes the village. More often, however, it is a hypothetical universe of all villages and interrelationships that could have existed under similar conditions (19, pp. 366–67; 123, pp. 441–44).

Level of Measurement

Observed phenomena can be classified according to their level of measurement (119). *Nominal* scales simply place observations into categories, *ordinal* scales rank observations, and *interval* scales specify the numerical differences between ranked observations. In a famous article, Stevens (119) argued that only nonparametric statistics (those that make no assumptions about distributions of the data) could be used on nominal and ordinal data. Parametric tests and measures such as the t-test, the Pearson correlation coefficient, and multiple regression could be applied only to interval data. The relationship between measurement scale and statistics proposed by Stevens has been accepted by many social scientists and statisticians (e.g., 5, 62, 115).

Sociocultural anthropologists applying statistics seem generally unaware that Stevens's ideas have not been universally accepted. Stevens has been challenged on the rather abstract grounds that measurement theory and statistics are unrelated since "the numbers do not know where they come from." (See 40 for a review of this literature.) More importantly, various empirical studies have been interpreted as showing that using parametric statistics on ordinal data does not always cause statistical problems (77, pp. 19–24); and in recent years statisticians have sometimes been willing to use parametric techniques on mixed nominal, ordinal, and interval data (see 18, pp. 171–211).

Distributions

Parametric statistical tests usually assume that the variables in the sample and the population are distributed normally. However, variables of interest to anthropologists are often nonnormally distributed. Marriage distances are sometimes leptokurtic (22, 65, 83, 103, 122), most wealth measures are lognormal (116), and the number of wives men have in African societies usually has a negative binomial distribution (118). Moreover, sociocultural anthropologists frequently have little information concerning the shape of the distribution of a particular variable. Since distributions are often either nonnormal or unknown, anthropologists make great use of nonparametric tests and measures such as chi-squares and Spearman correlations.

Parametric tests can often be used even when assumptions about distributions are not met. Assumptions underlying statistical tests can be classified according to their robustness. The more robust an assumption is, the less the interpretation of the results of the test must be altered when an assumption is not completely met. The assumptions of normality underlying many commonly used parametric tests are quite robust (139, pp. 263–66).

When either parametric or nonparametric tests can be used, parametric tests are usually preferable because they are less wasteful of data. Nonparametric tests, however, have the advantage of being easier to understand and present (97, pp. 161–62). Sociocultural anthropologists occasionally use complex parametric tests when they could make their point more easily with nonparametric tests. An excellent example of this is an acrimonious debate concerning (among other things) whether or not societies with warfare are more likely to have a higher percentage of male children (presumably because of female infanticide) than those without warfare (25, 26, 56, 57). Part of the argument hinges on whether or not data on sex ratios met the assumptions about distributions of the (parametric) t-test. Much of the vituperous and arcane debate that took place in several issues of the *American Anthropologist* could have been avoided if someone had recoded the sex ratio data into categories (e.g. high and low) and then used nonparametric tests and measures such as chi-square, Spearman, and gamma.

BIVARIATE METHODS

Most statistical analysis in sociocultural anthropology consists of descriptions of relationships between two variables. Such *bivariate analyses* often have two goals; testing independence and measuring association. Two variables are *independent* if a knowledge of the numerical value (or category in the case of nominal data) of one does not aid in the prediction of the value (or category) of the other. Tests of independence indicate the probability, given sample data, that in the *population* the two variables are independent. If two variables are not independent, they are said to be *related*. Measures of association describe the amount of relationship in the *sample* between the two variables.

The selection of an appropriate test of independence and measure of association is partially determined by the level of measurement of the data. Although many of the issues I examine pertain to interval and ordinal statistics, I restrict my discussion here to independence tests and measures of association for nominal level data. Sociocultural anthropologists very often use such data but are frequently unaware of certain fundamental analytic problems.

Tests of Independence

Cross-tabulations (contingency tables) of two variables are a staple feature of social science publications. Each variable is divided into two or more categories, and frequencies (counts) are presented of the numbers in the sample under examination that fall into each possible cross-classification of categories.

Either the chi-square or (less often) the Fisher exact test is ordinarily used to test independence.

If two variables are independent, fairly simple calculations (see any introductory statistics text) provide the expected frequencies in each cell of a contingency table. Observed frequencies ordinarily will not exactly match the expected frequencies because of chance fluctuations. If, however, observed frequencies differ enough from expected ones, the two variables are likely to be related. The familiar chi-square test indicates the probability that differences between observed and expected frequencies in a sample could be the result of chance fluctuations. Books on research methods (e.g. 97, pp. 162–63) usually recommend that a *significance level* be set prior to calculating the chi-square. If the probability of chance occurrence of differences between observed and expected frequencies in the sample is less than or equal to the significance level, the researcher concludes that the variables are related in the population. In practice, researchers often set no significance level in advance and report the probability (e.g. "significant at the .01 level") that a result could have occurred by chance.

There exists a vast literature on the use and abuse of significance tests (e.g. 19, 89), and common mistakes are routinely pointed out in introductory texts (e.g. 97, pp. 162–64; 123, pp. 459–68). Nevertheless, two errors are so prevalent in the anthropological literature that they bear yet another mention here.

The single most common error made by social scientists making statistical analyses of nominal data is the combined overemphasis on independence tests and underemphasis on measures of association. Independence (significance) tests provide information about whether differences from chance exist, but say little about the magnitude of such differences. The reason for this is that any fixed significance level means something quite different for a large sample than for a small one. Fairly minor proportional differences between observed and expected frequencies will be significant for large samples and fairly large proportional differences will not be significant for small samples. Nevertheless, of 19 articles in the *American Ethnologist* from 1974 to 1983 in which researchers used chi-square or Fisher tests on nominal data collected in the field, only 2 provided measures of association indicating the magnitude of differences between observed and expected frequencies.

Another pervasive mistake found in statistical analyses by anthropologists (and other social scientists) is an overemphasis on avoiding "Type I" error and an underemphasis on avoiding "Type II" error. Researchers making statistical tests examine data in attempts to reject a null hypothesis and accept an alternative hypothesis. A Type I error is incorrectly rejecting the null hypothesis, while a Type II error is incorrectly rejecting the alternative hypothesis (see 19 and 123, pp. 212–17 for lucid detailed discussions). Social scientists typically use chi-square and other statistical tests to calculate the level of significance, the probability that a Type I error has been made. By insisting that results attain a certain level of significance (usually .05), journal editors and article reviewers insure that not many Type I errors are made. Unfortunately, researchers, editors, and reviewers almost never comment on Type II error, the probability of being too conservative in interpreting results. For the small samples of 20–60 cases characteristic of much field research, a mandatory or recommended significance level of .05 insures that the probability of Type II error will be high. (The size of this probability depends on the "power" of the statistical test being used.) As Siegel notes (115, p. 10), researchers setting significance levels should reach some compromise that optimizes the balance between the probabilities of making Type I and Type II errors. Sociocultural anthropologists seem to make little effort to seek such a compromise.

Measures of Association

Since anthropologists frequently calculate Pearson and Spearman correlations for interval or ordinal data, their reluctance to calculate measures of association for nominal data cannot be entirely attributed to their overemphasis on tests of significance. Another reason for their reluctance may be the plethora of association measures of nominal data ["literally dozens" (105, p. 14)] and various theoretical and methodological problems associated with their use (for details see 43–46, 105).

Association measures can be either symmetric or asymmetric. If theory or common sense suggests that one variable causes the other, asymmetric measures should be used; otherwise, symmetric measures are preferable. Lambda (38, pp. 71–78), and tau (105, pp. 41–45) are examples of asymmetric measures; phi-squared (123, pp. 419–23), the odds ratio (105, pp. 20–27), and the contingency coefficient (115, pp. 196–202) are examples of symmetric measures. Association measures can also be classified according to their statistical basis. Some are based on the odds ratio, others on chi-square, and still others on how well cross-classifications can be predicted (105, pp. 29–45).

The principal difficulty of most measures of association for contingency tables is that marginal distributions (row and column totals) affect their numerical values. Two tables with different marginal distributions will not produce the same numerical value of association even when they record the same underlying relationship. Two common solutions to this problem are standardizing tables via an iterative procedure (4, pp. 83–102) and calculating the ratio of the numerical value to the maximum possible value, given the marginal distribution (105, pp. 18–19).

MULTIVARIATE METHODS

The holistic orientation characteristic of sociocultural anthropology often leads researchers to collect data systematically on many interrelated variables. Two related difficulties hamper efforts to analyze such data. First, there are problems in describing the relationships between pairs of variables because of the confounding effects of other lurking variables. Second, simplification of data frequently is useful since numerous variables on which information has been collected seem to measure the same thing.

The recent availability of "canned" computer packages has enabled an increasing number of anthropologists and other social scientists to employ a variety of complex multivariate techniques to control for confounding or lurking variables and to reduce or simplify data. *Multiple regression* and *path analysis* are the methods sociocultural anthropologists have most often used in their efforts to untangle interrelated variables, while *cluster analysis* (numerical taxonomy), *factor analysis,* and *multidimensional scaling* are the most commonly used data-reduction techniques.

Biological anthropologists and archaeologists have used multivariate techniques more extensively and for a longer time than sociocultural anthropologists. In both of these anthropological subfields articles appeared some years ago (74, 124) decrying the uncritical use of these methods. Problems were noted that arose from both the complexity of multivariate methods and the relative lack of statistical expertise among most biological anthropologists and archaeologists. Multivariate methods have been inappropriately or unnecessarily used, and the results of even well-done published analyses can often be understood by only a small fraction of the readers. As a result inept, pretentious, incomprehensible, and overly complicated analyses have frequently passed the not-so-critical scrutiny of journal and book referees and have been published. (See 60, 112, 124 for discussions of this issue.) Since sociocultural anthropologists as a group are less knowledgeable about statistics than their colleagues in biological anthropology and archaeology, the possibility of similar problems is obvious.

Although it would be easy to compile a catalog of abuses of multivariate statistics by sociocultural anthropologists, I have chosen not to do so here. I do agree with Thomas (124, p. 241), however, that multivariate techniques should be used only after simpler analytic methods have been fully investigated. The danger of using multivariate statistics to obfuscate rather than to clarify is ever present.

Controlling for Confounding Variables

Statisticians have devised three basic methods—randomization, elaboration, and residualization—to "control for" confounding variables when examining bivariate relationships (139, pp. 150–78). The use of randomization is ordinarily restricted to experimental research in which subjects can be assigned randomly to different experimental treatments. Although randomization is common in medicine and psychology, the nonexperimental nature of almost all sociocultural anthropological research generally rules out the use of this method. Elaboration, however, is frequently used in sociocultural anthropology (e.g. 15) and is the simplest and most straightforward way to control for the effects of specific confounding variables. Elaboration involves examining the association between two variables within separate categories of a third (and possibly confounding) variable. Suppose, for example, that a researcher wishes to examine the relationship between number of household consumers and annual cash income in a multiethnic community. Using elaboration, the researcher can control for any confounding effects of ethnicity by examining the bivariate relationship separately for each ethnic group.

Although elaboration makes possible perfect control of specific third variables, application of the technique to several third variables is difficult (139, p. 153). The number of tables required multiplies rapidly as the number of variables controlled for increases, and there may not be enough observations in every table to allow reliable conclusions to be drawn. This problem is especially important in sociocultural anthropology, where sample sizes are typically small.

In situations where there are too many confounding variables and/or too few cases for elaboration to be used, researchers can control statistically for the effects of several third variables by using "residualization" (139, pp. 154–78). Two techniques employing residualization frequently used by sociocultural anthropologists are *multiple regression* and *path analysis*. A third technique, which has not often been used by anthropologists despite certain advantages, involves the use of *log-linear models*.

MULTIPLE REGRESSION   Anthropologists commonly wish to analyze the relationship between a dependent variable and several independent (or *predictor*) variables. For example, a researcher might wish to compare the relative importance of number of consumers, land holdings, and ethnicity in predicting the annual cash income of a "peasant" household. The researcher might also want to determine how well a household's annual cash income can be predicted from a knowledge of these variables.

Multiple regression is a statistical technique that provides the linear equation of independent variables that best predicts the dependent variable. The *multiple correlation coefficient* is a measure of the predictive accuracy of this equation. The multiple regression equation is frequently calculated after all variables have been transformed so that each has a standard deviation of one. For such standardized multiple regression equations of the form $Y = A + b_1X_1 + b_2X_2 + \ldots + b_nX_n$ (where Y is the dependent variable, A a constant, and the X_is independent variables), the b_is are called *standardized regression coefficients*. The magnitude of any particular b_i is a measure of the relative importance of X_i in predicting Y.

Hirschfeld's (55) analysis of aesthetics among the San Blas Cuna of Panama illustrates well how multiple regression can be applied to anthropological questions. The Cuna produce *molas*, rectangular panels of reverse appliqué worn by women on the front and back of indigenously made blouses. One question Hirschfeld was interested in was the criteria Cuna used to rank the aesthetic quality of mola designs. He asked 20 women to view 34 color reproductions of molas and pick the three they liked best. The dependent variable in Hirschfeld's analysis was the number of times a particular mola was chosen. Most of the independent variables were various design features. Hirschfeld was able to generate a regression equation with a high multiple correlation coefficient. He also presented standardized regression coefficients showing that "density" (a measure of complexity) and asymmetry predicted mola preference better than most color features analyzed.

Sociocultural anthropologists have used multiple regression most often (35, 41, 82, 99, 100, 135) to examine the determinants of various measures of economic productivity or wealth. Somewhat controversial economic analyses employing multiple regression have also been made of the determinants of bride price in Nigeria (48) and the number of wives of Palestine men in the nineteenth and early twentieth centuries (95). Other sociocultural applications have been diverse, including examination of the determinants of leadership among Mayas in Chiapas (125), male bias in remembering kin among Belgrade factory workers (50), propensity to adopt innovations among Maine fishermen (1), "deferred gratification orientation" among the Buganda (102), and traditional beliefs about disease causation among "Rhodesian" students and teachers in training (86).

Although multiple regression has conventionally been restricted to intervally measured variables, in recent years statisticians have come to accept the use of the technique on ordinal and even nominal independent variables. This has been done through the use of dummy variables, in which one or more dichotomous variables (values at 0 or 1) are established for each nominal scale (see 18, pp. 171–211). The expansion of multiple regression to include variables measured nominally and ordinally has greatly increased the technique's applicability in sociocultural anthropology, where many variables of interest (e.g. ethnicity, place of residence, sex) cannot be measured intervally. Multiple regression, however, should not be used if the dependent variable is measured nominally. In such circumstances, *discriminant analysis*, an analytic method rarely employed by sociocultural anthropologists, is appropriate.

Multiple regression assumes that the underlying relationships among variables are linear and additive. Anthropologists (35, 41, 99) have sometimes borrowed techniques from economists to make logarithmic transformation of variables that convert nonlinear relationships into linear ones (see also 18, pp. 242–61). Although methods exist (18, pp. 291–337) to apply multiple regression in certain situations where relationships among variables are nonadditive, sociocultural anthropologists have generally assumed additivity even in situations where it might not be reasonable.

Several technical problems can arise when nonstatisticians attempt multiple regression analyses. Anthropologists and other social scientists often use the "shotgun approach," investigating a large number of independent variables in order to ensure that substantive issues are well covered and no important factors are overlooked. However, Cohen & Cohen (18, p. 160) note that "having more variables when fewer are possible increases the risks of both finding things that are not so and failing to find things that are." Another problem arises from *multicollinearity,* when some or all of the independent variables are highly intercorrelated. A paradoxical situation occurs. The more strongly related the independent variables are, the greater the need to control for confounding effects. However, the greater the intercorrelation of independent variables is, the less reliability can be placed on the relative importance indicated by the standardized regression coefficients (69, pp. 340–41). Finally, there are several methods of multiple regression analysis, each of which can give different results. The uncritical use of "stepwise regression," the method most often used by sociocultural anthropologists, has been cogently criticized (18, pp. 102–4).

PATH ANALYSIS   Social scientists examining the effects of several independent variables on a dependent variable are often willing to make fairly specific assumptions about causality. In such circumstances *path analysis* is more informative about relationships among variables than multiple regression. Path analysis was developed over 60 years ago by the geneticist Sewall Wright (137) and was introduced to sociologists by Boudon (8) and Duncan (30) and to anthropologists by Haddon & DeWalt (49). Within sociology the technique, described as being of "almost revolutionary importance" (10), has been applied extensively, if somewhat indiscriminately (84). Substantive applications in sociocultural anthropology (23, 24, 31, 51, 52, 63, 67, 94, 120, 125), while hardly routine, are not uncommon.

Path analysis requires that the researcher create a model of explicit causal relations among the variables being considered. This usually involves a series of weak causal orderings in which variable X_1 may or may not affect variable X_2, but X_2 cannot affect X_1. However, path analysis has also commonly been carried out when there is noncausal (within the confines of the model) correlation between certain variables (see some of the examples in 49) and occasionally (although not in sociocultural anthropology) where there is mutual causality among some variables (see 2, pp. 50–61). Path analysis assumes "causal closure" (see 69, p. 385), certain constraints on the direction of hypothesized causal effects or paths (see 2, p. 33; 138), and the same assumptions about linearity and additivity as multiple regression.

Path analysis has two major advantages when compared to multiple regression (49, p. 106). First, the technique forces a researcher to be more explicit about theoretical assumptions concerning causality. Second, path analysis allows systematic examination of the effects of intervening variables in a causal model. A bivariate correlation between variables X and Y (where X is causally prior to Y), for example, can be "decomposed" into three components (49, p. 112). There are *direct effects* of X on Y, *indirect effects* of X on Y via one or more intervening variables, and the *joint effects* arising either from unanalyzed correlation or when a single causally prior variable Z exerts direct or indirect effects on X and Y and thereby causes them to vary concomitantly.

Thomas's (125) study of the sociocultural determinants of political leadership in a Tojolabal community in Chiapas, Mexico, illustrates the advantages of path analysis. Using "action theory," Thomas assumed that wealth, family size, and number of friends were causally prior to leadership. Employing stepwise multiple regression, Thomas found that wealth was the most important of the independent variables in predicting leadership, followed by family size and number of friends. Thomas thought, however, that the multiple regression provided an incomplete picture of relationships among the variables because of the effects of family size and wealth on the number of friends a man had and the effects of family size on wealth. Using path analysis, Thomas not only was able to compare the direct effects of family size, number of friends, and wealth on leadership (as with multiple regression) but also could assess the indirect effects of family size on leadership via the intervening variables of wealth and number of friends. He concluded that family size, because of its substantial indirect causal effects via the intervening variables, was a more important determinant of leadership than was indicated by multiple regression.

Not long after path analysis was introduced to sociologists, enthusiasm in the field became so great that one editor announced his journal would not accept "mindless" applications of the technique (114, p. 13) and critics suggested many articles were more exercises in data manipulation than examinations of substantive, theoretically grounded models (84, p. 200). Similar problems have not arisen in sociocultural anthropology, where path analysis seems to be underused rather than overused.

LOG-LINEAR MODELS Social scientists often confront great difficulties in analyzing contingency tables involving more than two variables. Consider, for example, a situation in which a researcher wishes to examine the interrelationships among three nominal variables, A, B, and C. A few of the several possible relationships that might exist are: 1. All three variables are independent of one another; 2. A and B are related (not independent), but both are independent of C; 3. A and B are related for some categories of C, but are independent for other categories of C (this is called an "interaction" effect); and 4. A, B, and C are all related to one another, but there are no interaction effects.

Although techniques such as analysis of variance and multiple regression have enabled statisticians to unravel possible confounding relationships for interval-level data, until recently the prevailing methods (involving elaboration) for analyzing categorical data have not been satisfactory in situations where there are more than a few variables, especially when sample sizes are small (105, pp. 53–56).

In the past two decades statisticians have made great progress in analyzing discrete multivariate data (see 4, 34, 42, 105). One technique that has been developed, log-linear models, is said to "put the investigation of nominal data on a par with the study of interval-level variables" (105, p. 57). The goal of this analytic method is to develop a linear equation, with logarithmic terms, that accounts for the observed frequencies of cross-classifications. The results of a log-linear analysis allow a researcher to determine whether or not particular variables are independent of one another and whether or not interaction effects exist (for details see 4; 34; 105, pp. 57–81). They can also be used (with some difficulty) to evaluate the comparative strength of various relationships (105, p. 59).

Log-linear approaches are beginning to be used in sociocultural anthropology (36, 88, 121) to evaluate competing models of interrelationships among nominal variables. For example, Fleuret & Fleuret (36) were interested in the relationships among hereditary caste, father's occupation, and son's occupation for overseas Sikhs in Tanzania. They used log-linear methods to show that there are relationships between father's occupation and caste and between father's occupation and son's occupation, but not (controlling for the aforementioned effects) between son's occupation and caste.

Although log-linear analysis has clear advantages and should be considered by sociocultural anthropologists analyzing numerous categorical variables, the technique is not easy for nonstatisticians to use, present, and understand. Contingency tables used in elaboration, in contrast, can be understood by many anthropologists with little statistical background. When only three variables are being analyzed, simpler methods such as elaboration may be preferable to log-linear approaches.

Data Reduction

The goal of descriptive statistics is to summarize data by substituting a few measures for many numbers. Such reduction or simplification inevitably involves the loss of information but has the great advantage of enabling researchers to more readily see what is in the data (5, p. 4). Means, medians, and standard deviations are familiar descriptive statistics that reduce data to managebale proportions.

Multivariate descriptive statistics are most often used to reduce a data matrix, a rectangular array of cells. The rows of the matrix are *cases* (entities), while the columns are *variables* (attributes, characteristics) on which data have been collected for each case. The cell values consist of nominal, ordinal, or interval measurements for specific combinations of cases and variables. For a census, cases might be households, with four variables being the number of males, females, people over 18, and people under 18. One cell entry would be the number of females in a particular household censused.

Researchers using multivariate data-reduction techniques generally begin by constructing measures of similarity between pairs of rows or columns. Pearson correlation coefficients are commonly used when data are intervally measured, but there are many other measures of similarity (proximity). These measures are then used to divide cases or variables into fairly homogenous groups. Members of each group are similar to one another and dissimilar to members of other groups. Descriptive statistics are then used to measure the extent of intergroup and intragroup similarities and differences. Multidimensional visual representations ("maps") are sometimes also used to show the distances (amounts of dissimilarity) between all pairs of cases or variables.

Cluster analysis is the technique most commonly used in sociocultural anthropology to delineate groups of similar cases, while *factor analysis* is the method most often used to lump variables into groups. *Multidimensional scaling,* a method creating visual representations of distances, has frequently been used on both cases and variables.

CLUSTER ANALYSIS   The goal of cluster analysis (numerical taxonomy) is to subdivide a number of cases (or occasionally variables) into homogenous subgroups. These subgroups are frequently arranged hierarchically. The construction of nonintuitive typologies simplifies observations with a minimal loss of information and may contribute significantly to an understanding of the problem studied (79, pp. 3–4). Cluster-analytic techniques can be used on nominal, ordinal, and interval data and in situations where some attributes (variables) are measured nominally while others are measured on ordinal and interval levels.

When a cluster analysis is carried out, a similarity index is chosen that summarizes multiple measures of differences between cases. Using the matrix of similarity indexes of each pair of cases, a clustering technique is used to create groups of similar cases. There is no consensus about which similarity indexes and clustering techniques are most appropriate in particular situations, primarily because of different ideas about what forms an "acceptable" classification (6, p. 281).

Although cluster analysis was first used in sociocultural anthropology over 50 years ago (29), the technique was not widely employed in any social science until the 1960s (6, p. 28). Biological anthropologists (e.g. 9, 54, 93) rapidly began using the method after the publication of Sokal & Sneath's influential book (117) on the application of cluster analysis to biological taxonomy. Archaeologists (e.g. 17, 27, 104), no doubt because of their great interest in morphological typology, also were quick to adopt the technique. Although some archaeologists do not like cluster analysis (16, 124), numerical taxonomy is so common in the field that it has been (unenthusiastically) referred to as a "highly visible bandwagon" (124, p. 236).

In contrast to researchers in other subfields, sociocultural anthropologists have only occasionally applied cluster analysis to their field data. The method has been used to isolate Navajo household economic types (136) and to classify games in the Yucatan (129) and military pilot errors in the United States (108). Most applications (e.g. 37, 80, 128, 134), however, have been psychologically and linguistically oriented, often using a clustering technique developed by a psychological anthropologist (20). White's study (134) of psychological characteristics of status types on Santa Isabel in the Solomon Islands is a good example of this kind of application. White asked 29 middle-aged men about the personality traits associated with 10 types of "Big Men." From a corpus of 37 terms and phrases commonly used to describe personal traits, each informant selected 8 "appropriate" and 8 "inappropriate" attributes for each status type. White used the data to create a similarity index of status types. He then isolated two clusters that seemed to correspond to an overall contrast of mission- and government-related statuses and also isolated various subclusters (e.g. priest and bishop, catechist and teacher) within the larger clusters.

The results of a cluster analysis can be difficult to interpret. There is often no obvious label to put on the clusters of cases lumped together. These interpretive difficulties and the arbitrariness associated with choices of similarity indexes and clustering methods are the major nontechnical problems associated with the use of numerical taxonomy.

FACTOR ANALYSIS   Anthropologists and other social scientists frequently collect information about many interrelated variables for a number of cases. Researchers often suspect that some variables are redundant since they are measures of more or less the same thing or dimension. For example, a household economic survey in a peasant community might ask three separate questions about ownership of bicycles, radios, and kerosene stoves. The ownership of any one of these items might correlate highly with ownership of the other two and reflect overall wealth.

Factor analysis is the technique social scientists most often use to reduce data redundancy. Factor analysis was developed by the psychologist Spearman in an attempt to see how many dimensions underlie variables measured on so-called "intelligence tests." There exists a well-developed, mathematically sophisticated literature on the assumptions, methodology, and interpretation of factor analysis (e.g. 53, 70, 71, 111).

The fundamental assumption of factor analysis is that one or more underlying "factors" are responsible for covariation among variables (71, p. 12). Given an array of correlation coefficients for a set of variables (or occasionally cases), factor-analytic techniques reduce data to a smaller set of factors, which may be taken as source variables accounting for observed interrelationships (68, p. 469). The results of analysis include a list of factors, the "loadings" (correlations) between each individual variable and each factor, and the percentage of total variance accounted for or resolved by each factor.

Factor analysis has primarily been used in sociocultural anthropology to explore data (e.g. 23, 32, 52, 81, 86, 101, 102, 106, 107). The technique enables researchers to get some idea how much redundancy is in their data and to simplify statistical operations such as multiple regression by using factors instead of a myriad of confounding variables. After examining the particular variables loading highly on the different factors, researchers often attempt to improve their understanding of the data by labeling (giving names to) factors.

DeWalt's examination (23) of agricultural innovation in a peasant community in Mexico illustrates the exploratory use of factor analysis. "Development agents" had been working to increase productivity of corn and to change the region to a dairy economy. DeWalt therefore expected that innovations related to corn production (the use of fertilizers and tractors) would be adopted as a unit and that other innovations related to livestock production (e.g. sowing forage crops and vaccination of animals) would also be adopted as a set. A factor analysis of innovations, however, resulted in the identification of four factors (explaining 69% of the variance) rather than two. Furthermore, innovations associated with corn production were found in several factors, as were innovations associated with livestock. DeWalt was thus able to show via factor analysis that adoption strategies in the community were not what he had initially hypothesized.

Several serious problems limit the usefulness of factor analysis. There is no consensus about which of the many factor-analytic methods is most appropriate, and the results of the various methods differ. For instance, psychologists using different analytic techniques disagree sharply about the extent to which one factor (labeled "general intelligence") can explain the results of mental testing (47, pp. 234–320). The results of factor analysis, moreover, are often difficult to interpret. The labeling of factors is something of an art, and the literature is full of statements such as "this factor . . . link(s) such strange bedfellows as travel and brutality" (32, p. 239) and "the third factor is difficult to define . . . it seems to represent an alternate line to the classical gods of the Hindu pantheon" (107, p. 138). That factor analysis is not based in theory may be one cause of its hard-to-interpret results. As Gould (47, p. 316) notes, "the choice of factor analysis as method records the primitive state of knowledge in a field. Factor analysis is a brutally empirical technique, used when a discipline has no firmly established principles, but only a mass of crude data, and a hope that patterns of correlation might provide suggestions for further and more fruitful lines of inquiry."

MULTIDIMENSIONAL SCALING   The data used in multidimensional scaling consist of a number of items (either cases or variables) and measurements of the distances between all pairs of items. The goal of multidimensional scaling is to produce a map in which each item is represented by a point near the points of other similar items. When maps have three or fewer dimensions, visual representations are often made to aid researchers in their data interpretations.

Perfect correspondences between map distances at low dimensions and measurements of distances (proximities) are rare because of errors and noise in the data. Suppose, for example, that items are cities and proximities are averages of several informants' statements about the distances between pairs of cities. Informant disagreement and error will likely result in a two-dimensional map that does not quite match either mean perceived or real distances.

One measurement of how well a particular configuration of points fits the data is the *stress* associated with the configuration. The map of best fit in one dimension will have more stress than the map of best fit in two dimensions, which will have more stress than the map of best fit in three dimensions, and so forth. There are no fixed rules for selecting the number of dimensions, but two relevant considerations are that the amount of stress should not be "too high" and that dimensions should not be added if they do not reduce stress much (76, pp. 23–27).

Once a map is created, the researcher must choose the axis for each dimension. This choice can be handled objectively via multiple regression, but the interpretation of each dimension remains problematic. Although factor analysis and multidimensional scaling make different mathematical assumptions and yield different results (111, pp. 190–191, 507–513) the substantive meaning of and interpretive problems associated with factors and dimensions are similar.

Multidimensional methods have been developed for both metric (intervally measured) and nonmetric distances. One of the greatest attractions of multidimensional scaling for sociocultural anthropologists is the possibility of using the technique where distances can be compared in magnitude but not given numerical value. Multidimensional scaling, sometimes in conjunction with hierarchical cluster analysis (e.g. 20, 80, 108, 134), is the multivariate data-reduction method most often used in sociocultural anthropology.

Although multidimensional scaling can be applied to a variety of distance measures (see 76, 109), sociocultural anthropologists have almost always used the technique to analyze informants' perceptions of similarities and differences. Topics examined include disease terms (21, 39, 131), occupations, roles and statuses (11, 14, 134), kin terms (78, 110), personality traits (13, 72, 133,

134), pottery types (63), ethnic groups (113), and pilot errors (108). Attempts are sometimes made to compare the mental maps of various subgroups in the sample (e.g. 13, 21, 32, 72).

Lutz's analysis (80) of emotion words on Ifaluk in Micronesia is a clearly presented recent use of multidimensional scaling. She asked 13 informants to sort 31 emotion words (identified as "about our insides") into piles of similar words. Pairs of words were given a similarity score according to how many times they were put into the same pile. A multidimensional scaling of these scores gave a two-dimensional result with low stress. Lutz provides a visual representation of her results (80, p. 121), with circles around groups identified with a cluster analysis. She concludes from the position of terms on axes that one dimension represents a pleasant/unpleasant continuum while the other indicates ego's power or strength compared to other actors in an emotion-eliciting situation.

The major advantage multidimensional scaling has over other methods of multivariate data reduction is the possibility of visual representation when there are three or fewer dimensions. When analysis results in four or more important dimensions (e.g. 32, p. 226), this advantage disappears and factor analysis, with better-known mathematical properties, may be preferable.

FUTURE DIRECTIONS

The growing interest in intracultural variation (96) and systematic research design (62, 97), an increased demand for rigor by funding agencies and scholarly journals, and the availability of easily used computer packages all make it likely that sociocultural anthropologists will use statistics in the future more than they do now. The use of bivariate statistical methods to analyze data collected in the field is already routine in North America, if not elsewhere, and the application of multivariate methods is increasing rapidly. The lack of statistical expertise of most sociocultural anthropologists and the experiences of other anthropological subfields (74, 112, 124) suggest that multivariate applications will sometimes be incompetent and that researchers will occasionally overemphasize methodology and underemphasize substantive importance.

The eclectic methodology employed by sociocultural anthropologists makes it unlikely that they will ever use statistical methods as much as their colleagues in psychology and sociology. The heavy reliance by psychologists on laboratory experiments and by many sociologists on mass surveys has necessitated extensive and sophisticated use of statistical methods in those fields. Sociocultural anthropologists, however, rarely experiment, and they use surveys as only one of many research tools in their efforts to gain in-depth holistic understandings of particular cultural processes. The use of qualitative methods of data analysis such as the presentation of detailed case studies and life histories is one way in which sociocultural anthropology is distinct from other social sciences. Almost all sociocultural anthropologists, including those most committed to the use of statistical methods (e.g. 62, pp. 9-12; 97, pp. 67-77), regard qualitative data-analytic procedures as essential.

The diverse subject matter and theoretical breadth of sociocultural anthropology also insure that statistical methods will continue to comprise only part of the set of many useful research tools. Topics such as religion, law, and economic and political dependency are ordinarily not examined by statistical analyses of quantitative data. Moreover, theoretical approaches such as symbolism, structuralism, and Marxism make quite limited use of statistical analysis.

Nevertheless statistical methods are becoming increasingly important to sociocultural anthropologists. Many anthropology departments already require graduate students to take an introductory statistics course, and more are likely to do so in the future. Such requirements are reasonable since even sociocultural anthropologists who do not use statistics in their own work need to know something about them to understand much important current research.

ACKNOWLEDGMENTS

I thank Maeve Clark for research assistance and Chad McDaniel and June Helm for helpful comments on an earlier version of this paper.

Literature Cited

1. Acheson, J., Reidman, R. 1982. Technical innovations in the New England finfishing industry: An examination of the Downs and Mohr hypothesis. *Am. Ethnol.* 9:538-58
2. Asher, H. 1976. *Causal Modeling.* Sage Univ. Pap. Ser. Quant. Appl. in Soc. Sci. 07-003. Beverly Hills, Calif: Sage
3. Ballonoff, P. 1983. Theory of lineage organizations. *Am. Anthropol.* 85:70-91
4. Bishop, Y., Fienberg, S., Holland, P. W. 1975. *Discrete Multivariate Analysis.* Cambridge, Mass: MIT Press
5. Blalock, H. 1979. *Social Statistics.* New York: McGraw-Hill. 2nd rev. ed.
6. Blashfield, R. K., Aldenderfer, M. 1978. The literature on cluster analysis. *Multivar. Behav. Res.* 13:271-98
7. Boas, F. 1927. Anthropology and statistics. In *The Social Sciences and Their Interrelations*, ed. W. Ogburn, A. Goldenweiser, pp. 114-20. Boston: Houghton Mifflin
8. Boudon, R. 1965. A method of linear causal analysis: Dependence analysis. *Am. Sociol. Rev.* 30:365-74
9. Boyce, A. J. 1964. The value of some methods of numerical taxonomy with reference to homonoid classification. In *Phenetic and Phylogenetic Classification*, ed. V. Heywood, J. McNeill. London: Systematics Assoc. Publ. 6
10. Boyle, R. 1970. Path analysis and ordinal data. *Am. J. Sociol.* 75:461-80
11. Burton, M. 1972. Semantic dimensions of occupational names. See Ref. 109, pp. 55-71
12. Burton, M. 1973. Mathematical anthropology. *Ann. Rev. Anthropol.* 2:189-99
13. Burton, M., Kirk, L. 1979. Sex differences in Masai cognition of personality and social identity. *Am. Anthropol.* 8:841-73
14. Burton, M., Romney, A. K. 1975. A multidimensional representation of role terms. *Am. Ethnol.* 2:397-408
15. Chibnik, M. 1980. Working out or working in: The choice between wage labor and cash cropping in rural Belize. *Am. Ethnol.* 7:86-105
16. Christenson, A., Read, D. 1977. Numerical taxonomy, R-mode factor analysis

and archaeological classification. *Am. Antiq.* 42:163–79
17. Clarke, D. 1968. *Analytical Archaeology*. London: Methuen
18. Cohen, J., Cohen, P. 1975. *Applied Multiple Regression Correlation Analysis for the Behavioral Sciences*. Hillsdale, NJ: Erlbaum
19. Cowgill, G. 1977. The trouble with significance tests and what we can do about it. *Am. Antiq.* 42:350–68
20. D'Andrade, R. 1978. U-Statistic hierarchical clustering. *Psychometrika* 43:59–67
21. D'Andrade, R., Quinn, N., Nerlove, S. B., Romney, A. K. 1972. Categories of disease in American-English and Mexican-Spanish. See Ref. 109, pp. 9–54
22. Dannhaeuser, N. 1978. Regional patterns of marriage ties in North-Central Luzon, Philippines. *Am. Ethnol.* 5:733–47
23. DeWalt, B. 1979. Alternative adaptive strategies in a Mexican ejido: A new perspective on modernization and development. *Hum. Organ.* 38:134–43
24. DeWalt, B. 1979. *Modernization in a Mexican Ejido*. Cambridge: Cambridge Univ. Press
25. Divale, W., Harris, M. 1976. Population, warfare, and the male supremacist complex. *Am. Anthropol.* 78:521–38
26. Divale, W., Harris, M., Williams, D. 1978. On the misuse of statistics: A reply to Hirschfeld et al. *Am. Anthropol.* 80:379–86
27. Doran, J., Hodson, F. 1966. A digital computer analysis of Palaeolithic flint assemblages. *Nature* 210:688–89
28. Driver, H. 1953. Statistics in anthropology. *Am. Anthropol.* 55:42–59
29. Driver, H., Kroeber, A. 1932. Quantitative expression of cultural relationships. *Univ. Calif. Publ. Am. Archaeol. Ethnol.* 31:211–56
30. Duncan, O. D. 1966. Path analysis: Sociological examples. *Am. J. Sociol.* 72:1–16
31. Durrenberger, E. P. 1976. The economy of a Lisu village. *Am. Ethnol.* 3:633–45
32. Edgerton, R. B. 1971. *The Individual in Cultural Adaptation*. Berkeley: Univ. Calif. Press
33. Fairlie, J. 1927. Political science and statistics. See Ref. 7, pp. 279–98
34. Fienberg, S. 1977. *The Analysis of Cross-Classified Categorical Data*. Cambridge, Mass: MIT Press
35. Finkler, K. 1979. Applying econometric techniques to economic anthropology. *Am. Ethnol.* 6:675–81
36. Fleuret, A., Fleuret, P. 1980. Quantitative methods and the analysis of social change. *J. Anthropol. Res.* 36:231–44
37. Freeman, H., Romney, A. K., Ferreira-Pinto, J., Klein, R., Smith, T. 1981. Guatemalan and U.S. concepts of success and failure. *Hum. Organ.* 40:140–45
38. Freeman, L. 1965. *Elementary Applied Statistics: For Students in Behavioral Science*. New York: Wiley
39. Furbee, L., Benfer, R. 1983. Cognitive and geographic maps: Study of individual variation among Tojolabal Mayans. *Am. Anthropol.* 85:305–34
40. Gaito, J. 1980. Measurement scales and statistics: Resurgence of an old misconception. *Psychol. Bull.* 87:564–67
41. Gladwin, C. 1979. Production functions and decision models: Complementary models. *Am. Ethnol.* 6:653–74
42. Goodman, L. 1970. The multivariate analysis of qualitative data: Interaction among multiple classifications. *J. Am. Stat. Assoc.* 65:226–56
43. Goodman, L., Kruskal, W. 1954. Measures of association in cross-classification. *J. Am. Stat. Assoc.* 49:732–64
44. Goodman, L., Kruskal, W. 1959. Measures of association in cross-classification II: Further discussion and references. *J. Am. Stat. Assoc.* 54:123–63
45. Goodman, L., Kruskal, W. 1963. Measures of association in cross-classification III: Approximate sampling theory. *J. Am. Stat. Assoc.* 58:310–64
46. Goodman, L., Kruskal, W. 1972. Measures of association in cross-classification IV: Simplification of asymptotic variances. *J. Am. Stat. Assoc.* 67:415–21
47. Gould, S. J. 1981. *The Mismeasure of Man*. New York: Norton
48. Grossbard, A. 1976. An economic analysis of polygyny: The case of Maiduguri. *Curr. Anthropol.* 17:701–7
49. Haddon, K., DeWalt, B. 1974. Path analysis: Some anthropological examples. *Ethnology* 13:105–28
50. Hammel, E., Yarbrough, C. 1974. Preference and recall in Serbian cousinship: Power and kinship ideology. *J. Anthropol. Res.* 30:95–115
51. Handwerker, W. P. 1977. Family, fertility and economics. *Curr. Anthropol.* 18:259–89
52. Handwerker, W. P. 1981. Productivity, marketing, efficiency and price-support programs: Alternative paths to rural development in Liberia. *Hum. Organ.* 40:27–39
53. Harman, H. 1976. *Modern Factor Analysis*. Chicago: Univ. Chicago Press
54. Hiernaux, J. 1972. The analysis of multivariate biological distance between human populations: Principles and applications to SubSaharan Africa. In *The As-*

sessment of Population Affinities, ed. J. Weiner, J. Huzinga. Oxford: Clarendon
55. Hirschfeld, L. 1977. Cuna aesthetics: A quantitative analysis. *Ethnology* 16:147–66
56. Hirschfeld, L. 1979. A reply to Divale et al. *Am. Anthropol.* 81:349–51
57. Hirschfeld, L., Howe, J., Levin, B. 1978. Warfare, infanticide and statistical inference: A comment on Divale and Harris. *Am. Anthropol.* 80:110–15
58. Hobhouse, L., Wheeler, G., Ginsberg, M. 1915. *The Material Culture and Social Institutions of the Simpler Peoples: An Essay in Correlation*. London: Routledge & Kegan Paul
59. Hoffman, H. 1970. Mathematical anthropology. *Bien. Rev. Anthropol. 1969*, pp. 41–79
60. Hole, B. L. 1980. Sampling in archaeology: A critique. *Ann. Rev. Anthropol.* 9:217–34
61. Johnson, A. 1975. Time allocation in a Machiguenga community. *Ethnology* 14:301–10
62. Johnson, A. 1978. *Quantification in Cultural Anthropology*. Stanford, Calif: Stanford Univ. Press
63. Kaplan, F., Levine, D. 1981. Cognitive mapping of a folk taxonomy of Mexican pottery: A multivariate approach. *Am. Anthropol.* 83:868–84
64. Kaplan, P., Hsien Huang, C. 1974. Achievement orientation of small industrial enterprises in the Philippines. *Hum. Organ.* 33:173–82
65. Kashyap, L. K. 1981. Dynamics of marriage distances among the Ahmadiyyas. *Curr. Anthropol.* 22:572–73
66. Kay, P. 1971. Introduction. In *Explorations in Mathematical Anthropology*, ed. P. Kay, pp. xii–xvii. Cambridge, Mass: MIT Press
67. Kelley, J., Perlman, M. 1971. Social mobility in Toro: Some preliminary results from Western Uganda. *Econ. Dev. Cult. Change* 19:204–21
68. Kim, J. 1975. Factor analysis. In *Statistical Package for the Social Sciences*, ed. N. Nie et al, pp. 468–514. New York: McGraw-Hill. 2nd ed.
69. Kim, J., Kohout, F. 1975. Multiple regression analysis. See Ref. 68, pp. 320–67
70. Kim, J., Mueller, C. 1978. *Factor Analysis: Statistical Methods and Practical Issues*. Sage Univ. Pap. Ser. Quant. Appl. Soc. Sci. 07–014. Beverly Hills, Calif: Sage
71. Kim, J., Mueller, C. 1978. *Introduction to Factor Analysis: What It Is and How To Do It*. Sage Univ. Pap. Ser. Quant. Appl. Soc. Sci. 07–013. Beverly Hills, Calif: Sage
72. Kirk, L., Burton, M. 1977. Meaning and context: A study of contextual shifts in meaning of Masai personality descriptors. *Am. Ethnol.* 4:734–61
73. Kluckhohn, C. 1939. On certain recent applications of association coefficients to ethnological data. *Am. Anthropol.* 41:345–77
74. Kowalski, C. 1972. A commentary on the use of multivariate statistical methods in anthropometric research. *Am. J. Phys. Anthropol.* 36:119–32
75. Kronenfeld, D. 1981. Mathematical social-cultural anthropology. *Am. Anthropol.* 83:121–42
76. Kruskal, J., Wish, M. 1978. *Multidimensional Scaling*. Sage Univ. Pap. Ser. Quant. Appl. Soc. Sci. 07–011. Beverly Hills, Calif: Sage
77. Labovitz, S. 1972. Statistical usage in sociology: Sacred cows and ritual. *Sociol. Meth. Res.* 1:13–37
78. Lave, J., Stepick, A., Sailer, L. 1977. Extending the scope of formal analysis: A technique for integrating analyses of kinship relations with analyses of other dyadic relations. *Am. Ethnol.* 4:321–38
79. Lorr, M. 1983. *Cluster Analysis for Social Scientists*. San Francisco: Jossey-Bass
80. Lutz, C. 1982. The domain of emotion words in Ifaluk. *Am. Ethnol.* 9:113–28
81. McCracken, R. 1982. Cultural differences in food preferences and meaning. *Hum. Organ.* 41:161–66
82. McGuire, R., Netting, R. 1982. Leveling peasants? The maintenance of equality in a Swiss alpine community. *Am. Ethnol.* 9:269–90
83. Malhotra, K. C. 1980. Gene dispersion in man: The Indian case. *Curr. Anthropol.* 21:135–36
84. Miller, M., Stokes, C. S. 1975. Path analysis in sociological research. *Rural Sociol.* 40:193–201
85. Minge-Kalman, W. 1978. Household economy during the peasant-to-worker transition in the Swiss Alps. *Ethnology* 17:183–96
86. Mitchell, H. F., Mitchell, J. C. 1980. Social factors in the perception of the causes of disease. In *Numerical Techniques in Social Anthropology*, ed. J. C. Mitchell, pp. 49–68. Philadelphia: Inst. Study Human Iss.
87. Montgomery, E., Johnson, A. 1976. Machiguenga energy expenditure. *Ecol. Food Nutr.* 6:97–105
88. Morgan, K., Basehart, H. 1977. Concomitants of Matengo cultivation intensity: A discrete multivariate model. *Ethnology* 16:185–90

89. Morrison, D., Henkel, R., eds. 1970. *The Significance Test Controversy*. Chicago: Aldine
90. Murdock, G. 1949. *Social Structure*. New York: Macmillan
91. Naroll, R., Cohen, R., eds. 1970. *A Handbook of Method in Cultural Anthropology*. New York: Columbia Univ. Press
92. Ogburn, W. 1927. Sociology and statistics. See Ref. 7, pp. 378–92
93. Oxnard, C. 1973. *Form and Pattern in Human Evolution*. Chicago: Univ. Chicago Press
94. Palsson, G., Durrenberger, E. P. 1982. To dream of fish: The causes of Icelandic skippers' fishing success. *J. Anthropol. Res.* 38:227–42
95. Papps, I. 1983. The role and determinants of bride-price: The case of the Palestinian village. *Curr. Anthropol.* 24:203–17
96. Pelto, P., Pelto, G. 1975. Intra-cultural diversity: Some theoretical issues. *Am. Ethnol.* 2:1–18
97. Pelto, P., Pelto, G. 1978. *Anthropological Research*. Cambridge: Cambridge Univ. Press. 2nd ed.
98. Persons, W. 1927. Economics and statistics. See Ref. 7, pp. 161–77
99. Plattner, S. 1982. Economic decision making in a public marketplace. *Am. Ethnol.* 9:399–420
100. Poggie, J. 1979. Small-scale fishermen's beliefs about success and development: A Puerto Rican case. *Hum. Organ.* 38:6–11
101. Pollnac, R. 1975. Intra-cultural variability in the structure of the subjective color lexicon in Buganda. *Am. Ethnol.* 2:89–110
102. Pollnac, R., Robbins, M. 1972. Gratification orientations and modernization in rural Buganda. *Hum. Organ.* 31:63–72
103. Reddy, B. M. 1981. Marriage distances among migrants to Puri: More departures from leptokurtosis. *Curr. Anthropol.* 22:175–76
104. Redman, C. 1973. Multistage field work and analytic techniques. *Am. Antiq.* 38:61–79
105. Reynolds, H. 1977. *Analysis of Nominal Data*. Sage Univ. Pap. Ser. Quant. Appl. Soc. Sci. 07–007. Beverly Hills, Calif: Sage
106. Robbins, M., Pollnac, R. 1974. A multivariate analysis of the relationship of artificial to cultural modernity in rural Buganda. In *The Human Mirror: Material and Spatial Images of Man*, ed. M. Richardson, pp. 174–95. Baton Rouge: Louisiana State Univ. Press
107. Roberts, J., Chiao, C., Pandey, T. 1975. Meaningful god sets from a Chinese personal pantheon and a Hindu personal pantheon. *Ethnology* 14:121–48
108. Roberts, J., Golder, T., Chick, G. 1980. Judgment, oversight and skill: A cultural analysis of P-3 pilot error. *Hum. Organ.* 39:5–21
109. Romney, A. K., Shephard, R., Nerlove, S. B., eds. 1972. *Multidimensional Scaling*, Vol. 2. New York: Seminar Press
110. Rose, M., Romney, A. K. 1979. Cognitive pluralism or individual differences: A comparison of alternative models of American English kin terms. *Am. Ethnol.* 6:752–62
111. Rummel, R. 1970. *Applied Factor Analysis*. Evanston, Ill: Northwestern Univ. Press
112. Scheps, S. 1982. Statistical blight. *Am. Antiq.* 47:836–51
113. Schweizer, T. 1980. Multidimensional scaling of internal differences in similarity data: The perception of interethnic similarity in Indonesia. *J. Anthropol. Res.* 36:149–73
114. Short, J. 1974. Report of the editor of the American Sociological Review. *Footnotes* 2:12–13
115. Siegel, S. 1956. *Nonparametric Statistics*. New York: McGraw-Hill
116. Smith, C. 1978. Response to Thompson and Crandall. *Hum. Organ.* 27:103–10
117. Sokal, R., Sneath, P. 1963. *Principles of Numerical Taxonomy*. San Francisco: Freeman
118. Spencer, P. 1980. Polygyny as a measure of social differences in Africa. See Ref. 86, pp. 117–60
119. Stevens, S. 1946. On the theory of scales of measurement. *Science* 103:677–80
120. Stier, F. 1982. Domestic economy: Land, labor and wealth in a San Blas community. *Am. Ethnol.* 9:519–37
121. Strauss, D., Romney, A. K. 1982. Log-linear multiplicative models for the analysis of endogamy. *Ethnology* 21:79–99
122. Swedlund, A. 1972. Observations on the concept of neighbourhood knowledge and the distribution of marriage distances. *Ann. Hum. Genet.* 35:327–30
123. Thomas, D. 1976. *Figuring Anthropology*. New York: Holt, Rinehart & Winston
124. Thomas, D. 1978. The awful truth about statistics in anthropology. *Am. Antiq.* 43:231–44
125. Thomas, J. 1981. The socioeconomic determinants of political leadership in a Tojolabal Maya community. *Am. Ethnol.* 8:127–38
126. Tjon Sie Fat, F. E. 1981. More complex formulae of generalized exchange. *Curr. Anthropol.* 22:377–99

127. Tjon Sie Fat, F. E. 1983. Age metrics and twisted cylinders: Predictions from a structural model. *Am. Ethnol.* 10:585–604
128. Truex, G. 1977. Measurement of intersubject variations in categorizations. *J. Cross-Cult. Psychol.* 8:71–82
129. von Glascoe, C. 1979. Evidence for multiple cognitive realities in Yucatec game cognition. In *Ethnolinguisics: Boas, Sapir and Whorf Revisited*, ed. M. Mathiot, pp. 297–312. The Hague: Mouton
130. Weil, J. 1980. *The organization of work in a Quechua pioneer settlement: The adaptation of highland tradition in the lowlands of eastern Bolivia*. PhD thesis. Columbia Univ., New York, NY
131. Weller, S. 1983. New data on intracultural variability: The hot-cold concept of medicine and illness. *Hum. Organ.* 42:249–57
132. White, D. 1973. Mathematical anthropology. In *Handbook of Social and Cultural Anthropology*, ed. J. Honigmann, pp. 369–446. Chicago: Rand-McNally
133. White, G. 1978. Ambiguity and ambivalence in A'ara personality descriptors. *Am. Ethnol.* 5:334–60
134. White, G. 1980. Social images and social change in a Melanesian society. *Am. Ethnol.* 7:352–70
135. Winans, E., Haugerud, A. 1977. Rural self-help in Kenya: The Harambee Movement. *Hum. Organ.* 36:334–52
136. Wood, J. 1980. Rural Western Navajo household income strategies. *Am. Ethnol.* 7:493–503
137. Wright, S. 1921. Correlation and causation. *J. Agric. Res.* 20:557–85
138. Wright, S. 1934. The method of path coefficients. *Ann. Math. Stat.* 5:161–215
139. Zeller, R., Carmines, E. 1978. *Statistical Analysis of Social Data*. Chicago: Rand-McNally

TEXT AND DISCOURSE

Aaron V. Cicourel

Department of Sociology and School of Medicine, University of California San Diego, La Jolla, California 92093

Speaking, listening, writing, and reading are integral aspects of what we seek to convey by such notions as culture, symbolism, identity, and community when we examine human daily life across its folk-taxonomic "savage" and "domesticated" manifestations (15). The creation, analysis, storage, and growth of knowledge presuppose cognitive and linguistic processes for their sociocultural production and understanding. Knowledge is both a topic and a resource for the construction and understanding of human life, providing us with a framework for tracing changes in what often are called "traditional" and "modern" forms of social structure.

This chapter builds on several types of research, including an earlier paper by the author (7), and especially on the discussion by Goody (15) that writing, particularly alphabetic literacy, altered communication as a face-to-face activity, augmented our critical abilities and activities, and facilitated the accumulation of abstract knowledge. The reflexive or contemplative study of different textual materials, including those which were initially presented orally, made literacy a powerful resource for the reconstruction of history as well as giving us a better understanding of change and invariant conditions of knowledge accumulation and communication in preliterate and literate groups.

In his discussion of Robin Horton's (22) work comparing the relationship between African traditional thought and Western science, Goody distinguishes (a) comparisons of the religious thought of simple societies and the scientific thought of complex groups, from (b) the study of thought found in the development of contemporary science and the technical thinking found in traditional societies. The present chapter parallels Goody's concern by looking at the interaction of common sense and applied scientific reasoning in a contemporary medical setting.

I first present a review of some recent work on the study of literacy, thought, and meaning within a context of oral and written communication. This research does not always refer to the same or related topics or body of knowledge, but several themes can be identified, such as: differences in the way meaning is preserved in our understanding of oral versus written materials (21), the different linguistic styles that can be found in oral and written language (6), and the conditions under which oral and written language are used in daily life (20). Another general theme is the influence on oral and written language of bureaucratic activities in so-called postindustrial societies.

The latter portion of the chapter gives the reader brief examples of medical discourse in order to illustrate the interaction of common sense and applied scientific reasoning as constrained by organizational conditions. I examine elements of an original interview between a physician and patient and the way the interview is summarized in written medical history and physical examination reports. Observations of the transcript and tape of the original interview by a medical supervisor provide us with information on the adequacy or inadequacy of the questions used in the initial interview. Medical diagnostic inferences made by the first physician were also examined by the supervisor.

LITERACY IN A CULTURAL CONTEXT

An element often overlooked in discussions of literacy is the universal difficulty children experience in learning to read and especially to write. Literacy requires continual reproduction among adults to avoid problems with writing and reading, but with discourse, children and adults seem to flourish if the environment is perceived as appropriate.

Goody (15) challenges the ethnocentrism of writers who stress a bimodal pattern (particularly the work of Claude Lévi-Strauss) in the thought of the "savage" and "domesticated" mind. Idealized dichotomies tend to ignore the fundamental necessity of tacit knowledge and common-sense reasoning in everyday life *and* modern science (30, 35, 36).

The emergence of language and changes in communication are integral to the development of human thinking and everyday social interaction. The relation of orality and literacy is not simply the absence or presence of abstract thought, but it is the way abstractness is tied to daily life circumstances in oral rituals (4, 6) versus its communication in writing across time and space. Goody's reference to Bruner et al (5, p. 62) on the shift toward the decontextualization of knowledge calls attention to different forms of social organization. He points out, for example, the extent to which casual encounters in daily life and bureaucratic decontextualization yield observable differences in unplanned and planned conversation (28) and in written materials (7).

Oral cultures, according to Goody, tend to sustain "cultural homeostasis," or the absorption or rejection of the many relentless emergent mutations of culture during daily verbal interaction. But the mutation becomes a group change despite the contributions of individuals. With literacy, says Goody, there are commercial and political pressures that push and reward creative processes while bestowing recognition on individuals.

The theme of changes in human communications, notes Goody (15), was the consequence of the expansion of alphabetic literacy in Greece and the later introduction of the printed word during the Renaissance in Europe. He points out that Emile Durkheim ignored these factors in describing the shift from mechanical to organic solidarity while stressing the growth in the division of labor and its concomitant notion of role specialization.

For Goody, an essential aspect of writing is that it does not replace speech but enhances social action, particularly in bureaucratic politico-legal affairs. Writing provides an abstract form of social control over different groups without the necessity of continuous face-to-face exchanges where oral and nonverbal conditions dominate interaction. Goody briefly acknowledges the work of Max Weber here and the role of written documents in bureaucratic organizations. Writing influences daily work habits by making communication more formal or impersonal or depersonalized.

Goody points out that distinctions that refer to "primitive" versus "advanced" or "wild" versus "domesticated" thinking can be understood more clearly if we examine changes in the mode of communication and the introduction of different forms of writing. Accounting for the process of "domestication" becomes easier if we recognize the impact on daily life of devising different intellectual technologies. A major question becomes: How have changes in the means of communication transformed cognitive processes?

Changes in the means of communication not only lead to modes of thought that seem more closely tied to particular types of communication (such as the editing practices associated with writing), but also lead to changes in the extent and types of social interaction that can and will occur as, for example, when we become involved in interpreting documents or reports or prose in a group context (20).

The construction of documents occurs relentlessly in Western daily life. For example, oral activities often involve immediate or subsequently recorded experiences such as written medical histories, legal briefs, police reports, teachers' assessments of student oral performance (including reading aloud), and reports on business or other meetings. Such documentation is intended to summarize and provide details about the events that occurred. All such activities involve the preservation or transformation of meaning.

PROCESSING AND REPRESENTING KNOWLEDGE

Our ability to speak and write coherently and comprehend what we hear and read presupposes knowledge content and processes that have been characterized as mental structures, schemata, underlying representations, or folk models of the mind. Our perception and interpretation of objects, events, or general experiences are structured by schemata or folk models. Schemata are activated by environmental experiences and in turn guide and are influenced by our perceptions. As the environment produces new experiences or data there occurs an automatic, activated, interaction among schemata (27a).

A central feature of folk models is their use of a taken-for-granted knowledge base or "personal" (30) or "common sense" (35, 36) or "procedural" (1, 32–34, 43) construction by individual actors. The hallmark of procedural or commonsense knowledge is that comprehension is contingent on their embeddedness in, and sensitivity to, the settings in which their elements emerge and are used in daily life.

Constructed or schematized knowledge that is said to be governed by context free inference rules is often called "declarative" or "objective." The idea of declarative and procedural knowledge is meant to distinguish the "process" aspects of a representational system from its "data" aspects (43). Declarative systems consist of large numbers of facts and very few special purpose procedures. General rules are said to exist for making inferences in declarative systems, and these rules are not dependent on any particular set of facts (33). Declarative systems of knowledge are viewed as advantageous because they are supposed to receive new knowledge without having to develop new rules of inference, yet these same rules make it possible to create new inferences. Knowledge, in this idealized system, can be segmented into discrete statements that can be identified and made accessible fairly easily.

Procedural knowledge refers to processes and the knowledge embedded within these processes. Procedural knowledge consists of many special purpose procedures that contain knowledge of the kinds of contingencies that are an integral part of the special operators that make up the system. Each domain of knowledge is likely to be separate with little or no transfer from one to the other, hence making it difficult to add new knowledge (33). Procedural knowledge is an idealized notion that is always linked to special activities and settings.

The internal semantic structure of knowledge representation in the view of Rumelhart and Norman assumes importance under three sets of conditions. First, we are able to go beyond old knowledge to semantic domains that schemata were not designed to represent. Second, new knowledge becomes assimilated into the old structures. Third, elements of knowledge are compared with one another. The key issue here is that of learning or applying knowledge acquired in one domain to another through analogical reasoning. A central element of the Rumelhart and Norman schema theory is learning by analogy (how to specify new procedures from old ones). They seek to identify a mechanism that will bridge the differences between procedural and declarative perspectives.

The term "mental model" (23) is another way of explaining higher cognitive processes that are integral to oral and written communication and problem solving. The central activities of mental models are comprehension and inference. Johnson-Laird refers to the recursive procedures that must exist in order for individual actors to map propositional representations into mental models. An example would be the linguistic analysis of definite and indefinite descriptions, pronouns, and additional anaphoric expressions. Mental models enable us to interpret discourse and writing as coherent and plausible and to identify the speaker and reader's intentions. The recursive use of procedures with which to map propositions or to project images and thus create mental representations that go beyond the information given (i.e. create default values for missing information) enables individual actors to construct and revise mental models during action and communication.

SPOKEN VERSUS WRITTEN LANGUAGE USE

The literature on spoken and written language is quite large. A comprehensive review of what Tannen (38–40) calls oral and literate strategies is not possible here. Tannen's research on face-to-face conversation and expository prose pinpoints important differences between decontextualized written language and context-bound spoken language. She concludes that what is central is not spoken versus written modes, but the relative focus on interpersonal involvement that can usually be found in conversation, and the foregrounding of information that occurs in expository prose. Whereas written language achieves cohesion by lexicalization, notes Tannen, cohesion in spoken language depends on paralinguistic and nonverbal signals.

Subsequent remarks in this section will focus on a few writers in order to give the reader more details about the contrast between text and discourse than would be possible if only brief mention was made of the many empirical and theoretical studies of the subject. One of the consequences of my selective review of the literature is that I am unable to discuss the important work of Scribner and Cole (36a). Their attempts to isolate the effects of literacy from exposure to schooling lead Scribner and Cole to conclude that among the Vai of West Africa, literacy skills emerge independently of schools and teachers, and such skills transfer to other skills in a limited way. For Scribner and Cole, literacy per se does not foster abstract and logical thinking. Its use depends on the contexts in which it is used; literacy is viewed as a set of socially organized practices. The review that follows, therefore, is limited because it does not cover the comparative settings of the type described by Scribner and Cole.

Chafe (6, p. 36) distinguishes between 1. informal spoken language such as dinner table conversations, 2. formal spoken language as in lectures, 3. informal written language contained in letters, and 4. formal written language as used in academic papers. He also notes that a language with no written tradition can have different styles that parallel in some ways the differences between spoken and written language (6)—that a kind of "oral literacy" can exist in an "oral literature" (4).

A general conclusion reached by Chafe is that speaking is faster than writing and slower than reading. As might be expected, handwriting is the slowest form of communication, but writing by hand provides us with more time to integrate our thoughts than is possible when we speak some ten times faster. Thus the more integrated quality of writing contrasts with the fragmented nature of speaking where we string together various ideas without connectives. Common conjunctions like *and, but, so,* and *because* are used more often in speaking than in writing.

By the integration of writing, Chafe (6) means putting more information into an idea than would be the case for speaking. Everyday speaking is characterized by a single clause containing one predicative element such as a verb or predicate adjective plus noun phrases with subject or object. A fragmented notion in speech may only have a noun phrase or prepositional phrase.

Nominalizations, notes Chafe, are used as an integrative device in writing. For example, *treatment* is used instead of *treat*, or *development* and *operation* instead of *develop* or *operate*. Nominalization adds an essentialy predicative element to an idea unit in the role of a noun in the syntax of the phrase or unit expressed. As one of the arguments of the central predication, a nominalization not only adds more information per unit of writing, but also occurs considerably more frequently in writing than in speech. For a discussion of additional integrative devices see Chafe (6).

Speakers usually face a person or group, and they probably share common knowledge about the local environment, at the same time receiving feedback on the effects of the speech and the listener's understanding or need for clarification. Consistency is not so much an issue as is involvement with the audience and the need to get a point across. On the other hand, writers may know little or nothing about their audience, which is displaced in time and space. Here the concern is with consistency across different people on different occasions and places. So "detachment" rather than involvement is the way Chafe characterizes the difference between writing and speaking.

What are the detachment devices in written language? For example, devices which will put distance between language and specific concrete states and events include the passive voice in English and nominalizations. Nominalizations serve to integrate predications within larger sentences, but they also suppresses the writer's involvement in actions by using abstract reification.

The speaker's involvement with an audience can be observed in the occurrence of references to one's self and others. Other forms of involvement include the speaker's reference to her or his own mental processes ("I can recall my own reaction to . . .") and monitoring the listener's involvement or the flow of information ("So we . . . so we . . . you know, we have . . ."). Chafe notes the use of emphatic particles like *just* ("I *just* don't . . .") and *really* ("and he got . . . really furious"); the use of vagueness and hedges ("sort of," "and so on") and direct quotes ("and she said, 'Bill, can I . . .' ") are additional elements of involvement that are not usually found in written language of the type examined by Chafe.

The notion of oral literature, notes Chafe, seems to unite spoken and written language. Chafe provides the reader with examples from his research on an Iroquois language, Seneca, to illustrate the notion of oral literature. The distinction Chafe calls to our attention is that between colloquial and ritual language use in Seneca.

Ritual language is described by Chafe as having features similar to written language because its content, style, and formulaic structure remain constant from performance to performance. Ritual language is repeated because of its value to a group. The performer of a ritual, notes Chafe, is removed from an audience in a way that is similar to the writer because of stylized intonation that is formal and polished. Ritual language is a monologue that tends to have minimal feedback and no verbal interaction and therefore minimum involvement with an audience.

Seneca, however, does not have the language features of English that distinguish spoken and written use (nominalizers, participles, attributive adjectives, prepositions, and complementizers, to mention a few of the integrative devices). We cannot, therefore, count integrative features, but instead Chafe points to the fragmented quality of Seneca conversation and the integrative nature of ritual talk that unites phrases or clauses into a single sentence with internal cohesion where phrases and clauses depend on one another.

The idea of a continuum of language development, notes Heath (20), from an oral tradition to a literate one, is widespread. Some societies are depicted as having restricted literacy and are noted for specific characterizations of oral language usage, while others have particular features associated with written language because of a fully developed literacy.

The notion of a dichotomous view of oral and literate traditions has been associated with Goody (14), Goody & Watt (16), Havelock (19), and Ong (29), and is challenged by Heath, who believes that the distinction is not as clear-cut as many have assumed. She notes that a close reading of Goody (14) and Goody & Watt (16) does not point to invariant consequences of literacy for individuals and societies. In other words, there is no clear evolution from an oral tradition in which the meaning of information is contingent on the experiences of speakers and listeners to a tradition that makes meaning explicit in the text without reliance on the readers' experiences.

In all types of societies the key issue, notes Heath (citing Goody), is the actual setting in which written communication occurs and with what consequences. In a postindustrial society of automation, scientific management, microprocessors, and logical reasoning, where and when, asks Heath, are reading and writing accomplished, with or for whom, and how?

The notion of a "literacy event," as defined by Heath, refers to the relationships between spoken and written language and their literate functions such as reading, writing, or responding to an interview question. Heath states that many literacy events are ritualistic; they require appropriate knowledge about the nature of written materials such as contracts, applications, and regulations, and yet these events do not necessarily extend our reading or writing skills. Possessing basic level literacy skills as taught in school may not be linked to literacy events that require, but do not extend, minimal uses of an oral mode in order to respond to written materials.

The research context for Heath's paper (20) is a working-class all-black community in the Carolinas she calls "Trackton." Her ethnographic work in community and work settings confirmed different forms and functions of written and spoken language by members of the community.

In Trackton, adults did not read to children, there were no bedtime stories, no children's books, no special occasions for reading, and solitary reading was rare. Preschool children, however, were exposed to aspects of their environment that required limited reading such as distinguishing brand names from product descriptions on boxes or bags. The children were able to identify the price on a label in a context of other written information. The central point by Heath is that children learned to read for practical purposes deemed necessary for their daily lives in their community, including a knowledge of practical written formats.

Reading is a social activity for Trackton adults, notes Heath. Reading alone without expressing oneself was rare. Instead, several adults would interact about the meaning of written texts, using the occasions to socialize and inform each other. The occasion thus generated jokes, digressions, and narratives during the negotiated interpretation of the written material. The interaction had the practical consequence of creating a collective interpretation of a document while perhaps also helping one person prepare a response.

For Heath, the central point is that written materials in the community context of Trackton deviated from our usual sense of literacy; there was seldom reading for aesthetic or intellectual rewards, or reading to children as a way of supporting or socializing them to the practices they are likely to encounter in school such as psychometric testing and the use of formulaic question-answer strategies in the classroom.

Heath concludes her paper by citing research by historians on literacy: literacy could open many doors but did not always mean getting through them and receiving benefits often attributed to its possession. The historical materials summarized by Heath (10–12, 27, 31, 37, to cite a few) point to the necessity of linking literacy to job requirements and shifts thereof during different periods of technological change and sociocultural prescriptions and proscriptions. Heath suggests that the traditional literacy of the classroom may not translate into the requirements of the application forms and accounting procedures we face in everyday life, nor the kinds of literacy skills demanded by employers.

The linguistic and cognitive skills associated with modernity might be clarified if there are significant differences in the way written versus orally presented texts are understood. Reviewing several studies on the ability of listeners and readers to extract information from a text, Hildyard & Olson (21) note that listeners seem to recall the gist of a story, while readers do better at recalling verbatim features, irrelevant details, or the surface structure of a story. The key issue is the way meaning is preserved in oral and written language.

Hildyard and Olson refer to the speaker's meaning in oral language, or the listener's construction of the speaker's point or intention, or the significance of what is heard as preserved in the listener's memory. The general notion is that listening involves the idea of a construction or interpretation of what is being said, or what was earlier called schemata or mental model, but does not include actual words, syntax, and intonation (21). Many students of language would question the author's reference to intonation as "ephemeral." Prosodic clues are essential elements of a listener's ability to construct a model or interpretation of the speaker's intention (18).

The key to understanding written language is the "sentence meaning" of a sentence or the surface semantic elements derivable from lexical items and syntax. The reference to "sentence meaning" or "literal meaning" implies a self-conscious use of declarative or more context-free meanings for lexical items and phrases, and includes both the overall sense or meaning of the sentence and a reference to sentence meaning or underlying propositional structure (21).

Grice's (17) notion of implicature is a central notion here. Discourse and textual materials presuppose a class of inferences that must be constructed by the reader or listener in order to capture what is not contained in the "literal" meaning of an utterance but is conveyed nevertheless. The "literal" versus "derived meaning" distinction is useful but does not always make explicit the pragmatic elements from the local interactional context that permit the construction of meaning to occur. The Gricean maxims help us recover deleted elements of discourse under ideal conditions that are said to hold for normal speech exchanges. Emergent, local conditions that contribute to the understanding of discourse virtually always include differential knowledge attributions participants of discourse construct for each other and the knowledge each views as obvious or takes for granted.

Gricean notions suggest how we make inferences that link different premises in order to comprehend what is perceived. The reader or listener's general knowledge, therefore, is an essential ingredient in the construction of pragmatic inferences and the speaker's intentions. Hildyard and Olson ask: do readers and listeners process the different aspects of meaning outlined thus far in the same way? The upshot is that reading a text seems to direct us to the identification and remembering of sentence meaning or its content, while listening to discourse directs us to the identification and remembering of the speaker's meaning or what was intended or meant (21), or paying attention to utterances that help build a coherent interpretation.

Hildyard and Olson divided their subjects into good, average, and poor readers. Following current research on the comprehension of stories, the authors utilized stories whose constituents consisted of the setting, the characters, a plan of action, the action itself, and the final outcome. Prior research has shown that these constituents are more likely to be remembered because they introduce new events and hence information considered relevant and important in a narrative. Such structural information can be explicit or implicit and is said to be necessary for the coherence of a story's main theme. Incidental information is said to be least remembered and serves to elaborate an event or episode, but its removal would not alter the overall comprehension of a story.

Better readers performed at a higher level than average and poor readers regardless of whether the story was read or heard by them and whether the information was central or peripheral to the story. There was a developmental difference in the findings, with Grade 5 children performing better than Grade 3 children. In general, therefore, Hildyard and Olson conclude that readers and listeners seem to employ different strategies in the comprehension of narrative discourse. Acquiring literacy skills, however, seems to provide people with greater awareness of sentence meaning regardless of whether the subject reads or hears the narrative.

In our selective review of the literature on textual and discourse production and understanding, several types of literacy have been discussed. For example, Goody's (15) work provides us with a general framework and substantive examples of different types of literacy across cultures and time. Chafe (6) reveals some basic linguistic differences between oral and written forms of communication and literacy. Work by Heath (20) indicates that in home and work settings, literacy can take on variations that need not always be equivalent to the literacy we expect in the classroom or on individual-oriented tests. Hildyard and Olson (21) present us with experimental data on the way subjects preserve different meanings (i.e. they construct different schemata or mental models) when they are asked to listen to rather than read the same materials. The consequences of the development of writing systems are emphasized by Goody (15, pp. 36–51) in order to underscore the cognitive by-products of literacy: the emergence of logic, philosophy, and reflective thinking, the control of data by classification, and the refinement of modes of communication.

Oral language can mask inconsistency, ambiguity, and contradiction, making it difficult for the listener to clarify and analyze intentions, deceptions, and evasiveness. But there is also the danger that our use of classification schemes and symbolic systems can misrepresent the actor's point of view in nonliterate and literate societies, including subgroups within literate groups whose primary form of communication involves an oral delivery that is always embedded in the pragmatics of local interaction with its particular prosody, gestures, physical posturing, and local knowledge.

Goody suggests that our classification of oral communication and its pragmatic context into standardized categories brings order and control into our understanding and encourages the growth of knowledge. My thesis, however, is that we need to clarify the persistence of an oral tradition whose pragmatic context and commonsense reasoning can be found in all social interaction. The study of medical diagnostic reasoning in bureaucratic settings permits us to observe many of the conditions we associate with the notions of oral and written traditions. What is perhaps most striking about the applied scientific environments of modern medicine is their relentless reproduction of emotional displays or muted feelings, the use of fragmented and often ambiguous or confused communication in a local context where the linguistic environments can include technical, quite mundane, metaphorical, metonymic, anaphoric, and deictic expressions. The range of communicative expressions and mental models presupposed always occurs in a local context of variable dominance among the participants with respect to the larger system of stratification or power that prevails.

In the practice of modern medicine, we can identify many, if not most, of the conditions associated with the broad range of oral and written activities we associate with Goody's (15) cautious reference to "The Grand Dichotomy" of primitive and advanced societies. With Goody, we believe the discussion that follows views the dichotomy as an inadequate way to characterize text and discourse.

Another aspect of literacy is the ability to move from a *listening strategy* (with or without note taking), in which the individual perceives and constructs meanings, to a *written strategy* where these meanings are represented in a coherent text.

In the remaining sections of this chapter, I seek to supplement the literature review by first discussing the role of power, authority, and bureaucracy in modern society. Then I will show how the common bureaucratic activity of eliciting information in a physician-patient (or teacher-student, lawyer-client, researcher-informant, police-suspect) exchange leads to a written report that is supposed to summarize the discourse event that preceded the written description or interpretation. I will provide a few brief examples of practical professional literacy that is common to bureaucratic organizations. The examples from a medical case study illustrate a relationship between discourse and text that is pervasive in all types of literacy displays.

THE BUREAUCRATIC BASIS OF MEDICAL DISCOURSE AND TEXT

Our brief review of the literature often suggested that modern society epitomizes the production of objective knowledge. Enormous resources are devoted to the reproduction of abstract and detailed knowledge in public and private sectors of nation-states. The reproductive knowledge process occupies a central role in the way modern societies achieve stability and change. The reproduction and use of knowledge contributes to the creation, maintenance, and change of status systems and the acquisition and use of authority and power through the possession and/or control of communicative expertise and information. The physician's possession and use of medical knowledge within a limited professional group is also like the "scientific authority" described by Pierre Bourdieu (2). Physicians' power derives from their ability to create "objective" representations of the patient's health or illness.

Max Weber's work (42, p. 941) has been a continual reminder of the way structures of dominancy profoundly influence every aspect of social action. Domination, as a special case of power, is closely linked in modern societies to the possession and use of knowledge. This view of power is especially evident in the professional-client relationship, particularly the case of doctor-patient exchanges, where knowledge as power also translates into economic rewards.

Discussions of authority and power are not always empirically and methodologically clear. For example, a central feature of power is special knowledge and the ability to interpret this knowledge in circumstances that can favor the professional's ability to create and influence courses of action. How is the professional, in Weber's terms, able to dominate because of a monopoly or control over information or a constellation of interests? The physician is said to possess the authority to command, while making use of a Western cultural tradition that in its idealized form states that a patient's duty is to obey. The physician's knowledge base, professional status, and bureaucratic support become powerful resources that few patients can challenge. Theoretical discussions of domination often lack a specification of the way the doctor is able to sustain and justify his authority and power by his or her knowledge base and the sociocultural expectations and sanctions associated with health care delivery.

Weber's work tends to focus on the notion of domination as the "authoritarian power of command." But if Weber's notion is to become empirically viable, we must make theoretical modifications and create the methodological conditions needed for empirical clarification. In medicine, for example, we must look at communication strategies and their dominating implications to understand the way different interest constellations can operate. The cultural etiquette that prevails in medical settings makes it difficult to pinpoint the economic goals and constraints of patient and doctor during their actual exchanges.

The extent to which a patient complies with a cultural tradition to obey or follow the physician's wishes is contingent on several factors. For example, the fear of serious illness and death can be a strong motivating factor to be submissive with a physician. Patients' class and religious background and their mental models about medicine, illnesses, and remedies may be used to challenge the doctor's presumed monopoly over scientific medicine. Patients may appear to comply with the doctor's wishes throughout the medical interview but not pursue the physician's instructions for treatment. Patients may follow the physician's instructions but not believe in its effectiveness. Physicians may appear to dominate the interaction if patients are convinced that they cannot ask questions, or if they do ask, that they will not be answered. The doctor-patient relationship is often not only inhibited in these ways, but charged with latent and sometimes open emotion (8).

The local context of medical authority includes the emotionally charged thoughts that can flood a patient's consciousness at a time when a physician's detached communication can make any discrepancy in their respective knowledge resources appear even more exaggerated. Patients' "discourse literacy" or ability to use their own knowledge base or experiences can be markedly diminished during an interview and physical examination. For example, the patient can agree to symptoms suggested by the physician, or find it difficult to specify precise symptoms or events requested by the physician or experienced by the patient.

COMMUNICATION, KNOWLEDGE, AND LITERACY IN A MEDICAL SETTING

The medical setting of a university hospital or one of its clinics provides an arena for many forms of communication, knowledge, and literacy. Both highly technical and fairly mundane knowledge and discourse can be found, and an ability to "read" not only textual materials but also laboratory reports and radiological or various types of electronic outputs may be required. We can expect to find considerable variation in the forms and levels of "literacy" even among those with considerable education.

Before proceeding with a brief excursion into text and discourse in a particular medical setting, three general issues need to be stated that will provide a frame for the empirical excerpts that follow.

One general issue concerns the kinds of knowledge that characterize different human activities. To simplify matters, I will invoke the earlier distinction between schematized and local knowledge while recognizing that all human social interaction, including reading and writing, presuppose both of these broad categories. My intention here is simply to acknowledge the obvious distinction between the memorial knowledge brought to oral or written exchanges (speaking, listening, reading, writing) and the local production of knowledge as an emergent element of the particular setting and the way participants project and revise their immediate comprehension over the course of an exchange.

A second general issue is the following: how does writing about some event or interactional sequence differ from discourse about the same event or interactional sequence? A specific issue here is the kind of knowledge base each participant brings to the exchange and the text that accounts for the discourse.

The medical setting is nicely suited to examining the first two issues because of a bureaucratic requirement that medical histories and physical examinations must be summarized in written form. The existence of formal knowledge in textbooks about the biological and clinical medicine aspects of health care delivery provides us with a written cumulative knowledge base with which to compare the oral and written versions of a diagnostic interview and physical examination. Hence we have a basis for assessing the kinds of schematized or memorial basic science and clinical knowledge an intern, resident, or training fellow ("house staff") exhibits in asking questions of a patient and in writing up the medical history and physical examination. In the present case, therefore, we have the opportunity to assess the house staff's oral report to the medical supervisor and to obtain an additional assessment by examining the house staff's initial interview with the patient and the written report that summarizes this interview.

A third issue we must consider is the interaction between commonsense thinking or reasoning and applied scientific thinking or reasoning when the physician and patient elicit information from each other during the initial interview and when the physician (house staff) reports to the attending physician. What aspects of the discourse are to be found in the written report of the medical history and physical examination?

Our point is that we must confront the "Grand Dichotomy" noted by Goody and its oral/written contrast because of the necessary and ubiquitous role of commonsense reasoning in science, applied science, and all "rational" bureaucratic activities. Dichotomies do not examine adequately the conditions under which different modes of thought sustain their integrity despite the evolution of communication strategies and technology.

My concern in the pages that follow is with medical diagnostic reasoning as an interaction between basic and clinical science knowledge in a local, contextualized setting that forces the physician to recognize that a patient's knowledge base and reasoning can be orthogonal to the perspective of the doctor. Doctor-patient and physician-physician interactions presuppose and rely on knowledge sources that are embedded in their everyday life experiences, yet the use of technical language and reasoning pervades the exchanges that can be observed.

The observation that medical personnel rely on commonsense knowledge and reasoning with patients and among themselves underscores the interaction of schematized and local knowledge processes. Terms like subjective and objective knowledge do not capture this interaction of memorial and locally emergent knowledge. There is often a tendency to stress a strong deterministic or highly relativistic conception of knowledge processes and knowledge representation. If we are to avoid the reification of these idealized conceptions of knowledge processes and their abstract characterizations, we must examine the settings where on-line decision making occurs.

Aspects of Medical Literacy

The natural settings social scientists call formal organizations or bureaucratic institutions are rich resources for examining oral and written communication because they routinely exhibit states of affairs that reflect different modes of thought, apparent semantic consistency and clarity, confusion, ambiguity, and misinformation. We normally assume that organizational settings exhibit fairly clear and bounded oral and written semantic domains, but these domains often remain tacit resources to researchers and professionals and do not become topics of explicit research. The clinical practice of medicine is not an idealized application of literacy and declarative systems of knowledge learned in basic science courses, journals, medical clerkships and practice, but like other exchanges, it is an arena for constructing new schemata or mental models by intuitive and systematic analogical modifications of old domains of knowledge that interact with new experiences embedded in often mundane, emergent settings.

The impact of literacy and modes of communication is evident when the physician converts the often idiomatic and sometimes ambiguous language and personal beliefs or folk theories of the patient into statements with the appearance of unambiguous declarative knowledge and a systematic notation system. The process of creating elements of declarative knowledge by the physician integrates information elicited from the patient with existing concepts and categories whose semantic properties are assumed to be well known. Yet the patient's language reflects an uncertainty about how to reveal his or her knowledge about symptoms and their consequences, and these expressive problems are invariably embedded in confusing and often frightening emotions and feelings about his/her health condition.

All physicians possess at least a tacit level of awareness or proficiency in the use of different linguistic registers or codes. But the semantic aspects of these registers are not known uniformly and must be negotiated with respect to the sociocultural background of the doctor and patient. The medical setting, therefore, creates conditions under which everyday modes of communication and thinking initially take precedence over formal concerns with the production of objective medical knowledge.

The participants of medical organizational settings routinely reconstruct two universal features of bureaucracies: planned and unplanned verbal and nonverbal discourse and texts (reports, memoranda) that generate descriptive traces of the daily activities, decisions, and official actions of the organization. The physician's notes sometimes are cryptic and minimal, while on other occasions he or she may produce detailed and formal medical histories.

Medical decision making begins when the physician becomes aware of the reason for a referral. An oral or written communication about the patient's complaint may be given to a nurse or other personnel engaged in the initial screening and scheduling of an appointment. The physician poses indirect, direct, leading or probe-like questions and transforms the patient's responses into mental and/or written general or specific categories or facts that might lend support to general or specific hypotheses about a differential diagnosis. It is this historicized, interpretive, summarization process that can subsequently result in the production of a crisp and factually oriented oral or written account of the patient's medical history and physical status. Yet the initial interaction sequence virtually always contains elements of confusing, ambiguous, factually misleading or incorrect data in addition to information that is both helpful and necessary for a differential diagnosis (7–9).

The brief excerpts I present below from an original interview between a training fellow (TF) and the patient occurred in a small examining room in the regular clinic area of a university hospital. The setting in which the TF gives her account of the original interview to the attending (supervisory) physician is a small room a few doors away from the examining room.

Unlike the initial doctor-patient exchange where the TF is in control of the situation, the account the TF must give to the attending physician must contain topics or themes that can be perceived as coherent by the physician and that convey a command over a knowledge base both physicians may or may not take for granted during the exchange. The reader can obtain a minimal understanding of the kinds of information the TF must display as part of her competence by consulting the following excerpts taken from a slightly modified and partial handout given to medical students when they are introduced to rheumatological diseases in a course called An Introduction to Clinical Medicine. The handout closely resembles a textbook format and can be viewed as an instantiation of the discussion by Goody (15) and others on the way knowledge codification occurs.

Formal clinical description of rheumtoid arthritis (RA)*
1. Large *and* small joints of upper and lower extremities,
2. symmetrically (both sides of body).
3. Early joint problems can be transient or "migratory"—appear to
4. leave one joint, then involve another.
5. "Stiffness" or gel-like sensation in the morning or upon rising,
6. caused by inflammation.
7. Symptoms can wax and wane, but usually the arthritis is persistent
8. after a while.
9. Functionally: can produce difficulties in ambulation (because of
10. lower extremities) and in activities of daily living (upper
11. extremities such as shoulders, thumbs, etc).
12. Fairly constant, observable joint swelling, meaning involvement
13. of intra-articular structures (inside capsule of the joint).

Osteoarthritis (OA)
1. Degenerative process
2. (osteoar*throses,* emphasizes noninflammatory nature of
3. disease)
4. Can appear in 30s, but especially in women with history in
5. family with other women (mother, sisters).
6. Normally appears in middle age.
7. Two forms are common:
8. (*a*) Weight-bearing joints (knees, hips), low back and small
9.   joints of the hands. (Generalized OA)
10. (*b*) Fingers only (interphalangeal or inflammatory or erosive
11.   are the terms used). (OA of fingers)
12. Certain joints seldom involved; wrist, elbow, shoulders, and
13. ankles. When OA does occur in these joints, it means another
14. disease may be present (hyperparathyroidism, hemochromatosis).

The two partial descriptions of rheumatoid and osteoarthritis symptoms and characteristics are presented here to give the reader a minimal understanding of the way medical students and somewhat more advanced medical personnel like interns or residents may be introduced to aspects of two rheumatological diseases. The language used is fairly straightforward and not overly technical except in a few places where the following terms are used: "extremities," "inflammation," "ambulation," "intra-articular," "capsule of the joint," "interphalangeal," "hyperparathyroidism," and "hemochromatosis."

*From a handout prepared by Dr. Michael Weisman.

In the pages that follow, the reader will be able to see the way the TF employs some of these terms when speaking to the patient and attending physician and when writing up the medical history and physical examination.

The Interaction of Local and Schematized Knowledge

The occasion for a medical interview and physical examination signals the special nature of the exchange and activities that follow. We want to look for aspects of communication which we associate with spontaneous everyday encounters where we routinely take for granted the referents and topics to which we allude ambiguously or by default.

A central feature of everyday discourse is the pervasive use of anaphoric and deictic functions. The general topic here is the use of pronouns in discourse. A deictic use of pronouns occurs when the referent is contingent on context and the local circumstances in which the utterance is produced. Let us assume a doctor and patient have been talking about the pain the patient has been experiencing in her fingers. For example, the patient may state: "This is the one that kills!" The patient may point to a particular finger that is within the visual field of doctor and patient. The patient uses deictic expressions to identify a particular finger that perhaps has caused more pain than the others. "This is the one" refers to the particular finger, while "that kills" refers to the pain.

When a pronoun is used to refer to objects or persons that were introduced by other expressions in the discourse, the pronoun is often called an anaphoric function because it refers back to some object or person identified previously. For example, the patient may tell the doctor about a previous experience with a physician and say: "Dr. Jones said I had a tumor. He said it was benign." "He" and "it" exemplify the use of anaphoric functions.

The use of anaphora is economical; they enable us to presume that certain referents are clearly established and do not have to be repeated each time. Deictic elements force us to make inferences that are highly contingent on local circumstances in the production of meaning. Their occurrence is typical of everyday social interaction.

The interview between the doctor and patient opened with the TF asking:

1 TF: Umm, who sent you to arthritis?
2 P: Uh, Uh, oncology
   After a brief digression, in which the TF establishes the patient's age (44), the following exchange occurs:
8 TF: Okay (9 seconds) and (do you?) have any problems?
9 P: Oooooh, the whole body.
10 TF: Whole body.
11 P: Joints, really bad.
12 TF: Uhuh, yeah, okay.

13 P: And ummm, breakout in these big red spots, (mumbling)
14   tops and toes.
15 TF: Uhummm
16 P: But only when I sit in the hot water, they come out
17   quite a bit, my hands get, like this, they stiffen up.

The patient's general response (line 9) that her "whole body" is a problem, is followed by a more specific reference to her joints (line 11). The TF's encouraging reply in line 12 leads to further remarks (lines 13–14) by the patient about the "big red spots."

The opening lines of the initial doctor-patient interview provide us with deictic and anaphoric linguistic functions and take for granted referents like "tops and toes" that are characteristic of medical interviews and all discourse. For example, the reference to "tops and toes" could mean that red spots appear on the top parts of the hands and feet rather than the palms and soles. The reference to ". . . these big red spots . . ." in lines 13–14 above, presupposes elements of a common lexicon and knowledge base for the physician and patient, but where the deictic element "these" signals a past occasion and imagery that are unclear. The term "these" (line 13) implies a here and now, but there was no direct pointing to existing red spots. Local circumstances, therefore, help us infer that the patient has invoked procedural schematized knowledge from prior experiences and that her use of particular lexical items make sense to the physician.

The past nature of the red spots is underscored in lines 16–17 above when their appearance is said to occur ". . . only when I sit in the hot water . . ." The anaphoric function "they" of line 17 refers to the hands that ". . . get, like this," where the deictic "this" simulates a process that suggests a previous stiffening condition in the hands. We can confirm the patient's reference to past events because of the statement that the red spots only appear when she sits in hot water. Our local knowledge about the red spots stems from the observation of the lack of the same conditions in the patient's hands in the examining room. The planned circumstances of a bureaucratic interview reveal our necessary reliance on emergent, local, deictic or anaphoric expressions and the tacit knowledge they presuppose.

The use of lexical items or phrases such as "whole body," "joints really bad," "these big red spots," and "tops and toes," may appear meaningful for a nonmedical reader. The attending physician, however, stated that the red spots and hand stiffening that emerge when the hands and feet are placed in hot water are not diagnostic for rheumatological diseases and are not consistent with the information contained in the formal material presented above from the handout.

The TF attempts to establish a time frame for the red spots and hand stiffening in the following lines:

20 TF: Ummkay, so now how long has this been happening?
21 P: Oh, quite a while.
22 TF: Couple months? er,
23 P: Longer than that, cuz I was taking Dr. Blumberg
24   (Door/drawer slamming closed) up in San Miguel.
25 TF: But is he an arthritis doctor?
26 P: Mmhuh(?)
27 TF: Okay, what did Doc, now, so, it's maybe uh 9 months? or
28 P: No, it's been about a year'n a half.
29 TF: 'Bout a year an a'half.

The TF's remarks raised doubts for the attending physician about the stability and conciseness of her knowledge base. The time frame of 18 months should have told the TF that obvious rheumatoid arthritis symptoms should have been evident if this disease was confirmed by Dr. Blumberg and diagnostically relevant here. The symptoms described in the details from the handout above do not associate red spots with submersion in hot water. The reference to "joints really bad" remains ambiguous and would need considerable additional specificity to be of diagnostic value. Either the TF's knowledge base about the joints of the hands that are relevant for rheumatoid and osteoarthritis was not activated or we can suggest the knowledge is inadequately "crystalized" to be of value here.

The commonsense reasoning of the discourse is evident in line 20 of the original interview where the deictic "this" can refer to the red spots *and* hand stiffening. The anaphoric "it's" of lines 27 and 28 of the original interview refers back to the occurrence of red spots and stiffening in lines 13–19, and the remark ". . . how long has this been happening?" of line 20. When the TF asks if the time period had been a "couple of months" and then "9 months," her remarks could be motivated by a desire to explore schemata that could be linked to the handout material quoted above. The patient's reference to ". . . about a year'n a half" should have eliminated many diagnostic possibilities because her symptoms were too ambiguous for the amount of time that had elapsed.

The materials of the original interview are a vivid reminder of the necessary role of deictic and anaphoric functions in medical interviewing and all discourse ("they come out quite a bit," "my hands get, like this," "they stiffen up," "they stiffen all the way up," ". . . how long has this been happening"). These functions are an integral part of everyday communication and commonsense knowledge and reasoning and are also a routine part of the medical interview and physical examination.

Considerable attention has been given in recent years to the physician's communication with the patient and the extent to which the patient's emotional condition, social status, and uncertainty about what is wrong are taken into account when the physician and patient exchange questions and answers (13, 41). These studies of physician-patient communication, however, seldom examine the kinds of knowledge each participant presupposes in their questions and answers.

The TF and attending physician's remarks represent different levels of medical literacy. In order for the physician to obtain the information she needs, the patient's account of her experiences must activate associations the physician will perceive as relevant. The TF's knowledge base appears to lack stable information about disease categories, their possible symptoms, and the relevance of different drugs for relieving symptoms.

A Quick Look at a Professional Exchange

The medical training of house staff provides us with a convenient display of declarative-like and procedural-like schematized knowledge when the TF, in the present case, reports her findings to the attending immediately after the initial interview with the patient. This exchange enables us to observe an oral display of aspects of technical literacy that parallels the "oral literature" discussed by Chafe (6) in an earlier section.

The material presented in the following lines from the TF-attending physician exchange is fairly direct and objective, suggesting confidence about the information expressed.

Training Fellow-Attending Physician Exchange

1 TF: Ok, next is Elena Louis, (background voices) anyway,
2   she's 44 years of age and sent here from (the?)
3   oncology group.
4   So the past two years she has had episodes initially
5   of erythema followed by swelling involving the second
6   and third metacarpal and PIP joints of both hands,
7   alternating, one time this hand, one time this hand.
8   She's also had arthritis of her ankles, which includes
9   redness on a lateral border of the lateral malleolus
10   followed by swelling.
11   Comes on, first the redness, and she has pain and
12   swelling within 24 hours.
13   Lasts for several days, and then it goes away.
14   But when she has it, the pain is quite severe.
15   It greatly limits her hand function, and her walking
16   function.
17   Ummm, she really has minimal joint complaints other
18   than back stiffness and her other joints.
19   She has had no difficulty with her elbows really, or

20   her shoulders.
21   Uhh, she's not had any nodules.
22   She has no Raynaud's (disease).
23   She has no Sjogrens.
24   She is tired all the time.
25   She is now getting a lot of leg cramping.
26   Ummm, she has no family history of arthritis.
27   She has no occasional morning sickness, but it's
28   not real (?) . . .
29 AP: How long, has this been a problem?

    We do not observe the prior sometimes ambiguous and fragmented discourse with the patient that now has been integrated by the TF in a way that reminds us of Chafe's (6) discussion of ritual language. There are several deictic and anaphoric expressions (lines 2, 7, 13, 13, 15, 27). The concepts described in the material from the handout cited earlier are incorporated into the declarative-like statements of the TF. The order in which the information was obtained in the initial interview has been altered and reflects the kinds of symptoms which can be found in the handout material.

    Chafe (6), as noted earlier, points out that the notion of oral literature appears to combine spoken and written language. The language employed by the TF when speaking to the attending physician parallels the oral literature notion in the sense of combining technical and everyday terms such as "erythema" or redness, "swelling," "lateral border of the lateral maleollus" (a reference to the ankle), "back stiffness," "Raynaud's" (disease), and the like. The attending physician (AP) does not challenge the TF's remarks. They both take for granted the implied semantic domains of relevance. The remark, for example, "How long, has this been a problem?" asked by the AP (line 29) implies that the long narrative created by the TF (lines 1–28 of the TF-AP exchange) has been understood. The AP, however, told me that the opening remarks by the TF are not relevant diagnostically. The oral ritual is challenged indirectly by the AP later in the exchange, but the authority of the written medical history and physical examination was not seen by the AP and takes on a life of its own.

    The attending physician was critical of the way the TF had posed questions of the patient, stating that the TF misunderstood the patient's condition and hence was unable to pose appropriate questions. The AP stated that many of the questions used by the TF were designed to review various medical systems in the hope of encountering symptoms that might suggest relevant medical categories. The misdiagnostic reasoning attributed to the TF by the AP should be clarified for the reader.

    An examination of lines 8–10 of the TF-AP exchange could suggest that the patient has rheumatoid arthritis and not osteoarthritis. The ankles, notes the AP, are not usually part of osteoarthritis. The TF's diagnosis, however, was "DJD" or degenerative joint disease, or a form of osteoarthritis. The TF's remarks in lines 17–28 of the TF-AP exchange seek to rule out several major categories (not shown here) that are normally explored with rheumatology patients.

The attending physician stated that in addition to ruling out osteoarthritis, he also would have ruled out rheumatoid arthritis because the redness, swelling, and pain reported by the patient had not persisted in a way that would be characteristic of this disease. Privately, therefore, the AP claimed the TF had misdiagnosed the patient's condition and had not pursued certain signs adequately. For example, over what period of time did the symptoms or signs persist? The AP stated that the patient's responses revealed inconsistencies that an experienced rheumatologist should have recognized as not fitting any of the classical rheumatological categories.

The TF's written remarks (medical history and physical examination) are stated in a crisp, factual manner that expresses a confident medical literacy in the following excerpts.

Partial medical history symptoms as noted by the training fellow:

1 "For the past two years she has had episodes of pain
2 in her elbows, wrists, and hands which lasts for several
3 days and then resolves.
4 She has occasional hand stiffness.
5 Has a history of some low back pain.
6 For the past several months she has had episodes of pain
7 in her ankles.
8 With swelling particularly [in] her right ankle.
9 Which has limited her walking.
10 She states that most of the pain is in the 2nd and 3rd
11 MCP [metacarpal phalangeal] and PIP [proximal inter-
12 phalangeal] joints of both hands.

Partial description of patient based on physical examination

1 Examination of her neck, shoulders, and elbows are com-
2 pletely within normal limits.
3 Examination of her left wrist shows a small amount of
4 swelling on the dorsal side; however, there is no warmth
5 and it is nontender.
6 The patient states she fractured her left wrist some years
7 ago.
8 Examination of her hands including her MP, PIP, and DIP

9 [distal interphalangeal] joints are all completely within
10 normal limits.

The order of the written remarks are different from the initial interview and the TF-AP exchange and reflect the professional concern with an integrated, objective account.

The TF's questions of the patient, her account to the AP in their exchange, and the TF's written history and physical examination reveal considerable schematized knowledge about rheumatological diseases. The application of a more formal knowledge base, however, is contingent on the physician's clinical experience in the context of perceiving certain symptoms or physical conditions that cohere in a local setting. According to the attending physician, the TF refers to the redness and swelling of the ankle in her oral and written accounts but does not mention any tenderness or possible degeneration. The physical examination report does not state that the ankles were palpated in order to rule out tenderness and possible inflammation, but reports that "examination of her ankle is within normal limits."

CONCLUDING REMARKS

In our study of everyday, bureaucratic, and technical use of oral and written communication, we tend to view knowledge as if we are able to identify homogeneously bounded domains the researcher is privileged to know. In most field research, we often acquire enough technical knowledge to understand much of the routine activities of the persons and groups we observe and interview. But we seldom allow the reader to see the limitations in our knowledge base and how such limitations can influence our inferences and claims about those studied. A similar observation can be made of the comprehension and reification of scientific or objective knowledge. Our recursive, selective, and deft editing of written materials often obscures the rich and necessary legacy of an oral culture and the locally informed comprehension that is presupposed in producing and understanding more detached or objective types of literacy.

The technical and everyday language used in natural settings only partially reveal the schematized knowledge and environmental conditions they index. To clarify the level of detail required for a diagnosis, the clinician must link mental models or schemata of formal diagnostic categories, and the lexical elements associated with them, to intuitive clinical procedures and knowledge. The local setting, however, includes a commonsense communicative frame, taking for granted conceptual categories and lexical items associated with local sources of meaning.

Research based on data sources that are limited to single utterances, or conversational or discourse materials that are not ethnographically contextualized, or fragments of written texts do not clarify the interaction between schematized and locally produced knowledge and reasoning.

How do we assess the accuracy of interpretation in a medical environment that can be routinely ambiguous because of the way the patient presents her symptoms and the fluidity in the TF's knowledge base? The problem can be compounded in a context where the physician employs inadequate elicitation procedures and fails to perceive the limitations of the patient in what is often an emotionally charged local setting.

If we were historians of science, we might analyze the technical literacy of medical histories and physical examinations that were part of an archive of a large hospital of 50 years ago. But such written materials (and those of different historical periods) can mask the pervasive commonsense reasoning and analogic and tacit conditions of everyday communicative strategies that can be found in the TF-AP exchange and the earlier TF-patient exchange.

Our contacts with informants during field research are contingent on local circumstances that often include initial awkward communication and many intangibles such as our appearance, the way we are introduced and present ourselves to informants, and a host of emergent conditions.

Our ability to translate and transform daily planned and unplanned communication, casual physical and verbal contact, and systematic observations into field notes generates declarative-like statements that give our emotions, doubts, and facts an objective quality. We create formal schemata that are part of a written tradition in order to make claims about human sociocultural life. Our research process, therefore, recapitulates the modes of thought and communication we seek to understand: the historical reconstruction and evolution of orality and literacy across cultural and nation-state boundaries.

The reproduction of different kinds of knowledge (legal-rational, scientific, actuarial) is subjected to detached or impersonal written formats that seek to minimize the personal involvement of those producing organizational knowledge in bureaucratic settings (24). The bureaucratically filtered written language used to depict objective knowledge lends itself to a crisp, factual, historical analysis. The everyday, contingent, often vague circumstances that punctuate laboratory and field research, and the recursive editing practices, false starts, unexpected results and mistakes of scientific research, are purged in the construction of objective knowledge (3, 25, 26).

The writing activities we associate with formal schooling and bureaucratic literacy have enhanced our ability to think logically and reason in a reflexive declarative-like mode as we seek objective, context-free textual knowledge. But the development, comprehension, and use of objective, context-free textual knowledge always builds on and presupposes forms of communication and reasoning that derive from procedural and local knowledge conditions, analogical inference, and everyday language.

ACKNOWLEDGMENTS

I am grateful to Dr. Michael Weisman for his valuable help and suggestions. I would also like to thank Sondra Buffett for her helpful editorial suggestions.

Literature Cited

1. Bobrow, D. G., Norman, D. A. 1975. Some principles of memory schemata. In *Representation and Understanding: Studies in Cognitive Science*, ed. D. G. Bobrow, A. M. Collins, pp. 131–49. New York: Academic
2. Bourdieu, P. 1981. The specificity of the scientific field. In *French Sociology*, ed. C. Lemert, pp. 257–92. New York: Columbia Univ. Press.
3. Brannigan, A. 1981. *The Social Basis of Scientific Discoveries*. New York: Cambridge Univ. Press. 212 pp.
4. Bright, W. 1982. Poetic structure in oral narrative. In *Spoken and Written Language: Exploring Orality and Literacy*, ed. D. Tannen, pp. 171–84. New Jersey: Ablex
5. Bruner, J. S., Olver, R., Greenfield, P. M. 1966. *Studies in Cognitive Growth*. New York: Wiley. 343 pp.
6. Chafe, W. 1982. Integration and involvement in speaking, writing, and oral literature. See Ref. 4, pp. 35–53
7. Cicourel, A. V. 1975. Discourse and text: Cognitive and linguistic processes in studies of social structure. In *Versus: Quaderni di Studi Semiotici*. Sept/Dec: pp. 33–84
8. Cicourel, A. V. 1982. Language and belief in a medical setting. In *Contemporary Perceptions of Language: Interdisciplinary Dimensions*, ed. H. Byrnes, pp. 48–78. Georgetown University Round Table on Languages and Linguistics. Washington DC: Georgetown Univ. Press
9. Cicourel, A. V. 1985. Diagnostic reasoning in medicine: The role of clinical discourse and comprehension. In *Actes de la Recherche en Sciences Sociales* (in French). In press
10. Cressy, D. 1980. *Literacy and the Social Order: Reading and Writing in Tudor and Stuart England*. Cambridge: Cambridge Univ. Press. 246 pp.
11. Davis, N. 1975. Printing and the people. In *Society and Culture in Early Modern France*, pp. 189–226. Stanford, Calif: Stanford Univ. Press
12. Eisenstein, E. L. 1979. *The Printing Press as an Agent of Change*. 2 vols. Cambridge: Cambridge Univ. Press. 794 pp.
13. Fisher, S., Todd, A. D. 1983. *The Social Organization of Doctor-Patient Communication*. Washington DC: Cent. Appl. Ling. 269 pp.
14. Goody, J., ed. 1968. *Literacy in Traditional Societies*. Cambridge: Cambridge Univ. Press. 349 pp.
15. Goody, J. 1977. *The Domestication of the Savage Mind*. Cambridge: Cambridge Univ. Press. 179 pp.
16. Goody, J., Watt, I. 1963. The consequences of literacy. *Comp. Stud. Soc. Hist.* 5:304–45
17. Grice, H. P. 1975. Logic and conversation. In *Syntax and semantics*, Vol. 3: *Speech Acts*, ed. P. Cole, J. Morgan, pp. 41–58. New York: Academic
18. Gumperz, J. J. 1982. *Discourse Strategies*. Cambridge: Cambridge Univ. Press. 225 pp.
19. Havelock, E. 1963. *Preface to Plato*. Cambridge: Harvard Univ. Press. 328 pp.
20. Heath, S. B. 1982. Protean shapes in literacy events: Ever-shifting oral and literate traditions. See Ref. 4, pp. 91–117
21. Hildyard, A., Olson, D. R. 1978. Memory and inference in the comprehension of oral and written discourse. In *Discourse Processes* 1:91–117
22. Horton, R. 1967. African traditional thought and Western science. In *Africa* 37:50–71, 155–87
23. Johnson-Laird, P. N. 1983. *Mental Models*. Great Britain: Cambridge Univ. Press. 513 pp.
24. Kay, P. 1977. Language evolution and speech style. In *Sociocultural Dimensions of Language Change*, ed. B. G. Blount, M. Sanches, pp. 21–33. New York: Academic
25. Knorr-Cetina, K. D. 1981. *The manufacture of knowledge: An essay on the constructivist and contextual nature of science*. Oxford: Pergamon. 189 pp.
26. Latour, B., Woolgar, S. 1979. *Labora-*

tory Life. The Social Construction of Scientific Facts. Beverly Hills: Sage. 272 pp.
27. Lockridge, K. A. 1974. Literacy in Colonial New England. New York: Norton. 164 pp.
27a. McClelland, J. L., Rumelhart, D. E. 1981. An interactive activation model of context effects in letter perception, part 1: An account of basic findings. Psychol. Rev. 88:375–407
28. Ochs, E. 1979. Planned and unplanned discourse. In Discourse and Syntax, ed. T. Givon, pp. 51–80. New York: Academic
29. Ong, W. J. 1967. The Presence of the Word. New Haven: Yale Univ. Press. 360 pp.
30. Polanyi, M. 1958. Personal Knowledge. Chicago: Univ. Chicago Press. 428 pp.
31. Resnick, D. P., Resnick, L. B. 1977. The nature of literacy: An historical exploration. Harvard Educ. Rev. 47:370–85
32. Rumelhart, D. 1977. Understanding and summarizing brief stories. In Basic Processes in Reading Perception and Comprehension, ed. D. LaBerge, J. Samuels. pp. 265–303. Hillsdale, NJ: Erlbaum
33. Rumelhart, D. E., Norman, D. A. 1981. Analogical processes in learning. In Cognitive Skills and Their Acquisition, ed. J. R. Anderson, pp. 335–59. Hillsdale, NJ: Erlbaum
34. Rumelhart, D. E., Ortony, A. 1977. The representation of knowledge in memory. In Schooling and the Acquisition of Knowledge, ed. R. C. Anderson, R. J. Spiro, W. E. Montague, pp. 99–135. Hillsdale, NJ: Erlbaum
35. Schutz, A. 1945. On multiple realities. Philos. Phenomenol. Res. 5:533–75
36. Schutz, A. 1953. Common-sense and scientific interpretation of human action. Philos. Phenomenol. Res. 14:1–38
36a. Scribner, S., Cole, M. 1981. The Psychology of Literacy. Cambridge: Cambridge Univ. Press. 335 pp.
37. Stone, L. 1969. Literacy and education in England, 1640–1900. Past and Present 42:70–139
38. Tannen, D. 1982. Oral and literate strategies in spoken and written narratives. Language 58(1):1–21
39. Tannen, D. 1982. The oral/literate continuum in discourse. See Ref. 4, pp. 1–16
40. Tannen, D. 1985. Relative focus on involvement in oral and written discourse. In Literacy, Language and Learning: The Nature and Consequence of Reading and Writing, ed. D. Olson. New York: Cambridge Univ. Press
41. Waitzkin, H. 1984. Doctor-patient communication: Clinical implications of social scientific research. J. Am. Med. Assoc. 252:2441–46
42. Weber, M. 1968. In Economy and Society: An Outline of Interpretive Sociology, ed. G. Roth, C. Wittich. New York: Bedminster. 3 vols.
43. Winograd, T. 1975. Frame representations and the declarative/procedural controversy. In Representation and Understanding: Studies in Cognitive Science, ed. D. G. Bobrow, A. M. Collins, pp. 185–210. New York: Academic

MAYAN LINGUISTICS: WHERE ARE WE NOW?

Lyle Campbell

Department of Anthropology, State University of New York, Albany, NY 12222

Terrence Kaufman

Department of Anthropology, University of Pittsburgh, Pittsburgh, Pennsylvania 15260

In the last ten years the study of Mayan languages has seen both tremendous advances and setbacks. Lamentable political events in Central America, particularly in Guatemala, have stalled some Mayan specialists who launched their investigations in the 1970s, while others have reoriented their research to Mayan groups in Mexico. Our purpose in this paper is to survey recent developments in Mayan linguistics, both to update and characterize the field. Specifically, we consider the following: descriptive work, classification, Proto-Mayan (PM) reconstruction (both phonology and syntax), proposed distant genetic connections, diffusion, linguistic prehistory, Mayan hieroglyphic writing, and literature.

Descriptive Work

The Mayan family consists of 31 languages, spoken principally in Guatemala and southern Mexico. Two are now extinct: Chicomuceltec and Choltí. An impressive array of reference works (grammars and dictionaries) have recently appeared; examples of the languages involved include Quiché (44, 73, 74), Cakchiquel (95), Tzutujil (28), Sacapultec (30), Pokomam (88), Pokomchí (8), Kekchí (42, 89); Mam (33, 68), Ixil (2, 54); Jacaltec (26, 27), Motocintlec (50), Tojolabal (39, 65), Chuj (69); Chol (94, 1), Chontal (85); Choltí (36); Tzeltal (52, 18, 84), Tzotzil (43, 63, 46); Yucatec (4, 5, 6), Lacandon (9), Itza (45), Mopan (93); Huastec (72), and Chicomuceltec (18, 19).

Unpublished work is also done or in progress on Uspantec, Teco (cf 51), Aguacatec, Kanjobal, Acatec, and Chortí, as well as several of the languages cited above.

Classification

While Mayan subgrouping is now better understood than ever, the overall picture is still unclear, and some controversy remains. There is general agreement concerning the members of five subgroups of the family, listed here with comparative works cited in parentheses (see also Figure 1):

1. Huastecan (18, 57): Huastec and Chicomuceltec.
2. Yucatecan (34): Yucatec, Lacandon; Mopan, Itza.
3. Cholan-Tzeltalan (or Greater Tzeltalan) (59):
   a. Cholan (59): Chol, Chontal; Chortí, Choltí;
   b. Tzeltalan (53): Tzeltal, Tzotzil.
4. Kanjobalan-Chujean (or Greater Kanjobalan):
   a. Kanjobalan: Kanjobal, Acatec, Jacaltec; Motocintlec (Motocintlec and Tuzantec varieties);
   b. Chujean: Chuj, Tojolabal.
5. Quichean-Mamean (or Eastern Mayan):
   a. Quichean (14): Kekchí; Uspantec; Pokomchí, Pokomam; Quiché, Cakchiquel, Tzutujil, Sacapultec, Sipacapa;
   b. Mamean (cf. 51): Teco, Mam; Aguacatec, Ixil.

However, higher-level branchings are disputed. The most common current view has Huastecan splitting off first, then Yucatecan; then the remaining groups diverge (cf 55, 59). While this is plausible, it requires confirmation.

The position of Huastecan has been in dispute, but it now seems clear that it was the first to break off. Some had placed it closer to Greater Tzeltalan and/or Yucatecan based on what appeared to be shared innovations among these languages (cf 14, 37), but some of these reasons no longer exist. For example, Kaufman has recently discovered a dialect of Huastec, which he calls Otontepec (including among others the towns of Chontla and Chinampa in Veracruz), which preserves the distinct plural pronominal affixes inherited from PM. Other Huastec dialects have plural pronominal affixes composed of singulars plus a plural morpheme, a similarity to the Cholan pattern that had suggested a shared innovation. However, such plurals are now thought to have resulted from independent, parallel development. Other similarities are also not compelling. For example, the shared change of *q to k could easily have taken place independently. The change of *k to č actually happened under varied conditions in different contexts in the western subgroups (Huastecan, Greater Tzeltalan, Yucatecan, and some members of Greater Kanjobalan). Other similarities may be due to contact or parallel innovation. While the change from *r to y (Huastecan, Yucatecan, Greater Tzeltalan, most of Greater Kanjobalan) seems less subject to such an explanation, it alone is insufficient to confirm a higher-order subgrouping. Otherwise, Huastecan grammar and vocabulary are markedly different from other Mayan languages, a fact that could only be

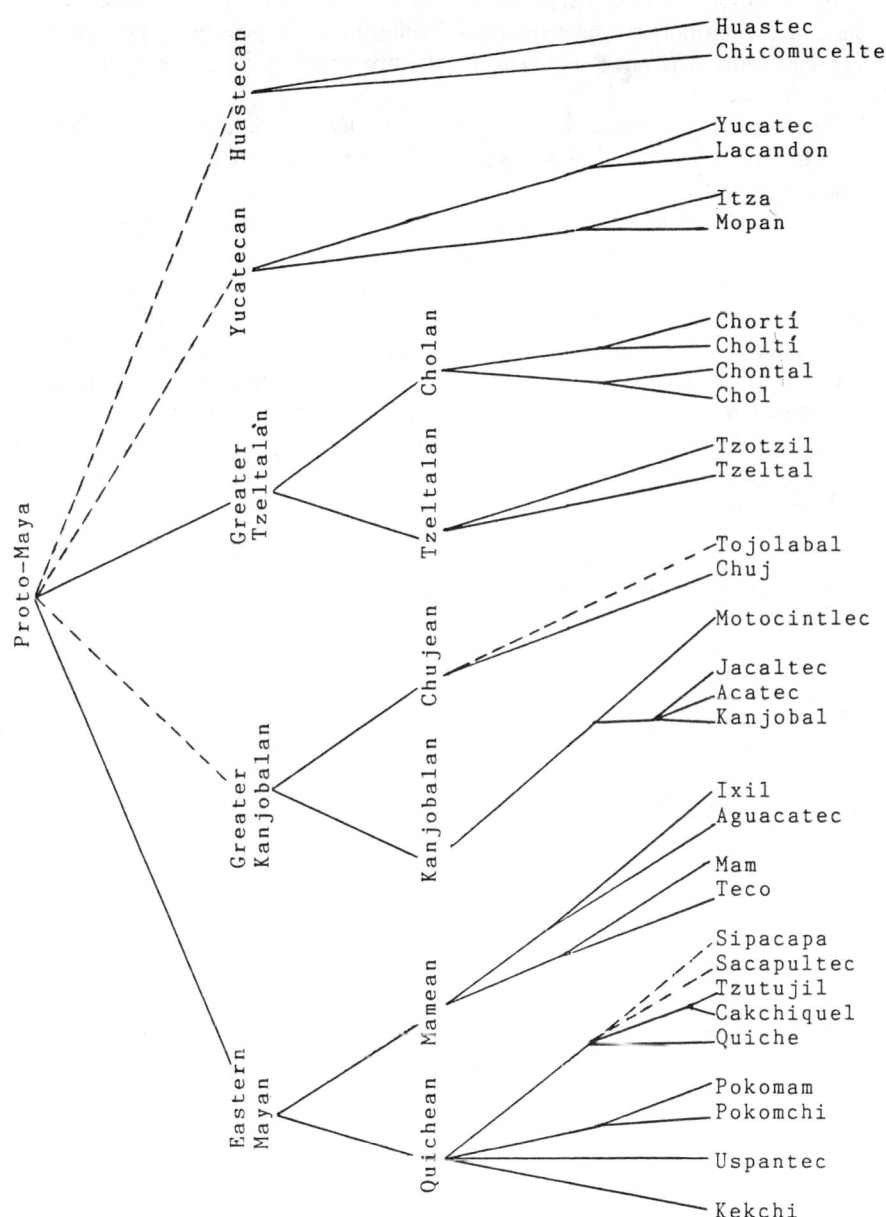

Figure 1 Classification of Mayan languages. Dotted lines represent less secure or more controversial groupings.

explained by either longer separation from the rest of the family or intensive influence from non-Mayan neighbors. While the latter possibility no doubt explains some differences and bears further investigation, it can hardly be the whole answer.

The place of Tojolabal has also been questioned, some placing it with Tzeltalan (cf 80). While the issue is open to further study, recent work indicates that it apparently belongs in Greater Kanjobalan, closer to Chuj (see 18, 58). The similarities shared with Tzeltalan appear to be due to intensive contact with Tzeltal; many Tojolabals are bilingual in Tzeltal and Tojolabal.

The testimony of phonology for Mayan subgrouping has largely been exhausted. Further refinements in the classification can be expected only as innovations in Mayan historical grammar come to be better understood. Clearly Greater Kanjobalan as the least studied subgroup is in need of comparative investigation and reconstruction, but all the subgroups could benefit from additional research of this kind (see Figure 1).

PM Reconstruction

Recent studies on PM have been undertaken by Campbell (14, 18), Fox (37), Kaufman (55, 56), Kaufman & Norman (59), and Norman & Campbell (78). The history of comparative Mayan studies is considered by Campbell (14) and Fox (37). Recent history has involved refinements of McQuown's (70, 71) and Kaufman's (49, 51) proposals. These refinements have led to the following phonemic inventory of PM:

```
p  t  t̰' ¢ č k q  ʔ         i        u   V:
b' t' t̰' ¢' č' k' q'           e    o
m  n         ŋ                  a
   s       š    x
   l
   r
w          y    h
```

Notable differences from earlier proposals are the absence of C̱ (retroflexed consonants), tone, ə, p̱', and ḵʸ, plus the presence of *ṟ.

PM Syntax

Good beginnings have been made towards a reconstruction of PM syntax (see 78, 81, 86). These studies reveal PM to have been an ergative language with all the traits expected of ergative typology, including an associated antipassive rule. A fundamental trait of ergative languages is that the subject of transitive verbs bears ergative case marking and is distinguished from the subject of intransitive verbs and the object of transitives, both of which bear absolutive case markings (see 5, 29, 62). Antipassive constructions, so characteristic of Mayan grammar, have the effect of playing up (emphasizing or focusing) the subject while playing down or eliminating the object of transitive sentences. That is, they are the antithesis of passive constructions, which play up the logical object and reduce the role of the logical subject (see, for example, 87). PM seems to have had VOS (Verb-Object-Subject) basic word order when the subject was higher than the object on the "animacy" hierarchy—with human highest, animate next, and inanimate lowest—but VSO order when subject and object were equal in animacy. PM nominal possession was of the form, for example, "his-dog the man" for "the man's dog". PM also had relational nouns for locative functions—i.e. a possessed noun root in construction (e.g. the equivalent of "my-head" for "on me," "his-stomach" for "in him").

Proposals for Distant Genetic Relationships

Proposals of distant genetic affiliation have attempted to link Mayan with Araucanian, Yunga, Chipaya-Uru, Penutian, Hokan, Tarascan, Huave, Mixe-Zoquean, and Totonacan, among others. Suffice it to say, none of these has been demonstrated, while most have been discredited. The initially impressive Chipaya-Uru proposal (see 79) has not held up under examination and ought now to be abandoned (16, 21, 22). The so-called Macro-Mayan hypothesis, which links Mayan with Mixe-Zoquean (henceforth MZ) and Totonacan, has received much attention (see 7, 21, 22). Despite a few supporters (7, 38), the evidence presented to date has been insufficient. Standard procedures for testing distant genetic relationships reveal this evidence to have other explanations (20–22). None of the other proposals comes even close to being convincing (16).

In short, the Mayan family has no known relatives beyond the 31 languages named herein. These hypotheses of remote linguistic relationship are at best preliminary proposals, none of which has general acceptance among linguists. Archaeological correlations or other historical or cultural inferences that rely on such unsubstantiated proposals are thus ill advised.

Contact and Diffusion

Under closer examination, many proposed cognates in the hypothesized remoter relationships turned out to be loan words (13, 15, 16, 20–22, 48, 57). Two other significant developments involving loans should be mentioned. First, loans help establish that the archaeological Olmecs spoke a MZ (not Mayan) language (20) and that Izapan culture was MZ in speech. Mayan languages have borrowed much from MZ under the influence of these two cultures, including many structural aspects of the writing system (48). Second, Greater Tzeltalan and Yucatecan languages participated in what is called the "Greater

Lowland Maya" linguistic area, where they borrowed extensively from one another. This interaction and mutual influence stemmed from Classic Lowland Maya culture. It is important to emphasize that "Lowland Maya" is not a genetic grouping, but rather refers to an area of much linguistic diffusion (see 48).

The Mayan languages also participate in the Mesoamerican linguistic area as an integral member. While the existence of a Mesoamerican linguistic (diffusion) area was once uncertain, the character and validity of the area are now firmly established (23). For example, Mayan shares with the rest of Mesoamerica the linguistic traits (sometimes called areal isoglosses) of a vigesimal numeral system, nominal possession of the form "his-dog the man," relational nouns (see above), non-verb-final basic word order, and several semantic calques (loan translated compounds).

Linguistic Prehistory

Linguistic prehistory (sometimes called linguistic paleontology) links the findings of historical linguistics with archaeology, ethnohistory, ethnographic analogy, and other sources of historical information for a fuller picture of prehistory. Linguists have contributed to cultural identifications, migrations, homeland, kinds of contacts, and much toward understanding the past social and material culture of different language groups. Kaufman (55) has hypothesized that PM was spoken in the Cuchumatanes Mountains of Guatemala, around Soloma, Huehuetenango at about 2200 BC, where its speakers exploited both highland and lowland ecological zones. Reconstructed vocabulary shows PM speakers to have been highly successful agriculturalists, with the maize complex at the core of a full range of Mesoamerican cultigens. PM diversified, ultimately occupying the areas of the present-day languages. After the early departure of Huastecan, the diversification and expansion brought Mayan speakers down the Usumacinta River into the Peten region around 1,000 BC, where Yucatecan and Greater Cholan are found. Later (about AD 200) the Tzeltalan branch went from this area up to the Chiapas highlands, formerly occupied by MZ speakers. The principal bearers of Classic Lowland Maya culture (AD 300–900) were first Cholan speakers, later joined by Yucatecans. The Lowland Maya linguistic area was formed during this period, contributing many loan words both within the Mayan family and to neighboring non-Mayan languages (13–15, 18, 20, 22, 48, 55, 57, 59). Quichean groups expanded into eastern and southern Guatemala quite late, after AD 1200. Pipil (Nahua) speakers did not arrive in Guatemala until after AD 800. Much of eastern Guatemala below the Motagua River was occupied by Xincan speakers, though Pokomam groups invaded their territory after the conquest of the Rabinal Valley by the Rabinal lineage of the Quiche had displaced the Pokomam, separating them from their Pokomchí cousins around AD 1250 (15).

Thus, speakers of Mayan languages had a much more limited distribution in earlier times than often thought by cultural historians. In effect, it has become clear that many Preclassic cultures and sites often thought to have been Mayan were in fact founded by non-Mayan groups. The archaeological Olmecs were MZ speakers (20), as were the bearers of greater Izapan culture, including Izapa itself (18, 48). It is still an open question as to who the builders of Preclassic Chalchuapa, Kaminaljuyu, and Abaj Takalic were, but it is by no means certain that they were Mayan, and MZ in many ways seems a better candidate. (For details of these arguments and the evidence upon which they are based, see 15, 18, 20, 48, 55.)

Mayan Hieroglyphic Writing

Until recently, few Mayan linguists had dedicated much serious attention to Mayan hieroglyphic writing. The exception was Floyd Lounsbury (e.g. 66), whose work, together with Kelley's (e.g. 60), may have attracted others. Efforts have been successful, and great progress has been made toward adequate reading of the texts.

The hypotheses of historicism and phoneticism are often-cited breakthroughs, and no serious student of the subject doubts these any longer. Historicism refers to the historical content of the texts, many of which contain dynastic histories of the births, offices, marriages, deaths, and kinship of rulers.

Phoneticism deals with the phonetic value of certain signs. Mayan writing is a mixed script. It began with strictly logographic signs, which have the value of whole morphemes. The use of rebuses made it more phonological, where something easier to depict could be employed for similar-sounding morphemes more difficult to represent graphically—e.g. a picture of an "eye" to represent English "I". Phonetic complements (or determiners) arose from logograms for morphemes of the form CVC (C = consonant, V = vowel), where the final C was "weak" (i.e. *h, ?,* rarely also *y* or *w*) and ignored in reading. Such phonetic determiners could be used to distinguish different semantic values of logograms. For example, most Mayan languages have two words for "house" (something like *nah* and *-otot*). The HOUSE logogram (T614)[1] sometimes bears as a phonetic complement T59, in origin a representation of a "torch," (cf Chol *tah,* with weak final C). The HOUSE sign plus the phonetic determiner *ta* specified that the value *-otot,* with final *t,* was intended, rather than *nah.* Later, the use of phonetic complements was expanded to contexts independent of the semantic value of logograms, employed in combinations solely for their phonetic value to spell words syllabically. Mayan words could be written either partly or totally with signs whose value is CV. Since Mayan roots are typically monosyllabic and of the form CVC, they could be spelled with two CV signs,

---

[1]Designations are from Thompson's 1952 catalog of Mayan hieroglyphs (91).

where the vowel of the second is silent but chosen to match the vowel of the root. For example, Yucatecan /ku:ȼ/ (turkey) was spelled *ku-ȼu* in the codices. Phoneticism in the script of this general form was discovered by Knorozov (61) and slowly accepted by Americanists (for details, see 17).

Other recent developments involving languages and linguistics are also significant. The Cholan hypothesis is a breakthrough. It is now clear that the script was originated by speakers of Cholan (or Greater Tzeltalan) and later passed on to Yucatecan speakers. Many of the monuments are demonstrably Cholan; the codices are in Yucatec. While there was significant MZ (Izapan) influence on the early form of Mayan writing and calendrics, they are Cholan linguistically. No highland Mayan language contributed to the script's development (47, 48).

The structure of the script is of considerable linguistic interest. It is significant that the development of phonetic values is understood only through Cholan (17). Glyph grammar is also now generally understood. It corresponds essentially to Cholan grammar. The word order is VOS (Verb-Object-Subject), often preceded by a date. It reflects split ergativity, gapping and conjunction reduction, verb classes (with distinct morphological patterns for transitives, intransitives, and positionals), and the paired couplets so typical of Mayan ritual discourse (47, 48, 59, 67, 82).

The above developments converge to facilitate decipherment efforts. For example, T644, the "seating" verb, refers to the *historical* event of rulers being "seated" in office. It frequently bears the suffixes T130.166, read *phonetically* as *wa* + *ni*. These make sense only in Cholan. The Mayan positional verbs (of which "seating" is a paradigm) take special morphology, and only in Cholan do we find the *-wan* 'completive' morpheme of positional verbs plus the *-i* 'completive' marker for intransitives (59, 67). T116, /ni/, /ne/, which looks like a tail, appears to come from Cholan **neh* (tail).

Mayan Literature

Mayan texts, both colonial and modern, have recently received considerable attention from linguists. These studies help to elucidate not only Mayan oral literature, but also folklore and oral tradition in general, ritual and religion, hieroglyphics, and Mayan life and thought (both ancient and modern). In addition, they make contributions to formal linguistics.

Mayan ritual language, both modern and old, is characterized by paired couplets, first described by Edmonson (31) for Quiche in the *Popol Vuh,* but found also across the languages of the Mayan family, including hieroglyphic texts. Moreover, this literary device is known throughout Mesoamerica, called *huehuetlatolli* in Nahuatl and *tz'onooj* in Quiche. This is illustrated in the following short sample taken from a prayer in the *Popol Vuh* (see 75, p. 96):

at tz'aqool, at b'itool
you shaper, you creator

k-oj-aw-ila', k-oj-a-ta'
see-us, hear-us

m-oj-a-tzoqoh, m-oj-a-pisk'aliij
don't-let-us-fall, don't-abandon-us

chi-kaaj, chi uleew
in-heaven, on earth

u-k'u'x ka:j, u-k'u'x uleew
heart of heaven, heart of earth

The *Popol Vuh*, the Quiche book of counsel, was found and first translated by Ximénez in about 1701 but is based on pre-Conquest sources. It has been the subject of considerable recent study (e.g. 25, 31, 75–77, 90). This research has revealed much about the structure of Mayan ritual language and about pre-Conquest Mayan mythology and cosmology. These findings are proving helpful in interpretation of Lowland Mayan hieroglyphic texts (90). In addition, Robert Carmack recently found the original Quiche text of the *Title of the Lords of Totonicapan,* and with James Mondloch has translated and analyzed it (24).

For ancient Yucatec Maya, significant are Barrera Vásquez's (3) study of the *Book of the Songs of Dzitbalché* and Edmonson's (32) treatment of the *Book of Chilam Balam of Tizimin.*

Modern Mayan texts are not essentially different in structure or content, though showing at times more effects of Spanish contact. A model for their investigation is Gossen's (41) collection, translation, and analysis of Chamula Tzotzil oral literature; see also Laughlin's (64) Zinacantan Tzotzil texts. The Lacandon texts in *The Book of Chan K'in* and in Bruce's other studies (10, 11) are significant for the information recorded on Mayan myth, religion and cosmology. It is not surprising that they have invited comparisons with the *Popol Vuh.* Also to be considered are Burns's (12) treatment of modern Yucatec oral literature, Fought's (35) collection and interpretation of Chortí tales, and the collections of texts analyzed and presented by Shaw (83), Furbee-Losee (40), and Townsend (92), among others.

Literature Cited

1. Aulie, H. W., Aulie, E. 1978. *Diccionario ch'ol-español, español-ch'ol.* Ser. Vocab. Diccion. Indígenas Mariano Silva y Aceves, Núm. 21. Mexico: Inst. Ling. de Verano. 216 pp.
2. Ayres, G. 1980. *Un bosquejo gramatical del idioma ixil.* PhD thesis. Univ. Calif., Berkeley. 384 pp.
3. Barrera Vásquez, A. 1965. *El Libro de los Cantares de Dzitbalché.* Ser. Invest. 9. Mexico: Inst. Nac. Antropol. e Hist. 89 pp. Republished 1980. Mérida: Ayuntamiento de Mérida. 141 pp.
4. Barrera Vásquez, A. 1980. *Diccionario maya cordemex.* Mérida: Ediciones Cordemex. (Maya-español 984 pp., español-maya 360 pp.)
5. Bricker, V. R. 1981. The source of the

ergative split in Yucatec Maya. *J. Mayan Ling.* 2:83–127
6. Bricker, V. R. 1981. Grammatical introduction. In *Yucatec Maya Verbs,* by E. Po'ot Yah. New Orleans: Tulane Univ. Cent. Latin American Stud. xcii, 35 pp.
7. Brown, C. H., Witkowski, S. R. 1979. Aspects of the phonological history of Mayan-Zoquean. *Int. J. Am. Ling.* 45:34–47
8. Brown, L. K. 1978. *Word formation in Pocomchí (Mayan).* PhD thesis. Stanford Univ., Stanford, Calif. 266 pp.
9. Bruce, R. D. 1968. *Gramática del lacandón.* Dept. Invest. Antropol., Publ. 21. Mexico: Inst. Nac. Antropol. e Hist. 152 pp.
10. Bruce, R. D. 1974. *El libro de Chan K'in.* Colección Científica, 12. Mexico: Inst. Nac. Antropol. e Hist. 385 pp.
11. Bruce, R. D. 1976. *Textos y dibujos lacandones de Najá/Lacandon Texts and Drawings from Naha'*. Colección Científica, 45. Mexico: Inst. Nac. Antropol. e Hist. 158 pp.
12. Burns, A. F. 193. *An Epoch of Miracles: Oral Literature of the Yucatec Maya.* Austin: Univ. Texas Press. 266 pp.
13. Campbell, L. 1976. The linguistic prehistory of the southern Mesoamerican periphery. In *Fronteras de Mesoamérica* (14ª Mesa Redonda, Vol. 1), pp. 157–84. Mexico: Soc. Mexicana Antropol.
14. Campbell, L. 1977. *Quichean Linguistic Prehistory.* Univ. Calif. Publ. Ling. 81. Los Angeles: Univ. Calif. Press. 132 pp.
15. Campbell, L. 1978. Quichean prehistory: linguistic contributions. In *Papers in Mayan Linguistics,* ed. N. C. England, pp. 25–55. Columbia, Mo: Dept. Anthropol. 311 pp.
16. Campbell, L. 1979. Middle American languages. In *The Languages of Native America: Historical and Comparative Assessment,* ed. L. Campbell, M. Mithun, pp. 902–1000. Austin: Univ. Texas Press. 1034 pp.
17. Campbell, L. 1985. The implications of Mayan historical linguistics for glyphic research. See Ref. 47, pp. 1–16
18. Campbell, L. 1985. *The Linguistics of Southeastern Chiapas.* (Pap. New World Archaeol. Found. No. 51. Provo Utah: Brigham Young Univ. Press. In press
19. Campbell, L., Canger, U. 1978. Chicomuceltec's last throes. *Int. J. Am. Ling.* 44:228–30
20. Campbell, L., Kaufman, T. 1976. A linguistic look at the Olmecs. *Am. Antiq.* 41:80–89
21. Campbell, L., Kaufman, T. 1980. On Mesoamerican linguistics. *Am. Anthropol.* 82:850–57
22. Campbell, L., Kaufman, T. 1983. Mesoamerican historical linguistics and distant genetic relationships: setting the record straight. *Am. Anthropol.* 85:362–72
23. Campbell, L., Kaufman, T., Smith-Stark, T. 1985. Mesoamerica as a linguistic area. *Language.* In press
24. Carmack, R. M., Mondloch, J. L. 1984. *El título de Totonicapan: su texto, traduccín y comentario.* Cent. Estud. Mayas, Fuentes Estud. Cult. Maya, 3. Mexico: Univ. Nac. Autóonoma de México
25. Carmack, R. M., Morales Santos, F., eds. 1983. *Nuevas Perspectivas sobre el Popol Vuh.* Guatemala: Editorial Piedra Santa. 428 pp.
26. Craig, C. G. 1977. *The Structure of Jacaltec.* Austin: Univ. Texas Press. 432 pp.
27. Day, C. 1973. *The Jacaltec Language.* Lang. Sci. Monogr., 12. Bloomington: Indiana Univ. Press. 135 pp.
28. Dayley, J. P. 1981. *Tzutujil grammar.* PhD thesis. Univ. Calif., Berkeley. 582 pp.
29. Dayley, J. P. 1981. Voice and ergativity in Mayan languages. *J. Mayan Ling.* 2:3–82
30. DuBois, J. W. 1981. *The Sacapultec language.* PhD thesis. Univ. Calif., Berkeley. 294 pp.
31. Edmonson, M. S. 1971. *The Book of Counsel: the Popol Vuh of the Quiche Maya of Guatemala.* Mid. Am. Res. Inst., Publ. 35. New Orleans: Tulane Univ. 273 pp.
32. Edmonson, M. S. 1982. *The Ancient Future of the Itza: the Book of Chilam Balam of Tizimin.* Austin: Univ. Texas Press. 220 pp.
33. England, N. C. 1983. *A Grammar of Mam, a Mayan Language.* Austin: Univ. Texas Press. 353 pp.
34. Fisher, W. M. 1973. *Towards the reconstruction of Proto-Yucatec.* PhD thesis. Univ. Chicago. 359 pp.
35. Fought, J. G. 1972. *Chorti (Mayan) Texts.* Philadelphia: Univ. Pennsylvania Press. 566 pp.
36. Fought, J. G. 1984. Choltí Maya: a sketch. In *Supplement to the Handbook of Middle American Indians, Vol. 2: Linguistics,* ed. M. S. Edmonson, pp. 43–55. Austin: Univ. Texas Press. 146 pp.
37. Fox, J. A. 1978. *Proto-Mayan accent, morpheme structure conditions, and velar innovations.* PhD thesis. Univ. Chicago, Ill. 315 pp.
38. Fox, J. A. 1984. Language and writing.

In *The Ancient Maya,* by S. G. Morley, G. W. Brainerd, R. J. Sharer, pp. 497–544. Stanford: Stanford Univ. Press. 708 pp. 4th ed.
39. Furbee-Losee, L. 1976. *The Correct Language, Tojolabal: a Grammar with Ethnographic Notes.* New York: Garland
40. Furbee-Losee, L., ed. 1976, 1979, 1980. *Mayan Texts I, II, and III.* Native Am. Text Ser., *Int. J. Am. Ling.* Chicago: Univ. Chicago Press
41. Gossen, G. H. 1974. *Chamulas in the World of the Sun: Time and Space in a Maya Oral Tradition.* Cambridge: Harvard Univ. Press. Reissued 1984. Prospect Heights, Ill: Waveland Press. 382 pp. Spanish translation 1979. *Los Chamulas en el Mundo del Sol.* Ser. Antropol. Soc. 58. Mexico: Inst. Nac. Indig. 455 pp.
42. Haeserijn, E. 1979. *Diccionario k'ekchi' español.* Guatemala: Editorial Piedra Santa. 489 pp.
43. Haviland, J. B. 1981. *Sk'op Sotz'leb: el Tzotzil de San Lorenzo Zinacantan.* Mexico: Univ. Nac. Autónoma de México. 387 pp.
44. Henne, D. 1980. *Diccionario quiché-español.* Guatemala: Inst. Ling. de Verano. 270 pp.
45. Hofling, C. A. 1982. *Itza Maya morphosyntax from a discourse perspective.* PhD thesis. Washington Univ., St. Louis, Mo. 377 pp.
46. Hurley Delgaty, A., Ruíz Sánchez, A. R. 1978. *Diccionario tzotzil de San Andrés con variaciones dialectales.* Ser. Vocab. Diccion. Indígenas Mariano Silva y Aceves, Núm. 22. Mexico: Inst. Ling. de Verano. 482 pp.
47. Justeson, J., Campbell, L., eds. 1985. *Phoneticism in Mayan Hieroglyphic Writing.* Inst. Mesoamerican Stud. No. 9. Albany: State Univ. New York. 393 pp.
48. Justeson, J., Norman, W., Campbell, L., Kaufman, T. 1985. *The Foreign Impact on Lowland Mayan Language and Script.* Mid. Am. Res. Inst., Publ. 53. New Orleans: Tulane Univ. 86 pp.
49. Kaufman, T. S. 1964. Materiales lingüísticos para el estudio de las relaciones internas y externas de la familia de idiomas mayanos. In *Desarrollo cultural de los mayas,* ed. E. Vogt, pp. 81–136. Spec. publ. Seminario de Cultura Maya. Mexico: Univ. Nac. Autónoma de México. 2nd ed. 1971.
50. Kaufman, T. S. 1967. *Preliminary Mochó Dictionary.* Lang. Behav. Res. Lab. Work. Pap. 5. Berkeley: Univ. Calif. 321 pp.
51. Kaufman, T. S. 1969. Teco—a new Mayan language. *Int. J. Am. Ling.* 35:154–74
52. Kaufman, T. S. 1971. *Tzeltal Phonology and Morphology.* Univ. Calif. Publ. Ling. 61. Berkeley: Univ. Calif. Press. 120 pp.
53. Kaufman, T. S. 1972. *El proto-tzeltal-tzotzil: fonología comparada y diccionario reconstruido.* Cent. Estud. Mayas, Cuaderno 5. Mexico: Univ. Nac. Autónoma de México. 162 pp.
54. Kaufman, T. S. 1974. *Ixil Dictionary.* Lab. Anthropol. Tech. Rep. 1. Irvine: Univ. Calif., Irvine. 1014 pp.
55. Kaufman, T. S. 1976. Archaeological and linguistic correlations in Mayaland and Associated Areas of Meso-America. *World Archaeol.* 8:101–18
56. Kaufman, T. S. 1978. The current state of Mayan comparative phonology. Presented at the 3rd Mayan Workshop, Cobán, Guatemala
57. Kaufman, T. S. 1980. Pre-Columbian borrowings involving Huastec. In *American Indian and Indoeuropean Studies, Papers in Honor of Madison S. Beeler,* ed. K. Klar, M. Langdon, S. Silver, pp. 101–12. The Hague: Mouton
58. Kaufman, T. S. 1984. Cross currents of grammatical innovation in the Mayan languages, with especial reference to Tojolabal. Presented at the symposium on the language of writing in the Mayan region, the Center for Latin American Studies, Univ. Chicago
59. Kaufman, T. S., Norman, W. 1985. An outline of Proto-Cholan phonology, morphology, and vocabulary. See Ref. 47, pp. 77–166
60. Kelley, D. 1976. *Deciphering the Maya Script.* Austin: Univ. Texas Press
61. Knorozov, Y. V. 1955. *La escritura de los antiguos mayas (ensayo de descifrado).* Moscow: Ed. Acad. Cienc. URSS. 79 pp.
62. Larsen, T., Norman, W. 1979. Correlates of ergativity in Mayan grammar. In *Ergativity: Towards a Theory of Grammatical Relations,* ed. F. Plank, pp. 347–70. New York: Academic. 569 pp.
63. Laughlin, R. M. 1975. *The Great Tzotzil Dictionary of San Lorenzo Zinacantan.* Smithsonian Contrib. Anthropol. 19. Washington, DC: Smithsonian Inst. 598 pp.
64. Laughlin, R. M. 1977. *Of Cabbages and Kings: Tales from Zinacantán.* Smithsonian Contrib. Anthropol. 23. Washington, DC: Smithsonian Inst. 427 pp.
65. Lenkersdorf, C. 1979. *B'omak'umal tojol ab'al-kastiya: Diccionario tojolabal-español,* Vol. 1. 429 pp.; *B'omak'umal kastiya-tojol ab'al: Diccionario español-*

tojolabal, Vol. 2. 817 pp. Mexico: Editorial Nuestro Tiempo
66. Lounsbury, F. 1973. On the derivation and reading of the 'ben-ich' prefix. In *Mesoamerican Writing Systems*, ed. E. Benson, pp. 99–143. Washington, DC: Dumbarton Oaks
67. MacLeod, B. 1983. *An epigrapher's annotated index to Cholan and Yucatecan verb morphology*. PhD thesis. Univ. Texas, Austin. 237 pp.
68. Maldonado Andrés, J., Ordoñez Domingo, J., Ortiz Domingo, J. 1983. *Diccionario de San Ildefonso Ixtahuacan Huehuetenango mam-español*. Hannover: Verlag für Ethnologie. 601 pp.
69. Maxwell, J. 1982. *How to talk to people who talk Chekel "different": the Chuj (Mayan) solution*. PhD thesis. Univ. Chicago
70. McQuown, N. A. 1955. The indigenous languages of Latin America. *Am. Anthropol.* 57:501–70
71. McQuown, N. A. 1956. The classification of the Mayan languages. *Int. J. Am. Ling.* 22:191–95
72. McQuown, N. A. 1984. A sketch of San Luis Potosí Huastec. See Ref. 36, pp. 83–142
73. Mondloch, J. L. 1978. *Basic Quiche Grammar*. Inst. Mesoam. Stud., Publ. 2. Albany: State Univ. New York. 222 pp.
74. Mondloch, J. L. 1981. *Voice of Quiche-Maya*. PhD thesis. State Univ. New York, Albany. 359 pp.
75. Mondloch, J. L. 1983. Una comparación entre los estilos de habla del quiché moderno y los encontrados en el Popol Vuh. See Ref. 24, pp. 87–108
76. Norman, W. M. 1980. Grammatical parallelism in Quiche ritual language. *Berkeley Ling. Soc.* 6:387–99
77. Norman, W. M. 1983. Paralelismo gramatical en el lenguaje ritual quiché. See Ref. 25, pp. 109–22
78. Norman, W. M., Campbell, L. 1978. Toward a Proto-Mayan syntax: a comparative perspective on grammar. See Ref. 15, pp. 136–56
79. Olson, R. D. 1964, 1965. Mayan affinities with Chipaya of Bolivia, I: correspondences, II: cognates. *Int. J. Am. Ling.* 30:313–24, 31:29–38
80. Robertson, J. S. 1977. A proposed revision in Mayan subgrouping. *Int. J. Am. Ling.* 43:105–20
81. Robertson, J. S. 1980. *The Structure of Pronoun Incorporation in the Mayan Verb Complex*. New York: Garland
82. Schele, L. 1982. *Mayan Glyphs: the Verbs*. Austin: Univ. Texas Press. 427 pp.
83. Shaw, M., ed. 1971. *According to Our Ancestors: Folk Texts from Guatemala and Honduras*. (Summer Inst. Ling. Publ. Ling. and Rel. Fields, No. 32. Norman: Univ. Oklahoma. 510 pp.
84. Slocum, M. C., Gerdel, F. L. 1965. *Vocabulario tzeltal de Bachajón*. Ser Vocab. Indígenas Mariano Silva y Aceves, Núm. 13. Mexico: Inst. Ling. de Verano. 216 pp.
85. Smailus, O. 1975. *El maya-chontal de Acalán: Análisis lingüístico de un Documento de los años 1610–12*. Cent. Estud. Mayas, Cuaderno 9. Mexico: Univ. Nac. Autónoma de México. 234 pp.
86. Smith-Stark, T. C. 1976. Some hypotheses on syntactic and morphological aspects of Proto-Mayan (*PM). In *Mayan Linguistics*, ed. M. McClaran, 1:44–66. Los Angeles: UCLA Am. Indian Stud. Cent. 267 pp.
87. Smith-Stark, T. C. 1978. The Mayan antipassives: some facts and fictions. See Ref. 15, pp. 169–87
88. Smith-Stark, T. C. 1983. *Jilotepeque Pocomam phonology and morphology*. PhD thesis. Univ. Chicago
89. Stewart, S. O. 1978. *Inflection in a grammar of Kekchi (Mayan)*. PhD thesis. Univ. Colo., Boulder. 217 pp.
90. Tedlock, D. 1985. *The Popol Vuh: a Mayan book of Myth and History*. New York: Simon & Schuster
91. Thompson, J. E. S. 1962. *A Catalog of Maya Hieroglyphs*. Norman: Univ. Okla. Press. 458 pp.
92. Townsend, P. G., ed. 1980. *Guatemalan Maya Texts*. Guatemala: Summer Inst. Ling. 231 pp.
93. Ulrich, M., Ulrich, R. 1976. *Diccionario Bilingüe, maya mopán y español, español y maya mopán*. Guatemala: Inst. Ling. de Verano. 393 pp.
94. Warkentin, V., Scott, R. 1980. *Gramática ch'ol*. Ser. Gramáticas de Lenguas Indígenas de México, Núm. 3. Mexico: Inst. Ling. de Verano. 134 pp.
95. Whalin, W. T. 1984. *Cakchiquel syntax*. M.A. thesis. Univ. Texas, Arlington. 133 pp.

MINING: ANTHROPOLOGICAL PERSPECTIVES

Ricardo Godoy

Harvard Institute for International Development, Harvard University, Cambridge, Massachusetts 02138

INTRODUCTION

Despite his antiquity, the miner, like Geertz's peasant, was recently discovered by anthropologists. This discovery, not fortuitously, came when the energy and environmental crisis made us all aware of the finite supply of nonrenewable natural resources and the limits of industrial growth. If interest in mining came late, systematic studies of mining have yet to arrive. Paraphrasing Geertz, one is not likely to find ideas, much less a coherent system of ideas, in anthropological studies of mining.

The aims of this essay are: (*a*) to review the anthropological literature on mining, drawing attention to the contributions of neighboring disciplines, and (*b*) to identify promising avenues for future research. The review deals with hard, nonfuel minerals. Oil, gas, coal, and uranium are dealt with only incidentally. Stress is placed on the extractive and not on the processing or marketing stages for the sake of coherence and brevity.

The review is divided into three sections. The first deals with mineral economics; the second contains a discussion of the demographic, social, and political characteristics of mining communities; the final section involves mining rituals, beliefs, and idcology. Implicit in this tripartite division is a view of mining consisting of an economic base and a derivative sociopolitical and ideological superstructure.

THE ECONOMICS OF MINING

Mining is a process composed of three major, logical, interrelated, and sequential phases: exploration, development, and production (189). Unique risks, economic considerations, and constraints characterize each stage.

Exploration

Exploration is the most important phase of a mining venture because most of the value added of a mineral deposit occurs at the moment of discovery. Most orebodies currently under exploitation were discovered through, and grew out of, enterprises initiated by small-scale producers (10, 151, 182). The strategies used by these people in locating deposits remain unknown. Phimister (155) discusses the formulas followed by the Shona of Southern Zambezia for finding reef outcrops. Arnold (5) probes the cognitive distinctions made by the Maya potters of Yucatan in classifying the physical properties of clay types and finds that folk distinctions match the mineral composition of the materials. Although he does not focus on how potters actually find mineral reserves, he pays attention to the criteria they use in making distinctions among clays of different qualities. Several mechanisms suggest themselves for sharing or shifting exploration risks (Figure 1).

Under scenario 1, the firm/miner receives a fixed fee or wage for exploration irrespective of the outcome and thus bears none of the geological risks. This contract structure does not contain built-in incentives to encourage exploration. Under scenario 3, the firm/miner bears all the exploration risks. If they are averse to risk, they may underexplore, as each party waits to see the outcome of a neighbor's discovery (48, 95, 152, 178). The economic intuition here is: wait until your neighbor strikes a vein, then explore in an adjacent area or else buy the property. In so doing one shifts prospecting risks to a neighbor or, more appropriately, the neighbor, having successfully borne the risks of exploration, gives one a free ride. Godoy (77) notes that among Bolivia's peasant miners the information spillover effect is more complicated and less detrimental than has been assumed by natural resource economists. Scenario 2 depicts a situation in which exploration risks are shared. This is the most common contractual format

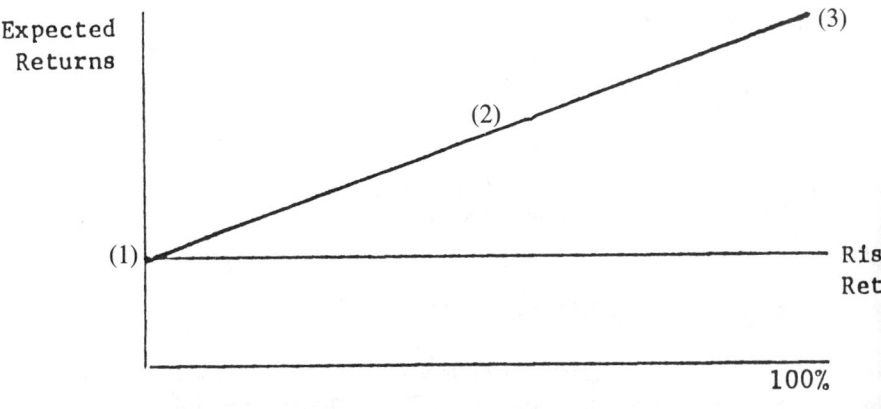

Figure 1 Exploration risk and expected returns.

for exploration, be it among individuals or firms, because it reduces the risks of failure in prospecting. Figure 1 suggests that the greater the share of exploration risks borne, the greater the expected return.

A firm undertaking a risk-free pursuit expects a minimum return equal to or greater than the next best alternative source of income. It expects a remuneration, R_1, greater than the opportunity cost of its capital. The future cash flow of its new activity, when discounted at R_1, should yield a net present value (NPV)$\geqslant$0. With inflation, the minimum discount rate includes an inflationary component, R_2. Further, if firms undertake a risky activity, such as exploration, they expect a compensation, R_3, for bearing the risk. The necessary premium varies according to the relative risk aversion of the firm; gamblers do not expect much above the opportunity cost of their investment. Prospectors thus expect a minimum return adjusted for the alternative uses of their efforts, inflation, and the share of exploration risk borne. Mathematically, the minimum discount rate can be expressed by:

$$MDR = R_1 + R_3 + (1 + R_1 + R_3) \times R_2$$

where,

MDR = minimum discount rate
R_1 = opportunity cost of capital
R_2 = expected future inflation rate
R_3 = risk compensation/premium

The Jukumani data of Bolivia (77), as well as scattered historical material (76), lend credence to this economic model, but more research is needed in establishing the causal links between the share of exploration risk borne and expected returns.

Several authors discuss the inherent instability of exploration contracts (77, 113, 126, 127, 128, 174, 197, 198). In mining, as in marriage, after one party makes an irrevocable first move, the other faces a reduced incentive to abide by the contract. Once a miner or a multinational corporation (MNC) sinks investments in a successful exploration venture, property holders or host nations have incentives to evict them or nationalize the venture. Moran (138), following Vernon, explains the nationalization of the Chilean copper industry under Allende. He also notes the growth of *dependencia* ideology as the outcome of a shift in bargaining power in favor of the host nation over the life of the contract.

Development and Production

After discovering the orebody, the firm/miner must measure reserves to decide on the best extractive and processing technology and the location of shafts and infrastructural facilities. Development risks, like exploration risks, are project-specific. The orebody, for example, may be of irregular mineralization and the original reserve estimates may have to be revised. Unfortunately, development risks have not been researched.

Tools for determining the financial/economic feasibility of developing a mineral reserve include benefit/cost ratios, internal rate(s) of returns, payback periods, and NPV. Benefit/cost ratios are of limited utility because of definitional problems. Internal rates of return are useful provided the cash flow remains positive after the initial investment. Payback periods are appropriate only for risk-averse firms with short investment horizons. Since the NPV approach allows one to transform a stream of cash into a stock of wealth, it provides the best basis for ranking and evaluating mining projects (25, 115, 165). Despite the growing popularity of the NPV approach, one caveat should be borne in mind: the NPV is as good as the price, costs, and inflation rate forecasts on which it rests.

If the feasibility study shows the mineral reserve to be worthy of exploitation, investments are made in building infrastructural facilities, shafts, and processing plants. Geological risks shrink during the production stage and are overshadowed by systematic marketing risks and country-specific political risks. Marketing risk refers to the unanticipated movement of metal prices, costs of inputs, or inflation rate. Under special circumstances, these risks can be shifted backwards to producers by metal traders through piece-rate systems of remuneration pegged to international quotations (77). The degree to which firms can shift marketing risks forward to consumers or backward to producers depends on the elasticity of demand and supply and the share of the market controlled by producers. A better hedge against these risks is portfolio diversification.

One of the most important political risks during the production phase involves expropriation (58, 106, 116). With fixed investments sunk, the conditions are ripe and the incentives are large for host nations to confiscate the holdings of mining firms. Mining expropriations in Less Developed Countries (LDCs) have risen dramatically during the past decade leading to many contract renegotiations (199). Zink (214) analyzes the causes and adaptation to political risk by MNCs in Peru. Although his emphasis is on the manufacturing sector, the strategies for political risk minimization are equally applicable to mining enterprises. Lax & Sebenius (113) propose innovative ways for hedging political risks in mining.

For heuristic ends, the production process can be categorized into its three most important factors: technology, capital, and labor.

TECHNOLOGY   Capital-intensive technology may be the "key to the mineral industry," because it has allowed the industry to reduce real unit costs (11) and exploit low-grade ores (186, pp. 191–200). The general opinion is that the decline of ore grades requires the deployment of increasingly more complex and expensive technology to find, extract, and purify mineral of leaner quality (24, p. 262; 36, pp. 129–37; 143, p. 26). The trend toward more automated operations and greater vertical integration is read as *prima facie* evidence for the effectiveness of economies of scale. Such a view is challenged by the growth of the artisanal mining sector in LDCs (1, 15, 145, 191, 192). Killick & During (104) and Godoy (78) argue that artisanal mining technology is as technically efficient as capital-intensive mining technology. Thoburn (188) compares the capital-intensive mining system of dredge mining versus the labor-intensive system of gravel pumping in Malaysia and finds little difference in profitability of linkages.

CAPITAL AND INVESTMENTS   Two types of capital are necessary for mining ventures: risk capital for exploration/development and business capital for actual production operations. Of the two, risk capital is the most difficult to secure, especially for small-scale firms with no significant collateral. The inability of mining firms to acquire risk capital has rendered the industry inordinately vulnerable to mergers and speculators. Lewis (114) was among the first to explore the implications of the capital requirements of the mining industry. He discussed the growing subordination of free miners in the tin mining areas of Cornwall and Devon ("the stannaries") to merchant monopolists who advanced risk capital and transported the tinner's ore to coinage towns. By early Tudor days the subordination of the independent tinner to the "tender mercies of the middleman and regrator" were complete. Freund (62) synthesizes the capital and labor strategies employed by the tin mining industry of Nigeria, and others (43, 44, 61, 96, 97, 109, 193) discuss the strategies used by mining firms in the Witwatersrand gold and diamond fields of South Africa to secure capital prior to World War I. Phimister & Van Onselen (156) note that one important factor hampering the development of the southern Rhodesian mining sector was the inability of mining industrialists to secure international capital and their reliance on local financial sources. Simmons (171) echoes the same theme in writing about the indigenous coal mining industry of colonial India.

Investment patterns in mining have changed significantly in the past two decades. Prior to the 1960s, most investments in LDC mining projects flowed from private, vertically integrated, capital- and technology-intensive, U.S.-based corporations. These firms controlled capital and a "package" of technological, marketing, and management skills (66, 121). The relationship led to the development of metropolitan economies, to the enrichment of mining firms, and to the pauperization and dependence of mineral-exporting LDCs (28, 71, 72, 108). During the 1960s a growing share of investments began to flow from European and Japanese MNCs. The past decade has seen the rapid growth of state-owned MNCs from LDCs, which account for a growing share of the market production (14, 57, 70, 98, 186). These developments were accompanied by the proliferation of new fiscal devices created by host countries to capture a larger share of rents from MNCs (66, 68, 69), as well as new and more complex contract structures between MNCs and host nations (174, 198). Due in part to the increasing risks of expropriation in LDCs and the emergence of state-owned MNCs, capital investments by the private mining sector of industrial nations into LDCs have shrunk (127) and have been rechanelled to low-risk developing countries (215).

DYNAMIC MODELS OF MINING   In contrast to static, numerical analysis of the mining industry (35, 169), dynamic models specify the allocation of capital and labor and the intertemporal path needed to optimally deplete an exhaustible reserve while maximizing the NPV (153). Using cost functions, growth or partial equilibrium models, several scholars (92, 93, 168, 175, 183, 201) conclude that the optimal extraction profile for perfect competitors involves extracting all the finest ore and best deposits first. Using linear programming techniques which incorporate geological, economic, and engineering variables, Conrad & Hool (40, 41) note that a profit-maximizing firm will not necessarily extract the richest ore first. Rather, the order of ore grades extracted should correspond to the ranking of discounted prices.

Distortionary variables in the optimal extraction profile include monopolies (102, 179, 183) and low interest rates (59, 169), both of which may accelerate the extraction pace. Taxes also have distortionary effects. Hotelling (95) and Peterson (152) note that *ad valorem* and *ad rem* severance taxes lead industry to shift extraction to later periods. McDonald (124) and Burnes (34) argue that shifting can be toward either later or earlier phases. Several economists (40, 41, 68, 111, 177) maintain that output-based taxes lower the level of reserves by raising the cut-off grade. Others (40, 67) argue that royalties, in addition to inducing selective exploitation, also lead to meager exploration and inefficient choice of technology since investments cannot be amortized or expensed when paying a tax defined as a proportion of unit value.

Restrictive assumptions may limit the utility of some of these models for understanding the behavior of miners. For example, some of the models assume known price cycles and grade distribution in the firm's profit-maximizing calculus. Mineral prices, costs, and tonnage are presumed to be the only cut-off grade determinants. Firms are expected to operate in an environment with clearly defined and enforceable private property rights; they can wait with equanimity until discounted metal prices peak before extracting the richest ore. Finally, most studies (40, 66, 68, 111, 177) assume output-based taxes raise the cut-off grade, thereby lowering the mineral reserves available to the nation.

The socioeconomic environment in which Third World miners operate may be sufficiently different to render these assumptions inoperative and the theories inapplicable. For instance, poor knowledge of ore-grade distribution and price cycles, coupled with poorly defined property rights and political uncertainty, may compel miners to extract all the finest ore first, irrespective of future discounted prices. In addition to cost/benefit calculations, the miner's cut-off grade may be influenced by contractual arrangements (76, 79, 160) and demographic and sociocultural variables. Finally, it is unclear to what extent, if any, shifting the cut-off grade upwards constitutes a waste of the nation's resources in a labor-glutted market with few alternative sources of employment (76).

The optimal extraction profile of nonrenewable stocks brings up the issue of the ultimate depletion of such resources. The Club of Rome (125) projected future rates of population growth and consumption of raw materials and concluded that the world would run out of minerals within the next century. They endorsed the use of royalties and progressive income taxes as a means of conservation. Marxists (186) disagree with the prognosis, arguing that the so-called shortage is induced by the irrational exploitation of the MNCs. More orthodox analysts find objectionable the Club of Rome's failure to incorporate rising prices which should encourage conservation and galvanize the search for substitutes (17, 102, 146).

SOCIAL ORGANIZATION OF MINING

The physical and social isolation of mining communities, coupled with the harsh working conditions and the labor requirements of the mining industry, give rise to recurrent patterns of population dynamics, labor recruitment practices, and political organization.

Demography

The notion that mining populations have high fertility was first set forth by the United Nations (190), taken up by Wrigley (210) in his study of Western Germany, North France, and Belgium, and irrefragably proved by Haines (89) for the 19th-century coal mining regions of Poland, England, Wales, and Pennsylvania. Nineteenth-century coal miners had higher fertility rates than rural dwellers from the surrounding countryside because of higher infant and adult debility/mortality, low levels of female labor force participation outside the home, low child-rearing costs, and early marriage for women. Although Haines's findings were independently corroborated by Friedlander (65), who used national and county data for England and Wales, the general thesis regarding high fertility of miners remains to be tested cross-culturally for contemporary populations.

Labor Recruitment and Migration

Mining, especially during the early phases, has been, and in many LDCs continues to be, a labor-intensive operation. Consequently, one of the first and most important requirements of the mining industry has been the procurement of an ample and reliable supply of inexpensive laborers. Some have stressed the coercive means employed by the industrial sector in securing a vast supply of miners (97, 194, 205). Recruitment mechanisms included taxation (3, 19, 39, 62, 133), quelching indigenous economic initiatives (3, 84), indebtedness to labor contractors or employers (50, 60, 163, 170, 172, 209), and the purchasing of entire landed estates with their tenants (129, 171). Revisionist scholars suggest that there may have been a voluntary element in the decision to enter the mining labor force (8, 9, 46, 64, 105, 164, 184, 185), such as the wish to build up cattle stock after epidemics (18, 19), to prove one's manliness (161, 167), to escape quarrels, witchcraft accusations, and arduous duties (134, p. 17), or, as in Indian coal mining, simply to meet seasonal subsistence shortages (173).

To minimize costs and avoid political liabilities, mining firms under the auspices of the state tended to pay workers below subsistence wages and took steps to preserve indigenous production systems, forcing miners to return home after their contract in the mine expired or once workers reached the age of retirement (90, 151). Indigenous societies thus bore much of the costs of reproducing and maintaining the mining labor force (6, 19, 50, 60, 208). The inadequacy and insecurity of the industrial wage, "repulsive" labor organization, and the difficulties of meeting subsistence needs in the rural sector underwrite a circular or "spiral" flow of migrants to and from the mining centers (49, 50, 56, 84, 132, 171, 176, 196, 200).

The early anthropological literature stressed the deleterious effects of migration upon indigenous patterns of political leadership and production. Richards (162) deplored the "hungry, manless areas" of Africa, and other anthropologists associated with the Rhodes-Livingstone Institute agreed that migration to the mines undermined traditional values and authority patterns (64, 74, 75, 133, 161, 206, 207). Chauncey (37) recently stressed the growth of the female population in the Zambian Copperbelt and the parallel rural decline brought about by the absence of women. Other work, however, suggests that the impact of migration on indigenous societies does not imply either factually or logically that there will be a rural decline; in fact, it may even reinforce traditional values and social organization (4, 55, 64, 196, 200).

Although the stabilization of the labor force brought about by the mechanization of the mining industry may bring about a complete or nearly complete breakage with the country (27, 50, 91, 108), active links with rural areas are maintained by migrant miners to keep rights to land, validate membership in the group, and mobilize political support (123, 176, 196). These links are nurtured though periodic visits, remittances (74), or ceremonial occasions (26). In the mining community itself, new cultural (75, 85, 131, 159), political (56, 200), and legal (180) forms emerge, cross-cutting tribal and ethnic group boundaries (75, 135, 137, 156).

The evidence suggests that migration to the mines of Africa, Latin America, and North America occurs on a more frequent basis and for longer periods of time (74, 119, 130, 148, 206). Until recently the net transfer of wealth flowed from the rural to the mining sector. In recent years, however, that subsidy has been reversed, with mining wages shoring up a rapidly decomposing indigenous subsistence structure (3, 18, 21, 49, 64, 118, 119, 140–142, 176).

Mining Communities and Political Organization

The location of mineral deposits in inaccessible areas gives rise to relatively self-contained communities, which can range from the open mining camps described by Luebben in Colorado (118, 119); Barrios de Chungara (12) and Harris & Albo (91) in northern Potosi, Bolivia; to the paternalistic company states of Northern Chile (157, 158), Toquepala, Peru (83, pp. 169–74), or Ajo, Arizona (181); to the hermetic, total institutions of the South African mining compounds (3, 84, 136, 139).

Given the capital immobility of the mining industry, a salient determinant of industrial strategy centers on cost minimization through the control and exploitation of labor (56, 97, 144, 186, 194, 205). The combination of low wages, coercive organization (29, 33, 85), dangerous but autonomous working conditions (82, 180), the economic leverage of miners flowing from the importance of mining exports to the health of the national economy (103), and the physical and social isolation of many mining enclaves (53, 103) underwrites the formation of intense forms of worker solidarity and radical labor movements (29, 33, 47, 86, 136, 137, 203) as well as the growth of new forms of political consciousness (139, 150, 194). The genesis and growth of radical mining movements is well analyzed in Bolivia (12, 117, 120, 144, 203), Chile (211, 213), Mexico (20, 22, 23, 147, 166, 212), Peru (16, 49, 50, 60, 107, 108, 110), Nigeria (2, 62), Zambia (13, 32, 33, 56, 99, 100), Ghana (42), and South Africa (149). As Phimister, Van Onselen, and Freund note, social protest can take informal hues such as ore theft (63), desertions (39), loafing, voluntary migration to the best labor markets, and deliberate wastefulness (60, 156, 194, 195). The origin of workers' political consciousness antedates the eruption of strikes or the creation of labor unions.

Ecological/Economic Impact of Mining

The mining industry requires not only capital and labor, but food for its workers and physical inputs for its operations. Consequently, mining activities tend to integrate surrounding regions into a single economic sphere. Several Africanists (6, 30, 151, 154) hold that the mining industry in South Africa created large demands for foodstuffs, which were initially met by African producers. By the 1920s, however, White Afrikaner farmers, with the backing of the state, succeeded in displacing native producers. The growing interest of mining capital in labor rather than in agricultural products made such a switch possible (208). In a more creative spirit, the Marxist historian Van Onselen (195), with his customary insights and warm humanity, has recently discussed in two tomes the effects of the Witwatersrand mines on the life of marginal segments of society such as liquor sellers, prostitutes, cab drivers, etc.

Assadourian and his colleagues (7) provide a theoretical framework for conceptualizing the interrelationship between the mining enclave and the surrounding rural Andean societies, while other Andeanists have explored the specific effects of the mining industry on transportation (38), fuels (80, 202), food (112), and other inputs (129).

Since national development policies traditionally give preference to mining enterprises in the exploitation of subsoil mineral wealth (31, 45), and mining codes are vague about indemnifying indigenous populations for ecological damages and land expropriation, mining projects often produce ecological alterations on the surrounding landscape. The environmental impact of mining can range from minor, subtle, imperceptible "shadow effects" involving noise, dust, run-off, seepage, and vibration (122) to major, permanent, and irreversable ecological transformations, rendering mining districts useless for subsequent economic developments (31). The range of impacts reflects the scale of operation and type of mining (52). Dewind (49) documents the effects of the smelter's smog of the Cerro de Pasco Corporation in Peru on the land and stock of surrounding peasant communities. Diamond (51) and Freund (62, pp. 156–73) note that tin mining produced extensive topsoil destruction in the land of the Birom-speaking peasantry of the Jos Plateau, Nigeria. Gjording (73) discusses some of the potential economic and ecological problems facing the Guaymi Indians of Panama if the Cerro Colorado copper project were to be carried out. Some international lending institutions now require a social and environmental impact statement before they fund mining projects in LDCs (81).

RITUAL AND IDEOLOGY

The seminal piece on miners' belief system is Eliade's *The Forge and the Crucible* (54). Eliade draws the analogy between obstetrics and mining, with ore equated to embryo, mine to uterus, shaft to vagina, and miner to obstetrician. Much in the same way embryos develop in the womb, so ores grow inside the earth until extracted by miners. Eliade's insights are interesting because they provide a framework for linking ideology to productive processes in mining. Unfortunately, anthropologists have not capitalized on Eliade's observations. The few contemporary pieces explicitly dealing with ideology lack both a sharply defined focus and the elegance of Eliade's simple but compelling thesis.

Chief among these works are Nash's *We Eat The Mines* (144), and Taussig's widely praised (e.g. 94, 204) *The Devil and Commodity Fetishism* (187), both of which deal with Quechua-speaking Bolivian miners. Nash and Taussig each attempt to explain the twin concepts of the devil *(el tio)* and the underground ritual libations *(ch'alla)* offered to this deity. Nash, perhaps unknowingly, follows Eliade's lead in suggesting that tin ores are a living substance, replenishable by the devil after receiving periodic libations. The devil assumes a pivotal role both for controlling the supply of ores and for monitoring underground safety. In this context, Nash suggests that the *ch'alla* is a ceremony designed to placate the devil and a forum for expressing worker solidarity. To Nash, rituals unify the group. (88).

Taussig distances himself from such a functionalist approach. In a message familar to students of contemporary symbolic anthropology, he asserts that the devil figure cannot be reduced to a psychological mechanism for coping with anxiety nor to a social device for displaying solidarity, because to do so is to reduce a rich cultural form to its functions and consequences. Such explanations can "tell us next to nothing" about detailed motifs, "precise configuration," vividness, and inner meanings of so rich a collective representation. Taussig's own "esoteric attempt" to clarify the devil belief system consists in viewing it in its own right, as a cultural/symbolic representation of alienation. His ultimate aim is thus not so much historical or explicative, as literary; namely, it is to "convey something of the 'feel' of social experience."

Explicit in Taussig's analysis is a dichotomization of modes of production into precapitalist (peasant) and capitalist. The precapitalist mode of production is characterized by use value, reciprocity, loose division of labor, satisfaction of need, and efficiency. Furthermore, precapitalist agriculture attempts to "replicate the natural ecology" and thus "preserves most of the pre-existing ecosystem." The capitalist mode of production, in contrast, is characterized by market (exchange) value, accumulation, unequal exchange, and rigid division of labor. As capitalist modes of production supplant precapitalist formations, social tensions arise, providing the groundwork for the emergence of the devil belief. More concretely, the transformation of the peasant mode of production generates conflict, suffering, and alienation, all of which concretize in the devil figure. As Bolivian peasants were transformed into proletarians, their rituals changed: the incorporeal mother earth spirit *pachamama* gave way to the devil, a virile and unpredictable figure. Unlike the *pachamama*, the devil is represented in idol form and requires frequent ritual libations. In agrarian rituals, peasants engage in balanced reciprocity with the *pachamama*; in mining rituals, on the other hand, miners are simple intermediaries between the devil and proprietors.

Despite Taussig's literary skills, his analysis remains unconvincing. Taussig critiques positivist orientations such as functionalism because they reduce social forms to the part they play in the maintenance of social systems. Despite his attempt to liberate himself from the fetters of so-called capitalist epistemology, Taussig's own "esoteric" approach does not amount to much more than a sophisticated form of symbolic neofunctionalism, in which belief systems serve the role of mediating between tensions, critiquing capitalist systems of production, or fetishizing evil. The functionalism of social structural interdependencies is replaced by the functionalism of interrelated symbols and meanings.

The book is premised on the notion that "neophyte proletarians" are "indifferent and outright hostile" to participation in the market economy. This is an empirical proposition, not a philosophical conclusion. As applied to Bolivia and other developing countries, it is wrong. It is wrong because peasants have often entered the mines during the first years of colonial rule to find, extract, and market the ore on their own free will. The Bolivian mines during the first half century of colonial rule, for example, were not run by Spaniards but by voluntary Indian workers who had been "attracted to the mines by the profits they could make from extracting and processing the richer ores" (8, 9, 184, 185). Taussig views the process of proletarianization as coercive, tyrannical, and unilineal, but this overlooks the fact that in Bolivia, as in Africa (46, 64, 105, 164), there was a voluntary dimension to this process. Furthermore, in contrast to Marxists' analyses, mining proletarianization may, in actuality, be a reversible process. In many mineral-exporting LDCs such as Malaysia, Sierra Leone, Brazil, and Bolivia, a substantial portion of the mining sector is undergoing a process of involution: more piece-rate workers, treatment of progressively lower ore grades, decapitalization, less machinery, and greater reliance on seasonal laborers to process ores of thinner and thinner quality. This involutionary process suggests, contrary to Taussig's claim, that miners in many LDCs may be currently shifting back and forth between precapitalist and capitalist relations of production with much less conflict, stress, and agony than he assumes.

CONCLUSIONS

Dividing the mining industry into an economic base, social organization, and ideology, one notes several important points about the contributions made by anthropologists to our understanding of mining. First, there is a paucity of anthropological writing about mineral economics. If, as several international organizations maintain, the small-scale, artisanal mining sector is expanding in mineral-exporting Third World nations, then anthropologists could make substantial contributions to mineral economics through the study of the small-scale sector. The questions that need to be explored include the methods and rules of thumb utilized by miners in localizing mineralized deposits. Having found the deposit, how do they categorize/conceptualize geological/mineral formations and different ore grades; and, based on native distinctions, how do miners decide where the cut-off grade is? Finally, the risk management strategies used in each mining phase deserve attention.

The paucity of research on mineral economics is matched by a lack of interest in the productive process and workplace itself. It is not unusual in a book-length monograph on miners for these topics to be treated in a page or two. This void may reflect simple lack of interest in production, difficulties inherent in conducting research underground, and management's objection to research conducted on its workforce. Godfrey Wilson's and Epstein's study of mining compounds in the Copperbelt of northern Rhodesia, for instance, were prematurely ended when management cancelled permission and withdrew facilities for research. Gordon's (84) fascinating account of a Namibian mine is all the more remarkable when one considers the hermetic and despotic nature of these totalitarian institutions.

Not surprisingly, anthropological contributions to mining tend to focus on social organization and migration. But even here serious gaps remain. We have noted the absence of demographic research on contemporary mining populations. In contrast, the causes, consequences, and meaning of migration to the mines have been examined *ad nauseam*, and it is unlikely that anything conceptually novel will emerge from further research on this topic, except, perhaps, for more unneeded case studies.

Since engineers, geologists, economists, political scientists, geographers, historians, and sociologists study mining, one might ask, what can anthropologists contribute to this field that will be new? At the risk of sounding trite, a truly anthropological study of mining will examine both the geological and economic infrastructure of the firm/industry as well as their secondary sociopolitical and ideological dimensions. This integrative perspective is currently missing, not only from anthropological studies, but also from research done in neighboring disciplines. The anthropologists' obsession with migration is matched by the economists' preoccupation with the effect of taxes on reserves and extraction rates, or with the political scientists' interests in the genesis of political consciousness. These seemingly disparate phenomena are interrelated if we examine the economic, social, and ideological dimensions of the production process as a whole. Given the anthropologists' penchant for, and strengths with, small-scale social systems, the major and first impact of anthropological contributions is likely to be made in the small-scale mining sector.

ACKNOWLEDGMENTS

I wish to thank Elizabeth Bangs and Sung Hee Suh for their help in preparing this chapter.

Literature Cited

1. AGID (Association of Geoscientists for International Development). 1982. *AGID News* 30
2. Akpala, A. 1965. Background of the Enugu colliery shooting incident of 1949. *J. Hist. Soc. Nigeria* 3:335–64
3. Alverson, H. 1978. *Mind in the Heart of Darkness*. New Haven: Yale Univ. Press
4. Anderson, C. 1983. Aborigines and tin mining in north Queensland: A case study in the anthropology of contact history. *Mankind* 13:473–98
5. Arnold, D. 1972. Ethnomineralogy of Ticul, Yucatan potters: Etics and emics. *Am. Antiq.* 36:20–40
6. Arrighi, G. 1970. Labour supplies in historical perspective. *J. Dev. Stud.* 6:157–234
7. Assadourian, C., Bonilla, H., Mitre, A., Platt, T. 1980. *Mineria y espacio economico en los Andes*. Lima: Inst. Estud. Peru
8. Bakewell, P. 1975. Registered silver production in the Potosi district, 1550–1735. *Jahrb. Gesch. Staat, Wirtsch. Ges. Lateinam.* 12:67–103
9. Bakewell, P. 1977. Technological change in Potosi: The silver boom of the 1570s. *Jahrb. Gesch. Staat, Wirtsch. Ges. Lateinam.* 14:57–77
10. Bancroft, J., Austen, J. 1961. *Mining in Northern Rhodesia*. London: Sidney
11. Barnett, H., Morse, C. 1963. *Scarcity and Growth*. Baltimore: Johns Hopkins Press
12. Barrios de Chungara, D. 1977. *Si me permiten hablar*. Mexico: Siglo Veintiuno
13. Bates, R. 1971. *Unions, Parties and Political Development*. New Haven: Yale Univ. Press.
14. Baumol, W. 1980. *Public and Private Enterprises in a Mixed Economy*. New York: St. Martin's
15. Baxter, M. 1975. *Garimpeiros of Poxoreo*. PhD thesis. Univ. Calif., Berkeley
16. Becker, D. 1983. *The New Bourgeoisie and the Limits of Dependency*. Princeton: Princeton Univ. Press
17. Beckerman, W. 1972. Economists, scientists, and environmental catastrophe. *Oxford Econ. Pap.* 24:237–44
18. Beinart, W. 1980. Labour migrancy and rural production: Pondoland c. 1900–1950. See Ref. 123, pp. 81–108
19. Beinart, W. 1982. *The Political Economy of Pondoland*. Cambridge: Cambridge Univ. Press
20. Bernstein, M. 1965. *The Mexican Mining Industry 1850–1950*. Albany: NY State Univ.
21. Berry, S. 1984. The food crisis and agrarian change in Africa. *Afr. Stud. Rev.* In press
22. Besserer, F., Diaz, J., Santana, R. 1980. Formacion y consolidacion del sindicalismo minero en Cananea. *Rev. Mex. Sociol.* 42:1321–54
23. Bizberg, I., Barraza, L. 1980. La accion obrera en Las Truchas. *Rev. Mex. Sociol.* 42:1405–42
24. Bosson, R., Varon, B. 1977. *The Mining Industry and the Developing Countries*. New York: Oxford Univ. Press
25. Brealey, R., Myers, S. 1981. *Principles of Corporate Finance*. New York: McGraw-Hill
26. Brown, J., Baldivieso, R., Uriarte, M. 1968. *Informe Cornell: el minero boliviano de Colquiri*. La Paz: Univ. Mayor de San Andres
27. Brown, M. 1976. Notas sobre la chonguinada de Junin. *Am. Indig.* 36:375–84
28. Brundenius, C. 1972. The anatomy of imperialism: The case of the multinational mining corporations in Peru. *J. Peace Res.* 9:189–207
29. Bulmer, M. 1975. Sociological models of the mining community. *Sociol. Rev.* 23:61–92
30. Bundy, C. 1972. The emergence and decline of a South-African peasantry. *Afr. Aff.* 71:369–88
31. Bunker, S. 1984. Modes of extraction, unequal exchange, and the progressive underdevelopment of an extreme periphery: The Brazilian Amazon, 1600–1980. *Am. J. Sociol.* 89:1017–64
32. Burawoy, M. 1972. Another look at the mineworker. *Afr. Soc. Res.* 14:239–87
33. Burawoy, M. 1976. The functions and reproduction of migrant labor. *Am. J. Sociol.* 81:1050–87
34. Burnes, H. 1976. On the taxation of non-replenishable resources. *J. Environ. Econ. Min.* 3:289–311
35. Carlisle, D. 1954. The economics of a fund resource with particular reference to mining. *Am. Econ. Rev.* 44:595–616
36. Carman, J. 1979. *Obstacles to Mineral Development*. New York: Pergamon
37. Chauncey, G. 1981. The locus of reproduction: Women's labour in the Zambian copperbelt 1927–1953. *J. S. Afr. Stud.* 7:135–64
38. Cobb, G. 1949. Supply and transportation for the Potosi mines, 1545–1640. *Hisp. Am. Hist. Rev.* 29:25–45
39. Cole, J. 1981. *The Potosi Mita under Hapsburg administration*. PhD thesis. Univ. Mass, Amherst
40. Conrad, R. 1978. *Taxation and the*

theory of the mine. PhD thesis. Univ. Wis., Madison
41. Conrad, R., Hool, B. 1981. Resource taxation with heterogeneous quality and endogenous reserves. *J. Public Econ.* 16:17–33
42. Crisp, J. 1983. Productivity and protest: Scientific management in the Ghanaian gold mines 1947–1956. See Ref. 142, pp. 91–130
43. Davis, R. 1976. Mining capital, the state and unskilled white workers in South Africa, 1901–1913. *J. S. Afr. Stud.* 3:41–69
44. Davis, R. 1979. *Capital, State and White Labour in South Africa 1900–1960.* New Jersey: Humanities Press
45. Davis, S. 1977. *Victims of the Miracle.* New York: Cambridge Univ. Press
46. Delius, P. 1980. Migrant labour and the Pedi, 1840–80. In *Economy and Society in Pre-Industrial South Africa,* ed. S. Marks, A. Atmore, pp. 293–312. Hong Kong: Longman
47. Dennis, N., Henriques, F., Slaughter, C. 1969. *Coal is Our Life.* London: Longman
48. Devarajan, S., Fisher, A. 1981. Hotelling's *Economics of Exhaustible Resources* fifty years later. *J. Econ. Lit.* 19:65–73
49. Dewind, A. 1975. From peasants to miners—Background to strikes in mines in Peru. *Sci. Soc.* 39:44–72
50. Dewind, A. 1977. *Peasants become miners.* PhD thesis. Columbia Univ., New York
51. Diamond, S. 1967. The Anaguta of Nigeria: Suburban primitives. See Ref. 129, pp. 361–505
52. Down, C., Stocks, J. 1977. *Environmental Impact of Mining.* London: Appl. Sci. Publ.
53. Edward, P. 1977. A critique of the Kerr-Siegel hypothesis of strikes and the isolated mass. *Sociol. Rev.* 25:551–74
54. Eliade, M. 1962. *The Forge and the Crucible.* London: Rider
55. Elkan, W. 1960. *Migrants and Proletarians.* London: Oxford Univ. Press
56. Epstein, A. 1958. *Politics in an Urban African Community.* Manchester: Manchester Univ. Press
57. Erickson, D., Gillis, M. 1980. High level enterprise and low-level radioactivity: Two hazards in LDC uranium concessions. *J. Energy Dev.* 6:39–60
58. Farber, M., Brown, R. 1980. Changing the rules of the game: Political risk, instability, and fairplay in mineral concession contracts. *Third World Q.* 2:100–19
59. Fisher, A., Krutilla, J. 1975. Resource conservation, environmental preservation, and the rate of discount. *Q. J. Econ.* 89:358–70
60. Flores Galindo, A. 1974. *Los mineros de la Cerro de Pasco.* Lima: Univ. Catolica del Peru
61. Frankel, S. 1967. *Investment and Return to Equity Capital in the South African Gold Mining Industry.* London: Oxford Univ. Press
62. Freund, B. 1981. *Capital and Labour in the Nigerian Tin Mines.* London: Harlow
63. Freund, B. 1982. Theft and social protest among the tin miners of northern Nigeria. *Radical Hist. Rev.* 26:68–86
64. Freund, B. 1984. Labor and labor history in Africa: A review of the literature. *Afr. Stud. Rev.* In press
65. Friedlander, D. 1973. Demographic patterns and socio-economic characteristics of the coal-mining population in England and Wales in the 19th century. *Econ. Dev. Cult. Change* 22:39–51
66. Gillis, M. 1982. Evolution of natural resources taxation in developing countries. *Nat. Resour. J.* 22:619–48
67. Gillis, M. 1982. Allocative and X-efficiency in state-owned mining enterprises: Comparisons between Bolivia and Indonesia. *J. Comp. Econ.* 6:1–23
68. Gillis, M., Beals, R. 1980. *Tax and Investment Policies Toward Hard Minerals.* Cambridge: Ballinger
69. Gillis, M., Buckovetsky, M., Jenkins, G., Petersen, U., Wells, L., Wright, B. 1978. *Taxation and Mining.* Cambridge: Ballinger
70. Gillis, M., Perkins, D., Roemer, M., Snodgrass, D. 1983. *Economics of Development.* New York: Norton
71. Girvan, N. 1970. Multinational corporations and dependent underdevelopment in mineral-exporting economies. *Soc. Econ. Stud.* 19:490–533
72. Girvan, N. 1971. Making the rules of the game: Company-country agreements in the bauxite industry. *Soc. Econ. Stud.* 20:378–419
73. Gjording, C. 1981. *The Cerro Colorado Copper Project and the Guaymi Indians of Panama.* Cambridge: Cultural Survival Occas. Pap. 3
74. Gluckman, M. 1941. *The Economy of the Central Barotse Plain.* Manchester: Rhodes-Livingstone Inst. Pap. 7
75. Gluckman, M. 1961. Anthropological problems arising from the African industrial revolution. In *Social Change in Modern Africa,* ed. A. Southall, pp. 67–82. London: Oxford Univ. Press
76. Godoy, R. 1984. *Bolivian Peasant Mining.* Unpublished manuscript
77. Godoy, R. 1984. Risk and moral contract in peasant mining in Bolivia. In *Research*

in Economic Anthropology, ed. B. Isaac. Greenwich: JAI Press. In press
78. Godoy, R. 1984. Technical and economic efficiency of Bolivian peasant miners. *Econ. Dev. Cult. Change.* In press
79. Godoy, R. 1984. Small-scale mining and agriculture in the Jukumani Ayllu, Northern Potosi, Bolivia. In *Debating the Dilemma: An Anthropological View of the Political Economy of Latin America,* ed. K. Yambert, B. Orlove. Submitted for publication
80. Godoy, R. 1984. Ecological degradation and agricultural intensification in the Andean highlands. *Hum. Ecol.* In press
81. Goodland, R. 1982. *Tribal Peoples and Economic Development.* Washington: World Bank
82. Goodrich, C. 1925. *The Miner's Freedom.* Boston: Marhall Jones
83. Goodsell, C. 1974. *American Corporations and Peruvian Politics.* Cambridge: Harvard Univ. Press
84. Gordon, R. 1977. *Mines, Masters and Migrants.* Johannesburg: Ravan Press
85. Gordon, R. 1978. The celebration of ethnicity: A 'tribal fight' in a Namibian mine compound. In *Ethnicity in Modern Africa,* ed. B. Du Toit, pp. 213–31. Boulder: Westview
86. Gouldner, A. 1954. *Patterns of Industrial Bureaucracy.* Glencoe: Free Press
87. Grayson, C. 1960. *Decisions Under Uncertainty.* Boston: Harvard Bus. Sch.
88. Gross, D. 1983. Fetishism and functionalism. *Comp. Stud. Soc. Hist.* 25:694–702
89. Haines, M. 1979. *Fertility and Occupation.* New York: Academic
90. Harris, M. 1959. Labour emigration among the Mozambique Thonga: Cultural and political factors. *Africa* 29:50–65
91. Harris, O., Albo, X. 1975. *Monteras y guardatojos.* La Paz: Centro de Investigacion y Promocion del Campesinado
92. Hartwick, J. 1978. Exploitation of many deposits of an exhaustible resource. *Econometrica* 46:201–7
93. Herfindahl, O. 1959. *Copper Costs and Prices: 1870–1957.* Baltimore: Johns Hopkins Press
94. Hobsbawm, E. 1982. Review of Taussig's *The Devil and Commodity Fetishism. NY Rev. Books* 163:142–43
95. Hotelling, H. 1931. The economics of exhaustible resources. *J. Polit. Econ.* 39:137–75
96. Innes, D. 1977. The exercise of control in the diamond industry of South Africa—Some preliminary remarks. In *Perspectives on South Africa,* ed. T. Adler, pp. 195–241. Johannesburg: Univ. Witwatersrand
97. Johnstone, F. 1976. *Class, Race and Gold.* London: Routledge & Kegan Paul
98. Jones, L., Mason, E., Vernon, R., eds. 1983. *Public Enterprises in Developing Countries.* New York: Oxford Univ. Press
99. Kapferer, B. 1976. Conflict and process in a Zambian mine community. In *Freedom and Constraint,* ed. M. Aronoff, pp. 50–82. Amsterdam: Van Gorcum, Assen
100. Kapferer, B. 1978. Structural marginality and the urban social order. *Urban Anthropol.* 7:287–320
101. Kauffman, G. 1963. *Statistical Decision and Related Techniques in Oil and Gas Exploration.* Englewood Cliffs: Prentice Hall
102. Kay, J., Mirrlees, J. 1975. The desirability of natural resource depletion. In *The Economics of Natural Resource Depletion,* ed. D. Pearce, J. Rose, pp. 140–76. New York Wiley
103. Kerr, C., Siegel, A. 1954. The interindustrial propensity to strike, an international comparison. In *Industrial Conflict,* ed. A. Kornhauser, R. Dubin, A. Ross, pp. 186–212. New York: McGraw Hill
104. Killick, A., During, R. 1969. A structural approach to the balance of payments of a low-income country. *J. Dev. Stud.* 5:274–93
105. Kimble, J. 1982. Labour migration in Basutoland, c. 1870–1885. In *Industrialization and Social Change in South Africa,* ed. S. Marks, R. Rathbone, pp. 119–41. London: Harlow
106. Kobrin, S. 1979. Political risk: A review and consideration. *J. Int. Bus. Stud.* 10:67–80
107. Kruijt, D., Vellinga, M. 1977. The political economy of mining enclaves in Peru. *Bol. Estud. Latinoam. Caribe* 23:97–126
108. Kruijt, D., Vellinga, M. 1980. Las huelgas en la Cerro de Pasco Corporation (1902–1974): los factores internos. *Rev. Mex. Sociol.* 42:1497–1590
109. Kubicek, R. 1979. *Economic Imperialism in Theory and Practice.* Durham: Duke Univ. Press
110. Laite, J. 1980. Miners and national politics in Peru, 1900–1974. *J. Lat. Am. Stud.* 12:317–40
111. Lane, K. 1964. Choosing the optimum cut-off grade. *Q. Colo. Sch. Mines* 59:811–30
112. Larson, B. 1982. *Explotacion agraria y resistencia campesina en Cochabamba.* Cochabamba: CERES

113. Lax, D., Sebenius, J. 1981. Insecure contracts and resource development. *Public Policy* 29:417–36
114. Lewis, G. 1915. *The Stannaries*. Cambridge: Harvard Univ. Press
115. Little, I., Mirrlees, J. 1974. *Project Appraisal and Planning for Developing Countries*. New York: Basic Books
116. Long, N. 1975. Resource extraction under uncertainty about possible nationalization. *J. Econ. Theory* 10:42–53
117. Lora, G. 1977. *History of the Bolivian Labour Movement*. Cambridge: Cambridge Univ. Press
118. Luebben, R. 1955. *A study of some off-reservation Navajo miners*. PhD thesis. Cornell Univ., Ithaca, NY
119. Luebben, R. 1958–59. The Navajo dilemma—A question of necessity. *Am. Indian* 8:6–16
120. Magill, J. 1974. *Labour Unions and Political Socialization*. New York: Praeger
121. Mamalakis, M. 1977. Minerals, multinationals, and foreign investment in Latin America. *J. Lat. Am. Stud.* 9:315–36
122. Marshall, I. 1982. *Mining, Land Use, and the Environment*. Ottawa: Lands Directorate Environment Canada
123. Mayer, P., ed. 1980. *Black Villagers in an Industrial Society*. Capetown: Oxford Univ. Press
124. McDonald, S. 1965. The effects of severance vs. property taxes on petroleum conservation. *Proc. Natl. Tax Assoc.*, pp. 320–27
125. Meadows, D., Randers, J., Behrens, W. 1972. *The Limits of Growth*. New York: Universe Books
126. Mikesell, R. 1975. *Foreign Investment in Copper Mining*. Baltimore: Johns Hopkins Univ. Press
127. Mikesell, R. 1978. Trends in foreign investment: Agreements in the resources industry. *Res. Policy* 8:194–99
128. Mikesell, R. 1980. Mining agreements and conflict resolution. In *Mining for Development in the Third World*, ed. S. Sideri, S. Johns, pp. 198–210. New York: Pergamon
129. Miller, S. 1967. Hacienda to plantation in northern Peru: The process of proletarianization of a tenant farmer society. In *Contemporary Change in Traditional Society*, ed. J. Steward, 3:135–225. Urbana: Univ. Ill. Press
130. Mitchell, J. 1954. *African Urbanisation in Luanshya and Ndola*. Lusaka: Rhodes-Livingstone Comm. No. 6
131. Mitchell, J. 1956. *The Kalela Dance*. Manchester: Rhodes-Livingstone Pap. 27
132. Mitchell, J. 1959. Migrant labour in Africa south of the Sahara. *Inter-Afr. Lab. Inst. Bull.* 6:8–47
133. Mitchell, J. 1961. Wage labour and African population movements in Central Africa. In *Essays on African Population*, ed. K. Barbour, R. Prothero, pp. 193–248. London: Routledge & Kegan Paul
134. Mitchell, J. 1968. Factors motivating migration from rural areas. In *Present Interrelations in Central African Rural and Urban Life*, ed. R. Apthorpe. Rhodes-Livingstone Inst, Conf. Proc. No. 11
135. Mitchell, J. 1970. Race, class and status in South Central Africa. In *Social Stratification in Africa*, ed. A. Tuden, L. Plotnicov, pp. 303–43. New York: Free Press
136. Moodie, D. 1980. The formal and informal social structure of a South African gold mine. *Hum. Relat.* 33:555–74
137. Moodie, D. 1983. Mine culture and miners' identity on the South African gold mines. In *Town and Countryside in the Transvaal*, ed. B. Bozzoli, pp. 176–97. Johannesburg: Ravan Press
138. Moran, T. 1974. *Multinational Corporations and the Politics of Dependence*. Princeton: Princeton Univ. Press
139. Moroney, S. 1978. The development of the compound as a mechanism of worker control. *S. Afr. Lab. Bull.* 4:29–49
140. Murray, C. 1980. Migrant labor and changing family structure in the rural periphery of Southern Africa. *J. S. Afr. Stud.* 6:139–56
141. Murray, C. 1981. *Families Divided*. Cambridge: Cambridge Univ. Press
142. Murray, C. 1983. Struggle from the margins: Rural slums in the Orange Free State. In *Struggle for the City*, ed. F. Cooper, pp. 275–318. Beverly Hills: Sage
143. Nankani, G. 1979. *Development Problems of Mineral-Exporting Countries*. Washington: World Bank Staff Work. Pap. 354
144. Nash, J. 1979. *We Eat the Mines*. New York: Columbia Univ. Press
145. Neilson, J., ed. 1982. *Strategies for Small-Scale Mining and Mineral Industries*. Bangkok: Assoc. Geoscientists for Int. Dev., Rep. No. 8
146. Nordhaus, W. 1973. World dynamics—Measurement without data. *Econ. J.* 83:1156–58
147. Novelo, V. 1980. De huelgas, movilizaciones y otras acciones de los mineros del carbon de Coahuila. *Rev. Mex. Sociol.* 42:1355–78
148. Ohadike, P. 1969. *Development of Factors in the Employment of African Mi-*

grants in the Copper Mines of Zambia 1940–65. Manchester: Manchester Univ. Press
149. O'Meara, D. 1975. The 1949 African mine worker's strike and the political economy of South Africa. *J. Commonw. Comp. Policy* 13:146–73
150. Parpart, J. 1983. *Labor and Capital in the African Copperbelt.* Philadelphia: Temple Univ. Press
151. Perrings, C. 1979. *Black Mineworkers in Central Africa.* New York: Africana Publ.
152. Peterson, F. 1975. Two externalities in petroleum exploration. In *Studies in Energy Tax Policy,* ed. G. Brannon, pp. 44–65. Cambridge: Ballinger
153. Peterson, F., Fisher, A. 1977. The exploitation of extractive resources: A survey. *Econ. J.* 87:681–721
154. Phimister, I. 1974. Peasant production and underdevelopment in southern Rhodesia, 1890–1914. *Afr. Aff.* 73:217–28
155. Phimister, I. 1976. Precolonial gold mining in southern Zambezia: A reassessment. *Afr. Soc. Res.* 3:1–30
156. Phimister, I., Van Onselen, C. 1978. *Studies in the History of African Mine Labour in Colonial Zimbabwe.* Gwelo: Mambo Press
157. Porteous, J. 1970. The nature of the company town. *Trans. Inst. Br. Geogr.* 51:127–42
158. Porteous, J. 1973. The company state: A Chilean case. *Can. Geogr.* 12:113–26
159. Powdermaker, H. 1962. *Copper Town.* New York: Harper & Row
160. Pzreworski, J. 1976. Mines and smelters: The role of the coal oligopology in the decline of the Chilean copper industry. *Nova Am.* 1:169–213
161. Read, M. 1942. Migrant labour in Africa and its effects on tribal life. *Int. Lab. Rev.* 45:605–31
162. Richards, A. 1939. *Land, Labour and Diet in Northern Rhodesia.* London: Oxford Univ. Press
163. Richardson, P. 1977. The recruiting of Chinese indentured labour for the South African gold mines, 1903–1908. *J. Afr. Hist.* 18:85–108
164. Rita Ferreira, A. 1963. *O movimento migratorio de trabalhadores entre Mocambique e a Africa do sul.* Lisbon: Junta de Investigacoes do Ultramar, Centro de Estudos Politicos e Sociais, No. 67
165. Roemer, M., Stern, J. 1975. *The Appraisal of Development Projects.* New York: Praeger
166. Sariego Rodriguez, J. 1978. *Los mineros de la Real del Monte.* Mexico: Cuadernos de la Casa Chata
167. Schapera, I. 1947. *Migrant Labour and Tribal Life.* London: Oxford Univ. Press
168. Schulze, W. 1974. The optimal use of non-renewable resources: The theory of extraction. *J. Environ. Econ. Min.* 1:53–73
169. Scott, A. 1955. *Natural Resources.* Toronto: Univ. Toronto Press
170. Siew, N. 1953. *Labour and Tin Mining in Malaya.* Data Pap. No. 7, Southeast Asia Prog., Dep. Far Eastern Stud. Ithaca: Cornell Univ.
171. Simmons, C. 1976. Indigenous entrepreneurship in the Indian coal mining industry c. 1835–1939. *Indian Econ. Soc. Hist. Rev.* 13:189–218
172. Simmons, C. 1976. Recruiting and organizing an industrial labour force in colonial India: The case of the coal mining industry c. 1880–1939. *Indian Econ. Soc. Hist. Rev.* 13:455–85
173. Simmons, C. 1979. Seasonal labour oscillation in the Indian coal mining industry before independence. In *South Asia,* ed. M. Gaborieau, A. Thorner, pp. 477–82. Paris: Centre National de la Recherche Scientifique
174. Smith, D., Wells, L. 1975. *Negotiating Third World Mineral Agreements.* Cambridge: Ballinger
175. Solow, R., Wan, F. 1976. Extraction costs in the theory of exhaustible resources. *Bell J.* 7:359–370
176. Spiegel, A. 1980. Rural differentiation and the diffusion of migrant labor remittances in Lesotho. See Ref. 123, pp. 109–68
177. Steele, H. 1967. Natural resource taxation: Resource allocation and distribution implications. In *Extractive Resources and Taxation,* ed. M. Gaffney, pp. 233–67. Madison: Univ. Wis. Press
178. Stiglitz, J. 1975. The efficiency of market prices in long-run allocations in the oil industry. See Ref. 152, pp. 82–105
179. Stiglitz, J. 1976. Monopoly and the rate of extraction of exhaustible resources. *Am. Econ. Rev.* 66:655–61
180. Stone, T. 1983. Atomistic order and frontier violence: Miners and whalemen in the 19th-century Yukon. *Ethnology* 22:327–39
181. Stucki, L. 1970. *The entropy theory of human behavior.* PhD thesis. Univ. Colorado, Boulder
182. SSTS (Subcommittee on Science, Technology, and Space). 1982. *An Assessment of Factors Affecting Small Mining and Custom Milling and Smelting Operations.* U.S. Senate, 97th Congress, 2nd Session. Washington: GPO
183. Sweeney, J. 1977. Economics of depletable resources: Market forces and in-

tertemporal bias. *Rev. Econ. Stud.* 44:125–42
184. Tandeter, E. 1981. La produccion como actividad popular: 'ladrones de minas' en Potosi. *Nova Am.* 4:43–65
185. Tandeter, E. 1981. Forced and free labour in late colonial Potosi. *Past & Present* 93:98–136
186. Tanzer, M. 1980. *The Race for Resources*. New York: Monthly Rev. Press
187. Taussig, M. 1980. *The Devil and Commodity Fetishism in South America*. Chapel Hill: Univ. North Carolina Press
188. Thoburn, J. 1977. Commodity prices and appropriate technology—Some lessons from tin mining. *J. Dev. Stud.* 14:35–52
189. Thomas, L. 1973. *An Introduction to Mining*. New York: Wiley
190. United Nations. 1953. *The Determinants and Consequences of Population Trends*. New York: UN
191. United Nations. 1972. *Small-Scale Mining in the Developing Countries*. New York: UN
192. United Nations. 1978. *Small-Scale Mining of the World*. New York: UN
193. Van Helten, J. 1980. Mining and imperialism. *J. S. Afr. Stud.* 6:230–35
194. Van Onselen, C. 1976. *Chibaro*. London: Pluto Press
195. Van Onselen, C. 1982. *Studies in the Social and Economic History of the Witwatersrand 1886–1914*. London: Longman. 2 vols.
196. Van Velsen, J. 1960. Labor migration as a positive factor in the continuity of Tonga tribal society. *Econ. Dev. Cult. Change* 8:265–78
197. Vernon, R. 1967. Long-run trends in concession contracts. *Proc. Am. Soc. Int. Law 61st Ann. Meet.*, pp. 81–89
198. Vernon, R. 1971. *Sovereignty at Bay*. New York: Basic Books
199. Walde, T. 1978. Revision of transnational investment agreements: Contractual flexibility in natural resources development. *Lawyer Am.* 10:67–93
200. Watson, W. 1958. *Tribal Cohesion in a Money Economy*. Manchester: Manchester Univ. Press
201. Weitzman, M. 1976. The optimal development of resource pools. *J. Econ. Theory* 12:351–64
202. West, T. 1983. *The burning bush: Exploitation of native shrubs for fuel in Bolivia*. Presented at 11th Int. Congr. Anthropol. Ethnol. Sci. Phase II, Vancouver, B.C.
203. Whitehead, L. 1980. Sobre el radicalismo de los trabajadores mineros de Bolivia. *Rev. Mex. Sociol.* 42:1465–96
204. Whitten, N. 1982. Review of *The Devil and Commodity Fetishism*. *Am. Anthropol.* 84:481–83
205. Wilson, F. 1972. *Labour in the South African Gold Mines*. Cambridge: Cambridge Univ. Press
206. Wilson, G. 1941–42. *An Essay on the Economics of Detribalization in Northern Rhodesia*. Rhodes-Livingstone Pap. No. 5/6
207. Wilson, G., Wilson, M. 1945. *The Analysis of Social Change*. Cambridge: Cambridge Univ. Press
208. Wolpe, H. 1972. Capitalism and cheap labour power in South Africa: From segregation to apartheid. *Econ. & Soc.* 1:425–56
209. Wright, T. 1981. "A Method of Evading Management"—Contract labor in Chinese coal mines before 1937. *Comp. Stud. Soc. Hist.* 23:656–78
210. Wrigley, E. 1961. *Industrial Growth and Population Change*. Cambridge: Cambridge Univ. Press
211. Zapata, F. 1979. *Los mineros de Chuquicamata*. Mexico: El Colegio de Mexico
212. Zapata, F. 1980. Trabajadores mineros. *Rev. Mex. Sociol.* 42:1321–1588
213. Zeilin, M., Petras, J. 1970. Working-class vote in Chile—Christian democracy versus Marxism. *Br. J. Sociol.* 21:16–29
214. Zink, D. 1973. *The Political Risks for Multinational Enterprises in Developing Countries*. New York: Praeger
215. Zorn, S. 1977. Conference review: The United Nations panel on international mining finance. *Nat. Res. For.* 1:239–50

THE INTERFACE OF NURSING AND ANTHROPOLOGY

Molly C. Dougherty

College of Nursing, University of Florida, Gainesville, Florida 32610

Toni Tripp-Reimer

College of Nursing, University of Iowa, Iowa City, Iowa 52242

Nursing in the Western world developed mainly as an applied field, and has contributed to social-cultural theory only in the past 30 years. The purpose of this presentation is to document (a) the contributions of nursing to medical anthropology, (b) the influence anthropology has had on nursing, (c) the differences between the interface of nursing and anthropology and that of medicine and anthropology, and (d) reasons that these differences have not been a focus in medical anthropology. We mean to draw attention to the special characteristics and aims of the nursing process and profession as they relate to the anthropological enterprise, but first we must describe the nature of nursing and how it differs from medicine.

THE NATURE OF NURSING

The interface of nursing and anthropology has a different focus than the interface of medicine and anthropology. While there are some similar areas of concern, there are also major and significant areas of divergence. That nursing is not subsumed by medicine is a point not widely understood in anthropology. In *Medical Anthropology*, Foster & Anderson (77) classically illustrated this point by titling a chapter "Professionalism in Medicine: Nursing." The term "health care" subsumes both nursing and medicine; unfortunately, anthropologists have frequently equated health care only with medicine.

Several factors account for the erroneous categorization of nursing as a part of medicine. First, there is considerable overlap in the contribution of each profession to client health, because all health professionals are generally concerned with the mental and physical well-being of clients. Second, anthropologists may be most familiar with nursing in university hospitals where the practice of nursing is least typical (131). Third, medicine, with the skillful promotion and protection of the American Medical Association, gained high visibility, social status, and authority in this century (169). This attracted anthropologists to the study of medicine.

The central concern of biomedicine is not general well-being, nor individual persons, nor simply their bodies, but their bodies in disease (110). Medicine is primarily (and properly) concerned with disease, its etiology, pathophysiology, and treatment. The medical frame of reference is based on models of normal and abnormal human conditions and of methods for diagnosing and treating diseases and pathologies.

Nursing, by contrast, is defined as "the diagnosis and treatment of human responses to actual or potential health problems" (10). There are important facets of this definition. Human responses to health problems are often multiple or continuous, and are less discrete than medical diagnostic categories. Examples of human responses on which nursing interventions focus include self-care limitations, pain, emotions related to disease and treatment, and changes related to life processes (birth, growth and development, and death). Thus, while physicians diagnose and treat pathology, nurses are concerned with actual and potential needs which emerge in response to illness or health states.

While physicians are identified as concerned with disease, clients are characterized as concerned with illness (110). This distinction defines a crucial domain for nursing. Nursing uses the model of illness and the model of disease and mediates the two, a distinction and relationship emphasized in nursing education. Nursing deals with treating disease, assisting the client in coping with discomforts, and in adapting lifestyles to the illness or treatment. Anthropologists have not recognized that nurses mediate the biomedical and client orientations; nursing has recognized this since at least 1932 (85).

Because nurses move flexibly between models, the nursing role is difficult to define. Using the disease/illness distinction, it is evident that the nebulous nature of nursing is a result of the differential importance given to each model in diverse clinical situations. When a situation is life threatening, the biomedical model takes precedence; during a cardiac arrest, little consideration is given to sociocultural dimensions. Conversely, when clients experience life changes that accompany many diseases, the illness model assumes primacy. The consistent orientation of professional nurses is the provision of care and nurturing that promotes well-being of sick and well people, individually and in groups.

NATURAL ALLIANCE

History of the Interface of Nursing and Anthropology

Focus on the client's culture has a long history in nursing, particularly in public health nursing. Early in the century, public health nurses worked with immigrant groups, and a series of articles in the *Public Health Nursing Quarterly* gave cultural overviews of groups such as Italians, Russians, and Portuguese. While an intent of this literature was to promote assimilation of immigrant groups, other authors (52, 67, 186) sought to improve understanding of their cultures. Yet, other than in public health nursing, inclusion of the cultural dimension was generally lacking until around the 1940s. Cultural content was introduced by nurses who had served with the military during World War II, and had learned the necessity of understanding cultural differences. After World War II, experienced public health nurses were added to nursing faculties and were able to teach from their experience with different ethnic groups (29).

At another level, anthropologists, other social scientists, and national organizations introduced cultural content into nursing, of which the early contribution of anthropologist Esther Lucille Brown (27) was particularly important. The National Nursing Council commissioned Brown to conduct a study of nursing education (28) which spearheaded midcentury educational reform in nursing. In university settings, behavioral science content gained importance (21, 129) and provided a theoretical base for practice that heretofore had been intuitive. As early as 1937 the National League of Nursing (NLN) recommended that nursing students take at least 10 semester hours in the social sciences. Inclusion of the social sciences was furthered by organization of the Joint Commission (118, 166), and anthropologists described the importance of social science, particularly anthropology, for nursing (18, 27, 28, 30, 112, 128, 133, 161). Studies of the culture of nursing included research on the societal view of the nurse (18), the history of women and the role of the nurse (56), change in the nursing profession (161), and socialization of the student nurse (191). Ethnographic studies of hospitals addressed nursing in an institutional setting (37, 49, 78, 185).

The importance of national foundations to social sciences in nursing was evident in a Russell Sage Foundation project at the Cornell University School of Nursing (1954–57) which featured lecturers from anthropology and sociology such as Margaret Mead, Renee Fox, Rhoda Metraux, and August Hollingshead (128). In 1948 Margaret Huger conducted a hospital study of Italian American patients' response to the nursing situation (Mead 133), initiating nursing research on the cultural component in the delivery of health care. Later research focused on cultural aspects of nursing care for black patients (132).

Under the federally funded Nurse Scientists Program in the 1960s, nurses obtained doctoral degrees in increasing numbers, and several obtained PhDs in anthropology. In 1968 the Council on Nursing and Anthropology (CONAA) was formed in relationship with the Society for Medical Anthropology. Later, other organizations were formed including the Transcultural Nursing Society (1974) and the American Nurses' Association's Council on Inter-Cultural Diversity (1980). Leininger's (120) work, an important milestone in the development of the relationship between nursing and anthropology, delineates the disciplines of nursing and anthropology, areas of common interest, and proposes common research interests.

In 1977 the NLN mandated the inclusion of cultural content in nursing curricula which triggered an explosion of interest. Cultural considerations in clinical practice and research have been featured in nursing journals (39, 113, 179). Texts have examined the common concerns of the two disciplines (14, 24, 123) and the inclusion of cultural content in nursing care (44, 143, 168).

Similarities Between Nursing and Anthropology

Since 1969, nurse anthropologists have identified the natural alliance between nursing and anthropology in a number of dimensions (14, 120, 144). Foster (76), moreover, has contrasted anthropological and sociological research on medical problems in at least four dimensions: (*a*) research topics, (*b*) basic conceptual approaches to problems, (*c*) research methodologies, and (*d*) identification with the actors in health dramas; these differences are discussed below.

RESEARCH TOPICS The basic approaches of nursing and anthropology as contrasted with medicine and sociology are reflected in research problems, data collection, and conclusions. One major difference is that nursing and anthropology tend to focus on normalcy while medicine and sociology focus on deviance. Much of anthropology has been concerned with shared beliefs, values, and behavior. Similarly, nursing practice addresses normal growth and development, wellness promotion and health education. During illness, the concern of nursing is in the client's behavioral response, and in enhancing modification of patterns of daily living to promote a return to a normal lifestyle. In a hospital setting, concerns of nursing are daily patterns of living which clients normally do for themselves: food, elimination, rest, sleep, diversions, and interpersonal relationships. When illness occurs, factors influenced by cultural patterns such as dependency, pain, fatigue, fear, personal physical care, diet modification, and stigma are the purview of nursing. In contrast, the sociological perspective is that illness is a form of deviance. This is analogous to the focus of medicine which has been identified as pathology or disease (68, 110). Medicine generally neglects social behavior and the social basis of disease (68). While these distinctions do not always hold (psychiatry, for example), the predominant orientations of sociology and medicine are similar.

Nursing differs from anthropology in the dominant level of analysis. Anthropological research focuses on cultural norms, a macro level of analysis; nursing concentrates on individuals, and uses cultural norms as a background from which to understand client behaviors. In nursing practice, cultural assessment includes an understanding of the values, beliefs, and behaviors of the client's reference group and the fit of the client to this normative pattern. The literature on ethnicity and health is deficient in its explication of intraethnic variation, and there are problems when materials that describe cultural norms are used to direct practical action with individuals from cultural or ethnic groups (89, 177).

METHODS Participant observation emphasizing qualitative data in the context of cultural systems has been the most productive research method in anthropology. In contrast, most medical sociologists use survey research as their primary method, augmented by statistical and other quantitative techniques (76).

While early nursing theory development was modeled on sociology, there has been a shift to other methods of inquiry. Nurses, as participant observers in home and hospital environments (34, 152), learn the intimate details of health and illness through their physical proximity and temporal relationships with patients; this parallels the fieldwork setting used by anthropologists. Presence with clients in ICUs for days or in nursing homes for months results in qualitative data; the nature of understanding is transformed by the intimacy of the interaction, a function of "being there." Like anthropologists, community health nurses have access to the natural environment of clients and their families (34). Nursing and anthropology rely on observation, on "being with" and "understanding other" (4).

The phenomenological approach is the method of inquiry in anthropology that is paralleled in nursing. Prolonged contact with subjects or patients yields different information from that generally collected by sociologists (117). The qualitative approach which clearly differentiates methods in anthropology from sociology similarly distinguishes nursing from medicine.

BASIC CONCEPTUAL APPROACHES Nursing and anthropology share a commitment to holism. Anthropology, insofar as it emphasizes the holistic study of human behavior, offers nursing and other fields information not available from any other discipline. Nursing incorporates theory on the connection between the affective, cognitive, and physical domains of health and illness, promoting the consideration of the environment, family, and individual in health, illness, and recovery. More than other professions, nursing is committed to the total care of the patient (144) which parallels the anthropological study of humankind. The contrast between the holistic approach of anthropology and nursing is in the level of analysis; it is used to study culture and individuals, respectively. The holistic orientation contrasts with sociology and medicine, which are more particularistic in orientation.

IDENTIFICATION WITH THE ACTORS Anthropologists identify with the people they study; research problems are rooted in the client perspective. By contrast, medical sociologists have taken the perspective of physicians and medical institutions (76). The social distance between physician and client is problematic, but nurses emphasize empathy, caring, and identification with the client, and are often a communication link between the client and the physician. Nurses are more often identified with lower status ethnic groups because of their social class origins and their status in the health care hierarchy (77). From this perspective, anthropology and nursing form a natural alliance that parallels the link between sociology and medicine.

DISCIPLINES: ACADEMIC AND PROFESSIONAL

Chrisman (42) states that a difference between anthropology and nursing is that anthropology is solely a discipline, while nursing is a discipline and a service profession. However, anthropology is an academic discipline with a professional aspect. The aim of academic disciplines is to know, and their theories are descriptive and explanatory in nature. Fields that apply research are more correctly termed applied disciplines, or applied branches of academic disciplines (57), rather than professional disciplines, which have prescriptive theories. For example, the nurse who deals with alleviating pain may choose from several alternatives, including talking to the patient to decrease anxiety, giving a back massage, or giving an ordered medication. Prescriptive theories characteristic of professional disciplines deal with application of knowledge in a practical sense. Prescriptive theory posits the ways practitioners should act in certain situations to achieve practical aims. Theory from academic disciplines is used to guide practice, but practitioners must select among competing or contradictory theories. Professional disciplines such as law, engineering, and nursing are directed toward practical aims and generate prescriptive theories. Applied research thus addresses questions about the applicability of basic theories rather than questions related to how basic theories are to be applied, which is the purview of professional disciplines. Basic and applied research are both needed in a professional discipline because each professional discipline has a practical aim. Failure to recognize the discipline's body of knowledge as separate from the activities of its practitioners has contributed to confusion about the role of research in nursing practice and the role of research in applied anthropology. The purview of academic nursing is the holistic study of health in humans including cultural influences; a practical aim is optimizing human environments to promote health. The contribution of medical anthropology is in theory and research on comparative analysis of human responses.

Some anthropologists who teach nursing students believe they translate anthropological principles in systematic and applicable ways; most, however, neglect the distinction of nursing as both an academic and professional discipline. The objectives of cross-cultural nursing courses are to help students make assessments and interventions which are astute and culturally appropriate, such as caring behaviors which conform to the patients' ethnosemantic description of what care "should be" in that particular subculture (174). Through translated anthropological perspectives, nursing students are taught to understand, and implicitly to accept, the sociocultural conditions which produce variation in life and in health. The anthropological conceptual perspectives which have been translated to nursing emphasize the relativist tradition of philosophical idealism which values people's ideas, health beliefs, and value orientations. This is an appropriate domain for professional nursing. However, there is another perspective of people's lives, the material reality, which includes the constraints of being poor, non-Caucasian, female, or old. Professional nurses must choose among competing prescriptive theories which include accepting the circumstances of clients or promoting change in those circumstances (174). Similar points are made about medicine (194).

The anthropologist clinician has evoked interest in recent years, but no clear direction has emerged. Some see a "bright future" (188), the use of intervention guided by moral judgment (9), and clinical anthropology as a new anthropological specialization (84). Issues to be resolved include: content of the program of instruction, selection of students, and supervision (164); licensure (99); certification (188); ethical standards of practice (164); and appropriate referral mechanisms. Each of these issues must be addressed by professional disciplines. However, professionals function on the basis of conflicting theories; medical anthropology has developed few prescriptive theories or practical aims.

The clinician functions within sets of alternatives, institutional restrictions, and legal constraints. Narrowing of employment opportunities pulled anthropologists toward clinical anthropology without a clear analysis of the compromises embodied in a clinical role. Issues that revolve around the definition and purpose of academic disciplines and professional disciplines are central to the interface of medical anthropology and nursing. Future progress depends on clarification of the roles filled by clinicians and academicians in the milieu of client encounters.

CONTRIBUTIONS OF GENERAL ANTHROPOLOGY TO NURSING

Theoretical formulations

A discipline is not global, but it is characterized by a unique perspective, a distinct way of viewing all phenomena which ultimately defines and limits the nature of its inquiry (57). This distinct perspective determines what phenomena are of interest and in what context such phenomena are to be viewed. In nursing, the theoretical base is partially self-generated and partially drawn from other fields. As a professional discipline, nursing uses the results of research and selects theories from other sciences on the basis of their explanatory power in relation to the phenomena nurses diagnose and treat.

There is general agreement concerning the phenomena of interest to the discipline of nursing. Leading writers on nursing theory have identified four critical elements in the domain of nursing: human nature, environment, health, and nursing care (40, 69, 73, 87). The way these four major components are conceptualized and interrelated frames the different theories of nursing. However, the conceptual structure of a discipline is subject to change and evolution.

Elements in a discipline can be extended by incorporating additional knowledge or can be narrowed or refined as more precise conceptualizations become possible. Information from other disciplines is incorporated into nursing knowledge and is transformed by the unique view of nursing science. Anthropological theory has been adopted and integrated into all four elements of nursing's disciplinary matrix.

HUMAN NATURE   Nursing models describe human nature in terms of individual attributes, wholeness, and integrity. Sociocultural anthropology conceptualizes humans through a focus on ethnocentrism and cultural relativism (61, 91) which posit differing ways of viewing human interactions and denote the perspective from which characteristics are interpreted. In nursing, this denotes whether data are interpreted from the perspective of the client or the nurse (19, 116, 160).

ENVIRONMENT   In nursing models the term environment refers to all the influences affecting the behavior and development of people. Here the major contribution of anthropology has been the concept of culture. Basic nursing texts address cultural affiliation as the background from which client values, beliefs, and practices can be anticipated, but nursing has also extended the concept of culture in cultural assessment models (2, 104, 121, 143, 177, 181). Assessment guides identify major cultural domains that are important to nurses in clinical situations or at the community level and delineate relevant values, beliefs, and behaviors. Cultural assessment models in nursing deal with three major aspects: what data to elicit, why it is important, and how to obtain it.

HEALTH   The concept of health in nursing has been enriched by the disease-illness distinction described in medical anthropology. Disease is defined in terms that are thought to be objective and quantifiable. Illness, however, is a personal phenomenon concerning an individual's altered perception of self (41, 47, 63, 68, 111).

Prior to the disease-illness distinction, health was conceptualized in nursing as: (*a*) a dichotomous variable (present or absent), (*b*) as a continuum (from wellness to death), or (c) as an inclusive holistic state. Health is perceived differently by the client and by the health professional, and the physiologically based definition of disease is inadequate for the discipline of nursing. These perspectives are reconciled through the concepts of illness and disease into the broader construct of health, which identifies areas of practitioner and client congruence and incongruence and posits different intervention strategies in these situations (178).

NURSING This element consists of nursing diagnosis and interventions, the latter influenced by anthropological theory. The nurse as mediator (49) or liaison (129) dates to 1929 (85). Along these lines, Brink (23) thinks of mediation in the relationships among the patient, doctor, and nurse as analogous to Freilich's (79) "natural triad." The construct "culture broker" (192) is applied to several roles which link various sectors of society (151) to health care delivery (189). As a nursing intervention, culture brokerage involves the nurse mediating between clients and health professionals (26, 156, 180). The unique perspective of nursing is enhanced by the contribution of anthropology to important constructs of this kind.

Anthropology Provides Theory For Nursing Research

The literature contributed by nurse anthropologists demonstrates that anthropological theory guides research on client belief systems, care in multicultural context, and nursing as a subculture. The majority of the research on client belief systems consists of descriptive accounts concerning the beliefs and practices of specific groups (36, 100, 103, 105, 137). An ethnographic study of low-income Anglos (13) described causes of illness, beliefs about ways to maintain good health, the definition of good health, and what constitutes deviations from good health. Later the study was extended to a population of middle-income Anglos (90). These studies provide baseline data on beliefs and point out the important differences between the subjective perception of the client's health state and objective pathology which may be evident.

Other investigations have focused on folk health beliefs of a specific group (13, 103) regarding specific conditions such as wind illness (138), evil eye (176), hypertension (7, 8, 17), and vitamin use (96). Contributions of the studies include (a) the integration of emic and etic perspectives to derive a complete understanding of a particular syndrome, (b) the importance of diversity within cultures when investigating traditional beliefs, (c) the importance of generational depth in studies of immigrant populations.

Refinements of the definition of folk health beliefs have resulted from an emphasis on syncretism (36, 101–103, 105, 137, 153, 154). Examination of the origins of health beliefs of Mexican-American women (101, 102), for example, led to the finding that there was a dominant and common source for what is currently considered "indigenous" medicine in the Southwest. The eighteenth century work, *The Florilegio Medicinal,* which combined herbal lore of American Indians with the materia medica and disease categories of European physicians, served to standardize terminology throughout the Greater Southwest.

Theory derived from anthropology has been adapted to guide nursing research. Lexemic change and semantic shift, for example, helped to demonstrate that the vocabulary of illness terms is affected by bilingualism and the coexistence of several health systems, and that illness terms are dynamic (105). Cognitive dissonance guides a study on factors associated with environmental stresses in hospital birth (15). Exchange theory was used in research on the care of the institutionalized elderly in Scotland and the United States (106). Still other work concerned cultural relativism and ethnocentrism that framed research on e.g. Appalachian and non-Appalachian health professionals' views of the behavior of Appalachian clients (175) in which the theoretical importance of considering synchronic and diachronic approaches when examining ethnic health patterns was demonstrated. Anthropological theory has served as the base for descriptive nursing research on various aspects of several cultures: Paiute Indians (22), Papago Indians (1), Salish Indians (92), and Appalachians (175). Studies have been conducted on cultures abroad by nurse anthropologists (25, 119, 167). A few studies (83, 145) specifically examined the relationship of health care behaviors to other aspects of the social structure. With few exceptions, these studies have little direct applicability to nursing practice, but they broaden nursing research into sociocultural analysis and bring together the approaches of the two fields.

Research in cross-cultural nursing has resulted in limited theoretical contributions because few investigators build progressively on research in one or two cultures. Cross-cultural nursing research is predominantly ethnographic and has neglected the comparative theory building of ethnology. However, some contributions (2, 122) provide a basis on which to pursue the ethnography of transcultural nursing and to develop a body of knowledge on which theory can be built. Anthropology provides rich description of ethnic groups and cultures; nursing is increasingly aware of the implications of providing care in a multicultural context, as seen by the research on this theme (8, 33, 38, 64, 92, 96, 127, 146, 150, 172, 183, 184, 187, 190).

Studies of culture and nursing include (*a*) the way in which nurses perceive clients from different ethnic groups, and (*b*) the culture of nursing. Contributions include the study of personality variables of the nurse (19) and nursing faculty (160). Comparisons of nurses in the United States and abroad on sick role, patient behavior (16), and nursing care (106, 107, 109) show that nurses from different cultures demonstrate differences in values, expectations, and caring behaviors. Studies of cross-cultural differences in nurses' assessment of physical pain and psychological stress (53–55) support the hypothesis that nurses in different cultures differ in the degree of suffering they infer. These studies show cultural variables that directly influence nursing care. Nurses as a subculture have been studied in a teaching hospital (173), a cancer unit (81), a neonatal intensive care unit (93, 139), and walk-in clinics (38). The results indicate that U.S. nurses have shared beliefs, values, and patterns of behavior. Ethnography and critical incidents (86) have high potential for the study of the culture of nursing. Although it is a relatively new area of investigation, important knowledge has been generated through cross-cultural nursing research.

Socialization of nurses has been studied extensively. Studies of socialization which take a broad view are conducted by social scientists employing qualitative methods (191). In particular, Olesen & Whittaker (140) demonstrate the complexity of socialization into a professional role, the importance of prior socialization, and the influence of societal values on the process.

In the decade of the 1970s, more than 102 research-based articles appeared (48), many of which emphasize differences between programs and psychosocial changes in students. Studies of socialization into the professional role after basic education is completed are lacking (48). The social science perspective goes beyond the educational process per se and is valuable for assessing the role of nursing society.

THE CONTRIBUTION OF NURSING TO ANTHROPOLOGY

The education of nurses in anthropology has been important for both disciplines. It has allowed nursing to profit from anthropological theory and research findings. Anthropology, in turn, has benefited from the understanding of health care delivery and applied physiology that nurses bring to anthropology.

Nursing Constructs for Anthropological Theory

Caring has been a major theoretical focus in cross-cultural nursing research. Utilizing research on the Papago Indians, Aamodt (5) developed the concept of care along four dimensions: (*a*) the fit in a cultural system of health and healing, (*b*) the applicability of a multicultural environment for care, (*c*) the power of belief, and (*d*) changes in mechanisms of care during the life cycle of human beings. These dimensions of care provide a basis for cross-cultural investigations and illustrate ways in which "taking care of" is a culturally relevant domain that organizes human experience. In these and other ways, the concept of care is viewed as the central focus of nursing behaviors, processes, and intervention modalities (121, 122, 124, 125). Exploration of the fit of health and healing in a cultural system and the multicultural environment of caring, for example, is seen in research on alternative healing systems in an Anglo-American subculture. The New Age Healers (36, 136) that emerged in opposition to Western medicine reveal syncretic belief systems that are characterized by flexibility and the ability to draw from several healing/caring traditions. Such emerging traditions survive on faith rather than science or one integrated theory of health and disease, as usually seen in Western medicine.

While literature on caring has been predominantly conceptual, a number of empirical studies have been reported (123–126). Leininger (125) defined care in a generic sense as "those assistive, supportive, or facilitative acts toward or for another individual or group with evident or anticipated needs to ameliorate or improve a human condition or lifeways" (p. 4). Aamodt (1) defines themes among the Papago which were important for understanding care as a culturally relevant domain. Elsewhere (3) she analyzes the important role of neighboring as a support system among Norwegian-American women; previously support networks had not been explored in research on caring. Other varieties of care preferences and networking appear to be characteristic of older order Amish, Czech, and Greek in Iowa, where the elderly do not necessarily prefer to be "cared for" in the home of a relative (182).

Conceptualization of care involves examining its significance in cultures that do not include the professional role of nurse. Three aspects of care found cross-culturally are (*a*) receiver of care, (*b*) giver of care, and (*c*) self-care (5). In the cycle of human development each person passes through periods in which one aspect or another is dominant. It may be that research on care has been deemphasized in anthropology because males in this culture are not attuned to its pervasive nature, and thus the importance of caring in social support has not been examined. Investigations of care in cultural context point to: (*a*) its role in promoting cohesion in society, (*b*) the range of activities that are caring, and (*c*) the reciprocal role that giving and receiving care has in culture.

Methodological Contributions

Anthropology traditionally has not validated theory, a difficult task insofar as researches are limited to single ethnographic settings. Nursing provides a useful arena for the application of medical anthropology theory (46, 71, 72, 175), given that the explication and implementation of qualitative methods have been major strengths of cross-cultural nursing studies. Methodology is best illustrated in cross-cultural nursing research through the use of ethnography (136). There are useful criteria for the evaluation of qualitative methods (32); ethnography, ethnoscience, and oral histories would be strengthened if investigators employed and stated their criteria for the development and evaluation of qualitative research.

Several investigators (3, 34, 36, 152) have emphasized the importance of the investigator's initial entry into the research setting and establishment of rapport with subjects. The issues and the dilemmas involved in participant observation have been well explicated (34) and refined (36).

A method and rationale for combining ethnographic methods with the use of historical materials was developed in studies of Italian Americans (152–154). This approach introduced a diachronic dimension to ethnography that is essential in settings where culture change is a factor; it is demonstrated in research on Mexican Americans in Arizona (100–103, 105). These studies begin with ethnography and proceed to precise, extensive examination of language and history. Important findings occur in the labeling of disease, with the direction of change being toward the scientific classification system.

A major difficulty in conducting cross-cultural nursing research has been precise definition and delineation of differences in such areas as ethnic identity, cultural differences, and caring behavior. Flaskerud (70) established the validity of an instrument which used vignettes to differentiate a minority group's normative behavior from the mainstream culture's deviant behavior; subsequently she developed a tool for comparing the perceptions of problematic behavior for use by other researchers (71, 72). Valid measures of ethnic differences require careful attention to respective ethnic entities if reliable, quantifiable differences are to be discovered. Clinton (46) succeeded in measuring ethnicity and evaluation of its influence on health-seeking behaviors in an integrative, multivariate, computer-assisted research design which proved successful in measuring European-origin ethnic identity. It was also used as a heuristic device for partitioning the analytical sample of health data.

Research Themes

THE ANTHROPOLOGY OF KNOWLEDGE   One area of inquiry is the anthropology of knowledge and anthropology of science (51, 134). As a relatively new academic field which is undergoing important conceptual changes, nursing represents an interesting setting in which to study a discipline shifting dominant paradigms from a biomedical model to a nursing model. In part, the structure of a discipline consists of the body of concepts which define the subject matter of that discipline and shapes its inquiries. The phenomena of interest to a discipline constitute elements of what is called its paradigm (114, 135) or metaparadigm (115, 130). The metaparadigm defines the domain of interest, determines the questions to be asked, and identifies the appropriate theories, methods, and instruments for answering the questions raised (87). The metaparadigm is the most global perspective of a discipline and is a framework within which more restricted structures develop. Most disciplines have a single metaparadigm but multiple conceptual models which incorporate the global concepts and propositions in a more restrictive yet abstract manner (60). The dominant nursing metaparadigm encompasses the conceptual elements of caring, human nature, environment, health, and nursing.

Since midcentury, U.S. nursing has shifted from the biomedical model to a focus on human responses and nursing process which resulted in increased attention to the psychosocial aspects of patient care. While this shift occurred in nursing in the U.S. during the 1950s, the shift in England began about 20 years later (12). The recent emphasis on communication and psychology suggests that English nursing succeeded in revising the identity of the patient, and consequently, the nurse. Chrisman (42) contends that nursing is dominated by the reductionistic, pathophysiological conceptual framework of biomedicine. He asserts this despite observing that caring and holism serve as key concepts in nursing, that the natural science bias found in medicine is not as strong in nursing, and that most nursing faculty have doctoral degrees in the behavioral sciences.

Since 1952, a number of competing conceptual nursing models have been developed (94, 108, 121, 142, 149, 157). The fact that not a single one has assumed primacy does not signal failure to establish a dominant paradigm that is distinct from biomedicine. There is consensus on the elements of the new nursing metaparadigm and these elements, as we have indicated, are different from those of biomedicine.

Some medical anthropologists observe that medicine could enter a paradigm shift toward a meaning-centered ethnomedical approach by using contributions from anthropology (43, 110). However, this evolution is unlikely, since the persistent development of medicine is toward increasing technical specialization (169). Anthropologists may study nursing as a discipline undergoing a paradigm shift, and compare developments in the United States, England, and other societies.

POLITICAL ANTHROPOLOGY AND GENDER   Nursing is a discipline represented by women. Among the 112,000 nursing students in the United States, 5 percent are male (11). In the past 30 years there has been a concerted effort to move nursing education into institutions of higher learning, especially universities. The embrace of academia may be seen as a way to improve social status, to employ science to separate nursing from medicine, and to establish a knowledge base distinguishing it as a discipline. The higher status ascribed to male-dominated professions suggests that professional disciplines disproportionately represented by women would embody characteristics of interest to anthropologists. Nursing provides a setting in which economic and political theory may be tested.

The practice of nursing in many cultures is on a continuum with indigenous care providers, including midwives. Of importance is the attention given to the cultural context of childbirth and the role of midwives cross-culturally (50, 58, 80, 88, 148). The study of care in indigenous populations, of care providers as represented by women, of the status of care providers cross-culturally, and the development of professional nursing in other cultures are all viable areas of inquiry.

Biases in anthropological theory built in from the male orientation of the discipline have come under scrutiny. There is a call for research on culture from the perspective of women, even women's culture as separate from men (155). Questions raised about male bias in anthropology include: (*a*) How is the ethnographer perceived by the people, and what kind of information is given and what kind denied? (*b*) How does the anthropologist's own culture act to structure perceptions and interactions in the field? (*c*) How do anthropological theory, hypotheses, and values direct the search for significant data and the analysis of what is discovered? (20). Fruitful areas of study have been the personal strategies that nurses use to manage the intensity of workplace stresses (93) and ways society place conflicting demands on women with regard to home and employment (128a, 155, 158).

PHYSIOLOGICAL REGULARITIES   The variety in ethnographic research reflects the difficulty that anthropologists have in agreeing upon points of comparison in cross-cultural research. Physiological regularities across human populations provide a basis for such comparison. Ironically, one of the unsung virtues of the medical model is that it begins with human biology and proceeds to the insight that the human body is one of our most potent symbols in all health/illness systems (170). There are physiological regularities in human experience surrounding birth, sexual maturity, sexuality, pregnancy, menopause, aging and death, and altered states of consciousness. A more rigorous approach to physiology and the ways culture is used to modify physiological regularities provides a useful way for anthropologists to approach cross-cultural research. In recent years there has been some attention to this approach (31, 62, 74, 88, 97, 98, 147).

A few studies by nurse anthropologists have focused on the interrelationship between cultural and biological variables. In particular, the influences of cultural patterns on fertility were addressed (82, 184, 187). Investigators have focused on the relationship of culture and disease transmission (35), blood pressure (163), and postsurgical convalescence (190). In our view, research combining physiological and social variables has high potential in that it combines the holistic approach of both anthropology and nursing.

SYMBOLIC ANTHROPOLOGY   The meanings and forms of language attached to nursing are a rich area of research in symbolic anthropology. In Western culture, those who care for the sick are identified with a lexicon which is profoundly female. The term "sister" is applied to the religious functionary, and, in many European languages, identifies the nurse, suggesting a personal closeness in the nurse-patient relationship (49). The expression, "nursing the sick" and "nursing the baby" denote a metaphorical similarity between care of the patient and nurturance of the child. This link to female role images has persisted throughout history, even though males have been involved in the performance of nursing tasks since the Crusades (131). Several investigations explored this symbolism in nursing. Schulman (162) contrasted two roles of the nurse-healer and mother surrogate. Healing activities center on those specifically necessary to treat the patient's affliction. In contrast, mother surrogate activities center about the everyday tasks of living which the patient must have others do. The mother surrogate role is analogous to care (131) or expressive role functions (95). Recently, Aamodt (6) has extended these ideas. Other fruitful lines of inquiry have been investigations of mythology in nursing (75), pretending to be the physician's handmaiden (171), the meaning nurses attach to their work (45), ritual and magic in practice (159), and the social and historical base of ideologies in nursing (191).

PROJECTIONS FOR THE FUTURE

There are striking similarities between nursing and anthropology in research topics, methods, conceptual approaches, and perspective. These features point to a natural alliance which was developed by certain anthropologists since midcentury and by contemporary nurse anthropologists. Nursing benefited from the social sciences and anthropology and has emerged with models for illness and health care different from medicine. The nursing paradigm itself reflects a unique body of knowledge.

Financial support affects the development of disciplines and the research that is conducted. Funding depends on the social environment as well as the ability of discipline leaders to assess societal priorities and influence legislative bodies and funding sources. Medicine has been especially successful in attracting private and public funds in this century. Medical anthropologists have been drawn to the prestige of medicine and to the availability of research funding in medicine. In comparison to medicine, nursing has had limited resources and fewer well-prepared researchers.

Major changes are afoot nationally. In the United States, growth of the for-profit health care sector and curtailment of insurance funding for hospitalization are resulting in changes that affect medical anthropology and nursing. For-profit hospital corporations, which are efficiently managed and provide services to the insured, employ professionals who historically have been self-employed (169). Increasingly, physicians are employees of conglomerate health corporations and are in greater supply. From the management perspective, and in terms of decision making surrounding patient care, medicine is becoming more like nursing. The provision of health services to the uninsured and underinsured is reverting to local agencies which are traditionally overextended and underfunded. With the advent of hospital care, nursing moved from home and community settings to hospitals. In hospitals nursing focused on institution-dependent practice. Local and religious hospitals gave physicians control in the workplace; a restricted supply of physicians results in their economic prosperity and authority. With recent federal regulations, including diagnostic related groups, nursing is returning to home and out-of-hospital settings and is resuming a more independent role, even though management is monolithic and centralized. The impact of these changes on the public and on the professions provides a focus for collaborative research in nursing and anthropology.

Changes in the age structure in the United States (fewer young adult college students) affects anthropology which will probably broaden its base to attract the adult learner and nonmajors. The rise of PhD programs in nursing promotes the development of nursing as an independent academic discipline; yet there will be opportunities for nurses with PhDs in anthropology for several years (59). The trend to prefer nurses with PhDs on a nursing faculty will eventually affect the number of nurses who pursue PhD degrees in anthropology. Nurses studying anthropology at the PhD level represent an important opportunity for anthropologists to influence nurse researchers, and for the anthropological perspective and methods to reach an audience whereby anthropological theory may be tested.

The interface of anthropology and nursing in research promotes the development of both disciplines. A significant number of nurse anthropologists are making important contributions to the research literature. The readiness with which nursing has incorporated theory from diverse academic disciplines reflects its vigor and provides an opportunity for anthropology to have a significant impact on this young academic discipline. More effective collaboration with anthropology would enhance the quality and volume of the research literature and the ability of the two disciplines to adapt to and thrive in a changing societal environment. Medical anthropology has not capitalized on the potential for collaboration with nursing; this review indicates that a closer relationship between these disciplines with many similarities would benefit both.

Literature Cited

1. Aamodt, A. M. 1972. The child view of health and healing. In *Communicating Nursing Research. The Many Sources of Nursing Knowledge*, ed. M. Batey, 5:38–54. Boulder, Colo: West. Interstate Comm. Higher Educ. 208 pp.
2. Aamodt, A. M. 1978. The care component in a health and healing system. See Ref. 14, pp. 37–45
3. Aamodt, A. M. 1981. Neighboring: Discovering support systems among Norwegian-American women. In *Anthropologists at Home in America: Methods and Issues in the Study of One's Own Culture*, ed. D. Messerschmidt, pp. 133–49. Cambridge, Engl: Cambridge Univ. Press. 310 pp.
4. Aamodt, A. M. 1982. Examining ethnography for nurse researchers. *West. J. Nurs. Res.* 4:209–21
5. Aamodt, A. M. 1984. Themes and issues in conceptualizing care. In *Care The Essence of Nursing and Health*, pp. 75–79. Thorofare, NJ: Slack. 266 pp.
6. Aamodt, A. M. 1984. *The sociocultural context and role of the prime practitioner of care: The Nurse.* Presented at Am. Anthropol. Assoc., Denver
7. Ailinger, R. L. 1981. Cultural factors in hypertension of Spanish-speakers. *Virginia Nurse* 49(3):14–17
8. Ailinger, R. L. 1982. Hypertension knowledge in a Hispanic community. *Nurs. Res.* 31:207–10
9. Alexander, L. 1979. Clinical anthropology: Morals and methods. *Med. Anthropol.* 3(1):61–107
10. American Nurses' Association. 1980. *Nursing—A Social Policy Statement.* Kansas City, MO: Am. Nurs. Assoc. 31 pp.
11. American Nurses' Association. 1983. *Facts about Nursing 82–83*, p. 1. Kansas City, MO: Am. Nurs. Assoc. 382 pp.
12. Armstrong, D. 1983. The fabrication of nurse-patient relationship. *Soc. Sci. Med.* 17:457–60
13. Bauwens, E. E. 1977. Medical beliefs and practices among lower-income Anglos. In *Ethnic Medicine in the Southwest*, ed. E. Spicer, pp. 241–70. Tucson: The Univ. Arizona Press. 291 pp.
14. Bauwens, E. E. 1978. *The Anthropology of Health.* St Louis: Mosby. 218 pp.
15. Bauwens, E. E., Anderson, S. V. 1978. Home births: A reaction to hospital environmental stressors. See Ref. 14, pp. 56–60
16. Bhanumathi, P. P. 1977. Nurses' conceptions of "sick-role" and "good patient" behaviour: A cross-cultural comparison. *Int. Nurs. Rev.* 24:20–24
17. Binn, M. 1980. Using the explanatory model to understand ethnomedical perceptions of hypertension and the resultant behaviors. In *Transcultural Nursing Care: Teaching, Practice and Research. Proc. 5th Natl. Transcult. Nurs. Conf.*, ed. M. Leininger, pp. 60–76. Salt Lake City: Univ. Utah Coll. Nurs. 135 pp.
18. Birdwhistell, R. 1949. *Social Science and Nursing Education.* 55th Ann. Rep. Natl. League Nurs. Educ., pp. 315–28. New York: NLN
19. Bonaparte, B. 1979. Ego defensiveness, open-closed mindedness, and nurses' attitudes toward culturally different patients. *Nurs. Res.* 28:166–72
20. Bourguignon, E. 1983. Sex bias ethnocentrism, and myth building in anthropology: The case of universal male dominance. *Cent. Issues Anthropol.* 5(1):59–79
21. Bridgeman, M. 1953. *Collegiate Education for Nursing.* New York: Sage Found. 205 pp.
22. Brink, P. J. 1971. Paviotso child training: Notes. *Indian Hist.* 4(1):47–50
23. Brink, P. J. 1972. Natural triad in health care. *Nurs. Outlook* 72:897–99
24. Brink, P. J., ed. 1976. *Transcultural Nursing: A Book of Readings.* Englewood Cliffs, NJ: Prentice Hall. 289 pp.
25. Brink, P. J. 1982. Traditional birth attendants among the Annang of Nigeria: Current practices and proposed programs. *Soc. Sci. Med.* 16:1883–92
26. Brink, P. J. 1984. Key issues in nursing and anthropology. *Adv. Med. Soc. Sci.* 2:107–46
27. Brown, E. L. 1936. *Nursing as a Profession.* New York: Sage Found. 157 pp.
28. Brown, E. L. 1948. *Nursing for the Future.* New York: Sage Found. 198 pp.
29. Brown, E. L. 1960. *Social Sciences in Nursing: Applications for the Improvement of Patient Care*, ed. F. C. MacGregor, pp. 5–8. New York: Sage Found. 354 pp.
30. Brown, E. L. 1963. Meeting patients' psychosocial needs in the general hospital. *Ann. Am. Acad. Polit. Soc. Sci.* 346:117–25
31. Brown, J. K. 1982. Cross-cultural perspectives on middle-aged women. *Curr. Anthropol.* 23(2):143–56
32. Bruyn, S. 1966. *The Human Perspective in Sociology: The Methodology of Participant Observation.* Englewood Cliffs, NJ: Prentice Hall. 286 pp.
33. Bush, M. T., Ullom, J. A., Osborne, O. H. 1975. The meaning of mental health: A report of two ethnoscientific studies. *Nurs. Res.* 24:130–38

34. Byerly, E. L. 1969. The nurse-researcher as participant-observer in a nursing setting. *Nurs. Res.* 18:230–36
35. Byerly, E. L., Molgaard, C. A. 1982. Social institutions and disease transmission. See Ref. 43, pp. 395–409
36. Byerly, E. L., Molgaard, C. A., Snow, C. T. 1979. Dissonance in the desert: What to do with the golden seal? In *Transcultural Nursing Care: Culture Change, Ethics and Nursing Care Implications. Proc. 4th Natl. Transcult. Nurs. Conf.*, ed. M. Leininger, pp. 114–33. Salt Lake City: Univ. Utah Coll. of Nurs. 173 pp.
37. Caudill, W. 1958. *The Psychiatric Hospital as a Small Society.* Cambridge, Mass: Harvard Univ. Press. 406 pp.
38. Chafetz, L. 1981. Aggressive behaviors in walk-in settings: Nursing responses. In *Developing, Teaching and Practicing Transcultural Nursing: Proc. 6th Transcult. Nurs. Conf.*, ed. P. Morley, pp. 96–114. Salt Lake City: Univ. Utah Coll. Nurs. and Transcult. Nurs. Soc. 156 pp.
39. Chinn, P. L., ed. 1982. From the Editor. Nursing and Culture. *Adv. Nurs. Sci.* 4(3):Xii–Xiiii
40. Chinn, P. L. 1983. Nursing theory development: Where we have been and where we are going. In *The Nursing Profession: A Time to Speak*, ed. N. L. Chaska, pp. 394–405. New York: McGraw-Hill. 914 pp.
41. Chrisman, N. J. 1977. The health seeking process: An approach to the natural history of illness. *Cult. Med. Psychiatry* 1:351–77
42. Chrisman, N. J. 1982. Anthropology in nursing: An exploration of adaptation. See Ref. 43, pp. 117–40
43. Chrisman, N. J., Maretzki, T. W., eds. 1982. *Clinically Applied Anthropology: Anthropologists in Health Science Settings.* Boston: Reidel. 437 pp.
44. Clark, A. L., ed. 1978. *Culture, Childbearing, Health Professionals.* Philadelphia: Davis. 190 pp.
45. Clarke, M. 1978. Getting through the work. In *Readings in the Sociology of Nursing*, ed. R. Dingwall, J. McIntosh, pp. 67–86. London: Churchill Livingstone. 201 pp.
46. Clinton, J. II. 1982. Ethnicity: The development of an empirical construct for cross-cultural health research. *West. J. Nurs. Res.* 4:281–300
47. Coe, R. 1970. *Sociology of Medicine.* New York: McGraw-Hill. 437 pp.
48. Conway, M. E. 1983. Socialization and roles in nursing. In *Annual Review of Nursing Research*, ed. H. H. Werley, J. J. Fitzpatrick, 1:183–208. New York: Springer. 238 pp.
49. Coser, R. 1962. *Life in the Ward.* East Lansing: Mich. State Univ. Press. 182 pp.
50. Cosminsky, S. 1977. Childbirth and midwifery on a Guatemalan finca. *Med. Anthropol.* 1(3):69–104
51. Crick, M. R. 1982. Anthropology of knowledge. *Ann. Rev. Anthropol.* 11:287–313
52. Davis, M., Haasis, B. 1920. The visiting nurse and the immigrant. *The Public Health Nurse*, pp. 823–34
53. Davitz, L. J., Davitz, J. R. 1978. Black and white nurses' inferences of suffering. *Nurs. Times* 74:708–10
54. Davitz, L. J., Davitz, J. R., Higuchi, Y. 1977. Cross-cultural inferences of physical pain and psychological distress—2. *Nurs. Times* 73:536–58
55. Davitz, L. J., Sameshima, Y., Davitz, J. R. 1976. Suffering as viewed in six different cultures. *Am. J. Nurs.* 76:1296–97
56. Devereux, G., Weiner, F. 1950. The occupational status of nurses. *Am. Sociol. Rev.* 15:628–34
57. Donaldson, S., Crowley, D. 1978. The discipline of nursing. *Nurs. Outlook* 26:113–20
58. Dougherty, M. C. 1982. Southern midwifery and organized health care. *Med. Anthropol.* 6(2):113–26
59. Dougherty, M. C. 1985. Anthropologists in nursing education programs. In *Technical Manual on Medical Anthropology*, ed. C. E. Hill. Washington, DC: Am. Anthropol. Assoc.
60. Eckberg, D. L., Hill, L. Jr. 1979. The paradigm concept and sociology: A critical review. *Am. Sociol. Rev.* 44:925–37
61. Edgerton, R. B. 1965. Cultural vs. ecological factors in the expression of values, attitudes and personality factors. *Am. Anthropol.* 67:442–47
62. Edwards, J. W. 1983. Semen anxiety in South Asian cultures: Cultural and transcultural significance. *Med. Anthropol.* 7(3):51–67
63. Eisenberg, L. 1977. Disease and illness: Distinctions between professional and popular ideas of sickness. *Cult. Med. Psychiatry* 1:9–23
64. Elms, R., Kevany, J., Thomson, C., Webb, M. 1979. Cross-cultural study of initial visits to psychiatric outpatient clinics. *Nurs. Res.* 28:81–84
65. Evaneshko, V., Bauwens, E. E. 1976. Cognitive analysis and decision-making in medical emergencies. In *Health Care Dimensions. Transcultural Health Care Issues and Conditions*, ed. M. Leininger, pp. 83–102. Philadelphia: Davis. 206 pp.

66. Evaneshko, V., Kay, M. A. 1982. The ethnoscience research technique. *West. J. Nurs. Res.* 4:49–64
67. Evans, C. 1917. The social aspect of public health nursing. *Public Health Nurse Quarterly*, pp. 175–79
68. Fabrega, H. 1974. *Disease and Social Behavior: An Interdisciplinary Perspective.* Cambridge, Mass: MIT Press. 341 pp.
69. Fawcett, J. 1980. A framework for analysis and evaluation of conceptual models of nursing. *Nurs. Educ.* 5:10–14
70. Flaskerud, J. H. 1979. Use of vignettes to elicit responses toward broad concepts. *Nurs. Res.* 28:210–12
71. Flaskerud, J. H. 1980. Perceptions of problematic behavior by Appalachians, mental health professionals, and lay non-Appalachians. *Nurs. Res.* 29:140–49
72. Flaskerud, J. H. 1980. Tool for comparing the perceptions of problematic behavior by psychiatric professionals and minority groups. *Nurs. Res.* 29:4–9
73. Flaskerud, J. H., Halloran, E. 1980. Areas of agreement in nursing theory development. *Adv. Nurs. Sci.* 3(1):1–7
74. Flint, M. 1975. The menopause: Reward or punishment? *Psychosomatics* 16:161–63
75. Ford, T. R., Stephenson, D. D. 1954. *Institutional Nurses: Roles, Relationships and Attitudes in Three Alabama Hospitals.* Tuscaloosa: Univ. Alabama Press. 165 pp.
76. Foster, G. M. 1974. Medical anthropology: Some contrasts with medical sociology. *Med. Anthropol. Newsl.* 6(1):1–6
77. Foster, G. M., Anderson, B. G. 1978. *Medical Anthropology.* New York: Wiley. 354 pp.
78. Freidson, E. 1963. *The Hospital in Modern Society.* New York: Free Press. 346 pp.
79. Freilich, M. 1964. The natural triad in kinship and complex systems. *Am. Sociol. Rev.* 29:183–200
80. Fuller, N., Jordan, B. 1981. Maya women and the end of the birthing period: Postpartum massage-and-binding in Yucatan, Mexico. *Med. Anthropol.* 5(1):35–50
81. Germain, C. 1979. *The Cancer Unit: An Ethnography.* Wakefield, Mass: Nursing Resources. 235 pp.
82. Glittenberg, J. E. 1977. Fertility patterns and child-rearing of the Ladinos and Indians of Guatemala. See Ref. 121, pp. 140–55
83. Glittenberg, J. E. 1981. Variations in stress and coping in three migrant settlements—Guatemala City. *Image* 13:43–46
84. Golde, P., Shimkin, D. B. 1980. Clinical anthropology—an emerging health profession? *Med. Anthropol. Newsl.* 12(1):15–16
85. Goodrich, A. 1932. *The Social and Ethical Significance of Nursing.* New York: Macmillan. 401 pp.
86. Gow, K. M. 1982. *How Nurses' Emotions Affect Patient Care: Self-Studies by Nurses.* New York: Springer. 336 pp.
87. Hardy, M. 1983. Metaparadigms and theory development. In *The Nursing Profession: A Time to Speak,* ed. N. L. Chaska, pp. 421–37. New York: McGraw-Hill. 914 pp.
88. Harrell, B. B. 1981. Lactation and menstruation in cultural perspective. *Am. Anthropol.* 83:796–823
89. Harwood, A., ed. 1981. *Ethnicity and Medical Care.* Cambridge, Mass: Harvard Univ. Press. 523 pp.
90. Hautman, M. A., Harrison, J. 1982. Health beliefs and practices in a middle-income Anglo-American neighborhood. *Adv. Nurs. Sci.* 4(3):49–64
91. Herskovits, M. 1972. *Cultural Relativism: Perspectives in Cultural Pluralism.* New York: Random House. 293 pp.
92. Horn, B. M. 1977. Transcultural nursing and child rearing of the Muckleshoot people. See Ref. 121, pp. 51–67
93. Hutchinson, S. A. 1984. Creating meaning out of horror. *Nurs. Outlook* 32(2):86–90
94. Johnson, D. E. 1980. The behavioral system model for nursing. In *Conceptual Models for Nursing Practice,* ed. Sister J. P. Riehl, C. Roy, pp. 207–16. New York: Appleton-Century-Crofts. 416 pp. 2nd ed.
95. Johnson, M. H., Martin, H. W. 1958. A sociological analysis of the nurse role. *Am. J. Nurs.* 58:373–77
96. Johnston, M., Sarty, M. E. 1978. Maternal beliefs about vitamin efficacy in four U.S. subcultures. *J. Cross-Cult. Psychol.* 9:327–37
97. Jordan, B. 1980. *Birth in Four Cultures.* Montreal: Eden Press Women's Publications. 109 pp.
98. Kaufert, P. A. 1982. Myth and the menopause. *Sociol. Health Illness* 4(2):141–66
99. Kaufman, L. 1980. Thoughts on clinical anthropology. *Med. Anthropol. Newsl.* 12(1):17–19
100. Kay, M. A. 1973. Disease concepts in the barrio today. In *Communicating Nursing Research: Collaboration and Competition,* ed. M. Batey, 6:185–94. Boulder, Colo: West. Interstate Comm. Higher Educ. 226 pp.

101. Kay, M. A. 1976. The fusion of Utoaztecan and European ethnogynecology in the Florilegio medicinal. *Proc. 41st Int. Congr. Americanists* 3:323–30
102. Kay, M. A. 1977. The Florilegio medicinal: Source of southwest ethnomedicine. *Ethnohistory* 24:251–59
103. Kay, M. A. 1977. Health and illness in a Mexican-American barrio. In *Ethnic Medicine in the Southwest,* ed. E. Spicer, pp. 99–166. Tucson: Univ. Arizona Press. 291 pp.
104. Kay, M. A. 1978. Clinical anthropology. See Ref. 14, pp. 3–11.
105. Kay, M. A. 1979. Lexemic change and semantic shift in disease names. *Cult. Med. Psychiatry* 3:73–94
106. Kayser-Jones, J. S. 1979. Care of the institutionalized aged in Scotland and the United States: A comparative study. *West. J. Nurs. Res.* 1:190–200
107. Kayser-Jones, J. S. 1982. Institutional structures: Catalysts of or barriers to quality care for the institutionalized aged in Scotland and the U.S. *Soc. Sci. Med.* 16:935–44
108. King, I. 1981. *A Theory for Nursing: Systems, Concepts, Process.* New York: Wiley. 181 pp.
109. Klein, H. E., Mosberger, M. M., Person, T. B., Vandivort, R. E. 1978. Transcultural nursing research with schizophrenics. *Int. J. Nurs. Stud.* 15:135–42
110. Kleinman, A. M. 1982. Clinically applied anthropology on a psychiatric consultation-liaison service. See Ref. 43, pp. 83–115
111. Kleinman, A. M., Eisenberg, L., Good, B. J. 1978. Culture, illness and care: Clinical lessons from anthropologic and cross-cultural research. *Ann. Intern. Med.* 99:25–58
112. Koos, E. 1950. *The Sociology of the Patient.* New York: McGraw-Hill. 266 pp.
113. Koshi, P. T., ed. 1977. Forward. *Nursing Clinics of North America* 12(1):1–3
114. Kuhn, T. S. 1962. *The Structure of Scientific Revolutions.* Chicago: Univ. Chicago Press. 210 pp. 2nd ed.
115. Kuhn, T. S. 1970. Reflections on my critics. In *Criticism and the Growth of Knowledge,* ed. I. Lakatos, A. Musgrave, pp. 231–78. Cambridge, Engl: Cambridge Univ. Press. 282 pp.
116. LaFarque, J. R. 1972. Role of prejudice in rejection of health care. *Nurs. Res.* 21:53–58
117. Landy, D. 1983. Medical anthropology: A critical appraisal. In *Advances in Medical Social Science,* ed. J. L. Ruffini, 1:185–314. New York: Gordon & Breach. 405 pp.
118. Leahy, K. M. 1947. *Integration of public health into basic curriculum.* Ann. Rep. Natl. League Nurs. Educ., pp. 181–92. New York: NLN
119. Leininger, M. 1967. The culture concept and its relevance to nursing. *J. Nurs. Educ.* 6(2):27–37
120. Leininger, M. 1970. *Nursing and Anthropology: Two Worlds to Blend.* New York: Wiley. 181 pp.
121. Leininger, M. 1977. Transcultural nursing and a proposed conceptual framework. In *Transcultural Nursing Care of Infants and Children: Proc. 1st Transcult. Nurs. Conf.,* ed. M. Leininger, pp. 1–18. Salt Lake City: Univ. Utah Coll. Nurs. 231 pp.
122. Leininger, M. 1978. Culturalogical assessment domains for nursing practices. See Ref. 123, pp. 85–106
123. Leininger, M., ed. 1978. *Transcultural Nursing: Concepts, Theories and Practices.* New York: Wiley. 532 pp.
124. Leininger, M. 1980. Caring: A central focus of nursing and health care services. *Nurs. Health Care* 1(3):135–43, 176
125. Leininger, M. 1981. The phenomenon of caring: Importance, research questions and theoretical considerations. In *Caring: An Essential Human Need. Proc. Three National Caring Conferences,* ed. M. Leininger, pp. 3–15. Thorofare, NJ: Slack. 157 pp.
126. Leininger, M., ed. 1984. *Care: The Essence of Nursing and Health.* Thorofare, NJ: Slack. 266 pp.
127. Lipson, J. G., Tilden, V. P. 1980. Psychological integration of the cesarean birth experience. *Am. J. Orthopsychiatry* 50:598–609
128. MacGregor, F. C. 1960. *Social Science in Nursing: Applications for the Improvement of Patient Care.* New York: Sage Found. 354 pp.
128a. Margolis, M. 1984. *Mothers and Such: Views of American Women and Why They Changed.* Berkeley: Univ. Calif. Press. 346 pp.
129. Martin, H. W. 1958. The behavioral sciences and nursing education: Some problems and prospects. *Social Forces* 37:61–67
130. Masterman, M. 1970. The nature of a paradigm. In *Criticism and the Growth of Knowledge,* ed. I. Lakatos, A. Musgrave. Cambridge, Engl: Cambridge Univ. Press. 282 pp.
131. Mauksch, H. O. 1972. Nursing: Churning for change. In *Handbook of Medical Sociology,* ed. H. E. Freemon, S. Levin,

L. G. Reeder, pp. 206–30. Englewood Cliffs: Prentice-Hall. 598 pp. 2nd ed.
132. McCabe, G. S. 1960. Cultural influences on patient behavior. *Am. J. Nurs.* 60:1101–4
133. Mead, M. 1956. Understanding cultural patterns. *Nurs. Outlook* 4(3):260–62
134. Mendelsohn, E., Elkana, Y. 1981. *Sciences and Cultures.* Boston: Reidel. 270 pp.
135. Merton, R. K. 1949. *Social Theory and Social Structure.* New York: Collier Macmillan. 423 pp.
136. Molgaard, C. A., Byerly, E. L. 1981. Applied ethnoscience in rural America: New Age health and healing. In *Anthropologists at Home in America: Methods and Issues in the Study of One's Own Culture,* ed. D. Messerschmidt, pp. 153–66. Cambridge, Engl: Cambridge Univ. Press. 310 pp.
137. Molgaard, C. A., Byerly, E. L., Snow, C. T. 1979. Bach's flower remedies: A New Age therapy. *Hum. Organ.* 38(1):71–74
138. Muecke, M. A. 1979. An exploration of "wind illness" in northern Thailand. *Cult. Med. Psychiatry* 3:267–300
139. Myers, L. 1982. *The Socialization of Neophyte Nurses.* Ann Arbor: Univ. Microfilms Int. 144 pp.
140. Olesen, V., Whittaker, E. 1968. *The Silent Dialogue: A Study in the Psychology of Professional Socialization.* San Francisco: Jossey-Bass. 312 pp.
141. Omery, A. 1983. Phenomenology: A method for nursing research. *Adv. Nurs. Sci.* 5(2):49–63
142. Orem, D. 1980. *Nursing: Concepts of Practice.* New York: McGraw-Hill. 232 pp.
143. Orque, M. S., Bloch, B., Monrray, L. A. 1983. *Ethnic Nursing Care: A Multi-Cultural Approach.* St. Louis: Mosby. 422 pp.
144. Osborne, O. H. 1969. Anthropology and nursing: Some common traditions and interests. *Nurs. Res.* 18:251–55
145. Osborne, O. H. 1972. Social structure and health care systems: A Yoruba example. *Rural Africana* 17:80–86
146. Osborne, O. H. 1977. Emic-etic issues in nursing research: An analysis of three studies. In *Communicating Nursing Research: Nursing Research in the Bicentennial Year,* ed. M. Batey, 9:373–80. Boulder, Colo: West. Interstate Comm. Higher Educ. 414 pp.
147. Palgi, P., Abramovitch, H. 1984. Death: A cross-cultural perspective. *Ann. Rev. Anthropol.* 13:385–417
148. Paul, L. 1978. Careers of midwives in a Mayan community. In *Women in Ritual and Symbolic Roles,* ed. J. Hoch-Smith, A. Spring, pp. 129–49. New York: Plenum. 289 pp.
149. Peplau, H. 1952. *Interpersonal Relations in Nursing.* New York: Putnam. 330 pp.
150. Powers, B. A. 1982. The use of orthodox and Black American folk medicine. *Adv. Nurs. Sci.* 4(3):35–47
151. Press, I. 1969. Ambiguity and innovation: Implications for the genesis of the culture broker. *Am. Anthropol.* 71:205–17
152. Ragucci, A. T. 1972. The ethnographic approach and nursing research. *Nurs. Res.* 21:485–90
153. Ragucci, A. T. 1977. The urban context of health beliefs and caring practices of the elderly women in an Italian-American enclave. In *Transcultural Nursing Care of the Elderly: Proc. 2nd Natl. Transcult. Nurs. Conf.,* ed. M. Leininger, pp. 33–51. Salt Lake City: Univ. Utah Coll. Nurs. 150 pp.
154. Ragucci, A. T. 1981. Italian Americans. See Ref. 89, pp. 211–63. Cambridge, Mass: Harvard Univ. Press. 523 pp.
155. Reiter, R. R., ed. 1981. *Toward an Anthropology of Women.* New York: Monthly Review Press. 416 pp.
156. Rimmer, L. M. 1975. *Brokerage in an experimental neighborhood health project.* PhD thesis. Univ. Kansas, Lawrence. 244 pp.
157. Rogers, M. E. 1970. *An Introduction to The Theoretical Basis of Nursing.* Philadelphia: Davis. 144 pp.
158. Rosaldo, M. Z., Lamphere, L., eds. 1974. *Woman Culture and Society.* Stanford, Calif: Stanford Univ. Press. 352 pp.
159. Roth, J. 1957. Ritual and magic in the control of contagion. *Am. Sociol. Rev.* 22:310–14
160. Ruiz, M. C. 1981. Open-closed mindedness, intolerance of ambiguity and nursing faculty attitudes toward culturally different patients. *Nurs. Res.* 30:177–81
161. Saunders, L. 1958. Culture and nursing care. In *Patients, Physicians and Illness,* ed. E. G. Jaco, pp. 538–48. Glencoe: Free Press. 479 pp.
162. Schulman, S. 1958. Basic functional roles in nursing: Mother surrogate and healer. See Ref. 161, pp. 528–37
163. Segall, M. E. 1965. Blood pressure and culture change. *Nurs. Sci.* 3:373–82
164. Shiloh, A. 1980. Therapeutic anthropology. *Med. Anthropol. Newsl.* 12(1):14–15
165. Silva, M., Rothbart, D. 1984. An analysis of changing trends in philosophies of science on nursing theory development and testing. *Adv. Nurs. Sci.* 6(2):1–13
166. Skooglund, C. C. 1943. Report of the

committee on the integration of the social and health aspects of nursing in the basic curriculum. *Proc. 49th Ann. Conv. Natl. League Nurs. Educ.*, pp. 100–3
167. Sohier, R. 1976. Gaining awareness of cultural difference: A case example. In *Transcultural Health Care Issues and Conditions: Health Care Dimensions*, ed. M. Leininger, pp. 67–81. Philadelphia: Davis. 206 pp.
168. Spector, R. E. 1979. *Cultural Diversity in Health and Illness*. New York: Appleton-Century-Crofts. 324 pp.
169. Starr, P. 1982. *The Social Transformation of American Medicine*. New York: Basic Books. 514 pp.
170. Stein, H. F. 1980. Clinical anthropology and medical anthropology. *Med. Anthropol. Newsl.* 12(1):18–19
171. Stein, L. 1967. The doctor-nurse game. *Arch. Gen. Psychiatry* 16:699–703
172. Sullivan, R. 1977. Some values, beliefs and practices of elderly women in the United States: Implications for health and nursing care. See Ref. 153, pp. 13–26
173. Taylor, C. 1970. *In Horizontal Orbit*. New York: Holt, Rinehart & Winston. 203 pp.
174. Thompson, J. A. 1981. Translation: The impact of reactionary perspectives in transcultural nursing. See Ref. 38, pp. 34–36
175. Tripp-Reimer, T. 1982. Barriers to health care: Perceptual variations of Appalachian clients by Appalachian and non-Appalachian health care professionals. *West. J. Nurs. Res.* 4:179–91
176. Tripp-Reimer, T. 1983. Retention of a folk healing practice (matiasma) among four generations of urban Greek immigrants. *Nurs. Res.* 32:97–101
177. Tripp-Reimer, T. 1984. Cultural assessment. In *Nursing Assessment: A Multidimensional Approach*, ed. J. Bellack, P. Bamford, pp. 226–46. Monterey: Wadsworth Health Sciences. 582 pp.
178. Tripp-Reimer, T. 1984. Reconceptualizing the construct of health: Integrating emic and etic perspectives. *Res. Nurs. Health* 7(2):101–9
179. Tripp-Reimer, T. 1984. Research in cultural diversity. *West. J. Nurs. Res.* 6(3):353–55
180. Tripp-Reimer, T., Brink, P. J. 1985. Culture Brokerage. In *Nursing Interventions: Treatments for Nursing Diagnoses*, ed. G. M. Bulechek, J. C. McCloskey, pp. 352–64. Philadelphia: Saunders. 414 pp.
181. Tripp-Reimer, T., Brink, P., Saunders, J. 1984. Cultural assessment: Content and process. *Nurs. Outlook* 32:78–82
182. Tripp-Reimer, T., Schrock, M. M. 1982. Residential patterns and preferences of ethnic aged: Implications for transcultural nursing. In *Focus on Transcultural Nursing: Arching the Domains of Practice. Proc. 7th Transcult. Nurs. Conf.*, ed. C. Uhl, J. Uhl, pp. 144–57. Salt Lake City: Transcult. Nurs. Soc. 177 pp.
183. Uhl, J. 1981. Caring as the focus of a multidisciplinary health center for the elderly. In *Caring: An Essential Human Need*, ed. M. Leininger, pp. 115–25. Thorofare, NJ: Slack. 157 pp.
184. Urdaneta, M. L. 1975. Fertility and the "pill" in a Texas barrio. In *Topias and Utopias in Health: Policy Studies*, ed. S. Ingman, A. Thomas, pp. 69–83. The Hague: Mouton. 548 pp.
185. von Mering, O., King, S. 1957. *Remotivating the Mental Patient*. New York: Sage. 216 pp.
186. Wald, L. D. 1921. A review of immigrant health and the community. *Public Health Nurse* 13:601
187. Wang, J. 1979. A cross-cultural study of educational level and family planning among Chinese in Pittsburgh, Pennsylvania and in Taipei, Taiwan. In *Transcultural Nursing Care: The Adolescent and Middle Years. Proc. 3rd Natl. Transcult. Nurs. Conf.*, ed. M. Leininger, pp. 96–124. Salt Lake City: Univ. Utah Coll. Nurs. 235 pp.
188. Weidman, H. H. 1980. Comments on "clinical anthropology". *Med. Anthropol. Newsl.* 12(1):16–17
189. Weidman, H. H. 1982. Research strategies, structural alterations and clinically applied anthropology. See Ref. 43, pp. 201–41.
190. Williams, M. A. 1972. A comparative study of post-surgical convalescence among women of two ethnic groups: Anglo and Mexican American. In *Communicating Nursing Research. The Many Sources of Nursing Knowledge*, ed. M. Batey, 5:59–73. Boulder, Colo: West. Interstate Comm. Higher Educ. 208 pp.
191. Williams, T. R., Williams, M. 1959. The socialization of the student nurse. *Nurs. Res.* 8:18–25
192. Wolf, E. 1956. Aspects of group relations in a complex society: Mexico. *Am. Anthropol.* 58:1065–78
193. Young, A. A. 1978. Rethinking the Western health enterprise. *Med. Anthropol.* 2(2):1–10
194. Young, A. A. 1982. The anthropologies of illness and sickness. *Ann. Rev. Anthropol.* 11:257–85

THE SOCIAL ANTHROPOLOGY OF WEST AFRICA

Keith Hart

Department of Social Anthropology, Cambridge University, Cambridge CB2 3RF, England

INTRODUCTION

Since World War II, West Africa has been the source of consistently innovative work, much of it relevant to the field of anthropology in general. British structural-functionalist ethnography, particularly the Cambridge school of Fortes and Goody, set theoretical and empirical standards which have rarely been matched anywhere. Again, briefly in the 1970s, anglophone social anthropology was almost overwhelmed by a school of French structuralist Marxists with its base in West African research. Moreover, the region has been a crucible for the emergent synthesis of anthropology and history; economic anthropology, the study of urbanization and economic development, and the politics of decolonization have all been prominent there; and West Africa's independent women have attracted the attention of numerous feminist anthropologists. For these and many other reasons, developments in the social anthropology of West Africa are of more than parochial interest.

This paper is an introduction to the best regional literature of the last four decades, paying most attention to the period since 1970. It cites many more books than articles. The subject matter is social anthropology, which means that much cultural anthropology and archaeology has been omitted. The bias in materials selected is toward anglophone writings. The majority of texts are introduced with only a few words each. The paper is therefore a discursive means of entry for interested outsiders rather than a critical addition to professional knowledge of the region. The presentation is divided into three main sections. The first of these covers the late colonial period (ca 1940–1960); the second addresses the immediate postcolonial decade (roughly the 1960s); and the third seeks to identify the trends of the last 15 years or so. The periods refer to date of publication, not to the time of original research, thereby lending a further indeterminacy to what is in any case only a rough mnemonic device. One major theme is the postcolonial shift in emphasis from ethnography to history.

This is no place to offer a brief guide to West Africa's history and geography (e.g. 113, chap. 2), but a few remarks are in order. West Africa has about 150 million people in a land area of 4 million km^2, much of it semidesert. More than half of that population lives in Nigeria, the rest in some 16 small states formed by decolonization 25 years ago. Within a single lifetime's span, West Africans experienced both their first collective conquest and incorporation into the United Nations as citizens of independent states. Whereas much of Northern Nigeria and Mali supported a complex, stratified civilization for many centuries, the majority of West Africans have never been subjected to class rule, have always had easy access to land, and have never lost control of the means of production, even during colonialism. In consequence, the West Africa of the 1980s is that region of the world least penetrated by capitalist production. This is reflected in the spirit of its peoples and in the chaos of its political economies. Much of the region's social anthropology has been inspired by the relative freedom and disorganization of West Africans; yet indigenous novelists and playwrights have captured the uniqueness of their forms of life most effectively.

THE LATE COLONIAL PERIOD (ca 1940–1960)

The British School of Structural-Functionalist Ethnography

The publication of *African Political Systems* (74) in 1940 marked the coming of a golden age in British social anthropology. Its aim was to announce a discovery (acephalous polities) and to celebrate the method responsible (ethnographic fieldwork). Political order was shown to be possible without the state, thereby undermining much in the history of Western political philosophy. Moreover, scientific investigations on the ground in Africa had revealed what speculation never could. The influential introduction by Evans-Pritchard and Fortes drew explicitly on theoretical contrasts made by Morgan and Durkheim, but preferred to stress the empirical basis of their ideas. There were two West African contributions to the volume—by Nadel and Fortes himself. Subsequent ethnographies were addressed not to a specific regional discourse, but to the wider project of a social anthropology dominated by works of African origin. A decade after *African Political Systems,* another volume brought together research on *African Systems of Kinship and Marriage* (180), introduced by a massive statement of conceptual elaboration and social classification by Radcliffe-Brown. Much of the work of this period traced the variable influence of unilineal descent on the organization of domestic groups formed through kinship and marriage. Anthropologists whose peoples had no lineages were obliged to explain their deviance from a model which had worked for the Greeks and Romans, for the Iroquois, and now for a rapidly expanding corpus of African ethnography.

Evans-Pritchard and Fortes were the standard bearers of British social anthropology at its height. They collaborated intimately in the years before and after World War II. Each wrote up his main research as two complementary monographs, one on political structure and one on kinship. Their ethnographic style and reach differed. Evans-Pritchard wrote over a broader front and with more explicit concern for intellectual history (73). But Fortes' two studies of the Tallensi (83, 84) arguably stand as the supreme synthesis of theory and description in British social anthropology. The first monograph on this stateless people of the Gold Coast's interior *(The Dynamics of Clanship)* struggles painfully with the canons of ethnographic writing which Fortes helped to invent. On the one hand the anthropologist must be true to the particularity of his sources—there are scores of proper names in the narrative. On the other hand he must address a general Western audience at a high analytical level. The resulting text has a unique honesty and power; it is also difficult to read. In most accounts of these societies the reader is left guessing how lineages and the like actually work; Fortes leaves out nothing of significance. The second monograph *(The Web of Kinship)* is much more accessible, being rich in detail and illuminated by simply expressed ideas. Here we see the stuff of interpersonal relations and the social rules inherent in their patterning. The life cycle of family groups is laid out in a tour de force of narrative and analytical skill. For Fortes the task was always to find the abstract in the concrete without losing the concrete along the way. British ethnography had discovered a new art form: the spirit of scientific inquiry was brought to observations made of exotic peoples living in their familiar social context. At first the intellectual and moral dilemmas posed by this method were far outweighed by the evident heuristic advantages.

Fortes's immediate successor in the Northern Territories of the Gold Coast was J. Goody. The LoDagaa were similar to the Tallensi and, as his first monograph shows (95), Goody did not have much new to say about them. Articles on incest, the mother's brother, earthcult shrines and much else (94, 96, 98) established Goody as a substantial anthropologist; but his main contribution at this time was to a volume on *The Developmental Cycle in Domestic Groups* (97). This arose out of Fortes' analysis of Tallensi kinship, which he had continued in a brilliant essay on Ashanti domestic organization (the title chapter of 85). The idea was to derive a picture of the ebb and flow of domestic life from a statistical cross-section, allowing extrapolations of a diachronic sort to be made from synchronic observations. Fortes showed that different phases of a common development cycle could be understood in terms of morphological features of family life, such as the accession and loss of members, particularly children. Goody's description of production, consumption, and residence in the LoDagaa farming economy captures well the fluidity of domestic arrangements; and Stenning's path-breaking account of Fulani domestic cycles [(208); see also his excellent monograph (209)] applied the model to pastoralist subsistence strategies with equal effect. The idea of a development cycle of domestic groups was not invented by Fortes and Goody, even though its impact on anthropology was both novel and deservedly widespread. A Russian economist, A. V. Chayanov (43), had come up with the idea some decades earlier in relation to an analysis of peasant economy. Fortes once told me that he had been inspired by the work of D'Arcy Thomson (217), but if so, he never acknowledged it in print. The development cycle concept introduced a temporal dimension to kinship studies without breaking ranks with British ethnography's concerted resistance to historical methods.

Further investigations into the stateless peoples of Southern Nigeria's forest and rivers revealed social organization owing little to the lineage principle. Forde's impact on West African anthropology was much greater than his writings alone would suggest. For a long time he was director of the International African Institute and head of anthropology at University College London. He shared his peers' preoccupation with kinship (77), but was also a leading exponent of social anthropology's affinity to economics, ecology, and geography. His comparative study, *Habitat, Economy and Society* (76), is a classic. Forde's writings on the Yakö (80) and on such peoples as the Efik (79) revealed the rich associational life of these cultures. Green's Igbo ethnography (106) and Little's study of the Mende of Sierra Leone (138) also confirmed the significance of secret societies in the organization of West African stateless polities and chiefdoms, a feature of the region highlighted earlier by the German anthropologist Frobenius (87). In the Cameroons, Kaberry carried out a pioneering study of women (126); and E. Ardener's demographic approach to bridewealth and divorce among the Bakweri (13) was unique for its time (the division between our periods) and well worth reading now.

The Tiv of Nigeria's middle belt, in the hands of L. and P. Bohannan, emerged as the clearest independent example of a segmentary lineage society after the Nuer and the Tallensi. At this stage the Bohannans owed more to their socialization in British anthropology than to their American origins. The result is an outstanding ethnographic record, published in several books and numerous articles (e.g. 30, 32, 33). But there is more to West Africa than stateless societies and forest chiefdoms. The vast civilization of Northern Nigeria forced a rather different approach on its ethnographers. (Hausaland alone contains one sixth of West Africa's population.) Remarkably enough, British anthropology found ethnographers equal to the task. Nadel's *A Black Byzantium* (159) is probably the most compendious monograph on a complex society ever produced by an anthropologist. Its subject is the Nupe Kingdom—its towns and villages, its political history, its colonial economy, and its variable culture. Nadel was a theorist of the first rank, who also worked in the Sudan. He now seems marginal to the mainstream of late colonial British anthropology, but his great work truly anticipated the focus on historical political economy which is such a prominent feature of the 1970s and 1980s.

At much the same time, Forde published (with Scott) a summary of Nigeria's "native economies" (82) which has never been surpassed. The best individual account of indigenous economic organization was M. G. Smith's report on the Hausa communities of Zaria (199). Here the subordination of peasants to state rule is laid out in stark detail, with due emphasis being placed on the political conditions of economic life. Smith's contribution to the debate on segmentary lineage systems was original, but not influential (200). The same could not be said of *Government in Zazzau* (201), a synthesis of ethnographic and historical method which leads directly to the postcolonial flood of interest in the history of African states. Like Nadel, Smith is a major theorist (with affinity to Weber). Finally, West Africa has a longstanding urban tradition in the coastal fort towns where European mercantilism generated creolized populations. Banton's study of Freetown (23) was the first in a growing body of urban anthropology. He and Little together made Edinburgh a center for urban research in the postcolonial period.

From this it can be seen that, even in its heyday, the British school responded to West Africa's complexity by addressing centralized polities and cities in addition to the stateless peoples of the countryside. The theory underpinning research in all areas, however, has been labeled "structural-functionalism" (179). Social structure was understood to be manifest in empirical social relations, and behavior was functional to the extent that it contributed to the coherence and integration of institutions forming a social structure. Customary behaviour was most likely to act as the repository of significant institutional forms. Historical statements by informants were of dubious value. In most cases it was assumed that documentary records did not exist. Armed with these assumptions, the ethnographer spent a year or two identifying the contemporary patterns of social life in one place, then a decade or more talking to his British colleagues before writing up a monograph. In both phases internal consistency was taken to be a powerful proof of veracity. This radical commitment to synchronic method has been subjected to much criticism since. Yet its best practitioners were more sophisticated than their latterday critics. Fortes lays out his reasons for abstracting Tallensi ethnography from its historical context (the precolonial situation and colonial rule) in the introduction to his first monograph (83). He believes that the conditions for structural transformation (e.g. the emergence of stratified classes) have not yet occurred, and he would be right to say the same now (112). His analysis of time and social structure in Ashanti (85), a state which had undergone profound changes in less than a century, demands subtle argumentation from anyone who seeks to reject the claims of structural-functionalism out of hand. Nadel (160) and M. G. Smith (202) offer equally complex methodological statements.

To be sure, the British ethnographers rarely were explicit about their relationship to the colonial state (18); and they were sometimes directed to politically troublesome areas. (Thus the Tallensi were being shelled by a British army as late as 1911 and the LoDagaa were part of a border dispute with the French.) They had little interest in the history of the precolonial period and scarely more in colonial structures and their imminent breakdown. One exception makes the general point. Busia was an Ashanti aristocrat and a future prime minister of Ghana. His book on the position of the chief in modern Ashanti politics (41) was in many ways exemplary of structural-functionalist method—too much so, according to his leftwing critics. But the format is explicitly historical, dealing with the colonial transformation and its possible aftermath. At least one African then used the approach to explore political alternatives to colonialism. Most ethnographers, however, wrote of their subjects as if the sun would never set. After the achievement of independence by the new West African states, such an orientation, whatever its virtues, became impossible to sustain.

French and American Contributions

Afrique Occidentale Française was an important crucible of modern French anthropology and its leading exponent was Griaule. A charismatic figure whose work covered the last three decades of the colonial period, Griaule is best known for his work on the Dogon and Bambara of Mali. His closest collaborator was Dieterlen, but their school contained several notable ethnographers who spanned decolonization—Paulme, Rouch and Griaule's daughter, Calame-Griaule (45). The turning point was the publication in 1948 of *Dieu d'Eau* or *Conversations with Ogotommêli* (107), a Dogon sage who was apparently deputed to reveal the secrets of his people. Dieterlen's *Essai sur la Religion Bambara* (60) and Griaule and Dieterlen's joint masterpiece *Le Renard Pâle* (108) are the highlights of a remarkable record. Griaule began as something of a collector, with an interest in documentation of all kinds, especially visual. But later he came to see the Dogon, even particular places or individuals, ". . . as privileged examples of *l'homme noir,* microcosms of 'African' thought, civilization, philosophy and religion" (45, p. 123). Ethnography became like initiation, a search for "deep knowledge." The style could not contrast more with the British fieldwork method. Griaule was incorrigibly idealistic and ahistorical, unconcerned with the details of practical existence. He relied throughout his life on translators and a few native informants; he discounted the significance of ordinary speech. His approach was an alternative to intensive participant observation; yet he was extremely self-conscious about interaction with the sources of his knowledge.

Whatever one's judgment of their anthropological merit, the corpus of writings produced by the Griaule school contains many fine examples of collaborative work in which Africans played an active role. Moreover, in Rouch the school generated an exceptional and prolific ethnographic film maker, whose work brings the ideals and standards of his mentors to modern audiences. Finally, the publication of *African Worlds* (78), a collection which included contributions by Dieterlen and Mercier under Forde's editorship, revealed a British interest in cosmology even when structural-functionalism flourished. As a footnote to this brief account, it should be pointed out that not all Frenchmen were seduced by the mysteries of African culture. Several writers pioneered the study of indigenous social organization and political economy. The most notable of these was Labouret's monograph on the peasants of Mali and Ivory Coast (130), a book which was cited, for instance, by Fortes and Goody in their Voltaic researches.

American anthropologists were slow to become involved in West Africa before the 1970s. The dominant figure was of course Herskovits, whose great work on Dahomey was published in 1938 (115). Herskovits's approach was essentially that of culture history; and his method resembled that of the semiprofessional colonial anthropologists who preceded the academic fieldworkers. Even so, his ethnography was compendious and is still valuable. Herskovits made Northwestern University for a time the leading center for African studies in America. We have seen how the Bohannans were converted to British social anthropology for their Tiv research. It is worth mentioning that L. Bohannan early on published an impressive comparative piece on West African marriage types (29) and, as "Eleanor Smith Bowen," wrote a sensitive, funny memoir of fieldwork (38) which easily bears comparison with more recent reflections on doing ethnography. Two other American studies during the colonial period were conducted in the region's dry savanna outposts. Miner's monograph on the medieval city of Timbuktoo (156) was based on research carried out during World War II in French territory; while R. Cohen (48, 49) set extremely high standards of empirical and analytical work in his ethnography of the Kanuri of Bornu State, Northern Nigeria. These disparate contributions do add up to an American presence in colonial West Africa; but it lacked the coherence of the schools led by Fortes and Griaule.

THE IMMEDIATE POSTCOLONIAL PERIOD
(ca 1960–1970)

The Modernization Decade

It is a truism to say that decolonization transformed West African anthropology. Apart from anything else, it was hard to sustain a synchronic, local level approach to societies whose wholesale reconstruction was so visible, month to month as it were. New nations wanted new histories—invented traditions and charters for the future. Anthropologists carried the bad smell of a reactionary colonial specialism, and many changed their label to that of sociologist, demographer, or whatever. Moreover, idealism was breaking out all over the Western world in the 1960s, and Africa was the repository of unrealistic hopes for a better political and economic order. This was the decade of modernization, an American theory of social improvement with insufficient connection to historical knowledge for its application to regions like West Africa to be seriously impeded. The postcolonial world was above all else the political kingdom; and its academic overlords were the political scientists, men such as Apter [whose Ghana monograph (12) is excellent] and Easton (70), whose impact was mainly theoretical. R. Cohen & Middleton's book, *From Tribe to Nation* (50), is a rare attempt by anthropologists to grapple with the heady politics of state formation. I have isolated the first years of independence because they were unusually confused. Much material published then was collected in the late colonial period; and new initiatives taken then really bore fruit in the 1970s. There was much unfocused excitement and optimism, but little genuine understanding of the structures that were evolving everywhere. Modernization theory itself was more an abstract psychology than a method for investigating social organization.

Anthropologists made an explicit attempt at this time to break new ground, addressing economic development, precolonial history, urbanization, the position of women, and belief systems. None of this, as we have seen, is without precedent in the colonial literature; and traditional ethnography of a high standard continued to be produced, much of it French. But if one man epitomizes the shift in the balance of anthropological effort after decolonization, it is J. Goody, whose work is considered below. At last West African creative writing burst on the scene to pose an indigenous challenge to anthropological representations of their societies. Given its unwelcome associations with the recent past, anthropology did not appeal to Africans as a vocation, so the vast bulk of work in the subject was carried out by the trinity of Western nations with which we are already familiar.

Economic Development

Export agriculture in West Africa is largely a peasant enterprise and local commerce is extremely lively. So, following on the work of Labouret, Forde, Nadel, and others, anthropologists and members of related disciplines set out around the time of decolonization to document the institutions of indigenous economic organization. Bohannan and Dalton's edited collection of essays on African markets (34) is notable for the quality of its case studies; but, more important in some ways, their introduction attempted a theory of economic development which was more complex than the models of one-way diffusion and static dualism then in vogue. Their idea was that peripheral marketplaces mediated between local economies and the forces of an exogenous capitalism.

It was crude and it has been much criticized (68), but this publication was a landmark in economic anthropology. The Bohannans' monograph on Tiv economy (31) further established the influence of the Polanyi school in the region, and Netting's fine study of the Kofyar of Nigeria (161) brought American cultural ecology to research on West African agriculture. Two works, however, stand out for their public impact in this field. Hill's investigations into the migrant cocoa farmers of Ghana stretched back to the mid 1950s, but her 1963 book (117) had enormous influence. Virtually singlehanded she recast the image of West African producers, revealing their pioneering role, entrepreneurial character, and continuing dynamism. Meillassoux's monograph on the Gouro of the Ivory Coast (151) is likewise concerned to a large extent with export agriculture, but its notoriety stems from its status as the first self-acknowledged Marxist ethnography. The Gouro book became for Marxists the equivalent of Evans-Pritchard's *The Nuer* (72), a canonical text through which savants expressed their competing opinions. Other studies, like Netting's, are superior as ethnography, but Meillassoux made West Africa a focal point for Marxist discourse. Mention should also be made of Pélissier's massive tome, *Les paysans du Sénégal* (173), an apparently exhaustive compilation of sources on the groundnut economy of the Senegambia. The proto-Marxist style of his analysis is not to everyone's taste; but this impressive book, along with Dupire's meticulous research on the Ivory Coast's cocoa farmers (66), makes for an outstanding record of indigenous rural economy in the 1960s. It seems likely that the development preoccupations of the new states and the relative absence of foreign capitalist producers combined to stimulate this quite remarkable achievement by West African anthropologists.

Precolonial Kingdoms

If the classical studies of the late colonial period were of stateless peoples such as the Tallensi or the Tiv, the 1960s saw an explosion in historical research (much of it by anthropologists) on West Africa's precolonial kingdoms. These states were an indigenous point of reference for self-government. The new ruling class was not looking to replicate their structure, but it needed national or regional histories to teach the school children. Anthropologists responded to the challenge, whether consciously or not; and a growing army of historians, many of them American, joined them in the task of rebuilding African studies. A collection edited by Forde and Kaberry, *West African Kingdoms in the Nineteenth Century* (81), captured this shift in emphasis. At that time the nineteenth century was simply taken to be the nearest precolonial era; but as African historiography matured, the period came to be understood as one of crisis and dislocation. Several notable monographs were published in the 1960s. Last (133) followed the lead of Nadel and M. G. Smith in Northern Nigeria to produce a more sophisticated historical account of the Sokoto

Caliphate. Jones's work (125) on the trading states of the Oil Rivers (the oil in question being of the palm) was a pioneering study of the highest quality. Bradbury's piecemeal historical ethnography of Benin belongs to this period; it epitomizes the best of the old and the new in West African anthropology. Polanyi's posthumous study of the Dahomean slave trade (177) never made as great an impact as his more general works. Wilks (e.g. 225) was beginning his great work on Akan history, helping to make Asante eventually the best-documented African kingdom; but his contribution will be considered below. Finally, historians such as Mauny (150) and Levtzion (136) put real time depth into West African history by bringing the medieval period into sharper focus. The result of these efforts was that anthropologists could no longer claim with conviction that the peoples they studied had no history. Ethnography in the region has never been the same since.

Urbanization

The growth of cities and associated migrations stimulated a great deal of research and publication immediately after decolonization. Kuper's collection (129) was interdisciplinary but restricted to West Africa; Miner's edited volume (157) extended to the continent as a whole. Banton's essay in the first of these (24) is perhaps the best single piece for anthropologists. This was a time when West African researchers were self-consciously engaged in a dialogue with the Manchester School of Central African research (223). Southall (204) reports on work from both areas and seeks to establish a suitable comparative typology. The main point of contrast was the relative freedom of settlement enjoyed by migrants to West Africa's cities compared with the more rigid regimes farther south. This is reflected in the work written and sponsored by Little (139). He emphasised continuities of identity among migrants whose adaptations to the city were facilitated by their own voluntary associations—a far cry from the mines of the Copperbelt, where Gluckman's team described sharp oscillations between the demands of rural and urban life. An outstanding product of this discourse was A. Cohen's influential study of Hausa traders in the Yoruba city of Ibadan (47). He described ethnicity (a new term for tribes and tribalism) as symbolically loaded political competition between groups for control of valued resources. The model would not seem dissonant in Chicago, but it was a breath of fresh air for Africanists. The Yoruba of Western Nigeria are a nation many millions strong, who live in a wide variety of towns. In the 1950s they were about as urbanized as France. The 1960s were the heyday of Yoruba research, much of it addressed to the specificity of their urban social organization. Lloyd (141, 142), Bascom (26), Morton-Williams (158), and Schwab (193) all contributed important studies; and Wheatley's massive comparison of city origins (224) endows the Yoruba with the status of being a primary (aboriginal) center for urbanization.

The Position of Women

The floodtide of feminist research had not reached West Africa in the 1960s, but several excellent studies of women were published then. Leith-Ross's *African Women* (135) is perhaps the slightest of these. Paulme's collection of essays entitled *Women of Tropical Africa* (171) belongs more to the colonial period than after, but its intellectual standard is very high. Much the best product of this period, however, is M. F. Smith's wonderful biography, *Baba of Karo* (198), a Hausa woman whose story is both moving and vivid. Kaberry's lead was thus taken up in the era of decolonization, but as yet only sporadically.

Belief Systems

An urgent priority of the new states was to shed Western cultural imperialism, to discover African ways of thinking, and to legitimize indigenous beliefs. Fortes and Dieterlen (86) brought together an impressive collection of British and French papers under the heading *African Systems of Thought* which, whether intentionally or not, showed that anthropologists could play a significant part in that process of intellectual decolonization. No anthropologist has done more in that respect than Horton (e.g. 121), whose papers on African thought, on religion, and science have helped to shape discourse on such matters far beyond the limits of his adopted Nigeria. Apart from reviving interest in traditional belief systems, the postcolonial era drew attention to the impact of modern changes on African religious movements and psychology. Lanternari (132) specifically set out to examine the historical context of millenarism in different places. Peel's intensive study of the Aladura movement in Western Nigeria (171b) addresses similar issues, but in a way that is more satisfying as ethnography. Finally, Field's eccentric but interesting studies of Southern Ghanaian psychology (e.g. 75) deserve wider exposure than they get. Above all, she and some of her peers felt obliged to examine the effects of contemporary forces on "the African mind," even as the social climate encouraged idealizations of traditional systems of thought. Nowhere was this last impulse realized more effectively than in the convergence of the Griaule school's researches (see above) and Senghor's advocacy of *négritude* (196). Anthropology did have a place in the postcolonial sun, after all.

Ethnography

Good ethnography of a traditional sort was not entirely eclipsed by the desire to be relevant. Much of it was French. Dupire's Fulani monograph (67) is outstanding even in an area which has attracted great ethnographers. Terray is well known as a theoretical Marxist of formidable analytical powers (214), but he is a fine historian and ethnographer too. His *L'Organisation Sociale des Dida* (213) describes a Southern Ivory Coast people coherently and in detail.

Nicolas's work on the Hausa of Niger peaked in the 1960s; apart from larger works, his many articles are accessible and original (e.g. 163, 164). In some ways the British tradition of fieldwork-based research was carried on more by French anthropologists after decolonization, some of them reacting against the idealism of the Griaule school and in the process reinventing the approach celebrated in *African Political Systems* (74). One British monograph, Ruel's study of a Cross River people in Cameroon (191), addresses a major topic in West African ethnology—the role of secret societies in indigenous political organization. Ruel's account of local politics on the eve of decolonization draws creatively on some of the ideas current in the modernization decade. On a larger scale, Skinner's politically oriented monograph, *The Mossi of Upper Volta* (197), provides an American example of the more traditional approach, but the tide of West African anthropology was not running with this style of research.

Jack Goody

If the years following decolonization saw anthropologists turning from fieldwork to history, one man's work encapsulates that transition. Jack Goody's finest achievement, *Death, Property and the Ancestors* (99), was published soon after independence. Partly an ethnography of funeral customs, it is in substance a wide-ranging comparative inquiry into the significance of property in kinship organization and social life, evoking the great Victorian jurists, such as Maine. Next he turned from studying a stateless people to the kingdom of Gonja (100, 101). Undoubtedly this experience emphasized the limits of conventional fieldwork and helped to push Goody toward those works of historical generalization for which he is perhaps best known. His output in the 1970s began with the catalytic *Technology, Tradition and the State* (102), a short collection of essays on the material foundations of state power in Africa, and extended to global contrasts between Eurasia and Africa, ranging from reproductive strategies to cooking (104, 105). Finally, these decades of research in Africa provided a launching pad for Goody's recent masterpiece on the historical origins of the European family (105a), a topic as far removed in methodology (if not in substance) from the tradition of Fortes and Radcliffe-Brown as it is possible to be. Goody's example in opening up the horizons of West African research (103) and in promoting links between the British and French schools was a central feature of the trend away from a more narrowly conceived fieldwork method in the postcolonial period.

West African Creative Writing

West Africans never played much of a part in the academic anthropology of their region, any more than indigenous populations elsewhere did, but in the 1960s a dazzling creative literature arose which ought to be seen as part of the region's anthropology. The main vehicle for this movement was the novel, a vast pyramid of popular writing with work of the highest international standard at its apex (165). The region has also produced major playwrights. And the lyrics of popular music, known as "highlife," have a poetry evocative of the tango songs of Argentina between the wars. Francophone West Africans, notably Sembane, have found an enthusiastic international reception for their films. Taken together, these phenomena constitute a distinctive modern culture as vital and original as any in our century. Their focal points are the countries which were enriched most by colonialism—Nigeria, Ghana, Senegal. Two writers, Achebe and Soyinka, both Nigerians, one a novelist, the other a playwright, are strong candidates for a Nobel prize (e.g. 1, 2, 205, 206). Achebe's work in particular is a remarkable account of the two or three generations which span the colonial conquest and today's military coups. His novel *Things Fall Apart* (1) is demoralizing for anthropologists who can only aspire to capture much less at greater length in their academic ethnography. Other notable artists, such as Ekwensi (71), Armah (16), and Tutuola (218), produce vivid descriptions which point up the abstraction, even aridity of our discipline's generalizations. No social anthropologist set out to emulate Turgenev; but the West African novel has brought a whole new perspective to our understanding of what makes the region's peoples unique. Perhaps in time something of that distinctive voice will rub off on our ethnographic literature, for West African writing, as much as modern politics, has undermined our ability to assume the positivist stance of confident scientific observer on which colonial anthropology thrived.

THE 1970s AND AFTER

Overview

After the incubation period of the immediate postindependence decade, the 1970s saw a genuine renaissance of West African anthropology, an efflorescence which tailed off badly in the 1980s, as world depression and political disaster took their toll. The most significant development was the consummation of the marriage between anthropology and history, for which the 1960s had been the engagement. Great works of synthesis flowed from the historians and compelled ethnographers to take notice; but several prominent anthropologists (e.g. Goody, M. G. Smith, Terray) insured that the traffic was two-way. This was the time when the fieldwork method lost its absolute primacy in West African anthropology. Although, as we will see, traditional ethnography still flourishes, and it is by no means obvious that recent approaches have effectively refuted the claims and methods of structural-functionalism.

A new generation of collections emerged to supplant *African Political Systems* (74) and the rest, most of them more narrowly focused on the region rather than on the continent as a whole. Moreover, they usually drew on collaboration between anthropologists, historians, geographers, and social scientists. Their titles speak of the shape of latter-day interests—slavery, migration, drought, gender. For a time it seemed that French structuralist Marxism was taking over anglophone anthropology (166); then it suddenly receded into a more minor, but still influential role. Once again West Africa was at the center of theoretical debate in the discipline. If the historians opened up the complexity of the region's precolonial structures, the longstanding interest of West Africans in urban and peasant economies became subsumed under the tidal wave of development studies which broke in this decade. The entry of the USA on a significant scale, after the Sahelian drought of the early 1970s, played a significant part in this. Anthropologists have never been strong in the analysis of national politics, but the evolving crisis of the postcolonial states may have begun to change this. Meanwhile, there is a persistent substratum of political studies in the periphery which deserves mention. Feminism has now found a secure place in West African studies, reflecting the rise of self-consciousness among Western academic women (which was not without precedent in earlier phases of the region's anthropology), as well as the distinctive attributes of West African women.

All of this lends support to the thesis that the old national schools of ethnography have broken up, the fragments being absorbed in an international melting pot of theoretical styles, each in its own way subordinating West African specificity to the elusive generalities of modern history. This seems to be particularly true of the British, who have been joined by many more Americans and who have been more open to the France of Lévi-Strauss and Althusser than at any time since they posthumously canonized Durkheim. French ethnography is more continuous with it earlier traditions, although here too a post-Griaule reaction has led some anthropologists to the structural-functionalism of Fortes. Be that as it may, it would be wrong to close this review without noting the richness of the ethnography still coming out of West Africa, rich both in empirical content and in theoretical significance. Three recent anglophone examples are chosen to illustrate the optimistic conclusions to be drawn from this survey.

The Rise of History

Everybody needs history. Stateless peoples like the Tallensi have their genealogies, and the new nations must have historical charters for their states. Social anthropologists traditionally adopted a radical empiricist stance toward history, choosing to find the past only in its manifestation as present actions and beliefs. Their scepticism (which made all history myth, if not bunk) was supported by the poverty of documentary evidence and the blatant manipulations of political culture. Now that the postcolonial dream has been punctured and in places has collapsed, ethnographic conservatism looks less reactionary than it once did. Nevertheless, it has become impossible to return to the days when a tribal ethnography could be extracted from West Africa on the basis of a single period of participant observation alone. Historians have proved that the region's past is knowable; and they have contributed vigorously to analytic debate. It is rare for two professions to operate in area studies on an equal footing, as here. West Africa's lack of a great indigenous literate tradition gave anthropologists a head start, which they are fast relinquishing to others; but for a time they have shared the stage with historians, so that many researchers have a foot in both camps and discourse is relatively open.

A major *History of West Africa* (5, 6) was produced in the mid-1970s. The coverage and standard of the contributions speak eloquently of the region's mature historiography. It is characteristic that the collection includes an interesting overview by Horton (122) of stateless societies, that is, of the peoples without history. Another synoptic landmark of this period was Hopkins' *Economic History of West Africa* (119). The book was criticized for its intellectual style and selective scope. But Hopkins' synthesis opened up a panorama which had previously been obscure, despite the existence of a great predecessor in McPhee's precocious doctoral dissertation of 1926 (149). West Africa's colonial era is quite well covered in English by Crowder's concrete and durable history (54a). The French Marxist historian Suret-Canale wrote two works on Afrique Occidentale Française (210a,b) dealing with the periods up to and after World War II. Of these the second is more impressive; but frequent revisions of left-wing historiography (which saw for a time the attempted rehabilitation of the 1930s Popular Front) have not left Suret-Canale's reputation unscathed.

Nowhere in Africa—perhaps in the world—has a precolonial polity been more thoroughly researched than the kingdom of Asante, political center of Ghana's Akan peoples. Wilks's monumental history (226) is in some ways the most significant publication of recent years. His account of Asante is rationalist, stressing the *real politik* of interests at the state capital and thereby lending to Asante protonationalism an air which would not seem out of place in eighteenth century Europe. Many others—McCaskie (146, 147), Arhin (15), Klein (127)—have fueled the spate of Akan historical studies. McCaskie's brilliant articles in particular have restored a richer blend of culture and political economy to Wilks's bureaucratic model. The Ivory Coast Akan have been as well served by French scholars. The smaller kingdom of Abron has been the object of massive researches by Terray, ranging from grand theoretical arguments with Coquery-Vidrovitch (54) over the primacy of trade in African polities (215) to minute documentation of the internal exchange of gold and slaves (prefigured in 216). And Perrot's monograph on kingship in Anyi-Ndenye is as masterly as it is beautifully produced (175). The Akan corpus is proof, if it were needed, that anthropology has benefited enormously from the postcolonial upsurge in historical work.

Apart from the forest kingdoms, the Moslem states of the dry savanna interior have also witnessed a boom in historical research. Baier's economic history of the area now known as Niger (22) offers a unique glimpse into the African end of the trans-Saharan trade, while Lovejoy's investigations into Hausa slavery culminated in a general survey of the topic (145). M. G. Smith's earlier history of Zaria (201) was intended to be part of a set on Hausa kingdoms. So far only one more volume has been published, on Daura (203); but it is remarkable for the analytical clarity and intellectual sweep of its organization. Samori was a freebooter of the late precolonial period whose exploits have been copiously documented by Person (176) in what must be the longest monograph ever written on a West African topic. Finally, the dean of American historians, Curtin, has capped a long attempt to establish a valid account of the Atlantic slave trade (55) with a monograph on one of its principal sources, the Senegambia (56). Here too the links with anthropology are explicit. The flowering of African history in the 1970s deserves more expansive treatment. It is the most significant change in the context of anthropological research since the academic fieldworkers first made their mark.

A New Generation of Collections

Perhaps the best indicator of trends in a diffuse subject like West African studies is the choice of topics for conferences, seminars, and collections. Several of these were sponsored by the International African Institute; perhaps the most influential of their publications was that on *The Development of Indigenous Trade and Markets in West Africa* (153). Comparison with Bohannan and Dalton's *Markets in Africa* (34) reveals the impact of just one decade of historical research. Meillassoux's introduction is a tour de force, showing that the nineteenth century was not the homogeneous culmination of an unbroken precolonial past, but rather a time of crisis, as local societies were submitted to the twin shocks of a declining slave trade and growing agricultural exports. The big topic of the last decade, however, has been slavery. Again Meillassoux (154) offered a seminal introduction to a strong collection of French essays, and Miers and Kopytoff (155) produced a worthy anglophone counterpart. Slavery focused attention on early relations between the colonizers and indigenous rulers; it also forced a reevaluation of domestic institutions which had previously been classed as an expression of consensual kinship systems. For the rest, the picture is dominated by the trials of West Africa's rural economies in the 1970s. Leftwing analysis was drawn in particular to the failures of agricultural development (11, 25, 116). The drought spawned an endless series of meetings and papers, some of which found their way into print (51, 52, 57, 58, 194). All these collaborative efforts on peasants and famine confirmed the conclusion that the contradictions of neocolonialism are to be found mainly in the countryside. The link with the cities was explored vigorously in Amin's collection on migration (10). His introduction mounts a comprehensive challenge to the liberal model of individual decision making and seeks to locate migrant flows in an alternative construction of West Africa's political economy. Taken together, these initiatives speak of a downbeat realism which contrasts somewhat with the euphoria of the 1960s and even with colonial efforts to depict indigenous societies as coherent and autonomous. It is not yet clear how the mood of despair so prevalent in the 1980s will be reflected in the output of West African studies; no doubt the books of conferences will not even be published.

Marxism

The French debate on Althusser and structuralist Marxism, which peaked in the late 1960s, hit the anglophone world in the early 1970s and acquired for five to six years a measure of intellectual dominance in anthropology and related subjects. Everyone, it seemed, tried to master the language of French Marxism. It was doubly impressive to our marginal profession that so many of the leading practitioners were anthropologists—and Africanists too! I have written a fuller discussion of this topic elsewhere (114). Terray's essay on Meillassoux's Gouro monograph (214) is still the best introduction to the issues, even though his is a most ahistorical version of historical materialism. Rey's contribution from the Congo (185)—including his seminal attack on Bohannan and Dalton (68)—is the indispensable third leg of this Althusserian trinity. Debate hinged on the power of elders over young men in West African societies. Meillassoux thought it came from their superior knowledge; Rey found a mechanism akin to class extraction of surplus labor; while Terray insisted on a functionalist interpretation of kinship as production organization. This ground was already familiar in substance to anglophone anthropologists who had identified the key role of marriage and the circulation of women in elder/junior relations (e.g. 32, 61, 93). The arguments may have seemed esoteric, but they were linked to the great issues of Parisian leftwing politics—on the Communist Party and China, for example. The intellectual standard was very high, although Terray's concern to emulate the empiricism of the British school was not widely shared.

Meillassoux progressed in the 1970s to an articulate overview of the region's political economy and to a sweeping general anthropology, unhappily translated into English as *Maidens, Meal and Money* (152). Rey, having pioneered an approach which came to be known as "the articulation of modes of production" (186), has recently advocated detailed studies of rural societies as a means of transcending facile talk of the African proletariat (134). On a broader front, much French writing in the 1970s was *marxisant* without achieving the clarity of the famous threesome. Copans' work on Senegal (53) falls into this category. He introduced an important collection of pieces in translation by French

Marxists (195) which includes several papers by Meillassoux and two fine ethnographic studies by Augé (20) and by Pollet and Winter (178). Augé's prolific contribution has been nearer to mainstream anthropology in many ways (19); a short work in English (21) provides an introduction to his ideas. Finally, Raynaut (181, 182) has published an impressive series of articles on the Hausa of Niger, which brings Marxist analysis to bear on contemporary social realities at a fairly specific level. Now that the honeymoon with French Marxism is over, we might ask what its initial appeal was. In the context of West African anthropology, the failure of structural-functionalism to survive decolonization left an intellectual gap which history, with its penchant for particular facts and concrete myths, could not fill. Marxism advertised itself as a materialist science of history, even when, as here, the logic and method of the specific approach were quite similar to those of structural-functionalism. By embracing structuralist Marxism, after their fashion, anglophone anthropologists could reject their past while retaining familiar ways of thinking. Later they were able to dispense with this crutch and return to a less theoretical eclecticism. Nevertheless, the French Marxists brought to West African studies a sense of wider purpose and a power of reasoning which has not been seen since the British school was at its height.

Development

The long tradition of urban and peasant studies in West African anthropology was continued in the 1970s. Once again the Yoruba received more than their fair share of attention. Eades's short overview (69) is an excellent guide to the Yoruba literature. Lloyd produced works on topics ranging from perceptions of inequality (143) to shanty towns (144). Peel's history of Ilesha is the best recent study of social change in the region (172). Berry's account of Southwestern Nigeria's cocoa farmers (27) is a worthy complement to Hill's Ghanaian work (117). Sudarkasa's research on Yoruba women at home and in Ghana (210) reflects her pioneering status as a black American female anthropologist. Peace's study of factory workers in a Lagos suburb (171a) has great originality; and Aronson's *The City Is Our Farm* (17) is a concrete study of migrants' lives. If Akan history is outstanding, Yorubology is much the most advanced sector of research into modern West Africa. Elsewhere in Nigeria, Hill's investigations into the Hausa peasantry near Kano have been first rate, especially *Rural Hausa* (118). Watts' recent monograph on a similar area (222) has justifiably attracted considerable attention. Uchendu's Igbo ethnography (219) is a rare example of work by a native anthropologist. Burnham's book on the Gbaya of Northern Cameroon (40a) makes a successful link between late precolonial history and the economic anthropology of the modern period. Two influential products of Cambridge's Ghana industry are Oppong's study of matrilineal marriage among Akan civil servants in Accra (167) and Schildkrout's *People of the Zongo* (192), the most significant work on ethnicity to emerge from West Africa since A. Cohen's Ibadan book (47). Gugler and Flanagan (108a) provide the most up-to-date review of urban studies in the region.

These painstaking ethnographies of West Africa's complex societies have been overshadowed—in publicity, if not in seriousness of context—by a deluge of studies oriented toward "development." This movement has three main strands: research financed by or closely connected to American aid; Marxist-influenced work often portraying itself as "political economy"; and studies carried out under the auspices of the French government, notably ORSTOM. The Institute for Development Anthropology at SUNY, Binghamton has sponsored a volume on the Sahel (39) which is representative of American applied anthropology. Much else in this field remains unpublished. Horowitz (120) and Swift (211) have greatly advanced our knowledge of West African pastoralism, the latter most recently in the Niger Livestock Development Project. A collection of agricultural case studies under Netting's direction (162) is of the highest quality. Amin's synthetic corpus on underdevelopment with an African face has inspired much critical writing on West Africa. His *Unequal Development* (9) contains the full theory, while a work specifically on West Africa (8) is rather less interesting than his early case study of the Ivory Coast (7). Some of the best *marxisant* writing has been on Senegal, where Copans (53) and Adams (3) deserve special mention. Derman's innovative study of Guinée (59) is a rare American example of ethnography influenced by Marxism. Gutkind and Wallerstein (109) present a number of papers on African political economy; and several of the collections referred to above lean in this direction. The output of French geographers, anthropologists, agronomists etc has been staggering. Gallais' work on the Inner Delta region of Mali (88) offers a consistent overview of relations between herders and peasants. Of many others, Boutillier (36), Dozon (62), Raynaut and Reboul (183) are conspicuous in having brought their ethnographic talents to bear on development problems. Finally, Rimmer's *The Economies of West Africa* (188) is the first regional survey of the national economies formed some 25 years ago.

What has all this activity meant for West African anthropology? First, it has provided jobs and research funds for ethnographers. Second, it has opened up our subject to explicit considerations of policy. Third, it has stimulated genuinely new understanding, of interactions between different specialist groups, for instance. "Development" is a catch phrase for our institutional equivalent of colonialism—directed change under Western leadership. In the 1970s, anthropologists came to terms with development in this sense as a necessary part of their collective existence in West Africa. It would be dishonest to pass over my own interest in the topic of this section. My original research into the economy of Accra's slums was undertaken as an exercise in the sociology of modernization (urban branch). An early publication (111) coined an expression "the informal sector" which helped to define a new bureaucratic interest in the Third World's urban poor. Eventually I turned to a historical survey of West Africa's political economy with the focus on agriculture (113); the annotated bibliography of this work would be a useful complement to the present paper. This personal shift from small-scale urban anthropology to the history of regional development reflects a major trend in West African studies. We are all global thinkers now, but can we still do the ethnography?

Politics on the Periphery

After the heady days of the 1960s, when political scientists like Apter wrote confident monographs on Africa's "new nations," much of the best work done on politics has looked at local realities in a national context. Dunn's excellent collection (64) offers short case studies of the principal countries; and the smaller anglophone states, such as Liberia and Sierra Leone, have lent themselves to encapsulated summary (44, 137). But it is the lower level studies that have been outstanding. Dunn's collaboration with the anthropologist A. Robertson (65) situates the remote Brong-Ahafo region in the wider framework of Ghana's political evolution. Cruise O'Brien's two monographs on an Islamic brotherhood in Senegal, the Mourides (54b, c), are of exceptional anthropological quality. Much the same could be said of Paden's *Religion and Political Culture in Kano* (170). Ladouceur's overview of politics in Northern Ghana (131) is indispensable to comprehension of the voluminous ethnographic literature on the area; while Staniland's Dagomba history exemplifies the progress made by political scientists in synthesizing the ideas and methods of several disciplines. As before, anthropologists have been backward in addressing a topic made for them—politics seen from below. The major exception to this is Owusu (169) who, like Busia in the colonial period (41), stepped out of the rut and studied politics in his own Akan area. The most prominent issue of our times is the crisis facing West Africa's postcolonial states. Since 1979 especially, Ghana and several other nations have been on the brink of collapse. Research is much more difficult under these conditions, but the moral and intellectual pressure on anthropologists to make sense of these phenomena should be overwhelming.

Gender Relations

Boserup's *Woman's Role in Economic Development* (35) gave feminist anthropology a systematic framework for linking West Africa's women to the developments of the postcolonial era. Later borrowings from Marxism invested these discussions with the importance of "political economy." I have summarized male/female relations elsewhere (113, pp. 142–45). The point is that women in many parts of the region strike outsiders as being unusually independent. This is especially true of the marketing sphere. Yet traditional social structure gave power unequivocally to men, as functionalist and Marxist analyses of marriage exchanges have repeatedly claimed. Both colonial and postcolonial societies have also been dominated by men at the top; but lower down the pecking order women often exercise more clout than Western housewives. Market women have been used as scapegoats for economic failure by male military regimes. It is an intriguing picture and one which attracted some of the best anthropological studies of gender relations anywhere. Oppong's collection (168) is up-to-date and rather uneven. It does, however, reveal the extraordinary variety of ethnographic findings in the region. Several of the contributors to this volume have written cogently on this and related topics: Ottenberg, Etienne, Sanjek, Schildkrout, Peil, and Brydon (whose paper is the best single contribution). The list of major writers on sex divisions in the last decade defies further description: Sudarkasa (210), Little (140), McCormack (148), Pellow (174), C. Robertson (190), Guyer (110), S. Ardener (14), Roberts (189), Vidal (221), Clignet (46), Bisilliat (28), just to name a few. Of these, Guyer's comparison of the Bete and Yoruba division of labor is part of a first-rate anthropological project; and Roberts has done more than most to integrate a feminist perspective with the critical line on political economy epitomized by the radical journal, *Review of African Political Economy* (e.g. 184).

It is hard to say what will be the long-term residue of this remarkable outpouring. Already enough doubt has been cast on traditional ethnographic models to undermine their grip on our minds. Thus, for example, it has been argued that the development cycle of domestic groups is biased toward males and that descent theory overstated the influence of rule-bound corporations dominated by men. Such challenges are bound to be salutary for the profession. On the other hand, the historical dependence of women's liberation on capitalist and socialist development tends to be overlooked by romantics searching for authentic precapitalist examples of female freedom in West Africa. The emancipation of women is a global force of greater political significance even than decolonization. The intellectual movement it has stimulated has just begun to transform West African anthropology.

What Happened to Ethnography?

The tradition of writing ethnography is far from dead in West Africa; and in some ways the French could be said to have done more to uphold that tradition in recent years than their anglophone counterparts. Much of their work is modeled on the Griaule school's method of cultural exegesis, modified perhaps to take more explicit account of psychology or linguistics. More remarkably, the British structural-functionalists have enjoyed a belated vogue in Paris, as several West African ethnographers took up the idea of fieldwork geared toward the analysis of concrete social organization. Dumas-Champion's monograph on the Masa of Chad (63) draws inspiration directly from *African Political Systems;* and Tardits' (212) combination of ethnography and history owes much to the Bohannans. As before, intensive collaboration in a few places has been more typical of French efforts than British. One organization, devoted to the study of systems of thought under the leadership of Cartry, produced an eight-volume series on sacrifice not long ago (42). Izard, one of the leading ethnographers, is a convert from history (123); and Adler's account of divine kingship in Chad (4) matches Perrot's Anyi history (175) but goes in for a rather more formal theoretical apparatus. From the outside it does seem that French anthropology, despite the original contributions of its Marxists and historians, has stayed closer to the concerns of colonial ethnography. In this sense, the shocks of decolonization have had less effect on the corpus of writing than has been the case for the British. It would be idle to ask why, when the proposition itself is so tenuous.

While J. Goody applied himself to the task of global comparison, the work of the Cambridge school, with its base in Northern Ghana, was carried on most notably by E. Goody. Her early work on Gonja (89) takes up the traditional concerns of kinship and marriage in an area where descent organization is weak. Since then she has branched out into a unique cluster of investigations, based partly on Gonja but also on research outside Africa. These include socialization, fostering, symbolic interaction, and craft occupations (90–92). An interest in social psychology is one source of underlying unity; but Goody's methods are extremely diverse, combining statistical and historical techniques with small-scale fieldwork observations. Brown's work on the rituals of Mamprusi kingship (40) is much nearer the interests of French researchers in the Voltaic area than to the current mainstream of British anthropology. Her mentor, Fortes, inspires more research these days in Paris than in his own university. This is not to deny that good ethnography still comes out of Britain—Jackson's sensitive study of the Kuranko of Sierra Leone (124) is one example. This section on the 1970s and after concludes with a selection of three monographs which keep alive the spirit of theoretically adventurous empiricism that has always marked the best anglophone work in West Africa.

Verdon's book on the Abutia Ewe of Southern Ghana (220) would not be a universal choice. His dedication to a method of "operational analysis," based on systematic reworking of old conceptual vocabulary, strikes some as unbendingly Cartesian—not for him the muddled realism of most British ethnography. Yet no individual has done more to sustain interest in the ideas of Radcliffe-Brown, Fortes, and the other founders of classical kinship theory. The Ewe lack a segmentary lineage system and this led Verdon into a reexamination of the "descent" concept. His fieldwork materials are well organized and his analysis is both original and rigorous. It may be that these problems no longer command a serious audience in anthropology. If so, it is a pity. Riesman's

Freedom in Fulani Social Life (187) is by far the most delightful monograph published in the last decade. It started out as a Sourbonne doctoral thesis *(Société et Liberté chez les Peuls)*, and it represents a unique synthesis of American and French elements. The topic is personal autonomy in a pastoralist culture. The method of exposition is remarkable—first a fairly conventional, "objective" account of social structure; then a variety of subjective approaches to the problem, experimenting with novel approaches for psychology, language, and philosophy. The freshness and idiosyncracy of this book make it one of a kind. Perhaps if more anthropologists conceived of their task as creative writing, our ethnography would be more humane and revealing. Finally, Peel's *Ijeshas and Nigerians* (172) addresses what is surely the pressing issue for West African anthropology today—the incorporation of local communities into new nation states. His canvas covers the whole modern period since long before colonialism. His method is historical narrative, but the spirit is ethnographic. Peel's meticulous scholarship and imaginative sweep do more to illuminate the complexities of Yoruba society than any other single work. Most of the great themes of postcolonial anthropology find a place here—forest kingdoms, urbanization, export production, trade, modern politics, ethnicity and so on. If any recent monograph offers a model that is likely to be imitated in coming years, this is it. The demands of ethnography and history are reconciled and a new art form, comparable to the scientific field report of colonial anthropology, struggles to emerge.

General Conclusions

The arrival of academic anthropology in West Africa during the late colonial period produced a creative outburst of great intellectual confidence. British structural-functionalism was an integrated theory and method; it yielded results; and it could be reproduced in universities. Its practitioners were well aware of the problems they faced in abstracting local societies from the wider arena of history and politics, but they counted the benefits of prolonged fieldwork more than adequate compensation. Their best monographs are a rare blend of concrete description and analytical rigor; they are a lesson on how to think through first-hand experience of the exotic. Decolonization ended all that, at least for the British. We have been overwhelmed by the sense of a world turned upside down, remaking itself almost by the day. We have lost any certainty that small-scale communities are valid subjects of study. We have turned to grand speculation about continental, even world history, and to the anxious paranoia of political economy. Who can deny the gains or would wish to restore an anthropology without history? Yet an uncomfortable feeling persists that the old ethnography may have been pushed to one side, but its claims have not been decisively refuted. Its vitality in recent French work suggests that the demise of structural-functionalism has been announced prematurely. (French neocolonialism is more alive in West Africa too.) The ethnographic canons of colonial anthropology are still compelling, however difficult to implement, and the weaknesses of speculative generalization have not been overcome by a new self-confident African history. There is some evidence that the pendulum, having swung between its antithetical extremes in the last two decades, may now be describing a narrower, more synthetic arc where history and ethnography are fruitfully combined. We cannot recapitulate the homogeneity of national schools in the 1940s; there are too many of us now. But the harsh climate of the 1980s forces us to take stock of the immediate postcolonial era and to concentrate our efforts on the future. West Africa will not become easier for anthropologists to study; but its peoples are still fundamentally free, and the region is likely to remain a crucible of original thought in our discipline for decades to come.

Literature Cited

1. Achebe, C. 1958. *Things Fall Apart*. London: Heinemann
2. Achebe, C. 1973. *No Longer at Ease*. London: Heinemann
3. Adams, A. 1977. *Le long voyage des gens du fleuve*. Paris: Maspero
4. Adler, A. 1982. *La mort est le masque du roi: la royauté sacrée des Moundang du Tchad*. Paris: Payot
5. Ajayi, A., Crowder, M., eds. 1974. *History of West Africa*, Vol. 2. London: Longman
6. Ajayi, A., Crowder, M., eds. 1976. *History of West Africa*, Vol. 1. London: Longman. 2nd ed.
7. Amin, S. 1967. *Le développement du capitalisme en Côte d'Ivoire*. Paris: Editions de Minuit
8. Amin, S. 1971. *L'Afrique de l'Ouest bloquée*, Paris: Editions de Minuit; transl. 1973, *Neocolonialism in West Africa*. Harmondsworth: Penguin
9. Amin, S. 1973. *Le développement inégal: essai sur les formations sociales du capitalisme péripherique*. Paris: Editions de Minuit; transl. 1976, *Unequal development*. New York: Monthly Review Press
10. Amin, S., ed. 1974. *Modern Migrations in Western Africa*. London: Oxford Univ. Press
11. Amin, S., ed. 1975. *L'agriculture africaine et le capitalisme*. Paris: Editions Anthropos
12. Apter, D. 1963. *Ghana in Transition*. New York: Atheneum
13. Ardener, E. 1962. *Divorce and Fertility: An African Study*. London: Oxford Univ. Press
14. Ardener, S., ed. 1975. *Perceiving Women*. London: Dent
15. Arhin, K. 1967. The structure of greater Ashanti (1700–1824). *J. Afr. Hist.* 8(1):65–85
16. Armah, A-K. 1972. *The Beautiful Ones Are not yet Born*. London: Heinemann
17. Aronson, D. R. 1978. *The City Is Our Farm: Seven migrant Ijebu Yoruba Families*. Boston: Hall
18. Asad, T., ed. 1973. *Anthropology and the Colonial Encounter*. London: Ithaca
19. Augé, M. 1975. *Théorie des pouvoirs et idéologie: étude de cas en Côte d'Ivoire*. Paris: Hermann
20. Augé, M. 1978. Status, power and wealth: relations of lineage, dependence and production in Alladian society. See Ref. 195, pp. 389–412
21. Augé, M. 1979. *The Anthropological Circle: Symbol, Function, History*. Cambridge: Cambridge Univ. Press
22. Baier, S. 1980. *An Economic History of Central Niger*. Oxford: Clarendon
23. Banton, M. P. 1957. *West African City: A Study of Tribal Life in Freetown*. London: Oxford Univ. Press
24. Banton, M. P. 1965. Social alignment and identity in a West African city. See Ref. 129, pp. 131–47
25. Barker, J., ed. 1984. *The Politics of Agriculture in Tropical Africa*. Beverly Hills: Sage
26. Bascom, W. R. 1969. *The Yoruba of Southwestern Nigeria*. New York: Holt, Rinehart & Winston
27. Berry, S. S. 1978. *Cocoa, Custom and Socio-economic Change in Rural West Nigeria*. Oxford: Clarendon
28. Bisilliat, J. 1983. The feminine sphere in the institutions of the Songhay-Zarma. See Ref. 168, pp. 99–106

29. Bohannan, L. 1949. Dahomean marriage: a revaluation. *Africa* 19:273–87
30. Bohannan, L., Bohannan, P. 1953. *The Tiv of Central Nigeria.* London: Oxford Univ. Press
31. Bohannan, L., Bohannan, P. 1968. *Tiv Economy,* Evanston, Ill: Northwestern Univ. Press
32. Bohannan, P. 1955. Some principles of exchange and investment among the Tiv. *Am. Anthropol.* 57:60–70
33. Bohannan, P. 1957. *Justice and Judgement among the Tiv.* London: Oxford Univ. Press
34. Bohannan, P., Dalton, G., eds. 1962. *Markets in Africa.* Evanston, Ill: Northwestern Univ. Press
35. Boserup, E. 1970. *Woman's Role in Economic Development.* London: Allen & Unwin
36. Boutillier, J. L. 1964. Les structures foncières en Haute-Volta. *Etudes Voltaiques,* No. 5
37. Deleted in proof
38. Bowen, E. S. 1964. *Return to Laughter.* New York: Doubleday
39. Brokensha, D., Horowitz, M. M., Scudder, T., eds. 1977. *The Anthropology of Rural Development in the Sahel: Proposals for Research.* Binghamton, NY: Inst. Dev. Anthropol.
40. Brown, S. D. 1975. *Ritual Aspects of the Mamprusi Kingship.* Cambridge: Afr. Res. Doc. No. 8, Afr. Stud. Cent.
40a. Burnham, P. 1980. *Opportunity and Constraint in a Savanna Society: The Gbaya of Meiganga, Cameroon.* London: Academic
41. Busia, K. A. 1951. *The Position of the Chief in the Modern Political System of Ashanti.* London: Oxford Univ. Press
42. Cartry, M., ed. 1976. Le sacrifice 1. *Systèmes de pensée en Afrique noire,* Vol. 2
43. Chayanov, A. V. 1966. *The Theory of Peasant Economy.* Homewood, Ill: Irwin
44. Clapham, C. 1976. *Liberia and Sierra Leone: An Essay in Comparative Politics.* Cambridge: Cambridge Univ. Press
45. Clifford, J. 1983. Power and dialogue in ethnography: Marcel Griaule's initiation. In *Observers Observed,* ed. G. W. Stocking, pp. 121–56. Madison: Univ. Wis. Press
46. Clignet, R. 1970. *Many Wives, Many Powers: Authority and Power in Polygynous Families.* Evanston, Ill: Northwestern Univ. Press
47. Cohen, A. 1969. *Custom and Politics in Urban Africa: A Study of Hausa Migrants in Yoruba Towns.* Berkeley: Univ. Calif. Press
48. Cohen, R. 1967. *The Kanuri of Bornu.* New York: Holt, Rinehart & Winston
49. Cohen, R. 1971. *Dominance and Defiance: A Study of Marital Instability in an Islamic African Society.* Washington, DC: Am. Anthropol. Assoc.
50. Cohen, R., Middleton, J. 1970. *From Tribe to Nation in Africa: Studies in Incorporation Processes.* Scranton, Pa: Chandler
51. Comité d'Information Sahel. 1975. *Qui se nourrit de la famine en Afrique? Le dossier politique de la faim au Sahel.* 2 vols. Paris: Maspero
52. Copans, J., ed. 1975. *Sécheresse et famines du Sahel.* 2 vols. Paris: Maspero
53. Copans, J., Couty, P., Roch, J., Rocheteau, G. 1972. *Maintenance sociale et changement économique au Sénégal.* 2 vols. Paris: Travaux et Documents de l'ORSTOM, No. 15
54. Coquery-Vidrovitch, C. 1969. Recherches sur un mode de production africain. *La Pensée* 144:61–78
54a. Crowder, M. 1968. *West Africa Under Colonial Rule.* Evanston, Ill: Northwestern Univ. Press
54b. Cruise O'Brien, D. B. 1971. *The Mourides of Senegal: The Politics and Economics of an Islamic Brotherhood.* London: Oxford Univ. Press
54c. Cruise O'Brien, D. B. 1975. *Saints and Politicians: Essays in the Organization of a Senegalese Peasant Society.* Cambridge: Cambridge Univ. Press
55. Curtin, P. 1969. *The Atlantic Slave Trade: A Census.* Madison: Univ. Wis. Press
56. Curtin, P. 1975. *Economic Change in Precolonial Africa: Senegambia in the Era of the Slave Trade.* Madison: Univ. Wis. Press
57. Dalby, D., Church, R. J. H., eds. 1973. *Drought in Africa.* London: School of Oriental and African Studies
58. Dalby, D., Church, R. J. H., Bezzaz, F., eds. 1977. *Drought in Africa II.* Afr. Environ. Spec. Rep. No. 6. London: Int. Afr. Inst.
59. Derman, W., Derman, L. 1973. *Serfs, Peasants and Socialists: A Former Serf Village in the Republic of Guinea.* Berkeley: Univ. Calif. Press
60. Dieterlen, G. 1951. *Essai sur la religion bambara.* Paris: Presses Univ. France
61. Douglas, M. 1967. Primitive rationing: a study in controlled exchange. In *Themes in Economic Anthropology,* ed. R. Firth, pp. 119–47. London: Tavistock
62. Dozon, J. P. 1977. Economie marchande et structures sociales: le cas de Côte d'Ivoire. *Cah. Etudes Afr.* 17(68):463–83
63. Dumas-Champion, F. 1983. *Les Masa du Tchad: bétail et société.* Paris: Cambridge Univ. Press

64. Dunn, J., ed. 1978. *West African States: Failure and Promise*. Cambridge: Cambridge Univ. Press
65. Dunn, J., Robertson, A. F. 1973. *Dependence and Opportunity: Political Change in Ahafo (Ghana)*. Cambridge: Cambridge Univ. Press
66. Dupire, M. 1960. Planteurs autochtones et étrangers en Basse-Côte d'Ivoire orientale. *Étude Eburnéennes*, No. 8. Abidjan: IFAN
67. Dupire, M. 1962. *Peuls nomades: étude descriptive des Wodaabe du Sahel Nigérien*. Paris: Travaux et Mémoires de l'Institut d'Ethnologie
68. Dupré, G., Rey, P.-P. 1978. Reflections on the relevance of a theory of the history of exchange. See Ref. 195, pp. 171–208
69. Eades, J. S. 1980. *The Yoruba Today*. Cambridge: Cambridge Univ. Press
70. Easton, D. 1959. Political anthropology. *Bien. Rev. Anthropol. 1959*, pp. 210–62
71. Ekwensi, C. 1963. *People of the City*. London: Heinemann
72. Evans-Pritchard, E. E. 1940. *The Nuer*. London: Oxford Univ. Press
73. Evans-Pritchard, E. E. 1951. *Social Anthropology*. London: Cohen & West
74. Evans-Pritchard, E. E., Fortes, M., eds. 1940. *African Political Systems*. London: Oxford Univ. Press
75. Field, M. J. 1963. *Search for Security: An Ethnopsychiatric Study of Rural Ghana*. London: Faber & Faber
76. Forde, C. D. 1934. *Habitat, Economy and Society*. London: Methuen
77. Forde, C. D. 1947. The anthropological approach to social science. *Adv. Sci.* 15: iv
78. Forde, C. D., ed. 1954. *African Worlds*. London: Oxford Univ. Press
79. Forde, C. D., ed. 1956. *Efik Traders of Old Calabar*. London: Oxford Univ. Press
80. Forde, C. D. 1964. *Yakö Studies*. London: Oxford Univ. Press
81. Forde, C. D., Kaberry, P., eds. 1967. *West African Kingdoms of the Nineteenth Century*. London: Oxford Univ. Press
82. Forde, C. D., Scott, R. 1946. *The Native Economies of Nigeria*. London: HMSO
83. Fortes, M. 1945. *The Dynamics of Clanship Among the Tallensi*. London: Oxford Univ. Press
84. Fortes, M. 1949. *The Web of Kinship Among the Tallensi*. London: Oxford Univ. Press
85. Fortes, M. 1970. *Time and Social Structure and Other Essays*. London: Athlone
86. Fortes, M., Dieterlen, G., eds. 1965. *African Systems of Thought*. London: Oxford Univ. Press
87. Frobenius, L. 1898. *Die Masken und Geheimbünde Afrikas*. Halle: Abh. der Kais. Leop.- Carol Deutschen Akad. Naturforsch. nova acta. 74, 1
88. Gallais, J., ed. 1977. *Stratégies pastorales et agricoles des sahéliens durant la sécheresse, 1969–1974*. Bordeaux: Centre d'Etudes de Géographie Tropicale
89. Goody, E. 1973. *Contexts of Kinship*. Cambridge: Cambridge Univ. Press
90. Goody, E. 1978. *Questions and Politeness: Strategies in Social Interaction*. Cambridge: Cambridge Univ. Press
91. Goody, E. 1982. *Parenthood and Social Reproduction: Fostering and Occupational Roles in West Africa*. Cambridge: Cambridge Univ. Press
92. Goody, E., ed. 1982. *From Craft to Industry*. Cambridge: Cambridge Univ. Press
93. Goody, E., Goody, J. R. 1967. The circulation of women and children in northern Ghana. *Man* 2(2):227–48
94. Goody, J. R. 1956. A comparative approach to incest and adultery. *Br. J. Sociol.* 7:286–305
95. Goody, J. R. 1956. *The Social Organization of the LoWiili*. London: HMSO
96. Goody, J. R. 1957. Fields of social control among the LoDagaba. *J. R. Anthropol. Inst.* 87:75–104
97. Goody, J. R., ed. 1958. *The Developmental Cycle in Domestic Groups*. Cambridge: Cambridge Univ. Press
98. Goody, J. R. 1961. The mother's brother and the sister's son in West Africa. *J. R. Anthropol. Inst.* 89:61–88
99. Goody, J. R. 1962. *Death, Property and the Ancestors: A Study of the Mortuary Customs of the Lodagaa of West Africa*. London: Tavistock
100. Goody, J. R., ed. 1966. *Succession to High Office*. Cambridge: Cambridge Univ. Press
101. Goody, J. R. 1967. The over-kingdom of Gonja. See Ref. 81, pp. 179–205
102. Goody, J. R. 1971. *Technology, Tradition and the State in Africa*. London: Oxford Univ. Press
103. Goody, J. R., ed. 1975. *Changing Social Structure in Ghana*. London: Int. Afr. Inst.
104. Goody, J. R. 1976. *Production and Reproduction: A Comparative Study of the Domestic Domain*. Cambridge: Cambridge Univ. Press
105. Goody, J. R. 1982. *Cooking, Cuisine and Class: A Study in Comparative Sociology*. Cambridge: Cambridge Univ. Press
105a. Goody, J. R. 1983. *The Development of the Family and Marriage in Europe*. Cambridge: Cambridge Univ. Press

106. Green, M. M. 1964. *Igbo Village Affairs.* London: Cass
107. Griaule, M. 1948. *Dieu d'eau: entretiens avec Ogotemmeli.* Transl. 1965, *Conversations with Ogotemmêli.* London: Oxford Univ. Press
108. Griaule, M., Dieterlen, G. 1965. *Le renard pale,* Tome 1. Paris: Inst. Ethnol.
108a. Gugler, J., Flanagan, W. 1978. *Urbanization and Social Change in West Africa.* Cambridge: Cambridge Univ. Press
109. Gutkind, P. C. W., Wallerstein, I., eds. 1976. *The Political Economy of Contemporary Africa.* Beverly Hills: Sage
110. Guyer, J. 1980. Food, cocoa and the division of labor by sex in two West African societies. *Comp. Stud. Soc. Hist.* 22:355–73
111. Hart, J. K. 1973. Informal income opportunities and urban employment in Ghana. *J. Mod. Afr. Stud.* 11(3):61–89
112. Hart, J. K. 1978. The economic basis of Tallensi social history in the early twentieth century. *Econ. Anthropol.* 1:185–216
113. Hart, J. K. 1982. *The Political Economy of West African Agriculture.* Cambridge: Cambridge Univ. Press
114. Hart, J. K. 1983. The contribution of Marxism to economic anthropology. In *Economic anthropology: Topics and Theories,* ed. S. Ortiz, pp. 105–44. Lanham, Md: Univ. Press of Am.
115. Herskovits, M. J. 1938. *Dahomey: An Ancient West African Kingdom,* 2 vols. Evanston: Northwestern Univ. Press
116. Heyer, J., Roberts, P., Williams, G., eds. 1981. *Rural Development in Tropical Africa.* London: Macmillan
117. Hill, P. 1963. *Migrant Cocoa Farmers of Southern Ghana.* Cambridge: Cambridge Univ. Press
118. Hill, P. 1972. *Rural Hausa.* Cambridge: Cambridge Univ. Press
119. Hopkins, A. G. 1973. *An Economic History of West Africa.* London: Longman
120. Horowitz, M. M. 1979. *The sociology of pastoralism and African livestock projects.* Washington, DC: AID program evaluation discussion paper No. 6
121. Horton, R. 1967. African traditional thought and Western science. *Africa* 37:50–71, 155–87
122. Horton, R. 1976. Stateless societies in the history of West Africa. See Ref. 6, pp. 72–113
123. Izard, M. 1965. *Traditions historiques des villages du Yatenga. 1. Cercle de Gourcy.* Paris: CNRS
124. Jackson, M. 1977. *The Kuranko: Dimensions of Social Reality in a West African Tribe.* London: Hurst
125. Jones, G. I. 1963. *The Trading States of the Oil Rivers.* London: Oxford Univ. Press
126. Kaberry, P. 1952. *Women of the Grassfields: A Study of the Economic Position of Women in Bamenda, British Cameroons.* London: Colonial Off. Res. Publ. No. 14
127. Klein, A. N. 1981. The two Asantes: competing interpretations of 'slavery' in Akan-Asante culture and society. In *The Ideology of Slavery in Africa,* ed. P. Lovejoy. Beverly Hills: Sage
128. Klein, M., ed. 1980. *Peasants in Africa: Historical and Contemporary Perspectives.* Beverly Hills: Sage
129. Kuper, H., ed. 1965. *Urbanization and Migration in West Africa.* Berkeley: Univ. Calif. Press
130. Labouret, H. 1941. *Paysans d'Afrique Occidentale.* Paris: Gallimard
131. Ladouceur, P. A. 1979. *Chiefs and Politicians: The Politics of Regionalism in Northern Ghana.* London: Longman
132. Lanternari, V. 1967. *Occidente e terzo mondo: incontri di civilita e religioni differenti.* Bari: Depalo
133. Last, D. M. 1967. *The Sokoto Caliphate.* London: Longman
134. Le Bris, E., Rey, P.-P., Samuel, M. 1976. *Capitalisme négrier: la marche des paysans vers le prolétariat.* Paris: Maspero
135. Leith-Ross, S. 1965. *African Women.* London: Routledge & Kegan Paul
136. Levtzion, N. 1976. The early states of the Western Sudan to 1500. See Ref. 6, pp. 114–51
137. Liebenow, G. 1969. *Liberia: The Evolution of Privilege.* Ithaca: Cornell Univ. Press
138. Little, K. L. 1951. *The Mende of Sierra Leone: A West African People in Transition.* London: Routledge & Kegan Paul
139. Little, K. L. 1970. *West African Urbanization: A Study of Voluntary Associations in Social Change.* Cambridge: Cambridge Univ. Press
140. Little, K. L. 1973. *African Women in Towns: An Aspect of Africa's Social Revolution.* Cambridge: Cambridge Univ. Press
141. Lloyd, P. C. 1962. *Yoruba Land Law.* Ibadan: Oxford Univ. Press
142. Lloyd, P. C. 1967. *Africa in Social Change.* Harmondsworth: Penguin
143. Lloyd, P. C. 1974. *Power and Independence: Urban Africans' Perceptions of Social Inequality.* London: Routledge & Kegan Paul
144. Lloyd, P. C. 1979. *Slums of Hope? Shanty Towns of the Third World.* Harmondsworth: Penguin
145. Lovejoy, P. E. 1983. *Transformations in*

Slavery, Cambridge: Cambridge Univ. Press
146. McCaskie, T. C. 1981. State and society, marriage and adultery: Some considerations towards a social history of precolonial Asante. *J. Afr. Hist.* 22:477–94
147. McCaskie, T. C. 1983. Accumulation, wealth and belief in Asante history. I. To the close of the nineteenth century. *Africa* 53(1):23–43
148. McCormack, C. P. 1972. Mende and Sherbro women in high office. *Can. J. Afr. Stud.* 6(2):151–64
149. McPhee, A. 1971. *The Economic Revolution in British West Africa*. London: Cass. 2nd ed.
150. Mauny, R. 1961. *Tableau géographique de l'ouest africain au moyen age*. Dakar: IFAN
151. Meillassoux, C. 1964. *Anthropologie économique des Gouro de Côte d'Ivoire*. Paris: Mouton
152. Meillassoux, C. 1975. *Femmes, greniers et capitaux*. Paris: Maspero. Transl. *Maidens, Meal and Money*. Cambridge: Cambridge Univ. Press
153. Meillassoux, C., ed. 1971. *The Development of Indigenous Trade and Markets in West Africa*. London: Oxford Univ. Press
154. Meillassoux, C., ed. 1975. *L'esclavage en Afrique précoloniale*. Paris: Maspero
155. Miers, S., Kopytoff, I., eds. 1977. *Slavery in Africa: Historical and Anthropological Perspectives*. Madison: Univ. Wis. Press
156. Miner, H. 1953. *The Primitive City of Timbuctoo*. Garden city, NY: Doubleday
157. Miner, H., ed. 1967. *The City in Modern Africa*. London: Pall Mall
158. Morton-Williams, P. 1967. The Yoruba kingdom of Oyo. See Ref. 81, pp. 36–39
159. Nadel, S. F. 1942. *A Black Byzantium*. London: Oxford Univ. Press
160. Nadel, S. F. 1967. *The Theory of Social Structure*. London: Oxford Univ. Press
161. Netting, R. McC. 1968. *Hill Farmers of Nigeria: Cultural Ecology of the Kofyar of the Jos Plateau*. Seattle: Univ. Wash. Press
162. Netting, R. McC., Cleveland, D., Stier, F. 1978. *The Conditions of Agricultural Intensification in the West African Savannah*. Abidjan: AID
163. Nicolas, G. 1971. Processus du resistance au 'développement' au sein d'une société africaine (Vallée de Maradi, Niger). *Civilisations* 21(1):45–66
164. Nicolas, G., Doumesche, H., Mouche, M. 1968. Etude socioéconomique de deux villages haussa: enquête en vue d'un aménagement hydro-agricole, Vallée de Maradi, Niger. *Etudes Nigériennes* 22. Niamey: CNRSH
165. Obiechina, E. N. 1975. *Culture, Tradition and Society in the West African Novel*. Cambridge: Cambridge Univ. Press
166. O'Laughlin, B. 1975. Marxist approaches in anthropology. *Ann. Rev. Anthropol.* 4:341–70
167. Oppong, C. 1974. *Marriage Among a Matrilineal Elite*. Cambridge: Cambridge Univ. Press
168. Oppong, C., ed. 1983. *Female and Male in West Africa*. London: Allen & Unwin
169. Owusu, M. P. 1970. *Uses and Abuses of Political Power—A Case Study of Continuity and Change in the Politics of Ghana*. Chicago: Univ. Chicago Press
170. Paden, J. 1973. *Religion and Political Culture in Kano*. Berkeley: Univ. Calif. Press
171. Paulme, D., ed. 1963. *Women of Tropical Africa*. Berkeley: Univ. Calif. Press
171a. Peace, A. J. 1979. *Choice, Class and Conflict: A Study of Southern Nigerian Factory Workers*. Brighton: Harvester
171b. Peel, J. D. Y. 1968. *Aladura: A Religious Movement Among the Yoruba*. London: Routledge
172. Peel, J. D. Y. 1984. *Ijeshas and Nigerians: The Incorporation of a Yoruba Kingdom, 1890s to 1970s*. Cambridge: Cambridge Univ. Press
173. Pélissier, P. 1966. *Les paysans du Sénégal: les civilisations agraires du Cayor au Casamance*. St. Yriex (Haute Vienne): Imprimerie Fabrègue
174. Pellow, D. 1977. *Women in Accra: Options for Autonomy*. Algonac, Mich: Reference Publ.
175. Perrot, C.-H. 1982. *Les Anyi-Ndenye et le pouvoir aux 18e et 19e siècles*. Paris: Ceda-Abidjan
176. Person, Y. 1970–71. *Samori: une revolution dyula*. 3 vols. Dakar: IFAN
177. Polanyi, K. 1966. *Dahomey and the Slave Trade*. Seattle: Univ. Wash. Press
178. Pollet, E., Winter, G. 1978. The social organization of agricultural labour among the Soninke (Dyahunu, Mali). See Ref. 195, pp. 331–56
179. Radcliffe-Brown, A. R. 1952. *Structure and Function in Primitive Society*. London: Cohen & West
180. Radcliffe-Brown, A. R., Forde, C. D., eds. 1950. *African Systems of Kinship and Marriage*. London: Oxford Univ. Press
181. Raynaut, C. 1972. *Structures normatives et relations electives: étude d'une communauté villageoise haoussa (Niger)*. Paris: Mouton
182. Raynaut, C. 1976. Transformation du système de production et inégalité économique: le cas d'un village haoussa

(Niger). *Can. J. Afr. Stud.* 10(2):279–306
183. Reboul, C. 1973. Structures agraires et problèmes du développement au Sénégal: les unités expérimentales du Siné-Saloum. *Tiers Monde* 54:403–16
184. Review of African Political Economy. 1984. Capital vs. Labour in West Africa. ROAPE No. 31
185. Rey, P.-P. 1971. *Colonialisme, néocolonialisme et transition au capitalisme: exemple de la Camilog au Congo-Brazzaville.* Paris: Maspero
186. Rey, P.-P. 1973. *Les alliances des classes.* Paris: Maspero
187. Riesman, P. 1977. *Freedom in Fulani Social Life: An Introspective Ethnography.* Chicago: Univ. Chicago Press
188. Rimmer, D. 1984. *The Economies of West Africa.* London: Weidenfeld & Nicholson
189. Roberts, P. 1979. The integration of women into the development process. *Inst. Dev. Stud. (Sussex) Bull.* 10:60
190. Robertson, C. 1974. Economic women in Africa: Profit-making techniques of Accra market women. *J. Mod. Afr. Stud.* 12:657–64
191. Ruel, M. 1969. *Leopards and Leaders: Constitutional Politics Among a Cross River People.* London: Tavistock
192. Schildkrout, E. 1978. *People of the Zongo.* Cambridge: Cambridge Univ. Press
193. Schwab, W. B. 1965. Oshogbo: An urban community? See Ref. 129, pp. 85–109
194. Scott, E., ed. 1984. *Life Before the Drought.* Boston: Allen & Unwin
195. Seddon, D., ed. 1978. *Relations of Production.* London: Cass
196. Senghor, L. S. 1970. *Négritude et humanisme gréco-latin.* Dakar: Ministère de la culture et de l'information
197. Skinner, E. P. 1964. *The Mossi of the Upper Volta: The Political Development of a Sudanese People.* Stanford: Stanford Univ. Press
198. Smith, M. F. 1963. *Baba of Karo: A Woman of the Moslem Hausa.* New York: Praeger
199. Smith, M. G. 1955. *The Economy of the Hausa Communities of Zaria.* London: HMSO
200. Smith, M. G. 1956. On segmentary lineage systems. *J. R. Anthropol. Soc.* 2:39–80
201. Smith, M. G. 1960. *Government in Zazzau, 1881–1950.* London: Oxford Univ. Press
202. Smith, M. G. 1974. *Corporations and Society.* London: Duckworth
203. Smith, M. G. 1978. *The Affairs of Daura: History and Change in a Hausa State, 1800–1958.* Berkeley: Univ. Calif. Press
204. Southall, A. W., ed. 1960. *Social Change in Modern Africa.* London: Oxford Univ. Press
205. Soyinka, W. 1973. *Collected Plays,* Vol. 1. London: Oxford Univ. Press
206. Soyinka, W. 1974. *Collected Plays,* Vol. 2. London: Oxford Univ. Press
207. Staniland, M. 1975. *The Lions of Dagbon: Political Change in Northern Ghana.* Cambridge: Cambridge Univ. Press
208. Stenning, D. J. 1958. Household viability among the pastoral Fulani. See Ref. 103, pp. 92–119
209. Stenning, D. J. 1959. *Savannah Nomads. A Study of the Wodaabe Pastoral Fulani of Western Bornu Province, Northern Nigeria.* London: Oxford Univ. Press
210. Sudarkasa, N. 1973. *Where Women Work: A Study of Yoruba Women in the Market Place and in the Home.* Ann Arbor, Mich: Museum Pap. No. 53
210a. Suret-Canale, J. 1971. *French Colonialism in Tropical Africa, 1900–1945.* London: Hurst
210b. Suret-Canale, J. 1972. *Afrique noire occidentale et centrale (1945–1960): crise du système colonial et capitalisme monopoliste d'état.* Paris: Editions sociales
211. Swift, J. 1977. Sahelian pastoralists: underdevelopment, desertification and famine. *Ann. Rev. Anthropol.* 6:457–78
212. Tardits, C. 1980. *Le royaume Bamoum.* Paris: Edisem
213. Terray, E. 1969. *L'organisation sociale des Dida de Côte d'Ivoire.* Dijon: Darantière
214. Terray, E. 1972. *Marxism and Primitive Societies.* New York: Monthly Review Press
215. Terray, E. 1974. Long-distance exchange and the formation of the state: The case of the Abron kingdom of Gyaman. *Econ. Soc.* 3(3):315–45
216. Terray, E. 1976. Classes and class consciousness in the Abron kingdom of Gyaman. In *Marxist Analyses and Social Anthropology,* ed. M. Bloch, pp. 85–135. New York: Wiley
217. Thomson, D. W. 1966. *On Growth and Form.* Cambridge: Cambridge Univ. Press
218. Tutuola, A. 1964. *My Life in the Bush of Ghosts.* London: Faber & Faber
219. Uchendu, V. C. 1965. *The Igbo of Southest Nigeria.* New York: Holt, Rinehart & Winston
220. Verdon, M. 1983. *The Abutia Ewe of West Africa—The Chiefdom that Never Was.* Berlin: Mouton

221. Vidal, C. 1977. Guerre des sexes à Abidjan: masculin, fémenin, CFA. *Cah. Etudes Afr.* 17(1):121–53
222. Watts, M. 1983. *Silent Violence: Food Famine and Peasantry in Northern Nigeria.* Berkeley: Univ. Calif. Press
223. Werbner, R. P. 1984. The Manchester school in South-Central Africa. *Ann. Rev. Anthropol.* 13:157–85
224. Wheatley, P. 1974. *The Pivot of the Four Quarters: A Preliminary Enquiry into the Origins and Character of the Ancient Chinese City.* Edinburgh: Univ. Edinburgh Press
225. Wilks, I. 1961. *The Northern Factor in Ashanti History.* Legon: Univ. Ghana Inst. Afr. Stud.
226. Wilks, I. 1975. *Asante in the Nineteenth Century.* Cambridge: Cambridge Univ. Press

ISSUES IN DIVINE KINGSHIP

Gillian Feeley-Harnik

Department of Anthropology, Johns Hopkins University, Baltimore, MD 21218

INTRODUCTION: THE DYING GOD

> I'm member and preacher to that church where the blind don't see and the lame don't walk and what's dead stays that way.
>
> Flannery O'Connor, *Wise Blood*

Most of the literature on divine kingship published since Frazer's first edition of *The Golden Bough* appeared in 1890 has been written from the point of view of Flannery O'Connor's preacher, Hazel Motes, and with the same results: what's meant to stay dead doesn't.

Frazer's immediate problem was the classical rule of succession whereby the priest of Diana's sacred grove at Nemi in southern Italy had to murder his predecessor and be murdered in turn. Frazer's broader questions concerned the relationship of murder to sacrifice: why should killing be required to sustain life, why should human sacrifice be so widespread, why, ultimately, did Jesus Christ have to be crucified to assure his followers of eternal salvation. His answer was to posit the existence, on a global scale, of a magico-religious (later these were sequential) stage of development characterized by a philosophy equating human life with the life of nature. The sacrifice of innumerable sorts of persons and things in whom that connection was embodied, archetypically "divine kings," was a way of regulating otherwise uncontrollable growth and decay in nature.

To Frazer, these ideas "savor(ed) of a barbarous age . . . (they were) like a primaeval rock rising from a smooth-shaven lawn" (56, 1(1):10). He argued that Europeans, now in the stage of science, had outgrown them, but as Hyman (78) pointed out and as Wood (168) has recently reiterated, the effect of *The Golden Bough* is profoundly equivocal. *The Golden Bough* was intended to shed light on the savage thoughts that compel people to kill in order to prosper. Owing to Frazer's own ambivalence about the course of human history, which deepened with the first world war (78, p. 246), the result of his argument is to reinforce the reader's awareness of the persistence of the "dark crimson stain" on the "web of thought" (56, 7(2):308).

Divine kingship is first and foremost the principal metaphor through which Frazer expressed his understanding of the irrationality and violence underlying the smooth surface of Christian ideals of progress in Victorian and Edwardian England. If the concept has any categorical integrity, it lies in this point, which vanished as Frazer himself removed his discussion of Christ's crucifixion from the body of the second edition of 1900 (56, 3:86–96) to the footnotes of the third of 1913–15 (56, 6:412–23), which he dropped from the abridged edition of 1922.

At the same time, classicists, historians, and anthropologists moved the problem from contemporary Europe to the ancient and primitive worlds, where the types multiplied in the past even as they vanished in the presence of colonial rule. Evans-Pritchard echoes Frazer's evaluation of the evidence in the preface to the abridged edition (56, p. vi) by concluding in his Frazer Lecture of 1948 on the African Shilluk case that "kingship everywhere and at all times has been in some degree a sacred office. *Rex est mixta persona cum sacerdote*" (44, p. 210). The very different approaches of Hocart (75), Needham (113; also 75, pp. xiii-xcix), Claessen & Skalnik (28a), Girard (62a), and Paul (116a) testify to the continuing vitality of the universalist perspective. But in 1922, Africa was already, as Frazer added, the source of "the most numerous and most similar cases" (to the Nemi priesthood) and the only ones still extant, leading Frazer to speculate on the influence of Africa, possibly migrant Africans, on southern Europe (56, p. vi).

The connection between these historical developments needs to be emphasized. Western scholars devised their ideas about power and prosperity in African polities as they were in the process of incorporating them, often forcibly, into their own. Fortes & Evans-Pritchard (55, p. 16) make it clear that the main issue in divine kingship, however narrowly or broadly it might be defined, was indigenous conceptions of power, legitimacy, and prosperity in which Europeans did not share. If the first lesson to be learned from the African data on divine kingship is, to generalize from Richards's summary of the Bemba case, that "there is no single divine ruler . . . but a divine king, divine princes with some supernatural powers, and secular chiefs, some with pretentions to ritual functions . . . call them gods, demi-gods, gods postulant or on probation and non-gods" (135, p. 26), then we must analyze these conceptions of power and prosperity in the context of changing social-cultural circumstances that include ourselves as aspirants as well as theorists.

This review attempts to combine particularist and comparative approaches to the literature on divine kingship by focusing on the way in which anthropologists and historians have used Frazer's metaphor of divine kingship attributed to exotic peoples, principally Africans, to explore questions about rationality and legitimacy in government, epitomized in the transformation of murder for personal gain into sacrifice for the common good, recognizing that the problem itself has roots in European relations with the Third World. I have organized the data around three main themes, which coincide with the "three functions" that Dumézil (e.g. 40) found at the root of Indo-European ideas about kingship: administration of the sacred, force, and prosperity. Dumézil did not include the *Śūdras,* or fourth caste obliged to serve the other three, in his tripartition, so (apart from some references) I have chosen to discuss force last and in two parts: the king's many bodies and regicide and revolution.[1]

ADMINISTRATION OF THE SACRED: THE KINGSHIP CAPTURES THE KING

Frazer's deeply equivocal picture of a divine king—an absolute ruler absolutely at the mercy of those who would kill him when his powers began to wane—is, as Frazer himself indicated, but less clearly with every edition, rooted in Christian imagery. As the Christian roots were removed, so the problem was trimmed down to size in the field by shifting from beliefs, requiring the interpretation of meaning, to the scientific analysis of behavior, resulting in an increasingly secularized picture of a divine king as a person/office who is more the casual by-product of social structural forces than a mystical being in his own right. Hocart (75, pp. 11–27) is a good example of this scientizing trend because his universalist perspective and emphasis on the priority of ideas are otherwise so unusual for the time.

Frazer himself recognized the need to ground his theories in scientifically collected facts and therefore attached himself to fieldworkers like Roscoe and Seligman, Meek, Palmer, and Talbot, who eventually provided him with his first living examples of divine kingship (56, 3:14–46; see 78, pp. 196–97, 203–4; 152). Nevertheless, Frazer soon became an embarrassment because most of his other evidence was as literary as his mode of explanation. Furthermore, regicide was so difficult to verify (170), and finally there were too many sorts of kings. Even as Seligman (141, pp. 5–7), in his Frazer Lecture of 1933, sought to specify what Frazer meant by "divine kings" in order to make his case for the Hamitic hypothesis, other anthropologists emphasized the variety of living examples. The first fieldwork on divine kingship, including that of Roscoe on the interlacustrine kingdoms of East Africa, Rattray on the Ashanti, Meek on the Jukun, Mair on Buganda, Richards on the Bemba, Kuper and Marwick on the Swazi, the Wilsons on the Nyakyusa and Ngonde,

---

[1]Given my definition of the problem, this review is restricted to African and some Southeast Asian, Polynesian, and European cases. Even so, the relevant literature is enormous; I discuss only a small portion of it here.

Evans-Pritchard on the Anuak, Nadel on the Nupe, and the Kriges on the Lovedu, ranging in publication from 1911 to 1943, called into question the absoluteness of divine kingship in conceptual, sociological, and historical terms. There is no absolute sovereign: "the king's power and authority are composite . . . their various components are lodged in different offices" (55, p. 11). African monarchies are therefore unstable and prone to civil war. They came into being only a few hundred years ago, owing to outside influences, and they are currently on their way out for the same reason.

The focus shifts in this period from the king and his royal prerogatives to his administration and the structural instability of African monarchies. The purest example of this shift—in icily objective style as well as in substance—is Evans-Pritchard's famous essay, The Frazer Lecture of 1948, on "The Divine Kingship of the Shilluk of the Nilotic Sudan," in which regicide, the core of Frazer's argument, is finally demolished as well. Shilluk have enough "moral density" to produce a common symbol, but not enough to stop quarreling about it. So they affirm their common interest in kingship "at the expense of the king's person." "Dogma" and "social facts" are not merely separate; they are, in the case of kingship, opposed. Regicide resolves the opposition because it is "the kingship and not the king who is divine," and then only in the sense that it transcends, from a purely social structural point of view, divisions among lineages (44, p. 211). Seligman (141) had made regicide the essential criterion of divine kingship. By doubting regicide and focusing on social structure, Evans-Pritchard moved the question of regicide from the vulnerability of persons to the frailty of African polities, and it stayed there for the next two decades.

The force of his argument can be measured not only in the echoes of innumerable successors, but in the dearth of subsequent research on regicide. Young (170) rebuts Evans-Pritchard's arguments on the grounds that he dismisses regicide too easily, that his social structural arguments do not apply to the Jukun case, and that he does not take Jukun beliefs into account. But Young does not put regicide at the center of divine kingship, as Frazer and Seligman did. He simply reiterates Fortes and Evans-Pritchard's (55, p. 16) description of the African monarch "at the apex of the state's structure, the permanent symbol of its unity and continuity, the embodiment of the culture's values and the guarantor of the society's prosperity" (170, p. 146).

Without regicide to reconcile the contradictions, scholars concentrated on either belief (e.g. 24, 52) or behavior, primarily the latter (e.g. 100). Their focus on social structural solutions to political instability was related to European preoccupations about the power of appointment to centralize colonial states. To paraphrase Evans-Pritchard, bureaucracy not kingship is transcendent in these studies. The personal sacrifice of the individual caught between his obligations to kin and country, which was an important theme (e.g. 26, 45), is the last whimper of regicide in a context in which African kings were being turned into European king's men.

Eventually, in the 1950s and early 1960s, the work drew attention to cases like Buganda, Asante, and the Nigerian emirates in which precolonial rulers had already begun to strengthen their positions through enslavement, bureaucratization, and militarization. These processes of acquiring power were typically expressed in metaphors about eating wealth, including humans, like food. [This idiom occurs much more widely, which accounts for its general use in Hocart's (75) analysis of the origins of government and Fortes's (54, pp. 18–19) analysis of installation rites.] But instead of investigating indigenous philosophies about power, wealth, and bureaucracy, scholars interpreted these processes in evolutionary terms, in which monarchy was simply a transitional form between acephalous polities and nation-states and force "the final arbiter . . . the fountainhead of power" (64, p. 25; see 65).

The study of Buganda by Fallers et al (46) is a good example of the limitations of social structural analysis in explaining even the role of force in a case where "civicide" not regicide seems to have been a critical factor (see Richards's essay in 46, p. 291, n. 46). In contrast to the emphasis on the weakness of descent-based monarchies, the *Kabaka*'s power is portrayed in such absolute terms that it is difficult to understand how Baganda learned "the art of being ruled" (Richards in 46, p. 273) well enough to account for either their famed social mobility or their adroit handling of the British administration [compare Albert's sociolinguistic analysis of rank and power in Burundi (4)]. Indigenous conceptions of power are not taken into account, except as concerns obedience. Fallers (46, p. 6) notes "the cultural tissue of arbitrary fierceness and power" woven around the body of the *Kabaka,* but killing is analyzed as a natural act in a brigand state, making it difficult to explain the connections between the role of violence in precolonial Buganda and more recent Ugandan politics, to which Mazrui (108) in particular has drawn attention [compare Weinstein (159) and Kuper (94) on the changing role of the military in Rwanda and Swaziland].

Walter (157, pp. 270–75) argues that Buganda was moving away from violent (but not despotic) rule in the late 19th century because the *Kabaka*'s power of appointment enabled him to suppress resistance without brutality. He wonders whether this transition was the result of indigenous factors, Gandan comparisons between Buganda and the Zulu state, or whether it was inspired by Islamic or Christian religious attitudes. Ray (127–129) examines indigenous conceptions of power and force in relation to royal funeral rituals and tombs. But, like other analysts of Buganda, he insists that the secular politics of the living were always separate from the sacred rituals involving the dead, so the connection between beliefs and actions involving violence has yet to be made. [In contrast, Pemberton (121) interprets the ritual violence of the Ogun festival in the Yoruba town of Ila-Orangun in relation to its political significance as acknowledging human violence while affirming the power of the king, and thereby society, to contain and transcend it; but see Peel (119, p. 47) and compare Girard (62a) and Muller (in 28a, pp. 239–50).]

The work of Fortes (53, 54), Richards (133–135), and Beidelman (16) in the 1960s on ritual and office marks the beginning of the reintegration of beliefs and social relations in the context of a broader comparative perspective that characterizes the best recent work on the "administration of the sacred." Even as social structuralists were emphasizing the secularization of power through bureaucratization, Fortes was asking the opposite question: why should secular processes be ritualized, a problem that Van Gennep's argument about rites of passage from profane to sacred statuses did not explain. Fortes (53, 54) argues that the individual is more complex than the office and needs to be socialized through ritual to assume the role and abide by its rules or be taken from it. Conversely, ritual is required to represent the office as a legitimate social entity that endures beyond the life of any one tenant.

Frazer's work inspired Fortes to expand his comparative perspective in *Oedipus and Job in West African Religion* (1959). In (53, p. 88) he refers to the potential value of Kantorowicz's (80) historical study of English political theology, *The King's Two Bodies*, recommended to him by Roman Jakobson. Kantorowicz's work on kingship in Tudor and Stuart England is, as Hocart (75, pp. 37–40) pointed out about the work of Marc Bloch (18a) on the healing powers of French and English kings, one of the few analyses of European monarchy to take beliefs seriously. Kantorowicz, arguing against Maitland (103), explains the legal fiction of "the king's two bodies" as the jurists' way of reconciling the contradictions between person and office in English kingship. The concept of "twin-born majesty," first derived from Christian symbolism, combined the king's natural body with the body politic. It served to harmonize ancient with contemporary law, personal with impersonal concepts of rule, and to provide continuity to government because "the king (in his corporate form) never dies."

Giesey (61), Kantorowicz's student, analyzes the development of embalming, effigies, processionals, and other features of French Renaissance royal funerals as means of prolonging power beyond the death of the king. The royal effigy, introduced "almost indirectly" (61, p. 143), eventually became the central focus of the ceremonial, and an important part of Giesey's argument has to do with the integration of structural and historical modes of analysis. Walzer (158) relies on Kantorowicz (80) to argue that the execution of the public person of the king as embodiment of the state, in contrast to the assassination of his private person, marked the end of monarchy first in England (when Charles I was executed in 1649) and then, in a second revolution modeled on the first, in France (when Louis XVI, forced first to abdicate, was executed as citizen Louis

Capet in 1793). As Saint-Just wrote in 1792, "The monarch [under the new constitution] does not reign, whatever be the sense of that word, he governs. . . . ." (cited in 158, p. 124; see 44, p. 200; 44a). Starkey (148) has applied Kantorowicz's insights in analyzing the changing role of the Lords of the Privey Chamber as symbols and stand-ins for the royal body in Tudor and Stuart England.

Fortes, in (54, p. 5; see p. 19, n. 1), draws attention to "that neglected pioneer A. M. Hocart," arguing that his analysis of installation rites is nothing more than a confirmation of what Hocart said in *Kingship*. Actually, Fortes disagrees with Hocart about the striking similarities among installation rites worldwide. He sees them as deriving from the social structural limitations of the situation, not from a common historical source, which was Hocart's argument. Furthermore, whereas Fortes (53, 54) analyzes the role of ritual in the mutual commitment of the individual and society, Hocart (74, 75) focuses on the ritual transformation of a person into a thing, the embodiment of an idea. As he puts it concerning the office of king: "Man *is* not a microcosm; he has to be *made* one in order that he may control the universe for prosperity. The ritual establishes an equivalence that was not there" (75, p. 69, his emphasis). In contrast to Fortes, his interpretation of the data on Tudor and Stuart kingship echoes the "table talk" of the best known historian (and lawyer) of that time, John Selden: "A king is a thing men have made for their own sakes, for quietness' sake. Just as in a family one man is appointed to buy the meat" (published posthumously in 1689; cited in Walzer 158, p. 16; compare Shakespeare in Hamlet IV, ii). Hocart says concerning interregna:

> To understand how a dead man can reign we have to go back to our principles of ritual. We insisted again and again that the principle need not be a man, or even a living being: it may be a stone, an image, the corpse of a whale; it may even be, as with our philosophers, an Idea (75, p. 135).

These different viewpoints are combined in the work of Richards (133–135) and Beidelman (16). Richards asks how to preserve charters of royal office in societies without written records (133); how to solve "the problems of centralization in a pedestrian state," given the proliferation of royal relatives (134); how to keep the king divine when he is really human (135). The solutions to these problems are always found in human beings who embody knowledge about royal history and traditions in themselves and in their relations with one another such that banning rituals is like burning books [a point that Richards made in 1939 about the royal tree-cutting ceremonies central to Bemba politico-religious economy (131)].

Beidelman's (16) essay on Swazi royal ritual is in part a response to Gluckman's (63, the Frazer Lecture of 1952) earlier analysis of the *ncwala* as a "ritual of rebellion" allowing for the open expression of social conflict and therefore strengthening kingship not weakening it. Beidelman argues that in taking a narrow focus on social structure and neglecting indigenous beliefs, Gluckman has misread the nature of the ceremony. Though Beidelman does not begin with the same question, his approach is like that of Richards in focusing on how to keep the king divine. Using Kuper's rich ethnography and other material on the Swazi (and Zulu), Beidelman analyzes the relationship of Swazi ideas about power embodied in the king to the complexities and contradictions of social life in which the king must participate and yet transcend as a political actor. An important part of the analysis concerns Swazi conceptions of force and the control of force at the heart of political legitimacy.

Richards and Beidelman are dealing with the same kinds of issues as their predecessors, but in terms that are at once more general than the culture-bound categories of "office," "bureaucracy," "modernization," and "state," and more particular in being grounded ethnographically in ways that lend themselves to historical rather than simply evolutionary or developmental analysis. They do this by analyzing the transformation of a person into a king as the creation of a "stranger." The process of estrangement is more relevant to the context of kinship in which the transformation takes place. It also draws attention to the discontinuity between kinship and kingship, despite the common hereditary principle. And it provides for consideration within the same framework of other kinds of strangers who serve to "fatten" the body of the king and widen the conceptual and social gap between kinship and kingship even as they expand the scale of the polity, e.g. slaves, soldiers, Europeans, traders, and so on. [See Feierman (51) and Fairley's and Kenny's essays in (11), which analyze the conceptual and social formation of the "stranger-king" in some East-Central African monarchies; and Feeley-Harnik (48), who examines the role of royal slaves as strangers in transforming kin into subjects of monarchy among the Sakalava of northwestern Madagascar.]

In addition, Richards and Beidelman show a strong sensitivity to material factors. Their work could be described as the perfect endpoint of the whole trend of secularization that began with the earliest field studies, in which the concept of divine kingship is finally reduced to its material essentials. But it is here in the raw ingredients that the turnabout lies. If Maitland's (103) point was that the English are too sensible to believe anything as silly as "the king's two bodies," then Richards and Beidelman assert the exact opposite: it is the fleshly medium that makes these "fictions" powerful. In this sense, their arguments also differ from those of Fortes and Kantorowicz in important respects. Where the latter focused on the role of ritual in transforming persons into offices, with the emphasis on the office, Richards and Beidelman (like Frazer in his theory of regicide) analyze the transformation of a person into a "stranger," never forgetting his humanity in indigenous terms.

Instead of conclusions about the secular nature of power, they provide insights into culturally specific ways in which abstractions are created out of homely materials; how "impersonal" (divine, transcendent, bureaucratic) creatures are created out of intensely human beings; how strangers are created out of kin. Their focus on the processes by which people make one another into things that are both more and less than persons helps to explain sociologically the transformation of persons into ideas, which was Hocart's point in 1936, and which is the foundation of current theory concerning the social construction of knowledge about such issues as power, leadership, citizenship, slavery, and prosperity in historical context. Their insights have been followed up in a variety of ways. For the moment we will concentrate on the *ncwala* rites.

The complex *ncwala* rites have continued to attract scholars working from a variety of theoretical perspectives. Kuper's earlier analyses identified the *ncwala* with the body of the king. The *ncwala* grew as he matured and took more extensive control of the kingdom. The rites reinforced kingship and dramatized currently important relations of rank. Kuper expands on these themes in recent work. In (89) she describes the changes in the ceremony during the reign of Sobhuza II, including variations in the participation of different groups that reflect the changing nature of political support for the monarchy. Her analysis of the continuing importance of the *ncwala* as a source of power shows that there are still many different parties interested in defining the body of the king for their own purposes. [Kuper's paper on "the language of sites" (90) makes similar points about changes in the politico-religious geography of Swaziland over the past several decades.] In (91, 92), she provides extensive new data on the indigenous significance of participants' costumes, especially the costume of the king, in relation to Swazi cosmology and social organization. As she puts it in (92), where she concentrates on the animal symbolism of the *ncwala,* these are the "ingredients" with which Swazi (as they see it) reinvigorate a king who epitomizes and stands outside and against Swazi society, a primordial wild thing that is ultimately brought under the control of the people.

Apter's (6) recent analysis of the *ncwala* as a joking relationship (in Radcliffe-Brown's definition) between the king and his subjects is intended to reconcile the interpretations of Gluckman and Beidelman. It has the value of drawing attention to the special intimacy in the relationship between king and people, but it does not negate the cosmic dimensions of the tension and conflict between them that Kuper and Beidelman emphasize.

Smith's (144) structuralist analysis turns on the correlation of the *ncwala* with the summer solstice, when the sun begins to move north again, and the waxing of the new moon in the Swazi lunar calendar. This is the period of intense hunger that served to explain psychobiologically the explosive release of tensions in Gluckman's (63) earlier argument. In Smith's view, the drama focuses on the king's heroism in bringing the Swazi through the critical and dangerous period between the death of the old year and rebirth of the new year in which their labors will be rewarded again with abundance. Like Kuper, he interprets the complexity of the *ncwala* as tied historically to the growth and development of the Swazi monarchy. But the essence of the ceremony lies not in its elaborate detail but in the structural connection between the power of the king as a warrior and as an agent of fertility, which is also fundamental to the royal ritual of Rwanda several thousand kilometers to the north (as presented in a text collected in 1945; see 69). Smith's analysis is valuable because it focuses on issues of military power and productive capacity that other writers have not dealt with so fully. But the sociological insights of Kuper and Beidelman must also be included to explain how ideas about prosperity and fertility are embodied in the person/office of the king and in the changing social structure of kingship, a topic to be discussed in more detail below.

De Heusch (72, pp. 244–306) analyzes the agricultural associations of the *ncwala* in much more detail. Like Kuper and Beidelman, he emphasizes that the connection between the social and natural worlds is made through the body of the king as created by diverse groups of people. His death and regeneration as the monstrous creature in whom these worlds are joined is the central feature of the ceremony [compare Muller's argument in (111) and in (28a, pp. 239–50)]. De Heusch focuses especially on the ideas and practices through which the single person of the king is infinitely enlarged through "twinning" (the king and his mother, the ritual queens of the left and right, the commoner *tinsila*, other male doubles of the left and right, and so on), a process that Swazi and other Bantu-speaking peoples of southern and eastern Africa associate with witchcraft and pollution (these connections between the Swazi and the Karange, Venda, and Lovedu of Zimbabwe and the Transvaal lead de Heusch to doubt Smith's hypothesis concerning Rwanda).

This emphasis on the duality of African kings who are at once the essence and opposite of the people they govern is the recurrent theme of de Heusch's work, which extends from his field research in Rwanda, beginning in 1949, to the present (e.g. 70–72). In consistently arguing that the sacralization of power is inseparable from political centralization, that politics is a branch of religion (most recently 72, pp. 13–28), and in combining structural with historical analysis, he is allied in his own view with Frazer and Dumézil. His publications are intended to provide the kind of integrated understanding of the Central African ethnography that Dumézil has provided for the Indo-European traditions of Eurasia.

De Heusch's analyses of the role of inversions like royal incest in the creation (sacralization) of power and of the relationship between symbolic patterns associated with royalty and with common practices (like the widespread *mukanda* circumcision ritual in (72, pp. 416–478) raise historical as well as sociological questions concerning the introduction or appropriation and transformation of custom as a means of domination that remain open to dispute. R.

Cohen (33) critiques de Heusch's interpretation of royal incest as an "Oedipal drama." His social structural analysis of the "queen mother" in Africa as the key element in the integration of potentially rival groups in a "proto-bureaucracy" stresses the continuities in state formation. Arens (10) combines de Heusch's insights on royal incest with Geertz's (58) arguments about charisma in his recent analysis of the installation of the Shilluk *reth,* which questions Evans-Pritchard's view that he "reigns but does not govern" (44, p. 200; see also 8). Van den Berghe and Mesher (154) propose a sociobiological explanation of royal incest worldwide.

The dual symbolism of African monarchy is also the subject of structuralist analyses by Yamaguchi (169) on the Jukun (inspired by Hocart), Adler (2, 2a) on the Moundang of Chad, Muller (111) on the Rukuba of Nigeria, and Tcherkézoff (151) on the Nyamwezi, the last of which is broadly comparative (owing to the influence of both Dumézil and Dumont). Gottlieb (in 11) explores the connections between kingship and witchcraft among the Beng of the Ivory Coast.

The role of regicide in the dualism of African monarchy remains open to question. Adler (1–2a) stresses regicide as the logic underlying Moundang royal ritual, regardless of whether or not it is actually practiced, which remains difficult to verify. MacGaffey (101a) emphasizes sociological factors as well, associating regicide with the requirements of kingship as a perpetual office. Ray (129) interprets Ganda installation rites as transforming regicide into homicide. Elam (43, p. 157, n. 2) finds no evidence of regicide in Ankole, but Ndayishinguje (112) documents the belief in Burundi, and Krige (86, pp. 55, 68) and Vaughan (156) confirm the practice among the Lovedu and Margi (Nigeria) respectively, which they see as substantiating Frazer's argument. Vaughan's analysis, in his words, combines Frazer's "why" with Evans-Pritchard's "how." Vaughan goes on to discuss Oedipal themes in the "divine king myth." These are the main focus of Paul's (116a) psychoanalytic approach to Tibetan traditions concerning kings and king-killings inspired by both de Heusch and R. Cohen, as well as Róheim's early work. Paul (116a, p. 305) suggests that Frazer "had an intuition that he was dealing with what we would now recognize as the Oedipal triangle" when he concluded *The Golden Bough* with these words: "*Le roi est mort, vive le roi! Ave Maria!*" (56, 7(2):309).

Huntington & Metcalf (77) and Arens (9) cite the reports of Lienhardt (99, pp. 275–77, 298–319) and Deng (36, p. 132, 146) on the ideally live burial of Dinka politico-religious leaders known as "masters of the fishing spear" in their reanalyses of the Shilluk, where the *reth*-ship continues to flourish. (Only the Ngok Dinka, to which Deng belongs, developed a centralized chieftaincy like that of the Shilluk; Deng describes the cases of his own great grandfather and grandfather.) They go on to compare Shilluk royal funeral ceremonies in the light of material from Kantorowicz (80) and Giesey (61) on the role of royal effigies in perpetuating the king's corporate body until his heir can be publicly installed in his place.

Ray's (129, pp. 57–58) discussion of the struggle in 1971 between the heir to the Ganda *kabaka*-ship and General Idi Amin for the body of the late *Kabaka* Sir Edward Mutesa II is also relevant in this context. Mutesa II died in exile in 1969 after Prime Minister Obote abolished the kingdoms of Buganda, Bunyoro, Ankole, and Toro in 1967. As a means of gaining Ganda support, Amin had the body returned from England for a state funeral shortly after he took over in January 1971. In Ganda custom, royal and common, possession of a person's corpse is required to legitimate succession to his social role. Amin received the corpse, conveyed it to the hill in Kampala where Uganda's independence ceremonies were celebrated nine years before, and later attended the funeral services at Namirimbe Cathedral. But the *Kabaka*'s heir was able to carry out the rites of succession to the *kabaka*-ship when the body was finally reburied in the royal tomb. Amin's government did not recognize his action, "the bark-cloth act being only a rite" (*Uganda Argus,* 6 April 1971, cited in 129, p. 58).

Ndayishinguje (112) deals with the burial of the Burundi king Mwazi Gisabo in 1908 and the installation of his successor, based on participants' accounts gathered by himself and J.-P. Chrétien. Whether or not the elderly Gisabo was poisoned, as widely rumored, regicide was associated with the time of year when he died (as among the Margi, see 156, pp. 131–32). Chrétien's analysis ("La royauté capture les rois," pp. 61–70) stresses the profoundly ambiguous position of the king as tyrant and scapegoat, using comparative data from Rwanda and Buha. Chrétien and Mworaha (28) and Gahama (57) analyze the funerary ritual and royal tombs associated with the kings and queen mothers of Burundi in the northwest and center of the country respectively. Gahama also deals with the powerful Bayange ("people of secrets"), two unrelated groups of Bahutu who carried out the funeral services for kings and queen mothers. They enjoyed autonomy, privileges, and wealth that rivaled that of royalty, but because Burundi royalty "ne meurt pas," they were also suspected of being murderers and cannibals. Their power was sustained over time because they continued to mediate between royalty and people in spirit cults that are still associated with the tombs.

Royal tombs and spirit cults, which are an important part of contemporary life in some parts of Madagascar, will be discussed later in the context of political dissent. It should be mentioned at this point that although the balance of powers between living and dead royalty in Madagascar might be described in terms of a contrast between person and office, focusing on the royal body, there is no evidence of regicide in Frazer's sense. The strangulation of the Merina king, Radama II (1861–1863), came closest to being a publicly sanctioned execution (at least according to some branches of the nobility). But it was widely rumored among the general populace to have failed [Delval (35) cites evidence to confirm the rumors]. The spirit possession ceremonies of the Sakalava of the northwest coast portray royal ancestors in the peak of death regardless of how they died. The dead in any form are considered to be more powerful than the living, at least in this century. Indeed, it could be said that Sakalava monarchy survived the French colonial period not by denying the death of kings, but by celebrating it (49).

These differences from the African ethnography raise questions that are not immediately solved by moving to other areas. Given the involvement, both unwitting and deliberate, of Western political theory and practice in their "discovery," it is difficult to evaluate the comparability of the dual/twin monarchies of Africa with "the king's two bodies" of Tudor and Stuart England, which Kantorowicz (80, pp. 42–86) himself felt to be related but not identical to the *persona mixta* and *gemina persona* of earlier European theorists. Asian concepts of sovereignty present the same problem. The dual monarchy of classical Indian theory that inspired Dumézil and Hocart suggested to Dumont (41, 42) that Indian kingship was above all secular. Yet Southeast Asianists, dealing with what are commonly called the "Indic," "Indianized," or "Hindu-Buddhist" states of Burma, Thailand, Cambodia, Java, Bali, and southern Sulawesi, find them to be above all unitary and sacred in character. Moreover, they are sacred in some unfamiliar ways, not least of which is (as in Madagascar, settled by Malayo-Polynesian speakers) the apparent absence of regicide (e.g. 5, 30, 58–60, 67, 110, 130, 150).

Given the influence of Asianists like Dumézil, Hocart, and Dumont on scholars of Africa and Madagascar, these differences should be noted. Gesick's preface to a recent collection of essays on "classic" Southeast Asian states, made for comparative purposes, provides a useful summary of their distinctive features. These include "the conviction that living beings were ordered along a continuum from the bestial to the sacred" (however that might be defined), and that status varied according to one's position on this continuum, that is, according to one's own sacredness or proximity to sacred people in whose power one might share. Associated with this continuum was a circular conception of space. A leader, constituting the center, was surrounded by people of progressively lesser sacred power and status, giving way at the periphery to realms of equal but opposite kinds of power (60, p. 2).

There is no evidence of Wittfogelian "hydraulic despotism" in the data (Geertz 59, pp. 68–86, makes the same point). Nor are there any Heine-Geldernian "god-kings" because "in a world in which the divine was everywhere immanent and the purpose of worship was to realize the divine in oneself by uniting it with the divine everywhere, the king was merely the most divine among humans, the most effective practitioner in the art of worship." The king's "work," as Geertz (59) argues at greater length in the case of Bali, was to convey this divine power to his people. The great politico-religious changes associated with the spread of Sinhalese Buddhism in the mainland and Islam in the islands seem to have come about not because commoners revolted against the divine despotism of their kings but because kings converted in their search for more potent forms of sacredness that would bring them still more followers (60, pp. 4–5). Alkire (4a, p. 492) makes a similar point in arguing that the ideas of order which Heine-Geldern (67) attributed to Hindu-Buddhist influences were indigenous to Southeast Asia and the Pacific Islands, where they were linked with quadripartite divisions and dual organizations. Winzeler (166; also 28a, pp. 455–67), also arguing against the Indicization of Southeast Asia, takes the approach of Goody (65) and Kottak (82) in emphasizing ecological and technological factors.

Geertz (59) examines these themes in the context of an historical "model" of the 19th century Balinese *negara,* which came to an end with the suicides of Balinese rulers in the face of Dutch conquest in the first decade of this century. He distinguishes royal ritual and politics on the grounds that royalty had no control over the irrigation system or the labor of kin groups, though he does acknowledge some connections with ports of trade, not very elaborate in Bali. Yet his analysis of the unceasing "centripetal" and "centrifugal" forces in Balinese social life, drawing people into royal centers and pulling them out again, will be familiar to Africanists [compare Tambiah's (150) concept of the "galactic polity" in Thailand].

Geertz's analysis of the *negara* as a "theatre state" is not meant to evoke Western images of ritual as the mask of force, but rather Balinese (generally Southeast Asian) conceptions of kingship as above all exemplary. Like many of the Africanists mentioned earlier (and ultimately Hocart), he concentrates not only on the indigenous features of these conceptions but also the material forms with which they are created (59, p. 124). These include the architecture of the palace, the royal regalia, and most important of all, royal funerals, including a wide variety of royal effigies besides the corpse. Balinese describe royal cremation as "king work"; it is "the quintessential royal ceremony . . . the most thoroughly dedicated to the aggressive assertion of status" (59, p. 117), as evident in a royal cremation in 1847, which included the suicide/cremation of three royal widows. [Given Geertz's theater analogy, the plays of writers Duro Ladipo and Wole Soyinka on this theme, inspired by a similar event in the early 1940s among the Yoruba, provide an interesting contrast; see also Huntington & Metcalf's comparison of Balinese and Thai royal funerals (77, pp. 123–32).]

Geertz (59, p. 115) considers the importance of the sacred weapons that embody the power of a Balinese king, and Tambiah also comments about Thai monarchy that "kings must be good killers before they can turn to piety and good works" (150, p. 522). Sahlins (138, pp. 107, 111) cites Dumézil's conviction about the correspondence between Indian and Polynesian modes of sovereignty, based in part on the research that Hocart did in Fiji (and elsewhere in Polynesia) before moving to Ceylon. But in practice, the Southeast Asian literature has tended to focus more on the pious, whereas the Polynesian literature marks a return to Dumézil's warrior king and to regicide.

Sahlins's (137) ironic account of how a British naval officer became a Frazerian god-king is in the Hocartian tradition of integrating structure with history. The structure is the annual reenactment of the rivalry for Hawaiian kingship between the peaceful god Lono, associated with agriculture, and the brutal god Kulaniopuu, associated with war and human sacrifice, in which Lono dies and the king, who represents Kulaniopuu, is reinstated. The event is Captain Cook's arrival in the Sandwich Islands in late 1778, about the time that Lono is due to reappear, and his inadvertant rearrival (having sprung a mast) after he is supposed to have gone for the rest of the year. So this time he is really killed (sacrificed), and his bones appropriated to legitimate the Hawaiian kingship. This is in keeping with the way in which the bones of one ruler are taken by his successor, who is assumed to have killed him, as a means of justifying his right to the throne (137, p. 24–25; see 153). Sahlins's more general argument is like Giesey's (61) in focusing on how people's efforts to reproduce their ideas of the world (which is the logic of Frazer's theory of regicide) result in its radical transformation. But it is unusual in also illuminating what might be considered historically and structurally the underside of Frazerian *praxis*.

The Fijian chief, in Sahlins's view (138, 139), is more like Cook than Kulaniopuu in that he is a "stranger-king," symbolically poisoned at his accession rite and in this way appropriated by his subjects. The kava he drinks is "grown from the leprous body of a sacrificed child of the native people" (138, pp. 125–26). Compare the cannibalism said to be required of a Yoruba king at his accession, an act that would kill him if he were not the rightful heir (121, pp. 104–5, n. 5); the Ganda coronation ceremony in which the "*kabaka* eats Buganda" (Young in 97, p. 199); and the Bunyoro installation ceremony in which the people "eat their king" (15, p. 115). Sahlins uses the Fijian case to explore a political philosophy that he associates with divine kingship as presented by Frazer, Dumézil, Hocart, and de Heusch, which differs from dominant Western political philosophy in seeing the power embodied in the "stranger-king" as a force of nature because it is foreign to society not inherent in its members. In the Fijian case, the stranger-king offers the indigenous settlers "cooked men," i.e. sacrificial victims as food, in exchange for their "raw women." He provides the feast, but as Sahlins points out (139, p. 87), he seems to be both "feeder of the people and their food."

KINGSHIP AND PROSPERITY

These images may serve as an andidote to the emphasis on harmony that otherwise pervades the literature on kingship and food. The purpose of this literature is essentially to answer the question of why people should create the means of their own oppression. But it may also provide some insight into indigenous ideas and practices concerning the relationship between power and prosperity.

Ritual and politics meet in food. This was Frazer's argument. This is essentially the argument of Hocart (75), Richards (131), and Fortes & Evans-Pritchard (55), for all their differences among themselves and their common antipathy to Frazer. And this is in many ways the viewpoint to which some anthropologists and historians are returning, if by a circuitous route. The question is what "food," "growth," "fertility," and "decay" mean in indigenous terms, and how "theor(ies) of prosperity," as Hocart (75, p. 290) put it, are embodied in the human and other materials with which kings and kingships are created, represented, and destroyed.

Hocart (75) contends that people invented government to assure themselves of "life," an undifferentiated concept for which Needham (in 75, pp. xxxii–xxxv) provides an interesting defense. Life-giving ritual, not politics, first brought people together in societies. As these increased in scale, government took over from ritual organization as the coordinating agency. The purpose of *Kings and Councillors* is to outline the stages by which this occurred. In the process, Hocart emphasizes what has since become a critical point to some current scholars: "theories of prosperity" must be seen in indigenous terms (implying that theories of life, growth, and so on, may in fact differ widely) to which Western distinctions between utilitarian and ritual action may be irrelevant (e.g. 75, pp. 215–25).

Fortes & Evans-Pritchard (55, pp. 1–23) echo both Frazer and Hocart on this issue. Like Hocart, they are dealing with fundamental questions of political organization and change. Like Hocart, they find no help in European political philosophy, though not for the same reasons (55, p. 4). Unlike Hocart, they vascillate between political, economic, and religious explanations for government. Finally, they fall back on mystical values concerning "life" (55, p. 18) that derive from private material interests, the true roots of social life, yet paradoxically transcend and outlast them (55, pp. 16–23).

Richards's (131) analysis of the Bemba provides the earliest and still the most systematic analysis of the relationship between indigenous ideas about wealth, food, and prosperity to the ideology and exercise of power and authority in kingship. Wealth, consisting in "rights over the services of others," is achieved by feeding people (131, p. 211). The "sacred kitchen" is the first building to be constructed on the site of a chief's new capital, and the installation of the "sacred hearth" climaxes the months-long ceremonies (131, pp. 48–50). Food is the language of social relations, and a fat and shining body is a powerful sign of prosperity and good fortune (131, p. 51). These qualities are epitomized in the Paramount Chief, who initiates and coordinates agricultural labor throughout the country by means of annual rites honoring the royal ancestors. The rites affirm the link between politico-religious and economic well-being (131, pp. 351–405). Richards analyzes these rites in terms of Bemba associations between chieftainship, fire, sex, and power over natural and social fertility, "powers (that) are hurt by blood, intercourse out of marriage, death, murder, lion-killing, and all cold, terrible, or 'bad things' " [(132, p. 36; in *Chisungu,* oddly like de Heusch, she explores these (royal) themes in the context of Bemba female initiation rites]. European perspectives on food as the fuel that energizes the laboring body/machine and on the connections between diet and development provide the framework of Richards's analysis [compare Gluckman's (63, pp. 131–35) explanation of why the Swazi *ncwala* is associated with the hunger period just before harvest]. In *Chisungu* (132), she emphasizes the importance that Bemba attribute to women as food producers, though she does not explore its political implications.

Richards's analysis of the Bemba case, where wealth consists in power over people, contrasts markedly with G. Wilson's (164) comparative analysis of the Ngonde and Nyakyusa published in the same year. He argues that it was the greater material wealth of the Ngonde, located on an ivory trade route, that accounted for why they, not the Nyakyusa, developed divine kingship. He points out that the belief in the *Kyungu*'s (Ngonde paramount chief) body as "the greatest magical object in the country" was associated with statements about regicide (164, p. 35). But the Nyakyusa comparison shows that material wealth was equally important. Abundance of food and generosity in feeding are "the supreme traditional marks of a chief" in Ngonde as among the Nyakyusa and in many other parts of Africa (164, p. 54). But Wilson does not analyze the relationship of food and fertility to the ivory trade or the indigenous significance of these factors in relation to one another.

Actually, M. Wilson (165) later analyzed Nyakyusa together with Ngonde political leadership as a kind of divine kingship, and Charsley's (27) reanalysis, using additional archival materials, supports her. In his view, "chiefship" was a European creation; indigenous politics were far more fluid. Yet Nyakyusa "princes" (as he calls them because of the tenuousness of their power and authority) were indeed killed by their headmen owing ostensibly to the connection between their well-being and that of the country. Charsley himself explains this in political terms having to do with headmen's interests in maintaining their personal positions and the competitive viability of their villages (27, pp. 92–93).

Most subsequent work on kingship and prosperity conforms to G. Wilson's focus on "mercantile divinity" (164, p. 71) rather than Richards's emphasis on "the magical potency of sex, fire, and blood" (132, p. 35). Southall (145) and Lonsdale (101) review studies that document in fine detail the connection between political, economic, and ecological factors in the growth and decline of centralized political systems in Africa over time. Nevertheless, the majority of these are "naturalistic" in Hocart's (74, pp. 32, 231) use of the term, resting on universal assumptions about human behavior. The indigenous significance of powerful substances like salt, ivory, gold, or cloth is rarely considered in depth. Curiously, this applies even to studies of slavery, where the substance is human and even the most naturalistic studies of political administration have demonstrated important connections in the positions of kings and slaves (see below).

Following the return of interest in indigenous conceptions of power signaled by Richards's and Beidelman's work in the 1960s, and in some cases influenced by their emphasis on the human and other materials with which abstractions like divinity are created and represented, scholars have begun to reexamine the connections between kingship and prosperity. The Igala kingdom of the Niger-Benue confluence was a key example in Seligman's (141, pp. 41–48) argument about the gradual evolution of divine kingship away from regicide, and yet another case in which a stranger-king is accepted as a ruler by local land-holding groups by virtue of his exotic origins. Boston's (23) reanalysis, based on new field research, examines the relationship between the two, which find their focus in the dual responsibilities of the king as clan head and territorial administrator, as head of the cult of the royal ancestors and the cult of the land, the one area where his powers are incomplete without the cooperation of commoners. [Compare, too, the analyses of Kuper (93) and Berg (17), which turn in part on the sacredness of land among the Swazi and the Merina of highland Madagascar respectively.]

Vansina's (155) recent history of the Kuba of central Africa explains the extraordinary development of Kuba monarchy as the result of ecological changes involved in migrations from one area to another, associated with the development of new tools. But Vansina also invokes the Kuba myth of the stranger-king who introduced new food crops together with new concepts about work that contributed through the reorganization of labor to the surpluses on which the kingdom grew fat. His work is distinctive among scholars of African political-economic history in incorporating the analysis of indigenous art forms into his argument.

Prins's (122) analysis of Lozi history from 1876–1896 is based on the argument that the Lozi "prize the moral economy more than trade and goods" (122, p. 283). He begins with detailed accounts of Lozi cosmology derived from oral traditions and archival data, then presents the historical events as the "acid test," which confirms the historiographical and sociological importance of taking beliefs into account, as he argues Gluckman did not do in his Lozi research. Packard's (116) purpose in analyzing chiefship and cosmology among the Bashu of eastern Zaire is to grasp the Bashu view of political competition after the model of Beidelman (16). This too involves the moral-political-economy of food: so-called "traditional" ideas about the connection between power and prosperity might appear to disappear because of European influence, but they reappear whenever disaster strikes (which was also Richards's point, 131, p. 351). Willis's (163) analysis of the development of the Fipa state (actually three related states) is also an effort to integrate structural and historical analysis focusing on food production. In this case, the "stranger-king" is a group of women who conquer an existing kingdom, transforming it into a dual monarchy. The transformation involves radically different relations between royalty and commoners, women and men, immigrants (laborers, traders, prospective affines) and indigenous settlers. Actually these changes seem to have occurred over a long period of political-economic and social reorganization in which Ufipa's unique mode of compost-mound cultivation and its central location on East-Central African trading routes were critical factors.

Historians Wilks and McCaskie have both written on the changing significance of the Asante Golden Stool and the Golden Elephant Tail over time. Wilks (161) follows his detailed analysis of Asante political history (160) by noting the dearth of references to money in Asante ethnography (this observation could be applied to any of the cases discussed in this review), despite the number of Asante proverbs expressing sentiments like "You cannot cook and eat nobility; money is what it is all about" (161, p. 2). He analyzes the concept of money (identified in part with gold) and its relationship to office and social status in Asante thought and practice since the 18th century. Death duties, said to have been instituted in ca. 1720–1750, were the most powerful means of appropriating wealth into the royal coffers and an important issue as late as 1930.

McCaskie (109), in the first of a two-part analysis of Asante ideas about wealth and accumulation, expands on these topics by arguing that the ideology of power embodied in gold [like excrement in the context of Asante ideas about nature and culture (102, pp. 27, 29–32)] must be analyzed in relation to religion as well as politics (109, p. 29). He argues that the ethic of "achievement by accumulation" embodied in the hierarchical relationship of the Golden Stool to the Golden Elephant Tail was transformed in the mid-19th century in part by the appearance of an alternative model of social and economic development. This was associated with the British occupation of the southern Gold Coast, but was probably seen in context not as foreign but as another African view having revolutionary consequences [the subject of the second as yet unpublished part of his analysis; see also (12)]. This article, which is one of several that

McCaskie has written on Asante social history, strongly emphasizes the need for integrating the "pseudo-rational" world constructed by historians with the " 'illogical' cultural densities" documented by ahistorical anthropologists (109, pp. 23–26). But in characterizing the results of this union as "conjectural history" (after Peel), he seems to reflect continued skepticism about whether beliefs, past or present, can ever be studied "scientifically" [for Vansina, this is "the problem posed by white porcelain clay," kaolin, the essence of sacredness for the Kuba (155, pp. 197–210)].

Peel's (117, 118) analyses of Yoruba concepts of development, also written with the aim of integrating belief with social structure in historical context, draw attention to the association that Ijesha make between knowledge and power, expressed in the concept of *ǫlaju* or "enlightenment" as the source of growth and change. Traditionally, knowledge held in secret as a scarce resource was not equally available to all. This changed with the introduction of mission schools, but as education came to be associated with new sources of power, new restrictions on access to knowledge have developed. The constant feature is Ijeshas' sense of peripherality to superior sources of power, first Oyo and Benin, later Europe. Peel suggests that the so-called "diploma disease" associated with underdevelopment should be seen in the context of cultural traditions of reflections on power and powerlessness (118, p. 160).

Recently, D. W. Cohen and Iliffe have dealt with these issues from different perspectives. Iliffe (79) argues against the myth that kinship ties and ample land precluded poverty in precolonial Africa. He discusses poverty in Yorubaland as expressed in categories of rich and poor and in asceticism, begging, and charity as recorded in missionary reports from the 19th century, though he does not put these ideas in the context of Yoruba religion or politics. D. W. Cohen's earlier work analyzed the changing influence of rival cultural traditions associated with Bunyoro (embodied in the legendary figure of Mukama) and Buganda (embodied in the figure of Kintu) on political competition in Busoga over the last several centuries and in the 19th century in particular (31). Recently (32), he has suggested that the appearance of enormous wealth in the Lakes Plateau region of east-central Africa that so attracted Europeans may have been the result of the draconian extractive strategies of the Ganda monarchy, particularly its control over the labor of neighboring groups which subsequent conquerors have failed to equal. Resistance, as expressed in emigration, opening up new areas for production, would simply have confirmed this illusion of plenty. Historical changes in relations of production should be taken into account in assessing the contemporary poverty of the region.

Like the study of food, the study of labor relations may prove to be one of the most fruitful ways of integrating different approaches to the relationship between power and prosperity. The organization of labor is one of the primary purposes of royal bureaucracies. Bureaucracies are living systems of classification, material expressions of ideologies about hierarchy or more usually about complex and constantly changing compromises between hierarchy and equality. They are also the instruments for extracting the surpluses on which the hierarchies are based. Substantial data show that people construct knowledge about kingship through rituals. The subject of royal work has not received the same attention, but there is some data to suggest that it may also be an important medium for the expression of ideas about domination and subordination.

In Madagascar, as in many parts of Africa and Southeast Asia, there is no distinction between royal ritual and royal work. The royal service of the Sakalava monarchy of northwestern Madagascar was (and still is) the chief instrument by which domestic labor was transformed into royal service. Since domestic labor was inextricably related to the network of exchange among kin, the process of alienating Sakalava from their labor was inseparable from the process of alienating them from one another, transforming them from kin into subjects of royalty. Sakalava express this as a process of enslavement, in which labor for monarchy is the most succinct expression of citizenship (48). The most important royal work involves the reconstruction of royal tombs that embody in the materials with which they remake the royal body theories about the growth and decline of communities based on kingship (49, 50).

Richards (131) documents the close relationship between labor and political loyalty among the Bemba and comments on the extensive use of "labour for labour's sake" among the Baganda where, given the extensive rights of the *Kabaka* over his subjects, the line between slave and free was not always clear (in 46, pp. 275–76). Swazi make a careful distinction between slaves and citizens; nevertheless, royal work is a major part of the *ncwala* ritual. Conversely, the imagery of slavery seems to have been central to the paradoxically powerless position of kings in the grip of the people [e.g. Arens (10); Feeley-Harnik (48); Henderson (68, pp. 273–74, 305); see also Richards (in 46, pp. 275, 285–86), who cites Kuper's data on the king as "child" of the people as well as "father" among the Baganda and Swazi]. Strickland's (149) argument about the "essential connection" between kingship and slavery in Africa relies too heavily on his logic rather than on data, despite his effort to test the hypothesis using the H.R.A.F. The connections between kingship, citizenship, and slavery, deriving from powerful ambiguities in the exercise of power and authority in hierarchical political systems that are hardly limited to Madagascar or Africa (as Frazer's own primordial case shows), require more extensive research from a comparative perspective.

One final point may be made in this context. The fact that materials like salt, ivory, cloth, gold, slaves, and money are universally traded, and that labor, both prior to and during the colonial period, was a major bone of contention between Europeans and indigenous peoples, raises the question of how the interaction of different theories of prosperity, power, and strength embodied in these common substances may be involved in the political-economic and social changes of recent decades. Data on the labor history of the Sakalava of Madagascar (49) suggests that what French colonists in Madagascar saw as "development," Sakalava saw as "death", both literally and metaphorically. Further research could be done on the French side of the dialogue. French explorers assessing the wealth of Madagascar during the late 19th and early 20th century (and finding it, like Europeans in East-Central Africa, to be full of promise) used metaphors of growth and decay derived from vitalistic theories about bodies and body politics that are strikingly similar to the organic metaphors of power and prosperity found in Malagasy and African monarchies. Some historians (e.g. 114, 123) are beginning to investigate ideas about growth, development, and decay and their incorporation into the conceptualization and organization of labor in late 19th century Europe. Ultimately it would be useful to find out how these ideas were incorporated into the labor policies of colonial governments, how they interacted with indigenous concepts of work, growth, and decline, and with what consequences for historical change and contemporary circumstances.

THE KING'S MANY BODIES: THE EXPRESSION OF DISSENT

In the process of trying to grasp the connections between ritual, office, and common welfare, scholars have returned to the analysis of indigenous concepts of power and prosperity. The other answer to the question of why people should create the means of their own oppression in the form of divine kings is that they do not. But the views of the indigenous on this issue are less well known. [A conspicuous exception is Codere's (29) collection of 48 Rwandan autobiographies, made in 1959–1960, when Hutu revolted against Tutsi, resulting in the exile of the king and elections in which 80% of the voters rejected the monarchy; see also Vansina (155, p. 209) on Kuba sceptics.]

Hocart (75, p. 299) ends by explaining oppression as the inadvertant consequence of purposive action: people intend to create life not despotism. Yet kings are killed as often as they are elevated to power. What scholars have found difficult to explain in the African context is why kingship is not killed: why there is ample evidence of assasinations and rebellions, but few revolutions. Studies like Gluckman's analysis of the Swazi *ncwala* that assume unquestioning acceptance of the social order (63, pp. 129, 135) were undoubtedly influenced by the colonial context in which most of them were carried out, but European historians make the same point. As Walzer says, it is peculiarly difficult to kill kingship. It took centuries in Europe, and the process is not clearly over (158, especially pp. 88–89). Walzer does quote Geertz as saying that the principle of kingly authority "was destroyed long before the king; it was to the successor principle that he was, in fact, a ritual sacrifice," but Walzer disagrees, contrasting Geertz's observation with Marat's comment after the execution of Louis XVI (as citizen Louis Capet): "I believe in the Republic at last!" (158, p. 88, n. 1).

Like Gluckman's (63) analysis of Swazi *simemo* songs, most studies of dissent other than succession wars focus on language. M. Wilson's (165) analysis (the Frazer Lecture of 1959) of the Nyakyusa concept of "the breath of men" is based on the connection that Nyakyusa make between anger and sickness and the necessity they see for "speaking out" as a form of political expression. One wonders how the "breath of men," expressed in "murmuring," is related to the "vitality, energy, physical vigour, force of character . . . life" at the core of Nyakyusa cosmology epitomized in the body and person of the king (165, pp. 5–8). Wilson applies her analysis to the *simemo* songs of Swazi royal ritual. Then she contrasts the Nyakyusa with the British view in which people speak openly in private but circumspectly in public, and speculates about the potential value of "the breath of men" for Nyakyusa as colonial subjects.

Apter's (6) analysis of the Swazi *ncwala* as a joking relationship interprets the *simemo* songs as songs of "dispraise" intended to mobilize support for the king where politically he is most vulnerable. Praise songs are more likely to contribute to rebellion because they constitute a standard against which, implicitly, a king may be criticized and found wanting (7). It might be mentioned in this context that the image of the Fool as antithesis and antidote to the wisdom of kingship is widespread. The European form derived (at least in part) from the same Christian sources as the European divine king (162). Kantorowicz (80, pp. 29–41) also points out that the Fool is "another human being . . . who is two-in-one".

Elam's (43) discussion of Ankole nomadism as a substitute for rebellion is unusual in drawing attention to the silent dissent of commoners in situations where more open forms of dissent are too dangerous. He argues that the marked absence of rebellions (despite recurrent succession wars) in the history of the lake kingdoms, typically Ankole, is not the result of "unquestioning obedience." Ethnographic data gathered in the 1950s, when the government installed water holes in an effort to stabilize pastoralists, suggests that nomadic movements were and are chronic "rebellions in miniature," even if pastoralists themselves speak about them in purely utilitarian terms. Elam also applies his analysis to Swazi royal ritual, although he finally argues, like Gluckman and Evans-Pritchard before him, that these movements around kings result in the affirmation of kingship (43, p. 156).

These studies have in common the effort to grasp the nature of political expression in circumstances in which neither servile consent nor revolution captures the complexity and ambiguity of hierarchical relationships. Elam's analysis of silent rebellion in particular is related to another line of reasoning on these issues that may prove especially useful for exploring the way in which values and practices concerning political expression may have been carried forth into the colonial and postcolonial eras. This has to do with the importance of specialized knowledge to politics, and conversely the importance of silence and secrecy, of nonverbal and covert means of preserving and transmitting politico-religious values that may help to explain their reemergence under changed circumstances.

Virtually every scholar of monarchy in Africa has commented on the importance of secrecy in the conduct of politico-religious affairs and the diverse forms it takes, from prohibitions on speech concerning particular topics (e.g. 25, p. 2; 49; 131, pp. 47–48, 351); to the beaded veil of Yoruba crowns, the principal symbol of royalty and embodiment of its power (13; 121, pp. 94–96, 99); to the eight "hidden kings" of the Onitsha Igbo (68, p. 267); and perhaps the fact that the chameleon is a widespread symbol of kingship in West Africa (68, p. 269); to the seclusion of the Lovedu queen (87). Rattray (126) is one of the few early writers who notes the way in which Africans used secrecy to protect themselves from European colonists, as in the case of the Asante Golden Stool. (His idealization of the anthropology section as the "Intelligence Department" of the colonial administration is the logical extension of these observations.) The Kriges stress this point in their discussion of relations between Lovedu and Europeans (87, p. 295; see also 86, p. 69).

Albert (4, pp. 90–91, 93–95) discusses "the survival value of discretion and falsehood" and "the pre-eminence of indirect reference" in Burundi, based on Rundi recognition of the power of language and silence as weapons, although she limits herself, except for a section on the consequences of sociolinguistic analysis for fieldwork, to the way in which these values operated within the kingdom.

The "politics of enlightenment" in Ilesha (118) derive from the importance of knowledge to power formerly epitomized in the secrecy surrounding the person of the king and currently manifest in the emphasis on education to which Ijesha have increasingly unequal access. Peel does not examine the role of other royal bodies in storing or hiding knowledge, but there are some data to suggest that royal tombs may continue to be valued for that reason. Nyikang, the first Shilluk *reth* and the spirit possessing all subsequent *reth,* is also associated with light and knowledge. Ceremonies honoring Nyikang and the royal house, the "main cult" of the Shilluk, are carried out at royal tombs and shrines located throughout Shillukland as well as at the capital of Fasoda (Lienhardt in 52, pp. 161–66).

Prins's (122) argument in *The Hidden Hippopotamous* [a phrase that derives from a Lozi proverb about how people protect the king by concealing him, whence too their power to kill him to keep kingship from dying (122, pp. 118–22)] concerns Lozi political strategies in dealing with Europeans that worked in part because of Europeans' ignorance of native values. Among the most hidden of Lozi royalty are the ancestors. Despite his historical focus, Prins found, like others before him, that Lozi royal tombs were among the most difficult topics to study "because of their continuing importance" (122, p. 123).

Cults focused on royal tombs are found not only throughout Africa but also in Madagascar (e.g. 14, 19, 20, 34, 47, 49, 50). In (19), Bloch cites Dumont's (42) separation between sacred and secular powers in traditional Indian kingship to argue for the separate consideration of the political-economic development of the Merina kingdom and its religious ideology, which served only to mask the exercise of force (see 17; 83; 84, pp. 58–87 for alternative views of state formation in highland Madagascar). In (20), Bloch continues this argument by suggesting that the inability of the Merina monarchy to break the power of local kin groups because of its dependence on their agricultural labor was reflected in their failure to appropriate successfully their funerary customs in the construction of royal tombs. In contrast, the capacity of Sakalava monarchy under different ecological conditions to swallow up local lineages is reflected in the dominance of royal tombs, associated here with spirit possession. Feeley-Harnik (49) argues that the proliferation of spirit mediums among the Sakalava is part of a larger shift in emphasis from living to dead royalty related to a shift in power from royalty to commoners and slaves in the context of encroachments from the Merina, then the French, and now the national government since the early 19th century. Sakalava sought to protect their political values in adverse circumstances by "hiding" them in royal ancestors, embodied in relics, entombed corpses, and commoners acting as mediums, forms that for different reasons were more resistant to military and legal controls that outside authorities were able to exercise over the living. That most mediums were and are female, like most Malagasy rulers since the early 19th century, may be related to their apparent political insubstantiality that permits them to assert political values with impunity in circumstances where their male counterparts cannot.

These are issues that could be explored on the basis of the African ethnography. One of the most striking features of the literature on divine kingship is the absence of attention to women. The early studies of bureaucracy focused on king's men, ignoring the role of women, as indeed, women were not incorporated into these new structures. [Compare Rattray's (126) account of Ashanti queen mothers with that of Busia (26), Roscoe's work with that of Fallers, and so on. Rattray (126, p. 89) is especially eloquent on the contrast between Ashanti and European views on this matter.] Even Kuper's (93) recent account of Swazi leadership focuses primarily on Sobhuza II rather than on both aspects of the Swazi dual monarchy, formerly complementary, as Kuper herself emphasized to Gluckman (63, pp. 257–58, n. 16).

While men forged ahead in secular politics, women were left with religion (e.g. Kuper 93, pp. 119–20). But to be content with this view would be to distort indigenous conceptions of political processes in which power was shared not only between royalty and commoners, living and dead, but also between men and women, whose cooperation as well as opposition in all these forms was the ultimate source of the fertile powers attributed to divine monarchy. In addition, it may distort some of the ways in which indigenous ideas about power and prosperity have been kept alive under conditions intended to eradicate them.

Lebeuf's (96) early survey of the role of women in African polities is confirmed by Albert's (3) case study in the same volume. Women in Burundi may "seem to be at a disadvantage in having to function in politics by indirect means and in secret (but) these are, in any case, the preferred methods of men in the delicate business of increasing wealth and power" (3, p. 181). Albert (4) expands on this in discussing the different educations that Tutsi men and women receive in speaking. Boys receive formal training from about their tenth year in a wide variety of methods of "speaking well". Girls are "also carefully trained, but to artful silence and evasiveness and to careful listening that will enable them to repeat nearly verbatim what has been said by visitors or neighbors" (4, pp. 76–77); nevertheless, Tutsi men are clearly seen as the masters in the use of silence as a weapon (p. 88). Albert emphasizes that given the complexity of the Burundi social hierarchy, both men and women learn a combination of verbal skills because there is no one (except those at the extreme top or bottom of the scale) superior in one position who is not inferior in another (3, p. 77; 4, p. 210).

Ethnographic data on marriage politics in African monarchies has emphasized the importance of ties through women as a means of concentrating wealth in royal clans, while integrating the community (e.g. 37, 85, 88, 98). R. Cohen (33) uses the case of the Pabir of northern Nigeria to refute structuralist explanations of divine kingship as derived from the power of incest to differentiate royalty from commoners (70, 71). He argues that the role of the queen mother is a direct development of the function of matrifiliation "to represent, contain and counter-balance the forces of opposition" to the integration of the kiń group, to the centralization of monarchy. The Pabir queen mother is chosen from a lineage segment that has just lost or is about to lose access to the throne to complete the process of deroyalization. She holds the royal relics and confers kingship, conceived as a process of giving birth to the new king.

The position of queen mothers in Asante (126; 160, p. 508), Burundi (57, pp. 15–20), and Swaziland (93) would confirm the power of women in this position, especially in their capacity as regents. Bonner's (21, p. 49) Swazi informants attributed the organization of nation-wide age-regiments associated with the expansion of the network of royal villages and innovations in royal ritual in the mid-19th century to the famous queen mother Thandile [but see

Kuper (93, p. 19), who says that the king Mswati, renowned as the greatest Swazi warrior-king, was responsible]. Nevertheless, the Swazi data also confirm the vulnerability implied in the lack of fortification around the queen mother's capital in the Pabir case, which Pabir explain by saying "it is a woman's town". Mswati's successor killed the queen mother who disagreed with him (93, pp. 21–22), but her crown was removed first.

The Lovedu monarchy (87) is still the best documented case of queens ruling in their own right. Like the queens of the Merina and the Sakalava, they came to power early in the 19th century (c. 1800), after a long line of male rulers [in the Lovedu case, as the result of father-daughter incest (87, p. 59)]. Krige (86) suggests that female rulers allowed the Lovedu monarchy to survive the turbulence of the 19th century, when male rulers were being killed off. Because, in the Lovedu view, "a woman does not fight," the Lovedu queens relied on diplomacy and strategy, especially the power derived from their control of rain medicines, intensified by secrecy epitomized in the seclusion of the ruler, a practice initiated with the first queen (86, pp. 60–61). Furthermore, the famed "woman-marriage" of the Lovedu provided the queen with a powerful means of incorporating people, including refugees from the wars of others, into the monarchy (86, pp. 62–66).

The role of women as queens, queen mothers, and king-makers should be compared with their roles as relic- and tomb-guardians and as spirit mediums, the principle means by which kingships are legitimated and kings kept alive after death. This might help to bring together what Ranger & Kimambo (125, pp. 4–9, 11–15) distinguish as the royal cults studied by historians and the popular cults studied by anthropologists. Schoffeleers (140) argues that the similarities in central African royal cults derive not from ideas and practices brought into the area by foreign conquerors, but from widespread similarities in popular cults taken over by royalty in the process of establishing their rule [Ottino (115) makes this argument about Sakalava spirit possession in Madagascar]. Mainga (102) suggests that indigenous cults may be incorporated differently or not at all, as when Lozi rulers chose to by-pass indigenous practices and establish their own cults based on royal tombs, not involving spirit mediums. Berger (18) examines the central role of female mediums in cults found throughout the Lakes Plateau region of East-Central Africa and in Unyamwezi, related in their common focus on the Abacwezi, Ryangombe, and other legendary figures, sometimes but not always associated with royalty. Berger argues that these cults concerned with the health, fertility, and prosperity of their suppliants were also a form of resistance to monarchy. The consistent features of these royal and common cults in Africa and Madagascar—the association between sickness and anger, the emphasis on physical/ social well-being, the implicit violence (the spirit will kill the unresponsive host), their regional spread, and their continuing vitality in the 20th century—

suggest that further research may help to clarify the range of opinion on power and prosperity in contemporary circumstances as well.

The king's many bodies draw attention to the multivocality of political expression involving indirect as well as direct modes of communication, the dead as well as the living, women as well as men, commoners and slaves as well as kings. They indicate ways in which diversity in communicative strategies may be involved in the persistence and change of political ideas and practices over time. The hidden bodies in particular suggest that closer attention might be paid to the connection between kingship and enlightenment, to which we now turn.

REGICIDE AND REVOLUTION

The core of Frazer's concept of divine kingship is the connection between the body of the king and the course of time. Paradoxically, regicide regenerates the world. Subsequent arguments about divine kingship, whatever else they may be, are inevitably arguments about the nature and course of human history. They are dominated by a surprisingly progressivist strain in which, as Frazer himself saw it, the transition from monarchy to popular sovereignty is inseparably associated with the transition from superstition to rational thought (e.g. 55, pp. 16–22; 63, pp. 129, 135–36; 74, p. 119; 164, preface). Yet even Walzer (158), who is most explicit on this point, expresses doubts about the consequences of killing kingship very like Frazer's doubts about the primeval rock lodged in the lawn. It took centuries for Europeans to revolt against kingship. Finally their revolt had to be "elevated" to the plane of ritual to have any chance of success, and even so, it was not clearly successful. Camus too argued in *The Rebel* that "the condemnation of the king is at the crux of our contemporary history." For him, it symbolized an attack against the moral structure of the universe, and Walzer himself is left with difficult distinctions between "good" and "bad" bloodshed. There is still a curious dearth of studies on this topic in Europe: "the destruction of kingship was a long and difficult process. . . . Much of this process remains hidden from view; the erosion of royalist ideology . . . still awaits its historian" (158, pp. 86–89).

Precisely the same points could be made about the overthrow of monarchy elsewhere. The African data substantiate the connection that Frazer made between royal bodies and human history. In addition to the ethnography on royal funerals, rites of installation, and rites of emergence, in which the reconstruction of the king (perhaps his death and rebirth) is associated with the recreation of time, there is also research on the concepts of history implicit in kinglists (146), the connection between embodiments of time and the politics of history as a scarce resource (47), and the transformation of concepts of time in the context of political-economic and social change (120). There are few studies of contemporary kingship or of the governments that succeeded monarchies in Africa and elsewhere that examine the consequences of these connections. The problem that Richards noted after revisiting the Bemba in 1957 remains: If "all rulers without standing armies or other institutionalized means of control have to balance on the knife edge of their people's belief" (if, she might have added, we killed kingship in Africa), then "the persistence of the whole ideology of divine kingship after some sixty years of colonial rule and strong mission influence itself requires some explanation" (134, p. 24).

If one were to apply the kind of regional analysis that Horton (76) pioneered in his study of state and stateless societies in precolonial West Africa, then one would analyze these apparently disparate political forms—relict kingdoms and Western style states—in precisely the same terms as the products of common historical forces rather than separately and sequentially. But this is not happening widely. In contrast to studies of African monarchy during the precolonial period, studies of kingship (and states) in contemporary circumstances have tended to perpetuate the old divide between ritual and politics. The contrast between two recent studies of neighboring kingdoms in northern Ghana, Staniland's study of the Dagomba and Brown's study of the Mamprusi, both published in 1975, is characteristic.

Staniland (147), a political scientist working primarily with archival material, documents the political history of Dagomba since the late 19th century, emphasizing the interaction between local and national affairs, in which traditions are invented to suit the circumstances. Brown's (25; also in 28a, pp. 117–31 anthropological analysis of the Mamprusi notes "the interdependence of the national authorities and the local traditional government" (25, p. 7), but focuses on the "cult of office" expressed in royal ritual. She concludes by summarizing the four features that the Mamprusi kingship has in common with kingship elsewhere in West Africa and perhaps more broadly: "The physical person of the king is 'sacred' (but there is no tradition of regicide) . . . the king does not rule alone . . . king-makers are ineligible for kingship . . . (and) political and ritual authority are inextricably related" (25, pp. 165–66).

Kilson's (81) anthropological and historical analysis of royal ritual among the Ga in southeastern Ghana shows a correlation between the decline of substantive power ("control over the allocation of resources") and the elaboration of ceremonies of office. Ga kingship "consumes energy, time, and money but it does not produce solutions to poverty, urban congestion and disease . . . (it) recreates a heroic tradition, but fails to create new worlds" (81, p. 421). Robertson (136) attributes the large number of deposition cases in Ghana in this century in part to the "pecuniary interests which have taken a stranglehold on the processes of accession and deposition" [(136, p. 419); compare (95) and Asiwaju's (13) analysis of the proliferation of Yoruba crowns]. Robertson argues that Ashanti deposition cases are like those brought against church and state officials in 17th century England (and against some contemporary politicians) in making a wide range of charges rather than one specific complaint. This does not represent a scattershot approach, but rather an astute understanding of the complexities and contradictions of the political system (including monarchies within states), which is required for the deposition to have any chance of success.

Gilbert (62) points out that it is hard to destool an Akan king because of his ancestral power, which may help to explain Robertson's concluding point that these depositions stand ambiguously both in and outside the law [compare also Walzer's (158) account of the legal issues involved in the trials of Charles I and Louis XVI]. Gilbert's analysis of the enstoolment and destoolment rites in the Akan kingdom of Akuapem in southern Ghana focuses on the nature of that ancestral power and the way it is put into the king through contact with the "black stool" of a predecessor and removed when he is deposed. The power of the "black stools" made during the 19th century (none have been made in this century) derived in part from human sacrifice. The purpose of the "40-day" *adae* and the annual *odwira* rites is in part to maintain the power of the ancestral stools by reannointing them. The *odwira* in particular is attended by thousands of Akuapem residents from all over Ghana.

Lemarchand's (97) collection of articles on the contemporary circumstances of monarchies elsewhere in Africa conforms to Staniland's approach. Six political scientists and one anthropologist provide fascinating details on the historical vicissitudes of what are distinguished as "theocratic kingship" (Ethiopia), "stratified kingships" (Rwanda, Burundi), "ethnic kingships" (Swaziland, Lesotho), and "incorporated kingships" (Buganda, Ankole, Ijeba). Yet Lemarchand (97, pp. 285–304) finally concludes that, broadly speaking, African kings had only two choices: to relinquish real power in order to retain the symbolic trappings of prestige or attempt to retain power, in which case they were sure to be destroyed, though some endured through sheer incompetence. [Doornbos's analysis of the decline of the Ankole monarchy as the result of its increasing "redundancy" and finally "irrelevance" in the political development of the colonial period is presented more fully in (38).] These alternatives do not account for either the Swazi case, as presented in Kuper's (93) recent biography of Sobhuza II, or the Ijesha (Yoruba) case analyzed by Peel (119).

Kuper's (93) official biography of Sobhuza II is a continuation of her argument in (89) that it is the king rather than the kingship which is divine in this case, and who by the force of his own personality has succeeded in revitalizing a dying office. Yet Kuper also shows how Sobhuza used indigenous conceptions of political legitimacy as his most powerful weapons in transforming the monarchy into a political party, regaining Swazi land lost to European concessions during the late 19th and early 20th centuries, and finally

(1973), in what was called the "King's coup," scrapping the "Westminster constitution" of 1968 and reassuming sole legislative, executive, and judicial powers.

Peel's (119) study, based on the premise that "political activity seems to be *the* major mode of society's self realization," especially in Africa (119, p. 7, his emphasis), focuses on the incorporation of Ijesha, residents of Ilesha, formerly capital of a kingdom with ties to Oyo, Benin, and Ekiti, into the Nigerian state (a process involving their becoming "Yoruba"). Like Tambiah (150, pp. 3–8), Peel found that his study became more historical than he originally intended as he sought to grasp the manifold ways in which Ijesha drew on their past experience in constructing models with which to guide and evaluate their current behavior in new circumstances. The study moves from a discussion of the precolonial kingdom centered on the town of Ilesha in the late 19th century to the 1970s, but in keeping with Ijesha perspectives on the meaning of history, it moves continually back and forth between the present and the past. These temporal relationships have their spatial counterpart in the movements of Ijesha (and their wealth) back and forth between the countryside and the town and between their "home town" and the larger community. All of these account for the increasing complexity of relations between ties of class and of community, rooted in alternative conceptions of power, authority, and prosperity that characterized the dynamics of the precolonial polity and continue to be central to Ijesha as Nigerian citizens.

Recent studies of the contemporary circumstances of some monarchies outside Africa in areas already considered in this review include, in addition to the Malagasy ethnography mentioned in previous sections, a collection of articles on kingship and royalist ideology in Madagascar (124), and work by Seneviratne on the Kandyan monarchy of Ceylon (142), Tambiah on the Thai monarchy (150), and Marcus on the contemporary kingdom of Tonga (105). The essays by Malagasy, French, and English scholars collected in Raison-Jourde's *Les Souverains de Madagascar* deal primarily with royal history, but also consider its "résurgences contemporaines." The unity of the collection is based on the hypothesis that the concept of *hasina,* the sacred power or force associated with kingship (see 34, pp. 139–63), derived from Malayo-Polynesian sources and spread throughout the island by means of Arab astrologers attached as spiritual advisers to kings. (Their role as traders, and indeed the role of economic factors generally, receives less attention.) This unity in turn accounts for the apparent success of the Merina in subduing most of the island during the 19th century (though historical data here and elsewhere suggest that Merina domination was contested everywhere outside the area surrounding the capital of Antananarivo). As with Ijesha, Malagasy views of the relevance of the past to the present are involved in the persistence of royalist ideology in the colonial and postcolonial periods. This theme is taken up in essays by Ellis,

Schlemmer, Randrianja, Althabe, and Chazan-Gillig on Malagasy resistance movements of the colonial period and the contemporary royal ritual of the Southern Sakalava of Menabe as practiced in 1968 (124, pp. 373–476).

Seneviratne (142) and Marcus (105) deal with relations between power and rank in Ceylon and Tonga respectively from two different viewpoints. Seneviratne focuses on the royal rituals at the Buddhist Temple of the Tooth at Kandy, as documented in historical accounts and his own contemporary ethnographic research. Hocart wrote on the Temple of the Tooth before turning to his more general work on ritual and politics (75), and part of the value of Seneviratne's account is in his demonstration of the ways in which these rituals (that participants saw as "work" not "worship") contributed to the prosperity of the polity. He also analyzes how and why some of these rituals were abandoned during the British colonial and postcolonial period whereas others—notably the annual Perahära ceremony involving the public display of the king's right to rule—were made central to the legitimacy of the contemporary state.

Marcus (105) is concerned with the position of the nobility in Tonga, one of the few Pacific polities besides Samoa and Fiji where indigenous chiefs still occupy politically important positions. Among these, Tonga is unique in having retained its kingship as well. As in his comparative study of land tenure in Tonga and Buganda, where differences in principles of kinship and appointment were critical factors (104), Marcus concentrates here on social structural issues involved in the formation of new elites including former commoners as well as former nobles. But he also deals with cultural factors, in particular the persistence of the concept of '*eiki* or "chiefly" values in relation to social organizational changes. Throughout his monograph and in (104, pp. 531–32), he suggests that the transformation of monarchical values and practices in Tonga and Buganda was complicated by the interest of British colonial officials in conceptualizing the processes involved in ways that conformed to their models of their own historical experience, an interest that indigenous political leaders were quick to turn to their own advantage.

The Thai monarchy was one of the few Third World polities to avoid European colonization altogether (Ethiopia is its African counterpart). Tambiah's (150) study, like those of fellow Southeast Asianists, combines structural with historical approaches to ritual and politics as integrated features of Thai social life. He begins in detail with an analysis of Buddhism as "a studied and ironic reversal of certain aspects of the brahmanical version of the world, society and kingship" (150, p. 19), epitomized in Asoka (c. 274–232 B.C.), the Indian emperor who, in converting to Buddhism, created the model for the Thai Buddhist polity (in which brahmans continued to participate in many capacities). He goes on to analyze the role of Buddhism in Thai monarchy as it developed and changed over several centuries in the context of structural constants, including the "galactic polity." The galactic polity, pulsating between centralization and dispersion, was the summation of the cooperation and opposition involved in relations between ruler and ruled at every level of the monarchy. It represented both the central place of the monarchy in the cosmos and the historical vicissitudes to which it was subject. The extraordinary statecraft of the 19th century Thai ruler Chulalongkorn is interpreted within this context as transforming the galactic polity into a "radial polity" through processes of bureaucratization comparable in some ways to those documented for Africa in the precolonial and colonial periods. (The increasing power of the king in this period is associated here with the elaboration of royal ritual.) One of the most interesting aspects of Tambiah's account of contemporary Thai politics has to do with Thai associations between enlightenment and growth (compare 117, 118) and the king's use of Buddhist monks in the political integration and economic development of the country along selectively Western lines. Tambiah concludes by putting the apparently more linear recent history of Thailand back into the context of recurrent "dialectical tensions" that summarize his understanding of Thai "religio-politics" as a total conceptual and historical as well as social fact.

All of these are studies of monarchies that, for reasons worth more investigation from a comparative perspective, slipped through the evolutionary net. There is almost no literature on the way in which political values associated with monarchy may be involved in the organization of only partially or nonmonarchical forms of government. Geertz dealt with some aspects of this problem in the Indonesian and Moroccan contexts in a series of articles published between 1963 and 1972 (in 57a, pp. 220–29, 243–49, 327–41). Mazrui's (107) analysis of African states deals with the efforts of secular African rulers to adopt monarchical styles through social ostentation, the personalization and sacralization of authority, and the creation of regal historical traditions. As such, his work is concerned, like the later collection of essays edited by Hobsbawm & Ranger (73), with "the invention of tradition" to cover political illegitimacy and reliance on force.

Hobsbawm's (73, pp. 1–14) distinction between "genuine" and "invented" traditions does not solve the hypothetical problem posed by such inventions, even as Wittgenstein (167, pp. 16–17) briefly formulated it in discussing Frazer's fire festivals. In any case, the data presented in the papers that follow are more complicated than this distinction supposes. Ranger's (124a) essay on Africa explores the ideology of "Imperial Monarchy" with which British and German colonists in particular sought to justify their rule. These "neotraditions" served to bring Africans into subordinate positions in colonial administrations, but also served as a means of asserting their own noble status, of redefining indigenous conceptions of hierarchy in their favor, and finally of challenging European authority. Cohn's (33a) essay on India shows that the imposition of British rule in India was characterized by fundamentally contradictory assumptions about what the consequences of that rule would be. He analyzes the political-ritual idiom in which these contradictions were embodied, epitomized in the Imperial Assemblage of 1876, noting that many of its features were later taken up by Indian nationalists. Cannadine's (26a) analysis of the changes in royal rituals during the growth and decline of the British empire (ca 1820–1977) is intended to demonstrate that rituals must be analyzed in their historical contexts. The first efflorescence of royal ritual in Britain during the 16th and 17th centuries was associated with the power of the monarchy; the second efflorescence of the Victorian and Edwardian periods was associated with its weakness. Apparently similar rituals differed widely in their conception and consequences.

Cannadine's account of Victorian royal ceremony might appear to support the relationship between the decline of political power and the elaboration of empty ceremonial expounded in Walter Bagehot's *The English Constitution*, published in this period (1865–67). Cannadine himself (26a, p. 107, n. 18) suggests that Bagehot's study was prescriptive rather than descriptive. Kuhn's (87a) analysis of Victorian attitudes toward the monarchy, focusing on Queen Victoria's Thanksgiving ceremony (for the Prince of Wales' recovery from illness) held in 1872, confirms that point and raises the question of why Bagehot's thesis should continue to be so influential. Hayden (66) analyzes the contemporary British monarchy from a different viewpoint. She suggests that the intimacy, even veneration, that many British citizens still feel for the monarchy is encouraged by Queen Elizabeth's deliberately frousy, middle-class style, which muffles the realities of social inequality and serves to support the position of the British upper classes for whom middle-class behavior is not the norm.

Cannadine's (26a, pp. 103–4) many references to political ceremonial in Tudor and Stuart England, Wilhelmine Germany, the French Third Republic and the Fascist and Communist regimes of the interwar period in Europe suggest that historians are beginning to reassess their own approaches to the relationship between ritual and politics in the European context. A reanalysis of Frazer's own work would make a valuable contribution to these efforts. Some recent essays concerning style in ethnographic writing mark an advance over narrow, sometimes ad hominem attacks that characterized many earlier appraisals of Frazer. Douglas (39) uses Gombrich's ideas about stylistic changes in the history of painting to analyze the changes in Frazer's reputation from his extraordinary popularity in the early part of this century to the disdain with which he is widely regarded now [see Smith's (143) recent critique in the tradition of Leach's debates with Jarvie in the 1960s, but compare Leach's (95a) Frazer Lecture of 1982 on "Kingship and Divinity" in first-second century A.D. Judaism]. Boon (22) points out that functionalist followers of Malinowski, who have criticized Frazer for his florid style, conform strictly to the rules of their own literary genre.

There are no studies of the way in which these disagreements about literature and science in social theory are themselves ensnarled in European associations between regicide in politics and rationalism in intellectual inquiry, beginning in England and France and carried into the Third World. Future research might heed Wittgenstein (167, pp. 16, 18) and cast a broader net, combining Hyman's (78) early work on Darwin, Marx, Frazer, and Freud as imaginative writers with an analysis of the political-economic context in which they wrote, then asking why it still matters.

Looking at a fraction of the relevant material published in the past few decades, I have argued that divine kingship involves several related issues: the barbarity of a world religion based on the ethic of love; indigenous conceptions of power, authority, and prosperity that Europeans did not share and that participants are unlikely to have shared equally; the natural science of government, which has vitiated rather than enhanced our understanding of social life; and rational government, as fantastic in conception as its antithesis. From a more universalist perspective, I have suggested that arguments about divine kingship are arguments about the course of human history, the transformation of superstition into logic and associated changes in the "opportunity costs," as it might now be phrased, of participating in social life. It is still an open question whether killing kingship has brought about more rational, less bloody forms of rule. Perhaps the fundamental issue remains as Mauss (106, p. 80) put it: "How to oppose one another without slaughter and to give without sacrificing (ones)self to others."

ACKNOWLEDGMENTS

I wish to thank T. O. Beidelman and Alan Harnik, who made valuable suggestions on earlier drafts of this review. I also benefited from discussions with members of a reading course on the topic: Pamela Feldman, Kenneth Newman, and Monica van Beusekom, and from comments received when some of the material was presented in the Anthropology Program at the Graduate Center of the City University of New York.

Literature Cited

1. Adler, A. 1978. Le pouvoir et l'interdit: aspects de la royauté sacrée chez les Moundang du Tchad. In *Systèmes des Signes: Textes Réunis en Hommage à Germaine Dieterlen*, pp. 25–40. Paris: Hermann. 519 pp.
2. Adler, A. 1979. Le dédoublement rituel de la personne du roi. In *La Fonction Symbolique: Essais d'Anthropologie*, ed. M. Izard, P. Smith, pp. 193–207. Paris: Gallimard. 346 pp.
2a. Adler, A. 1982. *La Mort Est le Masque du Roi: La Royauté Sacrée des Moundang du Tchad*. Paris: Payot. 427 pp.
3. Albert, E. M. (1960) 1963. Women of Burundi: A study of social values. In *Women of Tropical Africa*, ed. D. Paulme, pp. 179–215. London: Routledge & Kegan Paul. 308 pp.
4. Albert, E. M. (1964) 1972. Culture patterning of speech behavior in Burundi. In *Directions in Sociolinguistics: The Ethnography of Communication*, ed. J. J. Gumperz, D. Hymes, pp. 72–105. New York: Holt, Rinehart & Winston. 598 pp.
4a. Alkire, W. H. 1984. Concepts of order in Southeast Asia and Micronesia. *Comp. Stud. Soc. Hist.* 14:484–93

5. Anderson, B. R. O. G. 1972. The idea of power in Javanese culture. In *Culture and Politics in Indonesia*, ed. C. Holt, pp. 1–69. Ithaca: Cornell Univ. Press. 362 pp.
6. Apter, A. H. 1983. In dispraise of the king: Rituals 'against' rebellion in southeast Africa. *Man* (NS) 18:521–34
7. Apter, A. H. 1983. In praise of high office: The politics of panagyric among three Southern Bantu tribes. *Anthropos* 78:149–68
8. Arens, W. 1979. The divine kingship of the Shilluk: A contemporary reevaluation. *Ethnos* 3/4:167–81
9. Arens, W. 1984. The demise of kings and the meaning of kingship: Royal funerary ceremony in the contemporary southern Sudan and Renaissance France. *Anthropos* 79:355–67
10. Arens, W. 1985. The power of incest. See Ref. 11. In press
11. Arens, W., Karp, I., eds. 1985. *The Creativity of Power*. Bloomington: Indiana Univ. Press. In press
12. Arhin, I. 1983. Rank and class among the Asante and Fante in the nineteenth century. *Africa* 53:2–22
13. Asiwaju, A. I. 1976. Political motivation and oral historical traditions in Africa: The case of Yoruba crowns, 1900–1960. *Africa* 46:113–27
14. Baré, J.-F. 1980. *Sable Rouge: Une Monarchie du Nord-Ouest Malgache dans l'Histoire*. Paris: Harmattan. 383 pp.
15. Beattie, J. H. M. 1971. *The Nyoro State*. Oxford: Clarendon. 280 pp.
16. Beidelman, T. O. 1966. Swazi royal ritual. *Africa* 36:373–405
17. Berg, G. M. 1981. Riziculture and the founding of monarchy in Imerina. *J. Afr. Hist.* 22:289–308
18. Berger, I. 1981. *Religion and Resistance: East African Kingdoms in the Precolonial Period*. Tervuren: Musée Royal de l'Afrique Centrale. 181 pp.
18a. Bloch, M. L. B. 1924. *Les Rois Thaumaturges: Étude sur le Caractère Surnaturel Attribué à la Puissance Royale, Particulièrement en France et en Angleterre*. Strasbourg: Istra. 542 pp.
19. Bloch, M. 1977. The disconnection between power and rank as a process: An outline of the development of kingdoms in Central Madagascar. *Arch. Eur Sociol.* 18:107–48
20. Bloch, M. 1981. Tombs and states. In *Mortality and Immortality: The Anthropology and Archaeology of Death*, ed. S. C. Humphreys, H. King, pp. 137–47. New York: Academic. 346 pp.
21. Bonner, P. 1982. *Kings, Commoners and Concessionaires: The Evolution and Dissolution of the Nineteenth-Century Swazi State*. New York: Cambridge Univ. Press. 315 pp.
22. Boon, J. A. 1983. Functionalists write too: Frazer, Malinowski and the semiotics of the monograph. *Semiotica* 46:131–49
23. Boston, J. S. 1968. *The Igala Kingdom*. Ibadan: Oxford Univ. Press. 258 pp.
24. Bradbury, R. E. 1973. *Benin Studies*. London: Oxford Univ. Press. 293 pp.
25. Brown, S. D. 1975. *Ritual Aspects of the Mamprusi Kingship*. Leiden/Cambridge: African Studies Centre. 172 pp.
26. Busia, K. A. 1951. *The Position of the Chief in the Modern Political System of Ashanti*. London: Oxford Univ. Press. 233 pp.
26a. Cannadine, D. 1983. The context, performance and meaning of ritual: The British monarchy and the "invention of tradition," c. 1820–1977. See Ref. 73, pp. 101–64
27. Charsley, S. R. 1969. *The Princes of Nyakyusa*. Nairobi: East African Publ. 125 pp.
28. Chrétien, J.-P., Mworoha, E. 1970. Les tombeaux des bami du Burundi. *Cah. d'Études Afr.* 10:40–79
28a. Claessen, H. J. M., Skalník, P. 1981. *The Study of the State*. The Hague: Mouton. 535 pp.
29. Codère, H. 1973. *The Biography of an African Society: Rwanda, 1900–1960*. Tervuren: Musée Royal de l'Afrique Centrale. 399 pp.
30. Coedès, G. 1964. *Les États Hindouisés d'Indochine et d'Indonésie*. Paris: Bocard. 3rd ed. 494 pp.
31. Cohen, D. W. 1977. *Womunafu's Bunafu: A Study of Authority in a Nineteenth-Century African Community*. Princeton: Princeton Univ. Press. 216 pp.
32. Cohen, D. W. 1983. Food production and food exchange in the precolonial Lakes Plateau region. In *Imperialism, Colonialism and Hunger: East and Central Africa*, ed. R. I. Rotberg, pp. 1–18. Lexington: Heath. 270 pp.
33. Cohen, R. 1977. Oedipus rex and regina: The queen mother in Africa. *Africa* 47:14–30
33a. Cohn, B. S. 1983. Representing authority in Victorian India. See Ref. 73, pp. 165–209
34. Delivré, A. 1974. *L'Histoire des Rois d'Imerina: Interprétation d'une Tradition Orale*. Paris: Klincksieck. 448 pp.
35. Delval, R. 1972. *Radama II, Prince de la Renaissance Malgache, 1861–1863*. Paris: École. 959 pp.
36. Deng, F. M. 1972. *The Dinka of the*

Sudan. New York: Holt, Rinehart & Winston. 174 pp.
37. Derman, P. J. 1977. Stock and aristocracy: The political implications of Swazi marriage. *Afr. Stud.* 36:119–29
38. Doornbos, M. R. 1978. *Not All the King's Men: Inequality as a Political Instrument in Ankole, Uganda.* The Hague: Mouton. 232 pp.
39. Douglas, M. 1978. Judgements on James Frazer. *Daedalus* winter:151–64
40. Dumézil, G. 1977. *Les Dieux Souverains des Indo-Européens.* Paris: Gallimard. 268 pp.
41. Dumont, L. 1962. The conception of kingship in ancient India. *Contrib. Indian Sociol.* 6:48–77
42. Dumont, L. 1966. *Homo Hierarchicus: Le Système des Castes et ses Implications.* Paris: Gallimard. 449 pp.
43. Elam, Y. 1979. Nomadism in Ankole as a substitute for rebellion. *Africa* 49:147–58
44. Evans-Pritchard, E. E. (1948) 1962. The divine kingship of the Shilluk of the Nilotic Sudan. In *Social Anthropology and Other Essays,* pp. 192–212. New York: Free Press. 354 pp.
44a. Evans-Pritchard, E. E. 1971. Reigning and ruling. *MAN* (NS) 6:117–18
45. Fallers, L. A. 1956. *Bantu Bureaucracy: A Century of Political Evolution Among the Basoga of Uganda.* Chicago: Univ. Chicago Press. 283 pp.
46. Fallers, L. A., ed. 1964. *The King's Men: Leadership and Status in Buganda on the Eve of Independence.* London: Oxford Univ. Press. 414 pp.
47. Feeley-Harnik, G. 1978. Divine kingship and the meaning of history among the Sakalava (Madagascar). *Man.* (NS) 13:402–17
48. Feeley-Harnik, G. 1982. The king's men in Madagascar: Slavery, citizenship and Sakalava monarchy. *Africa* 52:31–50
49. Feeley-Harnik, G. 1984. The political economy of death: Communication and change in Malagasy colonial history. *Am. Ethnol.* 11:1–19
50. Feeley-Harnik, G. 1985. Ritual and work. In *Madagascar: Society and History,* ed. C. Kottak, A. Southall, P. Vérin. Durham: Carolina Academic Press. In press
51. Feierman, S. 1974. *The Shambaa Kingdom: A History.* Madison: Wisconsin Univ. Press. 235 pp.
52. Forde, D., ed. 1954. *African Worlds: Studies in the Cosmological Ideas and Social Values of African Peoples.* London: Oxford Univ. Press. 243 pp.
53. Fortes, M. 1962. Ritual and office. In *Essays on the Ritual of Social Relations,* ed. M. Gluckman, pp. 83–88. Manchester: Manchester Univ. Press
54. Fortes, M. 1968. Of installation ceremonies. *Proc. R. Anthropol. Inst.* 1967:5–20
55. Fortes, M., Evans-Pritchard, E. E., eds. 1940. *African Political Systems.* London: Oxford Univ. Press. 302 pp.
56. Frazer, J. G. 1913–15. *The Golden Bough: A Study in Magic and Religion.* London: Macmillan. 3rd ed., 12 vols. (1st ed., 2 vols. 1890; 2nd ed., 3 vols, 1900; abridged ed., 1922; *Aftermath: A Supplement to The Golden Bough,* 1936)
57. Gahama, A. 1979. *La Reine Mère et ses Prêtres au Burundi.* Nanterre: Laboratoire d'Ethnologie et de Sociologie Comparative. 78 pp.
57a. Geertz, C. 1973. *The Interpretation of Cultures: Selected Essays.* New York: Basic Books. 470 pp.
58. Geertz, C. 1977. Centers, kings, and charisma: Reflections on the symbolics of power. In *Culture and its Creators,* ed. J. Ben-David, T. N. Clark, pp. 150–71. Chicago: Univ. Chicago Press. 325 pp.
59. Geertz, C. 1980. *Negara: The Theatre State in Nineteenth-Century Bali.* Princeton: Princeton Univ. Press. 295 pp.
60. Gesick, L., ed. 1983. *Centers, Symbols and Hierarchies: Essays on the Classical States of Southeast Asia.* Yale Univ.: Southeast Asia Monogr. No. 26. 241 pp.
61. Giesey, R. E. 1960. *The Royal Funeral Ceremony in Renaissance France.* Geneva: Droz. 235 pp.
62. Gilbert, M. V. 1985. The quality of kingship: Ritual and power in a Ghanaian state. In *Pomp and Power: Royal Rituals in Pre-Industrial Societies,* ed. D. N. Cannadine, S. R. F. Price. Cambridge Univ. Press. In press
62a. Girard, R. *La Violence et le Sacré.* Paris: Grasset. 451 pp.
63. Gluckman, M. (1954) 1963. Rituals of rebellion in south-east Africa. In *Order and Rebellion in Tribal Africa: Collected Essays with an Autobiographical Introduction,* pp. 110–36. London: Cohen & West. 273 pp.
64. Goody, J. 1966. Introduction. In *Succession to High Office,* ed. Jack Goody, pp. 1–56. London: Cambridge Univ. Press. 181 pp.
65. Goody, J. 1971. *Technology, Tradition and the State in Africa.* London: Cambridge Univ. Press. 88 pp.
66. Hayden, I. 1985. *Cosmetics and Cosmology: Symbolic Domination and the Modern British Monarchy.* Tucson: Univ. Arizona Press. In press
67. Heine-Geldern, R. (1942) 1956. *Conceptions of State and Kingship in Southeast*

Asia. Cornell Univ., Dep. Asian Stud., SEA Program, Data Paper No. 18. 12 pp.
68. Henderson, R. N. 1972. *The King in Every Man: Evolutionary Trends in Onitsha Ibo Society and Culture*. New Haven: Yale Univ. Press. 576 pp.
69. d'Hertefelt, M., Coupez, A. 1964. *La Royauté Sacrée de l'Ancien Rwanda: Texte, Traduction et Commentaire de son Rituel*. Tervuren: Musée Royal de l'Afrique Centrale. 520 pp.
70. Heusch, L. de 1958. *Essai sur le Symbolisme de l'Inceste Royal en Afrique*. Bruxelles: Université Libre. 274 pp.
71. Heusch, L. de 1972. *Le Roi Ivre ou l'Origine de l'État: Mythes et Rites Bantous*. Paris: Gallimard. 331 pp.
72. Heusch, L. de 1982. *Rois Nés d'un Coeur de Vache: Mythes et Rites Bantous, II*. Paris: Gallimard. 537 pp.
73. Hobsbawm, E., Ranger, T., eds. 1984. *The Invention of Tradition*. London: Cambridge Univ. Press. 320 pp.
74. Hocart, A. M. 1927. *Kingship*. Oxford: Clarendon. 250 pp.
75. Hocart, A. M. (1936) 1970. *Kings and Councillors: An Essay in the Comparative Anatomy of Human Society*, ed., intro. R. Needham. Chicago: Univ. Chicago Press. 318 pp.
76. Horton, R. 1971. Stateless societies in the history of West Africa. In *History of West Africa*, ed. J. F. A. Ajayi, M. Crowder, I:78–119. London: Longman's. 568 pp.
77. Huntington, R., Metcalf, P. 1979. *Celebrations of Death*. London: Cambridge Univ. Press. 230 pp.
78. Hyman, S. 1962. *The Tangled Bank: Darwin, Marx, Frazer and Freud as Imaginative Writers*. New York: Atheneum. 492 pp.
79. Iliffe, J. 1984. Poverty in nineteenth-century Yorubaland. *J. Afr. Hist*. 25:43–57
80. Kantorowicz, E. H. 1957. *The King's Two Bodies: A Study in Mediaeval Political Theology*. Princeton: Princeton Univ. Press. 568 pp.
81. Kilson, M. 1983. Antelopes and stools: Ga ceremonial kingship. *Anthropos* 78:411–21
82. Kottak, C. P. 1972. Ecological variables in the origin and evolution of African states: the Buganda example. *Comp. Stud. Soc. Hist*. 14:351–80
83. Kottak, C. P. 1977. The process of state formation in Madagascar. *Am. Ethnol*. 4:136–55
84. Kottak, C. P. 1980. *The Past in the Present: History, Ecology and Cultural Variation in Highland Madagascar*. Ann Arbor: Univ. Michigan Press. 339 pp.
85. Krige, E. J. 1974. Woman-marriage with special reference to the Lovedu—its significance for the definition of marriage. *Africa* 44:11–37
86. Krige, E. J. 1975. Divine kingship, change, and development. In *Studies in African Social Anthropology: Essays Presented to Professor Isaac Shapera*, ed. M. Fortes, S. Patterson, pp. 55–74. London: Academic. 267 pp.
87. Krige, E. J., Krige, J. D. 1943. *The Realm of a Rain-Queen: A Study of the Pattern of Lovedu Society*. London: Oxford Univ. Press. 335 pp.
87a. Kuhn, W. M. 1985. *Dignity, efficiency and a royal thanksgiving: The British monarchy, 1871–72*. Presented at the General Seminar in Atlantic History, Culture and Society, Johns Hopkins University
88. Kuper, A. 1978. Rank and preferential marriage in southern Africa: the Swazi. *Man* (NS) 13:567–79
89. Kuper, H. 1972. Swazi royal ritual in a changing historical context. *Cah. d'Études Afr*. 12:593–615
90. Kuper, H. 1972. The language of sites in the politics of space. *Am. Anthropol*. 74:411–25
91. Kuper, H. 1973. Costume and identity. *Comp. Stud. Soc. Hist*. 15:348–67
92. Kuper, H. 1973. Costume and cosmology: The animal symbolism of the *ncwala*. *Man* (NS) 8:613–30
93. Kuper, H. 1978. *Sobhuza II: Nguenyama and King of Swaziland: The Story of an Hereditary Ruler and His Country*. New York: Holmes & Meier. 363 pp.
94. Kuper, H. 1978. The monarchy and the military in Swaziland. In *Social System and Tradition in Southern Africa: Essays in Honour of Eileen Krige*, ed. W. J. Argyle, E. Preston-Whyte, pp. 222–39. Cape Town: Oxford Univ. Press. 251 pp.
95. Kyerematen, A. 1969. The royal stools of Ashanti. *Africa* 39:1–10
95a. Leach, E. 1982. *Kingship and Divinity*. Frazer lecture of 1982. Presented at Oxford University
96. Lebeuf, A. M. D. (1960) 1963. The role of women in the political organization of African societies. See Ref. 3, pp. 93–119
97. Lemarchand, R. 1977. *African Kingships in Perspective*. London: Cass. 325 pp.
98. Lienhardt, G. 1955. Nilotic kings and their mothers' kin. *Africa* 25:29–42
99. Lienhardt, G. 1961. *Divinity and Experience: The Religion of the Dinka*. Oxford: Clarendon. 328 pp.
100. Lloyd, P. C. 1960. Sacred kingship and government among the Yoruba. *Africa* 30:221–37
101. Lonsdale, J. 1981. States and social pro-

cesses in Africa: A historiographical review. *Afr. Stud. Rev.* 24:139–225
101a. MacGaffey, W. 1985. African kingship cults. In *Encyclopedia of Religion*, ed. M. Eliade. New York: Free Press. In press
102. Mainga, M. 1972. A history of the Lozi religion to the end of the nineteenth century. In *The Historical Study of African Religions*, ed. T. O. Ranger, I. N. Kimambo, pp. 95–107. Berkeley: Univ. Calif. Press. 307 pp.
103. Maitland, F. W. 1901. The crown as corporation. *Law Q. Rev.* 17:131–46
104. Marcus, G. E. 1978. Land tenure and elite formation in the neotraditional monarchies of Tonga and Buganda. *Am. Ethnol.* 5:509–34
105. Marcus, G. E. 1980. *The Nobility and the Chiefly Tradition in the Modern Kingdom of Tonga*. Wellington: Polynesian Soc. 170 pp.
106. Mauss, M. (1925) 1967. *The Gift: Forms and Functions of Exchange in Archaic Societies.* New York: Norton. 130 pp.
107. Mazrui, A. A. 1967. The monarchical tendency in African political culture. *Br. J. Sociol.* 18:231–50
108. Mazrui, A. A. 1975. *Soldiers and Kinsmen in Uganda.* Beverly Hills: Sage. 325 pp.
109. McCaskie, T. C. 1983. Accumulation, wealth and belief. *Africa* 53:23–43, 79
110. Moertono, S. 1968. *State and Statecraft in Old Java: A Study of the Later Mataram Period, 16th to 19th Centuries.* Ithaca: Cornell Univ., Dep. Asian Studies, SEA program. 164 pp.
111. Muller, J.-C. 1980. *Le Roi Bouc Émissaire. Pouvoir et Rituel chez les Rukuba du Nigéria Central.* Québec: Fleury. 512 pp.
112. Ndayishinguje, P. 1977. *L'Intronisation d'un Mwami.* Nanterre: Lab. Ethnol. Sociol. Comp. 74 pp.
113. Needham, R. 1980. *Reconnaissances.* Toronto: Univ. Toronto Press. 120 pp.
114. Nye, R. 1984. *Crime, Madness, and Politics in Modern France: The Medical Concept of National Decline.* Princeton: Princeton Univ. Press. 367 pp.
115. Ottino, P. 1965. Le *tromba* (Madagascar). *L'Homme* 5:84–93
116. Packard, R. M. 1981. *Chiefship and Cosmology: An Historical Study of Political Competition.* Bloomington: Indiana Univ. Press. 243 pp.
116a. Paul, R. A. 1982. *The Tibetan Symbolic World: Psychoanalytic Explorations.* Chicago: Univ. Chicago Press. 347 pp.
117. Peel, J. D. Y. 1973. Cultural factors in the contemporary theory of development. *Arch. Eur. Sociol.* 14:283–303
118. Peel, J. D. Y. 1978. *Olaju:* a Yoruba concept of development. *J. Dev. Stud.* 14:135–65
119. Peel, J. D. Y. 1983. *Ijeshas and Nigerians: The Incorporation of a Yoruba Kingdom, 1890s–1970s.* New York: Cambridge Univ. Press. 346 pp.
120. Peel, J. D. Y. 1984. Making history: the past in the Ijesha present. *Man* (NS) 19:111–32
121. Pemberton, J. 1979. Sacred kingship and the violent god: The worship of Ogun among the Yoruba. *Berkshire Rev.* 14:85–106
122. Prins, G. 1980. *The Hidden Hippopotamus. Reappraisal in African History: The Early Colonial Experience in Western Zambia.* London: Cambridge Univ. Press. 267 pp.
123. Rabinbach, A. 1985. The European science of work: The economy of the body at the end of the nineteenth century. In *Representations of Work in France: Place, Practice, Organization and Meaning*, ed. S. S. Kaplan, C. Koepp. Ithaca: Cornell Univ. Press. In press
124. Raison-Jourde, F., ed. 1983. *Les Souverains de Madagascar: L'Histoire Royale et ses Résurgences Contemporaines.* Paris: Karthala. 476 pp.
124a. Ranger, T. O. 1983. The invention of tradition in colonial Africa. See Ref. 73, pp. 211–62
125. Ranger, T. O., Kimambo, I. N., eds. 1972. Introduction. See Ref. 102, pp. 1–26
126. Rattray, R. S. 1923. *Ashanti.* Oxford: Clarendon. 348 pp.
127. Ray, B. 1972. Royal shrines and ceremonies of Buganda. *Uganda J.* 36:35–48
128. Ray, B. 1977. Sacred space and royal shrines in Buganda. *Hist. Relig.* 16:363–73
129. Ray, B. 1977. Death, kingship and royal ancestors in Buganda. In *Religious Encounters with Death*, ed. F. Reynolds, E. Waugh, pp. 56–69. University Park: Penn. State Univ. Press. 247 pp.
130. Reid, A., Castles, L., eds. 1975. *Pre-Colonial State Systems in Southeast Asia.* Kuala Lumpur: Monogr. Malayan Branch of Royal Asiatic Soc., No. 6. 135 pp.
131. Richards, A. I. 1939. *Land, Labour and Diet in Northern Rhodesia: An Economic Study of the Bemba Tribe.* London: Oxford Univ. Press. 425 pp.
132. Richards, A. I. 1956. *Chisungu: A Girl's Initiation Ceremony among the Bemba of Northern Rhodesia.* London: Faber & Faber. 224 pp.
133. Richards, A. I. 1960. Social mechanisms for the transfer of political rights in some

African tribes. *J. R. Anthropol. Inst.* 90:175–90
134. Richards, A. I. 1961. African kings and their royal relatives. *J. R. Anthropol. Inst.* 91:135–50
135. Richards, A. I. 1969. Keeping the king divine. *Proc. R. Anthropol. Inst.* 1968:23–35
136. Robertson, A. F. 1976. Ousting the chief: Deposition charges in Ashanti. *Man* (NS) 11:410–27
137. Sahlins, M. 1981. *Historical Metaphors and Mythical Realities: Structure in the Early History of the Sandwich Islands Kingdom*. Ann Arbor: Univ. Michigan Press. 84 pp.
138. Sahlins, M. 1981. The stranger-king, or Dumézil among the Fijians. *J. Pacific Hist.* 16:107–32
139. Sahlins, M. 1983. Raw women, cooked men, and other 'great things' of the Fiji Islands. In *The Ethnography of Cannibalism*, ed. P. Brown, D. Tuzin, pp. 72–93. Washington, DC: Soc. Psychol. Anthropol. 108 pp.
140. Schoffeleers, M. 1972. The history and political role of the M'Bona cult among the Mang'anja. See Ref. 102, pp. 73–94
141. Seligman, C. G. 1934. *Egypt and Negro Africa: A Study in Divine Kingship*. London: Routledge. 61 pp.
142. Seneviratne, H. L. 1978. *Rituals of the Kandyan State*. London: Cambridge Univ. Press. 190 pp.
143. Smith, J. Z. 1973. When the bough breaks. *Hist. Relig.* 12:342–71
144. Smith, P. 1979. Aspects de l'organisation des rites. See Ref. 2, pp. 139–70
145. Southall, A. 1974. State formation in Africa. *Ann. Rev. Anthropol.* 3:153–65
146. Southwold, M. 1968. The history of a history: Royal succession in Buganda. In *History and Social Anthropology*, ed. I. M. Lewis, pp. 127–51. London: Tavistock, 307 pp.
147. Staniland, M. 1975. *The Lions of Dagbon: Political Change in Northern Ghana*. London: Cambridge Univ. Press. 241 pp.
148. Starkey, D. 1977. Representation through intimacy: A study in the symbolism of monarchy and court office in early-modern England. In *Symbols and Sentiments: Cross-Cultural Studies in Symbolism*, ed. I. Lewis, pp. 187–224. New York: Academic. 300 pp.
149. Strickland, D. A. 1976. Kingship and slavery in African thought: A conceptual analysis. *Comp. Stud. Soc. Hist.* 18:371–94
150. Tambiah, S. J. 1976. *World Conqueror and World Renouncer: A Study of Buddhism and Polity in Thailand Against a Historical Background*. New York: Cambridge Univ. Press. 557 pp.
151. Tcherkézoff, S. 1983. *Le Roi Nyamwezi, la Droite et la Gauche: Revision Comparative des Classifications Dualistes*. Cambridge: Cambridge Univ. Press; Paris: Maison des Sciences de l'Homme. 154 pp.
152. Thornton, R. 1983. Narrative ethnography in Africa, 1850–1920: The creation of an appropriate domain for anthropology. *Man* (NS) 18:502–20
153. Valeri, V. 1985. *Kingship and Sacrifice: Ritual and Society in Ancient Hawaii*. Chicago: Univ. Chicago Press
154. Van den Berghe, P. L., Mesher, G. M. 1980. Royal incest and inclusive fitness. *Am. Ethnol.* 7:300–17
155. Vansina, J. 1978. *The Children of Woot: A History of the Kuba Peoples*. Madison: Univ. Wisconsin Press. 406 pp.
156. Vaughan, J. H. 1980. A reconsideration of divine kingship. In *Explorations in African Systems of Thought*, ed. I. Karp, C. S. Bird, pp. 120–42. Bloomington: Indiana Univ. Press. 337 pp.
157. Walter, E. V. 1969. *Terror and Resistance: A Study of Political Violence, with Case Studies of Some Primitive African Communities*. New York: Oxford Univ. Press. 385 pp.
158. Walzer, M. (ed., intro.) 1974. *Regicide and Revolution: Speeches at the Trial of Louis XVI*. London: Cambridge Univ. Press. 219 pp.
159. Weinstein, W. 1977. Military continuities in the Rwanda state. In *The Warrior Tradition in Modern Africa*, ed. A. A. Mazrui, pp. 48–66. The Hague: Mouton. 260 pp.
160. Wilks, I. 1975. *Asante in the Nineteenth Century: The Structure and Evolution of a Political Order*. Cambridge: Cambridge Univ. Press. 800 pp.
161. Wilks, I. 1979. The golden stool and the elephant tail: An essay on wealth in Asante. In *Research in Anthropology*, ed. G. Dalton, I:1–36. Greenwich, Conn: JAI Press
162. Willeford, W. 1969. *The Fool and his Scepter: A Study on Clowns and Jesters and their Audience*. Evanston: Northwestern Univ. Press. 265 pp.
163. Willis, R. 1981. *A State in the Making: Myth, History and Social Transformation in Pre-Colonial Ufipa*. Bloomington: Indiana Univ. Press. 322 pp.
164. Wilson, G. 1939. *The Constitution of Ngonde*. Livingstone: Rhodes-Livingstone Inst. 86 pp.
165. Wilson, M. H. 1959. *Divine Kings and the 'Breath of Men'*. Cambridge: Cambridge Univ. Press. 27 pp.

166. Winzeler, R. L. 1976. Ecology, culture, social organization, and state formation in Southeast Asia. *Curr. Anthropol.* 17:623–39
167. Wittgenstein, L. 1979. *Bemerkungen über Frazers Golden Bough/Remarks on Frazer's Golden Bough.* rev. and ed., R. Rhees; transl. A. C. Miles. Atlantic Highlands: Humanities. 18/18e pp.
168. Wood, G. 1982. Frazer's magic wand of anthropology: Interpreting 'The Golden Bough'. *Arch. Eur. Sociol.* 23:92–122
169. Yamaguchi, M. 1972. *La Royauté et le symbolisme dualiste chez les Jukun de Nigeria.* Presented at École Pratique des Hautes Études, Paris
170. Young, M. W. 1966. The divine kingship of the Jukun: A re-evaluation of some theories. *Africa* 36:135–52

DENTAL EVIDENCE FOR THE DIET OF AUSTRALOPITHECUS

Richard F. Kay

Departments of Anatomy and Anthropology, Duke University, Durham, North Carolina 27710

INTRODUCTION

Explaining human structure in functional and adaptive terms and constructing a picture of behavioral changes in the course of human evolution are among the goals of evolutionary studies. Over the years many attempts have been made to interpret the behavior and ecology of *Australopithecus,* the earliest undoubted member of the human family. Such attempts have used information about environments of fossil deposition, the nature of the death assemblages, cultural associations, and the animals and plants with which australopithecines are found. One of the most important sources of information about australopithecine diets has been the anatomy of the animals themselves, especially the teeth. It is this last source that is examined critically here.

The basis for most reconstruction of the behavior of extinct animals is the analogical argument. We observe a pattern of behavior in a living species and note that such behavior is associated with an anatomical specialization. When a similar specialization is observed in an extinct species, that animal is inferred to have behaved in a similar way. By building up a catalog of such behavioral inferences, the broad patterns of behavior and ecology of a paleospecies emerge. Of course, this commonsense approach has difficulties, many of which are reviewed and debated in recent literature (3, 31, 58).

Many theories have been advanced about the dietary adaptations of *Australopithecus* and early *Homo*. Some of these theorics have utilized the evidence of australopithecine dental structure. J. T. Robinson (46) proposed that diets differed in the two species of *Australopithecus* then known. The larger species, *A. robustus,* was primarily a vegetarian whereas the smaller species, *A. africanus,* ate meat as well as vegetable foods. Largely in agreement with Robinson, Jolly (25) envisioned primitive *Australopithecus,* as exemplified by

A. robustus, shifting from a frugivorous diet to one centering on cereal grains. He saw "gracile" *Australopithecus (A. africanus)* as (*a*) the allometric equivalent of *A. robustus* at smaller size (and therefore also a seed-eater), (*b*) an even more primitive "prerobust" animal, possibly a frugivorous species, or (*c*) advanced over *A. robustus* in the direction of more meat eating, thus evolved toward the condition in earliest *Homo*. He argued that the last option was the most probable. Szalay (57) countered that the dental specializations of *A. robustus*, argued by Jolly as being adaptations for seed eating, make more sense if they are adaptations to meat tearing and bone crushing. He rejected Jolly's seed-eating hypothesis and argued that "*protohominids*" were hunters and scavengers. However, the relatively small, vertically implanted incisors of *Australopithecus*, upon which both Jolly's and Szalay's dietary hypotheses were based, are found as well in a variety of leaf-eating primate species (23, 33). It remained for Kay (30) to point out that the same cheek-tooth morphology featured in Jolly's and Szalay's scenarios is found in living arboreal primates that eat hard-shelled fruits and nuts. Kay argued that these last items may also have figured prominently in the diets of australopithecines.

In view of Hylander's and Kay's findings, it seems clear that Jolly's and Szalay's dietary scenarios for early hominids may need modification. Simply stated, it is difficult to argue convincingly that australopithecines were exclusively either seed-eaters or hunters and scavengers if such an argument is based on dental specializations found today in living primate species ranging from leaf-eaters to hard-fruit eaters. The purpose of this paper is to survey the evidence for australopithecine diets in light of current knowledge about the diet and dental anatomy of living primates, especially the apes. To provide a backdrop for the functional and adaptive interpretations which form the bulk of this paper, I first review briefly the diet and feeding behavior of the living apes. A second section concerns itself with the functional anatomy of the teeth of man and the apes. Finally, I consider some analytical approaches to the assessment of dental structure in terms of diet in living species.

DIETARY BEHAVIOR OF LIVING APES

The great apes are man's closest living relations; smaller "lesser apes" are more distantly related (the genera and species referred to here are enumerated in Table 1). Collectively with humans these animals are referred to as the Hominoidea or "hominoids," with three subgroups called Hominidae or "hominids" for *Homo*, plus *Australopithecus*, Pongidae for the great apes, and Hylobatidae for the lesser apes. This is not a cladistic classification. There is no implication that *Homo* is equidistant phylogenetically from all the living great apes. In fact, *Homo* probably shares a more recent common ancestor with the pongids *Pan* and *Gorilla* than with *Pongo*.

Table 1 Taxonomic groups of apes, humans, and prehumans[a]

Family/subfamily	Living forms	Extinct forms discussed
Hylobatidae (lesser apes)	*Hylobates* (gibbons) *Symphalangus* (siamangs)	
Pongidae (great apes)	*Pongo* (orangutan) *Pan* (common chimp and bonobo) *Gorilla* (gorilla)	none
Hominidae (humans and prehumans)	*Homo sapiens*	*Homo habilis* (earliest *Homo*) *Australopithecus* *A. afarensis* *A. africanus* (graciles) *A. robustus* (robusts) *A. boisei* (hyperrobusts)

[a] Phylogeny is not implied. Humans are recognized as being more closely related to some pongids than to others.

Among the great apes, the predominant food for common chimpanzees is fruit, which constitutes about 70% of the fresh weight of the diet on a yearly basis. Most of the rest of the diet is composed of more fibrous items: leaves, bark, and stems. These fibrous foods are thought to be the principal sources of protein in the diet. Although invertebrates and vertebrates are commonly foraged for and may be important sources of certain amino acids, these items taken together constitute 5% or less of the total yearly diet by weight (22, 73). The diet of bonobos is less well known but appears to be generally similar to that of the common chimpanzee (1). Both chimpanzees forage for food primarily in the trees. Gorillas sharply contrast with chimpanzees in being predominantly leaf-eating (folivorous), with a concentration on leaves, stems, and shoots. Fruits account for less than 5% of the diet (in terms of feeding time) in some areas but may be somewhat higher elsewhere. Food is eaten primarily on the ground (7).

Orangutans spend roughly 55% of their yearly feeding time eating fruits, although leaves and bark form the bulk of the diet in certain seasons (35). Feeding time underestimates the weight of fruit consumed if studies of chimpanzees are a guideline. Orangs are probably at least as frugivorous as common chimpanzees. More than any other living apes, orangutans will eat very hard-shelled fruits and nuts (8, 35). In one recent description, Galdikas (8) wrote:

> [There] seemed to be no fruit . . . which was so hard that adult orangutans of both sexes were not morphologically equipped to open it. . . . [They eat] hard nuts which are so difficult to

open that occasionally they defied nut-crackers and machetes. In fact the force exerted by orangutans in opening these nuts was so great that adult orangutans typically press their cheeks against tree trunks or branches to prevent the nuts from popping out of their mouths (8, p. 306).

The orangutan is the most arboreal of all the great apes in its feeding behavior. Most of the time feeding occurs in tree crowns.

Among the lesser apes, species of *Hylobates* inhabit South Asia as well as most of the Malay Archipelago. They are sympatric with *Symphalangus* in Sumatra and the Malay peninsula. Some species of gibbons are extremely frugivorous. *H. klossii* spends more than 90% of its feeding time eating fruits (68). Dietary percentages of fruits and leaves (including new and mature leaves as well as flowers) are roughly 60:40 for *H. lar* and *H. agilis;* a much larger component of the diet comes from leaves in siamangs (40:60). Siamangs also spend more time foraging for insects than do the gibbons (12). All hylobatids forage almost exclusively in the trees.

DENTAL FUNCTION AMONG HOMINOIDEA

A prerequisite for making dietary interpretations from dental evidence is a clear picture of the functional anatomy of primate, especially hominoid, teeth. In primates, two stages of oral food processing are recognized. Ingestion is the process whereby food is brought into the mouth and, if necessary, a bite is separated. The bite of food is "evaluated" and if suitable is swallowed. If not, it is masticated until the consistency is satisfactory for swallowing (21). Ingestion and mastication involve complex interactions of the masticatory apparatus as a whole, but only the teeth need concern us here. Ingestion can utilize the front teeth (incisors and canines), or food can be introduced into the side of the mouth and involve the cheek teeth (premolars and molars). Mastication ordinarily involves only the cheek teeth.

Ingestion

Because ingestion often involves the use of the front teeth, but much less commonly the molars, we should expect to find dental adaptations for ingestion in the incisors, canines, and perhaps the premolars. Generally, however, the structure of the anterior teeth represents a compromise of selective pressures for ingestive and social behaviors.

The incisors of hominoids are spatulate teeth that can be brought together edge to edge for the forceful separation of a bite of food. Generally occlusion occurs between all the lower incisors acting as a single edge and a corresponding edge of the upper incisors. This pattern is a hallmark of all living and fossil monkeys and apes and is seen as well in some Eocene prosimian groups. The major variations in this region among hominoids have to do with (*a*) the degree to which the upper lateral incisor and/or lower canine become incorporated into this slicing mechanism, and (*b*) the relative length of the incisor edge compared to body size. Variation in the latter has been shown to be related to feeding preference in living monkeys and apes and will be discussed later.

The canines of primitive pongids were robust pointed teeth. The upper canine could be occluded against the lower in a powerful stabbing mechanism or interdigitated into an embrasure behind the lower canine and against the mesial aspect of the front premolar. The distal edge of the upper canine was kept sharp by being ground against the lower premolar. Monkeys and apes use their large canine teeth for splitting and husking fruit, but an equally important role for the canines is as a weapon for intra- and interspecific conflicts.

In humans and australopithecines the canines are greatly reduced in size and the occlusal interdigitation deemphasized. In some *Australopithecus* the canines resemble incisors in appearance and functional role. The other major variation seen among monkeys and apes is in the relative size of male and female canines. This variation is most likely attributable to the changing role of the canines in defense and sexual competition (20).

Mastication

Mastication involving the cheek teeth is cyclical and rhythmic. In primates, including humans, it usually occurs on only one side of the mouth in any given cycle. Each cycle is arbitrarily divided into three strokes. Jaw movements begins at maximum jaw gape. In the closing stroke the jaws are shifted to the chewing side and the teeth approximated. The power stroke begins when contact occurs between the teeth or between tooth, food, and tooth, and continues as long as this contact persists. The opening stroke returns the jaws to maximum gape for the next cycle (21).

Masticatory cycles are divided into two broad types, "puncture-crushing" and "tooth-tooth contact." In puncture-crushing there is always food interposed between the teeth, so there is little precision during the power stroke; any wear produced on the teeth is smoothly rounded, and wear striations have no strongly preferred orientation. In tooth-tooth contact, the teeth interdigitate and the close contacts between matching tooth surfaces control and limit the movements occurring in the power stroke. The resultant wear surfaces tend to be sharply edged and planar; the striations found on these wear surfaces are often nearly parallel to the directions of jaw movement (13b, 32).

Two phases of the power stroke in chewing are recognized (2, 26, 32, 42). Phase I of the power stroke begins with the buccal cusps vertically aligned. The lower cheek teeth are moved upward and mesiolingually, the precise details of this movement being guided by the structure of the touching surfaces of the teeth. At the termination of this movement, the principal lingual cusps of the upper molars are seated upon the large lower molar platforms in centric occlusion. In Phase II, the lower cheek teeth are moved further mesiolingually and slightly downward until tooth contact ceases.

Phase I is dominated by the movement of matching pairs of sharp-edged crests past one another, an action which produces a cutting or shearing of resistant foods, especially those that contain fiber in the form of sheets or rods. As centric occlusion is approached, the cusps are approximated, crushing food interposed between them. Phase II is characterized by the movement of these crushing surfaces across one another in a grinding action (28).

Molar Occlusion

The pattern of molar occlusion among living and fossil hominoids has been quite stereotyped since Miocene times, i.e. for the past 20 million years (29, 37). Upper and lower molars are low-crowned with relatively little relief compared with most prosimians. Four principal cusps are present in all taxa and a fifth lower molar cusp, the hypoconulid, is often well developed. The cusps are low and rounded with flattened surfaces which appear to function primarily as crushing platforms in occlusion. They also support crests which function as cutting edges in the power stroke. The power stroke begins with the upper and lower buccal cusps vertically aligned. In Phase I the lower teeth are moved dorsally and lingually engaging the crests leading from the buccal cusps in such a way as to shear food interposed between them. Almost simultaneously at the beginning of Phase I the lingual cusps come into vertical alignment and their leading edges act as shearing devices. On each molar there are eight such pairs of cutting edges. Phase I continues as the trailing surfaces of these shearing crests are ground across one another. At the termination of this phase, principal upper molar cusps are lodged in lower molar basins in centric occlusion.

The power stroke continues in Phase II with the lower molar basins moving lingually and buccally across matching surfaces of protocone and hypocone in a grinding action. The direction of the jaw movement in the power stroke is powered by the muscles of mastication, but the details are controlled by the occlusal pattern. In relatively unworn teeth, Phase I involves a considerable dorsal component and Phase II includes a lesser but significant amount of ventral movement. However, with wear to the occlusal surfaces, Phases I and II come to be more parallel to the occlusal plane.

The principal differences in molar construction among the living apes are in the relative sizes of the cusps, the lengths of their accompanying crests, the areas of the basins, and the angles of attack of the lower molars in the power stroke. The largest part of this variation is attributable to changes in shape as a consequence of size (allometry) and adaptation to different diets.

All functional interpretations of molar structure presented to date assume that high levels of force are generated between the teeth throughout the power stroke. But recent studies by Hylander & Crompton (23b, described in 21), using in vivo strain gauges placed on mandibular bone, suggest that this may not be the case, at least in monkeys. Hylander and Crompton have found that strain in mandibular bone during mastication is greatest during Phase I, and often declines rapidly as the teeth approach centric occlusion. In Phase II, bone strain has declined considerably, suggesting that much less force is being transmitted between the teeth at this time. If these findings also hold for man and the apes, the significance of molar designs in Phase II activity has been greatly overstated. Further work is needed before Phase II activity is discounted, however, particularly in hominids. The presence of deep gouges and striations on the surfaces of ape molars that occlude in Phase II implies a powerful grinding action in some Phase II power strokes of some taxa (13a).

Occlusion in puncture-crushing is less precise since the teeth do not come into the intercuspal range. It has been suggested by various workers that pointed cusps could be an advantage for certain animals in puncturing the tough exoskeletons of insects (48, 49), but such an advantage is overweighed by other disadvantages in animals the size of humans or apes. In these larger animals there is increased risk that large stress concentrations generated at sharp cusps could lead to breakage. As a consequence, larger animals which do emphasize puncture-crushing tend to have relatively low crown relief.

ANALYTICAL TECHNIQUES

Allometry

Allometry describes the phenomenon of relative changes in shape during growth or relative differences in magnitude of dimensions in species of different sizes (14). The relationship between a pair of morphological or physiological variables X and Y can be expressed by the equation

$$Y = B \, (X)^\alpha$$

where Y is the dependent variable, X is the independent variable and (B) and (α) are constants. This equation can be linearized by transforming the data into logarithms to produce the equivalent equation

$$\text{Log } Y = B + \alpha \, (\text{Log } X)$$

where B and α (the Y-intercept and slope) are found from a least-squares fit to the data.

When the slope of the regression equation between two linear variables (X and Y) equals 1.0, Y is said to vary isometrically with respect to X. If the slope is less than 1.0, the Y is negatively allometric with respect to X. If it is greater than 1.0, we have positive allometry. When X is a linear dimension and Y an area, isometry refers to instances when the slope equals 2. When Y is a volume or weight, an isometric slope equals 3. Of course, when Y is a linear dimension and X is body weight, the slope (α) is 1/3; when Y is a surface area, (α) is 2/3.

Another common pattern seen among mammals is called metabolic scaling. For mammals, the total daily energy requirements (basal metabolism) in kilocalories is proportional to the 0.75 power of body weight. Thus the amount of energy in food that an animal must acquire must also be proportional to the 0.75 power of body weight (34). Dimensions of the body which change in size proportional to the 0.75 power of body weight often are said to be metabolically scaled.

Using Residuals to Compare Measurements

Once a regression equation is computed to express the relationship between two variables, it is useful to consider how individual pairs of measurements deviate from that regression. In the analysis of residuals, the expected value of Y (Ye), the dependent variable, is calculated from a given value of X. The empirically observed value of Y (Yo) is compared with that predicted by the equation using the equation

$$\text{Residual} = 100\ (Yo - Ye)/Ye$$

The residual is often referred to as the "percentage difference" value (52, 54). If X is body weight and Y the size of a tooth, an animal with a positive residual would be said to have a larger tooth than would be expected for its body weight.

Comparison of percentage-difference values has lead to some confusion in the literature. If the p-d value for one animal is $+10.5$ and another is $+21.0$, the first animal has a 9.5% larger value (121.0 divided by 110.5) not a 100% larger value.

APE MODELS AND AUSTRALOPITHECINE DIETS

Cheek-Tooth Area and Body-Size Scaling

Robinson (46, 47) first suggested that relative to body weight, robust australopithecines have proportionately larger cheek teeth than do gracile forms. Two conflicting hypotheses have been advanced to account for this observation. According to Robinson's dietary hypothesis, robust *Australopithecus* needed the additional molar surface over what would be expected for its body weight to support a diet of tough herbivorous foods, whereas gracile *Australopithecus*, being carnivorous in part, had less need for large grinding teeth. As will be seen, several other hypotheses about dietary differences between australopithecine species, working from the same observations, claim that the two species did differ in terms of diet but do not claim that the gracile form was more carnivorous (e.g. 25).

Pilbeam & Gould (43) countered Robinson with a hypothesis based on metabolic equivalence. They suggested that the two kinds of australopithecines were functionally equivalent in terms of the cheek tooth areas, and the relatively larger cheek teeth can be accounted for by the added energetic demands of a larger animal eating the same kinds of foods. [A variant of this argument had been considered and rejected by Jolly (25).] Gould later expanded this claim into a general rule of mammalian dental allometry (15).

The two hypotheses can be reformulated in terms of allometry. In the dietary hypothesis, it is assumed that different-sized animals eating similar foods will be geometrically scaled. The fact that the cheek teeth of the robusts are larger than what would be expected for simple geometric scaling (i.e. the slope of the equation relating crown surface area to body weight among australopithecines is greater than 0.67) is explained by the larger species having a different, tougher diet. In contrast, in the metabolic equivalence hypothesis, a slope greater than 0.67, namely one of 0.75, is predicted because of increased metabolic demands in a larger animal and may not involve a difference in diet.

To test these hypotheses, we can use data on living species of apes and other primates. For the metabolic equivalence hypothesis to be satisfied, in living primates having similar diets (or when a variety of dietary patterns are sampled at all body sizes) cheek-tooth area should scale to the 0.75 power of body weight (i.e. have slopes of 0.75 in the logistic equation above). Alternatively, if geometric scaling occurs, the same groups should have tooth area scaling to the 0.67 power of body weight. A number of studies of different groups of primates and other mammals have been made and all show slope values not significantly different from 0.67 and significantly less than 0.75 (e.g. 5, 11, 13, 27, 72).

Table 2 summarizes body weights and dental measurements of living apes and living and fossil humans on which the following accounts are based. Table 3 summarizes information pertaining to the metabolic equivalence hypothesis. Slopes are given for regressions with cheek-tooth area as the dependent variable and weight as the independent variable. None of these slopes is significantly different from 0.67, and in two cases the slope is significantly less than 0.75.

What accounts for the fact that, when diet is factored out, metabolic requirements scale to the 0.75 power of body weight whereas cheek-tooth size scales to approximately the 0.67 power of body weight? At least two other factors are presumably involved in the scaling of cheek-tooth size. To reduce food particles to optimal size and consistency, larger animals may simply chew more rapidly or spend more time chewing or both. For the equations to show metabolic scaling, the exponents of these factors must add up to 0.75, that is,

Table 2 Summary of data pertaining to dental anatomy of humans and living apes

Species	Body weight (kg) M	Body weight (kg) F	Cheek-tooth area (mm²) M	Cheek-tooth area (mm²) F	Lower second molar dimensions (mm) N	Lower second molar dimensions (mm) Length	Lower second molar dimensions (mm) Total shear	Lower second molar dimensions (mm) Crush surface	Lower second molar dimensions (mm) Hypoconid height
Hylobates									
agilis	5.82	(5.50)	119.7	(112.5)	5	6.53	14.72	16.23	3.38
H. klossii	—	(—)	100.2	(99.2)	5	5.85	12.96	12.95	3.35
H. lar	5.70	(5.30)	127.7	(126.0)	5	5.90	13.64	14.56	3.38
H. hoolock	6.90	(6.10)	155.8	(155.4)	5	7.70	17.71	24.15	4.63
H. moloch	5.81	(4.87)	152.5	(148.5)	5	6.32	14.06	16.70	3.63
Symphalangus									
syndactylus	11.1	(10.3)	[238.8]		6	8.71	20.49	31.60	5.12
Pongo									
pygmaeus	69.0	(37.0)	667.2	(563.1)	5	12.77	28.98	63.03	7.66
Pan									
troglodytes	49.0	(41.0)	407.3	(380.6)	10	11.68	24.74	55.25	6.58
P. paniscus	39.0	(31.0)	296.7	(308.8)	11	9.90	21.50	40.40	5.7
Gorilla									
gorilla	140.0	(70.0)	915.1	(780.8)	14	18.03	41.53	108.63	8.41
Australopithecus									
afarensis	[37]		[655.3]		—	—	—	—	—
A. africanus	[35]		[743.2]		—	—	—	—	—
A. robustus	[44]		[837.2]		—	—	—	—	—
A. boisei	[48]		[1084.5]		—	—	—	—	—
Homo habilis	[48]		[655.1]		—	—	—	—	—
Homo sapiens	60.0	(54.0)	[475.8]		—	—	—	—	—

Sources for body weight of living species are those cited in 10, 26, 43, 50.
Estimated body weights of fossil homonids are from 40.
Summed mandibular cross-sectional areas is m-d length × b-1 breadth for P4-M3.
Data from Kay (personal data; 24, 36, 67, 70). Data in square brackets is based on combined sexes or sexes not specified.
Lower second molar dimensions are from Kay (personal data):N = sample size; Length = mesiodistal length; Total shear = sum of the lengths of crests 1-8 which occlude in Phase I, see Kay (29); Crush surface = surfaces which occlude at centric occlusion, see Kay (27); Hypoconid height = the vertical height of the hypoconid cusp

the exponent of surface area plus the exponent of chewing rate plus the exponent of chewing time must equal the exponent of metabolic rate.

Actually, larger animals chew much more slowly than do small ones; data of my own and from the literature (27) suggest that the exponent of chewing rate is around −0.20 (the taxa are: *Tupaia, Galago crassicaudatus, Saimiri sciureus, Ateles* sp., and *Homo*). Substituting these numbers into the equation and solving for chewing time, the exponent of increase in chewing time as a function of body weight must be 0.26. The equation predicts that larger animals must spend more time chewing their food than do smaller ones eating foods of the same nutritional quality. "Foraging time" in primates does increase with increased size, lending some support to this hypothesis (4), but foraging time includes so many other activities besides mastication that the prediction cannot be tested rigorously as yet.

Taken separately, slope values for pongid and hylobatid males and females are considerably higher than those for apes as a whole (Table 3), although not

Table 3 Interspecific scaling of cheek-tooth area against body weight in hylobatids and pongids

Species groups:	Slope	95% confidence interval	Intercept	Correlation coefficient	N
Hylobatid plus pongid females:	0.620	0.47–0.79	1.677	0.960	9
Hylobatid plus pongid males:	0.572	0.46–0.68	1.696	0.974	9
Hylobatid and pongid males and females:	0.588	0.50–0.68	1.696	0.964	18
Pongid females: (*Pongo pygmaeus, Pan troglodytes, P. paniscus, Gorilla gorilla*)	0.998	−0.90–2.90	1.052	0.849	4
Pongid males: Hylobatid females: (*Hylobates agilis, H. hoolock, H. lar, H. moloch, Symphalangus syndactylus*)	0.861	0.06–1.66	1.153	0.958	4
	0.755	−0.76–2.28	1.600	0.836	5
Hylobatid males: (All the above plus *H. lar*)	0.905	0.58	1.432	0.944	5

Presented in the table are the least-squares slope, the 95% confidence interval for the slope, the Y-intercept, the coefficient of correlation (r), and the sample size (N) for equations in the form (log surface area = slope value (log body weight) + intercept value.

significantly different from 0.67, as Table 3 and Figure 1 show. Consideration of these apparent exceptions points to a significant dietary component to the scaling. *Symphalangus,* the largest hylobatid, and *Gorilla,* the largest pongid in these regressions, are each more folivorous than the other members of their respective families. Among noncercopithecoid primates generally, the more folivorous species have proportionally larger teeth (27, 28). In this case, the coincidence of the most folivorous species also being the largest one raises the value of the slope coefficient. One suspects that some similar dietary difference may have been at play among australopithecine species given that the slope of the regression between cheek-tooth area and body weight is much higher than geometric scaling would dictate (27, 41).

Thus, the available evidence of the scaling of cheek-tooth size in living animals suggests that larger australopithecines have proportionally larger cheek teeth than their smaller relatives because fiber was more emphasized in the

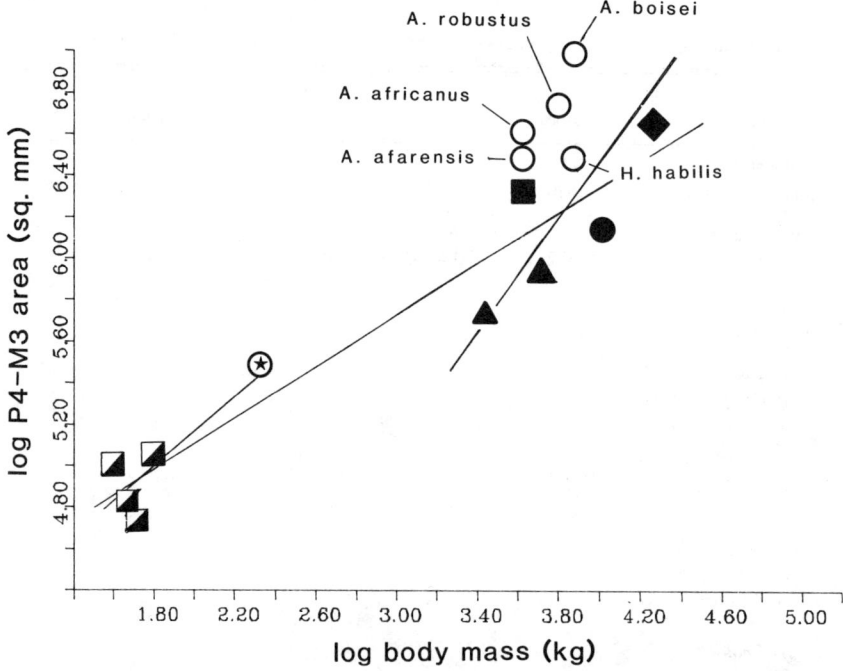

Figure 1 Log-log plot of mandibular cheek-tooth area vs. body weight. Three curves fit to the data represent Y on X for 1. all female apes: log area (sq mm) = 0.609 log weight (kg) + 1.692; 2. for female pongids: log area (sq mm) = 0.998 log weight (kg) + 1.052; and 3. for female hylobatids: log area (sq mm) = 0.755 log weight (kg) + 1.600. Symbols: closed triangles, *Pan;* closed diamond, *Gorilla;* closed square, *Pongo;* half-closed squares, *Hylobates;* circle with star, *Symphalangus;* closed circle, *Homo sapiens.* Open circle are extinct hominid taxa identified separately.

larger species and less so in the smaller (27). However, this is not necessarily evidence that gracile *Australopithecus* had more meat in its diet, as Robinson argued.

Cheek-Tooth Size

It is now generally accepted that australopithecines were "megadont" animals, that is, for their body weight the cheek teeth were particularly large compared with apes (71). Recently, McHenry (41) has confirmed this claim, employing the technique of percentage difference as a measure of relative cheek-tooth area and data from living great apes as a standard. The question can be reformulated to ask if there are living apes which are also megadont and could serve as a model for understanding that pattern in australopithecines. This problem has been approached here by calculating the least-squares regressions between mandibular P3-M3 cheek-tooth area as a function of body weight for males and females separately and computing the percentage-difference values for the individual species.

Table 4 gives the results of that analysis. Whether the model for male or female apes is chosen, it is clear that *Pongo,* the orangutan, stands out as having particularly large cheek teeth compared with other great apes. In terms of tooth size in both models, modern humans, as exemplified by Australian aborigines, have rather small cheek teeth, about the same as in *Pan troglodytes. Homo*

Table 4 Residuals (percentage deviations) from regressions characterizing the relative cheek-tooth area of hominids and living pongids

Species	Model A	Model B
Females only:		
Pongo pygmaeus	14.24	
Pan troglodytes	−7.85	
P. paniscus	−4.88	
Gorilla gorilla	−0.03	
Males only:		
Pongo pygmaeus		9.16
Pan troglodytes		0.19
P. paniscus		−4.88
Gorilla gorilla		−3.89
H. sapiens	−11.97	1.22
Australopithecus		
afarensis	22.04	36.75
africanus	32.06	47.49
robustus	25.90	42.53
boisei	35.71	54.44
Homo habilis	9.02	24.06

Calculated residuals are based on two models. In Model A the least squares regression is computed for all female pongids, in Model B for all male pongids. The equations used in these models are given in Table 3.

habilis apparently had cheek teeth about the same size relatively as those of orangutans by the female ape model. Australopithecines appear to have had even larger molars. On average the teeth were 13% larger by the model for female apes and 33% using the male ape model, assuming that body weight estimates for these animals made by McHenry (40) are correct. The analysis again suggests that there may have been dietary differences among the australopithecine taxa.

It is tempting to conclude that the same selective factors for megadonty operated in australopithecines, early *Homo,* and orangutans. The latter stand out among the great apes for being able to eat extremely hard food objects such as seeds and nuts. Perhaps early hominids were doing the same but even more so. It is well to remember, however, that early hominids did not live in the same sorts of environments as those where orangs live today; such analogies should be drawn only in terms of the mechanical properties of the food and not the actual foods consumed (42a). By this reasoning, *Australopithecus* was eating something very hard, but the precise nature of the food is not known.

Enamel Thickness

The enamel on the molar teeth of australopithecines was quite thick like that in *Homo* but unlike the much thinner enamel of gorillas or chimpanzees. Two explanations have been advanced for this. The terrestriality hypothesis (25, 51, 55) accounts for the presence of thick enamel by positing that a ground-foraging animal such as *Austalopithecus* specialized on some particularly hard, tough, or abrasive food item found commonly on the ground but not in the trees. (Three candidates for such a dietary item were cereal grains, meaty metapodials, and underground tubers.) Such an animal probably ate considerable amounts of grit along with its food. The food and the grit would produce rapid tooth wear, selecting for the evolution of thick enamel to prolong the life of the tooth. If this hypothesis is correct, we should expect to find thicker enamel in terrestrial animals than in their arboreal close relatives.

Critics of this idea (e.g. Kay, 30) feel that feeding on hard and brittle foods alone may have been the selective impetus responsible for evolving thick enamel. Dietary grit is an extraneous factor. They point out that several species of arboreal primates have evolved thick enamel. Thus, the evolution of this specialization need not have been "driven by," or even coincided in time with, the attainment of a terrestrial foraging pattern with a concomittant heavy-wear dietary regime (30). If they are right, irrespective of whether an animal is an arboreal or terrestrial forager, the thickest enamel might be expected in animals that eat hard, brittle foods. The thinnest enamel would be expected in leaf-eaters where forces are concentrated narrowly at cusp tips and along crests. Animals that eat softer, less brittle fruits should fall between these extremes. Dietary grit would have a neglible role in selecting increased enamel thickness.

Having thick enamel would not rule out an animal being a terrestrial forager, but it must not be taken as evidence that an animal was terrestrial or passed through a terrestrial stage in its evolution.

A study of comparative molar enamel thickness casts doubt on the terrestriality model and supports the dietary model (30). Up until now cheek-tooth dimensions have been considered in relation to body weight. It is also instructive to make comparisons of tooth shape. In the analyses that follow, the method of residuals is used to compare lower second molar shape with mesiodistal molar length treated as the independent variable. [There is no sound theoretical reason for the choice of length as the independent one instead of, say, length times breadth or breadth alone. Any of the other measurements could yield results somewhat different from those presented here, a problem discussed recently by Smith (53).]

The distribution of enamel thickness among living ape species bears little relation to what would be expected under a terrestriality hypothesis, but it closely mirrors what would be expected if selection for enamel thickness is based strictly on diet. Once differences in tooth size are accounted for by percentage-difference analysis, *Gorilla,* the most terrestrial species of apes, has the thinnest enamel not the thickest, contrary to what the terrestriality hypothesis would have predicted. Arboreal species run the gamut from having very thick to comparatively thin enamel. The same lack of correlation between enamel thickness and substratum preference occurs in arboreal and terrestrial species of monkeys (30).

Enamel thickness is highly correlated with diet preference. More leaf-eating species like the siamang and gorilla have thinner enamel than do more fruit-eating species like chimpanzee and gibbon. Orangutans stand out as having extremely thick enamel, much thicker than in other living apes. This accords well with field reports (see above) of orangutans eating extremely hard nuts. The same distribution is seen among monkey species: folivores have the thinnest enamel, hard-object frugivores the thickest, and other frugivores are intermediate.

What then best accounts for australopithecines having thick enamel? Thick enamel would suggest that australopithecines ate some very hard, brittle foods. Such an adaptation may well have evolved in the trees where hard-shelled fruits or nuts may have been abundant. Also, thick enamel may have been well suited for terrestrial food items like roots, tubers, or cereal grains. Enamel thickness by itself should not be taken as evidence for a terrestrial foraging strategy in earliest australopithecines or any other species (30, 61). Determination of whether earliest australopithecines spent considerable time in the trees should be left to analysis of paleoenvironments and postcranial anatomy.

An unresolved problem is why human molar enamel is so thick (9, 39). A dietary explanation in terms of hard food objects seems difficult to sustain, at least in modern populations. It may be that the thick enamel of humans today is a holdover from an earlier time when selection favored having thick enamel.

Molar Shape

Although there have been many ideas about what australopithecines ate, scant attention has been paid to what details of molar crown patterns might tell. [The work of Grine (18, 19) reviewed below is a striking exception to this generalization.] Most workers seem to believe that because the details of the molar crowns are soon obliterated by wear, any differences there might be are more likely the result of genetic drift or pleiotropic effects rather than natural selection for dietary specialization. Wallace (65) suggested that the primary function of tooth cusps in australopithecines was not to slice food but simply to facilitate the learning of a chewing pattern.

A series of measurements can be used to characterize various functional aspects of the molar crown. A measure of crushing and grinding development is the area of surfaces that contact at the termination of Phase I and are ground across those of the upper molars in Phase II. An impression of the importance of shearing or cutting to the overall design is gained by summing the lengths of eight cutting or shearing edges which are effective in Phase I. Additionally, the height of a principal lower-molar cusp, the hypoconid, was used as a measure of crown height to provide a crude indication of the longevity of the tooth crown in response to tooth wear. The detailed definitions of the measurements are presented elsewhere (26, 28). The raw measurements are summarized in Table 2 and analyzed in part in Table 5.

Surface area of living apes scales nearly isometrically with respect to tooth length (1.93 +/− 0.26) (surface dimensions should change by the square of linear dimensions in isometry). Percentage-difference values for the various taxa bear no apparent relationship to the dietary spectrum of living apes. Differences in the surface area for crushing and grinding may play a significant part in the adaptive strategy for feeding on different sorts of foods, but if so, the accentuation of crushing and grinding must be achieved by several alternative and not necessarily exclusive strategies. Some taxa show a greater proportion of the molar devoted to this task; others achieve the same effect by expanding the molar field, e.g. by molarizing the premolar surfaces.

The lower-molar-crown height is likewise isometric with respect to tooth length (0.95+/−0.14). The only interesting finding is that orangutans have rather high crowns relative to tooth length in comparison to chimpanzees or gorillas. The possible significance of this for resistance to wear is unclear. Whether other species of mammals that eat hard objects have relatively high crowns should be explored.

The summed lengths of shearing crests on the lower second molars (summarized in Table 5) is of considerable interest in relation to diet. Overall, shearing crests are isometric with respect to tooth length. Two models for shearing are outlined in the table. One model considers percentage difference for more folivorous species in relation to frugivores as a group; the other considers percentage difference for the more frugivorous species in relation to folivores as a group. In both cases, percentage differences for the more folivorous species are much higher than those of the frugivorous species.

Thus far, little attempt has been made to evaluate the teeth of fossil hominids in terms of the development of shearing, crushing, or crown height. Gregory & Hellman (17) noted that australopithecine molars wear nearly flat, not differing

Table 5 Residuals (percentage deviations) from least squares regressions characterizing the relative size of dental features in living apes and man

Species	Incisor % difference		Shearing % difference		Enamel thickness % difference
	Maxillary	Mandibular	Model A	Model B	
Primarily frugivorous species					
Pan					
troglodytes	4.60	11.10	−3.41	−9.09	−3.1
P. paniscus	2.51	5.65	−1.73	−7.28	—
Hylobates					
agilis	—	—	0.10	−4.97	—
H. klossii	—	—	−2.10	−6.90	6.3
H. lar	7.15	2.48	2.15	−2.88	−5.0
H. hoolock	—	—	2.91	−2.53	7.8
H. moloch	—	—	−1.25	−6.21	−7.9
Hard-object frugivore —folivore					
Pongo					
pygmaeus	13.83	18.99	4.02	−2.22	33.8
Primarily folivorous					
Gorilla					
gorilla	−10.35	−19.69	7.11	0.15	−23.4
Symphalangus					
syndactylus	−14.67	−13.60	5.92	0.13	−19.2

Calculations for residuals of incisor size are based on the regression equations as follows: log (mandibular incisor size in mm)= 1.830+ 0.381(log body weight in kilograms); log (maxillary incisor size in millimeters)= 2.270+ 0.346(log body weight in kilograms). Females only are used. Incisor data courtesy of Dr. William Hylander.

Calculations of residuals for shearing are based on two models. In the first, the least-squares regression is computed for all frugivorous species (N=8) producing the equation ln S = 0.953 (ln M2) + 0.90 where S is the summed lengths of eight shearing crests and M2 is lower second molar length. In the second, the regression is computed for folivorous species (N=2): ln S = 0.968 (ln M2) + 0.92.

Calculations of residuals for enamel thickness are summarized in Kay (30). The coefficient of correlation (r) between the two models of shearing is 0.988; a Spearman's rank correlation is 0.93.

greatly from those of modern man or the orangutan. They argued that this made possible a heavy grinding action and implied a diet of tough or gritty foods. They were more concerned however, to show the distinctions between australopithecines and apes, especially chimpanzees, and did not emphasize differences within the first group. Recently Grine (18, 19) has noted that robust australopithecines have teeth which wear into a relatively flat and featureless configuration, whereas the gracile form from South Africa has molars with considerably more occlusal relief and, in at least one population of graciles, possibly more emphasis on Phase I wear facets. This suggests that the *A. africanus* may have had relatively better development of shearing than did *A. robustus*, implying a dietary difference. Even the graciles appear to have much less shearing emphasis than any living folivorous apes. In light of this, it seems extremely unlikely that any species of *Australopithecus* could have had a high-fiber diet like that of *Gorilla*.

Incisor Proportions

Robinson (46, 47) observed that robust *Australopithecus* has proportionally smaller incisors than the gracile form from South Africa and proposed that this could be explained by dietary differences, the gracile form being more omnivorous. Pilbeam & Gould (43) also examined incisor size compared with cheek-tooth area. They agreed that the relatively and absolutely smaller size of the incisors between hyperrobust *Australopithecus boisei* and early *Homo* probably had a dietary explanation, perhaps even the same one originally formulated by Robinson (i.e. more meat in the diet of *Homo* than in *A. boisei*). However, they believed that all species of australopithecines were herbivores "of one kind or another." They hinted at the possibility for dietary differences among the herbivorous australopithecines but did not examine this critically.

Several more specific claims about the adaptive significance of the small incisors of *Australopithecus* have been advanced. Szalay (57) argues that *Australopithecus*' small vertically implanted incisors are reminiscent of the incisors of some scavenging Carnivora and may have been used for pulling and tearing meat from bones. Jolly (25) suggests that the incisors of *Australopithecus* are small because they were eating small food items which required little "preparation" before being masticated. He contrasted this with animals which use their incisors frequently while eating "fleshy fruits and other tree products (page 14)." The implication seems to be that small incisors might point to a terrestrial forager. Specifically, Jolly considers cereal grains as a likely dietary component.

In terms of incisor adaptations, it is well to ask first, as Pilbeam and Gould did, if early *Homo* and robust and gracile *Australopithecus* represent functionally equivalent incisor adaptations at different size, or whether the differences can be attributed to a more purely dietary explanation. To resolve this we might need to consider how incisors scale among hominoids with similar diets, and, when body size is controlled for, if the remaining differences allow a plausible adaptive interpretation.

The incisor size differences Robinson originally documented in early hominids were proportional ones between cheek-tooth size and incisor size, so it becomes difficult to tell if the relatively small incisors of the larger taxa are accounted for by their having relatively larger cheek teeth. To avoid this problem, incisor size is considered here in relation to body weight, as Hylander did in a study of this sort (23). Figures 2 and 3 are log plots of body weight vs incisor spans (a measure of the total breadth of the incisor cutting edge) for female apes (data courtesy of W. Hylander). Slopes of the regression equations with body weight as the independent value are 0.38 for mandibular-incisor size and 0.34 for maxillary-incisor size. The two are not significantly different (at the 95% confidence level) from one another nor are they significantly different from isometry (0.33). Percentage-difference values in Table 5 show that chimpanzee, gibbon, and orangutan have relatively large incisors, whereas siamang and gorilla have relatively small ones.

Folivorous species have smaller incisors than do the frugivorous ones in this analysis, so one is tempted to interpret these differences purely in terms of diet. However, as Hylander properly cautioned, such a conclusion is unwarranted. For example, the calculated value for incisor percentage difference in *Homo sapiens* (-32.0) is even smaller than that for *Gorilla*, but *Homo* is clearly not a folivore. Hylander proposed a more general explanation, one which is accepted here: the relative size of the incisors relates to the overall amount that they are employed in food preparation. Selection favors larger incisors among animals that use their incisors more extensively in food preparation because this might prolong the life of the tooth subjected to heavy wear. Hylander proposed that the small incisors of *Homo* might result from less incisal preparation of foods owing to the takeover of some of these functions by hand tools.

I have selected the values for maxillary-incisor span for single specimens of *Australopithecus afarensis* and *A. boisei* as measured from casts (see Figures 1–3 for details) as examples of where early hominids might be expected to fall on the above plots. Body weights again come from McHenry (40). If his weight estimates are correct, both *A. afarensis* and *A. boisei* had small incisors for their body weights. The percentage-difference values are -8.8 and -16.6 respectively. The difference between the maxillary-incisor spans of these two australopithecines is almost as great as that between pairs of living apes gorilla and chimpanzee, or between gibbon and siamang. Interestingly, however, there was further incisor reduction leading to *Homo*, suggesting a possible link with increased tool use at the *Australopithecus* to *Homo* transition (i.e. increased use of tools to prepare foods relieves the selective demands for large incisors to do the same job (23).

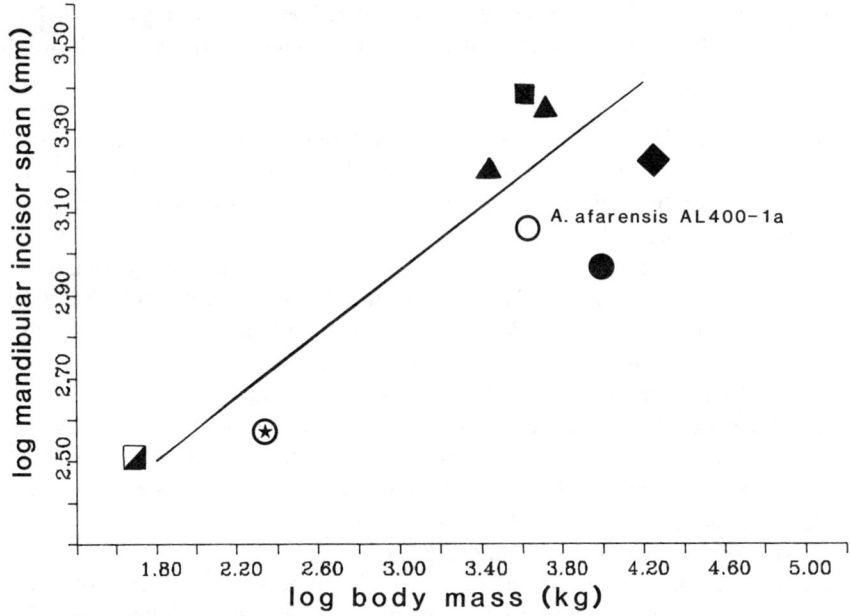

Figure 2 Log-log plot of mandibular incisor span vs body weight as measured in (23). The curve fit to the data represents Y on X for all female apes: log mandibular incisor span (mm) = 0.381 log weight (kg) + 1.830. Symbols as for Figure 1. Data from W. L. Hylander.

To summarize the above findings, australopithecines had small incisors compared with those of chimpanzees and orangutans but in the size range of gorilla. The study of living anthropoids shows that incisor size scales roughly isometrically with body size, although possibly the scaling is positively allometric for maxillary-incisor size. Thus, dietary or other behavioral factors being equal, we should expect the incisor span of the larger australopithecines to increase linearly with the cube root of body weight. The finding that larger australopithecine species have proportionally smaller incisors than do smaller species points to a difference in the way these species may have used their incisors. The difference between hyperrobust *(A. boisei)* and earliest australopithecines *(A. afarensis)* is of the same magnitude as between modern hominoids known to differ in their techniques of food incision. Whether the differences observed in the fossil hominids have to do with dietary differences or result from different food preparation techniques cannot be resolved at this point, although it is again clear as it was for enamel thickness that having small incisors need not imply that australopithecines were terrestrial foragers. Modern humans have even smaller incisors than did australopithecines, and the possibility of a link between incisor reduction and tool use since the australopithecine stage is a viable one.

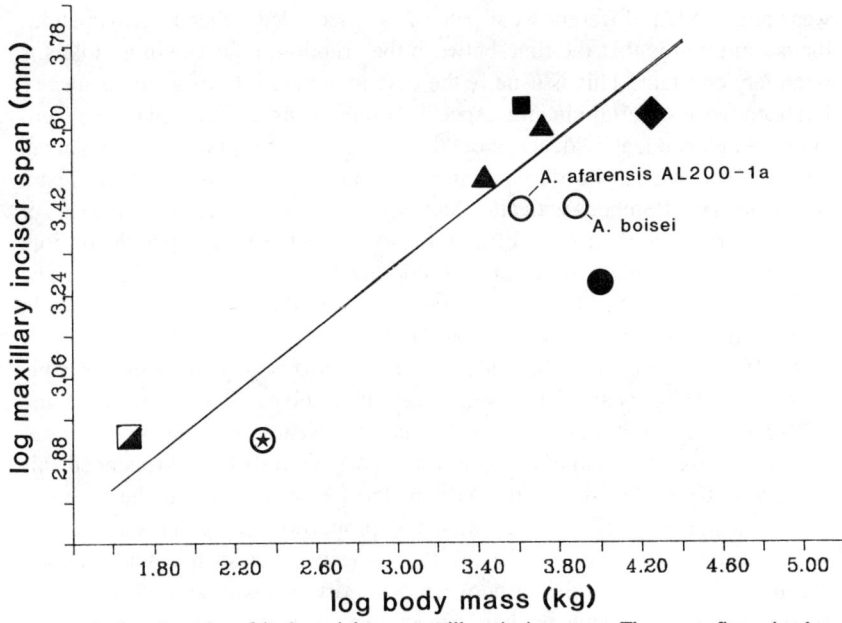

Figure 3 Log-log plot of body weight vs. maxillary incisor span. The curve fit to the data represents Y on X for all female apes: log maxillary incisor span (mm) = 0.346 log weight (kg) + 2.270. Symbols as for Figures 1, 2.

Tooth Wear

When the lower teeth are drawn across their counterparts in the power stroke of mastication, friction between occluding tooth surfaces as well as between food and the teeth produce patterns of scratching and pitting wear on the surfaces. For many years these patterns were used to reconstruct occlusal events during the power stroke (e.g. 2, 21, 32, 37). Additionally, inferences about the diet were drawn from the rate at which wear occurred. Recently it has also been suggested that surface wear patterns may be diagnosed as resulting from dietary preferences. The dietary interpretations thus involve either quantitation of the overall rate of wear on the teeth or the study of wear surfaces themselves.

The pattern of wear, especially the rate of attrition, has long been used as a source of information about diets of human archaeological samples. For example, dental attrition has been related to the use of stone tools for grinding grain (e.g. 16). Using a quantitative technique to estimate the difference in overall wear between adjacent molars, P. L. Walker (64) demonstrated a particularly high attrition rate in one human population which placed a heavy dietary emphasis on the use of maritime food resources, particularly shellfish, fish, and sea-mammal meat dried in the sand. Using a similar approach, Teaford (59) has inferred differences in wear rates between a folivorous and a frugivorous species of monkey (the frugivorous monkey was inferred to have a more rapid wear rate). When different wear patterns are accorded a dietary explanation, the assumption is that the time between the eruption of succeeding molars is relatively constant. This is usually the case in populations of a single species but becomes less certain in cross-species comparisons, as Teaford recognized. Without independent evidence about the timing of the eruption of the molars in australopithecines, any differences in wear gradients could equally be the result of (*a*) dietary differences with attendant differences in the rate of tooth wear, or (*b*) a difference in the timing of eruption events between the species, or both (69). Before the wear patterns of australopithecines and other hominids can be interpreted in terms of diet, more details are needed concerning wear rates in living primate species with different diets.

A different approach to the study of wear patterns is to quantify microscopic characters of the wear on the wear facets themselves. Rensberger (45) and Walker et al (63) were among the first to interpret wear facet patterns in terms of diet in herbivorous mammals. Teaford & Walker (60) have broadened this work recently to encompass the wear patterns of a spectrum of herbivorous monkeys and apes. They quantified the proportions of gouges, pits, and striations on homologous wear facets of species that span a wide dietary spectrum. They distinguished between primarily frugivorous and folivorous species as well as between hard-object feeders and soft-fruit eaters. The soft-fruit-eating species in their study *(Pan)* differed from such folivores as *Gorilla, Alouatta* (the howler monkey), and *Colobus* (the leaf monkey) in having proportionally more pits than striations on crushing wear facets. This difference in the proportions of pits to striations is carried to an extreme in *Cercocebus* (mangabey), *Cebus,* and *Pongo,* all of which occasionally or commonly eat nuts and other hard fruits.

Application of the above findings to australopithecine diets has not advanced very far. Puech and coworkers (44) briefly described some aspects of australopithecine tooth wear but drew no dietary conclusions. Walker (62) proposed tentatively that australopithecines may have been fruit eaters because their enamel microwear patterns were said to be similar to those of the extant frugivorous anthropoids *Pan* and *Mandrillus*. Grine (18, 19) found differences in the tooth microwear on the deciduous teeth of robust and gracile *Australopithecus* and suggested *A. robustus* in South Africa ate harder objects, material containing opaline phytoliths, and perhaps more extraneous "dust." As yet few generalizations about the dietary distinctions among australopithecines are possible using microwear data.

DISCUSSION AND SUMMARY

Study of the dental correlates of diet have been somewhat impeded by blanket a priori claims that dietary differences among apes, now quite thoroughly documented, are not matched by corresponding differences in tooth structure. If this were true, there would be no reason to seek the pattern of dietary evolution in the study of teeth. Such a point is made emphatically by Washburn & Ciochon (66) in referring to man's closest living relatives:

> The anatomy of [chimpanzees and gorillas] has been known for many years. . . . Yet the dietary differences between the chimpanzee and the gorilla were not anticipated. In general the dentitions are similar and the basis of the difference seems to be the issue of ground feeding vs. tree feeding. . . . Adaptation is through diversity rather than close correlation between items of the diet and the structure of the dentition (p. 777).

Although pessimism continues in some quarters (38, p. 14), this nihilist view is now refuted. Actually, as we have seen, the dentition of living apes gives a rather clear picture of some aspects of diet. I have attempted to use this information to reconstruct the diets of australopithecines. Let me comment first on the two most "robust" existing dietary theories.

The evidence of the dental anatomy mitigates against some aspects of Jolly's theory of the seed-eater. He likened the masticatory apparatus of robust australopithecines to the design of a flour mill, where small, hard, spherical grains are pulverized by a grinding action, but this does not account satisfactorily for the molar structure of australopithecines. Typically, grass-seed-eating mammals such as the gelada baboon, on which Jolly based his model, and many kinds of rodents have molar crowns which wear into a flattened surface made up of a series of cutting edges formed by complexly infolded enamel. This presumably allows thin-shelled grass grains and blades to be milled efficiently. By contrast, as Jolly recognized, australopithecines have flat, relatively featureless molars on which shearing is deemphasized unlike mammalian grass-seed eaters. To account for this difference, Jolly argued that (*a*) geladas and other grass-seed-eating mammals generally also eat grass blades; (*b*) it is the grass-blade constituent in the diet that is the agent selecting for a shearing design; and therefore (*c*) early hominids must have eaten grass seeds but not grass blades. This argument is difficult to accept because it is hard to imagine how an early hominid could have separated successfully grass seeds from fibrous grass stems and leaves. Besides, even if this were possible, cereal grains would still require milling. The mechanical requirements of breaking apart thin-shelled grass hulls are an equally likely selective agent for the shearing designs of the teeth of graminivorous mammals. Moreover, no known seed-eating mammals (except modern *Homo*) reach the body weight of australopithecines. It seems doubtful that australopithecines could find enough grass seed the year around to survive on a diet of this sort.

Likewise, there are some difficulties with Szalay's proposal of a meat-eating scavenging way of life for "protohominids." Szalay noted, as did Jolly, that the characteristically thick enamel and robustly constructed jaws of early hominids might indicate heavy mastication. He considered these adaptations most consistent with a meat-chewing or bone-cracking adaptation. However, the postcanine teeth of extinct early hominids do not resemble those of meat-scavenging mammals. Modern scavengers like hyenas and certain dasyurids have pointed postcanine teeth for producing great force concentrations on large food objects. By contrast, flat occlusal surfaces would tend to distribute and disperse rather than concentrate bite forces on large objects, the reverse of the desired effect in bone munching. As Jolly noted, flat-crowned teeth are effective stress concentrators only on objects small enough to be rolled between the teeth.

Many uncertainties remain about australopithecine diets, but several general conclusions can be drawn from the dental evidence:

1. Australopithecines were megadont animals, that is, for their body weight they had larger cheek teeth than do humans, chimpanzees, or gorillas. Only one species of living ape, the orangutan, approaches *Australopithecus* in tooth size. Orangutans can eat very hard foods. Perhaps australopithecines could do the same. Obviously, however, australopithecines were not eating the *same* hard food items as living orangutans: the two lived in very different habitats.

2. The largest *Australopithecus*, *A. boisei*, has proportionally larger cheek teeth than the smaller species *A. africanus* and *A. afarensis*. It is likely that such a difference is accounted for by dietary differences among the species. One possible difference would be that the larger species was more specialized to feed on hard objects than the smaller ones, a view that finds support in other masticatory structures (23a). Earliest *Homo*, *H. habilis* apparently was slightly megadont, but less so than any *Australopithecus*. Modern *Homo* has extremely small cheek teeth relative to body weight.

3. *Australopithecus* has relatively thick cheek-tooth enamel compared with living apes. Again, the most similar among living apes is the orangutan, and the probable explanation is that *Australopithecus* were also specialized for chewing hard food objects. *Homo* apparently retains this thick enamel but the reason is obscure.

4. Collectively, australopithecines have rather poorly developed molar cresting compared with most apes. The same is true of early *Homo*. There is some evidence that the larger species had comparatively less well-developed cresting than do the smaller ones. This specialization points to a diet containing relatively little fiber (i.e. a diet more like that of chimpanzee and orangutan than gorilla). Less crest development in *A. robustus* and *A. boisei* suggests even less fiber in their diets. Some have suggested that australopithecines have high-crowned cheek teeth, but this is not documented. If so, this would be an additional resemblance to orangutans.

5. For their body weight, australopithecine species apparently have smaller incisors than do chimpanzee or orangutan. The incisors are comparable in size to those of gorilla and siamang, both of which are folivorous, but this may not

imply a folivorous diet for australopithecines. It could mean a difference in the technique of oral food preparation. *A. robustus* and *A. boisei* have smaller incisors than do *A. africanus* or *A. afarensis,* the degree of difference being similar to that between chimp and gorilla. Several proposed explanations for the small size of the incisors (e.g. small-object feeding, bone-gnawing) are plausible but not confirmed on present evidence. Modern *Homo* has very small incisors compared even with *Australopithecus,* a trend begun with *H. habilis.* This further reduction may have been the result of tool use preempting incisor use.

6. There are differences in microscopic tooth wear on the molars of robust and gracile australopithecines. These could be interpreted to mean that *A. robustus* ate either harder objects, more opal phytoliths, or more grit than did *A. africanus.*

Taken together, the dental pattern of australopithecines suggests they were often eating hard foods containing relatively *small* amounts of fiber (compared with gorillas or siamangs) and requiring little incisal preparation. Fruits with hard husks or seeds in pods (like those of legumes) are among the plausible candidates.

ACKNOWLEDGMENTS

I thank Drs. William Hylander, Alan Magid, Ross MacPhee, Pascal Picq, and John Wible for constructive criticism. Ms. Pat Thompson helped in manuscript preparation.

Literature Cited

1. Badrian, N., Badrian, A., Susman, R. L. 1981. Preliminary observations on the feeding behavior of *Pan paniscus* in the Lomako forest of central Zaire. *Primates* 22:173–81
2. Butler, P. M. 1952. The milk molars of Perissodactyla with remarks on molar occlusion. *Proc. Zool. Soc. London* 121:777–817
3. Clutton-Brock, T. H., Harvey, P. H. 1979. Comparison and adaptation. *Proc. R. Soc. London Ser. B* 205:547–65
4. Clutton-Brock, T. H., Harvey, P. H. 1977. Species differences in feeding and ranging behaviour in primates. In *Primate Ecology,* ed. T. H. Clutton-Brock, 19:557–84. London/New York: Academic. 631 pp.
5. Corruccini, R. S., Henderson, A. M. 1978. Multivariate dental allometry in primates. *Am. J. Phys. Anthropol.* 48:203–8
6. Deleted in proof
7. Fosse, D., Harcourt, A. H. 1977. Feeding ecology of free ranging mountain gorilla *(Gorilla gorilla beringei).* See Ref. 4, 14:415–49
8. Galdikas, B. 1978. Orangutans and hominid evolution. In *Spectrum: Essays Presented to Sultan Takdir Alisjahbana on His Seventieth Birthday,* ed. P. Udin. Jakarta: Jian Rakyat
9. Gantt, D. G. 1977. *Enamel of primate teeth: Its thickness and structure with reference to functional and phyletic implications.* PhD thesis. Washington Univ., St. Louis, Mo. 403 pp.
10. Gaulin, S. J. C., Sailer, L. D. 1984. Sexual dimorphism in weight among the primates: The relative impact of allometry and sexual selection. *Int. J. Primatol.* 5:515–36
11. Gingerich, P. D., Smith, B. H., Rosenberg, K. 1982. Allometric scaling in the dentition of primates and prediction of body weight from tooth size in fossils. *Am. J. Phys. Anthropol.* 58:81–100
12. Gittins, S. P., Raemakers, J. J. 1980. Siamang, lar and agile gibbons. In *Malayan Forest Primates,* ed. D. J.

Chivers, 3:63–106. New York/London: Plenum. 364 pp.
13. Goldstein, S., Post, D., Melnick, D. 1978. An analysis of cercopithecoid odontometrics. I. Scaling of the maxillary dentition. *Am. J. Phys. Anthropol.* 49: 517–32
13a. Gordon, K. D. 1982. A study of microwear on chimpanzee molars: Implications for dental microwear analysis. *Am. J. Phys. Anthropol.* 59:195–215
13b. Gordon, K. D. 1984. The assessment of jaw movement direction from dental microwear. *Am. J. Phys. Anthropol.* 63:77–84
14. Gould, S. J. 1966. Allometry and size in ontogeny and phylogeny. *Biol. Rev.* 41:587–640
15. Gould, S. J. 1975. On the scaling of tooth size in mammals. *Am. Zool.* 15:351–62
16. Green, D. L., Ewing, G. H., Armelagos, G. J. 1967. Dentition of a Mesolithic population from Wadi Halfa, Sudan. *Am. J. Phys. Anthropol.* 27:41–56
17. Gregory, W. K., Hellman, M. 1939. The South African fossil man-apes and the origin of the human dentition. *J. Am. Dent. Assoc.* 26:558–64
18. Grine, F. E. 1981. Trophic differences between "gracile" and "robust" australopithecines: a scanning electron microscope analysis of occlusal events. *S. Afr. J. Sci.* 77:203–30
19. Grine, F. E. 1984. Deciduous molar microwear of South African australopithecines. In *Food Acquisition and Processing in Primates*, ed. D. J. Chivers, B. A. Wood, A. Bilsborough, 23:525–34. New York/London: Plenum. 576 pp.
20. Harvey, P. H., Kavanagh, M., Clutton-Brock, T. H. 1978. Sexual dimorphism in primate teeth. *J. Zool.* 186:475–85
21. Hiiemae, K. M. 1984. Functional aspects of primate jaw morphology. See Ref. 19, 11:257–81
22. Hladik, C. M. 1977. Chimpanzees of Gabon and chimpanzees of Gombe: Some comparative data on the diet. See Ref. 4, 16:481–503
23. Hylander, W. L. 1975. Incisor size and diet in anthropoids with special reference to Cercopithecidae. *Science* 189:1095–98
23a. Hylander, W. L. 1979. The functional significance of primate mandibular form. *J. Morphol.* 160:223–40
23b. Hylander, W. L., Crompton, A. W. 1980. Leading patterns and jaw movement during the masticatory power stroke in macaques. *Am. J. Phys. Anthropol.* 52:239
24. Johanson, D. C. 1974. Some metric aspects of the deciduous and permanent dentition of the pygmy chimpanzee *(Pan paniscus)*. *Am. J. Phys. Anthropol.* 41: 39–48
25. Jolly, C. J. 1970. The seed-eaters: a new model of hominid evolution based on a baboon analogy. *Man* 5:5–26
26. Kay, R. F. 1973. *Mastication, molar tooth structure, and diet in primates.* PhD thesis. Yale Univ., New Haven, Conn. 376 pp.
27. Kay, R. F. 1975. Allometry and early hominids (letter). *Science* 189:63
28. Kay, R. F. 1975. The functional adaptations of primate molar teeth. *Am. J. Phys. Anthropol.* 43:195–216
29. Kay, R. F. 1977. The evolution of molar occlusion in the Cercopithecidae and early cararrhines. *Am. J. Phys. Anthropol.* 46:327–52
30. Kay, R. F. 1981. The nut-crackers—a new theory of the adaptations of the Ramapithecinae. *Am. J. Phys. Anthropol.* 55:141–52
31. Kay, R. F., Covert, H. H. 1984. Anatomy and behaviour of extinct primates. See Ref. 19, 21:467–508
32. Kay, R. F., Hiiemae, K. M. 1974. Jaw movements and tooth use in recent and fossil primates. *Am. J. Phys. Anthropol.* 40:227–56
33. Kay, R. F., Hylander, W. L. 1978. The dental structure of mammalian folivores with special reference to Primates and Phalangeriodea *(Marsupialia)*. In *The Ecology of Arboreal Folivores*, ed. G. G. Montgomery, pp. 173–92. Washington DC: Smithsonian Inst. Press. 574 pp.
34. Kleiber, M. 1961. *The Fire of Life.* New York: Wiley. 454 pp.
35. MacKinnon, J. 1977. A comparative ecology of the Asian apes. *Primates* 18: 747–72
36. Mahler, P. E. 1973. *Metric variation in the pongid dentition.* PhD thesis. Univ. Mich. Ann Arbor. 467 pp.
37. Maier, W., Schneck, G. 1981. Konstruktionsmorphologische Untersuchungen am Gebiss der hominoiden Primaten. *Z. Morphol. Anthropol.* 72:127–69
38. Mann, A. 1981. Diet and human evolution. In *Omnivorous Primates*, ed. R. S. O. Harding, G. Teleki, 2:10–36. New York: Columbia Univ. Press. 673 pp.
39. Martin, L. B. 1983. *The relationship of the Later Miocene hominoidea.* PhD thesis. University College, London. 450 pp.
40. McHenry, H. M. 1982. The pattern of human evolution: Studies on bipedalism, mastication, and encephalization. *Ann. Rev. Anthropol.* 11:151–73
41. McHenry, H. M. 1984. Relative cheek-tooth size in *Australopithecus*. *Am. J. Phys. Anthropol.* 64:297–306

42. Mills, J. R. E. 1963. Occlusion and malocclusion of the teeth of primates. In *Dental Anthropology*, ed. D. R. Brothwell, pp. 29–52. Oxford: Pergamon
42a. Peters, C. R., O'Brian, E. M. 1981. The early hominid plant-food niche: Insights from an analysis of plant exploitation by *Homo*, *Pan*, and Papio in eastern and southern South Africa. *Curr. Anthropol.* 22:127–40
43. Pilbeam, D. R., Gould, S. J. 1974. Size and scaling in human evolution. *Science* 186:892–901
44. Puech, P.-F., Albertini, H., Serratrice, C. 1983. Tooth microwear and dietary patterns in early hominids from Laetoli, Hadar and Olduvai. *J. Hum. Evol.* 12: 721–29
45. Rensberger, J. M. 1978. Scanning electron microscopy of wear and occlusal events in some small herbivores. In *Development, Function and Evolution of Teeth*, ed. P. M. Butler, K. Joysey, 25:415–38. New York/London: Academic. 523 pp.
46. Robinson, J. T. 1954. Prehominid dentition and hominid evolution. *Evolution* 8:324–34
47. Robinson, J. T. 1972. *Early Hominid Posture and Locomotion*. Chicago: Univ. Chicago Press. 361 pp.
48. Rosenberger, A. L., Kinzey, W. G. 1976. Functional patterns of molar occlusion in platyrrhine primates. *Am. J. Phys. Anthropol.* 45:281–98
49. Seligsohn, D. 1977. Analysis of species-specific molar adaptations in strepsirhine primates. *Contrib. Primatol.* 11:1–116
50. Shea, B. T. 1983. Allometry and heterochrony in the African apes. *Am. J. Phys. Anthropol.* 62:275–89
51. Simons, E. L., Pilbeam, D. R. 1972. Hominoid paleoprimatology. In *The Functional and Evolutionary Biology of Primates*, ed. R. Tuttle, pp. 36–62. Chicago/New York: Aldine, Atherton. 487 pp.
52. Smith, R. J. 1980. Rethinking allometry. *J. Theor. Biol.* 87:97–111
53. Smith, R. J. 1981. On the definition of variables in studies of primate dental allometry. *Am. J. Phys. Anthropol.* 55:323–29
54. Smith, R. J. 1984. Determination of relative size: The "criterion of subtraction" problem in allometry. *J. Theor. Biol.* 108:131–42
55. Smith, R. J., Pilbeam, D. R. 1980. Evolution of the orangutan. *Nature* 284:447–48
56. Sussman, R. W. 1978. Foraging patterns of nonhuman primates and the nature of food preferences in man. *Fed. Proc.* 37:55–60
57. Szalay, F. S. 1972. Hunting-scavenging protohominids: A model for hominid origins. *Man* 10:420–29
58. Szalay, F. S. 1979. Phylogeny and the problems of adaptive significance: The case of the earliest primates. *Folia Primatol.* 36:157–82
59. Teaford, M. F. 1982. Differences in molar wear gradient between juvenile macaques and langurs. *Am. J. Phys. Anthropol.* 57:323–30
60. Teaford, M. F., Walker, A. C. 1984. Quantitative differences in dental microwear between primate species with different diets and a comment on the presumed diet of *Sivapithecus*. *Am. J. Phys. Anthropol.* 64:191–200
61. Temerin, L. A. 1980. Evolution of the orangutan. *Nature* 288: 301
62. Walker, A. C. 1981. Dietary hypotheses and human evolution. *Philos. Trans. R. Soc. London Ser. B* 292:57–64
63. Walker, A. C., Hoeck, H. N., Perez, L. 1978. Microwear of mammalian teeth as an indicator of diet. *Science* 201:908–10
64. Walker, P. L. 1978. A quantitative analysis of dental attrition rates in the Santa Barbara Channel area. *Am. J. Phys. Anthropol.* 48:101–6
65. Wallace, J. A. 1972. *The dentition of the South African early hominids: A study of form and function*. PhD thesis. Univ. Witwatersrand, South Africa. 244 pp.
66. Washburn, S. L., Ciochon, R. L. 1974. Canine teeth: notes on controversies in the study of human evolution. *Am. Anthropol.* 76:765–84
67. White, T. D., Johanson, D. C., Kimbel, W. H. 1981. *Australopithecus africanus*. Its phyletic position reconsidered. *S. Afr. J. Sci.* 77:445–70
68. Whitten, A. J. 1982. Diet and feeding behaviour of Kloss gibbons on Siberut Island, Indonesia. *Folia Primatol.* 37:177–208
69. Wolpoff, M. H. 1971. Interstitial wear. *Am. J. Phys. Anthropol.* 34:205–28
70. Wolpoff, M. H. 1971. *Metric Trends in Hominid Dental Evolution*. Case Western Reserve Univ., Stud. Anthropol. No. 2. 244 pp.
71. Wolpoff, M. H. 1973. Posterior tooth size, body size, and diet in South African gracile *Australopithecus*. *Am. J. Phys. Anthropol.* 39:375–94
72. Wood, B. A. 1979. An analysis of tooth and body size relationships in five primate taxa. *Folia Primatol.* 31:187–211
73. Wrangham, R. W. 1977. Feeding behaviour of chimpanzees in Gombe National Park, Tanzania. See Ref. 4, 17:504–38

HUMAN GENETIC DISTANCE STUDIES: Present Status and Future Prospects

L. B. Jorde

Department of Human Genetics, University of Utah School of Medicine, Salt Lake City, Utah 84132

Genetic distance methodologies have been reviewed extensively (27, 42, 72, 73, 76, 81, 84, 93, 100, 157, 175). This review does not attempt to duplicate these efforts, several of which are comprehensive. Rather, the basic families of genetic distances and display techniques are treated briefly, an update of several recent developments in the theory and methodology of genetic distances are given, some interesting new applications of genetic distances are discussed, and the potential for new developments via molecular genetic technology is addressed. Coverage is restricted primarily to monogenic traits. A review of distance studies based on polygenic traits has recently been published (159).

MAJOR FAMILIES OF GENETIC DISTANCES

Commonly used genetic distance methods can be partitioned into four basic families. Each of these is summarized briefly in this section, with special emphasis given to their respective advantages and disadvantages for studies in human populations. Mathematical formulae are not given here since they are readily available in the original papers and in other reviews.

Chi-square Distances

A large number of genetic distance measures belong to this class, including those of Sanghvi (169), Balakrishnan & Sanghvi (11), Morton et al (128; also 122), Harpending & Jenkins (77), Steinberg et al (181), and Kurczynski (97). In essence, all of these measures involve the calculation of some form of squared difference between gene frequencies in two populations, followed by a standardization of this difference. A commonly used standardization factor is the mean gene frequency $\bar{p}$ of the total population (this is thought to represent the gene frequency of a founding population) (128). The product $\bar{p}(1-\bar{p})$, which represents expected random genetic drift, is also used (77). The covariance matrix among alleles is used in the Mahalanobis approach, which eliminates redundancy due to correlated alleles (11).

These distance measures have been criticized because they do not originate from any particular biological model (136). However, Morton's measure is in fact derived from a model which assesses identity by descent of genes, although its success in actually doing so has been debated (191).

All of these approaches carry the assumption that gene frequency differences between subpopulations are not too large. When the inverse of the covariance matrix is used as a standardizing function, as in the Balakrishnan-Sanghvi measure, this assumption is explicit: a common covariance matrix is used, and covariance depends on gene frequencies. The other measures also depend implicitly on this assumption by invoking a common rate of expected drift among subpopulations, measured by some function of $\bar{p}$.

Angular Transformation Distances

Several closely related distance measures have been advanced by Edwards & Cavalli-Sforza (45, 47). These measures involve an arcsine transformation of gene frequencies in order to make gene frequency variances independent of the frequencies themselves. This accommodates a model of evolution in which gene frequencies change according to a pure drift process modeled by Brownian motion (see 65 for an especially lucid description of this model).

Angular transformation measures are often criticized on the grounds that the transformation fails to provide independence at extreme gene frequencies ($p <$ .05 and $p >$ .95) (12, 134). This is true to some extent, however, of all genetic distance measures (65). Since the drift model assumes equal sizes of all populations, it is not appropriate when widely divergent sample sizes are used.

Gene Substitution Approaches

Nei (133, 134, 136) proposed a set of genetic distances which are designed to measure the number of codon substitution differences between two populations. Equal sizes of subpopulations are assumed. Unlike most other distance methods, which assume a pure drift model, Nei's method also incorporates mutation, assuming equilibrium between mutation and drift. In contrast to Morton's approach, which assumes a fixed number of alleles per locus, Nei's methods assume an "infinite alleles" model. This model, based on current findings in molecular genetics, recognizes that most mutations will result in a unique nucleotide sequence at the locus under consideration. Latter (106, 107) has also devised methods designed to estimate codon substitution rates.

These distance methods are well suited to comparisons at and above the species level, since they are approximately linear with time (136). If there has been little or no gene flow between populations, and if a random sample of the genome is obtained for distance analysis, Nei's methods can be used to estimate the amount of time since the divergence of two populations (145). Since these assumptions are not met in studies of humans, such estimates of divergence times for human populations must be regarded with caution.

In contrast to many of the other genetic distances, the sampling distributions of Nei's distances have been studied extensively (118, 119, 131, 137, 143). This allows the estimation of standard errors and confidence limits for these distances. The interlocus sampling variance is much larger than the intralocus variance (unless the sample size is extremely small), so sampling variance is reduced more effectively by adding more loci rather than by adding more individuals (137, 143).

Nei's measures have been criticized because they are not metric distances [i.e. they do not satisfy the triangle inequality: for populations i, j, and k, $d(i,j) \leq d(i,k) + d(j,k)$, where d is the distance between pairs of populations] (55). However, this criticism applies only when a small number of loci are used. If a large enough number of loci are studied, these distances are asymptotically metric (64, 140, 150).

Information Measures

Several measures have been proposed which measure gene diversity based on an information-theoretic approach. Although not distance measures in a strict sense, these genetic diversity indices can be apportioned into within- and between-groups diversity, yielding an estimate of overall genetic distance among groups. Lewontin (110) first used this approach. He applied the Shannon-Wiener information index, $H = -\sum_i p_i \log_2 p_i$, to genetic data for human races. Similar approaches for measuring genetic diversity have been formulated by Nei and colleagues (31, 135), Latter (108), and Rao (157). In the best available review of these techniques, Rao (157) found that all information measures gave highly similar results at most gene frequencies. However, he noted that the Shannon-Wiener measure overestimated diversity at low gene frequencies, echoing an earlier criticism by Mitton (120).

Concordance of Genetic Distance Measures

It is by now a commonplace to state that the major types of genetic distances produce highly correlated results when applied to human populations. This has been demonstrated both by comparative statistical analysis (10, 65, 72, 80, 96, 170) and empirical experience (see 84, p. 143 for examples). However, when distances between different species are estimated, the correlations between various measures decrease substantially (33). This results in part from the fact that some distance measures, such as those of Nei and Latter, are linearly related to divergence time while others are not.

One difficulty in comparing various distance measures is the diversity of notation and styles of presentation used in the original publications. Rao (157) has overcome this problem by providing a unified notational and theoretical framework for all of the major distance measures.

SOME NEW GENETIC DISTANCE MEASURES

Although many researchers feel that genetic distance measures already exist in sufficient abundance, new ones continue to appear. Some of these are different enough from existing measures to warrant attention; their properties will be summarized here.

Nonparametric Methods

Karlin et al (90, 91) have devised an original set of approaches based on principles of exploratory data analysis. These techniques are not based on genetic theory. Instead, they employ nonparametric statistical procedures, placing primary importance on robustness and freedom from the distributional assumptions that usually accompany parametric methods. The approach basically involves comparing the gene frequencies of each subpopulation to those of a "standard" population (e.g. a founding population or the average of all subpopulations). A nonparametric sign test is used to determine if one subpopulation is closer to the standard than another. The subpopulations can thus be ordered in terms of their ordinal distances from the standard population, and statistical significance levels can be assigned to the order comparisons. In addition, Karlin et al have devised weighting functions to emphasize either rare or common alleles in the calculations.

These techniques were applied by Karlin et al to study the genetic structure of worldwide Jewish populations and to explore the extent of gentile contributions to the Jewish gene pool. Morton et al (126) have explored the same questions, using their own distance techniques with a partly different set of populations and loci. Although they conclude that there is "reasonable agreement" between the orderings of Karlin et al and their two-dimensional topologies, substantial disagreements are also presented. In the one case in which a direct comparison was made using the same loci and populations (29), a high degree of congruence was observed between the nonparametric and traditional genetic distance methods.

Coancestry Coefficient for Short-term Evolution

Using a pure drift model, Reynolds et al (160) have devised a distance statistic designed especially for studies of relatively small, closely related populations (such as those often studied by anthropologists). They compare their statistic with several others using simulation data and show that it tends to be more reliable in some circumstances. The authors demonstrate the use of a jacknifing procedure to estimate sampling variance, and a statistically satisfactory weighting technique is developed for summing loci. The measure is nearly identical to that of Rogers (165) when diallelic loci are used (65) but differs for multiallelic loci.

Distance Based on Presence or Absence of Alleles

Mickevich & Mitter (117) have proposed a unique distance measure in which alleles are coded 1 or 0 to denote whether or not they are present in a given subpopulation. Distances are then formed on the basis of the number of shared alleles. This distance measure has been shown to exhibit erratic behavior when applied to simulation data (65). Since most human populations differ in the frequencies, but not the presence, of alleles, this measure would not be appropriate for use in human genetic distance studies.

DISPLAY TECHNIQUES

Genetic Maps

Several techniques reduce distance matrices into a more manageable two-dimensional graphical representation. The first of these, principal coordinates analysis, is the method most commonly used to produce the familiar two-dimensional genetic "maps." This technique has been reviewed elsewhere (84, 100). With the exception of new interpolation techniques and color graphics (115, 155), little new methodological work appears to have been done since these reviews were published. The principal coordinates approach is mathematically sound, and the frequency of its use in the published literature indicates a high degree of consumer satisfaction.

Multidimensional scaling also generates genetic maps and can be performed on either metric or nonmetric data. It has the advantage of statistical robustness. Lalouel (100) reviews the technique extensively and discusses its application to both symmetric and asymmetric matrices.

Evolutionary Trees

In marked contrast to the two-dimensional maps, a great deal of work has been done on estimating the structure of evolutionary trees during the past several years (see 59 and 62 for thorough reviews). This reflects the fact that trees attempt to convey more information about relationships between populations than do maps. In spite of a substantial body of effort, it is still debatable whether tree methodologies really achieve this goal.

Many tree methods are based on the criterion of maximum parsimony: the tree which requires the fewest number of gene substitutions between branching points is found. This is equivalent to the "minimum evolution" method first used by Edwards & Cavalli-Sforza (46). The approach works best with populations that have diverged relatively recently, since back mutations and convergent evolution violate the assumptions of the model.

Other tree methodologies are based on the compatibility principle. Here an attempt is made to find the tree that is compatible with the largest number of variables (e.g. gene frequencies). The compatibility and parsimony approaches have been reviewed thoroughly and critically by Felsenstein (62).

A substantial amount of work has been done on maximum likelihood techniques for phylogeny estimation (56, 59, 60, 63, 190). The tree is chosen in which the statistical likelihood of a given data set is maximized, given the particular phylogenetic model under consideration. Felsenstein is the leading exponent of this approach, and he has developed a "restricted" maximum likelihood algorithm which avoids some of the pitfalls of earlier endeavors. In particular, the problem of singularities in the likelihood surface is overcome. This approach has the advantages of a solid statistical basis and the ability to estimate standard errors of branch lengths. Also, the likelihoods of various topologies are calculated, allowing a well-defined statistical evaluation of which topology is "best." Disadvantages include relatively slow computation and dependence on the assumptions of this parametric method. Also, it is possible to obtain only a local maximum when using this technique; thus it does not guarantee that the "best" tree will be found.

Templeton (187, 188) has proposed a highly original approach to tree estimation. His technique is intended for use with restriction site and/or DNA sequence data (which will be discussed below). A maximum parsimony tree is generated for each restriction enzyme used (these correspond roughly to loci or small sets of loci). Then the compatibility criterion is applied in order to select a single tree that corresponds most closely with the largest number of individual parsimony trees. A nonparametric sign test can be used to determine whether two trees differ significantly. This approach has the advantages of distribution-free robustness and relative ease of computation. If convergent evolution due to parallel mutations is probable (i.e. when $\lambda t > .05$, where λ is the gene substitution rate and t is the time since divergence between subpopulations), the method does not work well. In this case, Templeton advises resorting to the maximum likelihood approach cited above. An application of these methods to mitochondrial DNA data from humans and great apes (66) has yielded a provocative phylogeny. The human line splits before the chimp-gorilla divergence, which leads Templeton to conclude that bipedalism (or at least an incipient version of it) may have been the primitive state in the human-chimp-gorilla ancestor, while knuckle-walking is a derived state which evolved after humans split from the chimp-gorilla line.

Nei et al (150) have compared several tree-making algorithms, including Farris's (54) maximum parsimony approach and the unweighted paired-group method (UPGMA), a simple agglomerative clustering technique. The techniques were applied to simulated data where the true phylogeny was known. Interestingly, the UPGMA technique, which consumes very little computer time, gave the most accurate results. Recently, a method has been derived to estimate the standard errors of branching points in UPGMA trees (146), allowing statistical inference. It would be interesting to conduct a similar comparison between UPGMA and the maximum likelihood approach.

One of the most persistent problems in applying tree methods to human data is the omnipresence of gene flow between populations after their divergence. This vitiates any estimate of divergence times (145). A partial solution to this problem has been proposed by Lathrop (105), who presents a method that simultaneously calculates maximum likelihood estimates of phylogenies and admixture rates between populations. A critical assumption is that the duration of admixture is short relative to the period of isolation between two subpopulations. Often, not enough is known about the migration history of human populations to ensure that this assumption will be fulfilled. Still, the method should be useful in some cases.

As in any genetic distance methodology, tree estimation is more reliable when a large number of loci is used. Estimated trees are nearly always erroneous (i.e. the topological arrangement will be wrong) if the number of loci is less than 30 (145, 150). If populations are closely related (as in many anthropological studies), even trees based on 100 loci will usually be incorrect (140). This is because the error variance of genetic distances increases when the distances are small. In addition, adding more populations to the analysis increases the probability that the tree will be incorrect (92, 150). Thus, it is best to use as few populations as possible. One good rule of thumb is to use at least three to four times as many independent characters as populations (156).

Maps or Trees?

In deciding whether to estimate genetic maps or trees, the researcher must weigh the advantages and disadvantages of each. Maps offer computational ease and good statistical definition. Unlike comparisons at the species level, comparisons of human populations sometimes do not involve any type of hierarchical structure. Since trees imply hierarchy, they tend to be inappropriate in such situations. The ubiquity and complexity of human migration patterns guarantee that branching points in trees will nearly always be suspect, in spite of promising new advances in incorporating admixture into tree estimation. On the other hand, many tree methods now allow the estimation of confidence limits for branching points and branch lengths, while statistical error estimation is absent from map methods.

Statistical confidence has remained sadly neglected in nearly all distance studies. Whether by using tree methods that allow statistical inference, or by examining the standard errors of genetic distances themselves and using maps, more attention needs to be paid to statistical significance. It could well be that many controversies in human microevolution involve topologies (either maps or trees) that are not statistically different from one another.

Autocorrelation

A novel development in the display of genetic relationships is the application of spatial autocorrelation methods to gene frequency data (48a, 176–178). An autocorrelation is the correlation of a series of frequencies, in this case arranged along a spatial coordinate system, with itself. At a displacement distance of zero, the autocorrelation is of course 1.0, but it is expected to decrease as the displacement distance increases. For example, the correlation between the series and itself, displaced by 50 kilometers, might be 0.5. Autocorrelations at regular geographic distances are plotted against distance (displacement) in a correlogram. In a pure drift system, there should be no spatial pattern of gene frequencies, so all autocorrelations at non-zero displacement values should be zero. Autocorrelation patterns corresponding to environmental gradients could indicate natural selection, while others (especially if they are similar for all loci) could reflect patterns of gene flow. This method has been applied to data from Bougainville (176) and indicates, in agreement with earlier studies, that gene flow is the primary determinant of genetic variation here. As discussed below, it has also been applied to pan-European gene frequencies to test hypotheses regarding the spread of farming during the Neolithic period (177).

APPLICATIONS OF GENETIC DISTANCE ANALYSIS

There are at least three major areas in which genetic distance studies can be applied: 1. microevolution and history of local populations; 2. macroevolution of the human species; 3. medical applications. Microevolution is defined here as short-term changes in gene frequencies of populations in restricted geographic areas. These changes result almost exclusively from the action of random drift and gene flow. Following Dobzhansky's (44a) usage, macroevolution refers to evolution of the human species in a more global and long-term sense. Here the action of natural selection is of great importance, but it will be argued that random genetic drift and gene flow have also played important roles in human evolution.

The great majority of distance studies have concentrated on microevolution. However, a few studies have contributed to macroevolution and medical studies as well. This section will discuss some salient empirical findings in each area.

Microevolution and History

It would be impossible to summarize the vast number of studies that have been conducted on the microevolution of local human populations. Thus, the discussion which follows is necessarily personal, eclectic, and unrepresentative of the total literature. It will be shown that some historical questions have been answered satisfactorily, others may soon be answered, and others probably can never be answered. A larger sample of microevolutionary/historical studies can be found in several recent edited volumes (39, 41, 52, 79, 192).

Population geneticists have devoted much attention to the origin and genetic composition of modern Jewish populations. While most studies discern at least some degree of Middle Eastern affinity for Jewish populations, the amount of admixture between Jews and their gentile neighbors is the subject of continued disagreement. Most analyses reveal a fairly low amount of total gene flow between Jewish and other populations, although the European Jews tend to show higher rates of admixture than Oriental or African Jews. These conclusions have been reached by applying gene diversity analyses (158), cluster analysis (95), nonparametric distance techniques (91), discriminant analysis (28), F-statistics (94), maximum likelihood estimation of admixture (129), least-squares estimation of admixture (193), and other approaches (130).

Morton et al (126) reached different conclusions after applying kinship bioassay, isolation by distance, and admixture estimation techniques. They conclude that a high rate of admixture has persisted between most Jewish and gentile populations—on the order of 1% per generation. Over many centuries, this rate would nearly eliminate genetic differences between Jews and their neighbors. This constrasts with Motulsky's (129) *total* estimate of admixture of only about 12%. One reason for this disparity may be the extraordinary differences in admixture rates estimated using different loci. For example, Cavalli-Sforza & Carmelli (30) found almost 100% admixture when the ABO locus was used, but the HLA loci indicated nearly 0% admixture. Similar interlocus heterogeneity was detected by Wijsman (193) in her least-squares analysis of admixture. Since there is uncertainty regarding drift effects, ancestral gene frequencies, and possible convergent selection at some loci, the question of Jewish-gentile gene flow may never be answered completely.

A question which has been largely answered is that of the origin of the Romany Gypsies. This population had long claimed a northern Indian ancestry, but some skepticism prevailed until studies of the ABO locus in the 1920s showed that Hungarian Gypsies were indeed much more similar to northern Indians than to native Hungarians (18). Further studies using additional loci have corroborated this result for central European Gypsies, but many northern European Gypsy populations are not genetically similar to northern Indian populations (182). This could reflect drift effects as well as gene flow from surrounding populations. There has also been speculation that the Irish Tinkers have Gypsy origins, but genetic distance studies have shown no evidence for this (36).

Cavalli-Sforza and colleagues have used gene frequencies to study the diffusion of farming from the Near East across Europe. The question is whether farming spread by *cultural* diffusion (spread of the idea) or *demic* diffusion (spread of farmers themselves). A complex modification of the principal coordinates approach (115, 155) and an autocorrelation technique (177) have been applied to European gene frequencies. The studies demonstrate that spatial gene frequency patterns correspond closely with archaeological maps of the spread of agriculture, implying demic diffusion. A major difficulty with these studies is controlling for the numerous migrational events that took place both before and after the spread of agriculture. Also, the genetic data are not of uniformly good quality. Nonetheless, the congruence of genetic and archaeological maps is tantalizing. With better genetic data and more historical information, this question may be answered definitively.

An intriguing example of the insularity of some populations is given by Roberts et al (161–163), who studied six subpopulations in Cumbria, northwest England. One of the subpopulations, the Lake District, was genetically quite divergent from the others, although present-day migration data indicated it should not be. Noticing that many of the villages in this area had Norwegian names and recalling a Viking incursion into the region, genetic distances were calculated between the Cumbrian subpopulations and a composite Norwegian population. The Lake District was shown to be genetically more similar to Norway than to any of the other Cumbrian subpopulations. It is remarkable that in spite of the population movements that must have occurred during the past 1000 years, the Viking genetic influence is still so clearly observable. Apparently this population was very isolated during most of its past.

Many other recent applications of genetic distances to historical and microevolutionary questions could be discussed. Some examples include the genetic affinities of the American Indians (180), the genetic origin and history of the Icelanders (85, 189, 193), the origins of the Lapps (50), genetic relationships of Eskimos and Alaskan Indians (38, 183, 184), origins of the Åland Islanders (86), and the colonization of the South Pacific Islands (171).

Macroevolution

Genetic distance studies have not yet added a great deal to our understanding of human macroevolution. Due in part to discouraging results in trying to use gene frequencies to measure natural selection (e.g. 127), some population geneticists have concluded that genetic studies in the human can never advance macroevolutionary knowledge (76) [although this author has since softened his position somewhat (78)]. In this section, some recent examples are cited which show that distance studies can indeed provide macroevolutionary insights.

Several studies have examined human genetic variation at the level of major races. The consensus is that the majority (85–90%) of genetic variation lies within, rather than between, races (108, 110, 138, 144, 145). Nevertheless, it is possible to classify individuals quite accurately into major racial groups by using multiple-locus methods (175a).

Phylogenetic relationships among the major races have also been explored (138, 145, 156). Using an impressive number of loci (62 protein and 23 blood group loci), Nei and colleagues estimated the divergence time between the Caucasoid and Mongoloid races at 50,000 years and the divergence time between the Negroid and Caucasoid-Mongoloid groups at 120,000 years Before Present (BP). Further work of this type is being done using mitochondrial DNA polymorphisms (138, 139). As noted earlier, estimates of divergence times for human populations are fraught with difficulties, but they at least provide a good comparison of genetic similarity among races.

These studies show that some groups, such as the American Indians, Papuans, and Australian aborigines, appear to have had higher gene substitution rates than others (hindering further the estimation of divergence times). This may be because of drift effects (145), but it could also be the result of different selective environments.

With the exception of the highly divergent Lapps, all European populations are very closely related, a finding which could be attributed to high migration rates. In fact, the genetic distances between English populations and northern Indian populations are much lower than those of geographic neighbors like the Bushmen and Bantus or the Alaskan Indians and Eskimos.

Several good demonstrations of the effects of genetic drift on gene frequencies have been published. A study of HLA frequencies in the Dariusleut Hutterites has shown that this population, which had a founding size of only several hundred, has diverged markedly from its ancestral populations (121). A study of Utah Mormon gene frequencies demonstrated that this population, by contrast, is nearly identical genetically to its northern European founding populations (114). This reflects a founding population size of many thousands and a large amount of gene flow after colonization. In this study, Anabaptist Hutterite, Amish, and Mennonite groups were also compared with European populations. The divergence between the Amish and Hutterites, who were derived from the same ancestral stock, was greater than that between any two European populations. The Mennonites, who had somewhat higher population sizes, had diverged substantially less. A classic similar study is that of Glass (70) on the Dunkers of Pennsylvania. Again, substantial gene frequency divergence due to small population sizes was demonstrated.

What do these studies of racial variation and genetic drift tell us about human macroevolution? For one thing, random genetic drift has had powerful effects on human gene frequency variation. Considering the shifting-balance theory of Sewall Wright (198), such drift effects provide the genetic variance that facilitates location of "adaptive peaks" for climatic adaptation, disease resistance, etc. Such action of natural selection is reflected in possible latitudinal selection gradients for some gene loci (155) and in the immense morphological and immunological diversity of the human species. Gene flow, which counteracts the effects of drift, has also been an important force, as evidenced by the close genetic kinship of the European populations. Variation in gene flow and drift effects, coupled with natural selection, could account for the apparent differences in evolutionary rates noted in various human populations.

Studies of human populations can also make important contributions to macroevolutionary understanding because of the many types of data that are unique to the species. One has only to peruse the literature of animal population genetics to discover that written records afford a record of human gene flow that is far superior to that of animal capture-recapture studies. As discussed below, such data have led to several interesting theoretical developments concerning the relationship between genetic covariance matrices and migration matrices.

Another useful type of data which exists in abundance for humans is that of quantitative traits (e.g. anthropometrics and dermatoglyphics). These data can aid in learning more about the effects of evolutionary forces on traits determined by one versus many loci, as will also be discussed later.

Medical Applications

Genetic distance studies can be useful in helping to understand the distribution of genetic diseases in populations. A good example is given by McLellan et al (114) in their study of Utah Mormon gene frequencies. Hemochromatosis, a previously little-known recessive iron-storage disorder, has been found to occur with high frequency in this population (about one in 200 to 300 adults). Since the Mormons are similar genetically to other Caucasian U.S. and northern European populations, the disease is probably just as common in these populations and should be screened more carefully (it has heretofore been confused with several other diseases). Screening would allow early detection and prevention of life-threatening symptoms. The Mormon study also implies that the rates of cancer and heart disease in this population, among the lowest in the United States, are due to lifestyle factors rather than a unique genetic constitution.

In contrast to the Mormons, the Old Order Amish, who are genetically divergent from their forebears, exhibit high frequencies of genetic diseases that are rare elsewhere (113). Similar observations have been made in the Åland Islands (51) and in isolated Finnish mainland populations (151, 152). These findings reflect the influence of genetic drift and, in some cases, inbreeding.

Genetic distance analyses have just begun to contribute to medical studies. With the ascendancy of genetic epidemiology (92a, 124) and an ever-increasing appreciation of the importance of genetic diseases, there is considerable potential for further such contributions.

COMPARISONS OF DISTANCES BASED ON DIFFERENT TYPES OF DATA

Studies of distances based on gene frequencies are greatly enriched by comparisons with distances estimated from other types of data, such as migration, isonymy, pedigrees, linguistic affinities, or anthropometrics. A review of such comparisons was given several years ago (84). Here, new work on two areas of interest will be summarized: estimation of gene flow from genetic covariance matrices and the comparative value of monogenic and polygenic traits for evolutionary studies.

Migration and Genetic Distances

Felsenstein (61) recently defined several unsolved problems in population genetics. One of these was: "For any given [genetic] covariance matrix, is there a corresponding migration matrix which would be expected to lead to it? If so, how can we find it?." Several approaches have been developed to deal with this problem. They illustrate nicely how human genetic data can be used to test evolutionary predictions, and they will be summarized here.

The best-known effort in this direction is that of Harpending & Ward (78), who used extensive linear algebra to demonstrate a direct and predictable mathematical relationship between a genetic covariance matrix and an estimated symmetric Markov migration matrix. For the relationship to hold, the diagonal elements of the migration matrix (endogamy rates) must be greater than .5, which is usually reasonable for human populations. If systematic pressure (immigration from outside the population) is uniform across subdivisions, then their theory predicts a linear relationship between heterozygosity in each subpopulation and the subpopulation's distance from the gene-frequency centroid [given by $(p_i - \bar{p})^2/\bar{p}(1-\bar{p})$]. When heterozygosity is plotted against distance from the centroid, those subpopulations that deviate from the regression line are inferred to have received more or less than average immigration from outside the population. Such plots have been applied in several genetic distance studies (37, 40, 44).

Another approach to this problem is that of Wijsman et al (194). They derive a multivariate least-squares regression method to predict a migration matrix when genetic covariance matrices and population sizes are known for multiple time periods. The method differs from that of Harpending and Ward both in its mathematics and in its assumption that the population is closed to outside immigration (although they show that low immigration rates do not distort the results appreciably). Their method was applied to covariance matrices derived from isonymy data, but gene frequency covariance matrices could also be used.

A third method (163a; A. R. Rogers, submitted for publication) does not predict a full matrix of migration rates but predicts the overall migration rate and effective population size. Here Wright's (197) F_{st}, a standardized index of genetic variance, is calculated from the gene frequencies of adults and children in the same population. Since genetic drift occurs at reproduction, F_{st} should be lower in adults than in children. The difference between F_{st} in adults and children can be used to estimate both population size and migration rate.

The last approach of this type (125) uses the well-known Malécot isolation-by-distance equation, $\phi(d) = ae^{-bd}$, where $\phi(d)$ is kinship between subpopulations at distance d, a is an estimated parameter denoting local random inbreeding, and b is another estimated parameter that measures the decay rate of kinship with geographic distance. The terms a and b are estimated by fitting the equation to kinship coefficients estimated from gene frequencies. Since a and b have predicted equilibrium relationships to effective population size and effective migration rate, they can be used to estimate these parameters. A major weakness of this method is its dependence on the isolation by distance model, which has been the subject of controversy (57, 58, 98, 99, 123). However, an empirical test of this model revealed a fairly high degree of accuracy (125).

All four of these methods are quite new and require further theoretical evaluation and empirical testing. Trials with data will be especially useful, since unfulfilled predictions often lead to the most interesting explanations.

Value of Monogenic Versus Polygenic Traits for Distance Studies

Population distances based on monogenic serological data have been compared with distances based on polygenic anthropometric data in a number of studies (see 84 and 159 for examples). In general the correlations between the two types of data have not been very high, particularly at the level of major races (142, 145, 156). This appears to result from the fact that morphological traits are more responsive to the effects of natural selection than are most blood markers. The correlation between the two types of data would be expected to decrease as larger geographic areas, with greater environmental (and thus selective) variation, are studied.

Birdsell (14) suggested that genetic drift should have less impact on polygenic than monogenic traits, since he felt that the effects of drift at multiple loci cancel one another. Hence, the between-population divergence of polygenic traits would be slower and less subject to stochastic effects than that of monogenic traits. He concluded that polygenic traits, including dermatoglyphics and anthropometrics, should then be more useful than monogenic blood markers for deducing historical relationships between populations. This assertion has been repeated several times (68, 159, 167, 196), but it is based on inappropriate reasoning (A. R. Rogers and L. B. Jorde, in preparation). The quantity of interest for this question is the between-groups genetic variance. Sewall Wright (197) demonstrated that the expected value of the between-groups variance is equivalent in monogenic and polygenic traits (see also 7; 23, chap. 12; 32, 56, 101, and 102 for related work). Rogers & Harpending (164) have extended this analysis to the case in which multivariate normality and linkage equilibrium are not assumed. They verify Wright's conclusion for the expectation of between-groups variance, and they show that the *precision* of the estimate (measured by the variance of the between-groups variance) is the same for polygenic and monogenic characters. Thus, monogenic traits are just as useful as polygenic traits for distance studies.

One empirical test of Birdsell's assertion has been performed (68). Nine villages classified into three language groups were analyzed. The hypothesis was that if drift has less effect on polygenic traits than on monogenic traits, then an assessment of intervillage distances based on dermatoglyphic data should show tighter clustering of villages into historical language groups than would an assessment based on gene frequencies. Discriminant analysis was used to analyze the dermatoglyphic data, and principal components analysis was used to analyze the gene frequencies. Tighter clustering within language groups was observed when dermatoglyphic traits were analyzed, and the authors concluded that drift does have less effect on polygenic traits. However, discriminant analysis is designed specifically to yield maximum separation of defined groups, while principal components analysis is not. Thus, this result may well be explained by the use of two different techniques rather than differential sensitivity to drift.

Lewontin (110a) also addressed this question in a recent theoretical analysis. He showed that in certain cases a polygenic character will yield statistically significant between-population differences while a single monogenic trait will not. He also showed that the reverse result can obtain. However, Lewontin's analysis does not address the general statistical relationship between monogenic and polygenic traits and thus does not contradict Wright's (197) original conclusion (163b).

COMPARISONS OF GENETIC DISTANCES USING DIFFERENT TYPES OF LOCI

Several recent studies have shown disparities between results based on red cell antigens (blood groups) and those based on electrophoretic systems. McLellan et al (114) found that genetic distances based on HLA antigens and electrophoretic systems correlated highly with one another and yielded genetic maps that corresponded closely with geographic maps of populations. Distances based on blood groups had lower correlations with the HLA-derived and electrophoretically derived distances, and the congruence with geographic distances was substantially lower. Ryman et al (168), who assessed worldwide genetic variation using HLA, blood group, and electrophoretic loci, obtained similar results. Nei (139) compared results based on blood groups, electrophoretic loci, and actual DNA sequences from mitochondria in a recent study of major races. The DNA sequence results were better correlated with those of the electrophoretic data than with those of blood groups.

There are several possible explanations for this apparent lack of agreement between blood groups and other types of data: 1. The blood groups may be more subject to natural selection than the electrophoretic loci. A recent study of racial variation in heterozygosity and genetic distance (31a) lends support to this possibility. However, this would not explain the concordance between electrophoretic loci and the HLA system, since the latter is almost certainly influenced by selection (16). 2. Since electrophoretic alleles reflect differences in sizes and shapes of proteins, they reflect directly the amino acid sequences of proteins, and thus, to the extent that code redundancy and wobble can be disregarded, the responsible DNA codons. The properties of red cell membrane antigens, and their relationship to DNA sequences, are much more poorly understood. Again, this would not explain why HLA loci, which are observed as antigens, correlate highly with electrophoretic loci. 3. The electrophoretic as well as the HLA loci have codominant alleles, while the blood group loci often involve complex dominance relationships among alleles. This means that gene frequency estimation in blood groups is more difficult and more subject to error. This is particularly true in small populations, where loci are less likely to be in Hardy-Weinberg equilibrium and sampled individuals are more likely to be related to one another.

These findings are a cause for concern, since blood groups constitute much of the available data for genetic distance studies, and since they are the primary basis of many or most previous studies of human genetic structure. This problem underscores again the need to employ as many loci as possible in genetic distance studies. Studies based on only a few loci have no place in modern population genetics. In addition, the jacknifing procedure advocated by Rao & Boudreau (158), in which the distance analysis is repeated with a different locus omitted each time, should often be used. This can reveal the distorting influence of one badly behaved locus, a problem which can be especially severe when using parametric distance estimation techniques. Finally, some of the new types of genetic data to be outlined in the next section may offer a way out of this difficulty.

DISTANCE STUDIES OF THE FUTURE: NEW TYPES OF GENETIC DATA

Many of the problems now encountered in genetic distance studies reflect a paucity of appropriate data rather than deficiencies in methodology. Traditional approaches such as red cell antigen detection are still yielding new loci: over

170 red cell antigens are now known (145) (although not all are useful in distance studies). In addition, refinements and advances in electrophoresis, to be discussed in this section, hold promise. The most exciting possibilities for new data have been generated by recombinant DNA technology. These will be outlined at some length in this section.

Advances in Electrophoresis

Electrophoresis has been a mainstay of genetic distance studies for nearly 20 years. A number of variations in the technique allow the detection of additional alleles: denaturation by heat or urea, alteration of buffer pH, isoelectric focusing, and modification of gel concentration and composition [e.g. starch vs polyacrylamide (35)]. A classic example of the detection of additional alleles using such modifications is the study by Singh et al (174). Working with the *xdh* locus in *Drosophila*, they increased the number of detectable alleles from 6 to 27 and raised heterozygosity from 44% to 63%. A drawback of these approaches for distance studies is that they tend to increase the detection of rare alleles only (35). Alleles with low frequencies, as noted above, are less reliable for genetic distance estimation.

Another advance is two-dimensional electrophoresis (2DE) (see 35, 69, 71, and 132 for extended discussions). Here, two types of electrophoresis are executed sequentially in two different dimensions. The first dimension separates proteins by charge, and the second separates them by size. In contrast to one-dimensional electrophoresis, where one protein is analyzed on each gel, 2DE permits the simultaneous examination of many proteins on one gel. The first application of this technique in humans (112) revealed substantially *less* heterozygosity than traditional one-dimensional electrophoresis, a somewhat surprising finding. A half dozen subsequent studies (cited in 132) have corroborated this, usually yielding average heterozygosity estimates of about 2%, as opposed to the 6% value obtained by conventional techniques. This difference could result from the detection of a different class of proteins by the 2DE approach or from differences in the technique itself. One recent study on humans has in fact obtained a 6% heterozygosity estimate (166), but this may be attributed to the use of plasma proteins, which in general yield a high heterozygosity rate.

Distances Based on Nuclear DNA Polymorphisms

Recombinant DNA technology has led to some of the most significant biological discoveries of the past decade. Most current applications of this technology in human genetics involve gene mapping for medical genetic studies (116, 172), and spectacular results have been achieved (75, 195). Gene therapy—alteration of the genetic composition of somatic or even germ cells—is receiving increased attention (3). Recombinant DNA techniques can also be useful in generating polymorphisms for genetic distance studies. Although such applications are just beginning, they are a cause for optimism for the future of distance studies. Three techniques for assessing genetic distances using nuclear DNA will be discussed here. The interested reader is referred to (48) for a recent and readable introduction to recombinant DNA methods.

DNA-DNA HYBRIDIZATION   This technique is conceptually quite simple. Mechanically sheared pieces of single-stranded DNA from two different populations are allowed to associate. The more closely related the two populations are (i.e. the greater their sequence homology), the higher the number of bonds that form between the DNA strands. The hybridized DNA is then exposed to increasing levels of heat, a process which breaks the bonds and separates the DNA strands. Under standardized salt concentrations, the temperature at which the strands separate is an indication of the degree of homology of the DNA sequences, with separation at higher temperatures indicating greater similarity. An application of this approach to hominoid phylogeny (173) showed that the gorilla diverged before the chimpanzee-human divergence, with the two events occuring at 8–10 million BP and 6.3–7.7 million BP, respectively. This differs from the mitochondrial DNA phylogeny discussed above, generating predictable controversy (109). It agrees, however, with a phylogeny based on chromosome banding patterns (199). Unfortunately, DNA-DNA hybridization technology does not allow fine resolution of DNA sequence similarity, so, at least for the present, it is not useful for intraspecific comparisons.

ANALYSIS OF DNA SEQUENCES   Perhaps the ideal genetic distance would be based on the actual differences in nucleotide sequences between two populations. A variety of techniques exist for DNA sequencing (74, 111), and they are being applied with enthusiasm. Thus far, only a tiny fraction of the three billion nucleotides of the human genome has been sequenced. Several methods have recently been developed to estimate heterozygosity (185), genetic distances (as gene substitutions) (89, 185), and evolutionary trees (60, 63) using DNA sequence data. Since there are only four types of nucleotides, while there are 20 types of amino acids, DNA sequences are easier to analyze statistically than are protein sequences. A comparison of the standard errors of the branching points of trees based on amino acid sequences, electrophoretic loci, restriction site polymorphisms (discussed below), and DNA sequences showed that DNA sequences yielded the smallest error rate (139). Thus, DNA sequence data, when available in sufficient quantity, should prove useful for human genetic distance studies.

RESTRICTION SITE POLYMORPHISMS   Restriction site methods provide an indirect way of observing DNA sequences. Since they are now the

HUMAN GENETIC DISTANCE STUDIES   361

most popular and feasible approach to studying DNA polymorphism in the human, the techniques will be summarized briefly. Further details are given in (17, 48, 67, 172).

This technique is based on the use of restriction enzymes (synonymous with restriction endonucleases), which are extracted from prokaryotic organisms such as *Escherichia coli*. When exposed to DNA from another species, these enzymes cut, or cleave, the DNA at certain nucleotide sequences (recognition sequences or restriction sites). Most restriction enzymes recognize either a four-base or a six-base nucleotide sequence. In one method of restriction site analysis, purified DNA representing the entire genome of an individual is digested with a restriction enzyme, resulting in numerous DNA fragments of varying lengths. When subjected to agarose gel electrophoresis, shorter fragments will migrate faster than longer ones, allowing separation according to length. Digestion of all of the DNA of the genome yields millions of fragments which present an unintelligible "smear" on the gel; a method must be used to pick out only a few fragments of interest. To do this, the fragments are transferred to a filter membrane such as nitrocellulose, where they are exposed to a radioactively labeled probe consisting of a defined DNA sequence [this is a Southern transfer, named after its inventor (179)]. Under standardized hybridization conditions, only DNA fragments containing sequences homologous to the probe will be observable when exposed to X-ray film. Polymorphisms are identified when different individuals have different DNA sequences, causing the restriction enzymes to cut the DNA at different locations. The resulting variations in DNA fragment lengths are sometimes called "restriction fragment length polymorphisms." By using different restriction enzymes and different DNA probes, various polymorphic "loci" can be defined in a population. The polymorphisms can represent single-base substitutions as well as deletions, additions, or rearrangements (e.g. inversions) of multiple bases.

Some of the earliest and most commonly used statistical methods for estimating heteroyzgosity and genetic distances with restriction site data are those of Nei & Li (141). Extensions and corrections of this work are given by Nei & Tajima (147), and a maximum likelihood method for estimating substitution rates has been derived (148). A number of other approaches to estimating distances (87, 88) and heterozygosity (53) have been put forward. In general, these methods yield similar results.

Methods have also been devised to estimate the level of polymorphism using restriction site data (49, 53, 82). Although they give similar results, the last-cited approach has the lowest sampling variance.

An important assumption of these statistical methods is that the restriction sites are distributed randomly throughout the genome. Adams & Rothman (1) examined this assumption using 54 restriction enzymes with known sequences of human mitochondrial DNA. They found a markedly nonrandom distribution of restriction sites. This violation is apparently of consequence only if the expected total number of gene substitutions per site is greater than .3 (148) or if the expected average heterozygosity is near 1.0 (149).

As in traditional genetic distance studies, where it is important to use as many loci as possible, one should use as many restriction enzymes as possible in restriction site analyses (147, 186). Again, using more restriction enzymes lowers error variance more effectively than the use of more individuals.

Restriction site data offer several distinct advantages over traditional data for genetic distance studies. The number of restriction site loci, most of which are highly polymorphic, now exceeds 200 (see 34 for a recent partial enumeration), and it is increasing exponentially. Because virtually any part of the genome can be accessed, a truly random sample of the genome can likely be obtained for analysis. Also, DNA sequences with different functions can be analyzed. For example, regions that do not code for proteins (e.g. introns), and may thus be selectively neutral, can be analyzed and compared to sequences that do code for proteins.

All of these features could be tremendously useful in distance analyses. In fact, it has recently been suggested that DNA polymorphism data will soon replace blood groups and electrophoretic data altogether in genetic distance studies (65).

Thus far, this approach has been used little, if at all, in studying typical anthropological populations. This can be attributed to both the newness and unfamiliarity of the methodology as well as to its perceived cost. Once blood samples are obtained, a fully equipped DNA laboratory should be able to process 20 polymorphisms for roughly $100 to $200 per individual (M. Leppert and R. White, personal communication). This assumes that digests with six to eight different restriction enzymes would be performed, and several different probes would be used with each digest on reusable filters. Since so many loci are now known, it would be easy to obtain highly polymorphic ones. The cost of obtaining additional polymorphisms would not be additive, since much of the expense involves initial preparation and purification of DNA. By way of comparison, typing of eight to ten typical blood groups costs about $35 to $50, and electrophoretic analysis of 20 loci (not all of which would be highly polymorphic) costs about $100 (T. McLellan, personal communication). Thus, if an equipped DNA laboratory is available, the cost of obtaining DNA polymorphisms should not be substantially greater than that of traditional methods.

Distances Based on Mitochondrial DNA

About 1000 mitochondria exist in the cytoplasm of most mammalian somatic cells. These organelles, which are the sites of cellular respiration, may have originated from ancient bacteria that developed a symbiotic relationship with other cells and were eventually incorporated directly into their cytoplasm. Each mitochondrion has a small circular DNA molecule. The apparently universal nuclear DNA code does not apply to mitochondria: several of the mitochondrial DNA (mtDNA) codons produce amino acids that differ from those of their nuclear DNA counterparts (6, 13). The size of the molecule, 16,569 base pairs in the human, is highly conserved in mammals, as is the arrangement of genes along the mtDNA molecule (20). One human mtDNA molecule has been sequenced completely (2). Earlier studies concluded that most mtDNA sequence variation was due to single-base substitutions, but higher-resolution restriction site studies made possible by the sequenced human mtDNA molecule have shown that a large proportion of mtDNA mutations in noncoding regions are insertions and deletions of multiple bases (26). Recent reviews of the mtDNA literature are given by Avise & Lansman (8) and Brown (20).

Of particular interest for human evolutionary studies are the following features: (*a*) recombination does not occur in mammalian mtDNA (4); (*b*) in higher animals, mtDNA is inherited only through the maternal line (104); (*c*) the gene substitution rate of mtDNA is about ten times faster than that of nuclear DNA (21), although some segments of the molecule are constrained from rapid evolution (5). This high substitution rate could result from a higher intrinsic mutation rate, a lack of DNA repair mechanisms, shorter generation length, or other factors (20, 25, 26).

The maternal inheritance of and lack of recombination in mammalian mtDNA guarantee that mtDNA gene combinations will not be rapidly broken up by sexual reproduction as they are in nuclear DNA. This fact has been exploited to examine introgression and hybridization in mice (103) and sunfishes (9). Similar applications could be pursued in humans.

The rapid evolution of mtDNA should yield more finely tuned distance analyses in closely related populations. The statistical techniques cited above for nuclear DNA can also be used for mtDNA restriction site and sequence data. Some of the population genetic theory (effective population size, fixation rates of mutants) pertinent to mtDNA has been worked out by Birky et al (15).

Because the mtDNA genome is small and easy to isolate, it is more convenient to work with in the laboratory than is nuclear DNA. Laboratory methods for analyzing mtDNA restriction sites are similar to those of nuclear DNA, except that it is not necessary to hybridize the fragments with radioactive probes. This is because a typical digest will cleave the mtDNA in only a few places, producing only a few fragments. The fragments themselves can thus be radioactively labeled and visualized by exposure to X-ray film.

Several phylogenetic studies of the hominoid species have been done using mtDNA, including the one by Templeton (187) mentioned above, in which restriction site data were analyzed. Templeton's study was particularly instructive in that mtDNA was used to resolve the chimpanzee-gorilla-human phylogeny, but because of its high substitution rate, it was not useful to resolve the divergence date of the orangutan. This is because after about 15 million years, multiple substitutions at the same site begin to blur phylogenetic relationships. In order to estimate the orangutan divergence, nuclear DNA, which evolves more slowly, was used.

Brown et al (22) analyzed mtDNA nucleotide sequences and concluded, as did Templeton, that the human line diverged before the chimpanzee and gorilla lines did. Nei (139) reanalyzed these data, computing standard errors of branching points. He concluded that the standard errors were too high to allow resolution of the chimpanzee-gorilla-human divergence. A reanalysis of the data used by Templeton also led to the conclusion, contrary to Templeton's, that the standard errors were too high to permit resolution of the divergence question (139).

Several studies at the racial level have been done using mtDNA. An analysis of 235 individuals using only one restriction enzyme (43) led to the conclusion that since the apparently oldest fragment pattern was most common in Asian populations, humans radiated from Asia about 50,000 to 100,000 years ago. Brown (19) analyzed the heterogeneity of human mtDNA and estimated that existing heterogeneity could be accounted for by a monomorphic founding population (even a single mating pair) originating about 200,000 years ago. Cann et al (24) constructed an evolutionary tree based on restriction site data from 100 individuals. Their tree was dissimilar from that of Nei & Roychoudhury (145), which was based on protein polymorphisms. The most disturbing results derived from mtDNA data are those of Johnson et al (83), who estimated the divergence time of the Bushmen at 220,000 BP and that of Asians and Europeans at only 5500 BP (alternatively, the evolutionary rate of Bushman mtDNA might be much faster than that of Asian and European mtDNA). As they note, these divergence times conflict seriously with archaeological and fossil evidence.

A recent theoretical analysis of the error variance of distances based on mtDNA data (139) demonstrated that for populations as closely related as human races, the standard errors of the distances are larger than the distances themselves. This is because the tiny mtDNA genome contains very few genes. Thus, some of the results cited above may be unreliable. mtDNA data are still useful for species-level comparisons such as the hominoid phylogeny, and their unique features can provide added insights. Unless other statistical techniques can provide better resolution, it appears that mtDNA may be of limited use in human genetic distance studies.

DNA Polymorphisms on the Y Chromosome

Recently, DNA polymorphisms have been detected on the human Y chromosome (153, 154). About five Y chromosome polymorphisms are now known (D. Page, personal communication), and new ones are forthcoming. In some ways, these polymorphisms are the male counterpart of mtDNA polymorphisms: they are paternally inherited, and they are not subject to recombination. It will be particularly interesting to compare genetic distances based on Y chromosome polymorphisms with relationship matrices based on isonymy using the methods of Wijsman et al (194), since surnames in many populations are also inherited through males.

CONCLUSIONS

A review published in this series a decade ago (76) reached pessimistic conclusions regarding the future of human genetic distance studies. The reviewer found that such studies were of use primarily as an auxiliary tool in divining local history and that the field generally lacked direction. It is agreed here that some genetic distance studies lack testable hypotheses or directed analysis. They tend to be uninspiring descriptions that are readily forgotten. It is also agreed that natural selection, the primary driving force of macroevolution, is difficult to measure effectively in human populations.

In spite of these problems, this reviewer finds cause for optimism. The human species, because of its unique capacity to record its own history, provides ancillary data (e.g. migration, isonymy) that are unavailable for any other species. Such data are valuable for testing evolutionary predictions and for exploring the interface between biology and culture, an area of special interest to anthropologists. As this review attempts to demonstrate, microevolutionary studies can make singular contributions to the solution of thorny historical questions. It is argued that macroevolutionary contributions can also be made. And finally, there is considerable potential for genetic distance analyses to produce information of value in medical genetics. Consideration of these and other types of goals should help the researcher to guide analysis in interesting and worthwhile directions.

Another source of optimism is the development of vast new reserves of genetic data as a result of molecular genetic research. This review has shown that difficulties in human genetic distance studies are due more to a dearth of suitable data than a lack of statistical methods. As outlined above, this problem is rapidly being overcome with hundreds of new DNA polymorphisms. In addition to providing data of greater quantity and suitability, the DNA polymorphisms will allow researchers to pose completely new questions about human evolution.

Rapid advances in computer technology during the past decade provide another key component in the furtherance and improvement of genetic distance studies. Techniques such as maximum likelihood estimation, which were once prohibitively time-consuming, can now be done relatively quickly and cheaply. With powerful microcomputers on nearly every desk and several excellent population genetic software packages available, any researcher who learns the techniques has few limitations in applying them.

In conclusion, the future appears bright for human genetic distance studies. A host of interesting questions, new data, and useful statistical techniques present themselves. The potentials are many, and the boundaries are few.

ACKNOWLEDGMENTS

This review has benefited from discussions with Drs. Dorit Carmelli, Mary Dadone, John Endler, Henry Harpending, Mark Leppert, Tracy McLellan, Kenneth Morgan, David Page, Alan Rogers, Richard Sage, and Ray White. Any errors are my own. Financial support for this work was provided by NIH grant HD-16109 and NSF grant BNS-8319448.

Literature Cited

1. Adams, J., Rothman, E. D. 1982. Estimation of phylogenetic relationships from DNA restriction patterns and selection of endonuclease cleavage sites. *Proc. Natl. Acad. Sci. USA* 79:3560–64
2. Anderson, S., Bankier, A. T., Barrell, B. G., de Bruijn, M. H. L., Coulson, A. R., et al. 1981. Sequence and organization of the human mitochondrial genome. *Nature* 290:457–65
3. Anderson, W. F. 1984. Prospects for human gene therapy. *Science* 226:401–9
4. Aquadro, C. F., Greenberg, B. D. 1983. Human mitochondrial DNA variation and evolution: Analysis of nucleotide sequences from seven individuals. *Genetics* 103:287–312
5. Aquadro, C. F., Kaplan, N., Risko, K. J. 1984. An analysis of the dynamics of mammalian mitochondrial DNA sequence evolution. *Mol. Biol. Evol.* 1:423–34
6. Attardi, G., Chomyn, A., Montoya, J., Ojala, D. 1982. Identification and mapping of human mitochondrial genes. *Cytogenet. Cell Genet.* 32:85–98
7. Avery, P. J., Hill, W. G. 1977. Variability in genetic parameters among small populations. *Genet. Res.* 29:193–213
8. Avise, J. C., Lansman, R. A. 1983. Polymorphism of mitochondrial DNA in populations of higher animals. In *Evolution of Genes and Proteins*, ed. M. Nei, R. K. Koehn, pp. 147–64. Sunderland, Mass: Sinauer
9. Avise, J. C., Saunders, N. C. 1984. Hybridization and introgression among species of sunfish *(Lepomis)*: Analysis by mitochondrial DNA and allozyme markers. *Genetics* 108:237–55
10. Balakrishnan, V. 1974. Comparison of some commonly-used genetic distance measures. In *Human Population Genetics in India*, ed. L. D. Sanghvi, V. Balakrishnan, H. M. Bhatia, P. K. Sukumaran, J. V. Undevia, pp. 173–86. New York: Orient Longman
11. Balakrishnan, V., Sanghvi, L. D. 1968. Distance between populations on the basis of attribute data. *Biometrics* 24:859–65
12. Balakrishnan, V., Sanghvi, L. D., Kirk, R. L. 1975. *Genetic Diversity Among Australian Aborigines*. Canberra: Aust. Inst. Aboriginal Stud.
13. Barrell, B. G., Bankier, A. T., Drouin, J. 1979. A different genetic code in human mitochondria. *Nature* 282:189–94
14. Birdsell, J. B. 1950. Some implications of the genetical concept of race in terms of spatial analysis. *Cold Spring Harbor Symp. Quant. Biol.* 15:259–314
15. Birky, C. W., Maruyama, T., Fuerst, P. 1983. An approach to population and evolutionary genetic theory for genes in mitochondria and chloroplasts, and some results. *Genetics* 103:513–27
16. Bodmer, W. F. 1975. Evolution of HL-A and other major histocompatibility systems. *Genetics* 79:293–304
17. Botstein, D., White, R. L., Skolnick, M., Davis, R. W. 1980. Construction of a genetic linkage map in man using restriction fragment length polymorphisms. *Am. J. Hum. Genet.* 32:314–31
18. Boyd, W. C. 1963. Four achievements of the genetical method in physical anthropology. *Am. Anthropol.* 65:243–52
19. Brown, W. M. 1980. Polymorphism in mitochondrial DNA of humans as revealed by restriction endonuclease analy-

sis. *Proc. Natl. Acad. Sci. USA* 77:3605–9
20. Brown, W. M. 1983. Evolution of animal mitochondrial DNA. See Ref. 8, pp. 62–88
21. Brown, W. M., George, M., Wilson, A. C. 1979. Rapid evolution of animal mitochondrial DNA. *Proc. Natl. Acad. Sci. USA* 76:1967–71
22. Brown, W. M., Prager, E. M., Wang, A., Wilson, A. C. 1982. Mitochondrial DNA sequences of primates: Tempo and mode of evolution. *J. Mol. Evol.* 18:225–39
23. Bulmer, M. G. 1980. *The Mathematical Theory of Quantitative Genetics.* Oxford: Clarendon
24. Cann, R. L., Brown, W. M., Wilson, A. C. 1982. Evolution of human mitochondrial DNA: A preliminary report. In *Human Genetics, Part A: The Unfolding Genome,* ed. B. Bonne-Tamir, T. Cohen, R. M. Goodman, pp. 157–65. New York: Liss
25. Cann, R. L., Brown, W. M., Wilson, A. C. 1984. Polymorphic sites and the mechanism of evolution in human mitochondrial DNA. *Genetics* 106:479–99
26. Cann, R. L., Wilson, A. C. 1983. Length mutations in human mitochondrial DNA. *Genetics* 104:699–711
27. Cannings, C., Cavalli-Sforza, L. L. 1973. Human population structure. *Adv. Hum. Genet.* 4:105–71
28. Carmelli, D., Cavalli-Sforza, L. L. 1979. The genetic origin of the Jews: a multivariate approach. *Hum. Biol.* 51:41–61
29. Carmelli, D., Jorde, L. B. 1982. A nonparametric distance analysis of biochemical genetic data from the Åland Islands, Finland. *Am. J. Phys. Anthropol.* 57:331–40
30. Cavalli-Sforza, L. L., Carmelli, D. 1979. The Ashkenazi gene pool: interpretations. In *Genetic Diseases Among Ashkenazi Jews,* ed. R. M. Goodman, A. Motulsky, pp. 93–102. New York: Raven
31. Chakraborty, R. 1980. Gene diversity analysis in nested subdivided populations. *Genetics* 96:721–26
31a. Chakraborty, R. 1984. Relationship between heterozygosity and genetic distance in three races of man. *Am. J. Phys. Anthropol.* 65:249–58
32. Chakraborty, R., Nei, M. 1982. Genetic differentiation of quantitative characters between populations or species. I. Mutation and random genetic drift. *Genet. Res.* 39:303–14
33. Chakraborty, R., Tateno, Y. 1976. Correlations between some measures of genetic distance. *Evolution* 30:851–53
34. Cooper, D. N., Schmidtke, J. 1984. DNA restriction fragment length polymorphisms and heterozygosity in the human genome. *Hum. Genet.* 66:1–16
35. Coyne, J. A. 1982. Gel electrophoresis and cryptic protein variation. In *Isozymes: Current Topics in Biological and Medical Research,* ed. M. C. Ratazzi, J. G. Scandalios, G. S. Whitt, 6:1–32. New York: Liss
36. Crawford, M. H. 1975. Genetic affinities and origin of the Irish Tinkers. In *Biosocial Interrelations in Population Adaptation,* ed. E. S. Watts, F. E. Johnston, G. W. Lasker, pp. 93–103. The Hague: Mouton
37. Crawford, M. H., Devor, E. J. 1980. Population structure and admixture in transplanted Tlaxcaltecan populations. *Am. J. Phys. Anthropol.* 52:485–90
38. Crawford, M. H., Enciso, V. B. 1982. Population structure of circumpolar groups of Siberia, Alaska, Canada, and Greenland. See Ref. 39, pp. 51–91
39. Crawford, M. H., Mielke, J. H., eds. *Current Developments in Anthropological Genetics,* Vol. 2. *Ecology and Population Structure.* New York: Plenum
40. Crawford, M. H., Mielke, J. H., Devor, E. J., Dykes, D. D., Polesky, H. F. 1981. Population structure of Alaskan and Siberian indigenous communities. *Am. J. Phys. Anthropol.* 55:167–85
41. Crawford, M. H., Workman, P. L., eds. 1973. *Methods and Theories of Anthropological Genetics.* Albuquerque: Univ. New Mexico Press
42. Crow, J. F., Denniston, C., eds. 1974. *Genetic Distance.* New York: Plenum
43. Denaro, M., Blanc, H., Johnson, M. J., Chen, K. H., Wilmsen, E., et al. 1981. Ethnic variation in Hpa I endonuclease cleavage patterns of human mitochondrial DNA. *Proc. Natl. Acad. Sci. USA* 78:5768–72
44. Devor, E. J., Crawford, M. H., Bach-Enciso, V. 1984. Genetic structure of the Black Caribs and Creoles. In *Current Developments in Anthropological Genetics, Black Caribs: A Case Study in Biocultural Adaptation,* ed. M. H. Crawford, 3:365–80. New York: Plenum
44a. Dobzhansky, T. 1951. *Genetics and The Origin of Species.* New York: Columbia Univ. Press. 3rd ed.
45. Edwards, A. W. F. 1971. Distance between populations on the basis of gene frequencies. *Biometrics* 27:873–81
46. Edwards, A. W. F., Cavalli-Sforza, L. L. 1964. Reconstruction of evolutionary trees. In *Phenetics and Phylogenetic*

Classification, ed. V. E. Heywood, J. McNeill, pp. 67–76 Systems Assoc. Publ. No. 6. London: Systematics Assoc.
47. Edwards, A. W. F., Cavalli-Sforza, L. L. 1972. Affinity as revealed by differences in gene frequencies. In *The Assessment of Population Affinities in Man,* ed. J. S. Weiner, J. Huizinga, pp. 37–47. Oxford: Clarendon
48. Emery, A. E. H. 1984. *An Introduction to Recombinant DNA.* New York: Wiley
48a. Endler, J. A. 1977. *Geographic Variation, Speciation, and Clines.* Princeton: Princeton Univ. Press
49. Engels, W. R. 1981. Estimating genetic divergence and genetic variability with restriction endonucleases. *Proc. Natl. Acad. Sci. USA* 78:6329–33
50. Eriksson, A. W. 1973. Genetic polymorphisms in Finno-Ugrian populations: Finns, Lapps, and Maris. *Isr. J. Med. Sci.* 9:1156–70
51. Eriksson, A. W., Fellman, J. O., Forsius, H. R. 1980. Some genetic and clinical aspects of the Åland Islanders. See Ref. 52, pp. 509–36
52. Eriksson, A. W., Forsius, H., Nevanlinna, H. R., Workman, P. L., Norio, R. K., eds. 1980. *Population Structure and Genetic Disorders.* New York: Academic
53. Ewens, W. J., Spielman, R. S., Harris, A. 1981. Estimation of genetic variation at the DNA level from restriction endonuclease data. *Proc. Natl. Acad. Sci. USA* 78:3748–50
54. Farris, J. S. 1972. Estimating phylogenetic trees from distance matrices. *Am. Nat.* 106:645–68
55. Farris, J. S. 1981. Distance data in phylogenetic analysis. In *Advances in Cladistics. Proc. 1st Meet. Willi Hennig Soc.,* ed. V. A. Funk, D. R. Brooks, pp. 3–23. New York: New York Botanical Garden
56. Felsenstein, J. 1973. Maximum-likelihood estimation of evolutionary trees from continuous characters. *Am. J. Hum. Genet.* 25:471–92
57. Felsenstein, J. 1975. A pain in the torus: Some difficulties with models of isolation by distance. *Am. Nat.* 109:359–68
58. Felsenstein, J. 1979. Isolation by distance: Reply to Lalouel and Morton. *Ann. Hum. Genet.* 42:523–27
59. Felsenstein, J. 1981. Evolutionary trees from gene frequencies and quantitative characters: Finding maximum likelihood estimates. *Evolution* 35:1229–42
60. Felsenstein, J. 1981. Evolutionary trees from DNA sequences: A maximum likelihood approach. *J. Mol. Evol.* 17:368–76
61. Felsenstein, J. 1982. How can we infer geography and history from gene frequencies? *J. Theor. Biol.* 96:9–20
62. Felsenstein, J. 1982. Numerical methods for inferring evolutionary trees. *Q. Rev. Biol.* 57:379–404
63. Felsenstein, J. 1983. Inferring evolutionary trees from DNA sequences. In *Statistical Analysis of DNA Sequence Data,* ed. B. S. Weir, pp. 133–50. New York: Dekker
64. Felsenstein, J. 1984. Distance methods for inferring phylogenies: A justification. *Evolution* 38:16–24
65. Felsenstein, J. 1985. Phylogenies from gene frequencies: A statistical problem. *Syst. Zool.* In press
66. Ferris, S. D., Wilson, A. C., Brown, W. M. 1981. Evolutionary trees for apes and humans based on cleavage maps of mitochondrial DNA. *Proc. Natl. Acad. Sci. USA* 78:2432–36
67. Flaherty, L. 1983. Introduction to molecular genetics. In *Recombinant DNA and Medical Genetics,* ed. A. Messer, I. H. Porter, pp. 1–8. New York: Academic
68. Froehlich, J. W., Giles, E. 1981. A multivariate approach to fingerprint variation in Papua New Guinea: Perspectives on the evolutionary stability of dermatoglyphic markers. *Am. J. Phys. Anthropol.* 54:93–106
69. Garrels, J. I. 1983. Quantitative two-dimensional gel electrophoresis of proteins. *Methods Enzymol.* 100(B):411–23
70. Glass, B., Sacks, M. S., Jahn, E. F., Hess, C. 1952. Genetic drift in a religious isolate: An analysis of the causes of variation in blood group and other gene frequencies in a small population. *Am. Nat.* 86:145–59
71. Goldman, D., Merrill, C. R. 1983. Human lymphocyte polymorphisms detected by quantitative two-dimensional electrophoresis. *Am. J. Hum. Genet.* 35:827–37
72. Goodman, M. M. 1974. Genetic distances: Measuring dissimilarity among populations. *Yearb. Phys. Anthropol.* 1973, 17:1–38
73. Gower, J. C. 1972. Measures of taxonomic distance and their analysis. See Ref. 192, pp. 1–24
74. Grossman, L., Moldave, K., eds. 1980. *Methods in Enzymology,* Vol. 65, *Nucleic Acids, Part I.* New York: Academic
75. Gusella, J. F., Wexler, N. S., Conneally, P. M., Naylor, S. L., Anderson, M. A., et al. 1983. A polymorphic DNA marker genetically linked to Huntington's disease. *Nature* 306:234–38
76. Harpending, H. C. 1974. Genetic struc-

ture of small populations. *Ann. Rev. Anthropol.* 3:229–43
77. Harpending, H. C., Jenkins, T. 1973. Genetic distances among southern African populations. See Ref. 41, pp. 177–99
78. Harpending, H. C., Ward, R. H. 1982. Chemical systematics and human populations. In *Biochemical Aspects of Evolutionary Biology*, ed. M. H. Nitecki, pp. 213–56. Chicago: Univ. Chicago Press
79. Harrison, G. A., ed. 1977. *Population Structure and Human Variation.* Cambridge: Cambridge Univ. Press
80. Hedrick, P. W. 1975. Genetic similarity and distance: Comments and comparisons. *Evolution* 79:362–66
81. Howells, W. W. 1973. Measures of population distances. See Ref. 41, pp. 159–76
82. Hudson, R. R. 1982. Estimating genetic variability with restriction endonucleases. *Genetics* 100:711–19
83. Johnson, M. J., Wallace, D. C., Ferris, S. D., Rattazzi, M. C., Cavalli-Sforza, L. L. 1983. Radiation of human mitochondria DNA types analyzed by restriction endonuclease cleavage patterns. *J. Mol. Evol.* 19:255–71
84. Jorde, L. B. 1980. The genetic structure of subdivided human populations: a review. In *Current Developments in Anthropological Genetics, Theory and Methods*, ed. J. H. Mielke, M. H. Crawford, 1:135–208. New York: Plenum
85. Jorde, L. B., Eriksson, A. W., Morgan, K., Workman, P. L. 1982. The genetic structure of Iceland. *Hum. Hered.* 32:1–7
86. Jorde, L. B., Workman, P. L., Eriksson, A. W. 1982. Genetic microevolution in the Åland Islands, Finland. See Ref. 39, pp. 333–65
87. Kaplan, N., Langley, C. H. 1979. A new estimate of sequence divergence of mitochondrial DNA using restriction endonuclease mapping. *J. Mol. Evol.* 13:295–304
88. Kaplan, N., Risko, K. 1981. An improved method for estimating sequence divergence of DNA using restriction endonuclease mappings. *J. Mol. Evol.* 17:156–62
89. Kaplan, N., Risko, K. 1982. A method for estimating rates of nucleotide substitution using DNA sequence data. *Theor. Popul. Biol.* 21:318–28
90. Karlin, S., Carmelli, D., Bonné-Tamir, B. 1982. Analysis of biochemical genetic data on Jewish populations: III. The application of individual haplotype measurements for intra- and interpopulation comparisons. *Am. J. Hum. Genet.* 34:50–64
91. Karlin, S., Kenett, R., Bonné-Tamir, B.

1979. Analysis of biochemical data on Jewish populations: II. Results and interpretations of heterogeneity indices and distance measures with respect to standards. *Am. J. Hum. Genet.* 31:341–65
92. Kidd, K. K., Cavalli-Sforza, L. L. 1971. Number of characters examined and error in reconstruction of evolutionary trees. In *Mathematics in the Archaeological and Historical Sciences*, ed. F. R. Hodson, D. G. Kendall, P. Tautu, pp. 335–46. Chicago: Aldine-Atherton
92a. King, M. C., Lee, G. M., Spinner, N. B., Thomson, G., Wrensch, M. R. 1984. Genetic epidemiology. *Ann. Rev. Public Health* 5:1–52
93. Kirk, R. L. 1977. Genetic distance—a pragmatic approach. In *Human Genetics*, ed. S. Armendares, R. Lisker, pp. 244–54. Amsterdam: Excerpta Medica
94. Kobyliansky, E., Livshits, G. 1983. Genetic composition of Jewish populations: diversity and inbreeding. *Ann. Hum. Biol.* 10:453–64
95. Kobyliansky, E., Micle, S., Goldschmidt-Nathan, M., Arensburg, B., Nathan, H. 1982. Jewish populations of the world: Genetic likeness and differences. *Ann. Hum. Biol.* 9:1–34
96. Krzanowski, W. J. 1971. A comparison of some distance measures applicable to multinomial data, using a rotational fit technique. *Biometrics* 27:1062–68
97. Kurczynski, T. W. 1970. Generalized distance and discrete variables. *Biometrics* 26:525–34
98. Lalouel, J. M. 1977. The conceptual framework of Malécot's model of isolation by distance. *Ann. Hum. Genet.* 40:355–60
99. Lalouel, J. M. 1979. Comment on Felsenstein's reply to Lalouel and Morton. *Ann. Hum. Genet.* 42:529
100. Lalouel, J. M. 1980. Distance analysis and multidimensional scaling. See Ref. 84, pp. 209–50
101. Lande, R. 1976. Natural selection and random genetic drift in phenotypic evolution. *Evolution* 30:314–34
102. Lande, R. 1979. Quantitative genetic analysis of multivariate evolution, applied to brain:body size allometry. *Evolution* 33:402–16
103. Lansman, R. A., Avise, J. C., Aquadro, C. F., Shapira, J. F., Daniel, S. W. 1983. Extensive genetic variation in mitochondrial DNA's among geographic populations of the deer mouse, *Peromyscus maniculatus*. *Evolution* 37:1–16
104. Lansman, R. A., Avise, J. C., Huettel, M. D. 1983. Critical experimental test of the possibility of "paternal leakage" of

mitochondrial DNA. *Proc. Natl. Acad. Sci. USA* 80:1969–71
105. Lathrop, G. M. 1982. Evolutionary trees and admixture: Phylogenetic inferences when some populations are hybridized. *Ann. Hum. Genet.* 46:245–55
106. Latter, B. D. H. 1973. Measures of genetic distance between individuals and populations. In *Genetic Structure of Populations*, ed. N. E. Morton, pp. 27–37. Honolulu: Univ. Hawaii Press
107. Latter, B. D. H. 1973. The estimation of genetic divergence between populations based on gene frequency data. *Am. J. Hum. Genet.* 25:247–61
108. Latter, B. D. H. 1980. Genetic differences within and between populations of the major human subgroups. *Am. Nat.* 116:220–37
109. Lewin, R. 1984. DNA reveals surprises in human family tree. *Science* 226:1179–82
110. Lewontin, R. C. 1972. The apportionment of human diversity. *Evol. Biol.* 6:381–98
110a. Lewontin, R. C. 1984. Detecting population differences in quantitative characters as opposed to gene frequencies. *Am. Nat.* 123:115–24
111. Maxam, A. M., Gilbert, W. A. 1977. A new method for sequencing DNA. *Proc. Natl. Acad. Sci. USA* 74:560–64
112. McConkey, E. H., Taylor, B. J., Phan, D. 1979. Human heterozygosity: a new estimate. *Proc. Natl. Acad. Sci. USA* 76:6500–4
113. McKusick, V. A., ed. 1978. *Medical Genetic Studies of the Amish: Selected Papers*. Baltimore: Johns Hopkins Univ. Press
114. McLellan, T., Jorde, L. B., Skolnick, M. H. 1984. Genetic distances between the Utah Mormons and related populations. *Am. J. Hum. Genet.* 36:836–57
115. Menozzi, P., Piazza, A., Cavalli-Sforza, L. L. 1978. Synthetic maps of human gene frequencies in Europeans. *Science* 201:786–92
116. Messer, A., Porter, I. H., eds. 1983. *Recombinant DNA and Medical Genetics*. New York: Academic
117. Mickevich, M. F., Mitter, C. 1981. Treating polymorphic characters in systematics: A phylogenetic treatment of electrophoretic data. See Ref. 55, pp. 45–58
118. Mitra, S. 1975. On Nei and Roychoudhury's sampling variances of heterozygosity and genetic distance. *Genetics* 80:223–26
119. Mitra, S. 1976. More on Nei and Roychoudhury's sampling variances of heterozygosity and genetic distance. *Genetics* 82:543–45
120. Mitton, J. B. 1977. Genetic differentiation of races of man as judged by single-locus and multilocus analyses. *Am. Nat.* 111:203–12
121. Morgan, K., Holmes, T. M., Schlaut, J., Marchuk, L., Kovithavongs, T., et al. 1980. Genetic variability of HLA in the Dariusleut Hutterites. A comparative analysis of the Hutterites, the Amish, and other selected Caucasian populations. *Am. J. Hum. Genet.* 32:246–57
122. Morton, N. E. 1975. Kinship, information and biological distance. *Theor. Popul. Biol.* 7:246–55
123. Morton, N. E. 1977. Isolation by distance in human populations. *Ann. Hum. Genet.* 40:361–65
124. Morton, N. E. 1982. *Outline of Genetic Epidemiology*. Basel: Karger
125. Morton, N. E. 1982. Estimation of demographic parameters from isolation by distance. *Hum. Hered.* 32:37–41
126. Morton, N. E., Kennett, R., Yee, S., Lew, R. 1982. Bioassay of kinship in populations of Middle Eastern origin and controls. *Curr. Anthropol.* 23:157–67
127. Morton, N. E., Krieger, H., Mi, M. P. 1966. Natural selection on polymorphisms in northeastern Brazil. *Am. J. Hum. Genet.* 18:153–71
128. Morton, N. E., Yee, S., Harris, D. E., Lew, R. 1971. Bioassay of kinship. *Theor. Popul. Biol.* 2:507–24
129. Motulsky, A. G. 1980. Askhenazi Jewish gene pools: admixture, drift and selection. In *Population Structure and Genetic Disorders*, See Ref. 52, pp. 353–65
130. Mourant, A. E., Kopec, A. C., Domaniewska-Sobczak, K. 1978. *The Genetics of the Jews*. New York: Clarendon
131. Mueller, L. D. 1979. Comparison of two methods for making statistical inferences on Nei's measure of genetic distance. *Biometrics* 35:757–63
132. Neel, J. V. 1984. A revised estimate of the amount of genetic variation in human proteins: Implications for the distribution of DNA polymorphisms. *Am. J. Hum. Genet.* 36:1135–48
133. Nei, M. 1972. Genetic distance between populations. *Am. Nat.* 106:283–92
134. Nei, M. 1973. The theory and estimation of genetic distance. See Ref. 106, pp. 45–51
135. Nei, M. 1973. Analysis of gene diversity in subdivided populations. *Proc. Natl. Acad. Sci. USA* 70:3321–23
136. Nei, M. 1975. *Molecular Population Genetics and Evolution*. Amsterdam: North Holland

137. Nei, M. 1978. Estimation of average heterozygosity and genetic distance from a small number of individuals. *Genetics* 89:583–90
138. Nei, M. 1982. Evolution of human races at the gene level. See Ref. 24, pp. 167–81
139. Nei, M. 1985. Human evolution at the molecular level. In *Proc. Oji Conf. Popul. Genet. Evol.* In press
140. Nei, M. 1985. Genetic distance and molecular phylogeny. In *Population Genetics and Its Application to Fisheries Management*, ed. N. Ryman. In press
141. Nei, M., Li, W. H. 1979. Mathematical model for studying genetic variation in terms of restriction endonucleases. *Proc. Natl. Acad. Sci. USA* 76:5269–73
142. Nei, M., Roychoudhury, A. K. 1972. Gene differences between Caucasian, Negro and Japanese populations. *Science* 177:434–36
143. Nei, M., Roychoudhury, A. K. 1974. Sampling variances of heterozygosity and genetic distance. *Genetics* 76:379–90
144. Nei, M., Roychoudhury, A. K. 1974. Genic variation within and between the three major races of man, Caucasoids, Negroids, and Mongoloids. *Am. J. Hum. Genet.* 26:421–43
145. Nei, M., Roychoudhury, A. K. 1982. Genetic relationship and evolution of human races. *Evol. Biol.* 14:1–59
146. Nei, M., Stephens, J. C., Saitou, N. 1985. Methods for computing the standard errors of branching points in an evolutionary tree and their application to molecular data from humans and apes. *Mol. Biol. Evol.* 2:66–85
147. Nei, M., Tajima, F. 1981. DNA polymorphism detectable by restriction endonucleases. *Genetics* 97:145–63
148. Nei, M., Tajima, F. 1983. Maximum likelihood estimation of the number of nucleotide substitutions from restriction sites data. *Genetics* 105:207–17
149. Nei, M., Tajima, F., Gojobori, T. 1984. Classification and measurement of DNA polymorphism. In *Human Population Genetics, Pittsburgh Symp.*, ed. A. Chakravarti, pp. 307–29. New York: Van Nostrand/Reinhold
150. Nei, M., Tajima, F., Tateno, Y. 1983. Accuracy of estimated phylogenetic trees from molecular data. II. Gene frequency data. *J. Mol. Evol.* 19:153–70
151. Norio, R. 1981. Diseases of Finland and Scandinavia. In *Biocultural Aspects of Disease*, ed. H. Rothschild, pp. 359–415. New York: Academic
152. Norio, R., Nevanlinna, H. R., Perheentupa, J. 1973. Hereditary diseases in Finland: Rare flora in rare soil. *Ann. Clin. Res.* 5:109–41
153. Page, D., de Martinville, B., Barker, D., Wyman, A., White, R., et al. 1982. Single-copy sequence hybridizes to polymorphic and homologous loci on human X and Y chromosomes. *Proc. Natl. Acad. Sci. USA* 79:5352–56
154. Page, D. C., Harper, M. E., Love, J., Botstein, D. 1984. Occurrence of a transposition from the X-chromosome long arm to the Y-chromosome short arm during human evolution. *Nature* 311:119–23
155. Piazza, A., Menozzi, P., Cavalli-Sforza, L. L. 1981. Synthetic gene frequency maps of man and selective effects of climate. *Proc. Natl. Acad. Sci. USA* 78:2638–42
156. Piazza, A., Sgaramella-Zonta, L., Gluckman, P., Cavalli-Sforza, L. L. 1975. The fifth histocompatibility workshop gene frequency data: A phylogenetic analysis. *Tissue Antigens* 5:445–63
157. Rao, C. R. 1982. Diversity and dissimilarity coefficients: A unified approach. *Theor. Popul. Biol.* 21:24–43
158. Rao, C. R., Boudreau, R. 1984. Diversity and cluster analyses of blood group data on some human populations. See Ref. 149, pp. 331–62
159. Relethford, J. H., Lees, F. C. 1982. The use of quantitative traits in the study of human population structure. *Yearb. Phys. Anthropol.* 25:113–32
160. Reynolds, J., Weir, B. S., Cockerham, C. C. 1983. Estimation of the coancestry coefficient: Basis for a short-term genetic distance. *Genetics* 105:767–79
161. Roberts, D. F. 1982. Population structure of farming communities of northern England. See Ref. 39, pp. 367–84
162. Roberts, D. F., Jorde, L. B., Mitchell, R. J. 1981. Genetic structure in Cumbria. *J. Biosoc. Sci.* 13:317–36
163. Roberts, D. F., Mitchell, R. J., Creen, C. K., Jorde, L. B. 1981. Genetic variation in Cumbrians. *Ann. Hum. Biol.* 8:135–44
163a. Rogers, A. R. 1982. *Variation of neutral characters in subdivided populations*. PhD thesis. Univ. New Mexico, Albuquerque
163b. Rogers, A. R. 1985. Population differences in quantitative characters and gene frequencies. *Am. Nat.* Submitted for publication.
164. Rogers, A. R., Harpending, H. C. 1983. Population structure and quantitative characters. *Genetics* 105:985–1002
165. Rogers, J. S. 1972. Measures of genetic similarity and genetic distance. *Univ. Texas Publ.* 7213:145–53
166. Rosenblum, B. B., Neel, J. V., Hanash,

S. M. 1983. Two-dimensional electrophoresis of plasma polypeptides reveals "high" heterozygosity indices. *Proc. Natl. Acad. Sci. USA* 80:5002–6

167. Rothhammer, F., Chakraborty, R., Llop, E. 1977. A collation of marker gene and dermatoglyphic diversity at various levels of population differentiation. *Am. J. Phys. Anthropol.* 46:51–60

168. Ryman, M., Chakraborty, R., Nei, M. 1983. Differences in the relative distribution of human gene diversity between electrophoretic and red and white cell antigen loci. *Hum. Hered.* 33:93–102

169. Sanghvi, L. D. 1953. Comparison of genetical and morphological methods for a study of biological differences. *Am. J. Phys. Anthropol.* 11:385–404

170. Sanghvi, L. D., Balakrishnan, V. 1972. Comparison of different measures of genetic distance between human populations. See Ref. 47, pp. 25–36

171. Serjeantson, S. W., Ryan, D. P., Thompson, A. R. 1982. The colonization of the Pacific: The story according to human leukocyte antigens. *Am. J. Hum. Genet.* 34:904–18

172. Shows, T. B., Sakaguchi, A. Y., Naylor, S. L. 1982. Mapping the human genome, cloned genes, DNA polymorphisms, and inherited disease. *Adv. Hum. Genet.* 12:341–452

173. Sibley, C. G., Ahlquist, J. E. 1984. The phylogeny of the hominoid primates, as indicated by DNA-DNA hybridization. *J. Mol. Evol.* 20:2–15

174. Singh, R. S., Lewontin, R. C., Felton, A. A. 1976. Genetic heterogeneity within electrophoretic "alleles" of xanthine dehydrogenase in *Drosophila pseudoobscura*. *Genetics* 84:609–29

175. Smith, C. A. B. 1977. A note on genetic distance. *Ann. Hum. Genet.* 40:463–79

175a. Smouse, P. E., Spielman, R. S., Park, M. H. 1982. Multiple-locus allocation of individuals to groups as a function of the genetic variation within and differences among human populations. *Am. Nat.* 119:445–63

176. Sokal, R. R., Friedlaender, J. S. 1982. Spatial autocorrelation analysis of biological variation on Bougainville Island. See Ref. 39, pp. 205–27

177. Sokal, R. R., Menozzi, P. 1982. Spatial autocorrelations of HLA frequencies in Europe support demic diffusion of early farmers. *Am. Nat.* 119:1–17

178. Sokal, R. R., Wartenberg, D. E. 1983. A test of spatial autocorrelation analysis using an isolation-by-distance model. *Genetics* 105:219–37

179. Southern, E. M. 1975. Detection of specific sequences among DNA fragments separated by gel electrophoresis. *J. Mol. Evol.* 98:503–17

180. Spuhler, J. N. 1979. Genetic distances, trees, and maps of North American Indians. In *The First Americans: Origins, Affinities, and Adaptations*, ed. W. S. Laughlin, A. B. Harper, pp. 135–83. New York: Fischer

181. Steinberg, A. G., Bleibtreu, H. K., Kurczynski, T. W., Martin, A. O., Kurczynski, E. M. 1967. Genetic studies of an inbred human isolate. *Proc. 3rd Int. Congr. Hum. Genet.* ed. J. F. Crow, J. V. Neel, pp. 267–89. Baltimore: Johns Hopkins

182. Sunderland, E. 1982. The population structure of the Romany Gypsies. See Ref. 39, pp. 125–37

183. Szathmary, E. J. E. 1979. Blood groups of Siberians, Eskimos, Subarctic and Northwest Coast Indians: the problem of origins and genetic relationships. See Ref. 180, pp. 185–209

184. Szathmary, E. J. E., Ossenberg, N. S. 1978. Are the biological differences between North American Indians and Eskimos truly profound? *Curr. Anthropol.* 19:673–701

185. Tajima, F. 1983. Evolutionary relationships of DNA sequences in finite populations. *Genetics* 105:437–60

186. Tajima, F., Nei, M. 1982. Biases of the estimates of DNA divergence obtained by the restriction enzyme technique. *J. Mol. Evol.* 18:115–20

187. Templeton, A. R. 1983. Phylogenetic inference from restriction endonuclease cleavage site maps with particular reference to the evolution of humans and the apes. *Evolution* 37:221–44

188. Templeton, A. R. 1983. Convergent evolution and nonparametric inferences from restriction data and DNA sequences. See Ref. 63, pp. 151–79

189. Thompson, E. A. 1973. The Icelandic admixture problem. *Ann. Hum. Genet.* 37:69–80

190. Thompson, E. A. 1975. *Human Evolutionary Trees*. Cambridge: Cambridge Univ. Press

191. Thompson, E. A. 1976. Population correlation and population kinship. *Theor. Popul. Biol.* 10:205–26

192. Weiner, J. S., Huizinga, J., eds. 1972. *The Assessment of Genetic Affinities in Man*. Oxford: Clarendon

193. Wijsman, E. M. 1984. Techniques for estimating genetic admixture and applications to the problem of the origin of the Icelanders and the Ashkenazi Jews. *Hum. Genet.* 67:441–48

194. Wijsman, E., Zei, G., Moroni, A., Cavalli-Sforza, L. L. 1984. Surnames in

Sardinia. II. Computation of migration matrices from surname distributions in different periods. *Ann. Hum. Genet.* 48:65–78
195. Woo, S. L. C., Lidsky, A. S., Guttler, F., Chandra, T., Robson, K. J. H. 1983. Cloned phenylalanine hydroxylase gene allows prenatal diagnosis and carrier detection of classical phenylketonuria. *Nature* 306:151–55
196. Workman, P. L., Niswander, J. D. 1970. Population studies on Southwestern Indian tribes. II. Local genetic differentiation in the Papago. *Am. J. Hum. Genet.* 22:24–49
197. Wright, S. 1951. The genetical structure of populations. *Ann. Eugen.* 15:323–54
198. Wright, S. 1970. Random drift and the shifting balance theory of evolution. In *Mathematical Topics in Population Genetics*, ed. K. Kojima, pp. 1–31. New York: Springer-Verlag
199. Yunis, J. J., Prakash, O. 1982. The origin of man: A chromosomal legacy. *Science* 215:1525–30

SUSTENANCE AND SYMBOL:
Anthropological Studies of Domesticated Animals

Eugenia Shanklin

Department of Sociology-Anthropology, Trenton State College, Trenton, New Jersey 08625

> "Prometheus, when creating man, took the predominant characteristic of every animal, and from contradictory elements formed mankind"
>
> (La Fontaine 100, p. 8).

INTRODUCTION
Thinking about Animals

For nearly as long as anything can be inferred about human cognition, paleoanthropologists and archaeologists believe humans have thought carefully about animals, about the "predominant characteristic" of each animal, and about those "contradictory elements" that make up humankind. This careful thought has had many outcomes, some scientific, others not.

Among the scientific outcomes in the 19th century was evolutionary thinking about the causes and consequences of domestication, including Charles Darwin's study (32) of the mechanics of human (artificial) selection of domesticated animal and plant population characteristics. In the 20th century, theoretical refinements and the painstaking collection of empirical data have led to studies of such disparate phenomena as the physical consequences of keeping pets (12); the spread of antibiotic-resistant bacteria as a result of feeding antibiotics to livestock (117); and the evolutionary consequences of milk-drinking (99).

Speculation about the origins of human-animal interaction is not the exclusive province of scientists: religions and storytellers alike customarily try to account for the beginnings of human-animal interaction. Genesis does so assertively: "And God said: 'Let us make man in our image, after our likeness; and let them have dominion over the fish of the sea, and over the fowl of the air, and over the cattle and over all the earth, . . ." (Genesis 1.26). The story of Noah's ark reasserts the image of human dominion over animals. Rudyard Kipling explained domestication whimsically: . . ."the cozy Cave that the Man and the Woman went to after the Baby came . . . was their summer Cave, and they planted wheat in front of it. The man [rode] . . . the horse to find the Cow and bring her back to the Cave to be milked" (97, p. 32).

Early scientific speculation about the domestication of animals is not so different from these literary accounts as scholars might like; anthropological theories are often closer to what Tylor called "Myths of Observation" than to scientific constructs. Myths of observation, Tylor said, were "inferences from observed facts, which take the form of positive assertions, and they differ principally from the inductions of modern science in being much more generally crude and erroneous." Further, a myth of observation "may shape itself into the form of a historical tradition, and be all the more puzzling for the portion of scientific truth which it really contains" (159, p. 167). Gordon Childe's observations about the origins of milking are nearly as whimsical as Kipling's: "The process of milking can only have been discovered when men had had ample opportunity of studying at close quarters the suckling of calves and lambs and kids. But once the trick was grasped, milk would become a second staple . . ." (23, pp. 168–69).

There are many other speculations about changes in human perceptions of animals. Some authors have characterized past centuries according to the metaphors used for animals in each: 17th century paintings depict peaceful animals, mastered by humans (108). In the 18th century, animal dispersion was the thinly disguised means of elaborating chauvinistic viewpoints, as Cuvier and Thomas Jefferson debated the question of whether New World animals were punier and smaller than those of the Old World. Depictions in the 19th century were of the bestial in human nature; "man is a wolf among his fellows," declared Hobbes. Thus far, the 20th century view is schizoid, ranging between sentimental animal liberation movements (142) and sociobiological interpretations (102).

Anthropological Thinking About Animals

Although humans have thought long and carefully about their relations to animals, scientists have not considered these relations until very recently. Mythical and artistic outcomes of thinking about animals are only now being subjected to scientific scrutiny. Twenty millennia before domestication, humans painted superb pictures of animals on cave walls, leaving messages that scholars now investigate with a variety of tools and analogies. Leroi-Gourhan inventoried the placement and kinds of animals that appear in Paleolithic cave paintings and concluded that the care in choosing and placing the animals "suggests a system polished in the course of time—not unlike the older religions of our world" (104, p. 118). Ucko & Rosenfeld (161, pp. 150–223) stress the need for careful sifting of ethnographic parallels in understanding the meanings of the paintings. Mary Douglas suggests that these animal paintings, the only clues to what paleolithic men thought, tell us "something positive about his openness to commerce with his fellows. When he painted humans with antlers or animal masks it might say even more about his friendly relations with fellow humans of other groups" (41, p. 41). The ethnographic parallels have been available in the anthropological literature for many years, but only recently have they been carefully interpreted, for what we think of as a "scientific" approach to the study of animals is still being developed.

Whether in Upper Paleolithic cave paintings or religious emblems (the lion of Judah, the lamb of God), whether in Aesop's *Fables* or Orwell's *Animal Farm*, human thinking about animals reflects human needs and conceptualizations, and anthropologists have pondered those needs and conceptualizations for some time. In the history of the anthropological study of domesticated animals, there are many watersheds, but there is little reason and less room here to rehearse all the views and arguments pertaining to animals, fascinating and copious as the literature is.

The focus of this article is on recent anthropological insights into human-animal interaction, and I will use the function/meaning distinction now current in anthropology (95, p. 481; 118, p. xi) as a device for examining new findings about the functioning of animals as sustenance, in an ecological/ecosystemic perspective, and new findings about the meanings of animals as symbols, in structuralist and symbolic perspectives. I review only some of the progress made recently in the ecosystemic study of domesticated animals and explore some of the commonalities in human symbolic conceptions of domesticated animals. Like the study of women, which has provided corrective and sometimes alternative views of how societies operate at many levels, the study of animal-human interaction now offers a stimulating and specific view of how humans operate at many levels.

I begin by looking at some of the old questions that were posed and go on to the new answers that have been proposed. The questions are similar to that of Franz Boas in 1914, who said that the "essential problem" was to know why "human tales are preferably attached to animals, celestial bodies, and other personified phenomena of nature" (14, p. 490). In 1922 and again in 1952, Radcliffe-Brown raised a similar question: "Why do the majority of what are called primitive peoples adopt in their custom and myth a ritual attitude towards animals and other natural species?" (121, 122, p. 129). Despite Lévi-Strauss's best efforts, the questions are as yet unanswered—Tambiah (155) calls this a "haunting problem"—but anthropological attempts to answer the questions are now much more sophisticated than ever before.

Recent Anthropological Studies of Animals

Part of the problem, of course, with answering the questions has been in their phrasing. Anthropologists are and always have been better at answering "how" questions than "why" questions. It is a truism that anthropology is becoming more scientific, but, to summarize, these are the three identifiable trends I take as important in recent studies of domesticated animals: 1. a trend away from speculation about why animals were domesticated and just-so stories about the single-event origins of domestication toward more scientific formulations and the study of the implications of what is now called the domesticating process; 2. a trend toward the study of the many functions of domesticated animals in human adaptations, away from equilibrium assumptions involving environmental predicates and cultural outcomes, toward ecosystemic nondeterminist thinking about the variables involved in keeping different kinds of animals; 3. the study of the multiple meanings of domesticated animals in social and ritual contexts, away from whimsy and Durkheimian classifications of sacred and profane toward an understanding of the real, multivalent contrasts in human thinking about animals.

Early domestication theories drew many inferences from few facts. In addition, early anthropological theories of domestication also have in common a marked tendency to read functions as origins, i.e. if animals are important in the functioning of the ritual/economic systems, then animals must have originally been domesticated for ritual/economic reasons (cf 66). This interpretation is one that the archaeological evidence does not support, as can be seen in many recent articles on the origins of domestication. I will survey some of those newer arguments briefly.

The function of animals has been studied in ecological anthropology, largely as a question of animals as sustenance. The study of the interaction of environmental and cultural factors was partly a reaction to the cruder evolutionary typologies—hunter-gatherer/pastoralist/agriculturalist—formulated to explain human history, and partly a reaction to the overemphasis on environment or economy as determining factors in the "explanation" of human society and culture. Early on, those who advocated the ecological approach, a combination of environmental and cultural factors, for the study of domesticated animals were primarily concerned with the functions of animals as buffers or interactive factors between humans and the environment. Later the ecologists turned to more specific investigations of other aspects of animal-human interaction, such as ecological energetics or nutritional parameters. Recently the trend has been in the direction of ecosystemic studies.

Studies of what animals symbolize or signify is also a thriving field, though views within it have not changed much. Neither has it been subject to so many technological developments as ecosystemic analysis; what people think about their animals is still something that the ethnographer, armed with notebook and pencil, must record in much the same way the turn-of-the-century ethnographer did. Indeed, it is to the credit of those ethnographers that modern analysts such as Roy Willis (169), for example, can use their data. He remarks that his study of the meanings assigned to cattle in different East African societies did not suffer from a lack of first-hand experience of some of those societies.

It is nonetheless true that the study of what animals symbolize has moved a considerable distance from its beginnings at the hands of Boas (14) and Radcliffe-Brown (122), as a glance at the care with which animals are dealt with in recent studies will show (e.g. 64). The directions I examine are three: metaphor, taxonomy, and sacrifice. There is a wealth of data available, both in classic studies and in more recent summations, much of it unanalyzed in modern perspective. Evans-Pritchard's (61) ideas about the equivalences between humans and cattle have been examined often, and I look carefully, if quickly, at DeHeusch's (34) recent examination. Other ideas have not been systematically explored by the comparative case studies method that is the hallmark of the symbolic school.

Each area of study is itself a separate field, but there are a number of unexplored intersections between these fields. For example, why should one group of anthropologists explore the ways in which animals are good to eat and another group explore the ways in which they are good to think or to imagine? Or why is so little known about the symbolic attributes of the oldest domesticate, the dog, and the horse, symbol of conquest in so many societies? (cf 78). Or what happens to the conceptualizations of people who customarily assign attributes to animals they hunt when herding begins to be the method of subsistence instead? Too few anthropologists have sought to bridge the gap between the study of animals as sustenance and animals as symbols or between the functional and the symbolic value of domesticated animals.

In order to highlight the new developments, I have selected only a few of the issues pertaining to animals, issues that seem to me to incorporate much of the thinking of past decades as well as new insights, and I have ignored other well-trodden issues. Thus I will not discuss all 50 domesticated animals (89, p. 44), nor emphasize them according to their numerical strengths [chickens are numerically the largest group of domesticated animals in the world; for census data, see (24, 89)]. The disproportionate emphasis of this article parallels the disproportionate emphasis in the anthropological literature on the larger animals.

In the anthropological literature, much has been reported on how animals are used, how they function in various societies, and how their many meanings are derived, and recently anthropologists have provided new insights into old questions about human-animal interaction. I believe that the investigation of human and animal interaction may well be one of the most fruitful endeavors of anthropology.

THE DOMESTICATING PROCESS

In the 1950s, Carl Sauer and Gordon Childe were theoreticians of great influence in geography and archaeology, their respective fields. Sauer believed that humans first domesticated animals for nonmaterialistic ritual purposes, and he stated categorically that the evidence for domestication would not support an economic interpretation of early domestication: the profane use of animals, he believed, derived from their ritual origins (132, pp. 59–60). Sauer thought that domestication of animals, especially dogs, pigs, and fowls, had probably first occurred among unspecialized fishing folk, in the moist tropics around the Bay of Bengal (131).

Sauer's theory of the ritual basis of animal domestication, like Childe's of the economic basis, is based on very little evidence, but that seems not to have been the reason anthropologists failed to pursue it; theoreticians opted instead for Childe's materialist/economic ideas. Childe's interpretation, his "oasis" theory of domestication, hinged on a period of desiccation in the Middle East, followed by the gathering of humans and animals around oases. Climatic crises increased the dependence of the human population on the tame beasts that had also gathered at the oases, and eventually humans recognized the immense importance of the animals (23, pp. 168–69).

One of the first advances in studies of domestication came from the recognition that there were various steps involved in the domesticating process. Domestication is now seen not as a one-time event but as a process "extending over several thousand years . . . that . . . had its own special characteristics in different areas of the ancient world. [It] . . . has recurred time and time again in different parts of the world and at different times. Domestication as a process still continues" (160, p. xx). Flannery, one of a growing number of scientists who believe that animals were domesticated before plants, reviewed theories of domestication and stated categorically that one model cannot explain the origins of agriculture in different parts of the world (65); he also emphasized the need for processual models.

The one-time event of Childe's myth of observation has been largely discarded or reworked to include empirical archaeological evidence. One example is Hesse's recent article (90) on the origins of domestication, in which he compares slaughter patterns in early Holocene sites in Iran and finds a shift in subsistence strategy between early samples (goat hunting) and late (meat-focused goat pastoralism).

Definitions of what is a domesticated animal have also been redrawn so as to include different observational viewpoints and a recasting of terminology. New definitions of taming and herding have been suggested by Ingold (92), who separates the two according to whether animals are incorporated into human society (taming) or whether they are managed for meat, milk, or as a hedge against hardship (herding).

These careful operational definitions and recent empirically based formulations are replacing Childe's ideas in the anthropological literature, but the one-time, one-step notion, predominantly economic in origin, still echoes, as in Harris's (87) positing of two-time domestication, once in the Middle East and once in the New World. Animals figure heavily in Harris's theory of further developments in Old and New Worlds, but the assumption of one- or two-time domestication is no longer tenable in light of available archaeological evidence.

The processual emphasis has also led to new discoveries in unexpected places, e.g. from Africa, which was almost never mentioned in early theories of domestication. Among the archaeologists working on the empirical evidence for African domestication is Charles Nelson, who was part of a team that announced in 1980 the finding of bones of domesticated cattle in association with hunter-gatherers in North and East Africa (*New York Times*, August 21, 1980). The North African sites are dated at 8900–9600 B.P. and they contain evidence for the independent domestication of cattle from *Bos primigenus*, the wild progenitors of domestic cattle. Remains of the animals are associated with the seasonal occupation of village sites, suggesting that those doing the domesticating were affluent hunters and gatherers who added domesticated animals as a means of augmenting their economy (C. M. Nelson, personal communication; for earlier views see 59).

Definitions of domestication have changed considerably from the early "myths of observation," and recent evidence is still being gathered and considered (e.g. 120). The importance of domestication as an ongoing phenomenon and the importance of domesticated animals in human adaptation are being studied in earnest at present, with interesting results. Given new definitions of domestication and new ideas about what happens, for example, when humans change from hunting animals to herding them, it is noticeable and regrettable that so few anthropologists have studied the psychic or symbolic components of the change from wild to domesticated animals, nor has much attention been given to indigenous renderings of differences between tame and wild in these societies. McCall (115) has traced the equivalence of mating and hunting in Bushman thought, but there are many equivalences to be studied among people who are settling down and acquiring new domesticated animals.

ANIMALS AS SUSTENANCE

Two subfields of ecological thought may be distinguished: first, the subfield of cultural ecology within American anthropology, which got its impetus largely from Julian Steward (152), and second, the ecological school within British social anthropology, which initially took its cues from the writings of Daryll Forde (66; cf 57, 58). These two subfields have their parallels in other fields of anthropology, e.g. Bartholomew & Birdsell's (10) article provided the analytic model, based on interactions between population and environment, still in use by paleoanthropologists (137, p. 38). Additionally, ecological findings are often paralleled in social anthropology by those interested not so much in environment as in relationships between economic institutions and others.

There are several differences in the ways the two subfields studied domesticated animals. First, the cultural ecologists merged economic with environmental variables into the overriding concept of ecology, while the British school treated environment and economy as separate entities whose connections had to be examined. Cultural ecologists treated animals as part of production, and British anthropologists tended to separate animals into different aspects of their studies, e.g. as elements of production, distribution, and consumption or marketing. Another difference is that the social anthropologists emphasized connections between animals as part of the environment and other institutions, e.g. politics or kinship, more than the cultural ecologists, who were concerned with environment and a much more broadly drawn concept of culture. A third difference is that the cultural ecologists initially concerned themselves with what Forde called an internal, functional point of view, while the social anthropologists more often took external connections into account and were better able to deal with ethnicity as a consequence.

Because the cultural ecologists have spent more time debating the importance of domesticated animals, I will be concerned here with the overall thrust of that school and mention the social anthropologists largely in order to summarize some of their contributions to the study of animals. It should be noted that not all Americans subscribed to the American school of cultural ecology and not all British anthropologists followed Forde's direction, and some Europeans have taken the predicates of both schools and molded them into their own directions, e.g. Barth (7, 8), whose niche concept discredited and replaced the idea of culture area. Recently Barth (8, 9) has gone from ecology and political anthropology to an approach that one critic describes as "distinctly structuralist . . . [in] style" (119, p. 108). Barth was also one of the first ecologists to look carefully at the role of animals in ethnic identification, a problem that lately has occupied more and more anthropological attention (e.g. 21, 71, 93, 96). Ellen's excellent critique (58) deals with most of the directions ecological study has taken, and Schneider (133, 134) has tested a number of hypotheses about the relation between economy and social structure with intriguing results.

There are other views about the study of animals, ideas that cross many areas (e.g. 46, 74, 77) and studies in which ecology or economy are used as a backdrop for other notions, e.g. the psychology of herding (55, 168) or of herding and child-rearing practices (6).

Apart from structuralism, cultural ecology has probably given rise to more interesting hypotheses and controversies than any other single subspecialty of anthropology in recent decades. The "sacred cow" issue also seems to have generated more print pages than any other recent anthropological controversy, and it is by no means resolved. When it began, the primary issue under debate was environmental vs cultural determinism, or which was the causal factor in the development of the Hindu treatment of cows? To a very great extent, this was a chicken-egg controversy, resolvable only in Samuel Butler's pithy way: "the chicken is the egg's way of ensuring that there will be another egg" or, in Lévi-Strauss's paraphrase, "the culture is the society's way of ensuring that there will be another society." But the controversy has gone on to become one of the exemplars of the shift from ecological to ecosystemic thinking. The sacred cow controversy has also been an area in which the merits of the distinction between internal and external viewpoints were debated (5). The controversy has grown in the course of its 20-year history, and the issues now involve the delineation of the complex interaction of a multiplicity of factors. The interesting thing about this controversy, however, is not its resolution or the lack thereof: rather it is the increasingly sophisticated data that have been brought to bear to support one or another interpretation of animal-human interaction.

Whether in incorporating development theory, in controversies, or in English-American differences about the relative importance of environmental and sociocultural factors, the ecological/ecosystemic study of domesticated animals is a thriving field.

Ecology as a Subfield of Cultural Anthropology

In the American school, Wissler's descriptive culture area concept was in vogue among American anthropologists until the 1950s, when a new model for the study of interaction was presented by Steward (152). Following Leslie White in some particulars but with emphasis on interaction, not evolution, Steward offered cultural ecology as an "heuristic device for understanding the effect of environment upon culture" (152, p. 30) and as a counter to theories of environmental or economic determinism (152, p. 37).

Cultural ecology was both a problem and a method. Its problem was to explain the origin of particular cultural features and patterns that characterize different areas, using the supplementary concept of cultural core, i.e. features closely related to subsistence activities and economic arrangements. As a method, cultural ecology involved three procedures: study of the interrelationship of exploitative technology and environment; analysis of behavior patterns involved in exploitation by a given technology; and ascertaining the extent to which the behavior patterns affect other aspects of culture (152, pp. 40–41). In this way different levels of sociocultural integration could be taken into account, and cultural types, conceived of as constellations of core features, could be identified.

The extent to which this thinking in terms of origins and levels has disappeared from anthropology may be gauged from a look at changes in definitions of nomadic pastoralism from Steward's time to the present. Early definitions, such as Krader's (98), focused on origins and defined pastoralists as those dependent on herds of domesticated stock. Krader believed that nomadic pastoralism was developed "in the steppes of interior Asia at the beginning of the first millenium B.C. by the Iranian Scyths" (98, p. 499). He defined pastoralists as "those who are dependent chiefly on their herds of domesticated stock for subsistence; they inhabit today, or once inhabited, parts of Asia, Europe and Africa" (98, p. 499).

In 1973, Spooner defined nomadism by the orientation of the nomadic population toward its habitat or niche, i.e. "Nomadic societies typically make little or no capital investment in their natural habitat—in any case far less than settled populations—and they have technologically simpler material cultures" (148, p. 4). He suggested not origins or levels but generative principles: "The nomad exploits his territory by means of his animals, which he uses to convert the natural pasture into his nutritional or commercial requirements" (148, p. 17). Spooner also stressed the distinction between "populations that produce for an outside non-nomadic market, which links them economically with an urban or peasant society, and populations that produce primarily for their own consumption and have to feed everyone every day from their own production. . . . It is in populations of this latter category that a ritual interest tends to develop in the animal on which they place greatest emphasis" (148, p. 18). From this position, Spooner (149) has gone on to the study of ecosystemic variables, including development policies.

In 1980, Salzman (129, 130) reviewed definitions of nomadic pastoralism and, in the same year, the Dyson-Hudsons (51) found many formulations inapplicable or inaccurate or both and suggested that the best thing for the study of pastoral nomads would be to abandon definitional wrangles and to focus instead on empirical/ecosystemic studies (cf 72, 135).

Definitional wrangles about Steward's levels of integration may be over, but there are many issues left to debate within the ecological/ecosystemic school. There are a number of excellent reviews of the work of cultural ecologists after Steward (4, 47, 116, 163, 164), reviews that incorporate critical commentaries on the assumptions of this school. One of the most finely honed reviews is Anderson's (1), defining three main lines of interactional thought that followed Steward's guidelines. The first was cultural ecology, with its emphasis on adaptation and core features.

The second line, ethnoecology, emphasized the ethnographic endeavor. Environments might be permissive or prohibitive with respect to specific technologies but, in Steward's conception, primary attention was to be paid to "relevant environmental features, . . . only those features to which the local culture ascribes importance . . ." (152, p. 39). This statement was largely ignored by Steward's followers, just as it had been ignored when White suggested it. Ethnoecology has almost died out in ecological studies, and its principles have been taken up instead by the symbolic theorists, e.g. the extensive ethnoecological data of Harold Conklin has received more attention from Lévi-Strauss than from Steward's disciples (also see 58). Interest in the ethnoecological approach is periodically revived (e.g. 166), but it seems not to appeal to many materially oriented American ethnographers.

The third line Anderson mentioned was quasi-population or systemic ecology. These first and third lines have continued and converged in recent years as many cultural or human ecologists have turned to the study of ecosystems, at once a broader and a more fine-grained analytic apparatus. The Dyson-Hudsons, for example, began their studies of the Karimojong as cultural ecologists with interests in politics (50) and have gone on to the interdisciplinary study of ecosystemic variables in the South Turkana project (52–54, 110).

Anderson's heuristic categories are not mutually exclusive, and I have already mentioned that many anthropologists have switched emphases more than once. Although the switch from cultural ecology to ecosystemic considerations is the most current direction, it is by no means the only approach to interest anthropologists. Others have continued in the same line, e.g. Roy Rappaport, who stayed within the systemic school, began with a study of the energetics of pig-keeping (123) and went on to consider religious concepts in evolutionary cybernetic perspective (124, 125).

In each line of investigation, domesticated animals were treated differently. The cultural ecologists concerned themselves with internal questions about the regulatory effects of humans on animal populations (and vice versa). In the ecosystemic school, animals, like humans, were part of the overall picture.

The first interactionist studies carried out from the standpoint of cultural ecology assumed that animals were part of the functional "cultural core" through which humans adapted to their environment. Contributors to Leeds and Vayda's edited volume (103) pointed to correlations between animal populations and certain aspects of social organization. Sweet, for example, (154) focused on camel pastoralism and the minimal camping unit. Other common assumptions were: (*a*) that human interaction with animal populations had latent effects and functions that were waiting to be discovered, and (*b*) that the human population tended always toward equilibrium with its environment, making its adjustment by means of the animal population (cf 3).

Latent functions were deduced aplenty by the cultural ecologists, but the equilibrium assumption the model makes has probably been the main reason for its abandonment in recent years. Equilibrium models have been replaced by the study of ecosystems and precise balancing mechanisms, as well as long-term studies, but this replacement was not just a matter of flipping a coin over and studying dysfunction. Instead, the ecosystemic approach has significant effects for the study of changes in systems or for development.

One of the better examples of the study of balancing mechanisms is Rappaport's work on the energetics of pig-keeping among the Tsembaga Maring of New Guinea (123), a most ambitious and demanding project involving the tracing of energy flow, intake, input, and efficiency. Ellen has remarked (58, p. 110) that in so doing Rappaport traced "what proportion of the energy yield of a garden plot was consumed by pigs and what proportion by humans, and what proportion of food waste decomposed and what was consumed by scavengers such as domesticated dogs. These questions were important because the object of analysis was not simply the human population, but the system, whose functioning was regarded as having certain implications for humans whose behaviour, in turn, had implications for the functioning of the system." Friedman (70) has severely criticized both Rappaport's findings and his premises, but whatever one's view of equilibrium assumptions, it is clear that these very careful tracings of systemic interconnections led Rappaport in the direction of the study of ecosystems, as, in another connection, the study of the sacred cow also has done.

Chickens, Eggs, and Sacred Cows

The sacred cow controversy is best understood by tracing it from its beginnings through to the present. We can focus primarily on the writings of Marvin Harris because, unlike most polemicists, Harris does learn from his critics and has several times recast his arguments to provide documentation from many different sources (83–88).

In a 1965 article, Harris set out the hypothesis that there were latent functions to Hindu cow worship. The argument in the earliest version was that an ecological rationale underlay cow worship and that a better understanding of the cow complex could be gained by looking at the symbiotic relationship between humans and cattle. He concluded that "the power of the sacra surrounding the Indian cattle complex is thoroughly circumscribed by the material conditions under which both man and beast must earn their livings" (83, p. 226). What he did not say [and is usually careful to avoid saying, but see Harris (86)] was that cow worship was strictly a matter of technoenvironmental determinism. In fact, Harris is close here to Radcliffe-Brown's answer (122) to his own question about why certain animals become the focus of ritual attitudes. Radcliffe-Brown's simplistic and unitary response was that it had to do with the economic value of animals. It is a measure of the increasing sophistication of anthropology that Harris's answer, phrased in 1965 in terms of the energetics of cattle-keeping, was considered highly unsatisfactory little more than a decade after Radcliffe-Brown answered the question with a unitary shrug.

Critics of cultural ecology, as well as cultural ecologists themselves and the devotees of the religious school of thought in anthropology, quickly became embroiled in the controversy, which continues only slightly abated to the present (e.g. 140, cf. 139, 167). After critics responded to the 1965 article by calling upon historical factors, Harris drew history into his argument, and in a 1978 article (88), he traced the historical development of the concept of the sacred cow from ritual prescription in the 2nd millenium B.C. through a spiritual transformation that was beginning to be manifest ca 200 A.D. Then, "By 1000 A.D., all Hindus were forbidden to eat beef. Ahimsa, the Hindu belief in the unity of all life, was the spiritual justification for this restriction" (88).

In his 1978 article, Harris offered still more comparative information on American livestock production and its energy costs than he did in 1965. His assumptions about the origins of the sacred cow were phrased in terms of Darwinian selection:

> The practice arose to prevent the population from consuming the animal on which Indian agriculture depends. . . . It is probable that the elimination of meat eating came about in a slow, practical manner. The farmers who decided not to eat their cows, who saved them for procreation to produce oxen, were the ones who survived the natural disasters. Those who ate beef lost the tools with which to farm. Over a period of centuries, more and more farmers probably avoided beef until an unwritten taboo came into existence. . . . Only later was the practice codified by the priesthood (88, pp. 206–7).

In 1982, Harris and his collaborators (162) took a different approach, this time in terms of bovine sex and species ratios. The 1982 article might be said to be Harris's most quantified answer to his critics, but it, too, came under fire because of the use of government statistics and not material from what the Freeds (69) had earlier called analytical holistic ethnography. As mentioned, the controversy illustrates several anthropological points, not the least of which is the sophisticated data anthropologists are capable of calling into service (e.g. 35–37, 68, 69, 111, 112, 139, 140).

Thus, what began in 1965 as a somewhat naive, latent, or positive functioned argument, in two decades has become a sophisticated interchange about positive and negative functions, about energetics and sex ratios, and about the need for better (analytic holistic) ethnography. Whatever else one may say, the controversy over technique and data has had two, perhaps unintended, consequences: first, no anthropologist will ever again ignore animal-human interaction while working in India (and other parts of the world?). Second, while some of Harris's critics (e.g. 69) credit him with initiating a very interesting discussion, those of us interested in human-animal interactions can also express our gratitude to him for having—if not exactly guided, then prodded and shoved—the field of cultural ecology into the realm of scientific undertaking, though its still tenuous interpretations and conclusions are not necessarily those he might have preferred.

Ecology as a Subfield of Social Anthropology

In social anthropology, Forde (66) summarized the importance of environmental and cultural interactions and concluded that, given the complexity of human societies, a useful and meaningful theory of human society could not be based on ecological factors alone. This was true whether one dealt with economic/evolutionary stages, geographical determinism, or with "sociological determinism." Forde also warned against the dangers of functional assumptions:

> To approach the study of human society from an exclusively internal point of view may result in a very serious failure to appreciate the strength of cultural inertia. The belief that functional relations owe their existence to the needs they now fulfil, when they may be secondary by-products; the assumption that of two related elements neither could exist apart; in brief, the ascription of genetical significance to the existing functions of cultural traits and the neglect of any attempt to trace their history, can lead to a sociological determinism as invalid as environmentalism (66, pp. 471–72).

In addition to my view that there are two lines of development in ecological studies, I should add that I disagree with Ellen's assessment of Forde's contributions to ecological studies. I especially disagree with his characterization of Forde as occupying "a position equivalent to that of Kroeber" (58, p. 27). In my opinion, Forde advocated a much more sophisticated view of environment and social relations than Kroeber ever did. Forde also, both by his own work and that of his students, e.g. M. G. Smith (144) and M. Dupire (48, 49), sensitized a number of social anthropologists to the importance of collecting concrete data on the interaction of environmental and economic institutions. If Forde's students have not followed his directions precisely (e.g. 145), it is nevertheless true that some of Forde's "grand-students" [and one of Ellen's collaborators, P. Burnham, (20), "through" M. G. Smith] have used ecological data with sensitivity and distinction.

Although some social anthropologists have had no interest in matters ecological, nevertheless they have managed to raise and answer fascinating questions about human-animal interaction. Others, like Evans-Pritchard in *The Nuer* (60), have managed to confuse everyone about the extent of their interest in and belief in environmental factors as critical variables for social organization (95; cf 17).

I close this section by mentioning briefly some of the questions asked in social anthropology, especially the comparative work that has been done on different groups in the same environment or on groups with different environments and similar exploitation techniques. One work that considered environment, economy, and history was Winter's (172). He reiterated Forde's emphasis on cultural inertia in considering the effects of environment on subsistence:

> To put the matter briefly, the principal determinant in most areas is the cultural tradition of the people living there with environmental conditions exerting only a secondary influence. Thus, for example, if in a given locality one finds an Iraqw-speaking group of people, it is certain that they will be practicing agriculture while if one finds a group of Barabaig-speaking people in similar country, one will find them leading a purely pastoral existence (172, p. 459).

Asad contributed excellent analyses of the rationality of pastoral exploitation of resources (2), while Gray was one of the few who took the subject of goats seriously, considering them in relation to bride-price (80, 81) and documenting the Sonjo switch (82) from cattle-keeping to goats in the face of pressure from the Masai.

In 1962, Bohannan and Dalton edited what remains one of the best collections on the subject of livestock in economic contexts (15). Interestingly, a "regional" approach similar to that used in present day ecosystemic studies was apparent in the organization of this book, one section of which could well have been titled "The Masai and Their Neighbors," for it deals with differences in a number of groups in which pastoralism and agriculture occur in varying degrees. Many questions (and other areas) are also dealt with, including Dupire's raising of the question of cattle as repositories of value among the Fulani (48), as well as her survey of the ways in which different groups of Fulani use animals (cf 71, 134). With some few exceptions, e.g. Dupire (49), women's relation to pastoral production was not the subject of serious study.

Other considerations have included an interesting discussion of animal temperament as a factor in human settlement patterns. Spencer (147, p. 20) discussed the docility of camels as a factor in Rendille social organization, but after noting that camels are easier to handle in larger numbers, he came down firmly on the side of "cultural inertia" and concluded that "Rendille are accustomed to and prefer life in larger settlements associated with their clans" (147, p. 20). It is worth noting, too, that there are few discussions of animal temperament, real or imagined, in the anthropological literature.

The questions of the meaning of private property, sedentarization, and the rise of stratified societies have also been debated in terms of animals and markets. Dowling (45) refutes Barth's argument that pastoralist societies promote cultural patterns of private property through ascription of animals to individuals, and he argues that Barth's statements hold true for the Dobuans but not for the Basseri, who are market dependent. Dowling believes that patterns of sedentarization prevent Basseri society from rising to the climax seral stage by maintaining a compatible ratio of men and animals to pasture (45, p. 422), and he calls for comparative studies of property relations.

Schneider (134, p. 221) also takes up the argument about pastoralism and capital—the idea that it is capital and not land or labor that is central to the production of wealth in pastoral societies. Barth (9, p. 12) suggests that pastoral production determines the form and relation of nomads to other populations and makes savings and investment necessary in particular ways (cf 11). Another interesting question has been raised by Lincoln (109, p. 12), i.e. the extent to which archaeologists may attempt the elucidation of a religious system of a culture whose economy is based on the keeping of cattle.

The intersections of settlement (130) and stratification have intrigued scholars for a long time. Bates & Lees (11) discussed the adaptive responses of peasants and pastoralists, increasing and decreasing specialization or regrouping of peasant and nomad populations. Elam (56) discusses nomadism in Ankole as a form of political protest, a substitute for rebellion against kings.

Recently the effects of theft and raiding on herds and on social organization have been taken up in intriguing ways, with Cutshall (28) looking at the redistributive effects of theft as these pertain to the development of social divisions; Winter (173) considering the effects of Masai raiding among the Iraqw; and Dalleo (31) considering Somali poaching in historical context.

Stenning (150, 151) considered the tolerance of zebu cattle to tsetse fly in relation to Fulani transhumance. These "correlational" approaches, as Ellen calls them, within social anthropology have given way in recent years to the ecosystemic perspective. That perspective allows a number of views to be incorporated and also allows for the development of new subfields such as "veterinary anthropology" (146), but the efforts of the social anthropologists generally are a gold mine for those interested in human-animal interactions. I have mentioned here a few ideas that seem worthy of further exploration, but I have not mentioned some of the better-known debates concerning people with intimate relations to animals, e.g. the extensive literature on segmentary lineage systems, on the "identity" of the Nuer, and on the "cattle complex" (for recent reviews of these issues, see 16, 95, 109, 135).

Recent Ecosystemic Perspectives

The study of humans as part of the ecosystem, what Anderson called the quasi-population or systemic model, has come into prominence recently, partly as an artifact of development studies. To see the roles considered for domesticated animals in ecosystemic studies, a concrete example such as Richard's discussion of ecological change and African land use (126) is illuminating. Richards summarized the politics of domestic livestock keeping and pastoralism in Africa by noting the continuum between nomadic pastoralism and settled agricultural activities along with some of the disrupting factors, e.g. the rinderpest epidemic from the 1880s, and the expansion of tsetse fly belts, early in the colonial period, that caused people to move back and forth between the pastoral and agricultural ends of the available spectrum. He also points to the neglect of small domestic livestock in African agricultural research and says, "Only by ignoring small domestic livestock was it possible for colonial commentators to maintain the view that African cultivators knew nothing of mixed farming" (126, p. 38).

Richards cites Dahl & Hjort's study (30) showing that, for pastoralists, the mixing of small and large livestock is not dissimilar to intercropping in African agriculture. It is a means of withstanding ecological hazards and speeding recovery when drought reduces herd sizes. For recent views of goats and small stock, see especially Conant (25), DeBoer et al (33), Gatenby & Trail (75), Shanklin (136), Velez-Naur et al (165), Wilson (170, 171). Richards concludes by advocating the study of regional economic systems, in which pastoralism and hunting and gathering activities may be understood in their broader social contexts.

The ecosystemic approach has great promise for the understanding of the role of animals in human adaptation, but there are other new techniques and ideas that also show promise. New quantitative techniques (e.g. 153) have added greatly to the understanding of environmental and social interactions, e.g. Glatzer & Casimir (76) record a 10.1% increase in herds in a favorable year, but their most interesting data come from the use of remote "sensing" techniques, via satellite photographs, to predict (ecological) possibilities for the next year (cf 27).

Finally, I should mention the recent studies of famine and drought, in which animals are seen (by researchers and human subjects alike) as buffers against an uncertain environment. Torry's (156, 157) review articles summarize much of the research that has been done and call for more empirical social research to facilitate better understanding of famine vulnerability and coping strategies. Campbell (22), Dahl (29), and Dahl & Hjort (30) have also dealt with changes in pastoral societies as a result of drought in East Africa, while Franke & Chasin (67) have surveyed the effects of development and ecological destruction in the West African Sahel. Gambarotta (73) has looked at the future of the Sahel generally, and Maclachlan (112) has studied the process of decision making in potentially disastrous conditions, using Liebig's Law of the Minimum as the basis of his work.

In sum, then, those who have studied animals as sustenance have provided fine data on the interaction of humans and animals, with or without environmental correlates. Nonanthropologists who use the ecosystemic perspective—and study such things as animal bite-counts—often call for more information on the value systems of the peoples they incorporate (138, 141) in their regional perspective, and anthropologists are singularly well equipped to supply that information.

ANIMALS AS SYMBOLS

The several directions the symbolic study of animals has recently taken—directions such as the study of metaphor, of taxonomy, and very lately of sacrifice—have sprung mostly from the attempts of Lévi-Strauss to answer the questions of Boas and Radcliffe-Brown about why certain species are sacred, others not. Lévi-Strauss first (105) answered Radcliffe-Brown in *Totemism* by noting that the problem is resolved when one considers not the particular characteristic(s) of the species chosen but the whole classificatory system of similarities and differences that the society uses to "allow the natural and social universe to be grasped as an organized whole" (105, p. 135). Using totemism as a specific instance, Lévi-Strauss analyzed the general predilection in human thought toward categorizing, not resemblances between species—i.e. one animal species vs another animal species—but the resemblance between two systems of differences, e.g. animals and ancestors.

> ... The Nuer speak about natural species by analogy with their own social segments such as lineages, and the relation between a lineage and a totemic species is conceptualized on the model of . . . the relationship between collateral lineages descended from a common ancestor. The animal world is thus thought of in terms of the social world (105, p. 18).

Continuing along these lines in *The Savage Mind*, Lévi-Strauss stated his answer to Boas's question more succinctly: "The beings which native thought endows with significance are seen as exhibiting a certain affinity with man" (106, p. 37). He also noted that the principles underlying classifications could not be postulated in advance, that they must be discovered by ethnographic investigation and that two difficulties were posed in so doing: first, extrinsic difficulties from a lack of knowledge of the observations made by the classifiers, and second, intrinsic difficulties resulting from the "polyvalent nature of logics which appeal to several, formally distinct types of connection at the same time. . . ." (106, p. 61).

Lévi-Strauss's work was the jumping-off point for a number of scholars, including Stanley Tambiah (155), who believes that Lévi-Strauss does not adequately answer the questions he poses about the significance of animals; instead, Tambiah points out, Lévi-Strauss begs the question, discussing dietary prohibitions inadequately and the naming of animals delightfully. Lévi-Strauss also changes the question somewhat and focuses on the study of the passage from nature to culture, which he believes should be the central preoccupation of anthropology.

Animals as Metaphors

Following Lévi-Strauss, Edmund Leach (101) examined animal metaphors and obscenity, especially animal abuse "in which a human being is equated with an animal of another species" (101, pp. 42–43). Animal abuse, Leach found, was part of a wide field of study that includes animal sacrifice and totemism, but he was particularly concerned to demonstrate that verbal categories of edibility and marriageability correspond to categories of animals. In the structure of food, for example, Leach notes "a universal tendency to make ritual and verbal associations between eating and sexual intercourse," and hypothesizes that "the way in which animals are categorized with regard to edibility will have some correspondence to the way in which human beings are categorized with regard to sex relations" (101, pp. 59–60).

Then he examines the ambiguous, taboo-laden categories of pets and game, and makes some suggestions about the reasons for the monosyllabic names (in English) of house pets, farm and game animals, and the stretching of those monosyllables to describe the qualities of human beings, sometimes abusively, sometimes not. Leach concludes this tour de force by showing that, among the Kachin, the same kinds of discrimination and sexual metaphors are abundant, though the animals differ. "The more remote animals are the more edible, and the homonym meanings of the associated words become less taboo loaded as the social distance is increased. . . . Moreover, as remoteness is increased, we finally reach, as in English, a category of unknown and therefore inedible creatures, and the pattern is then reversed" (101, pp. 59–60).

Leach unequivocally assigned one meaning to one animal, but scholars who have followed his lead in the study of metaphor have been more equivocal, more concerned with a number of possible meanings for animals, not just domesticated ones as intermediaries or boundary breakers. Fernandez (63) advocated the systematic study of metaphors, involving the study of the movement they make in semantic space and specification of transformations, and he noted: "A cow in short is everything a rat is not and men are wise to draw the appropriate lessons that each nature has to teach. Men can be and are, through the diverse powers of culture, many things. Their choices are manifold. If they can look around and find some lessons in cows and calves, bears and rats, their choices are made easier" (63, p. 41). He added, "It will be enough if anthropologists pay attention in the field to the ways in which men are aided in conveying inchoate psychological experiences by appealing to a range of more easily observable and concrete events in other domains of their lives" (63, pp. 57–58).

To leave domesticated animals for wild/tame ones for a moment (in order to learn more about animal categories), Crocker (26) disagrees with some of Lévi-Strauss's statements about the relation of totemism to metaphor, and he examines the assertion Bororo make that they are brothers to parrots, finding many bases on which the affinity between animals and men rests (men is used in its specific sense). Among the matrilineal Bororo, ritual attitudes toward macaws involve synecdoche, "in that various attributes of macaws are considered aspects of clanship, and vice versa; other Bororo comparisons . . . rest on more purely syntagmatic contiguities, and reflect metonymy." But, Crocker adds, "neither the totemic nor the related cosmological realms of discourse are at all relevant to the case in question, which instead deals with the problem of man's nature rather than the clan's culture."

Brandes (18) recently has considered the problem of animal metaphors and the use of metaphoric clusters which he says "explain a host of otherwise irrational symbols," e.g. "an illegal migrant to the United States is called a *pollo* (chicken), not because there is anything about this animal itself to be compared with such men, but rather because the person who accompanies them safely across the border is a *coyote,* an animal who, like his human counterpart, wanders furtively through the night and carries off chickens" (18).

In Tzintzuntzan, Brandes believes, animal metaphors depend on the perception of parallels between human and natural worlds and are based on analogies between human relationships and animal-plant relationships. Exploration of observable or presumed qualities of the animals is the means of identifying specific symbolic meanings of the animals and, more particularly, of the human characteristics they are used to represent.

Brandes identifies three areas of conscious comparison between animals and humans: first, human character traits, e.g. the burro is considered stupid and stubborn and a person who exhibits those traits will be called a burro; second, physical qualities, e.g. oversized breasts may cause a woman to be likened to a milk-giving cow; and third, a category of functional equivalence in which animals and humans are equated, e.g. mules and barren women, neither of which can reproduce.

Brandes is careful to point out, however, the polysemic qualities of many terms, e.g. referring to someone as a burro may mean that the person is promiscuous or badly behaved generally. Cats, too, are polysemic, and humans may be brave or servile "like a cat." Similarly, the word "animal" may itself mean both sexual organs or poor manners, and Brandes finds that since sexuality is the most inherently bestial feature of humanity, animal terms are particularly evident among the metaphors.

Brandes disagrees with Leach about whether it is ambivalence in human-animal bonds that causes animal metaphors to be so prevalent. He believes instead that it is the ambivalent feeling of people about their own biological constitutions that determines the speech form, not their bonds with or feelings about the animal world. He concludes that animal metaphors have two uses: they can be used to criticize others or to form social bonds with them; and terms that are abusive in one context may be received amicably in another.

The Study of Taxonomy

In a different vein, Lévi-Strauss's ideas about taxonomy have been taken up seriously by a number of scholars, including Tyler (158), who provides an example of the ways in which American English linguistic categories may be broken down in his analysis of the component parts of the category, "livestock," and by Douglas, who uses Lévi-Strauss's notions in *Purity and Danger* (42) as a tool for considering the abominations of Leviticus and explaining why the pig was considered unclean by the ancient Hebrews: "Cloven hoofed, cud-chewing ungulates are the model of the proper kind of food for a pastoralist . . ." She then reviews some borderline cases, e.g. ruminants that are not cloven-hoofed and animals that are cloven-hoofed but not ruminant, i.e. the pig and the camel, and says: "I suggest that originally the sole reason for [the pig's] being counted as unclean is its failure as a wild boar to get in the antelope class, and that in this it is on the same footing as the camel and the hyrax, exactly as is stated in the book" (42, p. 69).

Bulmer (19) has taken issue with Douglas's suggestion, along much the same lines as Malinowski and Radcliffe-Brown debated the efficacy of magic in alleviating anxiety. Bulmer says that he would regard the statements as taxonomic rationalizations, made by very sophisticated professional rationalizers, and "It would seem equally fair, on the limited evidence available, to argue that the pig was accorded anomalous taxonomic status because it was unclean as to argue that it was unclean because of its anomalous taxonomic status" (19, p. 192).

In the course of his discussion, Bulmer elaborates the conclusions that Crocker also arrived at with respect to the use of metaphor. Bulmer, however, is concerned with the taxonomic distinctions that the Karam draw between themselves and cassowaries, including a forest-cultivation antithesis which is linked to kinship roles and rights. He illustrates these antitheses by referring to the characteristics of the dog and the pig, both of which cross the forest/cultivated area boundary but are treated differently. He sums up: "if cassowaries and dogs are quasi-humans, cassowaries the metaphorical cognates of men and dogs the distant potential affines and adopted children, pigs are not quasi-humans with a separate society of their own, but sub-human or non-human members of the human family: like women, only more so" (19, p. 191).

Douglas has used animals in other ways as well, quite apart from her famous discussion of the pangolin among the Lele (38–40, 44). In testing her grid/group model, she uses three Nilotic groups, the Dinka, the Nuer, and the Mandari, and compares them according to their beliefs about sin and spirit possession (43, p. 125 *et seq.*). She concludes that grid and group are strongest for the Mandari, weaker for the Nuer, and weakest for the Dinka, and that this formalist approach to religion and magic goes along with elaborate specifications of kinds of sin, illness, and appropriate sacrificial animals (according to color and thermal categories) for each offense. She concludes: "The weaker the social constraints, the more bodily dissociation is approved and treated as a central ritual adjunct for channelling benign power to the community. The stronger the social pressures, the more magicality in ritual and in the definition of sin" (43, p. 130). She goes on to note that the Dinka sense of living in an expanding economy may be derived from their successful cattle husbandry and cites Spencer's (147) comparative study of the Rendille and the Samburu as precedent for this idea.

Studies of metaphor and taxonomy have already produced a considerable amount of data on human-animal interactions, even though the answers that are made—and phrased in such nebulous terms as beliefs and feelings—are necessarily equivocal and variable. There is another recent approach, the study of sacrifice, that seems to me a most promising area for future studies. DeHeusch (34) has produced a masterful synthesis of viewpoints about animal sacrifice and suggested some new directions, which are worthy of detailed consideration.

The Study of Sacrifice

DeHeusch begins by reviewing Lévi-Strauss's comments on sacrifice and sacrificial ritual (as part of the problem of animal symbolism) in *The Savage Mind* (106), and Hubert and Mauss's description of sacrifice in Vedic India (91), finding both sets of ideas inapplicable or not helpful in understanding African sacrificial ritual. He considers the contradictions between Lévi-Strauss's (105) opposition of sacrifice and totemic representation (in which Lévi-Strauss claimed that totemic representation constituted a symbolic code that links social groups with the natural order through differentiation of animal species) and his (107) declaration that ritual functions to overthrow mythical thought, not to reinforce it.

In DeHeusch's view, Hubert and Mauss struggled ineffectively with the evolutionary view that animal sacrifice had originated in totemism, and he believes that Indo-European ethnocentrism marred Hubert and Mauss's definition of sacrifice as "a religious act which, through the consecration of a victim, modifies the condition of the moral person who accomplishes it or that of certain objects with which he is concerned" (91, p. 13).

DeHeusch then asks how certain domestic animals participate in the spirit world and proceeds to use some old distinctions in building his own grammar of the sacrificial rites, including major distinction between "sacralization" sacrifice and "desacralisation" sacrifice. In the first case, the movement is made from profane to sacred and the sacrificer is as closely associated as possible with the consecrated victim. After the departure of the spirit that resides in the victim, an alimentary communion takes place. "In desacralisation rites it is more a matter of ridding the sacrificer of any impurity contracted by the non-observance of a religious prescription or by the contact with impure things" (34, Chap. 3).

He notes that before proceeding with the analysis of sacrificial thought, it is necessary to investigate the status of the domestic animal in classificatory systems (opposing these ideas to Lévi-Strauss's interest in the difference between humans and wild animals and plants). He goes on to point out that symbolic designations and qualifications of species suitable for sacrifice, e.g. the dog, deserve greater attention, and call for new investigations of symbolic "substitutability," such as the Nuer substitution of the wild cucumber for an ox.

DeHeusch then breaks the problem down further:

> Different paradigms intersect within a topology which encompasses animal, man and the universe. The ritual killing of certain wild species cannot be dissociated from the sacrificial sphere. This killing adumbrates the other, more or less imaginary, side of sacrifice. Theoretically, the hornbill, python, etc. must be immolated bloodlessly; the same requirement is necessary when a black sheep is sacrificed in place of a man in order to put an end to sorcery. In all these cases, the sacrificed animal is truly a "person," sometimes representing a man, sometimes a cosmological divinity. This does not hold true for the ox or the goat in domestic rites. To this initial splitting of the problem, another kind of dialectic is added: the goat, which has been expelled and is laden with "blackness" after the extraction of the chyme, obviously does not have the same role as the one that is sacrificed to the ancestors with its special treatment of the entire digestive system. . . . Our problem is fragmented and open to different questions (34, Chap. 4).

These excerpts give an idea of the caliber of thought that DeHeusch brings to the problem of sacrifice, and an indication as well of the many directions in which he explores the question of animal sacrifices. In a number of case studies drawn from the anthropological literature, he also examines in detail the idea of human/animal substitutability; differentiates among the passages from an abusive "divinization" through a temporary "animalization" to the normal human state; and traces the animal's role in helping to construct a new personality. I will leave these ideas at this stage, for they are bound to generate controversy and new interpretations and that, as noted, is exactly what is needed in the anthropological study of domesticated animals.

In sum, then, the study of animals as symbols has produced, in the area of metaphor, the hypothesis, not very extensively tested, that domesticated animals occupy an intermediate position between humans (culture) and wild animals (nature) and a number of answers that are bound to be both equivocal and variable. The study of taxonomy has demonstrated a number of axes along which similarities and differences between animals and humans may be considered—and I think has led or will lead to more careful fieldwork than ever before, as well as to the comparative use of many ethnographic sources of data on human-animal interactions. Other ideas have not been well explored, e.g. Mbiti's tracing of ideas about Ankore time-keeping with cattle (113), in contrast to those suggested by Evans-Pritchard for the Nuer (62), and, in a different publication (114), Mbiti's provision of an inventory of African ideas about cows and wild animals used for sacrifice. The study of animal sacrifice, considered in a number of tantalizing ways, is both very old and very new, but promises to lead to even more discoveries.

CONCLUSIONS

I began by saying that while humans have thought very long and carefully about their relations to animals, scientists have not done so until quite recently. My intent in this article was to look at the directions that current studies are taking and to suggest some possibilities for study that have not been thoroughly explored. Thus I have looked "sideways," as it were, at the research being done on animals and suggested some intersections between these areas that still need exploration.

The identifiable thrusts of human-animal research may be broken down into two main directions—the study of the function(s) and the meaning(s) of animals. Of these, the study of the function of animals in human societies is the older, but new technological developments and interdisciplinary efforts have made possible many ways of exploring such old questions as, e.g. Forde's long ago mention of the dwarf goat found among central and West African cultivators, which, he said "has a much higher immunity to fly-borne diseases than has the larger brown goat of the African savanas" (66, p. 452). The functions of dwarf animals are being studied with ecosystemic techniques and such semantic techniques as the collection of the genealogies of dwarf cattle (79).

In contrast to the first, the second area of study, the meaning of animals, is a relatively unexplored field, though there is a wealth of available material, and this exciting and innovative area is a new "growth industry" within anthropology. A main point here is to ask what part domesticated animals play in metaphor and symbolic classifications or, to put it another way, what part animals play in what Rodney Needham calls "synthetic images." Sexuality, fertility, and lately color and thermal categories have become standard areas of investigation, but there are other possibilities to be explored, e.g. Karp's suggestion that "in polygynous African societies where large stock is inherited by the children of one mother, marriage will be imaged in metaphors equating women and stock" (94).

I believe there is a strong need for integration of some of the animal studies' perspectives developed within one field or the other, integration of different dimensions in a nondeterminist approach. Reading Ross (127), for example, as he takes issue with Sahlins (128) on the ascendancy of beef-eating in the U.S., makes one long for the subtle and delicate touch of Mary Douglas, or for an understanding brought by a combination of symbolic and ecological approaches, to explain why beef-eating apparently has become unfashionable of late among certain segments of the American population. The anthropological understanding of domesticated animals has been distorted long enough by studies that make all-encompassing claims. It is time to move toward a nondeterminist model of interpretation and explanation, such as that advocated by Karp and Maynard when they argue "that among the Nuer cattle . . . are essential to subsistence *and* can serve as metaphors of social relations [without] suggesting that the two relationships are equal" (95, p. 500; italics added).

ACKNOWLEDGMENTS

I am indebted to Rada Dyson-Hudson, Ivan Karp, and Charles M. Nelson for providing access to some of the unpublished or about-to-be-published material in this article as well as for discussion of many of the ideas contained herein. Other ideas were adumbrated in the introduction to a recent collection edited with Riva Berleant-Schiller (13). Responsibility for errors, however, is mine alone.

Literature Cited

1. Anderson, J. N. 1973. Ecological anthropology and anthropological ecology. In *Handbook of Social and Cultural Anthropology*, ed. J. J. Honigmann, pp. 179–239. Chicago: Rand McNally. 1295 pp.
2. Asad, T. 1973 [1964].[1] Seasonal movements of the Kababish Arabs of Northern Kordofan [Sudan]. See Ref. 143, pp. 143–58
3. Aschmann, H. 1965. Comments on the symposium "Man, Culture, and Animals." See Ref. 103, pp. 259–70
4. Bargatsky, T. 1984. Culture, environment, and the ills of adaptationism. *Curr. Anthropol.* 25(4):399–415
5. Barrett, R. A. 1984. *Culture and Conduct*. Belmont, Calif: Wadsworth
6. Barry, H. III, Child, I. L., Bacon, M. K. 1959. Relation of child training to subsistence economy. *Am. Anthropol.* 61:51–63
7. Barth, F. 1961. *Nomads of South Persia*. Boston: Little Brown
8. Barth, F. 1969. *Ethnic Groups and Boundaries*. Boston: Little Brown
9. Barth, F. 1975. *Ritual and Knowledge among the Baktaman of New Guinea*. New Haven: Yale Univ. Press
10. Bartholomew, G. A. Jr., Birdsell, J. B. 1953. Ecology and the protohominids. *Am. Anthropol.* 55(4):481–98
11. Bates, D. G., Lees, S. 1977. The role of exchange in productive specialization. *Am. Anthropol.* 79:824–41
12. Beck, A., Katcher, A. 1983. *Between Pets and People*. New York: Putnam
13. Berleant-Schiller, R., Shanklin, E., eds. 1983. *The Keeping of Animals*. Totowa, NJ: Allanheld, Osmun. 186 pp.
14. Boas, F. 1914. Mythology and folk-tales of the North American Indians. Reprinted in *Race, Language and Culture*, New York, 1940. [Quoted in Lévi-Strauss, p. 135; see Ref. 106)]
15. Bohannan, P., Dalton, G., eds. 1962. *Markets in Africa*. Northwestern Univ. Press. 762 pp.
16. Bonte, P. 1979. Pastoral production, territorial organisation and kinship in segmentary lineage societies. See Ref. 20, pp. 203–34
17. Bonte, P. 1984. On reading the Nuer. Comment on Karp & Maynard (See Ref. 95) *Curr. Anthropol.* 25(1):129–30
18. Brandes, S. 1983. Animal metaphors and social control in Tzintzuntzan. *Ethnology* 22(3):207–15
19. Bulmer, R. 1973. Why the cassowary is not a bird. See Ref. 44, pp. 167–93
20. Burnham, P. C., Ellen, R. F., eds. 1979. *Social and Ecological Systems*. New York: Academic. 314 pp.
21. Burton, J. W. 1981. Atutot ethnicity. *Africa* 51(1):496–507
22. Campbell, D. J. 1984. Response to drought among farmers and herders in southern Kajiado district, Kenya. *Hum. Ecol.* 12(1):35–64
23. Childe, V. G. 1951. *Man Makes Himself*. London: Watts
24. Clutton-Brock, J. 1981. *Domesticated Animals from Early Times*. Austin: Univ. Texas Press

[1]Square brackets indicate first publication date or publication quoted from.

25. Conant, F. P. 1982. Thorns paired, sharply recurved: Cultural controls and rangeland quality in East Africa. See Ref. 149, pp. 111–22
26. Crocker, J. C. 1977. My brother the parrot. In *The Social Use of Metaphor*, ed. J. D. Sapir, J. C. Crocker, pp. 164–92. Philadelphia: Univ. Penn. Press
27. Croze, H. J., Gwynne, M. D. 1981. A methodology for the inventory and monitoring of pastoral ecosystem processes. See Ref. 72, pp. 340–52
28. Cutshall, C. R. 1982. Culprits, culpability and crime: Stocktheft and cattle maneuvers among the Ila of Zambia. *Afr. Stud. Rev.* 25(1):1–26
29. Dahl, G. 1979. *Suffering Grass: Subsistence and Society of Waso Borana*. Stockholm: Univ. Stockholm, Dep. Soc. Anthropol.
30. Dahl, G., Hjort, A. 1979. *Pastoral Change and the Role of Drought*. Stockholm: Swedish Agency for Research Cooperation with Developing Countries
31. Dalleo, P. T. 1979. The Somali role in organized poaching in Northeastern Kenya, ca 1909–39. *Int. J. Afr. Hist. Stud.* 12(3):472–82
32. Darwin, C. 1868. *The Variation of Animals and Plants under Domestication*. London: Murray. 2 vols.
33. DeBoer, A. J., Fitzhugh, H. A., Hart, R. D., Sands, M. W., Job, M. O., Chema, S. 1984. Production of meat and milk from goats in mixed farming systems in the high potential tropics. See Ref. 141, pp. 335–59
34. DeHeusch, L. 1985. *Sacrifice in Africa*. Bloomington: Indiana Univ. Press. Joint publication with Manchester Univ. Press. In press
35. Diener, P. 1979. Comment on: "Questions in the sacred-cow controversy," by F. J. Simoons. *Curr. Anthropol.* 20:477–78
36. Diener, P. 1981. Comment on: "Sacred cows and water buffalo in India: The uses of ethnography," by S. A. Freed and R. S. Freed. *Curr. Anthropol.* 22:491
37. Diener, P., Nonini, D., Robkin, E. 1978. The dialectics of the sacred cow: Ecological adaptation versus political appropriation in the origins of India's sacred cattle complex. *Dialect. Anthropol.* 3:221–41
38. Douglas, M. 1957. Animals in Lele religious thought. *Africa* 27(1):46–58
39. Douglas, M. 1966. *Population control in primitive groups*. Presented to Assoc. Br. Zool., Jan. 1966. Reprinted 1982 in *In the Active Voice*, M. Douglas, pp. 135–47. London: Routledge & Kegan Paul
40. Douglas, M. 1972. Deciphering a meal. *Daedalus* 101(1):61–81
41. Douglas, M. 1972. Self-evidence. *Proc. R. Anthropol. Inst.*, pp. 27–44
42. Douglas, M. 1966 [1970]. *Purity and Danger*. London: Routledge & Kegan Paul (Harmondsworth, Middlesex, England: Penguin Books)
43. Douglas, M. 1973. *Natural Symbols*. New York: Vintage Books, Random House
44. Douglas, M., ed. 1973. *Rules and Meanings*. Harmondsworth, Middlesex, England: Penguin Educ. 319 pp.
45. Dowling, J. H. 1975. Property relations and productive strategies in pastoral societies. *Am. Ethnol.* 2(3):419–26
46. Downs, J. F. 1964. *Animal Husbandry in Navajo Society and Culture*. Berkeley: Univ. Calif. Publ. Anthropol., Vol. 1
47. Downs, J. F. 1973. *Human Nature*. New York: Glencoe
48. Dupire, M. 1962. Trade and markets in the economy of the nomadic Fulani of Niger (Bororo). See Ref. 15, pp. 335–62
49. Dupire, M. 1963. Women in a pastoral society. See Ref. 143, pp. 297–303
50. Dyson-Hudson, N. 1966. *Karimojong Politics*. Oxford: Clarendon. 280 pp.
51. Dyson-Hudson, R., Dyson-Hudson, N. 1980. Nomadic pastoralism. *Ann. Rev. Anthropol.* 9:15–61
52. Dyson-Hudson, R. 1983. Understanding East African pastoralism: An ecosystems approach. See Ref. 13, pp. 1–10
53. Dyson-Hudson, R., Little, M. A., eds. 1983. *Rethinking Human Adaptation: Biological and Cultural Models*. Boulder, Colo: Westview
54. Dyson-Hudson, R., McCabe, J. T. 1985. *South Turkana Nomadism: Coping with an Unpredictably Varying Environment*. New Haven: HRAFLEX. In press
55. Edgerton, R. B. 1965. 'Cultural' vs. 'ecological' factors in the expression of values, attitudes, and personality characteristics. *Am. Anthropol.* 67:442–47
56. Elam, Y. 1979. Nomadism in Ankole as a substitute for rebellion. *Africa* 49:147–58
57. Ellen, R. F. 1979. Introduction. See Ref. 20, pp. 1–18
58. Ellen, R. 1982. *Environment, Subsistence and System: The Ecology of Small-scale Social Formations*. Cambridge: Cambridge Univ. Press
59. Epstein, H. 1971. *The Origin of the Domestic Animals of Africa*. New York: Africana. 2 vols.
60. Evans-Pritchard, E. E. 1940. *The Nuer*. Oxford: Oxford Univ. Press
61. Evans-Pritchard, E. E. 1956. *Nuer Religion*. Oxford: Oxford Univ. Press

62. Evans-Pritchard, E. E. 1939. Nuer time-reckoning. *Africa* 12(2):189–216
63. Fernandez, J. W. 1972. Persuasions and performances: Of the beast in every body . . . and the metaphors of Everyman. *Daedalus* 101(1):39–60
64. Fernandez, J. W. 1982. *Bwiti*. Princeton: Princeton Univ. Press
65. Flannery, K. V. 1973. The origins of agriculture. *Ann. Rev. Anthropol.* 2:271–310
66. Forde, D. 1934 [1963]. *Habitat, Economy & Society: A Geographical Introduction to Ethnology*. London: Methuen; New York: Dutton
67. Franke, R. W., Chasin, B. H., eds. 1980. *Seeds of Famine: Ecological Destruction & the Development Dilemma in the West African Sahel*. Totowa, NJ: Rowman & Allanheld. 267 pp.
68. Freed, S. A., Freed, R. S. 1972. Cattle in a North Indian village. *Ethnology* 11:339–408
69. Freed, S. A., Freed, R. S. 1981. Sacred cows and water buffalo in India: The uses of ethnography. *Curr. Anthropol.* 22:483–502
70. Friedman, J. 1979. Hegelian ecology: Between Rousseau and the world spirit. See Ref. 20, pp. 253–70
71. Galaty, J. G. 1982. Being "Maasai": Being "People-of-Cattle": Ethnic shifters in East Africa. *Am. Ethnol.* 9(1):1–20
72. Galaty, J. G., Aronson, D., Salzman, P. C., Chouinard, A., eds. 1981. *The Future of Pastoral Peoples*. Ottawa: Int. Dev. Res. Cent.
73. Gambarotta, H. 1980. The Sahel region: splendour yesterday, famine today; what will happen tomorrow? *Afr. Dev.* 5(1):5–38
74. Garrison, V., Arensberg, C. M. 1976. The evil eye: Envy or risk of seizure? Paranoia or patronal dependency? In *The Evil Eye*, ed. C. Maloney, pp. 287–328. New York: Columbia Univ. Press. 335 pp.
75. Gatenby, R. M., Trail, J. C. M., eds. 1982. *Small Ruminant Breed Productivity in Africa*. Addis Ababa: Int. Livestock Cent. Africa
76. Glatzer, B., Casimir, M. J. 1983. Herds and households among Pashtun pastoral nomads: Limits of growth. *Ethnology* 22(4):307–25
77. Goldschmidt, W. 1969. *Kambuya's Cattle: The Legacy of an African Herdsman*. Berkeley: Univ. Calif. Press
78. Goody, J. 1971. *Technology, Tradition and the State in Africa*. Cambridge: Cambridge Univ. Press
79. Grandin, B. 1981. *Small cows, big money: Wealth and dwarf cattle production in southwestern Nigeria*. PhD thesis. Stanford Univ., Stanford, Calif. 260 pp.
80. Gray, R. F. 1960. Sonjo bride price and the question of African 'wife-purchase'. *Am. Anthropol.* 62:34–57
81. Gray, R. F. 1962. Economic exchange in a Sonjo village. See Ref. 15, pp. 469–92
82. Gray, R. F. 1963. *The Sonjo of Tanganyika*. Oxford: Oxford Univ. Press
83. Harris, M. 1965. The myth of the sacred cow. See Ref. 103, pp. 217–28
84. Harris, M. 1966. The cultural ecology of India's sacred cattle. *Curr. Anthropol.* 7:51–66
85. Harris, M. 1967. The myth of the sacred cow. *Nat. Hist.* 76:6–12
86. Harris, M. 1974. *Cows, Pigs, Wars and Witches*. New York: Vintage Books, Random House
87. Harris, M. 1977. *Cannibals and Kings*. New York: Random House
88. Harris, M. 1980 [1978]. India's sacred cow. In *Conformity and Conflict*, ed. J. P. Spradley, D. W. McCurdy
89. Heiser, C. B. Jr. 1981. *Seed to Civilization*. San Francisco: Freeman. 2nd ed.
90. Hesse, B. 1982. Slaughter patterns and domestication: The beginnings of pastoralism in western Iran. *Man* 17(3):403–17
91. Hubert, H., Mauss, M. 1968. [1898]. Essai sur la nature et la fonction du sacrifice. In *Oeuvres I*, ed. M. Mauss. Paris. (First published in *L'Annee Sociol.*, Vol. 2)
92. Ingold, T. 1980. *Hunters, Pastoralists and Ranchers*. Cambridge: Cambridge Univ. Press
93. Johnson, D. H. 1981. The fighting Nuer: Primary sources and the origins of a stereotype. *Africa* 51(1):508–27
94. Karp, I. 1986. Laughter at marriage: Subversion in performance. In *The Transformation of African Marriage*, ed. D. Parkin. London: Int. Afr. Inst. In press
95. Karp, I., Maynard, K. 1983. Reading *The Nuer*. *Curr. Anthropol.* 24(4):481–503
96. Kenny, M. G. 1981. A mirror in the forest: The Dorobo hunter-gatherers as an image of the other. *Africa* 51(1):477–95
97. Kipling, R. 1974 [1912]. *Just So Stories*. New York: New American Library, Signet Books
98. Krader, L. 1959. The ecology of nomadic pastoralism. *Int. Soc. Sci. J.* 11(4):499–510
99. Kretchmer, N. 1974 [1972]. Lactose and lactase. In *Biological Anthropology*, ed. S. H. Katz, pp. 310–18. San Francisco: Freeman. 494 pp.
100. La Fontaine, J. de. 1954 [1665]. *The

Fables of La Fontaine. Transl. M. Moore. New York: Viking
101. Leach, E. 1964. Anthropological aspects of language: Animal categories and verbal abuse. In *New Directions in the Study of Language,* ed. E. H. Lenneberg, pp. 23–63. Cambridge: MIT Press
102. Leach, E. 1982. *Social Anthropology.* Glasgow: Fontana Paperbacks
103. Leeds, A., Vayda, A. P., eds. 1965. *Man, Culture, and Animals: The Role of Animals in Human Ecological Adjustments.* Washington, DC: Am. Assoc. Adv. Sci., Publ. No. 78. 304 pp.
104. Leroi-Gourhan, A. (n.d.) *Treasures of Prehistoric Art.* New York: Abrams
105. Lévi-Strauss, C. 1963. *Totemism.* Boston: Beacon
106. Lévi-Strauss, C. 1966. *The Savage Mind.* Chicago: Univ. Chicago Press
107. Lévi-Strauss, C. 1971. *L' Homme Nu.* Paris: Librarie Plon
108. Lewinsohn, R. 1954. *Animals, Men and Myths.* New York: Harper
109. Lincoln, B. 1981. *Priests, Warriors & Cattle.* Berkeley: Univ. Calif. Press
110. Little, M. A. 1983. An overview of adaptation. In *Rethinking Human Adaptation: Biological and Cultural Models,* ed. R. Dyson-Hudson, M. A. Little, pp. 137–47. Boulder, Colo: Westview
111. Lodrick, D. O. 1984. A cattle fair in Rajasthan. *Curr. Anthropol.* 25(2):218–25
112. Maclachlan, M. D. 1983. *Why They Did Not Starve: Biocultural Adaptation in a South Indian Village.* Philadelphia: ISHI Press
113. Mbiti, J. S. 1969. *African Religions and Philosophy.* New York: Praeger
114. Mbiti, J. S. 1970. *Concepts of God in Africa.* New York: Praeger
115. McCall, D. F. 1970. *Wolf Courts Girl.* Athens, Ohio: Ohio Uni. Cent. Int. Stud. Afr. Prog. No. 7
116. Netting, R. McC. 1977. *Cultural Ecology.* Menlo Park, Calif: Benjamin-Cummings
117. Novick, R. P. 1981. The development and spread of antibiotic-resistant bacteria as a consequence of feeding antibiotics to livestock. *Ann. NY Acad. Sci.* 368:23–59
118. Parkin, D. 1982. Introduction. In *Semantic Anthropology,* ed. D. Parkin, pp. xi–li. London: Academic
119. Prattis, I. 1983. Barthing up the wrong tree. *Am. Anthropol.* 85:103–9
120. Price, T. D., Brown, J. A. eds., 1985. *Prehistoric Hunter-Gatherers.* New York: Academic. 480 pp.
121. Radcliffe-Brown, A. R. 1922 [1964]. *The Andaman Islanders.* New York: Free Press
122. Radcliffe-Brown, A. R. 1965 [1952]. *Structure and Function in Primitive Society.* New York: Free Press
123. Rappaport, R. A. 1969. *Pigs for the Ancestors.* New Haven: Yale Univ. Press
124. Rappaport, R. A. 1971. Ritual, sanctity and cybernetics. *Am. Anthropol.* 73(1):59–76
125. Rappaport, R. A. 1971. The sacred in human evolution. *Ann. Rev. Ecol. Syst.* 2:23–44
126. Richards, P. 1983. Ecological change and the politics of African land use. *Afr. Stud. Rev.* 26(2):1–72
127. Ross, E. B. 1980. Patterns of diet and forces of production: An economic and ecological history of the ascendancy of beef in the United States diet. In *Beyond the Myths of Culture,* ed. E. B. Ross, pp. 181–225. New York: Academic
128. Sahlins, M. 1976. *Culture and Practical Reason.* Chicago: Univ. Chicago Press
129. Salzman, P. C. 1980. Is 'Nomadism' a useful concept? *Nomadic Peoples* 6:1–7
130. Salzman, P. C., ed. 1980. *When Nomads Settle.* New York: Bergin/Praeger
131. Sauer, C. O. 1952. *Agricultural Origins and Dispersals.* Bowman Mem. Lect., Ser. 2. New York: Am. Geogr. Soc.
132. Sauer, C. O. 1971. Plants, animals and man. In *Man and His Habitat: Essays presented to Emyr Estyn Evans,* ed. R. H. Buchanan, E. Jones, D. McCourt, pp. 34–61. London: Routledge & Kegan Paul
133. Schneider, H. K. 1957. The subsistence role of cattle among the Pakot and in East Africa. *Am. Anthropol.* 59(2):278–300
134. Schneider, H. K. 1979. *Livestock and Equality in East Africa: The Economic Basis for Social Structure.* Bloomington: Indiana Univ. Press
135. Schneider, H. K. 1984. Livestock in African culture and society: A historical perspective. See Ref. 141, pp. 187–99
136. Shanklin, E., 1983. Ritual and social uses of goats in Kom. See Ref. 13, pp. 11–36
137. Shanklin, E., Mai, L. L. 1981. Joseph B. Birdsell: A conceptual biography. In *The Perception of Evolution: Essays Honoring Joseph B. Birdsell,* ed. L. L. Mai, E. Shanklin, R. W. Sussman, pp. 21–50. Los Angeles: *Anthropology UCLA,* Vol. 7. 273 pp.
138. Sidahmed, A. E., Koong, L. J. 1984. Application of systems analysis to nomadic livestock production in the Sudan. See Ref. 141, pp. 61–76
139. Simoons, F. J. 1968. *A Ceremonial Ox of India.* Madison: Univ. Wisconsin Press
140. Simoons, F. J. 1979. Questions in the

sacred-cow controversy. *Curr. Anthropol.* 20:477–78
141. Simpson, J. R., Evangelou, P., eds. 1984. *Livestock Development in Subsaharan Africa.* Boulder, Colo: Westview. 407 pp.
142. Singer, P. 1985. Ten years of animal liberation (review of 10 books on animal rights). *NY Rev. Books* (Jan. 17) 31(21–22):46–52
143. Skinner, E. P., ed. 1963. *Peoples and Cultures of Africa.* Garden City, NY: Nat. Hist. Press, Doubleday. 756 pp.
144. Smith, M. G. 1962. Exchange and marketing among the Hausa. See Ref. 15, pp. 299–334
145. Smith, M. G. 1965. *The Plural Society in the British West Indies.* Berkeley: Univ. Calif. Press
146. Sollod, A. E., Wolfgang, K., Knight, J. A. 1984. Veterinary anthropology: Interdisciplinary methods in pastoral systems research. See Ref. 141, pp. 285–302
147. Spencer, P. 1973. *Nomads in Alliance.* London: Oxford Univ. Press
148. Spooner, B. 1973. *The Cultural Ecology of Pastoral Nomads.* Addison-Wesley Module Anthropol. No. 45
149. Spooner, B., ed. 1982. *Desertification and Development.* London: Academic
150. Stenning, D. J. 1957. Transhumance, migratory drift, migration. *J. R. Anthropol. Inst.* 87:57–73
151. Stenning, D. J. 1959. *Savannah Nomads.* London: Int. Afr. Inst., Oxford Univ. Press
152. Steward, J. 1955. *Theory of Cultural Change.* Urbana: Univ. Ill. Press
153. Sullivan, G. M., Cartwright, T. C., Farros, D. E. 1981. Simulation of production systems in East Africa by use of interfaced forage and cattle models. *Agric. Syst.* 7:245–65
154. Sweet, L. E. 1965. Camel pastoralism in North Arabia and the minimal camping unit. See Ref. 103, pp. 129–52
155. Tambiah, S. J. 1969. Animals are good to think and good to prohibit. *Ethnology* 8(4):424–59
156. Torry, W. I. 1979. Anthropological studies in hazardous environments: Past trends and new horizons. *Curr. Anthropol.* 20(3):517–40
157. Torry, W. I. 1982. Social science research on famine: A critical evaluation. *Hum. Ecol.* 12(3):227–52
158. Tyler, S. A., ed. 1969. *Cognitive Anthropology.* New York: Holt, Rinehart & Winston. 630 pp.
159. Tylor, E. B. 1964. [1878] *Researches Into the Early History of Mankind and the Development of Civilization.* Chicago: Phoenix Books, Univ. Chicago Press
160. Ucko, P. J., Dimbleby, G. W., eds. 1969. *The Domestication and Exploitation of Plants and Animals.* Chicago: Aldine
161. Ucko, P. J., Rosenfeld, A. 1967. *Palaeolithic Cave Art.* New York: McGraw Hill
162. Vaidyanathan, A., Nair, K. N., Harris, M. 1982. Bovine sex and species ratios in India. *Curr. Anthropol.* 23(4):365–83
163. Vayda, A. P., ed. 1969. *Environment and Cultural Behavior: Ecological Studies in Cultural Anthropology.* Garden City, NY: Nat. Hist. Press. 485 pp.
164. Vayda, A. P., Rappaport, R. A. 1968. Ecology: Cultural and non-cultural. In *Introduction to Cultural Anthropology,* ed. J. A. Clifton, pp. 476–98. Boston: Houghton Mifflin
165. Velez-Naur, M. et al. 1982. Productivity of the West African dwarf goat at village level in southwest Nigeria. *Proc. 3rd Int. Conf. Goat Prod. Disease.* Scottsdale, Ariz: Dairy Goat J. Publ. Co.
166. Wallace, B. J. 1983. Plants, pigs, and people: Studying the food web in Pagan Gaddang. *Ethnology* 22(1):27–41
167. Westen, D. 1984. Cultural materialism: Food for thought or bum steer? *Curr. Anthropol.* 25(5):639–53
168. Whiting, B. B., Whiting, J. W. M. 1971. Task assignment and personality: A consideration of the effect of herding on boys. In *Comparative Perspectives on Social Psychology,* ed. W. W. Lambert, R. Weisbrod, pp. 33–45. Boston: Little, Brown
169. Willis, R. 1974. *Man and Beast.* London: Hart-Davis, MacGibbon
170. Wilson, R. T. 1982. Husbandry, nutrition and productivity of goats and sheep in tropical Africa. See Ref. 75, pp. 61–76
171. Wilson, R. T. 1983. Livestock production in central Mali: The Macina wool sheep of the Niger inundation zone. *Trop. Anim. Health Prod.* 15:17–31
172. Winter, E. H. 1962. Livestock markets among the Iraqw of northern Tanganyika. See Ref. 15, pp. 457–68
173. Winter, E. 1978. Cattle-raiding in East Africa with special attention to the Iraqw. *Anthropology* 2(1):53–59

CHICANO STUDIES, 1970–1984

Renato Rosaldo

Department of Anthropology, Stanford University, Stanford, California 94305

When asked, in the spring of 1981, to review anthropological writings on Chicanos for a conference at the University of California, Santa Barbara, I did some preliminary research, hoping to discover the magnitude of the job ahead of me. *Books in Print* yielded only two ethnographies (1, 35) and a few dissertations that had been printed (by Arno Press and R & E Research Associated) to meet the demand for Chicano studies course materials. A computer search with the keywords Chicano(s), Chicana(s), and Mexican American(s) provided, with duplication, exactly 710 titles, but anthropologists virtually never appeared on the printout, which was dominated by people from other disciplines writing on the topics of health care and bilingual education. So little appeared to have been published by anthropologists writing on Chicanos that I readily accepted the invitation and confidently took on what seemed a simple task.

Then I decided to write the few anthropologists known to me who did research on Chicanos. My letter requested lists of their writings, bibliographies on the subject, and the names of other researchers. Nobody sent a review article or bibliography of the field, but virtually everybody sent their own writings and the names of other people to contact. When my "chain letter" reached four removes (contacts of contacts of contacts of people initially contacted), diminishing returns set in. At last most of the people to contact were already known to me.

To make a long story short, thanks to the generous responses of the authors cited in this review, as well as the exceptionally able research assistance of Janice Stockard, I have now compiled a virtually exhaustive (as contrasted with the more selective list of works cited below) "Working Bibliography of Anthropological Writings on Chicanos, 1970–1983," which lists 321 books and articles (available, on request, from Stanford Center for Chicano Research, Stanford University, Stanford, CA 94305). During the period 1970–1983, the productivity in Chicano studies has followed a steadily rising curve from 1970 to 1981, when it has dropped off, perhaps reflecting the fate of affirmative action in the Reagan era. The exact numbers are: 31 entries for 1970–72, 36 for 1973–75, 77 for 1976–78, 101 for 1979–81, and 60 for 1982–84. Despite the field's productivity (and in marked contrast with such other Chicano studies disciplines as history, political science, sociology, and psychology), anthropological writings on Chicanos have never been reviewed [except in a working paper of mine (142)], and have proved difficult even to identify. Only nine anthropology books on Chicanos appeared during the period under review. The major anthropology journals have printed but four papers on Chicanos (68, 110, 211, 219), though *Human Organization,* the journal of applied anthropology, has 12 entries. Less visible journals in anthropology, Chicano studies, and other disciplines carried a certain number of other articles, but the majority were published in collections, conference proceedings, or as working papers with narrow distribution.

Evidently, as it now appears in retrospect, only my ignorance of its magnitude allowed me to embark on this project. Indeed, my ignorance was shared by the anthropologists studying Chicanos, who, in the absence of discipline-based review essays and conferences, have known themselves only partially, more as segments of networks than as a group. They have succeeded in being prolific without engaging in ongoing exchange with their fellow anthropologists, either in Chicano studies or in other areas of their discipline. This review essay attempts, as one step in a longer process, to make Chicano studies more visible, both to itself and to other anthropologists.

AN INITIAL ASSAULT

The characteristics of Chicano studies since the late 1960s in large measure date back to a series of papers by an anthropologist, Romano (137–141), and a sociologist, Vaca (173, 174), published at the beginning of the period under review. Publishing in *El Grito,* the Chicano journal they founded, Romano and Vaca set an agenda for the future and stridently attacked previous writings by Anglo anthropologists. Though they spoke of the social sciences in general, the writers most vilified for negative stereotyping prominently included such anthropologists as William Madsen, Arthur Rubel, Munro Edmonson, and Margaret Clark. Graduate students who read Romano and Vaca learned a litany of infamous names and were taught to protest against cultural determinism. They learned to recognize that anthropologists who assert that Chicanos suffer from their own alleged cultural values, such as passivity, fatalism, and *envidia,* have simply adopted the timeworn tactic of blaming the victim. The critique had the unintended consequence of so stigmatizing anthropology that one Chicano, who began his career in the early 1970s, called himself a behavioral scientist rather than acknowledge his anthropological identity.

Octavio Romano's voice, empowered as it was by the larger political movement in which he participated, has to be heard in all its late sixties flamboyance in order to appreciate its impact. He began with a telling critique of members of minority groups who exploit their own, such as "Mexican-American labor contractors who delivered and still deliver cheap Mexican labor (137, p. 7)." His tract claimed that such people not only exploit, but also stereotype their own by heaping upon them denigrating epithet after denigrating epithet, in the following manner:

> That is to say, once they [members of minority groups] occupy some position or role in society that is above abject poverty they all too often speak of those who remain in such straits as people who are fatalistic, resigned, apathetic, tradition oriented, tradition bound, emotional, impetuous, volatile, affected, non-goal-oriented, uncivilized, unacculturated, non-rational, primitive, irrational, unorganized, uncompetitive, retarded, slow learners, underachieving, underdeveloped, or just plain lazy (137, p.7).

The jist of his objection to this demeaning rhetoric comes in his next sentence:

> In using such words as these to describe other people they thereby place the reasons or causes of "inferior" status *somewhere within the minds, within the personalities,* or *within the culture* of those who are economically, politically, or educationally out of power (137, p. 7).

Romano, in other words, called for ex-victims to stop blaming present victims. He went on to assert that members of all American groups, whether ethnic, subcultural, or religious, have perpetuated the same mystique about the cultural reasons for their personal success versus the failure of others in their own group.

Romano extended his argument further and asserted that social scientists were not immune from the general American pattern of blaming the victim. In his words:

> This peculiar rationale has remained with us to this day, as witness the ubiquitous terminology of contemporary American social science that repeatedly describes people in the lower rungs of society as underachievers, retarded, fatalistic, tradition bound, emotional, etc., etc., etc. Good examples of this can be found in the Parsonian universal dichotomy which divides social systems into the instrumental-rational social systems (us, of course) *versus* the affective-emotional social systems (they, naturally) (137, pp. 8–9).

Here he touched a nerve. Social scientists thought they were too objective to participate in such shabby, even if culturally prevalent, rhetorical practices. Nor were they prepared for the onslaught that awaited them in future issues of the appropriately named *El Grito*.

The Romano-Vaca critique, if that is not too polite a term for so rude an assault, affirmed that social scientific notions about Chicanos developed during the 1950s and early 1960s simply reflected institutional racism and forms of domination prevailing in the society at large. Unwittingly laced with ideology, the anthropological writings attacked by Romano in retrospect do appear to be as often objectifying as objective. In any case, most researchers entering the field in the 1970s came with critique in hand, fully prepared to slay the by then doddering dragon who went by the name of passive-fatalistic-present-oriented-static-homogeneous-traditional culture.

A MORE DEVASTATING CRITIQUE

Writing about a decade after the Romano-Vaca onslaught, Paredes (129) revisited the terrain earlier so utterly demolished (see also 88, 154). He begins his essay with a tone of moderation, by stating the distressing facts in a matter-of-fact manner, as follows:

> We are well aware of the current quarrel in this country between minority groups and the social sciences. Nowhere has this quarrel reached greater proportions than between Chicanos and anthropology, with Chicanos bitterly attacking ethnographies made of their people by Anglo anthropologists. Octavio Romano, who himself received his doctorate in anthropology and did his fieldwork in a Chicano community, is perhaps the best known and most persuasive of these critics (129, p. 1).

In his next sentence, however, the tone shifts, becoming both more humorous and more pointed:

> The main target of Chicano wrath has been anthropologist William Madsen, Romano's erstwhile colleague, who has become a sort of *bête blanche* of the *movimiento*. Madsen's little book *Mexican-Americans of South Texas* is Exhibit A, to which all Chicanos point with disgust (129, p. 1).

This shift from Romano's relentless strident assault to Paredes's more modulated posture, now the voice of reason, now gentle humor, now irony with an edge, reflects a decade of changes in the broader political climate and in Chicano studies as a discipline.

In Paredes's hands, the critique of anthropology becomes both more devastating and more constructive. Paredes showed that the ethnographies of Madsen and Rubel erred less in overt prejudice than in the more subtle (and therefore more pernicious) unconscious perpetuation of stereotypes. In his words:

> [A]ttempting to be as objective as possible—and that is as much as one may expect either of anthropologists or the subjects of anthropologists—I must say that I find the Mexicans and Chicanos pictured in the usual ethnographies somewhat unreal (129, p. 2).

He further asserts, in the following passage, that his perceptions are shared by members of the communities under study:

> I am thinking especially of the reaction to studies such as those by Madsen, Arthur Rubel, and others on the part of the average Chicano student, especially those students coming from the communities studied by the Hogg Foundation Hidalgo County Project in 1957–1962. It is not so much a sense of outrage, that would betray wounded egos, as a feeling of puzzlement, that

this is given as a picture of the communities they have grown up in. Many of them are more likely to laugh at it all than feel indignant (129, p. 2).

His positive critique succeeds in being both more devastating and more constructive than his predecessors' because he elegantly dismantles specific analyses and builds convincing alternative interpretations. In one case, for example, he discusses how the anthropological folklorist, Munro Edmunson, has in part derived his analysis of Mexican fatalism from a mistranslation of the following stanza of a song:

> Guadalajara en un llano,
> México en una laguna;
> me he de comer esa tuna
> aunque me espine la mano.

In justifying his analysis of fatalism as a key Mexican cultural value, Edmonson renders these lines as follows:

> Guadalajara on a plain;
> Mexico on a lake.
> I have to eat this *tuna*
> even if it pricks me.

Paredes, however, suggests the following alternative translation:

> In these last two lines the first thing worth noting is the presence of *he,* a form of the helper verb *haber*. Bilingual dictionaries usually translate *haber de* as "ought to" or "must." But any Spanish speaker knows that *he de* denotes a strong determination to do something. What the singer is saying is, "No matter what, I *will* eat that prickly pear, even if I get my hand full of thorns." And the pear in question is not an actual fruit, of course, but a woman's favors (129, p. 7).

By comparing the lines with a speech by Shakespeare's Hotspur, Paredes suggests the following less literal, yet more telling translation:

> "Out of this thorny cactus, danger, I will pluck this *tuna,* beauty." Fatalism, indeed! (129, p. 7).

Suffice it to say that further examples in Paredes's essay are circumstancial, abundant, and convincing. Ethnographic errors in Madsen and Rubel include, among others, mistranslations, failing to see double meanings in speech, taking literally what people meant figuratively, and taking seriously what people meant as a joke. If ethnographers wish to move beyond stereotypes, Paredes suggests, they must acquire a deep grasp of the language, a fine understanding of social relations, and a rich sense of social context that minimally includes the ability to distinguish joking banter from deadly earnest.

Embodied in performance and embedded in social context, the concept of culture in Paredes's analysis no longer refers to that timeless, homogeneous essence: the monolithic Chicano. Paredes further enriches the notion of culture when he discusses how researchers can misinterpret what they hear if they fail to take into account their own positions in a field of interethnic and class conflict where certain people are dominant and others subordinate. Chicanos who in seeming earnest say, for example, that all Mexicans are stupid, lazy, and backward expect not agreement, but a response indicating that their friend, the researcher, differs from other Anglos who simply accept the dominant culture's racist stereotypes. How surprised they would be to learn that their remarks, meant to test the waters, have made their way into ethnographies as earnest self-descriptions, understood to be expressions of a cultural inferiority complex (129, pp. 20–21)! The meaning of people's words cannot be separated, in other words, from who is speaking to whom in what context. Paredes thus links cultural performance and power relations.

Always embedded in the analysis of particulars, Paredes's (121–133) theory of culture and power deserves a more general statement, even at the risk of excessive schematization. His view allows for a certain autonomy in people's patterned lifeways, suggesting that culture can both shape and reflect the larger political economy. His approach can be exemplified here in relation to the term "interests." Can one determine group interests simply by looking at their economic conditions? Or must one also discover how interests are culturally mediated, both reflected and created, through what people value and find worth struggling for? Crude idealist theories of culture, on the one hand, remove interests from factors that condition them. Such views ignore the practices through which interests achieve objective expression and undergo continual revision. Vulgar materialist theories of culture, on the other hand, reduce interests to socioeconomic formations. They fail to see how such conditions both enable and constrain the emergence of cultural conceptions. In Paredes's analysis, culture neither determines all human behavior nor dissolves into the economic base.

In this revised form the concept of culture allows for historical change and variation by region, class, city versus country, and time of immigration. It also permits one to stress tensions within and between cultures and classes, such as Mexican nationals, Chicanos, other American minorities, and Anglos. Analyses need not, in other words, generalize to Chicano culture as an eternal totality in a manner comparable to how scholars, according to Edward Said, have characterized the Orient.

THE POLITICS OF RESEARCH

The critical stance that has become prevalent in recent anthropological works on Chicanos faces in two directions. Looking inward toward the academic discipline itself, as Arvizu has said, "Chicanos continue to critique anthropology as a discipline which has developed through colonizing traditions (8, p.

119)." Looking outward toward Anglo American society, as Cuéllar asserts, insider studies stress "a critical dimension that centers on the rigorous analysis and critique of dominant perspectives and institutions (30, p. 70)." Anglo researchers in the field, to varying degrees, have adopted similar positions. Kutsche, for example, accounts for the reported factionalism of Hispano villages of northern New Mexico by affirming, "The simple and in my view adequate explanation [of factionalism] is oppression (84, p. 10)." Whether they take on their discipline or the dominant society, this shared critical posture both unifies researchers and enables them to ride off in widely divergent empirical and theoretical directions.

These writings have also explored what happens when so-called natives, the subjects of anthropological investigation, talk back, question research findings, and produce findings of their own. More often than not, the Chicanos talking back are also anthropologists with university teaching positions. This dual position, as Chicano and as anthropologist, particularly complicates the general debate about whether anthropologists and their subjects can engage in analytically productive exchange. In many, but not all cases Chicano anthropologists are not members of the particular communities for which they speak. Indeed, anthropologists who call themselves Chicanos on campus often do research among people of Mexican ancestry who call themselves, depending on context and region, Mexicanos, Mexicans, Mexican-Americans, and so on.

Let me hasten to say that in this essay Chicano (as is common in the literature) refers broadly to people of Mexican descent residing in the United States, rather than more narrowly to the urban (often university-based) political movement that emerged in the late 1960s. Readers who wish to learn about the etymology, political performance, and limits of the term Chicano should consult Limón (96). Paredes (130) has also insightfully explored contextual parameters of the enormously varied ethnic names in use among Americans of Mexican ancestry. His analysis stands as a cautionary tale against reifying a single term as an ethnic community's one and only self-designation.

Chicano anthropologists' identification with their subjects, whether or not they happen to have grown up in the community under study, includes a perception that ethnographer and informant share a common heritage. Thus the gap otherwise separating the pragmatic everyday uses of language among "natives" and the analytical projects of academic "anthropologists" seem less likely to confound matters when "native anthropologists" critique their own discipline on behalf of their subjects. Chicanos not trained as anthropologists have also commented on academic writings, and they have done so with insight (42, pp. 242–60; 176).

Both the engaged stance and Chicano responses to research have raised issues about the connections between power and knowledge. Who decides whether or not an ethnographic report is significant or accurate? Should the dialogue and debate about the validity of particular interpretations include only trained anthropologists, community members, or both? The anthropological discipline at large clearly should be (though it has not been) concerned with how vexing problems in the politics of research have been played out in the field of Chicano studies.

REGIONAL VARIATIONS

In what follows the literature surveyed, first by geographical region and then by analytical topic, has been shaped, among other signficant factors, by three relatively senior scholars. Paredes, just retired from the University of Texas, Austin, set a standard of creative scholarship in folklore and anthropology that has inspired younger scholars, foremost among others, his outstanding student, Limón. Kutsche, at Colorado College, has organized research projects and conferences that have shaped the regional vision that distinguishes studies of Hispanos in northern New Mexico and southern Colorado. Carlos, at the University of California, Santa Barbara, has published jointly with scholars from other disciplines, as well as with his two students, Gilbert and Keefe, in a substantial series of papers on social organization, health care delivery, and agricultural development.

Researchers have developed broad sketches of the boundaries and characteristics of regions and subregions within the area inhabited by people of Mexican ancestry. Spicer (148, 149; see also 91) provides a useful point of departure for the American southwest. His concept of plural society stands as a reminder that Chicanos cannot be understood in isolation. Although he proposes ethnic subdivisions (such as rural Norteño, urban Norteño, Hispano, and Mexican-American), Spicer notes that, unlike Native American groups, people of Mexican ancestry speak the same language and vary only by dialect and degrees of linguistic competence in Spanish (compare 135). The linguistic basis for Chicano unity probably seems so self-evident that only a comparative perspective can highlight its distinctive import. Spicer, on the other hand, speaks about the divisions separating Mexican-Americans, usually landless working class or peasant immigrants, from the Hispanos, who have resided continuously since the seventeenth century in northern New Mexico and southern Colorado. The latter identify with the land they own and inhabit, rather than with Mexican or Norteño culture. His distinction indicates the need for diverse sociohistorical accounts, rather than a single history, to explain how communities of Mexican descent in the United States have come to be as they are today.

Spicer's broad sketch of southwestern cultural types has been supplemented by Galarza's (43) more differentiated analysis of seven regional groupings: "the San Francisco Bay Basin, metropolitan Los Angeles, the Central Valley of California, the Salt River Valley of Arizona, the upper Rio Grande Valley of

New Mexico and Colorado, a less-defined area centering in Denver and Texas." He goes on to say, "There is an eighth which I will call the 'Border Belt' (43, p. 267)." Galarza's regions combine ecological, rural-urban, and cultural criteria. His classification implicitly calls for further research on the mutual influences of cultural forms and regional political economies.

The area most fully studied from a regional perspective has been the Hispano upper Río Grande Valley of northern New Mexico and Colorado. This area lends itself to anthropological study because the population, which owns the land it inhabits, resides in villages that make suitable units for community and comparative studies. Although only one ethnography of an Hispano village (88) has been published, historians, sociologists, and anthropologists have collaborated in illuminating comparative studies marked by an effort to understand the broader region (13–16, 55, 79–90, 135, 153a–157, 176–181, 222, 223). Van Ness and Kutsche (84, 88, 178, 179, 181) have together developed a broad ecological typology of three distinct subregions, including (*a*) a northern area of community land grants, small economic enterprises, high social solidarity, and relative social equality; (*b*) a southern area of individual land grants, large ranches, huge herds of sheep, and social inequality separating *patrón* [owner] and *peon* [laborer]; (*c*) and an eastern area settled only after 1848 and dominated by commercial cattle operations worked by cowboys.

The Hispano region has also been marked by a self-conscious pride in its own heritage. This awareness of traditional lore, which itself has a long distinguished history in the academic writings of Hispano folklorists, has been reflected in recent anthropological studies of folklore, religion, and local crafts (13–16, 207, 208). Among more recent writers, Briggs's published and forthcoming work appears especially promising. Paredes (127, 128, 133) has studied two Hispanos, one a psychologist and the other a novelist, who have written about the traditions of their homeland.

The most original contribution to cultural studies of the region is by Valdez (176), an Hispano intellectual who is not a university-based academic. In discussing *vergüenza* [shame], Valdez begins by contrasting the term with *sin vergüenza* [without shame, shameless], and convincingly shows that a person "with shame" has qualities of virtue and moderation. Such people are trustworthy and know how to keep a confidence. They appear more as paragons of self-control than as reflexes of social control. Valdez's analysis thus subverts the dominant view, current for the circum-Mediterranean and Spanish-speaking regions of the Americas, that "shame" is an external mechanism for doing the job that guilt, conscience, and inner control accomplish in "Western" cultures. Valdez himself stands as an exemplar of the Hispano region's remarkable cultural vitality, its capacity to produce what Antonio Gramsci called organic intellectuals.

Studies of the border region have only begun, but show considerable potential (6, 41, 130, 200–202, 225). Fernández Kelly has done pertinent research of high quality on *maquiladoras* working on the Mexican side of the border. In a fine oral history of his own extended family, Alvarez has shown the continuity in family relations and patterns of coordinated movement over the past two centuries on both sides of the southern-Baja California border.

Though a number of significant studies have focused on south Texas (92–104, 121–133, 224–227) and the Santa Barbara area (17, 18, 20, 50, 51, 66–76, 119, 120), this confluence reflects the inspiration of effective teachers, Paredes and Carlos respectively, more than an effort to analyze the regions as spatially organized systems. In part the absence of regional studies elsewhere should be attributed to the difficulties ethnographers face in attempting to discover the contours of historically and demographically complex areas. Such work would probably require an interdisciplinary team able to mix methodologies more diverse than those so successfully deployed in the Hispano region of northern New Mexico and southern Colorado.

TOPICS OF STUDY

Health care has been more extensively written about than any other topic in Chicano studies. One paper provides a profile of the health status of Chicanos in the United States (169). Another analyzes the status of Chicanas in the nursing profession (5). A number of articles offer outlines of ethnomedicine (4, 56–58, 61, 62, 115) and "traditional" curing practices (39, 45). Others study the interaction between ethnomedicine and modern medical health therapies (67, 71, 72, 116, 119, 120, 199, 204). These papers study the therapeutic effectiveness of traditional practices. They also ask about their role in supplementing, impeding, or promoting the use of other health care facilities.

The substantive issue that has received the most attention is fertility. Papers range from ethnographic descriptions of childbirth practices (60, 63), through menstruation (64) and menopause (65), to fertility rates (170) and fertility regulation (59, 168). Researchers also have treated the more politically volatile issue of involuntary sterilization (37, 186, 187). Vélez-Ibáñez effectively uses particular cases to make his analyses vivid.

Health care delivery and utilization is the explicit focus of a number of articles (21, 22, 67, 108, 116, 119, 120, 152). Much of this work, particularly that originating at the University of California, Santa Barbara, by Carlos and Keefe, uses network analysis to explore the interpersonal relations along which Chicanos seek help for their medical and mental afflictions. These researchers regard personal networks as support systems whose functions should be understood by institutions attempting to deliver mental health care (74–76, 118–120). This work's strength has been its systematic exploration of network analysis as a conceptual tool. It has not, however, attended sufficiently to cultural conceptions that shape the quality of social relations. What, for example, are the cultural notions of intimacy, friendship, *confianza* [trust], and helping?

Kinship and social organization have also been studied through network analysis, with similar strengths and weaknesses as in the health care field. Carlos (17) thus compares Mexican and Chicano *compadrazgo* [co-godparenthood, fictive kin relations]. Gilbert (50) and Keefe (68–70, 73) have used network analysis to study the extended family. The former (51) has also compared social structural variations in communities in the Santa Barbara area. In an analysis that nicely supplements studies by the Santa Barbara group, Vélez-Ibáñez (184, 189) has explored networks organized by exchange relations and the cultural conception of *confianza* [trust]. Trueba (161) uses life history materials to plead for less prejudiced accounts of Chicano and Mexican family life. Changing family relations in south Texas have been studied by Whiteford (227), and Wells (214) has perceptively characterized the rural Chicano family.

The two phases of the life cycle that have received the most attention are youth and aging. Among studies of youth, Vigil and his coworkers have studied gangs, particularly the relations between life style and educational performance (105, 113, 192, 195–198). Spielberg Benítez (150) has studied humor in youth gangs. Among studies of aging, Newton (117, 118) has given an overview, and Cuellar and his coworkers (12, 26, 28–30, 33, 34, 205) have studied the elderly from a variety of theoretical and empirical perspectives, including an extended case history of a senior citizens center, dilemmas of "insider" research, attitudes toward death among the elderly, and the political power of the aged. For both youths and the aged, researchers continually ask applied questions: how can the lives of their subjects be improved?

Feminist questions about gender have been the focus of two collections that include essays by anthropologists (109, 114). The former collection discusses childbirth (63), abortion (171), the nursing profession (5), and women as innovators (226). The latter collection provides a broad discussion of women in organizations (36), an overview of involuntary sterilization (37) plus a case study on the same topic (187), and a theoretical statement on class, nationality, and gender (38). Similar practical and political concerns underlie the writings on fertility and its regulation, discussed above under health care. Other feminist studies include Melville (107) on women's adaptation to migration, Geilhufe (47) on discrimination against women in San Jose jails, and Keefe (66) on gender and nationality in politics, with particular reference to Santa Barbara and Santa Paula, California.

Educational anthropology has been relatively well developed. Arvizu (7, 9) has discussed the creative potential in biculturalism and cross-cultural issues concerning parent participation in schools. The practical issue of bilingual education has received more attention than any other. It has been assessed both from philosophical (77) and policy perspectives (53). Anthropologists with central interests elsewhere have discussed the role of culture in bilingual education (3, 31). Trueba and his coworkers have given this topic broad sustained attention that includes general issues (158–160), assessment of language skills (166), models (162), adjustment problems (165), and ethnographic approaches (163, 164, 167).

Immigration has developed in lopsided fashion, more in demographic and sociological studies than in ethnographic ones. Cornelius's UC San Diego Center for U.S.-Mexican Studies has surveyed materials on immigration in southern California (23), and in the San Francisco Bay Area (24). In this connection, Chávez (21, 22) has written well on issues of health care delivery for undocumented workers. Elsewhere writers have explored explanations and theories of migration (143) and connections between ethnicity and migration (110). More specific studies include one on women's adaptation to migration (107), and another on retrained, relocated workers (172). Wells (210–212) has published a series of sophisticated studies on immigration in relation to factory labor in a Wisconsin small town.

Political economy has a small number of good studies. Carlos & Brokensha (19) have compared the effectiveness of government agencies for inducing socioeconomic and cultural integration among rural agrarian populations in California's San Joaquin Valley and Sinaloa, Mexico's Fuerte Valley. Moles (112) has shown how Mexican workers are replacing small farmers in the Sacramento Valley of northern California. Patricia Zavella has a good book forthcoming on cannery workers in San Jose, and a number of papers in preparation on women in the electronics industry of northern New Mexico. Vélez-Ibáñez (188, 189) has studied how rotating credit associations in the United States and Mexico have created and reflected cultural conceptions of *confianza* [trust] and socioeconomic exchange relations. Wells (213, 215–221) has developed a series of outstanding studies on the strawberry industry in the Salinas region of coastal northern California.

Urban life has been handled in a dispersed fashion that perhaps reflects the nature of the phenomenon under study. Cuéllar (25) formulated an early model for urban studies that should bear fruit in his forthcoming studies of Chicano and Mexican urban youth culture. Achor (1) has done an informative ethnography of a Dallas *barrio*. Davidson's (35) study of Chicano prisoners in San Quentin opens a field for further study. Geilhufe (46–48) has also studied women in jail, Chicanos and the police in San Jose, California, and urban life. Eiselein & Marshall (40) have reported on the effectiveness of public television programs designed for Chicanos in Tucson, Arizona. Weeks and Spielberg Benítez (206) have surveyed the cultural demography of Chicanos in the midwest, and the latter has explored Chicano work values and cultural traditions (151, 153).

The Chicano movement has been studied in a useful ethnography (42) of a south Texas community influenced by the *Raza Unida* movement in the early 1970s. This work has been innovative in using a historical perspective and by printing commentaries on the monograph by community members. Vigil's (193) superficial panoramic sketch, touching all from the Olmecs to the present, attempts to comprehend the Chicano movement in its most sweeping historical context. Other more focused essays on the Chicano movement include Kuroda (81), Vélez-Ibáñez (185), and Vigil (190). In a number of telling papers, Limón (92, 93, 96, 98) has studied the Chicano movement in its historical antecedents and among University of Texas at Austin students during the 1970s. His concerns have tacked back and forth between the "folk" and the university and between ideas and practical activities.

Cultural life has been explored in a number of studies that range from philosophy (78) and values (151), through nationalistic celebration (106), to mural art (52) and popular culture (54). Readers interested in folklore, particularly in its social context, should consult the fine works by Paredes (121–133) and Limón (92–104). Paredes (131, 133) and Limón (101, 104) have also written on Chicano literature, and Herrera is both a doctoral student in anthropology and a noted Chicano poet. García Castañón (44) has written an insightful interpretation of *Bernabé,* a work performed by the Teatro Campesino.

Theory and method have been developed in ways that reflect issues in the discipline and the exigencies of a politically committed anthropology. The concept of culture in relation to applied anthropology has received attention (10, 11, 49, 194). Poggie (134) has published a life history. The extended case method of the Manchester school has been used and explicated by Cuéllar (28, 32) and Vélez-Ibáñez (182). Marxist analysis has been invoked by Vigil (191) and given substantial formulation by Limón (103). Action research as method has been discussed in a number of papers (40, 111, 136, 144–147, 175).

Issues concerning insider research have been discussed by Aguilar (2) and Vélez-Ibáñez (183). Cuéllar (30) has compared insiders and outsiders in applied projects. Playing on Carlos Castañeda's *Teachings of Don Juan,* Cuéllar suggests that insiders face four enemies: fear, clarity, power, and fatigue. The privileged access that insiders can attain, in other words, creates its own characteristic dilemmas. Reflections on the position of Chicano anthropologists also notably include a report on minority participation in the profession coauthored by Weaver (203).

THE COMING GENERATION

Future anthropological writings on Chicanos will be significantly shaped by four scholars in their late 30s and early 40s. Their work has developed by combining, with varying degrees of emphasis, concerns at once political, applied, and theoretical. Each of these writers has a distinctive style and voice, reflecting their political commitments, research topics, and theoretical predilections.

Cuéllar (12, 25–34, 205) has studied Chicano gerontology and minority aging, often in collaboration with people from other disciplines and usually with an eye to applied interests. His distinctive methodological tool has been the analysis of generational cohorts. In doing cohort analysis, he includes historical factors and period of immigration from Mexico, with a view to studying the formative life experiences within age strata as well as the patterns of interaction between age strata. Recently, Cuéllar has turned from the aged to youth culture. He has embarked on a comprehensive investigation of the *cholo* style in urban culture, both in its homeland of east Los Angeles and as it has diffused to the American southwest and northwestern Mexico.

Vélez-Ibáñez (182–189) has done field research in Mexico City and Tucson, Arizona, concentrating on politics and economics, particularly rotating credit associations. His analyses combine concepts from economic anthropology with the Manchester School's extended case method. Recently, Vélez-Ibáñez has started a survey of relations of exchange and *confianza* in Tucson, Arizona, where he hopes to develop a community profile of social inequality and interpersonal alliances. This promises to be the most systematic study of a Chicano urban community to date.

Wells (209–221) has done field research on labor migration in the midwest, and on California's coastal strawberry industry. Her work draws creatively on neoclassical economics and Marxian analyses of political economy. Her study of the strawberry industry shows how labor has been empowered by the practical exigencies of production processes themselves. Strawberries, in a word, require extensive labor inputs that cannot be mechanized. Here ethnographic method illuminates a problem that aggregate statistical analysis cannot even discern. Following broader trends in Marxian thought, her work will probably devote more attention to political consciousness in the future. She is now writing a book that builds on the fine analyses in her articles on the strawberry industry.

Limón (92–104) has recently entered an especially creative phase. His studies of folklore have fruitfully combined symbolic anthropology and Marxian analysis, especially on the topics of culture, class, and ethnicity. His studies focus on local contexts such as student meetings, meals, or a restaurant, where folklore is practiced in everyday life situations. As he shows how folklore reveals class and ethnic conflict, he moves from specific practices to class relations and back again. Limón's studies have been theoretically explicit, employing and critiquing concepts authored by theorists ranging from Mary Douglas to Antonio Gramsci. Work of this caliber promises to make Chicano studies increasingly visible in the ongoing debates and dialogues of anthropology.

Anthropological writings on Chicanos over the past 15 years must be understood in relation to the politics of the late 1960s and early 1970s. As a direct outgrowth of that period, this subfield has developed a committed stance, engaged at once with the ideology of a broader political movement and concerned with applied problems involving migrant workers, health care delivery, and education. Unlike Thomas Kuhn's paradigm-bound scientists who systematically blind themselves to social problems, anthropologists studying Chicanos find that their research projects emerge from community politics and issues of social justice as often as from pressing conceptual puzzles in their discipline. Chicano studies, for the most part, share in the broader endeavor of combating ideological, political, and economic forms of oppression confronted by their research subjects.

ACKNOWLEDGMENTS

This essay began toward the end of my year (1980–1981) as a Fellow at the Center for Advanced Study in the Behavioral Sciences. That year was financially supported by a National Research Council Fellowship for Minorities, supplemented by National Science Foundation Grant #BNS 76 22943. Subsequent funds for institutional support from the National Research Council plus matching funds from Stanford University aided in completion of this project. Janice Stockard provided highly skilled help as a bibliographic research assistant. I am especially indebted to most of the people cited here for their active cooperation, correspondence, and conversation. I have learned much about Chicano studies from the following Stanford anthropology graduate students: R. R. Alvarez, Jr., S. F. Arvizu, L. R. Chávez, II, M. Díaz-Barriga, P. T. Espinosa, J. Garcia-Castañón, N. Geilhufe, J. F. Herrera, M. Menchaca, M. Ramírez, D. Reynolds, R. Rouse, and R. Sánchez. Mary Louise Pratt commented with insight on earlier drafts of the manuscript.

Literature Cited

1. Achor, S. 1978. *Mexican Americans in a Dallas Barrio.* Tucson: Univ. Arizona Press
2. Aguilar, J. L. 1981. Insider research: An ethnography of a debate. In *Anthropologists At Home in North America: Methods and Issues in the Study of One's Own Society,* ed. D. A. Messerschmidt, pp. 15–26. Cambridge: Cambridge Univ. Press
3. Aguilar, J. L., Vallejo, C. 1984. The "culture" in bilingual/bicultural education. In *Chicano Studies: A Multidisciplinary Approach,* ed. E. García, F. Lomelí, Y. Ortiz, pp. 227–35. New York: Columbia Univ. Teachers' Press
4. Alvarado, A. L. 1978. Utilization of ethnomedical practitioners and concepts within the framework of Western medicine. In *Modern Medicine and Medical Anthropology in the United States-Mexico Border Population,* ed. B. Velimirovic, pp. 17–21. Washington, DC: Pan Am. Health Organ. Sci. Publ. No. 359
5. Alvarado, A. L. 1980. The status of Hispanic women in nursing. See Ref. 109. pp. 208–16
6. Alvarez, R. R. Jr. 1984. The border as social system: The California case. *New Scholar* 9(1–2):119–34
7. Arvizu, S. F. 1974. Education for constructive marginality. In *The Cultural Drama,* ed. W. Dillon, pp. 123–35.

8. Arvizu, S. F. 1978. Critical reflections and consciousness. *Grito del Sol* 3(1):119–23
9. Arvizu, S. F. 1978. Home-school linkages: A cross-cultural approach to parent participation. In *Bilingual Education Training Series: A Cultural Approach to Parent Participation*. Sacramento: Calif. State Univ. Dep. Anthropol. Cross-Cult. Resource Cent.
10. Arvizu, S. F. 1978. Introductory comments. *Grito del Sol* 3(1):11–16
11. Arvizu, S. F., Snyder, W. A., Espinoza, P. T. 1978. *Demystifying the Concept of Culture: Theoretical and Conceptual Tools*. Sacramento: Calif. State Univ. Dep. Anthropol. Cross-Cult. Resource Cent. Monogr. 1
12. Bengston, V. L., Cuéllar, J. B., Ragan, P. K. 1977. Stratum contrasts and similarities in attitudes toward death. *J. Gerontol.* 32(1):76–88
13. Briggs, C. L. 1980. *The Wood Carvers of Cordova, New Mexico: Social Dimensions of an Artistic "Revival."* Knoxville: Univ. Tenn. Press
14. Briggs, C. L. 1983. A conversation with Saint Isidore: The teachings of the elders. See Ref. 208, pp. 103–15
15. Briggs, C. L. 1983. Questions for the ethnographer: A critical examination of the role of the interview in fieldwork. *Semiotica* 46(2–4):233–61
16. Brown, L. W., Briggs, C. L., Weigle, M. 1978. *Hispano Folklife of New Mexico: The Lorin W. Brown Federal Writers' Project Manuscripts*. Albuquerque: Univ. New Mexico
17. Carlos, M. L. 1975. Traditional and modern forms of Compadrazgo among Mexican Americans. In *Proc. Int. Congr. Americanists, 40th, Roma-Genova, 1972*. 3:469–83
18. Carlos, M. L. 1982. Chicano households, the structure of parental information networks, and family use of child-related social services. *Borderlands J.* 6(1):49–68
19. Carlos, M. L., Brokensha, D. 1972. Agencies, goals and clients: A cross-cultural analysis. *Stud. Comp. Int. Dev.* 7(2):130–55
20. Casas, J. M., Keefe, S. E., eds. 1978. *Family and Mental Health in the Mexican American Community*. Los Angeles: Univ. Calif. Spanish Speaking Mental Health Res. Cent. Monogr. 7
21. Chávez, L. R. II 1983. Undocumented immigrants and access to health services: A game of pass the buck. *Migration Today* 11:15–19
22. Chávez, L. R. II 1984. Doctors, Curanderos and Brujas: Health care delivery and Mexican immigrants. *Med. Anthropol. Q.* 15(2):31–37
23. Cornelius, W. A., Chávez, L. R. II, Castro, J. G. 1982. *Mexican Immigrants and Southern California: A Summary of Current Knowledge*. La Jolla: Univ. Calif. San Diego Cent. U.S.-Mex. Stud. Res. Rep. Ser. No. 36
24. Cornelius, W. A., Mines, R., Chávez, L. R. II, Castro, J. G. 1982. *Mexican Immigrants in the San Francisco Bay Area: A Summary of Current Knowledge*. La Jolla: Univ. Calif. San Diego Cent. U.S.-Mex. Stud. Res. Rep. Ser. No. 40
25. Cuéllar, J. B. 1971. Toward the study of Chicano urban adaptation: The multivariate environmental taxonomy. *Aztlan* 2(1):37–65
26. Cuéllar, J. B. 1976. Chicano power in old age. *Participant: The Pitzer College Magazine* 9(1):15–18
27. Cuéllar, J. B. 1977. Paradigms in ethnic studies: Notes on the Chicano experience. In *The Political Economy of Institutional Change: The Proceedings of the Ethnic Studies Symposium*, ed. D. Moreno, R. Torres, pp. 3–11. Irvine: Univ. Calif. Program Comp. Cult.
28. Cuéllar, J. B. 1978. El Senior Citizens Club: The older Mexican-American in the voluntary association. In *Life's Career—Aging: Cultural Variations On Growing Old*, ed. B. G. Myerhoff, A. Simic, pp. 207–29. Beverly Hills: Sage
29. Cuéllar, J. B. 1978. What is the history of minority senior programs? *Somos* 1(5):12–14
30. Cuéllar, J. B. 1979. Insiders and outsiders in minority aging. In *Minority Aging Research: Old Issues—New Approaches*, ed. E. P. Stanford, pp. 67–77. San Diego: Campanile Press
31. Cuéllar, J. B. 1980. A model for Chicano culture for bilingual education. In *Ethnoperspectives in Bilingual Education Research, Vol. II: Theory in Bilingual Education*, ed. R. V. Padilla, pp. 179–204. Ypsilanti: Eastern Mich. Univ.
32. Cuéllar, J. B. 1981. Social science research in the U.S. Mexican community: A case study. *Aztlan* 12(1):1–21
33. Cuéllar, J. B., Ragan, P. K. 1977. Stratum contrasts and similarities in attitudes toward death. *J. Gerontol.* 32(1):76–88
34. Cuéllar, J. B., Torres-Gil, F. 1978. A rationale for developing minority components in gerontological programs. In *Handbook for Training and Research in Minority Aging*, pp. 66–84. Washington, DC: Natl. Cent. on Black Aged
35. Davidson, R. T. 1974. *Chicano Prison-*

ers: The Key to San Quentin. New York: Holt, Rinehart & Winston
36. Del Castillo, A. R. 1980. Mexican women in organization. See Ref. 114, pp. 7–16
37. Del Castillo, A. R. 1980. Sterilization: An overview. See Ref. 114, pp. 65–70
38. Del Castillo, A. R., Mora, M. 1980. Sex, nationality and class: La obrera Mexicana. See Ref. 114, pp. 1–4
39. Edgerton, R. B., Karno, M., Fernández, I. 1970. Curanderismo in the metropolis. *Am. J. Psychother.* 24:124–34
40. Eiselein, E. B., Marshall, W. 1976. Mexican-American television: Applied anthropology and public television. *Hum. Organ.* 35(2):147–56
41. Fernandez Kelly, M. P. 1981. The U.S.-Mexico border: Recent publications and the state of current research. *Latin Am. Res. Rev.* 16(3):250–67
42. Foley, D. E., Mota, C., Post, D. E., Lozano, I. 1977. *From Peones to Politicos: Ethnic Relations in a South Texas Town 1900–1977.* Austin: Univ. Texas Cent. Mex. Am. Stud. Monogr. 3
43. Galarza, E. 1972. Mexicans in the southwest: A culture in process. In *Plural Society in the Southwest,* ed. E. Spicer, R. H. Thompson, pp. 261–97. New York: Interbook
44. García Castañón, J. 1978. Teatro Chicano and the analysis of sacred symbols: Towards a Chicano world-view in the social sciences. *Grito del Sol* 3(1):37–49
45. García Castañón, J. 1980. Witchy-Witchy: Estilo Chicano. *Metamorfosis* 3(1):11–12
46. Geilhufe, N. 1976. Urban life. In *The Study of Anthropology,* ed. D. Hunter, P. Whitten, pp. 408–27. New York: Harper & Row
47. Geilhufe, N. 1978. Discrimination against women in jail: An analysis of advocacy anthropology. *Hum. Organ.* 37(2):202–10
48. Geilhufe, N. 1979. *Chicanos and the Police: A Study of the Politics of Ethnicity in San Jose, California.* Washington, DC: Soc. Appl. Anthropol. Mongr. 13
49. Gibson, M. A., Arvizu, S. F. 1978. *Demystifying the Concept of Culture: Methodological Tools and Techniques.* Sacramento: Calif. State Univ. Dep. Anthropol. Cross-Cult. Resource Cent. Mongr. 2
50. Gilbert, M. J. 1978. Extended family integration among second-generation Mexican-Americans. See Ref. 20, pp. 25–48
51. Gilbert, M. J. 1980. Communities within communities: Social structural factors and variation in Mexican American communities. *Hispanic J. Behav. Sci.* 2(3):241–68
52. González, A. M. 1982. Murals: Fine, popular, or folk art? *Aztlan* 13(1 & 2):149–63
53. Hernández-Chávez, E., Alvarez, R. R., Arvizu, S. F., Llanes, J. 1982. *The Federal Policy Toward Language and Education: Pendulum or Progress?* Sacramento: Calif. State Univ. Cross Cult. Resource Cent. Monogr. 12
54. Herrera, J. F. 1980. On Cantinflas: Towards a concept of popular culture. *Metamorfosis* 3(1):2
55. Jiménez Núñez, A. 1974. *Los Hispanos de Nuevo Mexico.* Sevilla: Univ. Sevilla, Publ. Semin. Antropol. Am., Vol. 12
56. Kay, M. 1974. Disease concepts in the barrio today. In *Communicating Nursing Research,* ed. M. V. Batey, pp. 185–94
57. Kay, M. 1976. The fusion of Utoaztecan and European ethnogynecology in the Florilegio Medicinal. *Proc. Int. Congr. Americanists, 41st, Mexico, 1974,* 3: 323–30
58. Kay, M. 1977. Health and illness in a Mexican American barrio. In *Ethnic Medicine in the Southwest,* ed. E. H. Spicer, pp. 99–166
59. Kay, M. 1977. Mexican American fertility regulation. See Ref. 56, pp. 279–94
60. Kay, M. 1978. The Mexican American. In *Culture/Childbearing/Health Professionals,* ed. A. L. Clark, pp. 89–108. Philadelphia: Davis
61. Kay, M. 1979. The Florilegio Medicinal: Source of southwest ethnomedicine. *Ethnohistory* 24(3)1977:251–59
62. Kay, M. 1979. Lexemic change and semantic shift in disease names. *Cult. Med. Psychiatry* 3:73–94
63. Kay, M. 1980. Mexican, Mexican American, and Chicana childbirth. See Ref. 109, pp. 52–65
64. Kay, M. 1981. Meanings of menstruation to Mexican American women. In *The Menstrual Cycle,* ed. P. L. Komnenich, M. McSweeney, J. Noak, N. Elder, 2:114–23. New York: Springer
65. Kay, M., Voda, A., Olivas, G., Rios, F., Imle, M. 1982. Ethnography of the menopause-related hot flash. *Maturitas* 4(2):217–27
66. Keefe, S. E. 1976. Sex and ethnicity in politics: A minority group model of political interaction. *West. Can. J. Anthropol.* 6(3):213–42
67. Keefe, S. E. 1979. Mexican Americans' underutilization of mental health clinics: An evaluation of suggested explanations. *Hispanic J. Behav. Sci.* 1(2):93–115
68. Keefe, S. E. 1979. Urbanization, acculturation, and extended family ties: Mexi-

can Americans in cities. *Am. Ethnol.* 6(2):349–65
69. Keefe, S. E. 1980. Acculturation and the extended family among urban Mexican Americans. In *Acculturation: Theory, Models and Some New Findings*, ed. A. M. Padilla, pp. 85–110. Boulder, Colo: Westview. AAAS Selected Symp. 39
70. Keefe, S. E. 1980. Personal communities in the city: Support networks among Mexican Americans and Anglo Americans. *Urban Anthropol.* 9:51–74
71. Keefe, S. E. 1981. Folk medicine among urban Mexican Americans: Cultural persistence change and displacement. *Hispanic J. Behav. Sci.* 3(1):41–58
72. Keefe, S. E. 1982. Help-seeking behavior among foreign-born Mexican Americans. *Soc. Sci. Med.* 16:1467–72
73. Keefe, S. E. 1984. Real and ideal extended familism among Mexican Americans and Anglo Americans: On the meaning of "close" family ties. *Hum. Organ.* 43:65–70
74. Keefe, S. E., Casas, J. M. 1980. Mexican Americans and mental health: A selected review and recommendations for mental health service delivery. *Am. J. Community Psychol.* 8(3):303–26
75. Keefe, S. E., Padilla, A. M., Carlos, M. L. 1978. *Emotional Support Systems in Two Cultures: A Comparison of Mexican Americans and Anglo Americans.* Los Angeles: Univ. Calif. Spanish Speaking Mental Health Res. Occas. Pap. 7
76. Keefe, S. E., Padilla, A. M., Carlos, M. L. 1979. The Mexican-American extended family as an emotional support system. *Hum. Organ.* 38(2):144–52
77. Klor de Alva, J. J. 1974. Toward a philosophy of bilingualism. *Calif. J. Educ. Res.* 25(5):310–13
78. Klor de Alva, J. J. 1977. Critique of national character versus universality in Chicano poetry. *De Colores: J. Chicano Expression Thought* 3(3):20–24
79. Knowlton, C. 1975. Neglected chapters in Mexican-American history. In *Mexican-Americans Tomorrow*, ed. G. Tyler, pp. 19–59. Albuquerque: Univ. New Mexico
80. Knowlton, C. 1980. The town of Las Vegas community land grant, an Anglo American coup d'etat. *J. West* 19:12–21
81. Kuroda, E. 1978. The social and cultural characteristics of Spanish- and Mexican-Americans and the Chicano movement. In *Ethnicity and Cultural Pluralism in the U.S.A.*, ed. T. Ayabe, pp. 51–112. Fukuoka, Japan: Kyushu Univ. Faculty Educ. Res. Inst. Comp. Educ. Cult.
82. Kuroda, E. 1981. Ethnicity and ethnic culture in crisis: The struggles for existence of the Spanish-Americans in Taos, New Mexico. In *Ethnicity and its Identity in the U.S.A.*, ed. T. Ayabe, pp. 33–86. Ibaraki, Japan: Univ. Tsukuba Inst. Hist. Anthropol.
83. Kutsche, P. 1976. A New Mexico test of modernization theory. *Pap. Anthropol.* 17(2):138–49
84. Kutsche, P. 1979. Introduction: Atomism, factionalism and flexibility. In *The Colorado College Studies: The Survival of Spanish American Villages*, ed. P. Kutsche, pp. 7–20. Colorado Springs: Colo. Coll. Res. Comm.
85. Kutsche, P. 1983. Family and household in northern New Mexico. *J. Comp. Family Stud.* 14(2):151–65. Spec. issue
86. Kutsche, P. 1983. Theories of borders and frontiers. In *Borderlands Sourcebook: A Guide to the Literature on Northern Mexico and the American Southwest*, ed. E. R. Stoddard, R. L. Nostrand, J. P. West, pp. 16–19. Norman: Univ. Oklahoma Press
87. Kutsche, P., Gallegos, D. 1979. Community functions of the *Cofradía de Nuestro Padre Jesús Nazareño*. See Ref. 84, pp. 91–98
88. Kutsche, P., Van Ness, J. R. 1981. *Cañones: Values, Crisis, and Survival in a Northern New Mexico Village.* Albuquerque: Univ. New Mexico Press
89. Kutsche, P., Van Ness, J. R., Smith, A. T. 1976. A unified approach to the anthropology of Hispanic northern New Mexico: Historical archaeology, ethnohistory, and ethnography. *Hist. Archaeol.* 10:1–16
90. Lauderdale, M., Peterson, J., Swadesh, F. L. 1970. Sistemas Cuantitativos en el Estudio del Cambio Sociocultural. *Am. Indíg.* 30(1):107–34
91. Leon-Portilla, M. 1972. The Norteño variety of Mexican culture: An ethnohistorical approach. See Ref. 43, pp. 77–114
92. Limón, J. E. 1973. Stereotyping and Chicano resistance: An historical dimension. *Aztlan* 4(2):257–70
93. Limón, J. E. 1974. El Primer Congreso Mexicanista de 1911: A precursor to contemporary Chicanismo. *Aztlan* 5(1 & 2):85–117
94. Limón, J. E. 1977. Agringado joking in Texas-Mexican society: Folklore and differential identity. *New Scholar* 6:33–50
95. Limón, J. E. 1977. El Folklore y los Mexicanos en los Estados Unidos: Una Perspectiva Cultural Marxista. In *La Otra Cara de Mexico: El Pueblo Chicano*, ed. D. Maciel, pp. 224–42. México, D. F: Ediciones El Caballito

96. Limón, J. E. 1981. The folk performance of "Chicano" and the cultural limits of political ideology. In *"And Other Neighborly Names": Social Process and Cultural Image in Texas Folklore,* ed. R. Bauman, R. D. Abrahams, pp. 197–225. Austin: Univ. Texas Press
97. Limón, J. E. 1982. History, Chicano joking, and the varieties of higher education: Tradition and performance as critical symbolic action. *J. Folklore Inst.* 19:141–66
98. Limón, J. E. 1982. El Meeting: History, folk Spanish and ethnic nationalism in a Chicano student community. In *Spanish in the United States: Sociolinguistic Aspects,* ed. J. Amastae, L. Elías-Olivares, pp. 301–32. Cambridge: Cambridge Univ. Press
99. Limón, J. E. 1983. Folklore, social conflict, and the United States-Mexican border. In *Handbook of American Folklore,* ed. R. Dorson, pp. 216–26. Bloomington: Indiana Univ. Press
100. Limón, J. E. 1983. Legendry, metafolklore, and performance: A Mexican-American example. *West. Folklore* 42:191–207
101. Limón, J. E. 1983. A 'Southern Renaissance' for Texas letters. *Texas Observer* (Oct. 28):20–23
102. Limón, J. E. 1983. Texas Mexican popular music and dancing: Some notes on history and symbolic process. *Latin Am. Music Rev.* 4:229–46
103. Limón, J. E. 1983. Western Marxism and folklore: A critical introduction. *J. Am. Folklore* 96(379):34–52
104. Limón, J. E. 1984. Healing the wounds: Folk symbols and historical crisis. *Texas Humanist* 6(4):21–23
105. Long, J. M., Vigil, J. D. 1980. Cultural styles and adolescent sex role perceptions: An exploration of responses to the value picture projective test. See Ref. 109, pp. 164–72
106. Melville, M. B. 1978. The Mexican-American and the celebration of the Fiestas Patrias: An ethnohistorical analysis. *Grito del Sol* 3(1):107–16
107. Melville, M. B. 1978. Mexican women adapt to migration. *Int. Migr. Rev.* 12(2):225–35
108. Melville, M. B. 1978. Minority medical issues: Two views. See Ref. 4, pp. 73–76
109. Melville, M. B., ed. 1980. *Twice a Minority: Mexican American Women.* St. Louis: Mosby
110. Melville, M. B. 1983. Ethnicity: An analysis of its dynamism and variability focusing on the Mexican/Anglo/Mexican American interface. *Am. Ethnol.* 10(2):272–89
111. Melville, M. B., Melville, T. R. 1978. Anthropologists and political action. In *Anthropology for the Future,* ed. O. B. Shimkin, S. Tax, J. W. Morrison, pp. 214–93. Urbana: Univ. Ill. Dep. Anthropol. Res. Rep. 4
112. Moles, J. A. 1979. Who tills the soil? Mexican-American workers replace the small farmer in California: An example from Colusa County. *Hum. Organ.* 38(1):20–27
113. Moore, J., Vigil, J. D., García, R. 1983. Residence and territoriality in Chicano gangs. *Soc. Probl.* 31(2):182–94
114. Mora, M., Del Castillo, A. R., eds. 1980. *Mexican Women in the United States: Struggles Past and Present.* Los Angeles: Univ. Calif. Chicano Stud. Res. Cent. Occas. Pap. No. 2
115. Newton, F. C. 1978. The Mexican American emic system of mental illness: An exploratory study. See Ref. 20, pp. 69–90
116. Newton, F. C. 1980. Issues in research and service delivery among Mexican American elderly: A concise statement with recommendations. *Gerontologist* 20(2):208–13
117. Newton, F. C. 1981. The Hispanic elderly: a review of health, social, and psychological factors. In *Explorations in Chicano Psychology,* ed. A. Baron, pp. 29–49. New York: Praeger
118. Newton, F. C., Ruiz, R. A. 1981. Chicano culture and mental health among the elderly. In *Chicano Aging and Mental Health,* ed. M. R. Miranda, R. A. Ruiz, pp. 38–75. Rockville, Md: U.S. Dep. Health Hum. Sci.
119. Padilla, A. M., Carlos, M. L., Keefe, S. E. 1976. Mental health service utilization by Mexican Americans. In *Psychotherapy with the Spanish-Speaking: Issues in Research and Service Delivery,* ed. M. R. Miranda, pp. 9–20. Los Angeles: Univ. Calif. Spanish Speaking Mental Health Res. Cent. Monogr. 3
120. Padilla, A. M., Keefe, S. E. 1984. The search for help: Mental health resources for Mexican Americans and Anglo Americans in a plural society. In *The Pluralistic Society: A Community Mental Health Perspective,* ed. S. Sue, T. Moore, pp. 77–115. New York: Hum. Sci. Press
121. Paredes, A. 1970. Proverbs and ethnic stereotypes. *Proverbium* 15:95(511)–97 (513)
122. Paredes, A. 1972. The legend of Gregorio Cortez. In *Mexican-American Authors,* ed. A. Paredes, R. Paredes, pp. 35–50. Boston: Houghton Mifflin
123. Paredes, A. 1972. The United States,

Mexico and machismo. *J. Folklore Inst.* 8(1):17–37
124. Paredes, A. 1973. José Mosqueda and the folklorization of actual events. *Aztlan* 4(1):1–30
125. Paredes, A. 1976. The role of folklore in border relations. In *The International Border in Community Relations: Gateway or Barrier?*, ed. K. Skagen, pp. 17–22. San Diego: Fronteras
126. Paredes, A. 1976. *A Texas-Mexican Cancionero: Folksongs of the Lower Border.* Urbana: Univ. Ill. Press
127. Paredes, A., ed. 1977. *Humanidad: Essays in Honor of George L. Sanchez.* Los Angeles: Univ. Calif. Chicano Stud. Cent. Monogr. 6
128. Paredes, A. 1977. Jorge Isidoro Sánchez y Sánchez (1906–1972). See Ref. 127, pp. 120–26
129. Paredes, A. 1978. On ethnographic work among minority groups. In *New Directions in Chicano Scholarship,* ed. R. Romo, R. Paredes, pp. 1–32. La Jolla: Univ. Calif. San Diego, Chicano Stud. Program. Chicano Stud. Monogr. Ser.
130. Paredes, A. 1978. The problem of identity in a changing culture: Popular expressions of culture conflict along the lower Rio Grande border. In *Views across the Border: The United States and Mexico,* ed. S. R. Ross, pp. 68–94. Albuquerque: Univ. New Mexico Press
131. Paredes, A. 1979. The folk base of Chicano literature. In *Modern Chicano Writers: A Collection of Critical Essays,* ed. J. Sommers, T. Ybarra-Frausto, pp. 4–17. Englewood Cliffs, NJ: Prentice Hall
132. Paredes, A. 1982. Folklore, Lo Mexicano, and proverbs. *Aztlan* 13(1 & 2):1–11
133. Paredes, A. 1983. A sense of place. *Discovery* 8(2)(Austin: Univ. Texas):21–24
134. Poggie, J. J. Jr. 1973. *Between Two Cultures: The Life of an American-Mexican.* Tucson Univ. Arizona Press
135. Reich, A. H. 1979. Spanish American village culture: Barrier to assimilation or integrative force? See Ref. 84, pp. 107–13
136. Ríos, S. 1978. An approach to action anthropology: The community project, C.S.U.S. *Grito del Sol* 3(1):51–65
137. Romano-V, O. I. 1967. Minorities, history and the cultural mystique. *El Grito* 1(1):5–11
138. Romano-V, O. I. 1968. The anthropology and sociology of the Mexican-Americans: The distortion of Mexican-American history. *El Grito* 2(1):13–26
139. Romano-V, O. I. 1969. The historical and intellectual presence of Mexican-Americans. *El Grito* 2(2):32–46
140. Romano-V, O. I. 1970. Social science, objectivity and the Chicanos. *El Grito* 4(1):4–16
141. Romano-V, O. I. 1976. The scientists. *Grito del Sol* 1(1):85–108
142. Rosaldo, R. 1983. Anthropological perspectives on Chicanos 1970–1980. In *Chicanos and the Social Sciences: A Decade of Research and Development (1970–1980),* ed. I. D. Ortiz, pp. 59–66. Santa Barbara: Univ. Calif. Cent. Chicano Stud.
143. Sayers, R., Weaver, T. 1976. Explanation and theories of migration. In *Mexican Migration,* ed. T. Weaver, T. Downing, pp. 10–29. Tucson: Univ. Arizona Bur. Ethnic Res.
144. Schensul, S. 1973. Action research: The applied anthropologist in a community mental health program. In *Anthropology Beyond the University,* ed. A. Redfield, pp. 106–19. S. Anthropol. Soc. Proc. No. 7. Athens: Univ. Georgia Press
145. Schensul, S. 1974. Skills needed in action anthropology: Lessons from El Centro de la Causa. *Hum. Organ.* 33(2):203–9
146. Schensul, S., Bakszysz-Bymel, M. 1975. The role of applied research in the development of health services in a Chicano community in Chicago. In *Topias and Utopias in Health,* ed. S. Ingman, A. Thomas, pp. 425–43. The Hague: Mouton
147. Schensul, S., Schensul, J. 1978. Advocacy and applied anthropology. In *Social Scientists as Advocates: Views from the Applied Disciplines,* ed. G. H. Weber, G. McCall, pp. 121–65. Beverly Hills: Sage
148. Spicer, E. H. 1972. Introduction. See Ref. 43, pp. 1–20
149. Spicer, E. H. 1972. Plural society in the southwest. See Ref. 43, pp. 21–76
150. Spielberg Benítez, J. 1974. Humor in a Mexican-American palomilla: Some historical, social and psychological implications. *Revista Chicano-Riqueña* 2,3:41–50. Bloomington: Indiana Univ.
151. Spielberg Benítez, J. 1977. Dimensions for the study of work-related values in Mexican-American culture: An exploratory essay. In *American Minorities and Economic Opportunity,* ed. H. R. Kaplan, pp. 109–47. Itasca, Ill: Peacock
152. Spielberg Benítez, J. 1979. Systemic changes in health policy and health service delivery: The case of Chicanos. In *The Hispanics: A Missing Link in Public Policy,* ed. V. Correa-Jones, A. H. Benavides, M. A. Terán. Des Moines: Spanish-Speaking Peoples Commission of Iowa

153. Spielberg Benítez, J. 1980. The "little" cultural tradition of Hispanics. *Agenda: A Journal of Hispanic Issues* 10(3):30–36

153a. Stoller, M. L. 1980. Grants of desperation, lands of speculation: Mexican period land grants in Colorado. See Ref. 181, pp. 22–39

154. Swadesh, F. L. 1972. The social and philosophical context of creativity in Hispanic New Mexico. *Rocky Mt. Soc. Sci. J.* 9(1):11–18

155. Swadesh, F. L. 1974. *Los Primeros Pobladores: Hispanic Americans of the Ute Frontier*. Notre Dame, Ind: Univ. Notre Dame Press.

156. Swadesh, F. L. 1976. Archeology, ethnohistory and the first plaza of Carnuel. *Ethnohistory* 23(1):31–44

157. Swadesh, F. L. 1979. Structure of Hispanic-Indian relations in New Mexico. See Ref. 84, pp. 53–61

158. Trueba, H. T. 1976. Chicano bilingual/bicultural education. In *The Anthropological Study of Education*, ed. C. J. Calhoun, F. A. J. Ianni, pp. 299–309. The Hague: Mouton

159. Trueba, H. T. 1976. Issues and problems in bilingual bicultural education today. *J. Nat. Assoc. Biling. Educ.* 1(2):11–19

160. Trueba, H. T. 1977. Bilingual-bicultural education: An overview. In *Curriculum Handbook*, ed. L. Rubin, pp. 223–33. Boston: Allyn & Bacon. Abridged ed.

161. Trueba, H. T. 1978. The Mexican American family: A cultural dilemma. *J. Soc. Ethnic Spec. Stud.* 2(1):20–23

162. Trueba, H. T. 1979. Bilingual-education models: Types and designs. In *Bilingual Multicultural Education and the Professional: From Theory to Practice*, ed. H. Trueba, C. Barnett-Mizrahi, pp. 54–73. Rowley, Mass: Newbury House

163. Trueba, H. T. 1981. Bilingual education: An ethnographer's perspective. *J. Teacher Educ.* 8(3):15–41

164. Trueba, H. T. 1981. A challenge for ethnographic researchers in bilingual settings: Analyzing Spanish/English classroom interaction. *J. Multiling. Multicult. Dev.* 2(4):243–57

165. Trueba, H. T. 1983. Adjustment problems of Mexican and Mexican-American school children: An anthropological study. In *Learn. Disability Q.* 6(4):395–415

166. Trueba, H. T., Sridhar, K. K. 1979. Language assessment and evaluation. In *Bilingual Education for Latinos*, ed. L. A. Valverde, pp. 35–50. Washington, DC: Assoc. Supervision and Curriculum Dev.

167. Trueba, H. T., Wright, P. G. 1980–81. On ethnographic studies and multicultural education. *J. Nat. Assoc. Biling. Educ.* 5(2):29–56

168. Urdaneta, M. L. 1975. Fertility and the "pill" in a Texas barrio. See Ref. 146, pp. 69–83

169. Urdaneta, M. L. 1977. Health status profile of Chicanos in the United States. In *The Chicana Handbook*, ed. M. Cotera. Austin, Texas: Statehouse Press

170. Urdaneta, M. L. 1979. Fleshpots, faith, or finances? Fertility rates among Mexican Americans. In *The Chicano Experience*, ed. S. West, J. Macklin pp. 191–206. Boulder, Colo: Westview

171. Urdaneta, M. L. 1980. Chicana use of abortion: The Case of Alcala. See Ref. 109, pp. 33–51

172. Urdaneta, M. L., Aceves, J. B. 1970. Retrained, relocated workers from Rio Grande City: Three case studies. In *Mexican American Industrial Migrants*, ed. B. Reagan. Dallas, Texas: Southern Methodist Univ. Press

173. Vaca, N. C. 1970. The Mexican-American in the social sciences 1912–1970. Part I: 1912–1935. *El Grito* 3 (3):3–24

174. Vaca, N. C. 1970. The Mexican-American in the Social Sciences 1912–1970. Part II: 1936–1970. *El Grito* 4 (1):17–51

175. Valadez, S. 1978. In search of a perspective: An apology long overdue. *Grito del Sol* 3(1):67–74

176. Valadez, F. 1979. Vergüenza. See Ref. 84, pp. 99–106

177. Van Ness, J. R. 1976. Modernization, land tenure, and ecology: The costs of change in northern New Mexico. *Pap. Anthropol.* 17(2):168–78

178. Van Ness, J. R. 1976. Spanish-American vs. Anglo-American land tenure and the study of economic change. *West. Soc. Sci. J.* 13(5):45–52

179. Van Ness, J. R., Kutsche, P., Smith, A. 1979. Hispanic village organization in northern New Mexico: Corporate community structure in historical and comparative perspective. See Ref. 84, pp. 21–44

180. Van Ness, J. R., Kutsche, P., Smith, A. 1980. The Polvadera grant: Hispanic settlement in the canones region. In *Spanish Colonial Frontier Research*, ed. H. Dobyns, pp. 79–84. Albuquerque, NM: Cent. Anthropol. Stud. Spanish Borderlands Subser. No. 2

181. Van Ness, J. R., Van Ness, C. M., eds. 1980. *Spanish and Mexican Land Grants in New Mexico and Colorado*. Manhattan, Kansas: Sunflower Univ. Press

182. Vélez-Ibáñez, C. G. 1975. An evening in

Cuidad Reyes: A processual approach to Mexican politics. *New Scholar* 5(1):5–17
183. Vélez-Ibáñez, C. G. 1979. Ourselves through the eyes of an anthropologist. In *The Chicanos: As We See Ourselves*, ed. A. D. Trejo, pp. 37–48. Tucson: Univ. Arizona Press
184. Vélez-Ibáñez, C. G. 1980. Mexicano/Hispano support systems and confianza: Theoretical issues of cultural adaptation. In *Hispanic Natural Support Systems*, ed. B. Valle, W. Vega, pp. 45–54. Calif. Dep. Mental Health
185. Vélez-Ibáñez, C. G. 1980. Los Movimientos Chicanos: Problemas y Perspectivas de las Luchas Históricas al Norte del Río Bravo. *Las Relaciones México Estados Unidos*, ed. D. Barkin, G. Esteva, M. Kaplan, pp. 217–34. México: Nueva Imagen, Universidad Nacional Autónoma
186. Vélez-Ibáñez, C. G. 1980. The nonconsenting sterilization of Mexican women in Los Angeles. See Ref. 109, pp. 235–48
187. Vélez-Ibáñez, C. G. 1980. Se Me Acabó la Canción: An ethnography of nonconsenting sterilizations among Mexican women in Los Angeles. See Ref. 114, pp. 71–91. Occas. Pap. No. 2
188. Vélez-Ibáñez, C. G. 1982. Social diversity, commercialization, and organizational complexity of urban Mexican/Chicano rotating credit associations: Theoretical and empirical issues of adaptation. *Hum. Organ.* 41(2):107–20
189. Vélez-Ibáñez, C. G. 1983. *Bonds of Mutual Trust: The Cultural Systems of Rotating Credit Associations among Urban Mexicans and Chicanos*. New Brunswick, NJ: Rutgers Univ. Press
190. Vigil, J. D. 1974. *Early Chicano Guerrilla Fighters*. Upland, Calif: 915 W. 23 St. Private printing
191. Vigil, J. D. 1978. Marx and Chicano anthropology. *Grito del Sol* 3(1):19–34
192. Vigil, J. D. 1979. Adaptation strategies and cultural life styles of Mexican American adolescents. *Hispanic J. Behav. Sci.* 1(4):375–92
193. Vigil, J. D. 1980. *From Indians to Chicanos: A Sociocultural History*. St. Louis: Mosby
194. Vigil, J. D. 1981. Towards a new perspective on understanding the Chicano people: The Six C's model of sociocultural change. *Campo Libre: J. Chicano Stud.* 1(2):141–67. Los Angeles: Calif. State Univ.
195. Vigil, J. D. 1982. Chicano high schoolers: Educational performance and acculturation. *Educ. Forum* 47(1):59–73
196. Vigil, J. D. 1982. Human revitalization: The six tasks of victory outreach. *Drew Gateway* 52(3):49–59
197. Vigil, J. D. 1983. Chicano gangs: One response to Mexican urban adaptation in the Los Angeles area. *Urban Anthropol.* 12(1)
198. Vigil, J. D., Long, J. M. 1981. Unidirectional or nativist acculturation—Chicano paths to school achievement. *Hum. Organ.* 40(3):273–77
199. Weaver, T. 1970. Use of hypothetical situations in a study of Spanish American illness referral systems. *Hum. Organ.* 29(2):140–54
200. Weaver, T. 1975. The cultural ecology of a border town. In *The Douglas Report: The Community Context of Housing and Social Problems*, ed. T. Weaver, T. Downing, pp. 1–18. Tucson: Univ. Ariz. Bur. Ethnic Res.
201. Weaver, T. 1983. The social effects of the ecology and development of the U.S.-Mexico border. In *Ecology and Development of the Border Region. Proc. 2nd Binational Univ. Symp.-Border Stud.*, ed. S. Ross, pp. 233–70. Mexico: Anuies
202. Weaver, T. 1984. Visibilidad Etnica and Distancia Etnica. In *Estratificación Etnica y Relaciones Interétnicas*, ed. M. Nolasco, pp. 23–28. México, D. F: Instituto Nacional de Antropología e Historia
203. Weaver, T., Hsu, F. L. K., Jones, D. J., Lewis, D., Medicine, B., Gibbs, J. L. 1973. *The Minority Experience in Anthropology: Report of the Committee on Minorities and Anthropology*. Washington, DC: Am. Anthropol. Assoc.
204. Weaver, T., Hubbard, G. P. 1975. Health. See Ref. 201, pp. 236–54
205. Weeks, J. R., Cuellar, J. B. 1983. Isolation of older persons: The influence of immigration and length of residence. *Res. Aging* 5(3):369–88
206. Weeks, J. R., Spielberg Benitez, J. 1979. The cultural demography of midwestern Chicano communities. See Ref. 171, pp. 229–51
207. Weigle, M., ed. 1976. *Brothers of Light, Brothers of Blood: The Penitentes of the Southwest*. Albuquerque: Univ. New Mexico Press
208. Weigle, M., ed., with Larcombe, C., Larcombe, S. 1983. *Hispanic Arts and Ethnohistory in the Southwest*. Santa Fe: Ancient City Press and Univ. New Mexico Press
209. Wells, M. J. 1975. Ethnicity, social stigma and resource mobilization in rural America: Reexamination of a midwestern experience. *Ethnohistory* 22 (4):319–43
210. Wells, M. J. 1976. Immigrants from the

migrant stream: Environment and incentives in relocation. *Aztlan* 7(2):267–90
211. Wells, M. J. 1979. Brokerage, economic opportunity and the growth of ethnic movements. *Ethnology* 18(4):399–414
212. Wells, M. J. 1980. Oldtimers and newcomers: The role of context in Mexican-American assimilation. *Aztlan* 11(2):271–95
213. Wells, M. J. 1981. Alienation, work structure, and the quality of life: Can cooperatives make a difference? *Soc. Probl.* 28(5):548–62
214. Wells, M. J. 1981. Rural Mexican American familism: Continuity and variation. In *The Family in Rural Society*, ed. R. Coward, W. Smith, pp. 96–105. Boulder, Colo: Westview
215. Wells, M. J. 1981. Social conflict, commodity constraints, and labor market structure in agriculture. *Comp. Stud. Soc. Hist.* 23(4):679–704
216. Wells, M. J. 1981. Success in whose terms? Evaluations of a cooperative farm. *Hum. Organ.* 40(3):239–46
217. Wells, M. J. 1982. Political mediation and agricultural cooperation: Strawberry farms in California. *Econ. Dev. Cult. Change* 30(2):413–32
218. Wells, M. J. 1983. Collective goals and individual interests in agricultural production cooperatives. In *Values, Ethics, and the Practice of Policy Analysis,* ed. W. N. Dunn, pp. 151–71. Lexington, Mass: Heath
219. Wells, M. J. 1983. Mediation, dependency, and the goals of development. *Am. Ethnol.* 10(4):770–88

220. Wells, M. J. 1984. The resurgence of sharecropping: Historical anomaly or political strategy? *Am. J. Sociol.* 90 (1):1–29
221. Wells, M. J., Climo, J. 1984. Parallel process in the world system: Intermediate agencies and local factionalism in the United States and Mexico. *J. Dev. Stud.* 20(2):151–70
222. Whitecotton, J. W. 1970. The social history of a New Mexican region: A preliminary analysis. *Pap. Anthropol.* 11:1–20
223. Whitecotton, J. W. 1976. Tradition and modernity in northern New Mexico: An introduction. *Pap. Anthropol.* 17(2): 121–37
224. Whiteford, L. M. 1976. Context, a disambiguating factor in the study of migration. In *New Approaches to Migration Theory,* ed. J. D. Uzzell, D. Guillet, pp. 37–45. Houston: Rice Univ. Stud. 62 (3)
225. Whiteford, L. M. 1979. The border land as an extended community. In *Migration Across Frontiers: Mexico and the United States,* ed. F. Cámara, R. V. Kemper, pp. 127–37. Albany: State Univ. New York Press
226. Whiteford, L. M. 1980. Mexican-American women as innovators. See Ref. 109, pp. 109–26
227. Whiteford, L. M. 1982. Migrants no longer: Changing family structure of Mexican-Americans in south Texas. *De Colores: J. Chicano Expression Thought* 6(1 & 2):99–109

SEXUAL DIMORPHISM

David W. Frayer[1]

Department of Anthropology, University of Kansas, Lawrence, Kansas 66045

Milford H. Wolpoff

Department of Anthropology, University of Michigan, Ann Arbor, Michigan 48109

[1] Order of the authors is alphabetical.

INTRODUCTION

That the human species exhibits sexual dimorphism in size, shape, and behavior is an obvious conclusion from anyone's simple participation in society. It is common knowledge that males have a larger stature than females, more robust cranial and facial features, along with greater muscularity, strength, and speed. In all human groups, male tooth size exceeds that for females, females store more subcutaneous fat, males have proportionally more muscle fiber, pre- and postnatal hormonal levels differ, growth rates vary, and diseases affect the sexes differentially (122a, 278). The fact that most of these differences do not occur in infants, children, and subadults, but are typical primarily in the adult stage, indicates that many of the effects are the result of hormonal events occurring at puberty (23). Like the primary sexual characteristics (i.e. differences in external genitalia), secondary sexual characteristics are largely controlled or mediated by X-linked genes (247), although they differ in control from the primary ones in that the environment has a more direct influence on their expression. For example, muscular differences between males and females converge when comparing an athletically active female to a nonactive male. As another measure of plasticity, nutritionally deprived adolescent males have a greater reduction in realized stature than females suffering similar protein shortages. Differences in the plasticity of males and females, along with the underlying genetic differences, provide evidence for a long-term selection regime in which human males and females, each in their own ways, have responded to reproductive, environmental, and cultural factors. The intent of this review is to establish what can and cannot be said about human sexual dimorphism. We will examine this phenomenon in the context of primate and other mammalian dimorphism patterns and in the light of human evolutionary history. Our purpose, however, is not to document the variation but rather to attempt its explanation. Thus, our main focus will be on discussing, elaborating, and when possible testing the models that have been proposed to account for differing magnitudes of sexual dimorphism, and when possible we will use these models to help explain the human condition.

Dimorphism in the human skeletal system and in dentition is well established. It has been studied in detail because of the importance of accurate sex determination for archaeological remains (2, 20–22, 27, 30, 30a, 33, 43–45, 47, 51, 65, 66, 70–73, 75, 85, 101–105, 111–115, 133–137, 142, 145, 148, 149, 153, 154, 162, 166, 167, 174, 184, 209, 221, 225, 235, 237, 240, 248, 252, 260, 271–273, 284, 291–293, 294a, 295). These studies focus more on the determination of sex from various parts of the skeleton than on the degree of dimorphism. Even so, they provide, perhaps inadvertently, important information about the populational variability in the sex differences. This variation is great enough for the magnitude of sexual dimorphism itself to become one of the criteria used in establishing the region of origin for a skeletal sample. However, like so many other osteological criteria purporting to describe regional differences, the magnitude of sexual dimorphism may differ greatly from population to population, but it does not seem to differ on the average from region to region.

As a background to the sexual dimorphism in living groups, there is substantial evidence to show reduction of sexual dimorphism in the human lineage. Plio/Pleistocene hominids exhibit a level of dimorphism for tooth, cranial, and skeletal dimensions much greater than subsequent groups. Early *Homo* samples and other more recent Middle and Upper Pleistocene forms display levels of dimorphism intermediate between *Australopithecus* and extant groups (311). Similarly, when considered all together, European Upper Paleolithic groups have more dimorphism than their Mesolithic and Neolithic descendants (92, 93). Thus contemporary populations, as well as their fossil and more recent ancestors, consistently show sex differences. These appear to be greater in earlier populations.

Although sexual dimorphism is easily observed and well documented for fossil and extant groups, models accounting for its existence and persistence, as well as the trends for reduction, are varied and sometimes contradictory. Some of the confusion relates to the complexity of the underlying genetics and the interaction of environmental variables. As amply shown in anthropological genetics, traits of simple inheritance are much easier to analyze and interpret than those resulting from polygenic effects (200, pp. 21–22). Since the majority of sexually dimorphic traits are determined by polygenes, evolutionary explanations must consider nongenetic and genetic influences. In addition, the capacity of culture to override biological constraints and to substitute behavioral solutions makes it difficult to apply many of the models for sexual dimorphism deriving from nonhuman evolutionary biology. Moreover, uniformitarianism aside, there is no justification for assuming that the same factors controlling the maintenance of sexual dimorphism today are the same or at least related to the ones working in the past (25, 83, 89, 156, 213, 278, 297, 302).

In a broader context, studies of mammalian dimorphism, and specifically of dimorphism in the nonhuman primates, indicate that explanatory models must be more general than the human studies by themselves might suggest. Such a broader context is dictated by studies of dimorphism in groups as diverse as amphibians and reptiles (50, 251, 265, 270, 315), bats (220), rodents (78, 79, 178), decapods (3), insects (28, 90), and birds (9, 24, 74, 76, 234, 261, 262, 264, 279). The nonhuman primate literature is particularly extensive (7, 14, 17, 29, 56, 57, 69, 77, 96, 97, 107, 108, 116, 140, 144, 146, 161, 187, 188, 193, 195–197, 212, 224, 232, 233, 238, 239, 245, 253–258, 297, 298, 308, 314). While most of these establish some degree of dimorphism in particular primate species, and many relate this to specific evolutionary models, a few workers describe primates in which dimorphism is virtually or completely absent (59, 61, 172, 173, 217, 320, 322, 323). On the face of things, this diversity of fact and hypothesis suggests that if there is a general explanation of sexual dimorphism, it is likely to be complex (62, 83, 121, 242).

The literature on human sexual dimorphism can be viewed from the separate perspectives of proximate or ultimate causation. A proximate explanation considers sexual dimorphism as a response to nutritional stress or overall improvements in the environment of growing adolescents. Such nongenetic factors account for secular trends for increases in sexual dimorphism in recent groups or over periods of nutritional changes. Ultimate causation models view sexual dimorphism as a genetic adaptation to a variety of ecological, social, or economic factors, and traditionally incorporate selection as the primary explanatory mechanism. Though ultimate causation models have occupied a greater place in the literature, they do not necessarily explain short-term fluctuations in sexual dimorphism.

PROXIMATE CAUSATION

Numerous studies have documented a decrease in male/female differences in stature under conditions of nutritional stress and an increase in dimorphism with improved diet (39, 127, 131, 147, 176, 201, 274–278, 286, 303). Males are more susceptible to fluctuations in nutritional quality and show greater impairment in long bone growth. Females are less affected by nutritional shortages and prove to be more stable under the same food deficits, presumably because of reproductive demands, storage of more subcutaneous fat, and overall smaller body size. These differential growth vectors generally result in both a collapsing of the male and female mean adult statures and a reduction in the level of sexual dimorphism in body size. Nutritional factors, then, may explain trends for reduction in dimorphism in some horticultural and agricultural groups, since there is good documentation for the decline in dietary sufficiency in the shift from hunting and gathering to agriculture (185, 219, 228). However, we view this factor as a short-term consequence of deprivation and of little relevance for explaining patterns of reduction from australopithecines to early postglacial hunter-gatherers.

Proximate causation for sexual dimorphism changes are not without more ultimate (i.e. evolutionary) consequences. A possible long-term effect of nutritional shortages would be a shift toward smaller adult body size in both sexes. Should the dietary deficiencies become chronic, selection would operate to reduce body size with respect to energetic efficiency. Since males would be under more intense selection, sexual dimorphism should decrease. Furthermore, since body size is positively correlated with the degree of sexual dimorphism (53, 55, 195), any selection for smaller body size should result in reduced sexual dimorphism. Some evidence for this model is found for small body size and low levels of sexual dimorphism of agricultural groups in North America (40, 133), Mexico (228), Europe (94, 95, 170), India (168, 169), China, and Southeast Asia (37, 38, 205).

However, exceptions occur where nutritional patterns and sexual dimorphism are not correlated in modern populations (202) and where groups undergoing the transition from hunting and gathering to agriculture exhibit an increase in sexual dimorphism, because of greater reduction in female body size, as described by Larsen (185), or, as Tobias (286) has shown for the San, a greater increase in male stature. In the former case, Larsen argues that females have differential dependence on agricultural foods and show depressed nutritional status and growth retardation as a consequence. In the latter case, as Bushman groups become more sedentary and adopt "Neolithic" forms of subsistence, there has been a marked increase in male stature. These results present a stark contradiction to the nutritional hypothesis, given evidence for nutritional adequacies of hunting-gathering San (177, 290). As Eveleth (82) and Wolfe & Gray (305) have argued, it is difficult to demonstrate the relationship between nutritional status and sexual dimorphism in a worldwide sample. This must result at least in part from the interplay of proximate and ultimate causation for variation in sexual dimorphism. These clearly are not independent.

ULTIMATE CAUSATION MODELS

Because virtually all higher vertebrates exhibit sexual dimorphism, a great deal of effort has been made to explain the biological cause(s) and genetic mechanism of this underlying pattern of life. Unlike the proximate model discussed above, these models assume that environmentally mediated growth disruptions have little direct influence on adult body size, so that sexual dimorphism is related to different selection forces operating on males and females, according to Lande (182, 183). Ultimate causation models attempt to explain the conditions and existence of sexual dimorphism in relation to underlying genetic adaptations, which are tempered by selection forces. Historically, a number of ultimate causation models proposing to account for differences in sexual dimorphism have been published. Some of these are now understood to be based on faulty biological thinking, while others, such as the idea that female preference for male traits with no functional significance is a way of reducing or eliminating male sex chromosome parasitism (31), are undeserving of further comment. We will discuss what we believe are the four main ultimate causation models that have been seriously considered in recent years. These are 1. sexual selection and mating patterns, 2. body size, 3. economic patterns and the division of labor by sex, and 4. noneconomic role differences. The models are not necessarily mutually exclusive, and indeed it is the lack of clearly defined contradictions in the predictions generated from them that has made them so very difficult to decide between. It is possible that none of the causal models discussed here may be entirely irrelevant in the causation of sexual dimorphism.

Sexual Selection and Mating Patterns

Darwin (64) was the first to suggest that certain aspects of sexual dimorphism in humans and other animals could be attributed to selection occurring between members of the same sex (231). The critical factor in sexual selection is the reproductive advantage certain phenotypes have in attracting or acquiring mates, so that sexual selection is primarily invoked to explain selection operating on males (16). For example, Darwin ascribed gaudy coloration and ornamental plumage in some male birds and larger body size in most male mammals to intermale competition for females (64, pp. 210–211). However, it is also true that selection on or between females may play an important role in this relationship (52a, 294a).

Coupling female preference for better endowed males with the greater ability of large aggressive males to limit access of other males to females, these larger, more aggressive males would be more successful in leaving offspring (234). Thus, for sexual selection to promote differences between the sexes, certain social conditions must be met (32, 81). Principally, there must be unequal opportunities of access to females by males (some individual males can potentially have more offspring than females) which is established by a dominance system, a polygynous mating system (which results in a number of individual males having few or no offspring), and, probably, some operation of female discrimination or choice (4, 52, 57a, 98, 182, 183, 211). When such conditions are met, males compete with each other for control of females, and those with larger body size and a more aggressive personality, for example, have greater success in monopolizing their own breeding rights and territories, thereby contributing differentially to the next generation.

Numerous examples of mammals and other animals seem to corroborate these predictions, for example, a number of bird families (234), elephant seals (191), many ungulates (5, 157), langurs (150), macaques and baboons (26), orangutans (249), and other species (see 3, 4, 54, 56, 108, 122, 223) where male body size is considerably larger and more variable than body size in females, and have high male reproductive variance relative to female variance, at least when observed for individual mating seasons. The most extreme case is probably California elephant seals, where males are three times the size of females and the chance of any male leaving offspring is less than 10% (191, 192).

For mammals in general, correlations between sexual dimorphism and the mating system are also upheld when considering most monogamous species (5, 265). In monogamous groups, females are occasionally even larger than males, resulting in reverse dimorphism (241, 244), although monomorphism generally prevails so that body size, canine dimorphism, and other secondary sexual characteristics are not substantially different among males and females. Behavioral differences are also similar in that females can be equally aggressive and in some cases dominant to males (176). Male investment in offspring is greater in monogamous species (151, 152, 176, 181), which according to Trivers (289) and others (63, 106, 234) would reduce the competition between males. Moreover, in most monogamous species, males and females participate equally in defending young and territory, scent marking, vocalizations, grooming, and infant care (176).

Among the birds there does seem to be some sort of relationship between mating system, paternal care, perhaps even body size in some families, and the magnitude of sexual dimorphism (9, 74, 234, 242, 261, 262, 279). The mating system-dimorphism relation, in particular, seems particularly well founded in a recent study by Payne (234). This may be because the range of mating systems that can be analyzed in birds extends beyond the normal mammalian range. In his analysis of bird families, Payne discusses a scale of continuous mating behavior variation, ranging from monogamy through polygyny to lek and exploded arena systems. The later two permit no paternal care of the young and involve an important degree of female mate choice. With this magnitude of mating system variation, data clearly show a higher male success variance in lekking species than in monogamous ones. Yet it is unclear how far beyond the bird families studied this observation can be used since an analysis of Payne's data (234, table 2) also shows that polygynous males do not have a significantly greater variance in reproductive success than do the males of monogamous species (p = 0.15 using a student's *t* test). Even the basic observation that body size dimorphism differs with mating system was established only by comparing lek species with monogamous species. The more relevant comparison (for mammalian studies) of polygynous species with monogamous species shows a relation between dimorphism and these mating systems for only a few of the families discussed. Because the lekking species are characterized by more potential "causes" of dimorphism than male-male competition (for instance, an important element of female choice, the complete lack of male investment in offspring, and generally larger body size), it is unclear exactly what the bird data show. Specifically, while there might be a correlation between mating system and body size dimorphism among bird taxa, the nature of the relation (only significant between the extremes), the range of mating systems considered, and the number of independent variables make it difficult to establish cause clearly and problematic to extend the conclusions to the interpretation of mammalian variation. Thus, while these data bode well for the potential explanatory power of sexual selection in explaining the variation of sexual dimorphism among many bird species, between the lack of an unambiguous causal hypothesis accounting for the bird data and the greatly reduced variation in mammalian mating systems, it is not clear that the potential relation of sexual selection and sexual dimorphism in the primates can be illuminated.

Studies on primates have reported some weak and strong correlations between sexual dimorphism and mating systems. In numerous publications Leutenegger (195, 197–199) has argued for a small contribution of mating systems to levels of sexual dimorphism in primates, while an opposite position has been taken by Clutton-Brock (52a–56) and others (4, 16, 32, 50, 98, 107, 289). This inconsistency of interpretation is not surprising since some monogamous species (such as *Saguinus mystax*) show marked dimorphism while some polygynous species *(Propithecus verreauxi, Presbytis frontata)* show little dimorphism (52a, 54, 108). Moreover, selection acting on males and on females may be of fundamentally different origin. Even if male reproductive success is primarily a consequence of access to females, female reproductive success may be more dependent on female access to food supplies if food is a limiting resource (289). Finally, much of this difference in opinion and perspective relates to the nature of the statistics used and assumptions made, so that it is difficult to reach an easy answer to the controversy.

The problem with assuming a simple relationship between mating system and sexual dimorphsism within the primate is the breadth of the variation in the primate order. Although the common assumption is that monogamous primates are monomorphic and polygynous primates dimorphic, there are numerous exceptions to this "rule" which produce poor correlations between mating type and dimorphism (107) when all primates are considered. In some respects this should not be surprising since mating patterns are not easy to categorize nor to compare across different taxa. For example, both Leutenegger & Cheverud (198) and Gaulin & Sailer (107) include solitary species of prosimians in their analysis as nonmonogamous, yet this form of polygyny is not comparable to the more social prosimians let alone higher primates. At the same time, there are different intensities of polygyny in Old World monkeys and apes which call into question correlations across major taxa.

We have combined the data of Leutenegger & Cheverud (198) and Gaulin & Sailer (107) and reorganized the body weight dimorphism by major taxa (Table 1). On the surface, differences between the mating systems would appear to explain much of the variation in sexual dimorphism. Thus, in apes, the monogamous gibbons and siamangs have low dimorphism ($\overline{X} = 103.5$), while the more polygynous apes show increased levels ($\overline{X} = 144.4$). Similarly, New World monkeys that are monogamous have low levels of sexual dimorphism, while polygynous forms express marked sex differences. In the single monogamous species of prosimians (for which data exist), the *Indri* males and females are equal in size. Nonsolitary, polygamous prosimians show an average dimorphism of 110.6.

Despite these differences, there is a range of variation among the primates that detracts from any confidence in a strong relationship between weight dimorphism and mating system. Except for the prosimians, the monogamous species within each comparison are substantially smaller in body size than the polygynous species. They also tend to be more continuously arboreal. In addition, there is an incredible range of variation within each comparison according to the species presented in the summary tables of Leutenegger & Cheverud (198) and Gaulin & Sailer (107). In these tables (not reproduced here), gibbons and siamangs show a range from 93.5 *(H. moloch)* to 113.2 *(H.*

Table 1 Sexual dimorphism in body weight for living primates[a]

Species	Weight Dimorphism	Range	n
Monogamous			
Apes	103.5	93.5–113.2	7
OW monkeys (Mentawai langur)	101.6[b]		1
NW monkeys	101.6	95.0–112.5	7
Prosimians (indri)	100		1
Polygamous			
Apes	144.4	120.0–192.7	4
OW monkeys	143.7	98.9–236.4	37
NW monkeys	123.8	95.5–155.7	11
Prosimians	110.6	100.0–126.2	4

[a]Data are from Gaulin & Sailer (107), Leutenegger & Cheverud (198a), Tilson & Tenaza (285a), and Wrangham & Smuts (316). Weight dimorphism is the index of male weight/female weight × 100.
[b]Monogamy in the Mentawai langur is of recent origin (83).

lar) and chimpanzees, gorillas, and orangutans vary between 120.0 and 192.7. In New World monkeys, the monogamous forms range from 95.0 *(Callithrix jacchus)* to 112.5 *(Sanguinus mystax)*. The polygynous New World monkey species also show a great deal of variation and overlap at the bottom of the range with the monogamous forms. A similar pattern holds for the prosimians. Finally, among the Old World monkeys [which are all polygynous except the Mentawai langur (285a)], there is a remarkable spread in the range between the least and most dimorphic forms. From the data tables of Leutenegger & Cheverud (198) and Gaulin & Sailer (107), the least dimorphic is *Presbytis frontata* (98.9) and the most dimorphic *Mandrillus sphinx* (236.4). Between these endpoints is an array of arboreal and semiterrestrial, small- and large-bodied forms that show great variation. Ten species have indices of dimorphism below 110, while in six species the index exceeds 175.0. There appears to be no simple rule for predicting the cause of dimorphism among these polygynous Old World monkeys since some small-medium forms show great dimorphism (e.g. *Erythrocebus patas*-176.9) while others (e.g. *Colobus satanus*-111.1) show little dimorphism. Furthermore, some completely arboreal forms such as *Nasalis larvatus* show very marked dimorphism (206.0), while semiterrestrial forms such as *Macaca cyclops* exhibit much smaller male/female differences (121.3).

Perhaps this lack of patterning, or of an unambiguous association between the variables, should be expected. If body size dimorphism in a polygynous species is presumed to be causally linked to differential reproductive success in the males (resulting from increased intermale competition), the fact is that unlike the case for birds in which lekking and monogamous species could be compared, the actual variation in lifelong male reproductive success in polygynous mammalian species has never been shown to exceed the variation in lifelong reproductive success for males in monogamous species (52a). The presumed cause of this difference may not exist, a possibility not diminished by the analysis of the bird data that shows males of polygynous and monogamous species also do not differ significantly in the variance of their reproductive success. Thus, although it is a common notion in anthropology that polygamous species have great dimorphism and monogamous species have only small sex differences, there is no clear rule for predicting the degree of sexual dimorphism from mating patterns.

Evidence for a relationship between sexual selection, mating patterns, and degree of sexual dimorphism in humans is even less convincing. Alexander et al (5) reviewed data for sexual dimorphism in various mammals and argued that competition among males in polygynous systems led to proportionally greater selection for body size in males (compared to females) resulting in an increase in sexual dimorphism. Applied to sexual dimorphism of stature in human societies, they found an association between marriage patterns (monogamy and polygyny) and sexual dimorphism. In particular, those groups practicing polygyny and "socially imposed monogamy" showed greater sexual differences in stature than ones following what the authors described as "ecologically imposed" monogamous patterns, which led these authors to postulate that patterns of sexual dimorphism in humans resulted primarily from sexual selection relating to mating patterns. Subsequent, more comprehensive work by Gray & Wolfe (127, 304), using Murdock's *Ethnographic Atlas* and height data provided by a variety of sources, tested the correlation between sexual dimorphism and mating patterns in contemporary humans. Their results found only a weak correspondence between marriage patterns and level of dimorphism, so that "marriage systems explain very little of the variation of human sexual dimorphism of stature" (304, p. 226). Available nutrition shows higher correlation with sexual dimorphism than any mating form.

Although current research on modern humans and living primates refutes a strong relationship between mating patterns and sexual dimorphism, it is uncertain how appropriate these results are to fossil human samples. For example, human social arrangements in the ethnographic present probably bear little resemblance to patterns in Middle and Lower Paleolithic contexts. It is also problematic how patterns of mating in agricultural groups are at all relevant to Pleistocene hunters and gatherers, given differences in subsistence economy, diet and nutrition, and technology. We suspect that principles of uniformitarianism break down when considering human fossil assemblages, so that correlations in the present may be of little significance for fossil hominids.

It may be equally difficult to attribute patterns of correlation in a diverse group of primates (which uniformly lack a cultural adaptation) to fossil humans. For instance, variance in male investment in offspring is an important consideration in arguments that link monogamy and a low degree of sexual dimorphism in the primates. Yet "fathering," the extreme expression of male parental investment behavior, is virtually unique to humans among the primates (181, 300), and may well be fundamental to the human adaptation as it developed during the process of hominid origins (203). But fathering underlies important aspects of social relationships in all human societies, regardless of their marriage or mating patterns. Thus, if Lovejoy is correct in terms of the early appearance of fathering, the primate patterns of relationship simply may not apply at any stage of human evolution.

Similarly, if differential female access to food supplies dominates female reproductive success, the development of role expectations and the systematic reciprocal sharing of food resources would markedly reduce this differential in the hominids, and thereby reduce its potential for creating or maintaining sex differences.

Body Size

The possibility of a relation between the magnitude of sexual dimorphism and body size is one of the oldest alternatives to the mating pattern causation argument. Unfortunately, examination of this possibility is often confused by methodological considerations. The problem is how to examine the consequences of body weight differences for the magnitude of body weight dimorphism (or a measure of dimorphism related to it) and maintain the independence of the two variables compared. Recent discussions of this problem have centered on whether the ratio of means is a better measure of dimorphism than the difference between the means (107, 198, 198a), and there are numerous other ways of comparing the sexes in an attempt to describe the magnitude of dimorphism (66, 240, 246, 301). Allometry is also problematic in this context (161, 313). Finally, a possible relation between body weight and the magnitude of dimorphism may be confused by the influence of habitat differences (if arboreal primates are less dimorphic, for instance, they are likely to be smaller than terrestrial ones), and/or possibly differences in home range [there is a positive correlation between home range and diet in primates, more than likely resulting in the observation that range and dimorphism are related (222)].

Many studies indicate that with some exceptions, body size and sexual dimorphism are related to each other, but predictions concerning the amount of the contribution of body size alone varies from 83% of the variance in dimorphism (198) to less than 20% (107). Whatever the value, the generalization that a species overall size correlates with its level of sexual dimorphism has been said to hold for a great variety of animals from insects and other invertebrates [where reverse dimorphism often occurs (244)] to birds and mammals (234, 242) to primates (56, 195, 198, 198a). Although considerable variation occurs, in most animals there is a positive correlation between body size and sexual dimorphism. Among the nonprimates, when body size is large, sexual dimorphism is generally pronounced. Our review of the primate literature, however, suggests this relationship is not as strong as reported in other major taxa. We collected body size data for 80 different primate species, relying on data given by Leutenegger & Cheverud (198) and Gaulin & Sailer (107), supplemented by additional data for the common chimpanzees (161) and for pygmy chimpanzees (316). We used the ratio male/female body weight as our measure of sexual dimorphism and correlated this index with female body weight, as suggested by McCown (212). Unlike Leutenegger & Cheverud (198, 198a), we did not use the log of the absolute difference in weight between males and females, since this measure is clearly inappropriate (107).

Table 2 reviews our results, and it is clear that we find much lower correlations than are generally reported in the literature. For example, when all primates are considered, sexual dimorphism correlates significantly with female body weight ($r = .39$), which is well below the figures given by Leutenegger & Cheverud (198) and even lower than those reported by Gaulin & Sailer (107). When the total primate sample is divided into smaller units (cf 55), considerable variation occurs in the strength of the correlation. For example, prosimians, New World monkeys, and arboreal Old World monkeys all show low and insignificant correlations (two of which are negative). These deviate markedly from the condition in the terrestrial Old World monkeys and apes which show correlation coefficients of .514 and .816 respectively. In apes, the high correlation is partly due to the effect of comparing very small body size in *Hylobates* species with very large body size in gorillas and orangutans. In addition, there are few species in the ape comparison and much greater breadth in the range of body sizes represented. The smallest species are monogamous, are the most often arboreal, and have low levels of sexual dimorphism. The largest species are nonmonogamous, are the least arboreal of the apes, and are very dimorphic. Whether these associations occur by chance or whether they reveal an underlying pattern of relationship is unclear from this sample alone, but we find it suspicious that such a pattern cannot be found in any other primate groups.

As we view these data, we see no simple relationship between body size and degree of sexual dimorphism. There certainly is not a singular relationship which exists in primates, since there is no correlation among some major groups and high correlations among others. There is also considerable variation as is easily appreciated by inspecting the raw data tables given by Leutenegger & Cheverud (198) and Gaulin & Sailer (107). With respect to humans, as we discuss later, there is little reason to suspect that body size has much effect on the evolution of sexual dimorphism since there is only minor change of body size through time in the human lineage. Thus, we find little evidence of body

Table 2 Correlations between sexual dimorphism and female body weight for various groups of nonhuman primates[a]

	Correlation	n	Significance
All primates	.390	80	.001
Prosimians	−.101	15	ns
New World monkeys	.065	17	ns
All Old World monkeys	.404	37	.05
Arboreal Old World monkeys	−.050	23	ns
Terrestrial Old World monkeys	.514	14	.03
Apes	.861	11	.001

[a]Data are from Gaulin & Sailer (107), Jungers & Susman (161), Leutenegger & Cheverud (198a), and Wrangham & Smuts (316). With the kind help of R. W. Wrangham, we were able to resolve contradictions between the data sources, and corrections were made when necessary.

size as an important contributor to sexual dimorphism in either primates or fossil humans.

Economic Patterns and Division of Labor by Sex

Several models for development, maintenance, and reduction in sexual dimorphism have considered the adaptive importance of varying economic patterns based on the exploitation of different parts of the niche by males and females (267). Mechanisms that result in sex differences include differences in selection acting on females and males, sex differences in feeding behavior (262), and competition between the sexes for population-limiting resources (250, 267). One might consider the possibility that there are dimorphic niches, or perhaps bimodal niches differentially utilized by the sexes (251). Slatkin (267) emphasizes the importance of dimorphic niches, but discounts the model of bimodal niches differentially utilized by the sexes. Selander (261, 262) has discussed this factor in birds, and Galdikas & Teleki (99) suggest that different resource exploitation in baboons, orangutans, and chimpanzees foreshadow human patterns of division of labor by sex (155, 156, 181). This partitioning of resources reduces ecological competition between the sexes, which is expected when the variance of resource utilization ability is small relative to the width of the resource spectrum (267). Moreover, it carries another advantage, that of providing for a more efficient use of economic resources *if* there is reciprocal sharing.

The roles adopted by males and females in many species of higher primates often differ dramatically, resulting in nonoverlapping economic duties, and in some cases significant dietary differences (294, 294a). Besides the obvious and well-documented differences in mothering and troop defense, a common activity of higher primate males is hunting, especially hunting that takes males away from the confines of the social unit. For example, work by Strum (138, 280) has shown that male olive baboons were much more likely to participate in predatory behavior and were exclusively involved in hunting activities which took place outside the confines of the troop. The fact that these males completely dropped the cooperative hunting behavior when it conflicted with their reproductive effort (280) indicates that the dimorphic differences were related to something more than subsistence activities, but also that these differences between males and females established the preconditions for male hunting.

Similar patterns exist among some chimpanzees (215) in that males almost exclusively hunt small mammals (283), while female hunting is restricted to smaller prey that occurs in closer proximity to the troop and does not interfere with infant care. There are also sex differences in the techniques used in hunting (229). In the Mahale chimpanzees, females often hunt juvenile ungulates, taking them by seizure, while males chase adult monkeys (282). Another important sex difference in chimpanzee food procurement lies in the fact that females regularly share gathered plant foods with other females, but not with males (214, 216).

A parallel case for systematic sex differences in economic activities can be made for human hunter-gatherers where the economic roles of hunting males and gathering females are generally found (227, 227a), which may be closely associated with the requirements of female pre- and postnatal reproductive duties (41, 42). Thus for the higher primates, including humans, it seems there should be an association among dimorphism, economic patterns, and the division of labor by sex. Based on comparisons between hunting behaviors in nonhuman primate males, sexual dimorphism and differential reproductive factors preadapt males to more freely participate in cooperative hunting away from the social unit.

This presumed relationship between human sexual dimorphism and sexual division of labor in economic activities has been used to account for changes in the degree of sexual dimorphism in the hominid lineage (35–37, 86, 91–93, 95, 132, 310, 311). The theoretical basis for this relationship rests on assumptions concerning the separation of economic duties in hunter-gatherer groups and food-producing populations. Given the near exclusive involvement of males in long distance, multigame hunting and more equal sharing of economic duties in horticulturalists/agriculturalists (227a), Frayer (93, 95) has argued that reduction of sexual dimorphism in prehistoric European populations is related to changes in economic systems. A similar argument is implicit in Slatkin's work (267). He proposes that dimorphism will only result from differences in resource utilization when the variance in resource utilization ability for each sex is small relative to the total resource range. An important part of human evolution involves the expansion of this ability for both sexes. It follows that as the variance for resource utilization ability increases for each sex, the degree of sexual dimorphism would be expected to decrease. This explanation may account for sexual dimorphism decreases over much of human evolution, especially in the Lower and Middle Pleistocene. It would be reasonable to describe the pattern of changes in resource utilization during this time span as expanding for each sex (thereby increasing its proportional variance) because of technological improvements and increased knowledge about the habitat and the most effective means of utilizing its resources (156, 311).

However, differences in economic activities and sexual dimorphism in extant hunter-gatherers and food-producers do not corroborate this hypothesis. For example, Wolfe & Gray (305) have examined the correlation between sexual dimorphism in stature and economic patterns in a large sample of contemporary humans. They found agricultural groups no less dimorphic than hunter-gatherers, arguing against a relationship between economic patterns and sexual dimorphism. Unfortunately, Wolfe and Gray did not differentiate food-producing groups with respect to intensification of agriculture, which may be important since Ember (80) and Burton & White (48) have shown that women's contribution to agricultural work differs substantially between horticulturalists and intensive agriculturalists. These distinctions are, however, not easy to glean from the existing literature and are obviously open to conjecture in prehistoric groups.

To further test the economic model, we assembled data on mandibular canine and second molar breadths for a series of postglacial and recent hunter-gatherers, horticulturalists/agriculturalists, and modern urban populations (Tables 3 and 4). We selected the canine and second molar since these generally show the greatest dimorphism in human and primate groups and breadths, because they are not significantly reduced by occlusal wear. Other than showing that male canine and second molar breadths are *always* larger than female breadths, and that canine dimorphism is usually greater than second molar dimorphism (the only exception to this is the British sample), there is no other clearly emerging pattern. For the canine, the most dimorphic sample is the Czech Neolithic and the least the Danish Neolithic. In the second molar breadth, the Czech Neolithic sample shows much more sexual dimorphism than any hunter-gatherer population, and two of the Urban samples also exceed these in dimorphism. Overall differences among the three broad economic groups are absolutely nonexistent for either tooth. The differences in mean dimorphism are miniscule and not significant. On the basis of these data we concur with Gray and Wolfe's conclusions—modern differences in economic pattern have absolutely no influence on the magnitude of sexual dimorphism (127, 304, 305).

In sum, we note that even with the apparent bias toward sexing skeletons as males in skeletal samples (299), there are still no differences among the three economic categories, whether the data derive from skeletal or living samples (compare Tables 3 and 4 with 5). As with mating patterns and body size, a relationship between sexual dimorphism and economic systems is not demonstrable because of the great variation in recent human groups. Although this does not mean that such a relationship was unimportant in Pleistocene fossils, it does indicate the possibility that recent variation is not particularly useful in either *predicting* patterns of the past or *explaining* them because the fact remains that there are marked changes in economic systems through the Pleistocene, and hominids do greatly reduce in sexual dimorphism during this span of time. In addition, although we do not have body size data for all these groups, we suspect that the hunter-gatherer and urban samples have the greatest statures, yet they do not exhibit more dimorphism, negating any powerful relationship between sexual dimorphism and body size. The data for dental dimensions also lack a regional patterning with respect to the expression of sexual dimorphism (contra 82, 139). For instance, among hunter-gatherers the most and least dimorphic are Amerinds. In horticulturalists/agriculturalists, the

Table 3 Sexual dimorphism in mandibular canine breadth[a]

	Male x̄	n	Female x̄	n	% Dimorphism	Significance
Hunter-Gatherers						
Glacial Kame	8.0	20	7.2	18	111.1	.001
Libben	8.3	19	7.5	21	110.7	.001
Australian Aborigines						
Murray River	8.8	98	8.1	81	109.2	.001
Lapps	7.6	211	7.0	190	108.6	.001
Riviere aux Vase	7.9	11	7.3	13	107.4	.01
Indian Knoll	7.7	46	7.2	48	106.9	.01
Australian Walbiri	8.1	71	7.6	79	106.6	
Vlasac	7.8	16	7.4	11	106.1	.05
Jomon	7.5	62	7.1	25	105.6	.001
Ainu	7.5	32	7.1	20	105.4	.001
Nubian "Mesolithic"	8.4	17	8.0	15	105.0	.05
Aleuts	7.9	74	7.6	57	103.9	
St. Catherine's Island	7.8	25	7.5	29	103.9	.05
Horticulturalists/Agriculturalists						
Czech Neolithic	8.1	28	7.2	30	112.2	.001
Adena/Hopewell	7.9	42	7.1	52	111.3	.001
Swiss Neolithic	7.6	16	7.0	12	109.6	.01
Yayoi	8.2	13	7.5	40	109.3	.001
Leavenworth Arikara	8.3	21	7.6	23	109.0	.001
Nubian Agriculturalists	7.6	89	7.2	82	105.6	.05
St. Catherine's Island	7.9	44	7.5	45	105.1	.001
Nasioi	8.3	58	7.9	67	104.7	.001
Canaveral Indians	8.1	17	7.8	5	103.7	ns
Ticuna	7.5	27	7.2	27	102.9	ns
Danish Neolithic	8.0	12	7.8	9	102.6	ns

Urban Populations

Hungary Mediaeval (Zalavár)	7.9	49	7.2	40	.001
Koreans	8.3	11	7.6	5	.01
Ohio Whites	7.9	45	7.3	35	.001
Denmark Mediaeval	7.9	34	7.3	74	.001
Norwegians	8.1	78	7.5	87	.001
San Cristobal	7.9	49	7.5	27	.001
Japanese	7.1	114	6.7	158	.001
Javanese	7.9	139	7.2	42	
Tristan da Cunha	9.0	54	8.5	43	
North Chinese	8.1	80	7.7	10	.01
British	7.1	30	6.8	30	.01
Hong Kong Chinese	7.9	29	7.6	13	

	109.7
	109.2
	108.4
	108.2
	108.0
	106.5
	106.0
	106.0
	105.9
	105.2
	104.4
	103.9

[a] Data derive from 8, 19, 36, 37, 49, 123, 139, 185, 189, 206, 221, 226, 234a, 259, 263, 285, unpublished measurements kindly provided by C. L. Brace, and from our own measurements. The Leavenworth Arikara data were kindly provided by H. W. Case. "Ohio Whites" are from data provided by S. M. Garn, and differ significantly from the summary data published earlier (103).

Table 4 Sexual dimorphism in mandibular second molar breadth[a]

	Male $\bar{x}$	n	Female $\bar{x}$	n	% Dimorphism	Significance
Hunter-Gatherers						
Libben	11.3	19	10.7	20	105.6	.01
Vlasac	10.7	16	10.2	12	105.5	.01
Australian Aborigines						
Murray River	12.3	97	11.7	80	105.1	.001
Lapps	10.1	259	9.6	218	104.7	.001
Ainu	10.3	37	9.9	28	103.8	.001
Australian Walbiri	11.4	71	11.0	79	103.6	.001
Nubian "Mesolithic"	11.4	14	11.0	18	103.6	.05
Jomon	10.5	85	10.2	61	103.5	.001
Aleuts	10.6	45	10.3	37	102.9	
Glacial Kame	10.8	29	10.5	29	102.9	
Riviere aux Vase	11.0	10	10.7	10	102.5	ns
Indian Knoll	10.9	53	10.7	52	101.9	
St. Catherine's Island	10.9	23	10.7	43	101.9	ns
Horticulturalists/Agriculturalists						
Czech Neolithic	10.4	22	9.5	27	109.4	.001
Yayoi	11.0	32	10.4	13	105.8	.001
Nubian Agriculturalists	10.5	159	10.0	142	105.0	.05
Nasioi	11.0	66	10.6	65	103.9	.001
Adena/Hopewell	10.7	54	10.3	52	103.8	
Canaveral	10.8	17	10.4	5	103.4	ns
St. Catherine's Island	10.8	44	10.5	61	102.9	.01
Swiss Neolithic	10.0	13	9.7	12	102.8	ns
Ticuna	10.3	24	10.1	20	102.6	ns
Leavenworth Arikara	10.5	45	10.3	60	102.2	.01
Danish Neolithic	10.3	26	10.1	22	102.2	ns

Urban Populations					
Hungary Mediaeval (Zalavár)	10.0	55	9.4	42	106.4	.001
British	10.8	30	10.2	30	105.9	.001
Ohio Whites	10.6	31	10.1	22	105.2	.002
North Chinese	10.8	94	10.3	21	104.9	.001
Denmark Mediaeval	10.0	76	9.6	99	104.2	.001
Koreans	10.8	13	10.4	6	103.8	ns
Japanese	10.5	197	10.2	194	102.9	.005
Javanese	10.5	133	10.2	38	102.9	
Tristan da Cunha	10.8	108	10.5	92	102.9	.01
San Cristobal	10.8	29	10.5	20	102.9	.01
Norwegians	10.5	58	10.3	46	101.9	
Hong Kong Chinese	10.3	21	10.2	7	101.0	ns

^aData derive from 8, 20, 21, 36, 37, 49, 123, 139, 185, 189, 206, 221, 226, 234a, 259, 263, 285, unpublished measurements kindly provided by C. L. Brace, and from our own measurements. "Ohio Whites" are from data provided by S. M. Garn, and differ significantly from the summary data published earlier (103).

Table 5 Dental and body height percent sexual dimorphisms in living human populations[a]

	C̄ Breadth	n (m/f)	M₂ Breadth	n (m/f)	Femur length	n (m/f)
Bambandyanalo	110.1	5/2	112.9	6/2	110.7	2/2
Libben	110.7	19/21	105.6	19/20	109.7	37/41
Vlasac	106.1	11/16	105.5	16/12	109.2	11/4
Zalavár	109.7	49/50	106.4	55/42	109.1	65/41
Czech Neolithic	112.2	28/30	109.4	22/27	108.6	22/14
Japanese	106.0	114/158	102.9	197/194	107.6	20/25
Yuendumu	106.6	71/79	103.6	71/79	107.5	209/149
Nubian Neolithic	106.3	89/82	105.0	159/142	107.3	108/93
Leavenworth Arikara	109.0	21/23	102.2	45/60	107.2	25/19
St. Catherine's Island Agricultural	105.1	23/45	102.9	44/61	107.1	47/54
Ainu	105.4	32/20	103.8	37/28	106.7	44/25
Afalou/Taforalt	105.5	18/8	102.9	20/9	106.0	20/9
Nubian Mesolithic	105.0	17/15	103.6	14/18	105.9	11/10
St. Catherine's Island Hunter/Gatherer	103.9	25/29	101.9	23/44	103.3	9/19

[a]Data are from 21, 49, 65, 100, 185, and Abbie (1) for the Yuendumu femora, with the published lengths modified to approximate skeletal femoral lengths. Additional data were provided by C. O. Lovejoy, H. W. Case, T. Brown, and the authors.

most and least dimorphic samples for both teeth are Europeans, as is the case for the horticulturalists/agriculturalists. Finally, whether hunter-gatherers or horticulturalists/agriculturalists are considered, both monogamous and polygynous marriage systems are certainly represented, but it would be difficult to determine the mating preferences from the levels of dimorphism in canine and second molar breadths.

Thus, considering the economic pattern, our data confirm the generalization that most of the prehistoric groups spanning the transition from hunting and gathering to agriculture to urbanization do *not* show a pattern of decreased dimorphism (13, 49, 60, 133, 185, 243, 269), but either stability through time or a very slight increase. The only exceptions for this are Europe (91, 93, 95, 219), India (168, 169), and a group of Amerinds from Alabama (40). It remains to be demonstrated whether these are anomalies or are part of a pattern perhaps obscured by noneconomic factors.

Noneconomic Role Differences and the Division of Labor by Sex

Differences between female and male roles that are unrelated to economic activities provide a classic explanation for sexual dimorphism. Indeed, different social roles should probably be considered a special case of a dimorphic niche, as discussed by Slatkin (267). It has been argued that the energy requirements of sex roles predominate in controlling the degree of dimorphism expressed (74). The extent of sexual dimorphism resulting from role differences can range from a marked expression in baboons, presumably because of the male role in troop defense (62), to a weak expression in late Upper Paleolithic Europeans, presumably because of a decrease in male robustness following from improvements in hunting technology (93, 95), to an even weaker expression in some living groups which have virtually eliminated the differences in strength requirements between male and female roles (35, 37).

In a more complex model, Bridges (40) attributes a decrease in sexual dimorphism for skeletal strength measures associated with the transition to Mississippian agriculture in northwest Alabaman Amerinds to a number of cultural factors that result in more similar strength requirements in male and female roles. She argues that males retain their roles as hunters and become more involved in a variety of strenuous social and political activities (particularly warfare and sports), but do not contribute to agricultural chores as intensively as females. The pattern of male skeletal change involves the legs much more than the arms (although the right-left strength differences decrease, presumably as a consequence of the replacement of the spear by the bow and arrow). In females, the requirements of numerous new agricultural chores such as planting and grinding result in significant increases in the strength of the arm bones. Bridges concludes that in general the strength requirements of agriculture are greater than the requirements of hunting and gathering, and that the difference is greater for the females than for the males because their roles change more. Thus, there is a *decrease* in the magnitude of sexual dimorphism. However, the exact pattern of change differs according to whether the arms or the legs are considered, because different sorts of activities are involved in the patterns of change affecting males and females. One sure implication of Bridges' work is that the behavioral patterns underlying the magnitude of dimorphism are very complex, not necessarily reciprocal (i.e. males doing more or less of the same thing that females do), involve both economic and noneconomic roles, and affect different parts of the body in different ways.

Role differences are a much more productive way of looking at the consequences of division of labor by sex than is the more limited case of differences in economic pattern. However, a greater magnitude of role differences does not invariably lead to increased sexual dimorphism. For instance, increasing female specialization for long child dependency periods makes sex roles more distinct in humans as well as in other anthropoid primates. Yet the increased physiological demand on females in relation to reproductive requirements can result in selection for relatively larger female postcanine teeth and therefore a reduced sex difference in postcanine tooth size (313).

The hypothesis of increasing similarities in role requirements as a cause of decreasing sexual dimorphism is unique to human evolution (35, 311). However, the hominids are not the only lineage that shows sexual dimorphism reductions, and it is unlikely that role differences are a universal explanation of these reductions when all cases are considered. Indeed, one can question this explanation for the hominids themselves, since it rests on assumptions of behavioral differences in societies that no longer exist. Moreover, if explanations such as Bridges' (40) are correct, complex models of role differences and role difference changes as an explanation of changes in sexual dimorphism will always be untestable in the hominid fossil record. The inability to test a model does not invalidate it as an explanation, but it does render it meaningless as a scientific hypothesis.

Summary of Ultimate Causation Models

Review of the models of proximate and ultimate causation for sexual dimorphism leads to the uncomfortable conclusion that several of them have never been adequately tested, and moreover none of the models seem to be particularly successful in explaining patterns of dimorphism in humans and nonhuman primates. This may mean that factors other than those that have been traditionally considered may be of primary importance or, more likely, that sexual dimorphism in various species results from dissimilar and often complex causes. It may be true, for instance, that body size influences sexual dimorphism in some species, as Leutenegger and others have suggested, but this is not a universally applicable relationship. Similarly, mating systems and division of labor may contribute to differences in degree between males and females, although recognizing the possibility of a relationship between these may be of only limited application. Whatever model is appropriate, there is considerable reduction of sexual dimorphism in the hominid lineage.

DIMORPHISM IN EVOLUTION

Much of the recent thinking about sexual dimorphism and its role in the evolutionary process stems from the realization that the magnitude of human dimorphism was once much greater than it is today. Indeed, many workers now believe that the decrease in sexual dimorphism over the course of human evolution is at least as dramatic and significant as the increase in brain size and the decrease in posterior tooth size. Its explanation, then, must be at least as important and its role in the evolutionary process as critical as that of tooth size.

Apart from the primates, sexual dimorphism has only occasionally been considered to be an important aspect of the fossil record (58, 60, 118, 246, 301). Dimorphism has been noted and discussed in a number of fossil nonhuman primate species (11, 88, 119, 128, 129, 163–165, 210, 298, 312). By far the most work on fossil primate material has focused on sexual dimorphism in hominid evolution (6, 15, 34, 35, 37, 40, 46, 68, 84, 87, 91, 93–95, 109, 110, 143, 152, 158–160, 171, 175, 179, 180, 185, 186, 194, 207, 208, 228, 236, 268, 287, 288, 299, 306–312, 318, 321).

Among the primate fossils, the study of sexual dimorphism often focuses on whether the systematic differences between two specimens or two samples found at a site, or within an alleged taxon, differ because of sex or because of taxonomy. This question is often not resolved, and the sex vs taxonomic variation argument plagues the interpretation of the Proconsuls (compare 128 with 11), the ramapithecine remains (compare 129, 130, and 312 with 12, 163, 317), and many of the australopithecine fossils (compare 158 and 159 with 67, 190, 218, 230). Moreover, in those cases when the dimorphism itself is the object of study, there is often a similar lack of agreement. Even the fundamental issue of whether sexual dimorphism has changed substantially over the course of human evolution has evidently not been settled (compare 15, 37, 93, 309–311, with 194, 196, 319, 321).

In the primate fossil record, sexual dimorphism has been examined in the earliest unequivocal anthropoid fossils, and in the Fayum species most likely ancestral to the living hominoids—the *Aegyptopithecus zeuxis* remains from the later Oligocene of Egypt (88, 164). This is fortunate for an understanding of the evolution of sexual dimorphism since it provides insight into what may be the primitive condition for all anthropoid primates. This condition is one of very marked sexual dimorphism for all three of the Oligocene anthropoid species examined.

For the purposes of comparing sexual dimorphism in a number of fossil and living hominoid species, we settled on a limited number of metric features. These were dictated by our desire to make valid comparisons between different groups and to maximize the sample sizes for those individuals whose sex could be ascertained with reasonable likelihood. We have used the breadth of the mandibular canine, the breadth of the mandibular second molar, and the height of the mandibular corpus measured between the first and second molars in these comparisons.

Canine size is a traditional measure of sex difference in primates (73, 102, 103, 141, 296) because the canine is invariably the most dimorphic of the teeth (10, 120, 309). The second molar also shows a relatively considerable degree of sexual dimorphism in most human populations (102, 309), and dimorphism in the mandibular second molar is highly correlated with dimorphism in body size (104). The second molar also provides a measure of masticatory adaptation (306, 308, 309). Mandible corpus height was chosen because it is one of the best correlates of body height that is likely to be preserved in the fossils (117, 128). However, because of masticatory differences that characterize the course of human evolution, it is not clear that mandible height variation unambiguously reflects body size alone. In the recent and living human populations, femur length is substituted for mandibular corpus height as a more exact measure of body size.

Several authors have argued that there are really a number of quite different dimorphisms (83, 232, 233, 321), and thus that different measures of sexual dimorphism may reflect very different phenomena. To some extent this must be the case. For instance, when using multivariate procedures to examine numerous features simultaneously, patterns of skeletal dimorphism revealed in the primates are often different (197, 212, 232, 233, 314). Nevertheless, we believe that there is an important common factor underlying the sexual dimorphisms we have observed, and, minimizing variation in factors that strongly affect their independent variation, they covary to a surprising degree. With regard to the four characteristics we examined in living apes for comparisons with the fossil hominids (Table 6), there is generally covariation among the metric traits. Thus, the pygmy chimpanzees were found to be least dimorphic for all features, while the gorillas are most dimorphic for canine breadth, mandible corpus height, and femur length. Orangutans are most dimorphic for M_2 breadth. In the 14 human populations for which we could gather reliable data on three variables by sex (i.e. excluding mandibular height because femur length provides a better measure of body size dimorphism), using the small sample size modification, the correlation between dimorphism in femur length and dimorphism in the breadth of the mandibular canine is .763 while the femur length–M_2 breadth sexual dimorphism correlation is .770 (Table 5). These are high correlations, significantly different from 0.0 at better than the 0.001 level. We conclude that while these three characteristics in part reflect differing aspects of sexual dimorphism that may vary independently to some degree, they also strongly reflect a more general aspect of sexual dimorphism. To an important extent, then, these different measures actually measure the same thing.

In all the characteristics we examined (Table 7), *Aegyptopithecus* shows a dramatic magnitude of sexual dimorphism. Because the sample size is very small it is likely that the values we have determined are not exactly correct, but we believe it probable that this marked expression of sex difference is not merely an accident of small sample size. Canine dimorphism and the dimorphism reflected in mandible corpus height are extraordinary. The canine dimorphism cannot be matched in any living or fossil anthropoid species, while the mandibular height dimorphism may only be exceeded by several of the ramapithecine species. Because of the small sample sizes the conservative conclusion is that as a group the ramapithecines all reflect the primitive condition and probably do not actually differ substantially. Among the ramapithecines, the Ravin sample has the greatest likelihood of representing a real biological population. Mandibular corpus height dimorphism in this sample is the same as in *Aegyptopithecus*–the primitive state.

The dimorphism in M_2 breadth is also marked in *Aegyptopithecus*, although its absolute magnitude is not as great as the magnitude of dimorphism in other features. It is matched by the same level of dimorphism in *A. afarensis,* in the Ravin ramapithecines, and in living orangutans. One must assume that this too is the primitive condition. Thus, the *Aegyptopithecus* data indicate that the primitive condition for the anthropoids would seem to be very marked sexual dimorphism in the features we have chosen to examine. Interestingly, if no *Aegyptopithecus* were known, the dimorphism in this ancient species could be accurately reconstructed from the pattern of dimorphism in its fossil and living descendant species. If this were done, the only error would be an underestimate of the magnitude of canine dimorphism in the ancestral condition. Other than arguing that this level of dimorphism is the primitive state in the earliest apes, we offer no explanation for the degree of sexual dimorphism given the small size and arboreal habitat reconstructed for *Aegyptopithecus*.

For the earliest hominid species, *A. afarensis,* the magnitude of dimorphism is also considerable, exceeding all other hominids in measures of dental dimorphism. Mandibular body height dimorphism for this species, in contrast, does not appear to be the maximum for the hominids. However, we believe this reflects the small sample sizes, and we strongly suspect that dimorphism in this feature is the same for three of the australopithecine species *(afarensis, africanus, habilis)* and *H. erectus,* first reducing substantially in the Neandertals.

Table 6 Percent sexual dimorphisms in living ape species[a]

	C̄ Breadth	n (m/f)	M$_2$ Breadth	n	Femur length	n	Mandible height	n
Pan paniscus	118.3	23/25	100.0	24/33	101.2	10/10	100.0	12/17
Pan troglodytes	123.3	84/90	103.7	124/124	104.9	38/58	108.7	22/20
Pan gorilla	138.0	153/95	107.0	170/107	120.9	84/54	123.8	47/22
Pongo pygmaeus	126.6	48/59	112.0	69/73	115.0	32/29	117.0	12/16

[a]Dental data were collected by the authors. Mandibular data were provided by W. L. Jungers, A. Kramer, and measured by the authors. Postcranial data are from Schultz (253) and provided by W. L. Jungers.

Table 7 Percent sexual dimorphisms in fossil hominoid species[a]

	C̄ Breadth	n (m/f)	M₂ Breadth	n (m/f)	Femur length	n (m/f)	Mandible height	n (m/f)
Aegyptopithecus	149.9	3/1	111.4	4/6			135.1	4/7
Ravin Ramapithecines	130.3	3/2	112.3	5/3			136.4	2/1
Australopithecus afarensis	127.5	11/5	111.2	6/10			118.4	5/5
Australopithecus africanus	117.3	9/6	109.1	7/3			119.6	4/4
Homo habilis	125.4	4/7	107.9	4/8			126.9	5/10
Homo erectus	113.6	6/15	106.0	10/22			119.6	10/17
European Neandertals	115.8	13/9	104.8	12/10	108.1	4/1	115.5	7/8
European Early Upper Paleolithic	109.8	7/6	105.5	7/8	108.4	5/3	115.3	8/8

[a]*Aegyptopithecus* data are from Fleagle, Kay & Simons (88). The remaining data were measured by the authors.

Variation in mandibular corpus height dimorphism among the earlier hominid species confounds differences in both body size and in mastication. To the extent that these are independent of each other, the resulting variation is bound to be difficult to interpret.

The differences between the *afarensis* sample and the other australopithecine grade species are not great, and except for the decrease in M_2 breadth dimorphism, the differences among the australopithecine species are not statistically significant. If the dentition of *A. afarensis* seems to be the most dimorphic of the australopithecines, it should be seen in the context of the fact that all of the australopithecines are very dimorphic compared with later hominids. While it is possible that the magnitude of sexual dimorphism decreases through australopithecine grade evolution, such a decrease can only be demonstrated statistically for the M_2. If this decrease also occurred in other features, its extent was probably not great.

Finally, although the sample sizes are quite small, the differences in postcranial remains that seem to be attributable to sexual dimorphism appear to be large in both *A. africanus* (306, contra 194) and *A. afarensis* (158, 204). The data suggest that body size dimorphism was as marked in these australopithecines as one would expect from the dental and gnathic dimorphism. One of us (306) estimated that the sexual dimorphism in weight for *A. africanus* indicated males were twice the size of females. The larger postcranial sample now known for this species provides no basis for retracting this claim. Moreover, limb dimension comparisons at Hadar show *A. afarensis* to be equally dimorphic and comparisons of *H. habilis* postcranial remains from individuals as large as ER 1472 with remains from individuals as small as OH 13 also suggest marked dimorphism. Dimorphism in the earliest hominids may not be limited to size. It has been proposed that the Hadar australopithecines were also characterized by very significant sex differences in postcranial morphology which are said to reflect sex differences in locomotor behavior and habitat utilization (281). If true, this would be a good example of adaptation to a dimorphic niche, as discussed by Slatkin (267).

In the much larger *H. erectus* sample there is a drop in the magnitudes of dental sexual dimorphism. Canine breadth dimorphism is well below the australopithecine grade condition although still above most of the modern human populational means, while the dimorphism in M_2 size does not decrease as much (relative to the late australopithecines) although it falls to near the modern populational mean (about 105). In contrast, the mandibular corpus height dimorphism remains marked, and in fact is only exceeded by the *H. habilis* corpus height dimorphism value. Of course, all of the australopithecine mandibular sample sizes are small, and there is no reason to believe that any of the dimorphism values are significantly different. Thus, the conservative conclusion is that *erectus* mandibular corpus height dimorphism is probably unchanged from the australopithecine condition. The implications of this fact for estimations of body size dimorphism are unclear because there are too few postcranial remains known to be associated with or attributable to *H. erectus*. It is interesting that the newly discovered juvenile from west Turkana (WT-15000) is much larger than many workers expected. This probably does not indicate elevated dimorphism for the species, however, because an earlier discovered female of equal antiquity, ER 1808, is also very tall. If anything, these data would suggest that body size dimorphism in *H. erectus* is reduced compared with the australopithecines.

The European Neandertals are virtually identical to *H. erectus* in the magnitudes of dental sexual dimorphism, and the differences are not significant statistically. Here, body size dimorphism can be estimated by dimorphism in femur length. The value is well within the human populational range (143, 287), although according to the data we summarize here, it is above the mean. This might help confirm the suggestion of reduced body size dimorphism in *erectus* made above.

Looking at the European earlier Upper Paleolithic sample, the molar, femoral, and mandibular dimorphisms are virtually identical to the dimorphism values for the European Neandertals. In contrast, the canine dimorphism is much lower. Unlike the Neandertals, dimorphism of the canine in this European sample is within the range of modern populational means, although at its upper end.

We contend that these data show evidence for the persistent reduction of sexual dimorphism over the course of hominid evolution. The hominid lineage is not the only one showing reduction of sexual dimorphism. In making evolutionary comparisons, there is the inevitable problem of which similarities reflect the same condition in a common ancestor and which happened in parallel. Fortunately, the reinterpretation of phylogeny in the anthropoid primates makes it easier to distinguish these alternatives. The evidence that forces the particular interpretations of where the parallelisms in the hominoid radiation lie comes from a series of new evaluations of protein and DNA level variations as well as a reevaluation of morphological and paleontological information (18, 124–126, 130, 266, 312). These data combine to indicate clearly that it is humans and chimpanzees that form a sister group (i.e. that diverged most recently). This is a very differently composed sister group than the group defined by "great apes" (i.e. chimpanzees, gorillas, and orangutans), or even the group defined by "African apes" (gorillas and chimpanzees).

Without the fossil record (i.e. only comparing living species) one might suppose that the ancestral condition for this sister group is one of reduced sexual dimorphism. While this interpretation is possible, it leaves the pattern of variability and the systematic changes in this pattern over the course of human evolution as revealed by the fossil record inexplicable. If the bimodality in size (and to some degree morphology) was interpreted as the result of two sympatric hominid species with low levels of dimorphism and marked degrees of similarity, study of the course of Plio-Pleistocene evolution would show these "species" becoming more and more similar to each other. Such an interpretation is unlikely, and it is much more reasonable to interpret the differences as the result of dimorphism. This would mean that reduction of dimorphism in the chimpanzee and human lines is a homoplasy. The last common ancestor of these two lines, as well as the earlier ancestor of the monophyletic group of African hominoids, would both be markedly dimorphic on this interpretation. Thus, the reduction of sexual dimorphism in the hominids does seem to be parallel to the specific reductions in some of the other anthropoid primates. In the hominids this reduction seems to take place in three stages.

In the australopithecine grade, canine dimorphism is markedly reduced from the primitive anthropoid condition, although it remains very high compared to younger hominids. There is little difference in the canine breadth dimorphism between the australopithecines and common chimpanzees and orangutans (compare Tables 6 and 7). Breadth dimorphism is only slightly greater than this for the Ravin ramapithecines. Examination of the few unworn canines indicates that the same might also be true for the dimorphism in canine crown height. Parsimony, then, suggests that the degree of canine dimorphism in the early australopithecines, common chimpanzees, and orangutans reflects the primitive condition for the later hominoids, and that the expanded canine dimorphism of living gorillas is a characteristic unique to them. The idea that the early australopithecines show a reduction in sexual dimorphism of the canine (for instance 318) cannot be confirmed. This misinterpretation probably comes from a confusion of *dimorphism* reduction with *size* reduction, an entirely different matter! The subsequent reduction of canine dimorphism in the hominids is paralleled by a reduction in the pygmy chimpanzee lineage. These reductions are parallel and do not indicate that the reduced dimorphism in *Pan paniscus* is the primitive condition for the African hominoids (contra 61, 320). Indeed, it has become quite evident that little is primitive about the pygmy chimpanzee, and that it cannot validly serve as a model for the predivergence hominoid (186, 312).

In terms of molar size dimorphism, the primitive condition of marked dimorphism is evident in the *Aegyptopithecus* remains. This extreme is shared by the living orangutan, its likely ramapithecine ancestors, and the early australopithecines. Although all of the australopithecine species have marked dimorphism in molar size, this dimorphism does seem to decrease through the australopithecine span, and the latest species is considerably smaller in its molar sexual dimorphism than is the earliest species. At its largest the degree of australopithecine sexual dimorphism is equivalent to that of the orangutans, and it is very likely that this represents the primitive condition. Unlike the distribution of australopithecine canine breadth dimorphism, even the greatest molar breadth dimorphism is within the modern human range. At its smallest, the magnitude of sexual dimorphism in the australopithecine molars is slightly greater than that in gorillas and much greater than that in chimpanzees. Thus, the australopithecines are not the only lineage to show reduction in molar breadth dimorphism. The two African ape lineages also show a reduction in dimorphism, which is not only parallel to the hominid reduction but, according to the most recent phylogenetic reconstructions, must be parallel to each other because the earliest hominids have the greater magnitude of dimorphism that reflects the primitive condition. Interestingly, the orangutans (and the ramapithecines, which either are their ancestors or at least reflect the ancestral condition) show no such reduction.

Finally, the magnitude of sexual dimorphism in mandibular height varies among the australopithecines. This is almost certainly a consequence of small sample size, and it is likely that mandibular corpus height dimorphism in all of the australopithecine species does not differ significantly. In the Ravin ramapithecine sample, corpus height dimorphism is very marked, closely approximating the primitive condition as seen in *Aegyptopithecus*. By comparison, all of the later anthropoid primates are reduced in dimorphism. Gorillas and orangutans approximate the australopithecine condition, but if the Ravin ramapithecines reflect the ancestral condition for orangutans, this must be a parallel reduction. The further reduction in the two chimpanzee species is certainly a parallelism. Thus, mandibular corpus height, like canine breadth, is more dimorphic in the australopithecine grade than any living human population. There is some evidence that dimorphism in postcranial size is similarly extreme in this group.

Among the australopithecines, *A. afarensis* is the most dimorphic for the dentition. The differences in dimorphism within the australopithecines are not great. Yet it is interesting that if this early primitive species were unknown, variation in the other species would indicate that the earlier form should have been the most dimorphic in the genus.

The second stage is reflected by *H. erectus* and earlier populations of *H. sapiens*. It is characterized by an intermediate position for canine sexual dimorphism (between the australopithecine and the modern *H. sapiens* conditions), a reduction of molar sexual dimorphism to within the modern human range, but a retention of the australopithecine level of sexual dimorphism in mandibular corpus height. Comparison of these two stages provides some insight into other changes in sexual dimorphism that these variations reflect. In particular, sexual dimorphisms in other aspects of cranial morphology would seem to follow (i.e. be reflected in) the pattern of change in canine sexual dimorphism (212) better than these dimorphisms conform to the pattern of change in molar breadth or mandibular corpus dimorphism. Thus, sexual dimorphism in the cranial and facial features of the earliest australopithecines is dramatic (171, 311), and remains little changed in *H. habilis,* as comparison of male and female specimens such as ER 1470 and ER 1813 would indicate. The sexual dimorphism in *H. erectus* and Neandertal crania is reduced from this magnitude, although it remains well above the modern human range (208, 310, 311). Thus, like modern human crania, there is disproportionate sexual dimorphism in earlier hominid facial variation (153). In contrast, it is interesting that postcranial sexual dimorphism, insofar as it can be determined, seems to parallel sexual dimorphism in the molars. This dimorphism, at least in the Neandertal sample, is well within the modern human range (143, 287).

The third stage is the modern human condition, with its marked reductions compared with earlier human populations, its marked variability, and its unpatterned, intrapopulational variations. The sample of earlier Upper Paleolithic Europeans is really part of this stage in terms of reduction in sexual dimorphism, although it resembles the Neandertals in all but the reduction of canine dimorphism. Reduction in molar and body size dimorphism in humans and chimpanzees must be parallel evolutionary trends and cannot be due to their common ancestry. Reduction in canine dimorphism is unique to the human line, just as expansion in canine dimorphism is unique to the gorilla line. Explanations of the patterns of sexual dimorphism variation in humans and chimpanzees therefore need not be the same, while at the same time, explanations in both cases are required.

Patterns of sexual dimorphism for postglacial hunter-gatherers, agriculturalists, and modern groups were previously presented in Tables 3 and 4. Other than showing that male canine and second molar breadths are *always* larger than females and that the canine dimorphism is nearly always greater than the second molar breadth, there was no other clearly emerging pattern. Differences among the three broad economic types were not striking, nor statistically significant. In addition, although we do not have evidence for body size in all these groups, we suspect that the modern populations have the greatest stature, yet they show the least dimorphism which negates any powerful relationship between sexual dimorphism and body size. Finally, whether hunter-gatherers or agriculturalists are considered, both monogamous and polygynous marriage systems are represented, yet it would be difficult to determine the mating preferences from the levels of dimorphism present in the samples. Thus, when sexual dimorphism is considered in postglacial human samples, it is apparent that no consistent pattern appears and, moreover, that no single model is successful in describing the variation among and across samples. It may be that cultural factors interfere with biological (selection) forces that previously operated on the human fossil lineage.

SUMMARY

Explanations for these evolutionary trends, as is true for explanations of all paleontological phenomena, should be based on functional and/or adaptive models that can be tested. We have discussed a number of models that purport to account for differences in sexual dimorphism. Not all of these could account for the reduction of dimorphism in the hominids, and in fact primate dimorphism has proven to be more complex than is often realized (83). For instance, even if there were an important relation between sexual dimorphism and body size, the fact is that there is little change in average body size over most of the course of post-australopithecine hominid evolution. A rather different problem lies in applying the relation of sexual dimorphism to economic systems, since it was necessary to examine this relation over a range of economic systems that do not characterize most of the fossil hominid groups. All of these prehistoric populations were hunter/gatherers to some extent (although differing vastly in the relative importance of different food-procurement approaches). Habitat and dimorphism failed as an explanation for primate variation, and there are no arboreal humans to apply a primate-based habitat model to. Finally, dimorphism and mating system, however potentially explanatory in either primates or in living human populations, must always remain a speculative relation for fossil hominids (213). While some workers have argued for an early and perhaps critical appearance of monogamy as the original mating pattern in the hominids (203), others have argued that a polygynous system was more likely (6), while still others emphasize the idea that bonding, even if short lived, was the important aspect of male-female relationships early in hominid evolution (87). We simply shall never know. Nor can we easily clarify basic issues such as whether canine dimorphism reduced because of a reduction in aggression (presumably a reduction in male-male competition over mates or the replacement of the canines by improved technology during such competition—if it ever occurred), or whether canine dimorphism reduction is no more than a reflection of the reduction in sexual dimorphism related to a completely different cause. Similarly, there are no real prospects for linking warfare-related technology or aggressive behaviors to the magnitude of dimorphism. As in the cases above, if there was such a relationship, it was likely complex and interrelated with other factors that influence dimorphism as well.

One interesting complication results from the independent reduction of sexual dimorphism in the chimpanzee and human lineages. The fact is that the chimpanzees show a definite division of labor in how they acquire foods—a division that many think could act as a precursor for a human hunting/gathering adaptation. Yet little dimorphism in body size is shown in the two living chimpanzee species (the differences between them is not important in this regard). The differential resource exploitation is a common adaptation in chimpanzees and hominids, and this suggests that at least some of the dimorphism reduction in both of these lineages may be a consequence of the resource exploitation pattern; that is, of the economic adaptation that reduces the competition between the sexes.

Our tendency is to suspect that the systematic reduction in dimorphism over the course of human evolution is a consequence of a convergence in the requirements of male and female roles. We do not limit this contention to economic roles. This is because role requirements are complex in humans and involve far more than just those activities that can be directly related to the procurement and preparation of foods, as Bridges (40) and others (152, 213) have argued. Thus we contend that the hominids have adapted to a dimorphic niche which, over the course of human evolution, has become increasingly monomorphic. Males and females have each come to utilize a greater proportion of resources available to the population as a whole. Thus both the roles and the activities of the individuals change in such a way that would ultimately act to reduce the magnitude of sexual dimorphism and the extent of overlap between the sexes, according to this interpretation. Simply put, the problem with this contention is that we cannot test it in a convincing manner. If, as we believe, the causes of dimorphism are complexly interrelated, it is probable that specific changes in causation may never be discernible.

For some, conclusions which come to noncommittal positions may seem disconcerting and fruitless. Although we are convinced that sexual dimorphism reduces within the hominids, as well as in many other primate lineages, we are unable to determine any simple pattern of ultimate cause(s) and are unwilling to force the data into a particular model. Indeed, the models we presented in the first half of this paper are not particularly successful in explaining patterns of sexual dimorphism in the limited cases they cover. Applying them to fossil samples requires the acceptance of numerous assumptions about unknown factors of essentially unreconstructable social behavior. It is apparent from this review that sexual dimorphism reduces, but specifically why this takes place is still a unanswered problem. Most likely, simplistic, single cause models will not be effective in accounting for this common trend in evolution.

ACKNOWLEDGMENTS

We are grateful to a number of our colleagues who kindly provided data for our use: C. L. Brace, T. Brown, H. W. Case, S. M. Garn, W. L. Jungers, A. Kramer, and C. O. Lovejoy. R. Wrangham was very helpful in aiding our attempts to resolve contradictions between published sources of primate data. A number of colleagues helped edit the manuscript, and while admitting that we are responsible for its final form and content, we greatly appreciate the marked improvements suggested by M. Flynn, P. Holroyd-Vychodil, L. Schepartz, and K. Rosenberg. This manuscript was written jointly on the University of Michigan computer system (MTS) by using TELENET and logging on to the same ID from our terminals over 750 miles apart. This is an experience we urge our colleagues to try.

Literature Cited

1. Abbie, A. A. 1975. Studies in physical anthropology. *Aust. Inst. Aboriginal Stud.* 5:1–132
2. Acsadi, G., Nemeskéri, J. 1970. *History of Human Life Span and Mortality.* Budapest: Akademiai Kiado. 346 pp.
3. Adams, J., Greenwood, P. J. 1983. Why are males bigger than females in precopula pairs of *Gemmarus pulex? Behav. Ecol. Sociobiol.* 13:239–41
4. Alexander, R. D., Borgia, G. 1979. The origin and basis of the male-female phenomenon. In *Sexual Selection and Reproductive Competition in Insects,* ed. M. S. Blum, N. A. Blum, pp. 417–40. New York: Academic. 463 pp.
5. Alexander, R. D., Hoogland, J. L., Howard, R. D., Noonan, K. M., Sherman, P. W. 1978. Sexual dimorphisms and breeding systems in pinnipeds, ungulates, primates, and humans. In *Evolutionary Biology and Human Social Behavior: An Anthropological Perspective,* ed. N. A. Chagnon, W. Irons, pp. 402–35. North Scituate, MA: Duxbury. 623 pp.
6. Allen, L. L., Bridges, P. S., Evon, D. L., Rosenberg, K. R., Russell, M. D., et al. 1982. Demography and human origins. *Am. Anthropol.* 84:888–96
7. Almquist, A. J. 1974. Sexual differences in the anterior dentition in African primates. *Am. J. Phys. Anthropol.* 40:359–68
8. Alvesalo, L. 1970. *The influence of sex-chromosome genes on tooth size in man.* Academic dissertation. Univ. Turku, Finland. 52 pp.
9. Amadon, D. 1959. The significance of sexual dimorphism in size among birds. *Proc. Am. Philos. Soc.* 103:531–36
10. Anderson, D. L., Thompson, G. W. 1973. Interrelationships and sex differences of dental and skeletal measurements. *J. Dent. Res.* 52:431–38
11. Andrews, P. J. 1978. A revision of the Miocene Hominoidea of East Africa. *Bull. Br. Mus. Nat. Hist. Geol.* 30:85–224
12. Andrews, P. J., Tobien, H. 1977. New Miocene locality in Turkey with evidence on the origin of *Ramapithecus* and *Sivapithecus. Nature* 268:699–701
13. Angel, J. L. 1984. Health as a critical factor in the changes from hunting to developed farming in the Eastern Mediterranean. In *Paleopathology at the Origins of Agriculture,* ed. M. N. Cohen, G. J. Armelagos, pp. 51–73. Orlando: Academic. 601 pp.
14. Ankel-Simons, F. 1983. *A Survey of Living Primates and their Anatomy.* New York: Macmillan. 313 pp.
15. Armelagos, G. J., Van Gerven, D. P. 1980. Sexual dimorphism and human evolution: an overview. *J. Hum. Evol.* 9:437–46
16. Arnold, S. J. 1983. Sexual selection: The interface of theory and empiricism. In *Mate Choice,* ed. P. Bateson, pp. 67–107. Cambridge: Cambridge Univ. Press. 601 pp.
17. Ashton, E. H. 1957. Age changes in dimensional differences between the skulls of male and female apes. *Proc. Zool. Soc. London* 128:259–65
18. Baba, M. L., Darga, L. L., Goodman, M. 1982. Recent advances in molecular evolution of the primates. In *Advanced Views of Primate Biology,* ed. A. B. Chiarelli, R. S. Corruccini, pp. 6–27. Berlin: Springer-Verlag. 226 pp.
19. Bailit, H. L., DeWitt, S. J., Leigh, R. A. 1968. The size and morphology of the Nasioi dentition. *Am. J. Phys. Anthropol.* 28:271–88
20. Bailit, H. L., Hunt, E. E. Jr. 1964. The sexing of children's skeletons from teeth alone and its genetic implications. *Am. J. Phys. Anthropol.* 22:171–74
21. Bass, W. M. 1971. *Human Osteology.* Columbia: Missouri Archaeol. Soc. 281 pp.
22. Bass, W. M., Evans, D. R., Jantz, R. L., Ubelaker, D. H. 1971. *The Leavenworth Site Cemetery: Archaeology and Physical Anthropology.* Lawrence: Univ. Kansas Publ. Anthropol. No. 2. 200 pp.
23. Beach, F. A. 1978. Human sexuality and evolution. In *Human Evolution: Biosocial Perspectives,* ed. S. L. Washburn, E. R. McCown, pp. 123–53. Menlo Park, Calif: Cummings. 316 pp.
24. Becker, W. A., Sinha, S. P., Bogyo, T. P. 1964. The quantitative genetic relationship of sexual dimorphism of birds. *Genetics* 50:235 (Abstr.)
25. Benshoof, L., Thornhill, R. 1979. The evolution of monogamy and concealed ovulation in humans. *J. Soc. Biol. Struct.* 2:95–106

26. Berenstein, L., Wade, T. D. 1983. Intrasexual selection and male mating strategies in baboons and macaques. *Int. J. Primatol.* 4:201–35
27. Biggerstaff, R. H. 1975. Cusp size, sexual dimorphism, and heritability of cusp size in twins. *Am. J. Phys. Anthropol.* 42:127–40
28. Bird, M. A., Schaffer, H. E. 1972. A study of the genetic basis of sexual dimorphism for wing length in *Drosophila melanogaster*. *Genetics* 72:475–87
29. Black, E. S. 1970. Sexual dimorphism in the ischium and pubis of three species of South American monkeys. *J. Mammal.* 51:794–96
30. Black, T. K. II. 1978. Sexual dimorphism in the tooth-crown diameters of the deciduous teeth. *Am. J. Phys. Anthropol.* 48:77–82
30a. Black, T. K. II. 1978. A new method for assessing the sex of fragmentary skeletal remains: femoral shaft circumference. *Am. J. Phys. Anthropol.* 48:227–32
31. Blute, M. 1984. The sociobiology of sex and sexes today. *Curr. Anthropol.* 25:193–212
32. Borgia, G. 1979. Sexual selection and the evolution of mating systems. See Ref. 4, pp. 19–80
33. Boulinier, G. 1968. La détermination du sex des crânes humains à l'aide des fonctions discriminantes. *Bull. Mém. Soc. Anth. Paris* Sér. 12, 3:301–16
34. Brace, C. L. 1967. *The Stages of Human Evolution*. Englewood Cliffs, NJ: Prentice Hall. 110 pp.
35. Brace, C. L. 1973. Sexual dimorphism in human evolution. *Yearb. Phys. Anthropol.* 16:31–49
36. Brace, C. L., Nagai, M. 1982. Japanese tooth size, past and present. *Am. J. Phys. Anthropol.* 59:399–411
37. Brace, C. L., Ryan, A. S. 1980. Sexual dimorphism and human tooth size differences. *J. Hum. Evol.* 9:417–35
38. Brace, C. L., Shao, X., Zhang, Z. 1984. Prehistoric and modern tooth size in China. In *The Origins of Modern Humans: A World Survey of the Fossil Evidence*, ed. F. H. Smith, F. Spencer, pp. 485–516. New York: Liss. 590 pp.
39. Brauer, G. W. 1982. Size sexual dimorphism and secular trend: Indicators of subclinical malnutrition? In *Sexual Dimorphism in Homo sapiens: A Question of Size*, ed. R. L. Hall, pp. 245–59. New York: Praeger. 429 pp.
40. Bridges, P. S. 1985. *A biomechanical analysis of two prehistoric Amerind groups: Changes in habitual activities and the division of labor with the transition from hunting-and-gathering to agriculture*. PhD thesis. Univ. Mich., Ann Arbor
41. Brown, J. K. 1970. A note on division of labor by sex. *Am. Anthropol.* 72:1073–78
42. Brown, J. K. 1976. An anthropological perspective on sex roles and subsistence. In *Sex Differences*, ed. M. S. Teitelbaum, pp. 122–37. Garden City: Anchor Books. 232 pp.
43. Brown, P. 1981. Sex determination of Australian aboriginal crania from the Murray Valley: A reassessment of the Larnach and Freedman technique. *Archaeol. Oceania* 16:53–63
44. Brown, T., Barrett, M. J. 1964. A roentgenographic study of facial morphology in a tribe of central Australian Aborigines. *Am. J. Phys. Anthropol.* 22:33–42
45. Brown, T., Townsend, G. C. 1979. Sex determination by single and multiple tooth measurements. *Occas. Pap. Hum. Biol.* 1:1–16
46. Brues, A. 1959. The spearman and the archer: An essay on selection in body build. *Am. Anthropol.* 61:457–69
47. Burr, D. R., Van Gerven, D. P., Gustav, B. L. 1977. Sexual dimorphism and mechanics of the human hip: A multivariate assessment. *Am. J. Phys. Anthropol.* 42:273–78
48. Burton, M. L., White, D. R. 1984. Sexual division of labor in agriculture. *Am. Anthropol.* 86:568–83
49. Calcagno, J. M. 1984. *Human dental evolution in post-Pleistocene Nubia*. PhD thesis. Univ. Kansas, Lawrence. 220 pp.
50. Carothers, J. H. 1984. Sexual selection and sexual dimorphism in some herbivorous lizards. *Am. Nat.* 124:244–54
51. Carpenter, J. C. 1976. A comparative study of metric and nonmetric traits in a series of modern crania. *Am. J. Phys. Anthropol.* 45:337–44
52. Caspari, E. 1972. Sexual selection in human evolution. In *Sexual Selection and the Descent of Man*, ed. B. G. Campbell, pp. 332–56. Chicago: Aldine. 378 pp.
52a. Clutton-Brock, T. H. 1985. Size, sexual dimorphism, and polygyny in primates. In *Size and Scaling in Primate Biology*, ed. W. L. Jungers, pp. 51–60. New York: Plenum
53. Clutton-Brock, T. H., Harvey, P. H. 1977. Primate ecology and social organization. *J. Zool. Soc. London* 183:1–39
54. Clutton-Brock, T. H., Harvey, P. H. 1978. Mammals, resources, and reproductive strategies. *Nature* 273:191–95
55. Clutton-Brock, T. H., Harvey, P. H.

1984. Comparative approaches to investigating adaptation. In *Behavioral Ecology. An Evolutionary Approach*, ed. J. R. Krebs, N. B. Davies, pp. 7–29. Sunderland, MA: Sinauer
56. Clutton-Brock, T. H., Harvey, P. H., Rudder, B. 1977. Sexual dimorphism, socioeconomic sex ratio, and body weight in primates. *Nature* 269:797–800
57. Coelho, A. M. 1974. Socio-bioenergetics and sexual dimorphism in primates. *Primates* 15:263–69
57a. Cohen, J. A. 1984. Sexual selection and the psychophysics of female choice. *Z. Tierpyschol.* 64:1–8
58. Cook, D. C. 1984. Subsistence and health in the lower Illinois Valley: osteological evidence. See Ref. 13, pp. 235–68
59. Coolidge, H. J., Shea, B. T. 1982. External body dimensions of *Pan paniscus* and *Pan troglodytes* chimpanzees. *Primates* 23:245–51
60. Coombs, M. C. 1975. Sexual dimorphism in the chalicotheres (Mammalia, Perissodactyla). *Syst. Zool.* 24:55–62
61. Cramer, D. L., Zihlman, A. L. 1978. Sexual dimorphism in the pygmy chimpanzee *Pan paniscus*. In *Recent Advances in Primatology: Evolution*, ed. D. J. Chivers, K. A. Joysey, 3:487–90. London: Academic
62. Crook, J. H. 1972. Sexual selection, dimorphism, and social organization in the primates. See Ref. 52, pp. 231–81
63. Crook, J. H. 1980. *The Evolution of Human Consciousness*. Oxford: Clarendon. 178 pp.
64. Darwin, C. 1871. *The Descent of Man and Selection in Relation to Sex*. London: Murray. 668 pp.
65. Davivongs, V. 1963. The femur of the Australian Aborigine. *Am. J. Phys. Anthropol.* 21:457–67
66. Day, M. H. 1975. Sexual differentiation in the innominate bone studied by multivariate analysis. *Ann. Hum. Biol.* 2:143–51
67. Day, M. H., Leakey, M. D., Olson, T. R. 1980. On the status of *Australopithecus afarensis*. *Science* 207:1102–3
68. De Arsuaga, J. L., Alonso, J. 1983. Sexual variability and taxonomic variability in the innominate bone of *Australopithecus*. *Z. Morphol. Anthropol.* 73:297–308
69. Deblock, R., Fenart, R. 1973. Differences sexuelles sur crânes adultes chez *Pan paniscus*. *Bull. Assoc. Anat. (Nancy)* 57(157):299–306
70. Demoulin, F. 1972. Importance de certains mesures crâniennes (en particulier de la longueur sagittale de la mastoïde) dans la détermination sexuelle des crânes. *Bull. Mém. Soc. Anthropol. Paris* Sér. 12, 9:259–64
71. Derry, D. E. 1923. On the sexual and racial characters of the human ilium. *J. Anat.* 58:71–83
72. DiBennardo, R., Taylor, J. V. 1979. Sex assessment of the femur: A test of a new method. *Am. J. Phys. Anthropol.* 50:635–38
73. Ditch, L. E., Rose, J. E. 1972. A multivariate dental sexing technique. *Am. J. Phys. Anthropol.* 37:61–64
74. Downhower, J. F. 1976. Darwin's finches and the evolution of sexual dimorphism in body size. *Nature* 263:558–63
75. Dwight, T. 1905. The size of articular surfaces of the long bones as characteristic of sex: an anthropological study. *Am. J. Anat.* 4:19–32
76. Earhart, C. M., Johnson, N. K. 1970. Size dimorphism and food habits of North American owls. *Condor* 72:251–64
77. Eckhardt, R. B. 1975. The relative body weights of Bornean and Sumatran Orangs. *Am. J. Phys. Anthropol.* 42:349–50
78. Eisen, E. J., Hanrahan, J. P. 1972. Selection in sexual dimorphism for body weight of mice. *Aust. J. Biol. Sci.* 25:1015–24
79. Eisen, E. J., Legates, J. E. 1966. Genotype-sex interaction and the genetic correlation between the sexes for body weight in *Mus musculus*. *Genetics* 54:611–23
80. Ember, C. R. 1983. The relative decline in women's contribution to agriculture with intensification. *Am. Anthropol.* 85:283–304
81. Emlen, S. T., Oring, L. W. 1977. Ecology, sexual selection, and the evolution of mating systems. *Science* 197:215–23
82. Eveleth, P. B. 1975. Differences between ethnic groups in sex dimorphism of adult height. *Ann. Hum. Biol.* 2:35–39
83. Fedigan, L. M. 1982. *Primate Paradigms, Sex Roles, and Social Bonds*. St. Albans, Vt: Eden. 386 pp.
84. Ferembach, D. 1978. Sexe et adaptation au milieu. *La Recherche* 9(85):14–19
85. Ferembach, D., Schwidetzky, I., Stloukal, M. 1980. Recommendations for age and sex diagnoses of skeletons. *J. Hum. Evol.* 9:517–49
86. Fisher, E. 1979. *Women's Creation*. New York: McGraw-Hill. 484 pp.
87. Fisher, H. E. 1982. *The Sex Contract*. New York: Murrow. 253 pp.
88. Fleagle, J. F., Kay, R. F., Simons, E. L. 1980. Sexual dimorphism in early anthropoids. *Nature* 287:328–30
89. Fox, R. 1972. Alliance and constraint:

Sexual selection and the evolution of human kinship systems. See Ref. 52, pp. 282–331
90. Frankham, R. 1968. Sex and selection for a quantitative character in *Drosophila*. II. The sex dimorphism. *Aust. J. Biol. Sci.* 21:1225–37
91. Frayer, D. W. 1977. Dental sexual dimorphism in the European Upper Paleolithic and Mesolithic. *J. Dent. Res.* 56:871
92. Frayer, D. W. 1978. *The Evolution of the Dentition in Upper Paleolithic and Mesolithic Europe*. Lawrence: Univ. Kansas Publ. Anthropol. No. 10. 201 pp.
93. Frayer, D. W. 1980. Sexual dimorphism and cultural evolution in the Late Pleistocene and Holocene of Europe. *J. Hum. Evol.* 9:399–415
94. Frayer, D. W. 1981. Body size, weapon use, and natural selection in the European Upper Paleolithic and Mesolithic. *Am. Anthropol.* 83:57–73
95. Frayer, D. W. 1984. Biological and cultural change in the European late Pleistocene and early Holocene. See Ref. 37, pp. 211–50
96. Frisch, J. E. 1963. Sex differences in the canines of the Gibbon *(Hylobates lar)*. *Primates* 4:1–10
97. Frisch, J. E. 1973. The hylobatid dentition. *Gibbon Siamang* 2:55–95. Basel: Karger
98. Gadgil, M. 1972. Male dimorphism as a consequence of sexual selection. *Am. Nat.* 106:574–80
99. Galdikas, B. M. F., Teleki, G. 1981. Variations in subsistence activities of female and male pongids: New perspectives on the origins of hominid labor division. *Curr. Anthropol.* 22:241–56
100. Galloway, A. 1959. *The Skeletal Remains of Bambandyanao*. Johannesburg: Witwatersrand Univ. Press. 154 pp.
101. Garn, S. M., Cole, P. E., Van Alstine, W. I. 1979. Sex discriminatory effectiveness using combinations of root lengths and crown diameters. *Am. J. Phys. Anthropol.* 50:115–17
102. Garn, S. M., Lewis, A. B., Kerewsky, R. 1964. Sex differences in tooth size. *J. Dent. Res.* 43:306
103. Garn, S. M., Lewis, A. B., Kerewsky, R. 1966. Sexual dimorphism in the buccal lingual tooth diameter. *J. Dent. Res.* 45:1819
104. Garn, S. M., Lewis, A. B., Kerewsky, R. 1967. The relationship between sexual dimorphism in tooth size and body size as studied within families. *Arch. Oral Biol.* 12:299–301
105. Garn, S. M., Nagy, J. M., Sandusky, S. T. 1972. Differential sexual dimorphism in bone diameters of subjects of European and African ancestry. *Am. J. Phys. Anthropol.* 37:127–30
106. Gaulin, S. J. C. 1980. Sexual dimorphism in the human post-reproductive life-span: possible causes. *J. Hum. Evol.* 9:227–32
107. Gaulin, S. J. C., Sailer, L. D. 1984. Sexual dimorphism among the primates: The relative impact of allometry and sexual selection. *Int. J. Primatol.* 5:515–36
108. Gautier-Hion, A. 1975. Dimorphisme sexuel et organisation sociale chez les cercopithécinés forestiers Africans. *Mammalia* 39:365–74
109. Genovés, S. 1954. The problem of the sex of certain fossil hominids, with special reference to the Neandertal skeletons from Spy. *J. R. Anthropol. Inst.* 34:131–44
110. Genovés, S. 1969. Sex determination in earlier man. In *Science in Archaeology*, ed. D. Brothwell, E. S. Higgs, pp. 342–52. New York: Praeger. 595 pp.
111. Giles, E. 1964. Sex determination by discriminant function analysis of the mandible. *Am. J. Phys. Anthropol.* 22:129–36
112. Giles, E. 1966. Statistical techniques for sex and race determination: Some comments in defense. *Am. J. Phys. Anthropol.* 25:85–86
113. Giles, E. 1968. Sex determination by discriminant function analysis: Effects of age and number of variables. *Proc. 8th Int. Congr. Anthropol. Ethnol. Tokyo*, pp. 59–61
114. Giles, E. 1970. Discriminant function sexing of the human skeleton, In *Personal Identification in Mass Disasters*, ed. T. D. Stewart, pp. 99–109. Washington, DC: Smithsonian Inst. Press. 158 pp.
115. Giles, E., Elliot, O. 1963. Sex determination by discriminant function analysis of crania. *Am. J. Phys. Anthropol.* 21:53–68
116. Gingerich, P. D. 1972. The development of sexual dimorphism in the bony pelvis of the squirrel monkey. *Anat. Rec.* 172:589–95
117. Gingerich, P. D. 1977. Correlation of tooth size and body size in living hominoid primates, with a note on relative brain size in *Aegyptopithecus* and *Proconsul*. *Am. J. Phys. Anthropol.* 47:395–98
118. Gingerich, P. D. 1981. Variation, sexual dimorphism, and social structure in the early Eocene horse *Hyracotherium* (Mammalia, Perissodactyla). *Paleobiology* 7:443–55
119. Gingerich, P. D. 1981. Cranial morphology and adaptations in Eocene *Adapidae*. I. Sexual dimorphism in *Adapis magnus*

and *Adapis parisiensis*. *Am. J. Phys. Anthropol.* 56:217–34
120. Gingerich, P. D., Schoeninger, M. 1979. Patterns of tooth size variability in the dentition of primates. *Am. J. Phys. Anthropol.* 51:457–66
121. Glücksmann, A. 1974. Sexual dimorphism in mammals. *Biol. Rev.* 49:423–75
122. Glücksmann, A. 1978. *Sex Determination and Sexual Dimorphism in Mammals.* London: Wykeham. 179 pp.
122a. Glücksmann, A. 1981. *Sexual Dimorphism in Human and Mammalian Biology and Pathology.* London: Academic. 356 pp.
123. Gonda, K. 1959. On the sexual differences in dimensions of human teeth. *J. Anthropol. Soc. Nippon* 67:151–63
124. Goodman, M. 1976. Towards a genealogical description of the primates. In *Molecular Biology,* ed. M. Goodman, R. E. Tashian, pp. 321–53. New York: Plenum. 466 pp.
125. Goodman, M., Baba, M. L., Darga, L. L. 1983. The bearing of molecular data on the cladogenesis and times of divergence of hominoid lineages. In *New Interpretations of Ape and Human Ancestry,* ed. R. L. Ciochon, R. S. Corruccini, pp. 67–86. New York: Plenum. 888 pp.
126. Goodman, M., Braunitzer, G., Stangl, A., Shrank, B. 1983. Evidence on human origins from hemoglobins of African apes. *Nature* 303:546–48
127. Gray, J. P., Wolfe, L. D. 1980. Height and sexual dimorphism of stature among human societies. *Am. J. Phys. Anthropol.* 53:441–56
128. Greenfield, L. O. 1972. Sexual dimorphism in *Dryopithecus africanus*. *Primates* 13:395–410
129. Greenfield, L. O. 1979. On the adaptive pattern of *Ramapithecus*. *Am. J. Phys. Anthropol.* 50:527–48
130. Greenfield, L. O. 1980. A late divergence hypothesis. *Am. J. Phys. Anthropol.* 52:351–66
131. Hall, R. L. 1978. Sexual dimorphism for size in seven nineteenth century northwest coast populations. *Hum. Biol.* 50:159–71
132. Hamburg, B. A. 1978. The biosocial bases of sex difference. See Ref. 23, pp. 155–213
133. Hamilton, M. E. 1982. Sexual dimorphism in skeletal samples. See Ref. 39, pp. 107–63
134. Hanihara, K. 1958. Sexual diagnosis of Japanese long bones by means of discriminant function. *J. Anthropol. Soc. Nippon* 66:39–48
135. Hanihara, K. 1959. Sex diagnosis of Japanese skulls and scapulae by means of discriminant function. *J. Anthropol. Soc. Nippon* 67:191–97
136. Hanihara, K. 1978. Differences in sexual dimorphism in dental morphology among several human populations. In *Development, Function, and Evolution of Teeth,* ed. P. M. Butler, K. A. Joysey, pp. 127–33. London: Academic. 523 pp.
137. Hanna, R. E., Washburn, S. L. 1953. The determination of the sex of skeletons, as illustrated by a study of the Eskimo pelvis. *Hum. Biol.* 25:21–27
138. Harding, R. S. O., Strum, S. C. 1976. The predatory baboons of Kekopey. *Nat. Hist.* 85:46–53
139. Harris, E. F., Nweeia, M. T. 1980. Tooth size of Ticuna Indians, Columbia, with phenetic comparisons to other Amerinds. *Am. J. Phys. Anthropol.* 53:81–91
140. Harvey, P. H., Kavanagh, M., Clutton-Brock, T. H. 1978. Sexual dimorphism in primate teeth. *J. Zool. London* 186:475–85
141. Harvey, P. H., Kavanagh, M., Clutton-Brock, T. H. 1978. Canine tooth size in female primates. *Nature* 276:817–18
142. Hauser, G., Jahn, R. 1984. Sexual dimorphism in pelvic height. *J. Hum. Evol.* 13:589–92
143. Heim, J-L. 1983. Les variations du squelette post-crânien des hommes de Néandertal suivant le sex. *Anthropologie* 87(1):5–26
144. Heisler, P., Eastman, C., eds. 1982. *Behavioral and Morphological Aspects of Sexual Dimorphism in Primates.* New York: Plenum
145. Helmuth, H. 1968. Einige Masse des processus mastoideus beim Menschen und seine Bedeutung für die Geschlechtsbestimmung. *Z. Morphol. Anthropol.* 60:75–84
146. Hershkovitz, P. 1979. The species of sakis, genus *Pithecia* (Cebidae, Primates), with notes on sexual dichromatism. *Folia Primatol.* 31:1–22
147. Hiernaux, J. 1968. Variabilitié du dimorphism sexuel de la stature en Afrique Subsaharienne et en Europe. In *Anthropologie und Humangenetik,* ed. T. Bielicki, pp. 42–50. Stuttgart: Fischer. 195 pp.
148. Hoshi, H. 1962. Sex difference in the shape of the mastoid process in norma occipitalis and its importance to the sex determination of the human skull. *Okajimas Folia Anat. Jpn.* 38:309–13
149. Howells, W. W. 1973. Cranial variation in man. A study by multivariate analysis of patterns of difference among recent human populations. *Pap. Peabody Mus. Archeol. Anthropol.* 67:1–259

150. Hrdy, S. B. 1977. *The Langurs of Abu.* Cambridge: Harvard Univ. Press. 361 pp.
151. Hrdy, S. B. 1981. *The Woman That Never Evolved.* Cambridge: Harvard Univ. Press. 256 pp.
152. Hrdy, S. B., Bennett, W. 1981. Lucy's husband: What did he stand for? *Harvard Magazine* July/Aug:7–9
153. Hunter, W. S., Garn, S. M. 1972. Disproportionate sexual dimorphism in the human face. *Am. J. Phys. Anthropol.* 36:133–38
154. Iordanidis, P. 1961. Détermination du sex par les os du squelette. Eléments métrique des os. *Ann. Méd. LéG. Fr.* 42:117–34
155. Isaac, G. Ll. 1978. The foodsharing behavior of protohuman hominids. *Sci. Am.* 238(4):99–108
156. Isaac, G. Ll. 1981. The early development of proto-human sociocultural behavior. *Q. Rev. Archaeol.* 2:15–17
157. Jarman, P. J. 1974. The social organization of antelope in relation to their ecology. *Behaviour* 48:215–67
158. Johanson, D. C., Lovejoy, C. O., Kimbel, W. H., White, T. D., Ward, S. C., et al. 1982. Morphology of the Pliocene partial hominid skeleton (A.L. 288-1) from the Hadar formation, Ethiopia. *Am. J. Phys. Anthropol.* 57:403–51
159. Johanson, D. C., White, T. D. 1979. A systematic assessment of early African hominids. *Science* 202:321–30
160. Johanson, D. C., White, T. D. 1980. On the status of *Australopithecus afarensis*. *Science* 207:1104–5
161. Jungers, W. L., Susman, R. L. 1984. Body size and skeletal allometry in African apes. *The Pygmy Chimpanzee. Evolutionary Biology and Behavior,* ed. R. L. Susman, pp. 131–77. New York: Plenum
162. Kajanoja, P. 1966. Sex determination of Finnish crania by discriminant function analysis. *Am. J. Phys. Anthropol.* 24:29–34
163. Kay, R. F. 1982. Sexual dimorphism in Ramapithecinae. *Proc. Natl. Acad. Sci. USA* 79:195–216
164. Kay, R. F., Fleagle, J. F., Simons, E. L. 1981. A revision of the Oligocene apes from the Fayum Province, Egypt. *Am. J. Phys. Anthropol.* 55:293–322
165. Kay, R. F., Simons, E. L. 1983. A reassessment of the relationship between later Miocene and subsequent hominoidea. See Ref. 125, pp. 577–624
166. Keen, H. A. 1950. A study of sex differences in male and female skulls. *Am. J. Phys. Anthropol.* 8:65–79
167. Kelley, M. 1978. Phenice's visual technique for sexing the os pubis: a critique. *Am. J. Phys. Anthropol.* 48:121–22
168. Kennedy, K. A. R. 1984. Growth, nutrition, and pathology in changing paleodemographic settings in South Asia. See Ref. 13, pp. 169–92
169. Kennedy, K. A. R. 1984. Biological adaptation and affinities of Mesolithic South Asians. In *The People of South Asia,* ed. J. Lukacs, pp. 29–58. New York: Plenum. 465 pp.
170. Key, P. 1980. Evolutionary trends in femoral sexual dimorphism from the Mesolithic to the Late Middle Ages in Europe. *Am. J. Phys. Anthropol.* 52:244 (Abstr.)
171. Kimbel, W. H., White, T. D., Johanson, D. C. 1984. Cranial morphology of *Australopithecus afarensis:* A comparative study based on a composite reconstruction of the adult skull. *Am. J. Phys. Anthropol.* 64:337–88
172. Kinzey, W. G. 1972. Canine teeth of the monkey *Callicebus moloch:* Lack of sexual dimorphism. *Primates* 13:365–69
173. Kinzey, W. G. 1984. The dentition of the pygmy chimpanzee. See Ref. 161, pp. 65–88
174. Kiszely, I. 1974. On the possibilities and methods of the chemical determination of sex from bones. *Ossa* 1:51–62
175. Kitahara-Frisch, J. 1979. A note on sexual dimorphism in the early hominid dentition. *Ossa* 6:75–82
176. Kleiman, D. G. 1977. Monogamy in mammals. *Q. Rev. Biol.* 52:39–69
177. Kolata, G. B. 1974. !Kung hunter-gatherers: Feminism, diet, and birth control. *Science* 185:932–34
178. Korkman, N. 1957. Selection with regard to the sex difference in body weight in mice. *Hereditas* 43:665–78
179. Krantz, G. S. 1982. The fossil record of sex. See Ref. 39, pp. 85–106
180. Lancaster, J. B. 1979. Sex and gender in evolutionary perspective. In *Human Sexuality,* ed. H. Katchadourian, pp. 51–80. Berkeley: Univ. Calif. Press. 358 pp.
181. Lancaster, J. B., Lancaster, C. S. 1983. Parental investment: the hominid adaptation. In *How Humans Adapt,* ed. D. J. Ortner, pp. 33–65. Washington, DC: Smithsonian Inst. Press. 560 pp.
182. Lande, R. 1980. Sexual dimorphism, sexual selection, and adaptation in polygenic traits. *Evolution* 34:292–305
183. Lande, R. 1981. Models of speciation by sexual selection on polygenic traits. *Proc. Natl. Acad. Sci. USA* 78:3721–25
184. Larnach, S. L., Freedman, L. 1964. Sex determination of aboriginal crania from New South Wales. *Rec. Aust. Mus.* 26:295–308

185. Larsen, C. S. 1982. The anthropology of St. Catherine's Island. 3. Prehistoric human biological adaptation. *Anthropol. Pap. Am. Mus. Nat. Hist.* 57(3):157–270
186. Latimer, B. M., White, T. D., Kimbel, W. H., Johanson, D. C., Lovejoy, C. O. 1981. The pygmy chimpanzee is not a living missing link in human evolution. *J. Hum. Evol.* 10:475–88
187. Lauer, C. 1975. A comparison of sexual dimorphism and range of variation in *Papio cynocephalus* and *Gorilla gorilla* dentition. *Primates* 16:1–7
188. Lauer, C. 1975. The relationship of tooth size to body size in a population of rhesus monkeys *(Macaca mulatta)*. *Am. J. Phys. Anthropol.* 43:333–40
189. Lavelle, C. L. B. 1968. Anglo Saxon and modern British teeth. *J. Dent. Res.* 47:811–15
190. Leakey, R. E. F., Walker, A. C. 1980. On the status of *Australopithecus afarensis. Science* 207:1103
191. LeBoeuf, B. J. 1974. Male-male competition and reproductive success in elephant seals. *Am. Zool.* 14:163–76
192. LeBoeuf, B. J., Briggs, K. T. 1977. The cost of living in a seal harem. *Mammalia* 41:167–95
193. Leutenegger, W. 1973. Sexual dimorphism in the pelves of African Lorises. *Am. J. Phys. Anthropol.* 38:251–54
194. Leutenegger, W. 1977. Sociobiological correlates of sexual dimorphism in body weight in South African australopiths. *S. Afr. J. Sci.* 73:143–44
195. Leutenegger, W. 1978. Scaling of sexual dimorphism in body size and breeding system in primates. *Nature* 272:610–11
196. Leutenegger, W. 1982. Scaling of sexual dimorphism in body weight and canine size in primates. *Folia Primatol.* 37:163–76
197. Leutenegger, W. 1982. Sexual dimorphism in nonhuman primates. See Ref. 39, pp. 11–36
198. Leutenegger, W., Cheverud, J. M. 1982. Correlates of sexual dimorphism in primates. *Int. J. Primatol.* 3:387–402
198a. Leutenegger, W., Cheverud, J. M. 1985. Sexual dimorphism in primates. The effects of size. See Ref. 52a, pp. 33–50
199. Leutenegger, W., Kelley, J. T. 1977. Relationships of sexual dimorphism in canine size and body size to social, behavioral, and ecological correlates in anthropoid primates. *Primates* 18:177–86
200. Lewontin, R. C. 1974. *The Genetic Basis of Evolutionary Change.* New York: Columbia Univ. Press. 346 pp.
201. Lieberman, L. S. 1982. Normal and abnormal sexual dimorphic patterns of growth and development. See Ref. 39, pp. 263–316
202. Lopez-Contreras, M. E., Farid-Coupal, N., Landaeta de Jimenez, M., Laxague, G. 1983. Sex dimorphism of height in two Venezuelan populations. In *Human Growth and Development,* ed. J. Borms, C. Susanne, M. Hebbelinck, R. Sand, pp. 277–81. New York: Plenum. 836 pp.
203. Lovejoy, C. O. 1981. The origin of man. *Science* 211:341–50
204. Lovejoy, C. O., Johanson, D. C., Coppens, Y. 1982. Hominid lower limb bones recovered from the Hadar formation: 1974–1977 collections. *Am. J. Phys. Anthropol.* 57:679–700
205. Lukacs, J. R. 1984. Cultural variation and the evolution of dental reduction: An interpretation of the evidence from South Asia. *Proc. Ind. Stat. Inst.* 2:252–69
206. Lunt, D. A. 1969. An odontometric study of mediaeval Danes. *Acta Odont. Scand. Suppl.* 55(27):1–173
207. Mann, A. 1971. Hominid and cultural origins. *Man* 7:379–86
208. Mann, A. 1981. The significance of the Sinanthropus casts, and some paleodemographic notes. In *Homo erectus. Papers in Honor of Davidson Black,* ed. B. A. Sigmon, J. S. Cybulski, pp. 41–62. Toronto: Univ. Toronto Press. 271 pp.
209. Martin, E. S. 1936. A study of an Egyptian series of mandibles, with special reference to mathematical methods of sexing. *Biometrika* 28:149–78
210. Martin, R. D. 1980. Sexual dimorphism and the evolution of higher primates. *Nature* 287:273–75
211. Mayr, E. 1972. Sexual selection and natural selection. See Ref. 52, pp. 87–104
212. McCown, E. R. 1982. Sex differences: the female as a baseline for species description. See Ref. 39, pp. 37–84
213. McEachron, D. L. 1984. Hypothesis and explanation in human evolution. *J. Soc. Biol. Struct.* 7:9–15
214. McGrew, W. C. 1975. Patterns of plant food sharing by wild chimpanzees. In *Contemporary Primatology,* ed. S. Kondo, M. Kawai, A. Ehara, pp. 304–9. Basel: Karger. 522 pp.
215. McGrew, W. C. 1979. Evolutionary implications of sex differences in chimpanzee predation and tool use. In *The Great Apes,* ed. D. A. Hamburg, E. R. McCown, pp. 441–64. Menlo Park, Calif: Cummings. 554 pp.
216. McGrew, W. C. 1981. The female chimpanzee as a human evolutionary prototype. In *Woman the Gatherer,* ed. F.

Dahlberg, pp. 35–74. New Haven: Yale Univ. Press. 250 pp.
217. McHenry, H. M. 1984. The common ancestor: A study of the postcranium of *Pan paniscus, Australopithecus,* and other hominoids. See Ref. 161, pp. 201–32
218. McHenry, H. M., Corruccini, R. S. 1980. On the status of *Australopithecus afarensis. Science* 207:1103–4
219. Meiklejohn, C., Schentag, C., Venema, A., Key, P. 1984. Socioeconomic changes and patterns of pathology and variation in the Mesolithic and Neolithic of Western Europe. See Ref. 13, pp. 75–100
220. Meyers, P. 1978. Sexual dimorphism in the size of Vespertilionid bats. *Am. Nat.* 112:701–11
221. Mijsberg, W. A. 1931. On the sexual differences in the teeth of the Javanese. *K. Akad. Wet. Amsterdam Ser. B* 34:1111–15
222. Milton, K., May, M. L. 1976. Body weight, diet, and home range area in primates. *Nature* 259:459–62
223. Mitchell, G. 1979. *Behavioral Sex Differences in Nonhuman Primates.* New York: Van Nostrand/Reinhold. 515 pp.
224. Mobb, G. E., Wood, B. A. 1977. Allometry and sexual dimorphism in the primate innominate bone. *Am. J. Anat.* 150:531–38
225. Moeschler, P. 1966. Structures morphologiques et dimorphisme sexuel: esssai de différenciation métrique. Application à l'os coxal. *Arch. Suisses Anthropol. Gén.* 30:1–56
226. Moorrees, C. F. A. 1957. *The Aleut Dentition. A Correlative Study of Dental Characteristics in a Eskimoid People.* Cambridge: Harvard Univ. Press
227. Murdock, G. P. 1957. Comparative data on the division of labor by sex. *Soc. Forces* 15:551–53
227a. Murdock, G. P., Provost, C. 1973. Factors in the division of labor by sex: A cross cultural analysis. *Ethnology* 12:203–25
228. Nickens, P. R. 1976. Stature reduction as an adaptive response to food production in Mesoamerica. *J. Archaeol. Sci.* 3:31–41
229. Nishida, T. 1981. *The World of Wild Chimpanzees.* Tokyo: Choukoronsha
230. Olson, T. R. 1981. Basicranial morphology of the extant hominoids and Pliocene hominids: The new material from the Hadar Formation, Ethiopia and its significance in early human evolution and taxonomy. In *Aspects of Human Evolution,* ed. C. B. Stringer, pp. 99–128. London: Taylor & Francis. 233 pp.
231. Otte, D. 1979. Historical development of sexual selection theory. See Ref. 4, pp. 1–18
232. Oxnard, C. E. 1983. Sexual dimorphisms in the overall proportions of primates. *Am. J. Primatol.* 4:1–22
233. Oxnard, C. E. 1984. Interpretation and testing in multivariate statistical approaches to physical anthropology: The example of sexual dimorphism in the primates. In *Multivariate Statistical Methods in Physical Anthropology,* ed. G. N. van Vark, W. W. Howells, pp. 193–222. Dordrecht: Reidel. 433 pp.
234. Payne, R. B. 1984. Sexual selection, lek and arena behavior, and sexual size dimorphism in birds. *Ornithol. Monogr.* No. 33. Washington, DC: Am. Orinothol. Union
234a. Perzigian, A. J. 1976. The dentition of the Indian Knoll population: odontometrics and cusp number. *Am. J. Phys. Anthropol.* 44:113–22
235. Phenice, T. W. 1969. A newly developed visual method of sexing the *os pubis. Am. J. Phys. Anthropol.* 30:297–302
236. Pilbeam, D. R., Zwell, M. 1973. The single species hypothesis, sexual dimorphism, and variability in early hominids. *Yearb. Phys. Anthropol.* 16:69–79
237. Pons, J. 1955. Sexual diagnosis of isolated bones of the skeleton. *Hum. Biol.* 27:12–21
238. Post, D. G. 1979. Sexual dimorphism in primates: Some thoughts on causes and correlates. *Am. J. Phys. Anthropol.* 50:471–72 (Abstr.)
239. Post, D. G., Goldstein, S., Melnick, D. 1978. An analysis of cercopithecoid odontometrics. II. Body size, dimorphism, and diet. *Am. J. Phys. Anthropol.* 49:533–44
240. Potter, R. Y. 1972. Univariate versus multivariate differences in tooth size according to sex. *J. Dent. Res.* 51:716–22
241. Ralls, K. 1976. Mammals in which females are larger than males. *Q. Rev. Biol.* 51:245–76
242. Ralls, K. 1977. Sexual dimorphism in mammals: Avian models and unanswered questions. *Am. Nat.* 111:917–38
243. Rathbun, T. A. 1984. Skeletal pathology from the Paleolithic through the Metal Ages in Iran and Iraq. See Ref. 13, pp. 137–67
244. Reiss, M. 1982. Males bigger, females biggest. *New Sci.* 28:226–29
245. Rensch, B. 1950. Die Abhängigkeit der relativen Sexualdifferenz von der Körpergrösse. *Bonner Zool. Beit.* 1:58–69

246. Reyment, R. A. 1969. Statistical analysis of sexual dimorphism in some groups of living mammals. See Ref. 301, pp. 21–27
247. Rice, R. W. 1984. Sex chromosomes and the evolution of sexual dimorphism. *Evolution* 38:735–42
248. Richman, E. A., Michel, M. E., Schulter-Ellis, F. P., Corruccini, R. S. 1979. Determination of sex by discriminant function analysis of postcranial skeletal measurements. *J. Forensic Sci.* 24:159–67
249. Rodman, P. S., Mitani, J. C. 1985. Social systems and sexual dimorphism of orangutans. In *Primate Societies,* ed. D. Cheney, R. Seyfarth, B. Smuts, T. Struhsaker, R. Wrangham. Chicago: Univ. Chicago Press. In press
250. Schoener, T. W. 1969. Models of optimum size for solitary predators. *Am. Nat.* 103:277–313
251. Schoener, T. W. 1977. Competition and the niche in reptiles. *Biol. Reptiles* 7:35–136
252. Schranze, D. 1964. Morphologische untersheide männlicher und weiblichen Zähne. *Acta Morphol.* 12:401–6
253. Schultz, A. H. 1930. The skeleton of the trunk and limbs of higher primates. *Hum. Biol.* 2:303–438
254. Schultz, A. H. 1949. Sex differences in the pelves of primates. *Am. J. Phys. Anthropol.* 7:887–964
255. Schultz, A. H. 1962. Metric age changes and sex differences in primates. *Z. Morphol. Anthropol.* 52:239–55
256. Schultz, A. H. 1963. Age changes, sex differences, and variability as factors in the classification of primates. In *Classification and Human Evolution,* ed. S. L. Washburn, pp. 85–115. Chicago: Aldine. 371 pp.
257. Schultz, A. H. 1965. The cranial capacity and orbital volume of hominoids according to age and sex. In *Homenaje a Juan Comas en su 65 Anniversario,* Vol. 2. Mexico City: Libros de Mexico
258. Schultz, A. H. 1969. *The Life of Primates.* New York: Universe. 281 pp.
259. Sciulli, P. W. 1979. Size and morphology of the permanent dentition in prehistoric Ohio Valley Amerindians. *Am. J. Phys. Anthropol.* 50:615–26
260. Segebarth-Orban, R. 1980. An evaluation of the sexual dimorphism of the human innominate bone. *J. Hum. Evol.* 9:601–8
261. Selander, R. K. 1966. Sexual dimorphism and differential niche utilization in birds. *Condor* 68:133–51
262. Selander, R. K. 1972. Sexual selection and dimorphism in birds. See Ref. 52, pp. 180–230
263. Selmer-Olsen, R. 1949. An odontometric study of the Norwegian Lapps. *Skrifter Det Norvske Videnskaps-Akademi I Oslo, Mathematsk-Naturvidenskapelig Klasse* 65:1–168
264. Shaklee, W. E., Knox, C. W., Marsden, S. J. 1952. The inheritance of the sex difference of body weight in turkeys. *Poultry Sci.* 31:822–25
265. Shine, R. 1979. Sexual selection and sexual dimorphism in the Amphibia. *Copeia* 1979:297–306
266. Sibley, C. G., Ahlquist, J. E. 1984. The phylogeny of the hominoid primates, as indicated by DNA-DNA hybridization. *J. Mol. Evol.* 20:2–15
267. Slatkin, M. 1984. Ecological causes of sexual dimorphism. *Evolution* 38:622–30
268. Smith, F. H. 1980. Sexual differences in European Neanderthal crania with special reference to the Krapina crania. *J. Hum. Evol.* 9:359–75
269. Smith, P., Bar-Yosef, O., Sillen, A. 1984. Archaeological and skeletal evidence for dietary change during the Late Pleistocene/Early Holocene in the Levant. See Ref. 13, pp. 101–36
270. Stamps, J. A. 1983. Sexual selection, sexual dimorphism, and territoriality. In *Lizard Ecology,* ed. R. B. Huey, E. R. Pianka, T. W. Schoener, pp. 169–204. Cambridge: Harvard Univ. Press. 501 pp.
271. Steel, F. L. D. 1962. The sexing of long bones with reference to the St. Brides's series of identified skeletons. *J. R. Anthropol. Inst.* 92:212–22
272. Steele, D. G. 1976. The estimation of sex on the basis of the talus and calcaneus. *Am. J. Phys. Anthropol.* 45:581–88
273. Stewart, T. D. 1984. Sex determination in the skeleton by guess and by measurement. *Am. J. Phys. Anthropol.* 12:385–92
274. Stini, W. A. 1969. Nutritional stress and growth: Sex difference in adaptive response. *Am. J. Phys. Anthropol.* 31:417–26
275. Stini, W. A. 1972. Malnutrition, body size, and proportion. *Ecol. Food Nutr.* 1:121–26
276. Stini, W. A. 1975. Adaptive strategies of human populations under nutritional stress. In *Biosocial Interrelations in Populational Adaptations,* ed. E. Watts, F. E. Johnston, G. W. Lasker, pp. 19–41. The Hague: Mouton. 412 pp.
277. Stini, W. A. 1982. Sexual dimorphism and nutrient reserves. See Ref. 39, pp. 391–419
278. Stini, W. A. 1985. Growth rates and sexual dimorphism in evolutionary perspec-

tive. In *The Analysis of Prehistoric Diets*, ed. R. I. Gilbert, J. H. Mielke, pp. 191–226. Orlando: Academic. 436 pp.
279. Storer, R. W. 1966. Dimorphism and food in accipiters. *Auk* 83:423–36
280. Strum, S. C. 1981. Processes and products of change: Baboon predatory behavior at Gilgil. In *Omnivorous Primates*, ed. R. S. O. Harding, G. Teleki, pp. 255–302. New York: Columbia Univ. Press. 673 pp.
281. Susman, R. L., Stern, J. T., Jungers, W. L. 1984. Arboreality and bipedality in the Hadar hominids. *Folia Primatol.* 43:113–56
282. Takahata, Y., Hasegawa, T., Nishida, T. 1984. Chimpanzee predation in the Mahale Mountains from August 1979 to May 1982. *Int. J. Primatol.* 5:213–33
283. Teleki, G. 1981. The omnivorous diet and eclectic feeding habits of chimpanzees in Gombe National Park, Tanzania. See Ref. 280, pp. 303–43
284. Thieme, F. P., Schull, W. T. 1957. Sex determination from the skeleton. *Hum. Biol.* 29:242–73
285. Thomsen, S. 1955. *Dental Morphology and Occlusion in the People of Tristan da Cunha*. Oslo: Det Norvske Videnskap Akademi. 75 pp.
285a. Tilson, R. L., Tenaza, R. P. 1976. Monogamy and duetting in an Old World monkey. *Nature* 263:320–21
286. Tobias, P. V. 1962. On the increasing stature of the Bushmen. *Anthropos* 57:801–10
287. Trinkaus, E. 1980. Sexual differences in Neandertal limb bones. *J. Hum. Evol.* 9:377–97
288. Trinkaus, E. 1984. Neandertal pubic morphology and gestation length. *Curr. Anthropol.* 25:509–14
289. Trivers, R. L. 1972. Parental investment and sexual selection. See Ref. 52, pp. 136–79
290. Truswell, A. S., Hansen, J. D. L. 1976. Medical research among the !Kung. In *Kalahari Hunters and Gatherers*, ed. R. B. Lee, I. DeVore, pp. 166–94. Cambridge: Harvard Univ. Press. 408 pp.
291. Van Gerven, D. P. 1972. The contribution of size and shape variation to patterns of sexual dimorphism of the human femur. *Am. J. Phys. Anthropol.* 37:49–60
292. Van Gerven, D. P., Oakland, G. B. 1974. Univariate and multivariate statistical models in the analysis of human sexual dimorphism. *Statistician* 22:256–68
293. Vlček, E. 1971. *Symposium über die Alters- und Geschlechtsbestimmung an Skelettmaterial*. Prague: Narodni Muzeum v Praze. 180 pp.
294. Wade, M. J. 1979. Sexual selection and variance in reproductive success. *Am. Nat.* 114:742–46
294a. Wade, M. J., Arnold, S. J. 1980. The intensity of sexual selection in relation to male sexual behavior, female choice, and sperm precedence. *Anim. Behav.* 28:446–61
295. Washburn, S. L. 1948. Sex differences in the pubic bone. *Am. J. Phys. Anthropol.* 6:199–208
295a. Washburn, S. L. 1949. Sex differences in the pubic bone of Bantu and Bushmen. *Am. J. Phys. Anthropol.* 7:425–32
296. Washburn, S. L. 1968. On Holloway's 'tools and teeth'. *Am. Anthropol.* 70:97–101
297. Washburn, S. L. 1978. What we can't learn about people from apes. *Hum. Nat.* 1:70–75
298. Washburn, S. L., Ciochon, R. L. 1974. Canine teeth: Notes on controversies in the study of human evolution. *Am. Anthropol.* 76:765–84
299. Weiss, K. M. 1972. On the systematic bias in skeletal sexing. *Am. J. Phys. Anthropol.* 16:69–79
300. West, M. M., Konner, M. 1976. The role of the father: An anthropological perspective. In *The Role of the Father in Development*, ed. M. Lamb, pp. 185–218. New York: Wiley. 582 pp.
301. Westerman, G. E. G., ed. 1969. *Sexual Dimorphism in Fossil Metazoa and Taxonomic Implications*. Stuttgart: Nagele & Obermiller. 250 pp.
302. Wickler, W., Seibt, U. 1983. Monogamy: an ambiguous concept. See Ref. 16, pp. 33–50
303. Wolanski, N., Kasprzak, E. 1976. Stature as a measure of environmental change. *Curr. Anthropol.* 17:548–52
304. Wolfe, L. D., Gray, J. P. 1982. A cross-cultural investigation into the sexual dimorphism of stature. See Ref. 39, pp. 197–230
305. Wolfe, L. D., Gray, J. P. 1982. Subsistence patterns and human sexual dimorphism of stature. *J. Hum. Evol.* 11:575–80
306. Wolpoff, M. H. 1973. Posterior tooth size, body size and diet in South African gracile australopithecines. *Am. J. Phys. Anthropol.* 39:375–94
307. Wolpoff, M. H. 1975. Sexual dimorphism in the australopithecines. In *Paleoanthropology: Morphology and Paleoecology*, ed. R. H. Tuttle, pp. 245–84. The Hague: Mouton. 453 pp.
308. Wolpoff, M. H. 1976. Primate models for australopithecine sexual dimorphism. *Am. J. Phys. Anthropol.* 45:497–510

309. Wolpoff, M. H. 1976. Some aspects of the evolution of early hominid sexual dimorphism. *Curr. Anthropol.* 17:579–606
310. Wolpoff, M. H. 1980. Cranial remains of Middle Pleistocene European hominids. *J. Hum. Evol.* 9:339–58
311. Wolpoff, M. H. 1980. *Paleoanthropology.* New York: Knopf. 329 pp.
312. Wolpoff, M. H. 1982. *Ramapithecus* and hominid origins. *Curr. Anthropol.* 23:501–22
313. Wolpoff, M. H. 1985. Tooth size—body size scaling in a human population: Theory and practice of an allometric analysis. See Ref. 52a, pp. 273–318
314. Wood, B. A. 1976. The nature and basis of sexual dimorphism in the primate skeleton. *J. Zool. London* 180:15–134
315. Woolbright, L. L. 1983. Sexual selection and size dimorphism in anuran amphibians. *Am. Nat.* 121:110–19
316. Wrangham, R. W., Smuts, B. B. 1980. Sex differences in the behavioral ecology of chimpanzees in the Gombe National Park, Tanzania. *J. Reprod. Fert. Suppl.* 28:13–21
317. Wu, R., Xu, Q., Lu, Q. 1983. Morphological features of *Ramapithecus* and *Sivapithecus* and their phylogenetic relationships—morphology and comparison of the crania. *Acta Anthropol. Sin.* 2:1–10
318. Zihlman, A. L. 1976. Sexual dimorphism and its behavioral implications in early hominids. In *Les Plus Anciens Hominidés*, ed. P. V. Tobias, Y. Coppens, pp. 268–93. The Hague: Mouton. 464 pp.
319. Zihlman, A. L. 1978. Women and evolution. Part II: Subsistence and social organization among early hominids. *Signs* 4:4–20
320. Zihlman, A. L. 1979. Pygmy chimpanzee morphology and the interpretation of early hominids. *S. Afr. J. Sci.* 75:165–68
321. Zihlman, A. L. 1982. Sexual dimorphism in *Homo erectus*. In *L'Homo erectus et la Place de L'Homme de Tautavel parmi les Hominidés Fossiles,* ed. H. de Lumley, pp. 949–70. Nice: Louis-Jean
322. Zihlman, A. L. 1984. Body build and tissue composition in *Pan paniscus* and *Pan troglodytes,* with comparisons to other hominoids. See Ref. 161, pp. 179–200
323. Zihlman, A. L., Cramer, D. L. 1978. Skeletal differences between pygmy and common chimpanzees. *Folia Primatol.* 29:86–94

BIOANTHROPOLOGICAL RESEARCH IN DEVELOPING COUNTRIES

Rebecca Huss-Ashmore and Francis E. Johnston

Department of Anthropology, University of Pennsylvania, Philadelphia, PA 19104

INTRODUCTION

In recent years the number of biological anthropologists involved in research in developing countries has increased. This upsurge of interest can be traced in part to an increased awareness of the problems faced by populations in these countries and to an increased realization that anthropologists are well equipped to address those problems. Though the problems themselves are not new, the emphasis on short-term adaptation is new. Physical anthropology's traditional emphasis on long-term adaptation in racial studies, skeletal anatomy, and genetic adaptation involved a relative neglect of short-term biological problems and responses. The current shift in emphasis from prehistoric and modern industrialized populations to those of the Third World acknowledges the importance of short-term problems in understanding human adaptation.

Problems in Developing Countries

Developing countries, whatever their geographic location, can be defined by a series of common economic and social conditions. Most of their population is rural and is involved in small-holder subsistence agriculture. Industrialization is minimal and the opportunities for nonfarm employment few. Limited opportunities for formal education restrict the supply of technically trained manpower. The juxtaposition of an educated elite and a rural peasant majority produces a wide discrepancy in incomes.

Developing countries also share a number of environmental and social conditions that interest human biologists and bioanthropologists. These include problems of climate, disease, population, and resources. Although the precise nature of these problems varies from region to region, in general they have two properties that make them important for research. First, these environmental and social conditions are potentially stressful. As such, they pose a set of adaptive problems for human populations seeking to persist in their environment. Second, these conditions are not static. With modernization, many developing countries are experiencing unprecedented rates of change. This change may affect food supplies, disease vectors, and even social relationships. Thus traditional coping strategies may no longer be effective in preventing stress.

The effects of environmental stress and change are central problems in biological anthropology today. Following the example of biological ecologists, anthropologists have studied human adaptive strategies in terms of access to resources and avoidance of stress (23). However, unlike ecologists, biological anthropologists have dealt predominantly with environmental stressors, almost to the exclusion of resources and opportunities. Research in developing countries has concentrated attention primarily on *lack* of resources. An exception to this trend is the study of wild plant and animal resources used as food and medicine by both foraging and farming populations (124).

Change is also an important theme in current (as well as past) bioanthropological research. Changes in prehistoric subsistence ecology are presumed to account for large biological changes in the affected human populations. These biological changes include changes in dental and cranial morphology, changes in growth and nutritional status, and such genetic changes as the development of the sickle-cell trait in response to malarial exposure. Such changes may also have far-reaching demographic consequences—settled agriculture is believed to have increased rates of both mortality and fertility. In developing countries today, changes in diet, health care, and disease have altered mortality patterns, leading to unprecedented rates of population growth.

In this review, we concentrate upon the issues of childhood growth, food supply and nutrition, health and disease, and population processes. Such topics are the current focus of interest among biological anthropologists who work in these areas. It is obvious that these research interests are in no way the exclusive property of anthropologists. Rather, they are broad problem areas requiring the expertise of many disciplines for their eventual resolution. Physicians, nutritionists, demographers, public health workers, ecologists, economists, and planners, among others, have all contributed to the corpus of interdisciplinary work on these problems. Because of the dual nature of their training (both as biologists and as anthropologists), bioanthropologists can contribute in particularly valuable ways.

Because of the interdisciplinary nature of the research and the voluminous literature on each of these topics, we review the literature selectively. We have not included all material published in the last five years, nor have we limited ourselves to work done by anthropologists. Rather, we have concentrated on issues currently being explored by bioanthropologists who work in developing countries. We have ignored much of the work in such countries that might be of general anthropological interest but is unrelated to the issues of development (e.g. effects of hypoxia on growth). In choosing this approach, we hope to outline a series of problems that constitute research priorities for these countries in the near future.

Why Bioanthropology?

Bioanthropology is particularly suited to exploring the problems of less-developed countries. The complexity of problems in these areas requires the broad training and holistic approach long associated with anthropologists of all subdisciplines. Biological anthropologists, particularly those interested in biocultural problems, have adopted a number of methodological approaches that allow them to deal with this complexity (23, 257, 455). First, the strong ecological emphasis of many bioanthropologists results in a focus upon the interactions of populations with their physical and social environments. These researchers also tend to approach their research from a systems standpoint, emphasizing multiple causes and responses. As a result, their theoretical orientations are nonreductionist and their analytic methods multivariate.

Further, bioanthropologists are concerned with variability. This concern provides valuable balance to the more normative approaches often taken by economists and sociologists in studying the impact of development. Priorities in this field therefore often include the development of basic methodological tools for the description and quantification of variability among individuals and groups. Use of these tools by bioanthropologists (and others) in measuring growth and nutritional status has provided insight into the effects of economic and dietary change on children in the developing world.

The juxtaposition of macro- and micro-scale methodologies may prove to be one of the most valuable contributions of anthropology to the study of biological problems in less-developed countries. On the one hand, anthropologists have traditionally concentrated on the fine-grained study of disease dynamics in small populations. On the other hand they have also begun to use the epidemiological techniques and computer-assisted analyses of large-scale public health studies. The application of these dual approaches to problems of growth, nutrition, and population in the Third World is a positive step toward the integrated analysis of these complex problems.

GROWTH AND DEVELOPMENT

The Evaluation of Growth Status

The growth of children is widely recognized as one of the more sensitive and reliable indicators of health and nutritional status in human populations (243). Patterns of growth and development of children and youth have been described for most world regions containing developing countries, but the interpretation of these numerous studies is still problematic. Much of the data are questionable, usually because of small sample sizes, lack of sample characterization, or unknown reliability. In addition, the use of different reference standards has hindered comparability.

A controversial issue in the study of the growth of children and youth in less-developed countries concerns the selection of an appropriate data set to serve as a reference in the evaluation of growth. Though many investigators refer to such a set of "reference standards," the data are not intended to be a "norm"—i.e. a standard to be attained. Rather, reference data are measures to which growth may be compared.

The controversy arises over whether to use (a) a single international set of reference data or (b) local data, likely to be ethnically and geographically more similar to the study population than an international standard would be. This issue has been discussed by a number of authors (e.g. 167, 189, 231, 245, 246, 453).

It is important to remember that not all samples qualify as reference data. Reference values are not simply data of convenience, but are precise estimates of the means, the standard deviations, and the percentiles of the appropriate age and sex categories of a well-defined population (245). The numbers of individuals in each category should be large enough [Waterlow et al (453) argue for 200] and the statistical procedures sufficiently reliable to insure that values at least as far from the mean as the 5th and 95th percentiles are estimated accurately.

Many investigators have suggested that local samples, geographically and ethnically similar to the group being evaluated, should be used to provide reference values. By and large, such contentions result from a belief that differences in growth status among populations reflect, to a significant degree, genetic differences. Local standards of reference are seen to provide a better control over these genetic factors.

Theoretically speaking, an evaluation of growth status should be based on reference values reflecting shared climatic, historical, and ethnic determinants. However, the task of obtaining reference data that fulfill the necessary criteria is a formidable one. Virtually all who have considered this topic in its complexity have agreed that more is lost by relying on poorly constructed standards, derived from inadequate samples drawn from undefined population groups, than by the careful use of a single international set of reference values (245).

The efforts required to produce reference data are beyond the resources of all individual investigators and most nations. The data set most widely accepted as an international standard of reference is therefore that of the US National Center for Health Statistics (191). The NCHS data are based upon a national probability sample of children and youth from the continental United States with numbers in each age/sex cell ranging from 300 to 1600. Furthermore, the percentiles have been developed by smoothing techniques involving a cubic spline function. Virtually all international bodies concerned with growth assessment have recommended that the NCHS data be used as an international reference standard (230).

Descriptive Studies

One of the major ongoing studies of childhood growth in a developing country has been conducted in Guatemala City, sponsored by the *Colegio Americano de Guatemala* (American School) and, more recently, the *Universidad del Valle de Guatemala* (University of the Valley of Guatemala). From its beginning in 1953, this study has examined longitudinally the children and youth attending several schools in Guatemala City. The schools have been selected to provide a cross-section of the school-attending population, from the highest SES to the urban poor. Because of its design, and because of the large number of subjects followed serially (in the tens of thousands), this study provides a unique opportunity for the description and comparison of the growth of children of different SES levels within a developing country. In particular, this study permits the examination of the growth of a large sample of children and youth from a developing country who, as a group, are free of the stresses affecting the poor of such countries.

A number of papers have come from the American School study, beginning in 1973, when Johnston, Borden & MacVean presented descriptive statistics for the upper SES component of this population: (*a*) height and weight, by sex, between 6 and 17 years; and (*b*) whole-year velocities, centered on age as well as on peak velocities (247). Additional data are available for height and weight (43, 44, 248, 253) and for body composition (44, 245, 246, 249).

Together these studies indicate that upper-class Guatemalan school children, as would be expected, are taller, weigh more, and have greater stores of fat and lean tissue than their lower-SES age and sex peers. Furthermore, the growth of children in the upper-class samples is comparable to that of those in North American or European reference data. This suggests that the lower body size and smaller fat and muscle stores of the poor of less-developed countries (LDCs) are environmental in origin.

There is a continuum of body size in Guatemalan children according to the adequacy of their environments (e.g. 43). Johnston et al (245a) have compared the heights and weights of five samples of Guatemalan 7-year-olds. Two school samples are from the American School study. A third was drawn from a disadvantaged community on the outskirts of Guatemala City composed of refugees from the earthquake of 1976 (250a). Sample four was semiurban, from an indigenous Indian community located a few kilometers from the capital. The fifth, a rural sample, consisted of Ladino children from the countryside to the east of Guatemala City who were part of a nutritional supplementation study sponsored by the INCAP (Nutritional Institute of Guatemala and Panama). There was a clear and consistent gradation in the sample means of both males and females, from the high SES sample through the rural group.

Further insight into the growth of children from developing countries has been provided by the work of Malina and his colleagues in the Oaxaca Valley, Mexico. This project has gone on for some 15 years and has focused on measures of body size, composition, and maturation, and their relationships to environmental and secular variables (56, 209, 290, 291).

Zapotec-speaking children from a marginal agricultural community in the Valley are among the smallest reported for Mexico, and are significantly smaller than either rural Ladino or urban residents (56). Furthermore, the rural sample is larger in body size than the urban one, indicating that, in this instance, migration to the city has not resulted in improved growth (289).

Rates of maturation of Oaxaca children, as indicated by ages at menarche of the females, are delayed. The median age, estimated by probit-analysis, in 1972 was 14.3 years (291), which did not differ significantly from a rural Zapotec sample studied in 1978. These ages are more than 1.5 years greater than those reported for the four major urban centers of Mexico but are comparable to those reported for disadvantaged females elsewhere in the world (290).

Skeletal growth of children from Oaxaca has been described by Himes et al (209), who measured the dimensions of the second metacarpals of 364 6–14-year-olds on hand-wrist radiographs. Along with other investigators, they found a correlation between measures of compact bone and stature; and as would be expected from the reduced body size of Oaxaca children, they reported reduction in metacarpal dimensions. However, the reductions in compact bone mass were relatively greater than the reductions in stature, a finding also reported elsewhere in undernourished children.

Data on the growth and development of children from elsewhere in the world do not provide the comprehensiveness over time, combined with adequate sample sizes and subsample variability, that is found in the Guatemala City and the Oaxaca projects. Much of the less-current existing data are summarized by Eveleth & Tanner (112). In the remainder of this section, we review selected studies published since then for comparative purposes.

Recent descriptions of the growth of Southeast Asian children have been reported by Olness et al (350) and Bailey et al (19). Olness and her colleagues measured the heights and weights of 1650 Indochinese children, 9 months to 13 years old, living in Lao and Cambodian refugee camps and surrounding Thai villages. Children from the camps were generally free of acute illnesses. The authors compared their measurements to the reference data of the US National Center For Health Statistics (NCHS), as well as to published data on village children of "low or average economic status" from northern Thailand. Differences were expressed as Z-scores, or the number of standard deviation units from the reference mean. The children had small body sizes with mean Z-scores for weight or height for age always below -1.7. Weights for height were also below the US reference, but by not as much. Compared to village children from northern Thailand, the refugee groups showed some reduction in body size.

Bailey and his colleagues have reported on a longitudinal study of over 1000 infants and children from 29 villages in Thailand's northern Chang Mai province. The villages are described as socioeconomically homogeneous and free of marked food shortages (19). The rice consumed in the villages had been fortified with amino acids, thiamin, vitamin A, and iron. Compared to the NCHS data, the children grew in body length between the 5th and the 10th percentiles (corresponding to Zs of -1.3 and -1.6) until 18 months, falling considerably below the 5th percentile thereafter. Weight and head circumference showed a similar pattern, although the differences from NCHS values were not as great.

Data on body composition followed a similar pattern, with triceps skinfolds initially below the 3rd percentile relative to British reference data, climbing to the 25th–50th in early childhood, and then dropping back to the 10th–25th percentiles from ages 4 through 9. In a subsequent paper (20), these investigators report that, after infancy, subscapular fat is added more rapidly than triceps fat, a phenomenon similar to what has been reported for other nonwestern populations.

The study by Bailey and his colleagues also included skeletal age (SA), assessed by hand-wrist radiographs. The investigators report that, relative to chronological age, SA shows a steadily increasing lag in both sexes, reaching a maximum (at age 9) of 3 years in males and 4 in females (19).

Studies from other regions of the developing world also reveal a spectrum of small body size, reduced fat and lean tissue stores, and, in some instances, a low weight-for-height ratio (468). Delayed growth, relative to NCHS reference data, has been reported by El-Nofely (107) for Nubian children and by Sukkar et al (419) for rural Sudanese children from Khartoum. These two studies also reported reduced skinfold thicknesses and, for the sample from Khartoum, a median menarcheal age of 14.0, calculated by probit analysis. Menarche occurred 1–1.5 years later than is usually observed in developed nations.

Similar findings are reported for sub-Saharan Africa (205, 279, 374), India (200, 228), and South America (171). On a worldwide basis, Meredith (323) has compared the body size of 8-year-olds from different regions; as expected, samples drawn from less-developed countries reveal smaller means.

The study by Hauspie et al (200) is of particular interest since it applied a sophisticated mathematical model to longitudinal data. The Preece-Baines function (370) was fitted to the growth-in-height records of 303 males and 260 females from middle-class families near Calcutta. Of the differences in adult height between the Indian sample and British controls, Hauspie et al (200) found that, in males, all could be accounted for by preadolescent growth; in females the figure was approximately 60%.

Factors Responsible For Growth Variation

The growth of children and youth of developing nations is reduced relative to their age and sex peers from developed countries. This reduction is minimal in the first postnatal year; but then growth falls off sharply through 3 years, followed either by a parallel course or even a slight catch-up, depending upon the measurement and the sample. Linear measures are affected more than are measures of body mass and composition, and males are generally affected more than females. Maturation rates, indicated by either skeletal age or the age at menarche, are likewise affected, indicating that LDC children grow less and mature more slowly than children comprising the international reference standards. Greater differences are seen when measures are related to age (e.g. height-for-age) than when other indexes are used (e.g. weight-for-height). This indicates that children from LDCs are proportionately smaller than their peers from either developed nations or upper-SES groups in their own country.

HEREDITARY AND ENVIRONMENTAL FACTORS The interpretation of the data on growth and maturation is controversial. The primary issue concerns the relative contribution of hereditary and environmental factors to intergroup variation. The biggest obstacle in studies of heredity vs environment is the difficulty of designing research that will not be confounded by the interaction of genetic and environmental factors. Almost without fail, those inhabitants of any LDC who reflect most closely its indigenous gene pool experience the poorest environments.

Despite these problems, a body of data has now accumulated that provides a consistent set of answers to the question of the hereditary and environmental determinants of growth retardation among peoples of the world's developing countries. Environmental factors strongly regulate growth in body size and composition and the rate of biological maturation (120, 288).

In contrast, genetic determinants of body shape and proportion are more resistant to the environment. While environmental components of growth in shape can be demonstrated, the body proportions characteristic of ethnic groups seem to maintain themselves across a range of environmental conditions.

Evidence for the importance of the environment has come from several studies that used different designs. In one of the earliest, Habicht et al (189) analyzed the differences between mean height and weight of preschool children from a number of published studies. The differences among high-SES samples from developed and less-developed countries showed a range of variation of

3% in height and 6% in weight. In contrast, the differences between high- and low-SES samples within LDCs showed a range of 12% in height and 30% in weight. The authors concluded that differences between samples reflected environmental factors associated with SES and that ethnic differences in growth potential were, on a global basis, minor.

In 1976, Johnston et al (253) reported on a longitudinal analysis of the growth in height of a sample of participants in the American School of Guatemala study. All subjects were from the highest level of Guatemalan society. The sample was subdivided into individuals of Guatemalan ancestry and those of European and North American heritage who had lived in Guatemala for their primary and secondary school years. A third group, taken from the literature, consisted of children of North American ancestry, participants in the Berkeley Growth Study.

Growth records were fitted to a double logistic model, permitting the estimation of a number of parameters of growth for each individual. Of all parameters, however, differences were found in only two, growth during childhood and during adolescence. The Western European/North American children growing up in Guatemala differed from their genetically similar US peers in the amount of growth during childhood, but not in growth during adolescence. The authors interpreted these results as supporting the study of Habicht et al (189), indicating that growth during childhood at that SES level was regulated by environmental factors. However, population genetic factors seemed to predominate during the adolescent phase.

In a third study, Frisancho et al (144) examined this issue in Quechua and Mestizo children and youth living in a single community in Peru at an altitude of 1320 m. Within each group, subjects were classed as being of either good or poor nutritional status, and height was compared between nutritional status groups (matched for ethnicity) and between ethnic groups (matched for nutritional status). The results were similar to those of Johnston et al (253). During childhood, nutritional status differences were four to five times greater than differences by ethnicity. During the adolescent years, however, only a two- to threefold differential was observed.

Taken together, these studies indicate that growth differences between groups reflect environmental factors during childhood. However, during the adolescent years, genetic factors play a role and cannot be ignored. Adult size results from a blend of hereditary and environmental factors, though environmental determinants predominate.

Other studies find the environment crucial in the regulation of growth. Included among these are the many conducted around the world which have measured changes through time in the size of children (and adults) of the same age. Increasing body size has been documented over the past century in Europe and North America (324, 424). While other factors may contribute, the overwhelming weight of evidence indicates that environmental changes, especially improved health care and increased caloric intake (444, 445), are responsible for this trend. On the other hand, in LDCs, the few relevant studies conducted among the disadvantaged have failed to reveal a significant secular trend (208, 211).

Some authors have approached the problem of the regulation of growth by the analysis of heritability for human body measures, derived from parent/offspring correlations (335). They have postulated that, where the environments are poor, heritabilities would be reduced due to an increase in the environmental component of the variability (see 300 for a review). However, Martorell et al (300) found no reductions in parent-child or sib-sib correlations of malnourished Guatemalan children compared to those reported for European samples. Likewise, in their study of growth in a rural Colombian village, Mueller & Titcomb (336) found no reduction in such correlations, despite the fact that the villagers suffered from suboptimal nutriture. Mueller & Titcomb hypothesized that the existence of a correlation between offspring and parental environments would keep the heritability values high, even though the growth dimensions in question were affected by the environment. This hypothesis was supported by a study of the correlation of measurements at birth of Taiwanese siblings (365). Each mother had received a nutritional supplement during the pregnancy of the second sibling, but not the first. A control sample, where no supplementation had occurred, was also analyzed. Correlations were reduced where supplementation was a factor, suggesting the importance of the correlation of parental and offspring environments.

ENVIRONMENTAL FACTORS The role of disadvantaged environments in the small body size of inhabitants of LDCs seems well established. Furthermore, the crucial period for long-term environmental effects seems to be the years of childhood. What, then, are the environmental factors that have been identified?

Nutritient intake is, of course, crucial to the growth process. The malnutrition so prevalent in the developing world is widely accepted as the primary factor in poor growth. The role of nutrition as a specific variable is considered in a subsequent section of this review. In this section, we focus upon other factors, but it is important to keep in mind that none of these factors operates independently. Environmental components operate as part of an ecosystem, and the pathways by which they affect growth involve complex interactions with other components (78).

Socioeconomic status, a variable frequently used to characterize groups being compared, is composed of many factors—e.g. nutritional status, disease prevalence, health status, and life history. Because of its global nature, it is almost universally correlated to growth; in fact, growth status is frequently used as an indicator of socioeconomic inequity (38). In LDCs, socioeconomic correlates of growth have been demonstrated for urban Guatemalan children (43–45). Compared to upper-SES samples, lower-SES school students were smaller, had smaller stores of fat and muscle, and showed reduced IQs.

Similar findings come from other regions. Among rural Colombians, adults of higher SES show a slower reduction in stature with aging than those of lower status (211). Socioeconomic factors in growth in other populations have been reviewed by Susanne (420).

Seasonal variations related to growth among children of LDCs have also been reported. In the Oaxaca study, Malina & Himes (292, 293) have reported a seasonality of births and deaths. The seasonal distribution of births seems to reflect the annual agricultural cycle. The distribution of mortality indicated a particular risk associated with the rainy season. However, the major component of the seasonal distribution was an excess of deaths due to gastrointestinal disorders among 1–4-year-olds. There was no seasonal component in infant mortality, presumably due to the protection afforded by breast feeding.

Seasonal effects associated with the rainy season have also been shown in rural Taiwan and The Gambia of West Africa. In Taiwan, mothers weighed less during the rainy months, whether or not they were pregnant or lactating (3). The mean birth weights were also lower in this period, and the number of low birth weight infants was disproportionately high as well. In The Gambia, rates of growth in height and weight were lowest during the late rains (39). Migration status may also affect growth, largely through differences in socioeconomic status and its nutritional and health correlates; but the data are not clear. In their study of Guatemala City children, Bogin & MacVean (44) found that children of rural-born parents were shorter than those whose parents were urban-born, but children with one parent born in the city and one in the rural area were the tallest of all. In this study the length of time the migrant parents had lived in the city was not controlled.

Infectious disease, so prevalent in LDCs, is in theory an important factor in growth. However, most of the research purporting to demonstrate a relationship is confounded by one or more problems: (*a*) The synergistic effects of nutrition and disease are not controlled (396); (*b*) disease episodes are recorded from retrospective reports without identification of the responsible pathogens; and/or (*c*) many analyses are rendered invalid by failure to control for unreported periods. Nevertheless, the available research does suggest an effect of disease upon growth that is independent of a concomitant reduction in nutrient intake, or other nutritional effects (313). Episodes of diarrheal disease are associated with reduced growth, especially in weight. This has been reported for Guatemala (302), Mexico (73), Belize (238), and Taiwan (26). Baumgartner & Mueller (26) report a relationship to lower respiratory infections as well, but this has not been verified by other research.

The synergistic relationship of manutrition and disease has been investigated by Martorell et al (298), who examined the effects of illness upon dietary intakes of malnourished Guatemalan children. The presence of common symptoms of disease was associated with a reduction of nearly 20% in estimated food intake, equivalent to 175 kcal and 4.8 g protein. This suggests that infections have a marked impact upon nutritional status in children of LDCs.

NUTRITION AND MALNUTRITION IN LESS-DEVELOPED COUNTRIES

Countless books and articles in the popular and scientific press attest to the ubiquitous nature and numerous effects of human malnutrition in LDCs (24, 53, 79, 334, 421, 465). Perhaps because of their high visibility, nutritional problems in developing countries are currently a major focus of anthropologists who work there. Both biological and sociocultural anthropologists have become increasingly involved in the study of food systems and their consequences for nutritional status. Current work in Asia, Africa, and Latin America is aimed at documenting (a) traditional diets and their effects, and (b) the causes and consequences of dietary change. In addition, anthropologists have joined nutritionists and public health personnel in their search for the causes of childhood malnutrition.

Almost all societies in the developing world today base their subsistence on agriculture or an agro-pastoral adaptation. For most, the food production system now contains both traditional elements (cultigens, technology, labor patterns) and elements of modernization. The latter may show up as changes in agricultural technology (plows, tractors), changes in marketing strategy, and changes in crops or other products produced. The introduction of cash cropping, and the linking of pastoralists to international markets has in many cases profoundly affected local diets (91, 196, 432). While some of these changes are positive—increasing crop yields and household incomes—others appear to have had a negative effect on overall nutritional status.

The Assessment of Nutritional Status

Nutritional status refers to the state of nutriture of an individual or a specific group. The term may refer to a specific nutrient (e.g. zinc) or to a class of nutrients (as in the assessment of protein-energy malnutrition) and may apply to either nutritional deficiency or excess (235, 236, 402). Finally, nutritional status may be assessed in a laboratory, using precise instrumentation, or in the field, utilizing other appropriate methods.

Biological anthropologists have most frequently used field methods in assessing nutritional status. Such methods tend to focus either upon the evaluation of dietary intake or upon the measurement of growth and body composition status (i.e. nutritional anthropometry). Methods for determining and evaluating dietary intake have been discussed by nutritionists and nutritional anthropologists (325, 372).

Nutritional anthropometry is recognized widely as an effective means of assessing nutritional status, especially at the level of the population. The measurements taken are used to assess either physical growth or body composition (i.e. the amount of stored fat and protein). The former is a reflection of nutrient adequacy during development (425), the latter an indicator of the excess or deficit of energy and protein (140).

A number of papers have surveyed the applicability of anthropometry to the assessment of nutritional status (e.g. 188, 235, 244, 250, 296, 452, 471). In general, the authors agree that body measurements are especially sensitive indicators of chronic malnutrition, owing to the essential and cumulative role of nutrition in human development. However, the same measurements are generally low in specificity, since a number of environmental factors in addition to nutritional deficiency may drive an individual off his or her developmental course as well as affect the amount of stored fat and muscle.

The low specificity of nutritional anthropometry is not as serious a problem as it might seem. In nutritional ecosystems, such environmental factors as undernutrition, disease, and crowding tend to covary.

The measurements most often used to indicate nutritional status are height (length before 2 years of age) and weight, evaluated against age (see e.g. 453). As in studies of growth, deviations from the reference value are usually expressed in one of three ways: (*a*) as a percentage of the mean; (*b*) as a Z-score (i.e. a standard score); or (*c*) as a percentile. The percentage of the mean, frequently used (269, 317), is difficult to interpret, since the standard deviations of the measurements differ by age. Though some workers utilize percentile values, which permit the classification of an individual, without a program for estimating exact values, such percentiles are only approximations of relative size and cannot be manipulated statistically (452). Z-scores are thus the most useful descriptive statistic for the children of LDCs.

Of the anthropometric indexes available, weight-for-height is used most frequently. Although it is useful as a measure of wasting in acute malnutrition (452), it is not a sensitive indicator of chronic undernutrition, since in this condition both weight and stature tend to be affected similarly. Some investigators have used the ratio of head circumference to chest circumference in assessing nutritional status (235). However, in a study of 1119 Ladino Guatemalan children, Martorell et al (302) found this ratio "to have no power to discriminate either populations or individuals who are well nourished or moderately malnourished."

Reference data are available for evaluating body composition from anthropometry. For skinfolds of children and youth, NCHS data have been presented by Johnson et al (242), while Frisancho (142) has published NCHS data for skinfolds and arm-muscle circumference and area for a broader age range, 1–75 years. Reference data for skinfold thicknesses for Guatemalan children have been developed from American School data by Johnston et al (246).

The main criticism levelled at nutritional anthropometry is that, in identifying the small children of LDCs as chronically malnourished, it includes those who are genetically small. Scholl et al (392) analyzed the longitudinal records of a one-year cohort of 276 Mexican children who had been examined monthly from birth through 36 months of age. Of the total, 72 (26.1%) had been diagnosed from their records as experiencing growth failure due to chronic protein energy malnutrition (PEM). The authors found that, below 6 months of age, a single evaluation length or weight for age was not an adequate predictor of PEM. However, from 12 to 36 months, a single measurement taken at 12 months could identify up to 78% of future 2nd- and 3rd-year cases of PEM.

Effects of Malnutrition on Growth

The effects of malnutrition upon growth, and by extension upon adult body size, have been investigated by many researchers. Their studies have focused upon alterations of the growth process as a result of both chronic and acute PEM and upon the functional outcomes of those alterations. While there has resulted a large body of literature detailing the effects of malnutrition, our knowledge of the subject is not as specific as we would like, nor is it likely ever to be. The major reason lies in our inability to disentangle the covarying components of the environments of children in LDCs. For example, it is unclear to what degree the deserved effects may be attributed to malnutrition and to what degree to the infectious diseases always prevalent in such ecosystems. Researchers have turned increasingly to analytic techniques such as principle components or path analysis in their attempts to differentiate among correlated determinants (see e.g. 26, 143, 244, 251, 252).

Compared to children from nutritionally sound environments, children from LDC environments associated with chronic undernutrition display impaired growth and development (237, 391), body composition (44), and maturation of the skeleton (159, 160, 207, 210, 246, 268, 299), as well as the interrelationships between variables (161).

Malnutrition is associated also with behavioral effects, including impaired cognitive function. These findings are reported both for experimental animals and for children in their natural habitats (48, 79, 176, 177). There seems little doubt that, when malnutrition is severe and acute, neurological deficits may interfere with cognitive function. However, among children displaying mild-to-moderate PEM, the relative importance of nutritional factors and of the social-environmental factors that coexist with them is not completely clear. In such children, growth status correlates with indicators of mental ability.

However, cognitive development is regulated by both nutritional history and other environmental factors, and height and weight are indicators of both. In a comprehensive quasi-experimental study of growth and cognition among rural Guatemalan children, Freeman et al (137) report evidence that nutritional intake affects cognitive development independently of social factors. At the same time, Bogin & MacVean (45) have analyzed correlations among growth and maturation status, socioeconomic status, and cognitive development in urban Guatemalan school children. When SES was controlled, few correlations were found between physical growth and mental development. Finally, Pollitt, Mueller & Leibel (366) have analyzed the relationship between growth and cognition in United States children among whom malnutrition was negligible. In contrast to what is found in LDCs, Pollitt et al report a relationship only for weight-for-height. These authors suggest that in malnourished populations height and weight are measures of nutritional history. In well-nourished samples, height reflects only SES.

One part of the problem, of course, rests with the sensitivity of height and weight to both nutritional and other socioenvironmental variables, while another concerns the fact that nutritional factors can operate directly on the brain, or indirectly through interference with learning (78). In a comprehensive review of the entire subject, Pollitt & Thomson (367) caution against drawing hasty conclusions from studies of animals that may not be generalizable to humans, and from studies with disadvantaged societies in which the complexity of social and nutritional factors may not be controlled adequately. Excluding cases of severe, chronic, and early undernutrition, these authors conclude that even mild-to-moderately malnourished older children and early adolescents possess the structures necessary for appropriate cognitive functioning. What they lack are the "ontogenetic learning experiences and accumulation of information necessary for modernization and industrialization" (367, p. 300).

The long-term biological response of humans to malnutrition during infancy and childhood is a topic of interest to bioanthropologists. Anthropological theory tends, in general, to emphasize adaptive responses of human populations to environmental stress, through evolutionary, developmental, or cultural mechanisms. This theoretical stance has been carried by some workers into their nutritional studies in LDCs. As noted below, Adair (2) has described adaptive aspects of biological changes in pregnant Taiwanese women, emphasizing that, while a comparison to US dietary and anthropometric data would suggest the existence of malnutrition, an examination of pregnancy outcomes indicates that the population "is well adapted" (5).

Stini (414, 415) suggested that the altered growth patterns of populations under nutritional stress may be termed adaptive since they improve the chances for survival. Observations from his study in Colombia support this contention. First, a reduction of mean adult male body weight of 15% (70–60 kg) represents an energy savings of approximately 33% (3243–2351 kcal). Second, the savings may be even more, since the reduction is relatively greater in estimated protein stores than in body weight. Finally, males show a greater reduction than do females, which Stini interprets as adaptive in that the males, who are larger than females, could have their body size reduced without "serious loss of productivity."

Frisancho et al (149) have supported this view in a study of a low-SES community on the outskirts of Cuzco, Peru. They found a greater proportion of surviving offspring (through 19 years of age) for mothers who were below the sample's height mean than for those above the mean. The authors suggest that small body size is adaptive in adverse environments. However, they also stressed the need for prospective studies.

The issue of body size and malnutrition has been approached prospectively by Scholl and her associates (390, 391) in a one-year cohort of children from a rural Mexican village. The children were examined monthly from birth through 36 months, and every 4 months until 7 years. Chronic malnutrition in individuals was defined as failing growth from 6 through 36 months, relative to the overall sample. Of a total of 276 children, 72 developed growth failure and were classified as chronically malnourished. The authors tested two hypotheses: first that clinically severe PEM (i.e. kwashiorkor or marasmus) in the second and third years of life would be more likely among children who at 6 months were larger than among the smaller children, who were growing more slowly. The second hypothesis was that clinically severe PEM would be more frequent among children with chronic mild-to-moderate PEM.

The first hypothesis was rejected. The 19 children who developed clinically severe PEM showed no differences in body size at 6 months. The second hypothesis was accepted. Children who developed severe PEM were significantly more likely to come from the group with chronic malnutrition. The authors concluded that small body size could not be shown to be adaptive.

Other studies have also failed to support the hypothesis of small body size as adaptive. After adjusting for age and number of births in a study of 380 malnourished Guatemalan women, Martorell et al (297) found that the shortest mothers had the greatest infant mortality rate. Even though higher fertility rates compensated for this to a degree, shorter women were still at a slight disadvantage.

Reddy et al (375) investigated functional parameters involved in resistance to infection in children with varying grades of nutritional status. Shorter children were shown to have altered cell-mediated immune responses and impaired phagocytic function.

Thus the adaptive significance of small body size is still an issue. Physiological adaptive responses enable chronically malnourished populations to survive under their typical environmental conditions, but the small body size characteristic of such populations is associated with functional deficits. As a result, the numerically small differences in growth, body size, and body composition documented by biological anthropologists and others are valid indicators of adverse environments and impaired physiological and behavioral function.

Factors Influencing Nutritional Status

TRADITIONAL DIETS   The causes of nutritional imbalance in the developing world are complex (305). There is currently some question whether food systems in these areas have always been subject to failure or whether present nutritional problems are a legacy of colonial and postcolonial policy. Recent work suggests that dietary imbalance may be less a problem of the inherent productive capacity of traditional food systems than of poor storage, maldistribution, and unplanned dietary change (33, 98, 360). Evidence exists that despite occasional shortfalls, indigenous food systems left undisturbed can provide relatively well-balanced diets in sufficient quantity to meet the needs of the human population (163). Such systems may have developed over time as rational adaptations to local environmental and technological limitations. Nutrient balance in traditional systems is maintained partly by a complementary mix of cultigens and partly by the inclusion of wild plant and animal foods (124). In either case, diversity of dietary sources seems to be a key to maintaining nutritional balance.

Many of the best known examples of diets based on complementary domesticates involve a mix of grains and legumes, or the addition of animal protein to diets based on grain or tubers (115, 186). For example, the indigenous New World diet of maize, beans, and squash is generally considered nutritionally sound; the other components compensate for the vitamin and amino acid imbalances of the staple maize. Similarly, the wheat-pulse-yoghurt diet of the Near East and portions of India and the manioc-fish diet of the Amazon basin can provide a balanced human diet (96, 181, 358). Current problems of malnutrition in these societies are connected to larger ecological and economic problems, such as environmental degradation, drought, and resource inequalities attendant on an emerging cash economy.

Access to wild foods is an important element in maintaining the viability of many traditional agricultural systems. Inhabitants hunt small game, fish, and gather wild plant foods (278, 344, 376, 387). Of these, plant resources probably make the most important contribution to human diet. Leaves, stems, and inflorescence of *Amaranth, Chenopodium, Cucurbita, Dioscorea, Ipomoea, Manihot,* and *Vigna,* either wild or cultivated, are widely used as ingredients in relishes, soups, and stews that supplement the diet staple (124, 219, 343). These provide important nutrients otherwise missing in the diet, including significant amounts of protein, calcium, iron, and vitamins (353). In many cases, they have been shown to be more nutritionally valuable than the imported vegetable crops introduced by development officials. Among agricultural and pastoral peoples, the role of wild plants as famine foods has been well documented (124). However, many species are also part of the daily diet in these societies (34, 101, 123, 180, 222, 325, 387, 431, 447, 462).

While traditional food systems have generally been thought to provide adequate human diets, they are not without problems. Periodic famines have affected a wide variety of subsistence societies (75, 440) and continue to do so. Many such societies experience seasonal shortfalls in food supply (10, 60, 64, 86, 158, 163, 199, 222, 401, 446). This "hungry season" often occurs during the preharvest period when agricultural labor requirements are high. The classic studies of Fox (134) and Haswell (198) in the Gambia and of Hunter (217) for Northeast Ghana show a significant loss in body weights of both adults and children at that time. While some authors have argued that the hungry season is merely a matter of monotonous or less-desired diet (349, 377a), the seasonal weight loss of small children can have serious effects on their growth and development, as well as their continued survival (70, 388, 408).

Some traditional diets have also been shown to have dystrophic effects. Amounts of phytate in grain-based diets have been held accountable for specific zinc-deficiency syndromes (35, 381). Toxic effects have also been demonstrated for diets high in oxalates or lathyrogens (416). While these can interfere with mineral absorption and bone formation, their effects are less noticeable than those of other dietary toxins. Cyanogenetic glycosides, present in manioc and lima beans, have been implicated in some forms of tropical blindness and neural degeneration seen in West Africa, Jamaica, and Malaya. Using an animal model, Jackson & Jackson (231) have shown that the cyanide content of the Liberian manioc-based diet is sufficient to cause growth and behavior retardation, altered glucose metabolism, depressed thyroid activity, and hematological disturbances. Katz (258) has suggested that manioc consumption in the presence of the sickle-cell gene may be a positive adaptation to malarial conditions.

The adequacy of traditional diets also depends upon the degree to which humans can adapt to chronic low levels of energy and nutrient intake. Ample evidence supports the contention that humans adapt to both low and fluctuating energy intake by changing their energy requirements (11, 14, 81, 99, 102–104, 114, 162, 234, 418, 430). Research in New Guinea has also suggested that humans can adapt to very low protein intakes (119, 345, 352). The question of "adequate" diet thus becomes complicated, as the changing standards for FAO requirements reflect.

High variability among individuals and among populations in the rate of nutrient synthesis and metabolism makes it difficult to judge the adequacy of traditional diets simply from an inspection of foods ingested. A more meaningful criterion may be the ability of individuals to maintain function (e.g. growth and development, learning, work performance, reproduction). [While the effects of diet on learning ability and mental function are beyond the scope of this paper, other measures of biological functioning are classic (and current) research interests in physical anthropology (e.g. 178, 272, 280).] The relationship of energy intake and work performance is particularly important for developing countries. If dietary restriction impairs working ability, this has negative implications for economic growth and change. While humans adapt to low energy intake by decreasing requirements, they also do so by slower growth, smaller body size, and reduced levels of activity (135, 177, 226, 261, 384, 435). The relation of these factors to overall productive capacity is an important consideration in assessing the economic impact of nutrition programs (32, 74, 195, 271, 354).

SUBSISTENCE AND DIETARY CHANGE   The causes and consequences of dietary change are especially relevant questions in current situations of modernization and economic development. In most of the developing world, traditional diets have been influenced by either change in the system of food production or change in the amounts and types of foods available. The impact of modernization on diet varies widely, from change in only one staple (e.g. from sorghum to maize to bread in urbanizing Southern Africa, or from couscous to macaroni in parts of the Sahel) to a complete adoption of a Westernized diet. The nutritional consequences of change are accordingly varied, ranging from a net improvement in nutritional balance (with iodization of salt, for example, or parboiling of rice before milling) to increased incidence of diet-related disease and death.

Causes of malnutrition   On a worldwide basis, protein energy malnutrition (PEM) is the most common type of nutritional disease. Among those biological and cultural factors known to be important in the development of PEM are maternal nutritional status, patterns of breast feeding and weaning, interactions with infectious disease, and the sociodemographic profile of the household. All of these factors are susceptible to change with the impact of modernization.

One of the more important factors in the etiology of childhood malnutrition may be the nutritional status of the mother. Taller and better-nourished women have fewer obstetrical complications and lower perinatal mortality (438). Higher survival rates for the offspring of larger mothers are largely attributable to the decreased incidence of low birth weight (< 2500 g) infants in this group. Low birth weight may be the result not only of overall maternal nutritional status, but also of maternal diet during pregnancy. Delgado et al (84) have estimated that 13–43% of infants born to lower-SES parents in developing countries weigh less than 2500 g. Such infants have twice the risk of neonatal mortality and are more susceptible to infectious diseases. Dietary supplementation can result in higher birth weights, larger subcutaneous fat deposits, and better temperature regulation for offspring. Increased maternal food variety and vitamin supplementation have also been advocated in LDCs for their beneficial effects on fetal and infant nutrition (25, 41, 442).

Investigators have studied the effects of malnutrition of the mother upon infant status at birth, as well as upon subsequent lactational performance. To a significant extent, the fetus is buffered from the nutritional deficiencies of the environment by adaptive changes in the mother and the placenta. Adair (2, 5) has reported on Taiwanese women of a marginally nourished rural population. Despite energy intakes below recommended levels, these women produced infants with acceptable birth weights. Adair describes maternal skinfold changes during pregnancy and lactation that precede the periods of fetal demands upon maternal tissues and provide nutrient stores ready for mobilization. For example, there is a rapid gain in fat during early pregnancy when fetal demands are minimal, providing stores for the last trimester when the fetus is growing rapidly. Lechtig et al (274, 275) have studied this issue in rural Guatemalan women. They found mean birth weight to be low. Placental analyses revealed that the average placental weight was 15% less than high-SES controls, but that the biochemical composition of the placenta of the undernourished women did not differ. The administration of a caloric supplement raised the mean birth weight, largely by reducing the number of low birth weight neonates.

The risk to the fetus and neonate in LDCs is greater in younger mothers, especially young adolescents, 13–15 years old. Frisancho and his colleagues have investigated pregnancy outcome in a large sample of lower-SES urban females in Lima, Peru (146–148). They have reported that pregnant women with greater caloric reserves had fatter neonates, while mothers with greater protein stores had longer infants. Among the adolescent component of their sample, these investigators found thinner and smaller newborns than among older women matched for maternal nutritional status. Frisancho and his colleagues advanced two hypotheses, (not mutually exclusive): (*a*) that, since young adolescents are still growing, their nutritional needs may compete with those of the fetus, resulting in impaired prenatal growth; and (*b*) that the placenta of the adolescent cannot function adequately for normal fetal growth.

Infant feeding and weaning practices have also been shown to influence the development of PEM. Marasmus, or severe wasting, is connected to abrupt, early weaning (in the first year), bottle feeding, diarrhea, and witholding of food (316). Kwashiorkor, a protein-deficiency disease, appears to be related to weaning during the second year onto a high-carbohydrate, low-protein diet. Advocacy of breast feeding and improved weaning diets are based on their potential to lower the health risks for young children (61, 66, 141, 306). Thus both the decline in prevalence of breast feeding (213, 369) and factors that influence breast feeding (17, 184, 215) are of interest. Unfortunately, much of the information on this topic is based on survey data. There is currently a need to expand this information through anthropological studies of infant feeding practices in the developing world. Prospective, observational studies of infant diets could add materially to our understanding of childhood malnutrition under conditions of socioeconomic change (183).

It is widely accepted that the chronic malnutrition ubiquitous in LDCs is rooted in the environments within which at-risk populations live and their children develop. Not only are these environments responsible for the failing growth that strikes some 30% of children in their second and third years of life, they are also responsible for the maintenance of poor nutritional status and for a general lack of catch-up in growth and other indicators (246, 391). On the other hand, the identification of specific causal factors responsive to intervention is difficult. Humans and their feeding activities must be viewed in an ecological perspective, in order to understand factors that cause food systems to break down, resulting in both chronic and acute malnutrition.

Some authors have approached the identification of the causes of malnutrition by analyzing specific variables associated with nutritional deficiency. At the level of policy, Behar (30) has made a number of specific suggestions for nutritional intervention. At the research level, other writers have provided examples of attempts to identify particular variables as indicators (255, 274, 295).

Other authors have taken a systemic and ecological approach to this issue, emphasizing the complexity of the problem. The elegant charts of Cravioto and his colleagues (77, 78) are reminders of the difficulties involved. Mata's summary of his extensive work in Santa Maria Cauque, Guatemala, emphasizes the need to examine microenvironmental factors within the home (307).

Social and demographic factors that influence the development of PEM in children include family income, family size, parental education, parenting styles (affection, attention), and other measures of home environment. In general, PEM is most strongly associated with income. However, this relationship may hold only below a certain threshold value (21). Above this threshold, maternal education appears to be one of the most important variables separating households with malnourished children from those with adequate nutritional status (126, 332, 359). Maternal education and household income appear to have an interactive effect, such that improved income has more nutritional effect in households with a literate mother (21). Number of children in the family, birth order of the malnourished child, presence of printed matter and other intellectual stimulation in the home, and occupation of the father (wage-laborer vs subsistence) are all associated variables (126, 400, 448). With the increase of wage-labor employment and cash cropping under programs of development, the changing impact of these variables upon nutritional effect will need to be monitored.

Johnston et al (251, 252) applied principal component analysis to a correlation matrix of 38 × 38 environmental and parental-anthropometric variables. They extracted seven components: 1. socioeconomic status, 2. family demography, 3. child morbidity, 4. maternal body mass, 5. paternal body mass, 6. maternal linear size, and 7. paternal linear size. Component scores were calculated for the sample of 276 subjects. These scores were related to body size from birth to 36 months; in addition, the mean scores for each component were compared in children with and without chronic PEM. Three components were significant in these analyses: (*a*) SES, (*b*) the linear size of the mother, and (*c*) the linear size of the father. Children with chronic PEM came from poorer homes and had parents who were smaller than children without PEM. The two components summarizing parental linear dimensions were interpreted as reflecting the nutritional history of the parents when they themselves were children. The authors concluded that the parents had "recreated" their own childhood environments in their homes (252). This finding introduces a generational component into the problem of malnutrition.

The predictive strength of parental nutritional history was tested further by introducing all 38 variables into a stepwise discriminant function, with the contrast being children with and without chronic PEM. Five variables provided maximum differentiation of the groups: the hip and shoulder breadth of the father, the hip breadth of the mother, and the personal hygiene score of the father. These variables were sufficient to correctly identify approximately 77% of the children as malnourished or not malnourished. This analysis lent further support to the importance of the environments of the parents when they were children as determinants of malnutrition among their offspring.

Nutrition and agricultural development   One of the basic aims of international development efforts has been to improve the nutritional status of disadvantaged populations. The success of these efforts is currently disputed. The success of specific projects indicates that such direct interventions as feeding programs can make a temporary difference in nutritional status (8, 33). However the ability of such efforts to change health on a sustainable basis is questionable. In addition, the nutritional outcomes of such indirect programs of assistance as development of infrastructure, income generation, or intensification of agricultural inputs are still debated (33, 363).

The nutritional consequences of agricultural development and agricultural policy have recently emerged as a topic of anthropological interest. These policy-related studies are an outgrowth of a larger tradition in anthropology that has long been concerned with the outcomes of patterns of food production, consumption, and distribution. The shift in emphasis from traditional food systems to those undergoing modernization is a recognition that processes of economic change may impact nutritional status. The differences in impact for different portions of the population, and the reasons for these differences, are particularly critical problems.

Specifically, there is a current controversy over the nutritional effects of wage labor and agricultural commercialization (125). On the one hand, it is argued that these forces of socioeconomic change increase the purchasing power of rural households, thus enabling them to increase the security of food supply (68, 410). With sufficient cash, the effects of underproduction or crop failure can be offset through purchases of food. On the other hand, data from Africa, Asia, and Latin America indicate that commercial agriculture and labor migration may increase the incidence of malnutrition, primarily through changes in patterns of cropping, consumption, and household labor allocation (87, 90, 284, 389). In reviewing this controversy, Fleuret & Fleuret (124) conclude that commercial agriculture and attendant socioeconomic change may endanger the nutritional status of children in participating households. At issue here is the trade-off between (a) the perceived benefits that result from improved diets due to increased family incomes and (b) the increased risks to food supply that derive from the abandonment of subsistence agriculture for cash cropping (105, 434). Increased risk is at least partially a consequence of reduced variability, both in crop mix and in overall economic strategy. Many of the indigenous food systems studied have maintained their stability by flexible and varied strategies for food procurement (72, 87). Such strategies have acted to even out seasonal and long-term fluctuations in food supply. The nutritional success of commercial agriculture for developing countries will depend on its ability to provide access to essential dietary resources during times of economic or ecological crisis.

While there is still little empirical research on nutritional effects of cash cropping, existing literature indicates that commercial agriculture may interfere with nutritional status via at least four routes:

1. It may interfere with consumption patterns in the household. Gross & Underwood (182), for example, demonstrated that commercial sisal workers in Brazil required such large caloric intakes that nutritional resources were diverted to them from other household members, particularly children. Calorimetric work from other areas supports these findings (101, 185, 427).
2. It may interfere with either quantity or quality of food supply, through reduction of food production. Many authors (6, 88, 91, 127, 192, 361) have noted that crop diversity declines with a shift to cash cropping, and that foods no longer planted are replaced with commercial foods of inferior nutrient content.
3. It may interfere with both subsistence production and domestic processes of reproduction, through reallocation of household labor. This process may in-

crease the demands on labor time of women, thus changing cooking habits (125, 229, 266, 368). In addition, Huss-Ashmore (220–222) has shown that the seasonality of these demands can lead to seasonal problems in nutrition and health for rural women and their children.

4. Further, commercial agriculture may interfere with household acquisition of food by changing control of income, budgeting, and resource distribution. In traditional food systems, adult females often control distribution (if not production) of staple foods, particularly those produced by the household. They are thus gatekeepers for food flows (277a), in effective control of nutrient budgets for family members. With a shift to increased cash income, males may increasingly control resource flow. By allocating household resources (labor, land, cash) to purposes other than food acquisition, they may inadvertently reduce quantity or quality of food available to other family members.

Recent empirical studies suggest that some of these problems can be offset by diversification of economic strategies. Fleuret & Fleuret (125) found that East African households that supplemented either wage labor or commercial agriculture with household food production showed the best nutritional status. In Sonora, Baer (18) showed that nutritional status was improved for communities that combined cash and subsistence cropping. Best nutritional status, however, was seen in households that also had access to essential economic resources for production, such as irrigation water or outside income. Brown & Partridge (49, 355) showed similar results for a group of resettled farmers in southeastern Mexico.

Future research on the nutritional effects of agricultural and subsistence change should take account of these complex issues of access to resources and diversity of economic strategies. The assumption of a direct link between increased income and improved household nutrition has not been supported and needs to be rigorously investigated (351, 363). An ecological approach to household nutrition, which integrates physical, biotic, and social environment with human biological needs, may help to orient future research in this area (88, 239, 240).

Nutritional Intervention and Child Development

While anthropology is not usually identified as an applied science, much of the work of bioanthropologists in the world's LDCs aims to alleviate the problems of residents. In view of the importance attached to childhood malnutrition and its implication for later function, it is no wonder that a considerable effort has been devoted by workers in basic and applied fields toward programs designed to reduce malnutrition and its impact.

Biological anthropologists, as well as their colleagues in related disciplines, have played a number of roles in nutritional intervention. Much of their effort, discussed above, has been in basic research on the correlates of malnutrition that might be altered through specifically designed programs. Research designed to determine indicators of nutritional status enables effective screening programs to identify the malnourished (187, 298).

Bioanthropologists also help to evaluate the effectiveness of nutritional intervention programs. In some instances the interventions are local and specific; in others, the programs are large in scope and comprehensive in application. Unfortunately, "successful" intervention programs are all too few, and it is still impossible to develop models that may be applied broadly in the developing world (443).

Brozek, Coursin & Read (52) reviewed comparisons of six longitudinal studies (conducted in Bogota, Cali, Guatemala City, New York City, and Mexico City) on the effects of nutritional supplementation on growth and behavioral development. Supplementation of the mother can increase birth weight (perhaps by increasing gestation time), while supplementation of the child will improve growth rate; but "there is probably no true catch-up growth that will bring [children] to accepted norms for their age groups" (52). Greater behavioral changes are seen in motor than in cognitive skills. In all cases, socioeconomic variables also affect growth and cognition and may confound the evaluation of the nutritional effect.

Adair & Pollitt (4) have recently summarized a series of in-depth analyses of the Bacon Chow study, a comprehensive intervention with rural Taiwanese women conducted for some 15 years by Chow, just before his death in 1973. Eligible women were followed from before the birth of one child until 15 months following the birth of a second infant, with dietary supplementation from the first birth onward. The study was unique in that a woman could serve as her own control. Adair & Pollitt concluded that, while supplement effects could be seen, there were no clear differences between the first and the second children. As did Brozek et al (52), they emphasized the difficulties in isolating main effects from the array of endogenous and exogenous variables that interact with the treatment.

Other studies of the impact of nutritional intervention have dealt with improved diets of children (399), physical growth (8, 330, 331), and cognition (315). Each has shown some effects, but all emphasize the complexity of nutritional ecosystems and the problems in identifying a direct effect of the supplement from among other interacting variables.

STUDIES OF HEALTH IN DEVELOPING COUNTRIES

Disease Ecology

The concern with ecological studies in nutrition has its roots in the more general concept of the ecology of health and disease. As defined by May (308), this approach considers disease to be a product of the interaction of host, pathogen, and environment. For humans, this environment includes not only physical and biotic factors, but also cultural factors and the influence of other human groups. Audy & Dunn (15) expanded this framework to include insults of multiple origin as causes of disease. Much of the current work in medical anthropology is based on some form of this basic theoretical model (12, 132, 197).

The application of this model to health problems in developing countries has involved the work of anthropologists, medical geographers, and epidemiologists, among others. Much of their concern has centered around the conditions affecting transmission of and adaptation to infectious disease. The now classic study by Livingstone (281; see also 459) on malaria showed the importance of both cultural and genetic factors in the development of infectious disease. This pioneering ecological study was followed by the intensive studies of Blumberg and his co-workers on the hepatitis B virus (HBV) (42). A third landmark in studies of medical ecology was the investigation of kuru by Gadjusek and his colleagues (157). The association of a fatal neurological disease in highland New Guinea with a slow virus transmitted by cannibalism underscored the necessity of a holistic approach to medical problems.

While these studies have become models to emulate in biomedical anthropology, the problems investigated are still current concerns in developing countries. For example, malaria, once thought close to eradication, is now on the increase (165, 172). Resistance of the *Plasmodium* parasite to chloroquine and of the *Anopheles* mosquito to DDT has been blamed for much of the increase. The susceptibility of humans, especially children, to malaria, and its prevalence in developing countries, give it high priority for future biomedical research (59, 122, 329). Similarly, the hepatitis B virus continues to be a problem in the Third World. Studies from West Africa and eastern Asia have confirmed a link between HBV and primary hepatic carcinoma (154, 193, 270, 460). Other effects appear to be depression of fertility and an elevation of the offspring sex-ratio (95). Progressive neurological diseases of viral and parasitic origin, while much less prevalent in the developing world, continue to excite medical interest (155, 156, 441).

In addition to these classic "anthropological" disease problems, other infectious and parasitic conditions are currently under investigation in LDCs. Their impact on human populations varies greatly, ranging from major public health problems to obscure conditions of medical curiosity. Diarrheal and respiratory diseases are among those having greatest impact on the health of large portions of the human population. Diarrheal diseases are of particular interest because of their close association with malnutrition in children (301, 303, 306, 396). Negative effects of diarrhea are more pronounced in malnourished than in well-nourished children (85). While diarrhea is a common accompaniment to other childhood infections (383, 395), it is also associated with problems of poor water supply, food preparation, and personal hygiene (117). The amelioration of these problems in developing countries is a current priority of both national and international development-donor agencies. Success will require an understanding of both biological and cultural factors influencing the transmission of disease.

Respiratory infections are one of the chief causes of morbidity and mortality in young children (286, 314, 404). For Third World children, the synergism with malnutrition and complications from diarrhea make them especially dangerous. These infections often show a seasonal pattern, both in children and adults (64). Such infections are likely predisposing factors in subsequent weight loss and acute undernutrition, and they may cause adults to lose time from productive activities. Tuberculosis continues to be a highly prevalent and debilitating disorder in these societies (218, 326). Where large numbers of adults within a community are affected, social networks may have to be employed to compensate for lost work time (436).

A variety of other epidemiological problems are of potential interest to bioanthropologists working in development settings. These include schistosomiasis (241, 377, 456), arboviruses (31, 433), filarial infections (97, 166, 403), intestinal parasites (37, 256, 273), trypanosomiasis (133), endemic and epidemic fevers (69, 164, 263), rheumatic fever and rheumatic heart disease, and sexually transmitted diseases (STD) (339). The World Health Organization has assigned a priority status to STD (third after malaria and tuberculosis) among communicable diseases. Factors affecting their transmission are a potentially valuable area of bioanthropological research.

Health and Modernization

In addition to their long-term interest in infectious disease stress, anthropologists have also been concerned with the effects of change and modernization on human health. It has gradually become apparent that changes in life-style significantly affect disease patterns. Modernizing populations regularly exhibit a shift from infectious disease as a major stressor to a pattern of "civilized" diseases. These include obesity, diabetes, hypertension, coronary heart disease, ulcers, and certain cancers. The causes of these changes are presently an active concern.

Many of the diseases of modernization are hypothesized to be related to stress. Social stress resulting from both migration and internal culture change have been related to changing levels of urinary catecholamines and increased blood pressure (50, 232, 304). Other hypothesized causes include changes in diet, increased use of tobacco and alcohol, and changing activity patterns.

Increases in cardiovascular disease are of particular concern to health personnel in developing countries. Epidemiological studies have indicated that incidence of coronary heart disease (CHD) among black populations is generally lower than among whites, and lower in rural than in urban populations (417, 454). A similar distribution has been found for the frequency of arterial atherosclerotic lesions. In South Africa, whites and Asians showed significantly higher rates of ischemic heart disease than blacks (466). Low levels of CHD were associated with the maintenance of high levels of high-density lipoproteins into old age (449). The authors hypothesize that the lower risk for black populations may be associated with vigorous activity and a frugal traditional diet.

High blood pressure has also been identified as a risk factor in the development of CHD. In several developing areas of Africa, the Caribbean, and the Pacific Islands, chronic hypertension has become a prevalent endemic disease. Elevated blood pressure among adult Bahamians is the eighth leading cause of death for that population, and is associated with both genetic and life-style factors (190). Among the latter are elevated salt intakes, smoking, alcohol use, and use of oral contraceptives. Elevated blood pressures have also been found in children in a variety of populations. Tokelauan children migrating to New Zealand had higher blood pressures than nonmigrants (27). Mean systolic pressures were also found to be elevated in healthy Nigerian school children (1). No explanation for this finding has been offered. Religiosity (a presumed antagonist to social stress) has been examined for its effect on reducing blood pressure, but results have proved contradictory (225, 450).

Obesity in developing countries is associated with both hypertension and diabetes. Acculturation is associated with significant secular increases in body size and fat levels (139). These changes are associated with changes in diet and activity (40). Changes in activity also appear to be related to fluctuating insulin levels (347).

Probably the largest coordinated study of health and modernization in a single society is that of Baker and his associates in Samoa. In the last five years, a wealth of information has become available on the health status and associated factors for this population. While blood pressure is elevated, both for sedentary and migrant groups, coronary heart disease is generally lower than the US average (80, 194, 311, 312). High blood pressure is related to fatness and trunk dimensions (310). High levels of obesity in this population are similar among spouses, and are associated with migration, urban residence, and dietary change (51, 233, 357). However, neither energy intake nor dietary quality totally explains patterns of obesity. Further, patterns of fatness and changing activity levels have had a negative impact on aerobic capacity (179). This points to a significant role for activity levels in the etiology of diseases associated with modernization.

Other problems of modernization have been much less thoroughly studied. Surveys of cervical, bladder, and liver cancers have linked them to infectious conditions and cultural patterns (259, 285). Cigarette smoking, with the attendant risk of CHD and lung cancer, has only begun to receive attention in the developing world (69, 464). Other problems that have received only nominal attention are the influence of modernization on ulcers and other psychosomatic complaints (386), gynecological and skin diseases (106), and the health status of the elderly (168).

Anthropology and Health Care

Anthropologists (including bioanthropologists) have become increasingly involved in the study of health and health care. Much of this involvement has been directed toward the technological aspects of medicine, particularly traditional medicine. This has led to the production of a catalog of curing practices and indigenous medicines, and an evaluation of their efficacy. More recently, the concern with traditional medicine has become focused on its role as one alternative within a larger system of medical providers (276a). Attempts to integrate traditional medicine into the health care system of developing countries have begun to involve anthropologists in health planning and policy formulation. This role is likely to be expanded.

While the efficacy of traditional medicine continues to be debated, two decades of research on indigenous healing practices has produced the following anthropological wisdom. Extensive studies of traditional and indigenous pharmacopoeias indicate that a substantial portion of them are medically efficacious (16, 108, 260, 287, 380, 439). While both single plants and mixed herbal decoctions have physiologic effects, variation in concentration and dosage make it difficult to predict precise outcomes of treatment. The incorporation of medicinal plants or substances as part of the regular diet may have preventive health effects (110, 111, 260). In addition, healers themselves may play a significant role in aiding patients to recover from psychosomatic or self-limiting diseases (e.g. 393). Belief in their efficacy for curing specific classes of diseases (usually chronic or mysterious) may be found among all social classes (28, 109, 318, 328).

Since traditional healers are rarely the only source of medical care for any given population today, anthropologists have been concerned with the factors that lead people to choose traditional medicine, and circumstances under which they will do so. In general, the use of traditional versus modern medicine has been based on the perceived causes of disease (71, 113, 129, 170, 282), ethnic and social identity of the patient (76), acculturation level of the patient or his family (379), belief in the efficacy of care (92, 469), and the availability of different treatment types (201, 470). The extensive literature available on this subject reflects the initial concern of health planners and providers over the reluctance of modernizing populations to utilize Western care facilities. The acceptability of cosmopolitan medical care has therefore been disproportionately emphasized in this area of research.

While indigenous healers continue to play an important role in many developing countries, there is increasing evidence that they are no longer the preferred source of routine health care (13, 223). Demand for Western medical services has grown phenomenally in the Third World, such that national governments have found it difficult to keep pace. This has led health planners to consider the possible utilization of local healers as purveyors of health care (227, 319, 342, 356, 373). This suggestion has taken two forms—the recognition of traditional medicine as a legitimate form of therapy, and the retraining of local healers as primary health care providers. Official approval of these strategies by WHO was intended to facilitate implementation of national policies toward this end.

Using either approach, the integration of modern and traditional medicine has proved difficult. Physicians remain skeptical of indigenous therapies, while traditional healers are reluctant to give up their unique position in the community. The potential success of traditional healers in adapting to primary health care delivery (in the Western sense) is still largely untested (174); in those few countries where traditional medicine has been encouraged (China, India, Ghana, Indonesia, the Philippines), the performance of the traditional sector has not been evaluated. Indeed, there is some question even *how* to evaluate it. Some success has been achieved in upgrading the skills of traditional birth attendants (175, 362), but institutional and cultural barriers generally continue to discourage the use of traditional practitioners in national health systems (118, 267, 411).

The question of future research priorities for biological and medical anthropologists has received recent attention (89, 131, 206, 264, 265). In general, health planning in developing countries is seen as a potentially productive area for anthropological input. The need for developing countries to provide improved health care to more people at moderate cost is likely to dominate research priorities in this area for some time to come. Therefore, anthropologists concerned with health problems in the Third World may find themselves under increasing pressure to make their investigations policy-relevant. In particular, the organization and health impact of primary health care programs is an area needing attention (36, 67, 130, 136, 341, 463). Problems of infectious disease have been increasingly well contained, but difficulties remain, both in effective prevention of disease and in the ability to insure patient compliance with treatment. Problems of food and water sanitation continue to be important, but may be increasingly overshadowed by problems of chemical contamination as agricultural and industrial development proceed. In the long run, change itself may prove to be one of the most significant stressors for Third World populations. Examining adaptation to that change is an ongoing requirement for the understanding of human health issues.

POPULATION ISSUES

The rapid growth of human populations is a salient feature of currently developing countries. This rapid growth apparently began for most countries during the colonial period and has continued into the postcolonial era (340). This growth has been seen as both an obstacle to development and an eventual threat to the adequacy of the world's resources (382). The causes of this rapid growth and the possible regulating mechanisms for human population have accordingly interested demographers and demographic anthropologists. While much of the work in this area has been policy related, some (particularly among anthropologists) has been oriented toward ecological theories of population growth and regulation. Because the literature on Third World population processes is so vast, we limit our discussion here to an outline of the issues that are both development-related and pertinent to the interests of bioanthropologists. More general reviews of population studies in anthropology have been presented (22, 338, 340, 364, 409, 422, 457).

Much of the current research on population issues in LDCs has been stimulated by demographic transition theory. The applicability of this theory to developing countries has been questioned; but despite its drawbacks, the idea of orderly transitions in demographic rates has had wide appeal. Briefly stated, this theory attempts to explain population growth in developing countries through the use of a three-stage model (346, 432, 437). Derived from the European experience, this model was thought to characterize changes in mortality and fertility for all countries undergoing economic development and industrialization. In the first or preindustrial stage of the model, high mortality due to disease and famine is balanced by high fertility, such that population size remains stable. During the second stage of the transition, improvements in sanitation, medical care, and diet drastically reduce mortality. Fertility remains high, however, and the population experiences rapid growth. With the third or industrial stage, fertility regulation once again brings the two rates into balance. The low mortality and low fertility that characterize this stage once again dampen population growth.

As the theory was classically formulated, economic forces were postulated to be responsible both for the maintenance of high fertility in stages one and two and for its decline in stage three. Only when the economic value of large families had been negated by industrialization and compulsory education could a fertility decline be accomplished. Recent work has criticized these assumptions on several grounds. First, more intensive research on the conditions of fertility decline in Europe has shown that the stages of the demographic transition were not as clear-cut as had been assumed, even for the area where the theory was developed (262). Prior to the transition, levels of fertility in Europe were not uniformly high. Rather, birthrates showed considerable variation across geographic and cultural regions, even among groups practicing natural fertility.[1] Further, fertility did not decline everywhere at the same rate, nor in response to a given level of economic development. Instead, cultural setting or context appears to have been more critical in overall timing of fertility change.

The application of demographic transition theory to developing countries has proven to be particularly difficult (82, 432). Improvements in living standards and medical care have indeed decreased mortality in these countries. However, increasing modernization has not resulted in the predicted fertility decline. Much of the Third World thus appears to be stuck in the second stage of the transition, with its high rates of population growth. The timing of the next stage (or whether it will occur) is therefore a critical issue in population research. Much of this research is currently oriented toward discovering the determinants of Third World fertility, and by extension, how it might be changed.

Fertility Determinants in Developing Countries

Bulatao & Lee (54) have presented a conceptual framework for organizing knowledge about the factors that influence fertility in LDCs. This framework separates influences into three groups according to the channels through which they operate: demand for children, supply of children, and costs of regulation. Supply and demand are not used here in the strict economic sense, and no assumption is made that couples will make optimizing decisions about births. Rather, these factors are seen as macro-variables that may subsume a series of social and biological influences. "Demand" for children here refers to the family size and composition (number, gender, spacing) a couple might see as ideal. "Supply" refers to "the surviving children couples would have if they did not regulate their fertility, or their children's survival, in parity-specific ways" (54, p. 758). Supply therefore depends on all the factors that affect intercourse, conception, gestation, and birth. It also depends on child survival, and therefore on both parental behaviors and ecological circumstances that affect child health. Both supply and demand presumably enter into the decision to have or avoid a given birth. Whether or not a couple will take active steps to avoid a birth also depends on the "costs" of regulation, whether in money, effort, inconvenience, discomfort, violation of norms or beliefs, or perceived hazards to health.

Much of the extensive demographic literature on fertility determinants is concerned with factors that influence demand for children (see e.g. 29, 54, 57, 320). These include such things as education, socioeconomic status, rural-urban residence, costs and benefits of children, and local tastes and norms.

---

[1] Natural fertility is usually defined as fertility behavior that is not altered by the number of children desired or the number already born (204). It is thus fertility that is not regulated in parity-specific ways.

Despite the recognized importance of such factors in influencing fertility decisions, they have generally fallen outside the scope of biological anthropology. Instead, bioanthropologists have been concerned primarily with the factors that influence the supply of children. For our purposes, these factors can be divided into those that influence natural fertility and those that affect child survival. While the following discussion is not exhaustive, it outlines some of the more prominent concerns in this area.

DETERMINANTS OF NATURAL FERTILITY   Natural fertility prevails in the absence of deliberate parity-specific behavior limiting family size. That is to say, reproductive behavior is not altered by either the number of children already born or the number ultimately desired. In practice, this may be taken to mean the absence of deliberate contraception or abortion. Factors that affect natural fertility may be either sociocultural or biological, but are presumed to operate by affecting some portion of the reproductive cycle. The intervening variables through which external factors may affect fertility were originally defined by Henry (203) and Davis & Blake (83). These have since been modified by Bongaarts & Potter (47) to give an elegant model of the proximate determinants of fertility. Briefly, this model specifies that fertility determinants must operate upon (*a*) the period of postpartum infecundability, (*b*) waiting time to conception, (*c*) spontaneous intrauterine mortality, (*d*) age at marriage (or onset of exposure to intercourse) and amount of marital disruption, or (*e*) onset of permanent sterility. Any factor that impinges on one of these proximate determinants has the ability to alter natural fertility, and thus the supply of children.

Note that these proximate determinants include factors that affect the total length of the reproductive period, as well as those that affect the timing and spacing of births. While the reproductive period logically begins with puberty, in practice the timing of puberty has little effect on actual fertility. Age at marriage or entry into a stable sexual union has been shown to be a much more relevant factor for examining population dynamics. Economic and cultural variables that affect timing of family formation can therefore have considerable impact upon fertility performance (58, 212, 348, 407, 407a). However, in societies where marriage is closely tied to menarche, age at first menses may affect reproductive history. Katz (258) presents a series of biological factors that can affect age at menarche. These include genetic factors, nutrition, disease, altitude, temperature, light-dark cycles, and psychological trauma.

Of these factors, nutrition has probably received the most attention in recent years (333). Girls in well-nourished populations have been shown to achieve menarche at younger ages than those in poorly nourished populations (169, 426). In addition, Frisch has suggested that menarche occurs in American girls at an invariant mean weight or fatness level (150–152). Based on this observation, she has suggested that minimal levels of body fat are necessary for reproductive functioning. While this hypothesis has occasioned considerable controversy (216, 254, 394), it is likely that fat plays some role in the timing of overall growth and sexual maturation. Nutritional status may also be involved in the timing of menopause, in that this event appears to occur earlier in populations with marginal nutritional status (65). However, as a regulator of human fecundity and fertility, its impact is apparently negligible (46, 173, 219, 322).

In order for nutritional status (or any other biological variable) to have maximal impact on natural fertility, it is necessary that it operate upon some segment of the birth interval (47, 321). That is, it would be necessary for it to affect ovulation (and thus the period of fecundability), waiting time to conception, intrauterine mortality, or the birth process itself. Observations of amenorrhea in marathon runners and ballet dancers, all of whom have low fat levels, have led to the suggestion that minimal fatness levels may also be necessary for maintenance of ovulation and menstrual cycles (153, 451, 461). While this appears to be true in the case of female athletes, the fat levels involved are extremely low (245). For populations practicing natural fertility, lactation appears to be a much more powerful influence on ovulation and fecundability (9). Length of postpartum amenorrhea is closely correlated with length and intensity of breast feeding (276). Unsupplemented breast feeding can delay return of menses for up to 20 months (277). However, in order to assess the true impact of lactation upon fertility, it is necessary to control for the confounding effect of infant mortality (100, 432).

Nutritional status might theoretically operate upon other segments of the birth interval, as well. Waiting time to conception has been shown to be primarily a function of coital frequency (47). Therefore, if malnutrition lowers the frequency of intercourse, it could affect fertility. While data on coital frequency for different populations are notably lacking (but see 337), the classic studies of Keys et al (261) showed that loss of libido accompanied the weight loss of gradual starvation. There is also ample evidence that conceptions are reduced during periods of famine (412, 413). The precise impact of undernutrition on intrauterine mortality is unknown, but it is likely that it contributes to the 20% fetal wastage generally reported for developing countries (47). As discussed above, complications of the birth process and viability of newborns may also be a function of maternal nutritional status. The degree to which these factors alter actual fertility performance in developing countries has not been assessed.

For certain populations, disease may also act as a regulator of fecundity[2] and

[2]Fertility is defined here as actual reproductive performance, that is, the actual production of children. Fecundity, on the other hand, refers to the theoretical ability for conception, gestation, and live birth. Fecundability is more specifically defined as the probability of conception during a particular period.

natural fertility (116, 173, 406). For example, high rates of childlessness (up to 50% in women over 50) characterize large portions of sub-Saharan Africa (309). These high levels of subfecundity have been attributed to high prevalence of pelvic inflammatory disease resulting from sexually transmitted diseases (STD) and postpartum or postabortal infection. In addition, McFalls & McFalls (309) have called attention to the role of tuberculosis, particularly genital tuberculosis, in limiting fecundity. This disease may affect men or women, causing dyspareunia (painful intercourse), inflammation, and occlusion of the genital ducts. Other diseases which they show to reduce fecundity are malaria, filariasis, leprosy, schistosomiasis, sleeping sickness, and other fevers (e.g. in smallpox, influenza, pneumonia). Such diseases undoubtedly play a role in keeping fertility in LDCs below theoretical biological maximum.

It should be noted that cultural factors may also act to constrain levels of natural fertility, and thus the supply of children. For example, the long postpartum taboos on intercourse found in many African societies may prolong the interbirth interval by several years (385). Similarly, those Asian societies where it is considered unseemly for a woman to give birth after the marriage of her first child (or the birth of her first grandchild) may find the total reproductive span shortened by this practice (423). Endemic warfare may also lower fertility by removing husbands (either temporarily or permanently) and thus reducing exposure of fecundable women to intercourse (458). In all of these cases, the factors reducing fertility are not parity-specific (that is, not related to the number of children already born) and thus do not violate the assumption of natural fertility.

CHILD SURVIVAL   While nutritional status and disease make variable contributions to overall levels of natural fertility, they are undoubtedly the most critical factors affecting rates of child survival in the developing world. Rates of infant mortality in these societies are high, ranging from 33 per thousand live births in Panama to 142 per thousand in Nepal (443). Childhood mortality (0–5 years of age) is also high, ranging from 46 to 435 per thousand. Most of this mortality is estimated to be the result of the interaction between malnutrition and infectious disease. This pattern of childhood mortality may have a large effect on fertility in LDCs (100, 145, 327), in that declining rates of childhood mortality are one of the better aggregate predictors of lowered fertility rates (405). Two separate hypotheses have been advanced to explain this relationship. The child replacement hypothesis specifies that children who die will be replaced by another birth as rapidly as possible (351). The child survival hypothesis presumes that parents aim at a level of completed family size that will guarantee a certain number of children surviving to adulthood (428). When infant mortality drops, this desired number of survivors can be achieved with fewer actual births.

For individual populations, the idea of an invariable link between declining infant mortality and declining fertility has been challenged (398). Preston (371) has suggested that couples will not reduce their fertility until they are convinced that infant mortality has actually dropped. As with most other variables affecting fertility, the change in performance may take several generations to achieve, and the discrepancy between expected and actual survival rates can lead to substantial population growth. Other variables shown to affect child survival include mother's age and parity level, both parents' socioeconomic status (including education and income), drinking water and sanitation, and the availability of health care (55). The relative importance of technological change vs economic modernization in improving child survival continues to be debated.

While demographers have paid little attention to the role of infanticide in regulating the supply of children, there is evidence that for some societies it forms an important mechanism for population regulation (398). Although strictly defined as the willful destruction of infants, in practice infanticide includes the killing, exposure, neglect, or abandonment of both infants and young children. Data on the incidence of infanticide have proven difficult if not impossible to collect, but a wide variety of societies record the practice (62, 65, 94). Some, as among the Tikopia, have justified the practice in terms of food supply (121). Others, such as the Eskimo (138) and the McKenzie Dene (202), cite population control as a specific reason. Howell (214) records the use of infanticide among the !Kung as a means of spacing births, and thus of reducing overall fertility.

Where infanticide is consciously rationalized as a method of population control, it is easy to see this practice as an adaptation to scarce or uncertain food supply. The practice of selectively killing female infants has been explained on these grounds (93, 94). However, in many societies, the practice may not be explicitly recognized or may even be denied. In these cases, infanticide may take the form of benign neglect (63) or underinvestment in a particular infant (397). This type of passive infanticide probably plays a role in the high rates of mortality for high-parity children in developing countries (7, 467). By simply allowing such children to die when diseased, parents achieve a certain measure of fertility control. However, substantial further research will be needed before the impact of infanticide upon Third World population can be assessed.

Bioanthropology and Population Policy

As is the case with health policy in general, the potential contribution of bioanthropologists to population policy in the developing world is substantial. To date, this potential has been largely unrealized, partially due to the reluctance of physical anthropologists to define themselves as applied or practicing anthropologists, but also partially due to the political sensitivity of the issues involved. Population policy has generally been identified with programs of birth control. The notable failure of many of these programs (294) and the resultant criticism of their design and aims has made anthropologists understandably wary of involvement in further applied population activities.

However, the current recognition that population growth is a critical variable in development planning has led to an increased demand for anthropological insights into factors by which it may be influenced. The framework presented above outlines some of these influential variables, particularly those that affect fecundity and fertility through the supply of children. The interaction of fertility and mortality, particularly at the household level, may prove to be especially important for predicting future population trends.

Ford & Arcury (128) list a series of priority research needs for the formulation of population policy in the developing world. These include information on levels and trends in fertility, mortality, and migration; evaluation of demographic impact of development projects; development of theory for analyzing determinants and consequences of demographic behavior; analysis of the political process of population policy; and analysis of the relationships among development style, population policy, and population processes (128).

These priorities indicate the need for basic demographic information in developing countries, and for frameworks that link this information to the process of development. The broadly systemic and ecological orientation of most bioanthropologists seems ideally suited to deal with these needs. While classical demographic transition theory has engendered valuable research on population processes in the developing world, it is only a heuristic device. Its acceptance by planners as a model of the real world is potentially disadvantageous (and perhaps even dangerous) for the populations they serve (432).

Most demographers agree that population growth in LDCs must eventually be contained. However, there is no reason to believe that containment will be achieved through the decline of fertility to meet the low mortality levels characteristic of developed countries.[3] Alternatively, levels of mortality may rise to meet those of present high fertility. There is current evidence, particularly from Africa, that such an increase in mortality has already begun (185). A third scenario, one that seems likely for the near future, is that rising mortality and falling fertility may result in balanced but moderate rates for both. It is important that planners recognize the possibility and the implications of these alternatives.

We have not dealt here with the application of policy in terms of programs of conscious family limitation and population control. Anthropological participation in this area has been minimal but is likely to increase. Because of the

---

[3]The idea of alternative outcomes for the next demographic transition was suggested by S. Phillip Morgan, Population Studies Center, University of Pennsylvania (personal communication).

grounded nature of their research, anthropologists are in a good position to address questions of determinants and outcomes of contraception use and abortion. Household-level and community-level studies of these issues may prove to be critical in evaluating both the direct and indirect impact of development programs on demographic processes.

CONCLUSIONS

The bioanthropology of development does not currently exist as a unified field. However, those biological and biocultural anthropologists working in developing countries would recognize the concerns we have outlined here as central to adaptive success of populations in these regions. Nutrition, growth, health, and population change are all closely related concerns. All are responsive to conditions of modernization, and none can be understood in isolation.

Ecological conditions in developing countries play a large part in many of the problems we have discussed. Environmental factors that influence disease and food supply are particularly important to understand. The ecological orientation of many biological anthropologists has been one of their most important contributions to the analysis of problems in these regions. However, our discussion has also shown that a traditional analysis of adaptive response to environmental conditions would leave out some of those variables that most critically affect human persistence and functioning. In the process of modernization, political and economic processes may influence coping strategies and access to resources far more than the parameters of the natural environment.

Change itself has been identified here as one of the critical factors to which populations of LDCs must adjust. Modernization involves not only changes in technology, diet, and economic organization, but also changes in ideas, aspirations, and norms. Because populations in developing countries often have little control over the pace or style of development, such changes can be highly stressful. Studying the impact (and the potential alleviation) of such stress is truly an interdisciplinary undertaking. We have identified here several areas in which bioanthropologists are currently contributing to that effort. With their broad range of interests and training, their opportunities for future participation in development research should only expand.

ACKNOWLEDGMENTS

The assistance of Virginia Lathbury, George Armelagos, and Sophie Luzecky is gratefully acknowledged.

Literature Cited

1. Abdurrahman, M. B., Ochoga, S. A. 1978. Casual blood pressure in school children in Kaduna, Nigeria. *Trop. Geogr. Med.* 30:325–29
2. Adair, L. S. 1985. Marginal intake and maternal adaptation: the case of rural Taiwan. In *Energy Intake and Activity*, ed. E. Pollitt, P. Amante. New York: Liss
3. Adair, L. S., Pollitt, E. 1983. Seasonal variation in pre- and postpartum maternal body measurements and infant birth weights. *Am. J. Phys. Anthropol.* 62:325–31
4. Adair, L. S., Pollitt, E. 1985. Outcome of maternal nutritional supplementation: a comprehensive review of the Bacon Chow study. *Am. J. Clin. Nutr.* In press
5. Adair, L. S., Pollitt, E., Mueller, W. H. 1983. Maternal anthropometric changes during pregnancy and lactation in a rural Taiwanese population. *Hum. Biol.* 55:771–87
6. Adams, R. 1972. Some observations on the interrelations of development and nutrition programs. *Ecol. Food Nutr.* 3:85–88
7. Aguirre, A. 1966. Colombia: The family in Candelaria. *Stud. Fam. Plann.* 11:1–5
8. Anderson, J. 1982. *School Lunches in Lesotho*. Maseru: Food & Nutr. Coord. Off.
9. Anderson, J., Morris, L., Pineda, A., Santiso, R. 1980. Determinants of fertility in Guatemala. *Soc. Biol.* 27:20–35
10. Annegers, J. 1973. Seasonal food shortages in West Africa. *Ecol. Food Nutr.* 2:251–57
11. Apfelbaum, M., Bostsarram, J., Locatis, D. 1971. Effect of caloric restriction and excessive calorie intake on energy expenditure. *Am. J. Clin. Nutr.* 24:1405–9
12. Armelagos, G. J., Goodman, A., Jacobs, K. 1978. The ecological perspective in disease. In *Health and the Human Condition*, ed. M. Logan, E. Hunt, pp. 71–83. North Scituate, MA: Duxbury
13. Ashraf, A., Chowdhury, S., Streefland, P. 1982. Health, disease, and health care in rural Bangladesh. *Soc. Sci. Med.* 16:2041–54
14. Ashworth, A. 1968. An investigation of very low calorie intakes reported in Jamaica. *Br. J. Nutr.* 22:341–52
15. Audy, J. R., Dunn, F. L. 1974. Health and disease. In *Human Ecology*, ed. F. Sargent II, pp. 325–43. Amsterdam: North Holland
16. Ayensu, E. S. 1978. *Medicinal Plants of West Africa*. Algonac, MI: Reference Publ.
17. Baer, E., Winikoff, B., eds. 1981. Breastfeeding: Program, policy, and research issues. *Stud. Fam. Plann.* 12:123–206
18. Baer, R. 1984. Nutritional aspects of commercial agriculture. Presented at annual meetings, Am. Anthropol. Assoc., Denver
19. Bailey, S. M., Gershoff, S. N., McGandy, R. B., Nondasuta, A., Tantiwongse, P., et al. 1984. A longitudinal study of growth and maturation in rural Thailand. *Hum. Biol.* 56:539–58
20. Bailey, S. M., Gershoff, S. N., McGandy, R. B., Nondasuta, A., Tantiwongse, P. 1985. Subcutaneous fat remodelling in Southeast Asian infants and children. *Am. J. Phys. Anthropol.* In press
21. Bairagi, R. 1980. Is income the only constraint on child nutrition in Bangladesh? *Bull. WHO* 58:767–72
22. Baker, P. T., Sanders, W. T. 1972. Demographic studies in anthropology. *Ann. Rev. Anthropol.* 1:151–78
23. Baker, P. T., Weiner, J. S., ed. 1964. *The Biology of Human Adaptability*. Oxford: Clarendon
24. Balderston, J. B., Wilson, A. B., Freire, M. E., Simonen, M. S. 1981. *Malnourished Children of the Rural Poor*. Boston: Auburn House
25. Bashir, T., MacDonald, H., Peacock, M. 1981. Biochemical evidence of vitamin D deficiency in pregnant Asian women. *J. Hum. Nutr.* 35:49–52
26. Baumgartner, R. N., Mueller, W. H. 1984. Multivariate analyses of illness data for use in studies on the relationship of physical growth and morbidity. *Hum. Biol.* 56:111–28
27. Beaglehole, R., Eyles, E., Prior, I. 1979. Blood pressure and migration in children. *Int. J. Epidemiol.* 8:5–10
28. Beals, A. 1976. Strategies of resort to curers in South India. In *Asian Medical Systems*, ed. C. Leslie, pp. 184–200. Berkeley: Univ. Calif. Press
29. Becker, G. S. 1981. *A Treatise on the Family*. Cambridge, Mass: Harvard Univ. Press
30. Behar, M. 1977. Protein-calorie deficits in developing countries. *NY Acad. Sci.* 300:176–87
31. Belle, E. A., King, S. D., Griffiths, B. B., Grant, L. S. 1980. Epidemiological investigation for arboviruses in Jamaica, West Indies. *Am. J. Trop. Med. Hyg.* 29:667–75
32. Belli, P. 1971. The economic implications of malnutrition: The dismal science

revisited. *Econ. Dev. Cult. Change* 20(1):1–23
33. Berg, A. 1981. *Malnourished People: A Policy View*. Washington, DC: World Bank
34. Berlin, E., Markell, E. 1977. An assessment of the nutritional and health status of an Aguaruna Jivaro community, Amazonas, Peru. *Ecol. Food Nutr.* 6:69–81
35. Berlyne, G. M., Ben Ari, J., Nord, E., Shainkin, R. 1973. Bedouin osteomalacia due to calcium deprivation caused by high phytic acid content of unleavened bread. *Am. J. Clin. Nutr.* 29:910–11
36. Bessinger, C. D., McNeeley, D. F. 1984. A cooperative model for provision of regional health services in a developing nation. *J. Am. Med. Assoc.* 252:3149–51
37. Bhattacharya, S. K., Mukhopadhyay, B., Bharati, P., Gupta, R., Dey, B., Basu, A. 1981. Intestinal parasitic infestations in populations inhabiting similar and contrasting ecological zones. *Hum. Ecol.* 9:485–94
38. Bielicki, T., Welon, Z. 1982. Growth data as indicators of social inequalities: the case of Poland. *Yearb. Phys. Anthropol.* 25:153–68
39. Billewicz, W. Z., McGregor, I. A. 1982. A birth-to-maturity longitudinal study of heights and weights in two West African (Gambian) villages, 1951–1975. *Ann. Hum. Biol.* 9:309–20
40. Birkbeck, J. 1981. Obesity, socioeconomic variables and eating habits in New Zealand. *J. Biosoc. Sci.* 13:299–307
41. Black, S., Sanjur, D. 1980. Nutrition in Rio Pedras: A study of internal migration and maternal diets. *Ecol. Food Nutr.* 10:25–33
42. Blumberg, B. S. 1977. Australia antigen and the biology of hepatitis B. *Science* 197:17–25
43. Bogin, B. A., MacVean, R. B. 1978. Growth in height and weight of urban Guatemalan primary school children of low and high socioeconomic class. *Hum. Biol.* 50:477–87
44. Bogin, B., MacVean, R. B. 1981. Nutritional and biological determinants of body fat patterning in urban Guatemalan children. *Hum. Biol.* 53:259–68
45. Bogin, B., MacVean, R. B. 1983. The relationship of socioeconomic status and sex to body size, skeletal maturation, and cognitive status of Guatemala City schoolchildren. *Child Dev.*, 54:115–28
46. Bongaarts, J. 1980. Does malnutrition affect fecundability? A summary of the evidence. *Science* 208:564–69
47. Bongaarts, J., Potter, R. 1983. *Fertility, Biology, and Behavior*. New York: Academic
48. Brazier, M. A. B., ed. 1975. *Growth and Development of the Brain: Nutritional, Genetic, and Environmental Factors*. New York: Raven
49. Brown, A., Partridge, W. 1984. Agricultural policy and child health in rural Mexico. Presented at annual meetings, Am. Anthropol. Assoc., Denver, Colo.
50. Brown, D. 1981. General stress in anthropological field work. *Am. Anthropol.* 83:74–92
51. Brown, V., Hanna, J. M., Severson, G. 1984. A quantitative study of dietary change and modernization. *Am. J. Phys. Anthropol.* 63:142 (Abstr.)
52. Brozek, J., Coursin, D. B., Read, M. S. 1977. Longitudinal studies on the effects of malnutrition, nutritional supplementation, and behavioral stimulation. *Bull. Pan Am. Health Organ.* 11:237–49
53. Brozek, J., Schurch, B., eds. 1984. *Malnutrition and Behavior: Critical Assessment of Key Issues*. Lausanne: Nestle Found.
54. Bulatao, R., Lee, R., eds. 1983. *Determinants of Fertility in Developing Countries*, Vols. 1, 2. New York: Academic
55. Bulatao, R., Lee, R. 1983. An overview of fertility determinants in developing countries. In *Determinants of Fertility in Developing Countries*, ed. R. Bulatao, R. Lee, 2:757–87. New York: Academic
56. Buschang, P. H., Malina, R. M. 1983. Growth in height and weight of mild-to-moderately undernourished Zapotec school children. *Hum. Biol.* 55:587–97
57. Caldwell, J. 1982. *The Theory of Fertility Decline*. New York: Academic
58. Caldwell, J., Reddy, P., Caldwell, P. 1983. The causes of marriage change in South India. *Popul. Stud.* 37:343–61
59. Campbell, C. C., Martinez, J. M., Collins, W. E. 1980. Seroepidemiological studies of malaria in pregnant women and newborns from coastal El Salvador. *Am. J. Trop. Med. Hyg.* 29:151–57
60. Cappetta, M. 1983. Population, food, and nutrition: Swaziland, 1940–1982. In *The Swazi Rural Homestead*, ed. F. de Vletter, pp. 163–208. Soc. Sci. Res. Unit. Kwaluseni: Univ. Swaziland
61. Caribbean Food and Nutrition Institute. 1979. *Feeding the Weaning Age Group. Guidelines for the Caribbean*. Kingston, Jamaica: PAHO, WHO
62. Carr-Saunders, A. M. 1922. *The Population Problem. A Study in Human Evolution*. London: Clarendon
63. Cassidy, C. 1980. Benign neglect and toddler malnutrition. See Ref. 177, pp. 109–42

64. Chambers, R., Longhurst, R., Pacey, A., eds. 1981. *Seasonal Dimensions to Rural Poverty.* London: Pinter
65. Chavez, A., Martinez, C. 1973. Nutrition and development of infants from poor rural areas. III. Maternal nutrition and its consequences on fertility. *Nutr. Rep. Int.* 7:1–8
66. Chavez, A., Martinez, C., Bourges, H., Coronado, M., Lopez, M., et al. 1975. Child nutrition problems during lactation in poor rural areas. In *Nutrition,* ed. A. Chavez, H. Bourges, S. Basta, p. 90. Basel: Karger
67. Chen, P. C. 1984. Providing primary health care with non-physicians. *Ann. Acad. Med. Singapore* 13(2):264–71
68. Chernichovsky, D. 1978. *The Economic Theory of the Household and Impact Measurement of Nutrition and Related Health Programs.* World Bank Staff Work. Pap. No. 302. Washington, DC: World Bank
69. Cohen, M. S., Casals, J., Hsiung, G.-D., Kwei, H. E., Chin, C.-C., et al. 1980. Epidemic hemorrhagic fever in Hubei Province, The People's Republic of China: A clinical and serological study. *Yale J. Biol. Med.* 54:41–55
70. Cohen, N., Clayden, A. D. 1978. Seasonal variations in weight of children attending an under-fives clinic in Lesotho. *Acta Paediatr. Scand.* 67:25–31
71. Colson, A. 1971. The differential use of medical resources in developing countries. *J. Health Soc. Behav.* 12:226–37
72. Colson, E. 1979. In good years and in bad: Food strategies of self-reliant societies. *J. Anthropol. Res.* 35:18–29
73. Condon-Paoloni, D., Cravioto, J., Johnston, F. E., De Licardie, E. R., Scholl, T. O. 1977. Morbidity and growth of infants and young children in a rural Mexican village. *Am. J. Public Health* 67:651–56
74. Correa, H., Cummins, G. 1970. Contributions of nutrition to economic growth. *Am. J. Clin. Nutr.* 23:560
75. Cox, G. W. 1980. The ecology of famine: An overview. In *Famine: Its Causes, Effects, and Management,* ed. J. R. K. Robson, pp. 5–18. New York: Gordon & Breach Sci. Publ.
76. Crankshaw, M. E. C. 1980. *Changing Faces of the Achichilas: Medical Systems and Cultural Identity in a Highland Bolivian Village.* PhD thesis. Amherst: Univ. Mass.
77. Cravioto, J. 1970. Complexity of factors involved in protein-calorie malnutrition. *Bibl. Nutr. Dieta* 14:7–22
78. Cravioto, J., Birch, H. G., De Licardie, E. R., Rosales, L. 1967. The ecology of infant weight gain in a pre-industrial society. *Acta Paediatr. Scand.* 56:71–84
79. Cravioto, J., Hambraeus, L., Vahlquist, B., eds. 1974. *Early Malnutrition and Mental Development.* Uppsala: Almqvist & Wilksell
80. Crews, D. 1984. Predictors of cardiovascular mortality in American Samoa. *Am. J. Phys. Anthropol.* 63:149 (Abstr.)
81. Crowdy, J., Consolazio, C., Forbes, A., Haisman, M., Worsley, D. 1982. The metabolic effects of a restricted food intake on men working in a tropical environment. *Hum. Nutr. Appl. Nutr.* 36a:325–44
82. Cutright, P., Hargens, L. 1984. The threshold hypothesis: Evidence from less-developed Latin American countries, 1940–1980. *Demography* 21:459–74
83. Davis, K., Blake, J. 1956. Social structure and fertility: An analytic framework. *Econ. Dev. Cult. Change* 4:211–35
84. Delgado, H., Lechtig, A., Yarbrough, C., Martorell, R., Klein, R., Irwin, M. 1977. Maternal nutrition: Its effects on growth and development and birthspacing. In *Nutritional Impacts on Women throughout Life with Emphasis on Reproduction,* ed. K. Moghissi, T. Evans, pp. 133–50. Hagerstown, MD: Harper & Row
85. Delgado, H., Valverde, V., Belizan, J., Klein, R. 1983. Diarrheal diseases, nutritional status and health care: Analyses of their interrelationships. *Ecol. Food Nutr.* 12:229–34
86. deVletter, F. 1983. *The Swazi Rural Homestead Survey.* Soc. Sci. Res. Unit. Kwaluseni: Univ. Swaziland
87. Dewalt, K. M. 1983. Income and dietary adequacy in an agricultural community. *Soc. Sci. Med.* 17:1877–86
88. Dewalt, K. M., Pelto, G. H. 1977. Food use and household ecology in a Mexican community. In *Nutrition and Anthropology in Action,* ed. T. Fitzgerald, pp. 79–93. Assen, The Netherlands: Van Gorcum
89. Dewalt, K. M., van Willigen, J. 1984. Research priorities for medical anthropologists in the 1980's. *Soc. Sci. Med.* 18(10):845–46
90. Dewey, K. 1979. Agricultural development, diet, and nutrition. *Ecol. Food Nutr.* 8:265–73
91. Dewey, K. 1981. Nutritional consequences of the transformation from subsistence to commercial agriculture in Tabasco, Mexico. *Hum. Ecol.* 9(2):151–87
92. de Zoysa, I., Carson, D., Feachem, R.,

Kirkwood, B., Lindsay-Smith, E., Loewenson, R. 1984. Perceptions of childhood diarrhea and its treatment in rural Zimbabwe. *Soc. Sci. Med.* 19:727–34
93. Dickeman, M. 1979. Female infanticide, reproductive strategies, and social stratification: A preliminary model. In *Evolutionary Biology and Human Social Behavior: An Anthropological Perspective*. North Scituate, MA: Duxbury
94. Divale, W. T., Harris, M. 1976. Population, warfare, and the male supremacist complex. *Am. Anthropol.* 78:521–38
95. Drew, J., London, W. T., Blumberg, B. S., Serjeantson, S. 1982. Hepatitis B virus and sex ratio on Kar Kar Island. *Hum. Biol.* 54:123–35
96. Dufour, D. 1984. The food intake and nutritional status of the Tuanoan Indians in the Northwest Amazon. *Am. J. Phys. Anthropol.* 63(2):153 (Abstr.)
97. Duke, B. 1981. Onchocerciasis. *Br. Med. J.* 283:961–62
98. Dumont, R., Cohen, N. 1980. *The Growth of Hunger*. London: Boyars
99. Durnin, J. V. G. A., Edholm, O. G., Miller, D. S., Waterlow, J. C. 1973. How much food does man require? *Nature* 242:418
100. Dutt, J. 1980. Altitude and fertility: The confounding effect of childhood mortality—a Bolivian example. *Soc. Biol.* 27(2):101–13
101. Eder, J. 1978. The caloric returns to food collecting: Disruption and change among the Batak of the Phillipine tropical forest. *Hum. Ecol.* 6:55–69
102. Edmundson, W. 1977. Individual variations in work output per unit energy intake in East Java. *Ecol. Food Nutr.* 6:147–51
103. Edmundson, W. 1979. Individual variations in basal metabolic rate and mechanical work efficiency in East Java. *Ecol. Food Nutr.* 8:189–95
104. Edmundson, W. 1980. Adaptation to undernutrition: How much food does man need? *Soc. Sci. Med.* 14D:119–26
105. Eicher, C., Baker, D. 1982. *Research on Agricultural Development in Sub-Saharan Africa: A Critical Survey*. MSU Int. Dev. Pap. No. 1, Dep. Agric. Econ. East Lansing: Michigan State Univ.
106. Elegbe, I. A., Elegbe, I. 1983. Quantitative relationships of *Candida albicans* infections and dressing patterns in Nigerian women. *Am. J. Public Health* 73:450–52
107. El-Nofely, A. A. 1978. Anthropometric study of growth of Egyptian Nubian children. *Hum. Biol.* 50:183–208
108. Elvin-Lewis, M. 1983. The antibiotic and healing potential of plants used for teeth cleaning. See Ref. 380, pp. 201–20
109. Erinosho, O. 1977. Belief-system and the concept of mental illness among medical students in a developing country: A Nigerian example. *J. Anthropol. Res.* 33:158–66
110. Etkin, N., Ross, P. 1982. Food as medicine and medicine as food: An adaptive framework for the interpretation of plant utilization among the Hausa of Northern Nigeria. *Soc. Sci. Med.* 16:1559–73
111. Etkin, N., Ross, P. 1983. Malaria, medicine, and meals: Plant use among the Hausa and its impact on disease. See Ref. 380, pp. 231–59
112. Eveleth, P. B., Tanner, J. M. 1976. *Worldwide Variation in Human Growth*. Cambridge: Cambridge Univ. Press
113. Fabrega, H. 1977. Perceived illness and its treatment: A naturalistic study in social medicine. *Br. J. Prev. Soc. Med.* 31:213–19
114. FAO/WHO. 1978. *Requirements for Protein and Energy: An Examination of Current Recommendations*. Report of a group of consultants. Rome: FAO (Mimeo.)
115. Farb, P., Armelagos, G. J. 1980. *Consuming Passions: The Anthropology of Eating*. Boston: Houghton-Mifflin
116. Farley, R. 1970. *Growth of the Black Population: A Study of Demographic Trends*. Chicago: Markam
117. Feachem, R., Burns, E., Cairncross, S., Cronin, A., Cross, P., et al. 1978. *Water, Health, and Development*. London: Tri-Med Books
118. Ferguson, A. E. 1981. Commercial pharmaceutical medicine and medicalization: A case study from El Salvador. *Cult. Med. Psychiatry* 5(2):105–34
119. Ferro-Luzzi, A., Norgan, N., Durnin, J. 1975. Food intake, its relationship to body weight and age; and its apparent nutritional adequacy in New Guinean children. *Am. J. Clin. Nutr.* 28:1443–53
120. Fiawoo, D. K. 1975. Physical growth and the social environment: a West African example. See Ref. 455, pp. 353–66
121. Firth, R. 1961. *Elements of Social Organization*. Boston: Beacon
122. Fischer, M., Little, B. 1984. Socioeconomic, population structure, and migration effects on the epidemiology of malarial infection in an ethnically stratified relocation center near Lahore, Pakistan. *Am. J. Phys. Anthropol.* 63:157 (Abstr.)
123. Fleuret, A. 1979. The role of wild foliage plants in the diet: A case study from Lushoto, Tanzania. *Ecol. Food Nutr.* 8:87–93

124. Fleuret, P., Fleuret, A. 1980. Nutrition, consumption, and agricultural change. *Hum. Organ.* 39:250–60
125. Fleuret, P., Fleuret, A. 1983. Socioeconomic determinants of child nutrition in Taita, Kenya: A call for discussion. *Cult. Agric.* 19:8,16–20
126. Florencio, C. 1980. Comparison of the determinants of nutrient intake of rural and urban families. *Ecol. Food Nutr.* 10:97–104
127. Florencio, C., Smith, V. 1969. Efficacy of food purchasing among working-class families in Colombia. *J. Am. Diet. Assoc.* 55:239–45
128. Ford, T., Arcury, T. 1984. Population and health in the developing world: Research perspectives for medical anthropologists. *Soc. Sci. Med.* 18:855–59
129. Foster, G. M. 1978. Medical anthropology and international health planning. See Ref. 283, pp. 301–13
130. Foster, G. M. 1982. Community development and primary health care: Their conceptual similarities. *Med. Anthropol.* 6(3):183–95
131. Foster, G. M. 1984. Anthropological research perspectives on health problems in developing countries. *Soc. Sci. Med.* 18:847–54
132. Foster, G. M., Anderson, B. 1978. *Medical Anthropology*. New York: Wiley
133. Foulkes, J. 1981. Human trypanosomiasis in Africa. *Br. Med. J.* 283:1172–74
134. Fox, R. 1953. *A Study of the Energy Expenditure of Africans Engaged in Various Rural Activities, with Special Reference to Some Environmental and Physiological Factors Which May Influence the Efficiency of Their Work*. PhD thesis. London: Univ. London Press
135. Francois, P., Dubois, J., Yai, E. 1983. Energy cost and daily timed activities: An activity index based on Ivory Coast data. *Food Nutr.* 9:30–37
136. Frankenberg, R. 1980. Medical anthropology and development: A theoretical perspective. *Soc. Sci. Med. B* 14:197–207
137. Freeman, H. E., Klein, R. E., Townsend, J. W., Lechtig, A. 1980. Nutrition and cognitive development among rural Guatemalan children. *Am. J. Public Health* 70:1277–85
138. Freeman, M. 1971. A social and economic analysis of systemic female infanticide. *Am. Anthropol.* 73:1011–1018
139. Friedlaender, J., Rhoads, J. 1982. Patterns of adult weight and fat change in six Solomon Islands societies: A semilongitudinal study. *Soc. Sci. Med.* 16:05–15
140. Frisancho, A. R. 1974. Triceps skin fold and upper arm muscle size norms for assessment of nutritional status. *Am. J. Clin. Nutr.* 27:1052–1058
141. Frisancho, A. R. 1978. Nutritional influences on human growth and maturation. *Yearb. Phys. Anthropol.* 21:174–91
142. Frisancho, A. R. 1981. New norms of upper limb fat and muscle areas for assessment of nutritional status. *Am. J. Clin. Nutr.* 34:2540–45
143. Frisancho, A. R. 1984. Influence of growth status and placental function on birth weights of infants born to young still-growing teenagers. *Am. J. Clin. Nutr.* 40:801–7
144. Frisancho, A. R., Guire, K., Babler, W., Borkan, G., Way, A. 1980. Nutritional influences on child development and genetic control of adolescent growth of Quechuas and Mestizos from the Peruvian lowlands. *Am. J. Phys. Anthropol.* 52:367–76
145. Frisancho, A. R., Klayman, J. E., Matos, J. 1976. Symbiotic relationship of high fertility, high childhood mortality, and socio-economic status in an urban Peruvian population. *Hum. Biol.* 48(1):101–11
146. Frisancho, A. R., Klayman, J. E., Matos, J. 1977. Influence of maternal nutritional status on prenatal growth in a Peruvian population. *Am. J. Phys. Anthropol.* 46:265–74
147. Frisancho, A. R., Matos, J., Bollettino, L. A. 1984. Influence of growth status and placental function on birth weights of infants born to young still-growing teenagers. *Am. J. Clin. Nutr.* 40:801–7
148. Frisancho, A. R., Matos, J., Flegel, P. 1983. Maternal nutritional status and adolescent pregnancy outcome. *Am. J. Clin. Nutr.* 38:739–46
149. Frisancho, A. R., Sanchez, J., Pallardel, D., Yanez, L. 1973. Adaptive significance of small body size under poor socioeconomic conditions in southern Peru. *Am. J. Phys. Anthropol.* 39:255–62
150. Frisch, R. E. 1972. Weight at menarche: Similarity for well-nourished and undernourished girls at differing ages, and evidence for historical constancy. *Pediatrics* 50:445–50
151. Frisch, R. E. 1976. Fatness of girls from menarche to age 18, with a nomogram. *Hum. Biol.* 48:353–59
152. Frisch, R. E. 1978. Population, food intake, and fertility: Historical evidence for a direct effect of nutrition on reproductive ability. *Science* 199:22–29
153. Frisch, R. E., McArthur, J. 1974. Menstrual cycles: Fatness as a determinant of

minimum weight for height necessary for their maintenance or onset. *Science* 185:949–51
154. Froment, A., Larouze, B., Feret, E., Marinier, E., Sow, A. M., et al. 1981. Hepatitis B infection and the prevention of primary hepatocellular carcinoma: Studies in Senegal. *Prog. Med. Virol.* 27:133–36
155. Gadjusek, D. C. 1977. Unconventional viruses and the origin and disappearance of Kuru. *Science* 197:943–60
156. Gadjusek, D. C. 1977. Urgent opportunistic observations: the study of changing, transient, and disappearing phenomena of medical interest in disrupted primitive human communities. *Health and Disease in Tribal Societies*. Ciba Found. Symp. 49, pp. 69–101. North Holland: Elsevier
157. Gadjusek, D. C., Zigas, V. 1959. Kuru: clinical, pathological and epidemiological study of an acute progressive degenerative disease of the central nervous system among natives of the eastern highlands of New Guinea. *Am. J. Med.* 26:442–69
158. Galvin, K. 1984. Seasonal variation in diet of the nomadic, pastoral Turkana. *Am. J. Phys. Anthropol.* 63:159 (Abstr.)
159. Garn, S. M. 1966. Malnutrition and skeletal development in the pre-school child. In *Pre-school Child Malnutrition*, pp. 43–62. Washington, DC: Natl. Res. Council
160. Garn, S. M., Guzman, M. A., Wagner, B. 1969. Subperiosteal gain and endosteal loss in protein-calorie malnutrition. *Am. J. Phys. Anthropol.* 30:153–56
161. Garn, S. M., Rosenberg, K. R., Schaefer, A. E. 1983. Relationship between fatness level and size attainment in Central America. *Ecol. Food Nutr.* 13:157–65
162. Garrow, J. S. 1978. *Energy Balance and Obesity in Man*. Amsterdam: Elsevier
163. Gaulin, S., Konner, M. 1977. On the natural diet of primates, including humans. See Ref. 465, pp. 2–86
164. Germain, M., Francy, D. B., Monath, T. P., Ferrara, L., Bryan, J., et al. 1980. Yellow fever in the Gambia 1978–1979: Entomological aspects and epidemiological correlations. *Am. J. Trop. Med. Hyg.* 29:929–40
165. Gilles, H. 1981. Malaria. *Br. Med. J.* 283:1382–85
166. Godoy, G., Orihel, T., Volcan, G. 1980. *Microfilaria bolivarensis:* A new species of filaria from man in Venezuela. *Am. J. Trop. Med. Hyg.* 29:545–47
167. Goldstein, H., Tanner, J. M. 1980. Ecological considerations in the creation and the use of child growth standards. *Lancet* 1:582–85
168. Goldstein, M. C., Beall, C. M. 1982. Indirect modernization and the status of the elderly in a rural third world setting. *J. Gerontol.* 37:743–48
169. Gopalan, C., Naidu, A. N. 1972. Nutrition and fertility. *Lancet* 2:1077–79
170. Gould, H. 1965. Modern medicine and folk cognition in India. *Hum. Organ.* 24:201–8
171. Graham, G. G., MacLean, W. C. Jr., Kallman, C. H., Rabold, J., Mellits, E. D. 1980. Urban-rural differences in the growth of Peruvian children. *Am. J. Clin. Nutr.* 33:338–44
172. Gramiccia, G., Hempel, J. 1972. Mortality and morbidity from malaria in countries where malaria eradication is not making satisfactory progress. *J. Trop. Med. Hyg.* 75:187–92
173. Gray, R. 1983. The impact of health and nutrition on natural fertility. See Ref. 55
174. Green, E., Makhubu, L. 1984. Traditional healers in Swaziland: Toward improved cooperation between the traditional and modern health sectors. *Soc. Sci. Med.* 18:1071–79
175. Greenberg, L. 1982. Midwife training programs in highland Guatemala. *Soc. Sci. Med.* 16:1599–1609
176. Greene, L. S., ed. 1977. *Malnutrition, Behavior, and Social Organization*. New York: Academic
177. Greene, L. S., Johnston, F. E. eds., 1980. *Social and Biological Predictors of Nutritional Status, Physical Growth, and Neurological Development*. New York: Academic
178. Greksa, L. P. 1984. Maximal work capacity in European and Aymara boys at altitude. *Am. J. Phys. Anthropol.* 63:167 (Abstr.)
179. Greksa, L. P., Baker, P. T. 1982. Aerobic capacity of modernizing Samoan men. *Hum. Biol.* 54:777–88
180. Grivetti, L. 1979. Kalahari agropastoralist-hunter-gatherers: The Tswana example. *Ecol. Food Nutr.* 7:235–56
181. Gross, D. R. 1975. Protein capture and cultural development in the Amazon Basin. *Am. Anthropol.* 77:526–49
182. Gross, D. R., Underwood, B. A. 1971. Technological change and caloric costs: Sisal agriculture in Northeast Brazil. *Am. Anthropol.* 73:725–40
183. Gussler, J. D., Mock, N. 1983. A comparative description of infant feeding practices in Zaire, the Philippines, and St. Kitts-Nevis. *Ecol. Food Nutr.* 13:75–85
184. Guthrie, G. M., Guthrie, H. A., Fernandez, T. L., Estrera, N. 1983. Early termination of breastfeeding among Philip-

pine urban poor. *Ecol. Food Nutr.* 12: 195–202
185. Gwatkin, D. R. 1981. Signs of change in mortality trends—Is progress slowing? *Dev. Digest* 19:54–64
186. Haas, J. D., Harrison, G. G. 1977. Nutritional anthropology and biological adaptation. *Ann. Rev. Anthropol.* 6:69–101
187. Habicht, J.-P., Meyers, L. D., Brownie, C. 1982. Overview: indicators for identifying and counting the improperly nourished. *Am. J. Clin. Nutr.* 35:1241–54
188. Habicht, J.-P., Yarbrough, C., Martorell, R. 1979. Anthropometric field methods: criteria for selection. See Ref. 236, pp. 365–88
189. Habicht, J.-P., Yarbrough, C., Martorell, R., Malina, R. M., Klein, R. E. 1974. Height and weight standards for preschool children. *Lancet* 1:611–14
190. Halberstein, R. A., Davies, J. E. 1984. Biosocial aspects of high blood pressure in people of the Bahamas. *Hum. Biol.* 56:317–28
191. Hamill, P. V. V., Johnson, C. L., Reed, R. B., Roche, A. F. 1977. *NCHS growth curves for children birth–18 years*. Publ. (PHS)78–1650. Hyattsville, MD: Natl. Ctr. Health Stat.
192. Hanks, L. 1972. *Rice and Man.* Arlington Heights, IL: AHIM Publ.
193. Hann, H.-W., Kim, C., London, W. T., Whitford, P., Blumberg, B. S. 1982. Hepatitis B virus and primary hepatocellular carcinoma: Family studies in Korea. *Int. J. Cancer* 30:47–51
194. Hanna, J. M., Baker, P. T. 1979. Biocultural correlates to the blood pressure of Samoan migrants in Hawaii. *Hum. Biol.* 51:481–97
195. Harris, B., Harris, J. 1982. Development studies. *Progr. Hum. Geogr.* 6:584–92
196. Harvey, P. W., Heywood, P. F. 1983. Twenty-five years of dietary change in Simbu Province, Papua New Guinea. *Ecol. Food Nutr.* 13:27–35
197. Hasan, K. A. 1981. The ecology of health and disease: Some biological and cultural considerations. *Mankind Q.* 21: 315–25
198. Haswell, M. 1953. *Economics of Agriculture in a Savanna Village.* Colonial Res. Study No. 8. London: HMSO.
199. Hausman, A., Wilmsen, E. 1984. Impact of seasonality of food on growth and fertility. *Am. J. Phys. Anthropol.* 63:169 (Abstr.)
200. Hauspie, R. C., Das, S. R., Preece, M. A., Tanner, J. M. 1980. A longitudinal study of the growth in height of boys and girls of West Bengal (India) aged six months to 20 years. *Ann. Hum. Biol.* 7:429–40
201. Heller, P. 1982. A model of the demand for medical and health services in peninsular Malaysia. *Soc. Sci. Med.* 16: 267–84
202. Helm, J. 1980. Female infanticide, European diseases, and population levels among the McKenzie Dene. *Am. Ethnol.* 7:259–85
203. Henry, L. 1953. Fondements theoriques des mesures de la fecondite naturelle. *Rev. Inst. Int. Stat.* 21:135–51
204. Henry, L. 1961. Some data on natural fertility. *Eugen Q.* 8:81–91
205. Hiernaux, J. 1970. Interpopulation variation in growth, with special reference to sub-Saharan Africa. *Monogr. Soc. Res. Child Dev.* 37(7):74–77
206. Hill, C. 1984. The challenge of comparative health policy research for applied medical anthropology. *Soc. Sci. Med.* 18(10):861–71
207. Himes, J. H. 1978. Bone growth and development in protein-calorie malnutrition. *World Rev. Nutr. Diet.* 28:143–87
208. Himes, J. H., Malina, R. M. 1975. Age and secular factors in the stature of adult Zapotec males,. *Am. J. Phys. Anthropol.* 43:367–70
209. Himes, J. H., Malina, R. M., Stepick, C. D. 1976. Relationships between body size and second metacarpal dimensions in Oaxaca (Mexico) school children 6 to 14 years of age. *Hum. Biol.* 48:677–92
210. Himes, J. H., Martorell, R., Habicht, J.-P., Malina, R. M., Klein, R. E. 1975. Patterns of cortical bone growth in moderately malnourished preschool children. *Hum. Biol.* 47:337–50
211. Himes, J. H., Mueller, W. H. 1977. Aging and secular change in adult stature in rural Colombia. *Am. J. Phys. Anthropol.* 46:275–80
212. Hirschman, C., Rindfuss, C. R. 1982. The sequence and timing of family formation events in Asia. *Am. Sociol. Rev.* 47:660–80
213. Hofvander, Y., Petros-Barvazian, A. 1978. WHO collaborative study on breastfeeding. *Acta Paediatr. Scand.* 67: 556–60
214. Howell, N. 1979. *Demography of the Dobe !Kung.* New York: Academic
215. Huffman, S. 1984. Determinants of breastfeeding in developing countries: overview and policy implications. *Stud. Fam. Plann.* 15(4):170–83
216. Huffman, S. L., Chowdhury, A. K. M. A., Mosley, W. H. 1978. Postpartum amenorrhea: How is it affected by maternal nutritional status? *Science* 200:1155–57

217. Hunter, J. M. 1967. Seasonal hunger in part of the West African savanna: A study of Nangodi, Northeast Ghana. *Trans. Inst. Br. Geogr.* 41:167–85
218. Hunter, J. M., Arbona, S. 1984. Disease rate as an artifact of the health care system: Tuberculosis in Puerto Rico. *Soc. Sci. Med.* 9:997–1008
219. Huss-Ashmore, R. 1980. Fat and fertility: Demographic implications of differential fat storage. *Yearb. Phys. Anthropol.* 23:65–91
220. Huss-Ashmore, R. 1982. Seasonality in rural highland Lesotho: Method and Policy. In *A Report on the Regional Workshop on Seasonal Variations in the Provisioning, Nutrition, and Health of Rural Families*. Nairobi: AMREF
221. Huss-Ashmore, R. 1984. Food, health, and agricultural underdevelopment. Presented at annual meetings, Am. Anthropol. Assoc., Denver, Colo.
222. Huss-Ashmore, R. 1984. Seasonal cycles of nutrition and resource procurement in Lesotho. *Am. J. Phys. Anthropol.* 63(2):173 (Abstr.)
223. Huss-Ashmore, R. 1984. *Strategies for Health Care in Highland Lesotho*. PhD thesis. Amherst: Univ. Mass.
224. Deleted in proof
225. Hutchinson, J. 1984. Biocultural analysis of blood pressure variation among the Black Caribs of St. Vincent, West Indies. *Am. J. Phys. Anthropol.* 63:173 (Abstr.)
226. Immink, M., Viteri, F. 1981. Energy intake and productivity of Guatemalan sugarcane cutters: An empirical test of the efficiency wage hypothesis. *J. Dev. Econ.* 9:230–87
227. Imperato, P. J. 1975. Traditional medical practitioners among the Bambara of Mali and their role in the modern health care delivery system. *Trop. Geogr. Med.* 27:211–21
228. Indian Council of Medical Research. 1972. *Growth and Physical Development of Indian Infants and Children*. Tech. Rep. No. 18, Indian Coun. Med. Res., New Delhi
229. International Center for Research on Women. 1980. *The Productivity of Women in Developing Countries: Measurement Issues and Recommendations*. Office of Women in Development. Washington, DC: USAID
230. International Union of Nutritional Sciences. 1971. The creation of growth standards: a committee report of a meeting in Tunis. *Am. J. Clin. Nutr.* 25:218–20
231. Jackson, L., Jackson, R. 1984. Health implications of chronic dietary cyanide ingestion. *Am. J. Phys. Anthropol.* 63:174 (Abstr.)
232. James, G. D., Jenner, D. 1984. The association among blood pressure, stress, and lifestyle in Western Samoan men. *Am. J. Phys. Anthropol.* 63:174 (Abstr.)
233. James, G. D., McGarvey, S. T., Baker, P. T. 1983. The effect of modernization on spouse concordance in American Samoa. *Hum. Biol.* 55:643–52
234. James, W., Shettey, P. 1982. Metabolic adaptations and energy requirements in developing countries. *Am. J. Clin. Nutr.* 36C:331–36
235. Jelliffe, D. B. 1966. *The Assessment of the Nutritional Status of the Community*. Geneva: WHO
236. Jelliffe, D. B., Jelliffe, E. F. B., eds. 1979. *Nutrition and Growth*. New York: Plenum
237. Jenkins, C. L. 1981. Patterns of growth and malnutrition among preschoolers in Belize. *Am. J. Phys. Anthropol.* 56:169–78
238. Jenkins, C. L. 1982. Factors in the aetiology of poor growth in Belize. *Cajanus* 15:172–84
239. Jerome, N. W., Pelto, G. H., Kandel, R. 1980. An ecological approach to nutritional anthropology. See Ref. 240, pp. 13–46
240. Jerome, N. W., Kandel, R., Pelto, G. H., eds. 1980. *Nutritional Anthropology*. Pleasantville, NY: Redgrave
241. Jobin, W. 1980. Sugar and snails: The Ecology of Bilharziasis related to agriculture in Puerto Rico. *Am. J. Trop. Med. Hyg.* 29:86–94
242. Johnson, C. L., Fulwood, R., Abraham, S., Bryner, J. D. 1981. *Basic data on anthropometric measurements and angular measurements of the hip and knee joints for selected groups 1–74 years of age*. (PHS) 81-1669. Hyattsville, MD: US Dep. Health Human Resources
243. Johnston, F. E. 1981. Anthropometry and nutritional status. In *Assessing Changing Food Consumption Patterns*. Natl. Res. Coun., pp. 252–64. Washington, DC: Natl. Acad. Press
244. Johnston, F. E. 1981. Physical growth and development: epidemiological considerations. *Fed. Proc.* 40:2583–87
245. Johnston, F. E. 1985. Reference data for physical growth in nutritional anthropology. *Training Manual in Nutritional Anthropology*, ed. S. Quandt, C. Ritenbaugh. Washington, DC: Am. Anthropol. Assoc.
245a. Johnston, F. E., Bogin, B. A., MacVean, R. B., Newman, B. C. 1984. A comparison of international standards versus local reference data for the triceps and subscapular skinfolds of Guatemalan children and youth. *Hum. Biol.* 56:143–56

246. Johnston, F. E., Bogin, B. A., MacVean, R. B., Newman, B. C. 1984. A comparison of international standards versus local reference data for the triceps and subscapular skinfolds of Guatemalan children and youth. *Hum. Biol.* 56:157–71
247. Johnston, F. E., Borden, M., MacVean, R. B. 1973. Height, weight, and their growth velocities in Guatemalan private school children of high socioeconomic class. *Hum. Biol.* 45:627–41
248. Johnston, F. E., Borden, M., MacVean, R. B. 1975. The effects of genetic and environmental factors upon the growth of children in Guatemala City. See Ref. 455, pp. 377–88
249. Johnston, F. E., Dechow, P. C., MacVean, R. B. 1975. Age changes in skinfold thickness among upper class children of differing ethnic backgrounds residing in Guatemala. *Hum. Biol.* 47:251–62
250. Johnston, F. E., Lampl, M. 1984. Anthropometric assessment. See Ref. 53, pp. 51–70
250a. Johnston, F. E., Low, S. M., de Baessa, Y., MacVean, R. B. 1985. Growth status of disadvantaged urban Guatemalan children of a resettled community. *Am. J. Phys. Anthropol.* In press
251. Johnston, F. E., Newman, B., Cravioto, J., De Licardie, E. R., Scholl, T. O. 1980. A factor analysis of correlates of nutritional status in Mexican children, birth to 3 years. See Ref. 177, pp. 291–310
251a. Johnston, F. E., Roche, A. F., Susanne, C., eds. 1980. *Human Physical Growth and Maturation, Methodologies and Factors*. New York: Plenum
252. Johnston, F. E., Scholl, T. O., Newman, B. C., Cravioto, J., DeLicardie, E. R. 1980. An analysis of environmental variables and factors associated with growth failure in a Mexican village. *Hum. Biol.* 52:627–37
253. Johnston, F. E., Wainer, H., Thissen, D., MacVean, R. B. 1976. Hereditary and environmental determinants of growth in height in a longitudinal sample of children and youth of Guatemalan and European ancestry. *Am. J. Phys. Anthropol.* 44:469–76
254. Johnston, F. E., Roche, A., Schell, L. M., Wettenhall, N. 1975. Critical weight at menarche: A critique of a hypothesis. *Am. J. Dis. Children* 129:19–23
255. Kanawati, A. A., McLaren, D. S. 1973. Failure to thrive in Lebanon. II. An investigation of the causes. *Acta Paediatr. Scand.* 62:571–76
256. Kaplan, J. E., Larrick, J. W., Yost, J., Farrell, L., Greenberg, H. B., et al. 1980. Infectious disease patterns in the Waorani, an isolated Amerindian population. *Am. J. Trop. Med. Hyg.* 29:298–312
257. Katz, S. 1972. Biological factors in population control. See Ref. 409, pp. 351–69
258. Katz, S. 1982. Food, behavior, and biocultural evolution. *The Psychology of Human Food Selection*, ed. L. Barker, pp. 171–88. Westport, Conn: Avi
259. Keen, P., Fripp, P. J. 1980. Bladder cancer in an endemic schistosomiasis area: Geographical and sex distribution. *S. Afr. J. Sci.* 76:228–29
260. Keith, M., Armelagos, G. J. 1983. Naturally occurring dietary antibiotics and human health. See Ref. 380, pp. 221–30
261. Keys, A., Brozek, J., Henschel, A., Mickelson, O., Taylor, H. 1950. *The Biology of Human Starvation*. Minneapolis: Univ. Minn. Press
262. Knodel, J., van de Walle, E. 1979. Lessons from the past: Policy implications of historical fertility studies. *Popul. Dev. Rev.* 5:217–45
263. Kourany, M., Johnson, K. M. 1980. A survey of Q fever antibodies in a high risk population in Panama. *Am. J. Trop. Med. Hyg.* 29:1007–11
264. Kroeger, A. 1983. Anthropological and socio-medical health care research in developing countries. *Soc. Sci. Med.* 17(3):147–61
265. Kroeger, A. 1983. Health interview surveys in developing countries: A review of the methods and results. *Int. J. Epidemiol.* 12:465–81
266. Kumar, S. K. 1977. *Role of the Household Economy in Determining Child Nutrition at Low Income Levels. A Case Study in Kerala*. Occas. Pap. No. 95, Dep. Agric. Econ. Ithaca: Cornell Univ.
267. Kunstadter, P. 1980. Medical ethics in cross-cultural and multi-cultural perspectives. *Soc. Sci. Med.* 14B:289–96
268. Lampl, M., Johnston, F. E., Malcolm, L. A. 1978. The effects of protein supplementation on the growth and skeletal maturation of New Guinean school children. *Ann. Hum. Biol.* 5:219–27
269. Classification of infantile malnutrition. 1970. *Lancet* 2:302
270. Larouze, B., Blumberg, B. S., London, W. T., Lustbader, E., Sankale, M., Payet, M. 1977. Forecasting the development of primary hepatocellular carcinoma by the use of risk factors: Studies in West Africa. *J. Natl. Cancer Inst.* 58:1557–61
271. Latham, M. 1975. Nutrition and infec-

tion in national development. *Science* 188:589–93
272. Lau, R. M., Brown, D. E. 1984. Acclimatization and acute mountain sickness in shift workers at high altitude. *Am. J. Phys. Anthropol.* 63:182 (Abstr.)
273. Lawrence, D. N., Neel, J. V., Ababie, S. H., Moore, L. L., Adams, L. J., Healy, G. R., Kagan, I. G. 1980. Epidemiological studies among Amerindian populations of Amazonia. *Am. J. Trop. Med. Hyg.* 29:530–37
274. Lechtig, A., Delgado, H., Lasky, R., Yarbrough, C., Klein, R. E., et al. 1975. Maternal nutrition and fetal growth in developing countries. *Am. J. Dis. Child.* 129:553–56
275. Lechtig, A., Yarbrough, C., Delgado, H., Martorell, R., Klein, R. E., Behar, M. 1975. Effect of maternal malnutrition on the placenta. *Am. J. Obstet. Gynecol.* 123:191–201
276. Leridon, H. 1977. *Human Fertility: The Basic Components.* Chicago: Univ. Chicago Press
276a. Leslie, C. 1980. Medical pluralism in world perspective. *Soc. Sci. Med.* 14B(4):191–95
277. Lesthaeghe, R., Page, H. 1980. The post-partum non-susceptible period. Development and application of model schedules. *Popul. Stud.* 34:143–70
277a. Lewin, C. 1947. Group decision and social change. See Ref. 342a, pp. 330–44
278. Linares, O. 1976. "Garden hunting" in the American tropics. *Hum. Ecol.* 4:331–50
279. Little, M. A., Galvin, K., Mugambi, M. 1983. Cross-sectional growth of nomadic Turkana pastoralists. *Hum. Biol.* 55:811–30
280. Little, M. A., Johnson, B. R. 1984. Arm strength, muscle fatigue, and body composition in nomadic Turkana pastoralists. *Am. J. Phys. Anthropol.* 63:186 (Abstr.)
281. Livingstone, F. 1958. Anthropological implications of sickle cell gene distribution in West Africa. *Am. Anthropol.* 60:533–62
282. Logan, M. 1978. Humoral medicine in Guatemala and peasant acceptance of modern medicine. See Ref. 283, pp. 363–75
283. Logan, M., Hunt, E., eds. 1978. *Health and the Human Condition.* North Scituate, MA: Duxbury
284. Longhurst, R. 1981. *Rural Development Planning and the Provision of Improved Nutrition and Child Health.* Dep. Agric. Econ. Rural Sociol. Work. Pap. No. 1. Zaria, Nigeria: Ahmadu Bello Univ.
285. Lunt, R. 1984. Worldwide early detection of cervical cancer. *Obstet. Gynecol.* 63:708–13
286. Lusty, T. 1981. The child in the third world. *Am. J. Dis. Child.* 135:462–66
287. Makhubu, L. 1982. Interview. In *Science in Africa: Interviews with African Scientists,* ed. L. Nichols. Washington, DC: Voice of America
288. Malcolm, L. A. 1975. Some biosocial determinants of the growth, health, and nutritional status of Papua New Guinean preschool children. See Ref. 455, pp. 367–76
289. Malina, R. M., Buschang, P. H., Aronson, W. L., Selby, H. A. 1982. Childhood growth status of eventual migrants and sedentes in a rural Zapotec community in the Valley of Oaxaca, Mexico. *Hum. Biol.* 54:709–16
290. Malina, R. M., Chumlea, C. 1980. Reexamination of the age at menarche in Oaxaca, Mexico. *Ann. Hum. Biol.* 7:281–83
291. Malina, R. M., Chumlea, C., Stepick, C. D., Lopez, F. G. 1977. Age of menarche in Oaxaca, Mexico, schoolgirls, with comparative data for other areas of Mexico. *Ann. Hum. Biol.* 4:551–58
292. Malina, R. M., Himes, J. H. 1977. Seasonality of births in a rural Zapotec municipio, 1945–1970. *Hum. Biol.* 49:125–37
293. Malina, R. M., Himes, J. H. 1977. Differential age effects in seasonal variation of mortality in a rural Zapotec-speaking municipio, 1945–1970. *Hum. Biol.* 49:415–28
294. Mamdani, M. 1971. *The Myth of Population Control.* New York: Monthly Rev. Press
295. Marchione, T. J. 1980. The dynamics of malnutrition in Jamaica. See Ref. 177, pp. 201–22
296. Martorell, R. 1984. Comment. See Ref. 53, pp. 71–76
297. Martorell, R., Delgado, H., Valverde, V., Klein, R. E. 1981. Maternal stature, fertility, and infant mortality. *Hum. Biol.* 53:303–12
298. Martorell, R., Klein, R. E., Delgado, H. 1980. Improved nutrition and its effects on anthropometric indicators of nutritional status. *Nutr. Rep. Inter.* 21:219–30
299. Martorell, R., Yarbrough, C., Klein, R. M., Lechtig, A. 1979. Malnutrition, body size, and skeletal maturation: interrelationships and implications for catch-up growth. *Hum. Biol.* 51:371–89
300. Martorell, R., Yarbrough, C., Lechtig, A., Delgado, H., Klein, R. E. 1977. Genetic-environmental interactions in physical growth. *Acta Pediatr. Scand.* 66:579–84

301. Martorell, R., Yarbrough, C., Lechtig, A., Habicht, J.-P., Klein, R. E. 1977. Diarrheal diseases and growth retardation in preschool Guatemalan children. *Am. J. Phys. Anthropol.* 43:341–46
302. Martorell, R., Yarbrough, C., Malina, R. M., Habicht, J.-P., Lechtig, A., Klein, R. E. 1975. The head circumference/chest circumference ratio in mild-to-moderate protein-calorie malnutrition. *Environ. Child Health* 20:203–7
303. Martorell, R., Yarbrough, C., Yarbrough, S., Klein, R. E. 1980. The impact of ordinary illnesses on the dietary intakes of malnourished children. *Am. J. Clin. Nutr.* 33:345–50
304. Martz, J. 1984. Stress in daily life: Evidence from Samoa. *Am. J. Phys. Anthropol.* 63:190 (Abstr.)
305. Mata, L. J. 1977. Environmental determinants and origins of malnutrition. See Ref. 421, pp. 9–20
306. Mata, L. 1978. Breast feeding: Main promoter of infant health. *Am. J. Clin. Nutr.* 34:2058–65
307. Mata, L. 1978. *The Children of Santa Maria Cauque: A Prospective Field Study of Health and Growth.* Cambridge, MA: MIT Press
308. May, J. 1960. The ecology of human disease. *Ann. NY Acad. Sci.* 84:789–94
309. McFalls, J., McFalls, M. 1984. *Disease and Fertility.* New York: Academic
310. McGarvey, S. T. 1984. Subcutaneous fat distribution and blood pressure of Samoans. *Am. J. Phys. Anthropol.* 63:192 (Abstr.)
311. McGarvey, S. T., Baker, P. T. 1979. The effects of modernization and migration on Samoan blood pressures. *Hum. Biol.* 51:461–79
312. McGarvey, S. T., Schendel, D., Baker, P. T. 1980. Modernization effects on familial aggregation of Samoan blood pressure: A preliminary report. *Med. Anthropol.* 4:321–38
313. McGregor, I. A., Rahman, A. K., Thompson, B., Billewicz, W. Z., Thomson, A. M. 1968. The growth of young children in a Gambian village. *Trans. R. Soc. Trop. Med. Hyg.* 62:341–52
314. McGregor, I. A., Rahman, A. K., Thomson, A. M., Billewicz, W. Z., Thompson, B. 1970. The health of young children in a West African (Gambian) village. *Trans. R. Soc. Trop. Med. Hyg.* 64:48–77
315. McKay, H., Sinisterra, L., McKay, A., Gomez, H., Lloreda, P. 1978. Improving cognitive ability in chronically deprived children. *Science* 200:270–78
316. McLaren, D. 1976. *Nutrition and its Disorders.* Edinburgh: Churchill Livingstone. 2nd ed.
317. McLaren, D. S., Read, W. W. C. 1972. Classification of nutritional status in early childhood. *Lancet* 2:146–48
318. McLean, C. U. 1971. *Magical Medicine.* London: Allen Lane/Penguin
319. McLean, C. U., Bannerman, R. H. 1982. Utilization of indigenous healers in national health delivery systems. *Soc. Sci. Med.* 16:1815–16
320. Mendez Dominguez, A. 1980. *Culture Change and Differential Fertility.* Battelle Mem. Inst. Human Affairs Res. Center, Universidad del Valle de Guatemala. Final rep.
321. Menken, J., Bongaarts, J. 1978. Reproductive models in the study of nutrition-fertility interrelationships. See Ref. 333, pp. 261–312. New York: Plenum
322. Menken, J., Trussell, J., Watkins, S. 1981. The nutrition-fertility link: An evaluation of the evidence. *J. Interdisc. Hist.* 9:425–41
323. Meredith, H. V. 1969. *Body Size of Contemporary Groups of Eight Year Old Children. Studies in Different Parts of the World. Monogr. Soc. Res. Child Dev.* 34:1
324. Meredith, H. V. 1976. Findings from Asia, Australia, Europe, and North America on secular change in mean height of children, youths, and young adults. *Am. J. Phys. Anthropol.* 44:315–26
325. Messer, E. 1984. Anthropological perspectives on diet. *Ann. Rev. Anthropol.* 13:205–49
326. Micozzi, M. 1982. Skeletal tuberculosis, pelvic contraction, and parturition. *Am. J. Phys. Anthropol.* 58:441–45
327. Millard, A. 1982. Child mortality and lactation contraception in Mexico. *Med. Anthropol.* 6(3):147–64
328. Mitchell, H. F., Mitchell, J. C. 1980. Social factors in the perception of the causes of disease. In *Numerical Techniques in Social Anthropology,* ed. J. Mitchell, pp. 49–68. Philadelphia: ISHI
329. Molineaux, L., Storey, J., Cohen, J. E., Thomas, A. 1980. A longitudinal study of human malaria in the West African savanna in the absence of control measures. *Am. J. Trop. Med. Hyg.* 29:725–37
330. Mora, J. O., Herrera, M. G., Suescun, J., de Navarro, L., Wagner, M. 1981. The effects of nutritional supplementation on physical growth of children at risk of malnutrition. *Am. J. Clin. Nutr.* 34:1885–92
331. Mora, J. O., Sellers, S. G., Suescun, J.,

Herrera, M. G. 1981. The impact of supplementary feeding and home education on physical growth of disadvantaged children. *Nutr. Res.* 1:213–25
332. Moreno-Black, G. 1983. Dietary status and dietary diversity of native highland Bolivian children. *Ecol. Food Nutr.* 13:149–56
333. Mosley, W. H., ed. 1978. *Nutrition and Human Reproduction*. New York: Plenum
334. Moss, N. H., Mayer, J., eds. 1977. *Food and Nutrition in Health and Disease*. *Ann. NY Acad. Sci.* 300:1–474
335. Mueller, W. H. 1976. Parent-child correlations for stature and weight among school-aged children: a review of 24 studies. *Hum. Biol.* 48:379–97
336. Mueller, W. H., Titcomb, M. 1977. Genetic and environmental determinants of growth of school-aged children in a rural Colombian population. *Ann. Hum. Biol.* 4:1–15
337. Nag, M. 1972. Sex, culture, and human fertility: India and the United States. *Curr. Anthropol.* 13:231–37
338. Nag, M. 1973. Anthropology and population: Problems and perspectives. *Popul. Stud.* 27:59–60
339. Narayan, V., Singh, J. 1980. Sociocultural factors in sexually transmitted diseases. *East. Anthropol.* 33:271–76
340. Nardi, B. 1981. Modes of explanation in anthropological population theory: Biological determinism vs. self-regulation in studies of population growth in third world countries. *Am. Anthropol.* 83:28–56
341. Nations, M. K., Shields, D., Araujo, J., de Sousa, M., Guerrant, R. 1984. Care within reach: appropriate health-care delivery in the developing world (letter). *N. Engl. J. Med.* 310(24):1612
342. Neumann, A. K., Lauro, P. 1982. Ethnomedicine and biomedicine linking. *Soc. Sci. Med.* 16:1817–24
342a. Newcombe, M. T., Hartley, E. L., eds. *Readings in Social Psychology*. New York: Holt
343. Newman, J. 1980. Dimensions of Sandawe Diet. See Ref. 378, pp. 27–34
344. Nietschmann, B. 1972. Hunting and fishing focus among the Miskito Indians, Eastern Nicaragua. *Hum. Ecol.* 1:41–68
345. Norgan, N. G., Ferro-Luzzi, A., Durnin, J. V. G. 1974. The energy and nutrient intake and the energy expenditure of 204 New Guinean adults. *Trans. R. Soc. London Ser. B* 268:309–48
346. Notestein, F. W. 1953. Economic problems in population. In *Economic Problems of Food Supply Symposium*, pp. 13–31, 63–65. London: Oxford Univ. Press

347. O'Dea, K., Spargo, R. M., Akerman, K. 1980. Some studies on the relationship between urban living and diabetes in a group of Australian Aborigines. *Med. Anthropol.* 4(1):1–20
348. Odell, M. 1982. The domestic context of production and reproduction in a Guatemalan community. *Hum. Ecol.* 10(1):47–69
349. Ogbu, J. 1973. Seasonal hunger in tropical Africa as a cultural phenomenon. *Africa* 43(4):317–32
350. Olness, K., Yip, R., Indritz, A., Torjesen, E. 1984. Height and weight status of Indochinese refugee children: an anthropometric study of 1,650 children. *Am. J. Dis. Child.* 138:544–47
351. Omran, A. R. 1971. *The Health Theme in Family Planning*. Carolina Popul. Cent. Monogr. No. 16. Chapel Hill: Univ. North Carolina
352. Oomen, H. 1970. Interrelationship of the human intestinal flora and protein utilization. *Proc. Nutr. Soc. (Gr. Br.)* 29:197–206
353. Oomen, H., Grubben, G. 1981. Leaves: An underrated source of nutrients. *Dev. Digest* 19(2):49–58
354. Oshima, H. 1967. Food consumption, nutrition, and economic development in Asian countries. *Econ. Dev. Cult. Change* 15:385
355. Partridge, W., Brown, A., Nugent, J. 1982. The Papaloapan Dam and Resettlement Project: Human ecology and health impacts. In *Involuntary Migration and Resettlement*, ed. A. Hanson, A. Oliver-Smith. Boulder, Colo: Westview
356. Pearce, T. O. 1982. Integrating Western orthodox and indigenous medicine. *Soc. Sci. Med.* 16:1611–17
357. Pelletier, D. 1984. Dietary patterns and body fatness among young Samoan men. *Am. J. Phys. Anthropol.* 63:203 (Abstr.)
358. Pellett, P. 1976. Role of food mixtures in combatting childhood malnutrition. In *Nutrition in the Community*, ed. D. McLaren, pp. 185–202. Chichester: Wiley
359. Pellett, P. 1981. Malnutrition, wealth, and development. *Food Nutr. Bull.* 3(1):17–19
360. Pellett, P. 1982. Changing concepts on world malnutrition. *Ecol. Food Nutr.* 13:115–25
361. Picon-Reategui, E. 1976. Nutrition. In *Man in the Andes*, ed. P. Baker, M. Little. Stroudsberg, PA: Dowden, Hutchinson, & Ross
362. Pillsbury, B. L. 1982. Policy and evaluation perspectives on traditional health practitioners in national health care systems. *Soc. Sci. Med.* 16:1825–34

363. Pinstrup-Andersen, P. 1981. *Nutritional Consequences of Agricultural Projects: Conceptual Relationships and Assessment Approaches*. Staff Work. Pap. No. 456. Washington, DC: World Bank
364. Polgar, S. 1975. Population history and population policies from an anthropological perspective. *Curr. Anthropol.* 13:203–11
365. Pollitt, E., Mueller, W. 1982. Maternal nutrition supplementation during pregnancy interferes with physical resemblance of siblings at birth according to infant sex. *Early Hum. Dev.* 7:251–56
366. Pollitt, E., Mueller, W., Leibel, R. L. 1982. The relation of growth to cognition in a well-nourished pre-school population, *Child Dev.* 53:1157–63
367. Pollitt, E., Thomson, C. 1977. Protein-calorie malnutrition and behavior: a view from psychology. See Ref. 465, pp. 262–306
368. Popkin, B. M., 1980. Time allocation of the mother and child nutrition. *Ecol. Food Nutr.* 9:1–13
369. Popkin, B. M., Bilsborrow, R. E., Akin, J. S. 1982. Breast-feeding patterns in low-income countries. *Science* 218:1088–93
370. Preece, M. A., Baines, M. J. 1978. A new family of mathematical models describing the human growth curve. *Ann. Hum. Biol.* 5:1–24
371. Preston, S. 1978. *The Effects of Infant and Child Mortality on Fertility*. New York: Academic
372. Quandt, S. 1986. Methods for determining dietary intake. In *Nutrition in Biological Anthropology*, ed. F. E. Johnston. New York: Liss. In press
373. Rappaport, H., Rappaport, M. 1981. The integration of scientific and traditional healing. *Am. Psychol.* 36:774–81
374. Rea, J. N. 1971. Social and economic influences on the growth of pre-school children in Lagos. *Hum. Biol.* 43:46–63
375. Reddy, V., Jagadeesan, V., Ragharamulu, N., Bhaskaram, C., Srikantia, S. G. 1976. Functional significance of growth retardation in malnutrition. *Am. J. Clin. Nutr.* 29:3–7
376. Reichel-Dolmatoff, G. 1976. Cosmology as ecological analysis: A view from the rain forest. *Man* 11:307–18
377. Rice, K. 1984. Time use, diet, and productive output in a schistosomiasis-stressed environment. *Am. J. Phys. Anthropol.* 63:207 (Abstr.)
377a. Richard, P. 1983. Ecological change and the politics of African land use. *Afr. Stud. Rev.* 26:1–72
378. Robson, J. R. K., ed. 1980. *Food, Ecology, and Culture*. New York: Gordon & Breach
379. Romanucci-Ross, L. 1977. The heirarchy of resort in curative practices: The Admiralty Islands, Melanesia. In *Culture, Disease, and Healing*, ed. D. Landy, pp. 481–86. New York: Macmillan
380. Romanucci-Ross, L., Moerman, D., Tancredi, L., eds. 1983. *The Anthropology of Medicine from Culture to Method*. New York: Praeger
381. Ronaghy, H., Halsted, J. 1975. Zinc deficiency occurring in females: Report of two cases. *Am. J. Clin. Nutr.* 28:831–36
382. Sai, F. 1984. The population factor in Africa's development dilemma. *Science* 226:801–5
383. Salomon, J., Gordon, J. E., Scrimshaw, N. S. 1966. Studies of diarrheal disease in Central America X. Associated chickenpox, diarrhea, and kwashiorkor in a highland Guatemalan village. *Am. J. Trop. Med. Hyg.* 15:997–1002
384. Satyanarayana, K., Naidu, A. N., Chatterjee, E., Rao, B. S. N. 1977. Body size and work output. *Am. J. Clin. Nutr.* 30:322–25
385. Saucier, J. F. 1972. Correlates of the long postpartum taboo: A cross-cultural study. *Curr. Anthropol.* 13:238–67
386. Schlebusch, L., Levin, A., Moshal, M. G. 1981. The role of intelligence and depression in Indian and Black duodenal ulcer patients in South Africa. *S. Afr. Med. J.* 60:613–14
387. Schlegel, S., Guthrie, H. 1980. Diet and the Tiruray shift from swidden to plow farming. In *Food, Ecology, and Culture*, ed. J. Robson, pp. 9–20. New York: Gordon & Breach
388. Schofield, S. 1974. Seasonal factors affecting nutrition in different age groups and especially pre-school children. *J. Dev. Stud.* 11(1):22–40
389. Schofield, S. 1979. *Development and the Problem of Village Nutrition*. Inst. Dev. Stud., Sussex. London: Croom Helm
390. Scholl, T. O. 1975. *Body Size in Developing Nations. Is Bigger Better?* PhD thesis. Philadelphia: Temple Univ.
391. Scholl, T. O., Johnston, F. E., Cravioto, J., De Licardie, E. R., Lurie, D. S. 1979. The relationship of growth failure (chronic undernutrition) to the prevalence of clinically severe protein energy malnutrition and to growth retardation in protein-energy malnutrition. *Am. J. Clin. Nutr.* 32:872–78
392. Scholl, T. O., Johnston, F. E., Cravioto, J. C., De Licardie, E. R. 1983. The utility of cross-sectional measurements of weight and length for age in screening for

growth failure (chronic malnutrition) and clinically severe protein energy malnutrition. *Acta Paediatr. Scand.* 72:867–72
393. Schwabe, C., Kuojak, I. 1981. Practices and beliefs of the traditional Dinka healer in relation to provision of modern medical and veterinary services for the Southern Sudan. *Hum. Organ.* 40:231–38
394. Scott, E. C., Johnston, F. E. 1982. Critical fat, menarche, and the maintenance of menstrual cycles: A critical review. *J. Adoles. Health. Care* 2:249–60
395. Scrimshaw, N. S., Salomon, J., Bruch, H., Gordon, J. E. 1966. Studies of diarrheal disease in Central America VIII. Measles, diarrhea, and nutritional deficiency in rural Guatemala. *Am. J. Trop. Med. Hyg.* 15:652–31
396. Scrimshaw, N. S., Taylor, C., Gordon, J. 1968. *Interaction of Nutrition and Infection.* WHO Monogr. Ser. 57. Geneva: WHO
397. Scrimshaw, S. C. M. 1978. Infant mortality and behavior in the regulation of family size. *Popul. Dev. Rev.* 4:383–403
398. Scrimshaw, S. C. M. 1983. Infanticide as deliberate fertility regulation. See Ref. 54, pp. 245–66
399. Sellers, S. G., Mora, J. O., Super, C. M., Herrera, M. G. 1982. The effects of nutritional supplementation and home education on children's diets. *Nutr. Rep. Inter.* 26:727–40
400. Sheffer, M. L., Grantham-McGregor, S., Ismail, S. J. 1981. The social environment of malnourished children compared with that of other children in Jamaica. *J. Biosoc. Sci.* 3:19–30
401. Simmons, E. 1976. *Calorie and Protein Intakes in Three Villages in Zaria Province, May 1970–July 1971.* Samaru Misc. Pap. 55. Inst. Agric. Res., Ahmadu Bello Univ.
402. Simopoulos, A. P., ed. 1982. Assessment of Nutritional Status. *Am. J. Clin. Nutr.* 35:1089–1325 (Suppl.)
403. Singh, M., MacKinlay, L., Kane, G., Mak-joon-wah, Yap, E.-H., et al. 1980. Studies on human filariasis in Malaysia: The application of an indirect hemagglutination technique for immunodiagnosis. *Am. J. Trop. Med. Hyg.* 29:548–52
404. Sinnett, P. F., Whyte, H. M. 1973. Epidemiological studies in a highland population of New Guinea: Environment, culture, and health status. *Hum. Ecol.* 1:245–77
405. Sloan, F. 1971. *Survival of Progeny in Developing Countries: An Analysis of Evidence from Costa Rica, Mexico, East Pakistan, and Puerto Rico.* Report prepared for USAID. Santa Monica: Rand
406. Smith, D. G., Guinto, R. S. 1978. Leprosy and fertility. *Hum. Biol.* 50(4):451–60
407. Smith, P. C. 1983. The impact of age and marriage and proportions marrying on fertility. See Ref. 54, pp. 473–531
407a. Smith, P. C. 1980. Asian marriage patterns in transition. *J. Fam. Hist.* 5:58–96
408. Spencer, T., Heywood, P. 1983. Seasonality, subsistence agriculture, and nutrition in a lowlands community of Papua New Guinea. *Ecol. Food Nutr.* 13:221–29
409. Spooner, B., ed. 1972. *Population Growth: Anthropological Implications.* Cambridge: MIT Press
410. Srinivisan, T. 1980. *Malnutrition: Some Measurement and Policy Issues.* Staff Work. Pap. No. 373. Washington, DC: World Bank
411. Steffensen, M., Colker, L. 1982. Intercultural misunderstandings about health care. *Soc. Sci. Med.* 16:1949–54
412. Stein, Z., Susser, M. 1975. Fertility, fecundity, and famine: Food rations in the Dutch famine 1944/45 have a causal relation to fertility and probably to fecundity. *Hum. Biol.* 47:131–54
413. Stein, Z., Susser, M. 1978. Famine and fertility. See Ref. 333, pp. 123–45
414. Stini, W. A. 1969. Nutritional stress and growth: sex difference in adaptive response. *Am. J. Phys. Anthropol.* 31:417–26
415. Stini, W. A. 1975. Adaptive strategies of human populations under nutritional stress. See Ref. 455, pp. 19–42
416. Strong, F. 1976. Toxicants occurring naturally in foods. In *Present Knowledge in Nutrition,* ed. D. M. Hegsted, pp. 516–27. New York: Nutr. Found. 4th ed.
417. Strong, J. 1972. Atherosclerosis in human populations. *Atherosclerosis* 16:193–201
418. Sukhatme, P., Margen, S. 1982. Autoregulatory homeostatic nature of energy balance. *Am. J. Clin. Nutr.* 35:355–65
419. Sukkar, M. Y., Kemm, J. R., Ballal, M. A., Ahmed, T. A. 1980. Growth velocity in children in rural Khartoum, Sudan. *Ann. Hum. Biol.* 7:473–80
420. Susanne, C. 1980. Socioeconomic differences in growth patterns. See Ref. 251a, pp. 329–38
421. Suskind, R. M., ed. 1977. *Malnutrition and the Immune Response.* New York: Raven
422. Swedlund, A. C. 1978. Historical demography as population ecology. *Ann. Rev. Anthropol.* 7:137–73
423. Tan, J.-P. 1983. Marital fertility at older ages in Nepal, Bangladesh, and Sri Lanka. *Popul. Stud.* 37:433–44
424. Tanner, J. M. 1966. The secular trend

toward earlier maturation. *T. Soc. Geneesk.* 44:524–39
425. Tanner, J. M. 1976. Growth as a monitor of nutritional status. *Proc. Nutr. Soc.* 35:315–22
426. Tanner, J. M., Eveleth, P. 1975. Variability between populations in growth and development at puberty. In *Puberty.* ed. S. R. Berenberg, pp. 256–73 Macy Found. Int. Children's Cent. Leiden: Stenfert Kroese
427. Taussig, M. 1978. Peasant economics and the development of capitalist agriculture in the Cauca Valley, Colombia. *Latin Am. Perspect.* 5:27–37
428. Taylor, C. E., Newman, J. S., Kelley, N. U. 1976. The child survival hypothesis. *Popul. Stud.* 30:263–78
429. Deleted in proof
430. Taylor, H. L., Keys, A. 1950. Adaptation to calorie restriction. *Science* 112: 215–18
431. Teitelbaum, J. 1977. Human vs. animal nutrition: A "development" project among Fulani cattlekeepers of the Sahel of Senegal. In *Nutrition and Anthropology in Action,* ed. T. Fitzgerald, pp. 125–40. Assen The Netherlands: Van Gorcum
432. Teitelbaum, M. 1975. Relevance of demographic transition theory for developing countries. *Science* 188:420–25
433. Tesh, R., Gadjusek, D. C., Garruto, R., Cross, J. H., Rosen, L. 1975. The distribution and prevalence of Group A arbovirus neutralizing antibodies among human populations in Southeast Asia and the Pacific Islands. *Am. J. Trop. Med. Hyg.* 24:664–75
434. Testerink, J. 1984. *Agricultural Commercialization in Swaziland: Farmers Compared.* Res. Pap. No. 11, Soc. Sci. Res. Unit. Kwaluseni: Univ. Swaziland
435. Thomas, R. B. 1975. The ecology of work. In *Physiological Anthropology,* ed. A. Damon, pp. 55–79. New York: Oxford Univ. Press
436. Thomas, R. B., Carey, J., Leatherman, T., Haas, J. 1984. Consequences and responses to illness among small-scale farmers: A research design. (Abstract) *Am. J. Phys. Anthropol.* 63:227
437. Thompson, W. S. 1928. Population. *Am. J. Sociol.* 34:3–15
438. Thomson, A., Hytten, F. 1977. Physiological basis of nutritional needs during pregnancy and lactation. In *Nutritional Impacts on Women Throughout Life, with Emphasis on Reproduction,* ed. K. Moghissi, T. Evans, pp. 10–22. Hagerstown, MD: Harper & Row
439. Thomson, W. A. R., ed. 1978. *Medicines from the Earth.* New York: McGraw-Hill
440. Torry, W. 1984. Social science research on famine: A critical evaluation. *Hum. Ecol.* 12:227–52
441. Tsubaki, T., Toyokura, Y. 1979. Amyotrophic lateral sclerosis. *Proceedings of the International Symposium on Amyotrophic Lateral Sclerosis.* Tokyo: Univ. Tokyo Press
442. Underwood, B. 1980. Conferences review: New research. *Mothers and Children* 1(1):1–5
443. Underwood, B. A., ed. 1983. *Nutrition Intervention Strategies in National Development.* New York: Academic
443a. United Nations. 1984. *Mortality and Health Policy.* Proc. Expert Group Mortality and Health Policy, Popul. Stud. No. 91. Dep. Int. Econ. Soc. Affairs. New York: United Nations
444. van Wering, E. R. 1981. The secular growth trend on Aruba between 1954 and 1974. *Hum. Biol.* 53:105–16
445. van Wering, E. R. 1981. The anthropometric status of Aruban children—1974. *Hum. Biol.* 53:117–36
446. Waldemann, E. 1973. Seasonal variations in malnutrition in Africa. *R. Soc. Trop. Med. Hyg.* 67:431
447. Waldemann, E. 1980. The ecology of the nutrition of the Bapedi, Sekhukuniland. See Ref. 378, pp. 47–60
448. Wale, O., Rodrigues, A. M. 1980. Nutrition considerations in a cassava production program for Guyana. *Ecol. Food Nutr.* 10:87–95
449. Walker, A. R. P., Walker, B. F. 1978. High high-density lipoprotein cholesterol in African children and adults in a population free of coronary heart disease. *Br. Med. J.* 2:1336–38
450. Walsh, A. 1980. The prophylactic effect of religion on blood pressure levels among a sample of immigrants. *Soc. Sci. Med.* 14B:59–63
451. Warren, M. P. 1979. *Reproductive Dysfunction in Altered Nutritional States and Illnesses.* Presented to Popul. Assoc. Am., Philadelphia
452. Waterlow, J. C. 1984. Current issues in nutritional assessment by anthropometry. See Ref. 53, pp. 77–90
453. Waterlow, J. C., Buzina, R., Keller, W., Lane, J. M., Nichaman, M. Z., Tanner, J. M. 1977. The presentation and use of height and weight data for comparing the nutritional status of groups of children under the age of 10 years. *Bull. WHO* 55:489–98
454. Watkins, L. O. 1984. Coronary heart disease and coronary disease risk factors in black populations in underdeveloped countries: The case for primordial prevention. *Am. Heart J.* 108(3,Pt. 2):850–62

455. Watts, E. S., Johnston, F. E., Lasker, G. W., eds. 1975. *Biosocial Interrelations in Population Adaptation.* The Hague: Mouton
456. Webb, G. 1981. Schistosomiasis: Some advances. *Br. Med. J.* 283:1104–1106
457. Weiss, K. 1976. Demographic theory and anthropological inference. *Ann. Rev. Anthropol.* 5:351–81
458. Werner, D. 1983. Fertility and pacification among the Mekranoti of Central Brazil. *Hum. Ecol.* 11(2):227–45
459. Wiesenfeld, S. 1967. Sickle cell trait in human biological and cultural evolution. *Science* 157:1134–1140
460. Wills, W., Saimot, G., Brochard, C., Blumberg, B. S., London, W. T., et al. 1976. Hepatitis B surface antigen (Australia antigen) in mosquitoes collected in Senegal, West Africa. *Am. J. Trop. Med. Hyg.* 25:186–90
461. Wilmore, J. H., Brown, C. H., Davis, J. 1977. Body physique and composition of the female distance runner. *Ann. NY Acad. Sci.* 301:764–76
462. Woolfe, J., Wheeler, E. F., VanDyke, W., Orraca-Tetteh, R. 1977. The value of the Ghanaian traditional diet in relation to the energy needs of young children. *Ecol. Food Nutr.* 6:175–81
463. World Health Organization. 1983. New approaches to health education in primary health care. *Tech. Rep. Ser.* 690:7–44
464. World Health Organization. 1983. Smoking control strategies in developing countries. Report of WHO expert committee. *Tech. Rep. Ser.* 695:7–92
465. Wurtman, R., Wurtman, J., ed. 1977. *Nutrition and the Brain.* New York: Raven
466. Wyndham, C. H. 1979. Mortality from cardiovascular diseases in the various population groups in the Republic of South Africa. *S. Afr. Med. J.* 56:1023–1030
467. Wyon, J., Gordon, J. 1971. *The Khanna Study: Population Problems in the Rural Punjab.* Cambridge: Harvard Univ. Press
468. Yarbrough, C., Habicht, J.-P., Malina, R. M., Lechtig, A., Klein, R. E. 1975. Length and weight in rural Guatemalan Ladino children: birth to 7 years of age. *Am. J. Phys. Anthropol.* 42:439–48
469. Young, J. C. 1980. *Medical Choice in a Mexican Village.* New Brunswick: Rutgers Univ. Press
470. Young, J. C., Garro, L. Y. 1982. Variation in the choice of treatment in two Mexican communities. *Soc. Sci. Med.* 16:1453–65
471. Zerfas, A. J. 1979. Anthropometric field methods: general. See Ref. 236, pp. 339–64

CONTEXT AND CHRONOLOGY OF EARLY MAN IN THE AMERICAS

William N. Irving

Department of Anthropology, University of Toronto, Toronto, Ontario, Canada M5S 1A1

"It is a vulgar superstition, now fortunately being dispelled, that archaeology is an empirical discipline . . . archaeological interpretations are a function not only of the evidence at hand, but also of the ideas and assumptions . . . that the interpreter carries about with him."

(Trigger, 109, p. 30).

PREFACE

Unfortunately, the superstition to which Trigger refers is not being dispelled in the special field of Early Man studies, where authority may masquerade as a reasoned conclusion, boldly stated opinion may pass for authority, and intransigence may stand either for conservatism or for radical innovation (67). It is ironic that this field, which is so overwhelmingly dependent on results obtained by means of the "hard sciences," should be so beset with disagreement as to what really are the empirical data. This betrays the fact, perhaps at once our strength and our weakness, that we must somehow practice both as scientists and as humanists. Failure to recognize this may be responsible for some of the confusion that surrounds us and for the astonishing range of opinion that now exists on the time of arrival of the first humans to reach the Western Hemisphere. In any event, this essay deals with that range of opinion. I advocate a holistic approach to the study of Early Man as the best way to deal with this dilemma.

I present here three widely differing points of view on the subject, with what I deem their merits and faults, and by way of illustration I shall peremptorily ascribe them to certain colleagues. Lest I myself become guilty of masquerading, I will accept membership in what I will call Position III—"very early first arrival,"–and acknowledge that those in Position II—"fairly early first arrival"—have much to contribute. Those in Position I—"Clovis was first"—

enliven the debate, but in ways they neither intend nor appear to understand. Of course, most of us are uncertain, and with good reason; much of the available evidence is both equivocal and unclear and much of it is unfamiliar.

BACKGROUND

The question of just when Man first got to the Western Hemisphere appeared to have been settled, or at least rendered relatively uninteresting, early in this century after Holmes (45) discredited the recognition of Palaeolithic types of stone implements in the middle Atlantic states, and Hrdlicka (48; also in many later publications) asserted that there was no evidence for anatomically primitive Man in the New World. The latter assertion can be made today, with but one or two caveats; for our purposes it remains a true statement. It doesn't imply a date of arrival, but it still permits inference of an age of a very few thousand years.

Starting in the 1920s, it was shown at a number of sites in the North American Plains that projectile points of the Clovis and Folsom types occur in intimate association with the skeletons of now extinct Pleistocene mammals, particularly giant bison and mammoth.[1] At first this seemed to require extending the chronology of human occupancy backward by a significant amount, and perhaps a reconsideration of the chronological implications of Holmes' and Hrdlicka's judgments. But the giant bison and mammoth were among the last of the Pleistocene species to become extinct. This suggested a scenario in which humans first slipped across the Bering Land Bridge from Siberia into Alaska just before the "bridge" was covered by rising postglacial sea levels, at a time when the North American ice sheets had retreated far enough to allow quick passage south along the east flank of the Rocky Mountains (95).

The scenario seemed to become clearer and more detailed following the radiocarbon revolution that began around 1950; however, this apparent confirmation may have been illusory. The results of the first few years of radiocarbon dating produced many more dates representing Clovis and younger rather than older ages. Because of the possibilities of error in the method, it was not unreasonable to suspect that the few dates older than the 11,000–12,000 year-old Clovis were simply wrong. This permitted the Pleistocene "overkill" hypothesis to develop to account for the extinction of the giant fauna by immigrant Clovis people and their descendants about 10,000 years ago (e.g. 72–75). To round out the hypothesis, Martin proposed that the extinctions marked the arrival of a new predator, Man, among the "naive" native American fauna; he reasoned that these had to be the first human arrivals.

---

[1] But see Rogers & Martin (97), who reported a fluted point excavated from beneath an extinct bison scapula in 1905 in Kansas.

However, this is far too simple a view of the facts. Field research has tended to focus on the relatively conspicuous "big game hunters" such as Clovis; thus there probably are many more field data on these than on other less visible, early cultures. This, rather than the fact that they were the first to arrive here, may explain why there are many radiocarbon dates on Clovis and later cultures and so few on earlier ones.

The primacy of Clovis among New World archaeological cultures is just one of several opinions contending for acceptance. Another holds that Clovis developed in the Western Hemisphere from much older, much simpler cultures. The first North American archaeologists to make this specific proposal in modern terms were Krieger (61) and Chard (24). Renaud (77, 94) may have been a worthy precursor. His observations on the chronology of the Black's Fork culture of Wyoming may yet prove to have been soundly based, although they now evoke disdain because Renaud compared Black's Fork flint implements with Palaeolithic handaxes from France. This simply is not *comme il faut* among prehistorians; the distance between Black's Fork and the Somme is too great, and the intervening cultures and culture areas are too different.

In 1957 Carter, a geographer, had published his work in the San Diego, California, area (23; see also 59), which he interpeted to show that assemblages of tools coming from alluvial and colluvial (hillside) deposits were datable to interglacial times on the basis of correlation with former sea levels. Carter's influence may well have been greater than a citation index would show, but it does not figure prominently in reviews of the subject.

Krieger defined a "Pre-Projectile Point Stage" older than Clovis, evidence of which he recognized at a large number of sites in North and South America (61). A number of these occurrences produced radiocarbon dates consistent with Krieger's view, and some of them contained bones of extinct mammals as well. He considered an age of 35,000–40,000 years possible but not then demonstrable. Like most writers, he refrained from speculating on the origin of the succeeding "Palaeoindian Stage", with projectile points, the oldest examples of which were dated to around 12,000 or 13,000 years ago.

In the course of making a proposal of a New World origin for Clovis, Chard (24), depending on Movius (80, 82), commented on the apparent absence from the Far East of more advanced Middle Palaeolithic cultures that, had they been present, might have been seen as ancestors to Clovis. This led quickly to a rejoinder from Bushnell & McBurney (20), who stated that a technique known as "step flaking" was present in the newly described Fen Ho complex of North China, and that this technique marked the Fen Ho complex as Middle, not Lower Palaeolithic. In the spirited discussion that followed, some groundwork for current thought about Asian ancestral cultures was established (25).

This exchange was preceded and followed by Soviet publications that seemed to reveal a Middle Palaeolithic presence in Soviet Central Asia and farther east (e.g. 81, 83, 100). Syntheses by Bryan (12) and Müller-Beck (84, 85) were offered, which included something resembling the Middle Palaeolithic as the source of American bifaces in general and fluted points in particular. This point of view may have been encouraged by Francois Bordes, who observed that, on the basis of his experiments in the manufacture of stone tools, an artisan able to make Mousterian (Middle Palaeolithic) tools could have used the same skills to make Clovis points (personal communication; Les Eyzies Lithic Technology Conference, 1964; and earlier as well). Presumably the Clovis artisan would have needed a reason for making Clovis points, but this is getting ahead of the narrative.

Bordes's opinion came as a not very pleasant surprise to many Americanists, for whom the uniqueness of the fluted point had come to be a matter of hemispheric pride and a proof of our close relation to the mainstream of human evolution; that fluted points might have been made by persons not educated in Upper Palaeolithic ways was, and is, difficult to accept. Fortunately, Movius, Bordes, and others had for years previously issued warnings that just because some Middle Palaeolithic industries, such as Mousterian, were produced by Neandertals, it did not necessarily follow that the Middle Palaeolithic outside of Europe also was produced by this somewhat archaic variant of *Homo sapiens*. There was no need to look for Neandertals in North America where Hrdlicka could find none.

Bordes's work in flintknapping and that of Crabtree (58) ushered in an era of experimentation in the manufacture of stone tools that continues to enliven the discipline by providing new insights and analogies to help in the interpretation of early sites. The importance of their contributions cannot be overrated. They probably are directly responsible for the development of cognitive models for stone tool manufacture (9) and use wear studies (42), and they stimulated the experimental search for analogies to assist in archaeological interpretation (e.g. 106). However, most of the experimental work has been done in an attempt to replicate one or another of the Palaeolithic or Palaeoindian technologies, rather than to clarify fundamental principles of flint fracture.

Other improvements in methods of research and presentation of results in recent years have been uneven. On the one hand, great strides forward have been made in archaeometry, from the identification of materials to the dating of sites and individual objects (71), and in palaeoecology and geoarchaeology (e.g. 21, 92). But in spite of a few valiant efforts to go beyond it, the majority of our practitioners and interpreters continue to depend on a normative paradigm in the analysis of artifacts, in which newly found objects must fit in established categories or they cannot be accommodated.

This vignette is meant to provide a background against which to view the very wide divergence of opinion on the age of Early Man in the Americas.

Perhaps some of the historical trends mentioned can be used to help explain this divergence, but an inquiry into this possibility is far beyond the scope of the present essay. For a more comprehensive discussion of these, Krieger (61) is still the best source. Now I present the three points of view, with selected representatives.

POSITION I

Position I, which holds that Clovis represents the first human population ever to appear in the Western Hemisphere, is held by a staunch few (e.g. 35, 44, 73). It has little merit or support when it is considered in the light of the great variety of manufacturing technologies and environmental adaptations extant here during the 10,000–12,000 B.P. interval which contains Clovis (13, 14). None of these complex cultural phenomena, certainly none of those from Central or South America, cited by Bryan (15), has a plausible direct antecedent in Asia, despite the assertions of West (113), Mochanov (79), and Dikov (27). This opinion implies a significant (but unspecifiable) depth of time for divergent development in the New World prior to the appearance of Clovis, of which more can be said in relation to Position II.

The most often repeated argument made in support of Position I is based on the fact that questions may be asked about each of the putatively older sites, and that therefore "there is no definite proof" that they exist or are old (30, 88). The indiscriminate use of this form of argument has severely harmed the discipline in the name of conservatism by trivializing the processes of proof, criticism, and debate. As a case in point, the two articles just cited review a very large number of sites and accept quite uncritically all negative comments or expressions of doubt about their age or authenticity. If the same formula for authenticating evidence were applied to the sites of the Archaic, we would be left wondering whether or not anyone occupied the eastern part of North America between 2000 and 7000 B.C.

The argument that the extinction of Pleistocene megafauna was caused by rapacious human predators (72, 73) is an interesting one that deserves attention. However, this does not account for the extirpation of species seldom or never eaten by humans, which certainly occurred (34), so Man is not involved in all extinctions. This is not to say that Man had no part in these extinctions, but only that the fact of extinction does not prove the time at which Man first arrived. The changes in fauna at the end of the Pleistocene quite likely were caused, at least in part, by complex changes in seasonal weather patterns that resulted in changes in plant communities and the habits and survival of animals dependent on them (115). The Clovis horizon, which can be documented from northern Alaska to Guatemala, and from the west coast to the east, but which has not been found in Asia, remains a phenomenon of great intrinsic interest, but in my opinion it has no bearing on the first appearance of humans in the Western Hemisphere.

POSITION II

The most popular and attractive alternative to Position I is Position II, which is the view that humans reached North America between 20,000 and 70,000 years ago. The first figure is based on 14C-dated sites and will find favor among a fairly large number of archaeologists, some of whose papers are in recent symposia edited by Bryan (14, 17), Ericson et al (31), LeMoine & MacEachern (65), and Shutler (104). However, each of these symposia includes dissenters from Position II, and some who would qualify their support for it. (It is here that we begin to see something of the range of opinion mentioned earlier.) Dincauze (30, p. 82) has complained that proponents of pre-Clovis Man (most of whom I would list as supporting Position II) "refuse to stand together," meaning, I think, that they have not agreed on a dogma. I regard this refusal to stand together as an indication of good intellectual health among the Position II people. The data provide little support for dogma beyond such assertions as "Man did not originate in the Western Hemisphere, because there are no known non-human hominoids here from which he could have evolved." I take it as given that this banal but necessary assertion is accepted by adherents to all three positions.

The suggested lower limit of 70,000 years is somewhat arbitrary; it should not discomfit those who look for a first entry around 30,000–40,000 years ago. It may approximate the beginning of the Wisconsinan glaciation and thus have a certain attraction for those who think it was necessary to have dry land at Bering Strait for humans to cross between Siberia and Alaska; this would have been present during glacial but not interglacial stages. Certainly such a "land bridge" would be a convenience for humans and for migrating animals; perhaps it was essential if animals were to move from one continent to another. But in my view, humans capable of living in northeastern Siberia were capable also of crossing wet Bering Strait by boat. Thus, my use of 70,000 years is simply meant to accommodate all of those who eschew Position I, except for a few who have adopted Position III. MacNeish (69) suggested that 70,000 years ago, plus or minus 30,000, was a useful estimate of the time at which humans first crossed Bering Strait.

Bryan (15, 16) has assembled what I consider convincing evidence that Position I is no longer defensible and that some version of Position II or III will prevail in the long run. To the extent that he has focused much of his thinking on the origin of bifacially flaked projectile points, he appears to have passed over other clues that might also have been useful, and perhaps also for this reason he has given little attention to the possibility of Position III being supportable. For the present, a mastodon with an El Jobo point within its pelvic girdle, excavated by Bryan and his colleagues at Taima Taima in Venezuela and radiocarbon dated to a little more than 13,000 B.P., is the outstanding example of pre-Clovis differentiation (19). El Jobo points are not closely related to any known North American Palaeoindian projectile point (99), a judgment based on their thick cross section, absence of basal edge preparation, and style of flake removal. However, there are many other examples to substantiate the impression of a long period of technological and cultural divergence prior to the Clovis time horizon (36, 52a, 68, 70, 78, 96).

In addition to the evidence assembled by Bryan, mainly from South America and western North America, that recovered from the Meadowcroft Rockshelter near Pittsburgh, just south of the glacial ice limit in western Pennsylvania, provides very strong support for Position II (1, 22a). The shelter is in a narrow, steep-sided mountain valley; it was excavated during the 1970s by a large team of specialists, mainly from the University of Pittsburgh, who made an exemplary effort to apply state-of-the-art techniques to the recovery and interpretation of cultural, chronometric, stratigraphic, and palaeoecological data. The long sequence of over 40 radiocarbon dates, all in perfect stratigraphic order (within standard limits of precision), does not support Haynes' suggestions of contamination by coal particles unsuspected by the investigators (43). The sequence extends beyond 20,000 years; the oldest cultural date is just over 19,000 years B.P.; the oldest stone artifacts appear to be between 14,000 and 15,000 years old.

The absence of Pleistocene megafauna from this narrow, steep-sided, rugged valley, remarked on by Mead (76), is to be expected because of the terrain. The temperate character of the vegetation throughout the record of the shelter stratigraphy may well reflect accurately the local conditions, which need not have been harsh, even though during a part of this time the ice front probably was no more than 50 miles to the north. Wright (115) has brought together interpretations of the glacial age ecology of the American Middle West in a way that supports this view. His synthesis is of far greater interest and importance than this citation would imply, and I commend it to everyone with a general interest in this subject.

The stone implements from Meadowcroft are few, small, and so far not very informative. They suggest that many other sites dating from this time range may be relatively unproductive, and that archaeologists will have to refine their analytical skills for dealing with simple, hard-to-recognize artifacts in order to make anything out of the prehistoric record between 12,000 and 20,000 years ago and before.

Three radiocarbon dates on bone artifacts from the old Crow River, Yukon, support Position II, although perhaps northern Yukon Territory is as much a part of Asia as of North America. The three determinations were made on apatite samples from two large mammoth bone fragments, broken by percussion while still fresh, and one sample from a caribou leg-bone "flesher." The three dates range from 25,000 to 29,000 B.P., with standard deviations so large that the three specimens might be the same age (51a). The reliability of the mineral apatite for radiocarbon dating has been questioned (41b), but the apatite results still show these artifacts to be "old"—probably older than Clovis. I will discuss fractured bone from Old Crow in relation to Position III.

Müller-Beck (84, 85) has offered the most comprehensive hypotheses germane to Position II. In this scheme, "Mousteroid" or Middle Palaeolithic cultures were the first to occupy the North Temperate latitudes in Eurasia and thus were the earliest cultures that could have reached Bering Strait. Some of these cultures included bifacial "points" (*blattspitzen* and other forms) in their inventories; from these the well-known Palaeoindian forms developed. This hypothesis has had great influence among some North American scholars. It still has merit, but it needs to be reconsidered in the light of much new data on the early penetration of middle and possibly high latitudes by Man in Europe (e.g. 10, 11, 22, 54, 86), which clearly places this achievement prior to the Riss-Saale glaciation and long before the oldest Middle Palaeolithic industries now recognized. No clear examples of early Mousteroid bifaces are yet known from Beringia.

The second major element in Müller-Beck's scheme is the emergence of "Aurignacoid," or Upper Palaeolithic cultures with technologies for carving bone and for living on treeless tundra. These are relatively late, and perhaps have more bearing on the background of various Eskimoan, Na-Dene, and Paleo-Asiatic cultures than on our present topic, except for the puzzling occurrence of "blades" in some Clovis and perhaps other early sites. Whether these markers of the Upper Palaeolithic were introduced to the Western Hemisphere or developed here as an instance of culture-evolutionary convergence is one of the intriguing questions that remains unanswered.

It is alarming to realize that nearly 50 years after Nelson (87) began discussing blades and microblades in North America as indicators of contact with Asia, no major study aimed at evaluating their culture-historical significance has been completed (but see 101). We take for granted the near absence of these items from South America, and their sporadic occurrence in Palaeoindian and Archaic assemblages throughout many parts of North America, and short papers on them are so numerous as to be burdensome, but no detailed, comprehensive statement about them has been attempted. Their possible derivation from Eurasian antecendents, perhaps during the Clovis horizon period, suggests that an effort to make a comprehensive statement about them might prove rewarding.

The reasons for adopting some version of Position II rather than Position I appear to be these:

1. There now is a very large number of radiocarbon dates older than 12,000 years on archaeological materials excavated from sites throughout the hemisphere. These probably are not all erroneous; in many cases they are consistent with stratigraphy (for example, at Meadowcroft Rockshelter).
2. The great diversity of projectile point manufacturing techniques present 10,000–12,000 years ago precludes any possibility of a first migration here from Asia shortly (two or three millenia?) before 12,000 years ago. The variety of ecological adaptations already evident by 12,000 B.P., ranging from interior subarctic to coast-tropical, can be used in the same form of argument.
3. There is no demonstration, based on systematic comparative study, of a close, and thus plausibly generic, relationship between the typology of Clovis, or that of any other Palaeoindian culture south of the continental glaciers, with the typology of any Asian culture [cf Wormington (114, p. 192) for a similar opinion]. The similarities that can be shown, such as the sporadic occurrence of blades, could be explained either by convergent development or, more likely, by the diffusion of Asian traits and ideas through an already established American population.[2]

I believe that Position II is now widely regarded as a legitimate point of view, albeit one that could stand some additional verification. It opens a wide field of speculation about the Asian ancestry of the first Americans: their biological identity could link them with late *Homo erectus,* early *Homo sapiens,* or *Homo sapiens sapiens.* There simply is not enough evidence of the needed age from east Asia to give much of a hint about this. The precise cultural identity of the first arrivals is beyond our ability to speculate reasonably at this time, and we should expect to arrive at a recognition of this through study of Western Hemisphere collections rather than by extrapolation from the very diverse materials summarized by Serizawa (103), Ikawa-Smith (49, 50), Aigner (2, 3), and Powers (91), suggestive and useful though these are. None of these complexes resembles a Palaeoindian inventory.

The most stimulating new developments that bear on Position II appear to be taking place in South America, where Dillehay and his colleagues (29) have excavated in southern Chile a 13,000-year-old village at Monte Verde with semipermanent (log-based) rectangular houses, whose inhabitants hunted mastodons and made items of wood and stone not heretofore found (or recognized) in any archaeological site (see also 28). Dillehay (see 90) reports culture-bearing layers stratigraphically older than the houses at the same site. In eastern Brazil, Bryan (16) and Gruhn are excavating pre-Clovis rockshelters, and Guidon (40) reports radiocarbon results from stratified deposits that date

---

[2]The similarity of a projectile point from the Ushki Lake burial in Kamchatka to one from Marmes Rockshelter in Washington State (27), both of terminal Pleistocene age, is by itself uninformative.

artifacts to roughly 30,000 years ago (112); this report needs to be confirmed. It is to be hoped that these new finds will be published soon in the proceedings of a symposium recently led by Hopkins & Bryan (46). Reeves (93) will present a comprehensive summary of primary evidence that bears on Positions II and III, which the interested reader should consult.

POSITION III

The third position is the view that humans were in the Western Hemisphere long before the oldest dates considered so far: 80,000, 150,000, or more years ago. This is a position that most of us in North America either intuitively or through well-trained habit consider preposterous. It seems to violate common sense, and it implies the presence here of pre-sapiens Man, for which there is no evidence.

Nevertheless, there are reasons for thinking about the unthinkable. These are of two kinds: radiometric dates from stratified, excavated sites with putative artifacts, and the trajectory of human population expansion out of the Tropics and into the middle and high latitudes. Much of the relevant evidence is relatively new, and much of it is still poorly understood or highly controversial and thus difficult to summarize. Some of the specific pieces of evidence, and the interpretations linked to them, are more robust than others. I have chosen to discuss only those sites that I think cannot be disregarded without undermining the empirical basis of our discipline.

Before taking up these topics it is necessary to mention work in human biology. Studies using discrete traits as genetic markers are interpreted to show that observable variation in modern indigenous American populations can be explained by postulating a single group of immigrants which came here from Siberia about 15,000 years ago. [Eskimos, and perhaps Athabaskans, came here more recently (64, 110).] Turner (110) finds that a genetically regulated pattern of tooth morphology, different from any other in Eurasia, first appeared in the Far East around 40,000 years ago. Turner also finds this condition, "Sinodonty," to be characteristic of all Native American populations, from which he concludes that all of their ancestors came here from Asia no more than 40,000 years ago. These findings, although they might be accommodated in a version of Position II, seem to contradict Position III. However, one needs only to think of the probably sudden and still inexplicable transition from *H.S. neandertalensis* to *H.S. sapiens* in western Europe to be reminded that it is difficult to project from modern populations very far into the past, and still more difficult to anticipate the biological character of ancestral or antecedent populations before they have been found (when the processes of change are still quite unknown). Physical anthropological studies fail to support Position III, but they do not render it implausible. Position III does not stipulate what kind of continuity, if any, links the first arrivals with modern populations.

On the other hand, a good reason for entertaining the possibility that humans arrived here at a very early time is the fact that as early as 500,000 years ago *Homo erectus* had completed three quarters of the journey from the Tropics to Bering Strait by arriving in North China, at Choukoutien.[3] Certainly genus *Homo* reached Europe, and perhaps even northern Europe, not long after the end of the Matuyama reversed magnetic polarity stage (53, 54) about 700,000 years ago; some argue for still earlier dates. These findings constitute a very significant change in the data base, which a couple of decades ago seemed to show that humans had first learned to cope with northern climates in much later times, with the help of Middle Palaeolithic technology; this seemed to imply an age of 150,000 years at most for the appearance of Man in north temperate latitudes. Now, however, it seems reasonable to accept as a strongly supported working hypothesis that mankind had expanded its geographic range from the Tropics to include much, if not all, of the Eurasian temperate zone by about half a million years ago, if not before (53, 54).

In preparation, or preadaptation, for this dramatic extension of geographical range from the Tropics, it was necessary for humans to learn to cope with at least two environmental challenges that are only locally important in the Tropics, but which are everywhere the rule in middle and high latitudes. These are (*a*) intense seasonal fluctuations in the food supply brought about by seasonal migrations of prey species, and (*b*) winter cold. A third way in which temperate regions differ from the tropics as habitat for humans is in the decreased availability, as one moves toward higher latitudes, of vegetable food that can be eaten unprocessed. This increased the importance to northerners of hunting, a form of subsistence believed to have been well developed by the oldest Eurasian populations.

These environmental challenges presented a number of adaptive thresholds. All of them had to be crossed in a definitive way before humans could occupy the environment of Peking, which has climatic means and extremes close to those of Nebraska. Certainly these adaptations were primarily behavioral and cultural in their nature: they need not have entailed much biological modification of the essentially tropical *Homo erectus* or *Homo sp.*, for no significant physiological or anatomical adjustments to seasonal scarcity, cold, or the need to hunt can be seen in modern descendants of early *Homo*. Humans grow hair on occasion, but not fur.

The special behavioral characteristics necessary for the survival of our

---

[3]Recent Chinese work on the cave deposits dates the Lower Palaeolithic occupation to before the limit of uranium series dating, 350,000 years ago, but after the Matuyama-Brunhes magnetic event some 700,000 years ago (Alfred Latham, personal communication; see also 66, 116); 500,000 years is a plausible estimate, 600,000 is not unlikely.

tropical genus in middle and high latitudes must have been almost entirely cultural in nature. These include, for example, the manufacture of clothing, the storage of food surplus and protection of stores from carnivores, the building of shelters, and in many areas the hunting of fleet-footed prey in open country, apparently without missile weapons. The control of fire is documented by the very large hearths at Choukoutien, where the bones of animals testifying to hunting prowess also are found. The need for clothing at Choukoutien is patent, if we accept the improbability of even a very tough human population being able to survive the extremes of a North China winter without it.

It should not be surprising that these fairly sophisticated kinds of adaptive behavior were practiced by humans who made and used only the simplest kinds of stone implements, as at Choukoutien. There are many ethnographically known subarctic and tropical cases in which the imperishable hardware is so scarce and nonspecific in form that the less durable items made of skin, bark, wood, and bone with stone tools could not be reconstructed or inferred from observations on the hardware alone. This permits suggestion that the occupants of Choukoutien were capable of making clothes out of the skins of animals they had used for food, even if direct evidence for this does not exist. It suggests further that the notion embedded in parts of our discipline, that the history of technology can be written in terms of stone tools alone—which has no foundation either in ethnographic analogy or in modern experimentation—has been a crippling perceptual disability to prehistorians who harbor it. It is necessary to use a holistic approach to make sense of the few items of hard evidence at our disposal.

Humans—*Homo erectus* and/or *Homo* sp.—had learned to hunt for a living and to cope with cold and seasonal scarcity by half a million years ago, and probably much earlier (11), in north temperate Eurasia. In my interpretation, once humans had acquired the behavioral skills with which to live in North China, they already had crossed most of the major adaptive thresholds and needed only to improve their competence, rather than make major additions to it, in order to spread to the northern limit of forest and beyond.

If humans occupied temperate and northern Eurasia in Middle Pleistocene times, as few will now dispute, it is reasonable to ask if they did not also move into the Western Hemisphere at or shortly after that time, as did a large number of other mammalian species which make up part of the Holarctic fauna. Indeed, it is useful to think of North American Pleistocene humans as members of the Upper Pleistocene Rancho La Brean fauna, which included a large number of other genera newly arrived from Eurasia (63).

It appears possible that humans did venture into the Western Hemisphere in early Upper or even Middle Pleistocene time. Although evidence for such a finding would not greatly perturb the main course of evolution as it is now perceived, such evidence certainly would raise a great many difficult questions.

Examples of such evidence are results of excavations at sites in the Valsequillo area of Pueblo, Mexico; near San Diego and Calico Mountains in California; and in the Old Crow region of the Yukon. I have visited the Hueyatlaco locality in the Valsequillo region and briefly noted some of the sites near San Diego. I have not been to Calico. Old Crow has been the geographic locus of my research since 1965. For a much more comprehensive review of North American sites, see Reeves (93).

If it is not implausible that humans reached North America several hundred thousand years ago, one must ask what kind of evidence that they did so we should expect; the answer to this question is not readily forthcoming. The difficulty of specifying a list of items to look for is suggested by the typologically amorphous nature of much of the Lower Palaeolithic material known from Asia. This "amorphousness," of course, may be illusory: there may be more technical and stylistic differentiation in the Lower Palaeolithic than we can perceive. We must, in any event, prepare to encounter tool forms and technologies that are not well known in current literature on the Palaeolithic of Eurasia.

Whatever evidence for human presence there may be, it must satisfy certain conditions if it is to serve as a basis for inferring a very ancient human population. First, there must be tangible, unequivocal signs of manipulation or disturbance of the natural environment by humans, evidence which could not have been produced by another agency. This must be found in stratigraphic context that certifies its association with other materials that can be recognized and dated. Of course, a dated human skeleton would satisfy our curiosity in this matter very nicely, but it is unlikely that many people will search in the right places for such remains until they have more encouragement and guidance, and this will come only with the recognition of artifacts or other traces and the application to them of acceptable tests for establishing their age. There are no human skeletons of very great age in the Western Hemisphere yet.[4] Finally, the estimate of age must be consistent with the position of the evidence in the local stratigraphy.

Three of the groups of sites to be discussed have in common a long history of investigation by specialists in many kinds of Quaternary studies, including aspects of stratigraphy, radiometric dating, palaeontology, and preceramic archaeology (prehistory). Although a single artifact found in a dated context should establish the presence of humans at that time, the demonstration of this appears to be far beyond the abilities of a single investigator or a small research group. Excellent though the observation, analysis, and reporting may be at Santa Rosa Island (6), El Bosque (32), Tlapacoya (78), El Cedral (68), Yuha Pinto Wash, and many other sites, they lack the extensive supporting and

[4]See, e.g., Taylor et al (108) on southwestern U.S. skeletons; however, sample preparation for accelerator dating is a developing art. These dates should be viewed with caution.

complementary studies that have been done in the three I have chosen to discuss. This is not to suggest, however, that only large, long-term, programmed studies can produce good data, but rather that progress at this stage of research depends on the concordance of results from several kinds of investigation that confirm or modify the insight that sparked the inquiry. Only with such concordance can the confidence of nonspecialists be secured; ironically, all of us are nonspecialists in this field of study, or nonexperts, for none of us knows it all, and none of us can specify exactly what we should find.

SAN DIEGO

It is nearly impossible to characterize the finds in the San Diego region, because Carter (23) does not follow archaeological custom in the presentation of field data by giving dimensions of excavations and numbers of specimens recovered. He does not provide a classification of artifacts, and he does not present individual specimens that convince skeptics of their authenticity. His dating of occurrences on the basis of correlation of alluvial terraces with former high sea levels has been questioned, both for the assumption of local tectonic stability and for the world-wide sequence of sea levels which he uses (55). There are, however, stone fragments that may be artifacts, associated with discolored lenses of earth that may be hearths, in situations that probably mark them as old. This set of sites is now being investigated by Reeves (93), who appears to be making progress in the conversion of Carter's apparently perceptive but undisciplined early work to results that can be evaluated by archaeologists.

VALSEQUILLO

The Valsequillo area was known as a source of vertebrate fossils as long ago as 1905, but it was not until Armenta (4) found a stone implement in 1955 that archaeological sites were confirmed there as well. During the early 1960s, major excavations were undertaken there by Irwin-Williams (52b). Subsequent stratigraphic and geochronological work have been done by Steen-McIntyre et al (107). Armenta continued his research in the locality and published a summary of it in which his interpretation of fractured mammal bone is strikingly parallel to that of Old Crow students (see below). There is no published comprehensive report on the five sites excavated by Irwin-Williams.

Irwin-Williams recognizes a nine-unit stratigraphic sequence in which volcanic ash is prominent. In the upper five units she found bifacially chipped tools and weapons in some variety. In the lower levels, separated from the upper by an unconformity that represents an interval of unknown duration, she found only unifacially retouched flakes; in my view these might well be placed within a Lower Palaeolithic framework. Vertebrate fossils apparently were found in all levels; the faunal list fits well in the Rancho La Brean category, characteristic of the Upper Pleistocene.

The age of the lower artifact-bearing deposits is very much at issue. A marine shell from Caulapan produced a radiocarbon date of 21,850 ± 850 B.P. The Caulapan deposit contained but a single flake of stone; however, Irwin-Williams correlates it with the more productive lower levels at Hueyatlaco (52, 52b). An age of 22,000 years is consistent with the fauna, but it is possible that the Valsequillo fauna represents a very long interval of time, as suggested by the radiocarbon dates obtained by Armenta (4) on animal bones, which range from about 24,000 to greater than 35,000 years.

A profoundly different estimate of the age of the lower Hueyatlaco deposits—and of the enclosed artifacts—is proposed by Steen-McIntyre et al (107). Malde, a coworker, had participated in some of the excavations by Irwin-Williams. He and Steen-McIntyre (both are geologists experienced in stratigraphy and geochronology) later reopened the trenches and dug new ones; Irwin-Williams was prevented by bureaucratic considerations from being present.

Steen-McIntyre has applied several dating techniques to materials recovered from Hueyatlaco. In her view, the results are consistent with one another; they support an age estimate of several hundred thousand years: uranium series dates on bone, 250,000 years; fission track dates on volcanic ash, 370,000 to 200,000 years; hydration of volcanic glass, 200,000 to 600,000 years. It is possible to suggest an age of between 200,000 and 300,000 years, in my estimation, but Steen-McIntyre does not do this. Irwin-Williams (52b) does not accept any of the indications of a great age, citing as a reason the essentially late Upper Pleistocene character of the fauna. Clearly, it would be desirable to have more work done at Valsequillo. This would be difficult, because Hueyatlaco is flooded much of the time by a recently built reservoir, but Malde and Steen-McIntyre already have shown that it can be done during seasons of low water level.

To my knowledge, the identification of the stone artifacts has not been questioned, and as an innocent in radiometric dating, I can accept the dates arrived at by several techniques and cautiously interpreted by Steen-McIntyre and her associates as suggesting great age. At issue, however, still may be the assumptions underlying the dating methods and the association of the dated material with the artifacts. One way to approach this problem is to continue large-scale, careful excavations to reconfirm the presence of stone artifacts in or beneath dated material. Another way is to follow up the impressive results obtained by Armenta (4) in the study of animal bone. Quite independently of work being done in the United States and Canada on the percussion modification of bone, Armenta made a series of observations which are remarkably congruent with the North American findings. These studies should be encouraged, with the hope that specimens determined to be artifacts can be dated by the uranium series technique. In the absence of features such as hearths, post molds, and charcoal of any sort, this would be a promising approach to a solution of the dating problem at Valsequillo.

The uranium series disequilibrium dating technique depends on the assumption that, once charged, the dated material remains a closed system (102). In any particular case, the assumption may be shown to be unwarranted by inconsistencies; nevertheless, in some cases this technique produces results consistent with stratigraphy (see below). Fission track dating, provided the ash is suitable in terms of particle size, mineralogy, and uranium content, appears to be dependable (J. Westgate, personal communication).

CALICO

The Mojave Desert of eastern California has produced some of the most interesting and hotly debated evidence for Early Man. The center of attention in recent years has been the Calico Mountains, which became known in the 1940s as an area with potential for very early archaeological studies. This led R. D. Simpson in the 1950s to conduct an intensive regional survey of the Manix Lake area next to the Calico Mountains. The stone fragments she found in the neighborhood of the now inactive Yermo alluvial fan elicited enthusiasm from L. S. B. Leakey, who recommended a strategy of excavation that was implemented in 1964. The excavations were planned to expose primary sites within the now stabilized fan. They continued until 1972, the year of Leakey's death. A field conference in 1970 (104a) failed to result in a consensus, or even a majority view, that Simpson and Leakey had excavated genuine stone artifacts from within the fan—which was conceded by nearly everyone to be a "very old" deposit. Indeed, many thought that the fan matrix could have been deposited at almost any time. The human authorship of the artifacts also was questioned, as well as the basis for estimating their age. Funding all but ceased. The site has been incorporated in the Bureau of Land Management system, which protects it, and work there continues under Simpson and Budinger, the warden (8), and volunteer workers.

Calico illustrates some of the difficulties of pre-Clovis research. My generation of North American archaeologists is woefully unprepared to contemplate artifacts older than and different from the Palaeoindian tools and weapons that are reasonably well known. Indeed, most of us were trained on sites of quite recent date, and it is difficult for a person with only this experience to evaluate a site in such a strange environment as an ancient alluvial fan. The chronology of the fan itself is intimidating: most observers agree that it was separated from its source by faulting 50,000 or more years ago; some estimate 500,000 years. If its contents include artifacts, these apparently were buried before that time. But most difficult of all is the recognition and acceptance of the excavated stone fragments as evidence for human handiwork. The provenience of the putative artifacts recovered by carefully controlled excavation appears well documented; their authenticity is widely questioned.

This problem has been addressed in a number of ways at Calico. Simpson and her associates have classified some 3500 or 4000 stone tools and 6000 refuse flakes recovered by excavation, which they designate the Manix Lake Lithic Industry (104a). The collection has not yet been published, nor has the classification of artifacts been described and illustrated in detail. Individual specimens have been published, and others have been brought to professional meetings for examination. These have not met with general acceptance. Nevertheless, the collection and its classification should be published with extensive illustrations so that some objective opinion can be formed of their significance.

I am impressed by the complex and orderly arrangement of flake scars on some of the specimens from within the fan. To me, this indicates intent, and therefore a human agency, and not the effects of random natural forces. But for this argument to have force, I would need to know more about the broken specimens from the fan that are not artifacts, and intergrades between these and the "artifacts," for such intergrades surely must exist. There always will be specimens whose cultural status is doubtful. How many of these have been included in the tool count cannot be estimated until the entire range of "possibles" has been considered and the criteria illustrated.

Payen (89) has made a study of the Calico flints using the "Barnes test," a criterion developed in the 1930s to cope with the problem of "eoliths" in Britain. Barnes (5) noted the difference between the mean "platform angle"—the angle between the striking platform and the outer surface of the flake—on known Palaeolithic flakes and on those found by Reid-Moyer in very old situations, which led the latter to infer great age for the cultures responsible for them. Barnes found that the means of the angles in the two samples were different; the known Palaeolithic artifacts gave smaller values. Barnes concluded that humans made smaller platform angles on purpose in order to improve their control over the size and shape of flakes being struck off, whereas nature did not do so. The "eoliths" were declared to be the work of nature, not of Man.

This simple criterion served well in the case of this putative industry, which was found only (or mainly) along the wave-cut cliffs along the North Sea. Pounding surf was an acceptable alternative to primitive Man as the agent responsible for fracturing the flints. The situation at Calico is not quite so simple, for the forces of fan building are very unlikely to be locally so intense and concentrated that they break flints and produce flakes in large numbers.

I have other reservations about this use of the Barnes test at Calico. The comparative collections used by Payen to illustrate the characteristics of controlled fracture all, with but one exception, are from Clovis or later North American sites. More Palaeolithic collections should have been used. The series of flakes used to illustrate "uncontrolled" or natural fracture have mean edge angles that vary widely and significantly overlap the range of "controlled" samples. Also, the several samples from sources in and near the Calico fan give means that vary so widely that each must be considered separately; only one seems to be outside the range of variation for "controlled" flaking, and this is not claimed by anyone as including artifacts. Payen's conclusion "that the Calicoliths are geofacts, not artifacts" seems to me unwarranted by the data on which he bases it. Variability of values for platform angles remains to be explained, and until then the Barnes angle should not be used to evaluate either individual specimens or whole collections for authenticity as man-made flakes. Payen did not consider the possibility that there are both genuine artifacts and specimens that are questionable or spurious in the Calico collection.

I was intrigued to note that the observations on Denbigh (the Denbigh Flint complex of Alaska) provide a mean Barnes angle closer to the values for uncontrolled fracture (natural flaking) than any other sample in the controlled fracture group. Denbigh, however, is probably the most elaborate and sophisticated stone technology known from North America. Clearly, variation in the value of the Barnes angle is not a simple thing.

Another approach to the authenticity of the Calico specimens as artifacts is to examine them individually. If one of the excavated specimens is an artifact, then part of the problem has been solved. I am impressed by the regularity of flake removal on some of the specimens I have seen. I also am impressed by the photographs of a "denticulate" with continuously sharp, unrounded edges shown by Bryan (15) and Simpson (104a). Had the flakes been removed by natural forces to form the denticulate edge, the same forces would have altered the edge further in a recognizable way, and this is not evident.

On the whole, a very strong case has been made for the excavated Calico specimens to include among them indubitable artifacts (105) as well as doubtful ones. This is acceptable because one cannot expect to be able to discriminate in every case between an artifact and a "geofact." I am confident that in time a much stronger case can and will be made for artifacts at Calico.

The age of the excavated material at Calico has troubled observers and commentators. There is general acceptance that the contents of the Yermo Fan slid into their present position more than 50,000 years ago, and perhaps as much as 500,000 years ago. While this happened, there were interruptions (44), during which people apparently lived there. Therefore, the announcement of some uranium series dates of about 200,000 years (7) on calcium carbonate adhering to stones excavated from "artifact bearing" layers in the fan is not unexpected. It would seem to indicate an age for the accompanying artifacts. The reliability of the assumptions on which this rather complicated method of dating is based needs to be questioned in each case (102). We have reassurance from colleagues in archaeometry that their technique is working; the uranium-thorium and uranium-protactinium ratios are said to confirm this, and the results obtained at Calico are consistent with the empirically derived chronology of palaeosols (103a). The contents of the Yermo Fan appear to have been deposited and buried about 200,000 years ago.

OLD CROW

At this stage in the progress of Early Man research, the Old Crow evidence from northern Yukon appears especially significant. I have participated in research there and believe that the Old Crow studies provide some of the most robust evidence for "very early Man" in the Western Hemisphere. The Old Crow data show clearly (*a*) that stone implements may be *very* rare among Pleistocene artifacts, and (*b*) that the nature of ancient New World archaeological complexes cannot be anticipated by simply projecting patterns of Old World assemblages onto the North American landscape. These three inferences from the Old Crow data may be of more general significance for Early Man studies than the proposed ages of the artifacts.

The Old Crow Basin west of the Rocky Mountains was never glaciated, but it was filled with fine-grained sediments during several episodes of Upper Pleistocene (?) time, at least one of which can be correlated with a glacial advance, the Wisconsin Maximum (18,000 B.P.). In postglacial time, and apparently quite rapidly, the Old Crow River cut down through some 35 m of these clays and sands to its present level where it is stable. As it meanders across the valley it exposes tremendous quantities of vertebrate fossils preserved in the low-energy stream deposits consolidated by permafrost. Fossils are distributed in clusters in a number of different modern sedimentary environments; some have been excavated from the valley walls in stratigraphically ancient (Pleistocene) sedimentary contexts.

The great majority of the Old Crow fossils are of Upper Pleistocene (Rancho La Brean) age. It was in such an assemblage that Harington and Lord first recognized bone artifacts in possible association with such extinct mammals as mammoth and horse (41a). The one implement, a bone scraper, and two fractured pieces of mammoth bone were radiocarbon dated to about 27,000 B.P., using the apatite fraction of the bones (51a, *vide supra,* Position II).

The radiocarbon dates and the diagnosis of bone working, which was soon confirmed and elaborated by Bonnichsen (8a), together with the exceptional organic preservation and stratigraphy in fine-grained sediments, led to intensive multidisciplinary research during the late 1970s, some of the results of which are now just beginning to appear (e.g. 47, 51, 52, 56, 79a,b). This work, much of it still unfinished, entails intensive field study and studies of many tens of thousands of specimens recovered during many man-months of controlled excavation and reconnaissance by a large number of workers. A summary of results is necessarily tentative, but certainly not premature, in the light of the work that has been done.

It has been established beyond possible doubt, by experiment with the remains of the unfortunate Ginsberg, that elephant bones can be broken by percussion, in a controlled fashion, so as to produce forms nearly identical with those observed in mammoth bone from the Old Crow Basin (106). Force as great as that of a 20-pound boulder, hurled with all-out effort, is needed to make the first fracture in a fresh elephant bone; thereafter, skill enables the use of small cobbles or other bones to serve as hammers for driving off flakes. The process is similar in principle but not identical in execution to that of flaking stone. Cores were prepared from Ginsberg's bones and made to produce flakes which were used in the further dismemberment of the elephant.

The creation of this experimental analogy does not prove that any of the Old Crow specimens are really artifacts, but it shows that a large number of the inferences drawn from the Old Crow bones about the way in which they had been modified (e.g. 9, 51a, b) could be replicated by modern craftsmen and scientists in ways that natural forces could not emulate. Could natural forces operate in other ways to produce the alterations of Old Crow bones? Guthrie & Thorson (41) propose that they could, but they provide no illustrations or descriptions from their experiments that even approximate the systematic nature of flaking observed on Old Crow bone and in the Ginsberg experiment. I consider the Ginsberg analogy substantial proof, when considered in the larger context of our studies, that an Old Crow bone industry using percussion is both plausible and very strongly indicated by the observations at hand. There may be analogs—or homologs—to it in Eurasia (33), but this needs to be studied further.

Other methods of working bone (and ivory) are indicated in the Old Crow fossil collections: carving, scraping, and polishing have produced a small but significant number of artifacts. Examples of these are few, but among them are some that have been excavated from deposits that can be dated. This stratigraphic position is important.

The chronology of the Old Crow Locality 12 Upper Pleistocene sediments appears to be fairly straightforward and clear as far back as the Sangamonian Interglacial. Morlan and his colleagues have determined that the upper 10 m or so represent some 70,000 years of Early and Late Wisconsinan time (79a). A minor erosion surface ("Disconformity A") just above a volcanic ash layer ("the Old Crow tephra") estimated to date at Locality 15 to approximately 80,000 B.P., has produced a suite of small bone fragments which likely were deposited on a flood plain (57); among them are a long-bone shaft with a cut mark on it (79a), and a number of bone fragments, including a very thin flake showing both platform and core edge preparation (51, 57). These observations are cogent evidence for the presence of humans during the time represented by Disconformity A.

About 15 m directly below Disconformity A is a deposit of alluvium at least 50 m in extent which contains bone fragments and other detritus left by a very low-energy stream system. There is no possibility that Morlan is correct when he suggests that this deposit may be correlated with "Disconformity A" or some other post-Sangamonian event (79a). We have referred this and related low-lying deposits (together, Unit 1b) and their contents to the end of the Illinoian Glaciation (56). This assignment still appears plausible, but because the chronology of the Illinoian is poorly known elsewhere, and because Unit 1b may have had a complex and protracted depositional history, the age of the deposit is difficult to estimate.

Recent findings broaden the discussion of the age of Unit 1b. Bison, the hallmark of Rancho La Brean fauna in North America, are missing from the 10,000 bone specimens recovered by excavation. *Predicrostonyx,* a lemming antecedent to the *Dicrostonyx* of Sangamonian and later times, may be present. A suite of four uranium series determinations on bones excavated from Unit 1b indicates ages for these beyond the range of this technique, that is, more than 350,000 years (H. Schwarcz, A. Latham, personal communication and in preparation). The uranium-thorium and uranium-protactinium ratios are concordant, thus supporting the reliability of the age estimates.

In general, the emerging sequence of uranium series dates is consistent with local stratigraphy and with previous age estimates, but it may show Unit 1b to represent a significantly longer time interval than had been thought. The oldest uranium series dated bones are from a thin stratum in Unit 1b from which several dozen fragments of proboscidean and horse bone, broken while still fresh, were excavated. These strongly suggest the presence of humans at a time before 350,000 years ago (H. P. Schwarcz et al, in preparation).

Whether or not we accept the uranium series dates as they are given, if we accept the Old Crow bone industry, which I have referred to as a "paralithic technology" (51b), there are many tens of thousands of years of human activity in the Old Crow Basin represented almost exclusively by bone artifacts. This seems to mean either that our present reading of the evidence is totally wrong, or that there is a vast realm of material culture in, or absent from, the prehistoric record that has not been recognized or specified as important.

SUMMARY AND CONCLUSION

Position I, in my view, is overwhelmingly negated by sites dated older than Clovis and by the diversity of technology present in the New World at the time of Clovis. The evidence for this also argues strongly in favor of Position II, that is, a first arrival during some part of the Wisconsinan glaciation or within the last 70,000 years. This is entirely plausible from all points of view, and the stratigraphic and radiometric evidence support it; the cultural evidence, although real enough, does not at present encourage attempts at interpretation or synthesis. Some data from human biology and human genetics suggest a first appearance of American human populations about 15,000 to 40,000 years ago; however, the calibration of this age estimate has not been described.

The intractibility, from the viewpoint of systematics, of the cultural evidence from sites that support or fit with Position II is itself a matter of interest. Bryan (e.g. 15) has noted this variation as an indication of time required to differentiate technologies. Dillehay and his colleagues (29) have described early (Position II) cultures with architecture and technology dating to about 13,000 years ago which had not been anticipated by any previous investigators. Our archaeological systematics for the early American periods needs some rethinking, for there is much more diversity than our present taxonomy can accommodate.

If Position III, that humans came to the Western Hemisphere much more than 70,000 years ago, is considered seriously, it poses an enormous challenge. It implies that as much as several hundred thousand years of human prehistory in the Americas are almost totally unknown. It raises questions about human evolution that we cannot now adequately express, much less attempt to answer, because we do not know the biological identity of those suggested first immigrants who, if they existed, document Man's adaptation to northern environments. It also implies that very long episodes of prehistory may be unrecognized in other parts of the world because they are not represented by durable artifacts or by artifacts with which we are already familiar. The kinds of evidence for humans found at Old Crow, Calico, and Valsequillo are in many cases very difficult for even an experienced archaeologist to recognize.

It is the particular responsibility of archaeologists to address this paradox. Others will attend to stratigraphy and chronometric dating, but at least for the present, only archaeology as a discipline can approach the problem of equivocal or enigmatic evidence for culture.

In fact, few of us are now prepared by training to recognize a New World Early Palaeolithic or to describe it for properly skeptical colleagues. Thus, any presupposition about the present empirical nature of Early Man studies, insofar as the recognition of ancient cultures is concerned, is likely to be a delusion, not only of the vulgar but of the cultivated as well. Our discipline still is predominantly normative rather than empirical, as perhaps it should be. But our norms, set many years ago, now bear little relation to empirical knowledge. This, I think, is the true nature of "the problem of Early Man" at the present time. It will be solved only with the realization that we must undertake more basic research in the systematic nature of artifact manufacture and use, and in the interpretation of heretofore "unproductive" early sites from a holistic point of view.

ACKNOWLEDGMENTS

First must come the people of Old Crow; they are valued friends and associates and sources of wisdom. Next, but not in order of importance, Maxine Kleindienst read the manuscript and made trenchant comments which have improved the product; thanks. Ruth Gotthardt has continued as a critical reader and as an active colleague. My graduate seminar of 1984–1985 was both an audience and an advisory group. My collaborators, A. V. Jopling and I. Kritsch-Armstrong, and my colleagues, C. S. Churcher and B. F. Beebe, have advised me well. My undergraduate students of 1984–1985 were a stimulus to attempt clarity.

My research during the preparations of this article has been supported by the Donner Canadian Foundation and the Bickell Foundation and by the University of Toronto. This is contribution No. 59, Northern Yukon Research Programme, University of Toronto.

Literature Cited

1. Adovasio, J. M., Gunn, J. D., Donahue, J., Stuckenrath, R. 1978. Meadowcroft Rockshelter, 1977: An overview. *Am. Antiq.* 43(4):632–51
2. Aigner, J. 1973. Relative dating of North Chinese faunal and cultural complexes. *Arctic Anthropol.* 9:36–79
3. Aigner, J. 1978. Important archaeological remains from North China. In *The Early Palaeolithic in South and East Asia*, ed. F. Ikawa-Smith, pp. 193–232
4. Armenta, J. J. 1978. *Vestigios de Labor Humana en Heusos de Animales Extintos de Valsequillo, Pueblo, Mexico*. Pueblo: Offset Mabek. 125 pp.
5. Barnes, A. S. 1939. The difference between natural and human flaking on prehistoric flint implements. *Am. Anthropol.* 41(1):99–113
6. Berger, R. 1983. Woolly Mammoth Site, Santa Rosa Island, California. See Ref. 31, pp. 163–70
7. Bischoff, J. L., Shlemon, R. J., Ku, T. L., Simpson, R. D., Rosenbauer, R. J., et al. 1981. Uranium series and soil geomorphic dating of the Calico archaeological site, California. *Geology* 9:576–82
8. Bischoff, J. L., Ikeya, M., Budinger, F. E. 1984. A TL/ESR study of the hearth feature at the Calico archaeological site, California. *Am. Antiq.* 49(4):764–73
8a. Bonnichsen, R. 1979. Pleistocene bone technology in the Beringian Refugium. National Museum of Man *Mercury Series*, No. 89. Ottawa: Archaeol. Survey of Canada
9. Bonnichsen, R., Young, D. E. 1984. Understanding stone tools: A cognitive approach. *Peopling of the Americas*, Vol. 1. Orono: Univ. Maine Center for Study of Early Man
10. Bordes, F. 1978. Preface. See Ref. 14, pp. 5–6
11. Bordes, F., Thibault, C. 1977. Thoughts on the initial adaptation of Hominids to European glacial climates. *Quat. Res.* 8:115–27
12. Bryan, A. L. 1965. *Palaeoamerican Prehistory*. Pocatello: Occas. Pap. Idaho State Museum, No. 16
13. Bryan, A. L. 1975. Palaeoenvironments and cultural diversity in late Pleistocene South America: A rejoinder to Vance Haynes and a reply to Thomas Lynch. *Quat. Res.* 5:151–59
14. Bryan, A. L., ed. 1978. *Early Man in America from a Circumpacific Perspective*. Occas. Pap. No. 1, Dep. Anthropol., Univ. Alberta. Edmonton: Archaeol. Res. Int.
15. Bryan, A. L. 1978. An overview of Paleoamerican prehistory from a circumpacific perspective. See Ref. 14, pp. 306–27
16. Bryan, A. L. 1986. Palaeoamerican prehistory as seen from South America. See Ref. 17
17. Bryan, A. L., ed. 1986. *New Evidence for the Pleistocene Peopling of the Amer-*

icas. Peopling of the Americas Series. Orono: Univ. Maine Center for Study of Early Man. In press
18. Deleted in proof
19. Bryan, A. L., Casamiquela, R. M., Cruxent, J. M., Gruhn, R., Ochsenius, C. 1978. An El Jobo mastodon kill at Taima-Taima, Venezuela. *Science* 200:1275–77
20. Bushnell, G., McBurney, C. 1959. New World origins seen from the Old World. *Am. Antiq.* 33:93–101
21. Butzer, K. W. 1982. *Archaeology as Human Ecology.* Cambridge: Cambridge Univ. Press
22. Butzer, K., Isaac, G., eds. 1975. *After the Australopithecines.* The Hague: Mouton
22a. Carlisle, R. C., Adovasio, J. M. 1982. *Meadowcroft: Collected papers on the archaeology of Meadowcroft Rockshelter and the Cross Creek drainage.* Prepared for "The Meadowcroft Rockshelter Rolling Thunder Review: Last Act." 47th Ann. Meet. Soc. Am. Archaeol., Minneapolis, April 14–17
23. Carter, G. F. 1957. *Pleistocene Man at San Diego.* Baltimore: Johns Hopkins Press
24. Chard, C. S. 1959. New World origins: A reappraisal. *Am. Antiq.* 33:44–49
25. Chard, C. S. 1963. The Old World roots: Review and speculation. *Anthropol. Pap. Univ. Alaska* 10(2):225–34
26. Childers, W. M., Minshall, H. L. 1980. Evidence of Early Man exposed at Yuha Pinto Wash. *Am. Antiq.* 45(2):297–308
27. Dikov, N. N. 1978. Ancestors of Palaeoindians and Proto-Eskimo-Aleuts in the Palaeolithic of Kamchatka. See Ref. 14, pp. 68–79
28. Dillehay, T. D. 1984. A late ice age settlement in southern Chile. *Sci. Am.* 25(4):106–217
29. Dillehay, T. D., Mario Pino, Q., Mott Davis, E., Valastro, S., Varela, A. G., et al. 1982. Monte Verde: Radiocarbon dates from an Early Man site in south central Chile. *J. Field Archaeol.* 9(4):547–50
30. Dincauze, D. 1984. An archaeological evaluation of the case for pre-Clovis occupations. In *Advances in World Archaeology,* ed. F. Wendorf, A. Close, 3:275–323. New York: Academic
31. Ericson, J., Taylor, R. E., Berger, R., eds. 1982. *Peopling the New World.* Anthropol. Pap. No. 23. Los Altos, Calif: Ballena Press
32. Espinosa, J., ed. 1976. Excavaciones Arqueologicas en "El Bosque". Informe No. 1, Dep. Antropol. Hist. Managua, Nicaragua: Inst. Geogr. Nac.
33. Freeman, L. G. 1978. The analysis of some occupation floor distributions from earlier and middle Palaeolithic sites in Spain. In *Views of the Past,* ed. L. G. Freeman, pp. 57–116. The Hague: Mouton
34. Grayson, D. K. 1977. Pleistocene avifaunas and the overkill hypothesis. *Science* 195:691–93
35. Griffin, J. B. 1979. The origin and dispersion of the first American Indians in North America. See Ref. 64, pp. 43–55
36. Gruhn, R. 1961. *The Archaeology of Wilson Butte Cave.* Occas. Pap. No. 6, Idaho State Coll. Mus.
37. Gruhn, R. 1977. Earliest Man in the Northeast: A hemisphere-wide perspective. In *Amerinds and Their Palaeoenvironments in Northeastern North America,* ed. W. S. Newman, B. Salwen. *NY Acad. Sci.* 288:163–64
38. Gruhn, R., Bryan, A. L. 1977. Los Tapiales: A Palaeoindian campsite in the Guatemalan Highlands. *Proc. Am. Philos. Soc.* 121:235–73
39. Gruhn, R., Bryan, A. L. 1984. The record of Pleistocene megafaunal extinction at Taima-Taima, northwestern Venezuela. See Ref. 74, pp. 128–37
40. Guidon, N. 1986. Las undidades culturales de Sao Raimundo Nonato, Sudeste del Estadado de Piaui. See Ref. 17
41. Guthrie, R. D. 1984. The evidence for middle-Wisconsin peopling of Beringia: An evaluation. *Quat. Res.* 22:231–41
41a. Harington, C. R., Irving, W. N. 1967. *Some Upper Pleistocene middens near Old Crow, Yukon Territory.* Presented at Ann. Meet. Soc. Am. Archaeol., Ann Arbor, Mich.
41b. Hassan, A. A., Tremaine, J. D., Haynes, C. V. 1977. Mineralogical studies on bone apatite and their implications for radiocarbon dating. *Radiocarbon* 19:364–74
42. Hayden, B., ed. 1979. *Lithic Use-Wear Analysis.* New York: Academic
43. Haynes, C. V. Jr. 1980. Palaeoindian charcoal from Meadowcroft Rockshelter: Is contamination a problem? *Am. Antiq.* 45:582–88
44. Haynes, C. V. Jr. 1982. Were Clovis progenitors in Beringia? See Ref. 47, pp. 383–98
45. Holmes, W. H. 1897. Stone implements of the Potomac-Chesapeake tidewater province. *Smithsonian Inst. Bur. Am. Ethnol. Ann. Rep.* 15 (for 1893–94), pp. 1–152
46. Hopkins, D. M., Bryan, A. L. 1984. Time and circumstances of the peopling of South America. *Archaeol. Geol. Div. Symp. 97th Ann. Meet., Reno.* Geol. Soc. Am. (Abstr.)

47. Hopkins, D. M., Mathews, J. V. Jr., Schweger, C. E., Young, S. B. 1982. *Palaeoecology of Beringia.* New York: Academic
48. Hrdlicka, A. 1907. Skeletal remains suggesting or attributed to Early Man in North America. *Bur. Am. Ethnol. Bull. No. 33,* Washington, DC
49. Ikawa-Smith, F. 1978. Chronological framework for the study of the Palaeolithic in Japan. *Asian Perspect.* 19:61–90
50. Ikawa-Smith, F. 1982. The early prehistory of the Americas as seen from northeast Asia. See Ref. 31, pp. 13–34
51. Irving, W. N. 1982. Pleistocene cultures in Old Crow Basin. See Ref. 31, pp. 69–80. Interim report
51a. Irving, W. N., Harington, C. R. 1973. Upper Pleistocene radiocarbon-dated artifacts from the Northern Yukon. *Science* 179(4071):335–40
51b. Irving, W. N., Jopling, A. V., Kritsch-Armstrong, I. D. 1984. *Studies of paralithic technology and taxonomy, Old Crow Basin, Yukon Territory.* Presented at 1st Int. Conf. Bone Modification, ed. R. Bonnichsen. To appear in *Peopling of the Americas Series.* Orono: Univ. Maine, Center for Early Man Studies
52. Irwin-Williams, C. 1967. Association of early man with horse, camel and mastodon at Hueyatlaco, Valsequillo (Puebla, Mexico). In *Pleistocene Extinctions,* ed. P. S. Martin, pp. 337–47. New Haven: Yale Univ. Press
52a. Irwin-Williams, C. 1978. Summary of archaeological evidence from the Valsequillo region, Puebla, Mexico. In *Cultural Continuity in Mesoamerica,* ed. D. L. Browman, pp. 7–24. The Hague: Mouton
52b. Irwin-Williams, C. 1981. Letter to the editor: Commentary on geologic evidence for age of deposits at Hueyatlaco archaeological site, Valsequillo, Mexico. *Quat. Res.* 16:258
53. Isaac, G. L. 1975. Sorting out the muddle in the middle: An anthropologist's post-conference appraisal. See Ref. 22, pp. 875–88
54. Isaac, G. L. 1984. The archaeology of human origins: Studies of the Lower Pleistocene of East Africa, 1971–1981. *Advances in World Archaeology,* ed. F. Wendorf, A. Close, 3:1–87. New York: Academic
55. Johnson, F., Miller, J. P. 1958. Review of *Pleistocene Man at San Diego,* by G. F. Carter (see Ref. 23). *Am. Antiq.* 24(2):206–10
56. Jopling, A. V., Irving, W. N., Beebe, B. F. 1981. Stratigraphic, sedimentological and faunal evidence for the occurrence of pre-Sangamonian artefacts in northern Yukon. *Arctic* 34:3–33
57. Julig, P., Jopling, A. V., Beebe, B. F., Alcock, J., D'Andrea, C., Irving, W. N. 1983. Excavation report on an *in situ* bone assemblage from Locality 12, Old Crow River, northern Yukon. In *Carnivores, Human Scavengers and Predators: A Question of Bone Technology,* ed. G. LeMoine, A. MacEachern, pp. 15–37. Calgary: Univ. Calgary Press
58. Knudson, R. 1982. Don E. Crabtree, obituary and bibliography. *Am. Antiq.* 47(2):336–43
59. Krieger, A. D. 1958. Review of *Pleistocene Man at San Diego,* by G. F. Carter (see Ref. 23). *Am. Anthropol.* 60(5):974–78
60. Deleted in proof
61. Krieger, A. D. 1964. Early Man in the New World. In *Prehistoric Man in the New World,* ed. J. D. Jennings, E. Norbeck, pp. 28–81. Chicago: Univ. Chicago Press
62. Kuhn, T. S. 1979. The structure of scientific revolutions. *International Encyclopedia of Unified Science,* Vol. 2. Chicago/London: Univ. Chicago Press
63. Kurtén, B., Anderson, E. 1980. *Pleistocene Mammals of North America.* New York: Columbia Univ. Press
64. Laughlin, W. S., Harper, A. B., eds. 1979. *The First Americans: Origins, Affinities and Adaptations.* New York: Fischer
65. LeMoine, G., MacEachern, A., eds. 1982. *Carnivores, human scavengers and predators: A question of bone technology.* Proc. 15th Ann. Conf: Chacmool. Univ. Calgary Archaeol. Assoc.
66. Lieu, Ze Chun. 1985. Sequence of sediments at Locality 1 in Zhoukoudian and correlation with loess stratigraphy in northern China and with the chronology of deep-sea cores. *Quat. Res.* 33:139–53
67. Lorenzo, J. L. 1978. Early Man research in the American hemisphere: Appraisal and perspectives. See Ref. 14, pp. 1–9
68. Lorenzo, J. L., Mirambel, L. 1981. *El Cedral, S. L. P., Mexico: un sitio con presencia humana de mas de 30,000 A.P.* Presented at 10th *Int. Congr. Int. Union Prehist. Protohist. Sci., Mexico.* Commission 10
69. MacNeish, R. S. 1976. Early Man in the New World. *Am. Sci.* 64:316–29
70. MacNeish, R. S., Vierra, R. K., Nelken-Turner, A., Lurie, R., Garcia-Cook, A. 1983. *Prehistory of the Ayacucho Basin, Peru.* Vol. 4: *The Preceramic Way of Life.* Ann Arbor: Univ. Mich. Press

71. Maheny, W. C., ed. 1984. *Quaternary Dating Methods. Developments in Palaeontology and Stratigraphy*, No. 7. Amsterdam: Elsevier
72. Martin, P. S. 1967. Prehistoric overkill. See Ref. 75, pp. 76–120
73. Martin, P. S. 1982. The pattern and meaning of Holarctic mammoth extinction. See Ref. 47, pp. 399–408
74. Martin, P. S., Klein, R. G., eds. 1984. *Quaternary Extinctions: A Prehistoric Revolution.* Tucson: Univ. Arizona Press
75. Martin, P. S., Wright, H. E. Jr., eds. 1967. *Pleistocene Extinctions: A Search for a Cause.* Vol. 6, *Proc. 7th Congr. Int. Assoc. Quat. Res., Boulder.* New Haven: Yale Univ. Press
76. Mead, J. I. 1980. "Is it really that old? A comment about the Meadowcroft Rockshelter 'Overview' ". *Am. Antiq.* 45:579–82
77. Minshall, H. L. 1976. *The Broken Stones.* San Diego: Copley
78. Mirambel, L. 1978. Tlapacoya: A Late Pleistocene site in central Mexico. See Ref. 14, pp. 221–30
79. Mochanov, Y. A. 1978. The Palaeolithic of northeast Asia and the problem of the first peopling of the Americas. See Ref. 14, pp. 67–68
79a. Morlan, R. E. 1983. Pre-Clovis occupation north of the ice sheets. See Ref. 104, pp. 47–64
79b. Morlan, R. E., Cinq-Mars, J. 1983. Ancient Beringians: Human occupation in the Late Pleistocene of Alaska and Yukon Territory. See Ref. 47, pp. 353–82
80. Movius, H. L. Jr. 1948. The Lower Palaeolithic cultures in southern and eastern Asia. *Trans. Am. Philos. Soc.* 38:329–420
81. Movius, H. L. Jr. 1953. Palaeolithic and Mesolithic sites in Soviet Central Asia. *Proc. Am. Philos. Soc.* 97(4):383–421
82. Movius, H. L. Jr. 1954. Palaeolithic archaeology in southern and eastern Asia, exclusive of India. *J. World Hist.* 2:257–82
83. Movius, H. L. Jr. 1956. The new Palaeolithic sites near Ting-Tsun in the Fen River, Shansi Province, North China. *Quaternaria* 3:13
84. Müller-Beck, H. 1966. Palaeohunters in America: Origins and diffusion. *Science* 152:1191–1210
85. Müller-Beck, H. 1967. On migrations of hunters across the Bering Land Bridge in the Upper Pleistocene. In *The Bering Land Bridge*, ed. D. M. Hopkins, pp. 373–408. Stanford: Stanford Univ. Press
86. Müller-Beck, H. 1982. Late Pleistocene man in northern Alaska and the Mammoth Steppe biome. See Ref. 47, pp. 329–52
87. Nelson, N. C. 1937. Notes on cultural relations between Asia and America. *Am. Antiq.* 2:367–72
88. Owen, P. 1984. The Americas: The case against Ice-Age human population. In *The Origins of Modern Humans: A World Survey of the Fossil Evidence*, ed. F. H. Smith, F. Spencer, pp. 517–63. New York: Liss
89. Payen, L. A. 1982. Artefacts or geofacts at Calico: Application of the Barnes test. See Ref. 31, pp. 193–202
90. Pollard, G. C. 1985. Current research: The southern core. *Am. Antiq.* 50 (1):184–90
91. Powers, W. R. 1973. Palaeolithic man in northeast Asia. *Arctic Anthropol.* 10(2):1–106 (whole issue)
92. Rapp, G., Gifford, J., eds. 1985. *Archaeological Geology.* New Haven: Yale Univ. Press
93. Reeves, B. O. K. 1986. *Early Man in the Americas: Who, When and Why?* Festschrift for E. L. Davies. Los Altos, Calif: Ballena. In press
94. Renaud, E. B. 1939. The Black's Fork Culture of Southwest Wyoming. Univ. Denver Archaeol. Survey, *Western High Plains Rep. No. 10*
95. Roberts, F. H. H. Jr. 1940. Developments in the problem of the North American Palaeoindian. In "Essays in Historical Anthropology of North America, Published in Honor of John R. Swanton." *Smithsonian Misc. Collect.* 100:51–116
96. Rogers, R. A. 1985. Glacial geography and native North American languages. *Quat. Res.* 23:130–37
97. Rogers, R. A., Martin, L. D. 1984. The 12 Mile Creek site: A reinvestigation. *Am. Antiq.* 49(4):757–63
98. Rouse, I. 1976. Peopling of the Americas. *Quat. Res.* 6(4):581–96
99. Rouse, I., Cruxent, J. M. 1963. *Venezuelan Archaeology.* Yale Caribbean Ser. No. 6. New Haven: Yale Univ. Press
100. Rudenko, S. I. 1961. The Ust-Kanskaia Palaeolithic cave site, Siberia. *Am. Antiq.* 27(2):203–15
101. Sanger, D., ed. 1970. Papers from a seminar on North American blades and cores. *Arctic Anthropol.* 7(2):1–117
102. Schwarcz, H. P. 1980. Absolute age determinations of archaeological sites by uranium series dating of travertines. *Archaeometry* 22:3–24
103. Serizawa, C. 1978. The Early Palaeolithic in Japan. In *Early Palaeolithic in South and East Asia*, ed. F. Ikawa-Smith, pp. 287–97. The Hague: Mouton

103a. Shlemon, R. J., Bischoff, J. L. 1986. Soil-geomorphic and uranium series dating of the Calico site. See Ref. 17
104. Shutler, R., ed. 1983. *Early Man in the New World*. Beverly Hills: Sage
104a. Simpson, R. D. 1982. The Calico Mountains Archaeological Project: A progress report. See Ref. 31, pp. 181–92
105. Simpson, R. D., Patterson, L., Singer, C. A. 1986. Early Lithic technology of the Calico site, southern California. See Ref. 17
106. Stanford, D., Bonnichsen, R., Morlan, R. E. 1981. The Ginsberg experiment: Modern and prehistoric evidence of a bone flaking technology. *Science* 212:438–40
107. Steen-McIntyre, V., Fryxell, R., Malde, N. E. 1981. Geologic evidence for age of deposits at Hueyatlaco archaeological site, Valsequillo, Mexico. *Quat. Res.* 16(1):1–17
108. Taylor, R. E., Payen, L. A., Prior, C. A., Slota, P. J. Jr., Gillespie, R., et al. 1985. Major revisions in the Pleistocene age assignments for North American human skeletons by C-14 accelerator mass spectrometry: none older than 11,000 C-14 years B.B. *Am. Antiq.* 50(1):136–40
109. Trigger, R. B. 1970. The strategy of Iroquoian prehistory. *Ontario Archaeol.* 14:3–48
110. Turner, C. G. III. 1983. Dental evidence for the peopling of the Americas. See Ref. 104, pp. 147–58
111. Velichko, A. A. 1984. *Late Quaternary Environments of the Soviet Union*. Minneapolis: Univ. Minn. Press. 327 pp.
112. Weber, R. L. 1985. Current research: The Amazon, Eastern Brazil, and the Orinoco. *Am. Antiq.* 50(1):175–79
113. West, F. H. 1983. The antiquity of Man in America. In *Late Quaternary Environments of the United States*, ed. H. E. Wright Jr. Vol. 1: *The Late Pleistocene*, ed. S. C. Porter. Minneapolis: Univ. Minn. Press
114. Wormington, H. M. 1983. Early Man in the New World: 1970–1980. See Ref. 104, pp. 191–96
115. Wright, H. E. Jr. 1984. Sensitivity and response time of natural systems to climatic change in the Late Quaternary. *Quat. Sci. Rev.* 3:91–131
116. Wu, R., Olsen, J. W., eds. 1985. *Palaeoanthropology and Palaeolithic Archaeology in the People's Republic of China*. New York: Academic

STATUS AND STYLE IN LANGUAGE

Judith T. Irvine

Department of Anthropology, Brandeis University, Waltham, Massachusetts 02254

INTRODUCTION

This paper reviews recent literature on the linguistic expression of social status, particularly those studies relating forms of language use (social dialectology and style of speaking) to forms of social stratification. To place that literature in cross-cultural perspective, the principal question orienting the review is this: to what extent do the findings of sociolinguistic research on this topic in North America—notably the urban dialectology that has flourished in the past two decades—resemble or contrast with results for the rest of the world, especially the non-Western world? In other words, have studies of sociolinguistic patterns in American cities identified processes that occur in any or all societies exhibiting distinctions of social status, or have they identified processes that pertain only to a society of a certain kind (urban, industrial, class-based, speaking an Indo-European language)?

I first summarize the relevant American work, then outline some of the problems in comparing these studies with studies of other settings; then I review some of the major forms of the linguistic expression of social status that have been discussed for the non-Western world: social dialects, language levels, and systems of honorifics. While language levels and honorifics may seem to pertain more to language structure than to language use per se, the relation between structure and use is one of the problems this literature raises.

STUDIES OF AMERICAN CITIES

The inspiration and model for much sociolinguistic work has been William Labov's pioneering study of social dialectology in New York City (67). Drawing mainly upon an already existing social survey of the Lower East Side, Labov showed that linguistic behavior correlated systematically with the speaker's social class (position on the survey's ten-point social class index). The linguistic phenomena expressing a speaker's class affiliation were not limited to that meaning, however. Rather, they were shown to be variables that range over social groups and situations. A speaker's group affiliation was expressed by the *relative quantity* of occurrence of a linguistic trait, not categorically by its presence/absence; and the same variables that marked social groups also marked differences within the behavior of an individual speaker over a range of styles of speaking. One such variable, for example, was the occurrence of postvocalic /r/ in words like *car, floor,* and *fourth*. The frequency with which postvocalic /r/ occurred varied with the speaker's social class, age, and speech style, particularly (according to Labov) its degree of formality.

Labov thus linked linguistic variation concerning social categories to variation concerning contexts of talk, as a single sociolinguistic process reflecting the perception of social norms in a speech community. The behavior of prestigious groups becomes a norm for other groups who imitate, and sometimes even overshoot, this behavior in situations when they are paying most attention to their speech (Labov's interpretation of "formality" of style). At the same time, variants associated with nonprestigious groups may become stigmatized and avoided. The process of imitation, "hypercorrection," and avoidance of stigmatized forms results in a restructuring of the distribution of the sociolinguistic variable and represents, Labov argued (69, 129), a principal mechanism of linguistic change.

Although most of the linguistic phenomena examined in the Lower East Side study were phonological, a related study of the English of black and Puerto Rican speakers in New York (74) also examined some other aspects of linguistic structure, such as copula deletion. Both studies, too, investigated the linguistic reflections of ethnicity (Jews and Italians, in the Lower East Side), not only social class. This attention to social variables other than class recalls Labov's earlier study of Martha's Vineyard (69), which explored the role of speakers' regional identification (as Islanders vs mainlanders) in phonological change.

Since the New York City studies, research in what may be called a Labovian paradigm has taken two main directions. The first consists of refinements of quantitative techniques and of the concept of "variable rules" expressing the distribution of linguistic variables in the speech community (21, 68, 110). This line of work sparked a theoretical debate, raised notably by Derek Bickerton (12), on the status of quantitative statements in a grammar. Could variable rules be considered "psychologically real," characterizing the competence of an individual speaker, or were they only the byproduct of Labov's lumping together individual performances in his description of group behavior? Labov responded (70) that individuals actually behave *less* regularly than groups. Linguistic description, he maintained, ought to focus less on the competence of the individual than on the patterned performance of the speech community, which shares norms evaluating the prestige or stigma attached to particular linguistic phenomena. But although Labov and his associates have clearly shown that variability is not just an artifact of the way they have presented their data, Bickerton and some other Creolists have tended to go a separate way, describing the linguistic resources of a community in terms of distinct "lects" to which speakers do not all have equal access, rather than in terms of a uniform grammar studded with quantitative (and socially-marking) indices. Ranking the lects in an implicational hierarchy, however (4), returns this mode of description to a group level [see comments on this point by Guy (44)].

The other main line of research in the Labovian framework has been the attempt to extend the paradigm to other kinds of cases: to syntax and semantics (e.g. 19, 134); to historical materials (95, 107); and especially to other locales. Among the many such studies that now exist for North America, some of the most important, in terms of scale of endeavor and/or methodological significance, are the studies of Detroit (117, 133) and Philadelphia (71, 73; see also *Pennsylvania Working Papers on Linguistic Change and Variation*). Another large-scale effort is the study of Montreal French (110, 110a); further studies of Black English (5), and of Spanish in the US and Latin America, are also noteworthy (e.g. 20, 76, 102, 103). In the early 1970s the model was further extended to Britain, first in Trudgill's study of Norwich (122, 123), and then elsewhere, such as Glasgow (78) and Belfast (87). All these studies investigated relations between linguistic behavior (dialectal variation and style-shifting) and hierarchically ranked social categories such as class and ethnicity (also age and gender). Some also added the investigation of social networks to the social side of the material (73, 88, 89).

In the Philadelphia study, Labov somewhat revised his ideas about the locus of linguistic change within the class structure. Contrasting "older sound changes" with sound changes in progress, he argued (72, p. 254) that although the former might show a linear class stratification, with the lowest social class having the highest frequency of stigmatized variants, the latter always show "a curvilinear pattern of social distribution, where the innovating groups are located centrally in that hierarchy: the upper working class or lower middle class." Meanwhile, however, some of the current research being done in Britain and other sites distant from North America—research characterizing itself as a "post- or neo-Labovian sociolinguistics" (108, p. 2)—has challenged Labov's class-based explanation of sociolinguistic patterning. A major objection these scholars make is that the cities they have studied do not show the monotonic sociolinguistic variation, and shared model of linguistic standardness, attributed to New York City (78, 89, 108). Instead, they advocate a more multidimensional approach, which would recognize that there may be many social groups within a city that have their own linguistic norms. These groups pick and choose the sociolinguistic variables that are most meaningful to them: "sociolinguistic structure is woven in a complex way throughout the community, with different phonological elements being associated with various social groups" (89, p. 31; 108, p. 14).

Still, the degree of departure from Labov's work is less radical than it may appear to be. The patterning of sociolinguistic behavior in New York City does not look so monotonic when Labov's own studies of ethnicity are taken into account. His discussion of class differentiation, too, is more complex and thoughtful in the full-scale study (67) than his briefer summarizing papers might suggest [see criticisms by Robinson (106)]. And nobody wants to propose that a class structure has nothing to do with linguistic behavior or linguistic change. Perhaps the point is really this: we cannot assume that class is the *only* social variable structuring a community, nor even the only kind of ranked social category; and we cannot predict the full content of a cultural system (of which norms of sociolinguistic evaluation are a part) only from a consideration of structural variables such as class. We cannot assume, moreover, that the norms of sociolinguistic evaluation are all uniformly shared throughout a complex social system.

Greater difficulties arise for the concept of *style,* as Labov originally used it. Several recent papers have argued that paying increased attention to speech does not necessarily shift it always in the same direction (10); that "formality" is not a unidimensional variable (57); and that formality of speech style may not be what the Labovian sociolinguistic interview measures at all, but some other variable such as reading vs speaking style or degrees of literacy (77; 107, p. 119). Speakers do shift style in different situations, and their speech can come to resemble that of other social groups, but the pertinent characteristics of those situations have not yet been undisputedly identified. Bell's (10) discussion of perceived audience characteristics and the studies of speaker accommodation (convergence and divergence) by Giles and his colleagues (35, 36) are relevant to this issue.

SOME PROBLEMS OF COMPARISON

Although a considerable amount of research in a Labovian framework has been conducted outside North America, most of it concerns urban settings in western Europe and Latin America and so does not venture far outside the Western urban-industrial world. What research of this kind there is for other locales will be reviewed below. But many studies relating language to social status and social stratification in non-Western societies describe instead such phenomena as language levels, special registers, multilingualism, address forms, and honorifics. Why is there this disparity? Four different (but not mutually exclusive) hypotheses could be suggested to answer this question:

1. Practical difficulties stand in the way of conducting comparable research. The Labovian paradigm described above has several prerequisites before the

sociolinguistic research can be carried out: (*a*) a detailed analysis of the linguistic system, especially the phonology, within which the sociolinguistic variation takes place; (*b*) a detailed social survey identifying relevant social characteristics of consultants; and (*c*) widespread literacy (if Labov's interviewing technique is to be replicated). These prerequisites are less easily found in non-Western, especially rural, settings. We shall see that the studies of such settings that do attempt a variationist approach generally have to modify it significantly, e.g. by examining morphological variation instead of phonological (56), by classifying informants by education rather than by any directly economic criterion of social class (91), or by replacing reading tasks with repetition tasks and prayers (2).

2. The societies concerned are different. The literature includes several suggestions as to major contrasts in social structure that might make an important difference for sociolinguistic systems: (*a*) "traditional" or "modern" societies, differing especially in their ideologies of dependence or equality (92, 93); (*b*) the presence or absence of a royal court (130); (*c*) degrees of mobility and separation between groups (51, 81; 124, p. 36); (*d*) unilineal or bilateral kinship systems (125); (*e*) the folk-urban continuum (2); (*f*) and types of cities, those with established traditions of social pluralism being contrasted both with homogeneous communities and with unstable agglomerations of recent migrants (42). Some of these suggestions will be examined more carefully below.

3. The languages concerned are different. The relevant typological factor is the nature of morphological elaboration. As Neustupny (92) suggests, languages with strong honorific systems (i.e. where honorifics are embedded in the morphology) are either agglutinative or polysynthetic. Analytic languages elaborate the lexicon instead, the result being language levels—lexical sets whose members differ only in implied respect rather than in reference. But Neustepny considers linguistic typology as only one factor among several conditioning how respect is linguistically expressed. Moreover, the typological contrast applies mainly within the non-Western world, distinguishing the cases of Japanese and Javanese, for example, rather than distinguishing American and European cases from others.

4. Models of description are not comparable, or have not identified what kinds of phenomena would be comparable. As Bell (10) points out, where sociolinguistic variationists have concentrated on small-scale linguistic variables ("microstyle"), scholars of other persuasions have more often examined broader discourse phenomena, such as turn-taking, politeness strategies, address systems, and other manifestations of "macrostyle" or "conversational style" (121). Thus another reason for a lack of comparable research has been a focus on different linguistic subsystems.

The various strands of research have also approached their material from very different angles. A social dialectology approach centers firmly on the speaker: his/her differences from other speakers, in terms of a society-wide classification of more or less permanent social identities such as ethnic, class, or sect affiliation, gender, and age cohort. Intraspeaker variation or "style" in this approach has tended to focus on psychological states internal to the speaker (such as degrees of self-consciousness). In contrast, studies of honorifics, language levels, politeness phenomena, etc focus on the speaker's *relation* to addressee, referent, and setting. Other differences between approaches concern whether one starts from language structure or from language use, and what relation one sees between them; and how much one relies on a structure of native metalinguistic categories for the framework of one's description. Studies of language levels, for example, tend to start from the set of labels for the levels and then outline their contents as these might emerge in the classic forms of linguistic elicitation. It is only very recently that attention is paid to the implementation of these structures in the flow of actual conversation (26, 132).

Before turning to language levels, honorifics, etc, however, I consider studies of social dialectology, a framework closer to Labov's whether actually modeled after his work or not.

SOCIAL DIALECTOLOGY IN THE NON-WESTERN WORLD: INDIA

The study of social dialects in non-Western societies should, in principle, allow us to consider the effect of different types of social structures on sociolinguistic patterns. Of special interest with regard to social stratification are studies of language use in India, where there is a considerable tradition of research on language differences relating to caste, beginning with Jules Bloch's 1910 "Castes et dialectes en Tamoul" (14), and recently summarized in several works (6, 41, 116). It is sometimes claimed that a greater stability of ranking and a greater social distance between groups, in a caste system as compared to class, analogously stabilizes and segregates linguistic varieties. Trudgill's sociolinguistics textbook tells us (124, p. 36), for example, that caste dialects are easier to study, and the differences among them are more stable and clearcut than among class dialects. Hudson (51, p. 47) maintains that "in India, the village is divided into clearly distinct groups (castes), each of which can be identified by its language." To what extent are these generalizations supported by the literature?

First of all, it must be noted that the large number of endogamous, named occupational castes (*jati*) that exist on the local level are grouped into broad sets or categories of castes (the *varnas* and groups of *varnas*), and it is these, rather than the *jati,* that show any qualitative linguistic differentiation. In North India, the major sociolinguistic distinction is between Touchable and Untouchable categories, with Touchable including both Brahmin and non-Brahmin castes; in

South India the main distinctions are between the Brahmin, non-Brahmin, and Adi-Dravida (Untouchable). To the extent that distinct linguistic features attach to the *jati* at all, they usually concern the special lexicon connected with the caste's occupation, as for example the technical terms used by Kanyakumari fishermen (115); see also a description (11) of secret codes used by South Kanara devil dancers while officiating in the duties of their caste. Otherwise, any linguistic distinctiveness at the *jati* level is due only to special historical circumstances. If some particular *jati* happen to be migrants into the region where they now reside, they will diverge linguistically from other local *jati*, but largely as a byproduct of their divergent geographical origin—a distinctness now maintained by their social distinctness, however, and perhaps over several generations (3, 40, 98). As to whether *jati* differ from one another in the relative quantity of their use of linguistic variables (i.e. as do social classes in New York City), we do not yet know. An intensive variationist study that might show this has not been done [see, however, the pilot study of Mysore City Tamil by Gnanasundaram & Rangan (37), conducted under Labov's direction].

Two works that have been very influential on Indian sociolinguistics, especially with regard to caste, are Gumperz's study of a North Indian village (40) and the collection published by Ferguson & Gumperz in 1960 (29). Gumperz's village study describes phonological distributions and phonetic detail for a cross-section of castes. The phonological differences, involving such matters as vowel height and the distribution of neighboring vowel phonemes among word classes, do not seem vastly greater than the differences Labov observed in New York City. Moreover, the social contrasts that emerged as linguistically significant only partly involve caste. The distinction between Touchable and Untouchable castes is linguistically relevant, as is a distinction between the immigrant Sweepers and other Untouchable castes. A few apparently minor phonetic characteristics differentiate the untouchable Shoemakers and Chamar (a caste of landless laborers) as well. Otherwise, the main social distinction concerns whether a speaker's fellow-villagers considered him "old-fashioned" or "backward," whatever his caste. Although some Untouchables were more likely to be considered "backward" because of their more limited access to educational opportunities, the distinction has no intrinsic connection with ritual status.

Gumperz's study is unusual in that it considers the sociolinguistic structure of a community as a whole and that its site is in North India. Most other studies of the sociolinguistics of caste focus on South India and take a language (usually Tamil, Kannada, or Tulu) rather than a community as their starting point. Among these, two studies of caste dialects in Kannada (16, 82) from the Ferguson & Gumperz collection (29) set the stage for many subsequent works. Bright (16) examined the sources and motivations of linguistic innovation;

McCormack (82) investigated whether, and how much, castes are actually recognizable by their speech.

Comparing Brahmin and non-Brahmin dialects of Kannada, Bright found that Brahmin speech is more archaic grammatically but more innovative in lexicon because it is more receptive to foreign loan words. These loans may, in turn, introduce new sounds into the phonological system. Non-Brahmin speech, on the other hand, shows more shifts in the natively Dravidian phonology. Bright attributes the difference to the Brahmins' greater literacy.

Later works have partly confirmed, partly elaborated these findings. A study by Ramanujan (105) of caste dialects in Tamil shows that Brahmins and non-Brahmins innovate in different directions, the Brahmins by over differentiating, the non-Brahmins by leveling. Ramanujan suggests that the social motivation for change in the Brahmin dialects comes from their caste-internal communicative uses, including self-identification as Brahmins, while the generalizing tendencies of non-Brahmin speech forms come from their function as intercaste media of communication. McCormack (83), however, claims that changes in non-Brahmin speech come from attempts to imitate the speech of the higher-status Brahmins, and that non-Brahmin speech therefore shows greater diversity and more rapid change. Some other studies similarly maintain that Brahmin speech is more uniform and closer to a standard than is non-Brahmin speech (105, 113), but the suggestion that Brahmins are therefore more linguistically conservative can be criticized (116, p. 155) for failing to recognize that the standard is derived from Brahmin speech in the first place.

Meanwhile, McCormack (82) focused on the recognition of Kannada speakers' social level—Brahmin, non-Brahmin, or Harijan (Untouchable)—from tape-recorded speech. He found that the Brahmins were most easily identified, the Harijans almost never. Despite the fact that Harijan speech includes distinctive forms (largely in the phonemic shape of person-number verbal suffixes), Harijans tended to use "a mixture of Brahmin, Lingayat and literary forms which effectively masked their own distinctive class dialect" (p. 81). Thus the difficulty of identifying them from their speech was not so much the result of some greater variability in the Harijan dialects themselves, but the result of a greater degree of style-shifting. Considerable shifting has also been noted for lower-caste Tamil speakers (115), and indeed for all castes (40, 97).

Perhaps the only conclusion that can be drawn from these various studies is that the sociolinguistics of caste in India are much more complex than the remarks by Trudgill and Hudson would have it. Apart from the two-way Touchable/Untouchable distinction in North India and the three-way Brahmin/non-Brahmin/Adi-Dravida (Harijan) distinction in South India, one can make few generalizations, and even this does not always firmly identify speakers. Linguistic variation attaching to caste is complicated by geographical variation, style-shifting, and variation attaching to other social factors; and the degree of variation and the direction of change may also differ depending on the particular aspect of linguistic structure concerned (lexicon vs phonology, for example). Moreover, the fact that speakers attempt to "caste-climb" by using speech forms associated with higher ranks suggests a social (and sociolinguistic) dynamic at odds with the stereotypical picture of Indian castes as rigid, immutable strata, unchallengeable and unmanipulable. Like recent work in the sociology and anthropology of Indian caste, sociolinguistic research does not support a view of caste as simply class ossified. It is both more like class (in being fundamentally dynamic) and less like it (in being less directly socioeconomic).

But whether or not we understand what caste is about, in the last few years some authors have even suggested that caste has been overrated as a factor in Indian sociolinguistic variation. Krishnamurti (64) argues that caste is a much less important variable than educational level, particularly in the emergence of standards and the differentiation of speech styles. The differences among caste dialects are usually less extensive than the differences between formal and informal standards of speaking—a stylistic gulf wide enough in many South Asian languages to deserve the label *diglossia* (28, 32, 114). Unlike European cases of diglossia, however, in India (at least in the North) any particular set of local informal (L) varieties can be associated with several distinct prestige (H) styles, each used for a different purpose (43). The H styles are acquired through education, of which there are various kinds.

The relationships among diglossia, education, and caste are complex. Zvelebil (136) argues that the supposed three-way caste division of dialects in Tamil confuses caste with educational level, and that the dialect usually identified as Adi-Dravida is really a form of L style associated with uneducated people and thus not based on caste at all. Schiffman (111), on the other hand, proposes that the persistence of diglossia in Tamil is itself an effect of the purity-pollution complex that is such an important aspect of caste in South India. Possibly the relative importance of caste and education (including acquisition of H forms) may vary according to the speakers' milieu. For example, in a study of Bengali pronouns and demonstratives, Das (24) suggests that in rural areas caste and age predominantly determine patterns of linguistic usage, whereas in urban areas education and occupation prevail. Another study indicates, however, that different linguistic variables may be differentially affected by caste and education. In a pilot study of variation in Bazaar Hindi in Mysore City, Jaswal et al (62) show that speakers' educational background and the formality of their speaking style explain the loss of /h/ in certain linguistic environments but fail to explain variation in deaspiration.

Clearly, a great deal of work remains to be done in the sociolinguistics of social status and style in India, despite a relatively large bibliography compared with other non-Western regions. Shapiro & Schiffman (116) recommend systematic variationist studies of the kind instituted by Labov, Bickerton, DeCamp, and others, studies that admit quantitative variation and inherent variability in social dialects, and that put caste in its place as only one out of many social parameters that may be correlated with linguistic variation. To this recommendation I would add another: we need to see more studies that are community-based (like Gumperz's village research, and like the New York City study) rather than language-based. Solid grounding in a local social structure enables a study to distinguish among many possibly relevant social characteristics of speakers—as Gumperz's study did—and avoids the assumption that language itself establishes community. [As Apte shows (3) in a study of Marathi-speaking Brahmins and Tailors in Tamilnadu, the fact of speaking Marathi did not establish a focus of self-identity or of social contacts; religion, residence, and caste were more important.] It will also be useful to see studies that distinguish among several possibly different forms of style-switching: diglossic, caste-climbing, imitating "educated" speech, and other forms of status-climbing or situation-specific styles.

SOCIAL DIALECTOLOGY IN OTHER NON-WESTERN AREAS

Dialectological approaches to the linguistic expression of social status in other parts of the non-Western world are relatively few and scattered. They do present some interesting problems and findings, however, for both the social and linguistic sides of the problem. To start with, these studies cannot select a sample of speakers in quite the same way as Labov did in New York City, partly for reasons of practicality and partly for reasons of appropriateness. Detailed surveys of socioeconomic class such as the one Labov used are not generally available in the Third World; and it is not clear that class is best measured there by precisely the same criteria, or even whether class is the most relevant social variable.

Among variationist studies that have tried to apply the Labovian model most directly, some have treated speakers' level of education as a substitute for, or index of, socioeconomic class. For example, Jahangiri & Hudson (60) propose that educational level is one of the main influences on variation in Tehrani Persian, and that factors such as occupation, parents' education, place of birth, and place of residence will not normally conflict with it. Speakers whose occupation, residence, etc did not match what was usual for their educational attainment were excluded from their analysis. Educational level thus replaces class in their sample because it is taken as the most important measure of social status other than sex and age. Another study of Persian (91) also uses education instead of class, but mainly for convenience [see also an investigation (109) of Mombasa Swahili, discussed further below].

While education may well define status groups in a particular society, it certainly cannot be taken as a universal predictor of social strata, especially in societies where a Western style of education is not the only kind, or where an indigenous system of social stratification long predates its introduction. A variationist study of speech styles in Javanese (25) measured speakers' education separately from other social factors such as noble vs common descent, economic achievement, and occupation. As indices of stylistic usage these latter factors emerged as distinct from education and far outweighing it. (Note, however, that this study is not strictly comparable to others considered here since its data were drawn from the representation of speech in novels rather than from living speakers.) In a complex situation such as Platt (100) describes for Singapore, education may be available in more than one linguistic medium, even for members of the same ethnic group. Platt cites ethnicity and educational background as the most important factors controlling the verbal repertoires of Singaporean speakers, though "age, sex, and socioeconomic status may also be of significance" (p. 64); but education is clearly not a simple social variable (and not a purely nonlinguistic one), since the medium of education may be English, Chinese, Arabic, or another language, depending on the school and educational track.

To consider education as if it marked social status independently of language is also problematic in diglossic situations, as noted above for India. Persian, too, shows sharp differences between literary and colloquial styles, education being the domain in which literary styles are acquired. The difficulty of relating speech performances in Persian to nonlinguistic variables must therefore be compounded when an elicitation method involves reading tasks. Thus it is not surprising that more educated speakers differ from less educated ones in an interview that contrasts reading tasks with oral narrative and conversation (91). Borrowed from Labov, this interview format risks circularity if (as was not the case in Labov's own work) social status is represented only by educational attainment. Jahangiri & Hudson's (60) use of only the "unscripted" parts of the Labovian interview is more sensible. Their finding that more educated speakers of Persian always use more of the "standard" variants is hard to interpret, however, since they do not clarify the relationship between standard and literary forms.

Meanwhile, other descriptions of the linguistic situation in Iran argue that literary style is a less significant marker of status distinctions than is the use of "politeness levels," a different dimension of stylistic variation (48, 49). We have little information on whether speakers' educational level predicts their use of these other speech styles. Perhaps the best assessment would be that there is more than one status hierarchy in Iran—one linked with educational attainment and marked by the use of literary (and perhaps "standard") forms, the other based on some other social categorization and reflected in the use of politeness levels. However, politeness levels may well mark characteristics of social situations—such as intimacy or formality—rather than of speakers (8, 9).

If education has been taken to index or imply social status in some studies, others select quite different social variables. A study of social dialects in Baghdad, for example, emphasizes speakers' religious affiliation: varieties of Arabic differed sharply depending on whether the speaker was Muslim, Jewish, or Christian (13). Within these religious communities there were also some more subtle linguistic differences reflecting other social factors, including class, but the religious division was clearly paramount. Another study of variation in Arabic, this time in Bahrain (50), also focuses on religious communities, but within Islam (Sunni and Shi'i sects). Sect affiliation, literacy, and urban versus rural origin are cited as the principal social determinants of linguistic variation among speakers, and also the factors speakers themselves recognize. Although a class analysis of this social situation might well be possible, it would represent only indirectly the social groupings on which speakers model their linguistic behavior.

Another set of social categorizations to be considered in relation to stratification is local and ethnic identity. Probably the majority of sociolinguistic studies of non-Western locales focus on ethnic identity as it is reflected in multilingualism (e.g. 1, 31, 63, 75, 84, 96, 112). These cases of ethnic pluralism and multilingualism are not all of the same type, however. In many African cities, for example, pluralism is recent because the cities themselves are recent agglomerations. The relationship to an emerging class system is not yet clear, nor is the outcome of the linguistic situation. In Asia, on the other hand, pluralism and multilingualism have settled (at least in some areas) into a more stable social order that involves a long-term language loyalty. Gumperz (42, p. 205) terms this "community multilingualism,"

> "a linguistic phenomenon which is characteristic of urban agglomerates in the so-called 'plural societies' of the East. In these societies, groups of widely different regional and cultural background live together in close geographical proximity ... [Although] inter-group barriers are now slowly but steadily breaking down, we still have a society which tolerates and keeps distinct a wide variety of diverse modes of behavior."

Though often described in an idiom of ethnicity rather than class, "plural societies" are not unstratified societies, but classes per se may not be the primary frame of reference for individuals' linguistic behavior. The relevance of this point for sociolinguistics, and the relation between ethnicity and stratification, are far from universally agreed upon, especially for non-Western cases. Some sociolinguistic analyses treat ethnicity and class as cross-cutting social variables (100, 128), as (in effect) did Labov in the New York City study; many of the multilingualism studies do not. The issues are several: our understandings of what ethnicity and class are, including the difference between "class" as prestige category (and therefore involving speakers' frame of reference for evaluating and modeling linguistic behavior) and "class" as economic category (not necessarily psychologically salient to speakers); the many kinds and sources of prestige speakers might recognize (122); when ethnic identity involves language loyalty and when it does not (30, 53); and when and how it matters whether the linguistic differences distinguishing social groups are phonological details or entire linguistic systems.

Several variationist studies are concerned with ethnicity and local identity in non-Western societies (91, 109, 128). Russell's study of Mombasa Swahili (109) investigated the speech of Muslim Swahili-speaking Afro-Arabs, a core community within Mombasa residing mainly in its "Old Town." The social variables examined were incommunity/outcommunity identity, age, and sex (as well as situational variables and genre of talk—factors Russell emphasizes particularly); class was not included. Arguably, however, her sample of speakers was actually recruited from a single socioeconomic category or status group (namely, ex-slaveholders) because of the network technique she used to select them. [See comments by Wald (127) comparing Russell's single-network sample with the sampling methods used by the Milroys in Belfast, where identifying several networks permits both linguistic and social comparisons among them.] It is not clear, therefore, that Russell's sample represents a community in the same way that Labov's Lower East Side sample did, and her conclusion that the Mombasa data do not fit his model for sound change remains in question.

Two other studies, on Persian (91) and on Jakarta Malay (128), both document the emergence of a specifically urban linguistic variety that replaces or supplements older prestige standards. In addition to literary Persian, then, colloquial Tehrani Persian is becoming a second norm, both within Tehran itself (where the most innovative forms are spoken by younger, less educated persons) and in some other regions of Iran. In Jakarta, a new linguistic variety known as "Modern Jakarta Malay" is emerging as an urban working-class norm. Innovative forms are associated most strongly with immigrant ethnic groups—people whose relatives in other parts of Java speak Javanese or Sundanese—rather than with the Betawi, the core population historically occupying the Jakarta region. This distinction between core and immigrant populations recalls the Mombasa study too, and suggests that there may be some common sociolinguistic patterns accompanying the emergence of urban class affiliations.

Finally, a study of variation in Cochabamba Quechua (2) traces the relationship between rural speakers' involvement in a national Spanish- and urban-dominated social system and the influence of Spanish on their Quechua. Here measures of socioeconomic status used by Labov are replaced by a complex set of measures concerning lifestyle and access to urban centers, as well as the more familiar scales of occupation and education. These variables do concern status, but for a system in which ethnicity and a folk-urban continuum play an important role.

So far in this section I have spoken mainly about the social side of the sociolinguistic studies of stratification—problems in defining, relating, and indexing class, ethnicity, and other social groupings. On the linguistic side, one problem has been to identify the direction of linguistic change. What linguistic forms are older? Some authors apparently assume that literary forms are always older than colloquial forms; some rely on age-grading, assuming that the older the speaker, the older the speech form; some allude to informants' characterizations of particular social groups as "traditional" or "modern"; some use linguistic comparisons and historical documentation. Unfortunately, for many languages adequate historical and comparative data are lacking. When they are available, it is sometimes possible to test whether linguistic innovations really do coincide with age-grading and other social characterizations. A study of sociolinguistic variation in Wolof noun classification (56) used nineteenth-century Wolof linguistic materials to identify innovations in present-day speech. Two opposite trends were found, one representing a trend toward elaboration of the noun class morphology, the other a trend toward its reduction. Usually the elaborations were *thought* to be conservative, however, even though historically they were not. Moreover, the age-grading of innovations was not linear. Most innovations emerged in middle age. In this social system the timing of linguistic innovation in a speaker's life-cycle coincides with the time when a certain status achievement, if not true upward mobility, is possible. The sociolinguistic analysis does link linguistic change with speakers' efforts at social achievement, but it locates those efforts in terms of the time of life when they are made, not only in terms of particular social strata.

Another important linguistic question has concerned the independence of phonology from other parts of the linguistic system. Wallace's study of Jakarta Malay (128) found that phonological diversity was strongly conditioned by an item's syntactic or semantic class, sometimes even by its lexical identity. Holes (50) makes a similar argument for Bahrain: what appears at first sight to be phonological variation turns out (at least in part) to be lexical variation instead. Citing a parallel with Trudgill's findings in Norwich, Wallace writes:

> We wonder . . . whether urban dialectology might not have to face one of the problems encountered earlier in dialect geography and stated in its extreme form by the maxim: Every word has its own history. For it might well be true that in cities like Norwich and Jakarta each lexical item has a different probability of receiving one variant pronunciation or another . . . (128, p. 184)

Besides dialect geography, another interesting comparison—interesting because it also involves lexical variation—would be with language levels, to which I turn below. However, we should note that where linguistic variation is tied up with lexicon it is also tied to topic and, ultimately, to situation. The connection discussed at the beginning of this review, between linguistic variation concerning social categories and linguistic variation concerning contexts of talk, is suggested again here in the more linguistic side of the analysis.

LANGUAGE LEVELS AND HONORIFICS

Language levels are most often described for languages of East and Southeast Asia, especially Indonesia [but see also the respect vocabularies in Samoan (25a, 86) and Ponapean (33), politeness levels in Persian (8, 9, 48, 49), and vocabulary levels in Zuni (94).] I focus first on the Indonesian cases, where similar and elaborate language-level systems occur in Javanese, Sundanese, Madurese, Balinese, and Sasak (25–27, 34, 38, 101, 120, 126, 131, 132). Although the history of this phenomenon is poorly understood, its emergence in Indonesia is probably related to the importation of Hinduism. Much of the special vocabulary of the higher, most "polite" levels has a Sanskrit origin or follows semantic patterns found in Indian languages. For this reason, Wolff and Poedjosoedarmo suggest that the "polite" levels may have begun as a hybrid Sanskrit used with certain castes or for certain religious functions (132, p. 9). Zurbuchen (135, p. 90) notes that in Bali, the most elaborate language-level systems are traditionally found in regions having most contact with the Balinese courts after the influx of Hindu-Javanese priests and nobles.

Linguistically, the differences between levels consist mainly in lexical substitutions and a few special affixes [prosodic and morphophonemic differences exist too, however (26, p. 9), and deserve more attention than they have apparently received]. The lexical basis of the levels—that is, the occurrence in them of lexical items with variant forms, the variants being socially ranked—underlies my suggestion (above) that a comparison between language levels and the social dialects described as relying on lexical variation would be of interest. However, in language levels, the variant forms for a lexical item are usually suppletions or expansions rather than just phonologically shifted renderings. It is not clear that they are necessarily quite perfect synonyms either. (The various systems that have been called "language levels" may differ on this point. Persian, for instance, seems often to draw upon expressions referring to the exalted nature of the addressee or referent and the humble nature of the speaker.)

Perhaps one of the most important points about language levels is their psychological salience: language levels are named and highly accessible to their speakers' conscious contemplation, even if the conscious representation may be more regular and consistent than what actually emerges in speech. In the Indonesian systems there are two major named levels, Krama (polite) and

Ngoko (ordinary). Within these, further distinctions (e.g. "high Krama" and "humble Krama") are possible, as well as the intermediate level Madya. The lexical items that vary among the levels are all words referential of or predicable of persons; Errington (27) links this fact with native speakers' awareness of the alternants and their social significance in a notion of "pragmatic salience."

Apparently, speakers conceive of the language levels as registers, whose use depends on one's assessment of a situation, particularly the relationships among its personnel, and the appropriateness of displaying affect. The higher forms are considered depersonalized, governed by an ethic of proper order, peace, and calm; in them one "does not express one's own feelings" (132, p. 41). Ngoko, on the other hand, is the "language . . . one loses one's temper in" (26, p. 9). There is also a sense in which the language levels distinguish categories of speakers. Not everyone controls all levels equally well, especially Krama. Thus Geertz (34) describes Javanese social ranks (the *prijaji*, the traditional high rank; non-*prijaji*, urban, somewhat educated persons; and peasants and uneducated townspeople) as differing significantly in the range they control within the total repertoire. More recent studies have also revealed generational differences, with younger speakers increasing their use of Ngoko relative to Krama (132, p. 27), and differences relating to "modernization" and the emergence of a new urban educated elite (26). This ambiguity between characteristics of speakers and characteristics of situations is also revealed in informants' differences of opinion about the status of Madya. Madya has relatively few forms belonging specially to it, but instead it draws upon the other levels. Some of Errington's informants considered it "sloppy" speech used by an outgroup, while others thought of it as informal speech used in situations intermediate in their status connotations (26, p. 17).

Informants' opinions about the content and functioning of the language levels, and their relatively rich metalinguistic vocabulary for describing them (as compared, e.g. with the description of social class dialects), stand out in this literature as clearly important, both in the levels' "meaning" and as a starting point for linguistic investigation and description. Only recently have we begun to see detailed study of the implementation of these forms in actual behavior. It is these studies that show language levels as bound up in a sociolinguistic process involving the aspirations and changing attitudes of social groups (26, 132). In implementation the levels also show much more variability than might have been supposed. Wolff & Poedjosoedarmo (132) found that except in formal speeches and ceremonies, speakers constantly shifted level—because of change in topic or attitude, conflicts in the status parameters governing the situation, uncertainty about what people's relative statuses were, quoting statements or thoughts, shifting for "rhetorical effect," or just "lack of control." Evidently, the sociolinguistic situation in Indonesia is extremely complex.

Moreover, to identify language levels, and even to observe them in use, does not exhaust the repertoire of linguistic varieties available to speakers of Indonesian languages. Additional codes are available, such as Jakarta Malay and Bahasa Indonesian (128), as well as formal and informal stylistic variants and use of titles that are largely independent of the language levels (132).

If much work remains to be done on the languages of Indonesia, especially regarding observation of language use in natural contexts, the same is true for other systems of "honorifics." I shall discuss these only briefly, because the term has not been applied very systematically. It sometimes includes the language level systems described above, as well as Asian languages like Japanese, where degrees of politeness are reflected not only in lexical substitutions but also (and apparently to a greater degree than in the Indonesian cases) in morphology and syntax. Other systems of honorifics consist largely in politeness affixes and elaborated pronoun systems. Examples are areally and socially diverse, including languages of South Asia (7, 17, 22, 61); the Americas, principally Nahuatl (47, 99), though a somewhat similar affix pattern is found in Aymara (15); Africa (39, 80, 104); and Europe, where the "honorifics" are limited to the pronoun system and its reflexes. There the classic work by Brown & Gilman (18) on the expression of power and social solidarity in the pronouns of European languages, with its emphasis on the *relationship* between speaker and addressee (rather than permanent characteristics of either, or of a situation), has provided a useful analytical model for other studies of honorific phenomena, whether limited to pronouns or not. [See also a review of the expression of respect in pronoun systems worldwide (46).]

What order, if any, can be seen in this miscellany? One approach would be to focus on linguistic subsystems (as I have implicitly done above). This would be necessary if one wanted to examine the role of linguistic constraints, the patterning of honorific forms with language type, or the effects of lexicalization. In Japanese, for example, the relation between honorific lexicon, morphology, and syntax, including the dependence of honorifics on grammatical function, has been of particular interest (45, 54, 79, 90, 93, 130). Another approach would be areal/historical and would allow us to examine the role of particular political or religious centers in the crystallization and spread of honorific systems and their associated ideology. In a comparative study of honorifics focusing mainly on Asian systems, Wenger (130, p. 161) links the elaboration of honorific systems with the presence of a royal court, as did Brown & Gilman (18) in connecting European pronoun uses with historical developments in the Roman Empire.

A third approach (17, 23, 93, 130) has been to categorize honorifics on the basis of whether they express respect to an addressee, to a referent, or to a bystander. Some languages use more than one type. For example, according to

Wenger (130, p. 117), Kannada, Malayalam, Hindi, Dzonkha, and Tibetan include only reference honorifics, whereas Thai, Korean, Japanese, Madurese, and Javanese express respect to an addressee as well. Guugu Yimidhirr and other Australian languages having special "mother-in-law" varieties express respect to addressee and bystander (with linguistic forms varying when addressee or bystander fall in certain affinal relationships to the speaker). Javanese court language expresses respect on all three axes, while European languages use honorifics only when the addressee is referent at the same time (i.e. in pronouns and imperatives [93, p. 207]).

As Brown & Levinson point out (17, p. 184), the study of honorifics suffers from a lack of systematic comparison, consistent descriptive apparatus, and theory. It also suffers from a lack of observational data on the implementation of honorifics in actual discourse and from erratic handling of its indexical dimensions. For example, it seems possible that the typology described above, which appears to show that honorific systems do not express respect for addressee unless they somehow also express respect for referent, may reflect investigators' predilection for the referential more than an empirical fact. Although Neustupny suggests (93, p. 206) that there may be no languages expressing addressee distance only, perhaps it is rather that such cases are labeled differently (e.g. as cases of euphemisms, or "indirectness," or possibly even as formal or rhetorical styles).

For all these reasons a great many questions about honorifics remain little understood: their relation to other devices for displaying deference and politeness (17); their role in linguistic and sociolinguistic change (47, 93); the circumstances in which they crystallize into distinct levels or registers, and when these are named or otherwise salient to their speakers; and their relation to speakers' social status (better known for pronouns and for some of the Indonesian cases than for other systems).

One study that remedies some of these gaps is Hill & Hill's work (47) on honorific usage in modern Nahuatl. A trend toward reduction in referential usage of honorifics is linked, they argue, with a shift in speakers' relationship to the larger, Spanish-dominated society. During periods when Nahuatl-speakers were isolated from opportunities for social mobility in that larger society, status distinctions in Nahuatl underwent elaboration. Today, prestige roles are becoming associated with Spanish, and the use of Nahuatl is shifting toward the display of indigenist ethnic solidarity in a wider society. Because the Hills included observational data, and their sample of speakers spans a range of occupations, localities, and age groups, their study is more compatible with the variationist approach than most other studies of honorifics are. Yet we are still not quite in a position to relate honorific usages to phonology or to a broader conception of "style" or register.

STYLE, STATUS, AND CULTURAL SYSTEM

The works reviewed in this paper have concerned various ways in which a repertoire of linguistic varieties reflects or expresses a system of social ranking. Some have taken a dialectology approach, focusing on the performance of socially defined groups of speakers; others have focused on registers and other linguistic resources available to speakers regardless of rank. I have suggested that the differences between the sociolinguistic systems studied in these ways may be less great than the differences between approaches might imply. For example, variation across status groups and variation across situational styles appear to be closely linked wherever we have the information to investigate the connection, although there remain problems in identifying what status groups and what situations should be investigated. A connection between language change and social mobility, too, is not limited to postindustrial Western society, although for other societies we may need to conceive of social mobility in different ways.

A final case, drawn from my own work among rural Wolof of Senegal (55, 56, 58, 59), may also help illuminate the relations between status and style by showing their linkage in a cultural system—an ideology of rank. Rural Wolof society is organized in a complex system of social stratification usually described in the West African ethnographic literature as a system of castes. Two of these castes—the high-ranking "nobles" and the low-ranking griots (praise-singers and professional speechmakers)—are particularly important from a linguistic point of view: styles of speaking are named after them ("noble speech" and "griot speech"), and in some respects the relation between these two social categories typifies, for Wolof villagers, the relation between high and low rank as it is manifested in patterns of speaking. "Noble speech" is a laconic, bland, unelaborated and even grammatically unskillful mode of discourse, while "griot speech" is a dramatic, hyperbolic, rhetorically elaborate style. In addition to the contrast between terseness and verbosity, the two styles differ conspicuously in prosody and, though more variably, in other linguistic features (phonological, morphological, and syntactic (59). The two styles are consistent with a background of cultural ideas about the behavioral, moral, and even physical nature of social ranks. The high ranks are supposed to be naturally inclined toward restraint and control of physical movements and processes, including speaking, while the low ranks are supposed to have an inherent disposition toward unrestrained, excessive activity, including talk. High ranks are thought to be solid and stable but laconic, in need of a spark to get them going; low ranks, especially griots, are thought to be more volatile, excitable, and exciting of others in their interaction with them, but unstable on their own.

What I have just described looks at first like social dialects—distinct linguistic varieties associated with distinct social groups (the nobles and griots)—but the distinctness is a Wolof cultural notion, not an objective one. Linguistically the varieties actually constitute a continuum or range of possibilities where social rank is represented by relative values or quantities rather than discrete or categorical forms. In practice these varieties are used as a range of registers signaling *relative* rank (of speaker as compared to addressee) rather than absolute rank. Except for the extreme ends of the register continuum, all speakers use all the rest of the range depending on their relation to a particular addressee and situation. A person of noble rank uses a "griot-like" style of speaking when addressing a noble kinsman from whom he (or she) wants to ask a favor, for example. So the speech styles invoke a kind of metaphor of high and low rank in order to define (in this case) an act of petitioning. [See also findings on the importance of speaker-addressee relations and genre in governing variation in Mombasa Swahili (109)].

To suggest that these are probably not really social dialects in the Labovian sense should not obscure an important similarity between these findings and his work: that social status and linguistic style are closely linked in a single sociolinguistic process. The linguistic forms indexing social strata are not exclusive to them, but are used by all speakers to differentiate social situations. An added factor in this study, however, is the system of cultural ideas, a system that identifies which social categories it might be useful to focus on, and provides a rationale for the association of particular linguistic variants with particular status groups. Linguistic differences and social boundaries have a common conceptual basis in Wolof cultural assumptions about the inherent nature of persons of different ranks, and their behavior, including speech performance. The linguistic phenomena that distinguish "noble speech" from "griot speech" are phenomena that represent restraint and the minimizing of affectivity, redundancy, and surface elaboration.

Although the concept of "style" thus culturally identified does include the phonological, it ranges more broadly over linguistic subsystems and even into other modes of activity. A broader concept of style (121) has several advantages. We have already seen that phonological variation sometimes turns out to be syntactically and lexically governed and that language levels and honorifics—phenomena that seem at first glance not to concern phonology—may have a phonological dimension (via prosody and morphophonemics). Investigations of broader scope would make it easier to compare these systems and the "co-occurrence rules" that integrate them. Moreover, a focus on phonological variation alone may incur the misleading assumption that the social has only to do with language's implementation (i.e. by whom and when it is used—its indexical aspect) and not with its contents (its referential aspect). In contrast, the study of lexical variation, politeness phenomena, and their extensions into topic and discourse management lead us more directly toward the ways language and language use are involved in the maintenance and reproduction of a social system.

The cultural background of sociolinguistic systems in the sense of a framework of ideas "explaining" and evaluating the linguistic and other behavior of persons and groups has rarely been investigated explicitly in variationist studies, although the concepts of prestige and norms of sociolinguistic evaluation do in fact pertain to the cultural realm. A few recent works on social/political ideology of language and its effects on language change in our own society are of special interest, therefore (65, 66, 118). In particular, Silverstein's work on the language of gender (118)—a matter intimately linked with status—draws on a familiarity with ethnographic approaches to language and the culture of language in the non-Western world. Although I started this paper with studies of North American cities and later looked at works that have tried, to varying degrees, to apply those methods in more exotic locales, influences between the study of the Western world and the non-Western world need not, and should not, go in only one direction.

Literature Cited

1. Afendras, E., Kuo, E. C., eds. 1980. *Language and Society in Singapore*. Singapore: Singapore Univ. Press. 300 pp.
2. Albo, X. 1970. *Social Constraints on Cochabamba Quechua*. PhD thesis. Cornell Univ., Ithaca, N.Y. 448 pp.
3. Apte, M. 1979. Region, religion, and language: Parameters of identity in the process of acculturation. See Ref. 84, pp. 367–76
4. Bailey, C.-J. 1974. *Variation and Linguistic Theory*. Arlington, VA: Cent. Appl. Ling. 162 pp.
5. Baugh, J. 1983. *Black Street Speech*. Austin: Univ. Texas Press. 149 pp.
6. Bean, S. S. 1974. Linguistic variation and the caste system in South Asia. *Indian Ling.* 35:277–93
7. Bean, S. S. 1978. *A Kannada System of Address*. Chicago: Univ. Chicago Press. 163 pp.
8. Beeman, W. O. 1976. Status, style and strategy in Iranian interaction. *Anthropol. Ling.* 18:305–22
9. Beeman, W. O. 1977. The hows and whys of Persian style: A pragmatic approach. In *Studies in Language Variation*, ed. R. Fasold, R. Shuy. Washington, DC: Georgetown Univ. Press
10. Bell, A. 1984. Language style as audience design. *Lang. Soc.* 13:145–204
11. Bhat, D. N. S. 1968. The secret code of South Kanara devil dancers. *Anthropol. Ling.* 10(4):15–18
12. Bickerton, D. 1971. Inherent variability and variable rules. *Found. Lang.* 7:457–92
13. Blanc, H. 1964. *Communal Dialects in Baghdad*. Cambridge, MA: Harvard Univ. Press. 204 pp.
14. Bloch, J. 1910. Castes et dialectes en Tamoul. *Mém. Soc. Ling. Paris* 16:1–30
15. Briggs, L. T. 1981. Politeness in Aymara language and culture. In *The Aymara Language in Its Social and Cultural Context*, ed. M. J. Hardman, pp. 90–113. Gainesville: Univ. Presses of Florida
16. Bright, W. 1960. Linguistic change in some Indian caste dialects. See Ref. 29, pp. 19–26
17. Brown, P., Levinson, S. 1978. Universals in language usage: politeness phenomena. In *Questions and Politeness*. ed. E. Goody. pp. 56–289. Cambridge: Cambridge Univ. Press
18. Brown, R., Gilman, A. 1960. The pronouns of power and solidarity. In *Style in Language*, ed. T. A. Sebeok. pp. 253–76. Cambridge, MA: MIT Press
19. Carden, G. 1972. Dialect variation and abstract syntax. In *Some New Directions in Linguistics*, ed. R. Shuy. pp. 1–35. Washington, DC: Georgetown Univ. Press
20. Cedergren, H. 1973. *The interplay of social and linguistic factors in Panama*. PhD thesis. Cornell Univ., Ithaca, NY

21. Cedergren, H., Sankoff, D. 1974. Variable rules: performance as a statistical reflection of competence. *Language* 50:333–55
22. Chandrasekhar, A. 1977. Degrees of politeness in Malayalam. *Int. J. Dravidian Ling.* 6:85–96
23. Comrie, B. 1976. Linguistic politeness axes: speaker-addressee, speaker-referent, speaker-bystander. *Pragmatics Microfiche* 1.7:A3. Cambridge: Univ. Cambridge Dep. Ling.
24. Das, S. K. 1968. Forms of address and terms of reference in Bengali. *Anthrop. Ling.* 10(4):19–31
25. Djajaengwasito, S. 1975. *Javanese Speech Styles: A Multiple Discriminant Analysis of Social Constraints*. PhD Thesis, Cornell Univ. 198 pp.
25a. Duranti, A. 1984. *Lāuga* and *Talanoaga:* Two speech genres in a Samoan political event. In *Dangerous Words: Language and Politics in the Pacific*, ed. D. Brenneis, F. Myers, pp. 217–42. New York: New York Univ. Press
26. Errington, J. J. 1984. *Language and Social Change in Java*. Athens: Ohio Univ. Cent. Int. Stud.
27. Errington, J. J. 1985. On the nature of the sociolinguistic sign: describing the Javanese speech styles. See Ref. 85
28. Ferguson, C. A. 1959. Diglossia. *Word* 15:325–40
29. Ferguson, C. A., Gumperz, J. J., eds. 1960. *Linguistic Diversity in South Asia: Studies in Regional, Social and Functional Variation*. Bloomington: Indiana Univ. Res. Ctr. in Anthropol., Folklore, Ling., Publ. 13
30. Fishman, J. 1971. The sociology of language: An interdisciplinary social science approach to language in society. In *Advances in the Sociology of Language*, Vol. 1, ed. J. Fishman. The Hague: Mouton
31. Fishman, J., Ferguson, C. A., Das Gupta, J., eds. 1968. *Language Problems of Developing Nations*. New York: Wiley
32. Gair, J. W. 1968. Sinhalese diglossia. *Anthropol. Ling.* 10(8):1–15
33. Garvin, P. L., Riesenberg, S. H. 1952. Respect behavior on Ponape: An ethnolinguistic study. *Am. Anthropol.* 54:201–20
34. Geertz, C. L. 1960. *The Religion of Java*. New York: Free Press
35. Giles, H., Powesland, P. E. 1975. *Speech Style and Social Evaluation*. New York: Academic. 218 pp.
36. Giles, H., St. Clair, R., eds. 1979. *Language and Social Psychology*. Baltimore: Univ. Park Press. 261 pp.
37. Gnanasundaram, V., Rangan, K. 1978. Negation in Mysore Tamil. See Ref. 98, pp. 123–32
38. Gonda, J. 1948. The Javanese vocabulary of courtesy. *Lingua* 1:333–76
39. Gregersen, E. 1977. *Language in Africa*. New York: Gordon & Breach
40. Gumperz, J. J. 1958. Dialect differences and social stratification in a North Indian village. *Am. Anthropol.* 60:668–82
41. Gumperz, J. J. 1969. Sociolinguistics in South Asia. In *Current Trends in Linguistics, Linguistics in South Asia*, ed. T. A. Sebeok, 5:597–606. The Hague: Mouton
42. Gumperz, J. J. 1971. Hindi-Punjabi code-switching in Delhi. In *Language in Social Groups: Essays by John J. Gumperz*, pp. 205–19. Stanford, Calif: Stanford Univ. Press
43. Gumperz, J. J., Naim, C. M. 1960. Formal and informal standards in the Hindi regional language area. See Ref. 29, pp. 92–118
44. Guy, G. R. 1980. Variation in the group and the individual: The case of final stop deletion. See Ref. 71, pp. 1–36
45. Harada, S. I. 1975. Honorifics. In *Syntax and Semantics, Japanese Generative Grammar*, ed. M. Shibatani, 5:499–561. New York: Academic
46. Head, B. 1978. Respect degrees in pronominal reference. In *Universals of Human Language, Word Structure*, ed. J. Greenberg, 3:151–212. Stanford, Calif: Stanford Univ. Press
47. Hill, J. H., Hill, K. C. 1978. Honorific usage in modern Nahuatl. *Language* 54:123–55
48. Hillman, M. 1981. Language and social distinctions in Iran. In *Modern Iran: The Dialectics of Continuity and Change*, ed. M. Bonine, N. Keddie, pp. 327–40. Albany: SUNY Press
49. Hodge, C. 1957. Some aspects of Persian style. *Language* 33:355–69
50. Holes, C. D. 1983. Patterns of communal language variation in Bahrain. *Lang. Soc.* 12:433–57
51. Hudson, R. A. 1980. *Sociolinguistics*. Cambridge: Cambridge Univ. Press. 250 pp.
52. Hymes, D. H., ed. 1964. *Language in Culture and Society*. New York: Harper & Row. 764 pp.
53. Hymes, D. H. 1968. Linguistic problems in defining the concept of 'tribe'. In *Essays on the Problem of Tribe: Proc. 1967 Ann. Spring Meet., Am. Ethnol. Soc.*, ed. J. Helm, pp. 23–48. Seattle: Univ. Wash. Press
54. Inoue, K. 1979. Japanese: a story of language and people. In *Languages and Their Speakers*, ed. T. Shopen, pp. 241–300. Cambridge, MA: Winthrop

55. Irvine, J. T. 1973. *Caste and Communication in a Wolof Village*. PhD thesis. Univ. Penn., Philadelphia. 484 pp.
56. Irvine, J. T. 1978. Wolof noun classification: The social setting of divergent change. *Lang. Soc.* 7:37–64
57. Irvine, J. T. 1979. Formality and informality in communicative events. *Am. Anthropol.* 81:773–90
58. Irvine, J. T. 1982. Language and affect: Some cross-cultural issues. In *Contemporary Perceptions of Language: Interdisciplinary Dimensions*, ed. H. Byrnes, pp. 31–47. Georgetown Univ. Round Table on Language and Linguistics 1982. Washington, DC: Georgetown Univ. Press
59. Irvine, J. T. 1983. Wolof speech styles and social status. In *Case Studies in the Ethnography of Speaking*, ed. R. Bauman, J. Sherzer, pp. 1–12. Austin, TX: Southwest Educ. Dev. Lab.
60. Jahangiri, N., Hudson, R. A. 1982. Patterns of variation in Tehrani Persian. See Ref. 108, pp. 49–63
61. Jain, D. K. 1969. Verbalization of respect in Hindi. *Anthropol. Ling.* 11:79–97
62. Jaswal, S. C., Das, T., Acharya, K. P. 1978. Report on Bazaar Hindi of Mysore City. See Ref. 98, pp. 109–17
63. Koenig, E. L., Chia, E., Povey, J., eds. 1983. *A Socio-Linguistic Profile of Urban Centers in Cameroun*. Los Angeles: Crossroads Press. 149 pp.
64. Krishnamurti, B. 1979. Problems of language standardization in India. See Ref. 84, pp. 673–92
65. Kroch, A. 1978. Towards a theory of social dialect variation. *Lang. Soc.* 7:17–36
66. Kroch, A., Small, C. 1978. Grammatical ideology and its effect on speech. See Ref. 110, pp. 45–55
67. Labov, W. A. 1966. *The Social Stratification of English in New York City*. Arlington, VA: Cent. Appl. Ling.
68. Labov, W. A. 1969. Contraction, deletion, and inherent variability of the English copula. *Language* 45:715–62
69. Labov, W. A. 1972. *Sociolinguistic Patterns*. Philadelphia: Univ. Penn. Press. 344 pp.
70. Labov, W. A. 1972. Some principles of linguistic methodology. *Lang. Soc.* 1:97–120
71. Labov, W. A., ed. 1980. *Locating Language in Time and Space*. New York: Academic. 271 pp.
72. Labov, W. A. 1980. The social origins of sound change. See Ref. 71, pp. 251–65
73. Labov, W. A., Bower, A., Hindle, D., Dayton, E., Kroch, A., et al. 1980. *Social Determinants of Linguistic Change*. Philadelphia: U.S. Regional Survey
74. Labov, W. A., Cohen, P., Robins, C., Lewis, J. 1968. *A Study of the Non-Standard English of Negro and Puerto Rican Speakers in New York City*. U.S.O.E. Final Rep., Res. Proj. 3288
75. Ladefoged, P., Glick, R., Criper, C. 1971. *Language in Uganda*. Nairobi: Oxford Univ. Press
76. Lavandera, B. 1975. *Linguistic structure and sociolinguistic conditioning in the use of verbal endings in Si-clauses (Buenos Aires Spanish)*. PhD thesis. Univ. Penn., Philadelphia
77. Macaulay, R. K. S. 1970. Review of Wolfram's *A Sociolinguistic Description of Detroit Negro Speech* (See Ref. 133). *Language* 46:764–73
78. Macaulay, R. K. S. 1977. *Language, Social Class, and Education: A Glasgow Study*. Edinburgh: Edinburgh Univ. Press
79. Martin, S. E. 1964. Speech levels in Japan and Korea. See Ref. 52, pp. 407–15
80. Mbaga, K., Whiteley, W. H. 1961. Formality and informality in Yao speech. *Africa* 31:135–46
81. McBrian, C. 1978. Language and social stratification: The case of a Confucian society. *Anthropol. Ling.* 20:320–26
82. McCormack, W. C. 1960. Social dialects in Dharwar Kannada. See Ref. 29, pp. 79–91
83. McCormack, W. C. 1968. Occupation and residence in relation to Dharwar dialects. See Ref. 119, pp. 475–85
84. McCormack, W. C., Wurm, S., eds. 1979. *Language and Society: Anthropological Issues*. The Hague: Mouton. 771 pp.
85. Mertz, E., Parmentier, R., eds. 1985. *Signs in Society*. New York: Academic. In press
86. Milner, G. B. 1961. The Samoan vocabulary of respect. *J. R. Anthropol. Inst.* 91(2):296–317
87. Milroy, J., Milroy, L. 1978. Belfast: change and variation in an urban vernacular. In *Sociolinguistic Patterns in British English*, ed. P. Trudgill. pp. 19–37. London: Arnold
88. Milroy, L. 1980. *Language and Social Networks*. Oxford: Blackwell
89. Milroy, L., Margrain, S. 1978. Vernacular language loyalty and social network. *Belfast Work. Pap. Lang. Ling.* 3:1–59
90. Mochizuki, M. 1980. Male and female variants for 'I' in Japanese: cooccurrence rules. *Pap. Ling.* 13:453–74
91. Modarressi-Tehrani, Y. 1978. *A socio-*

linguistic analysis of modern Persian. PhD thesis. Univ. Kansas, Lawrence. 257 pp.
92. Neustupny, J. V. 1968. Politeness patterns in the system of communication. *Proc. 8th Int. Congr. Anthropol. Ethnol. Sci., Tokyo and Kyoto,* pp. 412–19
93. Neustupny, J. V. 1978. *Post-Structural Approaches to Language.* Tokyo: Univ. Tokyo Press. 307 pp.
94. Newman, S. 1964. Vocabulary levels: Zuni sacred and slang usage. See Ref. 52, pp. 397–406
95. Nunberg, G. 1980. A falsely reported merger in eighteenth-century English: A study in diachronic variation. See Ref. 71, pp. 221–50
96. Ohanessian, S., Kashoki, M. E., eds. 1978. *Language in Zambia.* London: Int. Afr. Inst.
97. Pattanayak, D. P. 1975. Caste and dialect. *Int. J. Dravidian Ling.* 4:97–104
98. Pattanayak, D. P., ed. 1978. *Papers in Indian Sociolinguistics.* Mysore: Central Inst. Indian Lang.
99. Pittman, R. S. 1948. Nahuatl honorifics. *Int. J. Am. Ling.* 14:236–39
100. Platt, J. 1980. Multilingualism, polyglossia, and code selection in Singapore. See Ref. 1, pp. 63–83
101. Poedjosoedarmo, S. 1968. Javanese speech levels. *Indonesia* 6:54–81
102. Poplack, S. 1979. *Function and process in a variable phonology.* PhD thesis. Univ. Penn., Philadelphia
103. Poplack, S. 1980. Deletion and disambiguation in Puerto Rican Spanish. *Language* 56:371–85
104. Pumphrey, M. E. C. 1937. Shilluk 'royal' language conventions. *Sudan Notes and Records* 20:319–21
105. Ramanujan, A. K. 1968. The structure of variation: A study in caste dialects. See Ref. 119, pp. 461–74
106. Robinson, W. P. 1979. Speech markers and social class. In *Social Markers in Speech,* ed. K. Scherer, H. Giles, pp. 211–50. Cambridge: Cambridge Univ. Press
107. Romaine, S. 1982. *Socio-Historical Linguistics.* Cambridge: Cambridge Univ. Press. 315 pp.
108. Romaine, S., ed. 1982. *Sociolinguistic Variation in Speech Communities.* London: Arnold. 179 pp
109. Russell, J. 1981. *Communicative Competence in a Minority Group: A Sociolinguistic Study of the Swahili-Speaking Community of the Old Town, Mombasa.* Leiden: Brill. 262 pp
110. Sankoff, G., ed. 1978. *Linguistic Variation: Models and Methods.* New York: Academic. 296 pp
110a. Sankoff, G. 1980. *The Social Life of Language.* Philadelphia: Univ. Penn. Press. 373 pp.
111. Schiffman, H. F. 1973. Language, linguistics, and politics in Tamilnad. In *Studies in the Language and Culture of South Asia,* ed. E. Gerow, M. Lang, pp. 125–34. Seattle: Univ. Wash. Inst. Comp. Foreign Area Stud.
112. Scotton, C. 1972. *Choosing a Lingua Franca in an African Capital.* Edmonton: Linguistic Res. 211 pp.
113. Shankara Bhat, D. N. 1967–1968. Dialects of Kannada in the Mysore district. *Bull. Daccan Coll. Res. Inst.* 28 (1/2):66–76
114. Shanmugam Pillai, M. 1960. Tamil—literary and colloquial. See Ref. 29, pp. 27–42
115. Shanmugam Pillai, M. 1968. Fisherman Tamil of Kanyakumari. *Anthropol. Ling.* 10(4):1–10
116. Shapiro, M. C., Schiffman, H. F. 1983. *Language and Society in South Asia.* Dordrecht, Holland: Foris. 293 pp.
117. Shuy, R., Wolfram, W., Riley, W. 1966. *A Study of Social Dialects in Detroit.* Final Rep., Proj. 6–1347. Washington, DC: Off. Educ.
118. Silverstein, M. 1985. Language and the culture of gender: At the intersection of structure, usage, and ideology. See Ref. 85
119. Singer, M., Cohn, B., eds. 1968. *Structure and Change in Indian Society.* New York: Wenner-Gren (Viking Fund Publ. Anthropol. 47)
120. Stevens, A. 1965. Language levels in Madurese. *Language* 41:294–302
121. Tannen, D. 1983. Conversational style. In *Psycholinguistic Models of Production,* ed. H. Deckert, M. Raupach. Hillsdale, NJ: Erlbaum
122. Trudgill, P. 1972. Sex, covert prestige and linguistic change in the urban British English of Norwich. *Lang. Soc.* 1:179–96
123. Trudgill, P. 1974. *The Social Differentiation of English in Norwich.* Cambridge: Cambridge Univ. Press
124. Trudgill, P. 1974. *Sociolinguistics.* Baltimore: Penguin. 189 pp.
125. Tyler, S. A. 1965. Koya language morphology and patterns of kinship behavior. *Am. Anthropol.* 67:1428–40
126. Uhlenbeck, E. M. 1970. The use of respect forms in Javanese. In *Pacific Linguistic Studies in Honour of Arthur Capell,* ed. S. A. Wurm, D. Laycock, pp. 441–59. Canberra: Aust. Natl. Univ.
127. Wald, B. 1983. Review of J. Russell's "Communicative Competence in a Mi-

nority Group" (See Ref. 109). *Lang. Soc.* 12:398–405
128. Wallace, S. 1976. *Linguistic and social dimensions of phonological variation in Jakarta Malay.* PhD thesis. Cornell Univ., Ithaca, NY. 209 pp.
129. Weinreich, U., Labov, W. A., Herzog, M. 1968. Empirical foundations of linguistic theory. In *Directions for Historical Linguistics*, ed. W. Lehmann, Y. Malkiel, pp. 95–108. Austin: Univ. Texas Press
130. Wenger, J. R. 1982. *Some universals of honorific language with special reference to Japanese.* PhD thesis. Univ. Ariz., Tucson. 185 pp.
131. Wessing, R. 1974. Language levels in Sundanese. *Man* (N.S.) 9:5–22
132. Wolff, J. U., Poedjosoedarmo, S. 1982. *Communicative Codes in Central Java.* Ithaca, NY: Cornell Univ. Dep. Asian Studies, Southeast Asia Program, Data paper 116. 197 pp.
133. Wolfram, W. 1969. *A Sociolinguistic Description of Detroit Negro Speech.* Arlington, VA: Cent. Appl. Ling.
134. Wolfram, W. 1980. *A*-prefixing in Appalachian English. See Ref. 71, pp. 107–42
135. Zurbuchen, M. S. 1981. *The shadow theater of Bali: Explorations in language and text.* PhD thesis. Univ. Michigan, Ann Arbor
136. Zvelebil, K. 1964. Spoken languages of Tamilnad. *Arch. Orientalni* 32:237–64.

AUTHOR INDEX

A

Aamodt, A. M., 223, 226, 228-31, 234
Ababie, S. H., 501
Abate, A., 55
Abbie, A. A., 448
Abdurrahman, M. B., 502
Abell, G. O., 117, 128
Abraham, S., 488
Abramovitch, H., 233
Aceves, J. B., 416
Acharya, K. P., 565
Achebe, C., 255
Acsadi, G., 430
Adair, L. S., 485, 489, 494, 499
Adams, A., 261
Adams, J., 431, 434
Adams, L. J., 501
Adams, R. M., 20, 497
Adas, M., 63, 65, 66, 70
Adler, A., 264, 283
Adler, M. J., 108
Adovasio, J. M., 535
Aguilar, J. L., 416, 417
Aguirre, A., 510
Ahlquist, J. E., 360, 457
Ahmed, T. A., 481
Aigner, J., 537
Ailinger, R. L., 227, 228
Ajayi, A., 257
Akerman, K., 502
Akin, J. S., 495
Akpala, A., 207
Albert, E. M., 277, 296, 298
Albertini, H., 336
Alberts, B., 125
Albo, X., 206, 207, 561, 569
Albright, W. F., 110, 111, 113
Alcock, J., 548, 549
Alden, W. C., 117
Aldenderfer, M., 148
Alexander, L., 225
Alexander, R. D., 433-35, 437
Alkire, W. H., 286
Allen, L. L., 451, 461
Almquist, A. J., 431
Alonso, J., 451
Alvarado, A. L., 414, 415
Alvarez, R. R. Jr., 413, 416
Alverson, H., 206, 207
Alvesalo, L., 445, 447
Amadon, D., 431, 434
Amin, S., 258, 259, 261
Anderson, B. G., 219, 224, 500
Anderson, B. O'G., 59-61
Anderson, B. R. O. G., 285
Anderson, C., 206
Anderson, D. L., 452
Anderson, E., 540
Anderson, J., 496, 499, 508
Anderson, M. A., 359
Anderson, S. V., 228, 363
Anderson, W. F., 359
Andrews, P. J., 451
Angel, J. L., 449
Ankel-Simons, F., 431
Annegers, J., 492
Apfelbaum, M., 492
Appadurai, A., 55
Apte, M., 563, 566
Apter, A. H., 280, 295
Apter, D., 250
Aquadro, C. F., 363
Araujo, J., 504
Arbona, S., 501
Arcury, T., 511
Ardener, E., 246
Ardener, S., 263
Arens, W., 280, 283, 293
Arensberg, C. M., 382
Arensburg, B., 351
Arhin, I., 291
Arhin, K., 257
Armah, A-K., 255
Armelagos, G. J., 335, 451, 491, 500, 503
Armenta, J., 542, 543
Armstrong, D., 232
Arnold, D., 52, 65, 66, 200
Arnold, S. J., 430, 433, 435, 441
Aronson, D. R., 260, 384
Aronson, M., 480
Arrighi, G., 206, 208
Arvizu, S. F., 410, 415-17
Asad, T., 248, 389
Aschmann, H., 385
Asher, H., 145
Ashraf, A., 504
Ashton, E. H., 431
Ashworth, M., 492
Asiwaju, A. I., 296, 301
Assadourian, C., 208
Astruc, J., 111
Attardi, G., 363
Audy, J. R., 500
Augé, M., 260
Aulie, E., 187
Austen, J., 200
Avery, P. J., 357
Avise, J. C., 363
Ayala, F. J., 123-25, 127
Ayensu, E. S., 503
Ayres, G., 187

B

Baba, M. L., 457
Babler, W., 483
Bach-Enciso, V., 355
Bacon, M. K., 383
Badrian, A., 316
Baer, E., 495
Baer, R., 498
Baier, S., 258
Bailey, C.-J., 559
Bailey, S. M., 480, 481
Bailit, H. L., 430, 445, 447
Baines, M. J., 481
Bairagi, R., 495
Baker, D., 497
Baker, P. T., 476, 477, 502, 505
Bakewell, P., 206, 210
Bakszysz-Bymel, M., 417
Balakrishnan, V., 343-45
Bald, S. R., 61
Balderston, J. B., 486
Baldivieso, R., 207
Balfet, H., 80, 82, 85, 88, 93, 97
Ballal, M. A., 481
Ballonoff, P., 136
Bancroft, J., 200
Banerjee, S., 53, 63
Bankier, A. T., 363
Bannerman, R. H., 504
Banton, M. P., 247, 252
Bar-Yosef, O., 449
Baré, J.-F., 297
Bareis, C. J., 16
Bargatsky, T., 384
Barker, D., 364
Barker, J., 258
Barnes, A. S., 545
Barnett, H., 202
Barraza, L., 207
Barrell, B. G., 363
Barrera Vásquez, A., 187, 195
Barrett, M. J., 430
Barrett, R. A., 383
Barrios de Chungara, D., 207
Barry, H. III, 383
Barth, P., 382, 390
Bartholomew, G. A. Jr., 382
Bartlett, P., 55
Bascom, W. R., 252
Basehart, H., 147
Bashir, T., 494
Bass, W. M., 430, 447, 448
Basu, A., 501
Batara-Goa, A. W., 55
Bates, D. G., 390

Bates, R., 207
Baugh, J., 559
Baumgartner, R. N., 485, 488
Baumol, W., 204
Bauwens, E. E., 222, 227, 228
Baxter, M., 203
Beach, F. A., 429
Beaglehole, R., 502
Beall, C. M., 503
Beals, A., 503
Beals, R., 204
Bean, S. S., 562, 573
Beattie, J. H. M., 287
Beatty, J. H., 128
Beck, A., 375
Becker, D., 207
Becker, G. S., 506
Becker, W. A., 431
Beckerman, W., 205
Beebe, B. F., 547-49
Beeman, W. O., 568, 571
Behar, M., 494, 495, 505
Behrens, W., 205
Behura, N. K., 77
Beidelman, T. O., 278, 279, 291
Beinart, W., 206, 207
Belasco, B. I., 55
Belizan, J., 500
Bell, A., 560, 561
Belle, E. A., 501
Belli, P., 493
Ben Ari, J., 492
Benfer, R., 151
Bengston, V. L., 415, 418
Benkov, J. L., 111, 119-21
Bennett, W., 434, 451, 462
Benoit, P., 108
Benshoof, L., 431
Berenstein, L., 434
Berg, A., 491, 496
Berg, G. M., 290, 297
Berger, I., 299
Berger, R., 534, 541
Berleant-Schiller, R., 399
Berlin, E., 492
Berlyne, G. M., 492
Bernstein, H., 65
Bernstein, M., 207
Berry, S., 207
Berry, S. S., 260
Besserer, F., 207
Bessinger, C. D., 504
Beyerlin, W., 113
Bezzaz, F., 258
Bhanumathi, P. P., 228
Bharati, P., 501
Bhaskaram, C., 490
Bhat, D. N. S., 563
Bhattacharya, S. K., 501
Bickerton, D., 558
Bielicki, T., 485
Biggerstaff, R. H., 430

Billewicz, W. Z., 485, 501
Bilsborrow, R. E., 495
Binn, M., 227
Birch, H. G., 484, 489, 495
Bird, M. A., 431
Bird, W. R., 120
Birdsell, J. B., 356, 382
Birdwhistell, R., 221
Birkbeck, J., 502
Birky, C. W., 363
Birmingham, J., 79, 80, 82, 88, 93
Bischoff, J. L., 544, 546, 547
Bishop, Y., 141, 147
Bisilliat, J., 263
Bizberg, I., 207
Black, E. S., 431
Black, G., 53
Black, S., 126, 494
Black, T. K. II, 430
Blake, J., 507
Blalock, H., 137, 138, 147
Blanc, H., 364, 568
Blashfield, R. K., 148
Bleibtreu, H. K., 343
Bliss, R. B., 105
Bloch, B., 222, 226
Bloch, J., 562
Bloch, M. L. B., 278, 297
Blumberg, B. S., 500
Blute, M., 433
Boadt, L., 107, 109, 110
Boas, F., 135, 377, 379
Bodmer, W. F., 358
Bogin, B. A., 478, 479, 485, 488, 489, 495
Bogyo, T. P., 431
Bohannan, L., 246, 249, 251
Bohannan, P., 246, 250, 251, 258, 259, 389
Bollettino, L. A., 494
Bonaparte, B., 226, 228
Bongaarts, J., 507, 508
Bonilla, H., 208
Bonner, P., 298
Bonné-Tamir, B., 346, 351
Bonnichsen, R., 532, 547, 548
Bonte, P., 388, 390
Boon, J. A., 306
Borden, M., 479
Bordes, F., 536, 540
Borgia, G., 433, 435
Borkan, G., 483
Boserup, E., 262
Bossert, T. J., 53
Bosson, R., 203
Boston, J. S., 290
Bostsarram, J., 492
Botstein, D., 361, 364
Boudon, R., 145
Boudreau, R., 351, 358
Boulinier, G., 430
Bourdieu, P., 170

Bourges, H., 495
Bourguignon, E., 233
Bourque, S. C., 62
Boutillier, J. L., 261
Bowen, E. S., 249
Bowen, T., 77, 79, 82
Bower, A., 559
Bowler, P. J., 123
Boyce, A. J., 148
Boyd, W. C., 351
Boyle, R., 145
Bozzoli, B., 64
Brace, C. L., 117, 432, 442, 445, 447, 449-51
Bradbury, R. E., 276
Braithwaite, M., 88
Brandes, S., 394
Brannigan, A., 183
Brauer, G. W., 431
Braunitzer, G., 457
Bray, D., 125
Brazier, M. A. B., 488
Brealey, R., 202
Bresnan, J., 25, 26, 42, 44-46
Bricker, V. R., 187, 191
Bridgeman, M., 221
Bridges, P. S., 432, 449-51, 461, 462
Briggs, C. L., 413
Briggs, K. T., 434
Briggs, L. T., 573
Bright, W., 160, 164, 563
Brink, P. J., 222, 226-28
Brochard, C., 500
Brokensha, D., 261, 416
Brose, D. S., 18
Brown, A., 498
Brown, C. H., 191, 508
Brown, D., 501
Brown, D. E., 493
Brown, E. L., 221
Brown, J., 207
Brown, J. A., 9, 381
Brown, J. K., 233, 442
Brown, L. K., 187
Brown, L. W., 413
Brown, M., 206
Brown, P., 430, 573, 574
Brown, R., 202, 573
Brown, S. D., 264, 296, 301
Brown, T., 430
Brown, V., 502
Brown, W. M., 348, 363, 364
Brownie, C., 499
Brozek, J., 486, 493, 499, 508
Bruce, R. D., 187, 195
Bruch, H., 500
Brues, A., 451
Brundenius, C., 203
Bruner, J. S., 160
Brush, S. C., 128
Bruyn, S., 231

AUTHOR INDEX 585

Bryan, A. L., 532-35, 537, 538, 546, 550
Bryan, J., 501
Bryner, J. D., 488
Buckovetsky, M., 204
Budinger, F. E. Jr., 544
Bujra, J., 62
Bulatao, R., 506, 510
Bulmer, M., 207
Bulmer, M. G., 357
Bulmer, R., 395
Bundy, C., 208
Bunker, S., 208
Bunzel, R. C., 78
Burawoy, M., 207
Burgon, J. W., 109
Burnes, H., 204
Burnham, P., 260
Burnham, P. C., 388
Burns, A. F., 195
Burns, E., 501
Burr, D. R., 430
Burton, J. W., 382
Burton, M., 136, 151, 152
Burton, M. L., 443
Buschang, P. H., 480
Bush, M. T., 228
Bushnell, G., 531
Busia, K. A., 248, 262, 276, 297
Butler, P. M., 319, 335
Butzer, K. W., 532, 536
Buzina, R., 478, 487
Byerly, E. L., 223, 227, 230, 231, 233

C

Cairncross, S., 501
Calcagno, J. M., 445, 447-49
Caldwell, J., 506, 507
Caldwell, P., 507
Calvin, M., 123, 124, 128
Campbell, C. C., 500
Campbell, D. J., 391
CAMPBELL, L., 187-98; 187, 188, 190-94
Canger, U., 187
Cann, R. L., 363, 364
Cannadine, D., 306
Cannings, C., 343
Caplan, P., 62
Cappetta, M., 492
Carden, G., 559
Carey, J., 501
Carlisle, D., 204
Carlisle, R. C., 535
Carlos, M. L., 414-16
Carmack, R. M., 195
Carman, J., 203
Carmelli, D., 346, 351
Carmines, E., 139, 142, 143
Carothers, J. H., 431, 435

Carpenter, J. C., 430
Carr, J. A., 117
Carr-Saunders, A. M., 510
Carson, D., 503
Carter, G. F., 531, 542
Carter, J., 103, 109
Cartry, M., 264
Cartwright, T. C., 391
Casals, J., 501, 503
Casamiquela, R. M., 535
Casas, J. M., 414
Casimir, M. J., 391
Caspari, E., 433
Cassidy, C., 510
Casson, S., 79, 82
Castles, L., 285
Castro, J. G., 416
Caudill, W., 221
Cavalli-Sforza, L. L., 343, 344, 347-49, 351-56, 364, 365
Cedergren, H., 558, 559
Cederroth, S., 58
Centlivres-Demont, M., 77, 79, 80
Chafe, W., 160, 163, 164, 168, 179, 180
Chafetz, L., 228, 229
Chakraborty, R., 345, 356-58
Chambers, R., 492, 501
Chandra, T., 359
Chandrasekhar, A., 573
Chard, C. S., 531
Charlesworth, A., 64
Charlton, T. H., 84, 93, 95
Charsley, S. R., 289
Chasin, B. H., 391
Chatterjee, E., 493
Chaudry, M. A., 55
Chauncey, R., 206
Chavez, A., 495, 508, 510
Chávez, L. R., 414
Chávez, L. R. II, 416
Chayanov, A. V., 246
Chema, S., 391
Chen, K. H., 364
Chen, P. C., 504
Cherdieu, P., 58
Chernichovsky, D., 497
Chevalier, J., 52
Cheverud, J. M., 435-37, 439, 440
Chia, E., 568
Chiao, C., 150
CHIBNIK, M., 135-57; 143
Chick, G., 149, 151, 152
Child, I. L., 383
Childe, V. G., 376, 380
Chin, C.-C., 501, 503
Chinchilla, N. S., 53
Chinn, P. L., 222, 226
Chomsky, N., 25, 26, 28, 29, 31, 32, 39, 40
Chomyn, A., 363

Chouinard, A., 384
Chowdhury, A. K. M. A., 508
Chowdhury, S., 504
Chrétien, J.-P., 284
Chrisman, N. J., 224, 226, 232
Christenson, A., 149
Chumlea, C., 480
Church, R. J. H., 258
CICOUREL, A. V., 159-85; 159, 160, 171, 174
Cinq-Mars, J., 547
Ciochon, R. L., 337, 431, 451
Claessen, H. J. M., 274, 278, 281, 286, 301
Clapham, C., 262
Clark, A. L., 222
Clark, J. G. D., 12
Clark, S., 64
Clarke, D., 149
Clarke, M., 234
Clausen, R. T., 127
Clayden, A. D., 492
Cleveland, D., 261
Clewlow, C. W. Jr., 78
Clifford, J., 248
Clignet, R., 263
Climo, J., 416
Clinton, J. H., 230, 231
Cloud, P., 123, 128
Clutton-Brock, J., 379
Clutton-Brock, T. H., 315, 319, 325, 431-35, 437, 439, 440, 452
Cobb, G., 208
Cockerham, C. C., 346
Codère, H., 294
Coe, R., 226
Coedès, G., 285
Coelho, A. M., 431
Cohen, A., 252, 261
Cohen, D. W., 292
Cohen, J., 138, 144, 145
Cohen, J. A., 433
Cohen, J. E., 500
Cohen, M. R., 105
Cohen, M. S., 501, 503
Cohen, N., 491, 492
Cohen, P., 138, 144, 145, 558
Cohen, R., 135, 249, 250, 283, 298
Cohn, B. S., 305
Cole, F.-C., 3, 120
Cole, J. R., 120, 206, 207
Cole, M., 163
Cole, P. E., 430
Cole, S. G., 105
Colker, L., 504
Collins, W. E., 500
Colson, A., 503
Colson, E., 497
Comrie, B., 573
Conant, F. P., 391
Condon-Paoloni, D., 485

Conneally, P. M., 359
Conrad, R., 204
Consolazio, C., 492
Contenau, G., 115
Conway, M. E., 229
Cook, D. C., 451
Coolidge, H. J., 431
Coombs, M. C., 449, 451
Cooper, D. N., 362
Cooper, J. M., 108, 109
Copans, J., 64, 258, 259, 261
Copland, I., 63
Coppens, Y., 456
Coquery-Vidrovitch, C., 257
Corlett, W. T., 4
Cormack, C. W., 77
Cornelius, W. A., 416
Coronado, M., 495
Correa, H., 493
Corruccini, R. S., 323, 430, 451
Corson, D. W., 123
Corwin, E. S., 119
Coser, R., 221, 227, 234
Cosminsky, S., 233
Coulson, A. R., 363
Coupez, A., 281
Coursin, D. B., 499
Couty, P., 259, 261
Covert, H. H., 315
Cowgill, G., 138, 140
Cox, G. W., 492
Coyne, J. A., 359
Cracraft, J., 125
Craig, C. G., 187
Cramer, D. L., 431, 458
Crankshaw, M. E. C., 503
Cravioto, J., 484-86, 488-90, 495, 496
Cravioto, J. C., 488
Crawford, M. H., 351, 352, 355
Creen, C. K., 352
Cressy, D., 167
Crews, D., 502
Crick, M. R., 231
Criper, C., 568
Crisp, J., 207
Crocker, J. C., 393
Crompton, A. W., 126, 320
Cronin, A., 501
Crook, J. H., 431, 434, 449
Cross, J. H., 501
Cross, P., 501
Crossland, L. B., 80, 87
Crow, J. F., 124, 343
Crowder, M., 257
Crowdy, J., 492
Crowley, D., 224, 225
Croze, H. J., 391
Cruise O'Brien, D. B., 262
Cruxent, J. M., 535
Cuéllar, J. B., 411, 415-18
Cummins, G., 493
Curtin, P., 258

Curtis, F., 77, 80, 84
Cutright, P., 506
Cutshall, C. R., 390
Cuvier, G., 123

D

Dahl, G., 391
Dalby, D., 258
Dalleo, P. T., 390
Dalton, G., 250, 258, 389
D'Andrade, R., 149, 151, 152
D'Andrea, C., 548, 549
Daniel, S. W., 363
Dannhaeuser, N., 138
Darga, L. L., 457
Darwin, C., 375, 433
Das Gupta, J., 568
Das, S. K., 565
Das, S. R., 478, 481, 482
Das, T., 565
Daub, E. R., 118
David, N., 79, 80, 82, 83, 86, 87, 89-91, 94
Davidson, A., 52, 65, 66
Davidson, R. T., 405, 416
Davies, J. E., 502
Davies, M., 62
Davis, J., 508
Davis, K., 507
Davis, M., 221
Davis, N., 167
Davis, R., 203
Davis, R. W., 361
Davis, S., 208
Davitz, J. R., 229
Davitz, L. J., 229
Davivongs, V., 430, 448
Day, C., 187
Day, M. H., 430, 439, 451
Dayley, J. P., 187, 191
Dayton, E., 559
Deal, M., 80, 89
Dean, S. D., 121
De Arsuaga, J. L., 451
de Baessa, Y., 479
Deblock, R., 431
DeBoer, A. J., 391
DeBoer, W. R., 79, 81, 82, 88, 89, 91, 94
de Bruijn, M. H. L., 363
DeCamp, L. S., 120
Dechow, P. C., 479
Deere, C. D., 53
Deetz, J., 78, 83
De Heusch, L., 281, 298, 379, 396, 397
Del Castillo, A. R., 414, 415
Delgado, H., 484, 486, 490, 493-95, 499, 500
De Licardie, E. R., 484, 485, 488-90, 495, 496
Delius, P., 206, 210

Delivré, A., 297, 303
Delval, R., 285
de Martinville, B., 364
Demoulin, F., 430
Denaro, M., 364
de Navarro, L., 499
Deng, F. M., 283
Dennis, N., 207
Denniston, C., 343
De Puy, N. R., 107
Derman, L., 261
Derman, P. J., 298
Derman, W., 261
Desai, A. R., 53, 63
de Sousa, M., 504
Devarajan, S., 200
DeVaux, R., 113
Devereux, G., 221
deVletter, F., 492
Devor, E. J., 355
Devos, R., 128
DeWalt, B., 145, 146, 150
Dewalt, K. M., 497, 498, 504
Dewey, K., 486, 497
Dewind, A., 206-8
DeWitt, S. J., 445
Dey, B., 501
de Zoysa, I., 503
Diamond, S., 208
Diaz, J., 207
DiBennardo, R., 430
Dickeman, M., 510
Diener, P., 387
Dieterlen, G., 248, 253
Dikov, N. N., 533, 537
Dillehay, T. D., 537, 550
Dimbleby, G. W., 380
Dincauze, D., 533, 534
Ditch, L. E., 430, 452
Divale, W., 139
Divale, W. T., 510
Djajaengwasito, S., 567, 571
Doar, B., 64
Dobzhansky, T., 123-25, 127, 350
Domaniewska-Sobczak, K., 351
Donahue, J., 535
Donaldson, S., 224, 225
Donnan, C. B., 78, 79, 82
Donnelly, J. S., 64
Doolittle, R. F., 128
Doornbos, M. R., 302
Doran, J., 149
DOUGHERTY, M. C., 219-41; 233, 235
Douglas, M., 259, 306, 377, 395, 396
Doumesche, H., 254
Dowling, J. H., 389
Down, C., 208
Downey, D. G., 113
Downhower, J. F., 431, 434, 449

Downs, J. F., 382, 384
Dozon, J. P., 261
Drew, J., 500
Driver, H., 135, 148
Drouin, J., 363
Dubois, J., 493
DuBois, J. W., 187
Dufour, D., 491
Duke, B., 501
Dumas-Champion, F., 264
Dumézil, G., 275
Dumont, L., 285, 297
Dumont, R., 491
Duncan, O. D., 145
Dunn, F. L., 500
Dunn, J., 262
Dupire, M., 251, 253, 388, 389
Dupré, G., 251, 259
Duranti, A., 571
During, R., 203
Durnin, J. V. G. A., 492
Durrenberger, E. P., 145
Dutt, J., 508, 509
Dwight, T., 430
Dykes, D. D., 355
Dyson-Hudson, N., 384, 385
Dyson-Hudson, R., 384, 385

E

Eades, J. S., 260
Earhart, C. M., 431
Eastman, C., 431
Easton, D., 250
Eckberg, D. L., 232
Eckhardt, R. B., 431
Eder, J., 492, 497
Edgar, J. W., 122
Edgerton, R. B., 150, 152, 226, 383, 414
Edholm, O. G., 492
Edmonson, M. S., 194, 195
Edmundson, W., 492
Edson, G., 77
Edward, P., 207
Edwards, A. W. F., 344, 348
Edwards, J. W., 233
Eicher, C., 497
Eiselein, E. B., 416, 417
Eiselen, F. C., 113
Eisen, E. J., 431
Eisenberg, L., 226
Eisenstein, E. L., 167
Ekwensi, C., 255
Elam, Y., 283, 295, 390
Eldridge, N., 125
Elegbe, I. A., 503
Eliade, M., 208
Elkan, W., 206
Elkana, Y., 231
Ellen, R. F., 79, 82, 87, 382, 385, 386, 388
Elliot, O., 430

Elms, R., 228
El-Nofely, A. A., 481
Elvin-Lewis, M., 503
Ember, C. R., 443
Emery, A. E. H., 360, 361
Emlen, S. T., 433
Enciso, V. B., 352
Endler, J. A., 350
Engels, W. R., 361
England, N. C., 187
Epstein, A., 206, 207
Epstein, H., 381
Erickson, D., 204
Ericson, J., 534
Eriksson, A. W., 351, 352, 354
Erinosho, O., 503
Errington, F., 63
Errington, J. J., 562, 571, 572
Espejo, A., 9
Espinosa, J., 541
Espinoza, P. T., 417
Esteva, G., 64
Estrera, N., 495
Etkin, N., 503
Evangelou, P., 391
Evans, C., 80, 221
Evans, D. R., 430
Evans, R. K., 78
Evans-Pritchard, E. E., 244, 245, 251, 254, 255, 274, 276, 279, 283, 288, 300, 379, 388, 397
Eveleth, P. B., 432, 443, 480, 507
Evon, D. L., 451, 461
Ewens, W. J., 361
Ewing, G. H., 335
Eyles, E., 502

F

Fabrega, H., 222, 226, 503
Fairlie, J., 135
Falcon, N. L., 116, 117
Fallers, L. A., 276, 277, 293
Falwell, J., 109
Fang, R., 128
Farb, P., 491
Farber, M., 202
Farid-Coupal, N., 432
Farley, R., 509
FARMER, A. K., 25-^8; 25, 26, 33-35
Farrell, L., 501
Farris, J. S., 345, 348
Farros, D. E., 391
Fawcett, J., 226
Feachem, R., 501, 503
Fedigan, L. M., 431, 436, 452, 461
FEELEY-HARNIK, G., 273-313; 280, 285, 293, 294, 296, 297, 300

Feierman, S., 280
Feinman, G., 78
Fellman, J. O., 354
Felsenstein, J., 344, 345, 347, 348, 355-57, 360, 362
Felton, A. A., 359
Fenart, R., 431
Ferembach, D., 430, 451
Feret, E., 500
Ferguson, A. E., 504
Ferguson, C. A., 563, 565, 568
Fernández, I., 414
Fernandez, J. W., 379, 393
Fernandez, T. L., 495
Fernandez Kelly, M. P., 413
Ferrara, L., 501
Ferreira-Pinto, J., 149
Ferris, S. D., 348, 364
Ferro-Luzzi, A., 492
Fiawoo, D. K., 482
Field, M. J., 253
Fienberg, S., 141, 147
Finegan, J., 113, 115, 117, 118
Finkler, K., 144
Firth, R., 510
Fischer, M., 500
Fisher, A., 200, 204
Fisher, E., 442
Fisher, H. E., 451, 461
Fisher, S., 179
Fisher, W. M., 188
Fishman, J., 568, 569
Fitzhugh, H. A., 391
Fitzmyer, J. A., 110, 118
Flaherty, L., 361
Flanagan, W., 261
Flannery, K. V., 380
Flaskerud, J. H., 226, 230, 231
Fleagle, J. F., 451, 455
Flegel, P., 494
Fleuret, A., 147, 476, 491, 492, 497, 498
Fleuret, P., 147, 476, 491, 492, 497, 498
Flint, M., 233
Flint, R. F., 115
Florencio, C., 495, 497
Flores Galindo, A., 206, 207
Fodor, J., 46
Fogel, R. B., 64
Foley, D. E., 411, 417
Fontana, B. L., 77
Forbes, A., 492
Ford, J. A., 7
Ford, T. R., 234, 511
Forde, C. D., 244, 246, 247, 249, 251
Forde, D., 276, 296, 378, 382, 388, 398
Forsius, H. R., 351, 354
Fortes, M., 244, 245, 247, 253-55, 274, 276-79, 288, 300
Fosse, D., 317

AUTHOR INDEX

Foster, G. M., 77, 79, 89, 93, 95, 97, 219, 222-24, 500, 503, 504
Fought, J. G., 187, 195
Foulkes, J., 501
Fox, J. A., 188, 190, 191
Fox, R., 431, 492
Francois, P., 493
Francy, D. B., 501
Franke, R. W., 391
Frankel, S., 203
Frankenberg, R., 504
Frankham, R., 431
FRAYER, D. W., 429-73; 430, 432, 442, 449, 451
Frazer, J. G., 109, 113-15, 273-75, 283
Freed, R. S., 387
Freed, S. A., 387
Freedman, L., 430
Freeman, H., 149
Freeman, H. E., 489
Freeman, L., 141
Freeman, L. G., 548
Freeman, M., 510
Freidson, E., 221
Freilich, M., 227
Freire, M. E., 486
Freund, B., 203, 206, 207, 210
Friedlaender, J. S., 350, 502
Friedlander, D., 205
Friedman, J., 386
Friedrich, C. J., 119
Friedrich, M. H., 82, 84-86
Fripp, P. J., 502
Frisancho, A. R., 483, 487-90, 494, 495, 509
Frisch, J. E., 431
Frisch, R. E., 507, 508
Frobenius, L., 246
Froehlich, J. W., 356, 357
Froment, A., 500
Fryxell, R., 542, 543
Fuerst, P., 363
Fuller, N., 233
Fulwood, R., 488
Furbee, L., 151
Furbee-Losee, L., 187, 195

G

Gadgil, M., 433, 435
Gadjusek, D. C., 500, 501
Gahama, A., 284, 298
Gair, J. W., 565
Gaito, J., 138
Galarza, E., 412, 413
Galaty, J. G., 382, 384, 389
Galdikas, B., 317, 318
Galdikas, B. M. F., 441
Gallais, J., 261
Gallay, A., 77, 80, 82
Gallegos, D., 413

Galloway, A., 448
Galvin, K., 481, 492
Gambarotta, H., 391
Gantt, D. G., 329
García, R., 415
García Castañó, J., 414, 417
Garcia-Cook, A., 535
Gardner, M., 108
Garn, S. M., 430, 445, 447, 452, 460, 488
Garrels, J. I., 359
Garrison, V., 382
Garro, L. Y., 503
Garrow, J. S., 492
Garruto, R., 501
Garvin, P. L., 571
Gasper, L., 105
Gasser, S. A., 77
Gatenby, R. M., 391
Gaulin, S. J. C., 324, 431, 434-37, 439, 440, 491, 492
Gautier-Hion, A., 431, 434, 435
Gebre-Medhin, J., 60
Geertz, C., 70, 283, 285, 286, 305
Geertz, C. L., 571, 572
Geilhufe, N., 415, 416
Genovés, S., 451
George, M., 363
Gerdel, F. L., 187
Germain, C., 229
Germain, M., 501
Gershoff, S. N., 480, 481
Geschiere, P., 64
Gesick, L., 285, 286
Ghua, R., 52, 63, 65
Gibbs, J. L., 417
Gibson, M. A., 417
Giesey, R. E., 278, 284, 287
Gifford, J., 532
Gilbert, M. J., 414, 415
Gilbert, M. V., 302
Gilbert, W. A., 360
Giles, E., 356, 357, 430
Giles, H., 560
Gilkey, L., 115, 126
Gilles, H., 500
Gillespie, R., 541
Gillis, M., 203, 204
Gilman, A., 573
Gingerich, P. D., 323, 431, 451, 452
Ginsberg, M., 135
Girard, R., 274, 278
Girvan, N., 203
Gish, D. T., 126
Gittins, S. P., 318
Gjording, C., 208
Gladwin, C. H., 144
Glass, B., 353
Glatzer, B., 391
Glick, R., 568
Glittenberg, J. E., 228, 233

Glover, I. C., 79, 82, 87
Gluckman, M., 205-7, 279, 280, 289, 294, 295, 300
Gluckman, P., 349, 353, 356
Glücksmann, A., 429, 431, 434
Gnanasundaram, V., 563
Goad, S. I., 18
Godfrey, L. R., 104, 128
Godoy, G. A., 501
GODOY, R., 199-217; 200-3, 205, 208
Gojobori, T., 362
Golde, P., 225
Golder, T., 149, 151, 152
Goldman, D., 359
Goldschmidt, W., 382
Goldschmidt-Nathan, M., 351
Goldstein, H., 478
Goldstein, M. C., 503
Goldstein, S., 323, 431
Gomez, H., 499
Gonda, J., 571
Gonda, K., 445, 447
González, A. M., 417
Good, B. J., 226
Goodland, R., 208
Goodman, A., 500
Goodman, L., 141, 147
Goodman, M. M., 343, 345, 457
Goodrich, A., 220, 227
Goodrich, C., 207
Goodsell, C., 207
Goodspeed, T. H., 127
Goody, E., 259, 264
Goody, J., 159-61, 165, 168, 169, 174, 277, 286, 379
Goody, J. R., 245, 254, 259
Gopalan, C., 507
Gordon, J. E., 485, 500, 510
Gordon, K. D., 319, 321
Gordon, R. M., 119, 121, 206, 207, 211
Gordus, A. A., 18
Gosse, P., 108
Gossen, G. H., 195
Gould, H., 503
Gould, R. A., 78
Gould, S. J., 125, 128, 150, 321, 323, 324, 332
Gouldner, A., 207
Gow, K. M., 229
Gower, J. C., 343
Grabiner, J. V., 120
Graham, G. G., 481
Gramiccia, G., 500
Grandin, B., 398
Grant, L. S., 501
Grantham-McGregor, S., 495
Graves, M. W., 80, 82-85
Graves, R., 114
Gray, J. P., 431, 432, 438, 442, 443

AUTHOR INDEX 589

Gray, R. F., 389, 508, 509
Grayson, D. K., 533
Greber, N., 18
Green, D. L., 335
Green, E., 504
Green, M. M., 246
Greenberg, B. D., 363
Greenberg, H. B., 501
Greenberg, J. H., 124
Greenberg, L., 504
Greenberg, M. M., 119, 121
Greene, L. S., 488, 493
Greenfield, L. O., 451, 452, 457
Greenfield, P. M., 160
Greenwood, P. J., 431, 434
Gregersen, E., 573
Gregory, W. K., 331
Greksa, L. P., 493, 502
Griaule, M., 248
Grice, H. P., 167
GRIFFIN, J. B., 1-23; 3, 4, 6, 7, 9-12, 14, 16-19, 533
Griffiths, B. B., 501
Grine, F. E., 330, 332, 336
Grivetti, L., 492
Gross, D., 209
Gross, D. R., 491, 497
Grossbard, A., 144
Grossman, L., 360
Groves, M., 77, 79, 80, 82, 84, 88
Grubben, G., 491
Gruhn, R., 535
Guerrant, R., 504
Guggenheim, S., 65
Gugler, J., 261
Guidon, N., 537
Guinto, R. S., 509
Guire, K., 483
Guiterrez, J., 64
Gumperz, J. J., 167, 561-65, 568
Gunn, J., 84
Gunn, J. D., 535
Gupta, A., 63
Gupta, R., 501
Gusella, J. F., 359
Gussler, J. D., 495
Gustav, B. L., 430
Guthe, C. E., 77
Guthrie, G. M., 495
Guthrie, H. A., 491, 492, 495
Guthrie, R. D., 548
Gutkind, P. C. W., 261
Guttler, F., 359
Guy, G. R., 559
Guyer, J., 263
Guzman, M. A., 488
Gwatkin, D. R., 497, 511
Gwynne, M. D., 391

H

Haas, J. D., 491, 501
Haasis, B., 221
Habicht, J.-P., 478, 481-83, 485, 487, 488, 499, 500
Haddon, K., 145, 146
Haeserijn, E., 187
Hailman, J. P., 109
Haines, M., 205
Haisman, M., 492
Halberstein, R. A., 502
Hale, K., 25
Hall, R. L., 431
Halloran, E., 226
Halsted, J., 492
Hambraeus, L., 486, 488
Hamburg, B. A., 442
Hamill, P. V. V., 478
Hamilton, M. E., 430, 432, 449
Hammel, E., 144
Hamsum, K., 1
Hanash, S. M., 359
Handwerker, W. P., 145, 150
Hanihara, K., 430
Hankey, V., 77
Hanks, L., 497
Hann, H.-W., 500
Hanna, J. M., 502
Hanna, R. E., 430
Hanrahan, J. P., 431
Hansen, J. D. L., 432
Harada, S. I., 573
Harcourt, A. H., 317
Hardin, M. A., 82, 86, 87
Harding, R. S. O., 441
Hardy, M., 226, 232
Hargens, L., 506
Harington, C. R., 536, 547, 548
Harman, H., 149
Harnish, R., 34, 36
Harpending, H. C., 343, 344, 352, 355, 357, 365
Harper, A. B., 538
Harper, M. E., 364
Harrell, B. B., 233
Harris, A., 361
Harris, B., 493
Harris, C. L., 104, 110, 126, 128
Harris, D. E., 343, 344
Harris, E. F., 443, 445, 447
Harris, J., 493
Harris, M., 139, 206, 381, 386, 387, 510
Harris, O., 206, 207
Harrison, G. A., 351
Harrison, G. G., 491
Harrison, J., 227
Harriss, J., 49, 51, 52, 57, 58, 63
Hart, J. K., 244, 247, 261, 262
HART, K., 243-72; 244, 247, 261, 262

Hart, R. D., 391
Hartl, D. L., 125
Hartwick, J., 204
Harvey, P. H., 315, 319, 325, 431, 432, 434, 435, 439, 440, 452
Harvey, P. W., 486
Harwood, A., 223
Hasan, K. A., 500
Hasegawa, T., 441
Hassan, A. A., 536
Haswell, M., 492
Haugerud, A., 144
Hauser, G., 430
Hausman, A., 492
Hauspie, R. C., 478, 481, 482
Hautman, M. A., 227
Havelock, E., 165
Haviland, J. B., 187
Hayden, B., 532
Hayden, I., 306
Haynes, C. V., 536
Haynes, C. V. Jr., 533, 535, 546
Head, B., 573
Healy, G. R., 501
Heath, S. B., 160, 161, 165, 166, 168
Hedrick, P. W., 345
Hefley, J. C., 122
Heidel, A., 109, 114, 115
Heim, J-L., 451, 457, 460
Heine-Geldern, R., 285, 286
Heiser, C. B. Jr., 379
Heisler, P., 431
Heller, P., 503
Hellman, M., 331
Helm, J., 510
Helmuth, H., 430
Hempel, J., 500
Henderson, A. M., 323
Henderson, R. N., 293, 296
Henkel, R., 140
Henne, D., 187
Hennig, H., 79, 80, 82, 83, 86, 87, 89, 91, 94
Henriques, F., 207
Henry, L., 506, 507
Henschel, A., 493, 508
Hentoff, N., 122
Herfindahl, O., 204
Hernández-Chávez, E., 416
Herrera, J. F., 417
Herrera, L. A., 61
Herrera, M. G., 499
Hershkovitz, P., 431
Herskovits, M., 226
Herskovits, M. J., 249
Herzog, M., 558
Hess, C., 353
Hesse, B., 380
Heyer, J., 258
Heywood, P. F., 486, 492

Hiernaux, J., 148, 431, 481
Higginbotham, J., 32, 33
Higuchi, Y., 229
Hiiemae, K. M., 318-20, 335
Hildyard, A., 160, 167, 168
Hill, C., 504
Hill, J. H., 573, 574
Hill, J. N., 78, 83, 84
Hill, K. C., 573, 574
Hill, L. Jr., 232
Hill, P., 251, 260
Hill, R. M. II, 77, 80, 95
Hill, W. G., 357
Hillman, M., 567, 571
Himes, J. H., 480, 484, 485, 488
Hindle, D., 559
Hinton, P., 55
Hirschfeld, L., 139, 143
Hirschman, C., 507
Hirshleifer, J., 124
Hjort, A., 391
Hladik, C. M., 317
Hobhouse, L., 135
Hobsbawm, E., 209, 305
Hocart, A. M., 274, 275, 277-79, 288, 290, 294, 300, 304
Hodder, I., 82, 86-88
Hodge, C., 567, 571
Hodson, F., 149
Hoeck, H. N., 336
Hoffman, H., 136
Hofling, C. A., 187
Hofvander, Y., 495
Hoji, H., 25
Holden, C., 103
Hole, B. L., 137, 142
Holes, C. D., 568, 570
Holland, P. W., 141, 147
Holmes, T. M., 353
Holmes, W. H., 530
Hoogland, E. J., 64
Hoogland, J. L., 434, 437
Hool, B., 204
Hopkins, A. G., 257
Hopkins, D. M., 538, 547
Horn, B. M., 228
Hornstein, N., 26, 27
Horowitz, M. M., 261
Horton, R., 159, 253, 257, 301
Horvath, J., 25
Hoshi, H., 430
Hotelling, H., 200, 204
Howard, R. D., 434, 437
Howe, J., 139
Howell, N., 510
Howells, W. W., 343, 430
Howry, J. C., 77, 80-82
Hrdlicka, A., 530
Hrdy, S. B., 434, 451, 462
Hsiung, G. D., 501, 503
Hsu, F. L. K., 417

Huang, C.-T., 25
Hubbard, G. P., 414
Hubert, H., 396
Hudson, R. A., 561, 562, 566, 567
Hudson, R. R., 361
Huettel, M. D., 363
Huffman, S., 495
Huffman, S. L., 508
Huizinga, J., 351
Hunt, D., 64
Hunt, E. E. Jr., 430, 447
Hunter, J. M., 492, 501
Hunter, W. S., 430, 460
Huntington, R., 283, 286
Hupfeld, H., 111
Hurley Delgaty, A., 187
Huskins, C. L., 126
HUSS-ASHMORE, R., 475-528; 491, 492, 498, 504, 508
Hussain, A., 51
Hutchinson, G. E., 103
Hutchinson, J., 502
Hutchinson, S. A., 229, 233
Huylebroeck, D., 128
Hylander, W. L., 316, 320, 333, 334, 338
Hyman, S., 273-75, 307
Hymes, D. H., 569
Hytten, F., 493

I

Ikawa-Smith, F., 537
Ikeya, M., 544
Ileto, R. C., 64, 68, 70
Iliffe, J., 292
Imle, M., 414
Immink, M., 493
Imperato, P. J., 504
Indritz, A., 480
Ingold, T., 381
Innes, D., 203
Inoue, K., 573
Iordanidis, P., 430
IRVINE, J. T., 557-81; 560, 561, 570, 575
IRVING, W. N., 529-55; 536, 547-49
Irwin, M., 493
Irwin-Williams, C., 535, 542, 543, 547
Isaac, G. L., 431, 441, 442, 536, 539
Ismail, S. J., 495
Izard, M., 264

J

Jackendoff, R., 26
Jackson, L., 478, 492
Jackson, M., 264

Jackson, R., 478, 492
Jacobs, J. B., 64
Jacobs, K., 500
Jacobsen, T., 115
Jagadeesan, V., 490
Jahangiri, N., 566, 567
Jahn, E. F., 353
Jahn, R., 430
Jain, D. K., 573
Jamal, N., 53
James, G. D., 501, 502
James, W., 492
Jantz, R. L., 430
Jarman, P. J., 434
Jaswal, S. C., 565
Jelliffe, D. B., 486, 487
Jelliffe, E. F. B., 486
Jenkins, C. L., 485, 488
Jenkins, G., 204
Jenkins, T., 343, 344
Jenner, D., 501
Jerome, N. W., 498
Jiménez Núñez, A., 413
Job, M. O., 391
Jobin, W., 501
Johanson, D. C., 324, 451, 456, 458, 460
Johnson, A., 135, 137, 138, 152, 153
Johnson, B. R., 493
Johnson, C. L., 478, 488
Johnson, D. E., 232
Johnson, D. H., 382
Johnson, F., 11, 542
Johnson, G. A., 78
Johnson, H., 65
Johnson, K. M., 501
Johnson, M. H., 234
Johnson, M. J., 364
Johnson, N. K., 431
Johnson-Laird, P. N., 163
JOHNSTON, F. E., 475-528; 477-79, 483, 485, 487, 488, 490, 493, 495, 496, 508
Johnston, M., 227, 228
Johnstone, F., 203, 206, 207
Jolly, C. J., 315, 323, 328, 332
Jones, D. J., 417
Jones, G. I., 252
Jones, L., 204
Jones, W., 124
Jopling, A. V., 547-49
Jordan, B., 233
JORDE, L. B., 343-73; 343, 345-47, 352-57
Jorstad, E. T., 106
Jose, A. V., 63
Joshi, P. C., 53, 63
Jou, W. M., 128
Jukes, T. H., 125
Julig, P., 548, 549

AUTHOR INDEX 591

Jungers, W. L., 431, 439, 440, 456
Justeson, J., 191-94

K

Kaberry, P., 246, 251
Kagan, I. G., 501
KAHN, J. S., 49-75; 60, 64
Kajanoja, P., 430
Kallman, C. H., 481
Kalven, H. Jr., 120
Kanawati, A. A., 495
Kandel, R., 498
Kane, G. J., 501
Kant, I., 124
Kantorowicz, E. H., 278, 284, 285, 295
Kapferer, B., 207
Kaplan, F. S., 79, 81, 84, 88, 145, 152
Kaplan, J. E., 501
Kaplan, N., 360, 361, 363
Kaplan, R., 42
Karlin, S., 346, 351
Karno, M., 414
Karp, I., 280, 283, 377, 388, 390, 398, 399
Karpenchenko, G. D., 127
Karson, M. J., 18
Kashoki, M. E., 568
Kashyap, L. K., 138
Kasprzak, E., 431
Katcher, A., 375
Katz, R. R., 93
Katz, S., 477, 492, 507
Kaufert, P. A., 233
Kaufman, L., 225
KAUFMAN, T., 187-98; 191-94
Kaufman, T. S., 187, 188, 190-94
Kavanagh, M., 319, 431, 452
Kay, J., 204, 205
Kay, M. A., 226-28, 231, 414, 415
Kay, P., 135, 136, 183
KAY, R. F., 315-41; 315, 316, 319, 320, 323-31, 335, 451, 455
Kayser-Jones, J. S., 228
Keefe, S. E., 406, 414, 415
Keen, H. A., 430
Keen, P., 502
Keith, M., 503
Keller, W., 478, 487
Kelley, D., 193
Kelley, J., 145
Kelley, J. T., 435
Kelley, M., 430
Kelley, N. U., 509
Kelly, A. R., 3
Kemm, J. R., 481
Kemp, C., 52, 63

Kenett, R., 351
Kennedy, K. A. R., 432, 449
Kennett, R., 346, 351
Kenny, M. G., 382
Kerewsky, R., 430, 445, 447, 452
Kerr, C., 207
Kevany, J., 228
Key, P., 432, 449
Keyes, C., 55
Keys, A., 492, 493, 508
Kidd, K. K., 349
Kidd, R., 63
Killick, A., 203
Kilson, M., 301
Kim, C., 500
Kim, J., 145, 149, 150
Kimambo, I. N., 299
Kimbel, W. H., 324, 451, 456, 458, 460
Kimble, J., 206, 210
Kimura, M., 125
King, I., 232
King, M. C., 354
King, S., 221
King, S. D., 501
Kinzey, W. G., 321, 431
Kipling, R., 376
Kirk, L., 151, 152
Kirk, R. L., 343, 344
Kirkby, M., 117
Kirkwood, B., 503
Kishwar, M., 61
Kiszely, I., 430
Kitahara-Frisch, J., 451
Klayman, J. E., 494, 509
Kleiber, M., 322
Kleiman, D. G., 431, 434
Klein, A. N., 257
Klein, H. E., 228
Klein, R., 149, 493, 500
Klein, R. E., 478, 481-90, 494, 495, 499, 500
Klein, R. G., 530
Klein, R. M., 488
Kleinberg, M. J., 77, 95
Kleindienst, M., 78
Kleinman, A. M., 220, 222, 226, 232
Klor de Alva, J. J., 416, 417
Kluckhohn, C., 104, 135
Knight, J. A., 390
Knodel, J., 505
Knorozov, Y. V., 194
Knorr-Cetina, K. D., 183
Knott, J. W., 64
Knowlton, C., 413
Knox, C. W., 431
Knudson, R., 532
Kobrin, S., 202
Kobyliansky, E., 351
Koenig, E. L., 568
Kohout, F., 145

Kolata, G. B., 432
Konings, P., 53
Konner, M., 438, 491, 492
Koong, L. J., 391
Koos, E., 221
Kopec, A. C., 351
Kopytoff, I., 258
Korkman, N., 431
Koshi, P. T., 222
Kottak, C. P., 286, 297
Kourany, M., 501
Kovithavongs, T., 353
Kowalski, C., 142, 152
Krader, L., 384
KRAMER, C., 77-102; 78
Kramer, S. N., 115
Krantz, G. S., 451
Kretchmer, N., 375
Krieger, A. D., 531, 533
Krieger, H., 352
Kriesberg, L., 65
Krige, E. J., 283, 296, 298, 299
Krige, J. D., 296, 299
Krishnamurti, B., 565
Kritsch-Armstrong, I. D., 548, 549
Kroch, A., 57, 559
Kroeber, A., 135, 148
Kroeger, A., 504
Krogman, W. M., 3
Kronenfeld, D., 137
Krotser, P. H., 80, 82, 93
Kruijt, D., 203, 206, 207
Kruskal, J., 151
Kruskal, W. A., 141
Krutilla, J., 204
Krzanowski, W. J., 345
Ku, T. L., 546
Kubicek, R., 203
Kuhn, T. S., 231
Kuhn, W. M., 306
Kumar, S. K., 498
Kunstadter, P., 504
Kuojak, I., 503
Kuper, A., 298
Kuper, H., 252, 277, 290, 297-99, 302
Kurczynski, E. M., 343
Kurczynski, T. W., 343
Kuroda, E., 413, 417
Kurtén, B., 540
Kutsche, P., 408, 411, 413
Kwei, H. E., 501, 503
Kyerematen, A., 301

L

Labouret, H., 249
Labov, W. A., 557-60
Labovitz, S., 138
Ladefoged, P., 568
Ladouceur, P. A., 262

LaFarque, J. R., 226
La Fontaine, J. de, 375
Laite, J., 207
Lakoff, G., 37
Lalouel, J. M., 343, 347, 356
Lamphere, L., 233
Lampl, M., 487, 488
Lancaster, C. S., 434, 438, 441
Lancaster, J. B., 434, 438, 441, 451
Landaeta de Jimenez, M., 432
Lande, R., 357, 433
Landy, D., 223
Lane, J. M., 478, 487
Lane, K., 204
Langdon, S., 116
Langley, C. H., 361
Lansman, R. A., 363
Lanternari, V., 253
Laplace, P. S., 124
Larcombe, C., 413
Larcombe, S., 413
Larnach, S. L., 430
Larouze, B., 500
Larrick, J. W., 501
Larsen, C. E., 116, 117
Larsen, C. S., 432, 445, 447-49, 451
Larsen, T., 191
Larson, B., 208
Lasker, G. W., 477
Lasky, R., 494, 495
Lasnik, H., 29, 32, 33, 39-41
Last, D. M., 251
Latham, R. M., 493
Lathrap, D., 79, 81, 82, 89, 91
Lathrap, D. W., 79, 84, 87, 94
Lathrop, G. M., 349
Latimer, B. M., 451, 458
Latour, B., 183
Latter, B. D. H., 344, 345, 352
Lau, R. M., 493
Lauderdale, M., 413
Lauer, C., 431
Lauer, P. K., 77, 79-82, 84, 93
Laughlin, R. M., 187, 195
Laughlin, W. S., 538
Lauro, P., 504
Lavandera, B., 559
Lave, J., 151
Lavelle, C. L. B., 445, 447
Lawrence, D. N., 501
Lax, D., 201, 202
Laxague, G., 432
Leach, E., 306, 376, 392, 393
Leahy, K. M., 221
Leakey, M. D., 451
Leakey, R. E. F., 451
Leatherman, T., 501
Leavitt, E. E. Jr., 77
Lebeuf, A. M. D., 298
LeBoeuf, B. J., 434
Le Bris, E., 259

Lechtig, A., 481, 484, 485, 487-89, 493-95, 500
Le Clercq, F. W., 118, 119, 121
Lee, G. M., 354
Lee, R., 506, 510
Leeds, A., 385
Lees, F. C., 343, 356
Lees, J. M., 116, 117
Lees, S., 390
Legates, J. E., 431
LeGrand, C., 64
Leibel, R. L., 489
Leigh, R. A., 445
Leininger, M., 221, 222, 226, 228, 230, 232
Leith-Ross, S., 253
Lemarchand, R., 287, 302
LeMoine, G., 534
Lenkersdorf, C., 187
Leon-Portilla, M., 412
Leridon, H., 508
Leroi-Gourhan, A., 377
Leslie, C., 503
Lesthaeghe, R., 508
Leutenegger, W., 431, 432, 435, 439, 440, 451, 452, 456
Levin, A., 503
Levin, B., 139
Levine, D., 145, 152
Levinson, S., 573, 574
Lévi-Strauss, C., 392, 396
Levtzion, N., 252
Levy, L. E., 119
Lew, R., 343, 344, 346, 351
Lewin, C., 498
Lewin, M., 64
Lewin, R., 360
Lewinsohn, R., 376
Lewis, A. B., 430, 445, 447, 452
Lewis, D., 417
Lewis, E., 113
Lewis, G., 203
Lewis, I. M., 60
Lewis, J., 125, 558
Lewis, S., 106
Lewontin, R. C., 106, 123, 125, 345, 352, 357, 359, 430
Li, W. H., 361
Lidsky, A. S., 359
Liebenow, G., 262
Lieberman, L. S., 431
Lienhardt, G., 283, 298
Lieu, Z-C., 539
Lightfoot, J., 118
Limón, J. E., 411, 414, 417, 418
Linares, O., 491
Linares de Sapir, O., 79, 80, 82-84, 94
Lincoln, B., 390
Lindsay-Smith, E., 503

Lines, P. M., 119, 120
Linné, S., 77
Lipson, J. G., 228
Lisse, O., 77, 79, 80
Little, B., 500
Little, I., 202
Little, K. L., 246, 252, 263
Little, M. A., 385, 481, 493
Litto, G., 77
Livingstone, F., 500
Livshits, G., 351
Llanes, J., 416
Llop, E., 356
Lloreda, P., 499
Lloyd, P. C., 252, 260, 276
Locatis, D., 492
Lockridge, K. A., 167
Lodrick, D. O., 387
Loewenson, R., 503
Lofgren, L., 78
Logan, M., 503
London, W. T., 500
Long, J. M., 415
Long, N., 202
Longacre, W. A., 78, 79, 82, 83, 85, 90-92
Longhurst, R., 492, 497, 501
Lonsdale, J., 290
Lopez, F. G., 480
Lopez, M., 495
Lopez-Contreras, M. E., 432
Lora, G., 207
Lorenzo, J. L., 529, 535, 541
Lorr, M., 148
Lotka, A. J., 114, 126
Louis, A., 77, 79, 80
Lounsbury, F., 193
Love, J., 364
Lovejoy, C. O., 438, 451, 456, 458, 461
Lovejoy, P. E., 258
Low, S. M., 479
Lozano, I., 411, 417
Lu, Q., 451
Luebben, R., 207
Lukacs, J. R., 432
Lunt, D. A., 445, 447
Lunt, R., 502
Lurie, D. S., 488, 490, 495
Lurie, R., 535
Lustbader, E., 500
Lusty, T., 501
Lutz, C., 149, 151, 152
Lyell, C., 124

M

Macaulay, R. K. S., 559, 560
MacDonald, H., 494
MacEachern, A., 534
MacGaffey, W., 283
MacGregor, F. C., 221
Macias, A., 62

AUTHOR INDEX 593

MacKinlay, L. M., 501
MacKinnon, J., 317
Maclachlan, M. D., 387, 391
MacLean, W. C. Jr., 481
MacLeod, B., 194
MacNeish, R. S., 534, 535
MacVean, R. B., 478, 479, 483, 485, 488, 489, 495
Magill, J., 207
Maheny, W. C., 532
Mahler, P. E., 324
Mai, L. L., 382
Maier, W., 320, 335
Mainga, M., 291, 299
Maitland, F. W., 278, 280
Mak, J. W., 501
Makhubu, L., 503, 504
Malcolm, L. A., 482, 488
Malde, N. E., 542, 543
Maldonado Andrés, J., 187
Malhotra, K. C., 138
Malina, R. M., 478, 480-85, 487, 488
Mallowan, M. E. L., 116
Mamalakis, M., 203
Mamdani, M., 511
Mann, A., 337, 451, 460
Mann, C. S., 110, 113
Marantz, A., 26
Marchetti, P., 53
Marchione, T. J., 495
Marchuk, L., 353
Marcus, G. E., 303, 304
Maretzki, T. W., 232
Margen, S., 492
Margolis, M., 233
Margrain, S., 559, 560
Marinier, E., 500
Mario Pino, Q., 537, 550
Markell, E., 492
Marks, R. B., 64
Marsden, S. J., 431
Marshall, I., 208
Marshall, W., 416, 417
Martin, A. O., 343
Martin, E. S., 430
Martin, H. W., 221, 227, 234
Martin, L. B., 329
Martin, L. D., 530
Martin, P. S., 530, 533
Martin, R. D., 451
Martin, S. E., 573
Martinez, C., 495, 508, 510
Martinez, J. M., 500
Martorell, R., 478, 482-88, 490, 493, 494, 499, 500
Martz, J., 501
Maruyama, T., 363
Mason, E., 204
Masterman, M., 231
Mata, L. J., 491, 495, 500
Mathews, J. V. Jr., 547
Matos, J., 494, 509

Matson, F. R., 77-82, 93
Mattelart, M., 62
Mauksch, H. O., 220, 234
Mauny, R., 252
Mauss, M., 307, 396
Maxam, A. M., 360
Maxwell, J., 187
May, J., 499
May, M. L., 439
May, R., 27
Mayer, J., 486
Mayer, P., 206
Mayer, W. V., 128
Maynard, K., 377, 388, 390, 399
Mayr, E., 105, 127, 433
Mazrui, A. A., 277, 305
Mbaga, K., 573
Mbiti, J. S., 397
McArthur, J., 508
McBrian, C., 561
McBurney, C., 531
McCabe, G. S., 221
McCabe, J. T., 385
McCall, D. F., 381
McCaskie, T. C., 257, 291, 292
McClelland, J. L., 162
McConkey, E. H., 359
McCormack, C. P., 263
McCormack, W. C., 563, 564, 568
McCown, E. R., 431, 439, 452, 459
McCracken, R., 150
McDonald, S., 204
McEachron, D. L., 431, 461, 462
McFadden, E. S., 127
McFalls, J., 509
McFalls, M., 509
McGandy, R. B., 480, 481
McGarvey, S. T., 502
McGregor, I. A., 485, 501
McGrew, W. C., 441, 442
McGuire, R., 144
McHenry, H. M., 326-28, 333, 431, 451
McKay, A., 499
McKay, H., 499
McKern, W. C., 12
McKim, P., 104
McKusick, V. A., 354
McLaren, D., 494
McLaren, D. S., 487, 495
McLean, C. U., 503, 504
McLellan, T., 353, 354, 357
McNeeley, D. F., 504
McPhee, A., 257
McQuown, N. A., 187, 190
Mead, J. I., 535
Mead, M., 123, 221
Meadows, D., 205
Medicine, B., 417

Megivern, J., 108
Meiklejohn, C., 432, 449
Meillassoux, C., 251, 258, 259
Mellits, E. D., 481
Melnick, D., 323, 431
Melnick, R. R., 119
Melville, M. B., 406, 414-17
Melville, T. R., 417
Mencken, H. L., 105
Mendelsohn, E., 231
Mendez Dominguez, A., 506
Menken, J., 508
Menozzi, P., 347, 350, 352, 354
Meredith, H. V., 481, 483
Merrill, C. R., 359
Merton, R. K., 231
Mesher, G. M., 283
Messenger, E. C., 109
Messer, A., 359
Messer, E., 487, 492
Metcalf, P., 283, 286
Meyer, J., 64
Meyers, L. D., 499
Meyers, L. R., 55
Meyers, P., 431
Mi, M. P., 352
Michel, M. E., 430
Mickelson, O., 493, 508
Mickevich, M. F., 347
Micle, S., 351
Micozzi, M., 501
Middleton, J., 250
Mielke, J. H., 351, 355
Miers, S., 258
Mijsberg, W. A., 430, 445, 447
Mikesell, R., 201, 204
Millard, A., 509
Miller, D., 80, 83, 88, 94
Miller, D. S., 492
Miller, G. L., 78
Miller, J. P., 542
Miller, M., 145, 146
Miller, P. D., 120
Miller, S., 206, 208
Mills, J. R. E., 319
Mills, S. K., 128
Milner, A. C., 63
Milner, G. B., 571
Milroy, J., 559
Milroy, L., 559, 560
Milton, K., 439
Miner, H., 249, 252
Mines, R., 416
Minge-Kalman, W., 137
Minshall, H. L., 531
Mirambel, L., 535, 541
Mirrlees, J., 202, 204, 205
Mitani, J. C., 434
Mitchell, G., 434
Mitchell, H. F., 144, 150, 503
Mitchell, J. C., 144, 150, 206, 207, 503
Mitchell, R. J., 352

Mitra, S., 345
Mitre, A., 208
Mitter, C., 347
Mitton, J. B., 345
Mobb, G. E., 431
Mochanov, Y. A., 533
Mochizuki, M., 573
Mock, N., 495
Modaressi-Tehrani, Y., 561, 566, 567, 569
Moeran, B., 77, 95
Moerman, D., 503
Moertono, S., 285
Moeschler, P., 430
Mohanan, K. P., 25, 43, 46
Moise, E., 54, 55
Moldave, K., 360
Moles, J. A., 416
Molgaard, C. A., 227, 230, 231, 233
Molineaux, L., 500
Monath, T. P., 501
Mondloch, J. L., 187, 194, 195
Monrray, L. A., 222, 226
Montgomery, E., 137
Montoya, J., 363
Moodie, D., 207
Moore, J. A., 88, 111, 120, 122, 415
Moore, J. R., 104-6
Moore, L. L., 501
Moorey, P. R. S., 116
Moorrees, C. F. A., 445, 447
Mora, J. O., 499
Mora, M., 415
Morales Santos, F., 195
Moran, T., 201
Moreno-Black, G., 495
Morgadant, T., 64
Morgan, K., 147, 352, 353
Morlan, R. E., 532, 547, 548
Moroney, S., 207
Moroni, A., 355, 365
Morowitz, H. J., 126
Morris, H. M., 110, 111, 126
Morris, L., 508
Morrison, D., 140
Morse, C., 202
Morse, P., 126
Morton, N. E., 343, 344, 346, 351, 352, 354, 356
Morton-Williams, P., 252
Mosberger, M. M., 228
Moser, E., 77, 79, 82
Moshal, M. G., 503
Mosley, W. H., 507, 508
Moss, N. H., 486
Mota, C., 411, 417
Mott Davis, E., 537, 550
Motulsky, A. G., 123, 351
Mouche, M., 254
Mourant, Λ. E., 351
Movius, H. L. Jr., 531, 532

Moyer, W. A., 128
Muecke, M. A., 227
Mueller, C., 149, 150
Mueller, L. D., 345
Mueller, W. H., 484, 485, 488, 489, 494
Mugambi, M., 481
Mukhopadhyay, B., 501
Muller, J.-C., 281, 283
Müller-Beck, H., 532, 536
Muntzing, A., 127
Murdock, G., 135
Murdock, G. P., 442
Murray, C., 207
Mworoha, E., 284
Myers, L., 229
Myers, S., 202

N

Nadel, S. F., 246, 248
Nag, M., 505, 508
Nagai, M., 442, 445, 447
Nagel, E., 105
Nagy, J. M., 430
Naidu, A. N., 493, 507
Naim, C. M., 565
Nair, K. N., 387
Nankani, G., 203
Narayan, V., 501
Nardi, B., 505
Naroll, R., 135
Nartsupha, C., 63
Nash, J., 61, 207, 209
Nathan, H., 351
Nations, M. K., 504
Naylor, S. L., 359, 361
Ndayishinguje, P., 283, 284
Nebelsick, H., 109
Needham, R., 274
Neel, J. V., 359
Nei, M., 344, 345, 348, 349, 352, 353, 356-62, 364
Neilson, J., 203
Nelken-Turner, A., 535
Nelkin, D., 122
Nelson, B. A., 92
Nelson, N. C., 536
Nemeskéri, J., 430
Nerlove, S. B., 151, 152
Netting, R., 144
Netting, R. McC., 251, 261, 384
Neumann, A. K., 504
Neustupny, J. V., 561, 573, 574
Nevanlinna, H. R., 351, 354
Newell, N., 117, 128
Newman, B. C., 478, 479, 488, 495, 496
Newman, J., 491
Newman, J. S., 509
Newman, S., 571
Newton, F. C., 414, 415

Nichaman, M. Z., 478, 487
Nickens, P. R., 432, 451
Nicklin, K., 77, 79, 82
Nicolas, G., 254
Nietschmann, B., 491
Nishida, T., 441
Niswander, J. D., 356
Noakes, J., 18
Nondasuta, A., 480, 481
Nonini, D., 387
Noonan, K. M., 434, 437
Nord, E., 492
Nordhaus, W., 205
Norgan, N., 492
Norgan, N. G., 492
Norio, R. K., 351, 354
Norman, D. A., 162
Norman, W., 188, 190, 191
Norman, W. M., 190, 195
North, L., 53
Notestein, F. W., 505
Noth, M., 113
Novelo, V., 207
Novick, R. P., 375
Nugent, J., 498
Nugent, S. L., 58
Nunberg, G., 559
Nweeia, M. T., 443, 445, 447
Nye, R., 294

O

Oakland, G. B., 430
Obiechina, E. N., 255
O'Brian, E. M., 328
Ochoga, S. A., 502
Ochs, E., 160
Ochsenius, C., 535
Ochsenschlager, E. L., 77, 80
O'Dea, K., 502
Odell, M., 507
Ogbu, J., 492
Ogburn, W., 135
Ohadike, P., 207
Ohanessian, S., 568
Ojala, D., 363
O'Laughlin, B., 256
Olesen, V., 229
Olivas, G., 414
Olness, K., 480
Olsen, J. W., 539
Olson, D. R., 160, 167, 168
Olson, R. D., 191
Olson, T. R., 451
Olver, R., 160
O'Meara, D., 207
Omran, A. R., 498, 509
O'Neil, R. M., 118
Ong, W. J., 165
Oomen, H., 491, 492
Oppenheim, A. L., 115
Oppong, C., 260, 263
Ordoñez Domingo, J., 187

AUTHOR INDEX 595

Orem, D., 232
Orihel, T., 501
Oring, L. W., 433
Orque, M. S., 222, 226
Orr, J., 106
Orraca-Tetteh, R., 492
Ortiz Domingo, J., 187
Ortony, A., 162
Osborne, O. H., 222, 223, 228
Oshima, H., 493
Ossenberg, N. S., 352
O'Toole, G. B., 108
Otte, D., 433
Ottino, P., 299
Overton, W. R., 120, 121
Owen, P., 533
Owusu, M. P., 262
Oxnard, C., 148
Oxnard, C. E., 431, 452

P

Pacey, A., 492, 501
Packard, R. M., 291
Paden, J., 262
Padilla, A. M., 414
Page, D., 364
Page, D. C., 364
Page, H., 508
Palgi, P., 233
Pallardel, D., 490
Palsson, G., 145
Pandey, T., 150
Papousek, D. A., 77, 81, 82, 93, 94
Papps, I., 144
Paredes, A., 408-11, 413, 414, 417
Park, M. H., 353
Parker, F., 120
Parker, P., 126
Parkin, D., 377
Parpart, J., 207
Parrot, A., 115
Partridge, W., 498
Pastron, A. G., 79, 92
Patai, R., 114
Pattanayak, D. P., 563, 564
Patterson, L., 546
Paul, L., 233
Paul, R. A., 274, 283
Paulme, D., 253
Pavlovsky, D., 127
Payen, L. A., 541, 545
Payet, M., 500
Payne, R. B., 431, 433, 434, 439
Peace, A. J., 260
Peacock, D. P. S., 80, 81, 83, 94
Peacock, M., 494
Peake, H., 115
Pearce, T. O., 504

Peaslee, A. J., 119
Peel, J. D. Y., 253, 260, 265, 278, 292, 296, 300, 302, 303, 305
Peletz, M., 54
Pelletier, D., 502
Pellett, P., 491, 495
Pélissier, P., 251
Pellow, D., 263
Pelto, G., 135-37, 139, 140, 152, 153
Pelto, G. H., 497, 498
Pelto, P., 135-37, 139, 140, 152, 153
Pemberton, J., 277, 287, 296
Peplau, H., 232
Perez, L., 336
Perheentupa, J., 354
Perkins, D., 204
Perlman, M., 145
Perrings, C., 200, 206, 208
Perrot, C.-H., 257, 264
Perry, E., 64, 67, 69
Person, T. B., 228
Person, Y., 258
Persons, W., 135
Perzigian, A. J., 445, 447
Peters, C. R., 328
Petersen, U., 204
Peterson, F., 200, 204
Peterson, J., 413
Petras, J., 207
Petros-Barvazian, A., 495
Phan, D., 359
Phenice, T. W., 430
Phillips, P., 7, 9
Phimister, I., 200, 203, 207, 208
Piazza, A., 347, 349, 352-54, 356
Picon-Reategui, E., 497
Pilbeam, D. R., 323, 324, 328, 332, 451
Pillsbury, B. L., 504
Pineda, A., 508
Pinstrup-Andersen, P., 496, 498
Pipho, C., 111
Pittman, R. S., 573
Platt, J., 567, 568
Platt, T., 208
Plattner, S., 144
Plog, S., 83
Poebel, A., 115
Poedjosoedarmo, S., 562, 571-73
Poggie, J., 144
Poggie, J. J. Jr., 417
Polanyi, K., 252
Polanyi, M., 160, 162
Polesky, H. F., 355
Polgar, S., 505
Pollard, G. C., 537
Pollet, E., 260

Pollitt, E., 484, 485, 489, 494, 499
Pollnac, R., 144, 150
Pons, J., 430
Pope John Paul II, 108, 109
Popkin, B. M., 495, 498
Popkin, S., 54
Poplack, S., 559
Porteous, J., 207
Porter, I. H., 359
Porter, J. W., 16
Posnansky, M., 80, 87
Post, D., 323
Post, D. E., 411, 417
Post, D. G., 431
Potter, R. Y., 430, 439, 507, 508
Povey, J., 568
Powdermaker, H., 207
Powers, B. A., 228
Powers, W. R., 537
Powesland, P. E., 560
Prager, E. M., 364
Prakash, O., 360
Prattis, I., 382
Preece, M. A., 478, 481, 482
Press, I., 227
Preston, S., 510
Price, G. M., 108
Price, J. E., 16
Price, T. D., 381
Prins, G., 290, 296, 297
Prior, C. A., 541
Prior, I., 502
Pritchard, J. B., 115
Provine, W. B., 105
Provost, C., 442
Puech, P.-F., 336
Pumphrey, M. E. C., 573
Puri, H. K., 53, 63
Pylyshyn, Z., 25
Pzreworski, J., 205

Q

Quandt, S., 487
Quinn, N., 151, 152

R

Rabinbach, A., 294
Rabold, J., 481
Radcliffe-Brown, A. R., 244, 247, 377, 379, 386
Raemakers, J. J., 318
Raff, M., 125
Ragan, P. K., 415, 418
Ragharamulu, N., 490
Ragucci, A. T., 223, 227, 231
Rahman, A. K., 485, 501
Raikes, R. L., 116
Raison-Jourde, F., 303, 304
Ralls, K., 431, 434, 439

AUTHOR INDEX

Ramanujan, A. K., 564
Randall, M., 61
Randers, J., 205
Rangan, K., 563
Ranger, T., 305
Ranger, T. O., 299, 305
Rao, B. S. N., 493
Rao, C. R., 343, 345, 346, 351, 358
Rapp, G., 532
Rappaport, H., 504
Rappaport, M., 504
Rappaport, R. A., 384-86
Rashid, M., 63
Rathbun, T. A., 449
Rattazzi, M. C., 364
Rattray, R. S., 296-98
Raup, D. M., 126
Ray, B., 277, 283, 284
Raynaut, C., 260, 261
Rea, J. N., 481
Read, D., 149
Read, M., 206
Read, M. S., 499
Read, W. W. C., 487
Reboul, C., 261
Reddy, B. M., 138
Reddy, M. N., 55
Reddy, P., 507
Reddy, V., 490
Redman, C., 149
Reed, R. B., 478
Reeves, B. O. K., 538, 541, 542
Reich, A. H., 412, 413
Reichel-Dolmatoff, G., 491
Reid, A., 285
Reidman, R., 144
Reina, R. E., 77, 80, 93, 95
Reinhart, T., 29, 39, 40
Reiss, M., 434, 439
Reiter, R. R., 233
Relethford, J. H., 343, 356
Renaud, E. B., 531
Renckens, H., 115
Rensberger, J. M., 336
Rensch, B., 431
Resnick, D. P., 167
Resnick, L. B., 167
Rey, P.-P., 251, 259
Reyment, R. A., 439, 451
Reynolds, H., 141, 147
Reynolds, J., 346
Rhoads, J., 502
Rice, K., 501
Rice, P. M., 77, 94
Rice, R. W., 429
Richard, P., 492
Richards, A., 206
Richards, A. I., 274, 278, 279, 288-91, 293, 296, 301
Richards, P., 390, 391
Richardson, P., 206

Richman, E. A., 430
Riddle, O., 105, 123
Riesenberg, S. H., 571
Riesman, P., 265
Riley, W., 559
Rimmer, D., 261
Rimmer, L. M., 227
Rindfuss, C. R., 507
Rios, F., 414
Ríos, S., 417
Risko, K. J., 360, 361, 363
Rita Ferreira, A., 206, 210
Robbins, M., 144, 150
Roberts, D. F., 352
Roberts, F. H. H. Jr., 530
Roberts, J., 149-52
Roberts, K., 125
Roberts, P., 258, 263
Robertson, A. F., 262, 301
Robertson, C., 263
Robertson, J. S., 190
Robins, C., 558
Robinson, J. T., 315, 322, 332
Robinson, K., 63
Robinson, W. J., 77
Robinson, W. P., 560
Robkin, E., 387
Robson, K. J. H., 359
Roch, J., 259, 261
Roche, A. F., 478, 508
Rocheteau, G., 259, 261
Rodman, P. S., 434
Rodrigues, A. M., 495
Roeder, P. G., 54
Roemer, M., 202, 204
Roessingh, H. K., 55
Rogers, A. R., 355, 357
Rogers, J. S., 347
Rogers, M. E., 232
Rogers, R. A., 530, 535
Romaine, S., 559, 560
Romano-V, O. I., 406, 407
Romanucci-Ross, L., 503
Romer, A. S., 126
Romney, A. K., 147, 149, 151, 152
Ronaghy, H., 492
Rosaldo, M. Z., 233
ROSALDO, R., 405-27; 406
Rosales, L., 484, 489, 495
Rose, J. E., 430, 452
Rose, M., 151
Roseberry, W., 52, 57
Rosen, L., 501
Rosenbauer, R. J., 546
Rosenberg, K., 323
Rosenberg, K. R., 451, 461, 488
Rosenberger, A. L., 321
Rosenblum, B. B., 359
Rosenfeld, A., 377
Rosenfeld, M., 119
Ross, E. B., 398
Ross, P., 503

Roth, J., 234
Rothhammer, F., 356
Rothman, E. D., 361
Rothstein, M., 111, 119-21
Rouse, I., 535
Rowley, H. H., 113
Roychoudhury, A. K., 345, 349, 352, 353, 356, 359, 364
Rudder, B., 431, 434, 435, 439
Rudenko, S. I., 532
Ruel, M., 254
Ruiz, M. C., 226, 228
Ruiz, R. A., 414, 415
Rúz Sánchez, A., 187
Rumelhart, D. E., 162
Rummel, R., 149, 151
Ruse, M., 121
Russell, B., 104
Russell, J., 566, 569, 576
Russell, M. D., 451, 461
Ryan, A. S., 432, 442, 445, 447, 449, 451
Ryan, D. P., 352
Rye, O. S., 79, 80
Ryman, M., 357

S

Sacks, M. S., 353
Saffa, H. I., 61
Saffer, M. E., 77
Sahlins, M. D., 287, 398
Sai, F., 505
Sailer, L., 151
Sailer, L. D., 324, 431, 435-37, 439, 440
Saimot, G., 500
Saito, M., 25
Saitou, N., 349
Sakaguchi, A. Y., 359, 361
Saligan, D. P., 80, 82
Salomon, J., 500
Salzman, P. C., 384, 390
Samanta, R. K., 55
Sameshima, Y., 229
Samuel, M., 259
Sanchez, J., 490
Sandeen, E. R., 105
Sanders, W. T., 505
Sands, M. W., 391
Sandusky, S. T., 430
Sanger, D., 536
Sanghvi, L. D., 343-45
Sanjur, D., 494
Sankale, M., 500
Sankoff, G., 558, 559
Santana, R., 207
Santiso, R., 508
Saraswati, B., 77
Sariego Rodriguez, J., 207
Sarty, M. E., 227, 228
Sassoon, J., 65

Sathyamurthy, T. V., 60
Satyanarayana, K., 493
Saucier, J. F., 509
Sauer, C. O., 380
Saunders, J., 226
Saunders, L., 221
Saunders, N. C., 363
Sayers, R., 416
Schaefer, A. E., 488
Schaffer, H. E., 431
Scheans, D. J., 77, 80, 82, 83, 93, 97
Scheid, D. E., 122
Schele, L., 194
Schell, L. M., 508
Schendel, D., 502
Schensul, J., 417
Schensul, S., 417
Schentag, C., 432, 449
Scheps, S., 142, 152
Schiffman, H. F., 562, 564, 565
Schildkrout, E., 261
Schlaut, J., 353
Schlebusch, L., 503
Schlegel, S., 491, 492
Schmidtke, J., 362
Schmink, M., 53
Schneck, G., 320, 335
Schneider, H. K., 382, 384, 389, 390
Schoener, T. W., 431, 441
Schoeninger, M., 452
Schoffeleers, M., 299
Schofield, S., 492, 497
Scholl, T. O., 485, 488, 490, 495, 496
Schranze, D., 430
Schrock, M. M., 230
Schull, W. T., 430
Schulman, S., 234
Schulter-Ellis, F. P., 430
Schultz, A. H., 431, 454
Schulze, W., 204
Schumacher, J. N., 64
Schurch, B., 486
Schutz, A., 160, 162
Schwab, W. B., 252
Schwabe, C., 503
Schwarcz, H. P., 544, 547
Schweger, C. E., 547
Schweizer, T., 152
Schwidetzky, I., 430
Sciulli, P. W., 445, 447
Scott, A., 204
Scott, E., 258
Scott, E. C., 508
Scott, R., 187, 247
Scott, W. H., 60, 63
Scotton, C., 568
Scribner, S., 163
Scrimshaw, N. S., 485, 500
Scrimshaw, S. C. M., 510
Scudder, T., 261

Sears, E. R., 127
Sebenius, J., 201, 202
Seddon, D., 260
Segall, M. E., 233
Segebarth-Orban, R., 430
Scibt, U., 431
Selander, R. K., 431, 434, 441
Selat, N., 58
Selby, H. A., 480
Seligman, C. G., 275, 276, 290
Seligsohn, D., 321
Sellers, S. G., 499
Selmer-Olsen, R., 445, 447
Seneviratne, H. L., 303, 304
Senghor, L. S., 253
Serizawa, C., 537
Serjeantson, S. W., 352, 500
Serratrice, C., 336
Severson, G., 502
Sgaramella-Zonta, L., 349, 353, 356
Shainkin, R., 492
Shaklee, W. E., 431
Shankara Bhat, D. N., 564
SHANKLIN, E., 375-403; 382, 391, 399
Shanmugam Pillai, M., 563-65
Shao, X., 432
Shapira, J. F., 363
Shapiro, M. C., 562, 564, 565
Shapley, H., 123
Shaw, M., 195
Shea, B. T., 324, 431
Sheffer, M. L., 495
Shepard, A. O., 78, 82
Shephard, R., 151
Sheridan, M., 55
Sherman, P. W., 434, 437
Shettey, P., 492
Shields, D., 504
Shiloh, A., 225
Shimkin, D. B., 225
Shine, R., 431, 434
Shlemon, R. J., 546, 547
Short, J., 146
Shows, T. B., 359, 361
Shrank, B., 457
Shutler, R., 534
Shuy, R., 559
Sibley, C. G., 360, 457
Sidahmed, A. E., 391
Siegel, A., 207
Siegel, S., 138, 141
Siew, N., 206
Sillen, A., 449
Silverstein, M., 57
Simmons, C., 203, 206
Simmons, E., 492
Simonen, M. S., 486
Simons, E. L., 328, 451, 455
Simoons, F. J., 387
Simopoulos, A. P., 486
Simpson, G. G., 123-25

Simpson, J. R., 391
Simpson, R. D., 544-46
Singer, C., 124
Singer, C. A., 546
Singer, P., 376
Singh, J., 501
Singh, M., 501
Singh, R. S., 359
Sinha, S. P., 431
Sinisterra, L., 499
Sinnett, P. F., 501
Skalník, P., 274, 278, 281, 286, 301
Skinner, E. P., 254
Skocpol, T., 65, 67
Skolnick, M., 361
Skolnick, M. H., 353, 354, 357
Skooglund, C. C., 221
Slatkin, M., 441, 442, 449, 456
Slaughter, C., 207
Sloan, F., 509
Slocum, M. C., 187
Slota, P. J. Jr., 541
Smailus, O., 187
Small, C., 57
Smith, A. D., 60
Smith, A. T., 413
Smith, B. H., 323
Smith, C. A., 64, 138
Smith, C. A. B., 343
Smith, D., 201, 204
Smith, D. G., 509
Smith, F. H., 451
Smith, H. I., 5
Smith, J. M., 125
Smith, J. Z., 306
Smith, M. F., 253
Smith, M. G., 247, 248, 258, 388
Smith, P., 280, 449
Smith, P. C., 507
Smith, R. J., 322, 328, 329
Smith, T., 149
Smith, V., 497
Smith-Stark, T., 192
Smith-Stark, T. C., 187, 190, 191
Smouse, P. E., 353
Smuts, B. B., 436, 439, 440
Sneath, P., 149
Snodgrass, D., 204
Snodgrass, R. M., 3
Snow, C. T., 227, 230, 231
Snow, T., 122
Snyder, W. A., 417
Soebardi, S., 63
Sohier, R., 228
Sokal, R., 149
Sokal, R. R., 350, 352
Solheim, W. G. II, 77
Sollod, A. E., 390
Solow, R., 204
Sonenscher, M., 64

Sorokin, P. A., 115, 123
Southall, A. W., 252, 290
Southern, E. M., 361
Southwold, M., 300
Sow, A. M., 500
Soyinka, W., 255
Spargo, R. M., 502
Specht, J., 77, 83, 84
Spector, R. E., 222
Speiser, E. A., 107, 110, 114, 115
Spencer, P., 138, 389, 396
Spencer, T., 492
Spicer, E. H., 412
Spiegel, A., 206, 207
Spielberg Benítez, J., 414-17
Spielman, R. S., 353, 361
Spinner, N. B., 354
Spooner, B., 384, 505
Spriggs, M., 80
SPUHLER, J. N., 103-33; 352
Sridhar, K. K., 416
Srikantia, S. G., 490
Srinivisan, T., 497
St. Clair, R., 560
Stamps, J. A., 431
Stanford, D., 532, 548
Stangl, A., 457
Staniland, M., 301
Stanislawski, B., 82-84
Stanislawski, M. B., 82-84, 85, 87, 89, 91
Stark, B., 80, 81
Starkey, D., 279
Starr, P., 220, 232, 235
Stebbins, G. L., 123-27
Steel, F. L. D., 430
Steele, D. G., 430
Steele, H., 204
Steen-McIntyre, V., 542, 543
Steffensen, M., 504
Stein, H. F., 233
Stein, L., 234
Stein, Z., 508
Steinberg, A. G., 343
Stenning, D. J., 246, 390
Stephens, J. C., 349
Stephenson, D. D., 234
Stepick, A., 151
Stepick, C. D., 480
Stern, J., 202
Stern, J. T., 456
Stevens, A., 571
Stevens, S., 138
Steward, J. H., 123, 382-85
Stewart, S. O., 187
Stewart, T. D., 430
Stier, F., 145, 261
Stiglitz, J., 200, 204
Stiles, D., 78
Stini, W. A., 429, 431, 489
Stivens, M., 62
Stloukal, M., 430

Stocks, J., 208
Stokes, C. S., 145, 146
Stokes, E. T., 63
Stoller, M. L., 413
Stolmaker, C., 79, 81, 93, 95
Stone, L., 167
Stone, T., 207
Storer, R. W., 431, 434
Storey, J., 500
Stow, S. H., 18
Strauss, D., 147
Streefland, P., 504
Strickland, D. A., 293
Strong, A. H., 106
Strong, F., 492
Strong, J., 502
Strum, S. C., 441
Stuckenrath, R., 535
Stucki, L., 207
Sudarkasa, N., 260, 263
Suescun, J., 499
Sukhatme, P., 492
Sukkar, M. Y., 481
Sullivan, G. M., 391
Sullivan, L. L., 120
Sullivan, R., 228
Sunderland, E., 351
Super, C. M., 499
Suret-Canale, J., 257
Susanne, C., 485
Suskind, R. M., 486
Susman, R. L., 316, 431, 439, 440, 456
Susser, M., 508
Swadesh, F. L., 408, 413
Swedlund, A., 138
Swedlund, A. C., 505
Sweeney, J., 204
Sweet, L. E., 385
Swift, J., 261
Szalay, F. S., 315, 316, 332
Szathmary, E. J. E., 352

T

Tai, H. H., 64, 68
Tajima, F., 345, 348, 349, 360-62
Takahata, Y., 441
Tambiah, S. J., 285-87, 303, 304, 377, 392
Tan, J.-P., 509
Tanabe, S., 64
Tancredi, L., 503
Tandeter, E., 206, 210
Tannen, D., 163, 561, 576
Tanner, J. M., 478, 480-83, 487, 507
Tantiwongse, P., 480, 481
Tanzer, M., 202, 204, 205, 207
Tardits, C., 264
Tareke, G., 64
Tateno, Y., 345, 348, 349

Taussig, M., 209, 497
Taylor, B. J., 359
Taylor, C., 229, 485, 500
Taylor, C. E., 509
Taylor, H., 493, 508
Taylor, H. L., 492
Taylor, J. V., 430
Taylor, M. F., 119, 121
Taylor, R. E., 11, 534, 541
Tcherkézoff, S., 283
Teaford, M. F., 335, 336
Tedlock, D., 195
Teitelbaum, J., 492
Teitelbaum, M., 486, 505, 506, 508, 511
Teleki, G., 441
Temerin, L. A., 329
Templeton, A. R., 348, 363
Tenaza, R. P., 436, 437
Terray, E., 253, 257, 259
Tesh, R., 501
Testerink, J., 497
Thaxton, R., 64, 67
Thibault, C., 536, 540
Thieme, F. P., 430
Thissen, D., 479, 483
Thoburn, J., 203
Thomas, A., 500
Thomas, D., 135-38, 140-42, 149, 152
Thomas, J., 144-46
Thomas, L., 199
Thomas, R. B., 493, 501
Thompson, A. R., 352
Thompson, B., 485, 501
Thompson, E. A., 344, 348, 352
Thompson, G. W., 452
Thompson, J. A., 225
Thompson, J. E. S., 193
Thompson, R. H., 78, 80, 81, 84, 93
Thompson, W. S., 505
Thomsen, S., 445, 447
Thomson, A. M., 485, 493, 501
Thomson, C., 228, 489
Thomson, D. W., 246
Thomson, G., 354
Thomson, W. A. R., 503
Thornhill, R., 431
Thornton, R., 275
Thorson, R. M., 548
Tilden, V. P., 228
Tillich, P., 115
Tilly, C., 65
Tilly, L. A., 65
Tilson, R. L., 436, 437
Titcomb, M., 484
Tjon Sie Fat, F. E., 136
Tobias, P. V., 431, 432
Tobien, H., 451
Todd, A. D., 179
Torjesen, E., 480

AUTHOR INDEX 599

Torres-Gil, F., 415, 418
Torry, W. I., 391, 492
Toth, A., 7
Townsend, G. C., 430
Townsend, J. W., 489
Townsend, P. G., 195
Toyokura, Y., 500
Trail, J. C. M., 391
Tremaine, J. D., 536
Tribe, K., 51
Trigger, R. B., 529
Trinkaus, E., 451, 457, 460
TRIPP-REIMER, T., 219-41; 222, 223, 226-28, 230
Trivers, R. L., 434, 435
Trudgill, P., 559, 561, 562, 569
Trueba, H. T., 415, 416
Truex, G., 149
Trussell, J., 508
Truswell, A. S., 432
Tschopik, H. Jr., 77, 81, 92, 95
Tsubaki, T., 500
Tsujimura, N., 25
Tuck, J., 64
Turner, C. G. II, 78
Turner, C. G. III, 538
Turton, A., 52, 55-57, 64, 65
Tutuola, A., 255
Tyler, S. A., 394, 561
Tylor, E. B., 376

U

Ubelaker, D. H., 430
Uchendu, V. C., 260
Ucko, P. J., 377, 380
Uhl, J., 228
Uhlenbeck, E. M., 571
Ullom, J. A., 228
Ulrich, M., 187
Ulrich, R., 187
Underwood, B. A., 494, 497, 499, 509
Urdaneta, M. L., 228, 233, 414-16
Uriarte, M., 207
Ussher, J., 117

V

Vaca, N. C., 406
Vahlquist, B., 486, 488
Vaidyanathan, A., 387
Valadez, F., 411, 413
Valadez, S., 417
Valastro, S., 537, 550
Valentine, J. W., 123-25, 127
Valeri, V., 287
Vallejo, C., 416
Valverde, V., 490, 500
Van Alstine, W. I., 430
Van den Berghe, P. L., 283
Van der Leeuw, S. E., 97

van de Walle, E., 505
van Dijk, C., 63
Vandivort, R. E., 228
VanDyke, W., 492
Van Gerven, D. P., 430, 451
Van Helten, J., 203
Vanita, R., 61
Van Ness, C. M., 413
Van Ness, J. R., 408, 413
Van Onselen, C., 203, 206-8
Vansina, J., 290, 292, 294
Van Velsen, J., 206
van Wering, E. R., 484
van Willigen, J., 504
Varela, A. G., 537, 550
Varon, B., 203
Vaughan, J. H., 283, 284
Vayda, A. P., 384, 385
Vélez-Ibáñez, C., 417, 418
Vélez-Ibáñez, C. G., 414-17
Velez-Naur, M., 391
Vellinga, M., 203, 206, 207
Venema, A., 432, 449
Verdon, M., 264
Verhoeyen, M., 128
Vernon, R., 201, 204
Vidal, C., 263
Vierra, R. K., 535
Vigil, J. D., 415, 417
Viteri, F., 493
Vlček, E., 430
Voda, A., 414
Volcan, G., 501
von Glascoe, C., 149
von Mering, O., 221
Voyatzoglou, M., 79

W

Waane, S., 79, 81-85, 87
Wade, M. J., 430, 433, 441
Wade, N., 120
Wade, T. D., 434
Wagner, B., 488
Wagner, M., 499
Wahlman, M., 77, 80, 82, 84
Wainer, H., 479, 483
Waitzkin, H., 179
Wald, B., 569
Wald, L. D., 221
Walde, T., 202
Waldemann, E., 492
Wale, O., 495
Walker, A. C., 336, 451
Walker, A. R. P., 502
Walker, B. F., 502
Walker, P. L., 335
Wallace, B. J., 385
Wallace, D. C., 364
Wallace, J. A., 330
Wallace, S., 568-70, 573
Wallerstein, I., 261
Walsh, A., 502

Walter, E. V., 277
Walthall, J., 18
Walzer, M., 278, 279, 294, 295, 300, 302
Wan, F., 204
Wang, A., 364
Wang, J., 228, 233
Ward, R. H., 352, 355
Ward, S. C., 451, 456
Warkentin, V., 187
Warren, K. B., 62
Warren, M. P., 508
Wartenberg, D. E., 350
Washburn, S. L., 337, 430, 431, 451, 452
Waterlow, J. C., 478, 487, 492
Watkins, L. O., 502
Watkins, S., 508
Watson, J. D., 125
Watson, P. J., 78
Watson, W., 206, 207
Watt, I., 165
Watts, E. S., 477
Watts, M., 260
Way, A., 483
Weaver, T., 413, 414, 416, 417
Webb, G., 501
Webb, M., 228
Weber, M., 170
Weber, R. L., 538
Weeks, J. R., 415, 416, 418
Weidman, H. H., 225, 227
Weigand, P. C., 79, 83-85, 89, 91
Weigle, M., 413
Weil, J., 137
Weinberg, S. L., 122
Weiner, F., 221
Weiner, J. S., 351, 476, 477
Weinreich, U., 558
Weinstein, W., 277
Weir, B. S., 346
Weiskel, T. C., 64
Weiss, K. M., 443, 451, 505
Weitzman, M., 204
Welbourn, A., 88
Weller, R., 65
Weller, S., 151
Wellhausen, J., 109, 113
Wells, L., 201, 204
Wells, M. J., 406, 415, 416, 418
Welon, Z., 485
Wenger, J. R., 561, 573, 574
Werbner, R. P., 252
Werner, D., 509
Werner, J. S., 64
Wessing, R., 571
West, F. H., 533
West, J. K., 111
West, M. M., 438
West, T., 208
Westen, D., 387

Westerman, G. E. G., 439, 451
Wettenhall, N., 508
Wexler, N. S., 359
Whalin, W. T., 187
Whallon, R. Jr., 78, 83
Wheatley, P., 252
Wheeler, E. F., 492
Wheeler, G., 135
White, A. D., 118, 128
White, D., 136
White, D. R., 443
White, G., 149, 151, 152
White, L. A., 123
White, R. L., 361, 364
White, T. D., 324, 451, 456, 458, 460
Whitecotton, J. W., 413
Whiteford, L. M., 413-15
Whitehead, A. N., 110
Whitehead, L., 207
Whiteley, W. H., 573
Whitford, P., 500
Whiting, B. B., 383
Whiting, J. W. M., 383
Whittaker, E., 229
Whitten, A. J., 318
Whitten, N., 58, 209
Whyte, H. M., 501
Wickler, W., 431
Wiesenfeld, S., 500
Wijsman, E. M., 351, 352, 355, 365
Wilks, I., 252, 257, 291
Willeford, W., 295
Williams, D., 139
Williams, G., 258
Williams, M. A., 221, 228, 229, 233, 234
Williams, M. C., 64
Williams, R. C., 109-11
Williams, T. R., 221, 229, 234
Willis, R., 291, 379
Wills, W., 500
Wilmore, J. H., 508
Wilmsen, E., 364, 492
Wilson, A. B., 486
Wilson, A. C., 348, 363, 364
Wilson, F., 206, 207
Wilson, G., 206, 207, 289, 290, 300
Wilson, M., 206

Wilson, M. H., 289, 295
Wilson, R. T., 391
Winans, E., 144
Winikoff, B., 495
Winograd, T., 162
Winter, E. H., 389, 390
Winter, G., 260
Winzeler, R. L., 286
Wipper, A., 64
Wish, M., 151
Witkowski, S. R., 191
Wittgenstein, L., 305, 307
Wobst, H. M., 88
Wolanski, N., 431
Wolf, E., 227
Wolfe, L. D., 431, 432, 438, 442, 443
Wolff, J. U., 562, 571-73
Wolfgang, K., 390
Wolfram, W., 559
Wolpe, H., 206, 208
WOLPOFF, M. H., 429-73; 324, 327, 336, 430, 431, 439, 442, 450-52, 456, 458, 460
Woo, S. L. C., 359
Wood, B. A., 323, 431, 452
Wood, G., 273
Wood, J., 64, 149
Wood, J. E. Jr., 104, 118
Woolbright, L. L., 431
Woolfe, J., 492
Woolgar, S., 183
Woolley, C. L., 116
Workman, P. L., 351, 352, 356
Wormington, H. M., 537
Worsley, D., 492
Wrangham, R. W., 317, 436, 439, 440
Wrensch, M. R., 354
Wright, B., 204
Wright, G. S., 18
Wright, H., 116
Wright, H. E. Jr., 530, 533, 535
Wright, P. G., 416
Wright, S., 123-25, 145, 353, 356, 357
Wright, T., 206
Wrigley, E., 205
Wu, R., 451, 539

Wurm, S., 568
Wurtman, J., 486
Wurtman, R., 486
Wyman, A., 364
Wyndham, C. H., 502
Wyon, J., 510
Wysong, R. L., 109

X

Xu, Q., 451

Y

Yai, E., 493
Yamaguchi, M., 283
Yanez, L., 490
Yap, E.-H., 501
Yarbrough, C., 144, 478, 481-85, 487, 488, 493-95, 500
Yarbrough, S., 500
Yee, S., 343, 344, 346, 351
Yip, R., 480
Yost, J., 501
Young, A. A., 225
Young, D. E., 532, 548
Young, J. C., 503
Young, K., 62
Young, M. W., 275, 276
Young, S. B., 547
Yunis, J. J., 360

Z

Zapata, F., 207
Zawawi, W., 58
Zei, G., 355, 365
Zeilin, M., 207
Zeller, R., 139, 142, 143
Zerfas, A. J., 487
Zetterberg, P., 104, 109, 110
Zhang, Z., 432
Zigas, V., 500
Zihlman, A. L., 431, 451, 452, 458
Zink, D., 202
Zorn, S., 204
Zurbuchen, M. S., 571
Zurndorfer, H. T., 64
Zussman, M. F., 55
Zvelebil, K., 565
Zwell, M., 451

SUBJECT INDEX

A

Abortion
  in Chicano studies, 415
  and population control, 511-12
Absolute rule
  components of, 276
  and divine kingship, 275
Abstract algebra
  and anthropology, 136
Accession rite
  and Fijian kingship, 287
Accumulation
  and wealth
    Asante ideas of, 291
Acephalous politics
  in late colonial period
    West Africa, 244
Adam
  origin of word, 114
Adam and Eve
  as a creation
    of the mind of God, 108
Adaptation
  items of the diet
    and structure of the dentition, 337
Adaptation
  and sexual dimorphism, 461
Adaptation
  and small body size, 490
Administration
  of the sacred
    divine kingship, 278
Adolescence
  growth during
    double logistic model, 483
  placenta of
    as inadequate for fetal growth, 494
  and sexual dimorphism, 431
Aegyptopithecus zeuxis
  and sexual dimorphism, 451
Aegyptopithecus
  and mandibular corpus height dimorphism, 453
Aerobic capacity
  and patterns of fatness, 502
Affirmative action
  in the Reagan era, 405-6
Agglutinative language
  and honorific systems, 561
Aging
  Chicano studies, 415
Agrarian peoples
  see Peasant ideologies
    in the Third World

Agricultural development
  failures of
    in West Africa, 258
  and nutrition, 496
  in West Africa, 258
Agriculture
  and bioanthropology in developing countries, 476
  and the Hawaiian God Lono, 287
  innovation
    in Mexico, 150
  origins of, 380
  and pottery production, 79
  precapitalist
    and the mining industry, 209
  and sexual dimorphism, 432
Akan civil servants
  among matrilineal marriage, 260
Alleles
  and HLA loci
    genetic distance studies, 358
  presence or absence of
    genetic distance studies, 347
Allometry
  and sexual dimorphism, 439
  teeth and diet
    in *Australopithecus*, 321
Allopolyploidy
  species formation by, 127
Alluvial mud
  and the biblical flood, 116
Amaranth
  contribution to human diet, 491
Ambiguity
  and oral language, 169
America
  see Early man in the Americas
American Archaeology
  1928-1985, 1-23
American Bottom Mississippi
  flood plain, 16
American fundamentalist movement
  and scientific creationism, 106
American livestock production
  energy costs, 387
Americans
  Asian ancestry of, 537
Amin
  collection on migration, 259
Amino acids
  and human genetic distance

studies, 363
  and organic evolution, 125
Analytical holistic ethnography
  and domesticated animal studies, 387
Anaphor
  and NP-trace, 28
  and PRO, 44
Anaphora phenomena
  in modular grammar, 35-8
  various hypotheses, 25
Anaphoric control
  in lexical functional grammar, 43
Anaphoric functions
  in discourse, 176
Anatomical specialization
  and behavior of extinct animals, 315
Ancestors
  annual rites honoring, 289
Anglophone writings
  in West Africa, 243
Angular transformation distances
  genetic distance measures, 344
Animal studies
  domesticated
    sustenance and symbol, 375-403
Animal temperament
  as a factor in human settlement patterns, 389
Animal-human interaction
  and how societies operate, 377
Animals
  as symbols, 392-8
  see also Animal studies
Antecedent
  and PRO
    in grammatical theory, 45
Anthropoid primates
  sexual dimorphism, 459
Anthropological theory
  nursing constructs for, 229-30
Antibiotics
  fed to livestock, 375
Anticolonialism
  prophet-inspired
    and rebellion, 66-7
Antigens
  and genetic distance studies, 357
Antimodernism
  in peasant consciousness, 62-9
Antecedents
  and binding theory, 29
Ape models

601

602 SUBJECT INDEX

Australopithecine diets, 322-36
Apes
  living
    dietary behavior, 316-18
    taxonomic groups of
      figure, 317
Apostasy
  and creationism, 110
Applied disciplines
  and nursing theory, 224
Archaeology
  an individual's participation in, 1-23
  and pottery, 77
Artarhasis
  and Babylonian version of the great flood, 116
Artifact
  and ageofact
    distinction between, 546
  Old Crow specimens, 548
Asante political history
  and money, 291
Asia
  and peasant ideology, 69
Assassinations
  and divine kingship, 294
Association
  measures of, 141
Assumptions
  in modular grammar theory, 36
Astronomy
  and evolution, 124
Athabaskans
  as immigrants from Siberia, 538
Audience
  and speaking, 164
Auringnacoid
  emergence of, 536
Australopithecine diets
  ape models, 322-36
Australopithecus
  and sexual dimorphism, 430
  see also Teeth and diet
Authority
  medical
    and knowledge base, 170
Autocorrelation
  and genetic relationships, 350
Automation
  and reading and writing, 166

B

Bacteria
  antibiotic resistant, 375
Balanced treatment acts
  creationist-evolutionist controversy, 121

Bali
  language level systems, 571
Balinese *negara*
  and divine kingship, 286
Barnes test
  and study of Calico flints, 545
Bayange (people of secrets)
  and funeral duties, 284
Behavior
  of extinct animals
    reconstruction of, 315
  linguistic
    and language status, 559
  scientific analysis of
    divine kingship, 275
Belief systems
  in evolution
    surveys on, 105
  in West Africa, 253
Bible
  as literal truth, 109-10
  study courses
    in public schools, 121
Bible belt
  as a region, 106
Binding Theory
  principles of, 29
Bioanthropology
  in developing countries, 475-528
Biology
  and evolution, 122-4
Biomedicine
  as human response
    and nursing intervention, 220
Birds
  sexual dimorphism, 435
Birth
  human response to
    and nursing intervention, 220
Birth attendants
  upgrading the skills of
    Third World, 504
Birth control
  supply/demand for children, 506
Birth weights
  seasonal effects associated with, 485
Birthrates
  and levels of fertility, 505
Bisexuality
  and the creation, 113
Bivariate analyses
  independence and association, 139
Bivariate statistics
  and research methods, 136
Black stool
  rites of
    Akan kingdom of

Akuapem, 302
Blacks
  nursing care for
    cultural aspects of, 221
Blood groups
  and genetic distance studies, 357
Bodily dissociation
  as central ritual adjunct, 395
Body height
  percent sexual dimorphisms
    figure, 448
Body mass
  and composition
    male/female, 482
Body size
  and length of incisor edge, 319
  and sexual dimorphism, 439
Body weight
  sexual dimorphism in
    figure, 436
  and teeth and diet, 323
Body-size scaling
  and Australopithecine diets, 322-7
Bone formation
  diets high in oxalates or lathyrogens
    in developing countries, 492
Bonobos
  diet of, 317
Bororo tribe
  and ritual attitudes toward animals, 393
Boxer Rebellion
  and peasant ideology, 64
Breakage
  ceramics lifespan, 89
Breast feeding
  and health risks for young children, 494-5
Bride-price
  and domesticated animal studies, 389
British social anthropology
  in West Africa, 245
Buddhism
  and society and kingship, 304
Bureau of Land Management
  and the Calico site, 544
Bureaucracy
  and divine kingship, 280
  and doctors' authority, 170
Bureaucratization
  African monarch's use of, 277
Burial
  of the Burundi king Mwazi Gisabo, 284
Burial practices
  Mayan, 2
Burro

SUBJECT INDEX 603

and human animal character
  traits, 394
Busia
  as an Ashanti aristocrat, 248

C

Canaanite myths
  and the biblical flood, 116
Calico
  and evidence of early man,
    544-7
Caloric intake
  and growth and development
    in children, 484
Caloric supplementation
  and birth weight, 494
Cancer
  see Primary hepatic carcinoma
Canine dimorphism
  dentition, 457
Cannibalism
  virus transmitted by, 500
Capital investments
  in mining ventures, 203
Capitalism
  and women's liberation, 263
Capitalist production
  and West Africa, 244
Capitalist transformation
  and the peasantry, 52
Caring
  multicultural environment
    and nursing, 230
Cash
  and ceramics use, 90
Cash cropping
  nutritional effects of, 497
Caste
  and education
    in India, 565
Caste system
  and father/son occupation, 147
  and linguistics, 562
Cattle
  meanings assigned to
    in East African societies,
      379
  as respositories of value, 389
Cattle-keeping
  energetics of, 387
Caulapan
  lower artifact-bearing deposits, 543
Causation models
  and sexual dimorphism, 432-51
Cell-mediated immune responses
  and nutritional status
    in PEM children, 490
Censorship
  and textbooks, 122
Ceramic complexes

Ohio Valley Area, 5
Ceramic Ethnoarchaeology, 77-102
  division of labor, 77
Ceramics
  Cape Denbigh, 12
Cereal grains
  and *Australopithecus robustus*,
    316
Change
  cumulative
    and evolution, 124
  as theme in bioanthropological
    reasearch, 476
Charles Darwin
  animal studies, 375
Charles I
  execution of
    and divine kingship, 278
Cheek-tooth area
  and body-size scaling
    Australopithecine diets,
      322-7
Chemical contamination
  in the Third World, 504
Chewing
  phases of the power stroke in,
    319
Chi-square
  in statistical analyses, 140
Chi-square distances
  genetic distance measures,
    343-4
Chicano studies
  1970-1984, 405-27
Chickens
  and domesticated animal studies, 386
  as the largest group of
    domesticated animals,
      379
Chiefdoms
  in West Africa, 246
Child dependency
  female specialization, 450
Child development
  and nutritional intervention
    in less developed countries,
      498
Child morbidity
  and nutritional status, 496
Child survival
  and overall levels of natural
    fertility, 509
Child-rearing practices
  and domesticated animal studies, 383
Childbirth
  in Chicano studies, 415
  cultural context of, 233
Childhood malnutrition
  nutritional status of the
    mother, 493

studies of infant diets, 495
Children
  childhood mortality, 509
  demographic literature
    on fertility determinants,
      506
  in the developing countries,
    477
  and genetic drift, 356
  learning
    literacy, 160-1
    reading to, 166
Chile
  government of Popular Unity,
    62
Chilean copper industry
  nationalization of, 201
Chimpanzees
  and division of labor, 461
China
  peasant rebellions, 64
Chinese Communist Party
  and peasant ideology, 64
Chloroquine
  resistance of *plasmodium* to,
    500
Cholan-Tzeltalan
  as Mayan language, 188
Chomsky's principles
  modular grammar theory, 39
Choukoutien
  and *Homo erectus*, 539
Christ
  establishment of birthdate,
    118
Christian ideals
  of progress, 274
Christian religious attitudes
  Islamic attitudes
    and divine kingship, 277
Christianity
  and collective consciousness
    Phillipines, 68
Chromosomes
  and experimental recreation,
    127
Church
  and state
    separation of, 103
Civil war
  African monarchies prone to,
    276
Clan head
  and divine kingship, 290
Clanship
  dynamics of
    Gold Coast's interior, 245
Class
  as cross-cutting social variable, 568
Class affiliation
  and speech, 557-8
Class consciousness

604 SUBJECT INDEX

Marxist approaches to, 51-3
and peasant ideology, 50
Class interests
  vs. economic
    peasant ideology, 54
Class structure
  and language, 559
Classical kinship theory
  and the Abutia Ewe of Southern Ghana, 264
Clay
  and the creation myths, 114
Clay bodies
  and availability of materials, 78-83
Clay storage
  and preparation, 80
Client belief systems
  and nursing, 227
Climatic crises
  and animal domestication, 380
Clovis
  as first human population
    in the Western Hemisphere, 533
  primacy of
    among New World
      archaeological cultures, 531
  projectile points of, 530
Club of Rome
  rates of population growth, 205
Cluster analysis
  in data with variables, 148
Coancestry coefficient
  short-term evolution
    genetic distance measures, 346-7
Cognates
  in the Mayan language, 191-2
Cognitive development
  height and weight as indicators of, 489
Cognitive processes
  and oral and written communication, 163
Coherence
  definition of
    in grammatical theory, 42-44
Coital frequency
  and malnutrition, 508
Cole
  Fay-Cooper
    ethnologist, 2
Collections
  West African, 258
Colonial rule
  in Vietnam, 54
Colonization
  gene flow after
    and human genetic distance

studies, 353
Commerical agriculture
  and household acquisition of food, 498
Common law
  and theistic concepts, 119
Communalism
  and peasant ideology, 68
Communication
  intercaste media of
    in India, 564
  in the medical setting, 171-82
  physician/patient, 173
  see also Text and discourse
Communism
  and peasant ideology, 54
Communities
  Chicano, 411
Community land grants
  Chicano studies, 413
Competition
  and interaction among tribal groups, 87
Completeness
  definition of
    in grammatical theory, 42-4
Comprehension
  in oral/written exchanges, 172
Computer technology
  and human genetic distance studies, 365
Configurational structure
  in Lexical functional grammar, 41-46
Confounding variables
  controlling for, 142-7
Conjunction reduction
  in Mayan grammar, 194
Consensual kinship systems
  in West Africa, 258
Constitutionalism
  historical origins of, 119
Consumption patterns
  in the household
    and commercial agriculture, 497
Contact and diffusion
  in the Mayan language, 191-2
Contingency tables
  in social science publications, 139
Contraception use
  and population control, 511-12
Contradiction
  and oral language, 169
Cooking habits
  and labor of women, 498
Cooperatives
  potters, 94
Copper and silver
  Middle Woodland, 18
Copula deletion

and language status, 558
Coreference
  various hypotheses, 25
Corn production
  statistical analysis, 150
Coronary heart disease
  in Samoa, 502
Coronation ceremony
  Ganda, 287
Corporate groups
  and ceramics production, 97
Corpus dimorphism
  H. habilis, 460
Cosatisfaction Principle
  in Modular grammar theory, 36
Cosmic matter
  Genesis creation story, 114
Cosmogony
  and the origin of the universe, 108
Costumes
  indigenous significance of
    and divine kingship, 281
Coyote
  and illegal immigrants, 394
Craft occupations
  and E. Goody's work on Gonja, 264
Craft specialization
  and ceramics, 78
Creation
  date of, 116
  stories
    literal interpretation of, 113-5
Creative writing
  West African, 245-5
Credit relationships
  and ceramics production, 97
Cross-classifications
  in log linear analyses models, 147
Cross-cultural comparisons
  and use of statistics, 135
Cross-cultural nursing
  research, 228
Crowding
  and nutritional ecosystems, 487
Cult
  and divine kingship, 290
  focused on royal tombs
    Africa, 297
Cultural artefacts
  nationalism as, 60
Cultural assumptions
  and speech performance, 576
Cultural behavior
  ceramics as transformative tool, 88
Cultural ecology
  and domesticated animal

SUBJECT INDEX 605

studies, 381
Cultural inferiority complex
  Chicano studies, 410
Cultural life
  in Chicano studies, 417
Cultural system
  and language style, 575-7
Cultural traditions
  and social change, 70
Culture
  and literacy, 160-1
  and nursing, 220-1
Cuneiform
  Babylonian
    and the flood story, 116
Curing practices
  traditional
    and the Chicano community, 414
Cyanogenetic glycosides
  in developing countries, 492

D

D-structures
  and binding theory in grammar, 31
Data collection
  multivariate, 141-52
Data reduction
  in descriptive statistics, 147-8
  methods, 151
Data redundancy
  and factor analysis, 149
Death
  as human response
    and nursing intervention, 220
  and lunar calendar transitions, 281
Decision making
  and patient/physician communication, 174
Declarative
  inferences in
    and knowledge, 162
Decolonization
  in West Africa, 243
Deictic functions
  in discourse, 176
Demic diffusion
  and genetic distance studies, 352
Demographic factors
  and development of PEM in children, 495
Demographic transition theory
  and research on population issues, 505
Demography
  and mining ventures, 205
Dental
  percent sexual dimorphism

figure, 448
Dental anatomy
  of humans and living apes
    figure, 324
Dentition
  and *A. afarensis* as dimorphic for, 459
  dimorphism in, 430
Descent concept
  and the Abutia Ewe of Southern Ghana, 264
Developing countries
  studies of health in, 499-501
  see also Bioanthropology in developing countries
Development
  of children
    as indicators of health/nutritional status, 477-86
  as human response
    and nursing intervention, 220
  study of origin and evolution, 123
Development production
  in mining ventures, 201-5
Diagnosis
  nursing
    and interventions, 227
Diagnostic interview
  comparison of oral and written versions, 172
Dialect geography
  and language style, 570
Diarrheal disease
  and reduced growth, 485
  and malnutrition
    in children, 500
Dicrostonyx
  recovered in North America, 549
Diet
  and divine kingship, 289
  and sexual dimorphism, 438
  see also Teeth and diet
Diet preference
  and enamel thickness, 329
Dietary change
  and children in the developing world, 477
  in the developing world, 493
Dietary grit
  and australopithecines, 328
Dietary toxins
  and children's development, 492
Diets
  traditional
    factors influencing nutritional status, 491
Dimorphism
  see Men
  see also Sexual dimorphism

see also Women
Disadvantaged environments
  and small body size, 484
Discount rate
  computation of
    in mining ventures, 201
Discourse
  see Text
Discriminant analysis
  genetic distance studies, 357
Discriminant analysis
  in multiple regression, 144
Disease
  perceived causes of, 503
  and sexual dimorphism, 429
Disease ecology
  in developing countries, 499-501
Disease vectors
  bioanthropology in developing countries, 476
Disjoint reference
  and binding theory, 32
  and Chomsky's Binding Condition, 40
  various hypotheses, 25
Disjoint Reference Principle
  in Modular grammar theory, 36
Disjointness
  in grammar theory, 41
Disposal
  of ceramic vessels, 89
Dissent
  expression of
    the king's many bodies, 294
Distribution system
  ceramic, 82
Divine Kingship
  issues in, 273-313
  see also Kingship
Divine spirit
  Genesis creation story, 114
Division of labor
  and ceramics, 94
Division of labor
  and sexual dimorphism, 441-9
DNA
  and *Escherichia coli*
    genetic distance studies, 361
  mitochondrial
    and genetic distance studies, 348
    and organic evolution, 125
  nuclear polymorphisms
    and genetic distance studies, 359
DNA level
  and sexual dimorphism, 457
DNA polymorphisms
  human genetic distance

studies, 353
   on the Y chromosome
      and genetic distance studies, 364-5
DNA sequences
   analysis of
      in genetic distance, 360
DNA-DNA hybridization
   and genetic distance studies, 360-2
Domestic groups
   in West Africa, 245
Domestic labor
   and enslavement, 293
Domesticated animal studies
   see Animal studies
Domestication
   and literacy, 161
Domination
   as authoritarian power of command, 170
   and peasant ideology, 55
   racial
      and Chicano studies, 407
   and the realization of class consciousness, 57
Drift effects
   and human genetic distance studies, 354
Dualism
   theory of economic development
      West Africa, 250
Dwarf cattle
   collection of the genealogies of, 398
Dynamic models
   of mining, 204-5

E

Early man
   in the Americas, 529-55
Earth
   and the creation myths, 114
   destruction of the, 115
   planetary age, 117
Earthcult shrines
   in West Africa, 245
Earthquake
   and studies of
      continuum of body size in, 479
East Africa
   interlacustrine kingdoms, 275
Ecological anthropology
   and function of animals, 378
Ecological competition
   between the sexes, 441
Ecology
   ceramic, 78
   and impact of mining, 207-8
   as a subfield of social anthropology, 388-90
Economic development
   in West Africa, 243, 250-1
Economic differentiation
   and ceramics, 78
Economic patterns
   and sexual dimorphism, 441
Economic rationality
   and peasant ideology, 50
Economic relations
   of gender hierarchies, 61
Economic systems
   and domestication of animals, 378
Economics
   and bioanthropology in developing countries, 475
   and Chicano studies, 407
   and impact of mining, 207-8
   of mining, 199-205
Economists
   natural resource
      and mining exploration, 200
Economy
   farming, 246
   peasant, 246
Ecosystemic perspectives
   animal domestication studies, 390-1
Education
   bilingual
      Chicano studies, 416
   and caste level
      relevance to language, 565
   and Chicano studies, 407
   demographic literature
      on fertility determinants, 506
   fundamentalist complaints about, 122
   McLean v. Arkansas Board of Education, 120-2
   recommended nursing curriculum, 221
   and the story of creation, 118
   see also McLean v. Arkansas Board of Education
Educational anthropology
   in Chicano studies, 415
Eggs
   and domesticated animal studies, 386
El Grito
   Chicano journal, 406
El Trapiche
   formative period site, 10
Elaboration
   as a control for confounding variables, 142
Electrophoresis
   human genetic distance studies, 359
Elohim
   and the Document Theory, 111
Embalming
   as means of prolonging power beyond the death of the king, 278
Emotion words
   use of multidimensional scaling, 152
Emotional condition
   and communication with physician, 178
   patient's
      and communication with physician, 178
Emotions
   as human response
      and nursing intervention, 220
Enamel thickness
   on the molar teeth
      of australopithecines, 328-30
Energy
   deficit of
      and nutrition in developing nations, 487
Energy expenditures
   and ceramics, 93
Engels
   and class consciousness, 51
English kingship
   person and office, 278
Enlightenment
   as source of growth and change, 292
Enslavement
   African monarch's use of, 277
   and domestic labor, 293
Environment
   challenges to Early Man, 539
   interaction with pathogens/host
      models of disease, 500
   northern
      man's adaptation to, 550
   in nursing models, 226
   and sexual dimorphism, 431
Environmental factors
   and growth variation, 482
Environmental variables
   and domestication of animals, 382
Escherichia coli
   and DNA, 361
Eskimos
   as immigrants from Siberia, 538
Ethnic conformity
   and interaction among tribal groups, 87
Ethnic differences
   and nursing research, 231

SUBJECT INDEX   607

Ethnic groups
   and body shape and proportion, 482
Ethnic identification
   role of animals, 382
Ethnicity
   as cross-cutting social variables, 568
   and language status, 558
   and peasant ideology, 68
Ethnoarchaelogy
   see Ceramic ethnoarchaelogy
Ethnographic fieldwork
   in late colonial period
     West Africa, 244
Ethnographic phenomena
   application of statistics to, 135
Ethnography
   and cross-cultural nursing research, 230
   early history, 2
   Southern Ivory Coast people, 253-4
   structural-functionalist
     West Africa, 243
Ethnomedicine
   and the Chicano community, 414
Europe
   and the genus *Homo*, 539
Evangelical churches
   and scientific creationism, 105
Eve
   Genesis creation story, 114
Evolution
   general theory of, 123-4
   molecular, 125
   organic, 124-5
   and scientific creationism, 103
   in sexual dimorphism, 451-60
   as a theory, 104
   see also Short-term evolution
Evolution Model
   supreme court ruling, 111
Evolutionary stages
   and domesticated animal studies, 388
Evolutionary thinking
   and domesticated animal studies, 375
Evolutionary trees
   and genetic distance studies, 347
Excavation
   archaeological evidence
     of the biblical flood, 116
Exploitation
   economic
     and feminism, 62
     liberation from, 59
Exploration
   in mining ventures, 200

Export agriculture
   of the Ivory Coast, 251

F

Fact
   bible as religion
     not science, 110
Factionalism
   oppression
     and Chicano studies, 411
Factor analysis
   and variables, 149-51
Faith
   and the literal nature
     of the creation, 109
Falwell
   Rev. Jerry
     on the creation, 109
Family demography
   and nutritional status, 496
Family incomes
   and improved diets, 497
Family relations
   and the Chicano community, 414
Family size
   as a determinant of leadership, 146
Fatalism
   as alleged cultural values
     Chicano studies, 406
   as a key Mexican cultural value, 409
Fathering
   as unique to humans, 438
Father-daughter incest
   Lovedu monarchy, 299
Feeding activities
   and acute malnutrition, 495
Female
   sexual dimorphism, 429
   see also Sexual dimorphism
   see also Women
Female initiation rites
   of Bemba, 289
Feminism
   in Chicano studies, 415
   and peasant ideologies, 61
   in West Africa, 243
Fertility
   balancing famine/disease, 505
   determinants in developing countries, 506-10
   increased rates of, 476
Film maker
   Rouch, 249
Financial support
   and the development of disciplines, 234
Fire
   and ceramic production, 81
First Amendment

   and establishment of religion, 104
Fisher tests
   in statistical analyses, 140
Flood
   in creation story, 109
   Post-Pleistocene cataclysmic, 117
Flood myths
   creationist theory, 111-8
Flood plains
   Mississippi, 16
Folk health beliefs
   and nursing research, 227
Folk models
   and knowledge, 162
Folklore
   and Chicano studies, 412
   and symbolic anthropology
     in Chicano studies, 418
Food
   and relationship to divine kingship, 288
Food procurement
   and sexual dimorphism, 441
Food production
   and commercial agriculture, 497
   and the Fipa state, 291
Food shortages
   bioanthropology in developing countries, 481
Food supplies
   bioanthropology in developing countries, 476
   female access to
     and sexual dimorphism, 435
   security of
     and malnutrition, 497
Food systems
   and nutritional status, 486
Food waste
   and domesticated animal studies, 386
Foodstuffs
   see also Animal studies
Forest
   Southern Nigeria, 246
Forest kingdoms
   and historical research
     in West Africa, 258
Forest-cultivation antithesis
   and kinship roles and rights, 395
Fossil hominoid species
   percent sexual dimorphisms figure, 455
Fossil record
   intermediate steps in creation-evolution controversy, 126
   and sexual dimorphism, 452
Fostering

and E. Goody's work on Gonja, 264
France
  in West Africa
    colonial period, 248
Freedom
  and American history
    the Scopes trial, 120
  in Fulani social life, 265
Friendship
  cultural notions of, 415
Frugivorous diet
  and *Australopithecus robustus*, 316
Fruit
  in the chimpanzee diet, 317
Functional structure
  f-structure
    in Lexical functional grammar, 41-6
Fundamentalism
  evangelical churches, 105
Funeral services
  for kings and queen mothers, 284

G

Galago crassicaudatus
  chewing time, 325
Galeopsis tetrahit
  experimental recreation of, 127
Gang of Four
  academic liberalization in China, 69
Gender
  and ceramic production, 84
  in Chicano studies, 415
  peasants and ideologies of, 58-62
  political anthropology
    in nursing, 232
Gender hierarchy
  and peasant ideology, 50
Gender relations
  in West Africa, 262-3
Gene flow
  and organic evolution, 125
Gene frequencies
  and genetic distance measures, 343-4
Gene substitution
  and genetic distances, 344-5
Gene therapy
  and recombinant DNA techniques, 359
General anthropology
  contributions
    to nursing, 225-9
Genesis
  origin and contraditions, 109
Genetic data

futures studies, 358-65
Genetic determinants
  of body shape and proportion, 482
Genetic differences
  bioanthropology in developing countries, 478
Genetic distance
  human genetic distance studies, 343-73
  and migration, 355-6
Genetic distance measures
  concordance of, 345-6
Genetic drift
  and organic evolution, 125
Genetic maps
  and genetic distance studies, 347
Genetic relationships
  distant
    in Mayan linguistics, 191
Genetics
  and calibration of age of Early Man, 550
  and sexual dimorphism, 432-3
Geofact
  artifact
    distinction between, 546
Geographical region
  and Chicano studies, 412
Geological risks
  in mining ventures, 202
Geographical determinism
  and domesticated animal studies, 388
Ghana
  and colonialism, 255
Gilgamesh epic
  and the biblical flood, 116
Glaciation
  Riss-Saale
    and dating the origin of man, 536
  Wisconsinan, 534
Glyph grammar
  and Mayan language, 194
Gold
  internal exchange of
    in West Africa, 257
Government Binding Theory
  comparison of
    with Modular grammar theory, 38-41
  in grammar, 25-33
  as modular theory, 25
Government intervention
  and ceramics production, 95
Grade determinants
  in mineral industry, 204
Grammar
  and the Brahmin caste
    in India, 564
  and language status, 559

modular theories of, 25-48
  see also Glyph grammar
Great Britain
  influence of
    on West Africa, 243-66
Gricean notions
  and inferences
    in perception, 168
Griot speech
  qualities of style, 575
Growth
  of children
    as indicators of health and nutritional status, 477
  and children in the developing world, 477
  and conditions of modernization, 512
Growth failure
  and chronic malnutrition, 490
Growth patterns
  of populations under nutritional stress, 489
Growth rates
  and sexual dimorphism, 429
Growth variation
  factors responsible for
    youth of developing nations, 482
Guatemala
  ceramic techniques, 79
  and Mayan languages, 187

H

Habitat utilization
  sex differences in, 456
Handwriting
  as form of communication, 164
Hasina
  associated with kingship, 303
Hawaiian kingship
  bones of the ruler, 287
Healing practices
  indigenous
    medical efficacy of, 503
Health
  concept of
    in nursing, 226
  and conditions of modernization, 512
  and infectious disease, 501
Health care
  and bioanthropologists, 503-4
  and growth and development
    in children, 484
  see also Nursing
Health care delivery
  and the Chicano community, 414
Hegemony
  and modern forms of national-

SUBJECT INDEX

ism, 60
Height
  growth in
    longitudinal analysis of, 483
Helping
  cultural notions of, 415
Hemoglobin
  evolutionary change in mammalian genes, 128
Hepatitis B virus(HBV)
  and medical ecology, 500
Herbal lore
  and indigenous medicine, 228
Herding
  domesticated animal studies, 381
Hereditary factors
  and growth variation, 482
Heritage
  in Chicano studies, 411
Heterozygosity
  and genetic distance, 358
Hieroglyphs
  animals on cave walls, 376
Hieroglyphic writing
  Mayan, 193-4
High blood pressure
  as risk factor
    in the development of CHD, 502
Hindu cow worship
  latent functions to, 386
Hispanos
  see also Chicanos
Historical change
  and concept of culture, 410
Historical materialism
  and Marxism
    in West Africa, 259
History
  and genetic distance analysis, 350-2
  national or regional
    West Africa, 251
  study of as policy guide, 303
HLA antigens
  and genetic distance studies, 357
Hogg Foundation Hidalgo County Project
  in 1957-1962
    Chicano studies, 408
Holism
  basic conceptual approaches, 223
Homicide
  transforming regicide into, 283
Hominids
  monogamy
    as the original mating pattern, 461

Hominoidea
  dental function among, 318-21
Hominoids
  dietary behavior of, 316-18
Homo sapiens
  and meat eating, 316
  and Middle Palaeolithic industries, 532
  and the origin of Western man, 534
Homogeneity
  and tribal pottery production, 88
Honorifics
  language levels, 571-4
  systems of
    and language structure, 557
Hopi-Tewa Tribe
  pottery, 84-5
Hormonal levels
  postnatal
    and sexual dimorphism, 429
Hospital
  out-of
    and home nursing, 235
Host
  interaction with pathogens/environment
    models of disease, 500
House construction
  A.D. 300 to A.D. 1450, 17
Household income
  and nutritional status, 495
Household size
  and ceramic vessels, 91
  and ceramics, 78
Huastecan
  as Mayan language, 188
Human (artificial) selection
  of domesticated animals/plants, 375
Human evolution
  and scientific creationism, 103
Human fossil lineage
  and biological (selection) forces, 460
Human genetic distance studies
  present and future, 343-73
  see also Genetic distance
Human nature
  nursing models, 226
Human occupancy
  see Early Man
Human Organization
  journal of applied anthropology
    Chicano studies, 406
Human responses
  and nursing process, 232
Human sacrifice
  relationship to murder, 273
Human settlement patterns
  and domesticated animal

studies, 389
  as a factor in
    animal temperament, 389
Human skeletal system
  dimorphism, 430
Humanism
  and the Marxist tradition, 52
  secular
    and common law, 119
Humans
  regulatory effects of
    on animal populations, 385
Hunger
  death of the old year
    and rebirth of the new year, 281
Hungry season
  and children's growth, 492
Hunters
  see Clovis
Hunting
  and *Homo erectus*, 540
  and sexual dimorphism, 432
Hybrids
  and scientific creationism, 127
Hydraulic despotism
  and divine kingship, 285
Hylobates
  and sexual dimorphism, 440
Hylobatids
  and chewing time, 326
Hypercorrection
  and language status, 558

I

Ideology
  and mining, 208
Igala kingdom
  connections between kingship and prosperity, 290
Igbo ethnography
  Uchendu, 260
Illinoian Glaciation
  and evidence of Early Man, 549
Illinois
  woodland complexes, 3
Illness
  and cultural patterns, 222
Imitation
  and language status, 558
Immigrant groups
  and nursing, 221
Immigration
  and Chicano studies, 416
Imperialism
  Western cultural
    in West Africa, 253
Incest
  father-daughter
    Lovedu tribe, 299

in West Africa, 245
Incisor proportions
  in *Australopithecus*, 332-4
Independence Principle
  in modular grammar theory, 36
Independence testing
  in statistical analyses, 140
Indexing arrays
  and binding conditions, 30
Indexing rules
  noun P with a c-commanding NP, 39
India
  social dialectology in, 562-6
  and tradition
    peasant political consciousness, 65-6
Indians
  see Iroquois
Industrial growth
  limits of
    and mining, 199
Industrialization
  and cognitive functioning, 489
Infanticide
  role of
    in regulating the supply of children, 510
  in warfare societies, 139
Infectious disease
  adaptation to, 500
  as factor in
    developing countries, 485
  and malnutrition, 488
Inference
  and Gricean notions
    in perception, 168
Inferential statistics
  assumptions of, 137-9
Inflation
  and mining ventures, 201
Influenza
  and evolutionary change, 128
Information
  and overall comprehension, 168
Ingestion
  and Homonoidea, 318-19
Innovation
  and ceramic production
    tribal, 93
Installation rites
  analysis of
    African kings, 277
Intellectual decolonization
  in West Africa, 253
Intellectual stimulation
  and malnourishment, 495
Interlocus sampling variance
  genetic distance studies, 345
International Union of Prehistoric and Protohistoric Science
  post WWII, 12

Interpretive anthropology
  and the recovery of peasant viewpoint, 63
Interval scales
  in inferential statistics, 138
Interview
  medical, 174
Intimacy
  cultural notions of, 415
  between king and people, 281
Intonation
  and Modular grammar theory, 40
Inversions
  role of
    in divine kingship, 282
Investment patterns
  in mining, 203
Iroquois indians
  artifacts, 3-4
Islamic attitudes
  and divine kingship, 277
Ivory coast
  peasants of, 249

J

Jack Goody
  and the transition from decolonization
    in West Africa, 254
Jakarta Malay
  phonological diversity in, 570
Japan
  World War II
    and folk ceramics, 95
Java War
  and anticolonialism, 66
Jehova
  and flood myths, 111
Jesus Christ
  and eternal salvation, 273
Jewish populations
  human genetic distance studies, 351
Job requirements
  and literacy, 167

K

Kalinga tribe
  as potters, 85
Kanjobalan-Chujean
  as Mayan language, 188
Kilns
  and ceramic production, 81
Kingship
  see Divine kingship
Kinship
  African systems of, 244
  and human genetic distance studies, 351
  role of
    in ceramic production, 85

Kinship bioassay
  and human genetic distance studies, 351
Kinship theory
  and the Abutia Ewe of Southern Ghana, 264
Knowledge
  local and schematized
    interaction of, 176-9
  processing and representing, 161-3
  secret
    and divine kingship, 292
Knowledge and literacy
  in the medical setting, 171-82
Korea
  liberation theology, 64
Kroeber, Alfred
  anecdote, 21
Kulaniopuu
  God of war and human sacrifice
    Hawaiian, 287
Kwashiorkor
  causes of
    and early weaning, 494

L

Labor
  division of
    and ceramic ethnoarchaeology, 77
  and exploitation of Chicanos, 407
Labor recruitment
  in the mining industry, 206-8
Labor relations
  and divine kingship, 292
Labovian model
  see Language status and style
Lactation
  impact on
    and fertility, 508
Language
  fine-tuned understanding of
    in Chicano studies, 409
  and literacy, 160
  power of, 296
  and studies of dissent, 295
  use
    spoken versus written, 163-70
  see also Oral language
  see also Ritual
Language levels
  and honorifics, 571-4
Language status and style
  linguistic expression of social status, 557-81
Lasnik's rule
  Modular grammar theory, 39
Late colonial period

SUBJECT INDEX 611

1940-1960
  in West Africa, 244
Leadership
  sociocultural determinants of, 146
Learning
  to read and literacy, 160-1
  and traditional diets, 493
Learning routines
  and pottery, 77
Lenin
  and class consciousness, 51
Less developed countries (LDC)
  mining expropriations in, 202
Lexemic change
  and illness terms, 228
Lexical functional grammar (LFG)
  as a modular theory, 25, 41-6
Lexical structure(LS)
  in Lexical functional grammar, 41
Lexical variation
  and language style, 570
Lexicalization
  and patterning of honorific forms, 573
  and spoken language, 163
Lexicon
  in modular theories
    in grammar, 27
  and understanding written language, 167
Liberalism
  and Third World, 70
Liberals
  and peasant modernism, 53-5
Liberation theology
  in Korea, 64
Liberationism
  obstacles to the development of, 61
Life cycle
  and Chicano studies, 415
Light
  Genesis creation story, 114
Lineage principle
  and social organization
    in West Africa, 246
Linguistic functions
  deictic and anaphoric, 177
Linguistic paleontology
  and cultural identifications, 192
  and linguistics, 192
Linguistic system
  definition of, 25
Linguistics
  and evolution, 124
  see also Language status and style
  see also Mayan linguistics
Listening strategy

  as aspect of literacy, 169
Literacy
  in a cultural context, 160-1
  medical
    aspects of, 173-6
  in the medical setting, 171-82
Literacy skills
  acquiring, 168
Literal meaning
  vs. derived meaning, 167
Literate tradition
  Africa's lack of, 257
Literature
  creationist, 107
  see also Mayan literature
Lithic industry
  stone tools from, 545
Little Ice Age
  A.D. 1300-1500, 14
Locomotor behavior
  sex differences in, 456
Log-linear models
  statistical analysis, 146
Logical form (LF)
  in modular theories
    in grammar, 26
Logical reasoning
  and reading and writing, 166
Logograms
  in the Mayan languages, 193
Longevity
  ceramic, 91
Lono
  the peaceful god
    Hawaiian kingship, 287
Louis XVI
  execution of
    and divine kingship, 278
Lovedu queens
  and survival of their diplomacy, 299
Lower Mississippi Valley
  sites, 11
Lower Palaeolithic
  materials
    technical and stylistic differentiation, 541
Lower Yazoo Basin
  Phillip's, 7
Lunar calendar
  and death of the old year
  and rebirth of the new year, 281

M

Macroevolution
  and genetic distance studies, 352
Maize, beans, squash
  New World diet of, 491
Maji Maji rebellion
  and anticolonialism, 66

Malaria
  susceptibility of humans to, 500
Male
  see Men
  see also Sexual dimorphism
Male bias
  and nursing theory, 233
Male doubles
  and divine kingship, 282
Male-male competition
  and sexual dimorphism, 435
Male/female relations
  West Africa, 262
Mali
  Inner Delta region of
    Gallais' work on, 261
  peasants of, 249
Malnourishment
  dietary intakes of
    Guatemalan children, 486
Malnutrition
  in the developing world, 484
  and diarrheal diseases
    in children, 500
  effects of
    on growth, 488
  in less developed countries, 486-99
Mammalian dental allometry
  and teeth and diet, 323
Mammalian dimorphism patterns
  see Sexual dimorphism
Mammoth bone fragments
  dating the origin of Man, 536
Man
  Genesis creation story, 114
Manpower
  and bioanthropology in developing countries, 475
Mandibular canine
  sexual dimorphism in
    figure, 444
Mandibular cheek-tooth area
  vs. body weight
    figure, 326
Mandibular incisor span
  vs. body weight
    figure, 334
Mandrillus sphinx
  sexual dimorphism, 437
Manioc-fish diet
  of the Amazon basin, 491
Manix Lake
  stone tools from, 545
Manufacture
  and ceramics, 82
Maps
  genetic distance studies, 349-50
Marasmus
  early weaning, 494
Market demand

and pottery production, 87
Marketing mechanisms
  and ceramics production, 97
Marriage
  African systems of, 244
  imaged in metaphors
    equating women and stock, 398
  and residential patterns, 83
Marriage exchanges
  analysis of, 263
Marriage politics
  in African monarchies, 298
Marriage systems
  and sexual dimorphism of stature, 438
Marriage types
  West African, 249
Marx
  and mining proletarianization, 210
Marxism
  and statistical analysis, 153
  in West Africa, 259-60
Marxist Ideology
  in Third World, 50
Marxists
  French structural
    and peasant ideology, 52
  French structuralist
    in West African research, 243
Masai
  and domesticated animal studies, 389
Mastication
  in Homonoidea, 319-20
Maternal body mass
  and nutritional status, 496
Maternal education
  and nutritional status, 495
Mating patterns
  and sexual dimorphism, 433
Matrilineal marriage
  among Akan civil servants, 260
Maturation
  rates of
    Oaxaca children, 480
Mayan languages
  classification of
    figure, 189
Mayan linguistics, 187-98
  see Linguistics
Mayan Literature
  folklore and oral tradition, 194-5
McLean
  vs. Arkansas Board of Education, 120-2
Meadowcroft Rockshelter
  dating origin of Man, 535
Measurement

teeth and diet, 322
Medical anthropology
  and collaboration with nursing, 235
Medical discourse
  bureaucratic basis of, 170
Medical ecology
  and hepatitis B virus(HBV), 500
Medical health therapies
  and Chicano community, 414
Medicine
  see Nursing
Men
  male investment in offsprings, 434
  in warfare societies
    percentage of, 139
  see also Sexual Dimorphism
Menarche
  biological factors affecting age at, 507
Menarcheal age
  bioanthropology in developing countries, 481
Mennonites
  and human genetic distance studies, 353
Mental ability
  growth status correlates, 488
Mental testing
  and factor analysis, 150
Mesoamerican linguistics
  the Mayan languages, 192
Messiah
  bible translations, 110
Metabolic equivalence
  and teeth and diet, 323
Metabolism
  and nutrient synthesis
    and adequacy of traditional diet, 492-3
Metaphor
  and domesticated animal studies, 379
  animals as, 392-4
Methodology
  nursing and anthropology, 222
Methods
  in Chicano studies, 417
  in nursing, 223
Mexican-American
  labor
    and exploitation of Chicanos, 407
  see also Chicanos
Mexico
  and Mayan languages, 187
MG Modular Grammar Theory
  in comparison with
    GB Government Binding Theory, 38-41
Microevolution

and genetic distance analysis, 350-2
Middle class
  and language status, 559
Midwives
  role of
    cross culturally, 233
Migration
  after decolonization
    in West Africa, 252
  from Asia to Western Hemisphere, 537
  Early Man, 534
  and genetic distances, 355-6
  and linguistics, 192
  in the mining industry, 206-8
  of prey species
    and Early Man, 539
  women's adaptation to, 415
Militarization
  African monarch's use of, 277
Military regimes
  and economic failure, 263
Milk drinking
  evolutionary consequences of, 375
Millenarianism,
  in peasant rebellion, 67-9
Mineral absorption
  diets high in oxalates or lathyrogens
    in developing countries, 492
Mineral reserve
  developing
    fianancial/economic feasibility, 202
Mining
  anthropological perspectives, 199-217
Mining communities
  and mining, 207
Minority groups
  and labor, 407
Mississippi River
  ethnohistory, 7
  see also Lower Mississippi Valley
Mississippi Valley
  A.D. 1300, 16
Mitochondrial DNA
  genetic distances based on, 362-3
Modernism
  ideological obstacles to, 55-8
  and peasant consciousness, 50-5
Modernist economics
  conditions for taking root, 55
Modernization
  bioanthropology in developing countries, 476
  and cognitive functioning, 489

and divine kingship, 280
and infectious disease, 501
Modernization decade
  in West Africa, 249-55
Modular Grammar (MG)
  as modular theory, 25, 33-41
Mojave Desert
  and evidence for Early Man, 544
Molar construction
  differences in
    among living apes, 320
Molar occlusion
  in Homonoidea, 320-21
Molar shape
  and australopithecine diet, 330-2
Molas
  statistical analysis of, 144
Molecular genetic research
  and genetic data, 365
Molecules
  evolution of, 125
Mombasa Swahili
  and language style, 569
Monarchies
  African, 276
  Swazi
    development of, 282
Money
  and Asante political history, 291
Monkey trial
  see Scopes' trial
Monogamy
  and male investment in offspring, 434
Monogenic traits
  genetic distance studies, 356
Moral economist
  and peasant ideology, 54
Moral judgment
  and nursing intervention, 225
Moral Majority
  and creationist theory, 106
Mortality
  increased rates of, 476
Moses
  and flood myths, 111
Moslem
  states in West Africa
    and historical research, 258
Mother surrogate
  nurse as, 234
Mousterian tools
  artisans, 532
mtDNA genome
  and human genetic distance studies, 363
Mukanda circumcision ritual
  as common practice, 282
Multicollinearity
  in regression analysis, 145

Multidimensional scaling
  creating a map, 151
Multilingualism
  and language status, 560
Multiple regression
  in data analysis, 143
Multivariate data collection
  methods, 141-52
Murder
  relationship of
    to sacrifice, 273
Museum of Anthropology
  establishment of, 20
Mutation
  and organic evolution, 125
Mythology
  comparative
    and the great flood, 113
Myths
  of observation
  and domestic animals, 376

N

National Center for Health Statistics
  and bioanthropology in developing countries, 478
National Nursing Council
  and nursing education, 221
Nationalism
  and peasant ideologies, 50, 59-62
Nationalization
  of the Chilean copper industry, 201
Natural fertility
  determinants of, 507-09
Natural resources
  nonrenewable
    and mining, 199
Natural selection
  and human genetic distance studies, 354
  and organic evolution, 125
Nature
  personified phenomena of, 377
Ncwala rites
  and divine kingship, 281
Neandertals
  sexual dimorphism in, 457
Neighboring
  role of
    and nursing, 230
Neocolonialism
  French
    in West Africa, 266
Neonatal mortality
  and birthweight, 494
Neural degeneration
  and children's development, 492

Neurological diseases
  of viral and parasitic origin, 500
New Christian Right
  and creationist theory, 106
Niger livestock development project
  agricultural case studies, 261
Nigeria
  and colonialization, 255
Noah
  flood myths, 115
Noble speech
  qualities of style, 575
Nomadic pastoralism
  and domestication of animals, 384
Nominal scales
  in inferential statistics, 138
Nominalizations
  as an integrative device in writing, 164
Noncoreference Principle
  in Modular grammar theory, 36
Nonfuel minerals
  and mining, 199
Nonmodernism
  and modernism
    dichotomy between, 58
  in peasant consciousness, 62
Nonparametric methods
  genetic distance measures, 346
Nonverbal signals
  and spoken language, 163
Noun class morphology
  present trends, 570
Noun P
  with ac-commanding NP, 39
Noun phrases
  and binding theory, 32
NP-trace
  and anaphor, 28
Nuclear DNA polymorphisms
  and genetic distance studies, 359
Nucleic acids
  and organic evolution, 124
Nucleotide sequences
  genetic distance studies, 361
Numerical taxonomy
  in data with variables, 148
Nursing
  and anthropology, 219-41
Nursing courses
  cross cultural, 224-5
Nursing profession
  in Chicano studies, 415
Nursing research
  anthropology providing theory for, 227-9
Nutrient intake

SUBJECT INDEX

and small body size, 484
Nutrient synthesis
  and metabolism
    and adequacy of traditional diet, 492-3
Nutrition
  and conditions of modernization, 512
  in less-developed countries, 486
Nutritional intervention
  and child development
    in less developed countries, 498-9
Nutritional parameters
  and animal domestication studies, 378
Nutritional status
  assessment of
    developing countries, 486-8
Nutritional stress
  and sexual dimorphism, 431
Nutritional supplementation study
  Guatemalan children, 480

O

Obesity
  in developing countries, 502
Obscenity
  and animal metaphors, 392
Obsidian
  and prehistoric immigrants, 18
Occlusal wear
  and sexual dimorphism, 443
Occlusion
  as hallmark of all living monkeys, 318
Occupation
  ceramics, 92
  and language style, 570
Office
  and divine kingship, 280
Old Crow
  and evidence of Early Man, 547-9
Old Testament
  and the flood story, 115-6
Oppression
  economic forms of, 419
  and factionalism
    and Chicano studies, 411
  in the form of divine kings, 294
Oral cultures
  and homeostasis, 160
Oral history
  and nursing research, 231
  use of techniques, 63
  in West Africa, 257
Oral literature
  Mayan, 194

Orangutans
  diet of, 317
Ordinal scales
  in inferential statistics, 138
Ornamentation
  in pottery, 86
Osteoarthritis(OA)
  formal clinical description of, 175

P

Pain
  as human response
    and nursing intervention, 220
  and nursing theory, 228-9
Palaeolithic period
  stone implements
    in the middle Atlantic states, 530
Pan paniscus
  and sexual dimorphism, 458
Parametric statistical tests
  and population, 138
Passivity
  as alleged cultural values, 406
Pastoralism
  West African, 261
Paternal body mass
  and nutritional status, 496
Paternal care
  and sexual dimorphism, 434
Path analysis
  and independent variables, 145
Pathogen
  interaction with host/environment
    models of disease, 500
Patient/physician relationship
  and commonsense thinking, 171-2
Patterning
  and social rules
    in West Africa, 245
Peasant ideologies
  in the Third World, 49-75
Peasant modernism
  and liberals, 53-5
Peasant rebellions
  and anachronistic belief systems, 63
  Chinese, 64
Peasant studies
  in West Africa, 260
Pelvic inflammatory disease
  limiting fecundity
    in the Third World, 509
Pentateuch
  development of
    in creationist theory, 111-8
Perceptions

human
  of animals, 376
Perinatal mortality
  and maternal nutrition, 493
Persian language
  and speech performance, 567
Phagocytic function
  and nutritional status
    in PEM children, 490
Phenotypes
  evolution of, 125
Philippines
  and peasant rebellion, 68
Philosophy
  and divine kingship, 279
Phonetic form(PF)
  in modular theories
    in grammar, 26
Phoneticism
  and Mayan writing, 193
Phonology
  and language style/status, 561
  for Mayan language, 190
Phylogenetics
  and molecular evolution, 125
Physician/patient relationship
  and commonsense thinking, 172
Physiological regularities
  in ethnographic research
    nursing, 233
Pig
  as considered unclean, 395
Pinata
  and ceramics production, 94
Plasmodium
  resistance of
    to chloroquine, 500
Plastic water jars
  and ceramics use, 90
Pleistocene Age
  and flood myths, 115
Pleistocene megafauna
  extinction of, 533
Pluralistic societies
  and the Hispanic community, 412
  pottery making in, 86
Politeness levels
  and language, 567
Political action
  and class struggle, 58
Political anthropology
  and gender
    in Nursing, 232
Political consciousness
  peasant
    in India, 65-6
Political culture
  in West Africa, 256
Political economy
  Chicano studies, 416
  with focus on agriculture

SUBJECT INDEX 615

West Africa, 262
  Marxist influenced
    in West Africa, 261
  and peasant ideology, 54
Political organization
  and mining, 207
Political protest
  and the Chinese Communist Party, 64
Political relations
  of gender hierarchies, 61
Political scientists
  monographs on Africa's "new nations", 262
Political systems
  African, 244
Political upheaval
  and peasant ideology, 62
Politics
  and Chicano studies, 407
  and divine kingship
    person and office, 278
  and the peasantry, 65
  and ritual
    and prosperity, 288
Pollution
  and divine kingship, 282
Polygenic traits
  for genetic distance, 356
Polygynous mating system
  and sexual dimorphism, 433
Polygynous society
  pottery making in, 85
Polysynthetic language
  and honorific systems, 561
Pongo
  cheek-tooth size, 327
Poor
  bioanthropology in developing countries, 479
Pope John Paul II
  address to the
    Pontifical Academy of Sciences, 108
Popol Vuh
  Quiche book of counsel, 195
Popular sovereignty
  transition from monarchy to, 300
Population change
  and conditions of modernization, 512
Population dynamics
  and age at marriage, 507
Population geneticists
  human genetic distance studies, 351
Population policy
  and bioanthropology, 510-12
Population regulation
  see also Infanticide
Postcranial sexual dimorphism
  Neanderthal sample, 460

Postindependence decade
  West African anthropology, 255
Postvocalic /r/
  and language status, 558
Pottery
  binomial typology, 9
  ethnoarchaeology, 77
  Neolithic, 13
  Southeastern, 6
  see also Siberian prehistoric pottery
Poverty
  in Yorubaland
    and divine kingship, 292
Power
  and divine kingship, 274
Power relations
  and cultural performance
    Chicano studies, 410
Powers Fort
  Missouri site, 15
Pragmatic component
  in modular grammar, 35-8
Praise songs
  contributing to rebellion
    divine kingship, 295
Pre-Projectile Point Stage
  older than Clovis
    evidence in North/South America, 531
Pre-sapiens Man
  in North America, 538
Preadolescent growth
  middle-class families near Calcutta, 482
Precolonial kingdoms
  West African, 251
Predicate Argument Principle
  in modular grammar theory, 36
Predicrostonyx
  recovered in North America, 549
Prehistoric subsistence ecology
  bioanthropology in developing countries, 476
Presbytis frontata
  and sexual dimorphism in, 437
Primary hepatic carcinoma
  and link to HBV, 500
Primate
  and sexual dimorphism, 431
Primitive peoples
  ritual attitude towards animals, 377
Primordialism
  and peasant ideology, 60
Private property
  and domesticated animal studies, 389
PRO

lexical functional grammar
  vs Government binding theory, 44-6
  as an unexpressed pronoun
    grammatical theory, 44
Probability samples
  in inferential statistics, 137
Production
  ceramics, 78-88
  peasant mode
    and centralizing capitalism, 66
  standardization of, 94
Proevolutionists
  and scientific creationism, 106
Professional disciplines
  and prescriptive theories, 224
Professional exchange
  and schematized knowledge, 179
Professional status
  and doctor's authority, 170
Projectile point
  manufacturing techniques, 537
  North American Palaeoindian, 535
  bifacially flaked
    origin of, 534
Projection Principle
  O-criterion
    in modular grammar theory, 34
Proletarian revolution
  and peasant ideologies, 59
Pronomials
  and PRO, 45
Pronouns
  and binding theory, 29
Prosimians
  and sexual dimorphism, 436
Prosperity
  and the African monarch, 276
  and divine kingship, 274, 288-94
Protein
  deficit of
    and nutrition in developing nations, 487
  and sexual dimorphism, 457
Protein energy malnutrition (PEM)
  causes of, 493
  and less developed countries, 488
Protein polymorphisms
  and genetic distance, 364
Protein shortages
  and sexual dimorphism, 429
Proteins
  coding for
    and genetic distance studies, 362
  and organic evolution, 124

Proto-Mayan reconstruction
  comparative studies, 190
Protohominids
  meat-eating scavenging lifestyle, 337
Proximate causation
  and sexual dimorphism, 431
Psychology
  Southern Ghanaian, 253
Puberty
  timing of
    effect on actual fertility, 507
Public schools
  study of bible in, 121

Q

Quantification,
  increasing emphasis
    in anthropology, 135
Quichean-Mamean
  as Mayan language, 188
Quinua tribe
  as potters, 86

R

R-expression
  binding theory
    grammar, 30
Racism
  institutional
    and Chicano studies, 407
Radiocarbon revolution
  and dates representing Clovis, 530
Rain medicines
  and Lovedu queens, 299
Random gentic drift
  distance measures, 344
Randomization
  as a control for confounding variables, 142
Rank
  and language style, 575
  and power
    in Ceylon and Tonga, 304
Raza Unida movement
  Chicano studies, 417
Reading
  as a function of language, 166
Reasoning
  and commonsense thinking, 172
Rebellions
  and divine kingship, 294
Reconstruction
  and decolonialization, 249
Recycling
  ceramic, 91
Referral
  and patient/physician communication, 174
Refugees
  and studies of continuum of body size in, 479
Regicide
  and divine kingship, 300-07
  Frazer's work on divine kings, 275
  role of
    in African monarchy, 283
    Shilluk of the Nilotic Sudan, 276
Relationships
  eliciting information during, 172
  and peasant ideology, 56
Relevance
  semantic domains of, 180
Religion
  advancement of
    court ruling, 120-1
  definitions of
    in evolution controversy, 104
Religions
  and human-animal interaction, 375
Religiosity
  effects on reducing blood pressure, 502
Religious communities
  and language style, 568
Religious doctrine
  scientific creationism, 110
Representation
  and semantic structure, 162
Reproduction
  and traditional diets, 493
Reproductive success
  sexual dimorphism, 437
Reproductive variance
  and sexual dimorphism, 434
Research
  and nursing
    as a professional discipline, 225-6
  politics of
    in Chicano studies, 410-12
Research topics
  nursing and anthropology, 222
Residential patterns
  in ceramic production, 83
Residualization
  as a control for confounding variables, 142
Resins
  and ceramic production, 82
Respiratory infections
  chief causes of morbidity
    in Third World children, 501
Restriction site polymorphisms
  and genetic distance studies, 360-2
Revolt
  and ideological domination, 56
Revolution
  and divine kingship, 300-07
Revolutionary ideology
  and Chinese peasantry, 67
Revolutionary movements
  peasants in, 53
Rheumatoid arthritis(RA)
  formal description of, 175
Rhodesia
  mining operations in, 211
Rinderpest epidemic
  animal domestication studies, 390-1
Rio Grande Valley
  and Chicano studies, 413
Ritual
  and divine kingship, 278
  and mining, 208-10
  politics
    and prosperity, 288
Ritual language
  features of, 165
  and fragmented discourse, 180
  Mayan, 194
Ritual transformation
  of a person into a thing, 279
Rivers
  Southern Nigeria, 246
Rocky Mountains
  see Old Crow
Role differences
  noneconomic
    and the division of labor by sex, 449-50
Romano
  and *El Grito*
    Chicano journal, 406
Romany gypsies
  origin of, 351
Royal incest
  in divine kingship, 282
Royal work
  and divine kingship, 293
Rural households
  purchasing power of
    and malnutrition, 497
Rural life
  agrarian peoples, 49
Rural producers
  and class consciousness, 56
Rwanda
  changing role of the military, 277

S

S-Structures
  binding theory

grammar, 30
Sacred cow
  and cultural determinism, 383
  and domesticated animal studies, 383
  latent functions to, 386
Sacred power
  associated with kingship, 303
Sacrifice
  and animal symbolism, 396
  and domesticated animal studies, 379
Saimiri sciureus
  chewing time in, 325
Sakalava
  and spirit mediums, 297
Sampling
  in inferential statistics, 137
San Diego
  findings of Early Man, 542
Scavengers
  and domesticated animal studies, 386
  teeth and diet, 338
Schemata
  and knowledge, 162
Schematized knowledge
  and professional exchange, 179
Schools
  and the story of creation, 118
Science
  definitions of, 104
  and legislation
    McLean vs. Arkansas, 121
  and religion
    interference with, 128
  and religious doctrine, 273
Scientific creationism
  and evolution, 103-33
Scopes
  vs. State of Tennessee, 119
Scopes trial
  and the six-day creation, 108
Seasons
  growth among children
    in developing countries, 485
Secrecy
  in the conduct of politico-religious affairs
    divine kingship, 296
Sectarianism
  in peasant rebellion, 67-9
Sedentarization
  and domesticated animal studies, 389
Selection
  and organic evolution, 125
  and sexual dimorphism, 433-8
Self esteem
  and potter's profile, 92
Self-control

cultural definition of
    Chicano studies, 413
Semantics
  and the cosatisfaction principle, 37
  and language status, 559
Senegal
  and colonialism, 255
Settlement
  and migrants
    in West Africa, 252
Sex divisions
  in West Africa, 263
Sexual dimorphism
  in the human species, 429-73
Sexual maturation
  nutritional status, 508
Sexual metaphors
  and animal studies, 393
Sexual reproduction
  in nuclear DNA
    and human genetic distance studies, 363
Sexual selection
  and sexual dimorphism, 433
Sexually transmitted diseases(STD)
  in the Third World, 501
Sherds
  discard sites, 90
Short-term evolution
  coancestry coefficient
    genetic distance measures, 346-7
Siberian prehistoric pottery
  see Pottery
Silence
  as weapons
    in Burundi, 296
Silver
  Middle Woodland, 18
Skeletal change
  and sexual dimorphism, 449
Skeleton
  maturation of
    and malnutrition, 488
Skill
  in ceramic production, 84
Slavery
  nineteenth century
    in West Africa, 258
  significance of powerful substances, 290
Slaves
  internal exchange
    in West Africa, 257
Slums
  Accra's, 261
Social categorizations
  ethnic identity, 568
Social change
  and cultural traditions, 70
Social conditions

and bioanthropology in developing countries, 475
Social dialectology
  India, 562-6
Social equality
  and Chicano studies, 413, 418
Social mobility
  and language change, 575
Social organization
  in ceramics, 78, 83-8
  in Chicano studies, 415
  of mining, 205
Social relations
  fine-tuned understanding of
    in Chicano studies, 409
  food as the language of, 289
Social relationship
  bioanthropology in developing countries, 476
Social status
  and communication with physician, 178
  and education, 567
  see also Status and style
Social stress
  and diseases of modernization, 501
Social structure
  ceramic vessels, 88
  and regicide, 276
  traditional/modern forms, 159
Socialist development
  and women's liberation, 263
Socialization
  and E. Goody's book on Gonja, 264
  of nurses, 229
Sociocultural anthropology
  use of
    statistics in, 135-57
Socioeconomic status
  demographic literature
    on fertility determinants, 506
  and growth process
    in developing nations, 484
  and nutritional status, 496
Sociolinguistic work
  of American cities, 557
Sorcery
  and ceramic production, 81
Space
  circular conception of
    Southeast Asian, 285
Spatial distribution
  of ceramic vessels, 89
Speaking
  see Language
Specialization
  in production
    ceramics, 96
  role of
    and literacy, 161

Species
  evolution
    creation-evolution controversy, 126-8
Speech
  as indices of stylistic usage, 567
Spirit mediums
  proliferation of
    among the Sakalava, 297
Spirit possession
  ceremonies
    of the Sakalava, 285
Spokane Flood
  Pleistocene period, 117
Standardized regression coefficients
  in data analysis, 143
Stasis
  and the creation, 123
State
  and divine kingship, 280
  separation of, 103
State formation
  politics of
    West Africa, 250
State rule
  subordination of peasants
    in West Africa, 247
Stateless peoples
  and Tallensi
    and history of, 256
Stateless politics
  in West Africa, 246
Statistics
  use of
    in sociocultural anthropology, 135-57
  see also Inferential statistics
Status
  cultural system
    and language style, 575-7
Stereotypes
  unconscious perpetuation
    Chicano studies, 408
Stigmatizing
  and language status, 558
Stone tools
  manufacture of, 532
Storytellers
  and human-animal interaction, 375
Stress
  and multidimensional scaling, 151
Structural-functionalism
  and Marxism
    in West Africa, 260
Structuralism
  and statistical analysis, 153
Style
  in ceramics, 83-8
  cultural system
    and language style, 575-7
Subsistence
  in the developing world, 493
Subsistence economy
  and ceramics production, 97
Subsistence strategy
  and slaughter patterns in early Holocene sites, 380
Subsoil mineral wealth
  and mining enterprises, 208
Suicides
  of Balinese rulers, 286
Summer solstice
  death of the old year
    and rebirth of the new, 281
Supplementation
  and birth weight
    and growth rate, 499
Suprafamilial kinship
  and ceramics production, 97
Supreme Court
  and creation, 112
Susquehanna Valley
  excavation, 4
Sustenance
  animals as, 381-91
Swazi
  and power embodied in the king, 280
Swaziland
  changing role of the military, 277
Symbolic anthropology
  forms of language, 234
Symbolic interaction
  and E. Goody's book on Gonja, 264
Symbolism
  in nursing, 234
  and ritual
    in mining, 210
  and statistical analysis, 153
Symbols
  and ceramic production, 88
Synchronic method
  in ethnography
    West Africa, 247
Syntactic structure
  and modular grammar theory, 40
Syntax
  and language status, 559
  in modular theories
    in grammar, 27
  Proto-Mayan, 190-1

T

Tajin
  excavation, 10
Tallensi
  and stateless people
    and history of, 256
Taming
  domesticated animals studies, 381
Taxation
  as recruitment mechanisms
    in mining, 206
Taxes
  and mining ventures, 204
Taxonomy
  and animal domestication studies, 394-6
  and domesticated animal studies, 379
Techniques
  and ceramics, 93
Technological development
  and peasant ideology, 69-70
Technology
  Capital-intensive
    in the industry, 202-3
  and ceramics, 93
  exploitive
    and domesticated animal studies, 383
  and sexual dimorphism, 438
Teeth and diet
  of *Australopithecus*, 315-41
Temperature regulation
  and dietary supplementation, 494
Temple of Solomon
  and biblical chronology, 117
Text
  see Medical discourse
Text and discourse, 159-85
  see Communication
Textbooks
  and the creation-evolution controversy, 122
Thai monarchy
  and Third World politics, 304
Thailand
  and non-class ideologies, 55
  social transformation in, 56
Theatre state
  negara as, 286
Theft
  effects of
    on herds and social organization, 390
Theistic beliefs
  and evolution, 103
Theory
  in Chicano studies, 417
Theory development
  in nursing, 223
Thermodynamics
  second law
    creationist arguments against evolution, 126
Thermoluminescence instrumentation
  for measuring ceramics' ages, 91

SUBJECT INDEX 619

Thinking
  trends
    and peasant ideologies, 49
Third World
  European influence on
    and divine kingship, 275
  peasant ideologies in, 49
  urban poor
    in West Africa, 262
Third World nations
  mineral-exporting, 210
Third World politics
  and Thai monarchy, 304
Thought
  African traditional
    and Western science, 159
Time
  and biblical chronology, 118
Time structure
  West Africa, 247
Tonga
  position of nobility in, 304
Tools
  artisans, 532
Tooth size
  and sexual dimorphism, 450
Tooth wear
  in australopithecines, 335-6
Topology
  and genetic distance studies, 348
Totality
  and class consciousness, 52
Totemic representation
  and sacrifice, 396
Totemism
  and animal studies, 392
Tradition
  in India
    and political consciousness, 65-6
  in peasant rebellion, 67-9
  and the political history of Dagomba, 301
Traditional culture
  and Chicano non-achievement, 407-8
Translation
  of the Bible, 107
Transport technology
  and ceramics production, 97
Transportation
  effects of the mining industry, 208
Tropics
  preadaptation of humans to, 539
Trust
  cultural notions of, 415
Tsetse fly belts
  animal domestication studies, 390-1
Tupaia
  chewing time in, 325

Twinning
  and divine kingship, 282

U

Untouchable caste
  and language, 562-3
Upper Pleistocene Age
  and the Old Crow fossils, 547
Urban studies
  in West Africa, 260
Urban life
  Chicano studies, 416
Urbanization
  of potters, 80
  in West Africa, 243, 252

V

Vaca
  and *El Grito*
    Chicano journal, 406
Valsequillo
  findings of Early Man, 542-4
Variables
  interrelated
    problems in analysis, 142
  and quantification, 136
  see also Confounding variables
Venezuela
  peasants
    in the nineteenth century, 57
Veterinary anthropology
  as new subfield, 390
Victim
  blaming of
    in Chicano studies, 407
Vietnam
  and peasant based political movement, 67
  peasant ideology, 54
Vikings
  and genetic distance studies, 352
Village settlement
  A.D. 300 - A.D. 1450, 17
Violence
  and the Chinese Communist Party, 64
  and Christian ideals of progress, 274
  human
    and divine kingship, 278
Virtue
  cultural definition
    Chicano studies, 413
Viruses
  evolutionary change in, 128
Vowel phonemes
  and caste system in India, 563

W

Wage labor
  and ceramics production, 97
Wage-labor employment
  and nutritional status, 496
Wage-labor relationships
  and peasant ideology, 56
Warmth
  as a general trend, 15
Wasting
  measure of
    in acute malnutrition, 487
Water sanitation
  in the Third World, 504
Wealth
  and ceramic vessels, 91
  and relationship to divine kingship, 288
Weight gains
  and fetal demands, 494
West Africa
  social anthropology of, 243-72
Wheat-pulse-yoghurt diet
  of the Near East, 491
Wheel
  in pottery making, 79
Wild animals
  used for sacrifice, 398
Winds
  and ceramic production, 81
Witchcraft
  and ceramic production, 81
  and divine kingship, 282
Woman-marriage
  of the Lovedu, 299
Women
  in adolescence
    placentas of, 494
  and breastfeeding, 494-5
  and child dependency, 450
  collective
    as ruler of Fipa state, 291
  effect of education
    on nutritional status, 495
  female initiation rites, 289
  and gender hierarchies, 61
  gender relations
    West Africa, 262-3
  as innovators
    in Chicano studies, 415
  liberation
    and socialist development, 263
  maternal nutrition, 493
  as non-human member of the family, 395
  and origins of health beliefs, 227
  pioneering study of
    in West Africa, 246
  position of
    in West Africa, 253

as potters, 80
the queen mother
  in state formation, 283
  and the reproductive cycle, 507
role of
  in African politics, 298
as scapegoats
  of military, 263
the strategy of
  the Lovedu queens, 299
support system among, 230
in West Africa, 243
see also Feminism
see also Fertility
see also Sexual dimorphism
Women's liberation
dependence of
  on capitalist socialist development, 263
Women's movement
  and Chilean liberation, 62
Woodland complexes
  archaeological beginnings, 3
Work performance
  and traditional diets, 493
Working class
  landless, 412
  and language status, 559
World War I
  mining ventures prior to, 203
Written strategy
  as aspect of literacy, 169

X

X-linked genes
  and sexual dimorphism, 429

Y

Yakutsk
  prehistoric collections, 13
Yoruba society
  complexities of
    Peel, 265
Youth
  and Chicano studies, 415
Youth culture
  chola style in urban culture, 418
Yucatecan
  as Mayan language, 188
Yukon
  and evidence of Early Man, 547-9

Z

Zinc-deficiency syndrome
  and phytate in grain-based diets, 492
Zulu
  and power embodied in the king, 280
Zuni
  vocabulary levels in, 571

CUMULATIVE INDEXES

CONTRIBUTING AUTHORS, VOLUMES 7–14

A

Abramovitch, H., 13:385–417
Acheson, J. M., 10:275–316
Adams, J. W., 10:361–92
Adams, W. Y., 7:483–532
Aikens, C. M., 7:71–87
Ammerman, A. J., 10:63–88
Aronoff, M., 12:355–75

B

Bailey, G. N., 12:165–92
Barlett, P. F., 9:545–73
Barnard, A., 12:193–214
Bar-Yosef, O., 9:101–33
Baugh, J., 12:335–54
Beals, R. L., 11:1–23
Bernard, H. R., 13:495–517
Birdsell, J. B., 8:417–30
Blok, A., 13:333–44
Boaz, N. T., 8:71–85
Boissevain, J. F., 13:333–44
Brown, C. H., 7:427–51
Brown, D. E., 12:259–84
Brown, P., 7:263–91
Buikstra, J. E., 9:433–70
Burawoy, M., 8:231–66

C

Campbell, L., 14:187–98
Casson, R. W., 12:429–62
Chambers, E. J., 8:45–69
Chibnik, M., 14:135–57
Cicourel, A. V., 14:159–85
Clark, G., 8:1–20
Clark, J. T., 7:293–319
Cohen, A., 8:87–113
Cohen, R., 7:379–403
Cook, D. C., 9:433–70
Cook, E-D., 10:253–73
Cordell, L. S., 13:301–32
Crick, M. R., 11:287–313
Cushman, D., 11:25–69

D

Davis, R. S., 12:403–28
DeBoer, M. M., 8:579–600
Decker, H. W., 8:503–41
Dixon, R. M. W., 8:431–43
Dougherty, M. C., 14:219–41

Du Bois, C., 9:1–13
Dyke, B., 10:193–207
Dyson-Hudson, N., 9:15–61
Dyson-Hudson, R., 9:15–61

F

Farmer, A. K., 14:25–48
Feeley-Harnik, G., 14:273–313
Fernandez, J. W., 7:195–234
Fix, A. G., 8:207–30
Flenniken, J. J., 13:187–203
Fortes, M., 7:1–30
Fought, J., 9:293–314
Frayer, D. W., 14:429–73
Freedman, D. G., 8:579–600

G

Garn, S. M., 9:275–92
Gilmore, D. D., 11:175–205
Giovannini, M. J., 10:317–60
Gmelch, G., 9:135–59
Godoy, R., 14:199–217
Griffin, J. B., 14:1–23
Gross, D. R., 13:519–58
Gudeman, S., 7:347–77
Gurr, D. L., 12:79–103

H

Hage, P., 8:115–36
Hahn, R. A., 12:305–33
Halpern, J. M., 12:377–402
Hanna, J. M., 12:259–84
Hart, K., 14:243–72
Hassan, F. A., 8:137–60
Heath, J. G., 13:367–84
Heath, S. B., 13:251–74
Hill, J. H., 7:89–112
Hinshaw, R. E., 9:497–522
Hoben, A., 11:349–75
Hole, B. L., 9:217–34
Holzberg, C. S., 10:317–60
Huffman, T. N., 11:133–50
Huss-Ashmore, R., 14:475–528

I

Irvine, J. T., 14:557–81
Irving, W. N., 14:529–55

J

Jacobson, J., 8:467–502
Johnston, F. E., 14:475–528
Jones, R., 8:445–66
Jorde, L. B., 14:343–73
Jorgensen, J. G., 8:309–31

K

Kaeppler, A. L., 7:31–49
Kahn, J. S., 14:49–75
Kaplan, A., 13:25–39
Kaufman, T., 14:187–98
Kay, R. F., 14:315–41
Keith, J., 9:339–64
Keller-Cohen, D., 7:453–82
Kennedy, A. R. K., 9:391–432
Kideckel, D. A., 12:377–402
Killworth, P., 13:495–517
King, T. F., 12:143–64
Klein, R. G., 12:25–48
Kleinman, A., 12:305–33
Klepinger, L. L., 13:75–96
Kohl, P. L., 10:89–118
Kopytoff, I., 11:207–30
Kramer, C., 14:77–102
Krech, S. III, 9:83–100
Kronenfeld, D., 8:503–41; 13:495–517
Kuper, A., 11:71–95

L

Laboratory of Comparative Human Cognition, 7:51–69
Lamendella, J. T., 8:373–91
Lancy, D. F., 9:471–95
Leach, E. R., 13:1–23
Leap, W. L., 10:209–36
Levy, R. S., 7:483–532
Linares, O. F., 8:21–43
Löfgren, O., 9:187–215

M

MacDougall, D., 7:405–25
Marcus, G. E., 11:25–69
Matheny, R. T., 12:79–103
Maxwell, M. S., 9:161–85
McDermott, R. P., 7:321–45
McHenry, H. M., 11:151–73
McIntosh, R. J., 12:215–58

621

McIntosh, S. K., 12:215–58
Mel'čuk, I. A., 10:27–62
Messer, E., 13:205–49
Moore, L. G., 12:285–304
Murra, J. V., 13:119–41

N

Nash, J., 10:393–432
Nichols, J., 13:97–117

O

Orlove, B. S., 9:235–73

P

Palgi, P., 13:385–417
Parkin, D., 13:345–65
Parrington, M., 12:105–24
Pauw, B. A., 9:315–38
Philips, S. U., 9:523–44
Pilbeam, D., 8:333–52
Plog, S., 12:125–42
Purifoy, F. E., 10:141–62

R

Regensteiner, J. G., 12:285–304

Reidhead, V. A., 8:543–78
Richard, A. F., 11:231–55
Rosaldo, R., 14:405–27
Roth, D. R., 7:321–45

S

Sailer, L., 13:495–517
Saunders, G. R., 13:447–66
Schacht, R. M., 10:119–40
Schulman, S. R., 11:231–55
Schwartz, N. B., 7:235–61
Shanklin, E., 14:375–403
Shuy, R. W., 13:419–45
Silver, H. R., 8:267–307
Smith, R. T., 13:467–94
Snow, C. C., 11:97–131
So, J K., 9:63–82
Spindler, G. D., 12:49–78
Spindler, L., 12:49–78
Spores, R., 9:575–603
Spuhler, J. N., 14:103–33
Stokoe, W. C., 9:365–90
Strathern, M., 13:41–73
Swedlund, A. C., 7:137–73

T

Terrell, J., 7:293–319
Trigger, B. G., 13:275–300
Tripp-Reimer, T., 14:219–41

V

Van Gerven, D. P., 7:483–532
Vincent, J., 7:175–94

W

Wagner, R., 13:143–55
Wang, W. S-Y., 8:353–71
Washabaugh, W., 10:237–52
Washburn, S. L., 12:1–24
Werbner, R. P., 13:157–85
Williams, B. J., 10:163–92
Witkowski, S. R., 7:427–51
Wolpoff, M. H., 14:429–73
Worsley, P., 11:315–48

Y

Yanagisako, S. J., 8:161–205
Yengoyan, A. A., 8:393–415
Young, A., 11:257–85
Young, P. D., 8:45–69

CHAPTER TITLES, VOLUMES 7–14

OVERVIEWS
An Anthropologist's Apprenticeship	M. Fortes	7:1–30
Archaeology and Human Diversity	G. Clark	8:1–20
Some Anthropological Hindsights	C. Du Bois	9:1–13
Fifty Years in Anthropology	R. L. Beals	11:1–23
Evolution of a Teacher	S. L. Washburn	12:1–24
Glimpses of the Unmentionable in the History of British Social Anthropology	E. R. Leach	13:1–23
An Individual's Participation in American Archaeology	J. B. Griffin	14:1–23

ARCHAEOLOGY
Archaeology of the Great Basin	C. M. Aikens	7:71–87
Archaeology in Oceania	J. T. Clark, J. Terrell	7:293–319
What is Lower Central American Archaeology?	O. F. Linares	8:21–43
Demography and Archaeology	F. A. Hassan	8:137–60
The Fifth Continent: Problems Concerning the Human Colonization of Australia	R. Jones	8:445–66
Recent Developments in South Asian Prehistory and Protohistory	J. Jacobson	8:467–502
Linear Programming Models in Archaeology	V. A. Reidhead	8:543–78
Prehistory of the Levant	O. Bar-Yosef	9:101–33
Archaeology of the Arctic and Subarctic Zones	M. S. Maxwell	9:161–85
Sampling in Archaeology: A Critique	B. L. Hole	9:217–34
New World Ethnohistory and Archaeology, 1970–1980	R. Spores	9:575–603
Surveys and Archaeological Research	A. J. Ammerman	10:63–88
Materialist Approaches in Prehistory	P. L. Kohl	10:89–118
Estimating Past Population Trends	R. M. Schacht	10:119–40
Archaeology and Ethnohistory of the African Iron Age	T. N. Huffman	11:133–50
Variation in Prehistoric Agricultural Systems of the New World	R. T. Matheny, D. L. Gurr	12:79–103
Remote Sensing	M. Parrington	12:105–24
Analysis of Style in Artifacts	S. Plog	12:125–42
Professional Responsibility in Public Archaeology	T. F. King	12:143–64
Concepts of Time in Quaternary Prehistory	G. N. Bailey	12:165–92
Current Directions in West African Prehistory	S. K. McIntosh, R. J. McIntosh	12:215–58
Theoretical Issues in Contemporary Soviet Paleolithic Archaeology	R. S. Davis	12:403–28
The Past, Present, and Future of Flintknapping: An Anthropological Perspective	J. J. Flenniken	13:187–203
Archaeology at the Crossroads: What's New?	B. G. Trigger	13:275–300
Southwestern Archaeology	L. S. Cordell	13:301–32
Ceramic Ethnoarchaeology	C. Kramer	14:77–102
Context and Chronology of Early Man in the Americas	W. N. Irving	14:529–55

BIOLOGICAL ANTHROPOLOGY
Historical Demography as Population Ecology	A. C. Swedlund	7:137–73
The Retreat from Migrationism	W. Y. Adams, D. P. Van Gerven, R. S. Levy	7:483–532

Hominid Evolution in Eastern Africa During the Pliocene and Early Pleistocene	N. T. Boaz	8:71–85
Anthropological Genetics of Small Populations	A. G. Fix	8:207–30
Recent Finds and Interpretations of Miocene Hominoids	D. Pilbeam	8:333–52
Physical Anthropology in Australia Today	J. B. Birdsell	8:417–30
Biological and Cultural Differences in Early Child Development	D. G. Freedman, M. M. DeBoer	8:579–600
Human Biological Adaptation to Arctic and Subarctic Zones	J. K. So	9:63–82
Human Growth	S. M. Garn	9:275–92
Palaeopathology: An American Account	J. E. Buikstra, D. C. Cook	9:433–70
Prehistoric Skeletal Record of Man in South Asia	K. A. R. Kennedy	9:391–432
Endocrine-Environmental Interaction in Human Variability	F. E. Purifoy	10:141–62
A Critical Review of Models in Sociobiology	B. J. Williams	10:163–92
Computer Simulation in Anthropology	B. Dyke	10:193–207
Forensic Anthropology	C. C. Snow	11:97–131
The Pattern of Human Evolution: Studies on Bipedalism, Mastication, and Encephalization	H. M. McHenry	11:151–73
Sociobiology: Primate Field Studies	A. F. Richard, S. R. Schulman	11:231–55
The Stone Age Prehistory of Southern Africa	R. G. Klein	12:25–48
Human Heat Tolerance: An Anthropological Perspective	J. M. Hanna, D. E. Brown	12:259–84
Adaptation to High Altitude	L. G. Moore, J. G. Regensteiner	12:285–304
Nutritional Assessment from Bone	L. L. Klepinger	13:75–96
Anthropology, Evolution, and "Scientific Creationism"	J. N. Spuhler	14:103–33
Dental Evidence for the Diet of Australopithecus	R. F. Kay	14:315–41
Human Genetic Distance Studies: Present Status and Future Prospects	L. B. Jorde	14:343–73
Sexual Dimorphism	D. W. Frayer, M. H. Wolpoff	14:429–73
Bioanthropological Research in Developing Countries	R. Huss-Ashmore, F. E. Johnston	14:475–528

LINGUISTICS

Apes and Language	J. H. Hill	7:89–112
Lexical Universals	S. R. Witkowski, C. H. Brown	7:427–51
Context in Child Language	D. Keller-Cohen	7:453–82
Language Change—A Lexical Perspective	W. S-Y. Wang	8:353–71
Neurolinguistics	J. T. Lamendella	8:373–91
The Nature and Development of Australian Languages	R. M. W. Dixon	8:431–43
Current Trends in Phonology: The Challenges of Validation and Heterogeneity	J. Fought	9:293–314
Sign Language Structure	W. C. Stokoe	9:365–90
Sex Differences and Language	S. U. Philips	9:523–44
Meaning-Text Models: A Recent Trend in Soviet Linguistics	I. A. Mel'čuk	10:27–62
American Indian Language Maintenance	W. L. Leap	10:209–36
Sign Language in its Social Context	W. Washabaugh	10:237–52
Athapaskan Linguistics: Proto-Athapaskan Phonology	E-D. Cook	10:253–73
A Survey of Afro-American English	J. Baugh	12:335–54
A Decade of Morphology and Word Formation	M. Aronoff	12:355–75
Schemata in Cognitive Anthropology	R. W. Casson	12:429–62
Functional Theories of Grammar	J. Nichols	13:97–117
Linguistics and Education	S. B. Health	13:251–74
Language Contact and Language Change	J. G. Health	13:367–84
Linguistics in Other Professions	R. W. Shuy	13:419–45

Modular Theories of Grammar	A. K. Farmer	14:25–48
Text and Discourse	A. V. Cicourel	14:159–85
Mayan Linguistics: Where Are We Now?	L. Campbell, T. Kaufman	14:187–98
Status and Style in Language	J. T. Irvine	14:557–81

REGIONAL STUDIES

Archaeology of the Great Basin	C. M. Aikens	7:71–87
African Religious Movements	J. W. Fernandez	7:195–234
Community Development and Cultural Change in Latin America	N. B. Schwartz	7:235–61
New Guinea: Ecology, Society, and Culture	P. Brown	7:263–91
Archaeology in Oceania	J. T. Clark, J. Terrell	7:293–319
What is Lower Central American Archaeology?	O. F. Linares	8:21–43
Mesoamerican Community Studies: The Past Decade	E. J. Chambers, P. D. Young	8:45–69
Hominid Evolution in Eastern Africa During the Pliocene and Early Pleistocene	N. T. Boaz	8:71–85
Economy, Society, and Myth in Aboriginal Australia	A. A. Yengoyan	8:393–415
Physical Anthropology in Australia Today	J. B. Birdsell	8:417–30
The Nature and Development of Australian Languages	R. M. W. Dixon	8:431–43
The Fifth Continent: Problems Concerning the Human Colonization of Australia	R. Jones	8:445–66
Recent developments of South Asian Prehistory and Protohistory	J. Jacobson	8:467–502
Human Biological Adaptation to Arctic and Subarctic Zones	J. K. So	9:63–82
Northern Athapaskan Ethnology in the 1970s	S. Krech III	9:83–100
Archaeology in the Arctic and Subarctic Zones	M. S. Maxwell	9:161–85
Historical Perspectives on Scandinavian Peasantries	O. Löfgren	9:187–215
Recent South African Anthropology	B. A. Pauw	9:315–38
Human Adaptations to Arctic Zones	E. F. Moran	10:1–25
Meaning-Text Models: A Recent Trend in Soviet Linguistics	I. A. Mel'čuk	10:27–62
Athapaskan Linguistics: Proto-Athapaskan Phonology	E-D. Cook	10:253–73
Recent Ethnology of the Northwest Coast	J. W. Adams	10:361–92
Anthropology of the Mediterranean Area	D. D. Gilmore	11:175–205
Anthropologists View American Culture	G. D. Spindler, L. Spindler	12:49–78
Anthropology of Eastern Europe	J. M. Halpern, D. A. Kideckel	12:377–402
Andean Societies	J. V. Murra	13:119–41
The Manchester School in South-Central Africa	R. P. Werbner	13:157–85
Contemporary Italian Cultural Anthropology	G. R. Saunders	13:447–66
The Social Anthropology of West Africa	K. Hart	14:243–72
Chicano Studies, 1970-1984	R. Rosaldo	14:405–27

CULTURAL-SOCIAL ANTHROPOLOGY

History, Theory, and Method

Ethnographic Film: Failure and Promise	D. MacDougall	7:405–25
Graph Theory as a Structural Model in Cultural Anthropology	P. Hage	8:115–36
Cross-Cultural Comparisons	J. G. Jorgensen	8:309–31
Structuralism	D. Kronenfeld, H. W. Decker	8:503–41
Ethnographies as Texts	G. E. Marcus, D. Cushman	11:25–69
Anthropology of Knowledge	M. R. Crick	11:287–313
Philosophy of Science in Anthropology	A. Kaplan	13:25–39
Anthropology in the Netherlands Puzzles and Paradoxes	A. Blok, J. F. Boissevain	13:333–44

The Problem of Informant Accuracy: The Validity of Retrospective Data	H. R. Bernard, P. Killworth, D. Kronenfeld, L. Sailer	13:495–517
Time Allocation: A Tool for the Study of Cultural Behavior	D. R. Gross	13:519–58
The Use of Statistics in Sociocultural Anthropology	M. Chibnik	14:135–57

Technology, Ecology, and Economics

Anthropological Economics: The Question of Distribution	S. Gudeman	7:347–77
Nomadic Pastoralism	R. Dyson-Hudson, N. Dyson-Hudson	9:15–61
Ecological Anthropology	B. S. Orlove	9:235–73
Adaptive Strategies in Peasant Agricultural Production	P. F. Barlett	9:554–73
Anthropology of Fishing	J. M. Acheson	10:275–316
Anthropological Perspectives on Diet	E. Messer	13:205–49
Anthropology and the Concept of Social Class	R. T. Smith	13:467–94
Mining: Anthropological Perspectives	R. Godoy	14:199–217
Sustenance and Symbol: Anthropological Studies of Domesticated Animals	E. Shanklin	14:375–403

Social and Political Relationships

Political Anthropology: Manipulative Strategies	J. Vincent	7:175–94
The Social Organization of Behavior: Interactional Approaches	R. P. McDermott, D. R. Roth	7:321–45
Ethnicity	R. Cohen	7:379–403
Political Symbolism	A. Cohen	8:87–113
Family and Household: The Analysis of Domestic Groups	S. J. Yanagisako	8:161–205
"The Best Is Yet To Be": Toward an Anthropology of Age	J. Keith	9:339–64
Ethnographic Aspects of the World Capitalist System	J. Nash	10:393–423
Lineage Theory: A Critical Retrospect	A. Kuper	11:71–95
Slavery	I. Kopytoff	11:207–30
Contemporary Hunter-Gatherers: Current Theoretical Issues in Ecology and Social Organization	A. Barnard	12:193–214
Marriage Exchanges: A Melanesian Comment	M. Strathern	13:41–73
Peasant Ideologies in the Third World	J. S. Kahn	14:49–75
Issues in Divine Kingship	G. Feeley-Harnik	14:273–313

World View and Psychology

Dance in Anthropological Perspective	A. L. Kaeppler	7:31–49
Cognition as a Residual Category in Anthropology	Laboratory of Comparative Human Cognition	7:51–69
Oral Literature	W. P. Murphy	7:113–36
Ethnoart	H. R. Silver	8:267–307
Play in Species Adaptation	D. F. Lancy	9:471–95
Ritual as Communication: Order, Meaning, and Secrecy in Melanesian Initiation Rites	R. Wagner	13:143–55

Cultural Change and Applied Anthropology

The Anthropology of Industrial Work	M. Burawoy	8:231–66
Return Migration	G. Gmelch	9:135–59
Anthropology, Administration, and Public Policy	R. E. Hinshaw	9:497–522
Anthropology and Industry: Reappraisal and New Directions	C. S. Holzberg, M. J. Giovannini	10:317–60
The Anthropologies of Illness and Sickness	A. Young	11:257–85

Non-Western Medical Systems	P. Worsley	11:315–48
Anthropologists and Development	A. Hoben	11:349–75
Biomedical Practice and Anthropological Theory: Frameworks and Directions	R. A. Hahn, A. Kleinman	12:305–33
Political Language	D. Parkin	13:345–65
Death: A Cross-Cultural Perspective	P. Palgi, H. Abramovitch	13:385–417
The Interface of Nursing and Anthropology	M. C. Dougherty, T. Tripp-Reimer	14:219–41

Annual Reviews Inc.   ORDER FORM
A NONPROFIT SCIENTIFIC PUBLISHER
4139 El Camino Way, Palo Alto, CA 94306-9981, USA • (415) 493-4400

Annual Reviews Inc. publications are available directly from our office by mail or telephone (paid by credit card or purchase order), through booksellers and subscription agents, worldwide, and through participating professional societies. Prices subject to change without notice.

- **Individuals:** Prepayment required on new accounts by check or money order (in U.S. dollars, check drawn on U.S. bank) or charge to credit card — American Express, VISA, MasterCard.
- **Institutional buyers:** Please include purchase order number.
- **Students:** $10.00 discount from retail price, per volume. Prepayment required. Proof of student status must be provided (photocopy of student I.D. or signature of department secretary is acceptable). Students must send orders direct to Annual Reviews. Orders received through bookstores and institutions requesting student rates will be returned.
- **Professional Society Members:** Members of professional societies that have a contractual arrangement with Annual Reviews may order books through their society at a reduced rate. Check with your society for information.

Regular orders: Please list the volumes you wish to order by volume number.
Standing orders: New volume in the series will be sent to you automatically each year upon publication. Cancellation may be made at any time. Please indicate volume number to begin standing order.
Prepublication orders: Volumes not yet published will be shipped in month and year indicated.
California orders: Add applicable sales tax.
Postage paid (4th class bookrate/surface mail) **by Annual Reviews Inc.** Airmail postage extra.

ANNUAL REVIEWS SERIES		Prices Postpaid per volume USA/elsewhere	Regular Order Please send: Vol. number	Standing Order Begin with: Vol. number
Annual Review of **ANTHROPOLOGY** (Prices of Volumes in brackets effective until 12/31/85)				
[Vols. 1-10	(1972-1981)	$20.00/$21.00]		
[Vol. 11	(1982)	$22.00/$25.00]		
[Vols. 12-14	(1983-1985)	$27.00/$30.00]		
Vols. 1-14	(1972-1985)	$27.00/$30.00		
Vol. 15	(avail. Oct. 1986)	$31.00/$34.00	Vol(s). _____	Vol. _____
Annual Review of **ASTRONOMY AND ASTROPHYSICS** (Prices of Volumes in brackets effective until 12/31/85)				
[Vols. 1-2, 4-19	(1963-1964; 1966-1981)	$20.00/$21.00]		
[Vol. 20	(1982)	$22.00/$25.00]		
[Vols. 21-23	(1983-1985)	$44.00/$47.00]		
Vols. 1-2, 4-20	(1963-1964; 1966-1982)	$27.00/$30.00		
Vols. 21-23	(1983-1985)	$44.00/$47.00		
Vol. 24	(avail. Sept. 1986)	$44.00/$47.00	Vol(s). _____	Vol. _____
Annual Review of **BIOCHEMISTRY** (Prices of Volumes in brackets effective until 12/31/85)				
[Vols. 30-34, 36-50	(1961-1965; 1967-1981)	$21.00/$22.00]		
[Vol. 51	(1982)	$23.00/$26.00]		
[Vols. 52-54	(1983-1985)	$29.00/$32.00]		
Vols. 30-34, 36-54	(1961-1965; 1967-1985)	$29.00/$32.00		
Vol. 55	(avail. July 1986)	$33.00/$36.00	Vol(s). _____	Vol. _____
Annual Review of **BIOPHYSICS AND BIOPHYSICAL CHEMISTRY** (Prices of Vols. in brackets effective until 12/31/85)				
(Formerly Annual Review of Biophysics and Bioengineering)				
[Vols. 1-10	(1972-1981)	$20.00/$21.00]		
[Vol. 11	(1982)	$22.00/$25.00]		
[Vols. 12-14	(1983-1985)	$47.00/$50.00]		
Vols. 1-11	(1972-1982)	$27.00/$30.00		
Vols. 12-14	(1983-1985)	$47.00/$50.00		
Vol. 15	(avail. June 1986)	$47.00/$50.00	Vol(s). _____	Vol. _____
Annual Review of **CELL BIOLOGY**				
Vol. 1	(1985)	$27.00/$30.00		
Vol. 2	(avail. Nov. 1986)	$31.00/$34.00	Vol(s). _____	Vol. _____
Annual Review of **COMPUTER SCIENCE**				
Vol. 1	(avail. late 1986)	Price not yet established	Vol. _____	Vol. _____
Annual Review of **EARTH AND PLANETARY SCIENCES** (Prices of Volumes in brackets effective until 12/31/85)				
[Vols. 1-9	(1973-1981)	$20.00/$21.00]		
[Vol. 10	(1982)	$22.00/$25.00]		
[Vols. 11-13	(1983-1985)	$44.00/$47.00]		
Vols. 1-10	(1973-1982)	$27.00/$30.00		
Vols. 11-13	(1983-1985)	$44.00/$47.00		
Vol. 14	(avail. May 1986)	$44.00/$47.00	Vol(s). _____	Vol. _____

ANNUAL REVIEWS SERIES	Prices Postpaid per volume USA/elsewhere	Regular Order Please send:	Standing Order Begin with:

Annual Review of **ECOLOGY AND SYSTEMATICS** (Prices of Volumes in brackets effective until 12/31/85)

[Vols. 1-12	(1970-1981).................	**$20.00/$21.00**]
[Vol. 13	(1982)......................	**$22.00/$25.00**]
[Vols. 14-16	(1983-1985).................	**$27.00/$30.00**]

| Vols. 1-16 | (1970-1985)................. | **$27.00/$30.00** | | |
| Vol. 17 | (avail. Nov. 1986)........... | **$31.00/$34.00** | Vol(s). _____ | Vol. _____ |

Annual Review of **ENERGY** (Prices of Volumes in brackets effective until 12/31/85)

[Vols. 1-6	(1976-1981).................	**$20.00/$21.00**]
[Vol. 7	(1982)......................	**$22.00/$25.00**]
[Vols. 8-10	(1983-1985).................	**$56.00/$59.00**]

Vols. 1-7	(1976-1982).................	**$27.00/$30.00**		
Vols. 8-10	(1983-1985).................	**$56.00/$59.00**		
Vol. 11	(avail. Oct. 1986)...........	**$56.00/$59.00**	Vol(s). _____	Vol. _____

Annual Review of **ENTOMOLOGY** (Prices of Volumes in brackets effective until 12/31/85)

[Vols. 9-16, 18-26	(1964-1971; 1973-1981)........	**$20.00/$21.00**]
[Vol. 27	(1982)......................	**$22.00/$25.00**]
[Vols. 28-30	(1983-1985).................	**$27.00/$30.00**]

| Vols. 9-16, 18-30 | (1964-1971; 1973-1985)........ | **$27.00/$30.00** | | |
| Vol. 31 | (avail. Jan. 1986)........... | **$31.00/$34.00** | Vol(s). _____ | Vol. _____ |

Annual Review of **FLUID MECHANICS** (Prices of Volumes in brackets effective until 12/31/85)

[Vols. 1-5, 7-13	(1969-1973; 1975-1981)........	**$20.00/$21.00**]
[Vol. 14	(1982)......................	**$22.00/$25.00**]
[Vols. 15-17	(1983-1985).................	**$28.00/$31.00**]

| Vols. 1-5, 7-17 | (1969-1973; 1975-1985)........ | **$28.00/$31.00** | | |
| Vol. 18 | (avail. Jan. 1986)........... | **$32.00/$35.00** | Vol(s). _____ | Vol. _____ |

Annual Review of **GENETICS** (Prices of Volumes in brackets effective until 12/31/85)

[Vols. 1-15	(1967-1981).................	**$20.00/$21.00**]
[Vol. 16	(1982)......................	**$22.00/$25.00**]
[Vols. 17-19	(1983-1985).................	**$27.00/$30.00**]

| Vols. 1-19 | (1967-1985)................. | **$27.00/$30.00** | | |
| Vol. 20 | (avail. Dec. 1986)........... | **$31.00/$34.00** | Vol(s). _____ | Vol. _____ |

Annual Review of **IMMUNOLOGY**

| Vols. 1-3 | (1983-1985)................. | **$27.00/$30.00** | | |
| Vol. 4 | (avail. April 1986).......... | **$31.00/$34.00** | Vol(s). _____ | Vol. _____ |

Annual Review of **MATERIALS SCIENCE** (Prices of Volumes in brackets effective until 12/31/85)

[Vols. 1-11	(1971-1981).................	**$20.00/$21.00**]
[Vol. 12	(1982)......................	**$22.00/$25.00**]
[Vols. 13-15	(1983-1985).................	**$64.00/$67.00**]

Vols. 1-12	(1971-1982).................	**$27.00/$30.00**		
Vols. 13-15	(1983-1985).................	**$64.00/$67.00**		
Vol. 16	(avail. August 1986).........	**$64.00/$67.00**	Vol(s). _____	Vol. _____

Annual Review of **MEDICINE** (Prices of Volumes in brackets effective until 12/31/85)

[Vols. 1-3, 5-15, 17-32	(1950-52; 1954-64; 1966-81)......	**$20.00/$21.00**]
[Vol. 33	(1982)......................	**$22.00/$25.00**]
[Vols. 34-36	(1983-1985).................	**$27.00/$30.00**]

| Vols. 1-3, 5-15, 17-36 | (1950-52; 1954-64; 1966-85)...... | **$27.00/$30.00** | | |
| Vol. 37 | (avail. April 1986).......... | **$31.00/$34.00** | Vol(s). _____ | Vol. _____ |

Annual Review of **MICROBIOLOGY** (Prices of Volumes in brackets effective until 12/31/85)

[Vols. 18-35	(1964-1981).................	**$20.00/$21.00**]
[Vol. 36	(1982)......................	**$22.00/$25.00**]
[Vols. 37-39	(1983-1985).................	**$27.00/$30.00**]

| Vols. 18-39 | (1964-1985)................. | **$27.00/$30.00** | | |
| Vol. 40 | (avail. Oct. 1986)........... | **$31.00/$34.00** | Vol(s). _____ | Vol. _____ |

Annual Review of **NEUROSCIENCE** (Prices of Volumes in brackets effective until 12/31/85)

[Vols. 1-4	(1978-1981).................	**$20.00/$21.00**]
[Vol. 5	(1982)......................	**$22.00/$25.00**]
[Vols. 6-8	(1983-1985).................	**$27.00/$30.00**]

| Vols. 1-8 | (1978-1985)................. | **$27.00/$30.00** | | |
| Vol. 9 | (avail. March 1986).......... | **$31.00/$34.00** | Vol(s). _____ | Vol. _____ |

ANNUAL REVIEWS SERIES		Prices Postpaid per volume USA/elsewhere	Regular Order Please send:	Standing Order Begin with:

Annual Review of **NUCLEAR AND PARTICLE SCIENCE** (Prices of Volumes in brackets effective until 12/31/85)

[Vols. 12-31	(1962-1981)	$22.50/$23.50]		
[Vol. 32	(1982)	$25.00/$28.00]		
[Vols. 33-35	(1983-1985)	$30.00/$33.00]		
Vols. 12-35	(1962-1985)	$30.00/$33.00		
Vol. 36	(avail. Dec. 1986)	$34.00/$37.00	Vol(s). _____	Vol. _____

Annual Review of **NUTRITION** (Prices of Volumes in brackets effective until 12/31/85)

[Vol. 1	(1981)	$20.00/$21.00]		
[Vol. 2	(1982)	$22.00/$25.00]		
[Vols. 3-5	(1983-1985)	$27.00/$30.00]		
Vols. 1-5	(1981-1985)	$27.00/$30.00		
Vol. 6	(avail. July 1986)	$31.00/$34.00	Vol(s). _____	Vol. _____

Annual Review of **PHARMACOLOGY AND TOXICOLOGY** (Prices of Volumes in brackets effective until 12/31/85)

[Vols. 1-3, 5-21	(1961-1963, 1965-1981)	$20.00/$21.00]		
[Vol. 22	(1982)	$22.00/$25.00]		
[Vols. 23-25	(1983-1985)	$27.00/$30.00]		
Vols. 1-3, 5-25	(1961-1963, 1965-1985)	$27.00/$30.00		
Vol. 26	(avail. April 1986)	$31.00/$34.00	Vol(s). _____	Vol. _____

Annual Review of **PHYSICAL CHEMISTRY** (Prices of Volumes in brackets effective until 12/31/85)

[Vols. 10-21, 23-32	(1959-1970, 1972-1981)	$20.00/$21.00]		
[Vol. 33	(1982)	$22.00/$25.00]		
[Vols. 34-36	(1983-1985)	$28.00/$31.00]		
Vols. 10-21, 23-36	(1959-1970, 1972-1985)	$28.00/$31.00		
Vol. 37	(avail. Nov. 1986)	$32.00/$35.00	Vol(s). _____	Vol. _____

Annual Review of **PHYSIOLOGY** (Prices of Volumes in brackets effective until 12/31/85)

[Vols. 19-43	(1957-1981)	$20.00/$21.00]		
[Vol. 44	(1982)	$22.00/$25.00]		
[Vols. 45-47	(1983-1985)	$27.00/$30.00]		
Vols. 19-47	(1957-1985)	$27.00/$30.00		
Vol. 48	(avail. March 1986)	$32.00/$35.00	Vol(s). _____	Vol. _____

Annual Review of **PHYTOPATHOLOGY** (Prices of Volumes in brackets effective until 12/31/85)

[Vols. 2-19	(1964-1981)	$20.00/$21.00]		
[Vol. 20	(1982)	$22.00/$25.00]		
[Vols. 21-23	(1983-1985)	$27.00/$30.00]		
Vols. 2-23	(1964-1985)	$27.00/$30.00		
Vol. 24	(avail. Sept. 1986)	$31.00/$34.00	Vol(s). _____	Vol. _____

Annual Review of **PLANT PHYSIOLOGY** (Prices of Volumes in brackets effective until 12/31/85)

[Vols. 13-23, 25-32	(1962-1972, 1974-1981)	$20.00/$21.00]		
[Vol. 33	(1982)	$22.00/$25.00]		
[Vols. 34-36	(1983-1985)	$27.00/$30.00]		
Vols. 13-23, 25-36	(1962-1972, 1974-1985)	$27.00/$30.00		
Vol. 37	(avail. June 1986)	$31.00/$34.00	Vol(s). _____	Vol. _____

Annual Review of **PSYCHOLOGY** (Prices of Volumes in brackets effective until 12/31/85)

[Vols. 4, 5, 8	(1953, 1954, 1957)	$20.00/$21.00]		
[Vols. 10-24, 26-32	(1959-1973, 1975-1981)	$20.00/$21.00]		
[Vol. 33	(1982)	$22.00/$25.00]		
[Vols. 34-36	(1983-1985)	$27.00/$30.00]		
Vols. 4, 5, 8	(1953, 1954, 1957)	$27.00/$30.00		
Vols. 10-24, 26-36	(1959-1973, 1975-1985)	$27.00/$30.00		
Vol. 37	(avail. Feb. 1986)	$31.00/$34.00	Vol(s). _____	Vol. _____

Annual Review of **PUBLIC HEALTH** (Prices of Volumes in brackets effective until 12/31/85)

[Vols. 1-2	(1980-1981)	$20.00/$21.00]		
[Vol. 3	(1982)	$22.00/$25.00]		
[Vols. 4-6	(1983-1985)	$27.00/$30.00]		
Vols. 1-6	(1980-1985)	$27.00/$30.00		
Vol. 7	(avail. May 1986)	$31.00/$34.00	Vol(s). _____	Vol. _____

ANNUAL REVIEWS SERIES		Prices Postpaid per volume USA/elsewhere	Regular Order Please send:	Standing Order Begin with:

Annual Review of **SOCIOLOGY** (Prices of Volumes in brackets effective until 12/31/85)

[Vols. 1-7	(1975-1981)	**$20.00/$21.00**]		
[Vol. 8	(1982)	**$22.00/$25.00**]		
[Vols. 9-11	(1983-1985)	**$27.00/$30.00**]		
Vols. 1-11	(1975-1985)	**$27.00/$30.00**		
Vol. 12	(avail. Aug. 1986)	**$31.00/$34.00**	Vol(s). _____	Vol. _____

Note: Volumes not listed are out of print

SPECIAL PUBLICATIONS		Prices Postpaid per volume USA/elsewhere	Regular Order Please Send:

Annual Reviews Reprints: **Cell Membranes, 1975-1977**

(published 1978) Softcover .... **$12.00/$12.50** _____ Copy(ies).

Annual Reviews Reprints: **Immunology, 1977-1979**

(published 1980) Softcover .... **$12.00/12.50** _____ Copy(ies).

History of Entomology

(published 1973) Clothbound .... **$10.00/$10.50** _____ Copy(ies).

Intelligence and Affectivity:
Their Relationship During Child Development, by Jean Piaget

(published 1981) Hardcover .... **$8.00/$9.00** _____ Copy(ies).

Some Historical and Modern Aspects of Amino Acids,
Fermentations, and Nucleic Acids: Proceedings of a
Symposium held in St. Louis, Missouri, June 3, 1981

(published 1982) Softcover .... **$10.00/$12.00** _____ Copy(ies).

Telescopes for the 1980s

(published 1981) Hardcover .... **$27.00/$28.00** _____ Copy(ies).

The Excitement and Fascination of Science, Volume 1

(published 1965) Clothbound .... **$6.50/$7.00** _____ Copy(ies).

The Excitement and Fascination of Science, Volume 2

(published 1978) Hardcover .... **$12.00/$12.50**
                  Softcover .... **$10.00/$10.50** _____ Copy(ies).

TO: **ANNUAL REVIEWS INC., 4139 El Camino Way, Palo Alto, CA 94306-9981, USA • Tel. (415) 493-4400**

Please enter my order for the publications checked above. California orders, add sales tax. Prices subject to change without notice.

Institutional purchase order No. _____

Amount of remittance enclosed $ _____

INDIVIDUALS: Prepayment required in U.S. funds or charge to bank card below. Include card number, expiration date, and signature.

Charge my account ☐ VISA   Acct. No. _____

☐ MasterCard ☐ American Express Exp. Date _____

Signature _____

Name _____
          Please print

Address _____
           Please print

Zip Code _____

_____ Send free copy of current **Prospectus** ☐

Area(s) of Interest _____